SCHAUM'S SOLVED PROBLEMS SERIES

3000 SOLVED PROBLEMS IN

ORGANIC CHEMISTRY

by

Estelle K. Meislich, Ph.D.

Professor Emeritus of Chemistry
Bergen Community College

Herbert Meislich, Ph.D.

Professor Emeritus of Chemistry
City College of CUNY

Joseph Sharefkin, Ph.D.

Professor Emeritus of Chemistry
Brooklyn College of CUNY

McGRAW-HILL, INC.
New York   St. Louis   San Francisco   Auckland   Bogotá   Caracas   Lisbon
London   Madrid   Mexico City   Milan   Montreal   New Delhi
San Juan   Singapore   Sydney   Tokyo   Toronto

Estelle K. Meislich, Ph.D.
Estelle K. Meislich earned a B.S. degree in Chemistry from Brooklyn College, and M.A. and Ph.D. degrees in Organic Chemistry from Columbia University. She held a Research Assistantship in the Dept. of Neurology at Columbia Medical School, where she designed and synthesized the first antidote for a nerve gas. After teaching at City College of CUNY for many years she moved to Bergen Community College, where she is now Professor Emeritus. She is the author of a laboratory manual for nursing and other allied health students as well as several papers in the Journal of Chemical Education.

Herbert Meislich, Ph.D.
Herbert Meislich holds a B.A. degree from Brooklyn College and an M.A. and Ph.D. from Columbia University. He is Professor Emeritus from the City College of CUNY, where he taught Organic and General Chemistry for forty years at both the undergraduate and doctoral levels. He received the Outstanding Teacher award in 1985 and has coauthored eight textbooks, three laboratory manuals in General and Organic Chemistry and 15 papers on his research interests.

Jacob Sharefkin, Ph.D.
Jacob Sharefkin is Professor Emeritus of Chemistry at Brooklyn College. After receiving a B.S. from City College of New York, he was awarded an M.A. from Columbia University and a Ph.D. from New York University. His publications and research interest in Qualitative Organic Analysis and organic boron and iodine compounds have been supported by grants from the American Chemical Society, for whom he has also designed national examinations in Organic Chemistry.

 This book is printed on recycled paper containing a minimum of 50% total recycled fiber with 10% postconsumer de-inked fiber. Soybean based inks are used on the cover and text.

3000 SOLVED PROBLEMS IN ORGANIC CHEMISTRY

Library of Congress Cataloging-in-Publication Data

Meislich, Estelle K.
  3000 solved problems in organic chemistry / by Estelle K.
Meislich, Herbert Meislich, Joseph Sharefkin.
      p.   cm.—(Schaum's solved problems series)
  Includes index.
  ISBN 0-07-056424-8
  1. Chemistry, Organic—Problems, exercises, etc.   I. Meislich,
Herbert.   II. Sharefkin, Joseph.   III. Title.   IV. Series.
QD257.M43   1993   92-23614
547′.0076—dc20   CIP

2 3 4 5 6 7 8 9 0 BAW / BAW 9 8 7 6 5 4 3

ISBN 0-07-056424-8

Sponsoring Editor: David Beckwith
Production Supervisor: Leroy Young
Editing Supervisor: Maureen Walker
Cover design by Wanda Siedlecka.

This book is dedicated to the late Professor David Davidson,
formerly professor of Chemistry at Brooklyn College of CUNY.

ACKNOWLEDGMENTS

The spectra in this text were obtained, with permission from the following sources:

[1]H nuclear magnetic resonance spectra from "The Aldrich Library of NMR Spectra," Volume I, first edition, C. J. Pouchert and J. R. Campbell, the Aldrich Chemical Company, 1975.

Infrared spectra from (1) "The Aldrich Library of IR Spectra," second edition, C. J. Pouchert, the Aldrich Chemical Company. (2) "Sadtler Handbook of IR Spectra," William W. Simons, Sadtler Research Laboratories, Inc., 1978.

Permission for the publication herein of Sadtler Standard Spectra® has been granted, and all rights are reserved, by Sadtler Research Laboratories, Divison of Bio-Rad Laboratories, Inc.

CONTENTS

vi ⫽ CONTENTS

TO THE STUDENT

Organic chemistry is best learned by solving problems—as many as is practical. This book provides you with 3000 opportunities. In each chapter the problems are presented in sequence to best develop your understanding of the theories and practice of this basic, very logical science. The authors do not just present the answers. Rather we make clear the thought processes you should go through to get the correct answers. Attempt the problems first before resorting to the answers. By challenging yourself first, you will solidify your understanding. Some problems, especially those involving syntheses, may have several solutions and you may find more than one approach given. If your solution is different but correct—don't fret, more power to you!

Most textbooks used today have a consistent underlying sequencing of topics, albeit with significant variations. The order of chapters in 3000 Solved Problems is an attempt to conform with most textbooks. However, you may have to resort to the Table of Contents to find a particular subject. The very thorough index should also prove helpful.

We would like to send our thanks and appreciation to Ms. Maureen Walker and Mr. Nick Monti for their careful and thorough proofreading.

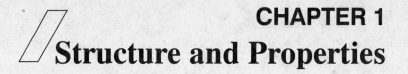

CHAPTER 1
Structure and Properties

DEFINITIONS

1.1 What is (*a*) organic and (*b*) inorganic chemistry?

▮ (*a*) With a few exceptions (i.e., carbonate salts and CO_2) *organic chemistry* is the study of carbon compounds. (*b*) *Inorganic chemistry* is the study of all other compounds.

1.2 What is the origin of the term *organic* chemistry?

▮ Prior to 1828, most carbon compounds had been found only in living matter and it was believed that their natural synthesis required a *vital force*. It was concluded that inanimate and living (organic) matter had different origins and were therefore completely different. In that year, Friedrich Wöhler converted the inorganic ammonium isocyanate $[(NH_4)^+(N\!=\!C\!=\!O)^-]$ to the known organic compound urea $[O\!=\!C(NH_2)_2]$, and the definitions of organic and inorganic chemistry changed.

1.3 What are the important differences between organic and inorganic compounds?

▮ In general, organic compounds
 (*1*) react more slowly and require higher temperatures for reaction;
 (*2*) undergo more complex reactions and produce more side products;
 (*3*) have lower melting and boiling points and are generally insoluble in water;
 (*4*) are less stable and therefore often decompose on heating to compounds of lower energy content;
 (*5*) are classified into families of compounds such as alcohols, which have similar reactive groups and chemical properties; and
 (*6*) are far more numerous than inorganic compounds.

1.4 Account for the large number of organic compounds.

▮ Carbon is in group IV of the periodic table and forms bonds with almost every other element (other than the noble gases). Carbon atoms bond to each other in single and multiple bonds, forming both long chains as well as ring compounds. Also, carbon compounds with identical molecular formulas but with different structural formulas are called *isomers*.

1.5 What are the three important classes of organic compounds?

▮ 1. *Aliphatic* compounds with C's bonded in chains are called *acyclic* to distinguish them from *cyclic* compounds, which have C's bonded in rings (not circular).
 2. *Aromatic* compounds, originally so named because of their pleasant odors, include derivatives of the parent hydrocarbon benzene (C_6H_6) and other ring systems with unusual stability.
 3. *Heterocyclics* are compounds with rings having at least one element other than C in the ring.

CHEMICAL BONDS

1.6 Why is it important to know about chemical bonds between atoms in a molecule?

▮ Since chemical reactions occur by breaking and making bonds, their energies and rates depend on the strength of these bonds.

1.7 What are the two important types of chemical bonds observed in organic molecules?

▮ (*1*) *Covalent bonds*, in which an electron pair is shared between the two atoms, A:B, and
 (*2*) *Ionic bonds*, formed by transfer of one or more e^-'s to form a positive cation and negative anion, i.e., $A^+:B^-$. Metallic (left side of the periodic table) elements usually form ionic bonds with nonmetallic (H and those on right side of the periodic table) elements. Nonmetallic elements form covalent bonds to each other and to themselves. All organic compounds have covalent bonds but some also have ionic bonds.

1.8 Specify the type of chemical bond in the compounds (*a*) Li_2O, (*b*) PH_3, (*c*) N_2O, and (*d*) CaF_2.

◢ (*a*) Ionic, (*b*) covalent, (*c*) covalent, and (*d*) ionic.

1.9 Predict the type of chemical bond in the following molecules from their physical properties:

	(*a*) Cl_2	(*b*) NaCl	(*c*) ICl	(*d*) H_2O
Melting Point:	$-101.6\ °C$	$800.4\ °C$	$27.2\ °C$	$0\ °C$
Boiling Point:	$34.6\ °C$	$1413\ °C$	$97\ °C$	$100\ °C$
Unit Particles:	molecules	ions	molecules	molecules

◢ (*a*) Covalent, (*b*) ionic, (*c*) covalent, and (*d*) covalent.

1.10 Explain the difference in melting point (mp) and boiling point (bp) of the covalent and ionic compounds in Problem 1.9.

◢ Melting and boiling require separation of the particles comprising the solid and liquid states, respectively. The ionic salt is a three-dimensional array of alternating cations (Na^+) and anions (Cl^-). Its mp and bp are high because the strong electrostatic forces of attraction between the oppositely charged ions must be overcome, and this requires considerable energy (high temperatures). In covalent compounds like H_2O, each H is covalently bonded to the O to give a discrete molecule, H_2O. In (*a*) and (*c*) the discrete particles are the molecules Cl_2 and ICl, respectively. These molecules are the unit particles that must be separated from each other during melting and boiling, and these processes require less energy (lower temperatures).

1.11 Can it be concluded from the answer in Problem 1.10 that covalent bonds are necessarily *weaker* than ionic bonds?

◢ No; covalent bonds are not broken when molecules are separated during melting and/or boiling. Breaking covalent bonds may require high temperatures (see Problem 1.12).

1.12 The mp of SiO_2, sand, is 1710 °C, and its bp is 2650 °C. (*a*) Describe the bonding in SiO_2. (*b*) Why are its mp and bp so high?

◢ (*a*) The relative positions of the elements in the periodic table indicate that the Si—O bond is covalent. (*b*) Each Si is bonded to four O atoms, and each O is bonded to two Si atoms in a three-dimensional array. There are no individual molecules of SiO_2. The entire grain of solid is considered a giant single molecule, often called a *network covalent* substance, with the empirical formula SiO_2. During melting and boiling, covalent bonds *between* atoms are broken. Much more energy is required to break covalent bonds than to separate molecules from each other.

1.13 Both diamond and graphite, two different crystalline allotropic forms of carbon, have extremely high mp's (> 3500 °C). Diamond is very hard while graphite is soft and slippery–it is used as a lubricant. Explain in terms of bonding.

◢ The high mp's point to a network covalent structure for both substances. The C to C bonds in graphite extend in sheets, two-dimensionally, with only weak forces of attraction between the sheets. Thus the layers can slide past each other easily, making graphite feel soft and slippery. The C to C bonds in diamond extend in three dimensions. Cracking a diamond crystal requires the rupture of a large number of stable C—C bonds, a process that takes much energy. Hence, diamond is the hardest known substance.

1.14 How does the Lewis–Langmuir octet rule explain the formation of chemical bonds?

◢ Individual atoms lose, gain, or share e^-'s to attain electronic configurations (stable outer shells with eight e^-'s) of the nearest noble gas. In ionic bonding an e^- is transferred to form a cation and an anion: $A\cdot + \cdot\ddot{B}\!: \rightarrow A^+ + :\ddot{B}\!:^-$. For example, Na· transfers the lone e^- in its outer (valence) shell to $:\ddot{F}\cdot$ with seven e^-'s in its outer shell, leaving both cation and anion with outer shells of eight (an octet) e^-'s.

$$Na(2,8,1) + F(2,7) \rightarrow Na^+(2,8) + F^-(2,8) \quad or \quad Na^+ :\ddot{F}\!:^-$$

Octets are also formed by transferring more than one e^-.

$$Mg(2,8,2) + 2\,Cl(2,8,7) \rightarrow Mg^{2+}(2,8) + 2\,Cl^-(2,8,8) \quad or \quad Mg^{2+}\ 2:\ddot{C}\!l\!:^- \ (or\ MgCl_2)$$

Noble gas configurations are attained during covalent bonding by sharing of e^- pairs, with each e^- having an opposite spin as required by the Pauli Exclusion Principle: $:\ddot{C}\!l\cdot + \cdot\ddot{C}\!l\!: \rightarrow :\ddot{C}\!l\!:\!\ddot{C}\!l\!:$.

1.15 (*a*) What is a *coordinate covalent bond* (dative bond)? (*b*) Once formed, how does it differ from a typical covalent bond?

◢ (*a*) In a coordinate covalent bond, the pair of e^-'s are furnished by one atom (the donor) for sharing with the acceptor atom:

$$:\ddot{\underset{\cdot\cdot}{Cl}}:^- + AlCl_3 \longrightarrow AlCl_4^- \text{ or } [:\ddot{\underset{\cdot\cdot}{Cl}}:\ddot{\underset{\cdot\cdot}{Al}}:\ddot{\underset{\cdot\cdot}{Cl}}:]^-$$

$$\underset{donor}{} \quad \underset{acceptor}{}$$

(*b*) Although it differs in mode of formation, once formed it is a typical covalent bond.

1.16 Identify donor and acceptor species in the formation of coordinate covalent bonds in the following:

$$(a)\ H_3O^+ \qquad (b)\ Cu(NH_3)_4^{2+} \qquad (c)\ AgCl_2^- \qquad (d)\ H_3N:BF_3$$

◢ *acceptor donor*

(*a*) $\quad H^+ \quad + \quad H:\ddot{O}:H \longrightarrow [H:\ddot{O}:H]^+$ (with H above O)

(*b*) $\quad Cu^{2+} \quad + \quad 4:NH_3 \longrightarrow [H_3N:\ddot{Cu}:NH_3]^{2+}$ (with NH₃ above and below Cu)

(*c*) $\quad AgCl \quad + \quad :\ddot{\underset{\cdot\cdot}{Cl}}:^- \longrightarrow AgCl_2^-$

(*d*) $\quad BF_3 \quad + \quad :NH_3 \longrightarrow F_3B:NH_3$

1.17 (*a*) Does the octet rule apply to H and Li? (*b*) Diagram the formation of (i) $HCl_{(g)}$, (ii) LiBr, and (iii) NaH.

◢ (*a*) H and Li form bonds to attain the stable *duet* of the noble gas He.

(*b*) (i) $H\cdot + \cdot\ddot{\underset{\cdot\cdot}{Cl}}: \rightarrow H:\ddot{\underset{\cdot\cdot}{Cl}}:$ (covalent bond)

(ii) $Li\cdot + \cdot\ddot{\underset{\cdot\cdot}{Br}}: \rightarrow Li^+:\ddot{\underset{\cdot\cdot}{Br}}:^-$ (ionic bond)

(iii) $Na\cdot + \cdot H \rightarrow Na^+:H^-$ (sodium hydride, ionic bond)

1.18 For the second period elements Be, B, C, N, O, and F give: (*a*) the number of e^-'s in the outer shell, (*b*) the number of covalent bonds formed, and (*c*) formulas of H compounds.

◢

	Be	B	C	N	O	F
(*a*)	2	3	4	5	6	7
(*b*)	2	3	4	3	2	1
(*c*)	BeH_2	BH_3	CH_4	NH_3	H_2O	HF

1.19 What are some of the exceptions to the octet rule?

◢ In addition to H and Li (Problem 1.17) Be and B form less than four bonds in many of their compounds, thus lacking an octet. The octet rule also does not apply to higher atomic number elements in the third and higher periods such as S, Si, and P, which can acquire more than eight e^-'s.

1.20 How many e^-'s make up (*a*) a single, (*b*) a double, and (*c*) a triple bond?

◢ (*a*) Two (one pair), (*b*) four (2 pairs), and (*c*) six (3 pairs).

1.21 Write *electron-dot* structures for the following covalent compounds: (*a*) F_2O, (*b*) H_2O_2, (*c*) PCl_3, (*d*) CH_3Cl, and (*e*) N_2H_4 (hydrazine).

◢ Electron-dot structures show all bonding and unshared valence e^-'s. First write the *skeleton* of the molecule, showing the bonding arrangement of the atoms. In molecules with three or more atoms there is at least one central atom, which has the highest covalency. If there is more than one multicovalent atom in the molecule [as in (*b*) and (*e*)], bond them to each other to get the skeleton; then bond the univalent atoms (H, F, Cl) to them in order to satisfy their normal multicovalencies. In their bonded state, second period elements should have eight e⁻'s, but not more. (Exceptions are Be and B which may have less than eight.) The number of e⁻'s in the Lewis structure should equal the sum of the valence e⁻'s of all the individual atoms.

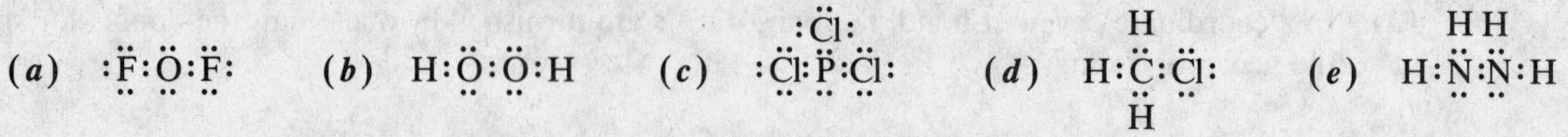

(a) :F̈:Ö:F̈:   (b) H:Ö:Ö:H   (c) :C̈l:P̈:C̈l: with :C̈l: above   (d) H:C̈:C̈l: with H above and below   (e) H:N̈:N̈:H with H H above

1.22 Provide electron-dot structures for the following multiple-bonded compounds: (a) H_2CO, (b) N_2, (c) CO_2, (d) HONO, and (e) HCN.

▮ If the number of univalent atoms available for bonding to the multicovalent atoms is insufficient for achieving normal covalencies, form multiple bonds (Problem 1.20).

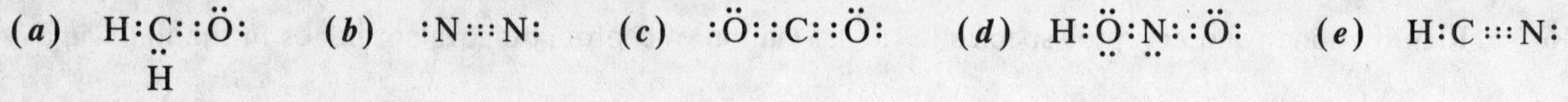

(a) H:C::Ö: with H below   (b) :N:::N: (c) :Ö::C::Ö: (d) H:Ö:N::Ö: (e) H:C:::N:

1.23 Provide electron-dot structures for the compounds whose molecular formulas are: (a) C_2H_6, (b) C_2H_4, and (c) C_2H_2.

▮ Carbon is tetravalent (Problem 1.18) and can form single and multiple bonds.

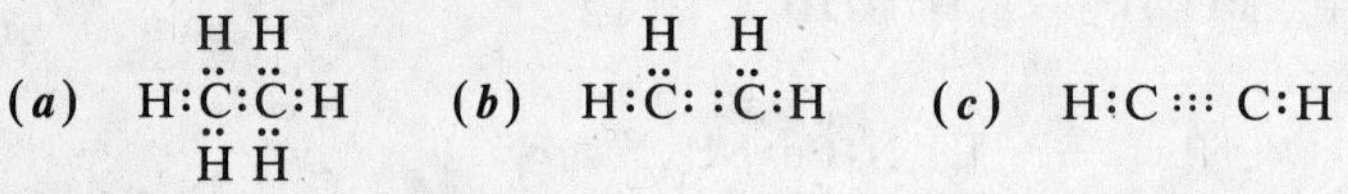

(a) H:C̈:C̈:H with H H above and H H below   (b) H:C̈::C̈:H with H H above   (c) H:C:::C:H

1.24 (a) Write an electron-dot structure for phosgene, $COCl_2$. (b) Why are all the following structures incorrect?

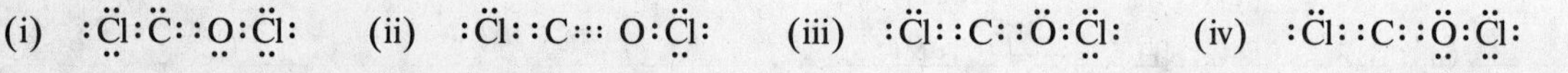

(i) :C̈l:C̈::Ö:C̈l: (ii) :C̈l::C:::O:C̈l: (iii) :C̈l::C::Ö:C̈l: (iv) :C̈l::C::Ö:C̈l:

▮ (a) The central atom C has the highest covalence. To satisfy the tetravalency of C and divalency of O, a double bond between them is required:

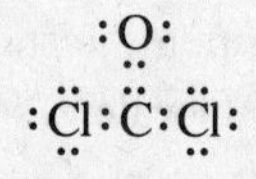

:O:
‖
:C̈l:C̈:C̈l:

(b) The total number of valence e⁻'s that must appear in the electron-dot structure is 24; 14 (two Cl's) + 4(C) + 6(O). In (i), C and O do not have their normal covalencies. Structures (ii) and (iii) are rejected because they each show only 22 e⁻'s. Also, in (ii) O has four rather than two bonds, and in (iii) and (iv) one Cl has two bonds. (iv) Is also rejected because O has 10 e⁻'s, yet it cannot have more than an octet.

1.25 Write electron-dot structures for the ionic compounds that also have covalent bonds: (a) K^+OH^-, (b) $Li^+NO_2^-$, (c) $H_3O^+Cl^-$, (d) $NH_4^+I^-$.

▮ Add an e⁻ for each − charge in the anion and subtract one for each + charge in the cation.

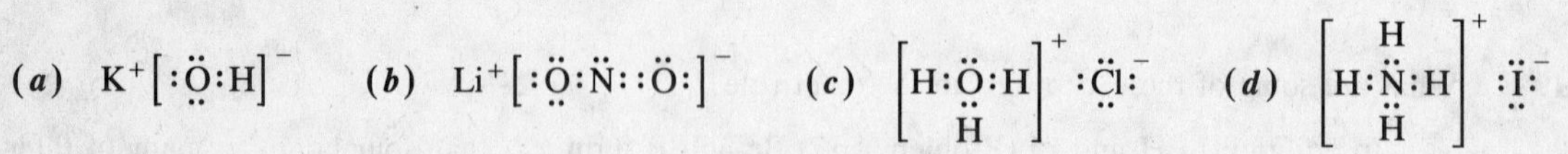

(a) K⁺[:Ö:H]⁻   (b) Li⁺[:Ö:N::Ö:]⁻   (c) [H:Ö:H with H below]⁺ :C̈l:⁻   (d) [H:N̈:H with H above and below]⁺ :Ï:⁻

1.26 Draw Lewis structures for (a) hydroxylamine, H_2NOH, (b) methanol, CH_3OH, (c) ClNO, (d) HOCN, and (e) CH_3NH_2.

▮ In Lewis structures a dash represents a shared electron-pair. Unshared outer shell (valence) e⁻'s are also shown.

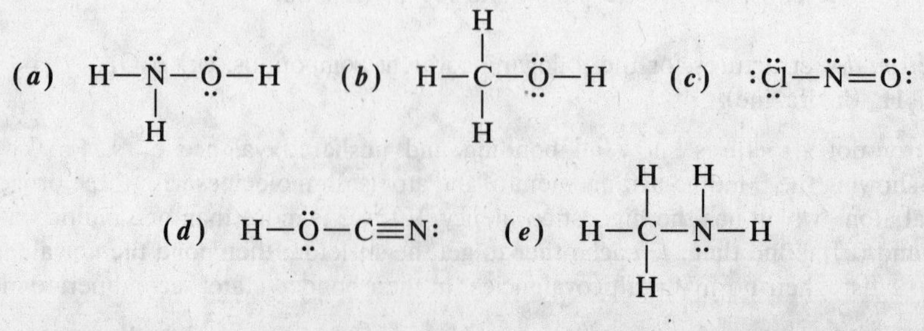

(a) H—N̈—Ö—H with H below   (b) H—C̈—Ö—H with H above and below   (c) :C̈l—N̈=Ö:

(d) H—Ö—C≡N: (e) H—C—N̈—H with H H above and H below

1.27 Determine the positive or negative charge, if any, on:

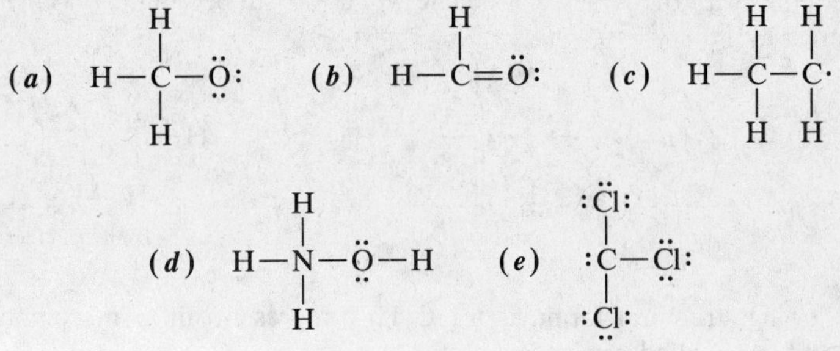

(*a*) H—C(H)(H)—Ö: (*b*) H—C(H)=Ö: (*c*) H—C(H)(H)—C·(H)(H)

(*d*) H—N(H)(H)—Ö—H   (*e*) :C(:Cl:)(:Cl:)—Cl:

▮ The charge on a species is numerically equal to the total number of valence electrons of the unbonded atoms, minus the total number of electrons shown (as bonds or dots) in the Lewis structure.

(*a*) The sum of the valence electrons (six for O, four for C, and three for three H's) is 13. The electron-dot formula shows 14 e⁻'s. The net charge is $13 - 14 = -1$ and the species is the methoxide anion, $CH_3\ddot{O}:^-$.

(*b*) There is no charge on the formaldehyde molecule, because the 12 e⁻'s in the structure equals the number of valence electrons; i.e., six for O, four for C, and two for H's.

(*c*) This species is neutral, because there are 13 e⁻'s shown in the formula and 13 valence electrons: eight from two C's and five from five H's.

(*d*) There are 15 valence electrons: six from O, five from N, and four from four H's. The Lewis dot structure shows 14 e⁻'s. It has a charge of $15 - 14 = +1$ and is the hydroxylammonium cation, $[H_3NOH]^+$.

(*e*) There are 25 valence electrons, 21 from three Cl's and four from C. The Lewis dot formula shows 26 e⁻'s. It has a charge of $25 - 26 = -1$ and is the trichloromethide anion, CCl_3^-.

1.28 Give Lewis structures for: (*a*) BrF_3, (*b*) PCl_5, (*c*) SF_6, (*d*) XeF_4, and (*e*) I_3^-.

▮ In these molecules the central atom is surrounded by more than eight e⁻'s. This *octet expansion* requires *d* orbitals, and is therefore only possible for elements below the second period. To determine the number of electron pairs in the valence shell of the central atom, add the number of e⁻'s contributed by it (its group number) to one e⁻ for each covalent bond and divide by 2. For anions, add the negative charge as well.

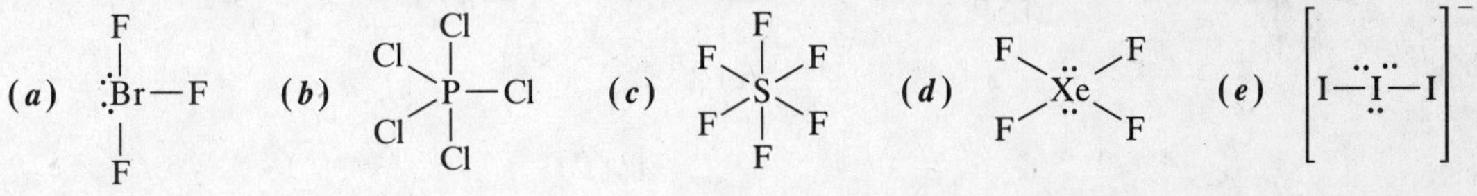

(*a*) :Br—F (with F above and F below)   (*b*) Cl, Cl / P—Cl, with Cl above and Cl below   (*c*) F, F, F, F, F, F around S   (*d*) F, F, F, F around Xe   (*e*) [I—I—I]⁻

The number of e⁻ pairs are: (*a*) $(7 + 3)/2 = 5$; (*b*) $(5 + 5)/2 = 5$; (*c*) $(6 + 6)/2 = 6$; (*d*) $(8 + 4)/2 = 6$; (*e*) $(7 + 2 + 1)/2 = 5$. (The three unshared pairs of e⁻'s on univalent halogens are omitted.)

STRUCTURAL FORMULAS AND ISOMERS

1.29 Write structural formulas for: (*a*) HOCl, (*b*) CH_3Br, (*c*) HONO, and (*d*) ClCN.

▮ Structural formulas omit the outer unshared e⁻'s of Lewis structures.

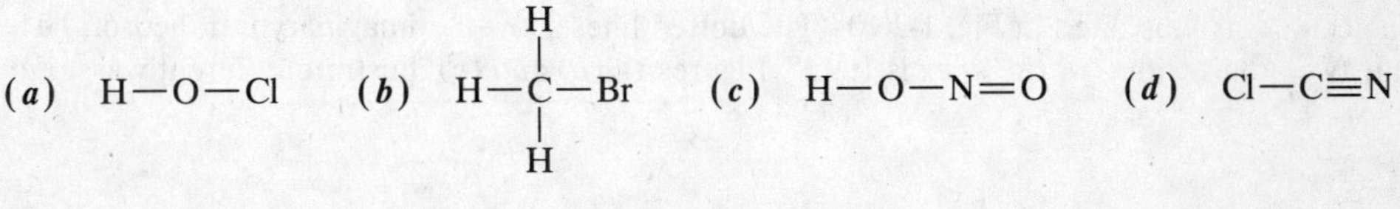

(*a*) H—O—Cl   (*b*) H—C(H)(H)—Br   (*c*) H—O—N=O   (*d*) Cl—C≡N

1.30 (*a*) Write two structures with the molecular formula CHNO. (*b*) What are these structures called?

▮ (*a*) Two structural formulas can be written with different skeletons corresponding to the compounds: H—O—C≡N (cyanic acid) and H—N=C=O (isocyanic acid). (*b*) Different compounds with the same molecular formulas are called *isomers*. Because in this case they differ in the order of arrangement of the atoms, they are *structural isomers*. They can be interconverted only by breaking bonds and forming new ones to other atoms.

1.31   Write two isomeric structures with the molecular formula C_2H_6O.

▮   The three atoms with the largest covalencies (C, C, O) can be bonded to each other in two ways, resulting in the two structures:

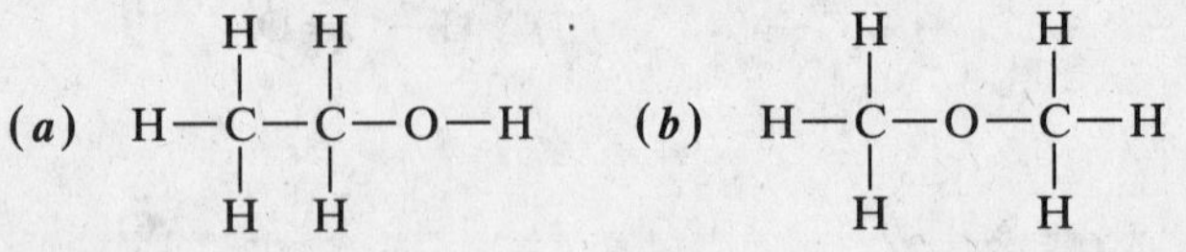

(*a*)   H—C—C—O—H   (*b*)   H—C—O—C—H

Ethyl alcohol   Dimethyl ether

1.32   (*a*) Do the following structural formulas for C_2H_5F represent different compounds? Explain.   (*b*) Illustrate your answer with the so-called *sawhorse* structures.

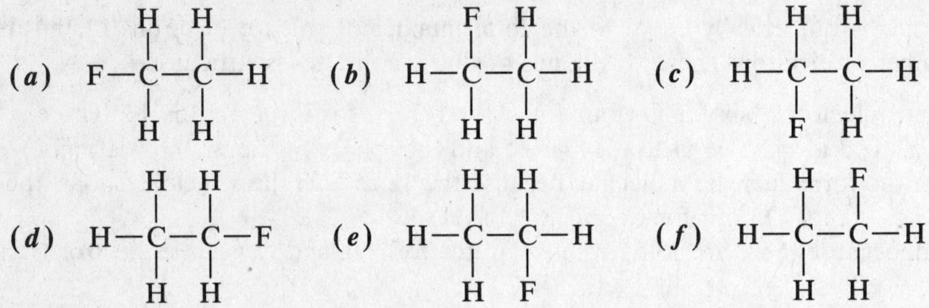

(*a*)   F—C—C—H   (*b*)   H—C—C—H   (*c*)   H—C—C—H

(*d*)   H—C—C—F   (*e*)   H—C—C—H   (*f*)   H—C—C—H

▮   No. There is only *one* compound C_2H_5F. Rotation about the C—C single bond brings the F to the different positions depicted in (*a*)–(*c*), and structures (*d*)–(*f*) are arrived at by turning structures (*a*)–(*c*) through 180° in the plane of the paper.   (*b*) See Fig. 1-1. In the three-dimensional *sawhorse (wedge) structure* a dotted line is a bond projecting below the plane of the paper and away from the viewer, and a darkened wedge is a bond projecting above the plane and toward the viewer. By rotating about the C—C bond, structures (*a*)–(*f*) appear.

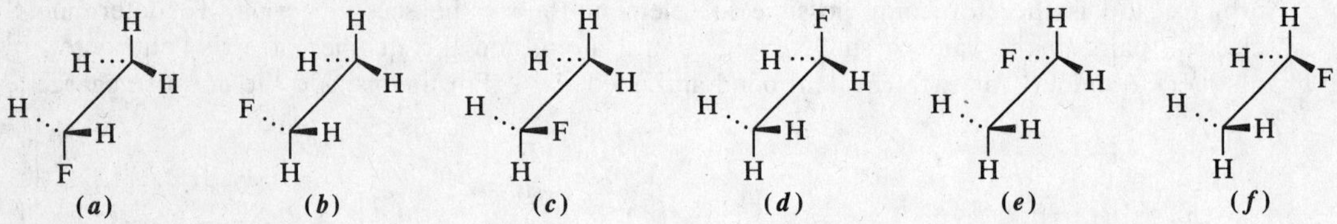

(*a*)   (*b*)   (*c*)   (*d*)   (*e*)   (*f*)

Fig. 1-1

1.33   Which, if any, of the structures (*a*)–(*d*) are isomers?

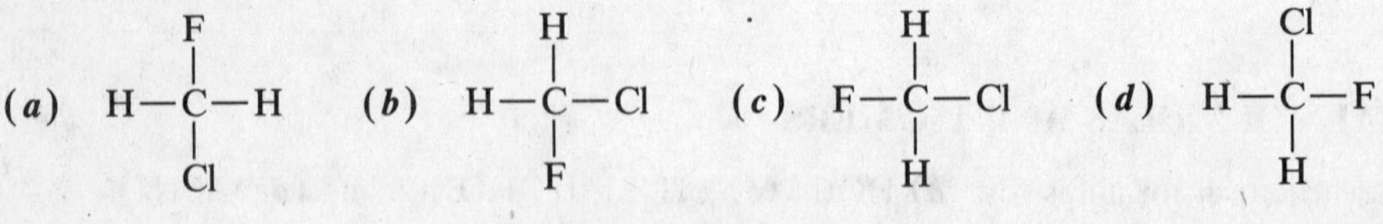

(*a*)   H—C—H   (*b*)   H—C—Cl   (*c*)   F—C—Cl   (*d*)   H—C—F

▮   None. They are all two-dimensional representations of one compound which is three-dimensional. The four single bonds of C are directed away from each other towards the corners of an imaginary tetrahedron, with C in the center, as illustrated in Fig. 1-2(*a*). (The dotted lines show the imaginary tetrahedron.) The angles separating any two atoms with C at the apex is 109.5°. Figures 1-2(*b*) and (*c*) illustrate different ways of depicting the spatial

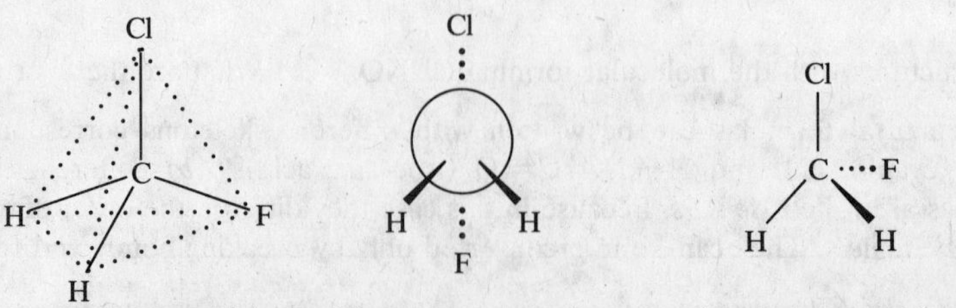

(*a*) Tetrahedron   (*b*) Newman projection   (*c*) Wedge projection   **Fig. 1-2**

relationship about a *tetrahedral* C. Structures (*a*)–(*d*) *appear* to be different; they do not accurately represent the space-filling molecule.

1.34   Which of the following represent the two isomers of $C_2H_4F_2$?

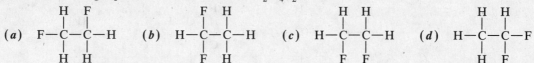

(*a*)   F—C—C—H   (*b*)   H—C—C—H   (*c*)   H—C—C—H   (*d*)   H—C—C—F

� Structures (*a*) and (*c*) represent one isomer (**A**), with an F on each C while (*b*) and (*d*) represent a second isomer (**B**) with both F's on the same C.

1.35   Explain how the introduction of a third F to form $C_2H_3F_3$ can help establish the structures of the two isomers in Problem 1.34.

▰ **A** affords *one* trifluoro product while **B** gives *two* trifluorides. The products from this *substitution method* also prove the structures of the two difluoro isomers inasmuch as these are predicted by deduction.

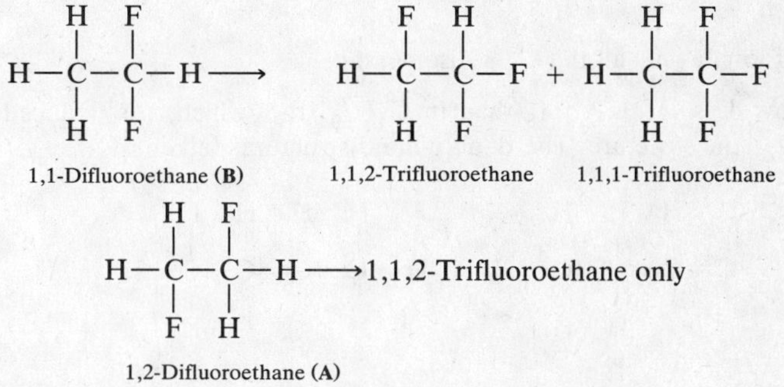

H—C—C—H ⟶   H—C—C—F + H—C—C—F

1,1-Difluoroethane (**B**)   1,1,2-Trifluoroethane   1,1,1-Trifluoroethane

H—C—C—H ⟶ 1,1,2-Trifluoroethane only

1,2-Difluoroethane (**A**)

1.36   Give structural formulas for the isomers of a compound $C_2H_2F_4$.

▰

F—C—C—F   F—C—C—F

1,1,1,2-Tetrafluoroethane (**C**)   1,1,2,2-Tetrafluoroethane (**D**)

1.37   Can the isomers in Problem 1.36 be distinguished by substituting (*a*) an F and (*b*) a Cl? Explain.

▰ (*a*)   No. Both isomers form the only possible pentafluoroethane, **E**, F—C—C—F.

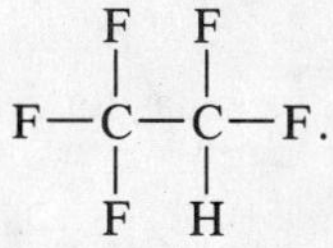

(*b*)   Yes, different compounds are formed as shown:

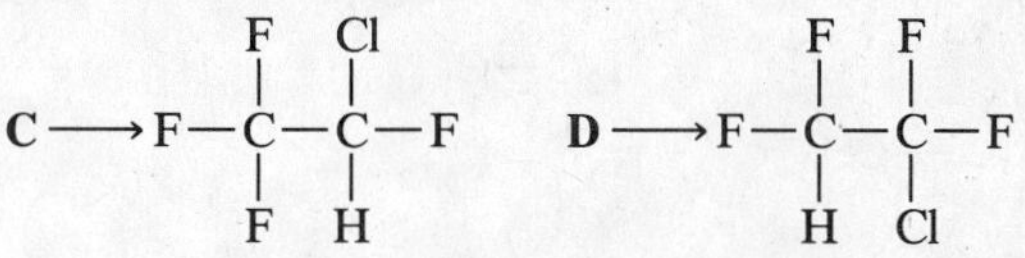

C ⟶ F—C—C—F   **D** ⟶ F—C—C—F

1.38   Derive all structural formulas for the isomers of (*a*) C_3H_8, (*b*) C_4H_{10}, and (*c*) C_5H_{12}.

▰ (*a*)   There is only one possible structure: H—C—C—C—H.

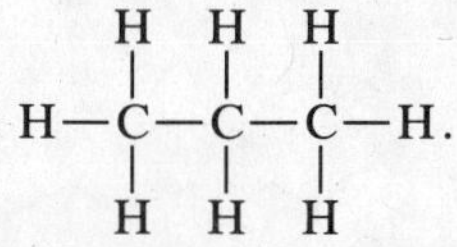

(*b*)   The four C's can lie in a straight (unbranched) or branched chain.

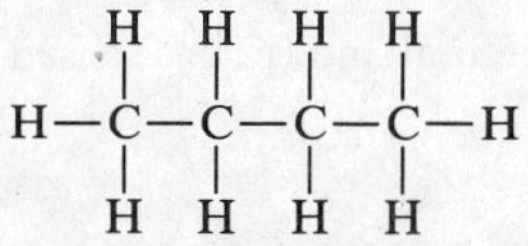

H—C—C—C—C—H

n-Butane

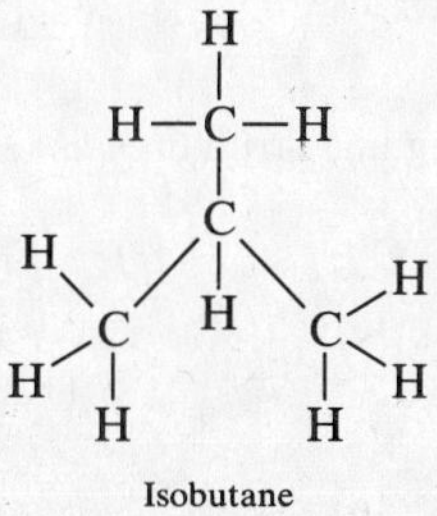

Isobutane

(*c*) The three isomers of pentane are:

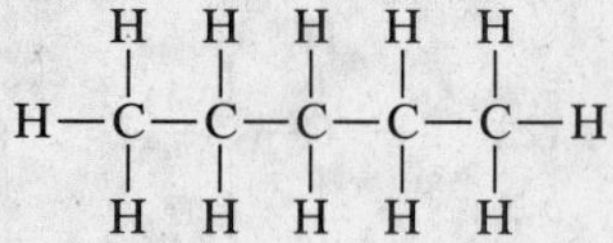

n-Pentane 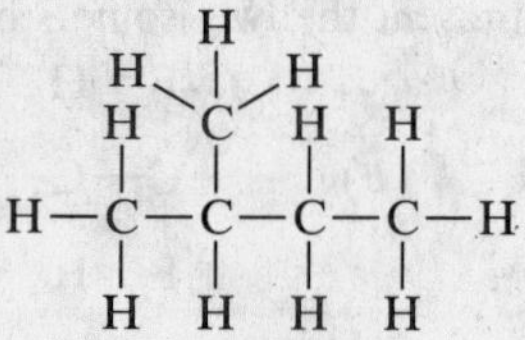   Isopentane 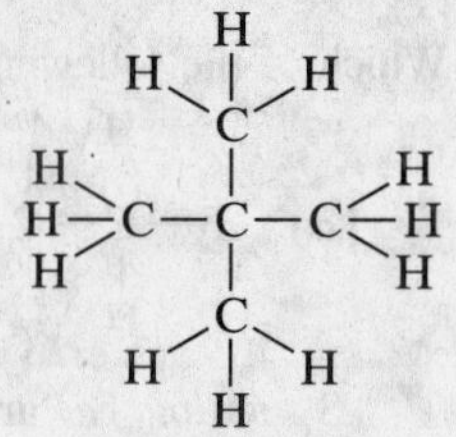   Neopentane

1.39 Write *condensed* structural formulas for the pentane isomers in Problem 1.38*c*.

▮ In condensed structural formulas parentheses are used for identical groups of atoms. *n*-Pentane, $CH_3(CH_2)_3CH_3$; isopentane $(CH_3)_2CHCH_2CH_3$; neopentane$(CH_3)_4C$.

1.40 Write structural formulas for all the C_4H_8 isomers.

▮ There are two less H's in C_4H_8 than in C_4H_{10} from which it is deduced that the isomers have either a double bond or a cyclic structure. The double bond structures (alkenes) are:

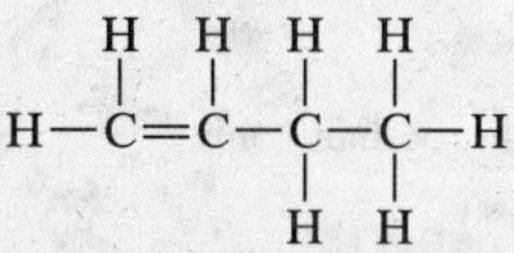

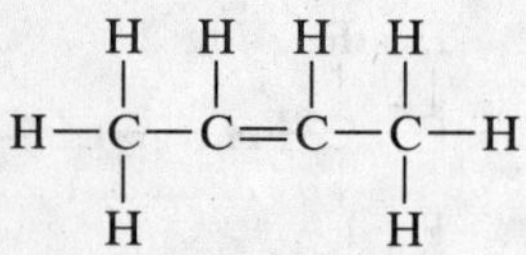

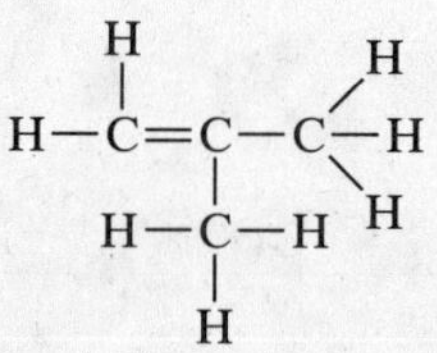

Two cyclic structures are possible: one is a four-C ring and the other is a three-C ring with an attached fourth C.

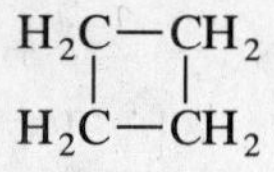

Cyclobutane 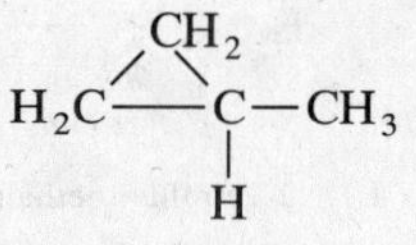   Methylcyclopropane

1.41 Give structural formulas for cyclic compounds having the molecular formula C_5H_{10}.

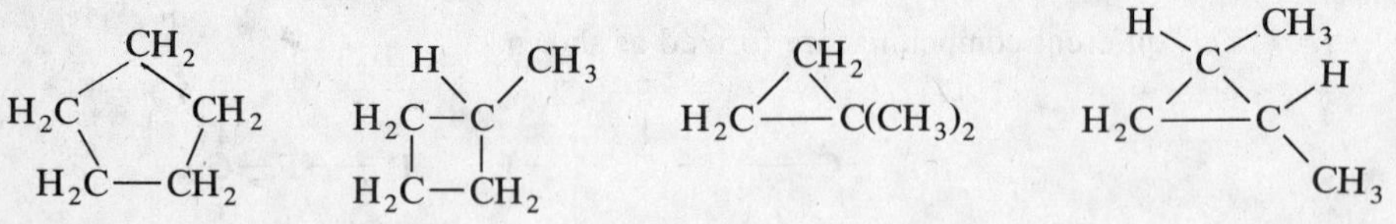

1.42 Draw simplified line or *carbon skeleton* structures for the compounds in Problems 1.38(*b*), 1.38(*c*), and 1.41.

▮ Problem 1.38(*b*):

Problem 1.38(*c*):

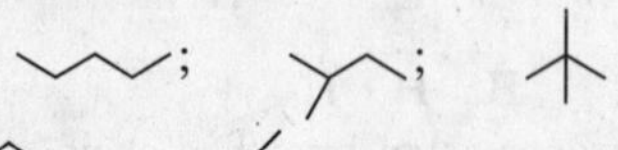

Problem 1.41:

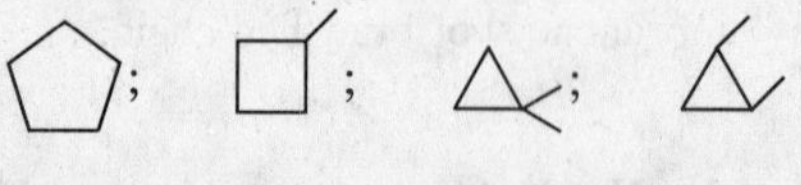

1.43 Write the following line structures as (i) structural and (ii) condensed structural formulas.

(*a*) HO   (*b*)   (*c*) H_2N

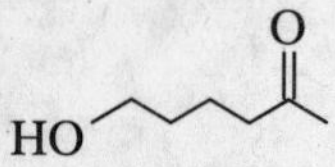

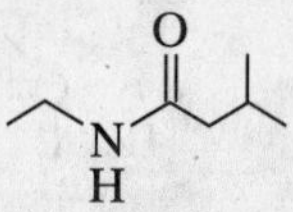

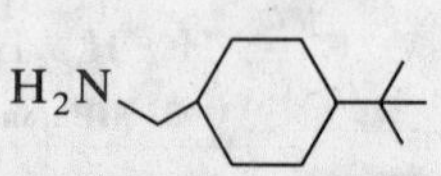

(a) (i)

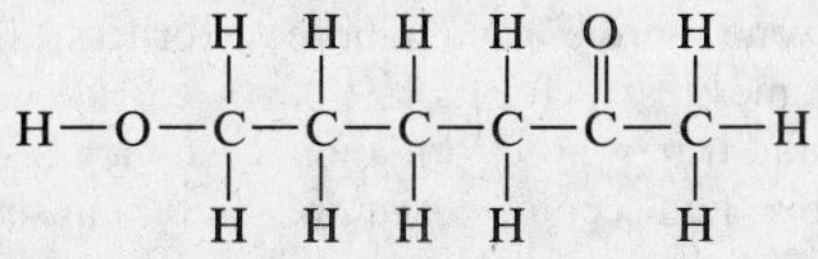

(ii) $HO(CH_2)_4COCH_3$

(b) (i)

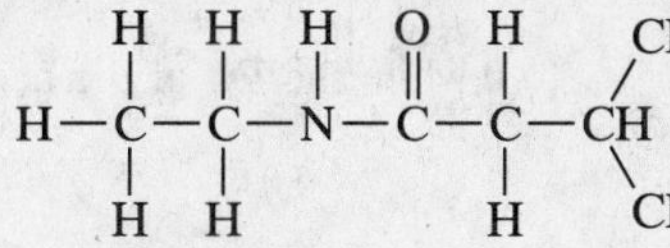

(ii) $CH_3CH_2NHCOCH_2CH(CH_3)_2$

(c) (i)

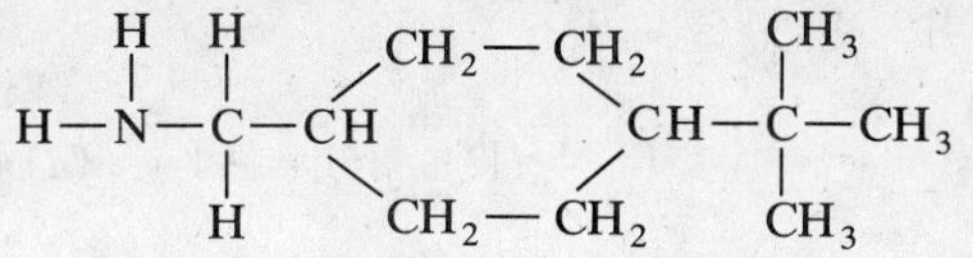

(ii)

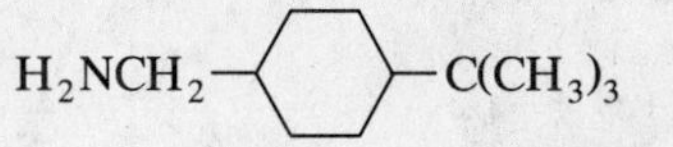

1.44 Explain why the following electron-dot structures are incorrect and write the correct structures: (a) $H\!:\!:\!\ddot{C}l\!:$, (b) $:C\!:\!:\!\ddot{O}\!:$, (c) $:N\!:\!:\!N\!:$, (d) $:\ddot{B}r\!:\!:\!\ddot{N}\!:\!:\!\ddot{O}\!:$.

   (a) H has four e⁻'s which is two more than it can accommodate; $H\!:\!\ddot{C}l\!:$

   (b) The C shell is incomplete since it has only six e⁻s, $:C\!:\!:\!:O\!:$.

   (c) There should be 10 e⁻s, five from each N; $:N\!:\!:\!:N\!:$.

   (d) N has 10 e⁻s, two more than required; $:\ddot{B}r\!:\!\ddot{N}\!:\!:\!\ddot{O}\!:$.

FORMAL CHARGE

1.45 (a) How is the *formal charge* on a covalently bonded atom determined? (b) How do formal charges differ from actual charges?

   (a) The formal charge (FC) is equal to the number of valence e⁻'s in the unbonded atom (its group number in the periodic table, G) minus the number of e⁻'s assigned to the atom in its bonded state. We presume that bonded e⁻'s are equally shared so that the assigned number is all the unshared e⁻'s plus one half the number of shared e⁻'s.

$$FC = G - \left[\text{unshared e}^-\text{'s} + \tfrac{1}{2}\text{ shared e}^-\text{'s}\right]$$

   The sum of the formal charges on all atoms in a molecule or ion equals the charge on the species.

   (b) Although called charges, they are *not* actual charges like those on an electron or ion. They are artificial charges based on an assumed, not actual, way or assigning e⁻'s.

1.46 Determine the formal charges on each atom in: (a) $H\!:\!O\!:\!Cl$, (b) NH_4^+, and (c) $H_2O\!:\!BF_3$.

   (a) $H = 1 - [0 + \tfrac{1}{2}(2)] = 1 - 1 = 0$; $O = 6 - [4 + \tfrac{1}{2}(4)] = 6 - 6 = 0$; $Cl = 7 - [6 + \tfrac{1}{2}(2)] = 0$.

   (b) Each $H = 1 - [0 + \tfrac{1}{2}(2)] = 0$; $N = 5 - [0 + \tfrac{1}{2}(8)] = +1$ (equal to charge on ion).

   (c) Each $H = 0$; $O = 6 - [2 + \tfrac{1}{2}(6)] = +1$; $B = 3 - [0 + \tfrac{1}{2}(8)] = -1$ (total FC = 0).

1.47 (a) Provide an isomeric Lewis structure for hydroxylamine [Problem 1.26(a)]. (b) How can it be determined which structure is more stable, lacking any other data?

   (a) Rearrange the skeleton and give the formal charges:

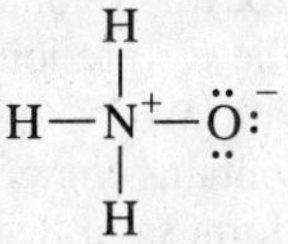

   (b) The most stable structure maximizes the number of atoms with normal covalencies. It will also have the least (or no) formal charge. Therefore the structure in Problem 1.26(a) is the more stable structure.

1.48 Explain the relationship of (a) normal covalency and formal charge of an atom, (b) coordinate covalent bonding and normal covalencies, and (c) coordinate covalent bonding and formal charge using (i) $H_3N\!-\!BF_3$ and (ii) $AlCl_4^-$ as examples.

   (a) Atoms showing their normal covalency have zero FC.

   (b) When atoms form coordinate covalent bonds they no longer have their normal covalencies.

(*c*) The acceptor atom is assumed to acquire one more e⁻ and a more − (or less +) FC. The donor atom is assumed to lose an e⁻ and its FC becomes less − (or more +).

   (i) N—B is a coordinate covalent bond during whose formation the donor N loses an e⁻ causing its FC to go from 0 to +1. Concurrently, the acceptor B acquires an e⁻ causing its FC to go from 0 to −1. Note the total charge is 0.

   (ii) The FC of the donor ion :$\ddot{\text{Cl}}$:⁻ goes from −1 to 0 while the FC of the acceptor Al goes from 0 to −1. The total charge from adding all FC's = −1.

1.49 Calculate the formal charge on C in: (*a*) a carbene, H_2C: ; (*b*) a carbocation, H_3C^+; (*c*) a carbanion, H_3C:⁻; (*d*) a radical, $H_3C\cdot$.

▮ (*a*) $4 - [2 + \frac{1}{2}(4)] = 0$ (*b*) $4 - [0 + \frac{1}{2}(6)] = +1$ (*c*) $4 - [2 + \frac{1}{2}(6)] = -1$ (*d*) $4 - [1 + \frac{1}{2}(6)] = 0$

1.50 Write Lewis structures with FC's for: (*a*) nitric acid, $HONO_2$; (*b*) sulfuric acid, $HOSO_2OH$.

▮ (*a*) H—O—N⁺=$\ddot{\text{O}}$: with :$\ddot{\text{O}}$:⁻ above N   (*b*) H—O—S²⁺—O—H with :$\ddot{\text{O}}$:⁻ above S and :$\ddot{\text{O}}$:⁻ below S

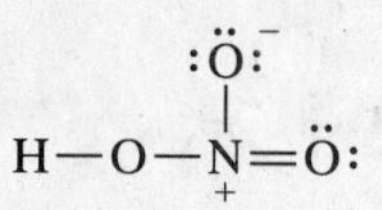

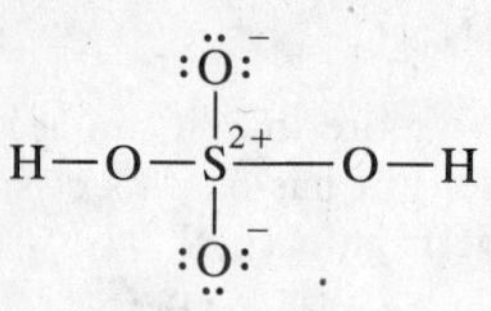

1.51 (*a*) Write a Lewis structure for sulfuric acid in which there are no formal charges.
(*b*) Why is it not possible to do this for nitric acid?

▮ (*a*) H—O—S—O—H with :O: double-bonded above S and :O: double-bonded below S

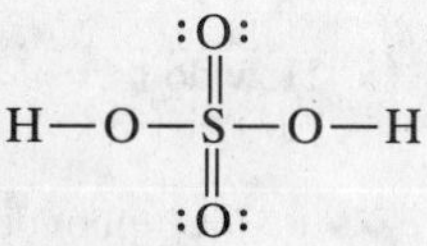

(*b*) S, a third period element, can expand its octet, accommodating more than eight e⁻'s. N, in the second period, has no *d* orbitals available and is limited to an octet.

1.52 With the aid of formal charges, determine which Lewis structure is more likely to be correct for each of the following molecules:

(*a*) Cl_2O: :$\ddot{\text{O}}$—$\ddot{\text{Cl}}$—$\ddot{\text{Cl}}$: *or* :$\ddot{\text{Cl}}$—$\ddot{\text{O}}$—$\ddot{\text{Cl}}$:   (*b*) N_2O: :N≡N⁺—$\ddot{\text{O}}$:⁻ *or* :$\ddot{\text{N}}$⁻=O⁺²=$\ddot{\text{N}}$:⁻ .

▮ (*a*) The first structure has FC's of −1 on O and +1 on the central Cl; the second structure, with no FC's is preferred.   (*b*) The second structure with *both* N's having a FC of −1 and O having a FC of +2 is unlikely. The first structure has less FC, the central N has a FC of +1 and O a FC of −1).

FUNCTIONAL GROUPS AND HOMOLOGOUS SERIES

1.53 Define the following terms: (*a*) *saturated* hydrocarbon and (*b*) *unsaturated* hydrocarbon.

▮ (*a*) A saturated hydrocarbon contains only C and H and all C—C bonds are single. In *alkanes* the C skeleton is open-chain; if the C's are joined to form a ring, it is called a *cycloalkane*. They are "saturated" with hydrogen, meaning that with a very few exceptions they do not undergo a reaction with hydrogen.   (*b*) An unsaturated hydrocarbon contains one or more C=C or C≡C bonds, which under proper conditions undergo a reaction with hydrogen to form saturated hydrocarbons.

1.54 (*a*) What is a *homologous series*?   (*b*) Give the general formula for the alkane homologous series.   (*c*) Give the molecular formulas for the first three members of the alkane series.

▮ (*a*) A series of compounds that can be represented by a general formula.   (*b*) The general formula is C_nH_{2n+2}.   (*c*) CH_4, C_2H_6, C_3H_8.

1.55 (*a*) Define a *functional group*.   (*b*) Why are functional groups important in organic chemistry?

▮ (*a*) A functional group is an atom or group of atoms in a compound that determines its chemical properties and in most cases is one of the sites of its chemical reactions.   (*b*) Organic compounds, while large in number, are classified into a relatively small number of categories whose properties are defined by their functional groups. Common functional groups are the double bond $\left(>C=C< \right)$, hydroxyl ($-OH$), and amine ($-NH_2$).

1.56 (*a*) How are molecules with a single functional group represented? (*b*) Write a general formula for: (i) an alkyl bromide, (ii) an alkyl alcohol, and (iii) an aromatic amine.

◢ (*a*) They are derived from a hydrocarbon by replacing one of its H atoms with a functional group. If the hydrocarbon is aliphatic, the rest of the molecule is an *alkyl group*, represented as R, and the molecule containing the functional group may be represented as RG. If the hydrocarbon is aromatic, the rest of the molecule is an *aryl* group, represented as Ar, and we abbreviate the whole molecule by ArG. (*b*) (i) RBr, (ii) ROH, and (iii) $ArNH_2$.

1.57 How do the compounds in a homologous series differ in (*a*) molecular formulas, (*b*) chemical properties, and (*c*) physical properties?

◢ (*a*) They differ by the number of CH_2 groups. (*b*) They undergo similar reactions whose rates depend on the size of the R group and shape of the molecule. (*c*) For compounds with similar carbon chains there is a regular change in physical properties such as an increase in boiling points or, in some cases, a decrease in water solubility.

1.58 (*a*) Give the structural formula for a three-carbon compound containing each of the following functional groups: (i) $>C=C<$, (ii) $-Cl$, (iii) $-C\equiv C-$, (iv) $-OH$, (v) $-O-$, (vi) $-\underset{H}{C}=O$, (vii) $-\overset{|}{C}=O$, and (viii) $-C\equiv N$. Give all isomers. (*b*) Name each functional group.

◢ (*a*) (i) $CH_3CH=CH_2$

(ii) $CH_3CH_2CH_2Cl$, $CH_3\underset{Cl}{\overset{|}{C}H}CH_3$

(iii) $CH_3C\equiv CH$

(iv) $CH_3CH_2CH_2OH$, $CH_3\underset{OH}{\overset{|}{C}H}CH_3$

(v) $CH_3CH_2OCH_3$

(vi) $CH_3CH_2\underset{H}{\overset{|}{C}}=O$

(vii) $CH_3\overset{\overset{O}{\|}}{C}CH_3$

(viii) $CH_3CH_2C\equiv N$

(*b*) (i) Alkene, (ii) alkyl chloride, (iii) alkyne, (iv) alcohol, (v) ether, (vi) aldehyde, (vii) ketone, and (viii) nitrile.

1.59 (*a*) Write the structure for a 3-C carboxylic acid. (*b*) Show structures for the following derivatives of this acid: (i) an ester, (ii) an acid chloride, and (iii) an amide.

◢ (*a*) $CH_3CH_2\overset{\overset{O}{\|}}{C}OH$ (*b*) (i) $CH_3CH_2\overset{\overset{O}{\|}}{C}OR$ where R is an alkyl group, (ii) $CH_3CH_2\overset{\overset{O}{\|}}{C}Cl$, and (iii) $CH_3CH_2\overset{\overset{O}{\|}}{C}NH_2$.

1.60 Write structures for the four isomeric amines with the formula C_3H_9N. Classify the functional group in each case.

◢ (i) $CH_3CH_2CH_2NH_2$ (ii) $(CH_3)_2CHNH_2$ (iii) $CH_3CH_2NHCH_3$ (iv) $(CH_3)_3N$

    1° amine ($-NH_2$)   1° amine ($-NH_2$)   2° amine ($-NH$)   3° amine ($-N$)

The three-C alkyl group can be unbranched (i) or branched (ii). The three C's can be attached to the N as part of one (primary, 1°), two (secondary, 2°), or three (tertiary, 3°) alkyl groups.

1.61 Provide a structural formula for the compound with the smallest number of C's that is (*a*) a cyclic alcohol, (*b*) an amide, (*c*) a cyclic ether, and (*d*) an alkenylcarboxylic acid.

◢ (*a*) [cyclopropanol structure with H and OH] (*b*) $H\overset{\overset{O}{\|}}{C}NH_2$ (*c*) $H_2C\overset{O}{\overset{\diagdown \diagup}{-}}CH_2$ (*d*) $H_2C=CH\overset{\overset{O}{\|}}{C}OH$

1.62   Identify the functional groups in Norethindrone, a synthetic derivative of progesterone.

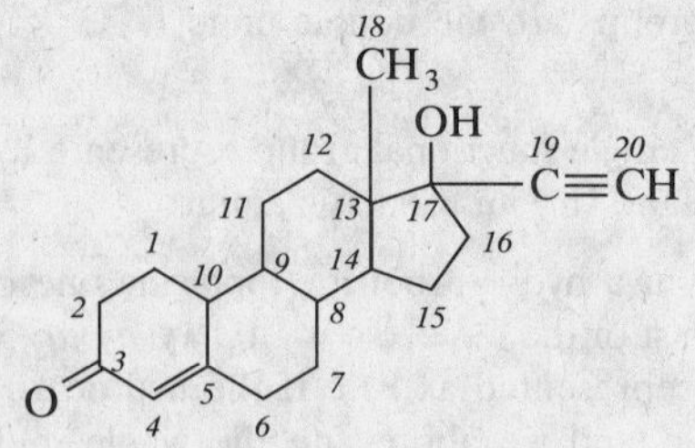

   ▰   A ketone at C^3, a double bond (alkene) at C^4 to C^5, an alcohol at C^{17}, and a triple bond (alkyne) attached at C^{17}.

1.63   (*a*) Name and give a general formula for the sulfur analogs of (i) alcohols, (ii) ethers, and (iii) peroxides, ROOR. (*b*) Give the names and general formulas for compounds in which P replaces N of amines.

   ▰   (*a*) The prefix *thio* usually but not always indicates the presence of S. (i) Thioalcohol, RSH; (ii) thioether, RSR; and (iii) disulfide, RSSR.   (*b*) Phosphines, RPH_2, R_2PH, and R_3P.

CALCULATIONS

1.64   Analysis of a compound **A** gives 92.25% C and 7.743% H. Calculate (*a*) its empirical formula and (*b*) its molecular formula. The molecular weight (MW) is determined to be 78.11 g/mol.

   ▰   (*a*)   Divide the % of each element by its atomic weight to give the mass ratio. Convert to the simplest whole number ratio to get the empirical formula.

$$C: 92.25 \div 12.01 \text{ g/mol} = 7.68 \text{ mol/g}   \qquad H: 7.743 \div 1.008 \text{ g/mol} = 7.68 \text{ mol/g}.$$

   The mass ratio is 1:1 and the empirical formula is (C_1H_1).
   (*b*)   The sum of the atomic weights in the empirical formula is 13.02. One molecular formula contains $78.11 \div 13.02 = 6$ (CH) units, or $(CH)_6$. The molecular formula is C_6H_6.

1.65   (*a*) Find the empirical formula of a compound whose analysis is 48.63% C, 8.18% H.   (*b*) What is the molecular formula if the MW is (i) 74.1 and (ii) 222.3?

   ▰   (*a*)   If the sum of the elements' percentages is significantly less than 100%, the difference is taken to be % oxygen. In this example, O = 43.19%. To simplify, units are omitted. Dividing each % by the atomic weight gives

$$C: 48.63 \div 12.01 = 4.05; \qquad H: 8.18 \div 1.01 = 8.10; \qquad O: 43.19 \div 16.00 = 2.70$$

   To get the ratio, divide by the smallest number (2.70):

$$C: 4.05 \div 2.70 = 1.5; \qquad H: 8.10 \div 2.70 = 2.99 \text{ (or 3)}; \qquad O: 2.70 \div 2.70 = 1$$

   The ratio of 1.5:3:1 is multiplied by 2 to get the smallest whole number ratio of atoms, giving 3:6:2, and an empirical formula of $C_3H_6O_2$.
   (*b*)   (i) Since the sum of the gram atomic weights (AW) from the empirical formula $C_3H_6O_2$ is 74, this is also the molecular formula. (ii) The MW of 222 contains $222 \div 74 = 3$ units of $C_3H_6O_2$. The molecular formula is $C_9H_{18}O_6$.

1.66   How are molecular weights determined experimentally?

   ▰   From freezing point depressions, boiling point elevations, vapor density measurements, and osmotic pressure measurements (for substances with high molecular weights). Today, most molecular weights are determined through *mass spectrometry* (see Chapter 12).

1.67   An 11.75-g sample of a hydrocarbon is volatilized at 1-atm pressure and 100 °C to a gas that occupies 5.0 L. What is its MW? ($R = 0.0821$ L · atm/mol · K)

   ▰   The ideal gas law, $PV = nRT$ is used, where $n = g/MW$ and $MW = g\ RT/PV$.

$$MW = \frac{(11.75 \text{ g})(0.0821 \text{ L} \cdot \text{atm/mol} \cdot \text{K})(373 \text{ K})}{(1 \text{ atm})(5.0 \text{ L})} = 72 \text{ g/mol}$$

Since the hydrocarbon contains only C and H, the maximum number of C's possible in a MW of 72 is five $(5 \times 12 = 60)$; the remainder of the molecule is 12 H's, or C_5H_{12}.

1.68 Complete combustion of 0.858 g of compound **X** gives 2.63 g of CO_2 and 1.28 g of H_2O. (*a*) Find the % composition of **X**. (*b*) What is the lowest MW it can have?

    (*a*) The mass of C in 2.63 g of CO_2 from the sample is

$$\frac{\text{AW of C}}{\text{MW of } CO_2} \times \text{mass of } CO_2 = \frac{12.01 \text{ g C/mol}}{44.01 \text{ g } CO_2/\text{mol}}(2.63 \text{ g } CO_2) = 0.718 \text{ g C}$$

which is $\dfrac{0.718 \text{ g C}}{0.858 \text{ g X}}(100\%) = 83.7\%$ of **X**.

The mass of H in 1.28 g of H_2O from the sample is

$$\frac{\text{AW of H}}{\text{MW of } H_2O} \times \text{mass of } H_2O = \frac{2.016 \text{ g H/mol}}{18.02 \text{ g } H_2O/\text{mol}}(1.28 \text{ g H}) = 0.143 \text{ g H}$$

which is 16.7% of **X**.

Since the sum of C and H %'s is 100.4%, O is absent.

    (*b*) C: $83.7 \div 12.01 = 6.97$; $6.97 \div 6.97 = 1$ H: $16.7 \div 1.01 = 16.5$; $16.5 \div 6.97 = 2.37$

Multiplying $1:2.37$ by 3 gives a ratio of $3.00:7.11$ and, if we round off, the empirical formula seems to be C_3H_7. But this formula doesn't fit any Lewis structure for a hydrocarbon, C_nH_{2n+2} (try it); a hydrocarbon cannot have an odd number of H's. The formula is thus C_6H_{14} and the MW is 86 g/mol.

1.69 The molal freezing point depression constant for camphor as a solvent is 40 °C kg/mol. Pure camphor melts at 179 °C. When 0.108 g of compound **A** is dissolved in 0.90 g of camphor, the solution melts at 166 °C. Find the molecular weight of **A**.

    Raoult's law gives the molality as

$$m = \frac{\Delta T_f}{K_{f.p.}} = \frac{179 \text{ °C} - 166 \text{ °C}}{40 \text{ °C} \cdot \text{kg/mol}} = 0.325 \text{ mol/kg}$$

0.325 mol of **A** is dissolved in 1 kg of camphor. Now, 0.108 g of **A** in 0.90 g camphor is the same concentration as 120 g of **A** in 1000 g camphor. Therefore, 120 g of **A** is 0.325 mol, and so the mass of one mole of **A** is

$$\frac{120 \text{ g}}{0.325 \text{ mol}} = 369 \text{ g/mol}$$

1.70 In a nitration of benzene, 10.0 g of benzene gave 13.2 g of nitrobenzene. (*a*) What is the *theoretical yield* of nitrobenzene? (*b*) What is the *percentage yield*?

    A balanced equation must be written first: $C_6H_6 + HNO_3 \xrightarrow{H_2SO_4} C_6H_5NO_2 + H_2O$.

(*a*) The equation shows that one mole of benzene (MW = 78 g/mol) would give one mole of nitrobenzene (MW = 123 g/mol) if the yield were 100% (the theoretical yield in %). Starting with 10.0 g of benzene, a 100% yield would be 10.0 g $\div$ 78.0 g/mol of nitrobenzene (0.128 mol), which is (10/78 mol)(123 g/mol) = 15.8 g of nitrobenzene, the theoretical yield in grams.

(*b*) The actual yield is 13.2 g, and the percentage yield = 13.2 g/15.8 g (100%) = 83.5%.

1.71 Phenol and P_2S_5 react to form thiophenol, C_6H_5SH

$$5C_6H_5OH + P_2S_5 \longrightarrow 5C_6H_5SH + P_2O_5$$

If 23.5 g of phenol and 10 g of P_2S_5 are reacted, what is the theoretical weight of thiophenol (PhSH) obtained?

    The balanced equation shows that five moles of phenol ($5 \times$ MW = 470) reacts with one mole of P_2S_5 (MW = 222) to give five moles of PhSH ($5 \times$ MW = 550). The reaction mixture has 23.5 g (0.25 mol) phenol and 10 g (0.045 mol) of P_2S_5. The ratio of five moles C_6H_5OH to one mole P_2S_5 is used to show that 0.25 mole of phenol requires $(0.25)/5 = 0.050$ mol of P_2S_5 for complete reaction. Inasmuch as only 0.045 mole of P_2S_5 is reacted, phenol is present in excess. The theoretical yield is based on P_2S_5, the "limiting" reactant. The amount of PhSH formed from 0.045 mole of P_2S_5 is 5×0.045 mol = 0.225 mol, or 24.8 g.

SUPPLEMENTARY PROBLEMS

1.72 Write Lewis structures for the following: (*a*) $CH_3NH_3^+$, (*b*) HO_2^-, (*c*) $POCl_3$, (*d*) $(CH_3)_2OH^+$, and (*e*) CH_3OSO_3H.

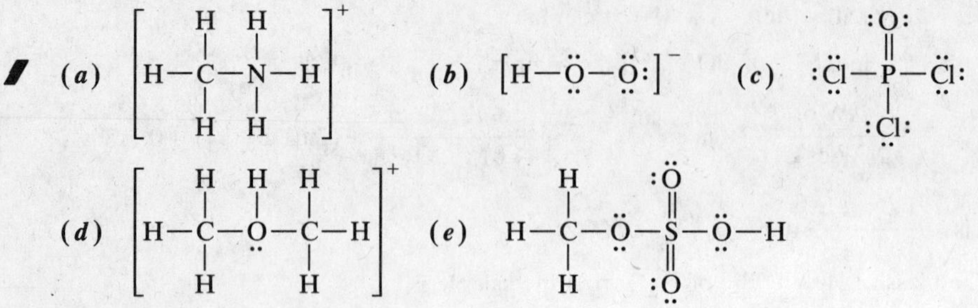

(*a*) $\left[\begin{array}{c} \text{H} \quad \text{H} \\ | \quad | \\ \text{H—C—N—H} \\ | \quad | \\ \text{H} \quad \text{H} \end{array} \right]^+$ (*b*) $\left[\text{H—Ö—Ö:} \right]^-$ (*c*) $\begin{array}{c} \text{:O:} \\ \| \\ \text{:Cl—P—Cl:} \\ | \\ \text{:Cl:} \end{array}$

(*d*) $\left[\begin{array}{c} \text{H} \quad \text{H} \quad \text{H} \\ | \quad | \quad | \\ \text{H—C—O—C—H} \\ | \quad | \quad | \\ \text{H} \quad \text{H} \end{array} \right]^+$ (*e*) $\begin{array}{c} \text{H} \quad \quad \text{:Ö} \\ | \quad \quad \| \\ \text{H—C—Ö—S—Ö—H} \\ | \quad \quad \| \\ \text{H} \quad \quad \text{:O:} \end{array}$

1.73 Find the formal charge on each atom in (*a*) CNO^-, (*b*) $H_2C{=}CH{-}\dot{C}H_2$, and (*c*) $H_2C{=}NH_2^+$.

First write each Lewis structure:

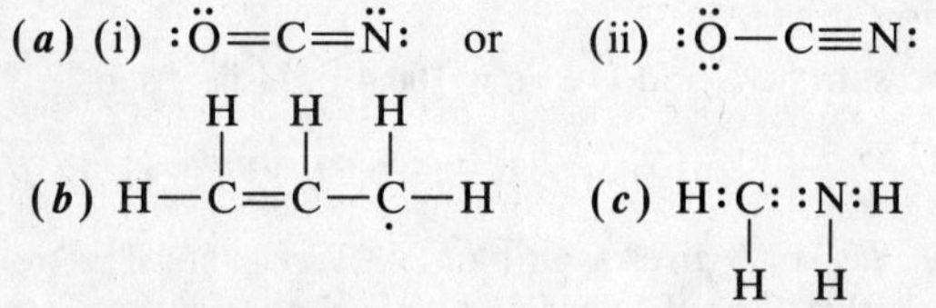

(*a*) (i) $:\ddot{O}{=}C{=}\dot{N}:$ or   (ii) $:\ddot{O}{-}C{\equiv}N:$

(*b*) $\begin{array}{c} \text{H} \quad \text{H} \quad \text{H} \\ | \quad | \quad | \\ \text{H—C=C—C—H} \\ \quad \quad \quad \cdot \end{array}$ (*c*) $\begin{array}{c} \text{H:C::N:H} \\ | \quad | \\ \text{H} \quad \text{H} \end{array}$

In (i) of (*a*) the FC on O and C are 0, and on N is −1. In (ii) O has a FC of −1, and C and N have FC's of 0. The decision as to which is the correct structure is discussed in 2.81. (*b*) None of the atoms have a FC. This species is a radical because the C with the odd e^- has only seven e^-'s. (*c*) N, with a covalency of four, has a FC of +1.

1.74 Provide simplified line structures for:

(*a*) $(CH_3)_2CHCH(OH)(CH_2)_2CH{=}O$ (*b*) $\begin{array}{c} \text{H}_2\text{C—CH}_2 \\ \diagup \quad \quad \diagdown \\ \text{O=C} \quad \quad \text{C(CH}_3)_2 \\ \diagdown \quad \quad \diagup \\ \text{HC=CH} \end{array}$

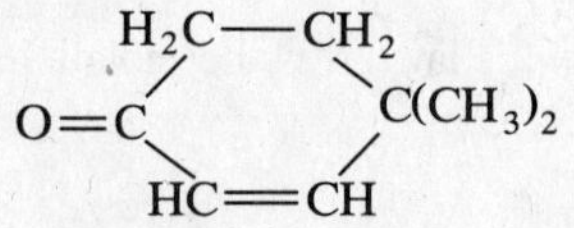

(*c*) $H_2C{=}C(CH_3)CH_2CH_2CH_2CONHCH_2CH(CH_3)_2$

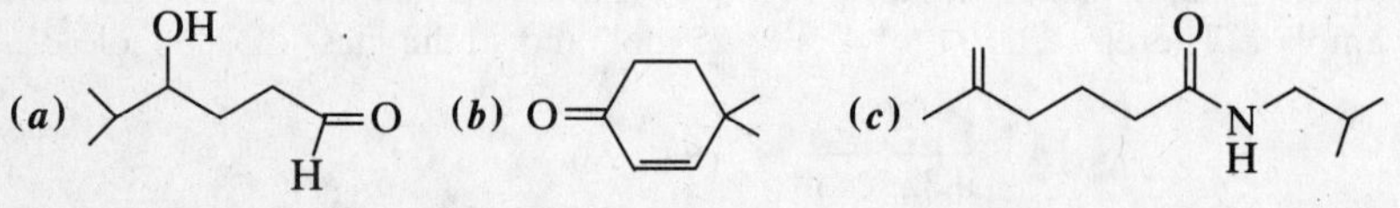

(*a*) [line structure with OH and =O, H]   (*b*) [cyclohexenone line structure]   (*c*) [line structure with O and N—H]

1.75 How many grams of cyclohexanol must be reacted to produce 20 g of cyclohexene, if the % yield is 54%? The equation is $C_6H_{11}OH \rightarrow C_6H_{10} + H_2O$.

One mole of cyclohexanol (MW = 100) would give one mole of cyclohexene (MW = 82) if the yield were 100%. The actual yield of cyclohexene in moles is 20 g/82 g·mol⁻¹ or 0.24 mol, which represents a 54% yield. The number of moles of cyclohexanol required to produce this amount of cyclohexene is thus 0.24 mol/0.54 = 0.44 mol; this is

$$0.44 \text{ mol}(100 \text{ g/mol}) = 44 \text{ g cyclohexanol}$$

1.76 What is the maximum amount of CH_3Cl that can be prepared from 20.0 g of CH_4 and 10.0 g of Cl_2 by the reaction $CH_4 + Cl_2 \rightarrow CH_3Cl + HCl$?

20.0 g of CH_4 is 1.25 moles and 10.0 g of Cl_2 is 0.141 mole, so Cl_2 is the limiting reactant. The reaction equation gives the molar ratio of $Cl_2 : CH_3Cl$ as 1:1. Thus the theoretical (maximum) yield is 0.141 mole of CH_3Cl, or

$$0.141 \text{ mol} \times 50.48 \text{ g/mol} = 7.12 \text{ g}$$

QUANTUM THEORY; ATOMIC ORBITALS

2.1   What is the main tenet of quantum theory concerning the energy of an electron that is (*a*) part or (*b*) free of an atom or molecule?

▟   (*a*) The energy of an electron in an atom or molecule is restricted to only certain fixed values; its energy is said to be *quantized*.   (*b*) An electron set free by ionization of an atom or molecule no longer has quantized energy levels; its energy is *continuous*.

2.2   Define the terms (*a*) ground state and (*b*) excited state.

▟   (*a*) The lowest energy state of a confined electron (or an atom or molecule) is called the *ground state*. (*b*) All other higher energy states are called *excited states*.

2.3   Describe the contributions to the electronic structure of atoms made by (*a*) de Broglie and (*b*) Schrödinger.

▟   (*a*) de Broglie postulated that an electron has properties of a standing wave as well as those of a particle. A standing wave vibrates in a fixed location, i.e., as in a plucked guitar string.   (*b*) Schrödinger then formulated an equation using the mathematics of wave motion to arrive at solutions, called wave functions indicated by the Greek letter psi (ψ). These wave functions are then used to calculate the quantized energies of an electron.

2.4   How does Heisenberg's uncertainty principle add to the understanding of the behavior of an electron in an atom or molecule?

▟   This principle states that it is not possible to determine *simultaneously* both the precise position and momentum of an electron. Hence, an exact path for an electron cannot be determined. The electron can just as well move irregularly in some space about the nucleus while maintaining a fixed energy.

2.5   (*a*) Draw diagrams showing crests ($+$) and troughs ($-$) for a standing wave with (i) the lowest energy and (ii) the next higher energy.   (*b*) Define a node and locate it in a diagram in part (*a*).

▟   (*a*) See Fig. 2-1. Note that the ends of linear standing waves are fixed. *Important*: the $+$ and $-$ signs are not electrical charges.   (*b*) A *node* is a point on the wave where actually there is no wave. It occurs whenever a crest ($+$) changes over to a trough ($-$) [see Fig. 2-1(ii)]. For an electron wave, the electron density (see Problem 2.7) at a node is zero because the electron can never be found there.

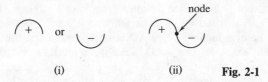

(i)   (ii)   **Fig. 2-1**

2.6   What is an atomic orbital (AO)?

▟   An *atomic orbital* is the region of space about the atomic nucleus where there is a high probability of finding an electron. The orbital is defined by ψ, and ψ^2 gives the *probability* of finding the electron in the orbital.

2.7   (*a*) How is the AO related to an electron cloud?   (*b*) What is meant by electron density?

▟   (*a*) The electron in the AO can be pictured as being smeared out to form a cloud called an *electron cloud*. (*b*) The negative charge dispersal of the electron cloud, which is related to the probability of finding the electron (ψ^2), is called the *electron density*. It is not uniform; in some regions of the AO the probability is higher than in others. These regions have a greater electron density.

2.8   What is the maximum number of electrons found in an AO?

▌   According to the Pauli exclusion principle, at most two electrons can occupy an orbital, and then only when they have opposite spins, designated $+1/2(\uparrow)$ and $-1/2(\downarrow)$.

2.9   Give the relationship between the principal energy level (shell), n, and (*a*) the maximum number of e⁻s in a shell and (*b*) the number of sublevels (subshells) in a shell.   (*c*) For the third shell ($n = 3$), give (i) the maximum number of electrons and (ii) the number of subshells.

▌   The values of n are whole numbers starting with 1.   (*a*) The maximum number of e⁻s in a shell, n, is $2n^2$. (*b*) The number of sublevels equals the value of n.   (*c*) (i) 18, (ii) 3.

2.10   (*a*) What is the relationship between the value of n and the number of the period in the periodic table?   (*b*) List the elements having an n value of 2 in increasing atomic numbers going from left to right.   (*c*) In which period of the periodic table are they found?

▌   (*a*) The period number is the value of n.   (*b*) Li, Be, B, C, N, O, F, Ne.   (*c*) The second period.

2.11   Give the letters used to designate the first three sublevels (a fourth sublevel is not encountered in organic chemistry) in increasing energy.

▌   First sublevel, s < second sublevel, p < third sublevel, d (rarely encountered)
   <u>increasing energy</u> →

2.12   (*a*) How many s orbitals can there be in a principal energy level?   (*b*) What information is given by the symbol $3s^2$?

▌   (*a*) Only one.   (*b*) The 3 indicates the principal energy level (in this case the third), s the first sublevel, and the superscript 2 is the number of electrons in this AO.

2.13   In terms of AO's, how is the energy of an electron indicated?

▌   There are four aspects of the energy: (1) the principal energy level (quantum number), n, related to the *size* of the AO; (2) the sublevel s, p, d, f, or g related to the *shape* of the AO; (3) except for the s, each sublevel has some number of equal-energy AO's differing in their *spatial orientation*; (4) the electron spin.

2.14   (*a*) Give the shape and draw the cross section of (i) a $1s$ and (ii) a $2p$ AO.   (*b*) How are these shapes determined?   (*c*) Can an electron ever be in the nucleus of an atom with (i) an s AO (ii) a p AO? (*d*) Respond to the question, "How can an e⁻ move from one lobe of a p AO to the other lobe without passing through the nucleus?"

▌   (*a*)   (i) A sphere [Fig. 2-2(i)]. (ii) Touching spheres or "dumbbell" [Fig. 2-2(ii)].
       To avoid using + and − signs that erroneously may be confused with electric charges, one p AO lobe (associated with the + sign) is shaded and one (associated with the − sign) is unshaded as shown in Fig. 2-2(ii).
   (*b*)   From solutions of the Schrödinger equation, the lowest energy AO, the s, has no trigonometric function, indicating that it has no angle dependency. The shape that fits this criterion is the sphere. The solution for the next higher energy AO has a trigonometric function, and a plot of the solutions give the "dumbbell" shape for the p AO. Since there are three solutions, there are three p AO's.
   (*c*)   (i) The s AO has no node and the e⁻ can be any place in the sphere *including* the nucleus. (ii) The p AO has one node at the nucleus; an e⁻ cannot be at the nucleus. This nodal point (the nucleus) lies on a nodal plane that separates the two lobes.
   (*d*)   The question is specious because it restricts the behavior of an e⁻ to being a particle. As a particle it could not make the questioned move but as a wave it can. The two lobes together form the electron cloud and each has the same amount of electron density. It is meaningless to talk about the e⁻ being in one lobe or the other; it is in both lobes.

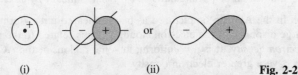

(i)   (ii)   **Fig. 2-2**

2.15 (*a*) Show with diagrams how the three *p* AO's differ. (*b*) Define *degenerate* orbitals.

    (*a*) They have the same energy and shape. They differ in their spatial orientation: p_x has its long axis on the *x* axis, p_y on the *y* axis, and p_z on the *z* axis (Fig. 2-3).

    (*b*) Different orbitals with the same energies are said to be *degenerate*.

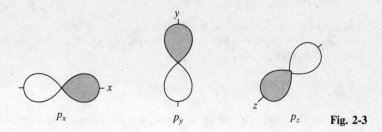

Fig. 2-3

2.16 (*a*) What is the relationship between *n*, the shell number, and the number of nodes present in the AO's of the shell? (*b*) Give the number of nodes in a 3*d* AO and illustrate with one of the four cloverleaf shapes (the fifth *d* AO looks like a *p* with a "lifesaver" around the nucleus). (*c*) Sketch (i) a 2*s* and (ii) a 3*p* AO, showing all nodes.

    (*a*) As the value of *n* increases, the number of nodes in the orbitals increases. The number of nodes in any AO is always one less than its *n* value.

    (*b*) The 3*d* AO has an *n* value of 3 and has two nodes present as nodal planes. In Fig. 2-4 the two perpendicular nodal planes through the nucleus are the *xz* and *yz* planes; the four orbitals are between the axes.

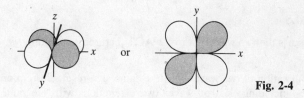

Fig. 2-4

    (*c*) (i) The 2*s* AO (*n* = 2) has one node present as a nodal sphere [Fig. 2-5(i)]. (ii) A 3*p* AO (*n* = 3) has two nodes, one a plane similar to that of the 2*p* [see Problem 2.14(*c*) (ii)], and the other a sphere through the lobes [Fig. 2-5(ii)].

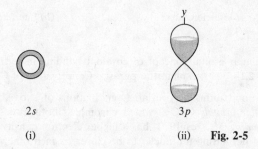

2*s*

(i)

3*p*

(ii)   Fig. 2-5

2.17 (*a*) State the *Aufbau* (German for building up) *principle* for filling orbitals with electrons. (*b*) State and explain *Hund's rule* for filling orbitals. (*c*) Give the electron distribution for a ground state C atom that (i) follows and (ii) does not follow Hund's rule. (*d*) If individual C atoms could be isolated (they cannot be), what different physical properties would separate the two electron distributions given in part (*c*)? (*e*) Which are the valence electrons?

   (*a*) The AO's are filled in order of increasing energies.
   (*b*) Each degenerate orbital [see Problem 2.15(*b*)] is half-filled before electrons are paired in an AO. There is less electrostatic repulsion between electrons in different orbitals than between paired electrons in a single orbital.

   (*c*) (i) $\dfrac{\uparrow\downarrow}{1s^2}\quad \dfrac{\uparrow\downarrow}{2s^2}\quad \dfrac{\uparrow}{2p_x^1}\quad \dfrac{\uparrow}{2p_y^1}\quad \dfrac{}{2p_z}$ (correct)

   Energies of orbitals increase from left to right. Large space between orbitals shows an increase in energy and less space is left between degenerate orbitals. The choice of p_x and p_y is arbitrary; any two *p* AO's can be used.

   (ii) $\dfrac{\uparrow\downarrow}{1s^2}\quad \dfrac{\uparrow\downarrow}{2s^2}\quad \dfrac{\uparrow\downarrow}{2p_x^2}\quad \dfrac{}{2p_y}\quad \dfrac{}{2p_z}$ (incorrect)

   (*d*) C atoms with the correct distribution, having some number of unpaired electrons, are *paramagnetic*; they are drawn into a magnetic field. C's with the incorrect distribution, having only paired electrons, would be *diamagnetic*; they would be somewhat repelled by a magnetic field.
   (*e*) The valence electrons for representative elements are those in the outermost shell, the one with the highest principal energy number, *n*. For C this is the second shell ($n = 2$) and there are four valence electrons in the $2s$ and the two $2p$ AO's.

2.18 (*a*) The atoms of which element in the second period of the periodic table ($n = 2$) would be the most paramagnetic if it could be tested? (*b*) Give the electron distribution of oxygen.

   (*a*) The element must have the maximum number of unpaired e⁻'s which would result if each *p* AO were half-filled. The electron distribution is $1s^2 2s^2 2p_x^1 2p_y^1 2p_z^1$. This element has an atomic number of 7 and is nitrogen.
   (*b*) $1s^2 2s^2 2p_x^2 2p_y^2 2p_z^1$

MOLECULAR ORBITALS

2.19 With sketches, discuss the two ways that two *s* AO's pictured as standing waves combine to (*a*) reinforce and (*b*) interfere.

   (*a*) The combination of two waves with the same sign results in reinforcement [Fig. 2-6(*a*)]. This is true for all standing waves, including electron waves (wave functions with the same sign). (*b*) The interaction of two waves of opposite sign (interference) gives a new higher-energy wave with a node [Fig. 2-6(*b*)].

(*a*) Reinforcement   (*b*) Interference   **Fig. 2-6**

2.20 (*a*) Explain the molecular orbital concept of covalent bonding in terms of the combination of standing waves discussed in Problem 2.19. (*b*) Explain the phrase "Conservation of Orbitals".

   (*a*) A covalent bond forms by overlap (combination) of two AO's—one from each atom. This overlap produces two *molecular orbitals* (MO's) which encompass both atoms. When orbitals with like signs overlap (reinforcement), a *bonding* MO results. It has a higher electron density between the two atoms, thus minimizing nuclear repulsion and permitting the nuclei to be closer to each other than in the unbonded state. The higher energy molecular orbital resulting from overlap of AO's with unlike signs (interference) is an *antibonding* MO (designated as MO*). It has a node (no electron density) in the region between the nuclei. The repulsion of its nuclei is high, and it has a higher energy than the individual separated atoms. (*b*) The number of molecular orbitals formed is equal to the number of AO's that overlap.

2.21 Draw an energy diagram showing the relationship between two AO's and the MO's resulting from their combination.

Two AO's combine (overlap) to form two MO's, one by reinforcement having a lower energy and the second by cancellation having a higher energy.

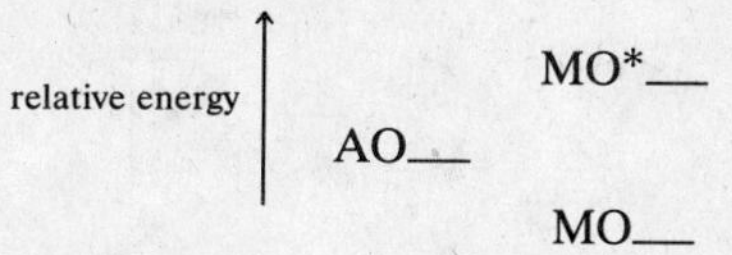

$$\text{relative energy} \uparrow \quad \begin{array}{ccc} & MO^*\_\_ & \\ AO\_\_ & & AO\_\_ \\ & MO\_\_ & \end{array}$$

2.22 (*a*) Describe how the mathematical method of *l*inear *c*ombination of *a*tomic *o*rbitals (LCAO) relates to the concept of bonding and antibonding molecular orbitals. Illustrate with A—B, where the wave function of each atom is the same. (*b*) What factor emerges from this method that relates to bond strength?

(*a*) Mathematically, AO's are combined in two ways: (1) by adding and (2) by subtracting the wave functions of the AO's to give the molecular orbital wave functions, Ψ_{MO} and Ψ_{MO}^* respectively. These combinations are squared to get the electron density probability between the bonded atoms. The values from these two calculations are then compared to the electron density between two uncombined isolated atoms.

Isolated atoms: $(\psi_A)^2 + (\psi_B)^2 = \psi_A^2 + \psi_B^2$
Addition: $(\psi_A + \psi_B)^2 = \psi_A^2 + 2\psi_A\psi_B + \psi_B^2 = \Psi_{MO}^2$
Subtraction: $(\psi_A - \psi_B)^2 = \psi_A^2 - 2\psi_A\psi_B + \psi_B^2 = \Psi_{MO^*}^2$

Addition gives a Ψ_{MO}^2 greater than that for the isolated atoms because of $2\psi_A\psi_B$ (the interaction term); addition gives the bonding MO. Subtraction gives a Ψ_{MO}^2 less than that of the isolated atoms because the interaction term is negative; subtraction gives the antibonding MO*.

(*b*) The more positive the interaction term, the greater is the electron density between the nuclei and the more stable is the bond. The greater the overlap of the AO's, the shorter and stronger is the bond.

2.23 Sketch the combination of the needed AO's to form (*a*) σ_s (sigma), (*b*) σ_{sp}, and (*c*) π_y (pi) MO's.

(*a*) The subscript *s* indicates that this MO comes from overlap of two *s* AO's. See Fig. 2-7(*a*).
(*b*) This σ MO comes from head-to-head overlap of an *s* and *p* AO. See Fig. 2-7(*b*).
(*c*) Side-to-side (lateral) overlap of two p_y AO's forms a π MO as shown in Fig. 2-7(*c*). Only one π bond is formed by the overlap of the top lobes with each other and the overlap of the bottom lobes with each other, as indicated by the tie-lines.

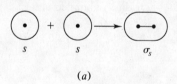

(*a*)

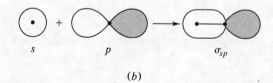

(*b*)

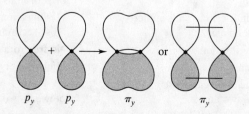

(*c*)   **Fig. 2-7**

2.24   Sketch the formation of (*a*) σ_s^*, (*b*) σ_{sp}^*, and (*c*) π_y^* MO's.

▮   The asterisks indicate that these are antibonding molecular orbitals. See Fig. 2-8.

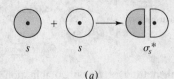

(a)

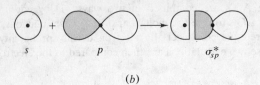

(b)

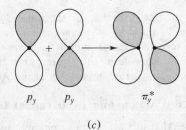

(c)   **Fig. 2-8**

2.25   Can a π bond be formed from lateral overlap of *s* and *p* AO's?

▮   No. Figure 2-9 shows that the bonding strength generated from the overlap between the $+s$ AO and the $+$ lobe of the *p* AO is canceled by the antibonding effect of the overlap between the $+s$ and the $-$ lobe of the *p*. Such interaction is no better than the individual unbonded atoms.

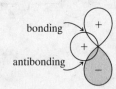

Fig. 2-9

2.26   (*a*) List the differences between sigma (σ) and pi (π) molecular orbitals.   (*b*) Why can these MO's be referred to as σ and π bonds?   (*c*) Why can free rotation occur easily around a σ bond but not around a π bond?

▮   (*a*)

σ Bond	π Bond
1. Formed by head-to-head overlap of AO's.	1. Formed by lateral overlap of *p* orbitals (or *p* and *d* orbitals).
2. Has cylindrical charge symmetry about bond axis.	2. Has maximum charge density in the cross-sectional plane of the orbitals.
3. Has free rotation.	3. No free rotation.
4. Lower energy.	4. Higher energy.
5. Only one bond can exist between two atoms.	5. One or two bonds can exist between two atoms.

(*b*) Although the molecular orbitals encompass the entire molecule, the electron density is highest between the bonding atoms. Hence these *localized* MO's are called bonds.   (*c*) Rotation around the bond axis of the σ bond does not change the overlap of the participating AO's. However, if one of the π-bonded atoms (along with its attached σ-bonded atoms or groups) is rotated, its p orbital must move out of the plane of the π bond. This prevents the overlap of the two p AO's and destroys the π bond.

2.27 Explain why two atoms cannot form three π bonds.

◢ When the three p AO's on one atom approach those on another atom, one of the p's, e.g., the p_x, must make a head-on approach with the p_x on the other atom to form a σ_p MO. Only the two other p's, the p_y and p_z, can overlap side-by-side to give π bonds, the π_y and π_z.

2.28 (*a*) How are electrons distributed in the MO's when two atoms interact to form a bond? (*b*) Illustrate (*a*) with H_2^+, H_2, H_2^-, HHe, and He_2. Give the symbolism for the molecular orbital electronic structure. (*c*) How can a MO electronic structure be used to predict whether or not these (or any species) can exist? (*d*) Which, if any, do not exist? (*e*) List each substance in decreasing order of stability.

◢ (*a*) The total number of electrons in the molecule or ion are placed in the molecular orbitals following the Aufbau principle and Hund's rule, discussed in Problem 2.17.

(*b*) The e^-'s are indicated with arrows representing the spins.

σ_{1s}^*		$\uparrow$	$\uparrow$	$\uparrow\downarrow$
σ_{1s} $\uparrow$	$\uparrow\downarrow$	$\uparrow\downarrow$	$\uparrow\downarrow$	$\uparrow\downarrow$
H_2^+	H_2	H_2^-	HHe	He_2
$(\sigma_{1s})^1$	$(\sigma_{1s})^2$	$(\sigma_{1s})^2(\sigma_{1s}^*)^1$		$(\sigma_{1s})^2(\sigma_{1s}^*)^2$

(*c*) Any species can exist if there are more e^-'s in MO's than in MO*'s. The greater the excess of e^-'s in MO's, the more stable is the molecule or ion.

(*d*) He_2 has an equal number of e^-'s in the MO and MO* and therefore does not exist.

(*e*) H_2 (two bonding e^-'s) > H_2^+, H_2^-, HHe (one excess bonding e^-) $\gg He_2$ (no excess bonding e^-). Since electrons exert some repulsive force, H_2^+ may be slightly more stable than H_2^- and HHe because it has fewer electrons.

2.29 Give an energy-level diagram showing energy levels of valence-shell molecular orbitals of diatomic molecules and ions arising by overlap of the valence-shell AO's of the second period elements: (*a*) For Li, Be, B, C, and N; (*b*) For O, F, and (hypothetically) Ne. The inner shell AO's ($n = 1$) are not included because they have no influence on bonding.

◢ (*a*)

		(*b*)		
___	σ_{2p}^*		___	σ_{2p}^*
___ ___	π_{2p}^* (π_y and π_z)		___ ___	π_{2p}^* (π_y and π_z)
___	σ_{2p}		___ ___	π_{2p} (π_y and π_z)
___ ___	π_{2p} (π_y and π_z)		___	σ_{2p}
___	σ_{2s}^*		___	σ_{2s}^*
___	σ_{2s}		___	σ_{2s}

2.30 Use the energy levels in Problem 2.29 to give the MO electronic structures for (*a*) C_2, (*b*) N_2 (*c*) O_2, (*d*) NO, and (*e*) CN^-. Give the number of valence e^-'s to be placed into the energy levels.

◢ (*a*) 8 e^-'s, 4 from each C. $\sigma_{2s}^2, \sigma_{2s}^{*2}, \pi_{y^2}, \pi_{z^2}$

(*b*) 10 e^-'s, 5 from each N. $\sigma_{2s}^2, \sigma_{2s}^{*2}, \pi_{y^2}, \pi_{z^2}, \sigma_{2p^2}$

(*c*) 12 e^-'s, 6 from each O. $\sigma_{2s}^2 \sigma_{2s}^{*2}, \sigma_{2p^2}, \pi_{y^2}, \pi_{z^2}, \pi_{y^1}^*, \pi_{z^1}^*$

(*d*) 11 e^-'s, 5 from N, 6 from O. $\sigma_{2s}^2, \sigma_{2s}^{*2}, \pi_{y^2}, \pi_{z^2}, \sigma_{2p^2}, \pi_{y^1}^*$

(*e*) 10 e^-'s, 4 from C, 5 from N and one from the $-$ charge. Isoelectronic with N_2.

In most cases the energy levels used for homodiatomic species (X_2) can be used for heterodiatomic species (XY), e.g., NO and CN^-

2.31 (*a*) Give the electronic structure for C_2 using the energy levels given in Problem 2.29(*b*). (*b*) How can the correct electronic structure be determined experimentally?

▰ (a) $\sigma_{2s^2}, \sigma_{2s^2}^*, \sigma_{2p^2}, \pi_{y^1}, \pi_{z^1}$. (b) This electronic structure predicts that C_2 would be paramagnetic since it would have two unpaired e$^-$'s. C_2 is not paramagnetic; therefore the electronic structure in Problem 2.30(a) is correct.

2.32 (a) Define the term *bond order*. (b) Give the bond order of each species in Problem 2.30.

▰ (a) Bond order $= \dfrac{\text{(number of e's in MO's)} - \text{(number of e's in MO*'s)}}{2}$

(b) For C_2 $4/2 = 2$; for N_2, $6/2 = 3$; for O_2, $4/2 = 2$; for NO, $5/2 = 2.5$; for CN$^-$, $6/2 = 3$

2.33 (a) Define the term *spin state*. (b) Give the spin states for (i) N_2, (ii) O_2, and (iii) NO.

▰ (a) Spin state $= 2$ (sum of all electron spin numbers) $+ 1$ where the spin numbers are either $+1/2$ or $-1/2$. (b) (i) For N_2 all electrons are paired and the sum of an equal number of $+1/2$ and $-1/2$ is zero. The spin state $= 2(0) + 1 = 1$. N_2 is a *singlet* molecule. (ii) O_2 has two unpaired e$^-$'s, each having a spin number of $+1/2$ for a total of one. The spin state $= 2(1) + 1 = 3$. O_2 is a *triplet* molecule. (iii) NO has one unpaired e$^-$. The spin state $= 2(1/2) + 1 = 2$. NO is a *doublet* molecule.

2.34 (a) Explain electron excitation in terms of molecular orbitals using (i) O_2 and (ii) $H_2C{=}CH_2$. (b) Can excited state $H_2C{=}CH_2$ undergo free rotation? (c) Account for the fact that the excited He$_2^*$ has been detected.

▰ (a) (i) Ground state triplet O_2 [see (ii) of Problem 2.33(b)] is excited to singlet O_2 when one of the highest energy (π^*) ground state electrons reverses its spin. There are two possible excited singlet states: the one with lower energy has an e$^-$ in each of the π^* MO*'s and the one with higher energy has a pair of opposite-spin e$^-$'s in one of the π^* MO*'s. (ii) $H_2C{=}CH_2$ illustrates the more commonly observed electron excitation whereby an e$^-$ in the *h*ighest *o*ccupied *m*olecular *o*rbital (HOMO) is excited to the *l*owest *u*noccupied *m*olecular *o*rbital (LUMO) while retaining its spin. In multiply-bonded molecules or ions the HOMO is invariably a π MO rather than the lower energy σ MO's. The LUMO is a π^* MO* rather than the higher energy σ^* MO*.

$$\underline{\quad}\ \pi^* \qquad\qquad \underline{\downarrow}\ \pi^* \text{ (LUMO)}$$

$$\xrightarrow{h\nu}$$

$$\underline{\uparrow\downarrow}\ \pi \qquad\qquad \underline{\uparrow}\ \pi \text{ (HOMO)}$$

(b) Yes. Excitation has broken the π bond since the p AO's no longer overlap and there is no resistance to free rotation.

(c) The electron distribution for He$_2^*$ is $\sigma_{1s^2} \sigma_{1s^1}^* \sigma_{2s^1}$. There is now an excess of e$^-$'s in bonding orbitals.

HYBRIDIZATION AND SHAPE

2.35 The BeH_2 molecule has two equivalent Be—H covalent bonds. (a) Can this bonding be explained by ground state Be bonding to two H atoms? (b) Account for this structure in terms of orbital hybridization.

▰ (a) No. Ground state Be ($1s^2\,2s^2$) does not have two half-filled AO's to overlap with an s orbital of each H atom. (b) To have two equivalent bonds, Be must use two identical AO's. These AO's arise from a mathematical process called *hybridization* which may be thought of as a blending of the $2s$ and any one of the $2p$'s to form two equivalent sp hybrid orbitals (called *diagonal*). They are degenerate; each one holds one electron and can now overlap with the s orbital of an H atom to form the two identical bonds. The Be atom retains two empty p AO's.

2.36 Account for (a) the three identical B—F bonds in BF_3 and (b) the four identical C—H bonds in CH_4 in terms of hybridization.

▰ (a) Ground state B is $1s^2\,2s^2\,2p^1$ and can form only one bond with its half-filled orbital. By hybridizing the $2s$ and two of the $2p$'s, three identical sp^2 hybrid orbitals (called *trigonal*) are formed, each containing one e$^-$ for bonding. B retains one empty p orbital. (b) Ground state C is $1s^2\,2s^2\,2p^1\,2p^1$ and can form only two bonds by using its half-filled orbitals. Hybridization of the $2s$ and the three $2p$ AO's creates four equivalent sp^3 hybrid orbitals (called *tetrahedral*), and each contains one e^- for bonding by overlap with the $1s$ AO of H.

2.37 (*a*) What are the relative energies of the sp, sp^2, and sp^3 hybrid orbitals (HO's) and the unhybridized s and p AO's? (*b*) Sketch the shape of the s-p type HO's. (*c*) What effect does hybridization have on the stability of bonds?

◢ (*a*) For a given atom, the more s character (or less p character) in an orbital, the lower is the energy of the electrons in that orbital, and the closer are the electrons to the nucleus. In terms of decreasing energy the order is: $p > sp^3 > sp^2 > sp > s$. (*b*) The three kinds of s-p HO's are p-like except that one lobe (the "head") is much larger than the other lobe (the "tail"). The large lobe does the overlapping. The shape is shown in Fig. 2-10. (*c*) An s-p type HO gives better overlap and a stronger bond than does a p AO because its "head" is larger than either lobe of the p AO.

"tail" → ← "head" **Fig. 2-10**

2.38 Account for the bond angles of (*a*) 180° in BeH_2, (*b*) 120° in BF_3, and (*c*) 109.5° in CH_4.

◢ Electron pairs in bonds repel each other. The electron pairs in bonds move as far away from each other as possible to minimize their mutual repulsion, and thus they assume the given angles. It should be noted that when hybridization is treated mathematically the hybrid orbital angles are predicted to be oriented toward these same angles.

2.39 (*a*) Account for the observed bond angles of (i) 107° in NH_3 and (ii) 105° in H_2O. (*b*) Could N and O use ground state AO's to form equivalent bonds? (*c*) Why do N and O use HO's for bonding?

◢ (*a*) (i) Since the bond angle is close to the tetrahedral angle, 109.5°, N must use three sp^3 HO's for bonding with H, and the unshared pair resides in the fourth sp^3 HO. The unshared pair exerts a greater repulsive force than do the shared pairs, which causes a contraction of the bond angles to somewhat less than 109.5°. (ii) H_2O also uses sp^3 HO's. Two of them are half-filled and are used for bonding with H's; the other two contain the unshared pairs. Since there are two unshared pairs, the repulsion is greater than in NH_3, and the bond angle shrinks even more to 105°.

(*b*) Yes. Ground state N has three half-filled p AO's $(1s^2 2s^2 2p_x^1 2p_y^1 2p_z^1)$ and O has two half-filled p AO's $(1s^2 s^2 2p_x^2 2p_y^1 2p_z^1)$ available for overlap.

(*c*) As discussed in Problem 2.37(*c*), HO's give stronger bonds than do p AO's. Furthermore, when p AO's form bonds, the bond angle should be close to 90°, the angle between the axes of any two p AO's. There is more repulsion between the bonding pairs of e^-'s with bond angles of 90° than there is in the tetrahedral angle.

Note that knowledge of the bond angle permits the prediction of the kind of orbital an atom uses for bonding.

2.40 (*a*) Suggest a method for determining the hybridized state of an atom from the structural formula of its compounds. (*b*) Give the bonding situation in which a C atom uses (i) sp^3, (ii) sp^2, and (iii) sp HO's.

◢ (*a*) For every σ bond and unshared pair of electrons, an atom uses an HO. An HO is not needed for an unpaired e^-. This is a statement of the *hybrid orbital number* (HON) rule. This rule is valid for second period elements and with few exceptions (see Problem 2.42) for elements in higher periods. Whether monovalent halogen atoms hybridize is indeterminant and certainly inconsequential.

(*b*) (i) Four σ bonds, $-\overset{|}{\underset{|}{C}}-$, or an anion with three σ bonds and an unshared pair of e^-'s, $-\overset{|}{\underset{|}{C}}\!:^-$.

(ii) Three σ bonds with either one π bond, $-\overset{|}{C}=$, or with a + charge, $-\overset{|}{C}^+$. The C could also have two σ bonds and an unshared pair of e^-'s, $-\overset{|}{C}\!:$. (iii) Two σ bonds and two π bonds either as a triple bond, $-C\equiv$, or as two double bonds, $=C=$, or one double bond and a + charge, $=\overset{|}{\underset{+}{C}}=$, or two unpaired e^-'s, $-\overset{\cdot}{\underset{\cdot}{C}}-$.

2.41 (*a*) Give the HO used by N and C and (*b*) predict its shape. For each of the following: (i) NH_4^+, (ii) CH_3NH_2, (iii) $H_2C=O$, (iv) $H_2C=NH$, and (v) $HC≡N$:

(*a*)

(i)

$$\overset{\displaystyle H}{\underset{\displaystyle H}{\overset{|}{\underset{|}{N}}}}\!\!-H^+$$

4 σ bonds, sp^3

(ii)

$$\overset{\displaystyle H \quad H}{\underset{\displaystyle H \quad H}{C\!\!-\!\!N\colon}}$$

C, 4 σ bonds, sp^3
N, 3 σ bonds + 1 lone pair, sp^3

(iii)

$$\overset{\displaystyle H}{\underset{\displaystyle H}{C}}\!\!=\!\!\ddot{\ddot{O}}\colon$$

3 σ bonds, sp^2

(iv)

$$\overset{\displaystyle H \quad H}{\underset{\displaystyle H}{C}}\!\!=\!\!N\colon$$

C, 3 σ bonds, sp^2
N, 2 σ bonds, 1 lone pair, sp^2

(v) $H\!\!-\!\!C≡N\colon$

C, 2 σ bonds, sp
N, 1 σ bond, 1 lone pair, sp

(*b*) (i) tetrahedral, 109.5° bond angles. (ii) The tetrahedral C is joined to a *pyramidal* N to give a nonplanar molecule. The bonds on N have a pyramidal shape because the lone pair replaces one of the tetrahedral bonds. A pyramid and terahedron have similar shapes except that in a pyramid the central atom is at a corner rather than in the center of the tetrahedron. All bond angles are approximately 109°. (iii) $H_2C=O$ is a planar trigonal molecule. The π bond is formed from lateral overlap of the p_z AO's of C and O, and the bond angles are 120°. (iv) Both the C and N have a trigonal array and bond through sp^2 σ bonds to give a planar molecule with 120° bond angles. The remaining p_z AO's on C and N overlap to give the π bond which has no effect on the shape. (v) Molecular shape is always dictated by the hybrid state of central atoms, in this case C, and never by terminal atoms, in this case N. The sp HO's of C are diagonal and HCN is a linear molecule.

2.42 Use the measured bond angles to suggest the type of orbitals used by P in (*a*) PH_3, 92°, and (*b*) PCl_3, 100°.

(*a*) The 92° bond angle suggests the use of the three $3p$ AO's for bonding with H, with the lone pair in the $3s$ AO. (*b*) The bond angle of 100° is just about midway between the 90° expected from the use of p AO's and the 109.5° from sp^3 HO's. This is a dilemma only if we insist that hybridization is an either-or choice of p, sp, sp^2, or sp^3. Rather, intermediate degrees of hybridization are possible so that the molecule achieves the lowest possible energy. The central atoms do not "know" about the pure hybrid states that we imagine. The terminology used for PCl_3 is that P uses sp^3 HO's which have considerably more p-character and that the sp^3 HO with the lone pair has considerably more s-character.

The central atoms of hydrides of period 3 (and higher) typically use p orbitals for bonding.

2.43 What kind of HO's are used by the C's and what are the bond angles in (*a*) ethane, $H_3C—CH_3$; (*b*) ethene, $H_2C=CH_2$; (*c*) ethyne, $HC≡CH$; (*d*) benzene, C_6H_6, ⬡; (*e*) allene, $H_2C=C=CH_2$?

(*a*) sp^3, 109°; (*b*) sp^2, 120°; (*c*) sp, 180°; (*d*) sp^2, 120°; (*e*) center C, sp, 180° and C^1 and C^3 sp^2, 120°.

2.44 What kind of hybrid orbitals are predicted for the underlined atom? (*a*) $H_2\underline{N}OH$, (*b*) $H_2\underline{S}$, (*c*) $\underline{B}F_4^-$, (*d*) $HO\underline{C}≡\underline{N}$, (*e*) $O=\underline{C}=O$, and (*f*) $H_2\underline{C}=\underline{C}=O$.

(*a*) sp^3; (*b*) p; (*c*) sp^3; (*d*) C, N, both sp; (*e*) sp; (*f*) C^1, sp^2, and C^2 (center C), sp.

ELECTRONEGATIVITY AND POLARITY

2.45 (*a*) Define electronegativity. (*b*) How does it differ from electron affinity? (*c*) How do electronegativity values of atoms relate to bond polarity?

(*a*) *Electronegativity* is the relative tendency of a bonded atom in a molecule to attract electrons. The atom with a higher electronegativity value attracts the electrons more effectively. (*b*) *Electron affinity* is the energy change that occurs when an electron is added to a gaseous *atom* in its ground state, and its value may be positive or negative. It does not refer to bonded electrons. (*c*) Atoms with different values of electronegativity form *polar* bonds to each other. The electron density is higher near the more electronegative atom. This atom is relatively negatively charged and is assigned a *partial negative charge*, δ−, while the less electronegative atom is given a *partial positive charge*, δ+. (These partial charges should not be confused with ionic charges.) A nonpolar covalent bond results when a bond forms between atoms having a very small or zero difference in electronegativity.

2.46 (*a*) Define a dipole moment. (*b*) Can a molecule have a dipole moment if it has no polar covalent bonds? (*c*) Can a molecule have polar bonds but no dipole moment? Justify your answer with an example.

◢ (*a*) The *dipole moment*, μ, of a polar molecule is the vector sum of all the individual bond moments. Mathematically, μ is the product of the magnitude of the partial charge, q, and the distance, d, between the centers of opposite charge, or $\mu = q \times d$. The unit for μ is the *debye* (D). (*b*) No. (*c*) Yes; if the individual polar bonds are arranged symmetrically so that the effect of any one bond is cancelled by the effect of the other(s), the net effect (dipole moment) will be zero. An example is $BeCl_2$, where the individual Be—Cl bonds are polar, but the two bond moments are equal and in opposite directions, and their vector sum is zero: Cl—Be—Cl. Note that polar bonds are indicated by $\leftrightarrow$ with the arrowhead pointing toward the more electronegative atom.

2.47 (*a*) Arrange the gaseous hydrogen halides in order of decreasing dipole moments and rationalize your order. (*b*) The dipole moments for the methyl halides are: CH_3F, 1.82 D; CH_3Cl, 1.94 D; CH_3Br, 1.79 D; and CH_3I, 1.64 D. Explain.

◢ (*a*) HF > HCl > HBr > HI. The electronegativities of the halogens decrease from F to I, which decreases the value of μ. (*b*) The order generally follows the decrease in electronegativity of the halogens with an exception. The apparent anomaly of CH_3F having a smaller μ than CH_3Cl is explained by the shorter C—F bond distance, which tends to decrease the value of μ even though F is more electronegative than Cl.

2.48 Explain why: (*a*) CO_2 has no dipole moment, but SO_2 does ($\mu = 1.60$ D); (*b*) NH_3 has a much greater dipole moment than NF_3 (1.46 D vs. 0.24 D); and (*c*) the unshared pair on P has little or no effect on the dipole moment of PH_3.

◢ In order to answer these questions, the electron-dot structures should be drawn, and the hybridization of the central atoms determined.

(*a*) C in CO_2 is *sp* hybridized, and the molecule is linear. The C—O bond moments oppose each other and cancel [Fig. 2-11(*a*)]. S in SO_2 is sp^2 hybridized, with two σ bonds to O and one with the unshared electron pair. The O—S—O bond angle is appr. 120°, and the S—O moments do not cancel [Fig. 2-11(*b*)].

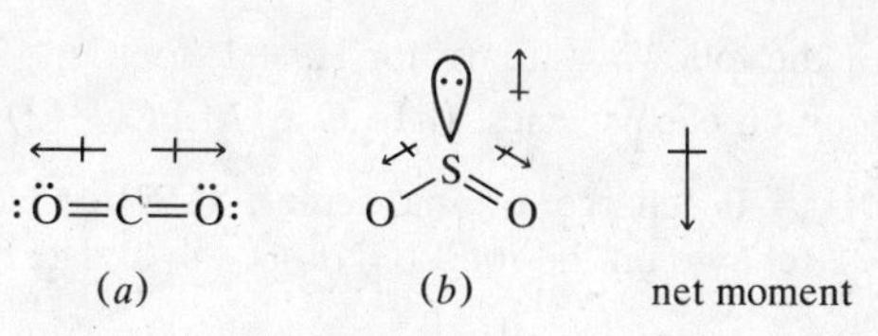

(*a*)   (*b*)   net moment   **Fig. 2-11**

(*b*) The unshared pair of electrons on N (which occupies an sp^3 HO) must be considered. In NH_3 the net moment of the N—H bonds and the contribution from the unshared pair are in the same direction and are additive [see Fig. 2-12(*a*)]. The net moment of the N—F bonds opposes the dipole effect of the unshared pair in NF_3. These opposing moments are approximately of the same size, and the resultant is a small moment of indeterminate direction [see Fig. 2-12(*b*)].

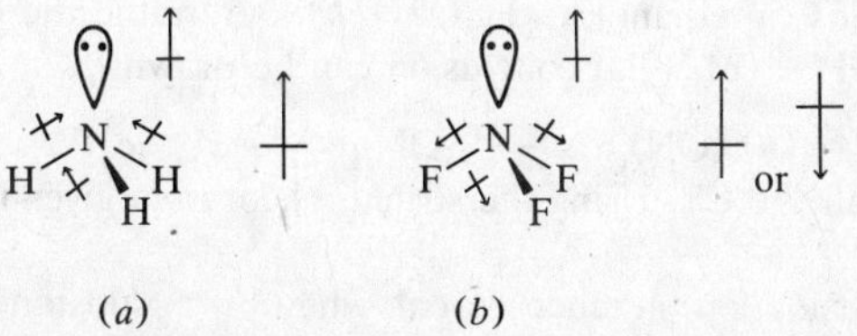

(*a*)   (*b*)   **Fig. 2-12**

(*c*) The unshared pair is in an *s* orbital [see Problem 2.42(*a*)] which is spherically symmetrical. In order to affect the polarity of the molecule, the electrons must be in a directional orbital.

2.49 Explain why the dipole moment of $CHCl_3$ is less than that of CH_2Cl_2.

▮ In CH_2Cl_2 all bond moments reinforce each other [Fig. 2-13(a)], while in $CHCl_3$ the bond moment of one of the Cl's opposes the net moment of the other two [Fig. 2-13(b)]. This effect is more apparent when the tetrahedral nature of the molecule is considered. (The actual μ values are: $CHCl_3$, 1.0 D, and CH_2Cl_2, 1.6 D.)

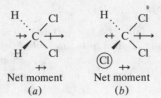

Net moment   Net moment   **Fig. 2-13**
(a)   (b)

2.50 *Organometallics* are compounds containing C—metal bonds. Metals typically have low electronegativity values, and the C—metal bond moment is toward the more electronegative C. (*a*) What generalization can be made as to the nature of the C—metal bond and the electronegativity of the metal? (*b*) What kind of a bond would you expect between C and (i) an alkali metal and (ii) a group 2 metal? Given an example of each. (*c*) Give an example of a C—metal bond that contains little or no ionic character. (Refer to a table of electronegativity values, if necessary.)

▮ (*a*) The smaller the electronegativity of the metal, the more likely its bond to C will be ionic. (*b*) (i) Ionic, $CH_3\ddot{C}H_2^-K^+$, (ii) highly polar covalent, $\overset{\delta-}{CH_3}-\overset{\delta+}{Mg}-\overset{\delta-}{CH_3}$. (*c*) Covalent, $(CH_3)_2Hg$, $(CH_3CH_2)_4Pb$.

OXIDATION NUMBER

2.51 (*a*) Define oxidation number. (*b*) How can the oxidation number be used to determine the charge on the species?

▮ (*a*) The *oxidation number* (ON) is a value assigned to an atom based on relative electronegativities. The bonding e^-'s are "given" to the more electronegative element of the bond, and all remaining e^-'s, including the unshared ones, are counted. The ON equals the periodic group number minus the counted e's. The ON is not a real charge, but nevertheless is useful for revealing whether reactions of covalent species are redox reactions (see Problem 2.55). (*b*) The sum of the oxidation numbers of all the atoms in a species is equal to its charge, which is zero in the case of a molecule.

2.52 Given the usual ON's of the following atoms: for H, $+1$; for O, -2; and for halogens (X), -1. Determine the ON of the underlined atom in each species: (*a*) $\underline{C}O_2$, (*b*) $\underline{P}Cl_3$, (*c*) $\underline{N}_2O_5$, (*d*) $\underline{S}O_3^{2-}$, and (*e*) $\underline{N}H_4^+$.

▮ (*a*) $(ON)_C + 2(ON)_O = 0$ (charge on molecule); $(ON)_C + 2(-2) = 0$; $(ON)_C = +4$, (*b*) $+3$, (*c*) $+5$, (*d*) $(ON)_S + 3(-2) = -2$ (charge on the ion); $(ON)_S = +4$; and (*e*) -3.

2.53 (*a*) Compare the ON's of the underlined atoms in the following pairs of compounds: (i) $H_2\underline{O}$ and $H\underline{O}-\underline{O}H$, (ii) $\underline{N}H_3$ and $H_2\underline{N}-\underline{N}H_2$, and (iii) $\underline{C}H_4$ and $H_3\underline{C}-\underline{C}H_3$. (*b*) What trend is noticed in ON values when like atoms are bonded to each other? (*c*) Account for the trend.

▮ (*a*) (i) For O, -2 and -1 respectively. (ii) For N, -3 and -2 respectively. (iii) For C, -4 and -3 respectively. (*b*) The ON becomes less negative (or more positive) by a value of one. (*c*) Each like bonded atom gets only half of the mutually shared e^-'s; consequently, each atom is assigned one less e^- than it would have were it bonded only to H's. Hence the difference in ON values in part (*a*).

2.54 (*a*) What is the ON of C in ethanol, C_2H_6O? (*b*) Determine the ON of each C in ethanol from the structural formula $C^2H_3C^1H_2OH$. (*c*) What conclusion can be drawn from the results of (*a*) and (*b*)?

▮ (*a*) $(ON)_C = -2$. (*b*) $(ON)_{C^1} = -1$, $(ON)_{C^2} = -3$. (*c*) When the molecular formula is used, an average ON is calculated for all the C's. Using the structural formula gives information about individual C's.

2.55 (*a*) How does the oxidation number reveal whether a substance has undergone oxidation or reduction? (*b*) Identify the following changes as oxidations, reductions, or neither.

    (i) $CH_4 \rightarrow CH_3OH$ (ii) $H_2CCl_2 \rightarrow H_2C=O$ (iii) $H_2C=CH_2 \rightarrow H_3CCH_3$

    (iv) $HC\equiv CH \rightarrow CH_3\underset{|}{C}=O$

                             H

◢ (*a*) An increase in ON (more positive or less negative) is an *oxidation*, and a decrease is a *reduction*. (*b*) (i) The ON of C goes from -4 to -2: oxidation. (ii) ON is zero for both: neither. (iii) -2 to -3: reduction. (iv) The ON of both C's has changed, one from -1 to -3, and the other from -1 to $+2$. Thus the average value must be compared (see Problem 2.54) for both reactant and product; this is -1, unchanged: neither.

2.56 Compare the assignment of e^-'s for formal charge (FC) (see Problem 1.45) and oxidation number (ON), neither of which is a real charge.

◢ For FC, the bond is assumed to be purely covalent and each atom gets half the number of bonded atoms. For ON, the bond is assumed to be completely ionic and the e^-'s are assigned to the more electronegative atom.

2.57 Give the structural formula for the simplest hydrocarbon in which C has a zero ON.

◢ The number of H's and C's must be the same so that their ON's with opposite signs will cancel. The simplest such hydrocarbon is C_2H_2, $HC \equiv CH$.

INTERMOLECULAR FORCES

2.58 Define the three types of intermolecular forces that can lead to interactions between neutral molecules, in order of decreasing strength.

◢ The strongest force is the *hydrogen-bond*, which consists of a bond between an H attached to a highly electronegative atom, X, and an electronegative atom bearing an unshared pair of electrons, either in another molecule or in a different part of the same molecule. It is considerably stronger than *dipole-dipole* interactions, which result from the attraction of the $\delta +$ end of one polar molecule for the $\delta -$ end of another polar molecule. *van der Waals* (*London*) *forces* are the weakest. They are present to some extent between all molecules, but are important only in nonpolar molecules when the other two forces are absent. They are a result of a momentary imbalance in charge distribution in neighboring molecules, resulting in a temporary dipole moment. Although constantly changing, these induced dipoles result in a weak net attractive force. Molecules with higher molecular weights engender greater van der Waals attractive forces because they have a greater number of electrons.

2.59 List the electronegative atoms, in decreasing order, that can participate in H-bonding.

◢ $F > O > N \gg Cl$.

2.60 What are the two kinds of attractive forces that can exist when ionic species are present?

◢ Cation-anion electrostatic and ion-dipole forces.

2.61 Give two properties of molecules that are affected by H-bonding and explain how H-bonding affects these properties.

◢ Boiling point, which increases with effectiveness of H-bonding between like molecules, and solubility, which increases with H-bonding between solute and solvent molecules.

2.62 Draw the H-bonding in (*a*) H_2O, (*b*) CH_3OH, and (*c*) HF.

◢ (*a*)

$$H-O \qquad \quad H$$
$$H---O \qquad \quad H$$
$$\quad \quad H---O$$
$$\qquad \qquad \quad H$$

(*b*)

$$H_3C-O \qquad CH_3$$
$$H---O \qquad \quad H$$
$$\quad \quad H---O$$
$$\qquad \qquad CH_3$$

(*c*) $H-F---H-F---H-F$

2.63 The boiling point of H_2O ($100°C$) is much higher than that of HF ($-83°C$), even though they both form H-bonds and have similar molecular weights. Explain.

◢ One molecule of HF H-bonds at the most with two other molecules, but each H_2O molecule contributes both H's for H-bonding with the O's of two other molecules, and uses its O for H-bonding with an H of a third molecule.

2.64   Draw the H-bonding in a solution containing (*a*) CH_3OH and H_2O, (*b*) NH_3 and H_2O, and (*c*) $H_2C{=}O$ and CH_3NH_2.

(*a*)

$$CH_3-O \qquad H \qquad\text{and}\qquad H$$
$$H\text{---}O \qquad\qquad O\text{---}H-O$$
$$H \qquad\qquad CH_3 \qquad H$$

(*b*)

$$H \qquad\qquad H$$
$$H-N \qquad H \qquad\text{and}\qquad O-H\text{---}N-H$$
$$H\text{---}O \qquad\qquad H \qquad H$$
$$H$$

(*c*)

$$\begin{array}{c} H \qquad H \\ C{=}\ddot{O}{:}\text{---}N-CH_3. \\ H \qquad H \end{array}$$ The H's on the C cannot H-bond; C is not sufficiently electronegative (see Problem 2.59).

2.65   The three isomeric pentanes, C_5H_{12}, have boiling points of 9.5, 28, and 36°C. Match each boiling point with the correct structure and give your reasons.

▰   The three pentanes and their corresponding boiling points are: *n*-pentane, $CH_3CH_2CH_2CH_2CH_3$, 36 °C; isopentane, $CH_3CH_2CH(CH_3)_2$, 28 °C, and neopentane, $(CH_3)_4C$, 9.5 °C. Alkanes are either very slightly polar or nonpolar. The forces holding nonpolar molecules to each other are thus weak van der Waals forces which exert themselves on the surface of the molecules only. The straight-chain isomer may be thought of as a zig-zag chain with the greatest surface area, and two such molecules can touch each other along the length of the chain. The more contact between molecules, the greater the van der Waals forces and the higher the boiling point. A branched-chain isomer such as isopentane may be regarded more as spherelike. Spheres touch only at a point and thus the van der Waals forces are smaller. This isomer has a lower boiling point than the straight-chain isomer. Neopentane with the most branching has the lowest boiling point since it has the least surface area.

2.66   Place the noble gases in order of increasing boiling point and justify your order.

▰   He (4 K) < Ne (27 K) < Ar (87 K) < Kr (120 K) < Xe (166 K) < Rn (211 K). As the atomic number increases, so does the number of electrons in each atom, and the van der Waals forces. The greater these forces, the higher the boiling point.

2.67   Account for the following facts: (*a*) the boiling point of NO (-152 °C) is much higher than that of N_2 (-195 °C); (*b*) acetone, $(CH_3)_2C{=}O$, and water are completely miscible; and (*c*) the boiling point of ethanol (78°C) is much higher than that of its isomer, dimethyl ether, CH_3OCH_3 (-24°C).

▰   (*a*) When both molecules have similar molecular weights the one with stronger intermolecular attractive forces will have a higher boiling point. NO is polar and its molecules are attracted intermolecularly by dipole-dipole forces; N_2 is nonpolar.   (*b*) The O in acetone H-bonds with the H of H_2O.   (*c*) The terminal H of one ethanol H-bonds with the O of another ethanol [see Problem 2.64(*a*)]. The H's in dimethyl ether are attached to C, and are not available for H-bonding.

2.68   Predict which of the following has a higher melting point, NaCl or CCl_4, and give your reason.

▰   NaCl has the higher melting point (801 °C). The crystal units are anions and cations, which are held together by strong electrostatic attractive forces. Hence much energy much be supplied to separate the ions. The crystal units in CCl_4 are nonpolar molecules, which are easily separated at a low temperature. CCl_4 melts at -24 °C.

2.69   Account for the following facts: (*a*) NaCl is soluble in water but not in pentane, and (*b*) mineral oil, a mixture of high molecular weight hydrocarbons, is soluble in hexane, but not in ethanol or water.

▰   (*a*) In addition to being highly polar, a solvent must have the ability to form strong bonds to stabilize the ions. Water H-bonds with anions, in this case Cl^-; and each Na^+ is attracted to additional H_2O molecules by the negative ends of the water dipole, via ion-dipole forces. Saturated hydrocarbons like pentane cannot stabilize ions in any way.   (*b*) The van der Waals forces between nonpolar molecules (as in mineral oil and pentane) are very weak and such molecules can dissolve into each other with relative ease. The H-bonding in ethanol or water is relatively strong, and most nonpolar molecules cannot overcome these attractive forces. These facts explain the adage "Like dissolves like."

2.70 Which of the following solvents would resemble water as a solvent: CCl_4, CH_3OH, liquified NH_3, $(CH_3)_2S{=}O$ (dimethylsulfoxide, DMSO)? Explain your choices.

▰ CH_3OH and liquid NH_3, like H_2O, are polar molecules capable of forming H-bonds, and so can separate and stabilize both anions and cations in solution. They are called *protic solvents*. While DMSO is also polar, its H atoms cannot H-bond. CCl_4 is nonpolar.

2.71 (*a*) Explain how a *polar aprotic solvent* acts to dissolve an ionic solute. (*b*) Draw a diagram of DMSO (Problem 2.70) solvating NaCl.

▰ (*a*) A polar aprotic solvent strongly solvates the cation by ion-dipole attraction using the negative end of its dipole which is exposed. Unlike a *protic* solvent it does not have the ability to solvate an anion through H-bonding. The anion is essentially "free" because it is only very weakly solvated by the positive end of the dipole which is buried deeply within the molecule. (*b*) The dipole moment of DMSO points toward the O, and the molecule can be regarded as having the shape shown in Fig. 2-14. Each Na^+ is surrounded by a shell of DMSO molecules, with the O's pointing toward the cation. The methyl groups shield the S, which is the positive end of the dipole, thereby preventing the approach to the Cl^-.

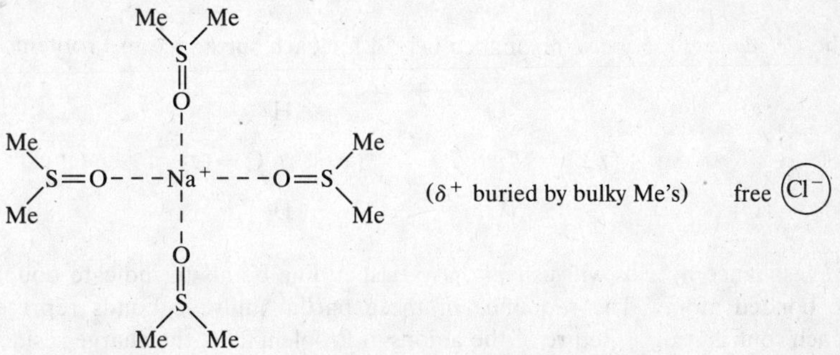

Fig. 2-14

2.72 (*a*) Define the term dielectric constant. (*b*) How is it related to the ability of a solvent to dissolve an ionic solute?

▰ (*a*) The *dielectric constant* measures the ability of a solvent to separate oppositely charged ions. Solvents with high dielectric constants tend to be more polar. (*b*) A good solvent for an ionic salt not only should have a high dielectric constant, but should be able to H-bond to the anion as well.

2.73 Explain why the reactivity of anions is greater in a polar aprotic solvent like DMSO or dimethylformamide (DMF, $HCONMe_2$) than in a protic solvent like ethanol or in a nonpolar solvent like benzene.

▰ Any factor that stabilizes the anion is expected to reduce its reactivity. Anions are H-bonded to a protic solvent like ethanol, thus their reactivity is diminished. They are impeded in benzene as well, because of the strong anion-cation attraction called *ion-pairing*. Polar aprotic solvents shield the cation effectively from the anion so that ion-pairing does not occur, but provide little or no solvation for the anion, which is considered to be "free".

2.74 Explain why glycerol, $CH_2OHCHOHCH_2OH$, is a very viscous liquid.

▰ Glycerol molecules, with three OH groups, H-bond with each other in long chains with many interlocking crosslinkages.

RESONANCE AND DELOCALIZED π ELECTRONS

2.75 (*a*) Differentiate between structural isomers and *contributing* (*resonance*) structures. (*b*) What is a resonance hybrid?

▰ (*a*) Structural isomers are real molecules whose atoms are linked together in different ways to form different "skeletons". *Contributing structures are not real*. They are written whenever one electronic structure cannot adequately represent the actual structure. Their atoms are σ-bonded to each other in the same way (same skeleton), but π bonds and unshared pairs are distributed differently, with the consequence that the presence and position of formal charges may be different. A double-headed arrow (↔) is written between them to indicate resonance, *not* equilibrium. (*b*) The *resonance hybrid* is the real structure that is considered to be a "blend" of the hypothetical contributing structures.

2.76 Write resonance structures for the following substances, showing all outer-shell electrons and formal charges when present: (*a*) formate ion, HCO_2^-, (*b*) nitrite ion, NO_2^-, (*c*) formaldehyde, H_2CO, and (*d*) nitrate ion, NO_3^-.

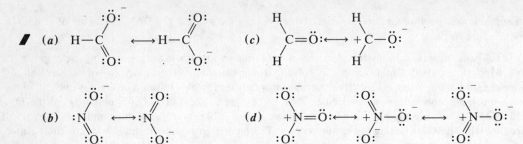

2.77 Represent the *delocalized n-bonded* resonance hybrid for each substance in Problem 2.76.

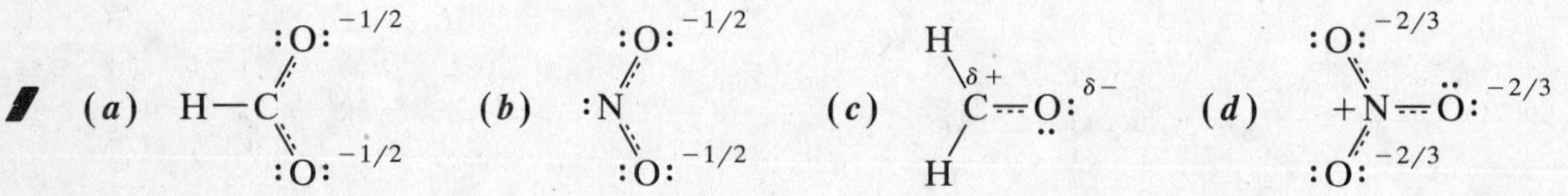

Structures of resonance hybrids will usually have dashed-line bonds to indicate double or triple bond character between the bonded atoms. The sequence of these partial multiple bonds represents the extended π-bond overlap. In each contributing structure of the anions in Problem 2.76, the charge resides on a different O atom. In the hybrid one might say that each O has a fractional − charge.

2.78 (*a*) Describe the resonance hybrid of (i) NO_2^- and (ii) NO_3^- in terms of overlapping atomic orbitals. (*b*) What is meant by the term *delocalization (resonance) energy*? (*c*) Compare the delocalization (resonance) energies (*stabilities*) of NO_2^- and NO_3^-.

(*a*) (i) N has three sp^2 HO's. Two form σ-bonds with the two O's and the third holds the unshared pair. Its *p* AO overlaps laterally with a *p* AO of *each* O, resulting in extended π-bond overlap encompassing both O's and the N. The charge is thus spread out over both O's. See Fig. 2-15(i). (ii) NO_3^- is much like NO_2^- except that a third O is involved in the extended π bond. The − charge is delocalized over three O's; each O has a −2/3 charge. See Fig. 2-15(ii).

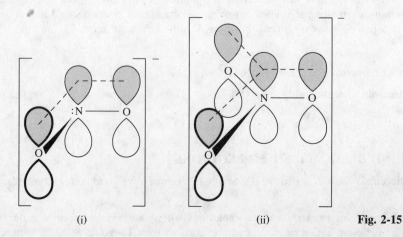

(i) (ii) **Fig. 2-15**

(b) The energy of the hybrid is always *lower* than that of any of the individual resonance structures. The greater the number of contributing structures with similar energies, the lower is the energy of the hybrid (more stable). The presence of more similar energy contributing structures results in more extended π bonding, permitting e^-'s to move in a larger space, thereby lessening electron repulsion. This difference between the energy of a "nonresonance" hypothetical structure, which can only be calculated, and the experimentally determined energy of the actual hybrid is the resonance or delocalization energy.

(c) The negative charge in NO_3^-, with three contributing structures, is delocalized over all three O's rather than over two O's as in NO_2^-, with two contributing structures. NO_3^- has more delocalization energy and, thus, is more stable than NO_2^-.

2.79 (a) Write contributing structures and the hybrid for N_2O (NNO). (b) Discuss how the N—N and N—O bond lengths in the hybrid compare with those in each contributing structure.

$\blacksquare$ (a) $:\overset{-}{\underset{..}{O}}-\overset{+}{N}\equiv N:$ $\longleftrightarrow$ $:\overset{..}{O}=\overset{+}{N}=\overset{-}{\underset{..}{N}}:$. The hybrid is $:\overset{\delta-}{\underset{..}{O}}\text{---}\overset{+}{N}\equiv N:^{\delta-}$.
   (i)   (ii)

(b) A specific bond length in the contributing structure has a standard single, double, or triple bond value. Bond lengths in the hybrid are intermediate in value between those of all the contributing structures. The O to N bond length in the hybrid is shorter than the single bond in (i) but longer than the double bond in (ii). The N to N bond length in the hybrid is longer than in (i) but shorter than in (ii).

2.80 (a) Write the contributing resonance structures and the delocalized hybrid for diazomethane, H_2CN_2, whose skeleton is H_2CNN. (b) Give the hybridized state for C and each N in each structure. (c) How does the H—C—H bond angle in the hybrid compare with the bond angles predicted from each contributing structure? (d) What generalization about hybrid conditions can be drawn from the answer to part (b)?

$\blacksquare$ (a) $H_2C=\overset{+}{N}=\overset{-}{\underset{..}{N}}:^-$ (A) $\longleftrightarrow$ $H_2\overset{..}{\underset{..}{C}}-\overset{+}{N}\equiv N:$ (B)   or $H_2\overset{\delta-}{C}\text{---}\overset{+}{N}\equiv \overset{\delta-}{N}:$ (C, resonance hybrid).
   (b) sp^2 sp sp^2 sp^3 sp sp sp^2 sp sp
   (c) The bond angle expected from **A** is 120°; that from **B** is 109.5°. Since the hybrid is a blend of each, the actual bond angle has some intermediate value.
   (d) To maximize extended π bonding, the atoms in the hybrid need p AO's. Consequently, the HO's used to form the σ-bonds have less p-character, i.e., C is sp^2-like rather than sp^3, and the terminal N is sp-like rather than sp^2.

2.81 Explain how the hybrid structure is related to the structures of each of the following pairs of contributing resonance structures:

(a) $^+CH_2-\overset{-}{\underset{..}{C}}H_2$ (A) $\longleftrightarrow$ $CH_2=CH_2$ (B)

(b) $H_2C=\overset{..}{\underset{..}{O}}:$ (C) $\longleftrightarrow$ $H_2\overset{+}{C}-\overset{..}{\underset{..}{O}}:^-$ (D)

(c) $R_2\overset{+}{C}-C=\underset{\underset{R}{|}}{\overset{..}{O}}:$ (E) $\longleftrightarrow$ $R_2C=C-\underset{\underset{R}{|}}{\overset{..}{O}}:^+$ (F)

(d) (acylium ion) $R-\overset{+}{C}=\overset{..}{O}:$ (G) $\longleftrightarrow$ $R-C\equiv O:^+$ (H)

(e) $R-C-\overset{..}{\underset{\underset{:O:}{||}}{O}}H$ (I) $\longleftrightarrow$ $R-C=\overset{+}{\underset{\underset{:O:^-}{|}}{O}}H$ (J)

(f) $R-\overset{..}{\underset{..}{C}}H-C-R$ (K) $\longleftrightarrow$ $R-CH=C-R$ (L)
       $\underset{:O:}{||}$ $\underset{:O:^-}{|}$

(g) $CH_3\overset{..}{\overset{+}{\underset{\underset{:O:^-}{|}}{S}}}-CH_3$ (M) $\longleftrightarrow$ $CH_3-\overset{..}{\underset{\underset{:O:}{||}}{S}}-CH_3$ (N)

$\blacksquare$ (a) Since the charged structure **A** has a high energy, the hybrid is the same as **B** and has practically no delocalization energy. Factors responsible for the high energy of **A** are: fewer number of covalent bonds, less than an octet on the C^+, and charge separation. (b) Even though **D** shows charge separation, this is reasonable because O is much more electronegative than C and strongly attracts the π electrons. The hybrid, $H_2\overset{\delta+}{C}\text{---}\overset{..}{O}:^{\delta-}$, is a good blend of both. (c) The hybrid more resembles **E**, the major contributor, because **F** has a higher energy. A + charge on an atom with less than an octet is better on the less electronegative atom, in this case C. (d) The hybrid more resembles **H**, the principal contributing structure, because both C and O have an octet and there is one more covalent bond. A + charge on an electronegative atom is not bad if the atom has an octet. **G** is possible, but has high energy because C has only six e^-'s. (*e*) Both have the same number of covalent bonds and make significant contribution to the hybrid. The hybrid more resembles **I** because **J** exhibits charge separation and has the higher energy. (*f*) Both have the same number of covalent bonds and make significant contribution. The hybrid more resembles **L** because the − charge is on the more electronegative O. (*g*) **M** has charge separation which is overcome in **N** when the S atom expands its octet by $p - d \pi$ bonding between one of its empty d AO's and a filled p AO of the O atom. This is a "trade-off", and the hybrid resembles both.

2.82 Explain why 1,3-pentadiene, $H_2C{=}CH{-}CH{=}CH{-}CH_3$, is more stable than 1,4-pentadiene, $H_2C{=}CH{-}CH_2{-}CH{=}CH_2$.

▮ The four doubly-bonded C's of the 1,3-isomer use sp^2 HO's for σ bonding, leaving a p AO on each C atom capable of lateral overlap to give an extended π system. The hybrid is $H_2C{\cdots}CH{\cdots}CH{\cdots}CHCH_3$. The 1,4-isomer cannot exhibit extended π bonding because C^3 is sp^3 hybridized and has no p AO.

2.83 Account for the fact that isocyanic acid, $HN{=}C{=}O$, and cyanic acid, $N{\equiv}C{-}OH$, have the same conjugate base.

▮ The conjugate bases of each acid are contributing structures of the same resonance hybrid.

$$H{:}\ddot{N}{=}C{=}\ddot{O}{:} \xrightarrow{-H^+} {:}\ddot{\ddot{N}}{=}C{=}\ddot{O}{:} \longleftrightarrow {:}N{\equiv}C{-}\ddot{\ddot{O}}{:} \xleftarrow{-H^+} {:}N{\equiv}C{-}\ddot{O}{:}H.$$ The hybrid is ${:}\overset{\delta-}{N}{\cdots}C{\cdots}\overset{\delta-}{\ddot{O}}{:}$.

2.84 (*a*) Explain why BF_3 exists whereas BH_3 does not. (*b*) Compare the B—F bond length in BF_3 and BF_4^-.

▮ (*a*) The delocalization of electrons from F to B in the former reduces the deficiency of electrons on B, leading to increased stability. This compensation does not occur in BH_3.

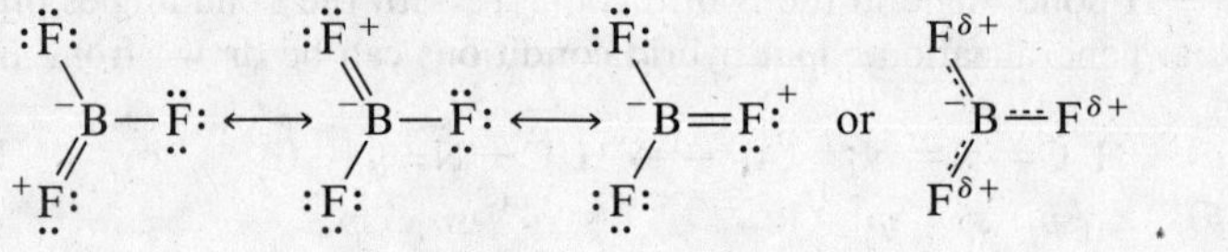

(*b*) Because of some double-bond character in BF_3 it has a shorter B—F bond than does BF_4^-.

2.85 Explain why each of the following structures is not a resonance form:

(*a*) ${:}\ddot{O}{=}\ddot{O}{:}$ and ${:}\ddot{O}{-}\ddot{O}{:}$ (*b*) $H_2\ddot{N}{-}O{-}H$ and $H_2\ddot{N}{=}O{-}H$

(*c*) $CH_3{-}\underset{\underset{OH}{|}}{C}{=}CH_2$ and $CH_3{-}\underset{\underset{O}{\parallel}}{C}{-}CH_3$

▮ (*a*) Contributing structures must have the same number of paired electrons. Singlet and triplet states (Problem 2.33) cannot be contributing structures. (*b*) The second structure cannot exist; N has ten electrons. (*c*) These isomers differ in the placement of the H atom; in this special case they are called *tautomers*.

CHAPTER 3
Chemical Reactivity and Organic Reactions

REACTION MECHANISM

3.1 What is a reaction mechanism and how does it differ from a balanced chemical equation?

 A balanced equation provides the number of moles of both reactants and products but does not show how the reaction proceeds. A *reaction mechanism* provides a detailed step by step description of a reaction.

3.2 What information is provided by a reaction mechanism?

 1. The bonds broken and formed.
 2. The discrete steps in the conversion of reactant (substrate) A to products D and E which may proceed through several steps. For example, A → D + E may proceed through steps i, ii, and iii as follows:

$$A \xrightarrow{\text{i}} [B] \xrightarrow{\text{ii}} [C] \xrightarrow{\text{iii}} D + E$$

 3. The reaction *intermediates*, i.e., [B] and [C], formed during the intermediate steps.
 4. The relative rates of the discrete steps, especially the slowest one.
     Note that once an intermediate is formed it must react further. If only some of it did, the balance would accumulate and become a product.

3.3 (*a*) Describe *heterolytic* (*polar*) covalent bond cleavage of (i) Ag:Ï:, (ii) $H_3\overset{+}{N}:\overset{-}{B}F_3$, and (iii) $Cu(:ÖH_2)_4^{2+}$. Focus on the indicated shared pair of e⁻'s. (*b*) What is the reverse of heterolytic cleavage called? (*c*) Describe *homolytic* covalent bond cleavage of $H_3CO:OCH_3$.

 (*a*) Both bonding electrons remain with the more electronegative atom.
 (i) Ag:Ï: → Ag⁺ + :Ï:⁻ When the bonded atoms have no charge, the more electronegative atom (or group) holding the pair of e⁻'s has a negative charge, the other atom is positive.
 (ii) $H_3\overset{+}{N}:\overset{-}{B}F_3 \to H_3N: + BF_3$ Bonded atoms with formal charges give uncharged products.
 (iii) $Cu(:ÖH_2)_4^{2+} \to Cu^{2+} + 4:ÖH_2$ For positively charged reactants, the less electronegative atom acquires the positive charge ensuring conservation of charge.
 (*b*) Coordinate covalent bonding.
 (*c*) Each bonded atom gets one unpaired electron to give species called *radicals*. Homolysis may be initiated by uv light or heat.

$$H_3CO:OCH_3 \longrightarrow 2\,H_3CO\cdot \text{ A radical}$$

REACTIVE CARBON INTERMEDIATES

3.4 For the reactive carbon intermediates *carbocation*, *carbanion*, *radical*, *singlet carbene*, *triplet carbene*, and *radical cation*, show in a table the simplified structure, calculation of formal charge, number of bonds, number of lone

Table 3-1 Reactive Carbon Intermediates

	Carbocation	Carbanion	Radical	Singlet*	Triplet†	Radical cation
				Carbene		
Structure	>Ċ—	—Ċ:⁻	—Ċ<	>C:	—Ċ—	—Ċ—
Formal charge	4 − 3 − 0 = +1	4 − 3 − 2 = −1	4 − 3 − 1 = 0	4 − 2 − 2 = 0	4 − 2 − 2 = 0	4 − 2 − 1 = +1
bonds	3	3	3	2	2	2
lone pairs	0	1	0	1	0	0
HON	3	4	3	3	2	2
HO's used	sp^2	sp^3	sp^2	sp^2	sp	sp
Shape	trigonal coplanar	pyramidal	trigonal coplanar	bent	linear	linear

*The singlet carbene has two unshared e⁻'s with opposite spins paired in one orbital.
†The triplet carbene has two e⁻'s with the same spin, each in a different orbital making it a diradical.

pairs of e⁻'s, HON, type of HO's used, and shape. In general for any element, a cation has a + charge, an anion a − charge and a radical has at least one unpaired e⁻.

3.5 (*a*) Typically in what kind of orbital can we find (i) an unshared pair of e⁻'s and (ii) an unpaired e⁻? (*b*) How are empty or half-filled *p* AO's oriented in space with respect to the array of *σ* bonds making up the geometry of the molecule?

◢ (*a*) (i) a hybrid orbital, (ii) a *p* AO. (*b*) At right angles. See Problem 3.6.

3.6 For each of the six carbon intermediates in Problem 3.4 draw (i) a wedge projection and (ii) an orbital diagram.

◢ See Fig. 3-1.

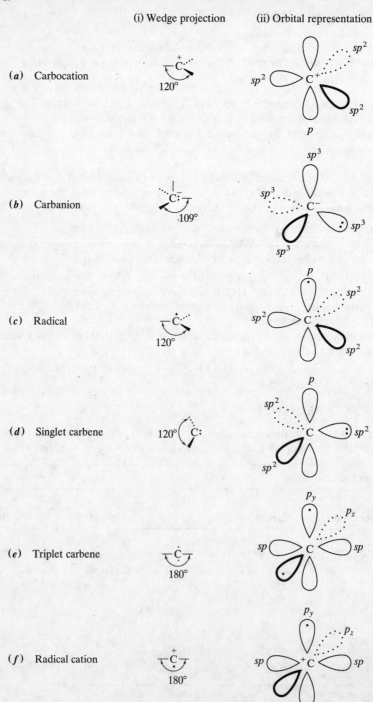

	(i) Wedge projection	(ii) Orbital representation
(*a*) Carbocation		
(*b*) Carbanion		
(*c*) Radical		
(*d*) Singlet carbene		
(*e*) Triplet carbene		
(*f*) Radical cation		

Fig. 3-1

3.7 (a) Discuss the origin of the designations (i) singlet and (ii) triplet. (b) Compare and account for the relative energies of a singlet and triplet (i) dialkylcarbene (R_2C) and (ii) dihalogenocarbene (X_2C). (c) Explain which X_2C (X = F, Cl, Br, I) is the most stable singlet as compared to the corresponding triplet.

    ◢ (a) (i) Since there are no unpaired e^-'s, S = 0 and 2S + 1 = 1 (the spin state equation, see Problem 2.33). The spin state is singlet. (ii) There are two unpaired e^-'s, each with a spin number of $+1/2$ so S = 1; 2S + 1 = 3 and the spin state is triplet.

    (b) (i) The triplet carbene has a lower energy because with two e^-'s in different orbitals there is less electrostatic repulsion than when both are in the same orbital. (ii) A p AO of X with a lone pair of e^-'s can overlap laterally with the empty p AO of the singlet carbene, thereby stabilizing the singlet state. This stabilization is not possible in the triplet state whose p AO's are not empty. The resonance structures are

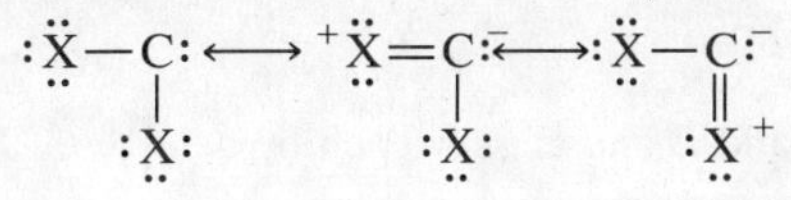

$$:\ddot{X}-\ddot{C}: \longleftrightarrow\ ^+\ddot{X}=\overset{..}{C}:^- \longleftrightarrow :\ddot{X}-\overset{..}{C}:^-$$
$$\underset{:\ddot{X}:}{|}\qquad\qquad \underset{:\ddot{X}:}{|}\qquad\qquad \underset{:\ddot{X}:^+}{\|}$$

    (c) $:CF_2$. Since F and C are in the same period of the periodic table, their p AO's are about the same size permitting more efficient overlap. Furthermore, of the X—C bonds, the F—C bond length is the shortest which again provides for more extensive lateral overlap of the respective p AO's.

3.8 Can the properties of O_2 be explained by (a) the Lewis structure and (b) the MO structure?

    ◢ (a) No. The 12 valence e^-'s of O_2, six from each O, could be assigned to give the structure $:\ddot{O}::\ddot{O}:$, having two complete shells of eight e^-'s. However, this structure does not account for the paramagnetism and bond strength (Problem 2.32) of 1.5 of O_2. (b) Yes [see Problem 2.30(c)]. This structure is consistent with the paramagnetism (O_2 is a diradical) and the bond strength of 1.5.

3.9 Compare and explain the difference in the ionization energy and electron affinity of $\cdot CH_3$.

    ◢ The electron affinity is less than the ionization energy. When $\cdot CH_3$ gains an e^- (electron affinity) to become a carbanion, C acquires a stable octet of e^-'s. When it loses an e^- (ionization energy) it becomes the unstable carbocation with only six e^-'s.

3.10 Classify each of the following carbon intermediates: (a) $C_2H_5\ddot{C}-H$, (b) $(CH_3)_3C\cdot$, (c) $CH_3\overset{-}{\ddot{C}}HCH_3$, and (d) $H_2C=CH-CH_2^+$.

    ◢ (a) A singlet carbene, (b) a radical, (c) a carbanion, and (d) a carbocation.

3.11 Give the product formed from the following reactions of intermediates: (a) $CH_3^+ + H_3C:^-$ and (b) $H_3C\cdot + \cdot CH_3$. Relate each reaction to homolytic and heterolytic bond cleavage.

    ◢ (a) H_3C-CH_3, the opposite of heterolytic cleavage. (b) H_3C-CH_3, the opposite of homolytic cleavage.

3.12 Give an orbital description of (a) carbocation in $H_2C=\underset{|}{C}^+$, and (b) carbanion in $H_2C=\underset{|}{\overset{..}{C}}:^-$.
$\qquad\qquad\qquad\qquad\qquad\qquad\qquad\qquad\quad H\qquad\qquad\qquad\qquad\qquad\quad H$

    ◢ (a) Removal of one substituent with its bonding electron pair leaves a carbocation with sp HO's. One remaining p AO is part of the π bond and the second empty p AO is in the plane of the molecule at right angles to the plane of the π bond. See Fig. 3-2(a). (b) Doubly bonded carbanions use sp^2 HO's, two for sigma bonds to the other unsaturated C and to a substituent. The third HO has the lone electron pair. The remaining p AO is part of the π bond in a plane at a right angle to the plane of three σ bonds. See Fig. 3-2(b).

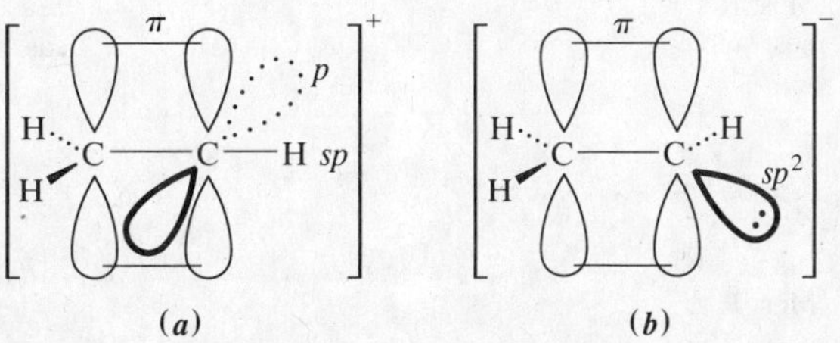

(a)   (b)   **Fig. 3-2**

3.13 Supply the structure and type for the intermediate species designated by ?.

(a) $CH_3CH(OH)CH_3 + H^+ \xrightarrow{heat} ? + H:\ddot{O}:H$

(b) $CH_3-CH=CH-CH_3 + H:\ddot{I}: \longrightarrow ? + :\ddot{I}:^-$

(c) $CH_3CH_2-N=N-CH_2CH_3 \xrightarrow{heat} ? + :N:::N:$

(d) $CH_3CHI_2 + Zn \longrightarrow ? + ZnI_2$

(e) $CH_3CH_2Cl + AlCl_3 \longrightarrow ? + [AlCl_4]^-$

(f) $CH_3-C\equiv C:H + Na^+:\ddot{N}H_2^- \longrightarrow ?\ Na^+ + H:\ddot{N}H_2$

(g) $CH_3-\overset{+}{\ddot{N}}\equiv N: \longrightarrow ? + :N:::N:$

▉ (a) $(CH_3)_2\overset{+}{C}H$, a carbocation; (b) $CH_3-\overset{+}{C}H-CH_2CH_3$, a carbocation; (c) $CH_3\dot{C}H_2$, a radical; (d) $CH_3\ddot{C}H$, a singlet carbene; (e) $CH_3CH_2^+$, a carbocation; (f) $CH_3-C\equiv C:^-$, a carbanion; (g) H_3C^+, a carbocation.

3.14 Write structures for **A** and **B** and classify each by type.

$$CH_3CH_2\ddot{O}H \xrightarrow{-e^-} A \longrightarrow \cdot CH_3 + B$$

▉ **A** is the radical cation $[CH_3CH_2\ddot{O}H]^+$. Loss of an *n* electron from O is most likely because it has a higher energy than bonded electrons. **B** is the resonance-stabilized cation $[CH_2=\overset{+}{O}H \leftrightarrow {}^+CH_2\ddot{O}H]$.

3.15 Give the structure for **C** in the following reaction and classify it by type. $Na + RC\equiv CR \rightarrow Na^+ + C$

▉ **C** is $R-\dot{C}=\ddot{C}-R$, a *radical anion*. One C is a typical vinyl carbanion [Problem 3.12(*b*)], while the other C is a vinyl radical.

3.16 (a) What is the major factor that influences the relative stabilities of carbanions, radicals, and carbocations? (b) Define the term inductive effect. (c) How does the inductive effect of an alkyl group affect the stability of these three intermediates?

▉ (a) Any diminution of + or − charge or of electron deficiency on the C stabilizes the intermediate. (b) The *inductive effect* of a substituent affects the charge or electron density on the C. Electronegative groups such as O, N, and halogens tend to withdraw electron density from the C whereas electropositive groups such as alkyl groups tend to increase its electron density. This effect is transmitted through the chain of σ bonds and diminishes with increasing chain length. (c) The carbanion C, with an unshared electron pair, has a high electron density. Electron-releasing alkyl groups make this electron density even higher, thus destabilizing the carbanion. Since the C's of the carbocation and radical are electron-deficient, these intermediates are stabilized by the electron-releasing inductive effect of an alkyl group, which diminishes their electron deficiency. The more R's attached to the C, the greater is the effect on the stability as shown:

Carbanions:

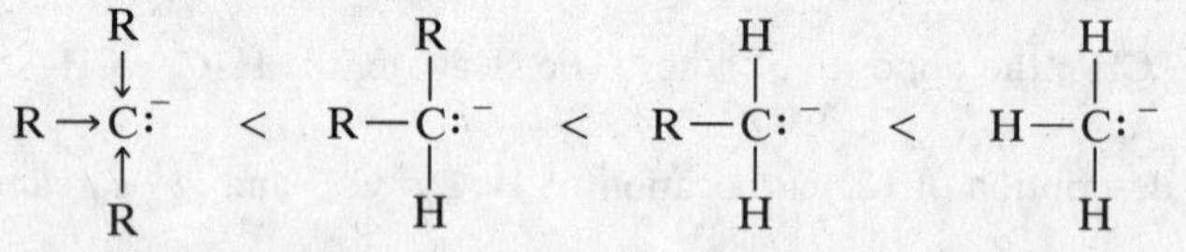

$$\begin{array}{ccccccc}
& R & & R & & H & & H \\
& \downarrow & & | & & | & & | \\
R\rightarrow &C:^- & < & R-C:^- & < & R-C:^- & < & H-C:^- \\
& \uparrow & & | & & | & & | \\
& R & & H & & H & & H
\end{array}$$

Most R's, least stable   Fewest R's, most stable

Radicals:

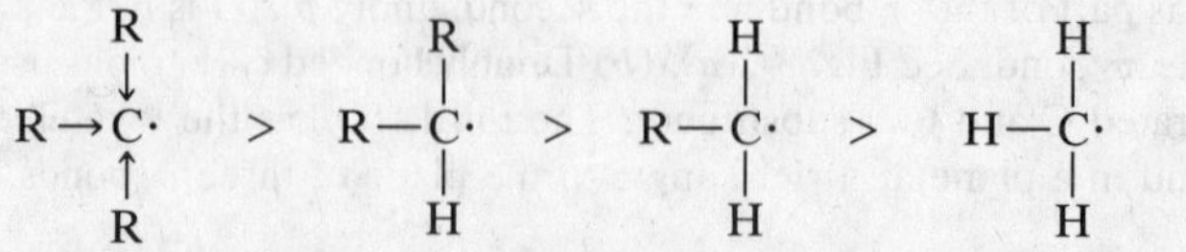

$$\begin{array}{ccccccc}
& R & & R & & H & & H \\
& \downarrow & & | & & | & & | \\
R\rightarrow &C\cdot & > & R-C\cdot & > & R-C\cdot & > & H-C\cdot \\
& \uparrow & & | & & | & & | \\
& R & & H & & H & & H
\end{array}$$

Most R's, most stable   Least R's, least stable

Carbocations:

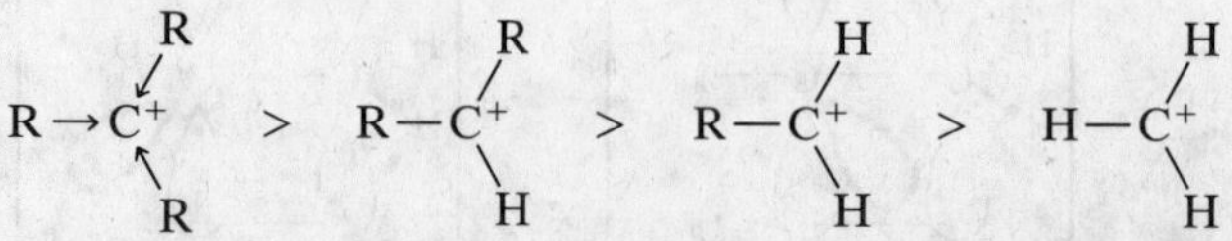

$$\begin{array}{ccccccc}
& R & & R & & H & & H \\
& \downarrow & & \diagup & & \diagup & & \diagup \\
R\rightarrow &C^+ & > & R-C^+ & > & R-C^+ & > & H-C^+ \\
& \diagdown & & \diagdown & & \diagdown & & \diagdown \\
& R & & H & & H & & H
\end{array}$$

Most R's, most stable   Least R's, least stable

3.17 Show how delocalization by extended π bonding (resonance) affects the stabilities of (*a*) a carbocation, (*b*) a radical, and (*c*) a carbanion. Illustrate with the H_2C=$CHCH_2$ (allyl) group.

▰ Extended π bonding can delocalize electron density by either electron contribution or withdrawal, depending on the charge or electron density on the C. As a result, extended π bonding *always* stabilizes these intermediates as shown by the following contributing structures:

(*a*) Carbocation:

$$
\begin{matrix} H & H & H \\ | & | & | \\ C::C:C & {}^{+} \\ | & & | \\ H & & H \end{matrix}
\longleftrightarrow
\begin{matrix} H & H & H \\ | & | & | \\ {}^{+}C:C::C \\ | & & | \\ H & & H \end{matrix}
$$

(*b*) Radical:

$$
\begin{matrix} H & H & H \\ | & | & | \\ C::C:C\cdot \\ | & & | \\ H & & H \end{matrix}
\longleftrightarrow
\begin{matrix} H & H & H \\ | & | & | \\ \cdot C:C::C \\ | & & | \\ H & & H \end{matrix}
$$

(*c*) Carbanion:

$$
\begin{matrix} H & H & H \\ | & | & | \\ C::C:\ddot{C}:{}^{-} \\ | & & | \\ H & & H \end{matrix}
\longleftrightarrow
\begin{matrix} H & H & H \\ | & | & | \\ {}^{-}:\ddot{C}:C::C \\ | & & | \\ H & & H \end{matrix}
$$

TYPES OF CHEMICAL REACTIONS

3.18 Define the following general types of chemical reactions: (*a*) Addition; (*b*) elimination: (i) β-elimination, (ii) α-elimination, and (iii) other than β- or α-; (*c*) displacement (substitution); (*d*) rearrangement; and (*e*) oxidation-reduction (redox).

▰ (*a*) *Addition*. Two reactants combine to yield one product. Addition frequently occurs with organic compounds at double or triple bonds and occasionally at small-sized rings.

(*b*) *Elimination* (*decomposition*). Elimination is the reverse of addition because two or more atoms or groups are removed from one molecule. (i) β-elimination involves removal from adjacent atoms and always leads to an increase in multiple bonding. (ii) α-elimination is the removal from the same atom and produces a carbene if this atom is carbon. (iii) If elimination is other than from adjacent atoms or the same atom, a ring results. For example, removal from atoms once removed (γ-elimination) affords a three-membered ring. Decomposition, a kind of elimination, is the energy-catalyzed breakdown of a molecule into at least two molecule without the intervention of any other reagent.

(*c*) *Displacement* (*substitution*). This is the replacement of one group by another. When an H is displaced, the reaction is called a substitution.

(*d*) *Rearrangement*. Bonds are scrambled to form an isomer.

(*e*) *Redox*. This involves transfer of electrons or change in oxidation number. Oxidation of a C is signaled by a decrease in the number of its bonded H's or an increase in its number of bonds to other atoms such as C, O, N, Cl, Br, F, and S.

Note that these names refer only to the net reaction as given by the chemical equation. For multistep mechanisms, individual steps may be of different types.

3.19 Give equations for the reactions of (*a*) H_3C^+, (*b*) H_3C:$^-$, (*c*) $H_3C\cdot$, (*d*) $H_2C\cdot^+$ with Br_2, and classify the reactions.

▰ (*a*) $H_3C^+ + :\ddot{B}r:\ddot{B}r: \longrightarrow H_3C:\ddot{B}r: + \ddot{B}r:^+$

(*c*) $H_3C\cdot + :\ddot{B}r:\ddot{B}r: \longrightarrow H_3C:\ddot{B}r: + :\ddot{B}r\cdot$

(*b*) $H_3C:^- + :\ddot{B}r:\ddot{B}r: \longrightarrow H_3C:\ddot{B}r: + :\ddot{B}r:^-$

(*d*) $H_2C\cdot^+ + :\ddot{B}r:\ddot{B}r: \longrightarrow H_2\dot{C}:\ddot{B}r: + \ddot{B}r:^+$

They all are displacement reactions in which the CH_3 displaces a Br from Br_2. The charge or odd e^- on Br is usually the same as on H_3C [see (ii) of Problem 3.20(*c*) for an exception].

3.20 (*a*) Give the final product from the reaction of each type of methylene carbene—singlet and triplet—with Br_2. (*b*) Identify the type of reaction. (*c*) In addition to a one-step reaction, both carbenes can proceed to a product by two steps. Show the steps for the (i) triplet and (ii) singlet.

◢ (a) H_2CBr_2

(b) This is an addition reaction because two species combined to form one.

(c) (i) $H_2C\cdot + :\ddot{Br}:\ddot{Br}: \xrightarrow{\text{step 1}} H_2C:\ddot{Br}: + \cdot\ddot{Br}: \xrightarrow{\text{step 2}} H_2C:\ddot{Br}:_2$

(ii) $H_2C: + :\ddot{Br}:\ddot{Br}: \xrightarrow{\text{step 1}} H_2\overset{-}{C}:\ddot{Br}: + \ddot{Br}:^+ \xrightarrow{\text{step 2}} H_2C:\ddot{Br}:_2$

$H_2C:$ acts as an electrophile towards Br_2 rather than a nucleophile (see Problem 3.25), because the product of step 1 has an octet. If it acted as a nucleophile, the intermediate ($H_2C:Br$) would have only a sextet.

3.21 Give the type of each of the following reactions. (A reaction may belong to more than one type.)

(a) $H_2C{=}CH_2 + Br_2 \longrightarrow H_2CBr{-}CH_2Br$

(b) $HO:^- + CH_3Cl \longrightarrow CH_3OH + Cl^-$

(c) $Me_2NH_2^+ + CH_3O^- \longrightarrow Me_2NH + CH_3OH$

(d) $CHCl_3 + OH^- \longrightarrow :CCl_2 + H_2O + Cl^-$

(e) $H_2C{-}CH_2 + H_2O \xrightarrow{H^+} H_2C{-}CH_2$ (with epoxide O, product with HO OH)

(f) $CH_3CHBrCHBrCH_3 + Zn \rightarrow CH_3CH{=}CHCH_3 + ZnBr_2$

(g) $(NH_4)^+(NCO)^- \longrightarrow O{=}C(NH_2)_2$

(h) $C_6H_6 + Cl_2 \xrightarrow{Fe} C_6H_5Cl + HCl$

(i) $BrCH_2CH_2CH_2Br + Zn \longrightarrow H_2C{-}CH_2 + ZnBr_2$ (with CH_2 ring)

(j) $H_3C{-}N{=}N{-}CH_3 \xrightarrow{\text{heat}} H_3CCH_3 + N_2$

(k) $H_2C{-}CH_2 \longrightarrow CH_3CH{=}CH_2$ (with CH_2 ring)

◢ (a) Addition and redox. The oxidation number (ON) of each C has changed from -2 to -1 (oxidation). The ON of each Br changed from 0 to -1 (reduction). (See Problem 2.55.) (b) Displacement. (c) Displacement. (d) α-elimination. (e) Addition. (f) β-elimination and redox. Zn is oxidized ($Zn \rightarrow Zn^{2+}$), the dihalide is reduced. (g) Rearrangement. (h) Substitution (an H is displaced) and redox Cl_2 is reduced and C_6H_6 is oxidized. (i) γ-elimination (a ring is formed) and redox [see (f)]. (j) Decomposition. (k) Rearrangement.

3.22 The reaction in [Problem 3.21(j)] may be a three-step reaction involving some homolytic decompositions. Suggest plausible steps.

◢ Step 1. $H_3C{-}\ddot{N}{=}\ddot{N}{-}CH_3 \longrightarrow H_3C{-}\ddot{N}{=}\ddot{N}\cdot + \cdot CH_3$ (A homolysis)

Step 2. $H_3C{-}\ddot{N}{=}\ddot{N}\cdot \longrightarrow H_3C\cdot + :N{\equiv}N:$ (A homolysis)

Step 3. $2\ H_3C\cdot \longrightarrow H_3C{-}CH_3$ (A combination or addition)

3.23 Categorize the reaction $CH_3CH_2Br + 2\ Na + BrCH_2CH_3 \rightarrow CH_3CH_2CH_2CH_3 + 2\ NaBr$.

◢ This is an example of a general reaction $2\ RX \xrightarrow{-2X^-} R{-}R$ which is called a *coupling* reaction because the individual R units are merged to give a larger molecule. It is a multistep reaction that proceeds through displacements, possibly as follows:

(1) $Na\cdot + R:\ddot{X}: \longrightarrow Na^+ + :\ddot{X}:^- + R\cdot$ (2) $R\cdot + Na\cdot \longrightarrow Na^+ + R:^-$ (3) $R:^- + R:\ddot{X}: \longrightarrow R:R + :\ddot{X}:^-$

3.24 The following equations represent the mechanistic steps for chlorination of methane:

Initiation step: 1. $:\ddot{Cl}:\ddot{Cl}: \xrightarrow{\text{energy}} :\ddot{Cl}\cdot + \cdot\ddot{Cl}:$

Propagation steps: 2. $H_3C:H + \cdot\ddot{Cl}: \longrightarrow H_3C\cdot + H:\ddot{Cl}:$

                         3. $H_3C\cdot + :\ddot{Cl}:\ddot{Cl}: \longrightarrow H_3C:\ddot{Cl}: + \cdot\ddot{Cl}:$

◢ (a) Write the equation for the overall reaction obtained from the sum of the propagation steps 2 and 3 and give its classification. (b) List the intermediates in all the steps. (c) Which steps are homolytic? (d) Classify step 1. (e) List the displacement steps. (f) Are any of the steps additions? (g) Which step follows step 3? (h) Name the reactions whose steps keep repeating themselves. (i) Write an equation for the formation of a byproduct from the collision of intermediates. Classify this reaction.

(a) $CH_4 + Cl_2 \rightarrow CH_3Cl + HCl$, a substitution reaction. (b) $H_3C\cdot$ and $:\ddot{Cl}\cdot$, each of which is consumed in ensuing steps. (c) All—each step involves formation of radicals. (d) Decomposition. (e) In step 2, $:\ddot{Cl}\cdot$ displaces $H_3C\cdot$ from an H. In step 3, a $:\ddot{Cl}\cdot$ is displaced from $:\ddot{Cl}:\ddot{Cl}:$ by $H_3C\cdot$. (f) No. (g) Step 2. (h) *Chain* reactions. (i) $H_3C\cdot + \cdot CH_3 \rightarrow H_3C:CH_3$, ethane, formed by a combination reaction.

ELECTROPHILES AND NUCLEOPHILES

3.25 (*a*) Define (i) a nucleophile or electron-donor and (ii) an electrophile or electron-acceptor.
(*b*) What structural units make a molecule (or ion) (i) a nucleophile or (ii) an electrophile?
(*c*) What kind of reaction occurs between a nucleophile and electrophile?

▰ (*a*) (i) Molecules having atoms with high electron density are called *nucleophiles* or *electron donors*. (ii) Molecules having atoms with low electron density are called *electrophiles* or *electron-acceptors*.
(*b*) (i) The atom in question, called a *nucleophilic* site, may be the negative $(\delta-)$ end of a polar covalent bond (see Problem 2.45), have an unshared electron pair, or be part of a π bond. It may also have a combination of these features. (ii) The atom in question, called an *electrophilic* site, may be capable of taking on more valence electrons or be the positive $(\delta+)$ end of a polar bond.
(*c*) Coordinate covalent bonding, $Nu\!:\, + E \rightarrow Nu\!:\!E$

3.26 Classify each of the following species as electrophile or nucleophile and explain your choice.
(*a*) $CH_3COO\!:^-$, (*b*) $CH_3\ddot{O}\!:^-$, (*c*) BF_3, (*d*) $:\ddot{C}l^+$, (*e*) $(CH_3)_3C\!:^-$, (*f*) $Cl_2C\!:$, (*g*) SiF_4, (*h*) $:\ddot{B}r\!:^-$, (*i*) $:P(CH_3)_3$, (*j*) $(CH_3)_2CH^+$, (*k*) $H_2C\!=\!CH_2$, and (*l*) HCl.

▰ *Electrophiles*: (*c*), (*d*), (*f*), and (*j*) have six valence e$^-$'s and can accept an electron pair from a nucleophile to acquire the stable octet. (*l*), typical of all Brönsted acids (Problem 3.30), is electrophilic because the H^+ it donates is electron deficient. Although (*g*) has eight valence e$^-$'s, it can nevertheless be an acceptor of a nucleophile's unshared pair by expanding its d shell to 12 e$^-$'s: $SiF_4 + 2\,:\!\ddot{F}\!:^- \longrightarrow SiF_6^{-2}$. This behavior is observed with elements in the third and higher periods of the periodic table that form covalent bonds.
Nucleophiles: (*a*), (*b*), (*e*), and (*h*) are anions, (*i*) has an unshared electron-pair, and (*k*) has two available electrons in a π bond.

3.27 Which of the following species behave as (*a*) a nucleophile, (*b*) an electrophile, (*c*) both, or (*d*) neither? $:\ddot{I}\!:^-$, $H_3N\!:$, $BeCl_2$, CH_4, Cr^{3+}, $CH_3C\!\equiv\!N\!:$, H_2, $SnCl_4$, $H_2C\!=\!\ddot{O}\!:$, and NO_2^+.

▰ (*a*) *Nucleophiles*: $:\ddot{I}\!:^-$, $H_3N\!:$. (*b*) *Electrophiles*: $BeCl_2$ (bonded Cl's are rarely nucleophilic), $SnCl_4$, Cr^{3+}, and NO_2^+ (the electrophilic character completely masks the potential nucleophilic behavior of the unshared electron-pairs on the O's). (*c*) *Both*: $CH_3C\!\equiv\!N\!:$, $H_2C\!=\!\ddot{O}\!:$. Since C in each of these species is π-bonded to a very electronegative atom, N and O respectively, C is an electrophilic site. The electronegative N and O also have unshared e$^-$ pairs and are nucleophilic sites. (*d*) *Neither*: CH_4, H_2.

3.28 Identify the species I and II as electrophiles (E) or nucleophiles (Nu) in the reactions:

	Species I	Species II	
(*a*)	$(CH_3)_2O\!:$	$+\,BMe_3$	$\longrightarrow (CH_3)_2\overset{+}{O} - \bar{B}Me_3$
(*b*)	$:CN\!:^-$	$+\,CH_3Br$	$\longrightarrow H_3C\!:\!CN + :\ddot{B}r\!:^-$
(*c*)	$H\!:\!C\!\equiv\!C\!:\!H + :\ddot{N}H_2^-$		$\longrightarrow H\!:\!C\!\equiv\!C\!:^- + H\!:\!\ddot{N}H_2$
(*d*)	C_2H_5Br	$+\,AlBr_3$	$\longrightarrow [C_2H_5]^+[AlBr_4]^-$
(*e*)	$CH_3CH\!=\!O + :SO_3H^-$ (bisulfite anion)		$\longrightarrow CH_3\underset{\overset{|}{O^-}}{CH}\!-\!SO_3H$

▰

Reaction	(*a*)	(*b*)	(*c*)	(*d*)	(*e*)
Species I	Nu	Nu	E	Nu	E
Species II	E	E	Nu	E	Nu

3.29 Formulate the following as a two-step reaction and designate the nucleophiles and electrophiles.

$$H_2C\!=\!CH_2 + Br_2 \longrightarrow H_2CBrCBrH_2$$

▰ $\underset{\text{nucleophile}}{H_2C\!=\!CH_2} + \underset{\text{electrophile}}{:\ddot{B}r\!:\!\ddot{B}r\!:} \overset{\text{step 1}}{\longrightarrow} \underset{\text{electrophile}}{H_2CBr\!-\!CH_2^+} + \underset{\text{nucleophile}}{:\ddot{B}r\!:^-} \overset{\text{step 2}}{\longrightarrow} H_2CBr\!-\!CH_2Br$

Br_2 is electrophilic since each electronegative Br prefers to have a full compliment of eight e$^-$'s.

ACIDS AND BASES

3.30 Compare (*a*) the Brönsted-Lowry and (*b*) the Lewis definitions of acids and bases.

◢ (*a*) Brönsted and Lowry defined an acid as a *donor* and a base as an *acceptor* of a proton (H^+). Central to this theory is the *conjugate* relationship between acids and bases since a base accepts a proton from an acid and is converted to its conjugate acid while the acid donates a proton and is changed to its conjugate base.

(*b*) In the *Lewis* concept, based on the electron-pair rather than the proton, a base is an electron-pair *donor* (a nucleophile) and an acid is an electron-pair *acceptor* (an electrophile) in the formation of a covalent bond.

3.31 (*a*) Identify the acids and bases and the conjugate acid-base pairs when (i) CH_3COOH and (ii) CH_3NH_2 dissociate in water. (*b*) What generalization can be made about the net direction of the acid-base equilibrium? (*c*) Draw a conclusion about the acid-base behavior of H_2O.

◢ (*a*) (i) $CH_3COOH + H_2O \rightleftharpoons H_3O^+ + CH_3COO^-$

$\qquad\qquad$ acid$_1$ $\qquad$ base$_2$ $\qquad$ acid$_2$ $\qquad$ base$_1$

$\qquad\qquad$ (weaker) (weaker) $\quad$ (stronger) (stronger)

(ii) $CH_3NH_2 + H_2O \rightleftharpoons OH^- + CH_3NH_3^+$

$\qquad\quad$ base$_1$ $\qquad$ acid$_2$ $\qquad$ base$_2$ $\qquad$ acid$_1$

$\qquad\quad$ (weaker) (weaker) $\quad$ (stronger) (stronger)

The conjugate pairs have the same subscript and are linked together.

(*b*) The net direction favors the formation of the weaker acid and base at the expense of the stronger acid and base as shown in the equations.

(*c*) H_2O can act either as a base (i) or as an acid (ii). Substances with such dual character are said to be *amphoteric*.

3.32 Give the conjugate acid of (*a*) $C_2H_5NH_2$, (*b*) CH_3O^-, (*c*) $H_2C:$, (*d*) $:\ddot{O}-\ddot{O}:^{2-}$, (*e*) CH_3OH, and (*f*) $H_2C=CH_2$.

◢ Add an H^+. (*a*) $C_2H_5NH_3^+$, (*b*) CH_3OH, (*c*) H_3C^+, (*d*) $H\ddot{O}\ddot{O}:^-$, (*e*) $CH_3OH_2^+$, and (*f*) $H_3C-CH_2^+$.

3.33 Give the conjugate bases, if any, of the substances in Problem 3.32.

◢ Subtract an H^+. (*a*) $C_2H_5NH^-$, (*b*) $:CH_2O^{2-}$, (*c*) $H\ddot{C}:^-$, (*d*) none, (*e*) CH_3O^-, and (*f*) $H_2C=CH^-$. The bases, (*b*) and (*c*), are extremely difficult to form and so we can say that CH_3O^- and $H_2C:$ have no conjugate bases.

3.34 Which of the following substances are amphoteric? (*a*) NH_3, (*b*) NH_4^+, (*c*) Br^-, (*d*) HCO_3^-, and (*e*) HF. Justify your choices.

◢ (*a*) Yes, it gives NH_4^+ and NH_2^-. (*b*) No. It cannot accept an H^+ because it has no unshared pairs of e^-'s. (*c*) No, cannot donate an H^+. (*d*) Yes, gives $H_2CO_3(CO_2 + H_2O)$ and CO_3^{2-}. (*e*) Yes, gives H_2F^+ and F^-.

3.35 Identify reactants I and II as a Lewis acid A or Lewis base B in the following:

Reactant I $\qquad$ Reactant II

(*a*) $CH_3CH=O + H^+$ (from a Brönsted acid) $\longrightarrow CH_3CH=OH^+$

(*b*) $H_2C=O \quad + :NH_3 \qquad\qquad\qquad \longrightarrow H_2C-O^-$
$\qquad\qquad\qquad\qquad\qquad\qquad\qquad\qquad\qquad |$
$\qquad\qquad\qquad\qquad\qquad\qquad\qquad\qquad NH_3^+$

(*c*) $O=C=O + OH^- \qquad\qquad\qquad \longrightarrow O=C-O^-$
$\qquad\qquad\qquad\qquad\qquad\qquad\qquad\qquad\qquad |$
$\qquad\qquad\qquad\qquad\qquad\qquad\qquad\qquad OH$

(*d*) $SiF_4 \qquad + 2 :\ddot{F}:^- \qquad\qquad\qquad \longrightarrow [SiF_6]^{2-}$

(*e*) $Ag^+ \qquad + 2 :NH_3 \qquad\qquad\qquad \longrightarrow [Ag(NH_3)_2]^+$

(*f*) $(CH_3)_3N: \quad + BF_3 \qquad\qquad\qquad \longrightarrow (CH_3)_3\overset{+}{N}-\bar{B}F_3$

Reaction	(a)	(b)	(c)	(d)	(e)	(f)
Reactant I	B	A	A	A	A	B
Reactant II	A	B	B	B	B	A

3.36 For the different reactions of H_2SO_4 with (i) $HONO_2$ and (ii) $HOClO_3$, (a) write the equations for the reactions and identify the conjugate acids and bases, and (b) explain the different behavior of H_2SO_4.

(a) (i) $H{-}OSO_2OH + H{-}ONO_2 \longrightarrow H{-}\overset{H}{\underset{+}{O}}NO_2 + {}^-OSO_2OH$

$\qquad$ acid$_1$ $\qquad$ base$_2$ $\qquad$ acid$_2$ $\qquad$ base$_1$

(ii) $H{-}OSO_2OH + H{-}OClO_3 \longrightarrow {}^-OClO_3 + H{-}\overset{H}{\underset{+}{O}}SO_2OH$

$\qquad$ base$_1$ $\qquad$ acid$_2$ $\qquad$ base$_2$ $\qquad$ acid$_1$

(b) (i) H_2SO_4, a stronger acid, gives a proton to HNO_3, a weaker acid now acting as a base.
(ii) H_2SO_4 is the weaker acid and acts as the base to accept a proton from $HClO_4$.

3.37 Discuss how (a) acid strength is related to K_a, the acid ionization constant, and to pK_a, and (b) base strength is related to K_b, the base ionization constant, and to pK_b. The values of pK_a and pK_b are defined as $-\log K_a$ and $-\log K_b$ respectively.

Acid and base strengths are measured by the position of equilibrium in reactions with water. The further the reactions go to the right, the greater the acid or basic strength.
(a) The equation for the acid equilibrium is: $H{:}A + H{:}OH \rightleftharpoons H_3O^+ + {:}A^-$. The expression for the equilibrium constant, K_a is

$$K_a = \frac{[H_3O^+][{:}A^-]}{[H{:}A][H_2O]} \quad \text{or simply} \quad \frac{[H_3O^+][{:}A^-]}{[H{:}A]}$$

The brackets indicate molar concentrations, mol/L. H_2O is always the solvent and its molar concentration, $[H_2O]$, equals $1000\,g/L \times 1\,mol/18\,g = 55.5\,mol/L$, a constant. This term is included in the K values and doesn't appear in the equilibrium expressions. The stronger the acid, the more it ionizes, the larger is the numerator and the larger is K_a. Then the *stronger* the acid, the *smaller* is the value for pK_a.
(b) The equilibrium for a base is: $B{:} + H{:}OH \rightleftharpoons B{:}H^+ + {:}OH^-$ and the equilibrium expression is

$$K_b = \frac{[B{:}H^+][{:}OH^-]}{[B{:}]}$$

Then, the *stronger* the base, the *smaller* is the value for pK_b.

3.38 (a) For acids and bases relate the terms (i) strong, (ii) feeble, and (iii) weak to H_3O^+, OH^-, and H_2O. (b) Give the arbitrary pK ranges for (i) intermediate and (ii) weak acids and bases which are found within the weak category.

(a) (i) A strong acid and base must be stronger than H_3O^+ (also a strong acid) and OH^- (also a strong base) respectively. (ii) Feeble acids and bases are weaker than H_2O. (iii) Weak acids are weaker than H_3O^+ but stronger than H_2O. Weak bases are weaker than OH^- but stronger than H_2O.
(b) (i) Intermediate acids and bases have pK's between 1 and 5. Weak acids and bases have pK's > 5 but less than 14. Most organic acids with carbon-containing functional groups and bases are weak.

3.39 Calculate the pK values of the following organic acids and bases from their given K constants:

(a) CH_3NH_2, $K_b = 4.5 \times 10^{-4}$; (b) CH_3COOH, $K_a = 1.8 \times 10^{-5}$; (c) CH_3OH, $K_a = 3.1 \times 10^{-16}$

(a) $pK_b = -\log(4.5 \times 10^{-4}) = 4 - 0.65 = 3.35$
(b) $pK_a = -\log(1.8 \times 10^{-5}) = 5 - 0.26 = 4.74$
(c) $pK_a = -\log(3.1 \times 10^{-16}) = 16 - 0.49 = 15.51$ (feeble)

3.40 (*a*) Write the equations for the (i) *self-ionization* of H_2O and (ii) K_w whose value is 10^{-14}. Also give the $[H_3O^+]$ and $[OH^-]$ in pure water. (*b*) Find pK_w. (*c*) Calculate the pK_{eq} of H_2O.

◢ (*a*) (i) $H:\overset{..}{\underset{..}{O}}:H + H:\overset{..}{\underset{..}{O}}:H \rightleftharpoons H:\overset{..}{\underset{\overset{|}{H}}{O}}:H^+ + :\overset{..}{\underset{..}{O}}:H^-$

$\qquad\qquad$ base$_1$ $\qquad$ acid$_2$ $\qquad\qquad$ acid$_1$ $\qquad$ base$_2$

$\qquad$ (ii) $K_w = [H_3O^+][OH^-] = 10^{-14}$ where K_w, called the *ion-product* of water, includes $[H_2O]^2$ [see (*c*) below].

$\qquad$ (iii)   For every H_3O^+ formed an OH^- is formed, and in pure water their concentrations are equal to 10^{-7} M, where M = mol/L.

(*b*) $pK_w = -\log 10^{-14} = 14$.

(*c*) The equilibrium constant, $K_e = \dfrac{[H_3O^+][OH^-]}{[H_2O]^2} = \dfrac{K_w}{55.5^2} = 3.25 \times 10^{-18}$. In this equation $[H_2O]$ is included.

3.41 Derive an equation relating the pK_a of an acid and the pK_b of its conjugate base *in water*.

◢ Ionization of $\qquad\qquad$ *acid* $\qquad\qquad\qquad\qquad\qquad\qquad$ *base*

$$H:B + HOH \rightleftharpoons H_3O^+ + :B^- \qquad :B^- + H:OH \rightleftharpoons H:B + :OH^-$$

$$K_a = \frac{[H_3O^+][:B^-]}{[H:B]} \quad (1) \qquad K_b = \frac{[H:B][:OH^-]}{[:B^-]} \quad (2)$$

Multiplying (1) and (2) and canceling identical terms gives

$$K_a K_b = \frac{[H_3O^+][:\cancel{B^-}]}{[\cancel{H:B}]} \frac{[\cancel{H:B}][:OH^-]}{[:\cancel{B^-}]} = [H_3O^+][:OH^-] = K_w = 10^{-14}$$

In summary, $K_a K_b = K_w$ or $pK_a + pK_b = pK_w = -\log 10^{-14} = 14$ (in water only!).

3.42 Using the relationship $pK_a + pK_b = 14$, (*a*) relate the relative strengths of acid-base conjugate pairs, (*b*) comment on the strengths of the conjugates of strong acids and bases, and (*c*) are the conjugates of weak acids and bases strong?

◢ (*a*)   As the acid gets stronger, pK_a gets smaller, the conjugate base gets weaker and pK_b gets larger.

(*b*)   The conjugates of a strong acid or base ($pK < -1$) are feeble, and $pK_b = 14 - pK > 15$.

(*c*)   No! The conjugates of weak acids or bases (i.e., $pK_a \cong 5$), are also weak ($pK_b = 14 - pK_a \cong 9$).

3.43 (*a*) Can the relationship $pK_a + pK_b = 14$ be used with solvents such as ethanol (C_2H_5OH)? (*b*) Why are some acid-base reactions studied in nonaqueous solvents?

◢ (*a*)   No. The value 14 is for water. Ethanol would have its own ion-product value (derived from $2\,EtOH \rightleftharpoons EtO^- + EtOH_2^+$) which is different from 14. Furthermore, the ionization of a base or acid and the K's would be different from that in water. Ethanol and water have different basicities, acidities and solvating abilities.

(*b*)   While H_2O is a superior ionizing solvent, it does not dissolve some organic acids or bases.

3.44 Account for the greater acidity of acetic acid, CH_3COOH (abbreviated HOAc), in water than in methanol, MeOH.

◢ The equilibrium

$$HOAc + H_2O \rightleftharpoons OAc^- + H_3O^+$$

lies more to the right than does

$$HOAc + MeOH \rightleftharpoons OAc^- + MeOH_2^+$$

This difference could result if MeOH were a weaker base than H_2O. However, this may not be so. The difference arises mainly from the solvents' abilities to solvate the product ions. The more polar water is a better solvator of ions than is MeOH, thereby shifting the equilibrium in water more to the right.

3.45 (*a*) Can the acid strengths of two strong acids, such as HY and HX, be compared in H_2O? Explain. (*b*) How are their acidities compared?

▰ (*a*) No. Strong acids, especially in dilute solutions, are practically completely ionized in H_2O so that the only acid present is H_3O^+. This is known as the *leveling effect*. (*b*) It is necessary to compare them in a solvent that is much less basic than water so that an equilibrium is established with both the unionized acids and their conjugate bases present. The solvent of choice is 100% (glacial) acetic acid (abbreviated HOAc).

$$\text{In } H_2O, \quad HX + H_2O \longrightarrow H_3O^+ + X^-; \quad \text{in HOAc,} \quad HX + HOAc \rightleftharpoons X^- + H_2\overset{+}{O}Ac$$

3.46 Give the conjugates of the compounds in Problem 3.39 and calculate their pK's.

▰ (*a*) $CH_3NH_3^+$, p$K_a = 14 - 3.35 = 10.65$
(*b*) $CH_3COO:^-$, p$K_b = 14 - 4.74 = 9.26$
(*c*) $CH_3O:^-$, p$K_b = 14 - 15.51 = -1.51$

3.47 How is base strength related to the availability of the electron-pair?

▰ Base strength depends on the ability of the basic site (which always has an unshared electron pair) to accept a proton. This ability depends on the charge in an anion or electron density in a molecular base. For species with an identical charge, dispersal or delocalization of the electrons from the basic site to other parts of the molecule results in decreased electron density and decreased base strength.

3.48 Illustrate the factors that affect delocalization of charge density by comparing the basicities of the following pairs of bases: (*a*) F^- and I^-, (*b*) $H_2\ddot{N}:^-$ and $H\ddot{O}:^-$, (*c*) $HC\equiv C:^-$ and $H_2C=\ddot{C}H^-$, (*d*) $:\ddot{O}=CH-NH_2$ and $CH_3\ddot{N}H_2$, (*e*) $:NH_2OH$ and $:NH_3$, and (*f*) $\ddot{C}l_3C:^-$ and $F_3C:^-$.

▰ Comparisons are best made with bases having the same charge.
(*a*) For elements in the same periodic group, the larger the basic site atom the more spread out (delocalized) is the charge (or electron density) and the weaker is the base. $I^- < F^-$.
(*b*) When the basic site elements are in the same period of the periodic table, the more lone pairs of e^-'s on the site atom, the more the charge is spread out and the weaker is the base. $H\ddot{O}:^-$, with three lone pairs, is a weaker base than $H_2\ddot{N}:^-$, with two lone pairs.
(*c*) The more *s-character* in the orbital with the unshared pair, the more localized are the e^-'s (the closer to C) and the less basic are bases.

$$\underset{sp}{HC\equiv C:^-} < \underset{sp^2 \text{ (less } s\text{-character)}}{H_2C=\ddot{C}H^-}$$

(*d*) Extended *p-p* π-bonding between the basic site atom and an adjacent π system (resonance) delocalizes electron density (Problem 3.17). $:\ddot{O}=CH-NH_2$ is less basic because it has extended *p-p* π bonding, as shown below with contributing structures, while CH_3NH_2 has none.

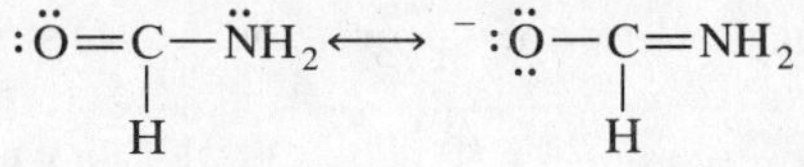

$$:\ddot{O}=\underset{H}{\overset{|}{C}}-\ddot{N}H_2 \longleftrightarrow {}^-:\ddot{O}-\underset{H}{\overset{|}{C}}=NH_2$$

Some more common π systems are:

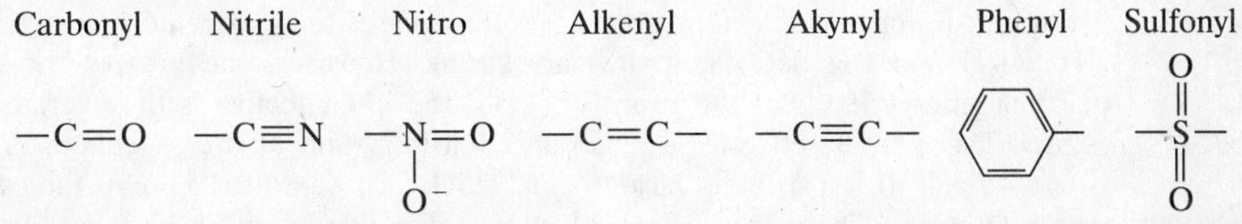

Carbonyl   Nitrile   Nitro   Alkenyl   Akynyl   Phenyl   Sulfonyl

$$-C=O \quad -C\equiv N \quad \underset{O^-}{\overset{|}{-N=O}} \quad -C=C- \quad -C\equiv C- \quad \langle\bigcirc\rangle- \quad \overset{O}{\underset{O}{\overset{\|}{-\overset{|}{\underset{\|}{S}}-}}}$$

(*e*) Electron-attracting inductive effects (Problem 3.16) of groups such as $-X$, $-OH$, $-OR$ (without π bonds), and all the π-bonded groups listed in (*d*), when not attached directly to the basic site, decrease electron density at a basic site and thus decrease base strength. Conversely, electron-releasing groups (R) increase electron density and base strength. Therefore, because of the electron-withdrawing and base-weakening OH, $HONH_2$ is less basic than NH_3.
(*f*) One might expect $F_3C:^-$ to be less basic than $Cl_3C:^-$ because F is more electron-withdrawing and base-weakening than Cl. However, in $Cl_3C:^-$ the unshared e^- pair of the C in the p orbital undergoes extended *p-d* π bonding into an empty d AO of each of the three Cl's as shown:

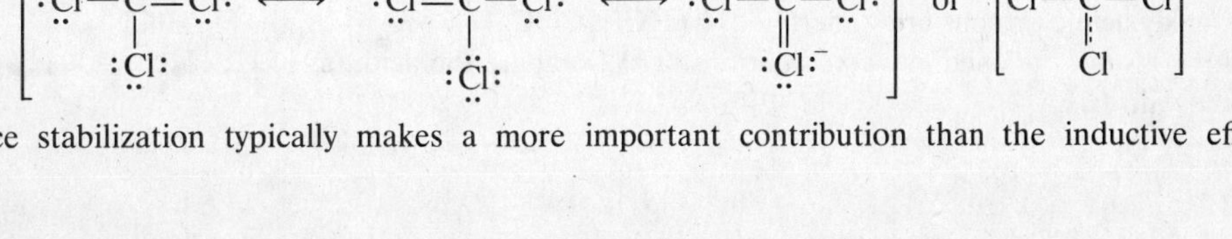

$$\left[\ddot{C}l-\overset{|}{\underset{:\ddot{C}l:}{C}}=\ddot{C}l:^- \longleftrightarrow {}^-:\ddot{C}l=\overset{|}{\underset{:\ddot{C}l:}{C}}-\ddot{C}l: \longleftrightarrow :\ddot{C}l-\overset{\|}{\underset{:\ddot{C}l:^-}{C}}-\ddot{C}l: \right] \text{ or } \left[Cl \cdots \underset{\underset{Cl}{\vdots}}{C} \cdots Cl \right]^-$$

Resonance stabilization typically makes a more important contribution than the inductive effect and

$Cl_3C:^-$ is the weaker base. Since F is in the second period with no d AO's, it can only exert an inductive effect. Note that in order to participate in extended π bonding the C must have a p AO for the lone pair and sp^2 HO's for its three σ bonds. As predicted by the HON rule (without modification for extended π bonding), the C in $F_3C:^-$ uses sp^3 HO's.

3.49 Are base strength and nucleophilicity, both involving reaction of an electron pair with a positive site, identical?

▰ No. While they are parallel quantities, they differ because strength is based on the K for the reaction of the base with a proton-donating Brönsted acid: $B:^- + H:A \rightleftharpoons B:H + :A^-$. *Nucleophilicity*, from the Lewis definition, is measured by the *rate* of reaction with an electrophile, usually a C atom as shown:

$$B:^- + -\overset{|}{\underset{|}{C}}-\overset{..}{\underset{..}{Br}}: \longrightarrow B-\overset{|}{\underset{|}{C}}- + :\overset{..}{\underset{..}{Br}}:^-$$

3.50 Compare (*a*) the acid strengths of CH_3COOH, $ClCH_2COOH$, $Cl_2CHCOOH$, and Cl_3CCOOH. (*b*) the base strengths of their conjugate bases.

▰ (*a*) The greater inductive effect of an increasing number of electron-attracting Cl's that is responsible for decreasing base strengths increases acid strengths. The relative order is: $Cl_3CCOOH > Cl_2CHCOOH > ClCH_2COOH$. (*b*) The order is reversed: $CH_3COO^- > ClCH_2COO^- > Cl_2CHCOO^- > Cl_3CCOO^-$.

3.51 Compare and explain the differences in base strengths of: (*a*) PH_3 (bond angle $\sim 90°$) and NH_3 (bond angle $= 107°$), (*b*) OH^- and SH^-, (*c*) CH_3O^- and CH_3COO^-, and (*d*) methanesulfonate, $CH_3SO_3^-$ and methaneselenate, $CH_3SeO_3^-$.

▰ (*a*) $NH_3 > PH_3$. Both P and N are in group 5 of the periodic table but P, a third period element, is larger. A clue to a much more significant reason is the difference in bond angles. The $90°$ H—P—H bond angle indicates that P uses p AO's for bonding, leaving the unshared pair in an s AO. The $107°$ N—H bond angle signals that N uses sp^3 HO's, in one of which is the lone pair. This orbital has less s-character than the corresponding one in PH_3, is more distant from the central atom, and more available for bonding to H. NH_3 is a much stronger base than PH_3.

(*b*) While O and S are in group VI, S is larger and its more dispersed charge causes SH^- to be a weaker base than OH^- and H_2S a stronger acid than H_2O.

(*c*) Resonance and charge dispersal over the two O's of CH_3COO^-, $\left[CH_3\overset{O^-}{\underset{|}{C}}=O \longleftrightarrow CH_3\overset{O}{\underset{||}{C}}-O^- \right]$,

make it a weaker base than CH_3O^- and CH_3COOH a stronger acid than CH_3OH.

(*d*) The S and Se atoms have p-d π bonds to three O's which bear some of the dispersed negative charge. This extensive charge delocalization causes these bases to be extremely weak and their conjugate acids, CH_3SO_3H and CH_3SeO_3H, to be very strong. However, the greater the difference between the principal energy levels of the p and d AO's, the less effective is the overlap and less delocalization occurs. There is less effective overlap and delocalization of the $-$ charge in $CH_3SeO_3^-$ because Se uses a $4d$ AO. It is a stronger base than $CH_3SO_3^-$ whose S uses a $3d$ AO to overlap with the $2p$ AO's of the O atoms. There is also less effective p-d π bond overlap because the Se—O bond is longer than S—O bond.

3.52 Assign and justify relative base strengths of (*a*) NH_3, (*b*) CH_3NH_2, and (*c*) NF_3.

▰ The strong electron-attracting inductive effect of the F's causes the electron density to be dispersed away from N and less available for bonding to an acid. CH_3 is electron-releasing and has the opposite effect. The relative basic strengths (*b*) > (*a*) > (*c*).

3.53 (*a*) Explain the relative magnitudes of the pK_a values and acid strengths of the following compounds whose weakly acidic protons are underlined: (i) $\underline{H}CH_2COC_2H_5$, $pK_a = 20$, (ii) $\underline{H}CH(CN)_2$, $pK_a = 11.2$. [The pK_a value for (i) is not obtained in water solutions.] (*b*) Compare the acidities of $\underline{H}CH_2CH{=}CH_2$ in Problem 3.17(*c*) with those in (*a*).

▟ Although an H bonded to C is usually not acidic these H's are, because of electron delocalization and resonance stabilization of their anionic conjugate bases:

(a) (i) $\quad$ H—CH$_2$—C(=O)—C$_2$H$_5$ $\xrightarrow{-H^+}$ $\left[{}^-:\text{CH}_2—\overset{\overset{:\ddot{O}:}{\|}}{C}—C_2H_5 \longleftrightarrow CH_2=\overset{\overset{:\ddot{O}:^-}{|}}{C}—C_2H_5 \right]$

(ii) $\quad :N\equiv C—CH_2—C\equiv N: \xrightarrow{-H^+}$

$[:N\equiv C—\ddot{C}H—C\equiv N: \longleftrightarrow {}^-:\ddot{N}=C=CH—C\equiv N: \longleftrightarrow :N\equiv C—CH=C=\ddot{N}:^-]$

Compound (ii) is more acidic than (i) because the $-$ charge of its conjugate base is delocalized to two N's whereas the charge in (i) is delocalized to only a single O atom.

(b) The compounds in (a) are much stronger acids because of the much greater effectiveness of the extended p-p π-bonding in their conjugate bases which delocalizes the charge to the more electronegative O in (i) and N in (ii). In $^-:$CH$_2$CH=CH$_3$ the charge is delocalized to a very weakly electronegative C atom: $[^-:$CH$_2$—CH=CH$_2$ $\leftrightarrow$ CH$_2$=CH—$\ddot{C}$H$_2$].

3.54 (a) Derive a relationship for pK_e of the reaction HA + B $\rightleftharpoons$ A$^-$ + BH$^+$ and the pK_a's of the acids HA and BH$^+$.

(b) Use this relationship to calculate pK_e and K_e for the following acid-base reactions:

(i) $\quad$ CH$_3$COOH (pK_a = 5) + CH$_3$NH$_2$ $\rightleftharpoons$ CH$_3$COO$^-$ + CH$_3$NH$_3^+$ (pK_a = 10)

(ii) $\quad$ CO$_3^{2-}$ + HCN (pK_a = 9.1) $\rightleftharpoons$ CN$^-$ + HCO$_3^-$ (pK_a = 10.2)

(iii) $\quad$ HCH$_2$NO$_2$ (pK_a = 10.2) + CH$_3$O$^-$ $\rightleftharpoons$ $^-$CH$_2$NO$_2$ + CH$_3$OH (pK_a = 16)

▟ (a) Acid-base reactions are competitions in which the extent of the equilibrium depends on the difference in the strengths of acid reactant pK_{ar} and product pK_{ap}. The equilibrium constant K_e is given by

$$K_e = \frac{[A^-][BH^+]}{[HA][B]} \qquad (1)$$

From the expressions for K_{ar} for the reacting acid, HA, and for the product acid, BH$^+$, are, respectively,

$$K_{ar} = \frac{[H^+][A^-]}{[HA]} \quad \text{and} \quad \frac{[A^-]}{[HA]} = \frac{K_{ar}}{[H^+]} \qquad (2)$$

$$K_{ap} = \frac{[H^+][B]}{[BH^+]} \quad \text{and} \quad \frac{[BH^+]}{[B]} = \frac{[H^+]}{K_{ap}} \qquad (3)$$

Substituting (2) and (3) into (1) gives

$$K_e = \frac{K_{ar}}{[H^+]}\frac{[H^+]}{K_{ap}} = \frac{K_{ar}}{K_{ap}}; \quad \text{or} \quad \text{p}K_e = \text{p}K_{ar} - \text{p}K_{ap}$$

A similar relationship may be derived from the pK_b's of the bases B (base reactant) and A$^-$ (base product): pK_e = pK_{br} - pK_{bp}.

(b) (i) pK_e = 5 - 10 = -5, and K_e = 10^5

(ii) pK_e = 9.1 - 10.2 = -1.1, and K_e = 10$^{1.1}$

(iii) pK_e = 10.2 - 16 = -5.8, and K_e = 10$^{5.8}$

3.55 Account for the fact that, unlike other amines (RNH$_2$), guanidine, H$_2$$\ddot{N}$—C(=NH)—$\ddot{N}H_2$, is a strong base.

▟ The cation formed by addition of H$^+$ has three equivalent contributing structures. This greatly stabilizes the conjugate acid making it very weak and the base strong.

$$\text{H}_2\ddot{\text{N}}—\overset{\overset{:\text{NH}}{\|}}{\text{C}}—\ddot{\text{N}}\text{H}_2 \xrightarrow{H^+} \left[\text{H}_2\ddot{\text{N}}—\overset{\overset{\text{NH}_2^+}{\|}}{\text{C}}—\ddot{\text{N}}\text{H}_2 \longleftrightarrow \text{H}_2\overset{+}{\text{N}}=\overset{\overset{:\text{NH}_2}{|}}{\text{C}}—\ddot{\text{N}}\text{H}_2 \longleftrightarrow \text{H}_2\ddot{\text{N}}—\overset{\overset{:\text{NH}_2}{|}}{\text{C}}=\overset{+}{\text{N}}\text{H}_2 \right]$$

THERMODYNAMICS AND BOND ENERGIES

3.56 (*a*) Which thermodynamic function is most often used in organic chemistry to express the heat of a reaction? (*b*) Give the sign of ΔH for an (i) exothermic and (ii) endothermic reaction. (*c*) Give the algebraic sign of the ΔH for a reaction involving (i) breaking and (ii) formation of covalent bonds. (*d*) Give the symbol used for change in enthalpy for reactions whose participating compounds are in their standard state.

◢ (*a*) The symbol for heat is q. For reactions at constant pressure the change in heat, q_p, is expressed as ΔH, called the change (the meaning of Δ) in *enthalpy*. At constant volume the change in heat, q_v, is expressed as ΔE. Since most organic reactions are performed at atmospheric pressure (constant), ΔH is used more frequently than is ΔE. The unit for ΔH is kcal/mol (kilocalorie/mole) or kJ/mol (kilojoule/mole).

(*b*) As is true for all thermodynamic functions, $\Delta H = H_{products} - H_{reactants}$. (We are never concerned about the individual H values, only about the ΔH values.) (i) For an *exothermic* reaction (heat is evolved), $H_{products} < H_{reactants}$, making ΔH negative ($-\Delta H$). (ii) For an *endothermic* reaction (heat is absorbed), the reverse is true and ΔH is positive ($+\Delta H$).

(*c*) (i) Bond-breaking is always endothermic; ΔH is positive. (ii) Bond formation is always exothermic; ΔH is negative. (*d*) The *standard state* of any pure substance is its stable state (gas, liquid, or solid) at a *pressure of one atmosphere* and a *standard temperature*, usually 25°C. Under these conditions, $\Delta H°$ is the symbol used. The ° superscript is always used for standard state functions and reactions.

3.57 (*a*) Define bond-dissociation energy. (*b*) What is the algebraic sign of the ΔH values used for (i) bond-dissociation energies, ΔH_d, and (ii) bond formation? (*c*) What is the difference between bond-dissociation energy and bond energy? (*d*) Which value is found in most tables? (*e*) How are bond strengths and ΔH values related?

◢ (*a*) *Bond-dissociation energy* is the energy needed for *homolytic* breaking of one mole of a covalent bond into one mole of particles in the gas phase: $A:B \rightarrow A\cdot + \cdot B$. Actually the term enthalpy rather than energy should be used since we use ΔH's. (*b*) (i) Bond-breaking is always endothermic and the sign of ΔH is positive. (ii) Bond formation is always exothermic and the sign of ΔH is negative. (*c*) In a molecule like CH_4 with four C—H bonds, ΔH for the process $CH_4 \rightarrow CH_3\cdot + H\cdot$ is the bond dissociation energy for breaking the first C—H bond *only*. The ΔH_d values for the stepwise breaking of each of the other three bonds are not the same. If it is necessary to break all four bonds in a reaction, the average value, calculated from the sum of all four individual ΔH's, called the *bond energy*, is used. (*d*) Since most reactions involve the breaking of a single bond, the values found in tables are bond-dissociation energies. However, these are often loosely (incorrectly) called bond energies. (*e*) The larger the ΔH_d value, the more energy is needed to break the bond, and the stronger is the bond.

3.58 Find the C—H bond energy from the following bond-dissociation energies, given in kJ/mol for the stepwise loss of an H· from CH_4: First, 435; second, 444; third, 444; fourth, 339.

◢ Add the four given values and divide by 4 since the bond energy is the average: $+1662/4 = +416$ kJ/mol. Note that the bond-dissociation energy for the first C—H bond is $+435$ kJ/mol.

3.59 (*a*) Use the bond-dissociation energy values, given in kcal/mol in parentheses, to calculate the heat of reaction ΔH_r for monobromination of methane:

$$H_3C—H \ (102) + Br—Br \ (46) \longrightarrow H_3C—Br \ (70) + H—Br \ (88)$$

(*b*) Is this reaction endothermic or exothermic?

◢ The *heat of reaction*, ΔH_r, is the sum of the ΔH_d values for the broken bonds plus the sum of the ΔH_d values for the bonds formed. When a bond is formed, a minus sign is placed in front of the bond-dissociation energies found in the tables (where the entries are always positive).

$$\Delta H_r = \Sigma[+\Delta H \text{ (bonds broken)}] + \Sigma[-\Delta H \text{ (bonds formed)}]$$

(*a*) The C—H and Br—Br bonds are broken and C—Br and H—Br bonds are formed. Therefore,

$$\Delta H_r = (+102 + 46) + [(-70) + (-88)] = -10 \text{ kcal/mol}$$

(*b*) Since ΔH_r is negative, the reaction is exothermic.

3.60 Find ΔH_r for the reaction CH_4 (435) + I_2 (151) → CH_3I (222) + HI (297), where the values in parentheses are the bond-dissociation energies, given in kJ/mol, for the broken or formed bonds. Is this reaction endothermic or exothermic?

$\blacktriangleright$ $$\Delta H_r = (435 + 151) + [(-222) + (-297)] = 586 - 519 = +67 \text{ kJ/mol}$$

A positive ΔH_r signals an endothermic reaction.

3.61 Find the ΔH_r for the following reaction and decide whether it is exothermic or endothermic. The values in parentheses are, as usual, in kJ/mol.

$$H_2C\!=\!CH_2 \text{ (590)} + H\!-\!H \text{ (435)} \longrightarrow H_3C\!-\!CH_3 \text{ (for C}\!-\!\text{C, 368; for C}\!-\!\text{H, 410)}$$

$\blacktriangleright$ The value 590 is for breaking both bonds of the $C\!=\!C$.

$$\Delta H_r = (590 + 435) + [(-368) + 2(-410)] = -163 \text{ kJ/mol}; \quad \text{exothermic reaction}$$

The $C\!-\!H$ value in CH_3CH_3 was doubled because two $C\!-\!H$ bonds were formed.

3.62 Why are the following bonds among those with the smallest bond-dissociation energies? $:\ddot{X}\!-\!\ddot{X}:$ (halogens), $-\ddot{O}\!-\!\ddot{O}\!-$, $-\ddot{N}\!-\!\ddot{N}\!-$, $-\ddot{O}\!-\!\ddot{X}:$, $-\ddot{N}\!-\!\ddot{X}:$

$\blacktriangleright$ Bonds between these atoms are weak because of repulsion due to their unshared electron pair(s).

3.63 Compare and account for the differences in bond-dissociation energies of:
(a) C bonded to F, Cl, Br, and I.
(b) $C\!-\!C$, $C\!=\!C$, and $C\!\equiv\!C$ bonds.
(c) Primary (1°), secondary (2°), and tertiary (3°) $C\!-\!H$ bonds in alkanes (see Problem 4.3). (i) $\underline{H}\!-\!CH_2C_3H_7$, (ii) $CH_3C\underline{H}_2C_2H_5$, (iii) $(CH_3)_3C\!-\!\underline{H}$.

$\blacktriangleright$ (a) The strength of a covalent bond decreases as the bond length increases and the polarity decreases. The relative electronegativities are F > Cl > Br > I and the relative bond distances to C are F < Cl < Br < I. Thus the relative bond strengths and relative ΔH values are: $C\!-\!F > C\!-\!Cl > C\!-\!Br > C\!-\!I$.

(b) With an increase in multiple bonding, there is an increase in the electron density between the bonded atoms permitting closer approach of C's. The shorter the bond distance, the stronger the bond, and the ΔH values are in the order $C\!\equiv\!C > C\!=\!C > C\!-\!C$.

(c) The stability of the incipient alkyl radical is reflected in the $C\!-\!H$ bond-dissociation energies. The greater the number of electron-releasing alkyl groups (R) attached to the C whose bond to H is broken, the more stable is the free radical intermediate ($R_3C\cdot > R_2CH\cdot > RCH_2\cdot$, see Problem 3.16) and the weaker is that $C\!-\!H$ bond. The order of decreasing bond dissociation energies is 1° > 2° > 3°.

3.64 (a) Define standard heat of formation, ΔH_f°. (b) Write the equation for the ΔH_f° formation of acetylene, C_2H_2. (c) Calculate ΔH_f° for C_2H_2 from the following thermochemical combustion equations (complete oxidations with O_2): where (g) and (l) are for gas and liquid respectively.

(1) $\qquad C_2H_2(g) + 2.5O_2(g) \longrightarrow 2CO_2(g) + H_2O(l) \qquad \Delta H^\circ = -1300 \text{ kJ/mol}$

(2) $\qquad C(graphite) + O_2(g) \longrightarrow CO_2(g) \qquad \Delta H^\circ = -394 \text{ kJ/mol}$

(3) $\qquad H_2(g) + 0.5O_2(g) \longrightarrow H_2O(l) \qquad \Delta H^\circ = 286 \text{ kJ/mol}$

Note that fractional numbers of moles of O_2 are used in these equations in order to have one mole of the compound oxidized. This is done because the ΔH°'s are given per mole of reactant oxidized. (d) What can be said about the chemical stability of acetylene?

$\blacktriangleright$ (a) The *standard heat of formation* ΔH_f° is the change in enthalpy when 1 mole of substance in its standard state (Problem 3.56) is formed from its elements in their standard states. By definition, ΔH_f° for any *element* in its standard state is zero.

(b) $2C(graphite) + H_2(g) \rightarrow C_2H_2(g)$.

(c) To find the ΔH_f° for the reaction in (b) that cannot be experimentally determined, equations (1), (2), and (3) in (c) are manipulated by using Hess' law. Units of ΔH° are in kJ/mol.

Transpose (1): $\qquad 2CO_2(g) + H_2O(l) \longrightarrow C_2H_2(g) + 2.5O_2(g) \qquad \Delta H^\circ = +1300$

Double (2): $\qquad 2C(graphite) + 2O_2(g) \longrightarrow 2CO_2(g) \qquad \Delta H^\circ = 2(-394)$

Rewrite (3): $\qquad H_2(g) + 0.5O_2(g) \longrightarrow H_2O(l) \qquad \Delta H^\circ = -286$

Adding these three equations gives the equation in (*b*). Adding the individual $\Delta H°$ values gives

$$\Delta H_f°\text{ for }C_2H_2 = 1300 + (-788) + (-286) = +226 \text{ kJ/mol}$$

(*d*) Acetylene is unstable because it has a positive $\Delta H_f°$. When heated it explodes.

3.65 Find the enthalpy of the following reaction using the $\Delta H_f°$ values given in kcal/mol:

$$CH_3CH_2CH_2CH_3(g)(-30.4) + H_2(g) \longrightarrow 2CH_3CH_3(g)(-20.2)$$

▮ The enthalpy of this reaction is $\Delta H_r°$ because the participants are in their standard states. For H_2, $\Delta H_f° = 0$ because it is an element in its standard state.

$$\Delta H_r° = \Sigma\Delta H_f°\text{ of products} - \Sigma\Delta H_f°\text{ of reactants}$$

$$= [2(-20.2)] - [(-30.4) + 0] = -10 \text{ kcal/mol; exothermic reaction}$$

3.66 Define and indicate the application to chemical reactions of:
(*a*) chemical thermodynamics, and (*b*) chemical kinetics.

▮ (*a*) *Chemical thermodynamics* determines energy changes in states of matter and it helps in predicting where equilibrium is established in chemical reactions. (*b*) *Chemical kinetics* considers rates (speed) of chemical reactions as well as their mechanisms.

3.67 What kinds of reaction occur under: (*a*) thermodynamic and (*b*) kinetic control?

▮ (*a*) Reactions under *thermodynamic control* lead to the most stable products. (*b*) Under *kinetic control*, the products are those formed most rapidly.

3.68 Predict the most stable state of H_2O in terms of (*a*) enthalpy (*H*) and (*b*) entropy (*S*). (*c*) Which thermodynamic function must be used to predict that water is a liquid at room temperature?

▮ (*a*) Since gas → liquid → solid are exothermic processes, ice has the least enthalpy. For this reason, ice should be the most stable state of H_2O. (*b*) Stabilities of systems also increase with an increase in randomness as measured by the *entropy*, *S*,—the more the randomness, the greater is *S*. Solid → liquid → gas shows increasing randomness (decreasing order) and therefore increasing entropy. On this basis steam should be the most stable state. (*c*) The trend to lowest enthalpy and highest entropy are in opposition and neither can be used independently to predict the favored state. The term that must be used for this purpose is *free energy*, *G*. It gives the balance between *H* and *S* according to the equation, $G = H - TS$ (*T* in degrees Kelvin). For chemical reactions, the equation used incorporates the changes in these terms: $\Delta G = \Delta H - T\Delta S$ where $\Delta S = S_p - S_r$ and $\Delta G = G_p - G_r$. The state with the lowest *G* or the reaction with most negative ΔG is favored. Reactions spontaneously proceed from higher to lower energy states with decrease in the free energy; larger differences lead to more complete reactions.

3.69 State whether the following reactions have a positive or negative ΔS and explain your choice.
(*a*) $H_2 + CH_3CH{=}CH_2 \longrightarrow CH_3CH_2CH_3$
(*b*) $H_2C{-}CH_2 \longrightarrow H_3C{-}CH{=}CH_2$
    $\quad\quad\backslash\,/$
    $\quad\quad CH_2$
(*c*) $CH_3COO^-(aq) + H_3O^+(aq) \longrightarrow CH_3COOH + H_2O$

▮ (*a*) Negative. Two molecules are combined into one molecule and there is more order (less randomness) in the product ($S_p < S_r$). (*b*) Positive. The rigid ring opens to a chain compound with free rotation about the C—C bond. ($S_p > S_r$). (*c*) Positive. The ions are solvated more than the molecule (CH_3COOH) and when they react they shed the solvating H_2O molecules thereby increasing the randomness ($S_p > S_r$).

3.70 The formation of liquid H_2O from gaseous H_2 and O_2 is exothermic:

$$H_2(g) + 0.5O_2(g) \longrightarrow H_2O(l) \quad \Delta H_r = -68.5 \text{ kcal/mol}$$

Why does the reaction not occur spontaneously when the reactants are mixed?

▮ ΔH's indicate only the energy difference between reactants and products but not the rate of the reaction. Under ambient conditions water formation is very slow and even though it is thermodynamically favorable the reaction does not occur spontaneously. [In this case, ΔH may be used because ΔS is insignificant (< 1 kcal) and ΔH and ΔG are about the same.]

3.71 (*a*) Write the expression for the *equilibrium constant*, K_e, for the generalized equilibrium reaction: $dA + eB \rightleftharpoons fX + gY$. (*b*) How is the magnitude of K_e related to the direction and extent of the equilibrium equation? (*c*) What is the value of ΔG at equilibrium? (*d*) Give the equation relating K_e to the change in free energy for this reaction. (*e*) How are G, S, and H related at equilibrium?

▱ (*a*) The equilibrium constant for this reaction is

$$K_e = \frac{[X]^f \, [Y]^g}{[A]^d \, [B]^e}$$

The brackets indicate molar concentrations and each reactant and product is raised to the power of the corresponding number of moles appearing in the chemical equation.

(*b*) Products are favored when K_e is large. Reactants are favored when K_e is small.

(*c*) At equilibrium $\Delta G = 0$.

(*d*) $\Delta G = \Delta G° + RT \log K_e$. At equilibrium $\Delta G = 0$, and so $\Delta G° = -RT \log K = -2.303RT \log K$ where R is the molar gas constant ($R = 1.987 \text{ cal/mol} \cdot \text{K}$ or $8.314 \text{ J/mol} \cdot \text{K}$).

(*e*) The Δ values used are those at standard states: $\Delta G° = \Delta H° - T\Delta S°$

3.72 Calculate $\Delta G°$ for monochlorination of methane (Problem 4.65) ($K_e = 4.8 \times 10^{18}$ at standard conditions and 25 °C).

▱ $\Delta G° = -2.30RT \log K_e = (-2.30)(2.00 \text{ cal/mol} \cdot \text{K})(1 \text{ kcal}/10^3 \text{ cal})(298 \text{ K})\left[\log(4.8 \times 10^{18})\right]$

$= (-26 \text{ kcal/mol})(4.18 \text{ kJ/kcal}) = -1.1 \times 10^2 \text{ kJ/mol}$

Since $\Delta G°$ is both negative and large, the forward reaction is favored.

3.73 How do ΔH and ΔS together determine the direction of a chemical reaction?

▱ Reaction is favored by a large negative value for ΔG, a result of a large negative ΔH, and a large positive ΔS. However, often ΔS may be disregarded because ΔH is larger and more dominant; in these cases predictions about the direction of a reaction can be made exclusively from ΔH (for example, Problem 3.70). ΔS becomes increasingly more significant as T increases.

3.74 Calculate $\Delta G°$ for the following standard state gaseous reaction and state whether it is favored.

$$CH_4 + Cl_2 \longrightarrow CH_3Cl + HCl$$

Given: $\Delta H° = -25 \text{ kcal/mol}$, $T = 298 \text{ K}$, $\Delta S° = +0.29 \times 10^{-3} \text{ kcal/mol} \cdot \text{K}$.

▱ $\Delta G° = \Delta H° - T\Delta S° = -25 \text{ kcal/mol} - (298 \text{ K})(0.29 \times 10^{-3} \text{ kcal/mol} \cdot \text{K})$

$= -25 \text{ kcal/mol} - 0.086 \text{ kcal/mol} = 24.914 \cong -25 \text{ kcal/mol}$ (2 sig. fig.)

The small ΔS term makes $T\Delta S$ negligible. ΔS is small because there are two moles of both gaseous reactants and products. Hence, the driving force of the reaction is the large negative ΔH. This value is consistent with the value calculated from K_e in Problem 3.72.

3.75 Predict the favored direction of the reaction: $H_3C:CH_3 \rightleftharpoons 2H_3C\cdot$ in terms of H and S.

▱ One CH_3CH_3 molecule forms two $H_3C\cdot$ radicals whose greater randomness makes ΔS positive and favorable for reaction. Nevertheless, this term is much smaller than the larger unfavorable positive ΔH (bond-dissociation energy), which favors the reverse reaction in which the CH_3CH_3 molecule is more stable than the two $H_3C\cdot$ radicals. As a result, ΔG is positive and the reverse reaction is favored.

3.76 What happens to the rates of the forward and reverse reactions and the concentrations of the participating substances when the state of equilibrium is attained?

▱ A reaction is in a state of equilibrium when both forward and reverse reactions proceed at the same rate and there is no change in concentrations of reactants and products.

3.77 Discuss the validity of the following statements: (*a*) If equilibrium is reached when the molar concentrations of each reactant and product is the same, K_e must be equal to one. (*b*) The value of K_e varies with temperature. (*c*) A value of $K_e > 10$ always indicates an exothermic reaction with $-\Delta H$ values.

▱ (*a*) This statement would be true *only* if (1) the number of reactants and products is the same, i.e., $A + B = C + D$, and (2) their coefficients are all equal to 1. (*b*) True. Rates of reactions change with temperature. The rates of the forward and reverse reactions change differently causing a shift in the equilibrium and a new K_e. (**c**) False. Such a K_e always indicates a $-\Delta G$ and often a $-\Delta H$ but not always. ΔH could be positive but overwhelmed by a very large $+\Delta S$ at a high T.

3.78 What changes could be made in the following reaction to increase the yield of $HCOOCH_3$?

$$HCOOH + CH_3OH \rightleftharpoons HCOOCH_3 + H_2O$$

/ The reaction must be shifted to the right. This is achieved by any combination of the following: add CH_3OH, add $HCOOH$ (reactants), remove H_2O, remove $HCOOCH_3$ (products).

3.79 Discuss the statement "Every reaction is reversible to some extent."

/ For many reactions, K_e is so large that from a practical point of view they are considered to go to completion. However according to the *Principle of Microscopic Reversibility* every reaction has some degree of reversibility.

3.80 Account for the relative K_e values for (**a**) the reaction in Problem 3.78 and (**b**):

$$(b) \quad \begin{array}{c} H_2C \\ H_2C \\ H_2C-OH \end{array} \!\!\! \begin{array}{c} COOH \end{array} \rightleftharpoons \quad \underset{O}{\bigcirc}\!\!=\!\!O + H_2O$$

/ Since the changes in bonding in both reactions are similar, the formation of the ester in (**a**) and the cyclic ester (lactone) in (**b**) have about the same ΔH_r. However, they differ in that (**a**) is *intermolecular* because two molecules react to form one molecule of product whereas (**b**) is an *intramolecular* cyclization wherein one molecule gives one molecule. Since reaction (**a**) loses more entropy (two molecules → 1 molecule), it has a less positive ΔS, a less negative ΔG, and a smaller K_e.

3.81 From the signs of ΔH and $T\Delta S$ tabulated below for reactions (**a**)–(**d**) predict the sign of ΔG, the direction the reaction proceeds, and whether K_e is more or less than one.

	ΔH	$T\Delta S$
(**a**)	−	+
(**b**)	+	−
(**c**)	−	−
(**d**)	+	+

/ (**a**) $-\Delta G$; forward; $K_e > 1$. (**b**) $+\Delta G$; reverse; $K_e < 1$. (**c**) If ΔH has a large negative value, it usually overwhelms a negative ΔS: $-\Delta G$; forward; $K_e > 1$. However, if T is very high, $T\Delta S$ can be high enough to overcompensate for a negative ΔH, and ΔG can become positive, the reaction is reversed, and $K_e < 1$. (**d**) If ΔH is very positive, it overrides the effect of a positive $T\Delta S$ term: $+\Delta G$; reverse; $K_e < 1$. At elevated T's, the positive $T\Delta S$ term becomes more important and it can cause a reaction to occur. A small positive ΔH with a large positive ΔS also results in $-\Delta G$, forward, and $K_e > 1$. Predictions cannot be made exclusively from the signs in (**c**) and (**d**) without knowing the actual values of ΔH, ΔS and T's.

CHEMICAL KINETICS

3.82 Define the rate of a reaction and express it mathematically.

/ The *rate of a reaction* is how fast a molar concentration changes. In terms of a reactant: rate $= -\Delta[\text{reactant}]/\Delta t(\text{time})$. A minus sign is used because concentrations of reactants must decrease with time. In terms of a product: rate $= \Delta[\text{product}]/\Delta t$. Now a plus sign is used because concentrations of products must increase with time.

3.83 (**a**) Give the *rate equation* for the general reaction: $aA + bB \rightleftharpoons cC + dD$. (**b**) Discuss the term k in the rate equation found in (**a**). (**c**) Discuss the relationship between the coefficients of the chemical equation and the exponents of the rate equation. (**d**) Must the exponents be positive integers? (**e**) How can the rate equation be used to compare reactions?

/ (**a**) For the given general reaction, the rate equation is

$$\text{Rate} = k_1[A]^x[B]^y \tag{1}$$

In most cases only concentrations of reactants appear in rate equations. In those rare cases when [product] appears, it will invariably be in the denominator.

(**b**) The *specific rate constant*, k_1, is a proportionality constant that is specific for each reaction. It changes with temperature but is independent of concentrations. It is not synonymous with rate–it equals rate only when the concentrations of all species appearing in the rate equation are 1M. The units for k_1 depend on the concentration factors, the exponents, and the unit of time.

(**c**) The exponents in (*1*), x and y, are determined experimentally and are not necessarily the coefficients a and b of the chemical equation.

(**d**) No. The exponents may be integers, fractions such as $1/2$, or zero.

(**e**) Since k_1 is independent of concentration, it is useful to compare k's for different reactants undergoing the same reaction at the same T, or for any one reaction at different T's.

3.84 (**a**) Give the rate equation for the reverse reaction in Problem 3.83. (**b**) How is K_e related to the rate constants for the forward and reverse reactions? (**c**) Define the terms *thermodynamic stability* and *kinetic stability* and apply them to the following situations: (i) $K_e = 10^{-40}/10^{-10}$, (ii) $K_e = 10^{-40}/10^{-50}$, and (iii) $K_e = 10^{10}/10^{40}$.

◢ (**a**) Rate $= k_{-1}[C]^p[D]^q$. Note the use of the -1 subscript to indicate a reverse reaction. (**b**) At equilibrium, the forward and reverse rates are equal and $K_e = k_f/k_r$ or k_1/k_{-1}. (**c**) A small K_e indicates thermodynamic stability, because ΔG for the reaction will be positive. A small k_1 compared to k_{-1} indicates kinetic stability; the reaction does not result in products because it is too slow. (i) $K_e = 10^{-30}$; the system is thermodynamically stable, but the very small value for k_1 indicates kinetic stability. (ii) $K_e = 10^{10}$; thermodynamically unstable but kinetically stable–a reaction with these values probably will not proceed to products. (iii) $K_e = 10^{-30}$; thermodynamically stable, but the large value for k_1 shows that the reactants are kinetically unstable. Note that the products are kinetically even more unstable ($k_{-1} \gg k_1$).

3.85 (**a**) How are concentrations related to rates? (**b**) List four other experimental factors that affect reaction rates.

◢ (**a**) Molecules must collide in order to react with each other. Increasing the concentration increases the number of collisions per unit time, resulting in a faster reaction. The rate equation (*1*) in Problem 3.83 expresses this relationship. (**b**) (1) *Temperature*. At high temperatures, molecules move faster, resulting in more collisions per unit time. A rough rule is that the rate (and value of k) doubles for every rise in temperature of 10°C. (2) *Particle size*. Increasing the surface area of solids (decreasing particle size) by pulverization increases the reaction rates by exposing more molecules to each other (increasing number of collisions). For example, very rapid exothermic oxidation of coal dust causes coal mine explosions. (3) *Catalysts and inhibitors*. Both substances affect rates but are recovered unchanged–catalysts speed up reactions, inhibitors slow them down. (4) *Solvent* used. Solvation often changes the reactivities of the reactants.

3.86 (**a**) How do the exponents x and y in the rate equation (*1*) in Problem 3.83 establish the order of a reaction? (**b**) How are they determined?

◢ (**a**) The *order of a reaction* is defined as the sum of the exponents x and y. We can also define the order of an individual reactant by its exponent. (**b**) Rate equations, with their exponents, and therefore their orders, are determined experimentally.

3.87 Give the orders of each of the following reactions and the orders of its individual reactants.
(**a**) $H_2 + I_2 \longrightarrow 2HI$; rate $= k[H_2][I_2]$
(**b**) $BrO_3^- + 5Br^- + 6H^+ \longrightarrow 3Br_2 + 3H_2O$; rate $= k[BrO_3^-][Br^-][H^+]^2$
(**c**) $Me_3CBr + H_2O$ (solvent) $\longrightarrow Me_3COH + HBr$; rate $= k[Me_3CBr][H_2O] = k[Me_3CBr]$
(**d**) $CHCl_3 + Br_2 \longrightarrow CBrCl_3 + HBr$; rate $= [CHCl_3][Br_2]^{1/2}$
(**e**) $CH_3CHO(g) \xrightarrow{\text{I}_2 \text{ (a catalyst)}} CH_4(g) + CO(g)$; rate $= [CH_3CHO][I_2]$

◢ (**a**) Second order $(1 + 1)$, first order in each reactant. (**b**) Fourth order $(1 + 1 + 2)$, first order in BrO_3^- and Br^- and second order in H^+. (**c**) Although solvents may be reactants, they never appear in rate equations. First order $(1 + 0)$, first order in Me_3CBr and an indeterminate order in H_2O. (**d**) 1.5 order $(1 + 0.5)$, first order in $CHCl_3$ and $1/2$ order in Br_2. (**e**) Second order, first order in each reactant. Note that a catalyst can appear in a rate equation.

3.88 (**a**) Use the experimentally-determined effect of changes in concentration on reaction rates to find the rate equation for each of the following two reactions of alkyl bromides with OH^-, carried out in an acetone-H_2O mixture as solvent.
    Reaction 1.

$$CH_3Br + OH^- \longrightarrow Br^- + CH_3OH$$

Doubling the molar concentration of either CH_3Br or OH^- doubles the reaction rate; doubling both quadruples the rate.

Reaction 2.

$$(CH_3)_3CBr + OH^- \longrightarrow Br^- + (CH_3)_3COH$$

The reaction rate is doubled when $[(CH_3)_3CBr]$ is doubled but is unaffected by changes in $[OH^-]$.

(*b*) Explain the difference in reaction orders of the two reactions since both are conversions of alkyl bromide to alcohol.

▟ (*a*) The data given for Reaction 1 show that the reaction rate depends on concentrations of both reactants raised to the first power. Had one of the concentrations been raised to the second power, doubling it would have resulted in quadrupling the rate when the other concentration is kept constant. The rate equation of Reaction 1 is rate $= k[CH_3Br][OH^-]$. This equation is of first order for each reactant but is of second order overall $(1 + 1)$.

The rate equation of Reaction 2 depends on $[(CH_3)_3CBr]$ raised to the power of one: rate $= k[(CH_3)_3CBr]$. It is of first order with respect to $[(CH_3)_3CBr]$, of zeroth order with respect to $[OH^-]$, and of first order $(1 + 0)$ overall.

(*b*) The rate equations are different because the reactions have different mechanisms.

3.89 Given the same set of conditions, find the three important factors that determine the rates of reactions.

▟ 1. *Frequency of collisions* [see Problem 3.85(*a*)].
2. *Activation energy*, E_{act}, or *enthalpy of activation*, $\Delta H^\ddagger$, at constant pressure, is the energy *in excess* of the average energy of the molecules necessary for them to react. More successful collisions and faster reactions are found with smaller values for $\Delta H^\ddagger$ ($\Delta H^\ddagger$ is never negative). The larger the value of $\Delta H^\ddagger$, the slower the reaction.
3. Not all collisions with the requisite $\Delta H^\ddagger$ result in a reaction. Often collisions must also occur in a certain *orientation* as reflected by the *entropy of activation*, $\Delta S^\ddagger$. The *more organized* or *less random* the required orientation of the colliding molecules, the *smaller* is the value of $\Delta S^\ddagger$ and the *slower* is the reaction. $\Delta S^\ddagger$ is also called the *probability factor*.

$\Delta H^\ddagger$ is often more significant than $\Delta S^\ddagger$ in comparing reactions. When they both have about equal weight, the *free energy of activation*, $\Delta G^\ddagger$, should be used, since $\Delta G^\ddagger = \Delta H^\ddagger - T\Delta S^\ddagger$. The more positive the value of $\Delta G^\ddagger$, the slower the rate.

3.90 Solvents can change reaction rates by increasing or decreasing either $\Delta H^\ddagger$, $\Delta S^\ddagger$, or both. Predict effect on rates from the following tabulated changes (*a*)–(*d*).

	(*a*)	(*b*)	(*c*)	(*d*)
$\Delta H^\ddagger$	Increase	Increase	Decrease	Decrease
$\Delta S^\ddagger$	Decrease	Increase	Increase	Decrease

▟ While the effect on rate will depend on the magnitude of each change, in most cases the change in $\Delta H^\ddagger$ is more significant than $\Delta S^\ddagger$.

(*a*) Decreased rate because of both changes. (*b*) Decreased rate because of $\Delta H^\ddagger$ but increased rate because of $\Delta S^\ddagger$. Hence, the prediction may be indeterminate. However, since the $\Delta H^\ddagger$ changes are usually more significant, there should be a rate decrease. (*c*) Both effects increase the reaction rate. (*d*) Decrease in $\Delta H^\ddagger$ should increase the rate while the decrease in $\Delta S^\ddagger$ should decrease it. The rate will probably increase for the reason given in (*b*).

TRANSITION STATES AND ENTHALPY DIAGRAMS

3.91 Define transition state.

▟ As reacting molecules with sufficient enthalpy and with the proper orientation begin to collide, they enter a transitory state in which there is a repositioning of certain atoms in the molecules while some bonds are breaking and others are forming. When this specific state is at its *maximum energy*, it is called a *transition state* (TS) or *activated complex*. Once TS is reached, it can proceed to products (or intermediates) or reform the reactants. When a structure is drawn for the TS, the breaking and forming bonds are shown with dashed lines because they actually are partial bonds.

3.92 Give equations for $\Delta H^{\ddagger}$, $\Delta S^{\ddagger}$, and $\Delta G^{\ddagger}$ in terms of the transition state.

▰ Although the TS is a *hypothetical* state, it nevertheless assumes thermodynamic functions, H_{TS}, S_{TS}, and G_{TS}, leading to the following relationships:

$$\Delta H^{\ddagger} = H_{TS} - H_{GS} \qquad \Delta S^{\ddagger} = S_{TS} - S_{GS} \qquad \text{and} \qquad \Delta G^{\ddagger} = G_{TS} - G_{GS}$$

where GS stands for the *ground state* which is the average condition of the reactants.

3.93 (*a*) At a given temperature, how do ground-state molecules attain the extra energy needed for a successful collision? (*b*) Must each colliding molecule have the extra energy? (*c*) Is the transition state a reaction intermediate? (*d*) How many transition states are there in a multistep mechanism?

▰ (*a*) During unsuccessful collisions between ground-state molecules, kinetic energy may be transferred from one to another causing one to slow down and the other to speed up. When superenergetic molecules now collide, they may have sufficient $\Delta H^{\ddagger}$. (*b*) No. The two together must have the extra energy, not necessarily individually. (*c*) No. Transition states are *not* true intermediates because they have no finite time of existence and have *energy maxima*, while intermediates are real and exist at *energy minima*, which indicate stability. Intermediates may be detected experimentally while transition states are theoretical constructs based *on experimentation*, not simply made up. (*d*) Each step in a multistep mechanism has its own transition state.

3.94 Write an equation showing the TS in the abstraction of an H· from CH_4 by Cl· to form H_3C· and HCl.

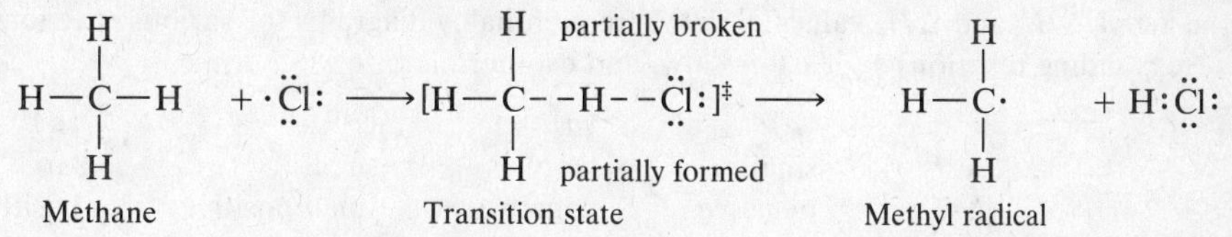

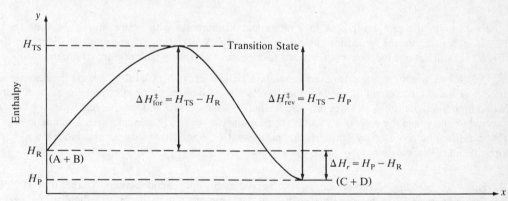

Methane   Transition state   Methyl radical

The brackets show the transient character of the TS that is further indicated by the symbol $\ddagger$.

3.95 (*a*) Draw an enthalpy (energy) diagram for a reversible one-step exothermic reaction: $A + B \rightarrow C + D$. (*b*) Compare the relative values of $\Delta H^{\ddagger}_{\text{forward}}$ ($\Delta H^{\ddagger}_{\text{for}}$) and $\Delta H^{\ddagger}_{\text{reverse}}$ ($\Delta H^{\ddagger}_{\text{rev}}$). (*c*) Are $\Delta H^{\ddagger}$ and ΔH_r related?

▰ (*a*) Enthalpy diagrams show the relationship between the enthalpies of reactants, transition state, and products along the y axis. The x axis shows the progress of the reaction. The y axis may indicate free energy or potential energy as well as enthalpy. See Fig. 3.3.

Progress of Reaction (Reaction Coordinate)   **Fig. 3-3**

Because the reaction is exothermic, $H_P < H_R$ ($\Delta H_r = H_P - H_R$). (*b*) Both reactions must proceed through the same TS. Since the reaction is exothermic and the enthalpy of the product is lower, $\Delta H^{\ddagger}_{\text{reverse}} > \Delta H^{\ddagger}_{\text{forward}}$. (*c*) They are rarely related. An exception is when the TS shows only the breaking of bonds.

3.96 Explain how the enthalpy diagram in Fig. 3.3 shows: (*a*) that the reaction is exothermic, (*b*) the number of steps in the reaction, and (*c*) the position of equilibrium.

▰ (*a*) H_P is lower than H_R and the difference ($\Delta H_r = H_P - H_R$) is negative as expected for an exothermic reaction. Had the reaction been endothermic, H_P would have been greater than H_R. (*b*) One transition state indicates a single step reaction involving both reactants. (*c*) The negative ΔH_r means the equilibrium favors the forward reaction providing ΔH_r is more significant than ΔS_r.

3.97 Draw an enthalpy diagram for the endothermic reaction in Problem 3.94 in which $\Delta H^{\ddagger} = 4$ kcal/mol and $\Delta H_r = 1$ kcal/mol.

▰ The transition state energy $\Delta H^{\ddagger}$ is greater by 4 kcal/mol than the ground state H_R. H_P is greater by 1 kcal/mol than H_R. See Fig. 3.4.

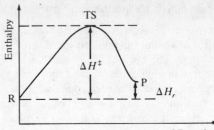

Fig. 3-4

3.98 Use the listed $\Delta H^{\ddagger}$ and ΔH_r values, derived from enthalpy diagrams for various reactions, to determine whether the corresponding reactions are fast or slow, and exothermic or endothermic.

	(*a*)	(*b*)	(*c*)	(*d*)
$\Delta H^{\ddagger}$	small	large	small	large
ΔH_r	negative	negative	small positive	positive

▰ (*a*) fast, exothermic; (*b*) slow, exothermic; (*c*) fast, endothermic; (*d*) slow, endothermic

3.99 Account for the behavior of a catalyst in terms of (*a*) H_{GS}, H_{TS}, and $\Delta H^{\ddagger}$ and, (*b*) S_{GS}, S_{TS}, and $\Delta S^{\ddagger}$.

▰ (*a*) Catalysts invariably speed up reactions by lowering $\Delta H^{\ddagger}$. This can be done by lowering H_{TS}, raising H_{GS}, or doing both. (*b*) Catalysts can also increase reaction rates by increasing $\Delta S^{\ddagger}$. This can be achieved by increasing S_{TS}, lowering S_{GS}, or doing both.

3.100 (*a*) Explain why the rate constant k in a rate equation increases with temperature. (*b*) State the drawback in increasing a reaction rate by raising the temperature? (*c*) What attempts are made to overcome this problem? (*d*) Why do all natural biochemical reactions take place at the body temperature of the organism?

▰ (*a*) Increasing the temperature increases the kinetic energy of molecules, making them move faster thereby increasing the number of collisions. More molecules now also have sufficient energy for more effective collisions. (*b*) At higher temperatures all rates increase, including those of *side* and *reverse* reactions. (*c*) Temperatures are selected to encourage the preferred reaction to take place at an acceptable rate with a minimum of side reactions. This can often be achieved by searching for catalysts. (*d*) Practically every natural biochemical reaction occurs with the aid of some catalyst, e.g., an *enzyme*.

3.101 (*a*) Draw an enthalpy diagram for an exothermic two-step reaction when (i) the first step is slow and rate-determining and (ii) the second step is rate-determining. Label the intermediate as I. (*b*) Compare the enthalpies of intermediates I_A and I_B with the transition states. (*c*) When may an intermediate be isolated? (*d*) Compare enthalpies of TS_1 and TS_2 in (*a*) and (*b*).

▰ (*a*) See Fig. 3.5.
   (*b*) In both (i) and (ii) the enthalpies of TS_1 and TS_2 are greater than the enthalpies of I_A and I_B.
   (*c*) If the $\Delta H^{\ddagger}_{rev}$ and $\Delta H^{\ddagger}_{for}$ for the intermediates are both large enough for the rates to be slowed sufficiently, the intermediate may accumulate permitting isolation. Under such circumstances the intermediate would be a byproduct.
   (*d*) (i) $TS_1 > TS_2$, (ii) $TS_2 > TS_1$. In both cases the TS of the slower (or slowest) step has the higher (or highest) H_{TS}.

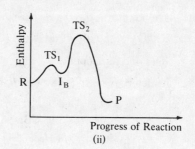

Fig. 3-5

3.102 (*a*) Define molecularity of a reaction. (*b*) What are the types of molecularity encountered and which type is rare? (*c*) Can molecularity be determined from the rate equation?

▮ (*a*) *Molecularity* is the number of reactant particles colliding in a step. Unlike the order of a reaction, the molecularity of a step must be an integer. (*b*) When one particle is the reactant in a step, the step is *unimolecular*. If a single species must collide with solvent molecules, the reaction will appear to be unimolecular because solvent does not appear in rate equations. Collision of two reacting particles is a *bimolecular* step. *Termolecular* reactions, involving the simultaneous collision of three species, are rare. (*c*) In multistep reactions, the molecularity of any single step is likely not to be related to the rate equation.

SUPPLEMENTARY PROBLEMS

3.103 Suggest a mechanism involving only unimolecular or bimolecular steps for the reaction

$$2A + 2B \longrightarrow C + D; \qquad rate = k[A]^2[B]$$

▮ In some combination, two A's and one B are needed to participate in the slow rate-determining step. The three do not collide simultaneously since termolecular steps are very rare and therefore disregarded. This dictates multisteps in which there are initial fast reactions to produce the intermediate necessary for the slow step. The second mole of B, which is in the chemical equation but not in the rate equation, is used in a fast step following the slow step. Two possible mechanisms are:

Mechanism 1	Mechanism 2
$A + B \xrightarrow{\text{fast}} AB$	$A + A \xrightarrow{\text{fast}} A_2$
$AB + A \xrightarrow{\text{slow}} A_2B$	$A_2 + B \xrightarrow{\text{slow}} A_2B$
$A_2B + B \xrightarrow{\text{fast}} C + D$	$A_2B + B \xrightarrow{\text{fast}} C + D$

The rate equation alone does not determine which is the correct mechanism.

3.104 For the following three-step exothermic reaction:

$$\text{Step 1: } A \xrightarrow{\text{fast}} B \qquad \text{Step 2: } B + C \xrightarrow{\text{slow}} D + E \qquad \text{Step 3: } A + E \xrightarrow{\text{fast}} 2F$$

(*a*) write the net chemical reaction, (*b*) list (i) reactants, (ii) intermediates, and (iii) products, and (*c*) give the molecularity of each step. (*d*) Which step is rate-determining?

▮ (*a*) Adding steps 1, 2, and 3 gives $2A + C \rightarrow D + 2F$. (*b*) (i) A and C, (ii) B and E, and (iii) F and D. (*c*) Step 1 is unimolecular; steps 2 and 3 are bimolecular. (*d*) The slow step is step 2, which is the rate-determining step.

3.105 Give the rate equation for the overall reaction in Problem 3.104. Explain.

▮ The rate equation for the slow step is rate = $k'[B][C]$. It has an intermediate, B, which is not permitted since only reactants and on rare occasions products are found. B can return to reactants at a faster rate than it can go on with C to D + E because $\Delta H^{\ddagger}$ for return is less than $\Delta H^{\ddagger}$ for step 2. We say that step 1 is fast and reversible; $A \rightleftharpoons B$; and $K_e = [B]/[A]$. It is now possible to express [B] in terms of [A], $[B] = K_e[A]$ and so rate = $k'K_e[A][C]$. But $k'K_e$ is a constant (k) and thus the required rate equation for the overall reaction is rate = $k[A][C]$.

3.106 From the rate equation, rate = $k[\text{Ag}^+][\text{Me}_3\text{CBr}]$, deduce a plausible two-step mechanism for the reaction

$$\text{Me}_3\text{CBr} + \text{Ag}^+ + \text{CH}_3\text{COO}^- \longrightarrow \text{Me}_3\text{COOCCH}_3 + \text{AgBr}$$

Indicate electrophiles and nucleophiles.

▎ The slow rate-determining step involves only Me_3CBr and Ag^+, not CH_3COO^- which must appear in an ensuing fast step.

$$Step\ 1:\quad \underset{\text{nucleophile}}{\text{Me}_3\overset{..}{\underset{..}{\text{C}}}\text{Br}:} + \underset{\text{electrophile}}{\text{Ag}^+} \xrightarrow{\text{slow}} [\text{Me}_3\text{C}^+] + \text{AgBr}$$

$$Step\ 2:\quad \underset{\text{electrophile}}{[\text{Me}_3\text{C}^+]} + \underset{\text{nucleophile}}{^-\text{OOCCH}_3} \xrightarrow{\text{fast}} \text{Me}_3\text{COOCCH}_3$$

3.107 A structural change is made in a reactant without affecting the reactive functional group. If this change increases the $H^\ddagger$ of the TS, is it accurate to say that the rate of reaction will decrease?

▎ Rate depends on $\Delta H^\ddagger$, not $H^\ddagger$. Since $\Delta H^\ddagger = H_{TS} - H_{GS}$, it is also necessary to evaluate the effect of the change on H_{GS} since there is likely to be a change. If H_{TS} is increased more than H_{GS}, $\Delta H^\ddagger$ increases and the rate will indeed decrease. This effect of the structural change is an example of *steric hindrance*. However, if H_{GS} is increased more than H_{TS}, $\Delta H^\ddagger$ decreases and the rate actually increases. This kind of structural change is an example of *steric acceleration*.

3.108 A and B can react at a certain temperature to give C, the rate-controlled product. At a higher temperature they give D, the thermodynamic-controlled product. Use an enthalpy diagram to explain this behavior and indicate the relative temperatures needed.

▎ See Fig. 3-6. The rate-controlled product, C, requires the smaller $\Delta H^\ddagger$, but has a higher H. Product C is isolated if the temperature is low enough to prevent the reverse of C to A and B. At higher temperatures the reversal takes place and some small number of A and B molecules can attain the higher $\Delta H^\ddagger$ to go on to D, the product with the lower H. This thermodynamic-controlled product cannot return to reactants because it is faced with a high $\Delta H^\ddagger$. As time goes on, more and more A's and B's take the high road and D accumulates as the major product.

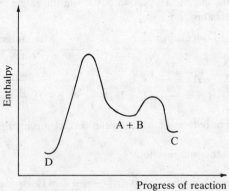

Progress of reaction   **Fig. 3-6**

3.109 The rate equations for the mechanistic steps for the pyrolysis of $\text{Ph}-\text{N}=\text{N}-\text{CPh}_3$ are:

$$\text{PhN}=\text{NCPh}_3 \underset{k_{-1}}{\overset{k_1}{\rightleftharpoons}} \underset{\text{caged radicals}}{\text{PhN}=\text{N}\cdot\cdot\text{CPh}_3} \overset{k_2}{\longrightarrow} \underset{\substack{\text{solvent-separated} \\ \text{radicals}}}{\text{PhN}=\text{N}\cdot//\cdot\text{CPh}_3} \overset{k_3}{\longrightarrow} \underset{\text{separated radicals}}{\text{Ph}\cdot + \cdot\text{CPh}_3} + :\text{N}\equiv\text{N}:$$

(*a*) Explain the differences between (i) caged, (ii) solvent-separated, and (iii) separated radicals. (*b*) If the rate of the reaction is decreased as the viscosity of the solvent or the pressure of the reaction is increased, which must be the slowest step?

▎ (*a*) (i) Radicals have not moved away from each other; they are almost at the bond length distance. They easily recombine and the step is reversible. (ii) Radicals have moved away from each other and are separated by a few solvent molecules as indicated by the two slash lines. They are still fairly close and feel the presence of each other. (iii) These are completely separated from each other by large numbers of solvent molecules. (b) These changes make it more difficult for the caged radicals to move away to give the solvent-separated radicals. Hence k_2 is the rate-controlling step because it is the step where the initial separation occurs.

3.110 The specific rate constant, k, at 25 °C is 0.013 s^{-1} for the first order reaction R—Br + H$_2$O → R—OH + HBr. (a) Explain the meaning of this constant. (b) Calculate $t_{1/2}$, the half-life, and explain its meaning.

✦ (a) For every mole of RBr present in the reaction vessel, 0.013 mole reacts per second. (b) For a first-order reaction, $t_{1/2} = 0.693/k$. Thus, $t_{1/2} = 53$ s. This means that exactly half the number of moles of RBr in the reaction vessel reacts in 53 seconds.

3.111 A reaction vessel contains 0.192 mole of RBr. (a) How many moles of RBr (Problem 3.110) will be left after 159 seconds of reaction? (b) How long will it take for 0.180 mole of RBr to react?

✦ (a) 159 s/53 s = 3 half-lives. After one half-life, 0.192/2 = 0.096 mol, after the second half-life, 0.096/2 = 0.048 mol, and after the third half-life, 0.048/2 = 0.024 mol remain. (b) The number of moles remaining is 0.192 − 0.180 = 0.012 mol. Hence, it is necessary to find the number of $t_{1/2}$'s needed to go from 0.192 to 0.012 mole. This would require one more half-life than in (a) since 0.024/2 = 0.012 mol, for a total of four half-lives or 4 × 53 = 212 s (3.5 min).

CHAPTER 4
Alkanes

NOMENCLATURE AND STRUCTURE

4.1 (*a*) What is the general formula for an alkane? (*b*) Give the molecular formulas for alkanes with (i) four C's, (ii) seven C's, (iii) 10 C's, and (iv) 22 C's. (*c*) Give the names of the alkanes having from 1 to 7 carbon atoms in a continuous chain.

◢ (*a*) The general formula is C_nH_{2n+2} where n is an integer. (*b*) (i) C_4H_{10}, (ii) C_7H_{16}, (iii) $C_{10}H_{22}$, and (iv) $C_{22}H_{46}$. (*c*) The alkanes having from 1 to 7 C's are, in order, methane, ethane, propane, butane, pentane, hexane, and heptane.

4.2 (*a*) Define an alkyl group. (*b*) Give the formula for each of the following two alkyl groups: (i) methyl (Me), and (ii) ethyl (Et). (*c*) Account for the two different alkyl groups derived from propane and write their structures.

◢ (*a*) An *alkyl* group is the structure remaining after one H is removed from an alkane.
(*b*) (i) CH_3— and (ii) CH_3CH_2—.
(*c*) Propane has two different kinds of H atoms. Removal of any one of the six H^a's attached to the terminal C's results in a propyl group (Pr), and removal of either of the two H^b's on the center C results in an isopropyl group (*i*-Pr).

$$CH_3CH_2CH_2-\;\xleftarrow{-H^a}\;H^a-\overset{\overset{\displaystyle H^a}{|}}{\underset{\underset{\displaystyle H^a}{|}}{C}}-\overset{\overset{\displaystyle H^b}{|}}{\underset{\underset{\displaystyle H^b}{|}}{C}}-\overset{\overset{\displaystyle H^a}{|}}{\underset{\underset{\displaystyle H^a}{|}}{C}}-H^a\;\xrightarrow{-H^b}\;CH_3\overset{\overset{\displaystyle |}{}}{C}HCH_3$$

Propyl group   Isopropyl group

4.3 (*a*) Provide a structural formula for $CH_3CH_2C(CH_3)_2CH_2CH(CH_3)_2$, and define and identify all the *primary* (1°), *secondary* (2°), *tertiary* (3°), and *quaternary* (4°) C's. (*b*) Identify all the 1°, 2°, and 3° H's. (*c*) Give the number of H atoms bonded to a 1°, 2°, 3°, and 4° carbon atom in an alkane. (*d*) Give the number of C atoms bonded to a 1°, 2°, 3°, and 4° carbon atom in an alkane.

◢ (*a*) In the condensed formula all atoms or groups written after a C are bonded to it.

$$a = 1°, \quad b = 2°,$$
$$c = 3°, \quad d = 4°$$

A 1 °C is bonded to only one other C, a 2 °C to two other C's, a 3 °C to three other C's, and a 4 °C to four other C's. (The C of CH_4 is super 1°.)
(*b*) 1 °H's are those attached to 1 °C's, 2 °H's to 2 °C's, and 3 °H's to 3 °C's. Other atoms or groups bonded to C, like halogen, are similarly identified. (A 4 °H cannot exist because all four bonds of a 4 °C are to other C's.)
(*c*) 3, 2, 1 and 0.
(*d*) 1, 2, 3, and 4.

4.4 Write condensed formulas for each of the following groups: (*a*) isobutyl (*i*-Bu), (*b*) *s*-butyl (*s*-Bu), (*c*) *t*-butyl (*t*-Bu), (*d*) isopentyl (isoamyl), and (*e*) *t*-pentyl (*t*-amyl).

◢ The prefix iso (or *i*-) may be used when there is a methyl group on the next-to-the-last C in the chain. Prefixes *sec*- or *s*- and *tert*- or *t*- indicate secondary and tertiary, respectively. (*a*) $(CH_3)_2CHCH_2$—,

(*b*) $CH_3CH_2\overset{|}{C}H(CH_3)$, (*c*) $(CH_3)_3C$—, (*d*) $(CH_3)_2CHCH_2CH_2$—, and (*e*) $CH_3CH_2\overset{|}{C}(CH_3)_2$

4.5 Write the structural formulas for each of the following compounds: (*a*) 3-Chloro-2-methylhexane, (*b*) 2,3,4-trimethylpentane, (*c*) 1,4-dibromo-2-methylbutane, (*d*) 2,2-dimethylpentane, and (*e*) 4-isopropylheptane.

(*a*) $CH_3 - \overset{\displaystyle |}{\underset{\displaystyle CH_3}{CH}} - \overset{\displaystyle |}{\underset{\displaystyle Cl}{CH}} - CH_2CH_2CH_3$ (*c*) $BrCH_2 - \overset{\displaystyle |}{\underset{\displaystyle CH_3}{CH}} - CH_2 - CH_2Br$

(*b*) $CH_3 - \overset{\displaystyle |}{\underset{\displaystyle CH_3}{CH}} - \overset{\displaystyle |}{\underset{\displaystyle CH_3}{CH}} - \overset{\displaystyle |}{\underset{\displaystyle CH_3}{CH}} - CH_3$ (*d*) $CH_3 - CH_2 - CH_2 - \overset{\displaystyle CH_3}{\underset{\displaystyle CH_3}{\overset{\displaystyle |}{\underset{\displaystyle |}{C}}}} - CH_3$

(*e*) $CH_3 - CH_2 - CH_2 - \overset{\displaystyle |}{\underset{\displaystyle CH_3CHCH_3}{CH}} - CH_2 - CH_2 - CH_3$

4.6 For each of the following state why the given names are incorrect, and then give the correct IUPAC (International Union of Pure and Applied Chemistry) names and write the corresponding condensed structural formulas. (*a*) 2-Dimethylbutane, (*b*) 3-chloro-4-methylpentane, (*c*) 2-ethylhexane, (*d*) 3-isopropylpentane, and (*e*) 1,1-dimethylbutane.

(*a*) Assuming that the "di" portion of the name is correct, each methyl group must have a numbered position even if they are both on the same carbon: 2,2-dimethylbutane, $(CH_3)_3CCH_2CH_3$. (*b*) In the incorrect name the chain of C's is numbered from the end that gives higher rather than lower numbers: 3-chloro-2-methylpentane, $CH_3CH(CH_3)CHClCH_2CH_3$. (*c*) The ethyl group should be part of the longest chain: 3-methylheptane, $CH_3CH_2CH(CH_3)CH_2CH_2CH_2CH_3$. (*d*) When there are two longest chains of the same length, select the one with the greater number of substituents: 3-ethyl-2-methylpentane, $CH_3CH(CH_3)CH(C_2H_5)CH_2CH_3$. (*e*) One of the methyl groups on C^1 is part of the longest chain: 2-methylpentane, $CH_3CH(CH_3)CH_2CH_2CH_3$.

4.7 Provide the IUPAC names for each of the following: (*a*) $(CH_3)_3CCH_2C(CH_3)_3$, (*b*) $C(CH_3)_4$, (*c*) $CH_3C(Cl)_2CH(CH_3)_2$, and (*d*) $(CH_3CH_2)_2CHCH(CH_3)CH_2CH_3$.

(*a*) 2,2,4,4-Tetramethylpentane, (*b*) 2,2-dimethylpropane, (*c*) 2,2-dichloro-3-methylbutane, and (*d*) 3-ethyl-4-methylhexane.

4.8 Draw simplified line structures for the compounds given in Problem 4.7.

In this method draw only the C—C bonds and all functional groups bonded to C. The approximate C—C bond angles are used.

4.9 Write structural formulas for the five isomeric hexanes and name them by the IUPAC system.

Start with the longest chain, hexane, $CH_3CH_2CH_2CH_2CH_2CH_3$. Going to a five-carbon chain, a CH_3 may be placed either on C^2 to produce 2-methylpentane, or on C^3 to give 3-methylpentane. Starting with a four-carbon chain, either a CH_3CH_2 or two CH_3's must be added as side chains for a total of six C's. The CH_3CH_2 cannot be placed anywhere on the chain because it would lengthen it. A CH_3 would also extend the chain if it were placed on either terminal C. Placing one CH_3 on each of the central C's gives 2,3-dimethylbutane, and if both are placed on the same central C, the isomer is 2,2-dimethylbutane. Note that each isomer has a distinctive name. If two structural formulas have the same correct names, they are identical even if they are drawn differently.

$\underset{\displaystyle CH_3}{\overset{\displaystyle |}{CH_3CHCH_2CH_2CH_3}}$ $\underset{\displaystyle CH_3}{\overset{\displaystyle |}{CH_3CH_2CHCH_2CH_3}}$ $CH_3 - \overset{\displaystyle |}{\underset{\displaystyle CH_3}{CH}} - \overset{\displaystyle |}{\underset{\displaystyle CH_3}{CH}} - CH_3$ $CH_3 - \overset{\displaystyle CH_3}{\underset{\displaystyle CH_3}{\overset{\displaystyle |}{\underset{\displaystyle |}{C}}}} - CH_2CH_3$

2-Methylpentane   3-Methylpentane   2,3-Dimethylbutane   2,2-Dimethylbutane

4.10 Identify as same or isomer the relationship between structure (*a*) and structures (*b*), (*c*), and (*d*).

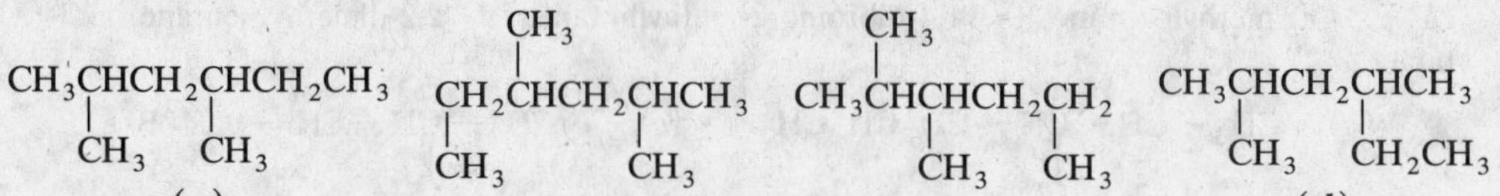

$$\underset{(a)}{CH_3CHCH_2CHCH_2CH_3} \quad \underset{(b)}{CH_2CHCH_2CHCH_3} \quad \underset{(c)}{CH_3CHCHCH_2CH_2} \quad \underset{(d)}{CH_3CHCH_2CHCH_3}$$

with side groups:
(a) CH_3 and CH_3; (b) CH_3 (top), CH_3 and CH_3; (c) CH_3 (top), CH_3 and CH_3; (d) CH_3 and CH_2CH_3

▟ (*b*) same, (*c*) isomer, and (*d*) same.

4.11 Write the structures and identify all the 1°, 2°, 3°, and 4° C's in (*a*) 2,2-dimethylpentane, and (*b*) 1-bromo-2,4-di-methylpentane.

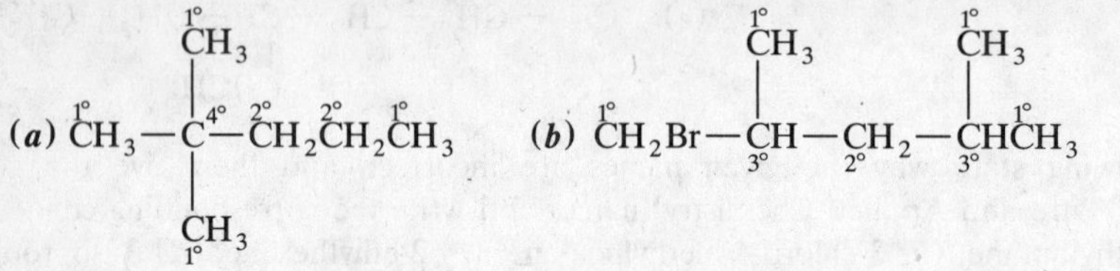

▟ (*a*)
$$\overset{1°}{CH_3} - \overset{4°}{C} - \overset{2°}{CH_2}\overset{2°}{CH_2}\overset{1°}{CH_3}$$
with $\overset{1°}{CH_3}$ above and $\overset{1°}{CH_3}$ below the central C

(*b*)
$$\overset{1°}{CH_2}Br - \overset{3°}{CH} - \overset{2°}{CH_2} - \overset{3°}{CH}\overset{1°}{CH_3}$$
with $\overset{1°}{CH_3}$ above the first CH and $\overset{1°}{CH_3}$ above the last CH

4.12 Write all isomers for the simplest alkane having only one 4°, one 3°, and one 2 °C.

▟ The three kinds of carbons can be represented respectively as: $-\overset{|}{\underset{|}{C}}-$, $-\overset{|}{\underset{|}{C}}-H$ and $H-\overset{|}{\underset{|}{C}}-H$. These units can be jointed in three orders, (i) $4° - 2° - 3°$, (ii) $4° - 3° - 2°$, and (iii) $2° - 4° - 3°$. (The reverse order gives the same isomer.)

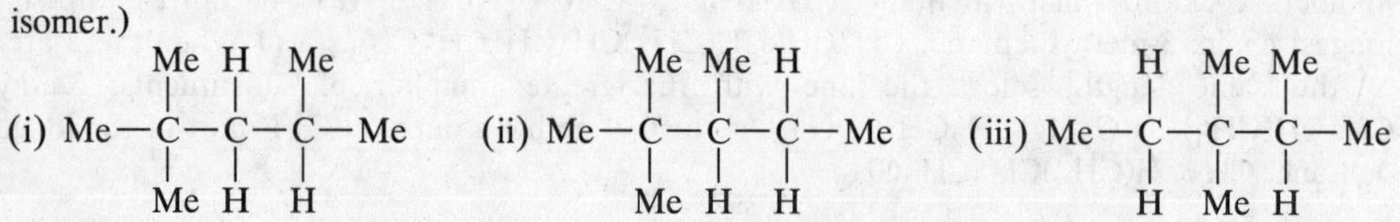

(i)
$$Me-\overset{Me}{\underset{Me}{C}}-\overset{H}{\underset{H}{C}}-\overset{Me}{\underset{H}{C}}-Me$$

(ii)
$$Me-\overset{Me}{\underset{Me}{C}}-\overset{Me}{\underset{H}{C}}-\overset{H}{\underset{H}{C}}-Me$$

(iii)
$$Me-\overset{H}{\underset{H}{C}}-\overset{Me}{\underset{Me}{C}}-\overset{Me}{\underset{H}{C}}-Me$$

4.13 Give the condensed formulas for the alkanes (*a*) C_8H_{18} and (*b*) $C_{11}H_{24}$ with the greatest number of methyl groups.

▟ (*a*) $(CH_3)_3C-C(CH_3)_3$, (*b*) $(CH_3)_3C-C(CH_3)_2-C(CH_3)_3$.

4.14 Derive the structural formulas and give the IUPAC names for all dibromo derivatives of propane.

▟ The two Br's are placed first on the same C and then on different C's.

$Br_2CHCH_2CH_3$	$CH_3CBr_2CH_3$	$BrCH_2CHBrCH_3$	$BrCH_2CH_2CH_2Br$
1,1-Dibromopropane	2,2-Dibromopropane	1,2-Dibromopropane	1,3-Dibromopropane

4.15 Repeat Problem 4.14 for all tribromo derivatives of propane.

▟ C^1 and C^3 are the same. All three Br's are placed on C^1 for the first structure. Two Br's go on C^1, and the third Br on C^2 for the second structure or on C^3 for the third structure. The next structure has one Br on C^1 and two on C^2, and the last has one Br on each C.

$Br_3CCH_2CH_3$	$Br_2CHCHBrCH_3$	$Br_2CHCH_2CH_2Br$	$BrCH_2CBr_2CH_3$	$BrCH_2CHBrCH_2Br$
1,1,1-Tribromo-propane	1,1,2-Tribromo-propane	1,1,3-Tribromo-propane	1,2,2-Tribromo-propane	1,2,3-Tribromo-propane

4.16 Why does carbon form no more than four *sigma* bonds?

▟ Hybridization of carbon's $2s$ and three $2p$ atomic orbitals (AO's) gives four sp^3 hybrid orbitals (HO's). Each orbital can form only one sigma bond.

PHYSICAL PROPERTIES

4.17 Place each of the following alkanes in order of corresponding increasing boiling point (bp °C), and give your reason for the order: pentane, hexane, and 2,3-dimethylbutane.

▟ C_5H_{12} with a lower molecular weight, has a lower bp than both C_6H_{14} isomers. The branched 2,3-dimethyl-butane has a lower bp than the straight chain isomer because it is a more compact molecule with less surface area, and thus has weaker intermolecular van der Waals attractive forces. The actual bp's are: pentane, 36 °C; 2,3-dimethylbutane, 58 °C; hexane, 69 °C.

4.18 (*a*) Predict which compound in each of the following pairs has the higher bp and give your reason: (i) pentane and 1-chloropentane and (ii) 2-methylhexane and 2,2-dimethylpentane. (*b*) Both CF_4 and hexane are nonpolar and have approximately the same molecular weight, yet CF_4 has a much lower bp ($-129\,°C$) than hexane ($68\,°C$). Explain.

▟ (*a*) (i) 1-Chloropentane. It is a more polar compound (the C—Cl bond has an appreciable dipole moment) and has a higher molecular weight. (ii) 2-Methylhexane. It has a longer less-branched chain. Less-branching leads to greater touchable surface area and, thus, greater van der Waals attractive forces.

(*b*) CF_4 is spherical and has less approachable surface area for intermolecular attractive forces than the unbranched hexane. Think of two balls that can touch only at a point and two strands of uncooked spaghetti in contact along their entire length.

4.19 What effect does branching of an alkane chain have on the melting point (mp)?

▟ For the same number of C's, increased branching leads to a more compact molecule that can pack more closely into a solid lattice. The intermolecular attractive forces are stronger, and the mp's higher.

4.20 Why are alkanes said to be *hydrophobic*?

▟ Alkanes are nonpolar. They are very insoluble in water because they lack polar groups that can H-bond or participate in dipole-dipole interactions with water molecules.

4.21 Why does an oil slick form on the surface of the ocean after a spill?

▟ Alkanes, the chief constituents of petroleum, are insoluble and have a lower density than water.

CONFORMATION

4.22 (*a*) Define the term conformation. (*b*) How many conformations of ethane are possible? (*c*) Name and draw the conformation with the lowest and the highest energies at room temperature. (*d*) What is the term used for low energy conformations? (*e*) How does the distribution of conformations change with rising temperature?

▟ (*a*) *Conformations* are structures arising from rotation about single bonds [or flipping of rings (see Problem 5.33)]. (*b*) There are an infinite number of conformations of ethane. (*c*) The two extreme conformations in (*b*) have the lowest and the highest energies at room temperature and are called *staggered* and *eclipsed* respectively. They are shown in Fig. 4-1. For simplicity we are concerned with these two extreme conformations. (*d*) *Conformer*. (*e*) The population of eclipsed-like conformations increases.

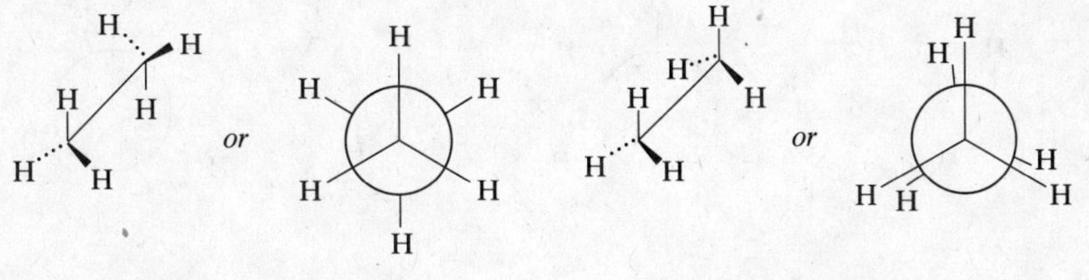

(i) Staggered (lowest energy)   (ii) Eclipsed (highest energy)   **Fig. 4-1**

4.23 The energy barrier (ΔH) to rotation about the C—C bond in ethane is about 3 kcal/mol at room temperature. (*a*) Draw a diagram showing the variation in energy with the rotation through $180°$ about the C—C bond of ethane. (*b*) Assuming the contribution to ΔG of the entropy is negligible, calculate the distribution of staggered and eclipsed conformations at 25 °C.

▟ (*a*) See Fig. 4-2.
(*b*) $\Delta G \cong \Delta H$, and so $\Delta G = -RT \ln K_{eq}$ for the equilibrium: eclipsed $\rightleftharpoons$ staggered.

$$K_{eq} = \frac{[\text{staggered}]}{[\text{eclipsed}]} \quad \text{and} \quad \ln K_{eq} = -\Delta G/RT = \frac{-3000 \text{ cal/mol}}{(1.99 \text{ cal/mol} \cdot \text{K})(298 \text{ K})} = 5.059; \quad K_{eq} = 157$$

A K_{eq} of 157 signifies that at 25 °C over 99% (157/158) of the molecules are in a staggered conformation, even though there is rapid rotation about the C—C bond.

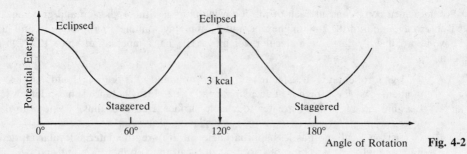

Fig. 4-2

4.24 Why is rotation about the C—C *sigma* bond in ethane not completely free?

▮ Small repulsive interactions between the electrons in eclipsed C—H bonds on adjacent C's do exist. These repulsive forces between bonds on adjacent atoms which restrict rotation are known as *torsional strains*.

4.25 (*a*) What structural features are necessary for a compound to exhibit conformational isomerism? (*b*) Determine which of the following compounds have conformations: (i) CH_3Cl, (ii) H_2O_2, (iii) H_2NOH, and (iv) $H_2C{=}CH_2$. (*c*) Draw three conformations for each compound.

▮ (*a*) There must be four atoms bonded sequentially only by *sigma* bonds, i.e., A—B—C—D.
(*b*) CH_3Cl has only three atoms bonded sequentially, and $H_2C{=}CH_2$ has a π bond in addition to a sigma bond between the two C's. Thus only (ii) and (iii) have conformations.
(*c*) See Fig. 4-3.

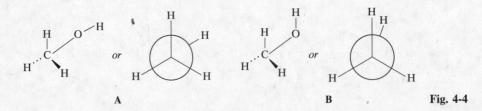

H_2O_2 H_2NOH **Fig. 4-3**

4.26 Draw the conformational isomers of methanol, CH_3OH, an organic alcohol.

▮ See Fig. 4-4. (The O is not visible, it is behind the C.)

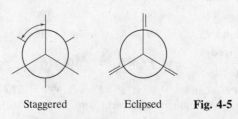

A   B   **Fig. 4-4**

4.27 (*a*) Define the dihedral angle. (*b*) What are the values of the dihedral angles in the staggered and the eclipsed conformations in ethane? (*c*) Draw *Newman-projection* structures of both conformations.

▮ (*a*) The *dihedral angle* is the angle formed from the H on one C and the H of the other C as sighted along the C—C bond. (*b*) The values of the angles in the staggered and the eclipsed conformations are 60° and 0° respectively. (*c*) See Fig. 4-5. H's are understood to be attached to each bond.

Staggered   Eclipsed   **Fig. 4-5**

4.28   (*a*) Compare the torsional strain in the *gauche* conformer of butane with the *anti* conformer.   (*b*) Draw Newman projections of both and indicate the values of the dihedral angles between Me's.

▮   (*a*) The *gauche* conformer has the Me groups on adjacent C's closer to each other, leading to greater torsional strain than in the *anti* conformer where they are separated as much as is possible.   (*b*) See Fig. 4-6.

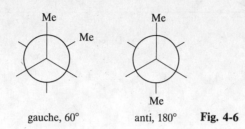

gauche, 60°   anti, 180°   **Fig. 4-6**

4.29   (*a*) Draw *sawhorse-wedge* projection formulas for the two eclipsed conformations of butane.   (*b*) Which conformation has greater torsional strain?   (*c*) What are the dihedral angles between adjacent Me's?

▮   (*a*) See Fig. 4-7.   (*b*) B has greater torsional strain because the two Me's are exactly eclipsing each other. (*c*) The dihedral angle is 0°. In A the Me's are farther apart and the dihedral angle is 120°.

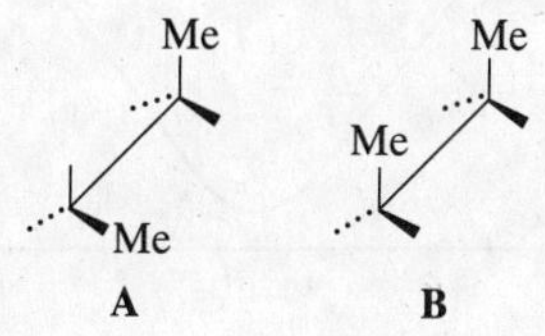

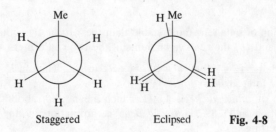

A   **B**   **Fig. 4-7**

4.30   Draw the $C^1 - C^2$ staggered and eclipsed conformations of propane.

▮   See Fig. 4-8.

Staggered   Eclipsed   **Fig. 4-8**

4.31   (*a*) Draw a graph relating potential energy to dihedral angle for propane and show the Newman projection for each maximum and minimum in the graph.

▮   See Fig. 4-9.

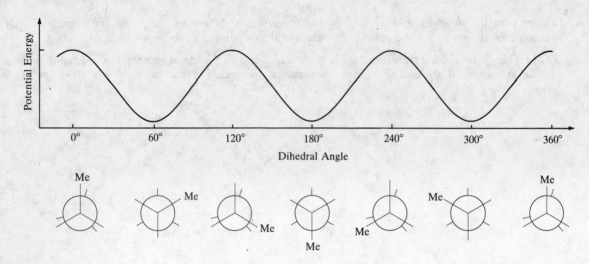

Fig. 4-9

4.32 Repeat Problem 4.31 for butane, about $C^2—C^3$. Label and draw the structure at each maximum and minimum.

⬛ See Fig. 4-10

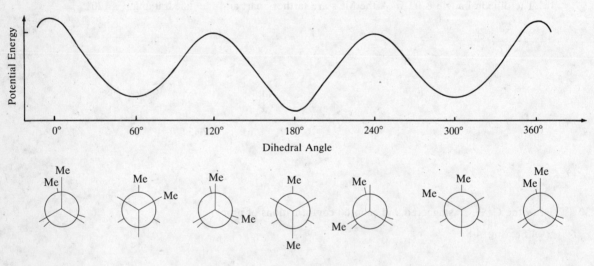

Fig. 4-10

4.33 The *anti* conformation of butane is more stable than the *gauche* by about 0.9 kcal/mol. (*a*) Calculate the K_e for the equilibrium, and (*b*) the relative amounts of the two conformers at room temperature (25 °C).

⬛ (*a*) Assume that $\Delta H = -900$ cal $\cong \Delta G = -RT \ln K_{eq}$. Then $\ln K_{eq} = 1.52$ and $K_{eq} = 4.57$ for *gauche* ⇌ *anti*.

(*b*) The ratio of *anti/gauche* is 4.6/1, which means that about 82% of the molecules are in the *anti* conformation and 18% in the *gauche* conformation at any one time, although they are rapidly interconverting.

4.34 What happens to the equilibrium in Problem 4.33 as the temperature increases?

⬛ As the temperature increases the $T\Delta S$ term in $\Delta G = \Delta H - T\Delta S$ becomes less easily ignored. Since there are two equivalent *gauche* and only one *anti* conformation, ΔS becomes more negative (or less positive) for the equilibrium as written: *gauche* ⇌ *anti*. The value of ΔG becomes less negative (or more positive) and K_{eq} is smaller. This means that the equilibrium shifts to the left, away from the *anti*, resulting in a larger concentration of the *gauche* conformer.

4.35 Draw the staggered conformations for 2-methylbutane in order of increasing energy.

  ▰ See Fig. 4-11

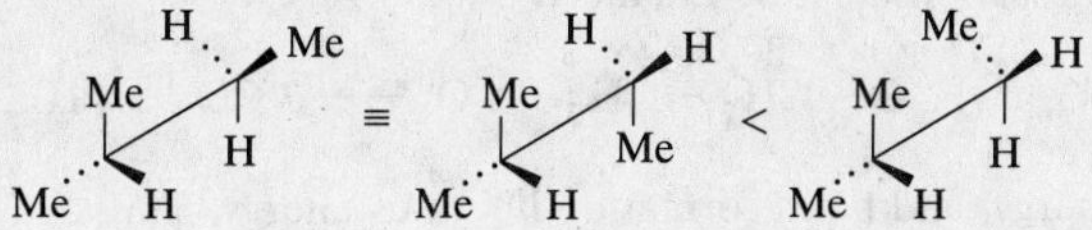

Fig. 4-11

4.36 Draw the eclipsed conformations for 2-methylbutane in order of increasing energy.

  ▰ See Fig. 4-12.

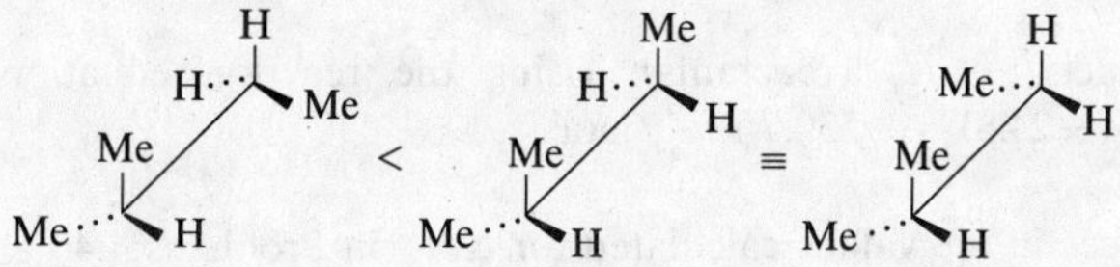

Fig. 4-12

4.37 Which has more torsional strain, butane or 2-methylbutane?

  ▰ 2-Methylbutane. It has two staggered conformer's with two Me's adjacent to each other and one Me at a distance. The third staggered conformer has all three Me's adjacent to each other, and has the highest energy. Butane has only two Me groups to consider. There are two conformers with adjacent Me's, and one lowest energy conformer, the *anti* form.

4.38 Draw the staggered conformations of 2,3-dimethylbutane in order of increasing energy.

  ▰ See Fig. 4-13.

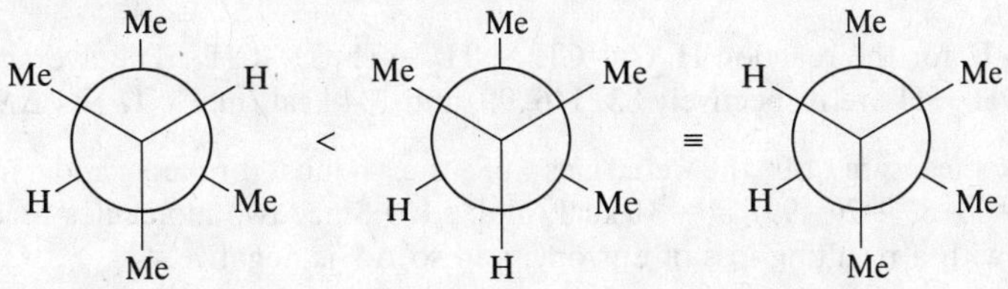

Fig. 4-13

4.39 Draw the eclipsed conformations of 2,3-dimethylbutane in order of increasing energy.

  ▰ See Fig. 4-14.

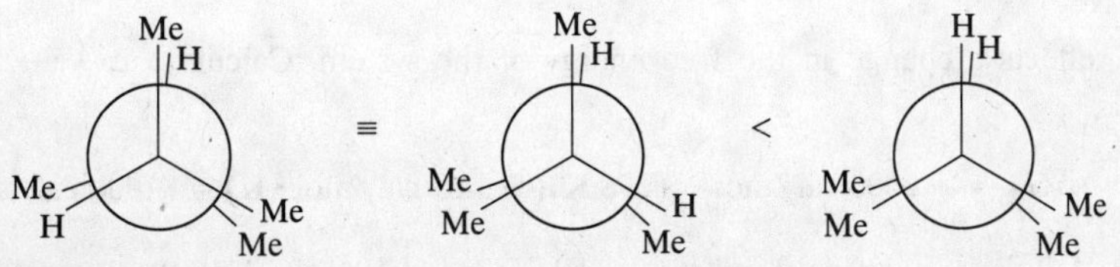

Fig. 4-14

THERMOCHEMISTRY

4.40   From the following average bond energies, given in kcal/mol at 25 °C, calculate the ΔH_c° (enthalpy of combustion) of propane: O=O, 119; C—C, 83; C—H, 99; O—H, 111; C=O from CO_2, 192.

   ▰ The equation for the reaction must be balanced first:

$$H_3C—CH_2—CH_3 + 5\,O_2 \longrightarrow 3\,CO_2 + 4\,H_2O$$

Bond breaking requires energy, and bond formation liberates energy. Thus

$$\text{Bonds broken: } 2\,C—C\,(166) + 8\,H—C\,(792) + 5\,O=O\,(595) = +1553 \text{ kcal/mol}$$

$$\text{Bonds formed: } 6\,C=O\,(-1152) + 8\,O—H\,(-888) = -2040 \text{ kcal/mol}$$

$$\Delta H_c^\circ = \text{bonds broken} + \text{bonds formed} = +1553 + (-2040) = -487 \text{ kcal/mol}$$

4.41   Calculate the ΔH_c° of propane from the ΔH_f°'s (standard enthalpy of formation) given in kcal/mol: C_3H_8, -24.8; CO_2, -94.1; H_2O, -68.3.

   ▰ $\Delta H_c^\circ = \Delta H_f^\circ$ (products) $- \Delta H_f^\circ$ (reactants). Using the reaction equation from Problem 4.40, we get $[3(-94.1) + 4(-68.3)] - (-24.8) = -530.7$ kcal/mol.

4.42   Account for the differences in the values calculated for ΔH_c^0 in Problems 4.40 and 4.41.

   ▰ Average bond energies are just that. Actual bond energies vary, depending on the rest of the bonds connected to the pertinent atoms. The value in Problem 4.41 is more accurate.

4.43   The ΔH_c°'s of butane and 2-methylpropane are -687.5 and -685.5 kcal/mol respectively. What does this say about the relative stabilities of the two isomers?

   ▰ Both isomers react to give the same number of moles of CO_2 and H_2O, so a direct comparison is possible. Butane liberates more heat on combustion than does 2-methylpropane, thus it contains relatively more potential energy, and must be thermodynamically less stable. (The higher the energy in a compound, the less stable that compound is relative to the products and to its isomer.)

4.44   Why is it not possible to calculate ΔH_f°'s for the C_4H_{10} isomers from average bond energies?

   ▰ Since isomers have the same number of C—C and C—H bonds, average bond energies will not reflect the differences in potential energy between the isomers.

4.45   (*a*) Calculate the ΔH for the reaction $H_2C=CH_2 + H_2 \rightarrow H_3C—CH_3$. The average bond energies for C—C, C=C, C—H, and H—H are respectively 83, 146, 99, and 104 kcal/mol.   (*b*) Is ΔS positive, negative or zero?

   ▰ (*a*) ΔH_r is the sum of the energies of the bonds broken and the bonds formed. Thus, $\Delta H_r = (146 + 104) + [-83 + 2(-99)] = -31$ kcal/mol.   (*b*) Since two molecules react to form one, there is less freedom of motion with a resulting loss of entropy; and so ΔS is negative.

4.46   For the equilibrium *n*-butane $\rightleftharpoons$ isobutane, $\Delta H = -2000$ cal/mol, and $\Delta S = -3.69$ cal/mol · K. Account for the observation that at 25 °C isobutane is the more stable isomer, but at 269 °C both isomers are present in equilibrium.

   ▰ Assume we start with 1 mol/L of *n*-butane. The change in

$$K_e = \frac{[\text{isobutane}]}{[n\text{-butane}]}$$

with temperature reflects a change in the free energy of the system. Calculate ΔG at 25 °C and 269 °C from $\Delta G = \Delta H - T\Delta S$.

$$\Delta G_{25} = -2000 \text{ cal/mol} - (298 \text{ K})(-3.69 \text{ cal/mol} \cdot \text{K}) = -900 \text{ cal/mol}$$

$$\Delta G_{269} = -2000 \text{ cal/mol} - (542 \text{ K})(-3.69 \text{ cal/mol} \cdot \text{K}) = 0 \text{ cal/mol}$$

At 25 °C the relation $\Delta G = -2.303\ RT \log K_e$ gives

$$-900 = -2.303(1.987)(298)\log K_e$$

whence $K_e = 4.57$, and

$$\frac{x}{1-x} = 4.57$$

where $x = $ [isobutane], $1 - x = $ [n-butane]. Solving, $x = 0.82$, i.e., 82% of the mixture is isobutane. At 269 °C, $\Delta G = 0$ and therefore $\log K_e = 0$ and $K_e = 1$. There is a 1-to-1 mixture of isomers. At temperatures higher than 269 °C, n-butane is more stable because ΔG is positive.

4.47 Place the three isomeric pentanes in order of increasing stability at room temperature.

❚ The stability of structural isomers generally increases with increased branching. Thus, pentane, $CH_3(CH_2)_3CH_3 < $ isopentane, $(CH_3)_2CHCH_2CH_3$, $<$ neopentane, $(CH_3)_4C$.

PREPARATION

4.48 Indicate the different ways that an alkyl halide can be converted to an alkane with the same skeleton.

❚ Reduction using (**a**) Zn, H^+, (**b**) $LiAlH_4$, (**c**) Mg/anh. ether followed by $\overset{+}{H}_2O$.

4.49 Give a method of preparation of propane from (**a**) an alkene and (**b**) an alkyl chloride.

❚ (**a**) $CH_3CH{=}CH_2 + H_2$ with a Pt, Pd, or Ni catalyst. (**b**) $CH_3CH_2CH_2Cl$ or $(CH_3)_2CHCl$ with Zn and H^+, or $LiAlH_4$.

4.50 Write the structure of all the alkenes that can be hydrogenated to form 2-methylpentane.

❚ The alkenes must have the same skeletal arrangement, $(CH_3)_2CHCH_2CH_2CH_3$. There are four different positions for the double bond; hence the four different alkenes are

4.51 (**a**) Write a balanced equation for the reaction of ethylmagnesium bromide, CH_3CH_2MgBr, with water and identify the conjugate acid-base pairs. (**b**) How is EtMgBr prepared?

❚ The $C{-}Mg$ (also $C{-}Li$) bond has considerable ionic character, which is emphasized in the equation to illustrate the acid-base character of the reaction.

(**a**) $(CH_3\ddot{C}H_2)^-(MgBr)^+ + H\ddot{O}H \longrightarrow CH_3CH_3 + (MgBr)^+ :\ddot{O}H^-$

   base$_1$ ...... acid$_2$ ...... acid$_1$ ...... base$_2$

(**b**) $CH_3CH_2Br + Mg \xrightarrow{\text{dry ether}} CH_3CH_2MgBr$

4.52 Write the reaction of CH_3CH_2MgBr with methanol, CH_3OH and identify the conjugate acid-base pair.

❚ $(CH_3\ddot{C}H_2)^-(MgBr)^+ + CH_3\ddot{O}H \longrightarrow CH_3CH_3 + (MgBr)^+CH_3\ddot{O}{:}^-$

   base$_1$ ...... acid$_2$ ...... acid$_1$ ...... base$_2$

4.53 Repeat Problem 4.52 using methyl magnesium iodide and deuterium oxide.

❚ $(\ddot{C}H_3)^-(MgBr)^+ + D\ddot{O}D \longrightarrow CH_3D + (MgBr)^+ :\ddot{O}D^-$

   base$_1$ ...... acid$_2$ ...... acid$_1$ ...... base$_2$

4.54 (*a*) Write the equation for the reaction of an alkyllithium compound, RLi, with an amine, $R'NH_2$. (*b*) Explain why *Grignard* or lithium reagents do not react with alkanes.

◢ (*a*) $R'\ddot{N}H_2 + R:^- Li^+ \longrightarrow Li^+(R'\ddot{N}H)^- + RH$
(*b*) The H in an alkane is not sufficiently acidic. In fact, it is one of the least acidic H's. H's attached to hetero atoms such as O, N, and S in H_2O, alcohols, acids, amines, and thiols do react.

4.55 Why is acid added to the product mixture in Problem 4.51(*a*)?

◢ Acid neutralizes and dissolves the basic magnesium salt:

$$(MgBr)^+OH^- + H^+X^- \longrightarrow Mg^{2+} + Br^- + X^- + HOH$$

4.56 Prepare 2-deuteropropane from isopropyl bromide.

◢ $(CH_3)_2CHBr + Mg/ether \longrightarrow (CH_3)_2CHMgBr \xrightarrow{D_2O} (CH_3)_2CHD$

4.57 Prepare butane from chloroethane using the *Wurtz* synthesis.

◢ $2\ CH_3CH_2Cl + 2\ Na \longrightarrow CH_3CH_2CH_2CH_3 + 2\ NaCl$

4.58 Why is the *Wurtz* synthesis not a good method for preparing propane?

◢ Two different alkyl halides must be used: ethyl and methyl chloride. When reacted in the presence of Na, three reactions occur, giving a mixture of three products: methyl couples with methyl to give ethane; methyl with ethyl to give propane; and ethyl with ethyl to give butane.

4.59 Discuss the limitations of the Wurtz reaction in terms of the structural requirements.

◢ The alkane to be synthesized must have an even number of carbons and the left and right-handed parts must be identical (symmetrical about a C—C bond). Only then can a single alkyl halide be used to couple with itself.

4.60 Which of the following alkanes cannot be synthesized by the Wurtz reaction in good yield? Explain.

$$(CH_3)_2CHCH_2CH(CH_3)_2\ (\mathbf{A}), (CH_3)_2CHCH_2CH_2CH(CH_3)_2\ (\mathbf{B}),$$

$$CH_3CH_2C(CH_3)_2CH_2CH_3\ (\mathbf{C}), (CH_3)_3CCH_2CH_2CH_3\ (\mathbf{D})$$

◢ Compounds **A** and **C** are symmetrical but they have an odd number of carbons and cannot be synthesized by coupling one molecule with itself. Compound **D** is not symmetrical and has an odd number of carbons.

4.61 Prepare butane from chloroethane using the *Corey–House* synthesis.

◢ $\underset{\text{Chloroethane}}{CH_3CH_2Cl} \xrightarrow[\text{2. CuI}]{\text{1. Li}} \underset{\text{Lithium diethylcuprate}}{(CH_3CH_2)_2LiCu} \xrightarrow{CH_3CH_2Cl} CH_3CH_2CH_2CH_3$

4.62 Starting with 1- and 2-bromopropane prepare 2-methylpentane.

◢ $(CH_3)_2CHBr \xrightarrow[\text{2. CuI}]{\text{1. Li}} \underset{\text{Lithium diisopropylcuprate}}{[(CH_3)_2CH]_2LiCu} \xrightarrow{CH_3CH_2CH_2Br} (CH_3)_2CHCH_2CH_2CH_3$

4.63 Prepare compounds **A**, **C**, and **D** from Problem 4.60 using alkyl halides of two or more C's.

◢ $(CH_3)_2CHBr \xrightarrow[\text{2. CuI}]{\text{1. Li}} [(CH_3)_2CH]_2LiCu \xrightarrow{(CH_3)_2CHCH_2Br} \mathbf{A}$

$CH_3CH_2C(CH_3)_2Br \xrightarrow[\text{2. CuI}]{\text{1. Li}} [CH_3CH_2C(CH_3)_2]_2LiCu \xrightarrow{CH_3CH_2Br} \mathbf{C}$

$(CH_3)_3CCH_2Br \xrightarrow[\text{2. CuI}]{\text{1. Li}} [(CH_3)_3CCH_2]_2LiCu \xrightarrow{CH_3CH_2Br} \mathbf{D}$

or $(CH_3)_3CBr \xrightarrow[\text{2. CuI}]{\text{1. Li}} [(CH_3)_3C]_2LiCu \xrightarrow{CH_3CH_2CH_2Br} \mathbf{D}$

4.64 Can compound **C** of Problem 4.60 be synthesized from the reaction of $(CH_3CH_2)_2LiCu$ with $CH_3CH_2C(CH_3)_2Br$?

◢ No, the alkyl halide which reacts with the lithium dialkylcuprate must be primary (RCH_2X) or secondary (R_2CHX).

REACTIONS .

4.65 Write a balanced equation for the reaction of chlorine with an excess of methane.

◢ $$CH_4 + Cl_2 \xrightarrow{h\nu} CH_3Cl + HCl$$

4.66 What are all the possible organic products in the reaction of methane with chlorine?

◢ The main product is CH_3Cl, but further reaction occurs, leading to CH_2Cl_2, $CHCl_3$, and CCl_4.

4.67 Experimentally, how can polychlorination of methane be minimized?

◢ The proportion of different chloromethanes produced depends on the relative amounts of the reactants and the reaction conditions. If a large excess of methane over chlorine is used, the chance of chlorine reacting with methane is greater than with any of the formed chloromethanes.

4.68 Why is monochlorination of ethane a more practical reaction than the monochlorination of propane?

◢ Only one monochlorinated product is possible from ethane, while propane forms two isomeric propanes, 1- and 2-chloropropane.

4.69 (*a*) Write the steps for the chain mechanism of the chlorination of methane. (*b*) What are the names of the steps?

◢ (*a*) Step 1. $Cl_2 \xrightarrow{\text{light or heat}} 2\ Cl\cdot$
Step 2. $CH_4 + Cl\cdot \longrightarrow CH_3\cdot + HCl$
Step 3. $CH_3\cdot + Cl_2 \longrightarrow CH_3Cl + Cl\cdot$
Then Step 2, then Step 3, etc.
(*b*) Step 1 is called the *initiation step*, followed by steps 2 and 3, called the *propagation steps*.

4.70 How is the chain reaction in Problem 4.69 terminated?

◢ *Termination* occurs whenever two radicals react with each other to give nonradical products. The reactions may be any or all of the following: $2\ Cl\cdot \rightarrow Cl_2$, $2\ CH_3\cdot \rightarrow CH_3CH_3$, $CH_3\cdot + Cl\cdot \rightarrow CH_3Cl$.

4.71 List the characteristics of the mechanism of free radical halogenation chain reactions.

◢ (*1*) The reaction is initiated by light or heat.
(*2*) The quantum yield, or the number of product molecules produced by one photon of light is typically high (about 10,000 in the chlorination reaction).
(*3*) If O_2 is present, there is an induction period, after which the reaction rate increases.
(*4*) Initiators, such as certain organic peroxides, can catalyze the reaction in the absence of light or heat.
(*5*) Reaction can be prematurely terminated by adding radical scavengers—i.e., substances that combine with free radicals, thus terminating a chain.

4.72 Why is light or heat necessary to initiate the chlorination reaction?

◢ The Cl—Cl bond must be broken to form $Cl\cdot$ radicals before the reaction with methane can commence. This homolysis requires energy, which is supplied either by heat or light.

4.73 Calculate the frequency of light required to break the Cl—Cl bond. The bond dissociation energy for chlorine is 58 kcal/mol. Use the following conversion factor and constants in solving: 1 kcal = 4.18×10^3 J; Planck's constant $h = 6.63 \times 10^{-34}$ J·s/particle; speed of light (c) = 3.00×10^{10} cm/s.

◢ First convert the bond energy to J/particle:

$$(58\ \text{kcal/mol}) \times (1\ \text{mol}/6.02 \times 10^{23}\ \text{particles/mol}) \times (4.18 \times 10^3\ \text{J/kcal}) = 4.03 \times 10^{-19}\ \text{J/particle}$$

Next substitute this value into Planck's equation: $\Delta E = h \times \nu$, where ν is frequency:

$$\nu = (4.03 \times 10^{-19}\ \text{J/particle})/6.63 \times 10^{-34}\ \text{J·s/particle} = 6.08 \times 10^{14}\ \text{s}^{-1}$$

For the wavelength (λ): $\lambda = c/\nu = [(3.00 \times 10^{-8}\ \text{m/s})/(6.08 \times 10^{14}\ \text{s}^{-1})] \times 10^9\ \text{nm/m} = 493$ nm. This wavelength is in the blue part of the visible spectrum.

4.74   Calculate ΔH for the two propagation steps in the reaction of methane with chlorine. The bond energies for: CH_3—H, CH_3—Cl, H—Cl, and Cl—Cl are respectively 105, 85, 103, and 58 kcal/mol.

▮   Step 1.   (Breaking the CH_3—H bond) + (forming the H—Cl bond) = $105 + (-103) = +2$ kcal/mol
    Step 2.   (Breaking the Cl—Cl bond) + (forming the CH_3—Cl bond) = $58 + (-85) = -27$ kcal/mol

4.75   Using the bond energies given in Problem 4.74, explain why the following sequence of steps is unlikely:

$$\text{Step 1. } CH_4 + Cl\cdot \longrightarrow CH_3Cl + H\cdot \; ; \quad \text{Step 2. } H\cdot + Cl_2 \longrightarrow HCl + Cl\cdot$$

▮ ΔH for step 1 = $105 + (-85) = +20$ kcal/mol. This is a much higher value than the value of ΔH calculated in step 1 of Problem 4.74; therefore this reaction will not occur, regardless of the value of ΔH for step 2 ($58 + (-103) = -45$ kcal/mol).

4.76   (*a*) Write the equations for the two propagation steps in the reaction of methane with bromine.   (*b*) Calculate ΔH for each step and the overall ΔH for the reaction. The bond energies for CH_3—H, CH_3—Br, H—Br, and Br—Br are respectively 105, 71, 87.5, and 46 kcal/mol.

▮   (*a*)   Step 1. $CH_4 + Br\cdot \longrightarrow HBr + \cdot CH_3$;   Step 2. $\cdot CH_3 + Br_2 \longrightarrow CH_3Br + Br\cdot$
    (*b*) $105 + (-87.5) = +17.5$ kcal/mol $46 + (-71) = -25$ kcal/mol
    ΔH for the reaction = step 1 + step 2 = $+17.5 - 25 = -7.5$ kcal/mol.

4.77   Compare the reactivity of the halogens towards alkanes.

▮   Fluorine (reacts explosively) $\gg$ chlorine > bromine > iodine (doesn't react).

4.78   The bond dissociation energies of the halogens F—F, Cl—Cl, Br—Br, and I—I are respectively 37, 58, 46, and 36 kcal/mol. Explain why we can eliminate the homolysis of the halogen molecule as the rate-determining step in the halogenation of alkanes from these data.

▮   If this step were rate-determining, the order of reactivity of alkanes should follow the order of homolysis of the halogens, e.g., $I_2, F_2 > Br_2 > Cl_2$. This is not the observed order.

4.79   The reaction $CH_4 + Cl\cdot \longrightarrow \cdot CH_3 + HCl$ has an activation enthalpy ($\Delta H^{\ddagger}$) of $+4$ kcal/mol and a ΔH° of $+2$ kcal/mol.   (*a*) Draw an energy profile diagram for the reaction.   (*b*) What is the value of $\Delta H^{\ddagger}$ for the reverse reaction?

▮   (*a*)   See Fig. 4-15.

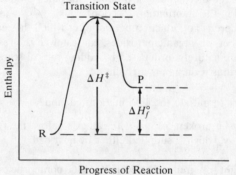

Fig. 4-15

(*b*) $\Delta H^{\ddagger}$ for the reverse reaction equals $\Delta H_f^{\ddagger}$ minus ΔH° for the forward reaction, or $+4 - 2 = +2$ kcal/mol.

4.80   (*a*) What is the activation energy for the reaction $Cl\cdot + Cl\cdot \rightarrow Cl_2$?   (*b*) Draw an energy profile diagram for this reaction.

▮   (*a*) In this case, no bonds are broken, only bonds are formed. This reaction has zero activation energy. Chain termination reactions, such as $2\cdot CH_3 \rightarrow CH_3CH_3$, also have zero activation energies.   (*b*) See Fig. 4-16.

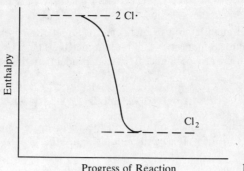

Fig. 4-16

4.81   (*a*) What is the order of stability of alkyl radicals?   (*b*) Place the following radicals in decreasing order of stability: $CH_3\overset{.}{C}HCH(CH_3)_2$, $\cdot CH_2CH_2CH(CH_3)_2$, $CH_3CH_2\overset{.}{C}(CH_3)_2$.

▮   (*a*) tertiary > secondary > primary > methyl.
   (*b*) $CH_3CH_2\overset{.}{C}(CH_3)_2 > CH_3\overset{.}{C}HCH(CH_3)_2 > \cdot CH_2CH_2CH(CH_3)_2$

4.82   Justify the order of stability of the alkyl radicals in Problem 4.81.

▮   Radicals are electron-deficient because carbon has only seven electrons. Since alkyl groups are electron-donating via induction, the more alkyl groups attached to the electron-deficient carbon, the more stable the radical is.

4.83   Describe the orbital structure of the methyl radical.

▮   A radical has only seven electrons in the valence shell of the carbon atom; therefore it is electron-deficient. The C uses sp^2 HO's and the odd electron is in the p AO perpendicular to the plane of the three C—H bonds (see Fig. 4-17).

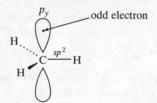

Fig. 4-17

4.84   Draw the reactants, transition state (TS), and products for $Br\cdot + CH_4 \rightarrow H—Br + \cdot CH_3$

▮   See Fig. 4-18.

REACTANTS   **TRANSITION STATE**   **PRODUCTS**

$$\underset{\substack{C \text{ is } sp^3 \\ (\text{tetrahedral})}}{\overset{\displaystyle H}{\underset{\displaystyle H}{\overset{\displaystyle |}{\underset{\displaystyle |}{H\!-\!\!\!\overset{\displaystyle \cdot\cdot}{C}\!-\!H}}}} + Br\cdot} \longrightarrow \underset{\substack{C \text{ is becoming } sp^2 \\ (\text{trigonal planar})}}{\left[\begin{array}{c} H \\ C\cdots H\cdots Br \\ H \quad H \end{array} \right]} \longrightarrow \underset{\substack{C \text{ is } sp^2 \\ (\text{trigonal planar})}}{\overset{\displaystyle H}{\underset{\displaystyle H \quad H}{\overset{\displaystyle |}{C\cdot}}} + H\!-\!Br}$$

bond forming / bond breaking   **Fig. 4-18**

4.85   The relative reactivity of 1°:2°:3° hydrogens to chlorination is 1:3.8:5.   (*a*) Calculate the relative amounts of all the monochlorobutanes obtained from the reaction of butane with Cl_2.   (*b*) Calculate the percentages of the different products

▰ (*a*) There are six equivalent H atoms which lead to formation of 1-chlorobutane (**A**) and four equivalent H atoms which lead to formation of 2-chlorobutane (**B**). The ratio of 1° to 2° H's is 3 to 2. The relative amounts of products are obtained from the product of the relative reactivity and the number of equivalent H's.

$$\mathbf{A} = 3 \times 1 = 3 \text{ and } \mathbf{B} = 2 \times 3.8 = 7.6, \text{ or 3 to 7.6.}$$

(*b*) The percentages are obtained by dividing the relative amount of each product by the sum of the relative amounts $(3 + 7.6 = 10.6)$ and multiplying by 100.

$$\text{Percentage of } \mathbf{A} = (3/10.6)100 = 28 \text{ and percentage of } \mathbf{B} = (7.6/10.6)100 = 72$$

4.86 Calculate the percentages of all the monochlorinated products obtained from the chlorination of 2-methylbutane, using the data from Problem 4.85.

▰ There are four different monochloro products:

$$\begin{array}{c} \text{CH}_3 \\ | \end{array}$$

ClCH$_2$CHCH$_2$CH$_3$ (**C**) resulting from the reaction of six equivalent 1° H's, $(CH_3)_2C(Cl)CH_2CH_3$ (**D**) resulting from the reaction of one 3° H, $(CH_3)_2CHCHClCH_3$ (**E**) resulting from the reaction of two equivalent 2° H's, and $(CH_3)_2CHCH_2CH_2Cl$ (**F**) resulting from the reaction of three equivalent 1° H's.

	relative amounts	percentages
C	$6 \times 1 = 6$	$6/21.6 = 28$
D	$1 \times 5 = 5$	$5/21.6 = 23$
E	$2 \times 3.8 = 7.6$	$7.6/21.6 = 35$
F	$3 \times 1 = 3$	$3/21.6 = 14$

4.87 Calculate the relative amounts of 1- and 2-bromopropane obtained from the bromination of propane. The relative reactivity of 1°:2°:3° H's to bromination is $1:82:1600$.

▰ The ratio of 1° to 2° H's is 6:2, or 3:1. 1-bromopropane: 3 H's $\times 1 = 3$; 2-bromopropane: 1 H $\times 82 = 82$. The percentages are: $3/85 = 3.5\%$ of 1-bromopropane and $82/85 = 96.5\%$ of 2-bromopropane. Bromination gives mostly 2-bromopropane.

4.88 Calculate the relative amounts of 1-bromo- and 2-bromo-2-methylpropane obtained from the bromination of isobutane. Refer to problem 4.87 for the relative reactivities.

▰
$$(CH_3)_2CHCH_3 \longrightarrow (CH_3)_2CHCH_2Br + (CH_3)_2CBrCH_3$$

| 1-Bromo-2- | 2-Bromo-2- |
| methylpropane (**E**) | methylpropane (**F**) |

For **E**: 9 H's $\times 1 = 9$, and $9/1609 = 0.6\%$

For **F**: 1 H $\times 1600 = 1600$, and $1600/1609 = 99.4\%$

Bromination occurs almost exclusively at the 3° position.

4.89 What is the reason for the higher selectivity in bromination compared to chlorination?

▰ The *Hammond postulate* states that, for comparable reactions, the more endothermic (or less exothermic) reaction has a transition state (TS) which more closely resembles the intermediate. The less endothermic (or more exothermic) reaction has a TS which less closely resembles the intermediate and may more closely resemble the ground state (reactants). Since attack by Br· on an alkane is more endothermic than attack by Cl·, its TS shows more C—H bond breaking and more H—Br bond formation. Any stabilization in the intermediate radical also occurs in the corresponding TS. Therefore, a TS leading to a 3° R· has a lower enthalpy than one leading to a 2° R·, which in turn has a lower enthalpy than one leading to a 1° R·; the relative rates of H-abstraction by Br· are 3° > 2° > 1°. The TS for H-abstraction by Cl· has less C—H bond breaking and less H—Cl bond formation; the nature of the incipient radical has less effect on the enthalpy of the TS and on the rate of its formation. Hence there is less difference in the rate of formation of the three kinds of R·'s. Bromination is thus more selective than chlorination.

4.90 Laboratory chlorination of alkanes is often done with sulfuryl chloride, SO_2Cl_2, instead of Cl_2 because of its convenience. What is the Lewis structure of SO_2Cl_2?

◢ The structure is

$$Cl-\overset{\overset{\displaystyle :\ddot{O}}{\|}}{\underset{\underset{\displaystyle :\ddot{O}}{\|}}{S}}-Cl \ .$$

4.91 When sulfuryl chloride is used to chlorinate an alkane, an organic peroxide, ROOR is used as an *initiator*. SO_2 is also a product. Write a mechanism for the chlorination, including the role of the peroxide.

◢ Step 1. $ROOR \longrightarrow 2\,RO\cdot$ Step 2. $RO\cdot + R'H \longrightarrow ROH + \cdot R'$
Step 3. $\cdot R' + SO_2Cl_2 \longrightarrow R'Cl + \cdot SO_2Cl$
Step 4. $\cdot SO_2Cl \longrightarrow SO_2 + Cl\cdot$
Step 5. $Cl\cdot + R'H \longrightarrow HCl + \cdot R'$

Steps 1 and 2 are initiation steps; steps 3, 4, and 5 are propagation steps.

4.92 Tetraethyl lead, $Pb(C_2H_5)_4$, initiates the chlorination of methane in the dark at 150 °C. Explain in terms of the mechanism.

◢ $Pb(C_2H_5)_4$ undergoes thermal homolysis of the C—Pb bond at 150 °C. $CH_3CH_2\cdot$ then generates $Cl\cdot$ which initiates the propagation steps.

$$Pb(C_2H_5)_4 \longrightarrow \cdot\dot{P}b\cdot + 4\,CH_3CH_2\cdot$$

$$CH_3CH_2\cdot + Cl_2 \longrightarrow CH_3CH_2Cl + Cl\cdot$$

$$CH_4 + Cl\cdot \longrightarrow \cdot CH_3 + HCl; \quad\text{and}\quad \cdot CH_3 + Cl_2 \longrightarrow CH_3Cl + Cl\cdot \quad\text{(propagation steps)}$$

4.93 (*a*) Write the propagation steps for the monofluorination of methane and calculate ΔH for each step. (*b*) Would you expect fluorination of an alkane to show selectivity between the 1°, 2°, and 3° substitution? Bond energies for HF, CH_3—F, F_2, and CH_3—H are respectively 136, 108, 38, and 105 kcal/mol.

◢ (*a*) Step 1. $F\cdot + CH_4 \longrightarrow HF + \cdot CH_3$ Step 2. $\cdot CH_3 + F_2 \longrightarrow CH_3F + F\cdot$
  $+105 - 136 = -31$ kcal/mol $+38 - 108 = -70$ kcal/mol

(*b*) The extreme exothermicity of the hydrogen abstraction step 1 means that the transition state has very little bond breaking, and thus there should be very little selectivity (see Problem 4.89).

4.94 Singlet methylene (Problem 3.4), $:CH_2$, generated by the decomposition of diazomethane, H_2CN_2, inserts between the C—H bond in an alkane. (*a*) Give the reaction of $:CH_2$ with ethane. (*b*) $:CH_2$ reacts with pentane to give the product distribution shown in the last column of Table 4-1. Calculate the theoretical percentage yields and then compare them with the observed percentage yields. What conclusion can be drawn about the reactivity and selectivity of $:CH_2$ from these data?

◢ (*a*)

$$H-\overset{\overset{\displaystyle H}{|}}{\underset{\underset{\displaystyle H}{|}}{C}}-\overset{\overset{\displaystyle H}{|}}{\underset{\underset{\displaystyle H}{|}}{C}}-H + :CH_2 \longrightarrow H-\overset{\overset{\displaystyle H}{|}}{\underset{\underset{\displaystyle H}{|}}{C}}-\overset{\overset{\displaystyle H}{|}}{\underset{\underset{\displaystyle H}{|}}{C}}-\overset{\overset{\displaystyle H}{|}}{\underset{\underset{\displaystyle H}{|}}{C}}-H$$

(*b*) Calculate the yields assuming that only the probability factor is important; i.e., that insertion occurs in a random fashion.

$$^1CH_3\,^2CH_2\,^3CH_2\,^2CH_2\,^1CH_3$$

insertion at ^1C → $CH_3CH_2CH_2CH_2CH_2CH_3$, hexane (**A**)
insertion at ^2C → $CH_3CH_2CH_2CH(CH_3)CH_3$, 2-methylpentane (**B**)
insertion at ^3C → $CH_3CH_2CH(CH_3)CH_2CH_3$, 3-methylpentane (**C**)

TABLE 4-1

Product	C—H insertion	Number of equivalent positions	Calculated % yield	Observed % yield
Hexane	^{1}C—H	6	$(6/12)100 = 50$	48
2-Methylpentane	^{2}C—H	4	$(4/12)100 = 33.3$	35
3-Methylpentane	^{3}C—H	2	$(2/12)100 = 16.7$	17

The fact that the experimental and calculated percentage yields are almost identical leads to the conclusion that insertion of $:CH_2$ is practically random. These results are consistent with the fact that $:CH_2$ is one of the most reactive and least selective species in organic chemistry.

4.95 Which of the following alkanes will give a single product with a methylene insertion?

$$(CH_3)_2CHCH(CH_3)_2, \quad CH_3CH_2CH_3, \quad (CH_3)_4C, \quad CH_3CH_3, \quad CH_3CH_2C(CH_3)_2CH_2CH_3.$$

Write the structure of the product in each case.

◢ Those alkanes having only equivalent H's will give one product; i.e., $(CH_3)_4C$ produces $(CH_3)_3CCH_2CH_3$, and CH_3CH_3 produces $CH_3CH_2CH_3$.

SYNTHESES

4.96 Synthesize $(CH_3)_3CCH(CH_3)_2$ (**A**) (*a*) from an alkene and (*b*) by a Corey-House synthesis using alkyl halides with more than one carbon. Show steps and catalysts.

◢ (*a*) The only alkene having the same carbon skeleton as **A** is $(CH_3)_3CC(CH_3)=CH_2$.

$$(CH_3)_3CC(CH_3)=CH_2 \xrightarrow{\text{H}_2,\ \text{Pt or Ni catalyst}} (CH_3)_3CCH(CH_3)_2$$

(*b*) $(CH_3)_3CBr \xrightarrow[\text{2. CuI}]{\text{1. Li}} [(CH_3)_3C]_2LiCu \xrightarrow{(CH_3)_2CHBr \uparrow}$

4.97 Using 1-bromo-3-methylbutane (**B**) and any other one or two carbon compounds, if needed, synthesize (*a*) 2-methylbutane, (*b*) 2,7-dimethyloctane, and (*c*) 2-methylhexane.

◢ (*a*) Both starting material and product have the same carbon skeleton.

$$CH_3CHCH_2CH_2Br \xrightarrow{\text{Mg/ether}} CH_3CHCH_2CH_2MgBr \xrightarrow{\text{H}_2\text{O}} CH_3CHCH_2CH_3$$
$$\underset{CH_3 \quad \mathbf{B}}{|} \qquad\qquad \underset{CH_3}{|} \qquad\qquad \underset{CH_3}{|}$$

or $\xrightarrow{\text{LiAlH}_4}$

(*b*) $\mathbf{B} \xrightarrow[\text{2. CuI}]{\text{1. Li}} [(CH_3)_2CHCH_2CH_2]_2CuLi \xrightarrow{\mathbf{B}} (CH_3)_2CHCH_2CH_2CH_2CH_2CH(CH_3)_2$

or 2 moles $\mathbf{B} \xrightarrow{\text{Na}}$ product (Wurtz reaction)

(*c*) $\mathbf{B} \xrightarrow[\substack{\text{2. CuI} \\ \text{3. CH}_3\text{CH}_2\text{Br}}]{\text{1. Li}} CH_3CH(CH_3)CH_2CH_2CH_2CH_3$

4.98 Using D_2O and the alkanes indicated, synthesize (*a*) $CH_3CHDCH_2CH_3$ (**C**) from butane, and (*b*) $(CH_3)_3CD$ (**D**) from 2-methylpropane.

◢ (*a*) $CH_3CH_2CH_2CH_3 + Br_2 \xrightarrow{\text{h}\nu} CH_3CHBrCH_2CH_3 \xrightarrow[\text{2. D}_2\text{O}]{\text{1. Mg/ether}} \mathbf{C}$

(*b*) $(CH_3)_3CH + Br_2 \xrightarrow{\text{h}\nu} (CH_3)_3CBr \xrightarrow[\text{2. D}_2\text{O}]{\text{1. Mg/ether}} \mathbf{D}$

In both cases bromination leads to the desired bromide because of the large differences in the rate of bromination of $3° > 2° > 1°$.

4.99 Prepare the following compounds using indicated starting materials and D_2O, D_2, and $^{14}CH_3I$. A compound once made can be used in a later synthesis.

(*a*) CH_3CHDCH_2D (**E**), from $CH_3CH=CH_2$ (*c*) $(CH_3)_2(^{14}CH_3)_2C$ (**G**), from $CH_3CH_2CH_3$

(*b*) $(CH_3)_2CH^{14}CH_3$ (**F**), from $CH_3CH_2CH_3$ (*d*) $(CH_3)_2CD^{14}CH_3$ (**H**), from $CH_3CH_2CH_3$.

◢ (*a*) $CH_3CH=CH_2 + D_2 \xrightarrow{\text{Pt}} \mathbf{E}$ (*b*) Propane $\xrightarrow[\text{h}\nu]{Br_2} CH_3CHBrCH_3 \xrightarrow[\substack{\text{2. CuI} \\ \text{3. }^{14}\text{CH}_3\text{I}}]{\text{1. Li}} \mathbf{F}$

(*c*) Prepare $\mathbf{F} \xrightarrow[h\nu]{Br_2} (CH_3)_2(^{14}CH_3)CBr \xrightarrow[\substack{2.\ CuI \\ 3.\ ^{14}CH_3I}]{1.\ Li} \mathbf{G}$

(*d*) $\mathbf{F} \xrightarrow[2.\ D_2O]{1.\ Mg,\ ether} \mathbf{H}$

4.100 Using $^{14}CH_3I$ as the only carbon source, prepare propane in which there are three ^{14}C's.

◢ (*1*) $^{14}CH_3I \xrightarrow[\substack{2.\ CuI \\ 3.\ ^{14}CH_3I}]{1.\ Li} {}^{14}CH_3{}^{14}CH_3$

(*2*) $^{14}CH_3{}^{14}CH_3 \xrightarrow[h\nu]{Cl_2} {}^{14}CH_3{}^{14}CH_2Cl \xrightarrow[\substack{2.\ CuI \\ 3.\ ^{14}CH_3I}]{1.\ Li} {}^{14}CH_3{}^{14}CH_2{}^{14}CH_3$

SUPPLEMENTARY PROBLEMS

4.101 (*a*) Why are alkanes so inert? (*b*) Why do the C—C rather than the C—H bonds break when alkanes are pyrolyzed (heated at high temperatures in the absence of O_2)? (*c*) Although combustion of alkanes is a strongly exothermic process, it does not occur at moderate temperatures. Explain.

◢ (*a*) A reactive site in a molecule usually has one or more unshared pairs of electrons, a polar bond, an electron-deficient atom or an atom with an expandable octet. Alkanes have none of these.

(*b*) The C—C bond has a lower bond energy ($\Delta H = +83$ kcal/mol) than does the C—H bond ($\Delta H = +99$ kcal/mol).

(*c*) The reaction is very slow at room temperature because of a very high $\Delta H^{\ddagger}$.

4.102 An alkane, C_6H_{14} gives two monochloroalkanes when chlorinated. What is the structure of the original alkane?

◢ There are five isomeric hexanes. Only one, 2,3-dimethylbutane can give two different monochlorinated compounds: 1-chloro-2,3-dimethylbutane, and 2-chloro-2,3-dimethylbutane.

4.103 An alkane, C_7H_{16}, is produced by the reaction of lithium di-(3-pentyl)cuprate with ethyl bromide. What is the structure of the alkane?

◢ This is a Corey–House synthesis $[(CH_3CH_2)_2CH]_2CuLi + CH_3CH_2Br \rightarrow (CH_3CH_2)_3CH$, triethylmethane, or 3-ethylpentane.

4.104 Explain why the free radical chlorination of methane occurs approximately twelve times faster than tetradeuteromethane, CD_4.

◢ Although D and H are chemically identical, C—D bonds are slightly stronger than C—H bonds. Therefore $\Delta H^{\ddagger}$ for abstraction of D is slightly greater than for H. Since abstraction is the slow step, removal of H will be faster.

4.105 (*a*) What is meant by "octane rating"? (*b*) Why does a high octane fuel have less tendency to knock in an automobile engine?

◢ (*a*) The term *octane rating* is based upon the performance of *n*-heptane, which is arbitrarily assigned an octane value of 0, and isooctane (2,2,4-trimethylpentane), which is given a value of 100 when used as an automobile fuel. A mixture of 85% isooctane and 15% heptane has an octane number of 85, as does any blend of gasoline with the same combustion performance in the engine. (*b*) Branched chain hydrocarbons burn more smoothly because, when they break down, they form more stable, less reactive 3° radicals. These radicals react more slowly and smoothly with oxygen than the 1° or 2° radicals which form from the breakdown of a straight chain hydrocarbon.

4.106 The following alkanes all react with chlorine to give only one monochloride. Give the structures of each alkane and its chloride: (*a*) C_5H_{12}, and (*b*) C_8H_{18}.

◢ An alkane must have all its hydrogens equivalent to form only one monohalide.

(*a*) $(CH_3)_4C \longrightarrow (CH_3)_3CCH_2Cl$ (*b*) $(CH_3)_3CC(CH_3)_3 \longrightarrow (CH_3)_3CC(CH_3)_2CH_2Cl$

4.107 (*a*) Calculate the $\Delta H°$'s for each step and the overall $\Delta H_r°$ for the reaction of I_2 with CH_4. (*b*) Give two reasons for the lack of reaction of I_2 with CH_4. Bond dissociation energies for I—I, H—I, CH_3—I, and

CH_3—H are respectively 36, 71, 57, and 105 kcal/mol.

▮ (a) $I\cdot + CH_4 \longrightarrow \cdot CH_3 + HI$ and $\Delta H^\circ = 105 + (-71) = +34$ kcal/mol

$\cdot CH_3 + I_2 \longrightarrow CH_3I + I\cdot$ and $\Delta H^\circ = 36 + (-57) = -21$ kcal/mol; $\Delta H_r^\circ = 34 + (-21) = +13$ kcal/mol
(b) The inertness of methane to iodination may be the result of a high $\Delta H^\ddagger$ for the first step, which would make this step too slow to be observable. Alternately, the large positive value of ΔH_r° points to unfavorable thermodynamics; i.e., the equilibrium constant is extremely small. The reason may be a combination of both factors. Actually the reverse reaction occurs:

$$CH_3I + HI \longrightarrow CH_4 + I_2$$

4.108 Tributylstannane, $(C_4H_9)_3SnH$, reduces an alkyl halide to the corresponding alkane by a free-radical mechanism. The initiator is an azo compound, $(CH_3)_2C(CN)-N=N-C(CN)(CH_3)_2$, which breaks down to N_2 and a radical. Give a plausible mechanism.

▮ The initiator gives the carbon radical $(CH_3)_2\dot{C}(CN)$, (Rad·) which abstracts an H· from the tin compound:
$$\text{Rad}\cdot + (C_4H_9)_3Sn-H \rightarrow (C_4H_9)_3Sn\cdot + \text{Rad}-H$$
The tributyltin radical abstracts a halogen atom from the alkyl halide, and the chain is propagated as follows:

$(C_4H_9)_3Sn\cdot + R-X \rightarrow (C_4H_9)_3Sn-X + R\cdot,$ then $R\cdot + (C_4H_9)_3Sn-H \rightarrow R-H + (C_4H_9)_3Sn\cdot$

4.109 t-Butyl peroxide is a radical initiator. When added to a mixture of 2-methylpropane and carbon tetrachloride, a reaction occurs at 130 – 140 °C, leading to 2-chloro-2-methylpropane and chloroform, $CHCl_3$. Give a reasonable mechanism for this reaction.

▮ $(CH_3)_3C-O-O-C(CH_3)_3 \rightarrow 2(CH_3)_3CO\cdot$
   $(CH_3)_3CO\cdot + (CH_3)_3CH \rightarrow (CH_3)_3COH + (CH_3)_3C\cdot$ initiation
   $(CH_3)_3C\cdot + CCl_4 \rightarrow (CH_3)_3CCl + \cdot CCl_3$ propagation step 1
   $\cdot CCl_3 + (CH_3)_3CH \rightarrow HCCl_3 + (CH_3)_3C\cdot$ propagation step 2

4.110 Alkanes are monochlorinated with t-butyl hypochlorite, t-BuOCl. The initiating step is the homolysis of the hypochlorite: $t\text{-BuOCl} \rightarrow t\text{-BuO}\cdot + Cl\cdot$. Give the propagation steps.

▮ $t\text{-BuO}\cdot + RH \longrightarrow t\text{-BuOH} + R\cdot$ then $R\cdot + t\text{-BuOCl} \longrightarrow RCl + t\text{-BuO}\cdot$

4.111 What bonding feature does O free radical sources like organic peroxides (ROOR), tetraethyl lead $[Pb(C_2H_5)_4]$, t-butyl hypochlorite $[(CH_3)_3COCl]$, and Cl_2 have in common?

▮ In each case, the bond broken is fairly weak. Some typical bond energies for Cl—Cl, O—O, and O—Cl, are respectively 58, 47, and 64 kcal/mol.

4.112 The species CH_5^+ has been detected in solution by Olah. It contains three identical bonds which differ from the other two identical bonds. Suggest a plausible bonding orbital structure.

▮ Three sp^2 HO's of C each overlap with an s AO of H, giving a trigonal planar geometry with bond angles of 120°. Each lobe of C's remaining p AO bonds weakly with an H above and below the plane of the C and three H's.

4.113 List and compare the differences in the properties of the transition states during chlorination and bromination that account for the different reactivities of 1°, 2°, and 3° H's.

▮ The differences may be summarized as follows:

	Chlorination	**Bromination**
1. Time of formation of transition state	Earlier in reaction	Later in reaction
2. Amount of breaking of C—H bond*	Less, $H_3\overset{\delta\cdot}{C}$--H----$\overset{\delta\cdot}{Cl}$	More, $H_3\overset{\delta\cdot}{C}$----H--$\overset{\delta\cdot}{Br}$
3. Free-radical character (δ·) of carbon	Less	More
4. Transition state more closely resembles	Reactants	Products

*Since chlorination is less endothermic than bromination, its TS is more like the GS and has less C—H bond breaking and less H—Cl bond formation. The TS of the more endothermic bromination is more like the intermediate and has more C—Br bond breaking and more H—Br bond formation (see Problem 4.89). See Fig. 4-19.

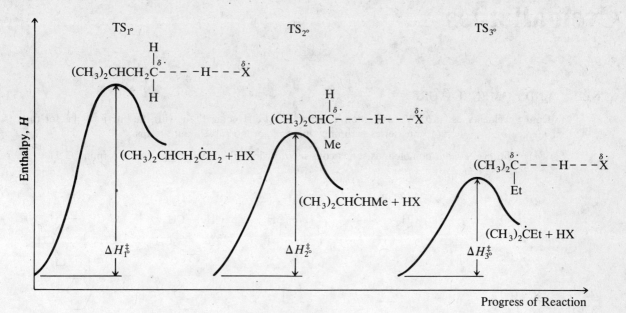

Fig. 4-19

4.114 In the halogenation of alkanes other than methane there is another chain terminating reaction that can occur called *disproportionation*. Write the mechanism for this reaction for $\cdot C_2H_5$.

$$\underset{\underset{H}{|}}{\overset{\overset{H}{|}}{CH_3C}}\cdot \ + \ H-\underset{\underset{H}{|}}{\overset{\overset{H}{|}}{C}}-\dot{C}H_2 \longrightarrow CH_3-CH_3 + H_2C{=}CH_2$$

CHAPTER 5
Cycloalkanes

GENERAL AND NOMENCLATURE

5.1 (*a*) Define cycloalkanes. (*b*) Write (i) the molecular, (ii) the structural, and (iii) the line formulas for the first four members of this homologous series with only one ring and no substituent groups.

◢ (*a*) The *cycloalkane* homologous series consists of hydrocarbons with the general formula C_nH_{2n}, where C—C bonds form a ring.

(*b*) (i) C_3H_6 $\qquad$ C_4H_8 $\qquad$ C_5H_{10} $\qquad$ C_6H_{12}

(ii)

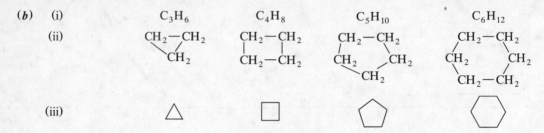

(iii)

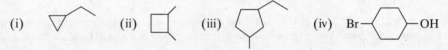

5.2 (*a*) Name the cycloalkanes in Problem 5.1. (*b*) Name each of the following substituted cycloalkanes:

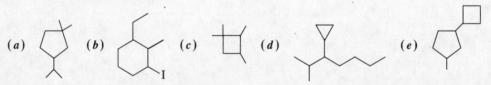

◢ (*a*) The prefix cyclo- is attached to the name of the alkane with the same number of C's giving respectively the names cyclopropane, cyclobutane, cyclopentane, and cyclohexane.

(*b*) Substituted cycloalkanes are named in the same way as alkanes.
(i) Ethylcyclopropane $\qquad$ (iii) 1-Ethyl-3-methylcyclopentane (not 1-methyl-3-ethylcyclohexane)
(ii) 1,2-Dimethylcyclobutane (iv) 4-Bromocyclohexanol (OH is understood to be on C^1.)

5.3 Name each of the following:

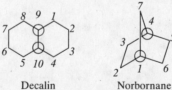

◢ (*a*) 1,1-Dimethyl-3-isopropylcyclopentane, (*b*) 3-Iodo-2-methyl-1-ethylcyclohexane, (*c*) 1,1,2,3-tetramethyl-cyclobutane, (*d*) 3-cyclopropyl-2-methylheptane, and (*e*) 1-cyclobutyl-3-methylcyclopentane.

5.4 Use the given line formulas of decalin and norbornane to define the following terms: polycyclic compounds, fused rings, bicyclic compounds, bridgehead C's, bridge C's, and bridged bicyclics.

Decalin $\qquad$ Norbornane

◢ Decalin and norbornane are *polycyclic* compounds because they have more than one ring. The rings of decalin share a common C—C bond and are said to be *fused*. Both are *bicyclic* compounds because they have two rings. The *bridgehead* C's, encircled in the structural formulas, are junction points for the rings. *Bridge* C's are in the chain connecting but not including the bridgehead C's. Norbornane is a *bridged* bicyclic because one or more C's separate the bridgehead C's whereas decalin is *not* a bridged bicyclic. The terms poly- and bicyclic are used mainly for fused and bridged system even though rings joined by single or double bonds are also polycyclic.

5.5   Give the IUPAC name for (*a*) decalin and (*b*) norbornane.

◢   The prefix *bicyclo-* is combined with a pair of brackets enclosing numbers separated by periods, which is followed by the name of the alkane whose number of C's equals the number of C's in the rings. The bracketed numbers show how many C's are in each bridge and are cited in decreasing order.
(*a*)   Bicyclo[4.4.0]decane. Note that a fused-ring system always has a 0 as one of the bracketed numbers.
(*b*)   Bicyclo[2.2.1]heptane.

5.6   Draw line formulas and give the IUPAC name for each of the following fused bicyclics:
(*a*) Bicyclobutane, (*b*) two isomers of bicycloheptane and (*c*) three isomers of bicyclooctane.

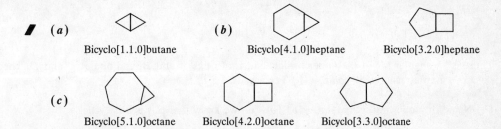

◢ (*a*)   Bicyclo[1.1.0]butane   (*b*)   Bicyclo[4.1.0]heptane   Bicyclo[3.2.0]heptane

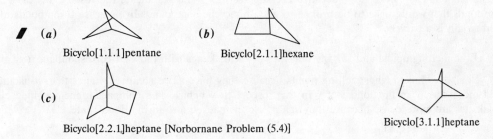

(*c*)   Bicyclo[5.1.0]octane   Bicyclo[4.2.0]octane   Bicyclo[3.3.0]octane

Check your answer by adding 2 for the bridgehead C's to the total of the numbers in the brackets. Your answer should be the same as the number of C's in the alkane name.

5.7   Draw line formulas and give IUPAC names for unsubstituted bridged (*a*) bicyclopentane, (*b*) bicyclohexane, and (*c*) two isomeric bicycloheptanes.

◢ (*a*)   Bicyclo[1.1.1]pentane   (*b*)   Bicyclo[2.1.1]hexane

(*c*)   Bicyclo[2.2.1]heptane [Norbornane Problem (5.4)]   Bicyclo[3.1.1]heptane

5.8   Draw line structures and show ring numbering for:
(*a*) 2-Ethyl-7-iodobicyclo[2.2.1]heptane, (*b*) 3-bromo-6-methylbicyclo[3.2.0]heptane, and
(*c*) 1,3,9-trimethyldecalin.

◢   To number bicyclics start at one bridgehead C and move along the longest chain to the next bridgehead C. Continue along the next longest chain to return to the first bridgehead C so that the shortest bridge is numbered last. For decalins, C^1 is next to a bridgehead C and is chosen so substituents have the lowest possible numbers—the bridgehead C's get the last numbers, *9* and *10* (Problem 5.4).

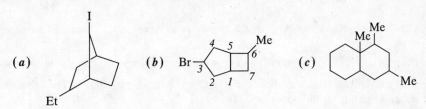

(*a*)   (*b*)   (*c*)

5.9   Define the term spirane and give two examples of spirooctanes with their corresponding names.

◢   *Spiranes* are polycylics that share only *one* C. Two examples of spirooctanes are

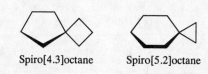

Spiro[4.3]octane   Spiro[5.2]octane

5.10 Give the general formulas of (*a*) bicyclalkanes and (*b*) tricycloalkanes.

▉ (*a*) With two rings, bicycloalkanes have 2° of unsaturation and the general formula is C_nH_{2n-2}. (*b*) Tricycloalkanes have three rings and 3° of unsaturation and the general formula is C_nH_{2n-4}.

5.11 (*a*) Draw the basic fused *steroid* ring system present in many important naturally occurring compounds such as cholesterol and designate the rings with letters. Show the location of the angular Me's. (*b*) Classify this polycyclic system.

▉ (*a*)

There is an angular Me at the upper bridgehead C of rings *A* and *B*, and one at *C* and *D*. The R indicates the position of an attached side chain. (*b*) Tetracyclic.

5.12 (*a*) Name the following compound. (*b*) How do we know that this is a tricyclic?

▉ (*a*) The name is tricyclo[4.2.2.0^{1,6}]decane. The superscripts *1* and *6* indicate the fused C's. (*b*) Find the number of bonds that would have to be broken to get a noncyclic compound. In this case three bonds must be broken and so this is a tricyclic.

5.13 Compare (*a*) the melting points and (*b*) the densities of cycloalkanes with those of corresponding *n*-alkanes.

▉ (*a*) Cycloalkanes have higher melting points because they have more compact shapes than *n*-alkanes and are packed more closely in the solid state. In this respect they behave like compact branch-chained alkanes. (*b*) Cycloalkanes are more dense because they can be closely packed also in the liquid state.

GEOMETRIC (*cis-trans*) ISOMERISM

5.14 Give the structural formulas and names of the three isomers of dimethylcyclopropane.

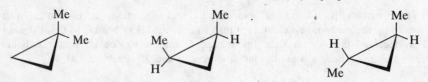

1,1-Dimethylcyclopropane (**A**)   *cis*-1,2-Dimethylcyclopropane (**B**)   *trans*-1,2-Dimethylcyclopropane (**C**)

5.15 Account for the existence of isomers **B** and **C** in Problem 5.14 and explain the terms *cis* and *trans*.

▉ The ring is rigid and rotation about the ring C—C bonds is prohibitive. The substituents can be on the same side of the ring (*cis*) or on the opposite sides (*trans*).

5.16 Use isomers **B** and **C** in Problem 5.14 as illustrations to define: (*a*) stereoisomers, (*b*) geometric isomers, (*c*) stereocenter, and (*d*) diastereomers.

▉ (*a*) Isomers **B** and **C** are examples of *stereoisomers*: they have the same sequence of covalent bonds but have different spatial arrangements. The phenomenon is called *stereoisomerism*. (*b*) A frequently used name for *cis-trans* isomers is *geometric isomers*. (*c*) If the exchange of the position of a pair of substituents (including an H) on an atom gives a different stereoisomer, the atom is called a *stereocenter*. In organic chemistry these atoms are most often C's as exemplified by each C bonded to Me and H in **B** and **C**.

(d) Compounds, such as **B** and **C**, that have more than one (in this case two) stereocenter are called *diastereomers*.

5.17 (a) Is geometric isomerism observed in 3,4-dimethylhexane, $CH_3CH_2CHMeCHMeCH_2CH_3$? (b) What structural features must be present in order for stereoisomers to exist?

▮ (a) No! We could write structures that resemble *cis-trans* isomers:

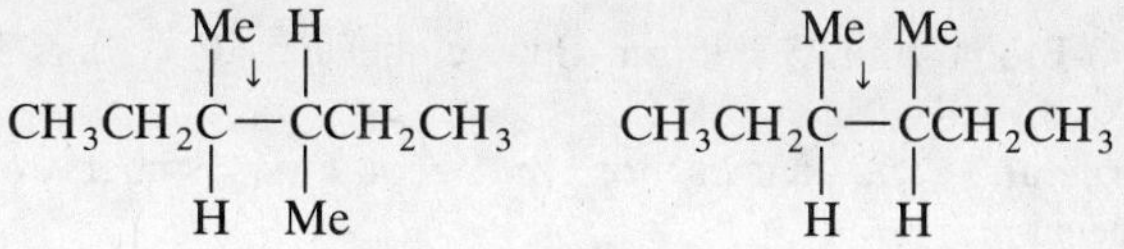

$$\underset{\underset{H}{|}}{\overset{\overset{Me\ \ H}{|\ \ \downarrow}}{CH_3CH_2C}}\!-\!\underset{\underset{Me}{|}}{\overset{}{C}}CH_2CH_3 \qquad \underset{\underset{H}{|}}{\overset{\overset{Me\ \ Me}{|\ \ \downarrow}}{CH_3CH_2C}}\!-\!\underset{\underset{H}{|}}{\overset{}{C}}CH_2CH_3$$

However, these are not isomers because they rapidly interconvert by rotation about the indicated bond and consequently they are not isolable. They are conformations.

(b) There must be a rigid site to preclude easy rotation which rapidly interconverts the structures. In cyclic compounds such a site is the ring.

5.18 Draw the structures for geometric isomers, if any; of (a) 1,1,2-trimethyl cyclopropane, (b) 1,2-dimethylcyclobutane, and (c) 1,3,5-trimethylcyclohexane.

▮ (a) None (b)

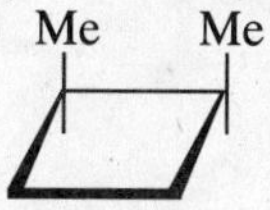

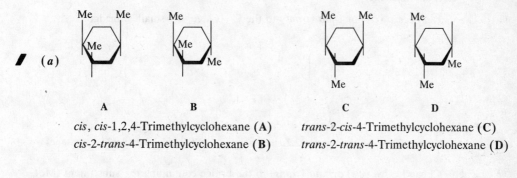

cis 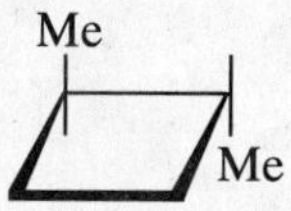   trans   cis, cis 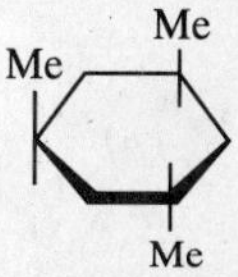   cis, trans

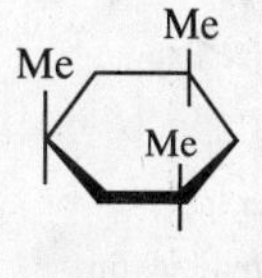

The stereochemical designations given in (c) indicate the positions of the substituents relative to the one at C^1.

5.19 Write the structures and give the names for the geometric isomers of (a) 1,2,4-trimethylcyclohexane, (b) 5-chloro-1,3 · dimethylcyclohexane, and (c) 3-bromo-5-chloromethylcyclohexane.

▮ (a)

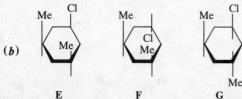

     A   B   C   D

cis, *cis*-1,2,4-Trimethylcyclohexane (**A**)   *trans*-2-*cis*-4-Trimethylcyclohexane (**C**)
cis-2-*trans*-4-Trimethylcyclohexane (**B**)   *trans*-2-*trans*-4-Trimethylcyclohexane (**D**)

(b)

     E   F   G

cis-5-Chloro-*cis*-1,3-dimethylcyclohexane (**E**)   *cis*-5-Chloro-*trans*-1,3-dimethylcyclohexane (**G**)
trans-5-Chloro-*cis*-1,3-dimethylcyclohexane (**F**)

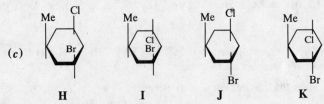

H   **I**   **J**   **K**

cis-3-Bromo-*cis*-5-chloromethylcyclohexane (**H**)   *trans*-3-Bromo-*cis*-5-chloromethylcyclohexane (**J**)
cis-3-Bromo-*trans*-5-chloromethylcyclohexane (**I**)   *trans*-3-Bromo-*trans*-5-chloromethylcyclohexane (**K**)

5.20   Give the structures and names for the geometric isomers of (*a*) decalin, (*b*) 9-methyldecalin, and (*c*) 2-methyldecalin.

▮   The two rings can be fused *cis* and *trans*.

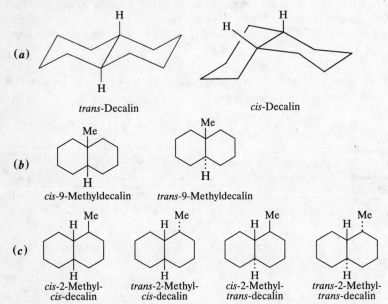

(*a*)

trans-Decalin   *cis*-Decalin

(*b*)

cis-9-Methyldecalin   *trans*-9-Methyldecalin

(*c*)

cis-2-Methyl-   *trans*-2-Methyl-   *cis*-2-Methyl-   *trans*-2-Methyl-
cis-decalin   *cis*-decalin   *trans*-decalin   *trans*-decalin

5.21   Give structures and IUPAC names for the geometric isomers of (*a*) 2-chloronorbornane (Problem 5.4), and (*b*) 2-methyl-7-chloronorbornane.

▮   (*a*)   The Cl can be *exo* (*cis*) or *endo* (*trans*) to the C⁷ bridge, the smallest bridge.

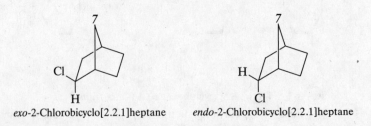

exo-2-Chlorobicyclo[2.2.1]heptane   *endo*-2-Chlorobicyclo[2.2.1]heptane

(*b*)   The C⁷Cl can be *syn* (*cis*) or *anti* (*trans*) to the bridge containing the substituent (Me).

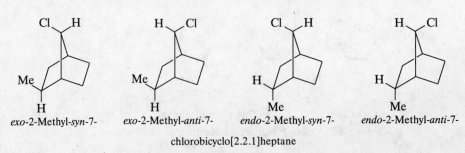

exo-2-Methyl-*syn*-7-   *exo*-2-Methyl-*anti*-7-   *endo*-2-Methyl-*syn*-7-   *endo*-2-Methyl-*anti*-7-

chlorobicyclo[2.2.1]heptane

5.22 Are the following compounds isolable?

(a)   (b)   (c)   (d)

(e)   (f)

▮ (a) Yes. Any sized rings can be fused *cis*. (b) Yes. Spiranes are known for any size ring if they are able to be at right angles. (c) No. A three- and a six-membered ring cannot be fused *trans*. The *trans* bonds on the potential bridgehead C's are too far apart to be bridged by a single carbon bridge. (d) No. As in (c) a four- and a five-membered ring cannot be fused *trans*. (e) Yes. Two five-membered (and larger) rings can be fused *trans* because the *trans* bonds on the bridgehead C's are in position for a 3-C bridge. (f) Yes. Large rings can be *trans*-fused.

RING STRAIN AND STABILITY

5.23 (a) How are enthalpies of combustion (ΔH_c) (see Problem 4.40) used to compare stabilities of different size cycloalkanes? (b) Calculate the ΔH_c per CH_2 unit for the first six cycloalkanes. The ΔH_c's, in kJ/mol, are: cyclopropane, -2090; cyclobutane, -2718; cyclopentane, -3288; cyclohexane, -3918; cycloheptane, -4632; cyclooctane, -5304. (c) How do the calculated values in (b) relate to the ring stability? (d) What factor causes rings to have different stabilities? (e) Generalize about ring size, ring strain, and stability for the first four cycloalkanes.

▮ (a) As is true for all homologous series, molecular formulas of successive members of the cycloalkanes differ by one CH_2. Their relative stabilities are determined by calculating and comparing their ΔH_c's per CH_2 unit. (b) Divide the given ΔH_c values by the number of CH_2 units in the ring (3, 4, 5, 6, 7, and 8, respectively), to obtain: cyclopropane, -697; cyclobutane, -680; cyclopentane, -658; cyclohexane, -653; cycloheptane, -662; cyclooctane, -663. (c) The larger, in this case the *less negative*, the value the more stable is the ring. (d) Different size rings vary in *ring strain*. (e) Ring strain decreases and stability increases with ring size up to cyclohexane. Larger rings, namely cycloheptane and cyclooctane, are slightly less stable.

5.24 (a) What assumptions can be made about the ring strain and stability of cyclohexane from its relative ΔH_c per CH_2 value (see Problem 5.23)? (b) Use the ΔH_c values to assess ring strain of the C_3-C_8 rings as compared with cyclohexane.

▮ (a) Cyclohexane has the least negative ΔH_c value per CH_2 unit and is assumed to be strain-free. (b) Using the ΔH_c per CH_2 value (-653) of cyclohexane as a standard, we calculate the ring strain in other cycloalkanes by multiplying 653 by the number of ring C's and subtracting this product from the ΔH_c of the cycloalkanes. For convenience, the $-$ sign in front of ΔH_c is dropped and ring strain per CH_2 unit is given as a positive number. The greater the difference the greater the ring strain.

Cycloalkane	Total ΔH_c (kJ/mol)		Ring Strain (kJ/mol)
Cyclopropane	2090	$-3(653) =$	131
Cyclobutane	2718	$-4(653) =$	106
Cyclopentane	3288	$-5(653) =$	23
Cyclohexane	3918	$-6(653) =$	0
Cycloheptane	4632	$-7(653) =$	61
Cyclooctane	5304	$-8(653) =$	80
Open chain	ΔH_c per CH_2 unit $= 653$		

5.25 Classify cycloalkanes by size and ring strain.

▮ 1. *Small rings* (C_3-C_4) have large ring strain. 2. *Common rings* (C_5-C_6) have little or no strain. 3. *Medium rings* (C_7-C_{12}) have little strain. 4. *Large rings* ($> C_{12}$) are strain-free.

5.26 Which factors influence the ring strain of cycloalkanes?

▮ *Bond-angle strain* is caused by distortion of the tetrahedral C angle in closing the ring. *Eclipsing (torsional) strain* results from eclipsing of adjacent pairs of C—H bonds. Other factors are *gauche interactions* which are similar to those in *n*-butane (Problem 4.24), and *transannular* (across the ring) *strain* arising from the proximity of H atoms not on adjacent C's.

5.27 How does the geometry of cyclopropane account for its ring strain?

▮ Alkane C's use sp^3 HO's whose bond angles are 109.5°. But the three C's in cyclopropane form an equilateral triangle so that their internal angles are 60°, which is 49.5° less than the normal tetrahedral angle. This deviation constitutes *angle strain*. In addition, the pair of H's on any given C eclipses a pair on each adjacent C introducing severe eclipsing strain [see Fig. 5-1(*a*)].

5.28 Compare the orbital overlap in cyclopropane with that in alkanes.

▮ The strongest covalent bonds result from maximum overlap of orbitals along the bond axis—this is achieved in alkanes by perfect head-on overlap of sp^3 HO's (Problem 2.37). For cyclopropane, head-on overlap of sp^3 HO's could not lead to ring closure because it would require bond angles of 109.5°. Instead, overlap is off the axis, giving less effective *bent* ("banana") bonds, as shown in Fig. 5-1(*b*).

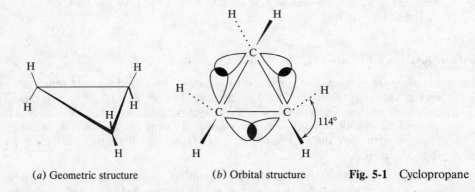

(*a*) Geometric structure   (*b*) Orbital structure   **Fig. 5-1** Cyclopropane

5.29 (*a*) In terms of hybridization, what assumptions are made to rationalize the observed H—C—H bond angle of 114° in cyclopropane?   (*b*) Compare the relative C—H bond lengths in cyclopropane and CH_2 in propane.

▮ (*a*) In order to minimize angle strain the C's develop more *p* character in the orbitals forming the ring (and consequently more *s* character in the external C—H bonds). Since bond angles generated from overlapping *p* orbitals are 90°, additional *p* character in the internal bonds decreases the ring strain. To get more *s* character the HO's for the external bonds are somewhere between sp^3 and sp^2, leading to enlargement of the angle. This is another example of deviations from pure p, sp, sp^2, sp^3 hybridization.   (*b*) The more *s* character in the HO used by C to form a bond, the shorter is the bond. The C—H bond in cyclopropane is shorter than in propane.

5.30 Use ring strain to predict the relative chemical reactivities of cyclopropane, cyclobutane, and cyclopentane, a typical cycloalkane with low ring strain.

▮ Cyclopentane with low ring strain withstands ring-opening reactions—chemically it behaves as an alkane. The large ring strain (131 kJ/mol) of cyclopropane (Problem 5.24) provides the driving force that increases its reactivity in ring-opening reactions. The less strained cyclobutane also undergoes ring-openings, but under more severe reaction conditions than for the more strained cyclopropane.

5.31 (*a*) Why is the ΔH_c of *cis*-dimethylcyclopropane greater than that of its *trans* isomer?   (*b*) Which isomer is more stable?

▮ (*a*) The *cis* isomer has more eclipsing strain because the Me's are closer.   (*b*) The *trans* is more stable.

5.32 Explain why the ring strain of cyclobutane is not much less than that of cyclopropane.

▮ Cyclobutane should have 90° bond angles if it is a square molecule. The deviation from 109.5° is considerably less than that for cyclopropane and there should be much less angle strain. However, this is somewhat offset by the additional eclipsing strain—cyclobutane has four pairs of eclipsing H's, one pair more than in cyclopropane.

5.33 Draw two conformations of cyclobutane that overcome the eclipsing strain.

▮ Cyclobutane is not a flat ring but rather exists as two equilibrating *puckered* ("folded") conformations (Fig. 5-2) in which eclipsing is eliminated and replaced by staggered H's. Puckering more than offsets the slight increase in angle strain because the new angles are 88°. The four boxed H's in Fig. 5-2 alternate between up-and-down, and the other four project outward from the perimeter of the ring.

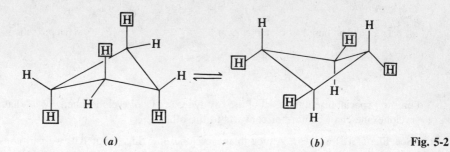

(*a*)   (*b*)   **Fig. 5-2**

5.34 Supply the terms for (i) and (ii) in the following statement. Boxed H's in Fig. 5-2(*a*) are called (i) and in Fig. 5-2(*b*) are called (ii).

▮ (i) *Axial*, (ii) *equatorial*.

5.35 Depict the puckered conformation of cyclobutane in a Newman projection.

▮ See Fig. 5-3.

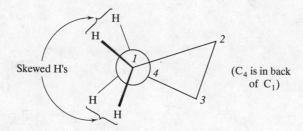

Fig. 5-3

5.36 Account for the small ring strain of cyclopentane.

▮ If a molecule of cyclopentane were a regular pentagon, it would have internal bond angles of 108°, very close to the 109.5° angles of a regular tetrahedron. Its angle strain would be insignificant. However, all five pairs of H's would be eclipsed, causing considerable eclipsing strain. This strain is reduced because cyclopentane has puckered "envelope" conformations in which a different C moves out of the ring plane. Very small energy changes are needed for twisting the C—C bonds needed to move individual C atoms above and below the ring plane. As this occurs, the out-of-plane C moves around the ring. The "envelope" conformation is

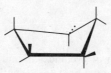

5.37 What factors make the cyclohexane ring the most stable, abundant and important ring structure in organic chemistry?

▮ Cyclohexane would not be stable if it had a planar hexagonal ring because of angle strain (bond angles of 120°, considerably larger than 109.5°) and eclipsing strain (from the six pairs of C—H bonds). Cyclohexane overcomes these strains by being puckered to give two rapidly equilibrating *chair conformations* in which (*a*) it achieves nearly tetrahedral angles with no angle strain, [see Fig. 5-4(*a*)], and (*b*) it eliminates eclipsing strain because all C—H bonds are staggered [see Fig. 5-4(*b*)].

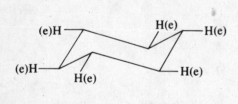

(a) Equilibrating chair conformations
(b) Newman projection

Fig. 5-4

5.38 (a) Based on their spacial orientation, label the two types of H's of cyclohexane. (b) What happens to these H's when one cyclohexane chair conformer converts to the other?

▮ (a) See Fig. 5-5(a) and (b). Although the cyclohexane ring is not flat, we can consider that the C's lie roughly in a plane for the purpose of identifying and naming the types of H's. Six H's are *equatorial* (e); they project out from the perimeter or equator of the ring. The other six H's are *axial* (a), alternating, perpendicularly, up from the ring plane (toward the north axis) and down (toward the south axis), hence the designation of the names axial and equatorial in Problem 5.34.

(b) Each C has one equatorial and one axial C—H bonds and in the conversion the equatorial bonds become axial while the axial bonds become equatorial [Fig. 5-5(c) and (d)].

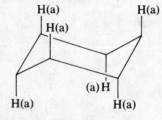

(a) Equatorial bonds
(b) Axial bonds

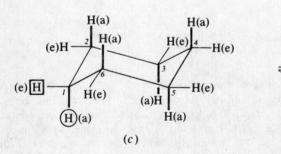
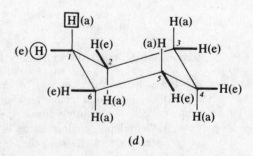

(c)
(d)

Fig. 5-5

5.39 (a) Draw (i) the *boat* conformation of cyclohexane and (ii) its Newman projection. (b) How does the chair conformation of Fig. 5-4(a) convert to the boat conformation? (c) Why is the boat conformation less stable than the chair conformation?

▮ (a) See Fig. 5-6.
(b) Flipping the chair conformer moves up C¹ to place it and C⁴ on the same side of the plane composing the remaining four C's, called the *gunwale* C's.
(c) Like the chair, the boat conformation has no angle strain but it has eclipsing strain from the two pairs of H's on each set of gunwale C's. There is also transannular strain from the crowding of the "flagpole" H's on C¹ and C⁴, which point towards each other and tend to occupy the same space.

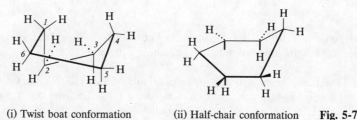

(i) Boat conformation   (ii) Newman projection   **Fig. 5-6**

5.40   (*a*) Draw (i) the *twist-* or *skew-boat* and (ii) the *half-chair* cyclohexane conformations.   (*b*) Explain why (i) the twist-boat conformation is more stable than the boat conformation, and (ii) the half-chair is the least stable conformation.

▰   (*a*)   See Fig. 5-7.

(i) Twist boat conformation   (ii) Half-chair conformation   **Fig. 5-7**

(*b*)   (i) Twisting the boat to the twist-boat conformation moves the "flagpole" H's away from each other and reduces eclipsing of the gunwale H's. Therefore, the twist-boat structure is more stable than the boat conformation.   (ii) The half-chair, formed by raising the footrest of the chair, has five of the six C's in a plane with one C out of the plane. It is reminiscent of the envelope conformation of cyclopentane (Problem 5.36). It is the least stable conformation of cyclohexane because of both angle and eclipsing strain.

5.41   (*a*) What are the relative populations of the cyclohexane conformations?   (*b*) Given the following strain energies, in kcal/mol; for: chair, 0; twist boat, 5.5; boat, 7.1; and half-chair, 11. Draw an energy diagram for the chair → half-chair → twist-boat → boat interconversions.

▰   (*a*) The largest number of cyclohexane molecules are, by far, in the chair conformation. The others are in the order: twist-boat > boat > half-chair. However, the low energy differences between the conformations permit rapid and frequent interconversions.
(*b*) See Fig. 5-8.

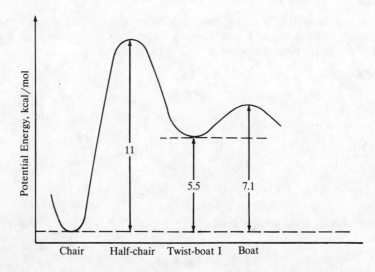

Fig. 5-8

SUBSTITUTED CYCLOHEXANES; CONFORMATIONAL ANALYSIS

5.42 (*a*) Draw the two equilibrating chair conformers of methylcyclohexane. (*b*) Give a conformational analysis of their relative energies.

▮ (*a*) See Fig. 5-9(*a*) and (*b*).

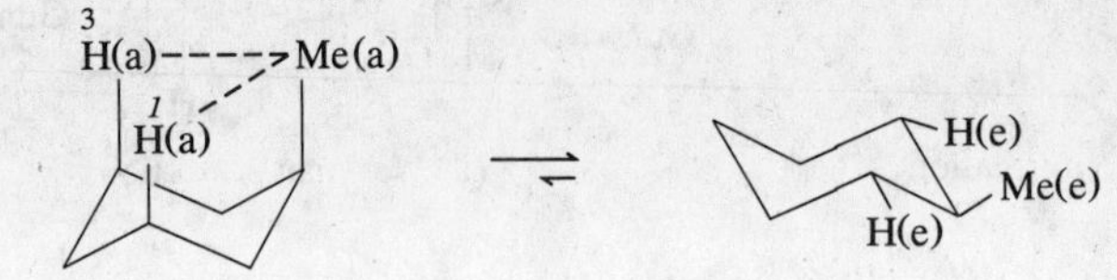

Methylcyclohexane, Me(a)   Methylcyclohexane, Me(e)
(less stable)   (more stable)

(*a*)   (*b*)   **Fig. 5-9**

(*b*) The conformer with $CH_3(e)$ dominates because it has less energy. An axial substituent has a less favorable spacial orientation than its equatorial mate because it is more crowded—a fact attributed to either.

(i) *Transannular strain* owing to the proximity of the axial CH_3 on C^1 to the axial H's on C^3 and C^5 [see Fig. 5-9(*a*)]; the equatorial CH_3 does not suffer from this *1,3-diaxial interaction*.

(ii) *Gauche interactions* of the $CH_3(a)$ on C^1 with the C^2-C^3 and C^5-C^6 ring bonds—the $CH_3(e)$ is *anti* to these ring bonds. Each gauche or 1,3-diaxial Me/H interaction increases the energy by 0.9 kcal/mol, to give a total increase of 1.8 kcal/mol. In calculations, use 0.9 per 1,3-interaction or per gauche interaction but do not use both.

5.43 (*a*) Calculate (i) K_e at 25 °C for the equilibrium in Problem 5.42, given the ratio $\Delta H_{(e)}/\Delta H_{(a)} = -1.8$ kcal/mol, and (ii) the percentage composition of the mixture. (*b*) Compare this ratio with that for *t*-butylcyclohexane and account for the difference.

▮ (*a*) (i) Since ΔS for this reaction is very small (1 mol ⇌ 1 mol), $\Delta G = \Delta H$ and $\Delta G = -1.8$ kcal/mol or -1800 cal/mol. Since $\Delta G = -2.303RT \log K_e$,

$-1800 = -2.303(2.00 \text{ cal/mol} \cdot \text{K})(298 \text{ K}) \log K_e$ from which $\log K_e = 1.313$ and $K_e = 20.6$

(ii) If the concentrations of (e) and (a) conformers are represented by [e] and [a], $K_e = [e]/[a]$. Calculating [e] from the equation $[e]/1 - [e] = 20.6$ gives the relative amounts of [e] = 0.954 and [a] = 0.046. The ratio of conformers is then 95 equatorial to 5 axial.

(*b*) A *t*-butyl group is bulkier than Me, and in the axial position it provides a larger transannular strain. The $\Delta H_{(e)}/\Delta H_{(a)} = 5$ kcal/mol and the ratio of [e]/[a] is so large ($10^5/1$) that practically only the equatorial conformer is present.

5.44 (*a*) Draw structures for the equilibrating chair conformers of *trans*- and *cis*-1,2-dimethylcyclohexane. Show all Me/H 1,3-diaxial interactions. (*b*) Select the more stable conformation for each diastereomer. (*c*) Compare the stabilities of the more stable conformer of each diastereomer.

▮ (*a*) See Fig. 5-10.

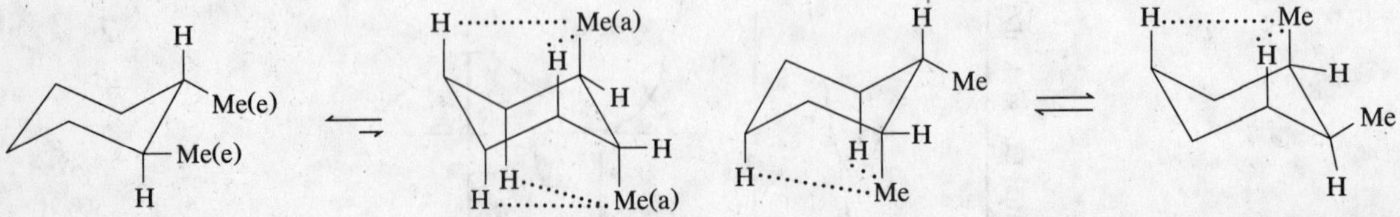

(Me's ee); more stable   (Me's aa); less stable

A   **B**   **C**   **D**

trans-1,2-Dimethycyclohexane   *cis*-1,2-Dimethylcyclohexane

(*a*)   (*b*)

Fig. 5-10

(b) (i) In **A** both Me's are equatorial (e, e) and **A** has no transannular strain. **B** has two axial Me's(a, a) with four 1,3-diaxial interactions. **A** predominates—**B** is practically nonexistent. (ii) **C** and **D** have an (e) and (a) Me, (e, a), and have the same energy.

(c) The axial Me of **C** introduces two 1,3-diaxial Me/H interactions and is less stable than **A** with no such interactions. *Trans* is more stable than *cis*.

5.45 (a) Draw structures for the two conformations of *trans-* and *cis*-1,3-dimethylcyclohexane. (b) Label the more stable conformer for each diastereomer and explain your choice. (c) Compare the stabilities of the more stable conformer of each diastereomer. (d) Before the advent of conformation theory (mid 40's) the greater stability of the *cis*-isomer was called an anomaly. Explain why it was so-called and how conformation theory explained the problem.

▰ (a) See Fig. 5-11.

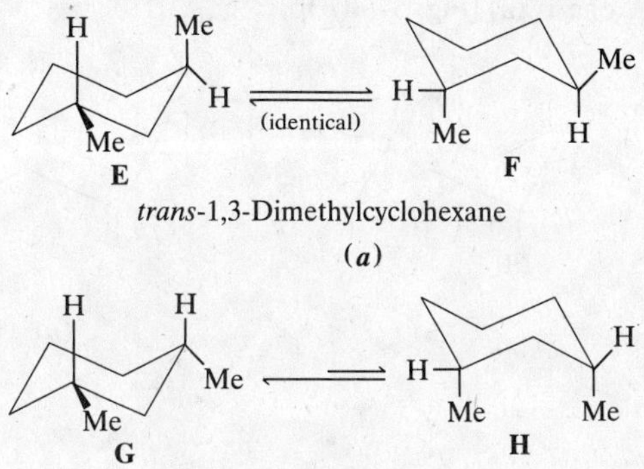

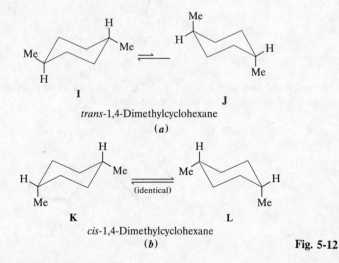

trans-1,3-Dimethylcyclohexane
(a)

cis-1,3-Dimethylcyclohexane
(b)   **Fig. 5-11**

(b) (i) **E** and **F** are identical (e, a) conformers with the same energy. (ii) **G** is (e, e) and is more stable than **H** (a, a).

(c) *cis*-**G** (e, e) is more stable than **E** or **F** [see Problem 5.44(c)].

(d) All *cis*-dialkylcycloalkanes were expected to be less stable because of steric interaction of the R's that were thought to be on the same side of the ring. Conformational analysis in terms of axial and equatorial orientations nicely explains the "anomaly".

5.46 Solve Problem 5.45 for *trans-* and *cis*-1,4-dimethylcyclohexane.

▰ (a) See Fig. 5-12.

trans-1,4-Dimethylcyclohexane
(a)

cis-1,4-Dimethylcyclohexane
(b)   **Fig. 5-12**

(b) (i) **I** (ee) is more stable than **J** (aa). (ii) **K** and **L**, both (ea) have the same energy.

(c) **I** (ee) is more stable than **K** or **L**.

5.47 Use 1,3-diaxial interactions to find the energy difference between the more stable conformers of (a) *cis-* and *trans*-1,3-dimethylcyclohexane, and (b) (e, e) and (a, a) *trans*-1,2-dimethylcyclohexane. Each Me/H 1,3-interaction imparts 3.75 kJ/mol (0.9 kcal/mol) of instability to a compound.

▮ (*a*) The *cis* isomer has (ee) Me's with no 1,3-interactions. The *trans* isomer (ea) has an axial Me with two Me/H 1,3-interactions, accounting for 2(3.75) = 7.5 kJ/mol of instability. The *cis* is more stable than the *trans* isomer by 7.5 kJ/mol.

(*b*) See Fig. 5-10; **A** (ee), with no 1,3-interactions, is more stable than **B** (aa) with four Me/H 1,3-interactions by 4(3.75) = 15 kJ/mol.

5.48 Which conformer of (*a*) *trans*-1-ethyl-3-isopropylcyclohexane and (*b*) *cis*-2-chloro-*cis*-4-chlorochlorocyclohexane is more stable?

▮ (*a*) All *trans*-1,3-isomers are (e, a) [see (i) of Problem 5.45(*b*)]. With identical substituents the equilibrating conformers have identical strain energy and stability. However, with different substituents the bulkier isopropyl group assumes the (e) position and the smaller ethyl group is (a) in the more stable conformer [Fig 5-13(*a*)]. (*b*) Two Cl's are (e) and Cl one is (a) [Fig. 5-13(*b*)].

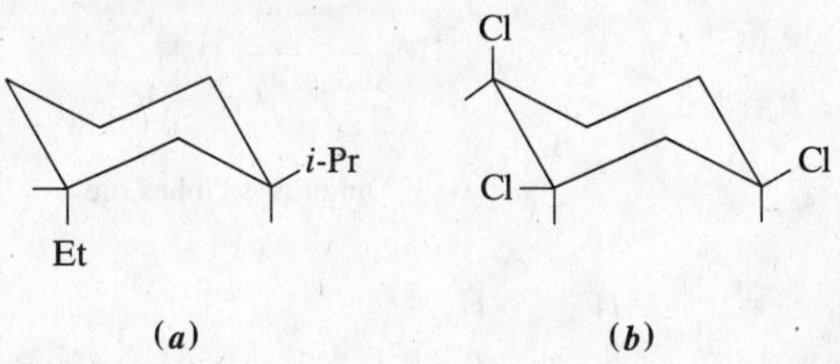

Fig. 5-13

5.49 Calculate and compare the energies of the more stable conformers for *cis*- and *trans*-1,1,3,5-tetramethylcyclohexane (**A** and **B**, respectively). A Me/Me interaction is 15.0 kJ/mol.

▮ See Fig. 5-14. **A** has three CH_3's (e) having no strain energy and one CH_3 (a) with two CH_3/H interactions giving 2(3.75) = 7.5 kJ/mol of strain energy. **B** has two CH_3's (a) involved in two CH_3/H interactions and one CH_3/CH_3 interaction whose total strain energy = 2(3.75) + 15 = 22.5 kJ/mol. The *cis* is more stable than the *trans* isomer by 22.5 − 7.5 = 15 kJ/mol.

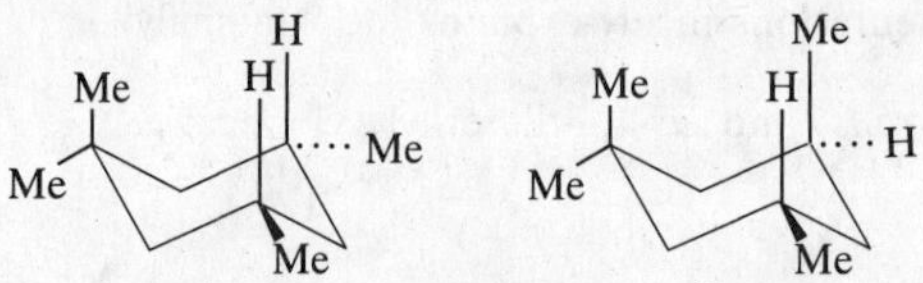

Fig. 5-14

5.50 Given the two alkylated cyclohexanes in Fig. 5-15, (*a*) draw the equilibrating chair conformations for each and (*b*) explain which is the more stable conformer for each.

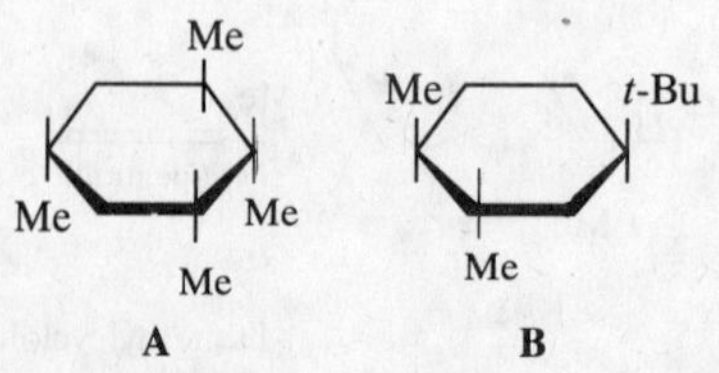

Fig. 5-15

▮ (*a*) See Fig. 5-16(*a*). (*b*) Conformers I and II of **A** each have two Me's (a) and two Me's (e). However the two axial Me's in conformer I are on the same side of the ring and engender a severe Me/Me 1,3-interaction besides two Me/H interactions. Conformer II is more stable because its (a) Me's are on opposite sides of the ring inducing four mild Me/H 1,3-interactions. In **B**, the ring strain from two (a) Me's and one (e) *t*-Bu of III is much less than that from one (a) *t*-Bu and two (e) Me's of IV; IV is much less stable [Fig. 5-16(*b*)].

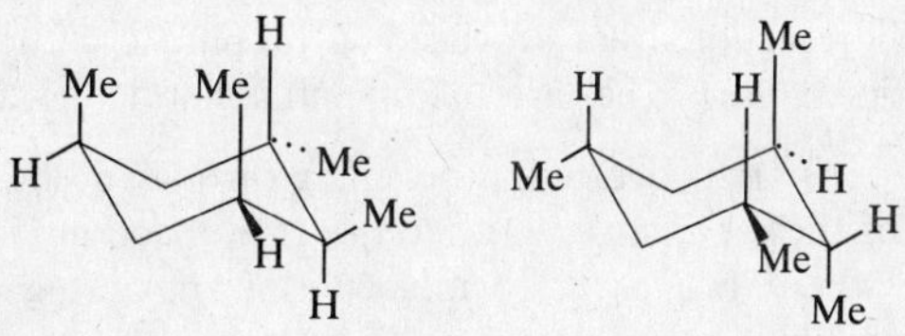

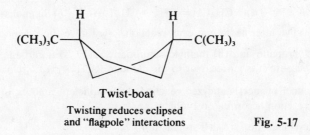

conformations: **I**   **II**

(*a*)

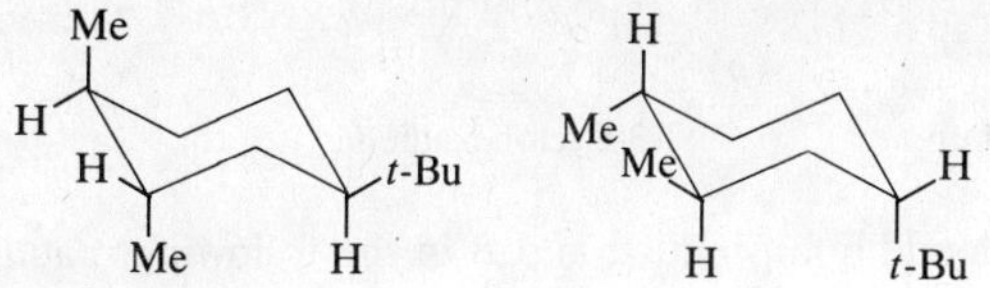

conformations: **III**   **IV**

(*b*)   **Fig. 5-16**

5.51   Draw the most stable conformation of *cis*-1,4-di-*t*-butylcyclohexane.

▮   Both chair conformations have an axial bulky *t*-butyl group [see Problem 5.43(*b*)] which is very unstable because of excessive ring strain. To overcome this ring strain, the molecule assumes a more stable twist-boat with a quasi-(ee) conformation (Fig. 5-17). In general, chair conformations with axial *t*-Bu groups do not exist.

$$(CH_3)_3C \quad\quad\quad\quad C(CH_3)_3$$

Twist-boat

Twisting reduces eclipsed
and "flagpole" interactions   **Fig. 5-17**

5.52   When *trans*-1,3 diRcyclobutane (R is COOMe) was equilibrated in base, a mixture of *cis*- and *trans*-isomers was isolated with *cis* dominating.   (*a*) In terms of a flat molecule, was this an expected result?   (*b*) Account for the observation.

▮   (*a*) No. Two R's on the same side of the ring should be destabilizing because of the crowding of the groups. (*b*) The puckered conformations (see Fig. 5-2) reveal that in its more stable conformation the *cis* R's are (ee) [Fig. 5-18(*a*)] and the *trans* R's are (ea) [Fig. 5-18(*b*)]. Hence, *cis* is more stable and is the major component of the equilibrium mixture. (This experimental finding gave credence to the conformational analysis for cyclobutane.)

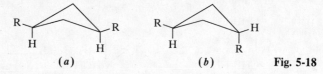

(*a*)   (*b*)   **Fig. 5-18**

5.53   Predict the relative stabilities of *trans*- and *cis*-1,2-dimethylcyclobutane.

▮   The *trans*-isomer has (ee) Me's and is more stable than the *cis*-isomer having (ea) Me's.

PREPARATION

5.54   Give two general approaches to synthesis of cycloalkanes.

▮   1. Conversion of available naturally-occurring cyclic compounds, often by hydrogenation (H_2 addition).
        2. Formation of rings from open chain compounds by either:
            (*a*)   Intramolecular cyclization of acyclic (noncyclic) compounds.
            (*b*)   Merging two or more acyclic compounds (cycloadditions).

5.55 (*a*) Define the pericyclic reactions that are used to prepare cyclic carbon compounds. (*b*) Give two general types of pericyclic reactions. (*c*) What are the essential characteristics of these reactions?

◢ (*a*) *Pericyclic* reactions are concerted, proceeding through cyclic transition states to form cyclic compounds. (*b*) Two general types of these reactions are: *electrocyclic* reactions in which a single molecule forms a ring and *cycloaddition* reactions where two or more molecules form a ring. (*c*) These reactions are initiated either thermally or photochemically, without catalysis. Their transition states have no partial charges. They are highly stereospecific (see Chapter 6).

5.56 Give the product of the electrocyclic reaction of: (*a*) 1,3-pentadiene and (*b*) 1,3,5-hexatriene

◢ (*a*)

3-Methylcyclobutene

(*b*)

1,3-Cyclohexadiene

5.57 (*a*) Identify **A**, a cycloaddition product, and **B** in the following reaction:

$$H_2C{=}CH{-}CH{=}CH_2 + H_2C{=}CH_2 \longrightarrow A \xrightarrow{H_2/Pd} B$$

(*b*) Name this very important cycloaddition.
(*c*) What size ring is always prepared by this type of synthesis?

◢ (*a*) **A** = cyclohexene, **B** = cyclohexane; (*b*) Diels–Alder (Problem 9.141); (*c*) six.

5.58 (*a*) Complete the following reactions:

$$(i) \quad H_2C{=}CH_2 + CH_2N_2 \text{ (diazomethane)} \rightarrow ?$$

$$(ii) \quad CH_3CH{=}CH_2 + CH_2I_2 \xrightarrow{Cu\text{-}Zn} ? \text{ (Simmons–Smith reaction)}$$

(*b*) What is the active intermediate in each reaction? (*c*) Give the reaction type.

◢ (*a*) (i) Cyclopropane and (ii) methylcyclopropane. (*b*) (i) a carbene, $:CH_2$ and (ii) ICH_2ZnI, called a carbenoid because it is a precursor to the carbene, $:CH_2$. (*c*) Cycloaddition.

5.59 (*a*) Give the product of metal-catalyzed reactions with sufficient amount of H_2 of toluene, a coal tar product. (*b*) Classify the reaction according to Problem 5.54.

◢ (*a*) Methylcyclohexane. (*b*) Hydrogenation.

5.60 Generate the following cyclopropanes in one step from any needed precursor: (*a*) 1,1-Dimethylcyclopropane and (*b*) 1,2-Dimethylcyclopropane (ignore *cis-trans* isomerism).

◢

(*a*)

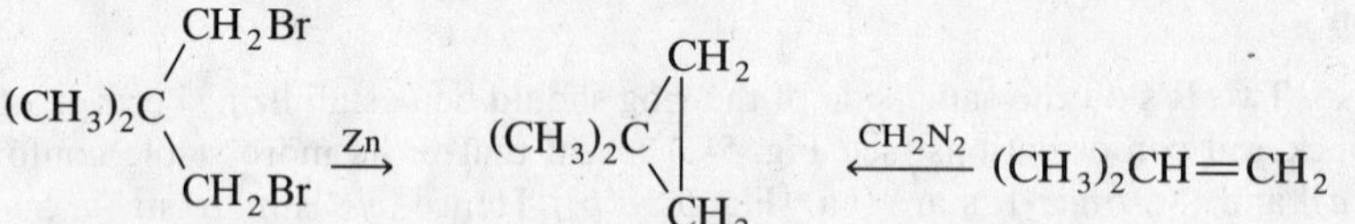

$(CH_3)_2C\big\langle{}^{CH_2Br}_{CH_2Br}$ $\xrightarrow{Zn}$ $(CH_3)_2C\big|{}^{CH_2}_{CH_2}$ $\xleftarrow{CH_2N_2}$ $(CH_3)_2CH{=}CH_2$

1,3-Dibromo-2,2-dimethylpropane   1,1-Dimethylcyclopropane

(*b*)

$CH_2\big\langle{}^{CHBrCH_3}_{CHBrCH_3}$ $\xrightarrow{Zn}$ $CH_2\big\langle{}^{CHCH_3}_{CHCH_3}$ $\xleftarrow{CH_2N_2}$ $CH_3CH{=}CHCH_3$

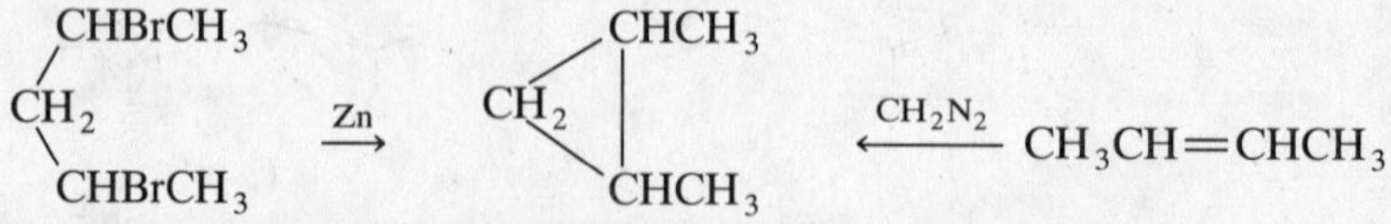

2,4-Dibromopentane   1,2-Dimethylcyclopropane

5.61 (*a*) Prepare 3,3-dichloro-1,1,2-trimethylcyclopropane (**A**) by a one-step cycloaddition. (*b*) Propose a mechanism for the formation of the dichlorocarbene.

◢ (*a*) $CHCl_3$ with a strong base ($Me_3CO^-K^+$) gives dichlorocarbene($:CCl_2$) which adds to the alkene precursor.

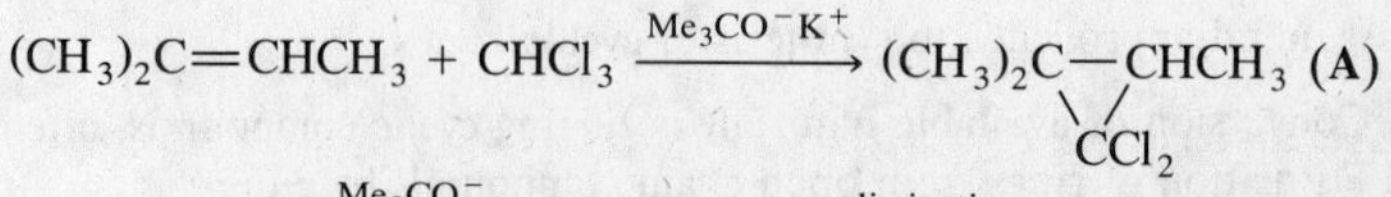

$$(CH_3)_2C{=}CHCH_3 + CHCl_3 \xrightarrow{Me_3CO^-K^+} (CH_3)_2C{-}CHCH_3 \text{ (A)}$$
$$CCl_2$$

(*b*) $H{:}CCl_3 \xrightarrow[-H^+]{Me_3CO^-} [:CCl_3]^- \xrightarrow{\alpha\text{-elimination}} Cl^- + :CCl_2 \quad (+Me_3COH)$

trichloromethyl-carbanion

5.62 Account for the following observations in syntheses by intramolecular cyclization:
   (i) Large rings with more than six C's are stable but difficult to prepare.
   (ii) Cyclopropanes have the greatest ring strain yet they are readily prepared.

   ▰ Formation of cycloalkanes by intramolecular cyclizations depends on two factors:
      1. Thermal stability which is determined by ring strain.
      2. The entropy factor (probability of bringing together the terminal C's) that decreases with chain length, making it successively more difficult to synthesize rings of increasing size.

5.63 (*a*) Using numbers to represent ring sizes, summarize the input of the two factors in Problem 5.62 for determining the ease of ring closure for cycloalkanes. (*b*) How do these account for the syntheses of cyclopropane and large rings?

   ▰ (*a*) 1. Thermal stability: $6 > 7, 5 > 8, 9 \gg 4 > 3$
            2. Entropy (probability) of ring closure: $3 > 4 > 5 > 6 > 7 > 8 > 9$
            Ease of synthesis (net effect of 1 and 2): $5 > 3, 6 > 4, 7, 8, 9$
      (*b*) In successful cyclopropane syntheses the favorable entropy factor is more important than thermal stability. With rings larger than six C's, ring stability is outweighed by the more important, highly unfavorable entropy factor.

5.64 Why are intramolecular cyclizations of rings with more than six C's better achieved at very low concentrations of reactant?

   ▰ Chains can also collide with each other to undergo *intermolecular* reactions forming longer chains. Unimolecular intramolecular reactions are ordinarily faster than bimolecular intermolecular reactions. The opposite is true for entropy-unfavorable intramolecular cyclizations leading to rings with more than six C's. Unfavorable intramolecular reactions are encouraged and intermolecular side reactions minimized by using high dilutions to decrease collisions between chains.

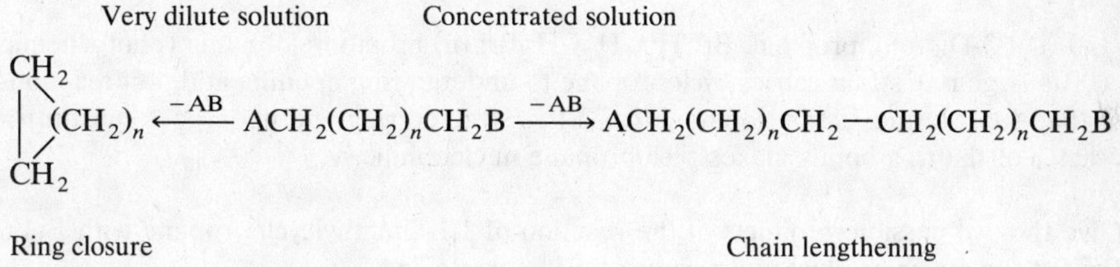

Very dilute solution   Concentrated solution

$$CH_2$$
$$|\ \ \ \diagdown$$
$$|\ \ \ \ (CH_2)_n \xleftarrow{-AB} ACH_2(CH_2)_nCH_2B \xrightarrow{-AB} ACH_2(CH_2)_nCH_2 - CH_2(CH_2)_nCH_2B$$
$$|\ \ \ \diagup$$
$$CH_2$$

Ring closure   Chain lengthening

5.65 (*a*) Complete the following reactions:
      (i) $ClCH_2CH_2CH_2Cl \xrightarrow{Mg} ?$ and   (ii) $ClCH_2CH_2CH_2CH_2Cl \xrightarrow{Mg} ?$

   (*b*) Give the reaction type (Problem 5.54) of (i).

   ▰ (*a*) (i) Cyclopropane (Freund reaction) and (ii) $ClMgCH_2CH_2CH_2CH_2MgCl$. See Problems 5.63 and 5.64 for a discussion of factors involved in ease of ring closure.   (*b*) Intramolecular ring closure.

5.66 (*a*) Prepare (i) cyclobutane (**A**) from any open chain compound and (ii) norbornane (**B**) from any monocyclic compound.   (*b*) Classify the cyclizations in (i) and (ii).

   ▰ (*a*) (i) $2\,H_2C{=}CH_2 \xrightarrow{h\nu} A$ or $H_2C{=}CHCH{=}CH_2 \xrightarrow{heat} \square \xrightarrow{H_2/Pd} A$

      (ii) 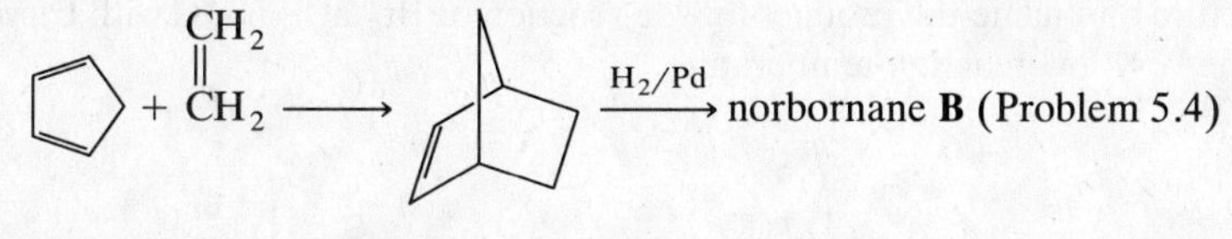 $\xrightarrow{H_2/Pd}$ norbornane **B** (Problem 5.4)

   (*b*) (i) Electrocyclic, (ii) cycloaddition.

CHEMICAL PROPERTIES

5.67 Relate the chemical properties of cycloalkanes and alkanes.

   ▰ With the exception of cyclopropane, the chemical reactions parallel each other.

5.68 (*a*) Give the product of the photochemical reaction of (i) cyclopentane and (ii) cyclohexane with Cl_2. (*b*) How is monochlorination ensured?

◢ (*a*) (i) Chlorocyclopentane and (ii) chlorocyclohexane. (*b*) An excess of the cycloalkane is used.

5.69 (*a*) Give the possible products with their names from monobromination of methylcyclohexane. (*b*) Predict the major product and explain your choice. (*c*) Discuss the distribution of monochlorination products.

◢ (*a*) The ring and the CH_3 are monobrominated giving a complex mixture of structural as well as the geometric isomers of the 2-, 3-, and 4-bromomethylcyclohexanes.

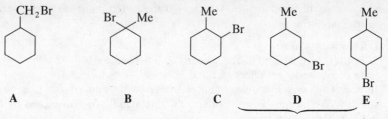

A is bromomethylcyclohexane; **B**, **C**, **D**, and **E** are 1-, 2-, 3-, and 4-bromomethylcyclohexanes, respectively. (*b*) The intermediate Br· is a selective radical and preferentially attacks the 3^0 H giving **B** as the major product (see Problem 4.87). (*c*) Cl· is much less selective (see Problem 4.85), and the statistical factor plays a significant role in determining the product distribution. There would be more of each isomer with none dominating.

5.70 (*a*) Give the product of the reaction of Br_2 with (i) cyclopropane and (ii) cyclobutane. (*b*) Rationalize the findings of (i) and (ii) above. (*c*) Classify the behavior of cyclopropane in the reaction with Br_2 in terms of its orbital representation.

◢ (*a*) (i) 1,3-Dibromopropane, $BrCH_2CH_2CH_2Br$; (ii) bromocyclobutane (photochemical). (*b*) See Problem 5.30. (i) Its large ring strain causes cyclopropane to undergo ring opening addition reactions. In this case Br_2 adds rather than substituting. (ii) Cyclobutane has a less strained ring and undergoes substitution. (*c*) The enhanced *p*-character of the ring bonds makes cyclopropane nucleophilic.

5.71 (*a*) Give the two possible products of the reaction of 1,1-dimethylcyclopropane with Br_2 (at room temperature). (*b*) Predict the major product and account for its formation.

◢ (*a*) $BrCMe_2CH_2CH_2Br$ (**C**) and $BrCH_2CMe_2CH_2Br$ (**D**). (*b*) A C—C bond breaks as the result of attack of the electrophilic Br^+ on one of the C's, generating a + charge on the other C. The more stable 3° $Me_2\overset{+}{C}CH_2CH_2Br$ leads to the major product, **C**.

5.72 Give the products, if any, and compare the experimental conditions for the hydrogenation of (*a*) $H_2C{=}CH_2$, (*b*) cyclopropane, (*c*) cyclobutane, and (*d*) cyclopentane and larger rings.

◢ CH_3CH_3. Alkenes readily undergo hydrogenation even at room temperature. (*b*) At higher temperatures (80 °C), the cyclopropane ring opens to relieve its strain and gives $CH_3CH_2CH_3$. (*c*) $CH_3CH_2CH_2CH_3$. The cyclobutane has sufficient ring strain to induce ring opening with H_2, which in this respect is a unique addendum. However, since the strain is less than that for cyclopropane, a higher temperature (200 °C) is required. (*d*) Cycloalkanes with five or more C's in their rings have little ring strain and are completely inert to H_2.

5.73 (*a*) Draw the structure and name the product for the reaction of Br_2 at -60 °C with tricyclo[3.2.1.0^{1,5}]octane (**A**). (*b*) Account for the very low reaction temperature.

◢ (*a*)

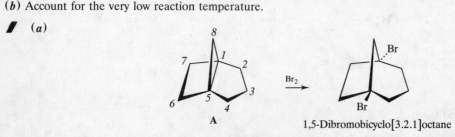

1,5-Dibromobicyclo[3.2.1]octane

(*b*) **A** has a strained 3- and 4-membered ring. Addition of Br_2 breaking the 3-membered ring is facile because the strain of both rings is relieved.

5.74 (*a*) Predict the product of the reaction of HBr with (i) cyclopropane and (ii) 1,1-dimethylcyclopropane. (*b*) Compare the rates of these reactions.

▮ (*a*) (i) $CH_3CH_2CH_2Br$ and (ii) $CH_3CH_2CBrMe_2$. (*b*) In (ii) the intermediate is a $3°R^+$, $HCH_2CH_2C^+Me_2$, formed when an H^+ adds to a ring CH_2 group. The addition of H^+ in (i) gives a much less stable $1°R^+$, $HCH_2CH_2CH_2^+$. Alkyl groups are also electron-releasing and increase the nucleophilicity and reactivity of the ring in electrophilic additions.

SUPPLEMENTARY PROBLEMS

5.75 Draw the structure and number the C's of tricyclo[3.3.1.1^{3,7}]decane (adamantane).

▮ See Fig. 5-19.

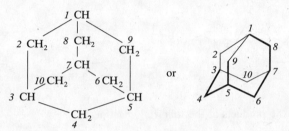

Fig. 5-19

5.76 Equal amounts of (a,a) and (e,e) conformers of *trans*-1,2-dibromocyclohexane exist in nonpolar solvents but the (e,e) conformer prevails in polar solvents. Explain.

▮ The 1,2-equatorial Br's cause some dipole-dipole repulsion, tending to partially destabilize the sterically more favored (ee) conformer but not the (aa) conformer whose Br's are further apart. Therefore the (ee) and (aa) conformations coexist because their energies are close. However, polar solvent molecules surround the Br's (by dipole-dipole attraction) and relieve the dipole repulsion between the Br's themselves. Hence, the lower-energy (ee) conformer now predominates. See Fig. 5-20.

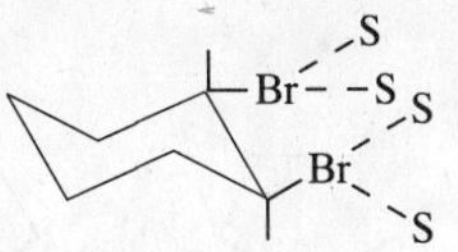

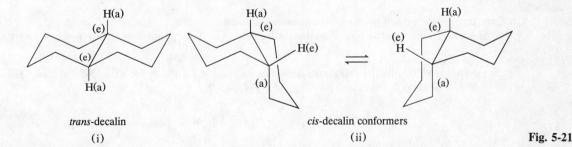

Fig. 5-20

5.77 (*a*) Draw the chair conformation for (i) *trans*- and (ii) *cis*-decalin. Compare their flexibilities. (*b*) Which isomer has the lower energy?

▮ (*a*) See Fig. 5-21. For each ring the other can be viewed as 1,2-substituents with respect to the bridgehead C's. For the *trans*-isomer only the rigid (ee) conformation is possible. Flipping to the (aa) orientation is impossible because the diaxial bonds point $180°$ away from each other and cannot be bridged by only four C's to complete the second ring. *Cis* fusion is (ea) and flipping can give the equilibrating (ae) conformer. The *cis* isomer is flexible. (*b*) *Trans* (ee) has a lower energy than *cis* (ea).

trans-decalin

(i)

cis-decalin conformers

(ii)

Fig. 5-21

5.78 You wish to determine the relative rates of an axial and an equatorial Br in some kind of organic reaction. Can you compare (*a*) *cis*- and *trans*-4-bromomethylcyclohexane, (*b*) *cis*- and *trans*-4-bromo-*t*-butylcyclohexane, (*c*) *cis*-,*cis*- and *trans*-,*trans*-3,5-dimethylbromocyclohexane, and (*d*) *cis*- and *trans*-3-bromo-*trans*-decalin?

▰ (a) No. The 1,4-*trans* substituents are (ee) and the *cis* substituents are (ea). Although the bulkier Me prefers to be (e) more than does Br, the difference in preference is small and an appreciable amount of conformers with Br(e)/Me(a) coexist with conformers Br(a)/Me(e). The *trans*-isomer has only (e)Br but at no time does the *cis* have conformers with only Br(a). (b) The very bulky *t*-butyl group can only be (e). In practically all the 1,4-*cis* molecules, Br must be (a) and in the *trans*-molecules Br must be (e). Because *t*-Bu "freezes" the conformation by preventing interconversion, these isomers can be used. The *t*-Bu is placed as far away from the Br as possible (1,4) so that it will not sterically hinder the reaction of the Br. (c) The *cis*-3,5-diMe's are almost exclusively (ee) to avoid severe Me/Me 1,3-diaxial interactions were they to be (aa). As does a *t*-Bu, these *cis* Me's freeze conformations. When Br at C^1 is *cis*, it is (e); when it is *trans*, it is (a). These isomers can be used. (d) *Trans*-decalin is rigid (Problem 5.77) and freezes the orientations of all substituents. In the *cis*-3-Br isomer, the Br is (e); in the *trans*-3-Br isomer, the Br is (a). The *cis/trans* notation refers to the relative juxtaposition of Br and the indicated (e) bond (see Fig. 5-22). These isomers can be used.

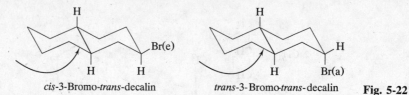

cis-3-Bromo-*trans*-decalin   *trans*-3-Bromo-*trans*-decalin   **Fig. 5-22**

5.79 Give the structures of the products of the following reactions:

(a) [cyclopentene with Me] + CHCl₃ $\xrightarrow{\text{Me}_3\text{COK}}$ **A + B**

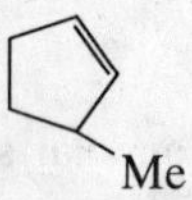

(b) [cyclopentene with Me] + CHClBr₂ $\xrightarrow{\text{Me}_3\text{COK}}$ **C + D**

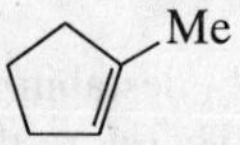

▰ (a) :CCl₂ adds *cis* to the C=C, but the resulting three-membered ring can be either *cis* or *trans* to Me (**A** and **B** in Fig. 5-23). (b) The anion formed, ClBr₂C:⁻, loses Br⁻, a better leaving group than Cl⁻, to give the carbene, ClBrC:, which adds to the C=C so that either Cl or Br is *cis* to Me (**C** and **D** in Fig. 5-23).

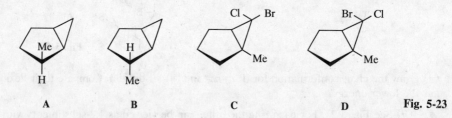

A   **B**   **C**   **D**   **Fig. 5-23**

5.80 Explain why cyclopropane has a greater acidity than propane in terms of its orbital representation. (See Problems 5.28 and 5.29).

▰ The C—H bonds of cyclopropane have more *s* character than those of an alkane. This causes the H's of cyclopropane to be more acidic.

5.81 (a) Give the structures and names of the products formed from the radical monobromination of a 2-C bridge -CH₂- of (i) norbonane and (ii) 7,7-dimethylnorbonane. (b) Select the more likely product and justify your choice.

▰ (a) The products are (i) *exo*- and *endo*-2-bromobicyclo[2.2.1]heptane [Fig. 5-24(a)]; and (ii) *exo*- and *endo*-2-bromo-7,7-dimethyl[2.2.1]heptane [Fig. 5-24(b)].

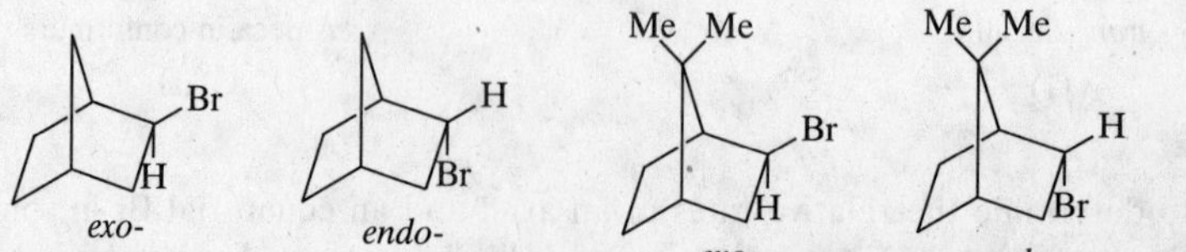

![structures of exo- and endo- bromobicyclo compounds]

exo-   *endo-*   *exo-*   *endo-*

(a)   (b)   **Fig. 5-24**

(*b*) (i) *Exo*. Br$_2$ approaches the intermediate norbornyl radical (see Problem 4.76 for the mechanism) from the *exo* rather than the *endo* side which is hindered by the transannular H's shown in the structure. (ii) *Endo*. The *exo* approach is more hindered by the *gem*-diMe's than the *endo* approach is by the H's.

5.82 Two geometric isomers, **A** and **B**, undergo the following reaction in which **A** gives one diastereomer and **B** gives two diastereomers. Identify **A** and **B**.

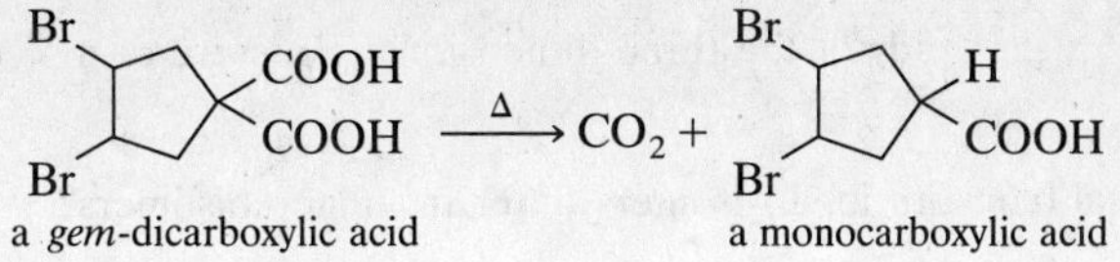

a *gem*-dicarboxylic acid   a monocarboxylic acid

◢ The Br's of the dicarboxylic acid may be *cis* or *trans*. **A** is *trans*—it reacts to yield a single product having one Br *cis* and one Br *trans* to COOH. **B** is *cis*; it reacts to yield two geometric isomers, one with the COOH *cis* and the other *trans* to the Br's.

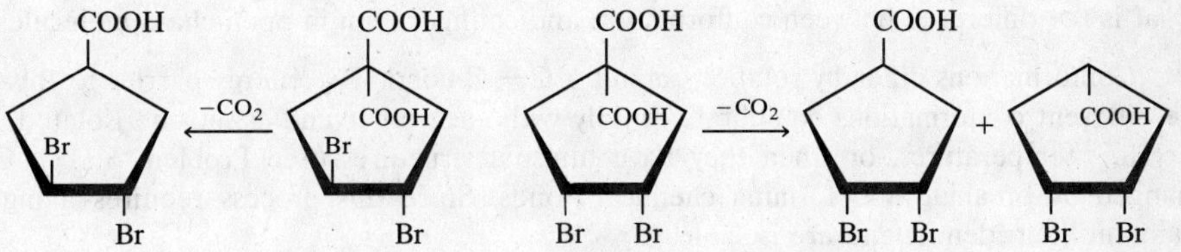

CHAPTER 6
Stereochemistry

DEFINITIONS

6.1   What is stereochemistry?

▮   *Stereochemistry* is the study of the three-dimensional structure of molecules.

6.2   (*a*) How do structural (constitutional) isomers differ from stereoisomers?   (*b*) What is meant by configuration?

▮   (*a*) Structural isomers have the same molecular formula but the atoms are joined in a different order. *Stereoisomers* have the same molecular formula, their atoms are attached in the same order, but they are arranged differently in space.   (*b*) *Configuration* is the spatial arrangement of stereoisomers.

6.3   What is the difference between conformation and configuration in open-chain molecules?

▮   Conformations differ by rotations about a C—C bond. The energy barrier to this rotation is so small that the different conformations equilibrate rapidly with each other and cannot be isolated, except in a few cases at very low temperatures, or when they have unusual structures (See Problem 6.111). Configurations are interchanged by breaking and forming chemical bonds. Since this process requires a high energy, stereoisomers maintain their identity and are isolable.

6.4   Define (*a*) enantiomer and (*b*) diastereomer.

▮   Stereoisomers consist of *enantiomers* (optical isomers) and *diastereomers*.   (*a*) *Enantiomers* are stereoisomers whose mirror images are not identical, i.e., they are not *superposable* on each other, in the same way that a left and right hand are not superposable.   (*b*) *Diastereomers* are stereoisomers which are not mirror images of each other, as for example *cis-trans* isomers in cycloalkanes (see Problems 5.15 and 5.16).

6.5   What is a racemic mixture?

▮   A *racemic mixture*, or racemate, is an equimolar mixture of enantiomers.

6.6   (*a*) What is a chiral molecule?   (*b*) How does it differ from an achiral molecule?

▮   (*a*) A *chiral* molecule is a stereoisomer whose mirror image is not superposable. It lacks a plane or center of symmetry.   (*b*) An *achiral* molecule has a superposable mirror image.

SYMMETRY ELEMENTS

6.7   Define (*a*) a plane and (*b*) a center (or point) of symmetry.

▮   (*a*) A *plane* of symmetry bisects a molecule so that one half of the molecule is the mirror image of the other half.   (*b*) The *center* of symmetry is invariably a point in the center of an object (or molecule). A line extended from any point (or atom) in the object (or molecule) through the center for the same distance meets a similar point (or atom) in the object (or molecule) at an equal distance from the center.

6.8   Identify which of the following objects possess at least one plane of symmetry: (*a*) a tree, (*b*) a glove, (*c*) an ear, (*d*) a nail, (*e*) a cup, (*f*) a filled spool of thread, and (*g*) an empty spool. Draw a mirror plane in all such symmetrical objects.

▮   The objects with at least one plane of symmetry are (*d*), (*e*), and (*g*) as shown in Fig. 6-1. For (*f*), a spool of thread has the thread wound on to it in either a clockwise or counterclockwise fashion.

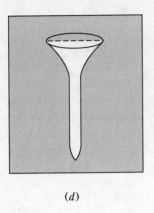

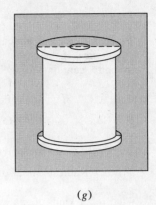

(d)   (e)   (g)

Fig. 6-1

6.9 Find and illustrate which of the following objects possess a center of symmetry: (*a*) a tree, (*b*) a six-pointed star, (*c*) a five-pointed star, (*d*) a dumbbell, (*e*) a nail.

The objects with a center of symmetry are (*b*) and (*d*) as shown in Fig. 6-2

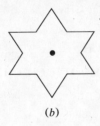
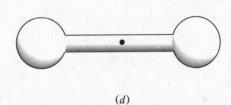

(*b*)   (*d*)   **Fig. 6-2**

6.10 Give the restrictions, if any, on the placement of (*a*) a plane and (*b*) a center of symmetry in a molecule.

(*a*) None. The plane of symmetry can cut atoms in half or cut bonds between atoms. (*b*) Yes. The plane must be at the center of the molecule, either in empty space, in an atom, or in the center of a bond between atoms.

6.11 Draw a hypothetical planar molecule with the formula A_2B_2X (X is the central atom) which has both a center of symmetry and at least two planes of symmetry.

See Fig. 6-3.

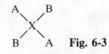

Fig. 6-3

6.12 How many planes of symmetry are present in the structural formula in Problem 6.11?

Three. They are (1) the plane through B—X—B and perpendicular to the plane of the paper, (2) the plane through A—X—A and perpendicular to the plane of the paper, and (3) the plane that cuts through all five atoms. This plane is the plane of the paper.

All planar molecules must be achiral because the plane of the atoms is a plane of symmetry.

CHIRALITY

6.13 What is a chiral center?

A *chiral center* is an atom bonded tetrahedrally to four different atoms or groups of atoms, called *ligands*. A chiral center is usually a C atom, but may be N, S, P, Si, etc. Chiral centers are indicated with an asterisk.

6.14   What is a stereocenter? How is a stereocenter related to a chiral center?

/   If two ligands attached to an atom are switched resulting in a new stereoisomer, the atom is called a *stereocenter*. If the new stereoisomer is an enantiomer, the stereocenter is a chiral center. Not all stereocenters are chiral centers but all chiral centers are stereocenters

6.15   Can the C^+ of a carbocation be a chiral center?

/   No. C^+ uses sp^2 HO's and has a flat geometry; thus it has a plane of symmetry.

6.16   Can a carbon radical be a chiral center?

/   No. Radicals are also sp^2 hybridized and have a plane of symmetry.

6.17   What other kinds of sp^2 hybridized C's cannot be chiral centers?

/ $C{=}C$ in alkenes, $C{=}O$ in aldehydes, ketones, and acid and acid derivatives, and $C{=}N$ in imines and oximes.

6.18   Identify the chiral center in each of the following compounds: (*a*) 2-chlorobutane, (*b*) 1,2-dichloropropane, (*c*) 3-bromo-1-pentene, and (*d*) ethylmethylpropylchlorosilane.

/

$$(a) \quad \underset{\underset{Cl}{|}}{\overset{\overset{H}{|}}{CH_3C^*}}{-}CH_2CH_3, \qquad (b) \quad ClCH_2\underset{\underset{H}{|}}{\overset{\overset{Cl}{|}}{C^*}}{-}CH_3,$$

$$(c) \quad H_2C{=}CH\underset{\underset{Br}{|}}{\overset{\overset{H}{|}}{C^*}}{-}CH_2CH_3, \qquad (d) \quad CH_3CH_2\underset{\underset{Cl}{|}}{\overset{\overset{CH_3}{|}}{Si^*}}{-}CH_2CH_2CH_3$$

Note that in (*d*) the chiral center is an sp^3 hybridized (tetrahedral) Si atom.

6.19   Give examples of N and P serving as stereocenters similar to C and Si.

/

$$\underset{\underset{CH(CH_3)_2}{|}}{CH_3CH_2\,\overset{\overset{CH_3}{|}}{{}^+N^*}}{-}CH_2CH_2CH_3 \qquad \underset{\underset{H}{|}}{CH_3CH_2\,\overset{\overset{CH_3}{|}}{{}^+P^*}}{-}CH_2CH_2CH_3 \qquad \underset{\underset{:\!\ddot{O}:^-}{|}}{CH_3CH_2\,\overset{\overset{CH_3}{|}}{{}^+N^*}}{-}CH_2CH_2CH_3$$

6.20   Can a tertiary amine ($R^1R^2R^3N{:}$) or a carbanion ($R^1R^2R^3C{:}^-$) exist as a pair of enantiomers?

/   Theoretically it can, but not in practice. A rapid "umbrella" type inversion converts either enantiomer to a racemic mixture. The energy required for this inversion is very low at room temperature, thus racemization is unavoidable and, typically, the enantiomers cannot be separated or isolated.

$$R^2\cdots\underset{R^3}{\overset{R^1}{N{:}}} \rightleftharpoons {:}\underset{R^3}{\overset{R^1}{N}}\cdots R^2 \qquad R^2\cdots\underset{R^3}{\overset{R^1}{C{:}^-}} \rightleftharpoons {}^-{:}\underset{R^3}{\overset{R^1}{C}}\cdots R^2$$

inversion

6.21   Tricovalent S and P compounds can be isolated as enantiomers. Explain why and give examples for each.

/   Trivalent S and P atoms have four sp^3 orbitals: three are used for bonding and the fourth for the unshared pair. When central S or P atoms are each bonded to three different ligands, they will be stereocenters. Unlike N and C (second period elements), the energy required for inversion about third period elements is sufficiently high so that the enantiomers can be separated.

$$\left[R^1{-}\underset{\underset{R^3}{|}}{\overset{\overset{+}{\ddot{S}}}{}}{-}R^2 \right] X^- \qquad R^1{-}\underset{\underset{:\ddot{O}:}{\|}}{\ddot{S}}{-}R^2 \qquad R^1{-}\underset{\underset{R^3}{|}}{\ddot{P}}{-}R^2$$

a sulfonium salt   a sulfoxide   a phosphine

6.22 Write the structural formulas for the simplest chiral (*a*) alkane, (*b*) alkene, (*c*) alkyne, (*d*) alcohol, (*e*) aldehyde, (*f*) ketone, (*g*) carboxylic acid, and (*h*) amine.

◢ (*a*)
$$\begin{array}{c} CH_3 \\ | \\ CH_3CH_2CHCH_2CH_2CH_3 \end{array} \text{ or } \begin{array}{c} CH_3 \\ | \\ CH_3CH_2CHCH(CH_3)_2 \end{array}$$
(*b*)
$$\begin{array}{c} CH_3 \\ | \\ CH_3CH_2CHCH{=}CH_2 \end{array}$$

(*c*)
$$\begin{array}{c} CH_3 \\ | \\ CH_3CH_2CHC{\equiv}CH \end{array}$$
(*d*)
$$\begin{array}{c} OH \\ | \\ CH_3CH_2CHCH_3 \end{array}$$
(*e*)
$$\begin{array}{c} CH_3 \\ | \\ CH_3CH_2CHCHO \end{array}$$

(*f*)
$$\begin{array}{c} O \\ \| \\ CH_3CCHCH_2CH_3 \\ | \\ CH_3 \end{array}$$
(*g*)
$$\begin{array}{c} CH_3 \\ | \\ CH_3CH_2CHCOOH \end{array}$$
(*h*)
$$\begin{array}{c} CH_3 \\ | \\ CH_3CH_2CHNH_2 \end{array}$$

OPTICAL ACTIVITY

6.23 Why are enantiomers sometimes called optical isomers?

◢ Enantiomers rotate the plane of polarized light through some angle. Because of this property they are also referred to as *optical isomers* and as being *optically active*.

6.24 (*a*) What is plane-polarized light? (*b*) How is it produced?

◢ A beam of ordinary light has electric and magnetic vibrations (at right angles to each other) in every plane perpendicular to its direction of propagation. Light becomes *plane-polarized* when it is passed through a polarizer (which may be a Nicol prism) and only the electric vibrations in one plane emerge.

6.25 How is plane-polarized light used in the analysis of enantiomers?

◢ Plane-polarized light is produced in an instrument called a *polarimeter*, and passes through a polarimeter tube containing either the liquid enantiomer or its solution. The angle through which the polarized light has been rotated is measured in an analyzer. The observed rotation, α_{obs}, is expressed in degrees. If the polarized light plane is rotated to the left (counterclockwise), the enantiomer is said to be *levorotatory*. A rotation to the right (clockwise) is called *dextrorotatory*. The symbols $(-)$ and $(+)$ designate rotation to the left and right, respectively.

6.26 (*a*) What factors affect the value of α_{obs}? (*b*) What is the specific rotation? (*c*) Can the sign and/or value of the specific rotation of a molecule be deduced from its structure?

◢ (*a*) Since the rotation of polarized light is caused by interaction of the photon of light with an enantiomeric molecule, the extent of rotation is a function of the structure of the molecules and their number in the path of the light beam; the latter depends on the concentration and the length of the tube containing the enantiomer. Other factors are: the solvent (if present), the temperature, and the wavelength of the light used. (*b*) The *specific rotation*, $[\alpha]_D$, defined to make it independent of these factors, is a true physical constant: $[\alpha]_D = \alpha_{obs}/\ell c$, where α_{obs} is the observed rotation, in degrees, in a sample cell whose path length, ℓ, is in decimeters (dm), and the concentration, c, is in g/mL. For pure liquids the density in g/mL is used. The subscript D tells us that the wavelength of light used is the D line of the sodium spectrum. The temperature is indicated by a superscript, and is usually 25 °C, thus $[\alpha]_D^{25°}$. (*c*) No!

6.27 (*a*) Calculate the specific rotation of coniine, the toxic component of poison hemlock, if a solution containing 0.75 g/10 mL is placed in a 1-dm polarimeter tube and its observed rotation at 25 °C (D line) is $+1.2°$. (*b*) What is the specific rotation of the enantiomer of coniine?

◢ (*a*) $[\alpha]_D = +1.2°/(1)(0.075) = +16°$. (*b*) $-16°$.

6.28 (*a*) Find the observed rotation of a solution of coniine (Problem 6.27) containing 0.35 g/mL as measured in a 5.0-cm tube (D line). (*b*) What is the observed rotation if (i) the concentration is doubled and (ii) the length of the tube is doubled? (*c*) What is the specific rotation if the concentration or the length of the tube is doubled?

◢ (*a*) $\alpha_{obs} = [\alpha]_D(\ell c) = +16°(0.50)(0.35) = +2.8°$. (*b*) (i) Doubling the concentration doubles the observed rotation because the number of molecules in the path of the light beam doubles, therefore $\alpha_{obs} = +5.6°$. (ii) Doubling the length of the tube also doubles the number of molecules encountered by the light beam; again $\alpha_{obs} = +5.6°$. (*c*) The specific rotation is a constant and is independent of concentration and path length.

6.29   Calculate the concentration of a solution of coniine (Problem 6.27) with an observed rotation of $+2.0°$ in a 1.0-dm tube (D line).

�/   Concentration = (observed rotation)/(specific rotation × length of tube) = $+2.0°/16° × 1.0 = 0.125$ g/mL or 0.13 g/mL

6.30   How can we decide whether an observed rotation of a solution of an optically active compound is $+170°$ and not actually $-190°$?

�/   If the tube length or the concentration is halved, a compound that is dextrorotatory will rotate the plane-polarized light to one half of its previous rotation, or $+85°$, but if it is levorotatory, the observed rotation will be $-95°$.

6.31   A newly discovered compound is thought to be chiral, but shows no rotation in a specific solvent. Does this mean that the compound is assuredly achiral?

�/   No. It might be racemic (Problem 6.5). If not, it may be fortuitous that there is no rotation in the solvent used. If there is no rotation in two other solvents, the compound is probably achiral. Also, if the wavelength of the light used is changed, rotation may occur.

6.32   The specific rotation of a pure enantiomer is $+12°$. What will be its observed rotation if it is isolated from a reaction with (**a**) 20% racemization and 80% retention and (**b**) 80% racemization and 20% inversion?

▲   (**a**) $\alpha_{obs} = 0.80(+12°) = +9.6°$; (**b**) $\alpha_{obs} = 0.20(-12°) = -2.4°$.

6.33   *Optical purity* (OP) $\equiv (\alpha_{obs}/[\alpha]_D) × 100\%$.   (**a**) What is the OP of a sample isolated from a reaction having an $\alpha_{obs} = +6.0°$ if $[\alpha]_D = +12°$?   (**b**) Calculate the molar % composition. (Assume all measurements are taken in a 1.0-dm tube at the same concentrations and with the same wavelength.)

▲   (**a**) OP $= (+6.0°/+12°) × 100\% = 50\%$.   (**b**) The mixture has 50% (+) and 50% (±), which is the same as 75% (+) and 25% (−).

6.34   What is the percentage composition of a mixture of the two enantiomers in Problem 6.32 whose rotation is $-9.0°$?

▲   The OP $(-9°/-12°) × 100\% = 75\%$ so 75% of the mixture consists of (−) enantiomer and 25% is the racemate. The total % of (−) is thus $75\% + \frac{1}{2}(25\%) = 87.5\%$, and the remaining 12.5% is (+).

ABSOLUTE AND RELATIVE CONFIGURATION

6.35   (**a**) Define the absolute configuration of an enantiomer.   (**b**) What are the rules for designating an enantiomer as R (from *rectus*, Latin for right) or S (from *sinister*, Latin for left)?   (**c**) Illustrate with 1-chloro-1-bromoethane, $ClBrCHCH_3$.

▲   (**a**) Absolute configuration is the special arrangement of substituents attached to a chiral center.   (**b**) A priority sequence (proposed by Cahn, Ingold, and Prelog) is assigned to the four ligands attached to the chiral center. The directly-attached atom having the highest atomic number has the highest priority, and the other ligand atoms follow in order of decreasing atomic numbers. When two ligands are isotopes, i.e., H and D, the one with the higher atomic weight has the higher priority. The molecule is then visualized with the ligand of lowest priority directed away from the viewer, behind the plane of the paper. The arrangement of the other ligands determines the classification: if the sequence from the highest to the lowest priority is clockwise, the molecule is specified *R*, and if the sequence is counterclockwise, the molecule is called *S*.   (**c**) The priority sequence is $Br > Cl > CH_3 > H$. The configurations and designations are:

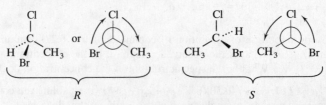

6.36   Assign priorities to the following pairs of ligands: (**a**) CH_3- and CH_3CH_2-; (**b**) $(CH_3)_3C-$ and $(CH_3)_2CH-$; (**c**) $(CH_3)_2CH-$ and $CH_2=CH-$; (**d**) $HC\equiv C-$ and $(CH_3)_3C-$; and (**e**) $O=CH-$ and $HC\equiv C-$.

(**a**) Since both ligands have a C bonded to the chiral atom, the priority is determined by moving to the next atom in the chain. In the case of $-CH_3$ these are H, H, and H. For the CH_2 portion of CH_3CH_2- these are H, H, and C, clearly a higher priority.

(**b**) Using the same approach, *t*-butyl has three methyl groups attached to the C giving it priority over isopropyl, which has two methyl groups and an H.

(**c**) Where there is a multiple bond, the multiply-bonded atoms are counted twice for a double bond and three times for a triple bond. Thus, $CH_2=CH-(C,C,H)$ has priority over $CH_3CH_2-(C,H,H)$. Isopropyl is also (C,C,H) and therefore we move to the next atom in the chain as shown:

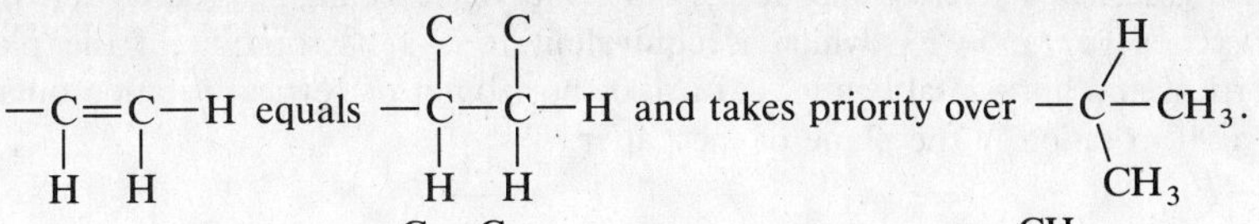

$$-C=C-H \text{ equals } -C-C-H \text{ and takes priority over } -C-CH_3.$$

(**d**) $HC\equiv C-$ equals $H-C-C-$ and takes priority over $-C-CH_3.$

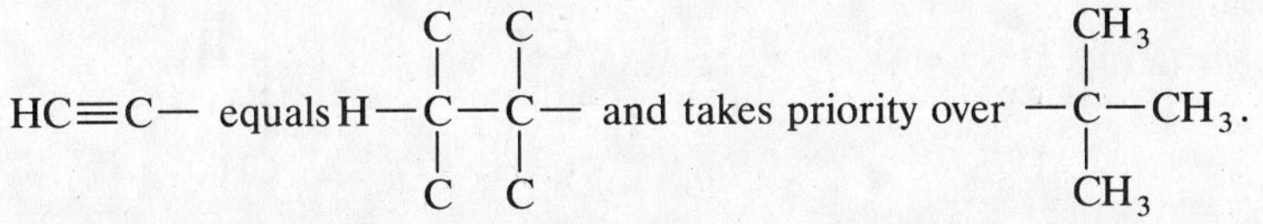

(**e**) $O=CH-$ equals $C-O-C$ and takes priority over $H-C\equiv C-.$

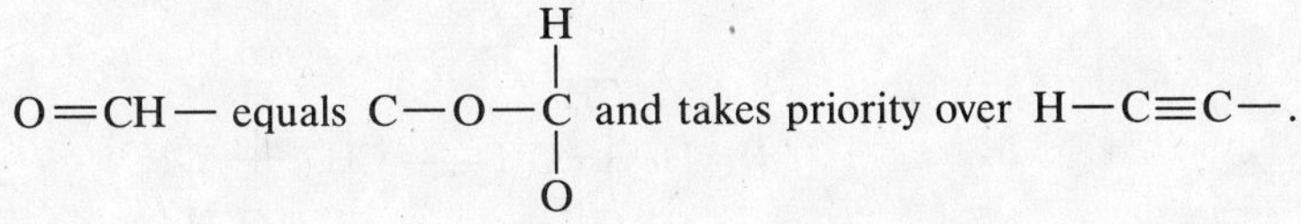

6.37 What is the priority sequence of the alkyl groups?

◢ $3° > 2° > 1° > CH_3.$

6.38 Arrange the following ligands in decreasing order of priority: (**a**) $-CH(OH)CH_3$, $-OH$, $-COOH$, $-CH_2OH$ and (**b**) $-CH_2NH_2$, $-NO_2$, $-C\equiv N$, $-NH_2$

◢ (**a**) $OH > COOH > CH(OH)CH_3 > CH_2OH$. (**b**) $NO_2 > NH_2 > C\equiv N > CH_2NH_2$.

6.39 Arrange the following ligands in decreasing order of priority: (**a**) $(CH_3)_2CH-$ and cyclohexyl, (**b**) cyclohexyl and phenyl, —⬡—, (**c**) phenyl and $(CH_3)_3C-$.

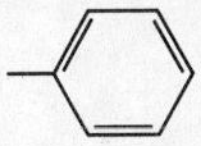

◢ (**a**) Cyclohexyl $> (CH_3)_2CH$, because the once-removed methyl C's each have three H's while the once-removed ring C's each have two H's and another ring C. (**b**) Phenyl $>$ cyclohexyl, because the phenyl C is doubly bonded and counted as attached to three C's (Problem 6.36). (**c**) Phenyl $> (CH_3)_3C$.

6.40 Assign *R* and *S* designations to the following compounds:

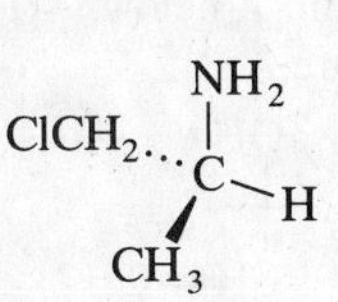

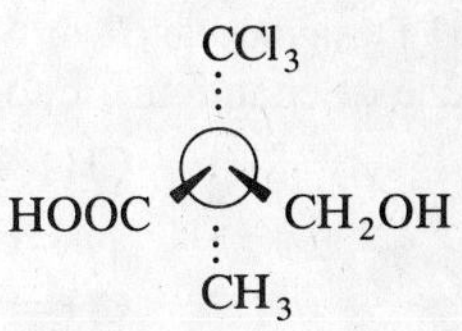

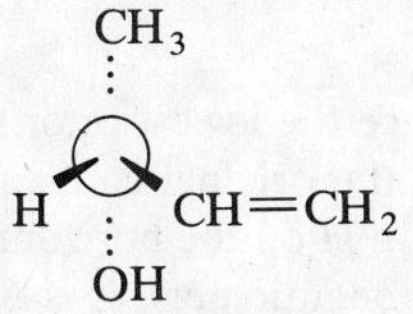

◢ (**a**) *R*, (**b**) *S*, (**c**) *S*, (**d**) *R*.

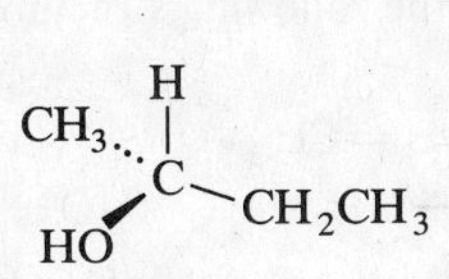

6.41 Convert the structures in Problem 6.35 to Fischer projection formulas.

◢ In the Fischer formula, the chiral atom is not drawn; it is at the crossing of a horizontal and a vertical line. The horizontal bonds project out of the plane of the paper, toward the viewer, and the vertical bonds project behind the plane of the paper, away from the viewer. Tip the Cl back so the H and Cl are behind the plane with the Cl on top and the H below. The Me and Br both project in front of the paper on the horizontal, the Me to the right and Br to the left of the viewer. For the S enantiomer the Cl is tipped to the back.

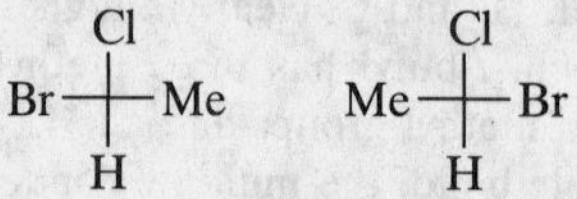

$$
\begin{array}{cc}
\text{Cl} & \text{Cl} \\
\text{Br}\!-\!\!\!+\!\!\!-\text{Me} & \text{Me}\!-\!\!\!+\!\!\!-\text{Br} \\
\text{H} & \text{H} \\
R & S
\end{array}
$$

6.42 Determine the effect, if any, on the configuration of (S)-2-butanol on performing each of the following operations: (*a*) exchanging ligands across the horizontal bond (*b*) exchanging ligands across the vertical bond, (*c*) making both switches (*a*) and (*b*) (which is equivalent to a 180° rotation in the plane of the paper), (*d*) exchanging a vertical and horizontal ligand, (*e*) a 180° horizontal or vertical rotation outside of the plane of the paper, and (*f*) a 90° rotation in the plane of the paper.

$$S \longrightarrow R \qquad\qquad\qquad S \longrightarrow R$$

(*a*) $\begin{array}{c}\text{CH}_3\\ \text{H}\!-\!\!+\!\!-\text{OH}\\ \text{C}_2\text{H}_5\end{array} \longrightarrow \begin{array}{c}\text{CH}_3\\ \text{HO}\!-\!\!+\!\!-\text{H}\\ \text{C}_2\text{H}_5\end{array}$
(*b*) $\begin{array}{c}\text{CH}_3\\ \text{H}\!-\!\!+\!\!-\text{OH}\\ \text{C}_2\text{H}_5\end{array} \longrightarrow \begin{array}{c}\text{C}_2\text{H}_5\\ \text{H}\!-\!\!+\!\!-\text{OH}\\ \text{CH}_3\end{array}$

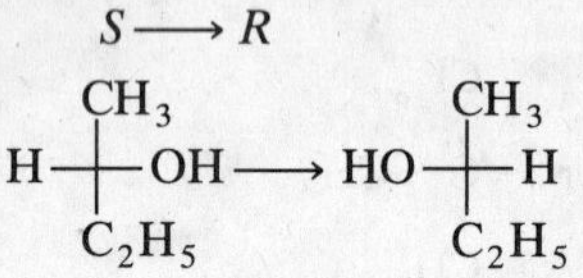

$$S \longrightarrow R$$

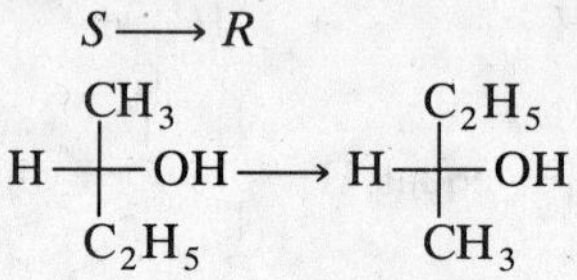

(*c*) no change
(*d*) $\begin{array}{c}\text{CH}_3\\ \text{H}\!-\!\!+\!\!-\text{OH}\\ \text{C}_2\text{H}_5\end{array} \longrightarrow \begin{array}{c}\text{H}\\ \text{CH}_3\!-\!\!+\!\!-\text{OH}\\ \text{C}_2\text{H}_5\end{array}$

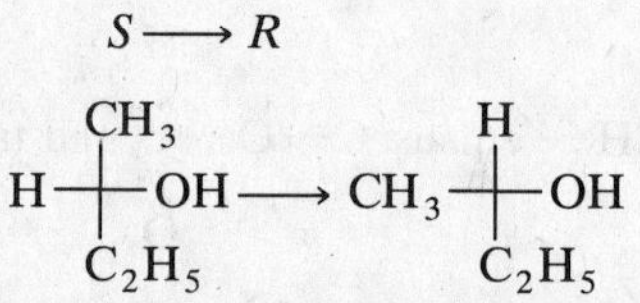

(*e*) Fischer projections cannot be used in this operation because in any flipping out of the plane of the paper (side-to-side or top-to-bottom) the ligands formerly projecting behind the plane of the paper end up projecting toward the viewer, and those formerly pointing to the viewer end up behind the plane of the paper. (*f*) This operation cannot be used with Fischer diagrams. Writing **A** as **A′** presumes that the H and OH project behind the plane, but a 90° (or any other) rotation in the plane does not change the projection of bonds toward or away from the viewer.

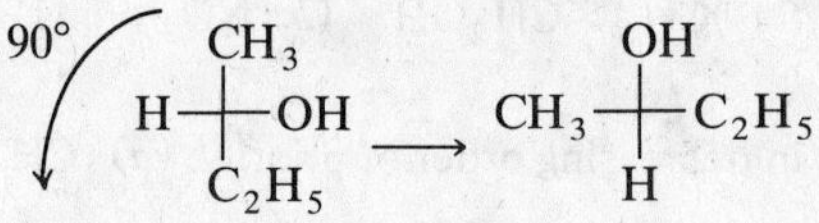

$$
90° \curvearrowleft \quad \begin{array}{c}\text{CH}_3\\ \text{H}\!-\!\!+\!\!-\text{OH}\\ \text{C}_2\text{H}_5\end{array} \longrightarrow \begin{array}{c}\text{OH}\\ \text{CH}_3\!-\!\!+\!\!-\text{C}_2\text{H}_5\\ \text{H}\end{array}
$$

$$\mathbf{A} \qquad\qquad \mathbf{A'}$$

6.43 What are the general rules for switching ligands or rotating Fischer structures?

(*1*) An even number of switches results in no change in the configuration. (*2*) An odd number of switches changes the configuration to that of the enantiomer. (*3*) The structure cannot be rotated out of the plane of the paper. (*4*) Any rotation of Fischer projections that interconverts horizontal and vertical ligands is not allowed. Hence, the structure can be rotated in the plane through 180°, but not through 90°.

6.44 (*a*) Designate as R or S the structure **A** below. (*b*) Identify the following structures **B**, **C**, and **D** as either the same or enantiomeric to the structure **A**.

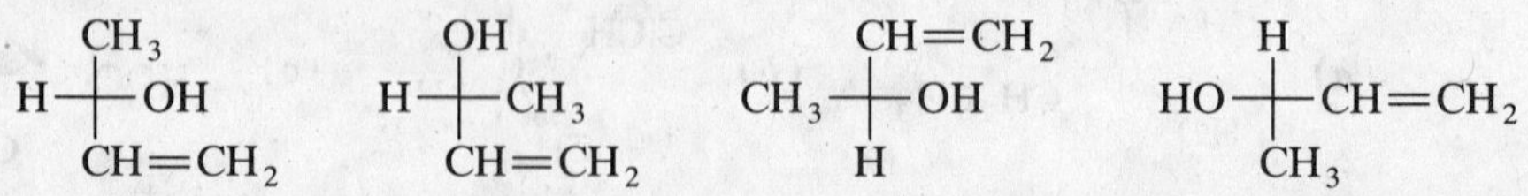

$$
\begin{array}{cccc}
\text{CH}_3 & \text{OH} & \text{CH}\!=\!\text{CH}_2 & \text{H}\\
\text{H}\!-\!\!+\!\!-\text{OH} & \text{H}\!-\!\!+\!\!-\text{CH}_3 & \text{CH}_3\!-\!\!+\!\!-\text{OH} & \text{HO}\!-\!\!+\!\!-\text{CH}\!=\!\text{CH}_2\\
\text{CH}\!=\!\text{CH}_2 & \text{CH}\!=\!\text{CH}_2 & \text{H} & \text{CH}_3\\
\mathbf{A} & \mathbf{B} & \mathbf{C} & \mathbf{D}
\end{array}
$$

(*a*) The priority order is OH > CH=CH$_2$ > CH$_3$ > H. Since the lowest priority (H) is on the horizontal, H is moved to the vertical by making any two switches preserving the original configuration. The structure is then found to be S. Alternately, the priority order in the original **A** with H on the horizontal is R, but this is wrong and the molecule is actually S. (*b*) Similarly, structure **B** is R (the enantiomer), **C** is S (identical), and **D** is R.

6.45 Identify each of the following as R or S:

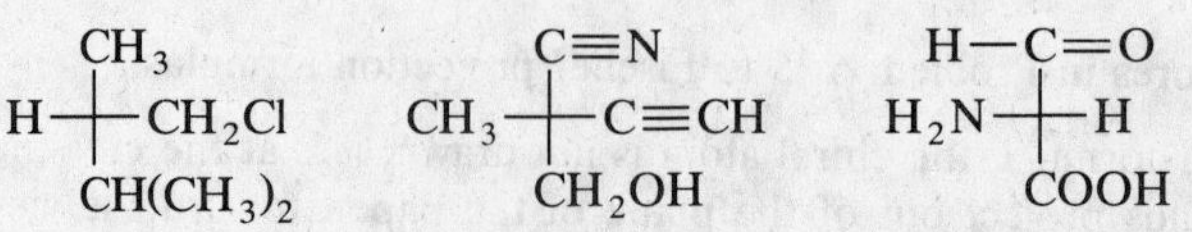

$$
\begin{array}{ccc}
\text{CH}_3 & \text{C}\!\equiv\!\text{N} & \text{H}\!-\!\text{C}\!=\!\text{O}\\
\text{H}\!-\!\!+\!\!-\text{CH}_2\text{Cl} & \text{CH}_3\!-\!\!+\!\!-\text{C}\!\equiv\!\text{CH} & \text{H}_2\text{N}\!-\!\!+\!\!-\text{H}\\
\text{CH(CH}_3)_2 & \text{CH}_2\text{OH} & \text{COOH}\\
\mathbf{E} & \mathbf{F} & \mathbf{G}
\end{array}
$$

In **E**, the priority order is $CH_2Cl > CH(CH_3)_2 > CH_3 > H$. The compound is S. In **F**, the priority order is $CH_2OH > CN > C\equiv CH > CH_3$. The compound is S. —CH_2OH has priority over $C\equiv N$ because one O counts before three N's. In **G**, the priority order is $NH_2 > COOH > CHO > H$. The compound is R.

6.46 Draw Fischer structures for (*a*) (*R*)- and (*S*)-2-butanol, $CH_3CH(OH)CH_2CH_3$ and (*b*) (*R*)- and (*S*)-glyceraldehyde (2,3-dihydroxypropanal, $HOCH_2CH(OH)CHO$).

∕   (*a*)
$$
\begin{array}{cc}
CH_3 & CH_3 \\
HO\!-\!\!\!\vert\!-\!H & H\!-\!\!\!\vert\!-\!OH \\
C_2H_5 & C_2H_5 \\
R & S
\end{array}
$$
(*b*)
$$
\begin{array}{cc}
HC\!=\!O & HC\!=\!O \\
H\!-\!\!\!\vert\!-\!OH & HO\!-\!\!\!\vert\!-\!H \\
CH_2OH & CH_2OH \\
R & S
\end{array}
$$

6.47 (*a*) What is the relationship, if any, between the sign of rotation of a chiral compound $(+)$ or $(-)$ and its designation as R or S?   (*b*) Give three ways of labeling a racemate.

∕   (*a*) None whatsoever. Sign of rotation is a molecular property unrelated to configuration.   (*b*) Racemic or *rac.*, (R,S), and $(\pm)$.

6.48 Esterification of $(-)$-lactic acid with methanol gives $(+)$-methyl lactate:

$$CH_3CH(OH)COOH + CH_3OH \xrightarrow{\text{HCl}} CH_3CH(OH)COOCH_3 + H_2O.$$

Has the configuration changed?

∕   No. Even though the sign of rotation changes, there is no changing of bonds to the chiral C.

6.49 The D, L method for assigning *relative configurations* (used mainly for sugars) uses glyceraldehyde [Problem 6.46(*b*)] as the reference molecule. Identify the R and S structures as D or L.

∕   As the molecule is shown [in Problem 6.46(*b*)], with the aldehyde group on the top and the primary alcohol group on the bottom, the R structure with an OH pointing out to the right is D and the S enantiomer, with the OH on the left side is L.

6.50 The naturally-occurring amino acids, the building blocks of proteins, are all L-amino acids. Identify the following Fischer formula for L-alanine (2-aminopropanoic acid) as either R or S.

$$
\begin{array}{c}
COOH \\
H_2N\!-\!\!\!\vert\!-\!H \\
CH_3
\end{array}
$$

∕   For L-amino acids, COOH is always placed at the top in the Fischer projection, the carbon chain runs vertically, and NH_2 is on the left. The compound is S. (Amino acids differ from one another by the nature of the alkyl group, in this case CH_3.)

6.51 Draw a Fischer projection for the naturally occurring amino acid, proline, and give its R/S designation.

∕   In proline the chiral C is part of a five-membered ring. It is attached to an N (the amino group) and this part of the ring has first priority. The carboxyl group is second and the C in the ring attached to the chiral C is third. The compound is S.

$$
\begin{array}{c}
COOH \\
HN\!-\!\!\!\vert\!-\!H \\
CH_2
\end{array}
$$

6.52 Does the R/S designation for the other naturally occurring amino acids differ from that of alanine if the only difference between them is the change from a methyl group to a different alkyl group?

∕   No. Regardless of the kind of the alkyl group the priority order will not change. The sequence will still be $NH_2 > COOH > R > H$.

$$
\begin{array}{c}
COOH \\
H_2N\!-\!\!\!\vert\!-\!H \\
R
\end{array}
$$

MOLECULES WITH MORE THAN ONE CHIRAL CENTER

6.53 (*a*) Draw all the stereoisomers of 3-chloro-2-pentanol, $CH_3CH(OH)CHClCH_2CH_3$. (*b*) Give the stereochemical relationships of the stereoisomers.

▮ (*a*) There are four stereoisomers. **A** and **B** are enantiomers, as are **C** and **D**. (*b*) **A** and **B** are diastereomers of **C** and **D**.

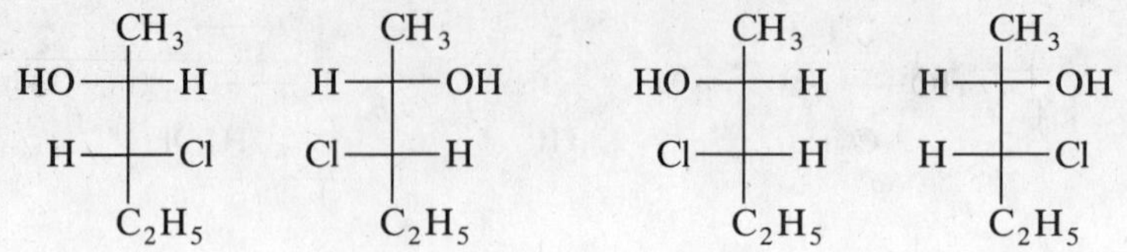

racemate₁ .... racemate₂

6.54 (*a*) How is the *R/S* designation of a compound with more than one chiral center determined? (*b*) Illustrate with the 3-chloro-2-pentanols shown in Problem 6.53.

▮ (*a*) The configuration about each chiral carbon is determined separately, and numbers are used to specify each carbon. (*b*) At C^2, the four ligands and their priority order are: OH > the carbon chain $CH(Cl)CH_3$ > CH_3 > H. The configuration is *R*. The priority order of the four ligands attached to C^3 are: Cl > the carbon chain $CH(OH)CH_2CH_3$ > CH_2CH_3 > H. The C^3 configuration is also *R*. The full name of **A** is (2*R*,3*R*)-3-chloro-2-pentanol, and **B**, its mirror image, is (2*S*,3*S*). **C** is (2*R*,3*S*), and its mirror image **D** is (2*S*,3*R*).

6.55 Give the *R/S* designation for each of the stereoisomers of 1,3-dibromo-2-methylbutane.

▮ There are two chiral C's (C^2 and C^3), and the four stereoisomers are shown below with their *R/S* designation.

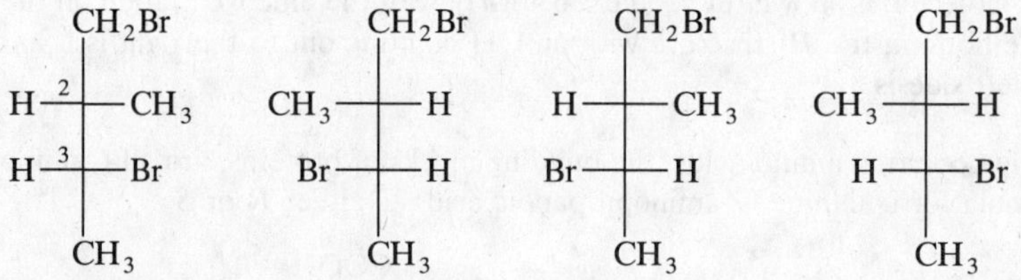

6.56 (*a*) Theoretically, what is the maximum number of possible stereoisomers of a compound having *n* dissimilar chiral atoms? (*b*) What is the maximum number of stereoisomers possible for a compound having (i) three and (ii) four different chiral centers?

▮ (*a*) A compound with *n* different chiral atoms can have 2^n stereoisomers. (*b*) (i) $2^3 = 8$ (four racemic pairs of enantiomers). (ii) $2^4 = 16$ (eight racemic pairs of enantiomers).

6.57 Compare the physical and chemical properties of diastereomers.

▮ Diastereomers have different physical properties, e.g., melting and boiling points, refractive indices, solubilities in different solvents, crystalline structures, and specific rotations. Because of their differences in solubility they often can be separated from each other by fractional crystallization; because of slight differences in molecular shape and polarity, they often can be separated from each other by chromatography. Diastereomers have different chemical properties toward both chiral and achiral reagents. Neither any two diastereomers nor their transition states are mirror images of each other and so will not necessarily have the same energies. The $\Delta H^{\ddagger}$'s will be somewhat different and thus the rates of reaction will differ. However, since the diastereomers have the same functional groups, their chemical properties are not too dissimilar.

6.58 Compare chemical and physical properties of (*a*) enantiomers and (*b*) an enantiomer and its racemic form.

▮ (*a*) The chemical properties of enantiomers are the same toward achiral reagents, solvents, catalysts, and conditions. Towards chiral reagents, solvents, catalysts, and conditions, enantiomers react at different rates. The transition states produced from the chiral reactant and the individual enantiomers are not mirror images. They are diastereomeric, and hence have different enthalpies; the $\Delta H^{\ddagger}$ values are different, as are the rates of reaction and the amounts of product formed. With the exception of rotation of plane-polarized light, enantiomers have identical physical properties. e.g., boiling and melting points, and solubility.   (*b*) The chemical properties are the same towards achiral reagents, but chiral reagents react at different rates. Enantiomers are optically active; the racemate is optically inactive–it does not rotate the plane of polarized light. Other physical properties, such as crystalline form, melting point, and solubility, of an enantiomer and its racemate may differ.

6.59   (*a*) How many stereoisomers of 2,3-butanediol, $CH_3CH(OH)CH(OH)CH_3$, are possible?   (*b*) Draw them.

◢   (*a*) We might expect that four stereoisomers are possible ($2^n = 4$). An allowed 180° rotation of **G** in the plane of the paper gives **H**; **G** and **H** are superposable and thus identical, and so there are only three stereoisomers. The stereoisomer **G** or **H** is called the *meso* form, and it is achiral and optically inactive.   (*b*) See Fig. 6-4.

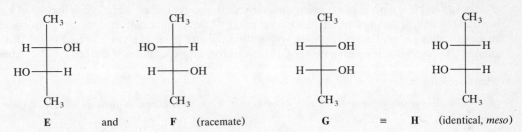

Fig. 6-4

6.60   (*a*) Why is a *meso* compound achiral?   (*b*) What structural feature must a *meso* compound have?

◢   (*a*) At least one conformer has either a plane or a point of symmetry, which makes it superposable upon its mirror image. (See, for example, **G** and **H** in Problem 6.59.) (*b*) It must have at least one pair of similar stereocenters.

6.61   Draw *meso*-2,3-butanediol (*a*) in the Fischer representation showing a plane of symmetry and (*b*) in the sawhorse representation showing (i) a plane in the eclipsed conformer, and (ii) a point in a staggered conformer.

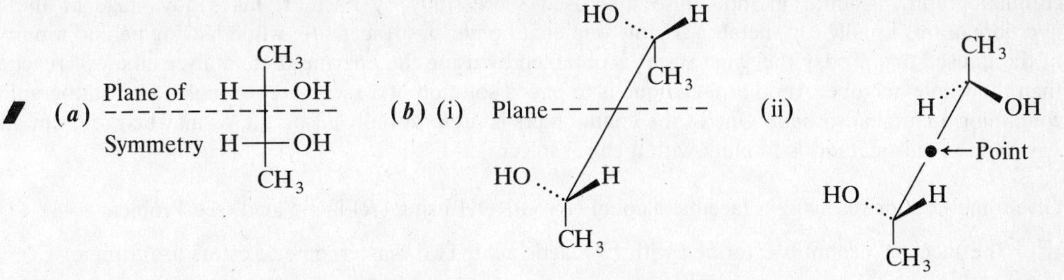

◢   (*a*)

```
           CH3
Plane of  H――OH
Symmetry  H――OH
           CH3
```

(*b*) (i) Plane ----/---- (ii)

6.62   (*a*) How can a *meso* compound be recognized in the Newman projection?   (*b*) Illustrate with *meso*-2,3-butanediol.

◢   (*a*) Rotate about the C — C bond to get a staggered conformer with a point of symmetry, **A**, or an eclipsed conformation with a plane of symmetry, **B**. (*b*) See Fig. 6-5.

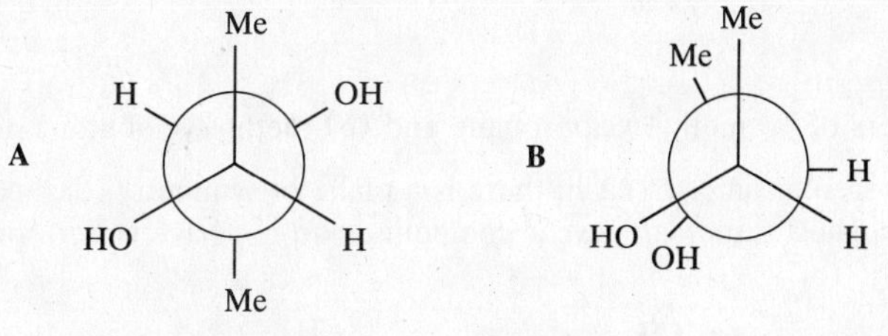

Fig. 6-5

6.63   What is the *R/S* designation for *meso*-2,3-butanediol?

◢   Since the $2R,3S$ structure is identical with the $2S,3R$ structure, it can be called either R,S or S,R. (Numbers are not necessary because the two designations are equivalent.)

6.64 Why are the following stereoisomers *meso*?

$$
\begin{array}{ccc}
& CH_3 & \\
H &\!\!\!-\!\!\!& Cl \\
(a)\quad Br &\!\!\!-\!\!\!& H \\
H &\!\!\!-\!\!\!& Cl \\
& CH_3 &
\end{array}
\qquad
\begin{array}{ccc}
& CH_3 & \\
H &\!\!\!-\!\!\!& OH \\
(b)\quad H &\!\!\!-\!\!\!& Cl \\
H &\!\!\!-\!\!\!& OH \\
& CH_3 &
\end{array}
\qquad
\begin{array}{ccc}
& Cl & \\
CH_3 &\!\!\!-\!\!\!& H \\
(c)\quad & (CH_2)_n & \\
CH_3 &\!\!\!-\!\!\!& H \\
& Cl &
\end{array}
$$

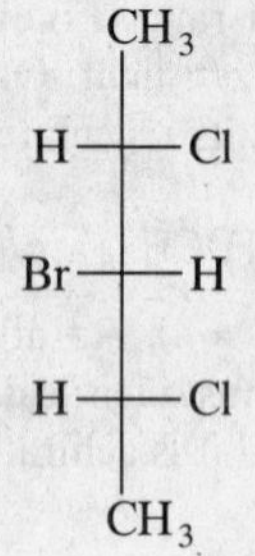

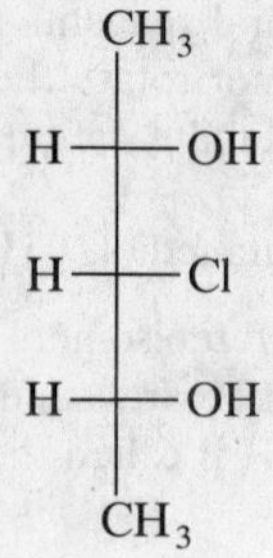

� In (*a*) and (*b*), a plane of symmetry cuts through the center carbon and the two horizontal ligands revealing that the top half of the molecule is the mirror image of the bottom half. It does not matter which ligands are attached to this carbon because they are within the symmetry plane. This is also true in (*c*) if $n = 1$ or an odd number. However, if n is an even number, the symmetry plane cuts through the central C—C bond.

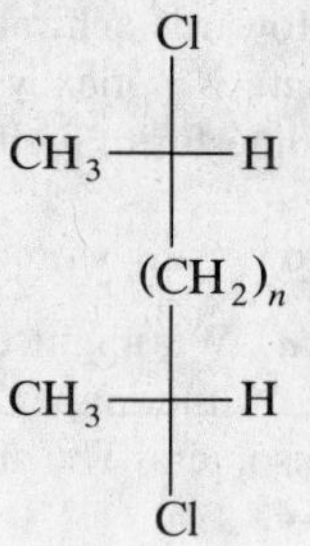

6.65 What is resolution?

▮ *Resolution* is the separation of two enantiomers from each other. A mixture of enantiomers is said to be *resolvable*.

6.66 Give methods for resolving a racemate.

▮ Both physical and chemical properties of enantiomers toward achiral reagents are identical (Problems 6.57 and 6.58). In rare cases the crystals of (+) enantiomer can be hand separated from those of the (−) enantiomer of the racemate. This is the method used by Louis Pasteur (the chiral agent) in 1848 with a microscope and a pair of tweezers, and it was possible only because he noticed that the sodium ammonium salt of racemic tartaric acid crystallized into mirror image crystals that were large and well formed. Pasteur was also the first investigator to resolve a racemate chemically, and his method is used today. An optically pure compound, for example, a (+) base, is reacted with a racemic acid, resulting in two salts: a (+)(+) salt and a (−)(+) salt. Since these are diastereomers, they have different solubilities and are separable by fractional crystallization, after which the enantiomers are recovered. If the diastereomers are liquids, they may be separable by fractional distillation, or chromatography. A third method, also first used successfully by Pasteur, takes advantage of the fact that microorganisms usually can metabolize only one enantiomer of a racemate, while leaving behind a pure solution of the unused one. Today the same result is obtained by using the enzyme that catalyzes the cell reaction rather than the whole microbe. Another technique is to pass a solution of a racemate through a chromatography column containing a chiral adsorbent. One of the enantiomers is preferentially adsorbed, or may be preferentially eluted. A variant of this method is to elute with a chiral solvent.

6.67 Give a method for resolving a racemic alcohol (R, S)-ROH using (R)-lactic acid (see Problem 6.48).

▮ The racemic alcohol is esterified with (R)-lactic acid. Two diastereomeric esters are formed:

$$(R)\text{-ROH} + (R)\text{-CH}_3\text{CH(OH)COOH} \longrightarrow \text{CH}_3\text{CH(OH)COOR} \,(R, R)$$
$$(S)\text{-ROH} + (R)\text{-CH}_3\text{CH(OH)COOH} \longrightarrow \text{CH}_3\text{CH(OH)COOR} \,(S, R)$$

These are separated by one of the methods in Problem 6.66. The separated alcohols are regenerated by hydrolyzing the separated esters with aq. NaOH to ROH and the acid.

CYCLIC COMPOUNDS

6.68 How many stereoisomers of (a) methylcyclopropane and (*b*) methylcyclobutane are possible? Draw them.

▮ See Fig. 6-6. One stereoisomer of each; there is a plane of symmetry (dashed line) through the CH_3 and H bisecting the ring. Monosubstituted carbocyclic compounds do not have stereoisomers.

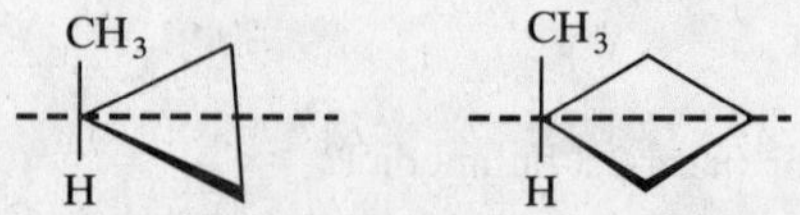

Fig. 6-6

6.69 Draw all the stereoisomers of (*a*) 1,2-dimethylcyclopropane, (*b*) 1,2-dimethylcyclobutane, and (*c*) 1,3-dimethyl-cyclobutane.

For (*a*) and (*b*) see Fig. 6-7. Three each: *cis*-1,2 are meso, and *trans*-1,2 exist as a pair of enantiomers in each case.

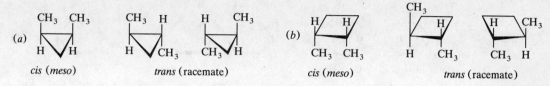

(*a*)   cis (meso)   trans (racemate)   (*b*)   cis (meso)   trans (racemate)

Fig. 6-7

(*c*) See Fig. 6-8. Two: *cis*-1,3 has a plane of symmetry; *trans*-1,3 has a plane and a center of symmetry. In both isomers C^1 and C^3 are stereocenters (Problem 6.14). Switching H and Me converts one stereoisomer to another.

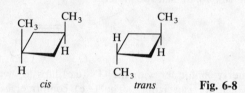

cis   trans   **Fig. 6-8**

6.70 Draw all the stereoisomers of 1,2- and 1,3-dimethylcyclopentanes.

See Fig. 6-9. Cyclopentane is best considered as a flat ring. All *trans*-isomers exist as a pair of enantiomers. All *cis*-isomers are *meso*.

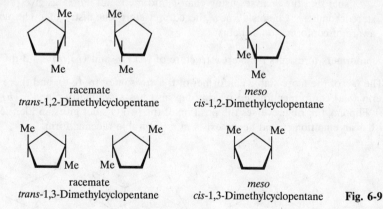

racemate
trans-1,2-Dimethylcyclopentane

meso
cis-1,2-Dimethylcyclopentane

racemate
trans-1,3-Dimethylcyclopentane

meso
cis-1,3-Dimethylcyclopentane   **Fig. 6-9**

6.71 (*a*) Make a general statement about the number of stereoisomers in disubstituted carbocyclic rings with *identical* ligands (both G). (*b*) Illustrate your statement with the disubstituted cyclohexanes.

(*a*) All *cis*-disubstituted cycloalkanes with the same ligands are achiral having a plane of symmetry. If the G's are not at opposite ends of the ring; i.e., 1,3 in a cyclobutane and 1,4 in a cyclohexane, the stereoisomer is *meso*. All *trans*-disubstituted cycloalkanes exist as a pair of enantiomers, unless the G's are at the opposite ends of a ring with an even number of C's. These and the *cis* compounds have no asymmetric C's, and the molecules are achiral. The correct number of stereoisomers is obtained by assuming the rings are flat, even though they may not be.

(*b*) See Fig. 6-10.

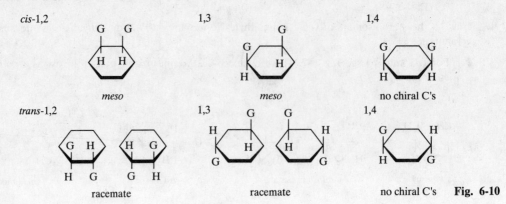

Fig. 6-10

6.72 Use chair conformers to discuss the stereochemistry of (*a*) *cis*- and (*b*) *trans*-1,2-diG-cyclohexanes.

 (*a*) In one conformer of the *cis*- isomer one (G) is (e) and the other is (a) (see Problem 5.38). Through ring flip this conformer is in rapid equilibrium with the other chair conformer, where the G's change position; the (e) becomes (a) and the (a) becomes (e). Although each equal-energy conformer is chiral, the molecule is achiral because these conformers are enantiomers comprising an optically inactive, nonresolvable *conformational racemate*.

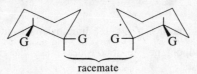

 (*b*) The lower energy conformer with the G's (e,e) flips to give the higher energy (less prevalent) (a,a) conformer which we can ignore. The (e,e) conformer, as well as the (a,a) conformer, has an enantiomer and hence exists as a resolvable racemate.

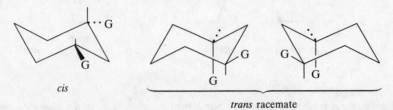

racemate

Note that the analyses using chair conformers and flat rings give the same answer about the ring stereochemistry. Chemists knew the correct stereochemistry of cyclic compounds before they were aware of conformational theory.

6.73 Use chair conformers to discuss the stereostructure of (*a*) *cis*- and (*b*) *trans*-1,3-diG-cyclohexanes.

 (*a*) The G's of the more stable conformer of the *cis*-isomer are (e,e), and there is a plane of symmetry. The higher energy (a,a) conformer formed by ring flip also has a symmetry plane. (*b*) Here one G is (e) and the other is (a). Flipping the ring reverses the position of the two G's but gives an identical structure. This *trans*-(e,a) conformer has an enantiomer and hence exists in a resolvable racemic form.

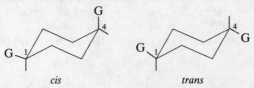

cis

trans racemate

6.74 Show that both *cis*- and *trans*-1,4-diG-cyclohexanes are achiral even though the ring is not flat.

 Both the *cis* and *trans*-1,4-isomers have a plane of symmetry bisecting the chair through ^{1}C and ^{4}C and their ligands. In addition, the *trans*-isomer with both G's in the (e) or (a) position has a center of symmetry. These diastereomers are both achiral. ^{1}C and ^{4}C are stereocenters (Problem 6.14) but neither is asymmetric.

6.75 How many stereoisomers of a disubstituted cyclohexane exist if the two ligands are different? Illustrate with ligands G and L.

◢ The 1,2- and 1,3-structural isomers each have two chiral C's and four stereoisomers ($2^n = 4$) as two pairs of enantiomers in two racemic forms. One racemate is *cis* and the other is *trans*. The 1,4-isomers exist as achiral *cis-trans* isomers. See Fig. 6-11.

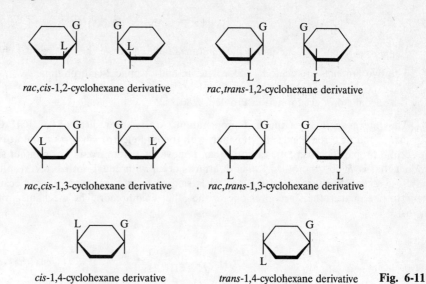

rac,cis-1,2-cyclohexane derivative   *rac,trans*-1,2-cyclohexane derivative

rac,cis-1,3-cyclohexane derivative   . *rac,trans*-1,3-cyclohexane derivative

cis-1,4-cyclohexane derivative   *trans*-1,4-cyclohexane derivative   **Fig. 6-11**

6.76 Draw the enantiomers of 3-bromocyclohexene and give R/S designation for each.

◢ See Fig. 6-12.

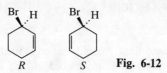

R S **Fig. 6-12**

DYNAMIC STEREOCHEMISTRY

6.77 What are the different ways in which the configuration of one enantiomer can be affected by a chemical reaction at the chiral C?

◢ If the product and starting material have *opposite* configurations, the reaction occurred with *inversion*. If the product has the same configuration, the reaction went with *retention* of configuration. If both processes occurred to the same extent, the product would be completely *racemized* (100% racemization) and if the two processes were not equal, partial racemization would occur.

6.78 What are the different ways in which the configuration of one enantiomer can be affected by a chemical reaction at a site *other* than the chiral C?

◢ Since the bonds to the chiral C are not disturbed, its configuration is unchanged. It is important to note however, that the R/S designation may change if there is a change in the order of priorities of the ligands. Occasionally chirality may disappear.

6.79 How can a reaction of one enantiomer at a site other than the chiral C result in an achiral product? Give an example.

◢ (1) If the reaction makes two identical ligands at the formerly chiral C, the product is achiral.

(1) $CH_3CH(OH)CH_2Cl \xrightarrow{\text{reduction}} CH_3CH(OH)CH_3$ achiral

(2) If the product molecule has a plane or center of symmetry, it is achiral.

(2)

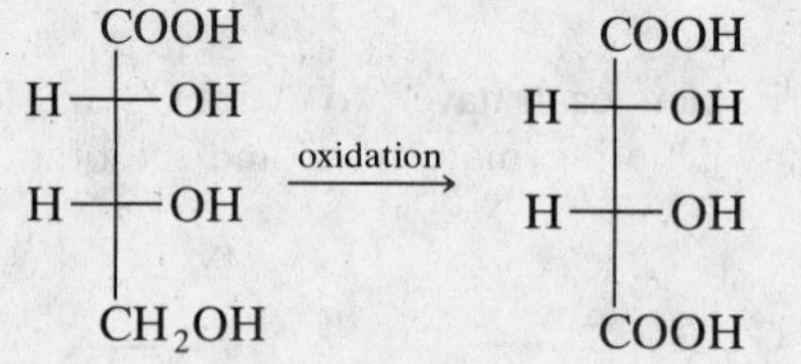

$$\begin{array}{c} COOH \\ H-\!\!\!\!-OH \\ H-\!\!\!\!-OH \\ CH_2OH \end{array} \xrightarrow{\text{oxidation}} \begin{array}{c} COOH \\ H-\!\!\!\!-OH \\ H-\!\!\!\!-OH \\ COOH \end{array} \quad meso$$

6.80 Give the stereostructure of the monochlorobutanes obtained from the free radical chlorination of butane.

▟ The two products are achiral 1-chlorobutane and racemic 2-chlorobutane.

6.81 Why is a racemic product formed in Problem 6.80?

▟ The intermediate from the first propagation step is the radical $CH_3\dot{C}HCH_2CH_3$. The radical C is sp^2 hybridized, and its three bonds are coplanar, with the odd electron in a p orbital at right angles to this plane. In the second propagation step, the radical C can remove a Cl atom from Cl_2 on either side of the plane to give one product that is R and the other S. These attacks occur with equal probability, resulting in equal amounts of R and S (a racemic mixture). The flat radical is said to have *enantiotopic faces* because attachment of a fourth ligand to one or the other face gives one or the other enantiomer. The mechanism of the formation is shown in Fig. 6-13.

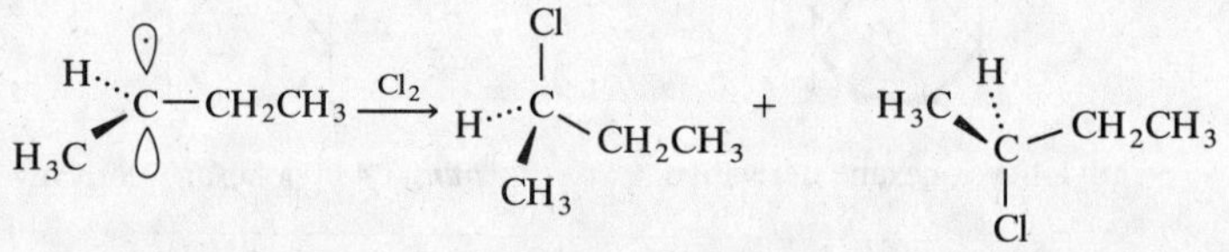

Fig. 6-13

6.82 (*a*) Identify all of the products possible from the radical monochlorination of (S)-2-chlorobutane. (*b*) Give their stereoidentity.

▟ (*a*)

$$(S)\text{-}CH_3CHClCH_2CH_3 \longrightarrow ClCH_2CHClCH_2CH_3 \ (\mathbf{D}) + CH_3C(Cl)_2CH_2CH_3 \ (\mathbf{E})$$
$$+ CH_3CHClCHClCH_3 \ (\mathbf{F}) + CH_3CHClCH_2CH_2Cl \ (\mathbf{G})$$

(*b*) **D** is still chiral and the C^2 configuration is unchanged because no bonds have been broken. However, because of the change in priorities ($CH_2Cl > CH_2CH_3$), it is R. **E** is achiral since C^2 with two Cl's has a plane of symmetry. Two diastereomers corresponding to **F** are formed. C^2 is still S, but C^3 can be R or S (see Problem 6.81). These diastereomers are 2S, 3S which is optically active, and *meso* 2S, 3R. Attack at C^4 does not affect the configuration at C^2, nor does the priority order change; **G** is S.

6.83 Define asymmetric induction. Give an example.

▟ *Asymmetric induction* is the use of a chiral reagent or catalyst to convert an achiral reactant to a chiral product having an excess of one enantiomer. In biochemistry the chiral catalyst is often an enzyme. For example:

$$CH_3COCOOH + coenzyme \xrightarrow{\text{reductase enzyme}} CH_3CH(OH)COOH + oxidized \ coenzyme$$

pyruvic acid $\qquad\qquad\qquad\qquad\qquad\qquad\qquad$ (S)(+)-lactic acid

6.84 Explain the reaction

$$(R)\text{-}CH_3CHIC_2H_5 + {}^{137}I^- \longrightarrow CH_3CHIC_2H_5 \ \text{containing 2\%} \ {}^{137}I.$$
$$\alpha_{obs} = -15.90° \qquad\qquad\qquad\qquad \alpha_{obs} = -15.26°$$

Note: Replacement of I with ^{137}I does not change the sign or value of the rotation.

▟ The optical purity of the recovered iodide is $(15.26/15.90)100\% = 96\%$. Hence, 4% of the iodide is racemic. This means that 2%, the same percentage that contains isotopic I, has been converted to the S. It is concluded that *every reaction with* $^{137}I^-$ *resulted in an inversion at* C^*.

6.85 Predict what would happen to optically active 2-iodobutane in the presence of I^-.

▟ Optically active RI should react with I^- with inversion at C^* and eventually be racemized.

6.86 Is it possible to predict the configuration of the product of the reaction of *cis*-3-iodo-1-methylcyclopentane with OH⁻? Explain.

▮ Assuming OH⁻ reacts with inversion the way the I⁻ does (see Problem 6.85), the product will be *trans*.

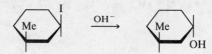

6.87 Predict the R/S designation of the product in each of the following reactions. If the starting material is optically active, should each resulting product be also optically active?

(*a*)   (*S*)-C₂H₅CHCH₃ + CH₃I ⟶ C₂H₅CHCH₃ + I⁻

(*b*)   (*S*)-C₃H₇CH(OH)CH=CH₂ + H₂ $\xrightarrow{\text{Pt catalyst}}$ C₃H₇CH(OH)CH₂CH₃

▮ In (*a*) the configuration is unchanged because the bonds to the chiral C are not disturbed. Since the priority order is unchanged, the product is *S*. The product is optically active. In (*b*) the bonds to the chiral C are undisturbed, but the priority sequence changes, and the product is *R*. The product is optically active. The products and reactants in (*a*) and (*b*) will have different specified rotations and their signs may differ. Specific rotations of reactants and products are independent of each other.

6.88 Predict whether the following reactions occur with racemization, retention, or inversion of configuration, and give your reason.

(*a*)   CH₃CH₂CH(OH)CH₂Br + OH⁻ ⟶ CH₃CH₂CH(OH)CH₂OH + Br⁻

(*b*)   CH₃CH₂CH=CH₂ + D₂ $\xrightarrow{\text{catalyst}}$ CH₃CH₂CH(D)CH₂D

(*c*)   CH₃CH₂CH(OH)CH(CH₃)₂ + CH₃COCl ⟶ CH₃CH₂CH(OCOCH₃)CH(CH₃)₂ + HCl

(*d*)   CH₃CH(NH₂)COOH + NaOH ⟶ CH₃CH(NH₂)COO⁻Na⁺ + H₂O

(*e*)   CH₃CH₂CH₂CH(Cl)CH₃ + OH⁻ ⟶ CH₃CH₂CH₂CH(OH)CH₃ + Cl⁻

▮ (*a*), (*c*), and (*d*) Retention; no bond-breaking occurs at the chiral C.   (*b*) Racemization; although the product has a chiral center (D being sufficiently different from H), both enantiomers are formed in equal amounts because D₂ adds to the enantiotopic faces of the alkene equally.   (*e*) Inversion (see Problems 6.84 and 6.85).

SUPPLEMENTARY PROBLEMS

6.89 State whether the following statements are true or false. Give your reason.
(*a*)   A compound with the *S* configuration is the (−) enantiomer.
(*b*)   An achiral compound can have chiral centers.
(*c*)   An optically inactive substance must be achiral.
(*d*)   In chemical reactions the change from an *S* reactant to an *R* product always signals an inversion of configuration.
(*e*)   When an achiral molecule reacts to give a chiral molecule the product is always racemic.

▮ (*a*) False; the sign of rotation is not related to the configuration.   (*b*) True; an example is a *meso* compound.   (*c*) False; a racemate shows no optical activity.   (*d*) False; the priority sequence of ligands may change.   (*e*) False; if an optically active chiral co-reactant, solvent, or catalyst such as an enzyme is used, the product will likely be optically active.

6.90 How many isomers (constitutional and stereoisomers) are possible for chloropiperidine (a C-chlorinated-6-membered nitrogen heterocyclic compound)? Draw them and characterize their stereochemistry.

▮ There are five isomers—one achiral and two pairs of enantiomers. See Fig. 6.14.

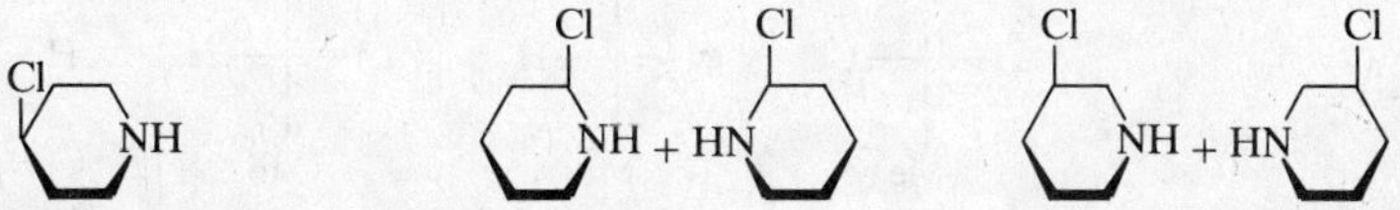

4-Chloropiperidine, achiral   (±)-2-Chloropiperidine   (±)-3-Chloropiperidine   **Fig. 6-14**

6.91   Optically active **A** has the molecular formula C_6H_{12} and catalytic hydrogenation converts it to achiral C_6H_{14}.
Give the structure of **A**.

⟋   A is 3-methyl-1-pentene, which is converted to achiral 3-methylpentane by addition of H_2.

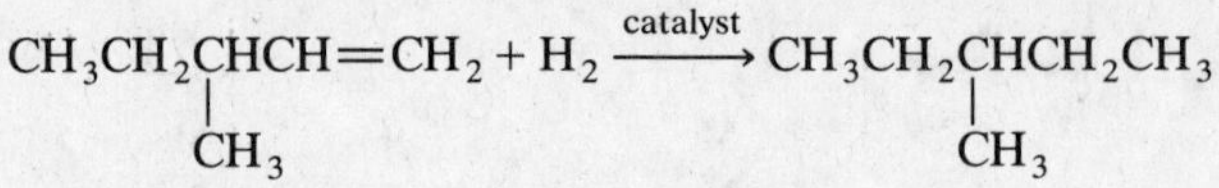

$$CH_3CH_2\underset{\underset{CH_3}{|}}{C}HCH=CH_2 + H_2 \xrightarrow{\text{catalyst}} CH_3CH_2\underset{\underset{CH_3}{|}}{C}HCH_2CH_3$$

$$\text{A}$$

6.92   Two optically active alkenes, **B** and **C**, have the same molecular formula, C_5H_9Cl. After addition of one mole of
H_2 to each, **B** is converted to **D** (achiral), and C forms E (optically active). Give the structures of **B**, **C**, **D**, and **E**.

⟋   In both **B** and **C**, one of the ligands on the chiral C must be $-CH=CH_2$ that adds H_2 to form a $-C_2H_5$
group. **B** already has a $-C_2H_5$ group on its chiral C, making the product achiral. However, since **C** does not
have an ethyl ligand, the product remains active.

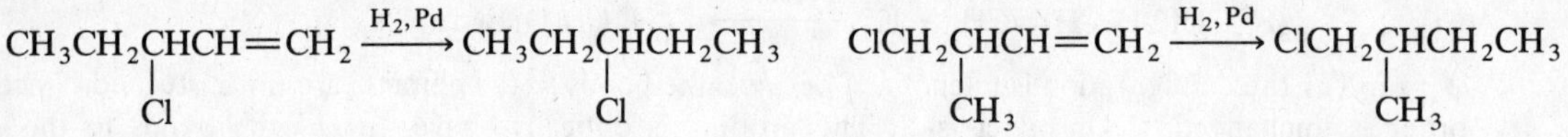

$$CH_3CH_2\underset{\underset{Cl}{|}}{C}HCH=CH_2 \xrightarrow{H_2,\,Pd} CH_3CH_2\underset{\underset{Cl}{|}}{C}HCH_2CH_3 \qquad ClCH_2\underset{\underset{CH_3}{|}}{C}HCH=CH_2 \xrightarrow{H_2,\,Pd} ClCH_2\underset{\underset{CH_3}{|}}{C}HCH_2CH_3$$

$$\text{B} \qquad\qquad\qquad\qquad \text{D} \qquad\qquad\qquad\qquad \text{C} \qquad\qquad\qquad\qquad \text{E}$$

6.93   How many stereoisomers can be obtained by catalytic hydrogenation of both double bonds in the following
compound **F**?

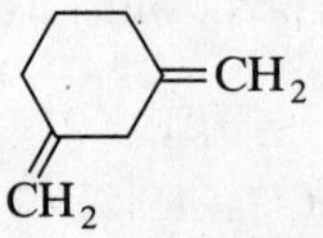

$$\text{F}$$

⟋   Three. If H_2 adds to both double bonds from the same face, the product will be *meso* **G**. If H_2 adds to the
double bonds from opposite faces, the product will be *rac* **H**, having both enantiomers in equal amounts.

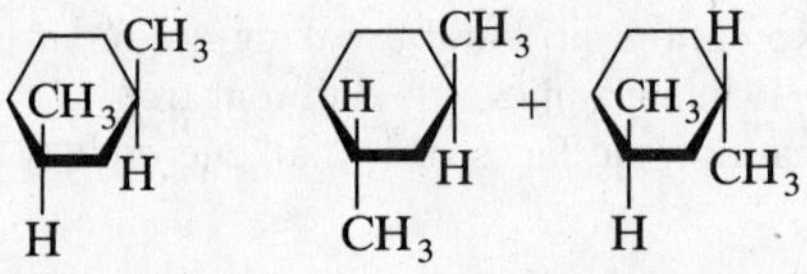

G (*meso*)   **H** (racemate)

6.94   What is the difference between *d* and *l* and D and L?

⟋   *d* and *l* stand for *dextrorotatory* (+) and *levorotatory* (−), respectively. These old symbols are rarely used
today. The D and L terminology is used mainly in carbohydrate chemistry to show the configuration of the bottom
2° OH group (to the left in the Fischer diagram for L and to the right for D). Historically, all D-sugars were related
structurally to the D-glyceraldehyde before absolute configurations were determined. Most naturally occurring
carbohydrates have the D configuration. (It is also used for amino acids, where it refers to the position of the NH_2
group, which is L, on the left side, in naturally occurring amino acids and proteins (Problems 6.50 and 6.51).

6.95   Define the terms erythro and threo and illustrate with Fischer diagrams using 3-chloro-2-butanol
($CH_3CH(OH)CHClCH_3$).

⟋   These terms are used to describe diastereomers with two chiral C's (usually adjacent), when both C's have
two sets of identical ligands. In Fig. 6-15 the identical ligands are H and Me. When the different ligands, in this

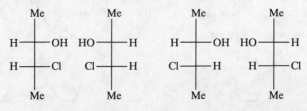

(*a*) *erythro* racemate   (*b*) *threo* racemate   **Fig. 6-15**

case OH and Cl, are on the same side of the vertical bonds as in Fig. 6-15(a), the molecule is called *erythro* (related to the sugar erythrose). When they are on opposite sides as in Fig. 6-15(b), the molecule is called *threo* (related to the sugar threose). The relationship of the *erythro* to a *meso* structure is apparent if we change OH to Cl.

6.96 Draw *erythro*- and *threo*-2,3-dibromopentane, $CH_3CHBrCHBrCH_2CH_3$.

▰ See Fig. 6-16.

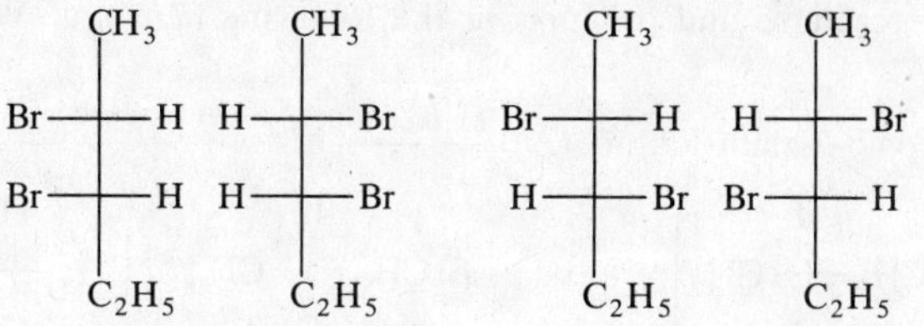

rac.-erythro   rac.-threo   **Fig. 6-16**

6.97 1-Chloro-1,2-butadiene, $CH_3CH{=}C{=}CHCl$ has no chiral C's, yet it is a chiral molecule (it has two enantiomers). Explain with the aid of orbital structures.

▰ C^2 is *sp* hybridized and has one *p* orbital overlapping in the *xy* plane with the *p* orbital of C^1, and the other overlapping in the *xz* plane with the *p* orbital of C^3 to form the two double bonds. The two ligands (H, Cl) attached to C^1 are therefore in a plane at right angles to the plane of the two ligands (H, CH_3) attached to C^3. The mirror images are not identical, as can be shown by rotating one of the structures, in this case **B** in Fig. 6-17(a), 180° out of the plane of the paper in order to superpose the H and Cl ligands in the plane of the paper. The ligands extending in back and in front of the plane of the paper will not match. See Fig. 6-17(b). This is an example of a chiral molecule that has two stereocenters (C^1 and C^3), but no chiral centers.

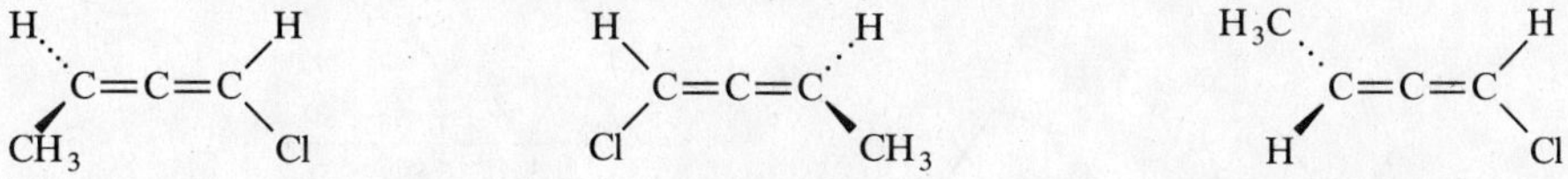

A   and   **B** enantiomers   **B** rotated out of the plane of the paper by 180°
(a)   (b)   **Fig. 6-17**

6.98 Draw the two enantiomers of 4-chloroethenylcyclohexane, **C**, shown in Fig. 6-18(a).

▰ This is best done by considering the ring to be flat. See Fig. 6-18(b).

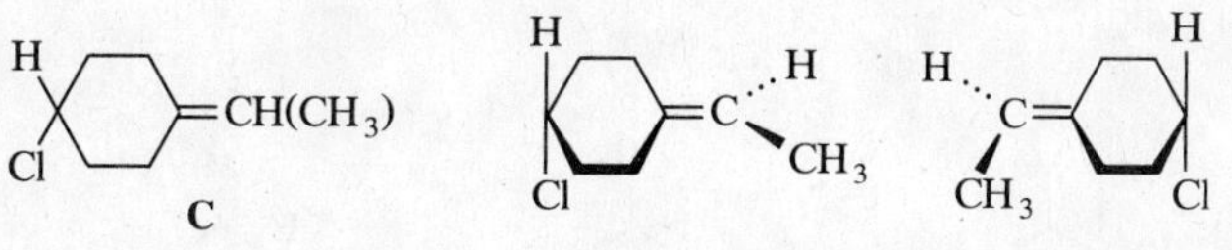

(a)   (b)   **Fig. 6-18**

6.99 Draw all the stereoisomers of 1,2,3-trimethylcyclohexane and give their stereoidentity.

▰ There are two *meso* structures (Problem 6.64) and one pair of enantiomers. See Fig. 6-19.

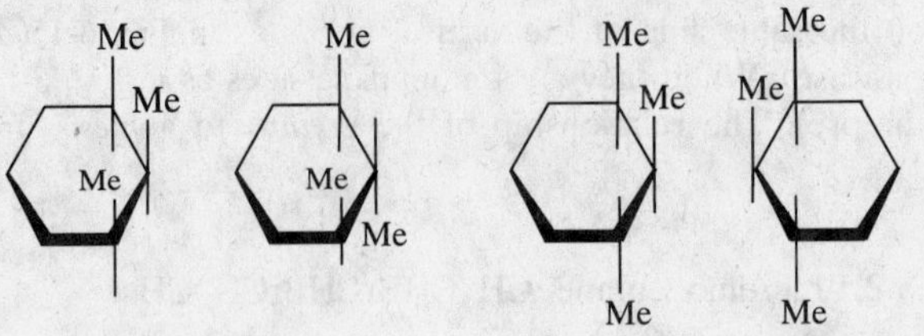

meso structures   enantiomers   **Fig. 6-19**

6.100 Write the structures of the reactants and products in the following reactions. What is the stereoidentity of **B** and **C**?

$$(R)\text{-1-bromo-2-methylbutane}(\mathbf{A}) \xrightarrow{\text{Li, then CuI}} \mathbf{B} \xrightarrow{(S)\text{-1-bromo-2-methylbutane }(\mathbf{D})} \mathbf{C}$$

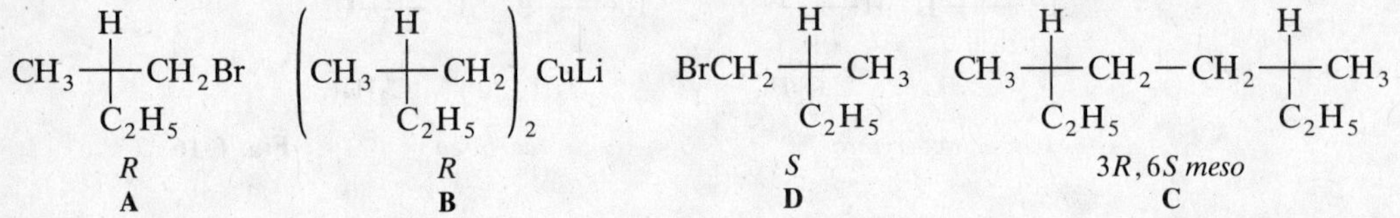

$$\begin{array}{ccccc}
CH_3\!-\!\overset{\overset{H}{|}}{\underset{\underset{C_2H_5}{|}}{C}}\!-\!CH_2Br & \left(CH_3\!-\!\overset{\overset{H}{|}}{\underset{\underset{C_2H_5}{|}}{C}}\!-\!CH_2\right)_{\!2}\!CuLi & BrCH_2\!-\!\overset{\overset{H}{|}}{\underset{\underset{C_2H_5}{|}}{C}}\!-\!CH_3 & CH_3\!-\!\overset{\overset{H}{|}}{\underset{\underset{C_2H_5}{|}}{C}}\!-\!CH_2\!-\!CH_2\!-\!\overset{\overset{H}{|}}{\underset{\underset{C_2H_5}{|}}{C}}\!-\!CH_3 \\
R & R & S & 3R,6S\ meso \\
\mathbf{A} & \mathbf{B} & \mathbf{D} & \mathbf{C}
\end{array}$$

6.101 How many 2,3,4,5-tetrahydroxyadipic acids, $HOOC(CHOH)_4COOH$ are possible? Give their R/S designations.

∥ Ten. There are four chiral carbons but two pairs are similar and some stereoisomers are *meso*. The following are enantiomeric pairs: *RRRR* and *SSSS*; *RRRS* and *SSSR*; *RRSR* and *SSRS*; *RSSR* and *SRRS*. *RSRS* and *RRSS* are two different *meso* diastereomers because the top and bottom halves have mirror images.

6.102 *Spiro* compounds are bicyclic compounds having one C common to both rings as shown below. Draw the enantiomers of (*a*) 2-chlorospiro[4,5]decane and (*b*) 8-chlorospiro[4,5]decane.

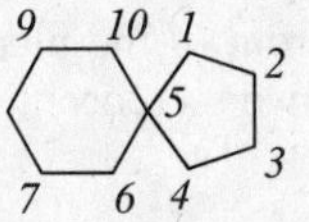

∥ See Fig. 6.20. The two rings are in different planes, making the situation reminiscent of the allenes.

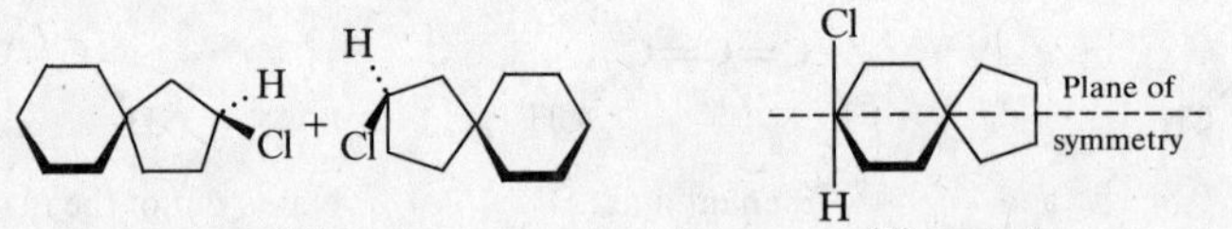

(*a*)   (*b*) achiral   **Fig. 6-20**

6.103 Use conformational theory to evaluate the validity of the following statement: "*Meso*-$CH_3CHClCHClCH_3$ is achiral because it has a plane of symmetry." Draw structures to illustrate your discussion.

∥ While one of the high-energy eclipsed conformations has a plane of symmetry, it represents only a very small part of the population of molecules. The most stable *anti* conformer has a center of symmetry. The infinite number of conformations between the eclipsed and anti (including the *gauche* conformers) are chiral. However, an equal number of R and S enantiomers exist for each conformation, and thus there are an infinite number of racemates. See Fig. 6-21.

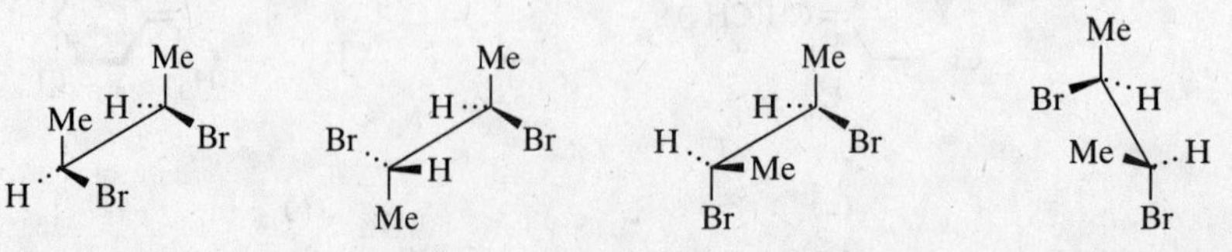

eclipsed   anti   gauche   enantiomeric gauche   **Fig. 6-21**

6.104 The enzyme *alcohol dehydrogenase* catalyzes the oxidation of CH_3CH_2OH to CH_3CHO. Explain why the optically active CH_3CHDOH remains when racemic CH_3CHDOH is similarly oxidized.

▮ The enzyme is a chiral catalyst that distinguishes between H and D on the chiral C, and in its presence only one of the enantiomers is oxidized. The unreacted, optically active enantiomer remains.

6.105 Draw the structure for each of the following: (*a*) $(2S,3S)$-$CH_3CHClCH(CH_3)C_2H_5$, (*b*) $(1R,3S)$-1-methyl-3-bromocyclopentane, and (*c*) an optically active stereoisomer of 1,3-dimethylcyclohexane. See Fig. 6-22.

▮

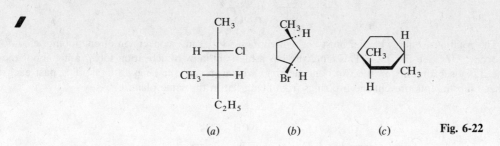

(*a*)   (*b*)   (*c*)   **Fig. 6-22**

6.106 (R)-$CH_2{=}CHCH(CH_3)C_2H_5$ adds D_2 in the presence of a catalyst. Draw the structure of the reactant and all the products. Give R/S designations. See Fig. 6-23.

▮

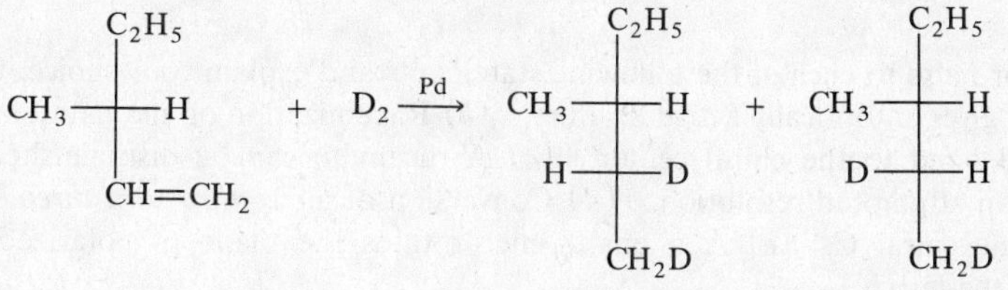

$$CH_3 \!-\!\!\!\!\overset{\displaystyle C_2H_5}{\underset{\displaystyle CH{=}CH_2}{|}}\!\!\!\!-\! H \;+\; D_2 \xrightarrow{\text{Pd}}\; CH_3\!-\!\!\!\!\overset{\displaystyle C_2H_5}{\underset{\displaystyle CH_2D}{\overset{|}{\underset{|}{\big|}}}}\!\!\!\!-\!H \;+\; CH_3\!-\!\!\!\!\overset{\displaystyle C_2H_5}{\underset{\displaystyle CH_2D}{\overset{|}{\underset{|}{\big|}}}}\!\!\!\!-\!H$$

R $(2R,3R)-$ $(2R,3S)-$
                                  1,2-Dideutero-3-methylpentane   **Fig. 6-23**

6.107 Tri-*sec*-butylmethane has four optically active stereoisomers. List the isomers in terms of R/S designation.

▮ Each *sec*-butyl group has a chiral C that can be R or S. Since all three alkyl groups are equivalent, the order of groups is immaterial: RSR is the same as SRR or RRS. The four isomers are: RRR and SSS; and RRS and SSR; they form two pairs of enantiomers.

6.108 Repeat Problem 6.107 with tetra-*sec*-butylmethane, which has four optically-active and one optically inactive stereoisomers.

▮ There are two sets of enantiomeric pairs: $RRRR$ and $SSSS$; and $RRRS$ and $SSSR$. The mirror image of $RRSS$ is the identical $SSRR$, making this the inactive *meso* diastereomer. The latter is a rare example of an achiral compound with no plane or center of symmetry—it has only an improper axis of symmetry.

6.109 Biochemists have used a "chiral" methyl group to investigate the mechanism of enzymatic reactions. What is a "chiral" methyl group?

▮ A C bonded to an H, a D and a T (tritium). Apparently enzymes can distinguish between the different isotopes of hydrogen.

6.110 Write the structures of the three *meso* diastereomers of $C_6H_{12}Cl_2$.

▮ Here *meso* structures can be identified easily by their plane of symmetry in at least one of their conformations, which divides them into mirror image halves, each with three C's. The isomers are:

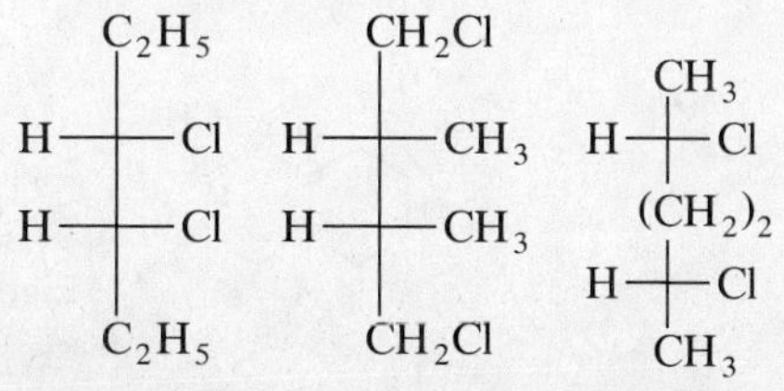

6.111 (*a*) What is the necessary condition for a pair of conformational enantiomers to be isolable? (*b*) Draw the enantiomers of the following compound and explain the structural feature which makes their isolation possible.

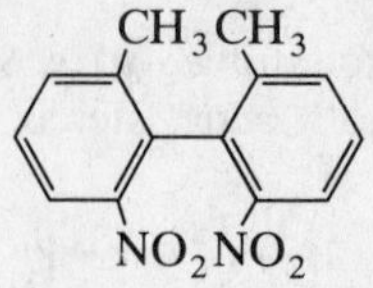

(*a*) The rotational energy barrier must be high enough so that interconversion of enantiomeric conformers does not occur. (*b*) See Fig. 6-24. This molecule has a high enthalpy of activation for rotating about the bond due to the bulky substituents on the two benzene rings which prevent the rings from slipping past each other. (Note: These substituents prevent the two rings from being flat in the same plane.)

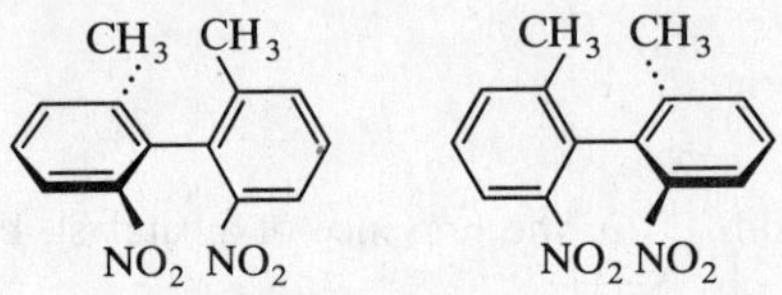

Fig. 6-24

6.112 Answer True or False to each of the following statements and explain your choice. (*a*) A reaction catalyzed by an enzyme always gives an optically active product. (*b*) Racemization of an enantiomer can only occur by breaking of at least one bond to the chiral center. (*c*) A racemate can be distinguished from a *meso* or an achiral compound by an attempted resolution. (*d*) Conversion of an *erythro* to a *threo* stereoisomer always occurs by inversion at one chiral C. (*e*) A D enantiomer rotates the plane of polarized light to the right and an L enantiomer to the left.

(*a*) False. The product could be *meso* or achiral.
(*b*) True. Only by breaking a bond can the configuration be changed. (Except as in Problem 6.111.)
(*c*) True. Unlike a racemate, *meso* and achiral compounds cannot be resolved because they do not consist of enantiomers.
(*d*) True. Changing the configuration at one of the chiral C's converts one diastereomer to the other.
(*e*) False. The terms D and L do not refer to the sign of rotation. They refer to the configuration of a stereoisomer relative to that of D-glyceraldehyde.

6.113 Are D and L stereoisomers enantiomers? Illustrate your response with a suitable compound.

Not necessarily. Consider the conversion of the D compound below to the L compound: a different diastereomer is formed. This statement is true only for a compound with one chiral C.

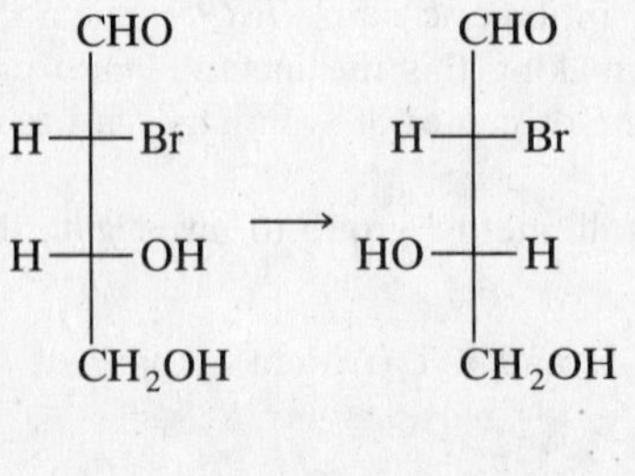

6.114 Point out all the chiral centers in 1-methyldecalin. How many stereoisomers exist?

The three chiral C's in Fig. 6-25 are encircled, and there are four racemic pairs of enantiomers or eight stereoisomers.

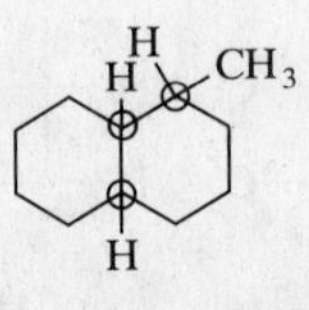

Fig. 6-25

6.115 Reproduce (*a*) The Fischer structure **A** below as a staggered sawhorse and (*b*) the Newman structure **B** as a Fischer structure.

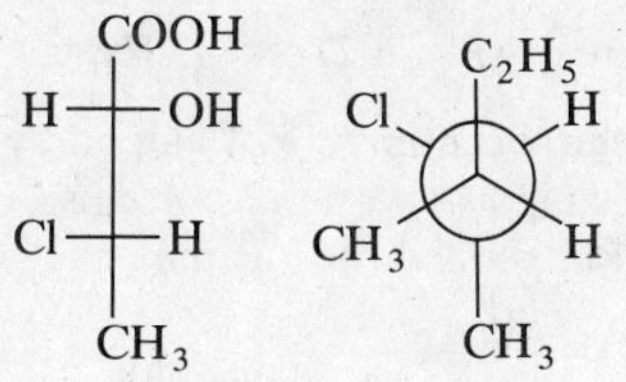

$$
\begin{array}{c}
\text{COOH} \\
\text{H}\!-\!\!\!-\!\text{OH} \\
\text{Cl}\!-\!\!\!-\!\text{H} \\
\text{CH}_3 \\
\textbf{A}
\end{array}
\qquad
\begin{array}{c}
\text{C}_2\text{H}_5 \\
\text{Cl} \quad\quad \text{H} \\
\text{CH}_3 \quad\quad \text{H} \\
\text{CH}_3 \\
\textbf{B}
\end{array}
$$

▰ (*a*) Fischer diagrams are easily converted to eclipsed conformations; rotation gives one of the staggered forms as shown. (*b*) The Newman structure is rotated to the eclipsed conformation and then converted to a Fischer diagram.

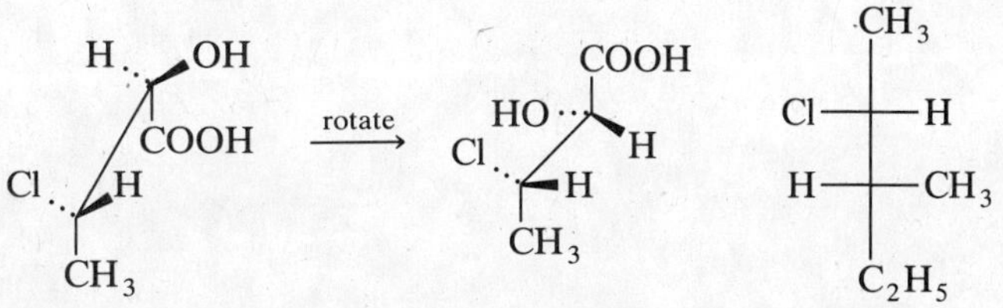

$$
\textbf{A} \qquad\qquad \textbf{B}
$$

6.116 Write the structures and give the stereochemical classifications of all dichlorinated compounds resulting from the free radical chlorination of (*R*)-2-methyl-3-chlorobutane.

▰ Four different structural isomers are formed. Chlorination at C^1 creates a new chiral center at C^2. Since this C can be *R* or *S*, two diastereomers are formed in unequal amounts: $2R, 3R$ (**D**) and $2S, 3R$ (**E**). Chlorination at C^2 gives **F**, which remains *R*. **G** results from reaction at C^3, and it is achiral since the chiral center is lost. **H** is the product of reaction at C^4. Although the configuration at C^3 is unchanged, the priority sequence changes, so **H** is *S*.

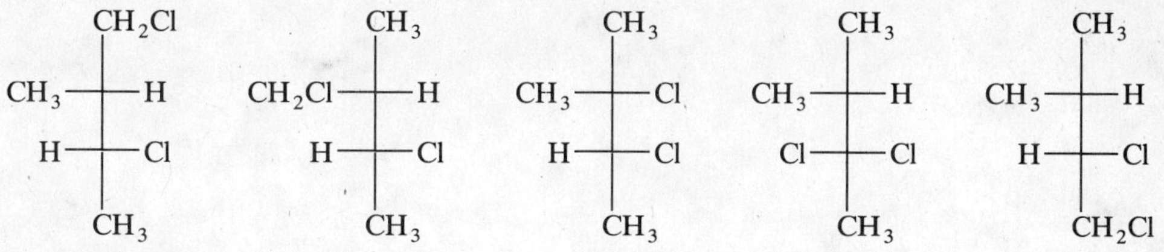

$$
\begin{array}{c}
\text{CH}_2\text{Cl} \\
\text{CH}_3\!-\!\!\!-\!\text{H} \\
\text{H}\!-\!\!\!-\!\text{Cl} \\
\text{CH}_3 \\
\textbf{D}
\end{array}
\quad
\begin{array}{c}
\text{CH}_3 \\
\text{CH}_2\text{Cl}\!-\!\!\!-\!\text{H} \\
\text{H}\!-\!\!\!-\!\text{Cl} \\
\text{CH}_3 \\
\textbf{E}
\end{array}
\quad
\begin{array}{c}
\text{CH}_3 \\
\text{CH}_3\!-\!\!\!-\!\text{Cl} \\
\text{H}\!-\!\!\!-\!\text{Cl} \\
\text{CH}_3 \\
\textbf{F}
\end{array}
\quad
\begin{array}{c}
\text{CH}_3 \\
\text{CH}_3\!-\!\!\!-\!\text{H} \\
\text{Cl}\!-\!\!\!-\!\text{Cl} \\
\text{CH}_3 \\
\textbf{G}
\end{array}
\quad
\begin{array}{c}
\text{CH}_3 \\
\text{CH}_3\!-\!\!\!-\!\text{H} \\
\text{H}\!-\!\!\!-\!\text{Cl} \\
\text{CH}_2\text{Cl} \\
\textbf{H}
\end{array}
$$

6.117 Draw the enantiomers of 4-bromocyclohexene.

▰ See Fig. 6-26.

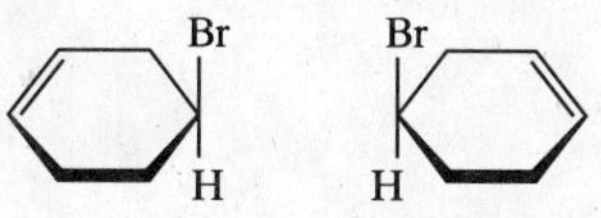

$$
S \qquad\qquad R \qquad \textbf{Fig. 6-26}
$$

6.118 Glyceraldehyde can be converted to lactic acid by the two routes shown below. These results reveal an ambiguity in the assignment of relative D, L configuration. Explain.

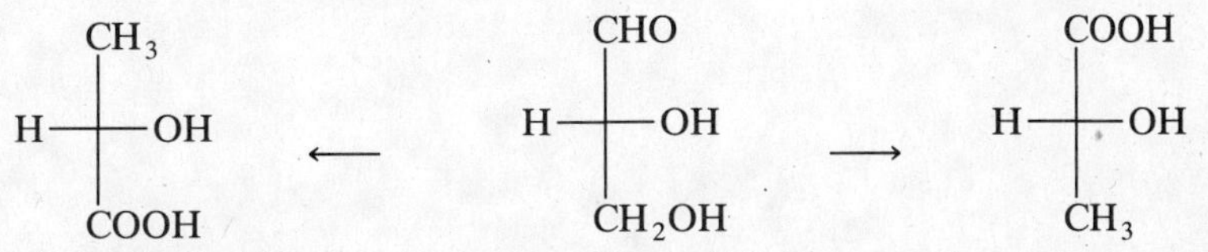

$$
\begin{array}{c}
\text{CH}_3 \\
\text{H}\!-\!\!\!-\!\text{OH} \\
\text{COOH} \\
(R)-(+)-\text{Lactic acid}
\end{array}
\quad\longleftarrow\quad
\begin{array}{c}
\text{CHO} \\
\text{H}\!-\!\!\!-\!\text{OH} \\
\text{CH}_2\text{OH} \\
\text{D}-(+)-\text{Glyceraldehyde}
\end{array}
\quad\longrightarrow\quad
\begin{array}{c}
\text{COOH} \\
\text{H}\!-\!\!\!-\!\text{OH} \\
\text{CH}_3 \\
(S)-(-)-\text{Lactic acid}
\end{array}
$$

▰ The bonds to the chiral C are unchanged in both routes. Since the starting material was D, both lactic acids should have the D configuration. However, since the COOH and CH_3 ligands are interchanged, the two lactic acids must be enantiomers. One is (+) and the other is (−). It is necessary to specify the reaction in the chemical change in order for the unambiguous assignment of D or L. Inspection of the Fischer diagram leads to the S assignment for the $(+)$ lactic acid, and the $(-)$ enantiomer is R. Unlike D/L, the R/S assignment is unambiguous.

6.119 (a) Indicate the chiral C's in camphor (Fig. 6-27). (b) Explain why only one racemic form is known.

◢ (a) Each bridgehead C is a chiral center. (b) Camphor, with two different chiral C's, might be expected to have 2^n or four stereoisomers existing as two racemic forms but only one is known. The bridge must be *cis* as shown in Fig. 6-27. The structural impossibility of a *trans* bridge eliminates a pair of enantiomers.

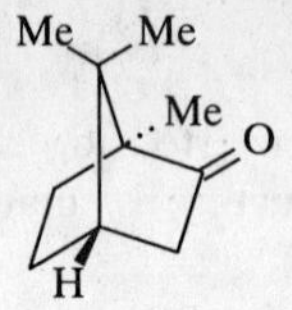

Fig. 6-27

CHAPTER 7
Alkenes

DEFINITIONS AND STRUCTURE

7.1 (*a*) Define alkenes by their (i) functional group and (ii) general formula. (*b*) They are isomeric with which class of compounds?

▮ (*a*) (i) They contain the functional group $>C{=}C<$. (ii) Alkenes have two fewer H's than alkanes and have the general formula C_nH_{2n}. (*b*) They are isomeric with cycloalkanes.

7.2 Give the condensed structural formula of the simplest alkene.

▮ Unlike the alkanes that can have a member with a single C (CH_4), the simplest alkene must have two C's; hence, $H_2C{=}CH_2$ (ethene or ethylene).

7.3 What is the importance of the double bond in alkenes?

▮ The double bond is the site of most of the chemical reactions of alkenes and also affects their shape and energy.

7.4 (*a*) Why are alkenes examples of *unsaturated* hydrocarbons? (*b*) Are cycloalkanes unsaturated?

▮ (*a*) Alkenes react to add two H's at the C=C to form alkanes. Alkanes are saturated hydrocarbons because they cannot react to add more H's. In general unsaturated compounds add some number of H's. (*b*) Except for cyclopropane (and cyclobutane at very high temperatures), cycloalkanes do not add H_2; they are saturated.

7.5 (*a*) Account for the greater bond dissociation energy of C=C (146 kcal/mol) compared to C—C (83 kcal/mol). (*b*) Does the greater bond dissociation energy of the double bond make alkenes less reactive than alkanes?

▮ (*a*) With C=C, two bonds are broken; with C—C, only one. (*b*) In most alkene reactions only one bond is broken; we assume it has a bond dissociation energy of 146 − 83 = 63 kcal/mol, which is less than the C—C single bond energy of 83 kcal/mol. Alkenes are more reactive than alkanes.

7.6 Relate the bond energies and bond lengths of C=C and C—C.

▮ Stronger bonds have shorter bond lengths. In the stronger C=C bond, four e^-'s shield the bonding C's permitting closer approach of their positively charged nuclei than in C—C shielded by only two e^-'s.

7.7 Determine the hybridized state and give the electronic configuration of the ground state and the hybridized state of each C of ethylene, $H_2C{=}CH_2$.

▮ Apply the HON rule (Problem 2.40). With three σ bonds and no unshared pairs, C uses sp^2 HO's and the remaining *p* AO. The ground and hybridized electronic configurations of the C's of C=C are:

$$\underset{\text{ground state}}{(1s)^2,(2s)^2,(2p_x)^1,(2p_y)^1,(2p_z)^0} \longrightarrow \underset{sp^2\text{ hybridized state}}{(1s)^2,(2sp^2)^1,(2sp^2)^1,(2sp^2)^1,(2p_z)^1}$$

7.8 (*a*) Discuss the bonding in ethylene in terms of orbital overlap. (*b*) Draw a figure showing all the overlapping orbitals. (*c*) Draw a simplified wedge projection formula without the overlapping orbitals for the σ bonds.

▮ (*a*) The three half-filled sp^2 HO's of each C form three σ bonds, two by overlapping with an *s* AO of each of two H's and the third from mutual overlap of each other's HO. The second bond between the two C's is a π bond formed by lateral overlap of the remaining $2p_z$ AO's. (*b*) See **Fig. 7-1(*a*)**. (*c*) See **Fig. 7.1(*b*)**.

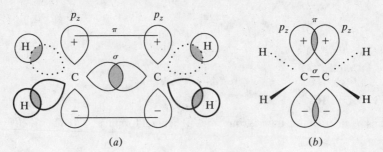

Fig. 7-1

7.9 (a) Describe the geometry of the σ bond skeleton. (b) Explain why the C=C—H bond angle is somewhat larger (121°) than the H—C—H bond angle (118°) in H_2C=CH_2. (c) In propylene, H_2C=$CHCH_3$, the C=C—C bond angle (124°) is larger than the corresponding C=C—H bond angle in ethylene. Explain.

◢ (a) The skeleton made up of the σ-bonded atoms is planar because the C's use sp^2 HO's. All bond angles are approximately 120°. (b) The pair of e⁻'s in the C—H bond is repelled more by the two pairs of e⁻'s in C=C than by the single pair in the other C—H bond, thereby causing a stretching of the angle from the expected 120°. (c) The CH_3 group has more electrons than H and is repelled more by the e⁻'s of the C=C.

7.10 (a) In terms of the HO's used for bonding explain why the C—H bond in ethylene is shorter and stronger than in ethane. (b) Use an asterisk to indicate the strongest C—C single bond in C—C=C—C=C—C.

◢ In general, an orbital with more s character forms a stronger and shorter bond because the shared e⁻'s are closer to and more strongly attracted by the positive nuclei. (a) The sp^2 C—H bond (more s character) in ethylene is stronger and shorter than the sp^3 C—H bond in ethane (less s character). (b) C—C=C $\overset{*}{-}$ C=C—C formed from overlap of two sp^2 HO's.

7.11 (a) Define degrees (or element) of unsaturation. (b) Find the degrees of unsaturation for (i) C_6H_{14}, (ii) C_4H_6, and (iii) C_6H_6. (c) What structural features induce degrees of unsaturation?

◢ (a) The number of pairs of H's a molecular formula lacks to be an alkane (C_nH_{2n+2}) is called the *degree* (or element) *of unsaturation*, sometimes called *index of hydrogen deficiency*. (b) (i) Zero. This molecular formula fits the alkane series. (ii) A molecule with four C's needs 10 H's to be an alkane. The formula with six H's lacks four H's or two pairs of H's and so it has 2° of unsaturation. (iii) A formula with six C's and only six H's lacks eight H's or four pairs of H's; it has 4° of unsaturation. (c) Rings and multiple bonds.

7.12 Draw structural formulas for all possible isomers of C_4H_6.

◢ C_4H_6 has 2° of unsaturation as follows: two double bonds, H_2C=$CHCH$=CH_2 or H_2C=C=$CHCH_3$; one triple bond: HC≡CCH_2CH_3 or CH_3C≡CCH_3; two rings ▱; one ring and one double bond;

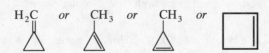

7.13 Find the degrees of unsaturation for (a) $C_3H_3Cl_3$, (b) C_3H_4O, and (c) C_4H_5N.

◢ (a) Count halogens as if they were H's; i.e., C_3H_6. The formula lacks two H's and has 1° of unsaturation. (b) Disregard O's. C_3H_4 lacks four H's and has 2° of unsaturation. (c) Disregard N but remove an H for each N. C_4H_4 has 3° of unsaturation.

7.14 (a) A hydrocarbon (**A**) has 2° of unsaturation. Describe a quantitative chemical reaction that can be used to determine whether **A** has two rings *or* one ring and one double bond *or* two double bonds *or* one triple bond. (b) Would this test be applicable if **A** had a cyclopropane ring?

◢ (a) Run a quantitative catalytic hydrogenation with one equivalent of **A**. If H_2 does not add (react), **A** has two rings. If one eq. of H_2 reacts, **A** has both a ring and a C=C. If two eq. of H_2 react, **A** has two double bonds or one triple bond. (b) No. Cyclopropanes react with (add) H_2.

7.15 (a) Compare (i) the dipole moments, (ii) the boiling points, and (iii) the solubilities of alkenes and corresponding alkanes. (b) Compare the dipole moments of $H_2C{=}CH_2$ and $H_2C{=}CHCH_3$.

▰ (a) (i) Alkenes and alkanes are nonpolar although some alkenes have very small dipole moments [see (b) below]. (ii) Since alkanes and the corresponding alkenes have approximately the same molecular weights and polarity, their boiling points are almost identical. (iii) They are not soluble in polar solvents such as water but are soluble in nonpolar solvents such as benzene and carbon tetrachloride, and weakly polar solvents such as ether. (b) The electron-donating CH_3, typical of R groups, induces a very small dipole moment making the C=C slightly negative:

$$\begin{array}{c} H_3C \diagdown \\[2pt] \qquad\nearrow C{=}C \diagup \\ H \qquad\qquad H \end{array}$$

NOMENCLATURE

7.16 (a) Write the structural formulas and give the common names for the alkenes (i) C_2H_4, (ii) C_3H_6, and (iii) C_4H_8 (three isomers). (b) Why do more structural isomers of alkenes exist than alkanes with the same number of C's?

▰ Replace the suffix -ane from the alkane name by the suffix -ylene.
(a) (i) $H_2C{=}CH_2$, ethylene; (ii) $CH_3CH{=}CH_2$, propylene; (iii) $H_2C{=}CHCH_2CH_3$, 1-butylene; $CH_3CH{=}CHCH_3$, 2-butylene; $H_2C{=}C(CH_3)_2$, isobutylene.
(b) Alkenes have more structural isomers mainly because of the several possibilities of positioning the double bond in the carbon chain.

7.17 Supply IUPAC names for:

(a) $CH_3CH{=}CHCH_2CH_3$, (b) $CH_3\underset{\underset{CH_3}{|}}{C}HCH{=}CHCH_3$, and (c) $CH_3CH_2CH_2\underset{\underset{CH{=}CH_2}{|}}{C}HCH_2CH_2CH_3$.

▰ Select the longest carbon chain or ring containing the largest number of double bonds and change the suffix of the parent alkane from -ane to -ene. The alkenes use the same prefixes as the alkanes. The chain is numbered from the end closer to the C=C, whose position is indicated by assigning the lower possible number to the first doubly-bonded C. Substituents are designated as for alkanes. (a) 2-Pentene; (b) 4-methyl-2-pentene; (c) named as a hexene, the longest chain with C=C, not as a heptane which is the longest C chain but does not include the C=C; thus 3-n-propyl-1-hexene.

7.18 Give the common and systematic names for the double-bond containing groups:
(a) $H_2C{=}CH{-}$, (b) $H_2C{=}CHCH_2{-}$, (c) $CH_3CH{=}CH{-}$, (d) $H_2C{=}C(CH_3){-}$, and (e) $H_2C{=}$.

▰ When named systematically these are alkenyl groups. (a) Vinyl and ethenyl, (b) allyl and 2-propenyl, (c) propenyl and 1-propenyl, (d) isopropenyl, and (e) methylene.

7.19 Name the following as substituted derivatives of ethylene: (a) $Cl_2C{=}CHCl$, (b) $CH_3CH{=}CHCH_3$, (c) $(CH_3)_2C{=}CH_2$, and (d) $(CH_2{=}CH)_2C{=}CH_2$.

▰ (a) Trichloroethylene, (b) sym-dimethylethylene, (c) unsym-dimethylethylene, and (d) unsym-divinylethylene. [Use sym (symmetrical) when each C of C=C has the same substituent and unsym (unsymmetrical) when both substituents are on the same C.]

7.20 Supply IUPAC names for

(a) $CH_3CH{=}C(NO_2)CH_2CH_3$,

(d) $H_2C{=}CHCH\underset{\underset{CH(Me)CH_2CH_3}{|}}{C}HClCH{=}CHCHMe_2$

(b) $Me_2C{=}C(Me)CH(Me)_2$

(e)

$$\begin{array}{c} CH_3 \\ \text{(ring with } C_2H_5 \text{ substituent)} \end{array}$$

(c) $(Me)_2CHCH{=}CHC\underset{\underset{Me}{|}}{H}CH{=}CH_2$

(f) $(H_2C{=}CH)_2CHCH_2CH{=}CHCH_3$.

▰ (*a*) 3-Nitro-2-pentene; (*b*) 2,3,4-trimethyl-2-pentene; (*c*) 3,6-dimethyl-1,4-heptadiene (note the use of *di* to indicate two C=C's); (*d*) 4-chloro-3-(1-methylpropyl or *s*-butyl)-7-methyl-1,5-octadiene; (*e*) 1-methyl-5-ethyl-1,3-cyclohexadiene; (*f*) the three C=C's cannot be incorporated into a single chain; pick the longest chain with two C=C's; 3-ethenyl-1,5-heptadiene.

7.21 Supply the structural formulas for (*a*) 3-Methylenecyclopentene, (*b*) 4-allyl-3-propenyl-1,3-cyclohexadiene, (*c*) bicyclo[2.2.1]2,5-heptadiene, and (*d*) 2-ethenylbicyclo[4.4.0]-1,5,8-decatriene.

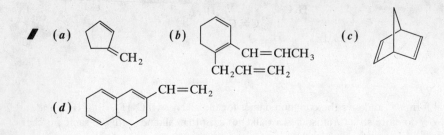

7.22 (*a*) Write the structural formulas from the following incorrect IUPAC names: (i) 2-Methylcyclohexene, (ii) 3-ethenyl-1-hexene, and (iii) 1,2,2-trichloro-4-pentene.· (*b*) Give the correct names in (*a*) and describe the given errors.

▰ (*a*) (i) [structure: cyclohexene with CH₃] (ii) $H_2C=CHCHCH_2CH_2CH_3$ with $CH=CH_2$ branch (iii) $ClCH_2CCl_2CH_2CH=CH_2$

(*b*) (i) 1-Methylcyclohexene. Number 1 is assigned to the C=C bond bonded to the Me; it can be omitted since it is understood when no number is given. (ii) 3-Propyl-1,4-pentadiene because the chain must include both double bonds. (iii) 4,4,5-Trichloro-1-pentene because C=C has priority and is assigned the smaller number even though the substituents acquire higher numbers.

GEOMETRIC (*cis-trans*) ISOMERISM

7.23 In (iii) of Problem 7.16(*a*) it was stated that there are three structural alkene isomers of C_4H_8. Actually there is a fourth isomer. Explain.

▰ 2-Butene has two diastereomers. *cis*-2-Butene has the Me's on the same side and *trans*-2-butene has the Me's on opposite sides of the double bond.

7.24 Illustrate the structures of *cis*- and *trans*-2-butene (*a*) in the plane of the paper and (*b*) perpendicular to the plane of the paper.

▰ (*a*) [structures of cis and trans 2-butene] (*b*) [structures of cis and trans 2-butene]

7.25 Use orbital theory to explain geometric isomerism in alkenes.

▰ The π bond (Problem 7.8) prevents free rotation about the C=C; thus the substituents on C=C remain fixed in their relative positions. In this respect alkenes and alkanes differ.

7.26 Which alkenes do not have geometric isomers?

▰ Alkenes with two identical groups on the same doubly-bonded C have no geometric isomers.

7.27   Determine which of the following alkenes have geometric isomers:

(a)
$$
\begin{array}{c}
H_3C \qquad\quad C_2H_5 \\
\diagdown\qquad\diagup \\
C{=}C \\
\diagup\qquad\diagdown \\
H_3C \qquad\quad H
\end{array}
$$

(b)
$$
\begin{array}{c}
H \qquad\quad Br \\
\diagdown\qquad\diagup \\
C{=}C \\
\diagup\qquad\diagdown \\
Cl \qquad\quad H
\end{array}
$$

(c)
$$
\begin{array}{c}
BrH_2C \qquad\quad CH_2I \\
\diagdown\qquad\diagup \\
C{=}C \\
\diagup\qquad\diagdown \\
IH_2C \qquad\quad CH_2Br
\end{array}
$$

(d)
$$
\begin{array}{c}
H_2C{=}CH \qquad\quad CH(CH_3)_2 \\
\diagdown\qquad\diagup \\
C{=}C \\
\diagup\qquad\diagdown \\
H_3C \qquad\quad CH(CH_3)_2
\end{array}
$$

▰   (a) No; one C has two Me's.   (b) and (c) Yes; each C has two different groups.   (d) No; one C has two $(CH_3)_2CH$ groups.

7.28   (a) Discuss the Cahn–Ingold–Prelog sequence rules (Problem 6.35) for specifying geometric isomers.   (b) When is this method preferable to the use of *cis-trans*?

▰   (a) The letter Z is used when the two high-priority substituents are on the same side of the double bond and the letter E is used when they are on opposite sides (from the German: zusammen, together, and entgegen, opposite), as shown:

$$
Z:\quad
\begin{array}{c}
High{-}C{-}Low \\
\| \\
High{-}C{-}Low
\end{array}
\qquad
E:\quad
\begin{array}{c}
High{-}C{-}Low \\
\| \\
Low{-}C{-}High
\end{array}
$$

(b) It is not practical to identify *cis* and *trans* isomers when the four groups on $C{=}C$ are different.

7.29   Assign E/Z configurations to each of the following alkenes:

(a)
$$
\begin{array}{c}
H_3C \qquad\quad CH_2CH_3 \\
\diagdown\qquad\diagup \\
C{=}C \\
\diagup\qquad\diagdown \\
H \qquad\quad H
\end{array}
$$

(b)
$$
\begin{array}{c}
BrCH_2 \qquad\quad CH_3 \\
\diagdown\qquad\diagup \\
C{=}C \\
\diagup\qquad\diagdown \\
H_3C \qquad\quad CH_2CH_3
\end{array}
$$

(c)
$$
\begin{array}{c}
Br \qquad\quad CH(CH_3)_2 \\
\diagdown\qquad\diagup \\
C{=}C \\
\diagup\qquad\diagdown \\
HOCH_2 \qquad\quad CH_2CH_2CH_3
\end{array}
$$

(d)
$$
\begin{array}{c}
H \qquad\quad CH_2Cl \\
\diagdown\qquad\diagup \\
C{=}C \\
\diagup\qquad\diagdown \\
CH_3CH_2 \qquad\quad COOH
\end{array}
$$

▰   (a) Z, (b) E, (c) Z, (d) E.

7.30   What paper and pencil change is made in the alkene structure to go from E to Z or from Z to E?

▰   Switch groups on the same C, never switch groups on different C's.

7.31   (a) Compare the relative stabilities of *cis* and *trans* isomers.   (b) How are these determined by equilibration experiments? (c) Explain the free energy difference.   (d) What happens to the relative stabilities of *trans* and *cis* diastereomers as the size of the R's increase?

▰   (a) In general, *trans* isomers are more stable than *cis*.   (b) A reaction is chosen that permits interconversion of the geometric isomers (alkenes and cyclic compounds). When equilibrium is reached the mixture is analyzed. The more abundant isomer is more stable. It is necessary to show that the same equilibrium mixture is attained starting with either pure diastereomer. For example, when either *cis*- or *trans*-2-butene is placed in a strong acid solution, each is converted to a mixture of 76% of the *trans* and 24% of the *cis* isomer. The ratio of isomers provides the equilibrium constant and the ΔG (Problem 3.72), showing the *trans* to be more stable than the *cis* by 0.66 kcal/mol. (c) The greater stability (lower free energy) of the *trans* isomer is attributed to steric strain in the *cis* isomer due to the van der Waals repulsion forces of large groups on the same side of the double bond.   (d) The *cis* becomes increasingly less stable because of the increasing repulsive force.

7.32 (*a*) Write the formula for the alkene hydrocarbon with the fewest number of C's that exhibits geometric *and* optical isomerism. (*b*) Provide the Fischer structural formulas and names for each stereoisomer.

◢ (*a*) MeCH=CHC*HMeEt. (*b*) There are four stereoisomers as shown:

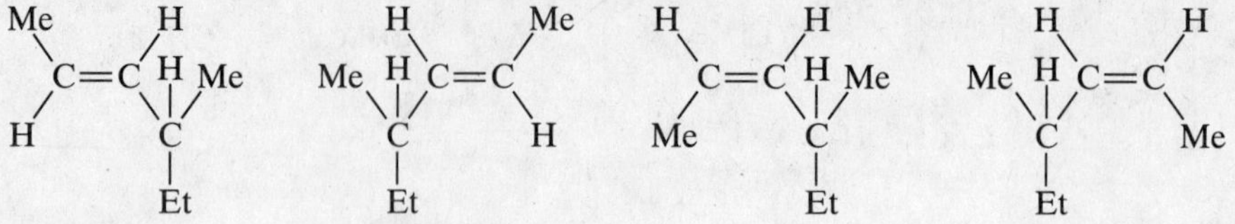

(*E*)(*S*)- (*E*)(*R*)- (*Z*)(*S*)- (*Z*)(*R*)-

4-Methyl-2-hexene

7.33 Write the structural formulas for: (*a*) (*E*)(*S*)-5-Bromo-2,7-dimethyl-4-nonene, (*b*) (*R*)-3-chloro-1-butene, and (*c*) (*E*)(*S*)-6-fluoro-3,7-dimethyl-3-octene.

◢ (*a*)

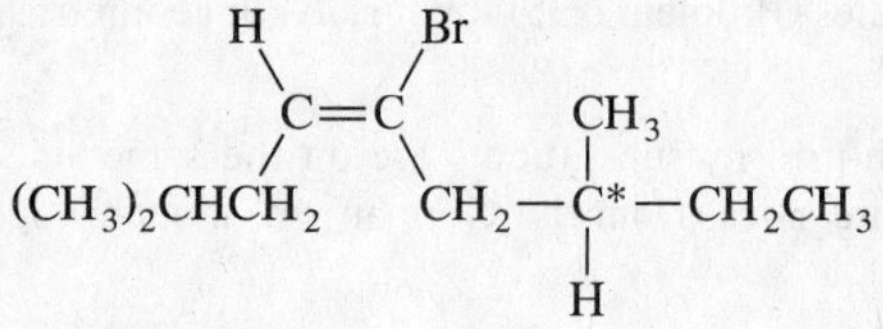

(*b*) $CH_3-\overset{Cl}{\underset{H}{C^*}}-CH=CH_2$

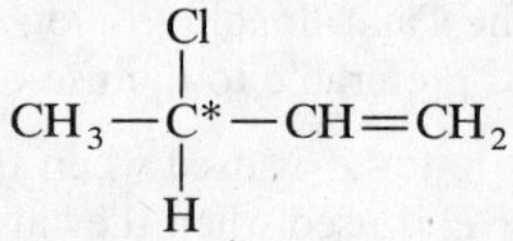

(*c*)

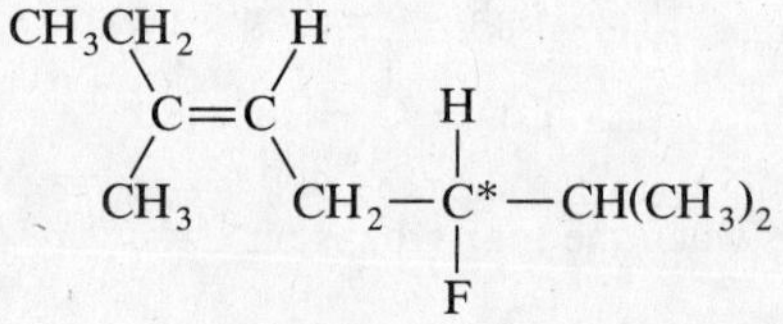

7.34 Give the structures and IUPAC names of the structural isomers and stereoisomers of pentene, C_5H_{10}.

◢ Alkene isomers are deduced by writing the carbon skeletons and then introducing the double bond. The possible skeletons are:

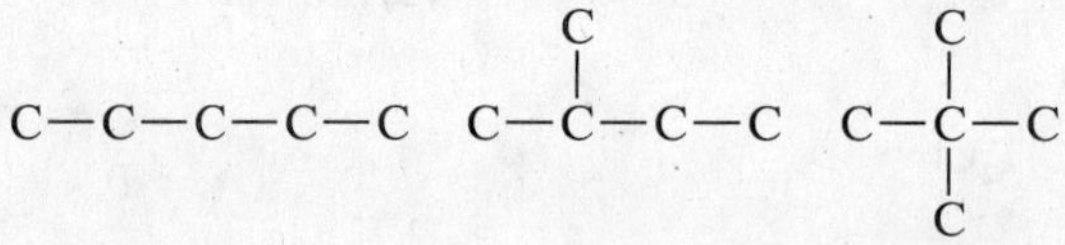

A B C

From **A** we get:

$H_2C=CHCH_2CH_2CH_3$ and

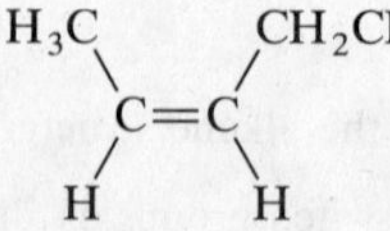

1-Pentene (*Z*)-2-Pentene (*E*)-2-Pentene

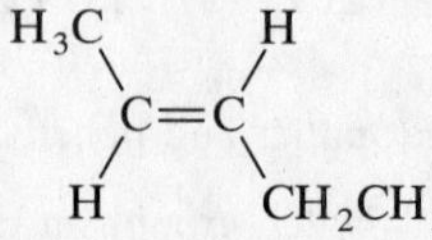

From **B** we get three structural isomers, none of which has geometric isomers.

$H_2C=C(CH_3)CH_2CH_3$ $(CH_3)_2C=CHCH_3$ $(CH_3)_2CHCH=CH_2$
2-Methyl-1-butene   2-Methyl-2-butene   3-Methyl-1-butene

The central C atom of **C** is quaternary and cannot form a double bond to give an alkene.

7.35 Compare the stabilities of 1-pentene, *cis*- and *trans*-2-pentene, and 2-methyl-2-butene.

◢ Since attached R's increase stability, the least stable isomer is 1-pentene with one R, and the most stable isomer is 2-methyl-2-butene with three R's. Among the isomers with two R's, *trans*-2-pentene is more stable than its *cis* isomer.

7.36 Compare the net dipole moments of (*a*) 1,1-, and *trans* and *cis*-1,2-dichloroethene, and (*b*) (*E*)- and (*Z*)-2,3-dichloro-2-butene.

◢ (*a*) The two Cl's of the *trans* isomer have equal and opposite bond moments leaving a net zero molecular dipole moment. 1,1-Dichloroethene has a smaller angle of separation of the two Cl's than has the *cis* isomer resulting in a greater dipole moment.

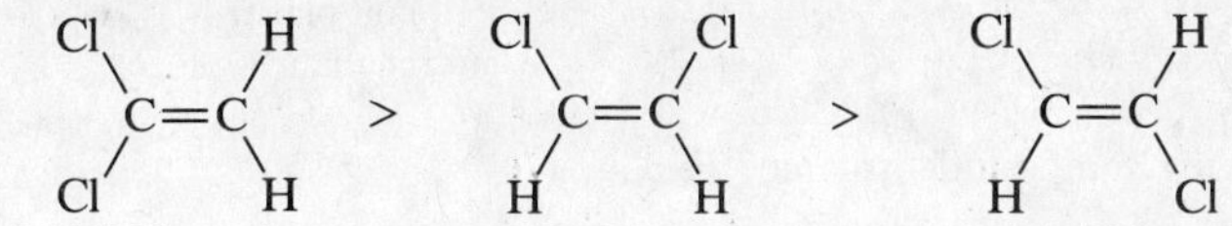

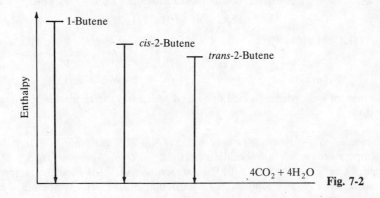

In the (*Z*) isomer the strongly electronegative Cl's on the same side of the π bond reinforce their electron-withdrawal. Likewise, the electron-donating Me's have a reinforcing effect. Electron-donation and electron-withdrawal on opposite sides of C=C enhance the dipole moment. The effects of Cl's and Me's on opposite sides in structure (*E*) cancel each other resulting in a smaller dipole moment.

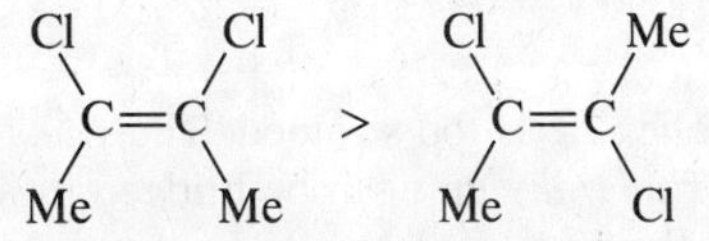

7.37 (*a*) With the aid of an enthalpy diagram show how heats of combustion (ΔH_c) can be used to compare stabilities of geometric isomers of hydrocarbon alkenes. (*b*) Is the conversion of a *cis* to a *trans*-isomer exothermic or endothermic? Why?

◢ (*a*) As shown in **Fig. 7-2**, the enthalpies of the products of alkene combustion, CO_2 and H_2O, are always less than those of the reactants, alkene and O_2. 1-Butene and *cis*- and *trans*-2-butene are arbitrarily chosen. All combustions are exothermic and have $-\Delta H_c$'s. Only isomeric hydrocarbons can be compared because only then will the equivalent amounts of reactants and products be the same. The most stable isomer has the smallest enthalpy, and the least negative ΔH_c. We can safely use ΔH_c instead of ΔG_c because ΔS_c is positive (eight moles of products from seven moles of reactants) and constant for combustion of each isomer. (*b*) The isomerization is exothermic because *cis* has a larger enthalpy than *trans*.

```
Enthalpy
|    — 1-Butene
|
|            — cis-2-Butene
|                   — trans-2-Butene
|
|
|
|                              4CO₂ + 4H₂O
|_____    Fig. 7-2
```

7.38 Account for the interconversion of *trans*- and *cis*-isomeric alkenes by ultraviolet radiation with a suitable photosensitizer.

◢ Radiation provides energy to excite a π e⁻ (Problem 2.34) into a π^*MO*, momentarily breaking the π bond. Rotation about the C—C bond of either excited *cis* or *trans* molecule gives a common nonplanar intermediate. When the electron returns to the ground state, the π bond reforms, and the same mixture of the two geometric isomers results from either starting isomer. Because the rate of return from the common intermediate to the *cis* ground state is faster, the *cis* predominates, even though it has the higher energy. The product ratio is kinetic-controlled, not thermodynamic-controlled.

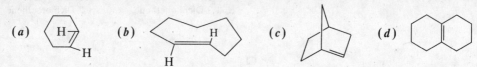

excited non-planar
intermediate

7.39 Are the following compounds isolable? Explain.

(*a*)   (*b*)   (*c*)   (*d*)

⬛ (*a*) No. A *trans*-cyclohexene is too strained. The *trans* unit C—C=C—C cannot be bridged by the two remaining C's. (*b*) Yes. This *trans* unit can be bridged by six C's. Eight-membered and larger rings can have a *trans*-substituted C=C in the ring. (*c*) No. A molecule cannot have a C=C at a bridgehead C if each bridge has at least one C and the bridges are not large. The C=C would require the bridgehead to flatten out—an impossibility. This is known as *Bredt's rule*. (*d*) Yes. Although there is a C=C at a bridgehead C, one of the bridges has no C and the bridgehead C's can flatten without ring strain.

PREPARATION

7.40 What is the major method for preparing alkenes by forming the double bond?

⬛ *Elimination* reactions whereby an atom or group is removed, with a net loss of 2 e⁻s, from each of two vicinal sp^3 C's so that a C—C becomes a C=C:

$$ \underset{\displaystyle |}{\overset{\displaystyle A}{\underset{\displaystyle -C-}{|}}}\ \underset{\displaystyle |}{\overset{\displaystyle B}{\underset{\displaystyle -C-}{|}}} \xrightarrow{\text{reagent}} \ \overset{\diagdown}{\underset{\diagup}{C}} = \overset{\diagup}{\underset{\diagdown}{C}} + A{:}B $$

Since the groups are eliminated from adjacent C's, these are called *β*- or 1,2-eliminations.

7.41 List the alkenes formed by the mainly industrial catalytic *dehydrogenation* ($-H_2$) at 500 °C of $CH_3CH_2CH_2CH_3$.

⬛ In this *β*-elimination, the two H's can be removed from C^1 and C^2 or C^2 and C^3. The two geometric isomers of 2-butene are formed. In addition, loss of four H's leads to a diene.

$H_2C{=}CHCH_2CH_3$

H_3C CH_3	H_3C H	
C=C	C=C	$H_2C{=}CHCH{=}CH_2$
H H	H CH_3	

1-Butene   *cis*-   *trans*-2-Butene   1,3-Butadiene

(A small amount of isobutylene, formed by rearrangement of the chain due to the severe reaction conditions, is also isolated.)

7.42 (*a*) Use the values $\Delta S = +28$ cal/mol · K and $\Delta H = +27.6$ kcal/mol to determine the most favorable of the following temperatures for dehydrogenation of butane to *trans*-2-butene: (i) 25 °C, (ii) 500 °C, and (iii) 1000 °C. (*b*) Why can a reaction occur even with the unfavorable ΔH? (*c*) Find the temperature at which $\Delta G = 0$ and discuss its significance. It is reasonable to assume that in the given temperature range ΔH, the difference in enthalpy between reactant and products, remains fairly constant.

⬛ Use Gibb's equation, $\Delta G = \Delta H - T\Delta S$. The best T has the most negative ΔG, as in (iii).
(*a*) (i) At 25 °C, $\Delta G = +27.6$ kcal/mol $- (298\ K)(2.8 \times 10^{-2}$ kcal/mol · K$) = +19.3$ kcal/mol.
(ii) At 500 °C, $\Delta G = +27.6$ kcal/mol $- (773\ K)(2.8 \times 10^{-2}$ kcal/mol · K$) = +6.0$ kcal/mol.
(iii) At 1000 °C, $\Delta G = +27.6$ kcal/mol $- (1273\ K)(2.8 \times 10^{-2}$ kcal/mol · K$) = -8.0$ kcal/mol.
(*b*) The $+\Delta H$ overwhelms the $+T\Delta S$ term at 25 °C, giving $\Delta G = +19.3$. As the temperature rises, the positive $T\Delta S$ term becomes larger and ΔG becomes less positive. At 1000 °C it predominates over the $+\Delta H$, ΔG becomes negative, and the reaction can occur.

(c) When $\Delta G = 0$, $\Delta H = T\Delta S$, and

$$T = \frac{\Delta H}{\Delta S} = \frac{27.6 \text{ kcal/mol}}{2.8 \times 10^{-2} \text{ kcal/mol} \cdot \text{K}} = 986 \text{ K} = 713 \,^{\circ}\text{C}.$$

Below this *crossover* temperature, ΔH dominates, ΔG is positive and there is no reaction. Above this temperature, $T\Delta S$ dominates, ΔG is negative, and the reaction occurs.

7.43 (a) Write a generalized equation for preparing alkenes from alkyl halides, $C_nH_{2n+1}X$, by *dehydrohalogenation* ($-HX$) using a base and heat. (b) Classify this reaction. (c) What is a commonly used base?

◢ (a) $H-\overset{|}{\underset{|}{C}}-\overset{|}{\underset{|}{C}}-X + :B^- \rightarrow \overset{\backslash}{\underset{/}{C}}=\overset{/}{\underset{\backslash}{C}} + B:H + :\overset{..}{\underset{..}{X}}:^-$

(b) An H^+ and an anion, X^-, are lost from adjacent C's; it is a β-elimination. (c) KOH in ethanol (abbreviated as alc. KOH), where ethoxide ion, EtO^- may be the active base.

7.44 (a) In general, what must be the nature of X in order for the substrate to lose an HX? (b) Explain why alcohols do not undergo base-induced dehydration ($-H_2O$) in the same way that RX's are dehydrohalogenated?

◢ (a) The anion lost, the *leaving group*, must be a very weak Brönsted base such as the halides Cl^-, Br^-, I^- (*not* F^-) and sulphonate esters, $RS(O_2)O^-$. The weaker the base, the better it is a leaving group. (b) In alcohols the leaving group would be OH^-, which is too strong a base for the reaction to proceed.

7.45 (a) What is the experimentally-determined rate expression for the base-induced β-elimination? (b) How many steps does this reaction have? (c) What symbol stemming from the rate expression is used to classify these types of reactions?

◢ (a) rate $= k[RX][B^-]$. (b) Since the rate expression has both RX and B^-, either a one-step reaction or a two-step reaction with a slow second step is possible. (c) E2 where E stands for elimination, and 2 for bimolecularity of the rate-determining step. (See Chapter 8 for a more detailed discussion of the E2 mechanism.)

7.46 (a) Give the structural formulas for the alkenes formed from the reaction of 2-bromobutane and alc. KOH. (b) Select the major and minor products and rationalize your choice. (c) What is the order of preferential removal of the type of H on dehydrohalogenation of alkyl halides? (d) In terms of R substitution, what general names are associated with these products?

◢ (a) $H_2C=CHCH_2CH_3$ (**A**), *cis*-$CH_3CH=CHCH_3$ (**B**), and *trans*-$CH_3CH=CHCH_3$ (**C**). (b) Alkene stability increases with increasing number of electron-releasing substituent R's bonded to the sp^2 C's, and the relative yields depend on their relative stabilities. **A** is the minor product because it has one R and is less stable than either 2-butene diastereomer having two R's. **C** is the major di-R alkene product because it is *trans*. (c) The order is $3^{\circ} > 2^{\circ} > 1^{\circ}$ (*Saytzeff rule*). If H's represent wealth, we say "the poor get poorer" because the H is best removed from the C with the fewest number of H's. **A** comes from removal of a 1° H from C^1 and **B** and **C** come from removal of a 2° H from C^3. (d) The more substituted alkene is the *Saytzeff* product, in this case **B** and **C**. The least substituted is the *Hofmann* product, in this case **A**.

7.47 (a) What happens to the relative yields of Saytzeff and Hofmann product alkenes when Me_3CO^- replaces EtO^- as the base for dehydrohalogenation? (b) Account for the change in relative yields.

◢ (a) The yield of 1-butene increases. (b) The bulkiness of $(CH_3)_3CO^-$ makes it more difficult for the more hindered 2° H to be abstracted, slowing the rate of formation of **B** and **C**, and favoring formation of **A** by removal of the less hindered 1° H.

7.48 (a) Use transition state theory to account for the relative yields of *cis* and *trans* alkenes in Problem 7.46. (b) Would it matter if the reaction showed kinetic or thermodynamic control? (c) How does replacing the Me's of 2-bromobutane by *t*-Bu's affect the ratio of product diastereomers?

◢ (a) In this one-step reaction the TS must begin to reflect the incipient alkene. Two TS's are possible, a *trans*-like and a *cis*-like. The *trans*-like TS, being more stable, has the lower $\Delta H^{\ddagger}$ and its formation is the preferred pathway. (b) No. The preferred product is both kinetically and thermodynamically controlled because the major stable product also has the lower enthalpy TS. (c) In 3-bromo-2,2,5,5-tetramethylhexane, $Me_3CCH_2CHBrCMe_3$, the repulsion of the bulkier groups causes a substantial increase in the $\Delta H^{\ddagger}$ of the *cis*-like TS as compared to the *trans*-like TS. Consequently, the *trans* diastereomer is practically the sole product.

7.49 List the possible products, in order of decreasing yield, from the reaction of 3-bromo-2,3-dimethylpentane with alc. KOH.

◢ $(CH_3)_2C=C(CH_3)CH_2CH_3$ $>$ $CH_3CH=C(CH_3)CH(CH_3)_2$

      tetrasubstituted, $R_2C=CR_2$ trisubstituted, $RHC=CR_2$

    $>$ $H_2C=C(CH_2CH_3)CH(CH_3)_2$

         disubstituted, $H_2C=CR_2$

7.50 Which isomers of C_4H_9Br yield only a single alkene on dehydrohalogenation? Give the structures of the alkenes.

◢   The 1° halides: $BrCH_2CH_2CH_2CH_3 \rightarrow CH_2=CHCH_2CH_3$
                       $BrCH_2CH(CH_3)_2 \rightarrow CH_2=C(CH_3)_2$
   The 3° halide (All vicinal H's are equivalent): $(CH_3)_3CBr \rightarrow CH_2=C(CH_3)_2$

7.51 Synthesize (*a*) cyclohexene from cyclohexane, and (*b*) propene from propane.

◢   (*a*)   Cyclohexane $\xrightarrow[hv]{Cl_2}$ chlorocyclohexane $\xrightarrow{alc.\ KOH}$ cyclohexene

    (*b*) $CH_3CH_2CH_3 \xrightarrow[hv]{Cl_2}$ mixture of $[CH_3CH_2CH_2Cl + CH_3CHClCH_3] \xrightarrow{alc.\ KOH}$ propene

      The mixture of chloropropanes need not be separated because they both give propene.

7.52 (*a*) Complete the following general reaction: $Br-\overset{|}{C}-\overset{|}{C}-Br + Zn/HOAc \xrightarrow{\text{(or NaI in acetone)}}$?

    (*b*) Classify this general reaction for preparing alkenes.

◢   (*a*) $\overset{\diagdown}{\underset{\diagup}{C}}=\overset{\diagup}{\underset{\diagdown}{C}}$ + $ZnBr_2$ (or $2NaBr + I_2$ if NaI is used).   (*b*) *Dehalogenation* of vicinal dihalides, a β-elimination.

7.53 In terms of oxidation-reduction and using ethane derivatives, compare dehalogenation, dehydrogenation, and dehydrohalogenation.

◢   Each C bonded to Br in CH_2BrCH_2Br has an oxidation number (ON) of -1. Each doubly-bonded C in the alkene has an ON of -2. This decrease in ON indicates that the dihalide is reduced and debromination is a reduction. (Zn is oxidized to Zn^{2+}). During dehydrogenation of CH_3CH_3, the C's that become doubly-bonded go from an ON of -3 to -2. This increase in ON (it becomes less negative) signals an oxidation of the hydrocarbon. (The H's are reduced; they go from an ON of $+1$ when bonded to C, to 0 in H_2.) In the alkyl halide, the C bonded to Br has an ON of -1 and the α-C has an ON of -3, for an average of -2, the same as in the alkene. Hence, dehydrohalogenation is not a redox reaction.

7.54 (*a*) Write a general equation for the reaction of an alcohol with concentrated acids such as H_2SO_4 or H_3PO_4 at about 170 °C.   (*b*) Classify this general reaction for preparing alkenes.   (*c*) Why is alcohol dehydration a useful reaction for alkene preparation?

◢   (*a*) $\overset{\diagup}{\underset{\diagdown}{C}}\overset{\overset{\displaystyle H}{|}}{-}\overset{\overset{\displaystyle OH}{|}}{\underset{\diagdown}{\overset{\diagup}{C}}} \underset{}{\overset{H_2SO_4}{\rightleftharpoons}} \overset{\diagdown}{\underset{\diagup}{C}}=\overset{\diagup}{\underset{\diagdown}{C}} + H_2O$

    (*b*)   Dehydration
    (*c*)   Complex alcohols are readily synthesized.

7.55 (*a*) Complete the reactions of the following alcohols with H_2SO_4 at ~ 170 °C: (i) $CH_3CH_2CH_2OH$, (ii) $CH_3CHOHCH_3$, and (iii) $(CH_3)_3COH$.   (*b*) Give the relative reaction rates of these alcohols.

◢   (*a*) (i) $CH_3CH=CH_2$, (ii) $CH_3CH=CH_2$, and (iii) $H_2C=C(CH_3)_2$.   (*b*) Since the order of reactivity of ROH is 3° > 2° > 1° > $-CH_3$, (iii) > (ii) > (i).

7.56 Give the alkene products of dehydration of $CH_3CHOHCH_2CH_3$ with their relative yields.

▮ Dehydration follows Saytzeff's rule. $CH_3CH{=}CHCH_3$ (*cis + trans*, major), $H_2C{=}CHCH_2CH_3$ (minor).

7.57 The rate expression for the acid-catalyzed dehydration of an alcohol is: rate $= k_1[ROH][H^+]$. (*a*) Write a three-step mechanism that is consistent with this expression, using $CH_3CHOHCH_3$ for ROH. (*b*) Identify the slow step and explain your choice. (*c*) Show how this rate expression is consistent with your mechanism. (*d*) Classify this elimination reaction.

▮ (*a*) *Step 1.*

$$CH_3\overset{H}{\underset{:\ddot{O}H}{CHCH_2}} + H_2SO_4 \rightleftharpoons CH_3\overset{H}{\underset{H:\overset{+}{\ddot{O}H}}{CHCH_2}} + HSO_4^-$$

base₁   acid₂   acid₁   base₂
an onium ion

Step 2.

$$CH_3\overset{}{\underset{H_2O^+\ \ H}{C{-}CH_2}} \longrightarrow CH_3\overset{+}{C}HCH_2 + H_2O$$
$$\overset{}{\underset{H}{}}$$

Isopropyl cation

Step 3.

$$CH_3\overset{+}{C}H{-}CH_2 + HSO_4^- \longrightarrow CH_3CH{=}CH_2 + H_2SO_4$$

very strong
acid₁   base₂   base₁   acid₂

Instead of HSO_4^-, a molecule of alcohol could act as the base in Step 3 to give ROH_2^+.

(*b*) Step 2 is rate determining and is the slow step. Bond-breaking requires energy because it leads to a high energy intermediate possessing a C with only six e⁻'s and a + charge.

(*c*) Since an intermediate cannot appear in a rate expression, ROH_2^+ is replaced by starting materials. Brönsted acid-base reactions are among the fastest known so the first step leading to formation of ROH_2^+ is fast and reversible. Hence,

$$K_e = [ROH_2^+]/[ROH][H^+] \quad \text{and} \quad [ROH_2^+] = K_e[ROH][H^+]$$

Substituting for $[ROH_2^+]$ in the rate expression for the slow second step, rate₂ $= k[ROH_2^+]$, gives

$$\text{rate} = kK_e[ROH][H^+]$$

$K_e k$ is a constant and the rewritten rate expression is as experimentally determined.

(*d*) E1. Again E stands for elimination and 1 for unimolecular since the slow step has only one species.

7.58 (*a*) Give the general and specific names for the intermediate formed in the slow step. (*b*) Explain why dehydration proceeds in acid but not in base.

▮ (*a*) The intermediate cation is called a *carbocation* (formerly called *carbonium ion*) and the name of the corresponding parent alkyl group is used. Me_2CH^+ is the *isopropyl* cation. (*b*) Under basic conditions the very poor leaving group OH^- (a strong base) would have to be eliminated. The essential role of the acid is to convert $-OH$ to $-OH_2^+$ so that the very good leaving group H_2O (a very weak base) is eliminated instead.

7.59 In terms of TS theory, with the aid of an enthalpy diagram, account for the relationship of the relative reactivities of RCH_2OH, R_2CHOH, and R_3COH and the stabilities of the intermediate carbocations.

▮ The order of reactivities is directly related to the order of stabilities of the incipient carbocations, $3° > 2° > 1°$ as shown in Fig. 7.3. Note that this is the same order of stabilities of radicals (see Problem 4.81). The lowest $\Delta H^{\ddagger}$ is required for the TS leading to the incipient carbocation of the 3° alcohol and the highest for the incipient C^+ of the 1° alcohol.

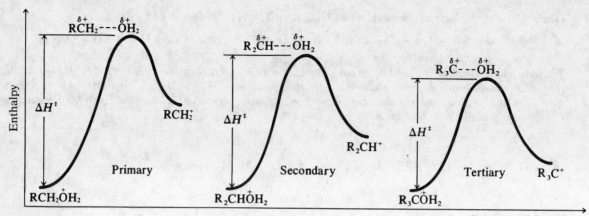

Fig. 7-3

7.60 (*a*) Supply mechanisms for the following acid-catalyzed dehydrations: (i) $HOCH_2CH_2CH_2CH_3$ to mainly *trans*-$CH_3CH=CHCH_3$ and (ii) $CH_3CH(OH)C(CH_3)_3$ to mainly $(CH_3)_2C=C(CH_3)_2$. (*b*) Why are the 1° alcohols poor starting materials for the synthesis of 1-alkenes?

◢ (*a*) (i) The 1° RCH_2^+ initially formed on the terminal C^1 is less stable than the 2° R_2CH^+ produced by the *hydride shift* of an H with its electron pair from C^1 to C^2. The hydride ion, $H:^-$ never forms. Instead it becomes attached to the new C (rearrangement terminus) as it breaks free from its old C (rearrangement origin) as shown in the TS for the hydride shift. (If a 1° RCH_2^+ is to be formed, it is likely the $:H$ begins to rearrange before the carbocation ever forms.) The reaction is completed when either the parent alcohol or the conjugate base of the acid removes the very acidic H^+ from C^3 of the 2° R^+ yielding 2-butene rather than the expected 1-butene.

$$CH_3CH_2\overset{\overset{H}{|}}{\underset{\underset{H}{|}}{C}}-\overset{\overset{H}{|}}{\underset{\underset{H}{|}}{C}}OH \xrightarrow[-H_2O]{H^+,\ heat} CH_3CH_2\overset{\overset{H}{|}}{\underset{\underset{H}{|}}{C}}-\overset{\overset{H}{|}}{\underset{\underset{}{}}{C}}^+ \xrightarrow{\sim\,:H}$$

1-Butanol   1° RCH_2^+

$$[CH_3CH_2HC\underset{\underset{H}{\overset{.\ .}{+}}}{-}CH_2]^{\ddagger} \longrightarrow CH_3CH_2\overset{\overset{H}{|}}{\underset{\underset{H}{|}}{C}}-\overset{\overset{H}{|}}{\underset{\underset{H}{|}}{C}}-H \xrightarrow{-H^+} trans\text{-}2\text{-Butene}$$

2° R_2CH^+

The hydride shift is indicated by $\sim :H$ over the reaction arrow.

(ii) Here a less stable 2° R_2CH^+ rearranges to a more stable 3° R_3C^+ by a *methide* ($:CH_3$ or $:Me$) *shift* whereby Me with its bonding electron pair moves from C^3 to C^2. $H_3C:^-$ is never set free but rather becomes partially bonded to the rearrangement terminus while still partially bonded to the origin.

$$CH_3\overset{\overset{H}{|}}{\underset{\underset{HO}{|}}{C}}-\overset{\overset{Me}{|}}{\underset{\underset{Me}{|}}{C}}CH_3 \xrightarrow[-H_2O]{H^+,\ heat} CH_3\overset{+}{C}H-\overset{\overset{Me}{|}}{\underset{\underset{Me}{|}}{C}}-CH_3 \xrightarrow{\sim\,:Me}$$

3,3-Dimethyl-   2° R_2CH^+
2-butanol

$$CH_3CH-\overset{\overset{Me}{|}}{\underset{\underset{Me}{|}}{\overset{+}{C}}}-CH_3 \xrightarrow{-H^+} CH_3-\overset{\overset{Me}{|}}{C}=\overset{\overset{Me}{/}}{C}-CH_3$$

3° R_3C^+ 2,3-Dimethyl-
2-butene

(*b*) The 1° RCH_2^+ would rearrange and a 2-alkene would result. Even if a 1-alkene were to form, it would tend to rearrange in acid to a 2-alkene.

7.61 Give the alkenes formed from acid-catalyzed dehydration of:

(*a*) $CH_3CH_2CH(OH)CH_2CH_3$,   (*b*) 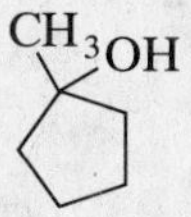 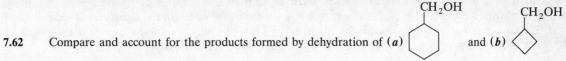   (*c*) $(CH_3)_3CCH_2OH$

▰ (*a*) *trans*-(major) and *cis*-(minor) 2-pentene. (*b*) 1-Methylcyclopentene. (*c*) $(CH_3)_2C\!=\!CHCH_3$ (major) $+ CH_2\!=\!C(CH_3)CH_2CH_3$ (minor). Neopentyl alcohol has no β-H's and it cannot be dehydrated without rearrangement. The incipient 1° neopentyl cation rearranges to the more stable 3° R_3C^+ by a :Me shift from the 4° β-C^2 to the 1° $RC^1H_2^+$. The H^+ loss gives the product.

7.62 Compare and account for the products formed by dehydration of (*a*) and (*b*)

▰ (*a*) 1-Methylcyclohexene. An :H shift converts the less stable 1° to a more stable 3° carbocation. The Saytzeff product dominates. (*b*) Cyclopentene. Rather than an :H shift from 1° to 3° carbocation, the side of the ring CH_2 shifts to give a 2° carbocation whose new five-membered ring is more stable than the old four-membered ring.

7.63 Which reaction gives 2,3-dimethyl-1-butene in the better yield: (*a*) dehydration of 2,3-dimethyl-1-butanol, or (*b*) dehydrohalogenation of 2,3-dimethyl-1-bromobutane? Explain.

▰ Dehydrohalogenation is preferred because dehydration is accompanied by a hydride shift leading to an intermediate 3° carbocation, which forms 2,3-dimethyl-2-butene.

7.64 (*a*) Give the products when $MeC\!\equiv\!CMe$ reacts with (i) one equivalent of H_2/Pd and (ii) Na/EtOH. (*b*) Use stereochemistry to classify the two reactions in (*a*). (*c*) Are these reactions thermodynamically controlled?

▰ (*a*) (i) *cis*-2-Butene, (ii) *trans*-2-butene. (*b*) These reactions, each giving *only* one of two possible stereomers, are called *stereoselective*. In this case they are more specifically called *diastereoselective* because the stereoisomers are diastereomers. (*c*) The reaction with H_2 is definitely not thermodynamically controlled because the *cis*-alkene is the less stable one. The reaction with Na/EtOH could be thermodynamically controlled because the *trans* alkene is more stable. However, it does not have to be. To be certain about the control of this reaction, an alkyne should be reduced with Na/EtOH to give an alkene whose *cis*-isomer is more stable. When this is done with special cycloalkynes, the less stable *trans*-cycloalkenes are isolated. The results of such experiments reveal that the reaction is not thermodynamically controlled.

7.65 (*a*) Give structures for compounds that will form 2-pentene (disregard stereoisomerism) in best possible yields when reacted with: (i) alc. KOH, (ii) Zn/HOAc, (iii) conc. H_2SO_4 + heat. (*b*) What is the best way to prepare only (i) *cis*- and (ii) *trans*-2-pentene?

▰ (*a*) (i) $CH_3CH_2CHClCH_2CH_3$. 2-Chloropentene would give some 1-pentene thereby reducing the yield. (ii) $CH_3CHBrCHBrCH_2CH_3$ (iii) $CH_3CH_2CHOHCH_2CH_3$ [See (i) for reasons why the 2-isomer should not be used.] (*b*) Reduce $CH_3C\!\equiv\!CCH_2CH_3$ using (i) H_2/Pd and (ii) Na/EtOH.

7.66 Provide the structural formula and the name of the principal product from each of the following reactions:

(*a*) $BrCH_2CH_2CH_2CH_2Br$ + alc. KOH   (*c*) $(CH_3)_3CBr + CH_3COO^-$

(*b*) $(CH_3)_2CHCH(OH)CH_3 + H_2SO_4$ + heat   (*d*) 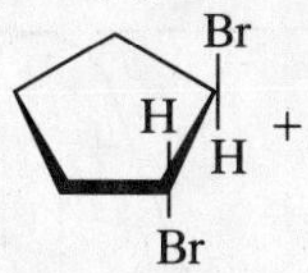   + Zn (in alcohol)

▰ (*a*) $H_2C\!=\!CH\!-\!CH\!=\!CH_2$, 1,3-butadiene; (*b*) $(CH_3)_2C\!=\!CHCH_3$, 2-methyl-2-butene; (*c*) $H_2C\!=\!C(CH_3)_2$, isobutylene (2-methylpropene); (*d*) cyclopentene.

CHEMICAL REACTIONS

1. Ionic (Polar) Additions

7.67 (*a*) Classify $C\!=\!C$ in terms of the Lewis acid-base concept. (*b*) With what type of reagents would $C\!=\!C$ be expected to react in polar reactions? (*c*) Show how the reaction of ethene with $AgNO_3$ substantiates the classification of $C\!=\!C$. (*d*) Use the molecular orbital concept to explain the bonding in the product in part (*c*).

▟ (a) The electron-rich π bond makes C=C a nucleophile capable of donating its electron-pair in polar (ionic) reactions. (b) Electrophiles. (c) The nucleophilic C=C reacts with the electrophilic Ag^+ to form a salt called a π *complex*:

$$H_2C \stackrel{\longrightarrow}{=\!=} CH_2$$
$$Ag^+ NO_3^-$$

The solid arrow indicates the donation of the π electron-pair from C=C to Ag^+. (d) The π bond overlaps head-to-head with the *s* orbital of Ag^+. In fact, Ag^+ is regarded as imbedded in the cloud on one side of the π bond. The broken arrow indicates the donation of an electron-pair of a filled *d* orbital of Ag^+ with the empty π* MO* of C=C. This *back-bonding* strengthens the π-complex bond even though it involves a MO*.

7.68 (a) Name the type of reactions of $\!\!>\!C\!=\!C\!<\!\!$ and electrophiles. (b) Write equations for a two-step ionic reaction of $\!\!>\!C\!=\!C\!<\!\!$ with E:Nu, where E is the electrophilic and :Nu is the nucleophilic portion. Show two possible structures for the intermediate cation R^+. (c) Classify the structures of R^+ in (b) as complexes.

▟ (a) *Addition reactions*, more specifically *1,2-additions*.

(b)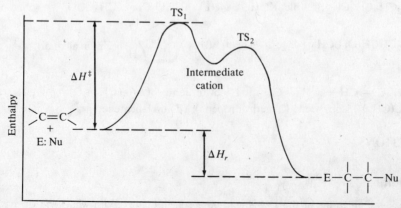

(c) Cation (**A**) is called a σ complex because of the σ bond between E and C. Cation (**B**) can be a π complex or a σ complex if there are practically full bonds between E and C.

7.69 Draw an enthalpy diagram for the mechanism of the ionic (polar) electrophilic addition in Problem 7.68.

▟ See Fig. 7-4. The first step is slow because it involves the formation of the unstable cation intermediate. The product has a lower enthalpy than the alkene because the π bond is gone.

Fig. 7-4

7.70 Give the number and structures of structural isomers that are possible when (*a*) a symmetrical adduct such as X_2 adds to (i) $CH_3CH=CHCH_3$, a typical symmetrical alkene, and to (ii) $CH_3CH=CH_2$, a typical unsymmetrical alkene. (*b*) Repeat (i) and (ii) for addition of an unsymmetrical adduct such as HX. Ignore stereoisomers.

⫸ (*a*) There is only one product in each case: (i) $CH_3CHXCHXCH_3$ and (ii) CH_3CHXCH_2X.

(*b*) (i) one product, $CH_3CHXCH_2CH_3$; (ii) two products, CH_3CHXCH_3 and $CH_3CH_2CH_2X$.

7.71 (*a*) Give the structure of the product formed when ethene reacts with (i) Br_2, (ii) HBr, (iii) H_2O (acidified), (iv) Cl_2 in H_2O (HOCl), and (v) H_2SO_4 (cold). Give specific names for reactions (i)–(iv). (*b*) For each addend in part (*a*) indicate the E and Nu portions (Problem 7.68).

⫸ (*a*) (i) CH_2BrCH_2Br (bromination), (ii) CH_3CH_2Br (hydrobromination), (iii) CH_3CH_2OH (hydration), (iv) CH_2ClCH_2OH (chlorohydrin formation), and (v) $CH_3CH_2OSO_3H$.

(*b*) The E's, assumed to add as E^+, are written first and the Nu's, assumed to add as Nu^- have parentheses: (i) Br(Br), (ii) H(Br), (iii) H(OH), (iv) Cl(OH), and (v) H(OSO$_3$H).

7.72 (*a*) Write the major product from the reaction of an unsymmetrical alkene, such as isobutylene, with the following unsymmetrical addenda: (i) HBr, (ii) $H_2O(H^+)$, and (iii) ClOH. (*b*) State the rule for getting the correct answers to part (*a*). (*c*) Give the general name for the reactions that give mainly one of several possible products.

⫸ (*a*) (i) $(CH_3)_3CBr$, (ii) $(CH_3)_3COH$, and (iii) $(CH_3)_2COHCH_2Cl$. (*b*) The *Markovnikov rule* states that E^+ adds to the double-bonded C that has more H's, followed by addition of $:Nu^-$ to the C with less H's. If E^+ is a proton, "the rich get richer". (*c*) *Regioselective*.

7.73 Predict the product of the reaction between $Me_2C=CH_2$ and ICl.

⫸ Cl is more electronegative than I making I the E^+ that, according to the Markovnikov rule, adds to the C with the greater number of H's. The product is 2-chloro-1-iodo-2-methylpropane, Me_2CClCH_2I.

7.74 (*a*) Give the alkene (there may be more than one) needed to prepare (i) 1-bromo-1-methylcyclohexane and (ii) 2-bromo-1-methylcyclohexane. (*b*) Which reaction in (*a*) would give the better yield of product? Explain.

⫸ This is an addition of HBr. (*a*) (i) 1-Methylcyclohexene or methylenecyclohexane, where the nucleophilic Br^- binds to the C with the Me (or fewer H's); and (ii) 3-methylcyclohexene (*b*) Both alkenes give the desired product. Since both doubly-bonded C's in 3-methylcyclohexene have one H, this reaction gives a mixture of 2-bromo and 3-bromocyclohexane.

7.75 (*a*) Give a mechanistic interpretation of the product formation in Problem 7.72 (from $Me_2C=CH_2$) using an enthalpy diagram. (*b*) Restate the Markovnikov rule using this interpretation.

⫸ See Fig. 7-5. The more stable cation ($3° > 2° > 1°$) has a lower $\Delta H^{\ddagger}$ for the transition state and forms more rapidly. TS_1, leading to the more stable $3°$ R^+, has a smaller $\Delta H^{\ddagger}$ than TS_2, leading to the less stable $1°$ R^+. Hence, the major product from the $3°$ R^+ forms more rapidly. (*b*) E^+ adds so as to furnish the more stable R^+.

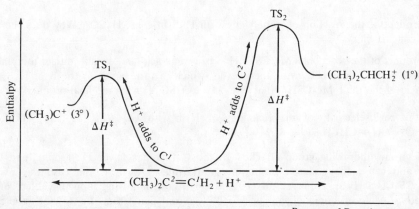

Progress of Reaction

7.76 Assuming the absence of any steric hindrance, list the following alkenes in decreasing order of reactivity towards electrophilic addition: (i) $ClCH_2CH=CH_2$, (ii) $Me_2C=CH_2$, (iii) $CH_3CH=CH_2$, (iv) $H_2C=CHCl$. Explain your order.

◢ Electron-donating groups such as R's make the π bond more electron-rich and more reactive. Conversely, electron-withdrawing groups such as halogens make the π bond more electron-poor and less reactive. The order is:

(ii) two R's > (iii) one R > (i) one R with a Cl > (iv) Cl on a doubly-bonded C.

7.77 (*a*) Why are hydrogen halides in the dry gaseous state or dissolved in inert nonpolar solvents used to convert alkenes to alkyl halides? (*b*) Compare and explain the relative rates (reactivities) of addition to alkenes of HCl, HBr, and HI.

◢ (*a*) Dry halogen halides are stronger acids and better electrophiles than H_3O^+, the only acid in their aqueous solutions. Furthermore, H_2O is a nucleophile that competes with the halide ion to give an alcohol. (*b*) The relative reactivities depend on the ability of an HX to donate H^+ (acidity) to give R^+ in the rate-controlling step. The acidity and reactivity order is HI > HBr > HCl. It is noteworthy that the nucleophilicity of the conjugate bases (X^-) has no effect on the rate because X^- participates in a second fast step.

7.78 Account for the formation of both 3-bromo-2,2-dimethylbutane and 2-bromo-2,3-dimethylbutane from the reaction of HBr with 3,3-dimethyl-1-butene.

◢ The predicted product from Markovnikov addition is 3-bromo-2,2-dimethylbutane.

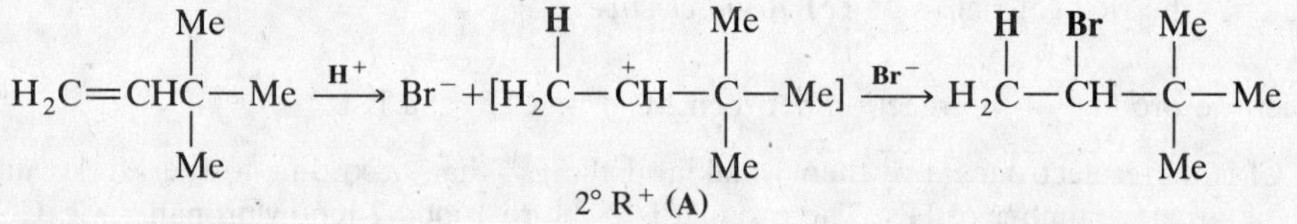

However, no matter how formed, an R^+ can undergo $:H$ or $:R$ shifts to a more stable R^+. In this case, the 2° R^+ intermediate undergoes a $:Me$ shift to a more stable 3° R^+ which adds Br^- to yield 2-bromo-2,3-dimethylbutane.

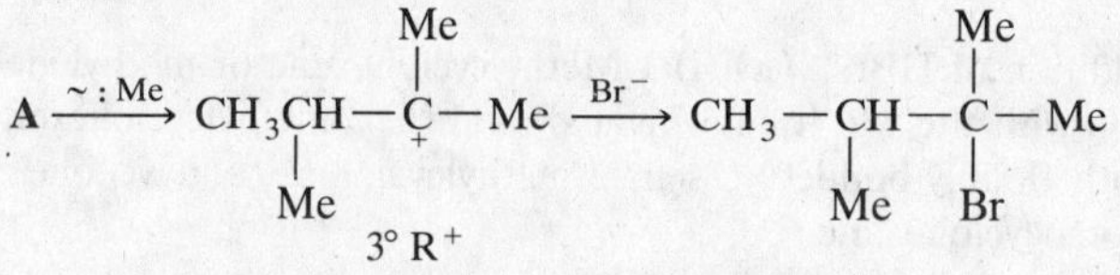

7.79 Isobutylene gas dissolves in 63% H_2SO_4 to yield a deliquescent white solid, **A**. When heated in water, the solid changes to a liquid, **B**, bp 83 °C. Give the structures of **A** and **B**.

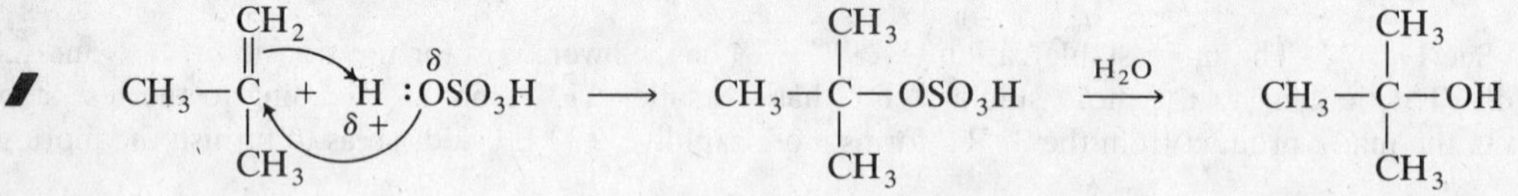

7.80 Give the product of the reaction of isobutylene with H_2S in conc. H_2SO_4. Why does the reaction fail in the absence of conc. H_2SO_4?

◢ The product of the reaction is Me_3CSH. H_2S is a weak acid and cannot initiate the reaction by adding H^+ to the C=C. H_2SO_4 adds H^+ giving the Me_3C^+ which in turn bonds to the S of H_2S. This results in the conjugate acid of the thiol, $Me_3CSH_2^+$, that loses H^+ to HSO_4^-, giving the final product.

7.81 Compare the regioselectivity of the reactions of HBr with (*a*) $CF_3CH=CH_2$, (*b*) $BrCH=CH_2$, and (*c*) $CH_3-O-CH=CHCH_3$.

◢ An electron-withdrawing group attached to the C that has fewer H's would tend to destabilize a + on this C and cause the addition to be anti-Markovnikov. Such is the case in (*a*), where the major product is $CF_3CH_2CH_2Br$. However, in (*b*) the electron-withdrawing inductive effect of Br is superseded by extended π delocalization of an unshared electron pair from Br to C^+, thereby stabilizing the R^+, $[:\ddot{B}r-CH-CH_3 \leftrightarrow :\ddot{B}r=CHCH_3]$. Thus, the Markovnikov product, Br_2CHCH_3, is formed.

(c) Protonation of either C of the C=C gives a 2° R⁺. However, the O behaves like Br in delocalizing a pair of e⁻'s to the adjacent C⁺, stabilizing the + charge, and H⁺ bonds almost exclusive to the carbon β to the O as follows: $[CH_3-\overset{..}{O}-\overset{+}{C}H-CH_2CH_3 \leftrightarrow CH_3-\overset{+}{O}=CH-CH_2CH_3]$. The product is $CH_3-O-CHBrCH_2CH_3$. In general, when the inductively electron-withdrawing group attached to the doubly-bonded C has an unshared pair of e⁻'s, Markovnikov addition is observed.

7.82 Account for the acid-catalyzed isomerization of *cis*-2-butene to *trans*-2-butene.

◢ H⁺ adds to C=C giving a flat R⁺, $CH_3CH_2\overset{+}{C}HCH_3$, that then loses an H⁺ from C to give mainly the more stable *trans*-alkene.

7.83 (a) Give the product(s) with the correct stereochemistry for the reaction of cyclohexene with (i) Br_2, (ii) Br_2 in the presence of NaCl, and (iii) Br_2 in CH_3OH. (b) Is Br_2 addition stereoselective and if so what course does it take?

◢ (a) (i) *trans*-1,2-Dibromocyclohexane (A), (ii) A + *trans*-1-bromo-2-chlorocyclohexane (no dichlorocyclohexane), and (iii) A + *trans*-1-bromo-2-methoxycyclohexane. (b) Yes, *trans* or *anti*. The addition is also said to be *antarafacial*, that is, groups of the addend bond from opposite faces of the double bond.

7.84 (a) Give the stereochemical structure of the reaction product of Br_2 with (i) *cis*-2-butene and (ii) *trans*-2-butene. (b) In terms of its stereochemistry, characterize this type of reaction.

◢ (a) (i) *rac*-2,3-Dibromobutane and (ii) *meso*-2,3-dibromobutane. (b) Diastereospecific.

7.85 (a) What mechanistic facts and interpretations emerge from the product formations in Problems 7.83 and 7.84? (b) Give a mechanism for the Br_2 addition. Illustrate with *cis*- and *trans*-2-butene.

◢ (a) (i) The addition is electrophilic, inferred from the absence of any 1,2-dichlorocyclohexane (which would require a source of Cl^+).

(ii) It is not a one-step reaction, inferred from the intrusion of the nucleophiles Cl^- and MeOH in formation of byproducts.

(iii) Addition is *anti* (*trans*); one Br adds to the face above the π bond, the second Br adds to the face below. *Anti* addition also precludes a one-step mechanism which would require the two Br's to approach from the same side of the π bond to give *cis*-1,2-dibromocyclohexane. Such an addition is called *cis*, *syn*, or *suprafacial*.

(iv) The diastereospecificity of the 2-butene reactions indicates the absence of an open carbocation intermediate [(i) in part (b) of Problem 7.68] whose p AO could be attacked from both the top and bottom giving a mixture of diastereomers. Furthermore, the same carbocation would form from both *cis*- and *trans*-2-butene and should then give the same product distribution. The intermediate must preserve the stereochemistry of the starting materials and is a bridged cation [(ii) in part (b) of Problem 7.68].

(b) The first step is the formation of a bridged cation, called a *bromonium ion*. In the second step, the nucleophile (mainly Br^- but also nucleophilic solvents or added anions) adds to the face away from the bridging group to yield the *anti* addition product.

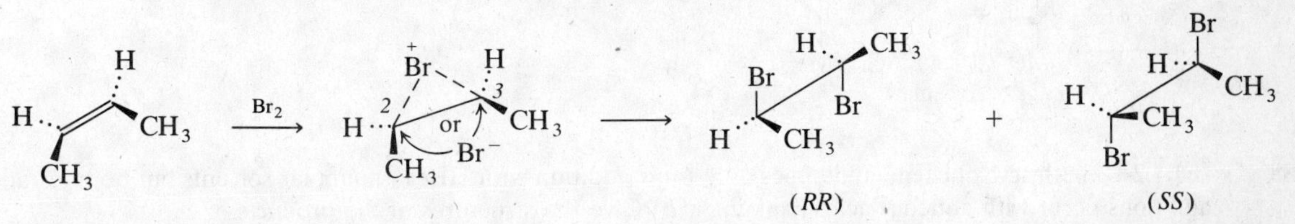

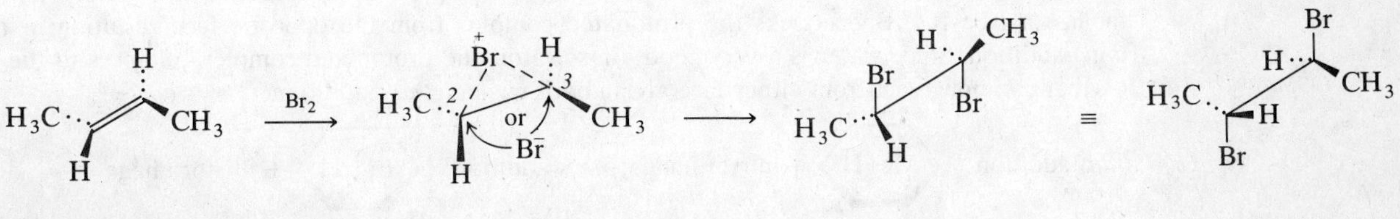

Formation of the bromochloro and bromomethoxy compounds (see Problem 7.83) requires attack on the bromonium ion by Cl^- and MeOH respectively. Br_2 does not ionize into Br^+ and Br^-. More likely, the π e^-'s attack one of the Br's displacing the other as Br^-, initially giving a π complex that moves on to a three-membered ring bromonium ion (Fig. 7-6).

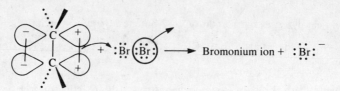

Fig. 7-6

7.86 (*a*) Give the product of the reaction of $(CH_3)_2C=CH_2$ with Br_2 in H_2O and account for its orientation in terms of the bromonium ion. (*b*) What intermediate ion is formed in the reaction of alkenes with Cl_2 and H_2O?

◢ (*a*) With this unsymmetrical alkene the X^+ adds to the terminal C with more H's to give the bromohydrin $(CH_3)_2C(OH)CH_2Br$, 1-bromo-2-methyl-2-propanol. The bromonium ion of this alkene has Br attached to two different C's and the product formation is a question of which C is the more active site toward bonding with the nucleophilic H_2O. When the nucleophile is poor (H_2O) and the solvent has a high polarity (H_2O), the C that can best be an incipient R^+ is the more reactive site. In this bromonium ion it is the 3° C to which the O of H_2O forms the bond, eventually giving the product. (*b*) Cl^+ replaces Br^+ to give a chloronium ion, another example of a halonium ion.

7.87 Give the product, indicating the stereochemistry when pertinent, for each of the following reactions: (*a*) cyclohexene + KI/H_3PO_4, (*b*) cyclopentene + Br_2 in H_2O, (*c*) *cis*- or *trans*-2-pentene + HBr, and (*d*) 1-methylcyclohexene + Cl_2 in H_2O.

◢ (*a*) Iodocyclohexane. This reagent is cheaper than using HI.
(*b*) *Anti* addition yields *rac*-*trans*-2-bromocyclopentanol.

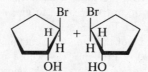

rac-*trans*-2-Bromocyclopentanol

(*c*) 3-Bromopentane and *rac*-2-bromopentane.

(*d*) 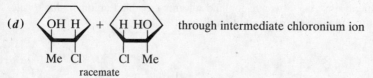 through intermediate chloronium ion

racemate

7.88 (*a*) 1,2-Dimethylcyclohexene undergoes only *trans* addition with HBr in nonpolar solvents but both *cis* and *trans* additions occur with aqueous acid. Explain. (*b*) Give the structures of the products.

◢ (*a*) This stereospecific reaction probably proceeds through a bridged cation like the bromonium ion where H replaces Br. The intermediate may actually be a π complex. In the absence of a solvent that can stabilize a free R^+, Br^- attacks the protonated complex from the opposite face resulting in *trans* (*anti*) addition. Since water is a very good ion-solvator, the protonated complex collapses to the free R^+ that can now react from either face giving both *cis* and *trans* addition.

(*b*) *trans* addition: 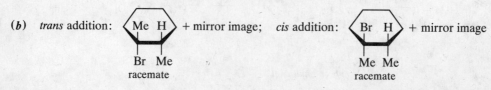 + mirror image; *cis* addition: + mirror image

Br Me   Me Me
racemate   racemate

7.89   (*a*) What principle relates the mechanisms of dehydration of alcohols and hydration of alkenes? (*b*) What experimental conditions favor dehydration rather than hydration?

▮   (*a*) The *principle of microscopic reversibility* states that every reaction is reversible, even if only to a microscopically small extent. Furthermore, the reverse process proceeds through the same intermediates and transition states, but in the opposite direction.

$$H^+ + RCH_2CH_2OH \rightleftharpoons RCH{=\!=}CH_2 + H_2O$$

(*b*) Low H_2O concentration and high temperature favor dehydration because the volatile alkene can be removed from the reaction mixture by distillation, thereby shifting the equilibrium to the right. Alkenes are hydrated at lower temperatures with *dilute* acid which provides a high concentration of the reactant H_2O to shift the equilibrium to the left.

7.90   (*a*) Supply the structures for **A** and **B** in the following two-step reaction:

$$C_3H_7CH{=\!=}CH_2 \xrightarrow[\text{THF/H}_2\text{O}]{\text{Hg(OAc)}_2} A \xrightarrow{\text{NaBH}_4/\text{NaOH}} B$$

(*b*) What is the net regiospecificity of this hydration? (*c*) Name (i) the first step and (ii) the second step. (*d*) Why is this hydration procedure superior to acid-catalyzed hydration of most alkenes? (*e*) What is the final state of Hg?

▮   (*a*) **A** is $C_3H_7CH(OH)CH_2{-}HgOAc$, an organomercurial alcohol; **B** is $C_3H_7CH(OH)CH_3$. (*b*) Markovnikov addition.   (*c*) (i) Oxymercuration (a type of solvomercuration) and (ii) demercuration.   (*d*) It precludes rearrangement.   (*e*) Reduction to Hg°.

7.91   (*a*) Give the stereoisomer formed when cyclohexene is oxymercurated.   (*b*) Suggest a mechanism for the oxymercuration step.

▮   (*a*) *Trans*.   (*b*) The electrophile of $Hg(OAc)_2$ is $AcOHg^+$ that adds to C=C to form a mercurinium ion similar to a bromonium ion. The mercurinium ion then reacts with H_2O (not OAc^-) at the more substituted C for the same reason and in the same way as does the bromonium ion (Problem 7.86).

mercurinium ion

7.92   (*a*) Supply the condensed formulas and names for the products from the reaction of three moles of propene and one mole of BH_3 in tetrahydrofuran (THF), a cyclic ether.   (*b*) Give the formulas of the intermediate products formed in this stepwise reaction.   (*c*) Name this addition reaction.   (*d*) Identify the electrophile and regiospecificity.   (*e*) Why must BH_3 be used in an ether solution and how is it made?

▮   (*a*) Pr_3B,tripropylborane, an organoborane.   (*b*) $PrBH_2$, propylborane, and Pr_2BH, dipropylborane. (*c*) Hydroboration.   (*d*) BH_3 is the electrophile and, since it adds to the C with the greater number of H's, it is a Markovnikov-type addition.   (*e*) BH_3 by itself does not exist. Its dimer B_2H_6 is known, but it is air and moisture sensitive. When B_2H_6 is dissolved in THF, it breaks down to BH_3, which is stabilized by forming a coordinate covalent bond with the O of the ether, $R_2\overset{+}{\underset{\cdot\cdot}{O}}{:}\bar{B}H_3$.

7.93   (*a*) Give the monoalkylborane formed from $Me_3CCH{=\!=}CH_2(E)$ and B_2H_6/THF.   (*b*) What mechanistic information about hydroboration is afforded by the isolation of the product in (*a*)?   (*c*) Provide a mechanism for the reaction.   (*d*) Can the trialkylborane of **E** be formed? Explain.

▮   (*a*) $Me_3CCH_2CH_2BH_2$.   (*b*) It cannot be a typical two-step reaction whose first step generates a 2° R^+, $Me_3C\overset{+}{C}HCH_2BH_2$, that would undoubtedly rearrange to the more stable 3° R^+, $Me_2\overset{+}{C}CHMcCH_2BH_2$.

(c) The addition is believed to occur in two steps. Step 1 is the formation of the π complex **A** between boron and the π bond. In step 2, **A** goes through a four-centered TS, **B**, to the product.

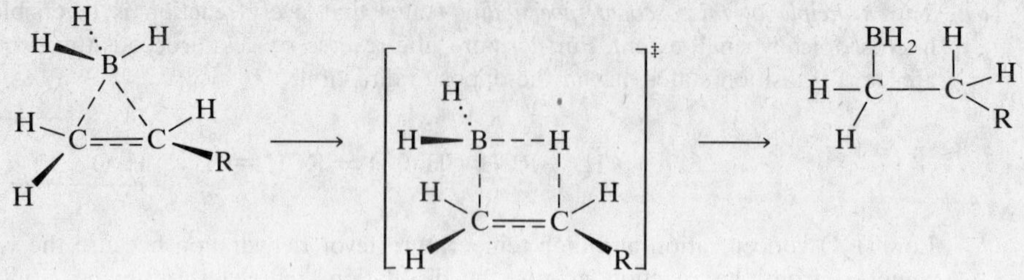

(d) The dialkylborane $(Me_3CCH_2CH_2)_2BH$ is too sterically hindered to add to the hindered alkene.

7.94 (a) Give the products from the reactions of tripropylborane, formed from propene and BH_3, with (i) $H_2O_2 + OH^-$ and (ii) Br_2. (b) What is the net regiospecificity of the addition to propene? (c) Name each type of reaction.

◢ (a) (i) $CH_3CH_2CH_2OH$ and (ii) $CH_3CH_2CH_2Br$. (b) Anti-Markovnikov. (c) (i) Hydroboration-oxidation and (ii) hydroboration-halogenation (specifically, bromination).

7.95 (a) Give the product from the hydroboration-oxidation of 1-methylcyclopentene. (b) Classify the mode of addition.

◢ (a)

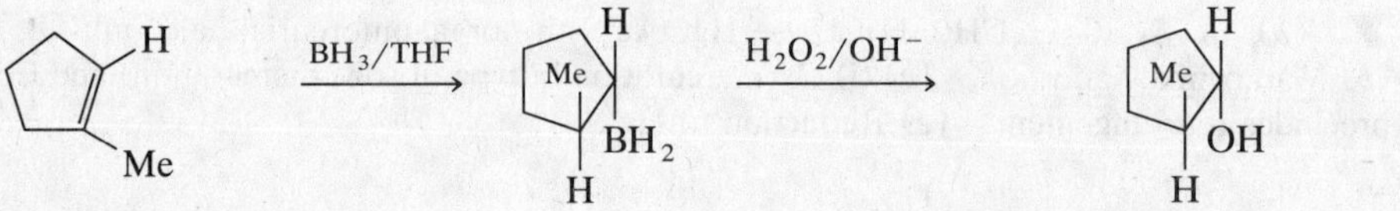

1-Methylcyclopentene   trans-2-Methylcyclopentanol

(b) Syn (cis, suprafacial)

7.96 Give, in tabular form, the major alcohol formed by (a) oxymercuration-demercuration, (b) H^+-catalyzed hydration, and (c) hydroboration-oxidation of: (i) 1-heptene, (ii) 1-methylcyclohexene, (iii) methylenecyclobutane, and (iv) bicyclo[2.2.1]heptene (norbornylene).

◢ See Table 7-1.
    In compound (iv), $AcOHg^+$ attacks from exo side, H_2O from the endo side (trans) to give the endo alcohol, while BH_3 approaches from the exo side to give the exo alcohol (syn addition). The intermediate R^+ from the H_3O^+ attack reacts to give the more stable product, which is the exo alcohol.

TABLE 7-1

	(a)	(b)	(c)
(i)	$C_5H_{11}CHOHCH_3$	$C_5H_{11}CHOHCH_3$	$C_6H_{13}CH_2OH$
(ii)	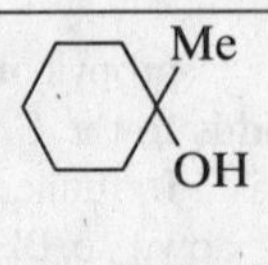	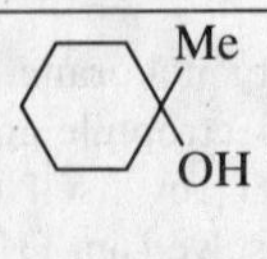	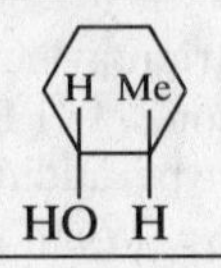
(iii)	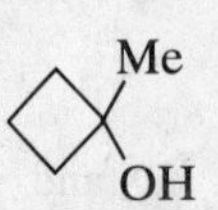	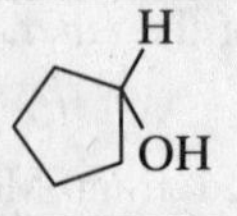	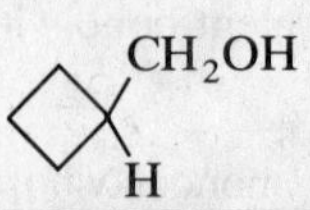
(iv)	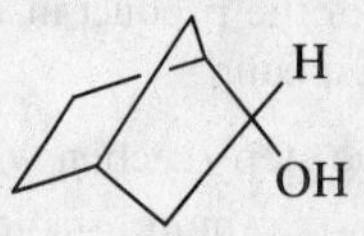	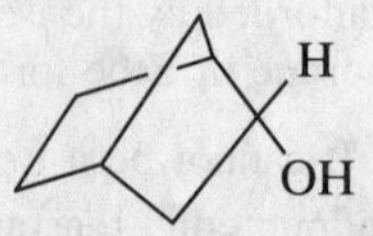	

7.97   Contrast (*a*) H$^+$-catalyzed hydration, (*b*) hydroboration-oxidation, and (*c*) oxymercuration-demercuration in terms of (i) regiospecificity, (ii) mode of addition, and (iii) susceptibility to rearrangement.

	(*a*)	(*b*)	(*c*)
(i)	Markovnikov	Anti-Markovnikov	Markovnikov
(ii)	No clear stereospecificity	*Syn*	No clear stereospecificity
(iii)	Yes	No	No

7.98   Deduce the structures of the products from hydroboration-bromination of: (*a*) (*Z*)- and (*E*)-2,3-dideutero-2-butene and (*b*) 1,2-dideuterocyclohexene.

▰   (*a*) *Syn*-addition gives a racemic mixture of the diastereomer **A** from the (*Z*)-alkene and **B** from the (*E*)-alkene.

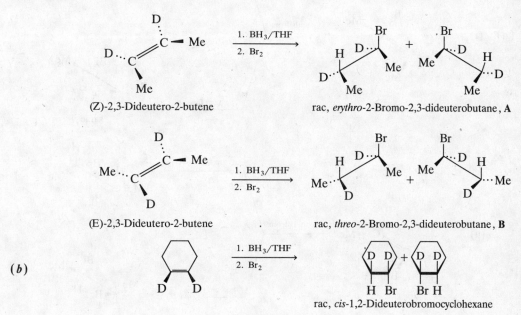

(Z)-2,3-Dideutero-2-butene   rac, *erythro*-2-Bromo-2,3-dideuterobutane, **A**

(E)-2,3-Dideutero-2-butene   rac, *threo*-2-Bromo-2,3-dideuterobutane, **B**

(*b*)

rac, *cis*-1,2-Dideuterobromocyclohexane

2. Reduction

7.99   (*a*) Complete the following reactions:

(i) $CH_3CH{=}CH_2 + H_2 \xrightarrow{\text{Pd, Pt, or Ni}} ?$ (ii) $CH_3CH{=}CH_2 + H_2 \xrightarrow{\text{RhCl[(Ph}_3\text{P)}_3]} ?$

The catalyst in (ii) is *Wilkinson's* catalyst. (*b*) In terms of the catalysts used, classify these two reactions. (*c*) Show the steps in the mechanism of reaction (ii) involving the catalyst.

▰   (*a*) (i) and (ii) $CH_3CH_2CH_3$.   (*b*) Both reactions are catalytic hydrogenations (addition of H_2).
(i) Heterogeneous catalytic hydrogenation in which the solid catalyst is in a different phase from the reactants. (ii) Homogeneous catalytic hydrogenation because reactants and catalyst are in the same phase.   (*c*) In step 1 an H_2 adds to the rhodium complex and one Ph_3P ligand (L) is lost, resulting in a five-coordinate rhodium complex, **A** (L = Ph_3P). In this *oxidative addition*, the Rh changes oxidation state from +1 to +3. In step 2 the alkene reacts with **A** to form a π complex, **B**, which undergoes rearrangement (step 3) of an H to one of the C's of the double bond, the other C forming a σ bond to the Rh (**C**).

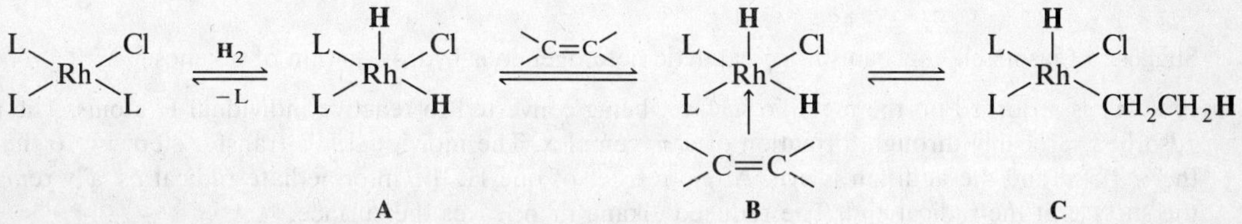

In the last step, a second H is transferred to the other C, and the alkane is lost with simultaneous regeneration of the metal catalyst: $C \overset{+L}{\rightleftharpoons} Rh(Ph_3P)_3Cl + HCH_2CH_2H$. The catalysis depends on the ability of rhodium, a transition metal, to form a π complex with $\overset{}{C}=\overset{}{C}$ (Problem 7.67).

7.100 (*a*) Give the products from catalytic hydrogenation of: (i) *cis*-2,3-dibromo-2-butene, (ii) *trans*-2,3-dibromo-2-butene, and (iii) 1,2-dimethylcyclohexene. (*b*) Classify the mode of addition.

(*a*) (i) H₂ adds from top face → / bottom face → same, *meso*

(ii) H₂ adds from top face → + bottom face → enantiomers

(iii) H₂ adds from top face → / bottom face → same, *meso*

In (i) and (iii), the same *meso* product is formed whether H₂ adds from the top or bottom face of the π bond. (*b*) *Syn* (*cis*).

7.101 Suggest a reasonable mechanism for catalytic heterogeneous hydrogenation of alkenes.

H₂ is adsorbed on the metallic surface, being converted to reactive individual H atoms. The alkene is also adsorbed, probably through formation of a π complex. The individual H's transfer stepwise to the open face of the π bond and the addition is *syn*. After transfer of one H, the intermediate radical usually remains bound to the surface at the radical end. The reduced alkane then leaves the surface.

7.102 Account for the isolation of some *trans*- and *cis*-2-butene from the incomplete reaction of 1-butene with H_2/Pd.

    ▟ Alkene isomerization proves that addition of the individual $H\cdot$'s is reversible. An $H\cdot$ adds to C^1 in the first step, leaving C^2 as a radical still bonded to the catalyst. Addition of $H\cdot$ is reversible, so 1-butene can be regenerated. However, either of two H's on C^3 can also return to the catalyst, leading to formation of *cis*- and *trans*-2-butene which can leave the metal surface (Fig. 7-7).

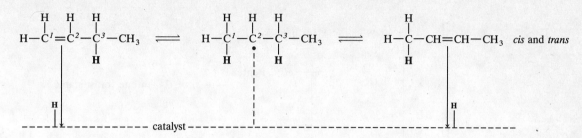

Fig. 7-7

7.103 Give the products and explain their formation when (*a*) cyclohexene and two equivalents of 1-hexene are heated in the presence of Pd but in the absence of H_2, and (*b*) 1,2-dimethylcyclopentene is heated with H_2NNH_2 (hydrazine) and an oxidant (H_2O_2). (*c*) What advantage does the reaction in part (*b*) have over catalytic hydrogenation?

    ▟ (*a*) Hexane and benzene. The reaction is called transfer hydrogenation. The catalyst removes two pairs of H's from cyclohexene, the reducing agent, forming the very stable benzene (see Problems 10.6 and 10.7). These H's then transfer to the two $>C=C<$'s to complete the reduction.

    (*b*) *cis*-1,2-Dimethylcyclopentane + N_2. H_2NNH_2 is oxidized to the unstable intermediate, $H\ddot{N}=\ddot{N}H$ (diimide), that donates its H's to $>C=C<$ in a concerted fashion through a six-membered transition state. The mode of addition is *syn*,

$$\left[\begin{array}{c} \ddot{N}\equiv\equiv\ddot{N} \\ \big| \quad \quad \big| \\ H \quad \quad H \\ \big| \quad \quad \big| \\ >C\equiv\equiv C< \end{array} \right]^{\ddagger} \longrightarrow \quad \begin{array}{c} :N\equiv N: \\ + \\ \begin{array}{c} H \ \ H \\ >C-C< \end{array} \end{array}$$

    (*c*) Diimide only reduces $C=C$'s and not multiple bonds between C and heteroatoms.

7.104 Give the structural formulas for **A** and **B** in the following sequence:

$$CH_3CH=CH_2 \xrightarrow{BH_3/THF} A \xrightarrow{CH_3COOH} B$$

    ▟ **A** is $(CH_3CH_2CH_2)_3B$; **B** is $CH_3CH_2CH_3$.

7.105 From 1-pentene (**A**) prepare (*a*) $CH_3CH_2CH_2CHDCH_3$ (**B**), (*b*) $CH_3(CH_2)_3CH_2D$ (**C**), (*c*) $CH_3CH_2CH_2CHDCH_2D$ (**D**) (use 3 methods).

    ▟ (*a*) $A \xrightarrow{BD_3/THF} (CH_3CH_2CH_2CHDCH_2)_3B \xrightarrow{HOAc} B$.

    (*b*) $A \xrightarrow{BH_3/THF} (CH_3CH_2CH_2CH_2CH_2)_3B \xrightarrow{DOAc} C$.

    (*c*) React **A** with (1) D_2/Pd, (2) $D_2NND_2 + H_2O_2$, (3) BD_3/THF, then DOAc → **D**.

7.106 Given the following heats of hydrogenation, $-\Delta H_h$, in kJ/mol: 1-pentene, 125.9; *cis*-2-pentene, 119.7; *trans*-2-pentene, 115.5. (*a*) Use an enthalpy diagram to derive two generalizations about the relative stabilities of alkenes. (*b*) Would the ΔH_h of 2-methyl-2-butene be helpful in making your generalizations? (*c*) The corresponding heats of combustion, $-\Delta H_c$, are: 3376, 3369, and 3365 kJ/mol. Are these values consistent with your generalizations in part (*a*)? (*d*) Would the ΔH_c of 2-methyl-2-butene be helpful in your comparison? (*e*) Suggest a relative value for the ΔH_c of 2-methyl-2-butene.

◢ (*a*) See Fig. 7-8. The most stable alkene has the largest ΔH_h. (1) The alkene with more R groups on the double bond is more stable; 2-pentene > 1-pentene. (2) The *trans* isomer is usually more stable than the *cis*. Bulky alkyl groups are *anti*-like in the *trans* isomer and eclipsed-like in the *cis* isomer.

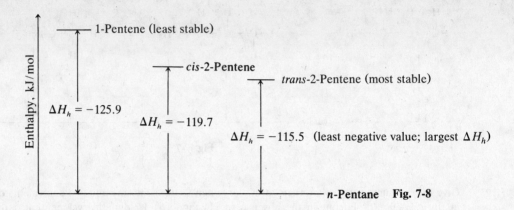

n-Pentane   **Fig. 7-8**

(*b*) No. The alkenes being compared *must* give the same product on hydrogenation.
(*c*) Yes. Again the most negative value indicates the least stable isomer.
(*d*) Yes. On combustion all four isomers give the same products, H_2O and CO_2.
(*e*) Less than 3365 kJ/mol, since this isomer is a trisubstituted alkene and the 2-pentenes are disubstituted.

3. Oxidation

7.107 (*a*) Give the product of the reaction of a peroxyacid such as peroxybenzoic acid, $PhC(=O)OOH$, with (i) cyclopentene, (ii) *cis*-2-butene, and (iii) *trans*-2-butene. (*b*) Consider the reaction as an electrophilic addition.

◢ (*a*) The product is a 3-membered ring ether called an *epoxide* or *oxirane*. The epoxide has the same geometry as the alkene reactant. The epoxide can be considered as the oxygen analog of a bromonium ion without a + charge. However, it is isolable unlike the bromonium ion.

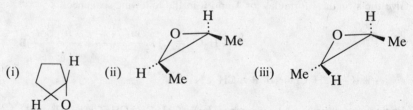

(*b*) The HO of the peroxyacid can be considered as an E^+. However, the $:Nu^-$ portion, $RCOO^-$, removes the H from OH as the O bonds to the C=C, giving the epoxide directly.

7.108 (*a*) Give the products from the reaction at room temperature of peroxyformic acid (from 35% H_2O_2 and formic acid, HCOOH) with the same three reactants in (*a*) of Problem 7.107. (*b*) What is the net addition and the mode? (*c*) Provide a mechanism using *cis*-2-butene. (*d*) Name the overall addition in part (*c*).

(a) (i) *trans*-1,2-Cyclopentanediol, (ii) *rac*-, and (iii) *meso*-CH$_3$CHOHCHOHCH$_3$.

(b) Two OH's add *anti*.

(c) HCOOH in the reaction mixture has sufficient acidity to catalyze the opening of the epoxide ring by H$_2$O in the same *anti* fashion as does the bromonium ion ring:

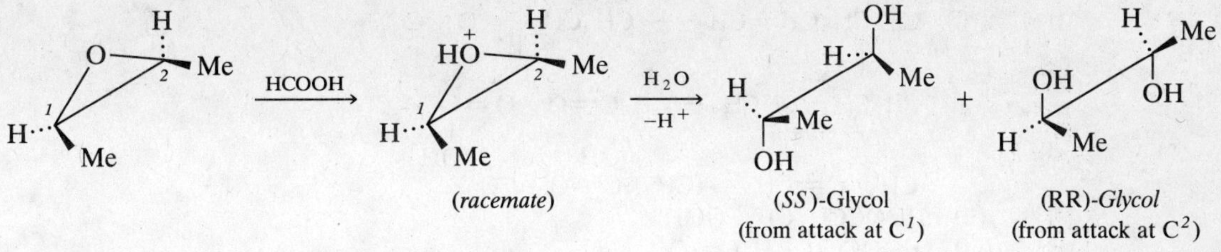

(racemate)

(SS)-Glycol
(from attack at C^1)

(RR)-Glycol
(from attack at C^2)

(d) Hydroxylation.

7.109 (a) Give the products from the reactions of the same three reactants in (a) of Problem 7.107 at room temperature with basic aqueous KMnO$_4$ or with catalytic amounts of OsO$_4$ (osmium tetroxide) in H$_2$O$_2$. (b) What is the net addition and the mode? (c) Provide a mechanism using *trans*-2-butene. (d) Why is KMnO$_4$ preferred to OsO$_4$?

(a) (i) *cis*-1,2-Cyclopentanediol, (ii) *meso*-, and (iii) *rac*-CH$_3$CHOHCHOHCH$_3$.

(b) *Syn* hydroxylation.

(c)

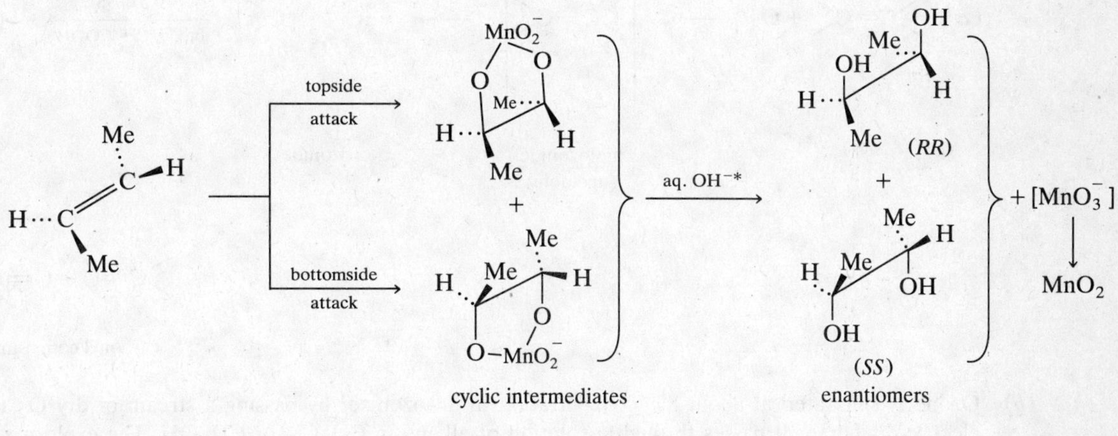

cyclic intermediates

enantiomers

*OH$^-$ is used to hydrolyze the Mn complex; H$_2$O$_2$ oxidatively cleaves the Os complex. A similar metal complex is formed in both cases. When M is Mn, the complex has a $-$ charge delocalized to the lone O's. There is no charge on the isolable osmate complex. In the breakdown of the cyclic complexes, the C—O bonds are not broken, their geometry is not disturbed, and the *syn* addition is preserved.

(d) OsO$_4$ is expensive and very toxic; it causes blindness. This problem can be minimized by using a catalytic amount of OsO$_4$ with H$_2$O$_2$ which regenerates the OsO$_4$ by oxidizing the reduced form of Os resulting from the hydroxylation.

7.110 (a) How does the reaction of a hot acidified KMnO$_4$ (or K$_2$Cr$_2$O$_7$) solution with alkenes differ from hydroxylation? (b) Summarize the relationship between the R substitution on C=C and the products formed on oxidative cleavage. (c) Give the expected products formed from hot KMnO$_4$ oxidation of (i) the C$_4$H$_8$ alkenes, (ii) cyclobutene, (iii) 1-methylcyclobutene, and (iv) 1,2-dimethylcyclobutene.

(*a*) This vigorous oxidative cleavage converts the $>C{=}C<$ to $>C{=}O + O{=}C<$. Any H on a doubly-bonded C is further oxidized to OH.

(*b*) A terminal $=CH_2$ is oxidized to unstable carbonic acid, $O{=}C(OH)_2$, that decomposes to CO_2 and H_2O. The $=CHR$ grouping is converted to HOOCR, a carboxylic acid, while $=CR_2$ and $=CRR'$ go to ketones, $O{=}CR_2$ and $O{=}CRR'$, respectively. A glycol is likely to be the intermediate that actually undergoes cleavage.

(*c*) (i) $CH_3CH_2CH{=}CH_2 \longrightarrow CH_3CH_2C(OH){=}O + CO_2$

$CH_3CH{=}CHCH_3$ (*cis* or *trans*) $\rightarrow CH_3C(OH){=}O + O{=}C(OH)CH_3$

$(CH_3)_2C{=}CH_2 \rightarrow (CH_3)_2C{=}O + CO_2$

(ii) $HOOCCH_2CH_2COOH$

(iii) $HOOCCH_2CH_2C(CH_3){=}O$

(iv) $O{=}C(CH_3)CH_2CH_2C(CH_3){=}O$

7.111 (*a*) Show steps for reductive ozonolysis (reaction with O_3) of an alkene. (*b*) What are the experimental conditions for this reaction? (*c*) What is the main utility of this reaction and why is it superior to $KMnO_4$ cleavage for this purpose?

(*a*)

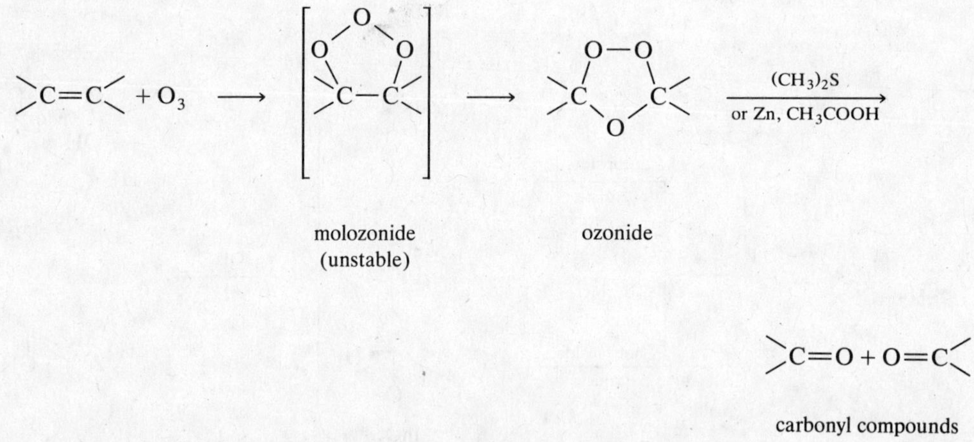

(*b*) Ozone is generated at about 8% concentration in an ozonizer by passing a stream of dry O_2 through an electric discharge. It passes through a solution of alkene in CH_2Cl_2 or CH_3OH. The explosive ozonide is reduced with Me_2S or Zn and HOAc without being isolated.

(*c*) It locates the position of C=C's in molecules. $KMnO_4$ cleavage is more vigorous and can oxidize other groups, i.e., OH.

7.112 Write the structures for the products from reductive ozonolysis of: (*a*) 3,5-Dimethyl-4-octene, and (*b*) 1,2-dimethylcyclohexene.

(*a*) $CH_3CH_2CH(CH_3)CH{=}C(CH_3)CH_2CH_2CH_3 \xrightarrow[2.\ Zn,\ HOAc]{1.\ O_3} CH_3CH_2CH(CH_3)CH{=}O + O{=}C(CH_3)CH_2CH_2CH_3$

2-methylbutanal (an aldehyde) 2-pentanone (a ketone)

(*b*) $CH_3\overset{O}{\overset{\|}{C}}(CH_2)_4\overset{O}{\overset{\|}{C}}CH_3$. A cycloalkene gives only a dicarbonyl compound.

7.113 Give the products formed on oxidative-ozonolysis (ozonide is cleaved with H_2O_2) from the compounds in Problem 7.112.

▟ The aldehydic group, $-CH=O$, is oxidized to the carboxylic acid group, $-\overset{\overset{\displaystyle OH}{|}}{C}=O$.
    (*a*) $CH_3CH_2CH(CH_3)COOH + O=C(CH_3)CH_2CH_2CH_3$, (*b*) no change.

7.114 Write structural formulas for the compounds which yield the following products on reductive ozonolysis:
  (*a*)   two moles of $O=C(CH_3)CH_2CH_3$ (*d*) $(C_2H_5)_2C=O + O=CHCH=O + O=CHCH_2CH_3$
  (*b*) $H_2C=O + O=CHCH(CH_3)CH(CH_3)_2$ (*e*)   two moles $O=CHCH_2CH=O$
  (*c*) $O=CHCH_2CH_2CH_2CH=O$

▟ (*a*)   The formation of a single carbonyl compound signals a symmetrical alkene. Write twice the structural formula of the ketone with the $C=O$ groups facing each other. Omit the O's and join the C's with a double bond.

$$CH_3CH_2\overset{\overset{\displaystyle CH_3}{|}}{C}=O \quad O=\overset{\overset{\displaystyle CH_3}{|}}{C}CH_2CH_3 \longleftarrow CH_3CH_2\overset{\overset{\displaystyle H_3C}{|}}{C}=\overset{\overset{\displaystyle CH_3}{|}}{C}CH_2CH_3 \ (cis \ \text{or} \ trans)$$

(*b*)   Two different carbonyl compounds means the alkene is unsymmetrical.

$$H_2C=O \quad O=CHCH(CH_3)CH(CH_3)_2 \longleftarrow H_2C=CHCH(CH_3)CH(CH_3)_2$$

(*c*)   The presence of two $C=O$'s in the same product indicates a cycloalkene, in this case cyclopentene.

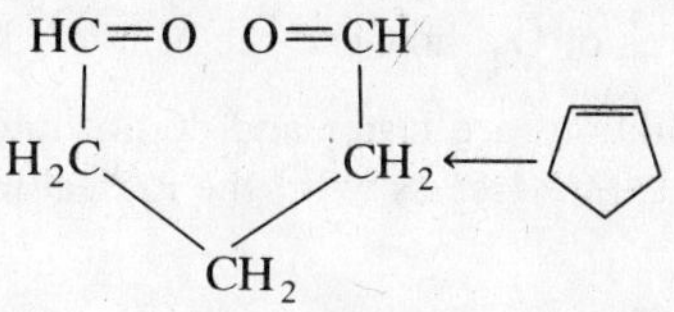

(*d*)   A total of four $C=O$'s in the products indicates a diene, a compound with two $C=C$'s.

$$(C_2H_5)_2C=O + O=CHCH=O + O=CHCH_2CH_3 \longleftarrow (C_2H_5)_2C=CHCH=CHCH_2CH_3$$

(cis or trans)

(*e*)   Two moles of a dicarbonyl compound signal a symmetrical cycloalkadiene

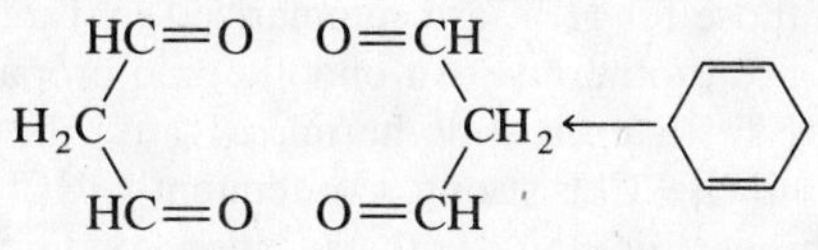

4. Free Radical Additions

7.115 (*a*) Compare the products from the addition of HBr to propene in (i) the absence and (ii) the presence of O_2 or peroxides, ROOR.   (*b*) What is the essential mechanistic difference between these two reactions?

▟ (*a*) (i) $CH_3CHBrCH_3$, Markovnikov adduct; (ii) $CH_3CH_2CH_2Br$, anti-Markovnikov adduct.
  (*b*) The product in (i) above is a typical ionic electrophilic addition whereas (ii) is a radical addition.

7.116 Outline a general mechanism for the radical addition of HBr to $\overset{}{>}C=C\overset{}{<}$.

▟ *Initiation steps*: $\cdot O—O\cdot$ (a diradical) $+ H:Br \rightarrow H:O—O\cdot + \cdot Br$ *or*

                   $RO—OR \overset{\Delta}{\longrightarrow} 2RO\cdot$ and $RO\cdot + H:Br \rightarrow ROH + \cdot Br$

Propagation step 1: $Br\cdot + \ >C=C< \ \rightarrow Br:\overset{|}{\underset{|}{C}}—\overset{|}{\underset{|}{C}}\cdot$

Propagation step 2: $Br:\overset{|}{\underset{|}{C}}—\overset{|}{\underset{|}{C}}\cdot \ + H:Br \rightarrow Br:\overset{|}{\underset{|}{C}}—\overset{|}{\underset{|}{C}}:H + \cdot Br$

$Br\cdot$ propagates the chain by repeating step 1 which is followed by step 2.

7.117 Give the termination steps in Problem 7.116.

▮ The chain is terminated whenever two radicals form a bond.

$$\text{(i) } 2Br\cdot \longrightarrow Br_2, \quad \text{(ii) } Br\cdot + \cdot\overset{\displaystyle |}{\underset{\displaystyle |}{C}}-\overset{\displaystyle |}{\underset{\displaystyle |}{C}}Br \rightarrow Br\overset{\displaystyle |}{\underset{\displaystyle |}{C}}-\overset{\displaystyle |}{\underset{\displaystyle |}{C}}Br, \quad \text{(iii) } Br\overset{\displaystyle |}{\underset{\displaystyle |}{C}}-\overset{\displaystyle |}{\underset{\displaystyle |}{C}}\cdot + \cdot\overset{\displaystyle |}{\underset{\displaystyle |}{C}}-\overset{\displaystyle |}{\underset{\displaystyle |}{C}}Br \rightarrow Br\overset{\displaystyle |}{\underset{\displaystyle |}{C}}-\overset{\displaystyle |}{\underset{\displaystyle |}{C}}-\overset{\displaystyle |}{\underset{\displaystyle |}{C}}-\overset{\displaystyle |}{\underset{\displaystyle |}{C}}Br$$

Another termination process is disproportionation, a kind of autooxidation-reduction:

$$2\ Br\overset{\displaystyle |}{\underset{\displaystyle |}{C}}-\overset{\displaystyle |}{\underset{\displaystyle |}{C}}\cdot \longrightarrow Br\overset{\displaystyle |}{\underset{\displaystyle |}{C}}-\overset{\displaystyle |}{\underset{\displaystyle |}{C}}H\ +\ Br\overset{\displaystyle |}{C}=C{\overset{\displaystyle <}{}}$$

In order for disproportionation to occur, there must be at least one H on the C adjacent to $\cdot$C.

7.118 Account for the anti-Markovnikov radical addition of HBr to $CH_3CH=CH_2$.

▮ Just as an electrophile adds to $C=C$ to give the more stable R^+, a radical adds to give the more stable $\cdot R$. Since the order of stability of radicals is $3° > 2° > 1° > CH_3$, $Br\cdot$ adds to the less substituted C to give the radical intermediate with the more substituted C.

7.119 (*a*) In addition to regiospecificity, how do electrophilic and radical additions differ? (*b*) Since it is difficult in practice to remove all traces of O_2, how can the Markovnikov product be encouraged?

▮ (*a*) These radical additions are faster and do not undergo H or alkyl group rearrangements. (*b*) Add an inhibitor (antioxidant) that traps (reacts with) the radical initiators and thereby prevents chains from starting.

7.120 Use the following bond energies, in kcal/mol, to predict whether HI and HCl exhibit the "peroxide effect". C—C, 83; C=C, 146; C—H, 98; C—Cl, 81; C—Br, 69; C—I, 56; H—Cl, 103; HBr, 88; H—I, 71.

▮ Determine the ΔH's for the two propagation steps (Problem 7.116) using the equation $\Delta H = \Sigma$ (bond energies of bonds broken) $- \Sigma$(bond energies of bonds formed).
  For step 1: $\Delta H = $ (bond energy of $C=C$) $-$ (bond energies of $C-X + C-C$)
  For step 2: $\Delta H = $ (bond energy of $H-X$) $-$ (bond energy of $C-H$)
The results, including those for HBr, are summarized in Table 7-2. Radical chain reactions are successful when the propagation steps are exothermic. An endothermic propagation step ($+\Delta H$) is reversible and would break the chain. With HI, the first step is endothermic because the $C-I$ bond is weak. With HCl, the second step is endothermic because the $H-Cl$ is strong. Consequently, HCl and HI do not show the peroxide effect. In fact HI is oxidized to I_2 (by the peroxide) under the reaction conditions. With HBr, both steps are exothermic and HBr does add to $C=C$ by a free radical mechanism.

TABLE 7-2

HX	Step 1	Step 2
HCl	-18	$+5$
HBr	-6	-10
HI	$+7$	-27

7.121 CH_3SH, $BrCCl_3$ and $HCCl_3$ each adds to $C=C$ with the aid of peroxide catalysis. Give equations for the initiation steps affording the radicals needed for the first propagation steps.

▮ $RO\cdot$, formed from decomposition of the peroxide, ROOR, reacts with the reactants to give the necessary radical for chain propagation.
  $RO\cdot + HSCH_3 \rightarrow ROH + \cdot SCH_3$
  $RO\cdot + BrCCl_3 \rightarrow ROBr + \cdot CCl_3$ (The weaker $C-Br$ bond is broken.)
  $RO\cdot + HCCl_3 \rightarrow ROH + \cdot CCl_3$

7.122 Supply structures and names for the products of the following peroxide-catalyzed reactions: (a) $Me_2C=CH_2 + CH_3SH$, (b) $CH_3CH=CH_2 + BrCCl_3$, and (c) methylenecyclopentane + $HCCl_3$.

◢ (a) $Me_2CHCH_2SCH_3$, isobutylmethyl sulfide; (b) $CH_3CHBrCH_2CCl_3$, 3-bromo-1,1,1-trichlorobutane;

(c) , 2,2,2-trichloroethylcyclopentane.

7.123 Referring to Problem 7.120, predict and justify the product from the uv-induced reaction of ICF_3 with $Me_3C—CH=CH_2$.

◢ $Me_3CCHICH_2CF_3$. The uv radiation supplies the energy to break the I—C bond homolytically to give I· + ·CF_3. As shown in Problem 7.120, the addition of I· to C=C is endothermic and consequently ·CF_3 adds in the first propagation step:

(1) $Me_3C—CH=CH_2 + ·CF_3 \longrightarrow Me_3C—\overset{·}{C}H—CH_2CF_3$
(2) $Me_3C—\overset{·}{C}H—CH_2CF_3 + ICF_3 \rightarrow Me_3C—CHI—CH_2CF_3 + ·CF_3$

7.124 (a) Rule out the following mechanism for the peroxide-induced addition of HBr to a symmetrically R-substituted alkene such as RHC=CHR:

Initiation step: $RO· + HBr \rightarrow ROBr + H·$
Propagation step 1: $RCH=CHR + H· \rightarrow R\overset{·}{C}HCH_2R$
Propagation step 2: $R\overset{·}{C}HCH_2R + HBr \rightarrow RCHBrCH_2R + H·$

(b) Why is this mechanism inappropriate for an unsymmetrically R-substituted alkene such as $R_2C=CH_2$?

◢ (a) The actual initiation step, $RO· + HBr \rightarrow ROH + Br·$, is thermodynamically more favorable because O—H has a much greater bond energy than the very weak O—Br. Also, step 2 is endothermic; $\Delta H =$ (bond energy of H—X) – (bond energy of C—Br) = 88 – 69 = +19 kcal/mol. (b) This mechanism would lead to the unobserved Markovnikov addition.

7.125 (a) (i) Give the two observed products from the peroxide-catalyzed reaction of $H_2C=CHCCl_3$ with HBr. (ii) Rationalize the formation of the unexpected product. (b) Offer a mechanism for the disproportionation of $CH_3\overset{·}{C}HCH_3$ (Problem 7.117).

◢ (a) (i) $BrCH_2CH_2CCl_3$ (expected) + $BrCH_2CHClCHCl_2$ (unexpected)
(ii) Although H and R do not rearrange in radicals, halogens can, and so

$$BrCH_2\overset{·}{C}HCCl_2 \xrightarrow[\text{step 1}]{\sim Cl·} BrCH_2CH\overset{·}{C}Cl_2 \xrightarrow[\text{step 2}]{HBr} BrCH_2CHClCHCl_2 + ·Br$$
$$\quad\quad\;\; |\quad\quad\quad\quad\quad\quad\quad\quad |$$
$$\quad\quad\;\; Cl\quad\quad\quad\quad\quad\quad\quad\;\; Cl$$

The rearranged intermediate reacts with HBr in step 2 to give the unexpected product.
(b) One radical abstracts an adjacent **H** from another radical forming the alkane and leaving the alkene.

$$CH_3\overset{·}{C}HCH_3 + CH_3\overset{·}{C}HCH_2 \longrightarrow CH_3CHCH_3 + CH_3CH=CH_2$$
$$\quad\quad\quad\quad\quad\quad\quad\quad\quad\;\; |\quad\quad\quad\quad\quad\;\; |$$
$$\quad\quad\quad\quad\quad\quad\quad\quad\quad\; H\quad\quad\quad\quad\; H$$

5. Addition Dimerization and Polymerization

7.126 The reaction of $Me_2C=CH_2$ with H_2SO_4 or HF gives two isomers, C_8H_{16}. (a) Give their structural formulas and designate the major isomer. (b) What is the general name for this reaction? (c) Account for the unexpected product ratio. (d) Provide a mechanism. (e) Why cannot HCl, HBr, or HI be used as acid catalysts?

◢ (a) $Me_3C—CH=CMe_2$ (minor) (**A**); $Me_3C—CH_2C(Me)=CH_2$ (major) (**B**)
(b) The reaction is called dimerization.
(c) The expected Saytzeff product **A** is sterically hindered because the bulky *t*-butyl group is *cis* to a Me.
(d) *Step 1.* $Me_2C=CH_2 + H^+ \longrightarrow Me_3C^+$

Step 2. $Me_3C^+ + \quad H_2C=CMe_2 \quad \longrightarrow Me_3C—CH—\overset{+}{C}—CH_2$
$$\quad\quad\quad\quad\quad\quad\quad\quad\quad\quad\quad\quad\quad\quad\quad\quad\quad |\quad\; |\quad\; |$$
$$\quad\quad\quad\quad\quad\quad\quad\quad\quad\quad\quad\quad\quad\quad\quad\quad\quad H\; Me\; H'$$
$$\quad\text{electrophile} \quad\text{``tail''} \quad\text{``head''} \quad\quad\quad\quad 3° \text{ dimeric } R^+$$
$$\quad\quad\quad\quad\quad\quad\quad\text{nucleophile}$$

Step 3. $R^+ \xrightarrow{-H^+} \textbf{A}$ and $R^+ \xrightarrow{-H'^+} \textbf{B}$

Step 2 is a Markovnikov addition of an electrophile. Attack at the "tail" gives the 3° R$^+$; attack at the "head" would give the much less stable 1° carbocation Me$_3$C—CMe$_2$CH$_2^+$.

(*e*) The acid catalyst must have a weakly nucleophilic conjugate base to avoid addition of HX to C=C. Cl$^-$, Br$^-$, and I$^-$, the conjugate bases of HCl, HBr, and HI respectively, are good nucleophiles that bind to R$^+$.

7.127 What is the industrial utility of the mixture of the dimeric alkenes (Problem 7.126) from isobutylene?

▰ The mixture ("diisobutylenes") is heterogeneously hydrogenated to the so-called "isooctane" (wrongly named), 2,2,4-trimethylpentane, CH$_3$C(Me)$_2$CH$_2$CHMeCH$_3$, used as a standard for octane ratings of gasolines.

7.128 (*a*) Give the products of the reaction of four moles of isobutylene. (*b*) Indicate the *mer*, the repeating unit in the product. (*c*) What process occurs to the alkene at high temperatures and pressures?

▰ (*a*) Me$_3$C(CH$_2$CMe$_2$)CH$_2$CMe$_2$CH=CMe$_2$ (C) + Me$_3$CCH$_2$CMe$_2$CH$_2$CMe$_2$CH$_2$CMe=CH$_2$. (*b*) The mer, —CH$_2$CMe$_2$—, is shown in parentheses in C. (*c*) The starting alkene, called the *monomer*, undergoes *polymerization* whereby thousands of alkene molecules are strung together. The general equation for formation of the isobutylene polymer is

$$n \; \text{Me}_2\text{C}=\text{CH}_2 \xrightarrow[\Delta]{\text{H}^+,\text{pr.}} \text{H}-(\text{CH}_2\text{CMe}_2)_{n-1}\text{CH}_2\text{CMe}=\text{CH}_2$$

where *n* is a very large number. Again the mer is shown in parentheses. Notice that polymerization stops when the intermediate R$^+$ loses H$^+$ to form a C=C.

7.129 Discuss the first step when BF$_3$ with a trace of H$_2$O is used as the catalyst to initiate polymerization of H$_2$C=CMe$_2$.

▰ BF$_3$ reacts with H$_2$O to give the very strong Brönsted acid, HBF$_3$OH, which initiates the polymerization by contributing H$^+$ to the alkene to form the R$^+$. This polymerization occurs at −200 °C.

7.130 (*a*) Is the polymer of propene chiral? Explain. (*b*) Give the three classes of stereoisomers based on the arrangements of the branching CH$_3$ (R) groups relative to the long "backbone" chain of the polymer.

▰ (*a*) Yes. Each C of the mer bonded to CH$_3$ (or any group, G) is chiral, giving millions of stereoisomers depending on the size of the polymer:

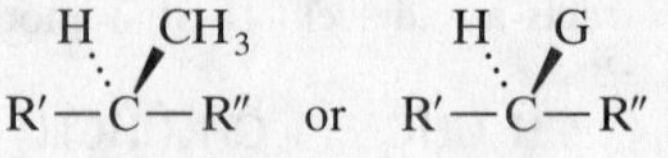

$$\begin{array}{cc} \text{H} \quad \text{CH}_3 & \text{H} \quad \text{G} \\ \text{R}'-\text{C}-\text{R}'' \quad \text{or} & \text{R}'-\text{C}-\text{R}'' \end{array}$$

(*b*) See Fig. 7-9.

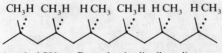

CH$_3$H CH$_3$H CH$_3$H CH$_3$H CH$_3$H CH$_3$H

Isotactic (CH$_3$ or R all on same side)

CH$_3$H H CH$_3$ CH$_3$H H CH$_3$ CH$_3$H H CH$_3$ CH$_3$ H

Syndiotactic (CH$_3$ or R on alternate sides)

CH$_3$H CH$_3$H H CH$_3$ CH$_3$H H CH$_3$ H CH$_3$

Atactic (CH$_3$ or R randomly distributed)   **Fig. 7-9**

7.131 (a) Show the combination of two mers in the polymer of (i) vinyl chloride, $H_2C{=}CHCl$, (ii) acrylonitrile, $H_2C{=}CHCN$, (iii) $Cl_2C{=}CH_2$, and (iv) $F_2C{=}CF_2$. (b) Give the commercial name for each polymer. (c) For the unsymmetrical alkenes indicate the "head" and the "tail".

◢ (a)

(i) $-(CH_2\underset{\underset{Cl}{|}}{CH})CH_2\underset{\underset{Cl}{|}}{CH}-$ (ii) $-(CH_2\underset{\underset{CN}{|}}{CH})CH_2\underset{\underset{CN}{|}}{CH}-$ (iii) $-(CH_2\underset{\underset{Cl}{|}}{\overset{\overset{Cl}{|}}{C}})CH_2\underset{\underset{Cl}{|}}{\overset{\overset{Cl}{|}}{C}}-$

(iv) $-(\underset{\underset{F}{|}}{\overset{\overset{F}{|}}{C}}-\underset{\underset{F}{|}}{\overset{\overset{F}{|}}{C}})-\underset{\underset{F}{|}}{\overset{\overset{F}{|}}{C}}-\underset{\underset{F}{|}}{\overset{\overset{F}{|}}{C}}-$

The mer is in parentheses.

(b) (i) polyvinyl chloride (PVC), (ii) orlon, (iii) saran, and (iv) teflon.

(c) In (i), (ii), and (iii) CH_2 is the "tail", the other C of C=C is the "head".

7.132 Describe (a) *radical-induced* and (b) *anion-induced* polymerization of alkenes. (c) What kinds of alkenes undergo anion-induced polymerization?

◢ (a) A radical initiator, RO· from decomposition of ROOR, adds according to Markovnikov's rule as shown with $MeCH{=}CH_2$

$$RO· + H_2C{=}CHMe \longrightarrow H_2C\underset{\underset{RO}{|}}{-}\underset{\underset{Me}{|}}{\overset{\cdot}{C}H} \xrightarrow{H_2C{=}CHMe} H_2C\underset{\underset{RO}{|}}{-}\underset{\underset{Me}{|}}{CH}{-}CH_2\underset{\underset{Me}{|}}{\overset{\cdot}{C}H}$$

This process continues with thousands of monomeric molecules. The polymerization chain terminates when two long chain intermediate radicals either combine, $R· + R· \rightarrow R{-}R$, or disproportionate.

(b) Anions such as $R:^-$, generated from organometallics or $:NH_2^-$ (from $LiNH_2$), initiate the polymerization by adding to one end of the monomer.

$$R:^- + H_2C{=}CHX \longrightarrow \left[RCH_2\underset{\underset{X}{|}}{\overset{\cdot\cdot}{C}H}\right]^- \xrightarrow{H_2C{=}CHX} \left[RCH_2\underset{\underset{X}{|}}{CH}{-}CH_2\underset{\underset{X}{|}}{\overset{\cdot\cdot}{C}H}\right]^-$$

(c) Since ordinary alkenes do not undergo nucleophilic addition, the alkene must have a functional group, such as $-C{\equiv}N$ or $O{=}\underset{|}{C}OR$, on C=C that can stabilize the negative charge by delocalization (Problem 18.6). These polymers show the controllable stereochemistry discussed in Problem 7.130.

7.133 Account for the fact that radical-induced polymerizations in CCl_4 leads to shortened chains containing small amounts of Cl.

◢ After many monomer molecules polymerize, the intermediate radical (P·) reacts with CCl_4 to terminate the chain while producing ·CCl_3 to start another chain (chain transfer):

$$P· + CCl_4 \longrightarrow PCl + ·CCl_3 \quad \text{A termination step that initiates a chain transfer:}$$

$$Cl_3C· + H_2C{=}CHR \longrightarrow Cl_3CCH_2\overset{\cdot}{C}HR \xrightarrow{n\,H_2C{=}CHR} \text{polymer with same mer}$$

7.134 (a) What happens when a mixture of two or more monomers, i.e., $CH_2{=}CHPh$ and $CH_2{=}C(Me)COOMe$, polymerizes? (b) Name this type of polymerization. (c) Give four types of polymers that can be formed in such a process.

◢ (a) Both monomers become part of the polymer:

$$-(CH_2CHPh)(CH_2\underset{\underset{COOMe}{|}}{\overset{\overset{Me}{|}}{C}})-$$

(b) *Copolymerization.* (c) The monomeric units can be distributed randomly to give a random copolymer $(-MMM_1MM_1M_1MM_1-)$ or they can alternate to give an alternating copolymer $(-MM_1MM_1MM_1-)$. Block copolymers have groups of one monomer alternating with groups of the other monomer

(—MMMMMM$_1$M$_1$M$_1$M$_1$M$_1$—). Graft copolymers have a branch of one kind grafted to a chain of another kind:

$$(-\text{MMMMMM}-) \quad \text{chain}$$
$$|$$
$$(\text{M}_1\text{M}_1\text{M}_1\text{M}_1\text{M}_1) \quad \text{branch}$$

6. Miscellaneous Additions

7.135 Compare the reactions of $H_2C{=}CH_2$ and $F_2C{=}CF_2$ with NaOEt in EtOH.

▰ Nucleophiles such as EtO$^-$ do not ordinarily add to alkenes because they are repelled by the π e$^-$'s. However, nucleophilic additions occur if electron-withdrawing groups, such as F's, are attached to C=C because they diminish the electron-density of the π bond and stabilize the intermediate carbanion.

$$F_2C{=}CF_2 + EtO^- \longrightarrow \underset{\overset{|}{EtO}}{F_2C}{-}CF_2 \xrightarrow[-EtO^-]{HOEt} \underset{\overset{|}{EtO}}{F_2C}{-}\underset{\overset{|}{H}}{CF_2}$$

7.136 (*a*) Write the structural formula for the radiation-induced reaction of diazomethane, H_2CN_2 with a generalized alkene, C=C, and explain the reaction. (*b*) How does this product compare with the other three-membered ring species formed on bromination, mercuration, and epoxidation?

▰ (*a*) Heating H_2CN_2 generates a singlet carbene (Problems 3.4 and 3.7), :CH$_2$. The carbene is electron-deficient and adds to the electron-rich π bond to give a cyclopropane ring:

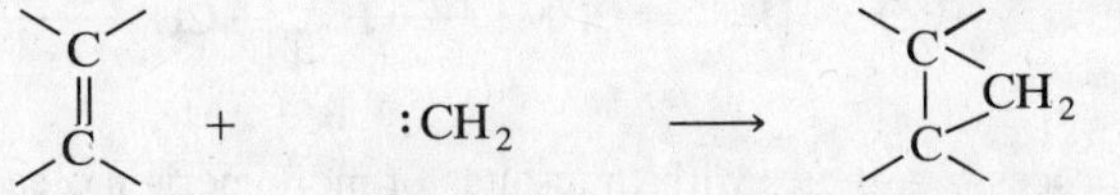

C=C (drawn)   +   :CH$_2$ ⟶   cyclopropane (drawn) CH$_2$

a singlet carbene   a cyclopropane

(*b*) The additions are similar one-step processes. Epoxides and cyclopropanes are stable isolable entities whereas bromonium and mercurinium ions are not.

7.137 Give the products with names from the reactions of (*a*) *cis*-2-butene and (*b*) *trans*-2-butene with H_2CN_2 irradiated with uv (i) in the absence and (ii) in the presence of a large amount of N$_2$.

▰ Addition of singlet carbenes is stereospecific and *syn*, while addition of triplet carbenes, $>\!\dot{C}\cdot$, is not stereospecific. H_2C: generated from CH_2N_2 is always singlet. However, in an atmosphere of the inert N$_2$, the singlet carbene collides with an N$_2$ molecule and loses energy to give the lower energy triplet carbene. The products are 1,2-dimethylcyclopropanes (**A**).
(*a*) (i) *cis*-**A**, (ii) a mixture of *cis*- and *trans*-**A**.
(*b*) (i) *trans*-**A**, (ii) a mixture of *cis*- and *trans*-**A** (not the same mixture of stereoisomers as in (ii) of part (*a*) because some singlet methylene also reacts).

7.138 (*a*) Complete the following reaction: *cis*-2-pentene + CH$_2$I$_2$ with Zn/Cu → ? (*b*) How does this reaction compare with the one with H_2CN_2 in Problem 7.137? (*c*) Why is the reaction in (*a*) preferred?

▰ (*a*) *cis*-1-Ethyl-2-methylcyclopropane. (*b*) They are both *syn* stereospecific additions. In this *Simmons–Smith* reaction a free carbene is not formed as with H_2CN_2. Instead, an organometallic complex, ICH$_2$ZnI, referred to as a *carbenoid*, is considered to transfer its CH$_2$ to the π bond, creating the cyclopropane ring. ZnI$_2$ is the inorganic product. (*c*) H_2CN_2 is very toxic and explosive—it is usually distilled with ether from the mixture in which it is prepared. Furthermore, free :CH$_2$ inserts in $>\!C{-}H$ bonds giving $>\!CCH_2H$.

7.139 Complete the following reactions: (*a*) cyclohexene + H_2CN_2 and (*b*) *trans*-2-butene + HCCl$_3$ + KOH.

▰ (*a*)   (*b*) See Problem 5.61 for the preparation of :CCl$_2$.

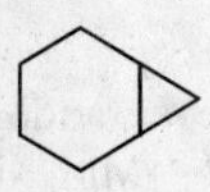

Bicyclo[4.1.0]heptane   *trans*-1,2-Dimethyl-3,3-dichlorocyclopropane
(norcarane)

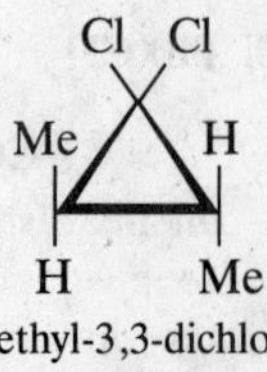

7.140 Complete the following reactions: (*a*) *cis*-2-butene + HCBr$_2$Cl + KOH (2 products), (*b*) *trans*-2-butene + HCBr$_2$Cl + KOH, and (*c*) 3-methylcyclopentene + H$_2$CI$_2$ + Zn/Cu(c).

(*a*)

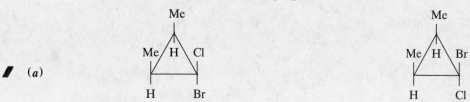

cis-2,3-Dimethyl-*cis*-1-chlorobromocyclopropane   cis-2,3-Dimethyl-*trans*-1-chlorobromocyclopropane

(*b*) *trans*-2,3-Dimethyl-1-chlorobromocyclopropane. Each halogen is *cis* to one Me and *trans* to the other.
(*c*) Two diasteromers:

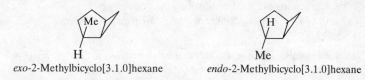

exo-2-Methylbicyclo[3.1.0]hexane   *endo*-2-Methylbicyclo[3.1.0]hexane

7.141 Complete the following reaction:

$$Me_2C{=}CH_2 + HCMe_3 \xrightarrow[0\,°C]{HF} ?$$

Me$_2$CHCH$_2$CMe$_3$, 2,2,4-trimethylpentane (see Problem 7.127 for its industrial utility).

7.142 Suggest a mechanism for the reaction of Problem 7.141.

See Problem 7.126. Steps 1 and 2 lead to the formation of the 3° dimeric R$^+$. In step 3 an intermolecular transfer of a 3° hydride (H:) from the alkane to the R$^+$ occurs, as shown:

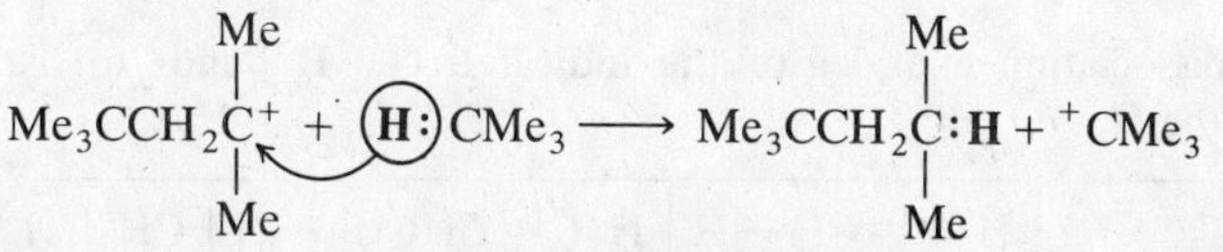

$$Me_3CCH_2\overset{Me}{\underset{Me}{C^+}} + \text{(H:)}CMe_3 \longrightarrow Me_3CCH_2\overset{Me}{\underset{Me}{C}}{:}H + {}^+CMe_3$$

The propagation steps in this chain reaction continue when Me$_3$C$^+$ adds to a molecule of isobutylene to form the same 3° R$^+$ which accepts a H: from another alkane molecule.

7.143 Ethylene is alkylated with Me$_3$CH using HF to give chiefly Me$_2$CHCHMe$_2$, not Me$_3$CCH$_2$CH$_3$. Account for the product.

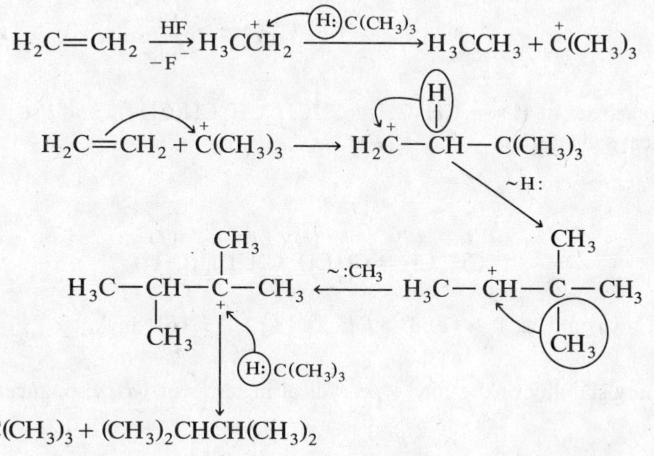

$$H_2C{=}CH_2 \xrightarrow[-F^-]{HF} H_3C\overset{+}{C}H_2 \xrightarrow{\text{(H:)}C(CH_3)_3} H_3CCH_3 + \overset{+}{C}(CH_3)_3$$

$$H_2C{=}CH_2 + \overset{+}{C}(CH_3)_3 \longrightarrow H_2C{-}CH{-}C(CH_3)_3$$

~H:

$$H_3C{-}CH{-}\overset{CH_3}{\underset{\overset{+}{C}H_3}{C}}{-}CH_3 \xleftarrow{\sim:CH_3} H_3C{-}\overset{+}{C}H{-}\overset{CH_3}{\underset{CH_3}{C}}{-}CH_3$$

$$\downarrow \text{(H:)}C(CH_3)_3$$

$${}^+C(CH_3)_3 + (CH_3)_2CHCH(CH_3)_2$$

7. Allylic Substitution

7.144 Compare the reactions of H$_2$C=CHCH$_3$ with Cl$_2$ or Br$_2$ (X$_2$) at (*a*) room temperature, (*b*) high temperature, or with uv radiation, or low concentrations of X$_2$.

(*a*) H$_2$CXCHXCH$_3$ by normal addition.   (*b*) H$_2$C=CHCH$_2$X by substitution at the allylic C.

7.145 Give the products of the reactions of cyclohexene in CCl_4 with (*a*) sulfuryl chloride, Cl_2SO_2, (*b*) *t*-butyl hypochlorite, Me_3COCl, and (*c*) *N*-bromosuccinimide (NBS).

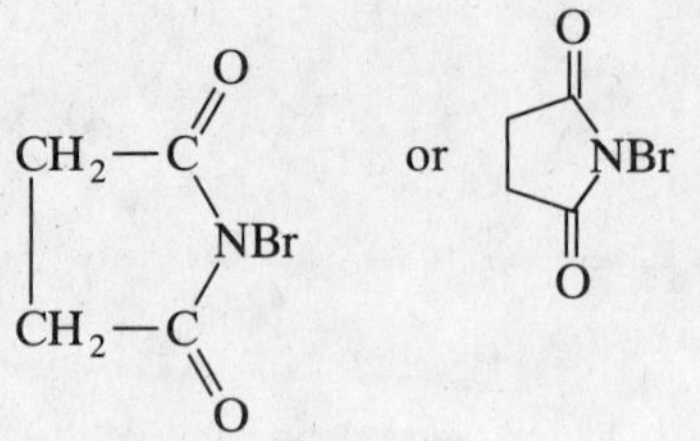

N-Bromosuccinimide

▟ All three reactions are allylic substitutions.
   (*a*) and (*b*) 3-Chlorocyclohexene. (*c*) 3-Bromocyclohexene.

7.146 (*a*) Write a mechanism for the uv-induced allylic halogenation of $RCH_2CH=CH_2$ with X_2. (*b*) Why does substitution become the favored reaction at high temperatures?

▟ (*a*) Induction by uv signals a homolysis, forming radical intermediates that participate in a chain reaction. Formation of an allylic $R\cdot$ is favored because it is resonance-stabilized (Problems 7.147, 7.148, and 7.149).

Initiation step: $X_2 \xrightarrow{uv} 2X\cdot$ (X is Cl or Br)
Propagation step 1: $RCH_2CH=CH_2 + X\cdot \longrightarrow$
  $[R\dot{C}HCH=CH_2 \longleftrightarrow RCH=CH\dot{C}H_2] + HX$
Propagation step 2: $[R\dot{C}HCH=CH_2 \longleftrightarrow RCH=CH\dot{C}H_2] + X_2 \longrightarrow RCHXCH=CH_2 + X\cdot$

(*b*) ΔS of the addition reaction is negative, two molecules forming one. At high temperatures, the unfavorable $T\Delta S$ term overshadows the favorable ΔH making ΔG positive; addition does not occur.

7.147 Use the bond dissociation energies of the indicated C—H bonds to list the relative reactivities in radical substitutions of the **H**.

	H_3C-H	$H_2C=CH-H$	$H_2C=CHCH_2-H$	$CH_3CH_2CH_2-H$	Me_2CH-H	Me_3C-H
Type of H	methyl	vinyl	allyl	1°	2°	3°
ΔH, kcal/mol	104	108	88	98	94.5	91

▟ The less positive is ΔH, the more reactive is **H**. The decreasing order of reactivity is

$$\text{allyl} > 3° > 2° > 1° > \text{Me} > \text{vinyl}$$

7.148 Designate the type of each set of H's in $CH_3CH=CHCH_2CH_2CH(CH_3)_2$ and list them in decreasing order of reactivity towards radical substitution.

▟ Labeling the H's as

$$\overset{(a)\ \ (b)\ \ \ \ \ (b)\ (c)\ \ (d)\ \ (e)\ \ (f)}{CH_3CH=CHCH_2CH_2CH(CH_3)_2}$$

we have: (*c*) allylic, 2° > (*a*) allylic, 1° > (*e*) 3° > (*d*) 2° > (*f*) 1° > (*b*) vinyl.

7.149 Explain the extraordinary stability of the allyl-type radical in terms of (*a*) resonance and (*b*) π orbital overlap (delocalization).

▟ (*a*) Since two equivalent resonance structures can be written

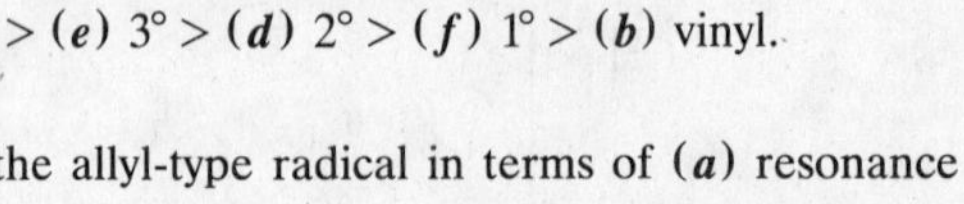

$$\left[>C=C-\dot{C}< \longleftrightarrow >\dot{C}-C=C< \right],$$

the allyl-type radical has considerable resonance energy and is relatively stable.

(b)   Each of the three sp^2 hybridized C's in the allyl unit has a p AO in a common plane (Fig. 7-10). They overlap to create an extended π system in which the odd e^- is delocalized thereby stabilizing the radical.

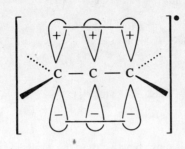

Fig. 7-10

7.150   (a) Show how NBS, written in abbreviated form as $\!\!>\!\!N\!-\!Br$, produces small concentrations of Br_2, the actual allylic bromination reagent.   (b) Account for the fact that small concentrations of Br_2 are conducive to allylic substitution while high concentrations give addition.

▌   (a)   In order for NBS to react, a small amount of H_2O must be present to generate (by hydrolysis) trace amounts of HBr. HBr reacts with NBS to give trace amounts of Br_2 rather than adding to $C\!=\!C$.

$$>\!\!N\!-\!Br + HBr \longrightarrow\ >\!\!N\!-\!H + Br_2$$

(b)   When Br_2 acts as an electrophile to give the bromonium ion, Br^- is produced. In nonpolar solvents, such as CCl_4, such an ion needs to be stabilized, a feat accomplished by another molecule of Br_2, giving the more stable Br_3^-. The rate expression for addition is second order in Br_2: rate = k[alkene][Br_2]^2. With very low concentrations of Br_2 the [Br_2]^2 term becomes negligible and the rate of addition becomes extremely small; substitution predominates.

7.151   Show the initiation and propagation steps for allylic substitutions with (a) Cl_2SO_2 and (b) Me_3COCl (Problem 7.145).

▌

$$(a)\qquad\qquad\qquad\qquad\qquad (b)$$

Initiation step: $Cl_2SO_2 \xrightarrow{\text{uv}} 2Cl\cdot + SO_2$ $Me_3COCl \xrightarrow{\text{uv}} Me_3CO\cdot + \cdot Cl$

Propagation steps: $>\!\!CH\!-\!\overset{|}{C}\!=\!C\!<\ + Cl\cdot \longrightarrow$ $>\!\!CH\!-\!\overset{|}{C}\!=\!C\!<\ + Me_3CO\cdot \longrightarrow$

(1)

$>\!\!\dot{C}\!-\!\overset{|}{C}\!=\!C\!<\ + HCl$ $>\!\!\dot{C}\!-\!\overset{|}{C}\!=\!C\!<\ + Me_3COH$

$>\!\!\dot{C}\!-\!\overset{|}{C}\!=\!C\!<\ + Cl\!-\!SO_2Cl \longrightarrow$ $>\!\!\dot{C}\!-\!\overset{|}{C}\!=\!C\!<\ + ClOCMe_3 \longrightarrow$

(2)

$>\!\!\underset{Cl}{\overset{|}{C}}\!-\!\overset{|}{C}\!=\!C\!<\ + \cdot SO_2Cl$ $>\!\!\underset{Cl}{\overset{|}{C}}\!-\!\overset{|}{C}\!=\!C\!<\ + \cdot OCMe_3$

$\cdot SO_2Cl \longrightarrow SO_2 + Cl\cdot$ then step 1   then step 1

7.152   (a) Account for the isolation of 1-bromo-2-octene in 80% yield from the reaction of 1-octene with NBS/CCl_4. (b) What is the other product formed?   (c) Give the general name for this kind of reaction.

▌   (a) From Problem 7.151 we saw that the allyl radical has radical character on each terminal C of the three carbon unit, [$R\dot{C}HCH\!=\!CH_2 \leftrightarrow RCH\!=\!CH\dot{C}H_2$]. Often the major brominated product results from introduction of Br on the methylene C so as to get the more substituted brominated alkene.   (b) 3-Bromo-1-octene. (c) This shift of the double bond is an example of an *allylic rearrangement*.

7.153   (a) Give all possible products from the reaction of NBS with 4-methyl-2-pentene. (Disregard geometric isomerism.)   (b) Predict the relative yields with an explanation.

▌   (a) H^a and H^b in $H_3^a CCH\!=\!CHCH^b Me_2$ are allylic.

1. Removal of H^a $\xrightarrow{\text{NBS}}$

$$[\text{H}_2\dot{\text{C}}\text{CH}=\text{CHCHMe}_2 \longleftrightarrow \text{H}_2\text{C}=\text{CH}\dot{\text{C}}\text{HCHMe}_2] \begin{cases} \longrightarrow \text{BrCH}_2\text{CH}=\text{CHCHMe}_2 \ (\textbf{A}) \\ \\ \longrightarrow \text{H}_2\text{C}=\text{CHCHBrCHMe}_2 \ (\textbf{B}) \end{cases}$$

2. Removal of H^b $\xrightarrow{\text{NBS}}$

$$[\text{H}_3\text{CCH}=\text{CH}\dot{\text{C}}\text{Me}_2 \longleftrightarrow \text{H}_3\text{C}\dot{\text{C}}\text{HCH}=\text{CMe}_2] \begin{cases} \longrightarrow \text{H}_3\text{CCH}=\text{CHCBrMe}_2 \ (\textbf{C}) \\ \\ \longrightarrow \text{H}_3\text{CCHBrCH}=\text{CMe}_2 \ (\textbf{D}) \end{cases}$$

(*b*) Since H^b is 3° allylic, it is more reactive than the 1° allylic H^a and consequently path 2 and its ensuing products dominate over path 1 and its products. The decreasing order of yields is **D** (path 2, more substituted) > **C** (path 2, less substitute) > **A** (path 1, more substituted) > **B** (path 1, less substituted).

7.154 Give all the products of the reaction of 3-methylmethylenecyclohexane with NBS.

▰ There are six products, including two pairs of *cis-trans* diastereomers that arise from allylic rearrangement and two products that do not.

1-Bromomethyl-3-methyl-
cyclohexene

cis- and *trans-*2-Bromo-3-methyl-
methylenecyclohexane

1-Bromomethyl-5-methyl-
cyclohexene

cis- and *trans-*2-Bromo-5-methyl-
methylenecyclohexane

7.155 Discuss the ^{14}C (indicated by **C**) labeling in the product from the reaction of NBS with $\text{CH}_2=\text{CHCH}_3$.

▰ The resonance hybrid of the intermediate allyic radical, $[\text{CH}_2\text{---}\text{CH}\text{---}\text{CH}_2]$, can bond to Br at either terminal carbon. Two nonseparable radioisotopic isomers can be formed:

$$\text{BrCH}_2\text{CH}=\text{CH}_2 \quad \text{and} \quad \text{CH}_2=\text{CHCH}_2\text{Br}$$

A degradation of this single isolated product shows labeling on both C^1 and C^3 and, therefore, the labeled product is $\text{CH}_2=\text{CHCH}_2\text{Br}$. This reaction is said to cause ^{14}C *scrambling*.

SYNTHESES

7.156 Outline the reactions for converting $\text{HOCH}_2\text{CH}_2\text{CH}_2\text{CH}_3$ to $\text{CH}_3\text{CH(OH)CHBrCH}_3$.

▰ $\text{HOCH}_2\text{CH}_2\text{CH}_2\text{CH}_3 \xrightarrow[150\,°\text{C}]{\text{H}_2\text{SO}_4} \text{H}_2\text{C}=\text{CHCH}_2\text{CH}_3 \xrightarrow{\text{dil. H}_2\text{SO}_4} \text{CH}_3\text{CH(OH)CH}_2\text{CH}_3$

$\xrightarrow[120\,°\text{C}]{\text{H}_2\text{SO}_4} \text{CH}_3\text{CH}=\text{CHCH}_3 \xrightarrow{\text{Br}_2/\text{H}_2\text{O}} \underset{\text{3-Bromo-2-butanol}}{\text{CH}_3\text{CH(OH)CHBrCH}_3}$

7.157 From propene, prepare (*a*) 2-chloropropane, (*b*) 1-chloropropane, (*c*) hexane, (*d*) 2-methylpentane, and (*e*) 2,3-dimethylbutane. Later syntheses can use products made earlier.

▰ (*a*) $\text{CH}_3\text{CH}=\text{CH}_2 + \text{HCl} \longrightarrow \text{CH}_3\text{CHClCH}_3$ (**A**)

(*b*) $\text{CH}_3\text{CH}=\text{CH}_2 \xrightarrow{\text{Cl}_2\text{SO}_2} \underset{\text{allyl chloride}}{\text{ClCH}_2\text{CH}=\text{CH}_2} \xrightarrow[\text{2. HOAc}]{\text{1. BH}_3/\text{THF}} \text{ClCH}_2\text{CH}_2\text{CH}_3$ (**B**)

Catalytic hydrogenation of allyl chloride would hydrogenolyze the C—Cl bond and give propane.

(c) The product hexane has twice as many C's as the starting material. Therefore, couple two 3-carbon derivatives of propane:

$$B \xrightarrow[\text{2. CuI}]{\text{1. Li}} Pr_2CuLi \xrightarrow{B} CH_3(CH_2)_4CH_3$$

(d) $A \xrightarrow[\text{2. CuI}]{\text{1. Li}} i\text{-}Pr_2CuLi \xrightarrow{B} Me_2CHCH_2CH_2CH_3$

(e) $A \xrightarrow[\text{2. CuI}]{\text{1. Li}} i\text{-}Pr_2CuLi \xrightarrow{A} Me_2CHCHMe_2$ (C)

7.158 Give the steps required for the following transformations using any needed solvents and inorganic reagents. (a) 1-Chloropentane (A) to 1,2-dichloropentane; (b) A to 2-chloropentane; (c) A to 1-bromopentane; (d) 1-bromobutane to 1,2-dihydroxybutane; and (e) Me_2CHCH_2Cl to $Me_3CCH_2CMe_2I$.

▮ Syntheses are best done by working backwards, keeping in mind your starting materials.

(a) The desired product is a *vic*-dichloride made by adding Cl_2 to the appropriate alkene, which in turn is made by dehydrochlorinating the starting material.

$$ClCH_2CH_2CH_2CH_2CH_3 \xrightarrow[\text{KOH}]{\text{alc.}} H_2C=CHCH_2CH_2CH_3 \xrightarrow{Cl_2} ClCH_2CHClCH_2CH_2CH_3$$

(b) To get a pure product add HCl to 1-pentene as made in part (a).

$$H_2C=CHCH_2CH_2CH_3 + HCl \longrightarrow H_3CCHClCH_2CH_2CH_3$$

(c) An anti-Markovnikov addition of HBr to 1-pentene [part (a)].

$$H_2C=CHCH_2CH_2CH_3 + HBr \xrightarrow{\text{peroxide}} BrCH_2CH_2CH_2CH_2CH_3$$

(d) Glycols are made by mild oxidation of alkenes.

$$BrCH_2CH_2CH_2CH_3 \xrightarrow[\text{KOH}]{\text{alc.}} H_2C=CHCH_2CH_3 \xrightarrow[\text{RT}]{KMnO_4} HOCH_2CHOHCH_2CH_3$$

(e) The product has twice as many C's as does the starting material. The skeleton of C's in the product corresponds to that of the dimer of $(CH_3)_2C=CH_2$.

$$(CH_3)_2CHCH_2Cl \xrightarrow[\text{KOH}]{\text{alc.}} (CH_3)_2C=CH_2 \xrightarrow{H_2SO_4} \underbrace{(CH_3)_3CCH=C(CH_3)_2 + (CH_3)_3CCH_2\overset{\overset{\displaystyle CH_3}{|}}{C}=CH_2}$$

$$\downarrow HI$$

$$(CH_3)_3CCH_2CI(CH_3)_2$$

7.159 Provide reactions for converting 1-methylcyclohexanol to: (a) 1-bromo-1-methylcyclohexane, (b) *cis*-1-bromo-2-methylcyclohexane, (c) *trans*-2-methylcyclohexanol, (d) *trans*-1,2-dibromo-1-methylcyclohexane.

▮ Dehydration with H_2SO_4 forms 1-methylcyclohexene (B) which reacts with the indicated reagents.

(a) $B \xrightarrow{HBr}$

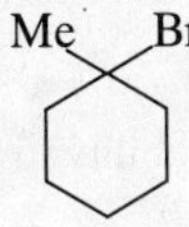

(b) $B \xrightarrow{HBr, ROOR}$ 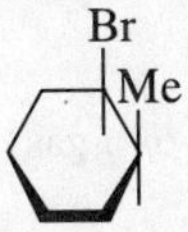 ; HBr addition in ROOR with cycloalkenes goes *trans*.

(c) $B \xrightarrow[\text{2. } H_2O_2, OH^-]{\text{1. } BH_3/\text{THF}}$ (d) $B \xrightarrow{Br_2}$

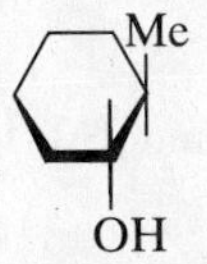

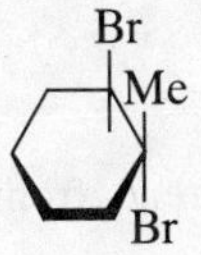

7.160 Devise a synthesis of (a) 3-bromocyclopentene and (b) 3,5-dibromocyclopentene from cyclopentanol.

▮ (a)

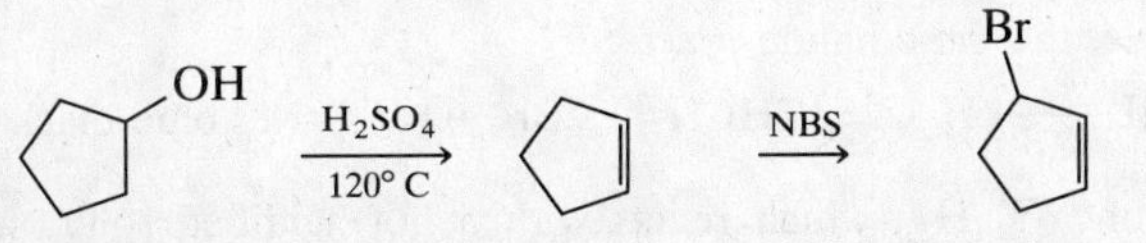

Cyclopentanol   Cyclopentene   3-Bromocyclopentene (C)

(*b*) **C** + NBS ⟶ 3,5-dibromocyclopentene. Since the allylic H of —CHBr— is deactivated by the Br, radical abstraction of the allylic H of —CH$_2$— occurs to give the desired product.

7.161 From any C$_4$H$_8$ alkene, prepare (*a*) *meso*-2,3-dihydroxybutane and (*b*) *rac*-2,3-dihydroxybutane. Do not use the same mode of addition.

▮ (*a*) *cis*-2-Butene (A) + cold KMnO$_4$ (*syn* addition).   (*b*) **A** + HCOOOH (*anti* addition).

7.162 From PrOH, prepare (*a*) 1,2,3-trichloropropane, (*b*) 1,3-dibromo-2-chloropropane, (*c*) 1-bromo-2-chloro-3-iodopropane, (*d*) 1,1,2-tribromopropane, and (*e*) BrCH$_2$CHOHCH$_2$Cl.

▮ For each synthesis dehydrate PrOH with conc. H$_2$SO$_4$ to CH$_3$CH=CH$_2$ (**B**).

(*a*) **B** $\xrightarrow{\text{Me}_3\text{COCl/peroxide}}$ ClCH$_2$CH=CH$_2$ $\xrightarrow{\text{Cl}_2}$ ClCH$_2$CHClCH$_2$Cl

(*b*) **B** $\xrightarrow{\text{NBS}}$ BrCH$_2$CH=CH$_2$ $\xrightarrow{\text{BrCl}}$ BrCH$_2$CHClCH$_2$Br

(*c*) BrCH$_2$CH=CH$_2$ $\xrightarrow{\text{ICl}}$ BrCH$_2$CHClCH$_2$I

(*d*) **B** $\xrightarrow{\text{Br}_2}$ BrCH$_2$CHBrCH$_3$ $\xrightarrow{\text{alc. KOH}}$ BrCH=CHCH$_3$ $\xrightarrow{\text{Br}_2}$ Br$_2$CHCHBrCH$_3$

Little H$_2$C=CBrCH$_3$ is formed because (*1*) the 1° H of —CH$_2$Br is more acidic and more easily removed by OH$^-$ than the 2° H of —CHBr, (*2*) the 1° H is less sterically hindered, and (*3*) there is twice as much of a chance to remove a 1° H, since there are twice as many of them. Little allyl bromide is formed because (*1*) the 1° H of C<u>H</u>$_3$ is less acidic than <u>H</u>—C—Br and (*2*) the vinyl bromide is more stable by virtue of delocalization of e$^-$'s from Br to C=C.

(*e*) BrCH$_2$CH=CH$_2$ + Cl$_2$/H$_2$O ⟶ BrCH$_2$CHOHCH$_2$Cl

ANALYSIS AND STRUCTURE PROOF

7.163 List four chemical tests to distinguish an alkene from an alkane.

▮ A positive test is indicated by one or more detectable events such as a color change, appearance of an insoluble solid or liquid, evolution of a gas, uptake of a gas or evolution of heat.

$$\text{C=C} + \text{Br}_2 \text{ (red)} \xrightarrow{\text{CCl}_4} \underset{\text{Br Br (colorless)}}{-\text{C}-\text{C}-} \quad \text{(loss of color)}$$

$$\text{C=C} + \text{KMnO}_4 \text{ (purple)} \longrightarrow \underset{\text{OH OH (colorless)}}{-\text{C}-\text{C}-} (+\text{MnO}_2) \quad \begin{matrix}\text{(loss of color and formation}\\\text{or precipitate)}\end{matrix}$$

brown-black precipitate

$$\text{C=C} + \text{H}_2\text{SO}_4 \text{ (conc.)} \longrightarrow \underset{\text{H}}{-\overset{}{\text{C}}-\overset{+}{\text{C}}-} + \text{HSO}_4^- + \text{heat} \quad \text{(solubility in sulfuric acid)}$$

$$\text{C=C} + \text{H}_2 \xrightarrow{\text{Pt}} \underset{\text{H H}}{-\text{C}-\text{C}-} \quad \text{(uptake of a gas)}$$

Alkanes give none of these tests.

7.164 Give a simple test to distinguish (*a*) 1-butene from the 2-butenes and (*b*) 1,3-dibromopropane from 1,2-dibromopropane.

▮ (*a*) Heat with acidified KMnO$_4$ and lead any evolved gas into limewater, Ca(OH)$_2$. If a white precipitate of CaCO$_3$ appears, it comes from 1-butene whose terminal C is emitted as CO$_2$:

$$\text{CO}_2 + \text{Ca(OH)}_2 \longrightarrow \text{CaCO}_3(\text{s}) + \text{H}_2\text{O}$$

(*b*) On adding NaI in acetone, the *vic*-dihalide reacts:

$$\text{H}_2\text{CBrCHBrCH}_3 + 2\text{I}^- \longrightarrow \text{H}_2\text{C}=\text{CHCH}_3 + 2\text{Br}^- + \text{I}_2 \quad \text{(gives blue-black color with starch.)}$$

7.165 Deduce the structure of a compound C$_{10}$H$_{20}$ which reacts with a hot acidified solution of KMnO$_4$ to form hexanoic acid, CH$_3$(CH$_2$)$_4$COOH, and isobutyric acid, CH$_3$CH(CH$_3$)COOH.

◢ The molecular formula has two less H's than an alkane $C_{10}H_{22}$ and must be a ring compound or an alkene. Oxidative cleavage indicates a double bond whose position is determined by writing the two acids with COOH groups (whose C's are site of the double bond) facing each other. Now erase the COOH's and join the C's with a double bond.

$$CH_3CH_2CH_2CH_2CH_2CH = CHCH(CH_3)_2 \quad \longleftarrow \quad CH_3CH_2CH_2CH_2CH_2COOH \quad HOOCCH(CH_3)_2$$

2-Methyl-3-nonene (cis or trans)

7.166 Supply a structural formula for C_6H_{10} which reacts with hot $KMnO_4$ to form adipic acid, $HOOC(CH_2)_4COOH$.

◢ With four fewer H's than the alkane C_6H_{14}, the 2° of unsaturation suggests either one triple bond, two double bonds, two rings or one double bond and one ring. Formation of only a single oxidation product with two COOH's indicates a ring and one double bond, namely a cycloalkene.

Cyclohexene

7.167 Three isomeric alkenes **A**, **B**, and **C**, C_5H_{10}, are hydrogenated to yield 2-methylbutane. **A** and **B** give the same 3° ROH on oxymercuration-demercuration. **B** and **C** give different 1° ROH's on hydroboration-oxidation. Supply the structures of **A**, **B**, and **C**.

◢ The isomers must have the same skeleton as 2-methylbutane and it becomes a question of placing the double bond. Since **A** and **B** give a 3° ROH, they have the $=CMe_2$ or $H_2C=C\!\!\!\underset{\underset{Me}{|}}{}$ grouping. Since **B** and **C** give 1° ROH's, they are terminal alkenes having the $H_2C=$ grouping.

$$\textbf{A is } Me-\underset{\underset{Me}{|}}{C}=\underset{\underset{H}{|}}{C}-Me; \qquad \textbf{B is } H_2C=\underset{\underset{Me}{|}}{C}-CH_2CH_3; \qquad \textbf{C is } H_2C=\underset{\underset{H}{|}}{C}-CHMe_2$$

7.168 (*a*) Two isomers, $C_7H_{13}Br$, are formed when either 1,2- or 2,3-dimethylcyclopentene (**A** and **B**) react in the dark with HBr in the absence of peroxides. What are these isomers? (*b*) Which isomers are formed when the same two cyclopentenes in part (*a*) react with HBr in the presence of peroxides?

◢ (*a*) There is a Markovnikov addition to give racemic diastereomers with the Me's *cis* or *trans*:

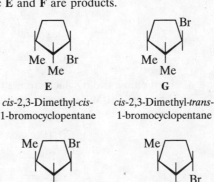

cis-1,2-Dimethyl-1-bromocyclopentane   *trans*-1,2-Dimethyl-1-bromocyclopentane

(*b*) The product is anti-Markovnikov. However, since ROOR catalyzes mainly *anti* addition of HBr to cycloalkenes, the major product from **A** is **D**. The bromo products from **B** have the vicinal Me and Br *cis*. With three stereocenters, eight stereoisomers (2^3), comprising four racemic diastereomers, exist (**E-H**), of which only racemic **E** and **F** are products.

E
cis-2,3-Dimethyl-*cis*-
1-bromocyclopentane

G
cis-2,3-Dimethyl-*trans*-
1-bromocyclopentane

F
trans-2,3-Dimethyl-*trans*-
1-bromocyclopentane

H
trans-2,3-Dimethyl-*cis*-
1-bromocyclopentane

7.169 3,3-Dimethyl-1-butene and HI react to give two products, $C_6H_{13}I$. On reaction with alc. KOH one isomer, **I**, gives back 3,3-dimethyl 1-butene. The other, **J**, gives an alkene that is reductively ozonized to $Me_2C=O$. Give the structures of **I** and **J** and explain the formation of the latter.

◢ **I** is the expected Markovnikov addition product, $MeCHICMe_3$. Two molecules of $Me_2C=O$ are formed from $Me_2C=CMe_2$ whose precursor is **J**, $Me_2CHCIMe_2$. Addition of H^+ to the original alkene gives $Me\overset{+}{C}HCMe_3$ that undergoes $\sim H_3C:$ giving $Me_2CHC\overset{+}{C}Me_2$ that then bonds to I^- to form **J**.

7.170 An unknown compound, C_6H_{12} (**K**), decolorizes Br_2 and is oxidized by hot acidified $KMnO_4$ to a resolvable carboxylic acid, C_4H_9COOH. Explain.

◢ Since **K** decolorizes Br_2, it is an alkene. The missing sixth C comes off as CO_2 during the oxidation so that **K** is a terminal alkene. Since the acid is resolvable, **K** has a chiral carbon

$$H_2C=CH-\overset{*}{\underset{|}{C}}H-CH_2CH_3 \xrightarrow{KMnO_4/H^+} O=C=O + HOOC-\overset{*}{\underset{|}{C}}H-CH_2CH_3$$
$$\underset{Me}{} \qquad\qquad\qquad\qquad\qquad\qquad\qquad \underset{Me}{}$$

K

7.171 (*a*) An unknown compound **L** contains 85.60% C and 14.40% H. Catalytic hydrogenation of 0.500 g at 0 °C and 1 atm consumed 100 mL of H_2. Find the molecular formula.   (*b*) Reductive ozonolysis gave $CH_3CH_2CH_2CHO$. Deduce the structure of **L**.   (*c*) What structural feature is still indeterminate?   (*d*) Discuss the results of some chemical reactions that would permit the definitive assignment of a structure.

◢ (*a*)   To find the ratio of atoms (empirical formula):
C: $85.60 \div 12.00 = 7.13$; H: $14.40 \div 1.008 = 14.3$. Thus, the C:H ratio is 1:2, the empirical formula is CH_2, and the molecular formula is $(CH_2)_n$. This is the formula of an alkene.
To find the gram molecular weight (GMW) in g/mol, we have

$$H_2 \text{ absorbed} = 0.100 \text{ L} \div 22.4 \text{ L/mol} = 4.46 \times 10^{-3} \text{ mol}$$

$$GMW = (0.500 \text{ g})/(4.46 \times 10^{-3} \text{ mol}) = 112 \text{ g/mol}$$

Divide the GMW by the gram empirical weight of CH_2 to get *n*: 112 g/mol $\div 14$ g/(CH_2 unit) = 8 CH_2 units/mol; the molecular formula is $(CH_2)_8$, or C_8H_{16}.
(*b*) $CH_3CH_2CH_2CH=O$ $O=CHCH_2CH_2CH_3$ tells us that **L** is $CH_3CH_2CH_2CH=CHCH_2CH_2CH_3$.
(*c*)   **L** may be *cis* or *trans*.
(*d*)   Hydroxylate **L** with $KMnO_4$ at room temperature. If the glycol is resolvable, it must be racemic, and since this hydroxylation is *syn*, **L** is *trans*. If the glycol cannot be resolved after several attempts by different methods, it must be *meso* and **L** is *cis*. This assignment can be confirmed by hydroxylating **L** with $HCOOOH$, which should give the racemic, resolvable glycol via *trans*-hydroxylation.

7.172 Find the structure of the compound C_9H_{12} (**M**) that reacts with two eq of H_2 and on reductive ozonolysis gives two eq of $H_2C=O$ and one eq of

◢ Compound **M** has 4° of unsaturation, two of which are multiple bonds (uptake of two eq of H_2) and two are rings. Obtaining two eq of $H_2C=O$ tells us **M** has two methylene groups attached, where the $C=O$'s are in the diketone ozonolysis product. The structure of **M** is

The following Problems 7.173 to 7.176 relate to unknowns with molecular formulas $C_{10}H_{16}$.

7.173 Write all possible structures for a compound $C_{10}H_{16}$ (**N**) that undergoes reductive or oxidative ozonolysis to yield two moles of the same compound C_5H_8O (**O**). **N** reacts with three eq of H_2/Pd at 120 °C. Neither **N** nor **O** is resolvable.

◢ Compound $C_{10}H_{16}$ lacks six H's for being an alkane $C_{10}H_{22}$—it has 3° of unsaturation. **N** is symmetrical (ozonolysis yields two moles of a single carbonyl compound), has only one C=C and two rings. The reaction with three eq of H_2 at elevated temperatures means that the two rings in **N** are cyclopropyl. The 2° of unsaturation in **O** are due to a cyclopropyl ring and a C=O which must be a ketone, since it results from either reductive or oxidative ozonolysis. The alkene type is RR′C=CRR′. Inability to be resolved means an absence of chiral atoms in **N** and **O**. The possible structures are

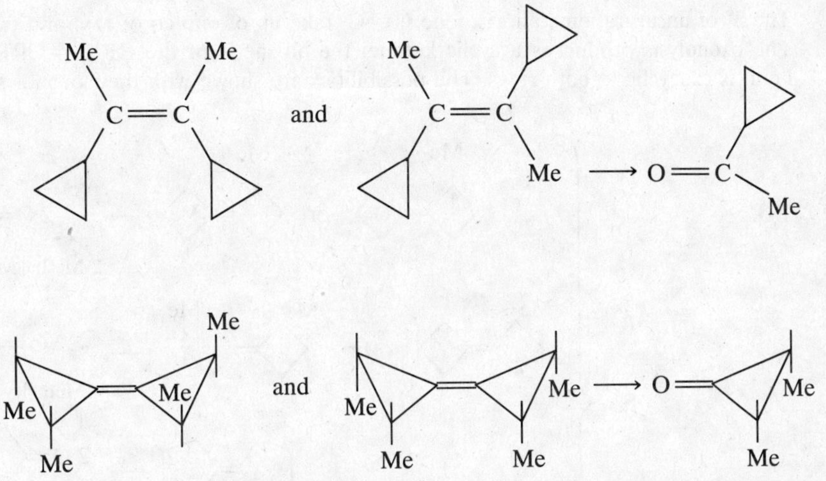

possible **N**'s   corresponding **O**'s

7.174 Give the structure of **P** that has the same hydrogenation and ozonolysis characteristics as its isomer **N**. However, **P** and its ketonic ozonolysis product **Q** are resolvable.

◢ Like **N**, **P** is of the RR′C=CRR′ type (**Q** is a ketone). For both **P** and **Q** to be resolvable, each cyclopropyl ring must be substituted and the double bond must be exocyclic to each ring. The substituents are either two *trans* ME's or one Et. *Cis* or *gem* di-Me's would give achiral molecules. Arrange the *trans* Me's to avoid planes and points of symmetry to preclude the unknown being *meso*. The possible structures are

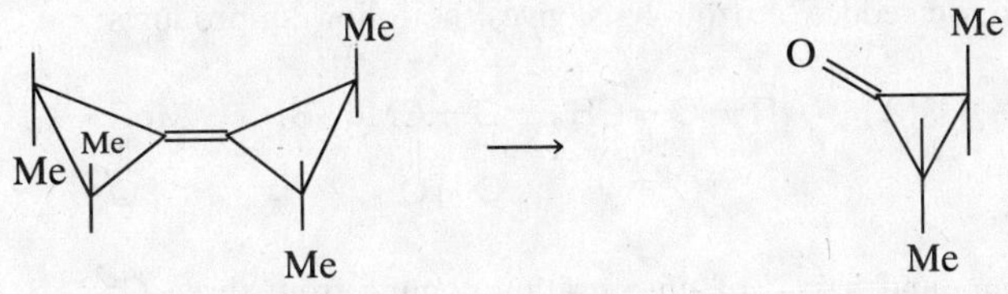

rac,trans-Dimethylcyclopropanone

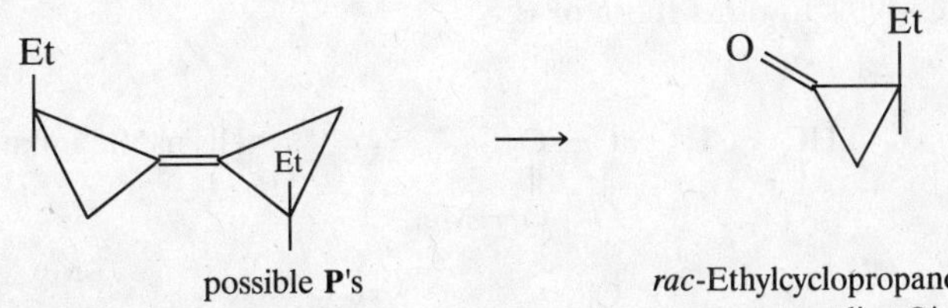

possible **P**'s   *rac*-Ethylcyclopropanone
                          corresponding **Q**'s

7.175 A nonresolvable isomer **R** has the same hydrogenation properties as **P** but gives one product on reductive ozonolysis and a different single product on oxidative ozonolysis. Neither ozonolysis product is resolvable. Give the possible structures of **R**.

▰ Again we have a dicyclopropyl alkene. The reductive ozonolysis product is an aldehyde, RCHO, while the oxidative product is a carboxylic acid, RCOOH. These facts indicate the symmetrical alkene is of the RHC=CHR type. The R's cannot be methylcyclopropyl groups because then the ozonolysis product would have to be a resolvable racemate of chiral enantiomers. **R** is either *cis*- or *trans*-cyclopropyl-CH_2CH=$CHCH_2$-cyclopropyl.

7.176 (*a*) An isomer **S** reacts with one eq of H_2/Pd (not three eq) and gives the same compound **T** on both reductive and oxidative ozonolysis. List all possible structures for **S** and **T** if (i) they are both resolvable, (ii) both irresolvable, and (iii) **T** is resolvable, **S** is not. (*b*) An isomer **U** also reacts with one eq of H_2/Pd but gives one product on reductive ozonolysis and a different single product on oxidative ozonolysis. Give all isomers of **U**.

▰ (*a*) The 3° of unsaturation comprise one C=C (take up of one eq of H_2) and two noncyclopropyl rings. The ozonolysis product is a cyclic ketone; the alkene is of the RR'C=CRR' type; and the double bond is exocyclic to both rings. The possibilities are shown with their ozonolysis products.

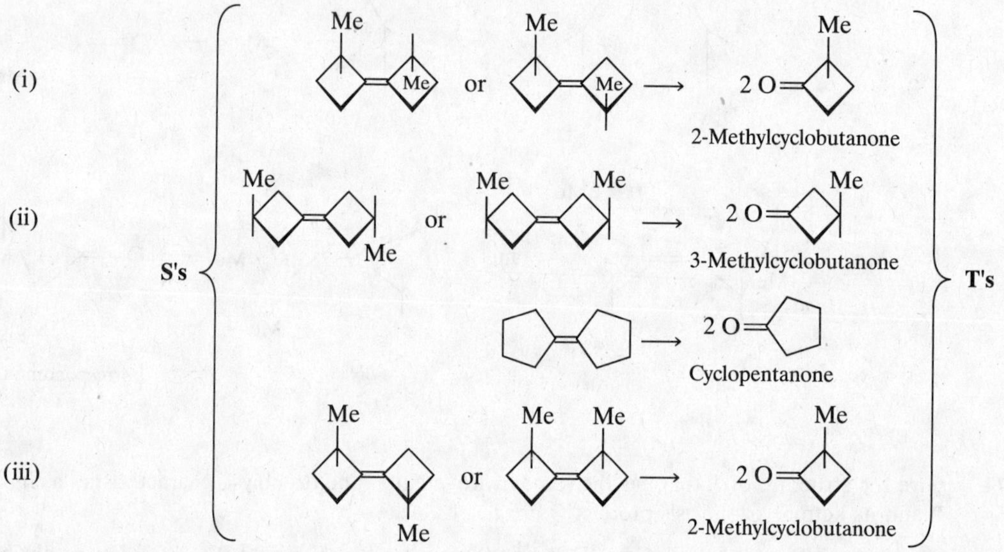

(*b*) The bicycloalkene must be of the RHC=CHR type. Compound **U** is either *cis*- or *trans*-1,2-dicyclobutylethene, cyclobutyl—CH=CH—cyclobutyl.

7.177 Deduce the structure of a compound $C_{10}H_{14}$ that is hydrogenated with three eq of H_2/Pd to give 1-isopropyl-4-methylcyclohexane, and, on reductive ozonolysis, gives the following products:

▰ The unknown compound has 4° of unsaturation coming from three C=C's and one cyclohexane ring. **A** comes from a terminal =CH_2 group that must be outside of the ring. The Me's must also be outside the ring, one attached to C^4, the other is part of the *i*-Pr group on C^1. The terminal =CH_2 cannot be the precursor of Me in the reduced product and must also be part of the *i*-Pr skeleton. This is shown by merging **A** to **B** and pointing the remaining C=O's towards those of **C**:

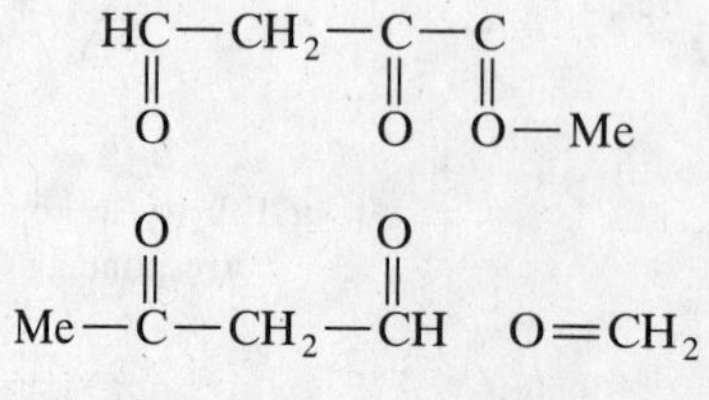

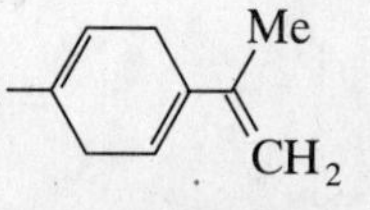

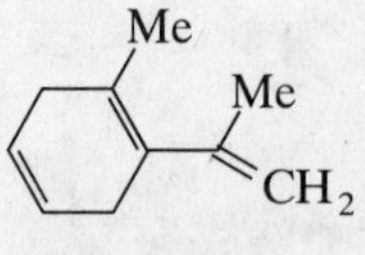

SUPPLEMENTARY PROBLEMS

7.178 Illustrate five reactions observed for intermediate carbocations.

(i) reacts with an ionic or uncharged nucleophile:

$$-\overset{|}{\underset{|}{C^+}} + :Nu^- \longrightarrow -\overset{|}{\underset{|}{C}}:Nu \quad \text{or} \quad -\overset{|}{\underset{|}{C^+}} + :Nu \longrightarrow -\overset{|}{\underset{|}{C}}:Nu^+$$

(ii) loses the very acidic H from the adjacent C (one of the most acidic known) to give an alkene:

$$-\overset{|}{C}H-\overset{|}{\underset{|}{C^+}} \longrightarrow -\overset{|}{C}=\overset{|}{C}-$$

(iii) rearranges by 1,2 H: or R: shift to give a more substituted (stable) R^+:

$$R_2CH-\overset{|}{\underset{|}{C^+}} \xrightarrow{\sim H:} R_2\overset{|}{\underset{+}{C}}-\overset{|}{C}H \quad \text{or} \quad R_3C-\overset{|}{\underset{|}{C^+}} \xrightarrow{\sim R:} R_2\overset{|}{\underset{+}{C}}-\overset{|}{C}R$$

(iv) adds to C=C, a nucleophilic site (because of its π e$^-$'s):

$$-\overset{|}{\underset{|}{C^+}} + \;>C=C< \longrightarrow -\overset{|}{\underset{|}{C}}-\overset{|}{\underset{|}{C}}-\overset{|}{\underset{|}{C^+}}$$

(v) accepts an :H from an alkane (hydride transfer), leaving a more stable R^+:

$$-\overset{|}{\underset{|}{C^+}} + RH \longrightarrow -\overset{|}{\underset{|}{C}}H + R^+$$

7.179 Effect the following transformations: (*a*) $CH_3CH_2CH_2CH_2I$ to $CH_3CH_2CH_2CH_2Br$, (*b*) $CH_3CHBrCH_3$ to $CH_3CHClCH_2Br$, (*c*) $CH_3CH_2CH_2OH$ to $CH_3CH(OH)CH_2Cl$, (*d*) $(CH_3)_2CHCH_2Cl$ to $(CH_3)_3CCH_2CBr(CH_3)_2$, (*e*) cyclopentene to 6,6-dichlorobicyclo[3.1.0]hexane, and (*f*) cyclobutene to *trans*-1,2-dihydroxycyclobutane

(*a*) $CH_3CH_2CH_2CH_2I \xrightarrow{\text{alc. KOH}} CH_3CH_2CH=CH_2 \xrightarrow[\text{ROOR}]{\text{HBr}} CH_3CH_2CH_2CH_2Br$

(*b*) $CH_3CHBrCH_3 \xrightarrow{\text{alc. KOH}} CH_3CH=CH_2 \xrightarrow{\text{BrCl}} CH_3CHClCH_2Br$

(*c*) $CH_3CH_2CH_2OH \xrightarrow[\text{heat}]{H_2SO_4} CH_3CH=CH_2 \xrightarrow{\text{HOCl}} CH_3CH(OH)CH_2Cl$

(*d*) $(CH_3)_2CHCH_2Cl \xrightarrow{\text{alc. KOH}} (CH_3)_2C=CH_2 \xrightarrow{H_2SO_4 \text{ (dimerization)}} (CH_3)_3CCH_2\overset{\overset{\displaystyle CH_3}{|}}{C}=CH_2 +$
$(CH_3)_3CCH=C(CH_3)_2 \xrightarrow{\text{HBr}} (CH_3)_3CCH_2CBr(CH_3)_2$

(*e*) Cyclopentene $\xrightarrow{\text{HCCl}_3/\text{KOH}}$

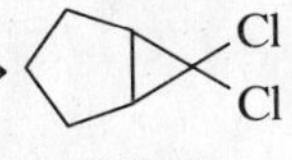

(*f*) Cyclobutene $\xrightarrow{\text{HCOOOH}}$

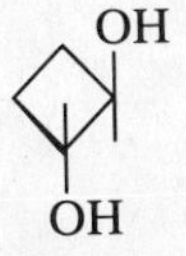

7.180 Give the products from the peroxide catalyzed reactions of 1-butene with (*a*) MeCH=O, (*b*) NH_3, (*c*) Cl_3SiH, (*d*) EtOH, and (*e*) MeCOOH. In each case indicate the radical intermediate that starts the chain propagation.

(*a*) $CH_3CH_2CH_2CH_2-\overset{\overset{\displaystyle O}{\|}}{C}Me$, $Me\overset{\overset{\displaystyle O}{\|}}{C}\cdot$; (*b*) $Bu-NH_2$, $\cdot NH_2$; (*c*) $Bu-SiCl_3$, $\cdot SiCl_3$;

(*d*) $Bu-OEt$, $EtO\cdot$; and (*e*) $Bu-O\overset{\overset{\displaystyle O}{\|}}{C}-Me$, $Me-\overset{\overset{\displaystyle O}{\|}}{C}-O\cdot$

7.181 Account for the formation of 1,2-dimethylcyclohexene (**A**) and isopropylidenecyclopentane (**B**) on dehydration of 2.2-dimethylcyclohexanol.

▰ Removal of the OH group during dehydration forms a 2° R^+ which rearranges to a more stable 3° R^+ by (*a*) a :CH_3 shift to **A'**, the precursor of **A** (path 1), or (*b*) a shift of the ring bond between C^2 and C^3 to C giving **B'**, the precursor of **B** (path 2). Both 3° R^+'s then lose an H^+ to form the two alkenes.

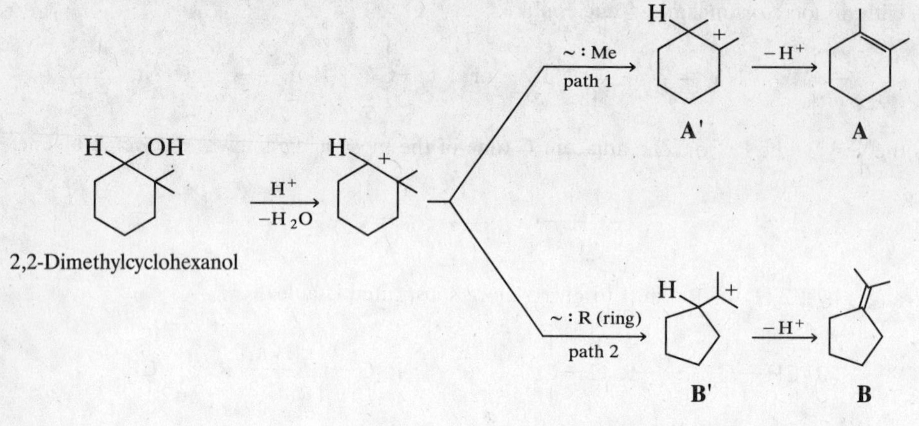

2,2-Dimethylcyclohexanol

7.182 Explain the following: (*a*) $Cl_2C{=}CCl_2$ (**A**) does not add Cl_2 under usual reaction conditions. (*b*) A small amount of $AlCl_3$ catalyzes the addition. (*c*) **A** adds Cl_2 in the presence of uv light. (*d*) O_2 inhibits the uv reaction.

▰ (*a*) Four electron-attracting Cl's decrease the nucleophilicity of the π e$^-$'s of the alkene.

(*b*) $AlCl_3$ reacts with Cl_2 to increase the electrophilicity of Cl^+ sufficiently to react.

$$Cl_2 + AlCl_3 \longrightarrow Cl^+ + AlCl_4^-$$

$$Cl_2C{=}CCl_2 \xrightarrow{Cl^+} Cl_3C{-}\overset{+}{C}Cl_2 \xrightarrow{AlCl_4^-} Cl_3C{-}CCl_3 + AlCl_3$$

(*c*) The uv light initiates the reaction by forming two Cl· atoms. The propagation steps are:

(i) Cl· + $Cl_2C{-}CCl_2 \longrightarrow Cl_3C{-}\dot{C}Cl_2$ and   (ii) $Cl_3C{-}\dot{C}Cl_2 + Cl_2 \longrightarrow$ Cl· + $Cl_3C{-}CCl_3$

(*d*) O_2, a diradical (·O—O·) reacts with Cl· to give the unreactive Cl—O—O· radical.

7.183 (*a*) Indicate the product of hydroboration of 3-methyl-2-pentene at (i) 25 °C and (ii) 160 °C. (*b*) Predict and explain the isomerization of the product in part (*a*) at (i) when heated to 160 °C. (*c*) Give the two trialkylboranes from the reaction of *cis*-4-methyl-2-pentene (**B**) with $BH_3\cdot THF$. (Just show the bonding to the B atom.) Predict the major R_3B product and explain your choice. (*d*) At which C does hydroboration occur when **B** reacts with a bulky dialkylborane, R_2BH? What is the synthetic utility of using bulky boranes for hydroboration?

▰ (*a*) At 25 °C, addition is typically *anti*-Markovnikov to form **C**.

(*b*) At higher temperatures, R_2B isomerizes to the terminal C forming **D** to minimize steric crowding.

$$CH_3CH{=}C(CH_3)CH_2CH_3 + BH_3\cdot THF$$

$$\overset{\overset{\displaystyle R_2B}{\displaystyle |}}{CH_3CHCH(CH_3)CH_2CH_3} \xleftarrow{\text{25 °C}} \qquad \xrightarrow{\text{160 °C (via C)}} R_2BCH_2CH_2CH(CH_3)CH_2CH_3$$

$$\mathbf{C} \xrightarrow{\text{160 °C}} \mathbf{D}$$

(*c*)   *i*-PrCH$_2$—CHMe (major, 57%)   *i*-PrCH—CH$_2$Me (minor, 43%)
                  | |
                —B—   —B—

When both C's are 2° as in **B**, preferential attack is on the C with the smaller R.

(*d*) The exclusive product arises from bonding at the C with the smaller R because the bulky borane is more sensitive to steric effects. The yield of the desired alcohol can be better controlled on oxidation of the borane.

7.184 Account for the interconversion of *cis* and *trans* alkenes on heating with I_2.

▰ I_2 has a weak bond (151 kJ/mol) and forms 2I· when heated. I· adds to C=C and the new radical can now rotate about its σ bond to form different conformations. However, the C—I bond is easily broken. When I· is lost, the C=C is reformed, and a mixture of *cis* and *trans* isomers is produced from the two extreme conformations.

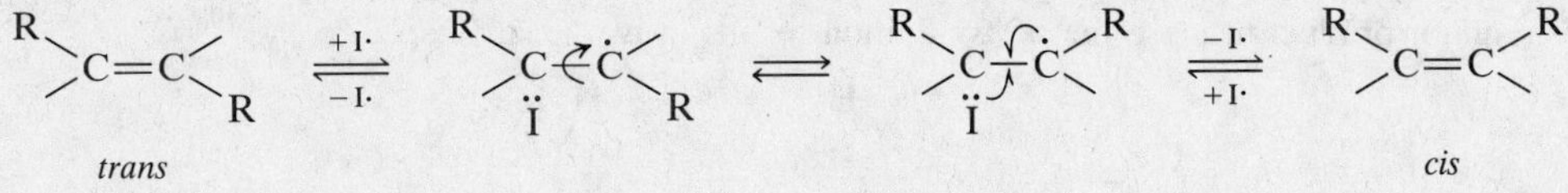

7.185 (*a*) $Me_2C^1{=}C^2HC^3H_2C^4H_2C^5H{=}C^6HMe$ reacts with H_2SO_4 to give four structural isomers, C_9H_{18}, that react with one eq of H_2/Pd. Give their structural formulas and account for their formation (the C's are numbered to simplify the explanation).   (*b*) On repeating the reaction with $Me_2C^1{=}C^2HC^3H_2C^4H{=}C^5HMe$, only two structural isomers are obtained. Give their structures and explain the fewer number.

(*a*) Since the products have 2° of unsaturation but add only one eq of H_2/Pd, they must have one ring and one C=C. H^+ adds to C^2 making C^1 a 3° R^+ that then adds intramolecularly to the other C=C in the same molecule. (These steps are reminiscent of the bimolecular-intermolecular dimerization.) Addition to C^6 (path 1) generates a six-membered ring R^+ that loses either of two protons giving products **A** and **B**. Addition to C^5 (path 2) generates a five-membered ring R^+ that loses either of two protons giving products **C** and **D**:

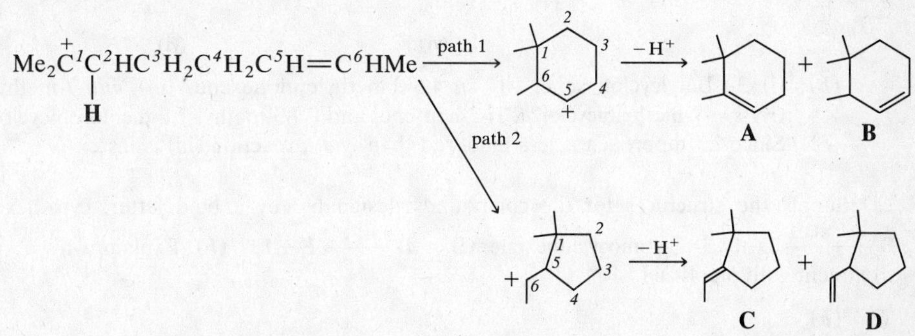

A and **C** are the major Saytzeff products for each ring size.

(*b*) Addition of H^+ gives a 3° R^+ which adds to C^5, giving a five-membered ring that loses H^+ to form **E**, the more favored Saytzeff product, and **F**. An unlikely four-membered ring would result from addition to C^4.

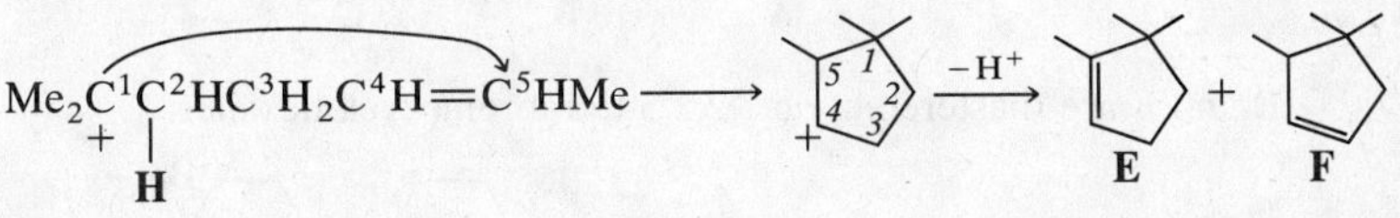

7.186 (*a*) Give the conformational structure for the major product from each of the following reactions:

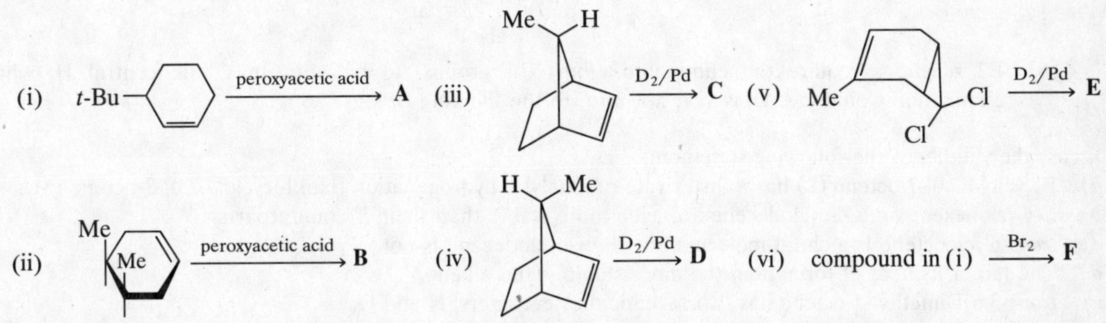

(*b*) Name the reactant compounds in reactions (i) to (v).   (*c*) Compare the rates in reactions (iii) and (iv).

(*a*) In reactions (i) and (ii) the peroxyacid approaches the C=C from the less hindered face. In reactions (iii), (iv), and (v) the less hindered face of the C=C is adsorbed on the surface of the metal catalyst, resulting in the introduction of D_2 at that face. If the starting material and all reagents and solvents are optically inactive, so will be the products even though they may have stereocenters—they will be racemic or *meso*.

(i) The epoxide ring is *trans* to the bulky *t*-Bu (**A**). (ii) The epoxide ring is *trans* to the two *cis* Me's (**B**). (iii) *Exo* approach is less hindered (**C**). (iv) The *syn* Me hinders the *exo* approach—the D's are *endo* (**D**). (v) D₂ adds to the face away from the cyclopropyl ring (**E**). (vi) Br₂ adds *trans* to give mainly **F**, in which all groups are *trans*. **F′** is a minor product because the *trans*-addition results in two axial Br's.

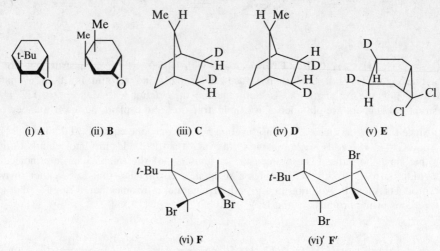

(i) **A**   (ii) **B**   (iii) **C**   (iv) **D**   (v) **E**

(vi) **F**   (vi)′ **F′**

(**b**) (i) 3-*t*-Butylcyclohexene, (ii) *cis*-4,5-dimethylcyclohexene, (iii) *anti*-7-methylbicyclo[2.2.1]-2-heptene, (iv) *syn*-7-methylbicyclo[2.2.1]-2-heptene, and (v) 3-methyl-7,7-dichlorobicyclo[4.1.0]-3-heptene.

(**c**) Since *exo* approach is less hindered than *endo*, reaction (iii) is faster.

7.187 (**a**) Supply the structures for the compounds designated by a bold letter: cyclohexene $\xrightarrow{\text{NBS}}$ **A** $\xrightarrow{\text{Br}_2}$ **B** + **C**; **B** $\xrightarrow{\text{alc. KOH}}$ **D** + 1,3-dibromocyclohexene (**D′**); **D** $\xrightarrow{\text{Br}_2}$ **E** + **F**. (**b**) Explain why **C** won't give **D** or **D′** on treatment with alc. KOH.

(**a**)

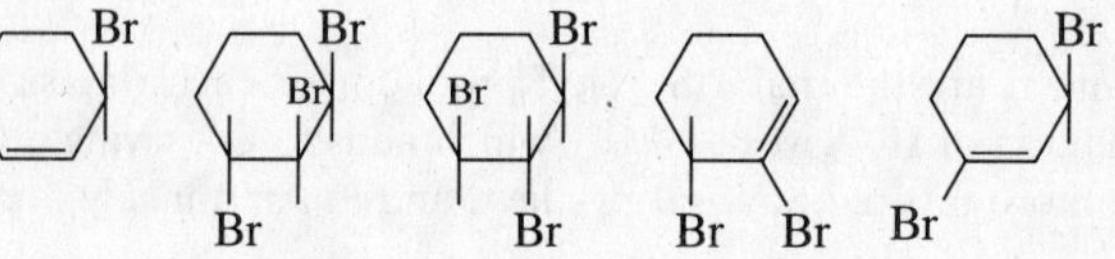

A   **B**   **C**   **D**   **D′**

E and F are diastereomeric 1,2,2,3-tetrabromocyclohexanes.

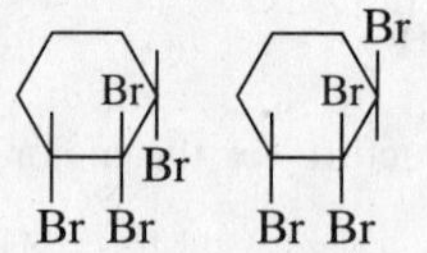

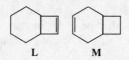

E and F

(**b**) E2 reactions require the eliminated atoms (or groups) to be *anti*. In **C** the central H, whose elimination would give **D**, is *syn*, not *anti*, to the flanking Br's.

7.188 Discuss the validity of the following statements:
(**a**) Bicyclo[4.2.0]-7-octene (**L**) has a faster rate of catalytic hydrogenation than bicyclo[4.2.0]-3-octene (**M**).
(**b**) Z-Cyclohexene and Z-cyclodecene are each more stable than their *E* counterparts.
(**c**) *trans*-Cyclooctene is a chiral molecule but *trans*-cyclodecene is not.
(**d**) The larger its heat of formation, the more stable is the alkene.
(**e**) *trans*-3,6-Dimethyl-4-octene has two racemic diastereomers, **N** and **O**.

(**a**) True. There is little change in ring strain when the cyclohexene ring of **M** is reduced. However, **L** has a cyclobutene ring whose strain, on going to the less strained cyclobutane ring, is reduced on hydrogenation.

L   **M**

(*b*) False. The statement is true for cyclohexene which cannot be *E* (*trans*) (see Problem 7.39). The eight C's of cyclodecene are capable of bridging a C=C from a *trans* juxtaposition. Cyclodecene is a typical alkene in that the *E* (*trans*) isomer is more stable than the Z and for the same steric effect reasons.

(*c*) True. *trans*-Cyclodecene is a flat molecule devoid of chirality. *trans*-Cyclooctene is not flat and it has two puckered conformations which are isolable enantiomers (Fig. 7-11).

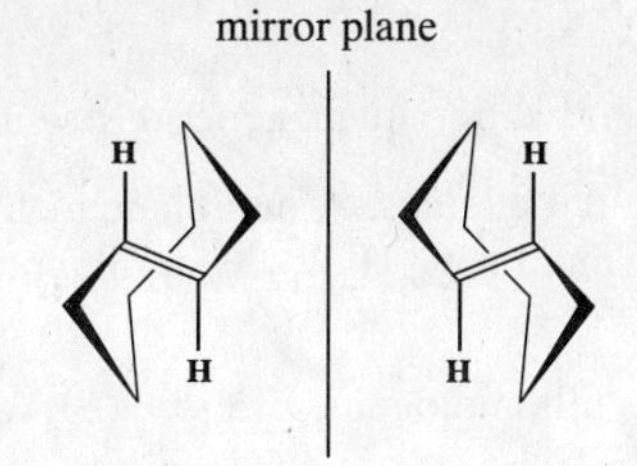

Enantiomers of *trans*-cyclooctene **Fig. 7-11**

(*d*) False. When dealing with negative numbers, we must be careful when expressing magnitudes. A less negative value is larger than a more negative one. With ΔH_f^0, the more negative (the smaller) the value, the more stable is the molecule.

(*e*) False. One diastereomer (**O**) has a center of symmetry.

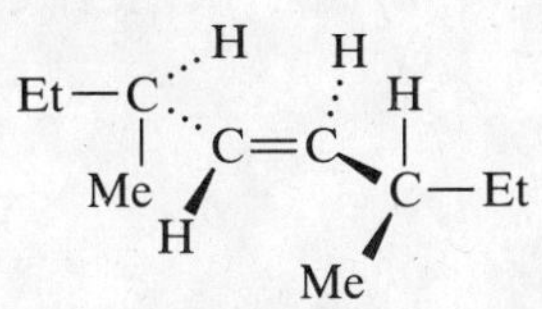

N (racemic)

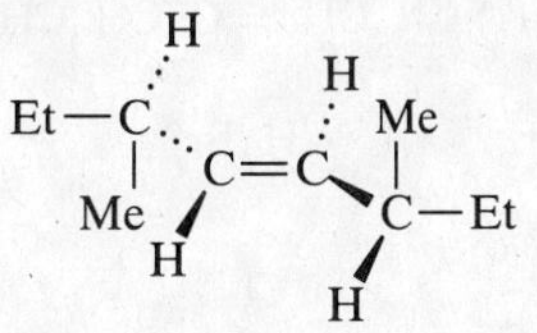

O

7.189 Deduce the structure of natural rubber from the 90% yield of $CH_3-\underset{\underset{O}{\|}}{C}-CH_2-CH_2-CH{=}O$ obtained from reductive ozonolysis. Indicate the mer.

■ The structure is written so that the double bonds show where the C=O groups are formed and the mer (the repeating unit) is indicated within the parentheses.

$$-CH_2-CH{=}\overset{\overset{CH_3}{|}}{C}-CH_2-(CH_2-CH{=}\overset{\overset{CH_3}{|}}{C}-CH_2)-CH_2-CH{=}\overset{\overset{CH_3}{|}}{C}-CH_2-CH_2-CH{=}\overset{\overset{CH_3}{|}}{C}-CH_2-$$

CHAPTER 8
Alkyl Halides

STRUCTURE AND NOMENCLATURE

8.1   Define alkyl halides (or haloalkanes) and supply their general formula.

▮   *Alkyl halides* are halogen-substituted alkanes. A monohaloalkane is written as RX, where X is any halogen atom (F, Cl, Br, or I). The general formula is $C_nH_{2n+1}X$. A dihaloalkane has the formula $C_nH_{2n}X_2$.

8.2   (*a*) Why are alkyl halides classified as a homologous series? (*b*) Why are they important?

▮   (*a*) They are characterized by a general formula and have a functional group, X, that has characteristic chemical properties under a prescribed set of conditions. Their physical properties tend to show progressive changes. (*b*) Because alkyl halides undergo elimination and many substitution reactions, they are useful in direct syntheses and as intermediates in preparing other functional groups.

8.3   (*a*) How do alkyl, allyl, and vinyl halides differ? (*b*) Classify the following halides.

$$\text{(i) } CH_3CH=CFCH_2CH_3, \qquad \text{(ii) } (CH_3)_2CClCH_2CH_3, \qquad \text{(iii) } H_2C=CHCH_2I,$$

(iv) cyclopentene ring with CH_2Br and Cl substituents

▮   (*a*) The X in an alkyl halide is bonded to an sp^3 hybridized C of an alkyl group. In an allyl halide, there is a C=C bonded to the C bearing the X. In vinyl halides, X is bonded to an sp^2 hybridized C of an alkene. (*b*) (i) vinyl fluoride, (ii) alkyl chloride because the C is sp^3 hybridized. (iii) This allyl iodide is an alkyl halide because I is bonded to sp^3 C. (iv) Vinyl chloride and allyl bromide.

8.4   (*a*) Classify alkyl halides on the basis of the bonding environment of the C of C—X. Illustrate with general formulas. (*b*) Use $C_2H_4Br_2$ to classify dihalides.

▮   (*a*) They are classified by the type of C to which X is bonded: *primary* (1°), *secondary* (2°), or *tertiary* (3°). Their definitions and corresponding general formulas are
    (i)   Primary: C is bonded to only one C; RCH_2X.
    (ii) Secondary: C is bonded to two C's; R_2CHX.
    (iii) Tertiary: C is bonded to three C's; R_3CX.
CH_3X is unique because the C is bonded only to H's. It is simply called a *methyl halide*.
    (*b*) The prefix *gem* (geminal) is used for two X's on the same C and *vic* (vicinal) for two X's on adjacent C's; CH_3CHBr_2 is a *gem*-dibromide and $BrCH_2CH_2Br$ is a *vic*-dibromide.

8.5   Supply (*a*) common and (*b*) IUPAC names for the C_4H_9I isomers and classify them as to whether they are 1°, 2°, or 3°.

▮   Common names have the alkyl group name followed by the halide name, i.e., ethyl bromide, C_2H_5Br. In the IUPAC system alkyl halides are named as haloalkanes. The longest alkane chain is numbered so that the smallest numbers are used to indicate the positions of substituents. Several substituents are named alphabetically.

$$CH_3CH_2CH_2CH_2I \qquad CH_3CH_2CHICH_3 \qquad CH_3\underset{\overset{|}{CH_3}}{\overset{CH_3}{C}}HCH_2I \text{ or } Me_2CHCH_2I \qquad CH_3\underset{\overset{|}{CH_3}}{\overset{\overset{\displaystyle CH_3}{|}}{C}}{-}I \text{ or } Me_3C{-}I$$

1°	2°	1°	3°
(*a*) *n*-Butyl iodide	*sec*-Butyl iodide	Isobutyl iodide	tert-Butyl iodide
(*b*) 1-Iodobutane	2-Iodobutane	1-Iodo-2-methylpropane	2-Iodo-2-methylpropane

8.6   Write structural formulas, give IUPAC names for and classify the isomers of: (a) $C_5H_{11}Cl$ and (b) $C_4H_8F_2$.

� First write the isomeric parent hydrocarbons (Problem 4.7) and then replace one of each type of equivalent H by X. Duplication of isomers is avoided by assigning IUPAC names.

(a)   The three isomeric pentanes showing their numbers of different kinds of equivalent H's are

$$CH_3^aCH_2^bCH_2^cCH_2^bCH_3^a \qquad (CH_3^a)_2CH^bCH_2^cCH_3^d \qquad C(CH_3^a)_4$$
Pentane (3)   Isopentane (4)   Neopentane (1)

Three isomers have the pentane skeleton:

$$ClCH_2CH_2CH_2CH_2CH_3 \qquad CH_3CHClCH_2CH_2CH_3 \qquad CH_3CH_2CHClCH_2CH_3$$
1-Chloropentane (1°)   2-Chloropentane (2°)   3-Chloropentane (2°)

Four isomers have the isopentane skeleton:

1-Chloro-2-methyl-butane (1°)   2-Chloro-2-methyl-butane (3°)   2-Chloro-3-methyl-butane (2°)   1-Chloro-3-methyl-butane (1°)

One isomer has the neopentane skeleton: $(CH_3)_3CCH_2Cl$, 1-chloro-2,2-dimethylpropane (1°).

(b)   Dihalogenated n-butanes and isobutanes are derived by systematically first placing the two F's on the same C and then on different C's. n-Butane affords two *gem*-difluoro isomers:

$$F_2CHCH_2CH_2CH_3 \qquad CH_3CF_2CH_2CH_3,$$
1,1-Difluorobutane   2,2-Difluorobutane

There are four isomers with two F's on different C's:

$$FCH_2CHFCH_2CH_3 \qquad FCH_2CH_2CHFCH_3 \qquad FCH_2CH_2CH_2CH_2F \qquad CH_3CHFCHFCH_3$$
1,2-Difluorobutane(*vic*)   1,3-Difluorobutane   1,4-Difluorobutane   2,3-Difluorobutane(*vic*)

The isobutane skeleton affords three difluoro isomers:

$$F_2CH-CH(CH_3)-CH_3 \qquad FCH_2-CF(CH_3)-CH_3 \qquad FCH_2CH(CH_3)CH_2F$$
1,1-Difluoro-2-methyl propane (*gem*)   1,2-Difluoro-2-methyl propane (*vic*)   1,3-Difluoro-2-methyl propane

8.7   Give IUPAC names for: (a) $BrCH_2CHClCHCl_2$, (b) $(CH_3)_3CCHClCH(CHBrCH_3)CH_2CH_2CH(CH_3)_2$,

(c) [structure], (d) [structure], and (e) $(CH_3)_2C=CHCH_2Cl$.

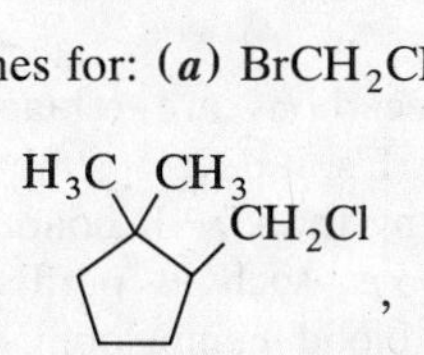

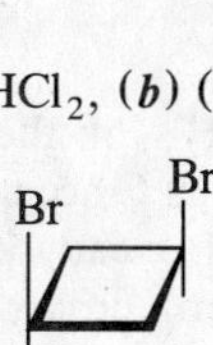

▶ (a) 3-Bromo-1,1,2-trichloropropane; (b) 4-(1-bromoethyl)-3-chloro-2,2,7-trimethyloctane; (c) 2-chloromethyl-1,1-dimethylcyclopentane; (d) *cis*-1,3-dibromocyclobutane, and (e) 1-chloro-3-methyl-2-butene.

8.8   (a) Write structural formulas and IUPAC names for: (i) methylene bromide, (ii) chloroform, (iii) allyl bromide, (iv) t-amyl chloride, and (v) neopentylbromide.   (b) Illustrate the use of the suffix "form" in naming trihalogen and trinitromethanes.

▶ (a) (i) CH_2Br_2, dibromomethane; (ii) $CHCl_3$, trichloromethane; (iii) $H_2C=CH-CH_2Br$, 3-bromo-1-propene; (iv) $(CH_3)_2CClCH_2CH_3$, 2-chloro-2-methylbutane; and (v) $(CH_3)_3CCH_2Br$, 1-bromo-2,2-dimethylpropane. (b) The "form" method is used for the HCX_3 type of compounds: HCF_3, fluoroform; $HCCl_3$, chloroform; $HCBr_3$, bromoform; HCl_3, iodoform; $HC(NO_2)_3$, nitroform.

8.9   Give the structure of each of the following compounds: (a) 2,3-dibromo-3-ethylheptane, (b) cis-2-bromochloromethylcyclohexane, (c) 1-bromo-2-iodocyclobutene, (d) trans-9-chlorodecalin, and (e) 2-exo-3-endo-dichlorobicyclo[2.2.2]octane.

(a) $CH_3CHCHCH_2CH_2CH_2CH_3$ with C_2H_5 substituent and Br Br

(b) cyclohexane ring with CH_2Cl and Br substituents

(c) cyclobutene ring with I and Br substituents

(d) decalin structure with H and Cl

(e) bicyclic structure with Cl, H H, Cl

PHYSICAL PROPERTIES

8.10 Describe the orbital overlap of the C—X bond in alkyl halides.

▮ The C of the C—X bond is tetrahedral and uses sp^3 HO's, one of which overlaps head-to-head with an HO of X that has mostly, but not only, p-character.

8.11 Give the decreasing order of the following factors for the halogens: (a) electronegativity, (b) size, (c) C—X bond lengths in Me—X, (d) vapor phase dipole moments in Me—X, (e) polarizability, and (f) bond strength in MeX.

▮ (a) F > Cl > Br > I (Problem 2.45). (b) I > Br > Cl > F. (c) MeI > MeBr > MeCl > MeF. (d) We might expect that the dipole moment should vary with electronegativity. This is not the case because μ also depends on bond lengths (Problem 2.46). The order is MeCl > MeF > MeBr > MeI (Problem 2.47). (e) The polarizability of an atom is the ability to have its electron cloud distorted toward the positive charge of its bonding partner. As a result, the atom becomes more elliptical (cigar-shaped), not spherical. The farther away the valence electrons are from the nucleus, the more polarizable is the atom. Hence, polarizability decreases with decreasing size: I > Br > Cl > F. (f) Bond strength increases with increasing bond polarity and decreasing bond length. Furthermore, on going from F to I, the volume of the bonding orbital used by X increases making its electron cloud more diffuse and the C—X bond weaker. The order is MeF > MeCl > MeBr > MeI.

8.12 (a) (i) What are perfluorohydrocarbons? (ii) Account for their remarkable stability and chemical inertness. (iii) What role do they play in blood chemistry? (b) (i) What are "Freons"? (ii) What are some of their industrial uses? (iii) Why is their use now restricted?

▮ (a) (i) The prefix *per* means that all H's of the hydrocarbons are replaced by F's. For example, perfluorooctane is $CF_3(CF_2)_6CF_3$. (ii) As C accumulates F's, it develops more δ^+ and exerts a greater electrostatic attraction for the δ^- F's, greatly increasing the C—F bond strength. As a result, the molecule is chemically inert. (iii) Perfluorohydrocarbons, such as perfluorooctane and perfluoro-decalin, are capable of transporting O_2 as does the blood hemoglobin. Research is underway to examine the efficacy of these compounds as blood substitutes when used under special conditions.

(b) (i) Freons are the trade names for commercial fluorochloromethanes, CF_xCl_y and $(x + y = 4)$ ethanes. Freon 12, CF_2Cl_2, is a major refrigerant. (ii) They are physiologically safe and chemically inert under ordinary conditions, and are used as solvents and cooling fluids in refrigerator systems. (iii) Because of their inertness, they reach the upper atmosphere where they finally react to destroy the essential ozone layer. In addition, they absorb infrared radiation, thereby contributing to the greenhouse effect.

8.13 (a) What conclusions can be drawn from the following rotational barriers (given in parentheses in kcal/mol) about the sizes of F and Cl compared to H: $H_3C—CH_3$ (3.0), $H_3C—CH_2F$ (3.3), $H_3C—CH_2Cl$ (3.7)? (b) Explain how the comparative sizes of H and F are used in drug design.

▮ (a) F is slightly larger and Cl is much larger than H. (b) Fluoro derivatives of essential biochemicals have been synthesized with the idea that although a fluoro compound having about the same size as the unfluorinated compound, can be absorbed by a cell, it cannot function as does the essential unfluorinated compound; it inhibits cell development. A good example is the anticancer drug fluorouracil, which has a greater inhibitory effect on the rapidly growing and multiplying cancer cells than normal cells.

8.14 Account for (*a*) the same energies of the *anti* and *gauche* conformers of 1,2-dichloroethane; (*b*) the following $-\Delta G°$ values (in kcal/mol at 25 °C) for the equilibrium, $X_{ax} \rightleftharpoons X_{eq}$ for halocyclohexanes: F (0.25), Cl (0.50), Br (0.50), I (0.45); and (*c*) the largest $-\Delta G°$ for the equilibrium in part (*b*) when X is Me (1.7).

◢ (*a*) Based on size and the repulsion between the two C—Cl dipoles, we would expect the *anti* conformer to have a lower energy. However, another counterbalancing factor must be considered. The *gauche* Cl's mutually polarize each other, making one somewhat positive and the other negative. This resulting *van der Waals attraction* stabilizes the *gauche* conformer. The net result is a balance—the conformers have equal energies. (*b*) The more negative is the value for $\Delta G°$, the larger is K_e and the more favored is the equatorial conformer. Based on size alone, we might expect equatorial preference to increase with atom size as is the case in going from F to Cl. However, we must also consider bond length and polarizability. As X gets larger, the C—X bond gets longer, the axial substituent becomes more distant from the 1,3-transannular H's, and this conformation is less unfavorable. For this reason, I_{ax} is not as bad as Br_{ax}. Also, the larger the atom, the more it is polarized, the more "cigar-shaped" rather than spherical it becomes, and the less susceptible it is to 1,3-transannular interactions. (*c*) Me is larger than F and Cl, and about the same size as Br, but smaller than I. It has a longer bond than C—F but shorter than the other C—X bond. In view of these variations, the dominant reason is that Me is not polarized.

8.15 (*a*) What two factors influence the boiling points of alkyl halides (as well as other compounds)? (*b*) Explain the trends in the following boiling points (in °C): (i) MeI (42.4) > MeBr (3.56) > MeCl (-24.2) > MeF (-78.4) > CH_4 (-161.7), (ii) PrBr (71.0) > *i*-PrBr (59.4), (iii) CCl_4(76.8) > $HCCl_3$ (61.3) > H_2CCl_2 (40.1) > H_3CCl (-24.2), and (iv) C_2F_6 (-79) > C_2H_6 (-89).

◢ (*a*) (1) Van der Waal (London) forces of attraction depend on the overall shapes and sizes of molecules and on their molecular weights. Linear molecules have more surface contact and enhanced attraction than branched-chain molecules, while spherically shaped molecules have very slight tangential contacts. (2) Dipole-dipole attraction is a significant factor for RX's, but not at all for alkanes. (*b*) (i) All alkyl halides boil at a higher temperature than the parent alkane. In this sequence the increases in molecular weight and size lead to increasing bp's. At the same time, dipole-dipole attractions decrease and this change should decrease the bp's. Clearly the effect of increasing van der Waal forces of attraction dwarfs the effect of decreasing dipole-dipole attraction. (ii) As with alkanes (Problem 4.17), branched C chains are more spherical-like and their smaller surface area results in lower boiling points. (iii) Accumulation of Cl's on CH_4 increases the molecular weight and size, causing the bp to increase. Notice that the Δbp gets smaller as more Cl's are introduced, a fact that may be due to an increase in the spherical nature of the molecule. (iv) The perfluoroalkane, a fluorocarbon, is predicted to have the higher bp because it has the larger molecular weight. What is surprising is the small difference in bp, a result due to F being only slightly larger than H (Problem 8.13) and having a low polarizability.

8.16 (*a*) List the densities of alkyl halides, water, and alkanes in decreasing order. (*b*) List in decreasing order the densities of the chloromethanes in (ñi) of part (*b*) of Problem 8.15 and H_2O. (*c*) Water is mixed with an immiscible liquid **A** in a separatory funnel to give two layers. Describe what can be done to tell which layer is water and which is **A**. (Do not solve the problem by taste or smell, it may not be healthy.)

◢ (*a*) RI > RBr > H_2O > RCl > RF > RH. (*b*) CCl_4 > $HCCl_3$ > H_2CCl_2 > H_2O > H_3CCl. (*c*) Let a small amount of the lower (denser) layer drop into a test tube containing an equal volume of H_2O. If it dissolves (one layer is observed), it is H_2O. If two layers form, the lower layer is **A**.

8.17 Discuss the ability of alkyl halides to dissolve (*a*) in H_2O, (*b*) in organic solvents, and (*c*) salts.

◢ (*a*) They are insoluble in H_2O, probably because there is little (in the case of RF) to no H-bonding to H_2O. (*b*) They are soluble in alcohol, ether, and benzene. (*c*) Although they are polar, they do not dissolve salts.

8.18 Discuss four major industrial uses of alkyl halides, other than as starting materials for the synthesis of other organic compounds.

(1) Industrial and household solvents. Once the most popular solvent for dry cleaning, CCl_4, has been shown to be toxic and cancer-causing and has been replaced by 1,1,1-trichloroethane, which should be used only in well-ventilated spaces. H_2CCl_2 is still used to decaffeinate coffee and tea, but is a suspected carcinogen. (2) Anesthetics. The first one used was $HCCl_3$, but it is no longer used because it was found toxic and carcinogenic. Halothane, $CF_3CHClBr$, which is nonflammable as well as nontoxic, is now widely used. C_2H_5Cl acts as a local anesthetic when sprayed as a liquid on the skin. It evaporates rapidly, causing a numbing effect by cooling the injured area. (3) Pesticides. Many, e.g., DDT, are now banned because of their deleterious environmental effects, and others because of their demonstrated ability to cause cancer, birth defects, and nerve damage in animals. Some are still used on a small scale (not agriculturally) under careful control as a last resort. (4) Refrigerants.

PREPARATION

8.19 (*a*) Which alkyl halides can be made by free radical halogenation of alkanes? (*b*) Why is this method seldom used for laboratory syntheses of alkyl halides? (*c*) How may polyhalogenation be minimized? (*d*) Explain the industrial use of free radical halogenations.

◢ (*a*) RCl and RBr, not RF or RI. (*b*) Several isomeric monosubstituted halides are formed because most alkanes have different types of H's. Furthermore, substitution of more than one H yields polyhalogenated compounds. (*c*) Polysubstitution is avoided by reacting the halogen with an excess of alkane. For this reason, the hydrocarbon should be relatively inexpensive. (*d*) Industrial halogenations are used when (i) all H's are equivalent, or if not, one is much more reactive, or (ii) any mixture of products can be used in the next step or readily separated by distillation.

8.20 Select the halides that can be made in good yields by free radical halogenation of the parent hydrocarbon. Explain. (*a*) CH_3CH_2Cl, (*b*) $CH_3CH_2CH_2CH_2Cl$, (*c*) Me_3CCH_2Cl, (*d*) Me_3CCl, (*e*) Me_3CBr, (*f*) chlorocyclopropane, (*g*) $H_2C\!\!=\!\!CHCH_2Cl$, and (*h*) $CH_3CHBrCH\!\!=\!\!CHCH_2CH_3$.

◢ To get single monohalogenated products, all the reactive H's of the parent hydrocarbon must be equivalent. This is true for (*a*) CH_3CH_3, (*c*) Me_3CCH_3, (*f*) cyclopropane, and (*g*) $H_2C\!\!=\!\!CHCH_3$. Although (*g*) has two types of H's, the allylic H's are much more reactive than the inert vinylic H's (Problem 7.147). The precursors for (*b*) and (*d*), which are $CH_3CH_2CH_2CH_3$ and Me_3CH respectively, have two kinds of H's and on chlorination give a mixture of monochloro products. However, (*e*) can be made in good yield even though there is more than one type of H, because bromination (Problems 4.87 and 4.88) is much more selective than chlorination and the 3° H is replaced almost exclusively by Br. Even though the parent hydrocarbon for (*h*), $CH_3CH_2CH\!\!=\!\!CHCH_2CH_3$, has only one kind of equivalent H and might be expected to give a single halogenated product, it actually gives two products. The first propagation step produces an allylic radical whose resonance hybrid can react with Br_2 in the second propagation step at either of two radical sites to form two monobromo substituted products.

$$CH_3CH_2CH\!\!=\!\!CHCH_2CH_3 \xrightarrow{\ Br\cdot\ }$$

$$[CH_3\overset{\delta\cdot}{CH}\!-\!CH\!-\!\overset{\delta\cdot}{C}HCH_2CH_3] \xrightarrow[-Br\cdot]{Br_2}$$

→ $CH_3CHBrCH\!\!=\!\!CHCH_2CH_3$
2-Bromo-3-hexene

→ $CH_3CH\!\!=\!\!CHCHBrCH_2CH_3$
4-Bromo-2-hexene

4-Bromo-2-hexene is formed through an allylic rearrangement (Problem 7.152).

8.21 Which hydrocarbon is consistent with the following information? ' (*a*) MW = 72 gives a single monochloride and two dichlorides on photochlorination, and (*b*) MW = 70 gives a single monochloride. Give the formulas for the chloro derivatives.

◢ To get the number of C's in the molecular formulas divide MW by 12 making sure that there are enough mass units for the H's. (*a*) $72 \div 12 = 6$ but this leaves no room for H's. Therefore, there are five C's and the molecular formula is C_5H_{12}. Since there is only one monochloro derivative, the compound has twelve equivalent H's present in four equivalent CH_3's. The compound is $(CH_3)_4C$ and the chloro derivatives are: $(CH_3)_3CCH_2Cl$, $(CH_3)_3CCHCl_2$ and $(CH_3)_2C(CH_2Cl)_2$. (*b*) Again there are five C's but now only ten H's. The molecular formula is C_5H_{10} and the compound has 1° of unsaturation. No alkene with five C's has only equivalent H's and so the compound is a nonsubstituted cycloalkane, i.e., cyclopentane, and the monochloride is chlorocyclopentane.

8.22 From alkenes prepare: (*a*) 2-iodo-2-methylpentane (**A**), (*b*) 3-methyl-1-bromobutane (**B**), and (*c*) 1-chloro-1-methylcyclohexane (**C**).

◢ These syntheses require addition reactions (see Problems 7.70 and 7.73).
(*a*) There are two parent alkenes:

$$\overset{\cdot}{M}e_2C\!\!=\!\!CHCH_2CH_3 \xrightarrow{\ HI\ }$$

→ $Me_2CICH_2CH_2CH_3$ (**A**)

$$H_2C\!\!=\!\!CMeCH_2CH_2CH_3 \xrightarrow{\ HI\ }$$

(*b*) $H_2C{=}CHCHMe_2 \xrightarrow[\text{ROOR}]{\text{HBr}} BrCH_2{-}CH_2CHMe_2$ (**B**)

(*c*) There are two parent alkenes:

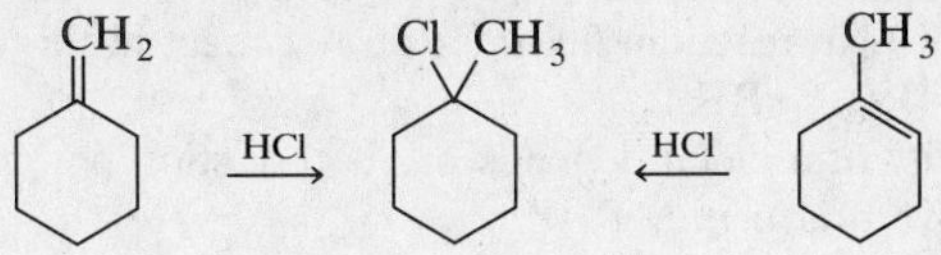

8.23 Suggest alkene addition reactions to prepare the dihalogen compounds:

(*a*) 2,3-Dimethyl-2,3-dibromobutane   (*c*) 1-Iodo-2-bromo-2-methylpentane   (*e*) 1,1-Dichloro-*cis*-2,3-dimethylcyclopropane

(*b*) *trans*-1,2-Dibromocyclopentane   (*d*) 2,2-Dibromobutane   (*f*) 1,3-Dibromopropane

(*a*) $Me_2C{=}CMe_2 \xrightarrow{Br_2} Me_2CBr{-}CBrMe_2$

(*b*)

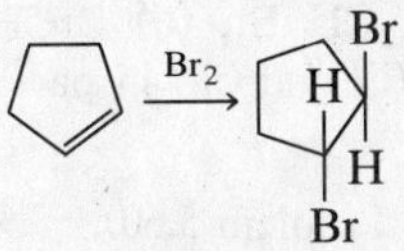

(*c*) $H_2C{=}\overset{\overset{\displaystyle Me}{|}}{C}CH_2CH_2CH_3 \xrightarrow{IBr} ICH_2\overset{\overset{\displaystyle Me}{|}}{C}BrCH_2CH_2CH_3$

(*d*) $H_2C{=}CBrCH_2CH_3 \xrightarrow{HBr} CH_3CBr_2CH_2CH_3$

(*e*) $\textit{cis-}CH_3CH{=}CHCH_3 + CHCl_3 + (CH_3)_3CO^-K^+ \longrightarrow \textit{cis-}CH_3CH{-}CHCH_3$ with CCl_2 bridging

(*f*) $H_2C{=}CHCH_2Br \xrightarrow[\text{ROOR}]{\text{HBr}} BrCH_2CH_2CH_2Br$

8.24 Alkyl halides are most often prepared from alcohols, rarely by direct halogenation. Supply structural formulas for the alkyl halides synthesized in the reactions:

(*a*) $CH_3CH_2CH_2CH_2OH \xrightarrow[\Delta]{\text{NaBr, H}_2\text{SO}_4}$ (*d*) $CH_3CH_2CH_2OH \xrightarrow{\text{PI}_3 \text{ (from P} + \text{I}_2)}$

(*b*) $(CH_3)_3COH \xrightarrow[\text{room temp.}]{\text{conc. HCl}}$ (*e*) $Me_2CHCH_2OH \xrightarrow{\text{SOCl}_2}$

(*c*) $CH_3CH(OH)CH_2CH_2CH_3 \xrightarrow{\text{PBr}_3}$

(*a*) $CH_3CH_2CH_2CH_2Br$. (*b*) $(CH_3)_3CCl$. (*c*) $CH_3CHBrCH_2CH_2CH_3$. (*d*) $CH_3CH_2CH_2I$.
(*e*) Me_2CHCH_2Cl.

8.25 Supply reactions for the preparation from propene of (*a*) allyl iodide and (*b*) allyl fluoride:

(*a*) $CH_3CH{=}CH_2 \xrightarrow{\text{Cl}_2 \text{ (h}\nu)} ClCH_2CH{=}CH_2 \xrightarrow{\text{NaI}} ICH_2CH{=}CH_2 + NaCl_{(s)}$. Allyl chloride is readily converted to the iodide with NaI in acetone because less soluble NaCl precipitates and is removed by filtration. This drives the reaction to completion.

(*b*) $ClCH_2CH{=}CH_2 + AgF \longrightarrow FCH_2CH{=}CH_2 + AgCl(s)$.

REACTIONS

1. Organometallics

8.26 (*a*) Give the products for the viable reactions: (i) *n*-PrCl + Mg/THF, (ii) MeBr + Li/Et$_2$O, (iii) cyclohexyl fluoride + Mg/Et$_2$O, (iv) *n*-BuI + Zn, and (v) *n*-BuCl + Zn. (*b*) Give the decreasing order of reactivity of alkyl halides in reactions with metals to give *organometallics*. (*c*) Discuss the role of metal reactivity in the viability of the reactions.

(*a*) (i) *n*-PrMgCl. (With RCl and especially ArCl, THF (tetrahydrofuran) is better than Et$_2$O.)
(ii) MeLi. (iii) No reaction; fluorides do not react in this case. (iv) *n*-BuZnI. (v) No reaction.
(*b*) RI > RBr > RCl ≫ RF.
(*c*) The reactivity of a metal depends on its reduction potential; the more easily a metal is reduced, the more reactive it is, e.g., Mg > Zn.

8.27 (*a*) (i) Complete the reaction *n*-BuLi + ClCH=CH$_2$ ⟶ ? (ii) Name this type of reaction. (iii) Which organometallic compound is favored in this reversible reaction? (iv) When is this type of reaction synthetically useful? (*b*) Complete and name the type of the following reaction: Me$_2$CHMgCl + HgCl$_2$ → .

(*a*) (i) LiCH=CH$_2$ + *n*-BuCl. (ii) Halogen-metal exchange. (iii) The compound with metal attached to the more electronegative C, in this case the sp^2 hybridized vinyl C. (iv) Vinyl halides, especially chlorides, react sluggishly with Mg. Since *n*-BuLi can be purchased, this reaction is easier to perform than direct reaction with Mg. (*b*) Me$_2$CHHgCl + MgCl$_2$; a metal-metal exchange.

8.28 (*a*) Give the product from the reaction of Mg/Et$_2$O with (i) BrCH$_2$CH$_2$Br, (ii) BrCH$_2$CH$_2$CH$_2$Br, and (iii) BrCH$_2$CH$_2$CH$_2$CH$_2$Br. (*b*) Discuss the difference in behavior of (ii) and (iii) in part (*a*). (*c*) Give the product of the reaction of CBr$_4$ + MeLi + cyclohexene.

(*a*) (i) H$_2$C=CH$_2$ (elimination of *vic* X's), (ii) cyclopropane (see Problem 5.60),
(iii) BrMg(CH$_2$)$_4$MgBr.
(*b*) Unlike compound (ii), compound (iii) does not react intramolecularly because a 4-membered ring does not form as readily as does a 3-membered ring.
(*c*)

$$CBr_4 + MeLi \xrightarrow[\text{exchange}]{\text{halogen-metal}} [Br_3CLi] + MeBr; \quad Br_3CLi \longrightarrow Br_2C: + LiBr$$
Dibromocarbene

The carbene then adds to the alkene in the typical fashion giving

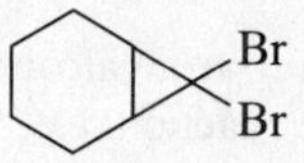

7,7-Dibromo[4.1.0]-bicycloheptane

2. Nucleophilic Displacements

8.29 (*a*) Give the structure of the product from the reaction of each of the following anionic nucleophiles (Nu:⁻) with CH$_3$CH$_2$Br, a typical alkyl halide, and classify the introduced functional group: (i) :Ï:⁻, (ii) :ÖH⁻, (iii) :ÖR⁻, (iv) ⁻:ÖCOR, (v) :CN⁻, (vi) ⁻:C≡CR (from NaC≡CR), (vii) R:⁻ (from RLi), (viii) HS:⁻, and (ix) :H⁻ (from LiAlH$_4$). (*b*) Classify these reactions. (*c*) Define the terms (i) substrate and (ii) leaving group.

(*a*) (i) EtI, alkyl iodide; (ii) EtOH, alcohol; (iii) EtOR, ether; (iv) EtOCOR, ester; (v) EtCN, nitrile; (vi) EtC≡CR, alkyne; (vii) EtR, alkane; (viii) EtSH, thiol (mercaptan); and (ix) EtH, alkane (reduction of RX). (*b*) *Nucleophilic displacements.* (*c*) (i) The *substrate* is the species undergoing displacement, in this case the alkyl halide, EtBr. One of its atoms, usually a C, is attacked by the nucleophile which is often a molecule but may be an anion. (ii) The *leaving group* is the displaced species which leaves the attacked C with an unshared pair of e⁻'s; it is also a nucleophile. The leaving group is often an anion but may be a molecule.

8.30 (*a*) Give the structure of the immediate product from the reaction of RX with the molecular nucleophiles (HNu:) and identify the functional group: (i) :ÖH$_2$, (ii) R'ÖH, (iii) :NH$_3$, (iv) :NH$_2$R', and (v) :P(C$_6$H$_5$)$_3$. (*b*) What is the major difference between these products and those in Problem 8.29?

(*a*) (i) [ROH$_2$]⁺, the onium ion of an alcohol, ROH. (ii) [R'OR]⁺, the onium ion of an ether.
|
H
(iii) [RNH$_3$]⁺, the ammonium ion of a 1° amine, RNH$_2$. (iv) [RR'NH$_2$]⁺, the ammonium ion of a 2° amine, RR'NH. (v) [RP(C$_6$H$_5$)$_3$]⁺:X⁻, a phosphonium salt.
(*b*) The species formed from the displacement are cations, not uncharged molecules.

8.31 Account for the fact that reaction of RX with H_2O and MeOH yield the neutral final products ROH and ROMe but reaction with NH_3 and $R'NH_2$ give the cations RNH_3^+ and $RR'NH_2^+$ as Cl^- salts.

▐ The onium ions in (i) and (ii) of part (a) of Problem 8.30 are strong acids and donate H^+ to their respective solvents as follows:

$$ROH_2^+ + H_2O \rightarrow ROH + H_3O^+ \quad \text{and} \quad ROR'H^+ + R'OH \rightarrow ROR' + R'OH_2^+.$$

The amines RNH_2 and $RR'NH$ are stronger bases than either H_2O or CH_3OH and their conjugate acids are too weak to donate H^+ to the solvent.

8.32 Supply formulas for the organic products from the reaction of:

(a) $CH_3C \equiv C:^- K^+ + CH_3CH_2CH_2Cl$ (e) $Me_2CHBr + Et\ddot{S}:^- Na^+$

(b) $(CH_3)_2CHO^- Na^+ + CH_3CH_2CH_2Cl$ (f) $MeI + EtNH_2$

(c) $CH_3CHClCH_2CH_3$ + aq. NaOH   (g) $MeI + Et_2NH$

(d) Bromocyclopentane + NaI (acetone)   (h) $CH_3CH_2CH_2Br + Me_2S$

▐ (a) $CH_3C \equiv C-CH_2CH_2CH_3$. (b) $(CH_3)_2CHO-CH_2CH_2CH_3$. (c) $CH_3CH(OH)CH_2CH_3$. Aqueous NaOH gives mainly displacement; alc. KOH gives mainly elimination. (d) Iodocyclopentane. (e) Me_2CHSEt. (f) $EtMeNH_2^+I^-$. (g) $Et_2MeNH^+I^-$. (h) $[CH_3CH_2CH_2SMe_2]^+Br^-$.

8.33 (a) In terms of X, what factors influence the rate of reaction (reactivity) of RX in nucleophilic displacements? (b) Give the decreasing order of reactivities of RX with change in X. (c) Nucleophilic displacements are microscopically reversible. In what way do the relative base strengths of reactant and product nucleophiles influence the direction of the reaction?

▐ (a) The weaker the Brönsted basicity of X^-, the better leaving group is X^- and the more reactive is RX. Within a periodic group the weakest base will also be the most polarizable (see part (e) of Problem 8.11). Consequently, the bonding to C persists while X is leaving, stabilizing the TS. It is also beneficial if the C—X bond is polar so that in the ground state there is some δ^+ on C. (b) Since the order of basicities of X^- is $I^- < Br^- < Cl^- \ll F^-$, the order of reactivity of RX is RI > RBr > RCl $\gg$ RF. (c) The stronger Brönsted base displaces the weaker one. If the potential leaving group is a stronger base than the attacking nucleophile, reaction will not take place.

8.34 (a) In terms of the Lewis theory, categorize the reaction site C of RX. (b) Does the rate of the reaction depend on the amount of δ^+ on the attacked C of RX? Explain.

▐ (a) The C is an electrophilic site that participates in bond formation with the nucleophilic atom of the attacking species. Its electrophilicity originates from the polarization of the $^{\delta^+}C-X^{\delta^-}$ bond (b) No. The amount of δ^+ on the C decreases with decreasing electronegativity of X in the order of F > Cl > Br > I, yet this is the reverse of the reactivities of RX. RI is the most and RF is the least reactive.

8.35 (a) Account for the suitability (or lack of) of the following underlined substituents as potential leaving groups in nucleophilic displacements. (i) R-H, (ii) R-Me, (iii) R-OMe, (iv) R-OH, (v) R-OH$_2^+$, (vi) R-OMeH$^+$, (vii) R-OCOMe (an ester), (viii) R-OSO$_2$Ar(R) (an ester of a sulfonic acid, ArSO$_3$H), (ix) R-OSO$_2$OR (an ester of alkyl sulfuric acid, ROSO$_2$OH), and (x) R-CN. (b) Illustrate with a general equation for R-OSO$_2$Ar.

▐ (a) Except for (v) and (vi), all underlined groups have to depart the C as anions. Only those that are conjugate bases of very strong acids are weak enough bases to be good leaving groups. For (i) and (ii), the anions are powerful bases because their conjugate acids, H_2 and MeH respectively, are among the weakest acids known. They are extraordinarily poor leaving groups. OMe$^-$ of (iii) and OH$^-$ of (iv) are very poor leaving groups because they are strong conjugate bases of the feeble acids, HOH and ROH respectively. $^-$OCOMe of (vii) and $^-$CN of (x) are poor leaving groups because they are conjugate bases of weak acids, MeCOOH and HCN respectively. H_2O of (v) and ROH of (vi) are molecules, not anions. They are weak bases and good leaving groups. ArSO$_3^-$ of (viii) and ROSO$_3^-$ of (ix) are exceptionally good leaving groups because they are extremely weak conjugate bases of the very strong acids mentioned above. These acids are strong like H_2SO_4. In summary, the increasing order of "leaveability" (*fugicity*) of the anions is

$$H^-, R^- \ll MeO^-, OH^- < CN^- < MeCOO^- < ROSO_2^-, ArSO_2O^-$$

(b) $:Nu^- + R-OSO_2Ar \longrightarrow Nu-R + {}^-OSO_2Ar$

arylsulfonate   Arylsulfonate
ester   anion

8.36   (a) Compare the effectiveness of CH_3COO^- (acetate), Cl_3CCOO^- (trichloroacetate), PhO^- (phenoxide), and $PhSO_3^-$ (benzenesulfonate) anions as leaving groups (fugicity) if the pK_a values of their conjugate acids are 4.5, 0.9, 10.0, and -2.6, respectively.   (b) Which is a better leaving group, $MeSO_3^-$, methanesulfonate ("mesyl"), or $F_3CSO_3^-$, trifluoromethanesulfonate ("triflate")?

◢   (a) The strongest acid has the smallest pK_a—its conjugate base is the weakest and is the best leaving group. The fugicity order is $PhSO_3^- > Cl_3CCOO^- > CH_3COO^- > PhO^-$.   (b) The strongly electron-withdrawing F's cause $F_3CSO_3^-$ to be a much weaker base and a better leaving group than $MeSO_3^-$.

8.37   Complete, if possible, each of the following reactions and explain each case. You may need to know some pK_a's which are found in tables such as in *Handbook of Physics and Chemistry*, Chemical Rubber Company. In each case the potential reaction occurs on Me.

   (a)   Dimethyl sulfate, $(MeO)_2SO_2 + EtS^-$;   (c) $MeCN + HS^-$ and,
   (b)   Methyl nitrate, $MeONO_2 + N_3^-$ (from NaN_3);   (d)   Methylfluorosulfonate, $MeOSO_2F + I^-$.

◢   (a) $EtSMe + MeOSO_3^-$ (**A**). **A** is a very good leaving group because it is the very weak conjugate base of a very strong acid, methyl sulfuric acid, $MeOSO_2OH$—the kin of H_2SO_4.   (b) MeN_3 (an azide, methyl azide) + NO_3^- (**B**). **B** is a very good leaving group because it is the weak conjugate base of a strong acid, HNO_3.   (c) No reaction. H_2S is a stronger acid than HCN and its conjugate base, HS^-, is weaker than CN^-, the conjugate base of HCN. A weaker base cannot displace a strong base.   (d) $MeI + FSO_3^-$ (**C**). **C** is one of the weakest known bases because its conjugate acid, fluorosulfuric acid, $HOSO_2F$, is one of the strongest known acids. Although I^- is a very weak base, it is stronger than fluorosulfate.

8.38   Give the organic products of the following reactions:

   (a) $n\text{-PrBr} + \overset{\overset{\displaystyle :O:}{\|}}{:N-\ddot{O}:}^- \longrightarrow$ (d) $ClCH_2CH_2CH_2I + CN^-$ (one mole each) $\longrightarrow$

   (b) $i\text{-PrBr} + \left[:\ddot{S}C\equiv N:\right]^-$ (isocyanate) $\longrightarrow$ (e) $H_2NCH_2CH_2CH_2CH_2Br \xrightarrow{-H+}$

   (c) $EtBr + \left[:\ddot{S}SO_3\right]^{2-}$ (thiosulfate) $\longrightarrow$

◢   The nucleophiles in (a), (b), and (c) are ambident since they each have more than one reactive site. In each case, the more nucleophilic atom reacts even though the other atom may bear a more negative charge. (a) $n\text{-PrNO}_2$ (b) $i\text{-PrSCN}$ (c) $[EtSSO_3]^-$ (with its cation it is called a Bünte salt). (d) $ClCH_2CH_2CH_2CN$. I^- is a better leaving group than Cl^-. (e) (pyrrolidine structure). When the nucleophilic and leaving groups are part of the same molecule, an intramolecular displacement occurs if a three-, a five-, or a six-membered ring can form.

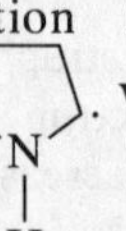

8.39   Define nucleophilicity as used for nucleophiles. Is it synonymous with basicity?

◢   *Nucleophilicity* is defined by a reaction of a :Nu with an electrophilic C, and it influences the rate of reaction as reflected by the rate constant, k_r. Basicity is the ability to remove H^+ from an acid as represented quantitatively by the equilibrium constant K_b. Basicity of the nucleophile determines the thermodynamics (equilibrium) of the reaction, $Nu:^- + RX \rightleftharpoons NuR + X:^-$; nucleophilicity the kinetics (rate).

Nucleophilicity   *Basicity*

$Nu:^- + \overset{|}{\underset{|}{C}}:L \longrightarrow Nu-\overset{|}{\underset{|}{C}} + :L^-$ $B:^- + H:A \rightleftharpoons B:H + :A^-$

8.40   Generalize about the relationship of basicity and nucleophilicity from the following relative rates of nucleophilic displacements:

   (a) $H\ddot{O}:^- \gg H_2\ddot{O}:$ and $H_2\ddot{N}:^- \gg H_3N:$ (d) $Me\ddot{O}:^- > H\ddot{O}:^- > MeC\ddot{O}O:^-$

   (b) $H_3C:^- > H_2N:^- > H\ddot{O}:^- > :\ddot{F}:^-$ (e) $HO\ddot{O}:^- > H\ddot{O}:^-$ and $H_2N\ddot{N}H_2 > H_3N:$

   (c) $:\ddot{I}:^- > :\ddot{B}r:^- > :\ddot{C}l:^- > :\ddot{F}:^-$ and $H\ddot{S}:^- > H\ddot{O}:^-$

◢   (a) Bases are better nucleophiles than their conjugate acids.   (b) In going from left to right across the periodic table, basicity and nucleophilicity are directly related—they both decrease.   (c) In going down a group in the periodic table, they are inversely related—nucleophilicity increases while basicity decreases.   (d) When the nucleophilic and basic sites are the same atom (here an O), nucleophilicity parallels basicity. (*e*) These relative rates are counter to relative basicities. When the atom bonded to the nucleophilic site also has an unshared pair of e⁻'s, e.g., $\ddot{G}$—Nu:, nucleophilicity of the species increases.

8.41 (*a*) Define soft and hard bases (nucleophiles). (*b*) Which have the greater nucleophilicity? (*c*) Discuss the relationship of polarizability and nucleophilicity.

▮ (*a*) *Soft bases* have larger, more polarizable basic site atoms (e.g., I, Br, S, and P). *Hard bases* have smaller, more weakly polarizable sites (e.g., N, O, and F). (*b*) Soft bases have enhanced nucleophilicities; hard bases have diminished nucleophilicities. (*c*) Distortion of the electron cloud of the active site atom [polarizability, see Problem 8.11(*e*)] concentrates electron density at its head as it approaches the C. The approach is more facile even though these are larger atoms.

8.42 (*a*) Distinguish between *soft* and *hard* acids (*electrophiles*). (*b*) Which combinations of soft and hard acids and bases give the best reactions? (*c*) Is the attacked C of RX a soft or hard electrophilic site?

▮ (*a*) The more polarizable electrophilic sites are soft, while the less polarizable sites are hard. (*b*) Soft bases (nucleophiles) bind best with soft acids (electrophiles). The same is true for hard bases and acids. This is known as the SHAB (*S*oft and *H*ard *A*cid-*B*ase) *principle*. (*c*) Since the softer bases react best in displacement reactions, the attacked C must also be soft-like.

8.43 Compare the following displacement reactions and account for any difference.

$$(a)\ ROH + NaBr \longrightarrow \qquad (b)\ ROH + HBr \longrightarrow$$

▮ (*a*) No reaction. The extremely weak base Br⁻ cannot displace the very strong base OH⁻. (*b*) This reaction occurs in two steps: $ROH + HBr \rightarrow ROH_2^+ + Br^- \rightarrow RBr + H_2O$. Displacement is on the onium ion of ROH whose good leaving group is the very weakly basic H_2O.

8.44 Explain the fact that a small amount of NaI catalyzes the general reaction

$$RCl + R'O{:}^- Na^+ \rightarrow ROR' + NaCl$$

▮ With I⁻ the overall reaction occurs in two steps, each of which is faster than the uncatalyzed reaction.
Step 1. $RCl + I^- \rightarrow RI + Cl^-$. This step is faster because I⁻, a soft base, has more nucleophilicity than OR⁻, a hard base.
Step 2. $RI + R'O{:}^- \rightarrow ROR' + I^-$. This step is faster because I⁻ is a better leaving group than Cl⁻.

8.45 Explain why the nucleophilicity order of X⁻ of Problem 8.40(*c*) prevails in nonpolar, weakly polar aprotic, and polar protic solvents, but is reversed in polar aprotic solvents.

▮ In nonpolar and weakly polar aprotic solvents, the salts of Nu:⁻ are present as ion-pairs (or ion-clusters) in which nearby cations (counterions) diminish the reactivity of the anion. Since ion-pairing is strongest with the smallest anion, F⁻, and weakest with the largest anion, I⁻, the reactivity of X⁻ decreases with decreasing size. In polar protic solvents, H-bonding attenuates the reactivity of the anion, more so with the smallest anion, again making it the least reactive. Polar aprotic solvents solvate only cations, leaving free, unencumbered ("naked") anions. The reactivities of all anions are greatly enhanced but more so for the smallest one because it is the most basic. The order in Problem 8.40(*c*) is reversed, F⁻ > Cl⁻ > Br⁻ > I⁻, and nucleophilicity and basicity are directly related. Apparently, the inverse relationship of nucleophilicity and basicity demonstrated in Problem 8.40(*c*) is a solvent-induced phenomenon.

8.46 (*a*) Rationalize the orders of relative rates for reactions carried out by the following nucleophiles in a weakly polar aprotic solvent, such as acetone. (i) LiI > LiBr > LiCl ≫ LiF, (ii) CsF > RbF > KF > NaF > LiF, and (iii) $Bu_4N^+Cl^- > Bu_4N^+Br^- > Bu_4N^+I^-$. (*b*) Show how the results in (i) are a good application of the SHAB principle (Problem 8.42).

▮ (*a*) In weakly polar aprotic solvents, ion-pairing influences the reactivity of Nu⁻. The more pervasive is ion-pairing, the less nucleophilic is Nu⁻. The countercation plays an important role in ion-pairing. (i) The − charge on the largest anion, I⁻, is the most diffused; I⁻ least readily forms ion pairs. The − charge on the smallest anion, F⁻, is the least diffused; F⁻ most readily forms ion pairs. (ii) As the alkali metal cation gets smaller, ion-pairing to a given X⁻ gets stronger and the nucleophilicity of X⁻ diminishes. The order given for diminishing nucleophilicity of F⁻ is the same as the order of reducing the size of M⁺. (iii) Bu_4N^+ has the positively charged N at its center, surrounded by four

Bu's, and consequently has practically no tendency to ion-pair with X^-. With no encumberance from ion-pairing or H-bonding, the reactivity of X^- is directly related to the order of basicity.

(b)   The smallest M^+ is the "hardest" acid and the smallest X^- is the "hardest" base. They combine to give the strongest bond—the most effective ion-pair.

8.47   (a)   What experimental conditions should be used to study the intrinsic nucleophilicity of halide ions? (b)   Predict the relative decreasing order of nucleophilicities of X^- in the following reaction: $(C_5H_{11})_4N^+X^-_{(s)}$ (where X^- is Cl, Br, I) $\xrightarrow{\Delta}$ $(C_5H_{11})_3N + C_5H_{11}X$.

▰   (a) Run without solvent; use the gaseous or solid state, in which there is no ion-pairing.   (b) This reaction fits the conditions suggested in part (a). The order of nucleophilicities should fit the order of basicities: $Cl^- > Br^- > I^-$.

8.48   (a)   Suggest three logical pathways for the following general nucleophilic displacement to occur:

$$Nu\colon^- + GX \longrightarrow NuG + \colon X^-$$

(Disregard the viability in terms of actual chemistry.)

(b)   Discuss the viability of each suggested pathway in (a) assuming G is an alkyl group with X bonded to a C, using sp^3 HO's.

(c)   What kind of atom can be attacked by the pathway not available to C in RX?

▰   (a)   *Path 1.*   Two steps $\colon X^-$ leaves first, then the remaining cation, G^+, bonds to $Nu\colon^-$.

$$G\colon X \to G^+ + \colon X^-; \text{ then } G^+ + Nu\colon^- \longrightarrow NuG$$

Path 2.   Two steps: $Nu\colon^-$ bonds first, then X^- leaves.

$$GX + Nu\colon^- \longrightarrow [NuGX]^- \longrightarrow NuG + \colon X^-$$

Path 3.   A one-step synchronous, concerted process, in which $\colon X^-$ begins to leave as $Nu\colon^-$ begins to bond.

(b)   When displacement occurs on C, paths 1 and 3 are possible. Path 2 does not occur because C cannot have five covalent bonds which would give C ten valence e^-'s.

(c)   Path 2 can occur when G is an atom in the third period of the periodic table, e.g., Si.

8.49   Classify paths 1, 2, and 3 in Problem 8.48(a) and predict their rate expressions and molecularities. Justify your predictions.

▰   Path 1.   Elimination-addition. Bond-breaking (step 1) is always slower than bond-forming (step 2). Since rate-determining step 1 involves only a single molecule, $rate_1 = k_1[GX]$ and this reaction is unimolecular.

Path 2.   Addition-elimination. $Rate_2 = k_2[Nu\colon^-][GX]$, regardless of which step is slow. However, the reaction is bimolecular if step 1 is slow, and unimolecular if step 2 is slow. It is reasonable to predict that step 1 is slow because it leads to loss of the normal covalency of the atom bonded to X. Predictably the reaction is bimolecular.

Path 3.   Concerted reaction. Both reactants participate in the single step and $rate_3 = k_3[Nu\colon^-][GX]$. The reaction is bimolecular.

8.50   (a)   Analyze the following generalized rate data and write the rate expression for the reaction: $RX + Nu\colon^- \to NuR + \colon X^-$, where R is 1° or 2°.

	[RX]	[Nu:⁻]	rate
(i)	0.10	0.10	1.2×10^{-4}
(ii)	0.20	0.10	2.4×10^{-4}
(iii)	0.10	0.20	2.4×10^{-4}
(iv)	0.20	0.20	4.8×10^{-4}

(b) What is the order and molecularity of the reaction?   (c) Suggest two experimental methods for studying the kinetics if the reactants are $RCl + OH^-$.

▰   (a) Doubling the molar concentrations of either reactant doubles the rate. Doubling the concentration of both reactants quadruples the rate, which therefore is directly related to each reactant: $rate = k[RX][Nu\colon^-]$. (b) It is a second-order reaction, first order in each reactant. Of the two possible pathways available for displacement on C, (3) of Problem 8.48(*a*) is the only one that has both reactants in the rate-controlling step; hence it is a bimolecular reaction. (*c*) Very small samples of the reaction mixture, kept at constant temperature, are removed periodically, quenched to stop the reaction, and quantitatively analyzed. The increasing concentration of Cl^- is determined by a standard method. In the other method, the decreasing concentration of OH^- is detected by standard acid-base titrations. The samples removed and analyzed are so very small that the only significant change in the concentrations of the reactants is due to the reaction itself.

8.51 Discuss the symbol S_N2, introduced by the British chemist Sir C.K. Ingold for this one-step nucleophilic substitution.

◢ S stands for *substitution*, $_N$ for *nucleophilic*, and 2 for *bimolecular*. The British call this reaction a substitution. It could also have been called D_N2 where D stands for displacement.

8.52 (*a*) Give the transition states for the two extreme juxtapositions of the approaching nucleophile and the leaving group when Nu:⁻ reacts the RX. Explain the stereochemical consequences of each mode of attack. (*b*) Explain which is the energetically preferred S_N2 mechanism.

◢ (*a*) In this one-step reaction, no matter how Nu:⁻ approaches the C, there must be a synchronous departure of X⁻. Nu:⁻ can approach the C from the same side (frontside) of the C—X bond, leading to *retention* of the configuration about C, Fig. 8-1(*a*). Nu:⁻ can also approach the C as far away as possible from the C—X bond (backside), leading to *inversion* of configuration about C, Fig. 8-1(*b*).

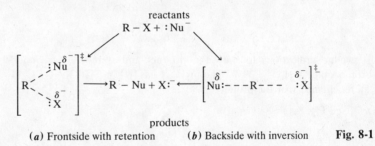

(*a*) Frontside with retention   (*b*) Backside with inversion   **Fig. 8-1**

(*b*) It is energetically more favorable for the approaching :Nu⁻ and departing X:⁻, both negatively charged groups, to have the maximum angle of separation to minimize electrostatic repulsion between them. The backside approach in which :Nu⁻ and X:⁻ are 180° apart (maximum angle of separation) has the lower enthalpy of activation and is the preferred mode of reaction. Practically every S_N2 attack goes with inversion.

8.53 (*a*) Is the S_N2 reaction exothermic or endothermic? (*b*) Draw an enthalpy diagram for an exothermic S_N2 reaction.

◢ (*a*) The reaction is thermochemically favorable only when a stronger base displaces a weaker base. Hence, successful displacements are exothermic. (*b*) See Fig. 8-2. This one-step reaction has one transition state and no intermediate.

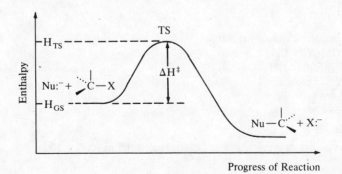

Fig. 8-2

8.54 (*a*) Use the general reaction between (*S*)-RCHDX and :Nu⁻ to illustrate and explain with the aid of orbital representations the stereochemical consequences of the S_N2 reaction. (*b*) Discuss the charge distribution in the transition state of this S_N2 reaction.

▮ (*a*) See Fig. 8-3. In the TS, the attacked C is sp^2 hybridized with a p AO available for overlapping one of its lobes with an orbital of the incoming :Nu⁻ while the other lobe overlaps with an orbital of the leaving group X⁻. These overlaps account for the partial bonds drawn in Fig. 8-1(*b*). The reaction is initiated by :Nu⁻ beginning to overlap with the small lobe (tail) of the sp^3 HO bonding with X. In order to provide more bonding volume to give a stronger bond, the tail becomes the larger lobe (head) and the head becomes the tail, inverting the configuration of C. The configuration of the OH compound is the opposite of that of the X compound. (*b*) As :Nu⁻ starts to bond to C, it loses some of its full charge and in the TS has a δ^- charge, as does X as it begins to leave as an anion. There is little + charge on the C which becomes sp^3 hydridized in the product.

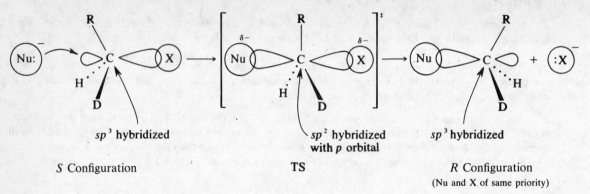

sp³ hybridized   *sp² hybridized*   *sp³ hybridized*
                                    with *p* orbital

S Configuration   **TS**   *R* Configuration
                                                        (Nu and X of same priority)

Fig. 8-3

8.55 (*a*) Use wedge projections to show the product and stereochemical course of the reaction of NaOH with (*R*)-2-bromooctane, $[\alpha]_D = -39.6°$. The product has $[\alpha]_D = +10.3°$ ($R = C_6H_{13}$).   (*b*) Is the sign of $[\alpha]_D$ related to the stereochemistry of the product?

▮ (*a*) See Fig. 8-4.

$$\underset{(R)\text{-2-Bromoctane, }[\alpha]_D = -39.6°}{\overset{\text{Me}}{\underset{R}{\underset{|}{C}}}-Br} \xrightarrow{\text{NaOH}} \underset{(S)\text{-2-Octanol, }[\alpha]_D = +10.3°}{HO-\overset{\text{Me}}{\underset{R}{\underset{|}{C}}}}$$ **Fig. 8-4**

(*b*) No.

8.56 Give the products of the following displacement reactions:

(*a*) (*R*)-CH₃CHBrCH₂CH₃ + MeO⁻
(*b*) (*S*)-CH₃CHBrCH₂CH₃ + MeO⁻
(*c*) *rac*, *cis*-4-iodoethylcyclohexane + OH⁻
(*d*) (*S*)- $\underset{H}{\overset{CH_3}{Br-\!\!\!-\!\!\!-COEt}}$ + CN⁻   (with $\overset{||}{O}$ on COEt)

▮ These S_N2 reactions invert configuration.
(*a*) (*S*)-CH₃CH(OMe)CH₂CH₃
(*b*) (*R*)-CH₃CH(OMe)CH₂CH₃
(*c*) *rac*, *trans*-4-ethylcyclohexanol
(*d*) (*S*)- $\underset{O \; H}{\overset{CH_3}{EtOC-\!\!\!-\!\!\!-CN}}$ (with $\overset{||}{O}$).

Although inversion occurs, the priority order changes and the product is (*S*).

8.57 Are S_N2 reactions stereospecific and/or stereoselective?

▮ They are *stereospecific* because stereoisomeric reactants give stereochemically different products. They are also *stereoselective* because they form exclusively or predominantly only one of a possible pair of enantiomers or one of the possible diastereoisomers.

8.58 (*a*) List the following types of alkyl halides in order of decreasing S_N2 reactivity: MeX, R₃CX, RCH₂X, and R₂CHX.   (*b*) How does the S_N2 mechanism account for this order?

▮ (*a*) MeX > RCH_2X > R_2CHX > R_3CX or methyl (superprimary) > 1° > 2° > 3°

(*b*) Replacement of the H's on the attacked C by R's makes backside approach more difficult, the transition state more crowded, $\Delta H^{\ddagger}$ higher, and the reaction rate slower.

8.59 (*a*) List the following alkoxide nucleophiles in order of decreasing order of S_N2 reactivity: Me_3CO^-, MeO^-,

$MeCH_2O^-$, Me_2CHO^-, and ⬠$-O^-$. (*b*) How does the S_N2 mechanism account for this order? (*c*) Criticize the generalization that for a given nucleophilic site atom nucleophilicity parallels basicity.

▮ (*a*) MeO^- > $MeCH_2O^-$ > ⬠$-O^-$ (**A**) > Me_2CHO^- > Me_3CO^-. (*b*) As R's accumulate on the C bonded to O^-, the nucleophile becomes bulkier and its backside approach to the displacement site is retarded, causing a decline in rate. Although **A** is an R_2HCO^- alkoxide, its R's are the sides of the ring and are "tied back" away from the $-O^-$. This arrangement permits a more facile approach than by Me_2HCO^-. Note that S_N2 reactivity is susceptible to steric hindrance by the nucleophile as well as by the R's around the site of displacement. (*c*) As will be discussed in Chapter 14, Me_3CO^- is a stronger base than MeO^- in solution. Yet in this reaction, because of its bulkiness, Me_3CO^- is a poorer nucleophile. Because of steric hindrance, basicity and nucleophilicity may diverge.

8.60 (*a*) Account for the following observations when an acetone solution of (R)-$CH_3CH_2CH_2CHDI$ is warmed with NaI (*a*) (i) The enantiomer is racemized, and (ii) with an excess of I^- (radioactive I^-), the rate of racemization is twice the rate of the incorporation of I^- in the product. (*b*) What definitive conclusion can be drawn from these experiments?

▮ (*a*) (i) I^- can displace I from RI as I^- by a typical S_N2 reaction as shown:

$$I^- + CH_3CH_2CH_2 \overset{D}{\underset{H}{-\!\!\!\!\mid\!\!\!\!-}} I \underset{\text{inversion}}{\overset{\text{inversion}}{\rightleftharpoons}} I \overset{D}{\underset{H}{-\!\!\!\!\mid\!\!\!\!-}} CH_2CH_2CH_3 + I^-$$

$$\qquad\qquad\qquad\quad (R) \qquad\qquad\quad (S)$$

One way of detecting the reaction is to use an optically active RX. Since enantiomers have identical energies, the reaction proceeds in both directions until arriving at a racemic equilibrium mixture. But don't forget, once equilibrium is reached, the reactions do not stop—they continue endlessly in both directions.

(ii) Incorporation of each I^- in the molecule forms one molecule of the inverted enantiomer. One molecule of the inverted enantiomer, resulting from reaction with I^-, and one unreacted molecule form a racemic modification. Since two molecules are racemized every time one I^- is incorporated, the rate of racemization is twice that of the rate of insertion of radioactivity in the product.

(*b*) Every displacement results in an inversion of configuration

8.61 (R)-n-$C_3H_7CH(OH)CH_3$ (**A**) is converted to its ethyl ether n-$C_3H_7CH(OC_2H_5)CH_3$ by two pathways: Path 1 is a reaction with K to form the alkoxide which then reacts with ethyl tosylate (C_2H_5OTs), and in path 2, **A** reacts first with tosyl chloride (TsCl) and then with $K^{+-}OC_2H_5$. [Tosyl (Ts) is p-$MeC_6H_4SO_2$.] When TsCl reacts with ROH, the R—O bond is not broken; thus the configuration about the chiral C is unchanged in the product R—O—Ts. (*a*) Use Fischer projections to show the stereochemistry of intermediates and products in each pathway and give their R,S designations. (*b*) Starting with optically pure **A**, determine the relative signs of $[\alpha]$ of the ether products.

▮ (*a*) *Path 1*:

$$\xrightarrow{K} \quad n\text{-}Pr \overset{CH_3}{\underset{H}{-\!\!\!\!\mid\!\!\!\!-}} O^-K^+ \xrightarrow{C_2H_5OTs} n\text{-}Pr \overset{CH_3}{\underset{H}{-\!\!\!\!\mid\!\!\!\!-}} OC_2H_5$$

$$(R) \qquad\qquad\qquad (R)$$

(**A**) $n\text{-}Pr \overset{CH_3}{\underset{H}{-\!\!\!\!\mid\!\!\!\!-}} OH$

$$(R)$$

Path 2: $\xrightarrow{TsCl}$ $n\text{-}Pr \overset{CH_3}{\underset{H}{-\!\!\!\!\mid\!\!\!\!-}} OTs \xrightarrow{K^{+-}OEt} EtO \overset{CH_3}{\underset{H}{-\!\!\!\!\mid\!\!\!\!-}} n\text{-}Pr$

$$(R) \qquad\qquad\qquad (S)$$

In both paths the nucleophile is an alkoxide anion. In path 1 the chiral center is in the nucleophile and none of its bonds are broken, resulting in retention of the configuration in the ether. Path 2 differs in that ethoxide attacks the chiral C backside in an S_N2 reaction with inversion of configuration and formation of the (S) enantiomer.

(*b*) They are equal and opposite, respectively.

8.62 Discuss the effect on S_N2 rates of having R's on the βC, by comparing 1-bromopentane (**A**), 1-bromo-2-methylbutane (**B**), neopentyl bromide (**C**).

◢ Replacing H's by R's on the βC increases the steric hindrance towards backside attack on the αC bonded to X. The decreasing order of reactivity is

$$\mathbf{A}(\text{one } \beta R) > \mathbf{B}(\text{two } \beta R\text{'s}) > \mathbf{C}(\text{three } \beta R\text{'s})$$

In fact neopentyl bromide is inert toward S_N2 reactions notwithstanding that it is a 1° RX.

8.63 Give examples of the four charge-types of S_N2 reactions that differ in charges on the nucleophile and substrate. Use Me derivatives.

◢ (1) $\text{Me:I} + \text{OH}^- \longrightarrow \text{Me:OH} + \text{I}^-$ (3) $\text{Me}_2\overset{+}{\text{S}}\text{:Me} + \text{OH}^- \longrightarrow \text{Me:OH} + \text{Me}_2\text{S}$

(2) $\text{Me:I} + \text{NH}_3 \longrightarrow \text{Me:NH}_3^+ + \text{I}^-$ (4) $\text{Me}_2\overset{+}{\text{S}}\text{:Me} + \text{NH}_3 \longrightarrow \text{Me:NH}_3^+ + \text{Me}_2\text{S}$

8.64 In terms of the $\Delta H^\ddagger$ of the S_N2 reaction in Problem 8.53 (Fig. 8-2), generalize about the effect of changes in the polarity of the solvent on the rate.

◢ In general, any change in solvent that increases $\Delta H^\ddagger$ decreases the rate. An increase in $\Delta H^\ddagger$ can be achieved by decreasing the H_{GS} or increasing the H_{TS} or doing both. Conversely, any change in solvent that decreases $\Delta H^\ddagger$ increases the rate. A decrease in $\Delta H^\ddagger$ can be achieved by raising H_{GS} or decreasing H_{TS} or doing both.

8.65 Show the TS with all partial charges for each reaction-type in Problem 8.63.

◢ (1) $\left[\text{HO}^{\delta-} \text{----} \overset{\overset{\displaystyle H \quad H}{\diagdown \diagup}}{\underset{\displaystyle |}{\text{C}}} \text{---} \text{I}^{\delta-} \right]^{-}$ (3) $\left[\text{HO}^{\delta-} \text{----} \overset{\overset{\displaystyle H \quad H}{\diagdown \diagup}}{\underset{\displaystyle |}{\text{C}}} \text{---} \text{S}^{\delta+}\text{Me}_2 \right]$

(2) $\left[\text{H}_3\text{N}^{\delta+} \text{----} \overset{\overset{\displaystyle H \quad H}{\diagdown \diagup}}{\underset{\displaystyle |}{\text{C}}} \text{---} \text{I}^{\delta-} \right]$ (4) $\left[\text{H}_3\text{N}^{\delta+} \text{----} \overset{\overset{\displaystyle H \quad H}{\diagdown \diagup}}{\underset{\displaystyle |}{\text{C}}} \text{---} \text{S}^{\delta+}\text{Me}_2 \right]^{+}$

8.66 Discuss the effect on the S_N2 rates for each reaction-type in Problem 8.63 on increasing the polarity of the solvent.

◢ It is essential to know the charge condition of the TS in each case. Increasing the polarity of the solvent stabilizes any charged ground state species, lowering H_{GS}. Such a change also stabilizes any charged transition state that would tend to lower H_{TS}. The enthalpy of a fully charged ion is lowered more than a species, such as a TS, with diffused charge.

(1) The charge in the TS (Fig. 8-3) is more diffuse than the charge on the anionic nucleophile; hence, an increase in the polarity of the solvent lowers H_{GS} more than H_{TS}. This net change increases $\Delta H^\ddagger$ and decreases the rate. (See Fig. 8-2 in Problem 8.53.)

(2) The ground state has no charged ions but the TS has δ charges. Hence, an increase in solvent polarity lowers H_{TS} but not H_{GS}. $\Delta H^\ddagger$ decreases and the rate increases.

(3) An increase in solvent polarity considerably lowers the enthalpy of the two fully charged GS reactants but only marginally the H of the TS, whose charge is much more diffuse. There is a large net increase in $\Delta H^\ddagger$ and a sharp decrease in rate.

(4) This situation is similar to (1). There is a charged reactant and a diffuse charged TS and the rate is decreased.

8.67 Determine the relative S_N2 reactivity with NaCN in aprotic DMSO of the alkyl halides:

(a) $CH_3CHClCH_2CH_3(\mathbf{A})$, $CH_3CHBrCH_2CH_3(\mathbf{B})$, $CH_3CHICH_2CH_3(\mathbf{C})$

(b) $CH_3CH(CH_3)CH_2CH_2I(\mathbf{D})$, $CH_3CH(CH_3)CHICH_3(\mathbf{E})$, $CH_3CI(CH_3)CH_2CH_3(\mathbf{F})$

(c) 4-Bromo-1,1-dimethylcyclohexane (**G**), 1-bromo-*cis*- or *trans*-1,4-dimethylcyclohexane (**H**), *cis*- or *trans*-2-bromo-*cis*-1,3-dimethylcyclohexane (**I**)

    (a) Group leavability is $I^- > Br^- > Cl^-$ and the order is $\mathbf{C} > \mathbf{B} > \mathbf{A}$.

    (b) Steric factors make the reactivity $1° > 2° > 3°$, giving the order $\mathbf{D} > \mathbf{E} > \mathbf{F}$.

    (c) **H** is $3°$ and the slowest. **I** suffers from ß substitution. The order is $\mathbf{G} > \mathbf{I} > \mathbf{H}$.

8.68 Compare the rates of reaction of *trans*- and *cis*-4-iodo-*t*-butylcyclohexane with radioactive I^-, noting that the TS is the same, whether starting with an equatorial or an axial I.

    Since the TS is the same, any rate difference must stem from the difference in the ground state enthalpies. The *cis* isomer with the axial I has the higher H_{GS}, the smaller $\Delta H^‡$, and the faster rate.

8.69 (a) Compare the reaction of Na^+ ^-SR in H_2O/acetone with (i) MeI and (ii) Me_3CBr. The acetone is used to solubilize the organic substrates. (b) In terms of the reactant, name the type of reaction in (ii) above.

    (a) (i) MeSR, the typical S_N2 product; (ii) Me_3COH. The 3 °C of Me_3CBr reacts with the nucleophilic solvent (H_2O), not with the better nucleophile (RS^-). (b) The reaction is an example of a *solvolysis* since the solvent helps break the $C-X$ bond and is the reactant. More specifically, this reaction is a hydrolysis.

8.70 (a) Analyze the following generalized rate data and write the rate expression for the reaction $R_3CX + Nu^- \xrightarrow{NuH} NuCR_3 + X^-$, where R_3CX is $3°$.

	$[R_3CX]$	$[Nu^-]$	rate
(i)	0.10	0.0010	1.3×10^{-2}
(ii)	0.20	0.0010	2.6×10^{-2}
(iii)	0.10	0.0020	1.3×10^{-2}
(iv)	0.30	0.0030	3.9×10^{-2}

(b) Why are low Nu^- concentrations used? (c) What is the designation for this type of reaction?

    (a) Changes in $[Nu^-]$ do not affect the rate, providing $[R_3CX]$ is constant. The rate is directly proportional only to $[R_3CX]$, i.e., rate $= k_1[R_3CX]$. The subscript of k indicates a first-order reaction. (b) Higher $[Nu^-]$ would cause an E2 reaction to give an alkene (Problem 8.116). (c) The designation of the mechanism for this type of reaction is S_N1, where S and $_N$ again stand for substitution and nucleophilic, respectively, and 1 for unimolecular.

8.71 (a) What conclusions can be drawn about the transition state of the rate-determining step from the rate equation in Problem 8.70? (b) Propose a mechanism for the S_N1 reaction of Me_3CBr and MeOH.

    (a) Since the rate does not depend on $[Nu^-]$, Nu^- *is not a part of the TS of the rate-determining step*. This is an example of the two step bond-breaking, bond-forming mechanism (see path 1 of Problem 8.48).

    (b) 1. The first and slow rate-determining step is ionization to a carbocation.

$$Me_3C:\ddot{Br}: \xrightarrow{slow} Me_3C^+ + :\ddot{Br}:^-$$

       2. The fast second step is attack by nucleophilic MeOH on the carbocation to form the protonated ether, and is followed by rapid loss of its proton to a second molecule of nucleophile to form an ether.

$$Me_3C^+ + H-\ddot{O}Me \xrightarrow{fast} Me_3C-\overset{+}{\underset{|}{\ddot{O}}Me} \xrightarrow{H\ddot{O}Me} H_2\overset{+}{\ddot{O}}Me + Me_3C-\ddot{O}Me$$

$$\text{an ether}$$

To generalize:

$$R-L \xrightarrow{slow} :L^- + R^+ \xrightarrow[fast]{:NuH} R:NuH^+ \xrightarrow[fast]{-H^+} RNu$$

8.72 Draw a reaction-enthalpy profile for an S_N1 reaction and compare it with that for the S_N2 reaction (Fig. 8-2).

    See Fig. 8-5. While S_N2 reactions have one TS and no intermediate, S_N1 reactions have two TS's and an intermediate carbocation. In the first and higher energy TS, (ii), the $C-L$ bond is stretching, $R_3C^{\delta+}---L^{\delta-}$.

In the second lower energy TS, bond-formation between a carbocation intermediate (iii) and a nucleophilic solvent molecule, NuH, is occurring, $R_3C^{\delta+} --- :NuH^{\delta+}$ (iv). As is the case with S_N2 reactions, S_N1 reactions are exothermic because a stronger base displaces a weaker one. This is indicated by having the enthalpy of the products $R_3C—Nu + :L^-$, (v), lower than the enthalpy of the reactants, $R_3C—L + :Nu^-$ (i).

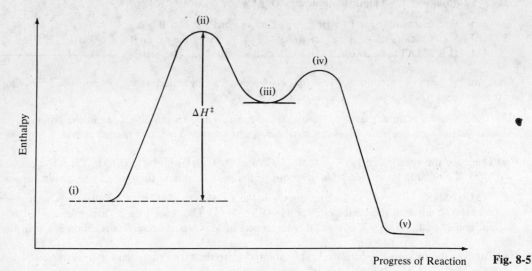

Fig. 8-5

8.73 Give the structural features of RX that most influence the relative S_N1 rates.

1. The fugicity (leavability) of X; the more weakly basic is X^-, the more reactive is RX. Therefore, RI > RBr > RCl.
2. The stability of the intermediate R^+; the more stable is R^+, the more reactive is RX. Therefore, the order of reactivity of RX is 3° > 2° > 1°. Note this order is the reverse of that in S_N2 reactions.

8.74 (*a*) Compare the TS's of the first step of the S_N1 reactions of 1°, 2°, and 3° RX's with the aid of enthalpy diagrams. (*b*) Apply the Hammond principle to justify the relative H_{TS}'s.

(*a*) See Fig. 8-6. (*b*) The reaction is endothermic so the TS more nearly resembles the carbocation. Any structural feature that lowers the H_{R^+} lowers the H_{TS} and speeds up the reaction.

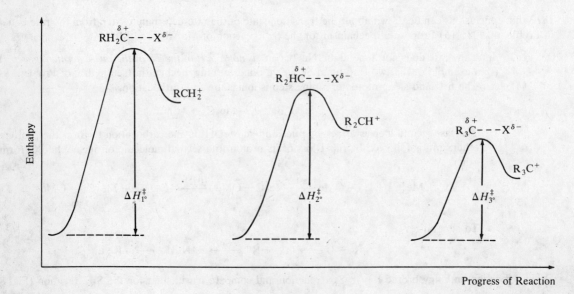

Fig. 8-6

8.75   Account for the relative stabilities of 3°, 2°, 1° and Me carbocations.

Several factors are deemed to play a role:

1. Electron-donating inductive effect of R's dissipate some of the positive charge on C. The more R's attached to the C, the greater is the stabilizing effect.

2. There is a steric effect, especially with large bulky R's. In the substrate, the R's, separated by 109° angles, are more crowded than in R^+, where they are separated by 120° bond angles arising from use by the C of sp^2 HO's. The more and larger the R's, the greater is this *steric acceleration*.

3. By *hyperconjugation* some charge delocalization occurs between the p AO of C^+ and the σ bond of the ßC—H as shown in Fig. 8-7. The more *beta* C's there are with H's, the more stable is the R^+.

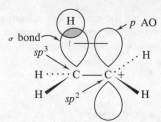

Fig. 8-7

8.76   (*a*) Explain how the stereochemistry of S_N1 and S_N2 reactions differ.   (*b*) Account for the detection of about 60% inverted and 40% racemic product from a typical S_N1 reaction.   (*c*) What is the actual distribution of product from inversion and retention in the typical S_N1 reaction?

(*a*) S_N2 gives complete inversion of configuration of the attacked C. If a free R^+ were to form in the S_N1 reaction, it would be achiral because it would possess a plane of symmetry incorporating its three σ bonds. Its p AO could be attacked equally well at either of its faces, giving a completely racemic product.

(*b*) The actual mechanism does not involve a free R^+. It is believed that as X leaves and the bond angles open up from 109° to 120° there is room for a solvent molecule (HS) to approach from the rear. The anion is also solvated by H-bonding as it leaves R.

$$HS: ---\overset{|\,\delta+}{\underset{|}{C}}---\overset{\delta-}{X}-\overset{\text{H-bond}}{---}HS:$$

Solvent-assisted S_N1 TS

This TS passes on to a di-solvated *intimate ion-pair* intermediate: $HS---R^+X^----HS$. If the solvation bond to C gets stronger and X^- leaves completely, an inverted product is obtained. In addition, some of these intermediate species can react with solvent to give a *solvent separated ion-pair*:

$$HS---R^+---SH---X^----HS \qquad \text{often simply written as} \qquad R^+\|X^-$$

backside   frontside

(*c*) From this intermediate, bonding by the backside solvent molecule causes inversion, while bonding by the frontside solvent molecule causes retention. The stages of intermediates in the ionization and dissociation of 3° RX free of participating solvent molecules are

$$\underset{\text{substrate}}{RX} \underset{\text{ionization}}{\rightleftharpoons} \underset{\text{intimate ion-pair}}{R^+X^-} \underset{-HS}{\overset{HS}{\rightleftharpoons}} \underset{\text{solvent-separated ion-pair}}{R^+\|X^-} \underset{\text{dissociation}}{\rightleftharpoons} \underset{\text{dissociated (free) ions}}{R^+ + X^-}$$

Note that each step is reversible. Each intermediate would have its own TS.

8.77   (*a*) In terms of the role of solvent discussed in Problem 8.76, account for the following facts: (i) The reaction is first order. (ii) Most frequently, R^+ reacts with solvent, not with the more nucleophilic anion.   (*b*) Under what experimental conditions would the rate expression be more than first order? What is the order? What would be the molecularity?

(*a*) (i) Although solvent molecules are present in the rate-determining TS, they do not appear in the rate expression. In such cases the reaction is often said to be *pseudo first order*, the implication being that solvent molecules intervene in the rate-determining TS. (ii) The solvating solvent molecules are close to bonding distance as R^+ forms and they form the new bonds, not the more distant $Nu:^-$. (b) Use an inert solvent (benzene) with small amounts of nucleophilic protic molecules such as MeOH. Now MeOH is a reactant whose molar concentrations can be changed. Then the rate expression is rate $= k_3[RX][MeOH]^2$ with k_3 indicating third order. If all three molecules were to come together at the same time, the reaction would be termolecular. *Termolecularity* is extremely rare. More likely the solvating molecule that helps remove X^- will appear first, followed by the backside attacking molecule. Each of these events would be bimolecular.

8.78 (a) Define dielectric constant. (b) How does the dielectric constant affect S_N1 rates? (c) Explain why solvolyses are much faster in EtOH than in acetone even though both solvents have about the same dielectric constant.

◢ (a) The *dielectric constant* determines the ability of a solvent to reduce the electrostatic attraction between oppositely-charged ions. With higher dielectric constants there is less ion-pairing. (b) The S_N1 mechanism requires the ionization of a covalent bond which is encouraged by solvents with high dielectric constants. (c) In addition to its dielectric constant, the ability to form H bonds with X makes EtOH the better S_N1 solvent than acetone which cannot form H bonds.

8.79 (a) Give an orbital diagram for the rate-determining TS of an S_N1 reaction leading to the solvated intimate ion-pair (Problem 8.76). (b) Give (i) the similarities and (ii) the differences for this TS and the S_N2 TS (Problem 8.54). (c) Give the main factors that control the relative rates of S_N1 and S_N2 reactions and compare their driving forces.

◢ (a) See Fig. 8-8.

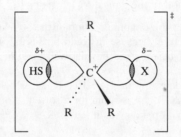

Fig. 8-8

(b) (i) They both have an sp^2C with a p AO, one of whose lobes partially overlaps with an orbital of the leaving group atom. The other lobe overlaps with the orbital of the nucleophilic atom of the solvent in S_N1, and with the attacking nucleophilic site atom in S_N2. (ii) For S_N2 the nucleophile and leaving group are closer to the C which therefore has little or no positive charge. Furthermore, the S_N2 TS suffers more from crowding. Because the partial bonds are longer in the S_N1 TS, there is a considerable amount of positive charges on the C and the TS is not crowded.

(c) For S_N1 the rate is directly related to the stability of the incipient R^+; the more stable the R^+, the faster is the rate. For S_N2, the rate is influenced by steric hindrance either from R's around the attacked C or from the bulkiness of Nu^-. The driving force for S_N2 is the rear-side approach of the nucleophile; for S_N1, it is the ionization of the $C-X$ bond.

8.80 (a) With the aid of the enthalpy diagram discuss the effect on the rate of solvolysis of t-BuCl of increasing the polarity of the solvent. (b) Give the equation for the methanolysis of $[Me_3CSMe_2]^+Br^-$. (c) Does the effect in part (a) prevail for solvolysis of $[Me_3CSMe_2]^+$? Explain.

◢ (a) See Fig. 8-9.
Since the ground state has no charge and the TS does, an increase in solvent polarity decreases H_{TS} and $\Delta H^{\ddagger}$, causing an increase in rate.

(b)

$$[Me_3C-SMe_2]^+Cl^- + 2MeOH \xrightarrow{-HCl} Me_3COMe + Me_2S + MeOH$$

a sulphonium salt   a sulfide

(c) No! The GS sulphonium cation has a full $+$ charge. H_{GS} is lowered more than H_{TS}, since in the TS the $+$ charge is more diffused. The rate is slower.

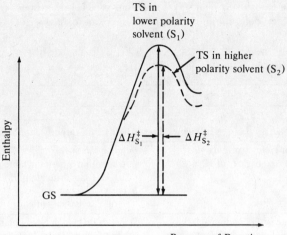

Fig. 8-9

8.81 Hydrolysis of 2-bromo-3-methylbutane (2°) yields only 2-methyl-2-butanol (3°). Explain.

⬛ During an S_N1 solvolysis, ionization produces an intermediate 2° R^+ which rearranges, here by a hydride shift, to more a stable 3° R^+ that reacts with H_2O to form the 3° ROH.

$$CH_3-\underset{\underset{Br}{|}}{CH}-\underset{\underset{H}{|}}{\overset{\overset{CH_3}{|}}{C}}-CH_3 \xrightarrow[\text{slow}]{-Br^-} CH_3-\overset{+}{C}H-\underset{\textcircled{\overset{..}{H}}}{\overset{\overset{CH_3}{|}}{C}}-CH_3 \xrightarrow{\sim \, :H}$$

2°

$$CH_3-\underset{\underset{H}{|}}{CH}-\overset{\overset{CH_3}{|}}{\underset{+}{C}}-CH_3 \xrightarrow[\underset{\text{fast}}{-H^+}]{+H_2O} CH_3-\underset{\underset{H}{|}}{CH}-\underset{\underset{OH}{|}}{\overset{\overset{CH_3}{|}}{C}}-CH_3$$

3°

8.82 Compare S_N1 and S_N2 reactions of RL with respect to the following mechanistic factors: number of steps; rate and order; molecularity; TS of slow step; stereochemistry; nucleophile.

⬛ See Table 8-1.

TABLE 8-1

		S_N1	S_N2
(a)	Number of steps	Two*: (1) $R{:}L \xrightarrow{\text{slow}} R^+ + {:}L^-$ (2) $R^+ + {:}NuH \xrightarrow{\text{fast}} R{:}Nu + H^+$	One: $R{:}L + {:}Nu^- \rightarrow R{:}Nu + {:}L^-$ *or* $R{:}L + {:}NuH \rightarrow R{:}NuH^+ + {:}L^-$
(b)	Reaction rate & order	Rate $= k_1[RL]$; first order	Rate $= k_2[RL]\,[{:}Nu^-]$; second order
(c)	Molecularity	Unimolecular	Bimolecular
(d)	TS of slow step	$HNu{:}---C^{\delta+}---^{\delta-}L---HNu{:}$	$^{\delta-}Nu{:}---C---{:}L^{\delta-}$ (with $:Nu^-$) $^{\delta+}HNu{:}---C---{:}L^{\delta-}$ (with $HNu{:}$)
(e)	Stereochemistry	Inversion and retention	Inversion (backside attack)
(f)	Reacting nucleophile	Nucleophilic solvent; stable R^+ may react with added nucleophile	Added nucleophile

*The simplified mechanism has two steps; the ion-pair concept has more steps.

8.83 Compare the effects on rates of S_N1 and S_N2 reactions of RL with respect to: structure of R and L; nature of nucleophile; solvent effect; determining factor; rearrangement; catalysis.

▟ See Table 8-2.

TABLE 8-2

		S_N1	S_N2
(a)	Structure of R	$3° > 2° > 1° >$ Me	Me $> 1° > 2° > 3°$
(b)	Nature of L	Weakest base is best leaving group, i.e., I $>$ Br $>$ Cl $>$ F	
(c)	Nature of nucleophile	For HNu: (solvent), rate α basicity of HNu:	*In protic solvents* (i) within a periodic table group, rate α polarizability of Nu (ii) for same site atom, rate α basicity of Nu *In aprotic solvents* rate α basicity of Nu
(d)	Solvent effect	Rate α H-bonding ability and dielectric constant	Depends on charge type. Polar aprotic solvents leaves "freest" most reactive Nu.
(e)	Determining factor	Stability of R^+	Steric hindrance
(f)	Rearrangement	Observed	Not observed, except for allylic (Problem 8.95)
(g)	Catalysis	Lewis and Brönsted acids: Ag^+, $AlCl_3$, and strong HA	Phase transfer (Problem 8.131), Crown ethers (Problem 14.13)

8.84 Explain the following observations in S_N1 reactions: (a) $AgNO_3$ increases the rates of solvolyses. (b) The more acidic the nucleophilic solvent, the faster is the rate of solvolysis. (c) The more stable the R^+, (i) the less inversion and more racemization occurs, and (ii) the more it reacts with the anionic nucleophile rather than the solvent, notwithstanding the fact that the rate of RNu formation is still first order.

▟ (a) Ag^+ has a stronger affinity for X^- than has a solvent molecule; the precipitation of AgCl accelerates the dissociation of X^-. This is an example of *electrophilic catalysis*. (b) The effectiveness of the H bonding, a factor that accelerates dissociation, increases with the acidity of the H. (c) The more stable the R^+, (i) the more chance it has to proceed to the solvent-separated ion pair from which racemization occurs, and (ii) the more selective it is and the more likely it will react with the nucleophilic anion. Unimolecular dissociation (step 1 of Table 8-1) is still slow and rate-determining.

8.85 Describe the experimental conditions needed for R^+ to survive long enough to be detected.

▟ The *counteranion*, An^-, must be so very weakly basic or nucleophilic that it would not combine with R^+ once the two species are formed. In practice, antimony pentafluoride (SbF_5) dissolved in liquid SO_2 at low temperatures is used in the dissociation of RX:

$$RX + SbF_5 \longrightarrow R^+ + [SbF_5X]^- \text{ (counteranion)}$$

SbF_5 has a greater affinity for X^- than does R^+, and is called a Lewis *superacid*. The acidic reagent $HSbF_6$ has powerful proton-donating power and consequently its conjugate base lacks basicity or nucleophilicity.

8.86 Write structures for the organic reaction products from solvolysis of Et_3CCl with (a) MeOH, (b) MeCOOH, and (c) HCOOH.

▟ (a) Et_3COMe, an ether; (b) $Et_3CO\overset{O}{\overset{\|}{C}}Me$; (c) $Et_3CO\overset{O}{\overset{\|}{C}}H$. Note that (b) and (c) are esters.

8.87 (a) Predict and account for the effect on reaction rate of increasing the percentage of H_2O in the acetone-H_2O solvent mixture in: (i) S_N1 solvolysis of Me_3CBr, and (ii) S_N2 reaction of KI and EtCl. (b) Predict the relative yields of the solvolysis products of Me_3CBr in 80% EtOH and 20% H_2O.

▟ (a) (i) Adding more water increases the polarity of the solvent and the rate increases. (ii) The rate decreases because of better solvation of I^- (with a full negative charge) in the GS through H-bonding with H_2O. (b) Although there is much more EtOH than H_2O, the latter solvates R^+ much better and more alcohol, Me_3COH, than ether, Me_3COEt, should form.

8.88 Optically pure (*S*)-(+)-2-bromooctane, $[\alpha]_D^{25°} = +36°$, reacts with aqueous NaOH in acetone to give optically pure (*R*)-(−)-2-octanol, $[\alpha]_D^{25°} = -10.3°$. With partially racemized bromo compound whose $[\alpha]_D^{25°} = +30°$, the $[\alpha]_D^{25°}$ of the alcohol product is −6.0°. Calculate: (*a*) the percent optical purity of partially racemized bromo compound and alcohol, (*b*) percentages of inversion and racemization, and (*c*) percentage of frontside and backside attack.

◢ (*a*) To find the percentage of optical purity (optically active enantiomer), divide the observed specific rotation by that of the pure enantiomer and multiply the quotient by 100%. The optical purities are

$$\text{Bromide} = \frac{30°}{36°}(100\%) = 83\% \qquad \text{Alcohol} = \frac{-6.0°}{-10.3°}(100\%) = 58\%$$

(*b*) The percentage of inversion is calculated by dividing the percentage of enantiomer of alcohol by that of reacting bromide and multiplying the quotient by 100%. The percentage of racemization is the difference between this percentage and 100%.

$$\text{Percentage inversion} = \frac{58\%}{83\%}(100\%) = 70\%$$

$$\text{Percentage racemization} = 100\% - 70\% = 30\%$$

(*c*) Inversion involves only backside attack, while racemization results from equal backside and frontside attack. The percentage of backside attack is the sum of the inversion and one-half the percentage of racemization. The percentage of frontside attack is the remaining half of the percentage of racemization.

$$\text{Percentage of backside attack} = 70\% + \tfrac{1}{2}(30\%) = 85\%$$

$$\text{Percentage of frontside attack} = \tfrac{1}{2}(30\%) = 15\%$$

8.89 (*a*) What inferences can be drawn from the data in part (*b*) of Problem 8.88 about the mode of reaction of 2° alkyl halides? (*b*) Give the rate expression. (*c*) In terms of the rate expression, describe the experimental changes for encouraging (i) S_N1 and (ii) S_N2.

◢ (*a*) The large percentage of inversion shows that 2° RX's react typically and predominantly by S_N2 and the smaller percentage of racemization indicates some S_N1 reaction.

(*b*) The rate expression is composed of an S_N1 and an S_N2 term:

$$\text{rate} = k_1[2° \text{ RX}] + k_2[2° \text{ RX}][\text{OH}^-]$$

(*c*) At very low [OH⁻] the k_2 term becomes insignificant and the S_N1 pathway predominates. At higher [OH⁻] the k_2 term becomes more significant and the S_N2 pathway predominates.

8.90 (*a*) Account for the trend in relative rates observed for the formation of alcohols from the listed RX's in H_2O/EtOH at 25 °C: MeBr, 2140; MeCH₂Br, 171; Me₂CHBr, 4.99; Me₃CBr, 1010. (*b*) Why is EtOH added to the water?

◢ (*a*) The first three halides react mainly by the S_N2 pathway and their rate decline as Me's replace H's on the attacked C, because of steric hindrance. H_2O is the nucleophile. A change to the S_N1 pathway accounts for the sharp rise in the reactivity of Me₃CBr.

(*b*) Water is a poor solvent for alkyl halides and EtOH is added to aid in their solution.

8.91 Account for the following observations: (*a*) *t*-BuF is solvolyzed only in very acidic solutions. (*b*) *t*-BuCl is solvolyzed more slowly than 2-chloro-2,3,3-trimethylbutane (**A**). (*c*) *t*-BuCl is solvolyzed much faster than 2-chloro-1,1,1-trifluro-2-methylpropane (**B**). (*d*) *t*-BuCl is solvolyzed more slowly in 90% D_2O-10% dioxane than in 90% H_2O- 10% dioxane solution.

◢ (*a*) F⁻ is a poor leaving group but H-bonding with a strong acid encourages its departure. This is an example of electrophilic catalysis.

(*b*) Formation of $\text{Me}_3\text{C}\!-\!\overset{\overset{\displaystyle \text{Me}}{|}}{\underset{\underset{\displaystyle \text{Me}}{|}}{\text{C}}}{}^+$ alleviates some of the steric crowding in **A** induced by the 2 Me's and the *t*-Bu on the αC. This is another example of steric acceleration.

(*c*) $\text{F}_3\text{C}\!-\!\overset{\overset{\displaystyle \text{Me}}{|}}{\text{CH}}{}^+$ is destabilized by the strongly electron-withdrawing F_3C group, making the solvolysis of **B** slower.

(*d*) D bonds are not as stabilizing as H bonds.

8.92 Compare the nucleophilic displacement products from *trans*-3-bromomethylcyclopentane with OH⁻ in H$_2$O by (*a*) S$_N$2 and (*b*) S$_N$1 mechanisms.

▰ (*a*) *Cis*-3-Methylcyclopentanol. There is complete inversion of configuration of the attacked C. In cyclic compounds, this means isomerization from *cis* to *trans* and *vice versa*.   (*b*) A mixture of *trans*- (from retention) and *cis*-3-methylcyclopentanol (from inversion).

8.93 Compare (*a*) the reactions of aq. HBr with (i) *n*-BuOH (**A**), (ii) Me$_3$COH (**B**), (*b*) Give the different techniques used.

▰ (*a*)   (i) uses S$_N$2: $\mathbf{A} + HBr \overset{fast}{\rightleftharpoons} Br^- + [n\text{-BuOH}_2]^+ \xrightarrow{slow} n\text{-BuBr} + H_2O$

   (ii) uses S$_N$1: $\mathbf{B} + HBr \underset{-Br^-}{\overset{fast}{\rightleftharpoons}} [Me_3C{-}OH_2]^+ \underset{-H_2O}{\xrightarrow{slow}} Me_3C^+ \overset{Br^-, fast}{\rightleftharpoons} Me_3CBr$

(*b*) **B** reacts when merely shaken with the HBr solution in a separatory funnel; **A** requires refluxing, usually with a mixture of NaBr and H$_2$SO$_4$ that supplies HBr *in situ*. In general S$_N$1 rates of 3° RL's are usually faster than the S$_N$2 rates of 1° RL's.

8.94 (*a*) Compare the rates of (i) S$_N$1 and (ii) S$_N$2 reactions of allyl chloride and *n*-Pr chloride. Explain your answers. (*b*) Account for the formation of HOCH$_2$CH=CHMe from the hydrolysis of H$_2$C=CHCH(Me)Cl.

▰ (*a*)   (i) Allyl chloride is much more reactive than *n*-PrCl, although it is also a 1° RX. The + charge of its intermediate R$^+$ is stabilized by extended π-bonding: $[H_2C{=}CH{-}CH_2^+ \leftrightarrow {}^+CH_2{=}CH{-}CH_2]$ or $[H_2^{\delta+}C \cdots CH \cdots C^{\delta+}H_2]^+$. (See Problem 7.149 for the corresponding allyl-type radical—replace the dot in Fig. 7-10 by a +.) The + is shared equally by the terminal C's. (ii) Allyl chloride is again more reactive, but not to the extent of the S$_N$1 reaction. The *p* AO of the TS can overlap with the parallel π bond, stabilizing the TS (Fig. 8-10, uncharged Nu is used).

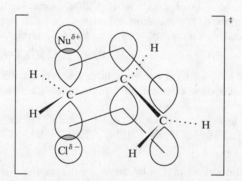

Fig. 8-10

(*b*) The intermediate R$^+$, $[H_2\overset{\delta+}{C^1} \cdots CH \cdots \overset{\delta+}{C^3}HMe]^+$ can react with H$_2$O at either C^1 or C^3, each of which has δ^+ charge. Reaction at the 1° C^1 affords the more substituted alkenol although 2° C^3 has more δ^+. This reaction is an example of an *allylic rearrangement*.

8.95 Account for the formation of CH$_3$CH=CHCH$_2$CN (**C**) and CH$_3$CH(CN)CH=CH$_2$ (**D**) from the reaction of CH$_3$CH=CHCH$_2$Cl with CN⁻.

▰ Unlike in Problem 8.94, the allylic rearrangement leading to **D** proceeds by an S$_N$2, not an S$_N$1 mechanism. **C** results from the expected S$_N$2 reaction at C^1. However, CN⁻ can also bond to C^3 with the nucleophilic πe⁻'s, displacing Cl⁻ as the allylic rearrangement occurs.

$$N\equiv C:\curvearrowright CH_3 {-}CH{=}CH{-}CH_2 \curvearrowleft Cl \longrightarrow CH_3{-}\underset{\underset{CN}{|}}{CH}{-}CH{=}CH_2 + :\ddot{Cl}:^-$$

This is called an S$_N$2-*prime* (S$_N$2′) mechanism.

8.96 Compare the rates of S$_N$1 and S$_N$2 reactions of (*a*) cyclopropyl and cyclopentyl chloride and (*b*) 1-chlorobicyclo[2.2.2]octane and 9-chlorodecalin (**A**).

▰ (a) Cyclopropyl chloride is much less reactive than cyclopentyl chloride in each type of reaction because the sp^2C (120° bond angle) created in each TS augments the ring strain. (b) The bridgehead halide is inert by both reaction types. A flat R^+ cannot form at the bridgehead C, making S_N1 impossible, and the three bridges prevent the backside attack necessary for S_N2. Furthermore, inversion is impossible. **A** is a typical 3° halide, and reacts rapidly via S_N1, but poorly via S_N2.

8.97 (a) Discuss the C—Cl bond of vinyl chlorides. (b) Predict the (i) S_N1 and (ii) S_N2 reactivities of vinyl halides.

▰ (a) The C—Cl bond of vinyl chlorides is shorter and stronger than the C—Cl bond of alkyl halides for two reasons: (1) Bond lengths at C_{sp^2} are shorter than at C_{sp^3}; and (2) delocalization of e^- density from Cl to C=C by extended π bonding, $H_2^{\delta-}C\text{---}CH\text{---}Cl^{\delta+}$, induces some double bond character in the C—Cl bond, making it shorter and stronger. The contributing resonance structures are: [$CH_2=CH—\ddot{C}l\!:\ \leftrightarrow\ ^-\!:CH_2—CH=\overset{..}{\underset{..}{C}}l\!:^+$].

(b) Vinyl halides are inert toward both types of displacement reactions.

(i) In S_N1 reactions they would have to ionize to vinyl cations which are very unstable because of their sp hybridization. The more s-character in the C^+, the less stable is the R^+.

(ii) 1. Backside approach is difficult because it must proceed in the plane of the alkene where it is repelled by the e^- density in the π bond. If C^2 is monoalkylated or dialkylated, steric hindrance to the approach of the Nu occurs.

2. Inversion of C^1, that must pass through an unfavorable sp-hybridized state, is energetically very difficult.

3. The stronger C—X bond is difficult to break.

8.98 Account for the rapid rate of ethanolysis of $ClCH_2OCH_2CH_3$, although the substrate is a 1° halide.

▰ The rapidity of this S_N1 reaction is attributed to the stability of a C^+ bonded to $—\ddot{O}—$. The empty p AO on C^+ can overlap sidewise with a filled p AO on O, thereby delocalizing and stabilizing the positive charge. The C^+ then reacts with EtOH, giving an ether.

$$CH_3CH_2—O—CH_2Cl \longrightarrow Cl^- + \begin{bmatrix} CH_3CH_2—\overset{..}{\underset{..}{O}}—CH_2^+ \\ \updownarrow \\ CH_3CH_2—\overset{+}{\underset{..}{O}}=CH_2 \end{bmatrix} \xrightarrow[-H^+]{C_2H_5OH} CH_3CH_2—O—CH_2OC_2H_5$$

8.99 (a) Provide the products of the reactions of the following substrates with $NaNO_2$ in EtOH: (i) n-BuCl and (ii) $ClCH_2OCH_2CH_3$. (b) Generalize about the mode of reaction of ambident ions, such as $:NO_2^-$, and the extent of positive charge on the attacked C. (c) Apply the SHAB principle (Problems 8.41 and 8.42) to your generalization.

▰ (a) (i) n-Bu—NO_2 and (ii) ONO—$CH_2OCH_2CH_3$ + EtO—$CH_2OCH_2CH_3$. (b) The less the positive charge on the attacked C, the more likely it will bond to the less electronegative nucleophilic site of the ambident ion (N). This happens in the S_N2 reaction in (i), where a C—N bond forms. The greater the positive charge on the attacked C, the more likely it will bond to the more electronegative nucleophilic site of the ambident ion (O). This happens in the S_N1 reaction in (ii), where a C—O bond forms. Since the R^+ in (ii) is so stable, it has a long enough half-life to react with any added nucleophile as well as nucleophilic solvent. (c) The more positive the charge on C, the "harder" it is, as in S_N1, and the more readily it bonds to the harder nucleophilic site, here the more electronegative O. In S_N2, C has little positive charge, is softer and preferentially bonds to the less hard and less electronegative N.

3. Elimination Reactions

8.100 (a) Give the products from the reactions of KOH in alcohol with (i) $CH_3CH_2CH_2CH_2Br$, (1°); (ii) $CH_3CH_2CHBrCH_3$, (2°); and (iii) $(CH_3)_3CBr$, (3°). (b) Give the relative order of reactivities of the RBr's in (a). (c) What structural factor determines the major product when more than one isomeric alkene is possible?

▰ These are alkene-forming elimination reactions: (i) $CH_3CH_2CH=CH_2$, (ii) $trans$-$CH_3CH=CHCH_3$ mainly, and (iii) $(CH_3)_2C=CH_2$. (b) 3° > 2° > 1°. (c) The most substituted alkene is produced with the highest yield as predicted by the Saytzeff rule, with $trans$ dominating over cis.

8.101 Provide structural formulas of the alkenes from the reactions: (i) Bromocyclopentane + $CH_3CH_2O^-K^+$, (ii) 2-bromopentane + $CH_3CH_2O^-Na^+$ (3 products), and (iii) 4-iodo-4-n-propylheptane

    (i)  ⬠

    (ii) *trans*- and *cis*-$CH_3CH=CHCH_2CH_3 + H_2C=CHCH_2CH_2CH_3$. *trans*-2-Pentene has the highest yield, 1-pentene the smallest.

    (iii) $CH_3CH_2CH=C(CH_2CH_2CH_3)_2$

8.102 (*a*) Name the property a reagent must have to promote a β-elimination (as in Problem 8.101). (*b*) List the following substances in decreasing order of reactivity for such eliminations: HO^-, RO^-, $RCOO^-$, CN^-, NO_3^-.

    (*a*) The reagent should be a strong Brönsted base. (*b*) The order decreases with the decreasing order of basicities: $RO^- > HO^- > CN^- > RCOO^- > NO_3^-$.

8.103 (*a*) Suggest three logical ways for the following general elimination to occur:

$$B:^- + -\overset{|}{C}H-\overset{|}{C}X \longrightarrow {\displaystyle \setminus \atop /}C=C{\displaystyle / \atop \setminus} + BH + X^-$$

(Disregard the viability in terms of actual chemistry.) (*b*) Predict the rate expressions, orders, and molecularities of the reactions in part (*a*). Justify your predictions. (*c*) What symbols are used to denote the three elimination pathways based on their molecularities?

    (*a*) 1. *Two steps*. X^- leaves first, then the remaining R^+ loses an adjacent H^+ to $:B^-$.

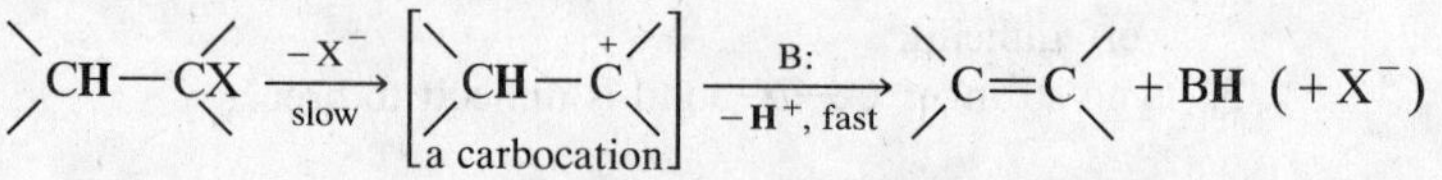

$$CH-CX \xrightarrow[\text{slow}]{-X^-} [CH-\overset{+}{C}] \xrightarrow[-H^+,\text{ fast}]{B:} C=C + BH\ (+X^-)$$
a carbocation

    The first step is slow because it is an ionization giving the very high energy R^+.
    2. *Two steps*. H^+ leaves first followed by X^- from the intermediate carbanion.

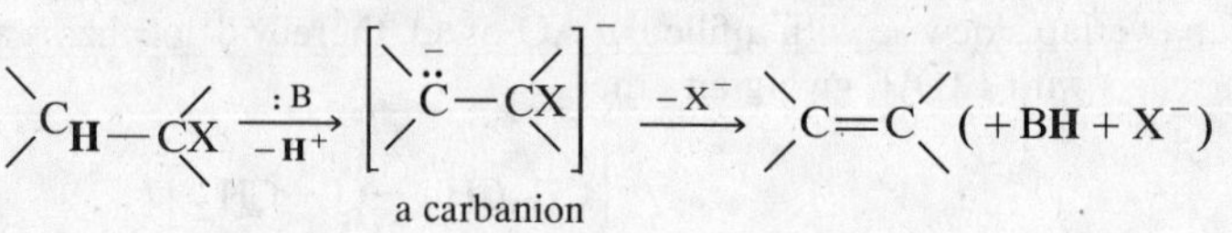

$$CH-CX \xrightarrow[-H^+]{:B} [\overset{..}{C}-CX]^- \xrightarrow{-X^-} C=C\ (+BH+X^-)$$
a carbanion

    Except for those few cases where the substrate has a very acidic H^+, the first step is slow.
    3. A *one step* concerted departure of X^- and H^+.

    (*b*) 1. The slow step has only one species, the substrate, and the first order rate $= k_1$ [RX] for this unimolecular reaction.
    2. Regardless of which step is rate-controlling, the second-order rate $= k_2[RX][:B^-]$. However, if the first step is slower, the reaction is bimolecular because both reactants are involved. If the second step is slower, only the carbanion is involved and the reaction is unimolecular.
    3. Both reactants participate in the single step, and the second order rate $= k_2[RX][:B^-]$ for this bimolecular reaction.
    (*c*) 1. **E1** (elimination, unimolecular).
    2. **E1$_{cb}$** (elimination, unimolecular of the conjugate base).
    3. **E2** (elimination, bimolecular).

8.104 (*a*) Give the order of decreasing reactivity for eliminations with strong bases of RX, when X = F, Cl, Br, I. (*b*) Explain how this information is necessary to decide between E2 and E1$_{cb}$.

    (*a*) For any type of reaction, whenever the rate-determining TS involves breaking of the C—X bond (S_N2, E2), the rate is directly related to the leavability of X^- which, in turn, is indirectly related to its basicity. The weakest base is the best leaving group: $I^- > Br^- > Cl^- > F^-$. The order of reactivity is RI > RBr > RCl > RF. (*b*) If E1$_{cb}$ prevails, expulsion of X^- occurs in the fast second step and the rate of the overall reaction is independent of the leavability of X—all RX's should then react at about the same rate. In E2, expulsion of X^- occurs in the rate-determining step and the nature of X influences the rate.

8.105 (*a*) What is the best stereospecific conformation for E2 eliminations? Explain. (*b*) If this conformation cannot be attained, what is the next best?

    (*a*) The base attacks the H from the rear by an S_N2-type process. An anti-coplanar conformation [Fig. 8-11(*a*)] with H and L 180° apart permits the approaching electron-rich base to be at a maximum distance from the electron-rich leaving group. (*b*) If the structure of the substrate precludes the attainment of this preferred conformation, the *syn*-coplanar conformation with eclipsed H and L is the next best [Fig. 8-11(*b*)].

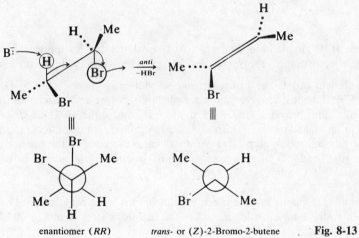

(*a*) *anti*-coplanar   (*b*) *syn*-coplanar   **Fig. 8-11**

8.106 (*a*) Draw the *anti*-coplanar TS for the E2 mechanism. Show all partial bonds and charges. (*b*) Compare the charge dispersal in the E2 and S_N2 TS's [(1) of Problem 8.65] for the reaction of RX with Nu⁻. (*c*) Discuss how increasing the polarity of the solvent affects the relative rates of these two reactions.

◢ (*a*) See Fig. 8-12.

B:$^{\delta -}$
|
H
|
L$^{\delta -}$ --- HS   **Fig. 8-12**

(*b*) Charges in the E2 TS are more diffuse than in the S_N2 TS. (*c*) The TS's both have the same ground state whose enthalpy is lowered by increasing the solvent polarity. Since the charge in the E2 TS is more diffuse than in the S_N2 TS, the E2 H_{TS} is lowered less than the S_N2 H_{TS}, causing the E2 $\Delta H^{\ddagger}$ to be greater and its rate to decrease more than that of the S_N2.

8.107 With the aid of wedge-sawhorses and Newman projections illustrate the stereochemistry of the products from the E2 dehydrobromination of (*a*) (*R, R*), and (*b*) *meso*-(*R, S*)-2,3-dibromobutane.

⬜ (*a*) See Fig. 8-13.

enantiomer (*RR*)   *trans*- or (*Z*)-2-Bromo-2-butene   **Fig. 8-13**

(*b*) See Fig. 8-14.

meso   *cis*- or (*E*)-2-Bromo-2-butene

Fig. 8-14

8.108 (a) From which conformation of bromocyclohexane is the E2 dehydrobromination best achieved? (b) Give the products from the reactions with $CH_3O^- Na^+$ of (i) *cis-* and (ii) *trans-*2-bromomethylcyclohexane.

▮ (a) Boat conformations can be disregarded because of their very high energies and infinitesimally small populations. The more stable chair conformer has Br_{eq} which, however, cannot assume an *anti*-coplanar juxtaposition with a vicinal H. *Anti*-coplanarity can be achieved only in the chair conformation with Br_{ax} and the orientation with the lost H is *trans-diaxial*.

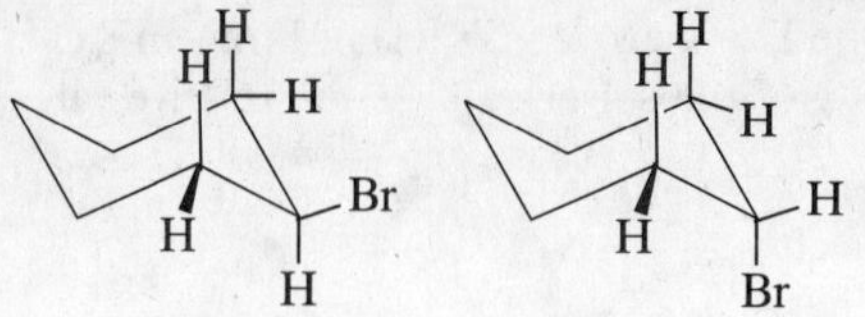

Br_{eq}(not *trans-diaxial*) Br_{ax}(*trans-diaxial*)

As the Br_{ax} conformation reacts, the equilibrium keeps shifting from Br_{eq} to Br_{ax} until all the Br_{eq} is consumed. This is another example of a reaction with the less stable conformation.

(b) (i)

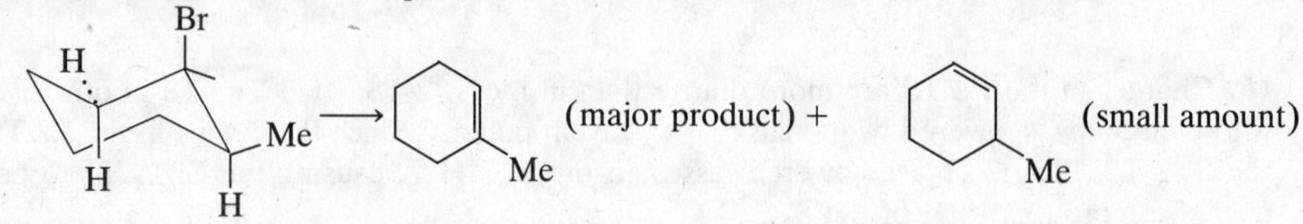

(major product) + (small amount)

1-Methylcyclohexene (**A**)   3-Methylcyclohexene (**B**)

(ii)

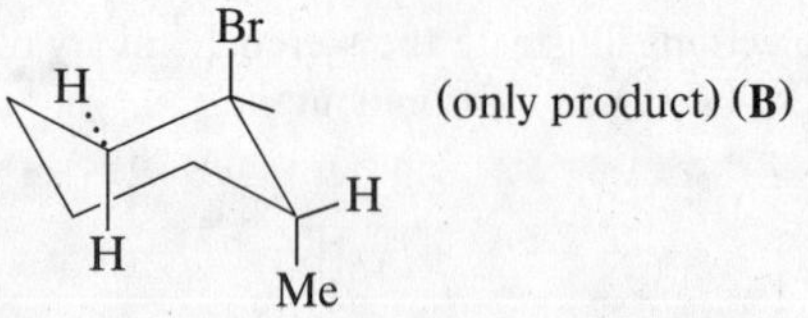

(only product) (**B**)

8.109 (a) Define the H/D kinetic isotope effect. (b) If a reaction has an appreciable isotope effect, what conclusion can be drawn about its mechanism? (c) Are isotope effects observed only for H and D?

▮ (a) Deuterium (D) is the hydrogen isotope with mass number 2. C—D bonds are almost chemically identical to C—H bonds; however, they are slightly stronger and react more slowly. The ratio of the rate constants, k_H/k_D, for breaking the C—H and C—D bond is the *H/D kinetic isotope effect*. A *primary isotope effect* is ≈ 2 or more, and can be as high as 8. (b) A primary isotope effect indicates that the bond departing H breaks in the rate-controlling step. (c) No. In all cases the bond to the heavier isotope is slightly stronger and breaks less easily. The H/D effect is more substantial because of the greater percentage difference in the masses of the isotopes.

8.110 In terms of the H/D kinetic isotope effect, explain (a) the more rapid loss of HI from CH_3CH_2I than DI from D_3CCH_2I, when strong base is added; and (b) the slightly faster rate of S_N1 or E1 reactions of $(CH_3)_3CCl$ than that of $(CD_3)_3CCl$.

▮ (a) The alkenes are $H_2C=CH_2$ and $D_2C=CH_2$, respectively. Since the elimination reaction of CH_3CH_2I is faster than that of CD_3CH_2I, it follows that the rate-determining step in E2 reactions is breaking a C—H or C—D bond. (b) S_N1 and E1 involve the formation of the same intermediate R^+ by the same rate-controlling ionization step. This step does not involve any C—H bond breaking so the H/D isotope effect is not primary. Rather it is a smaller *secondary isotope effect*, where $k_H/k_D = 0.7/1.5$. The deutereocarbocation, $(CD_3)_3C^+$, is not as stable as its proton analog because CD_3 is not as good an electron-donator as CH_3, nor is the C—D as good a hyperconjugative participant (Problem 8.75) as C—H.

8.111 (a) Draw the diastereomers of 2-chloro-1,3-dimethylcyclohexane and indicate the diastereomers that cannot undergo an E2 reaction. Give the product from those that do react. (b) Give the E2 product of compound **D**.

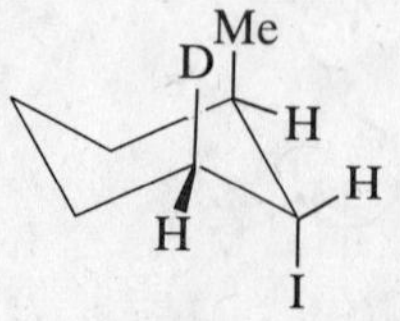

D

(c) Why is not the H/D kinetic isotope effect important here?

(*a*)   There are three diastereomers:

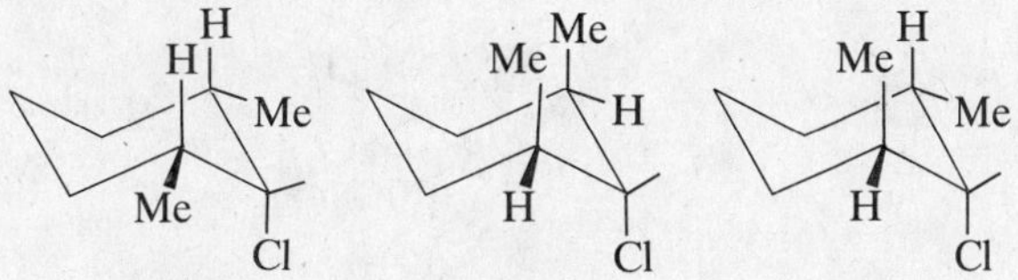

A   B   C

B cannot react because the vicinal H on each side is *cis*, and *anti*-coplanarity with Cl cannot be achieved. Neither can a Cl$_{eq}$ and an H$_{ax}$ be *syn* and coplanar. **A** and **C** can each achieve *anti*-coplanarity with Cl and a neighboring H to give 1,3-dimethylcyclohexene.

(*b*)

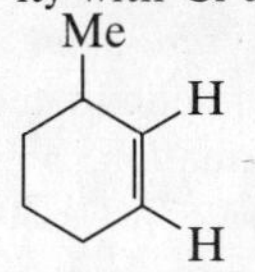

(*c*)   D is coplanar to Cl, and this requirement outweighs the H/D isotope effect.

8.112   Account for the formation of the same product from an E2 reaction of both *threo*- and *erythro*-2,2,3,5,5-pentamethyl-4-bromohexane.

In the *threo* diastereomer H and Br can be *anti*-coplanar with the bulky *t*-Bu's *anti* to each other. The TS is unencumbered by any steric hindrance from the *t*-Bu's. The product is the alkene with *trans t*-Bu's. In the *erythro* isomer *anti*-coplanarity of Br and H can only be attained if the bulky *t*-Bu's are *cis*-like in a prohibitively high enthalpy TS. However, *syn*-coplanarity of Br and H can be attained with *trans*-like bulky *t*-Bu's in a much lower enthalpy TS, giving **A**.

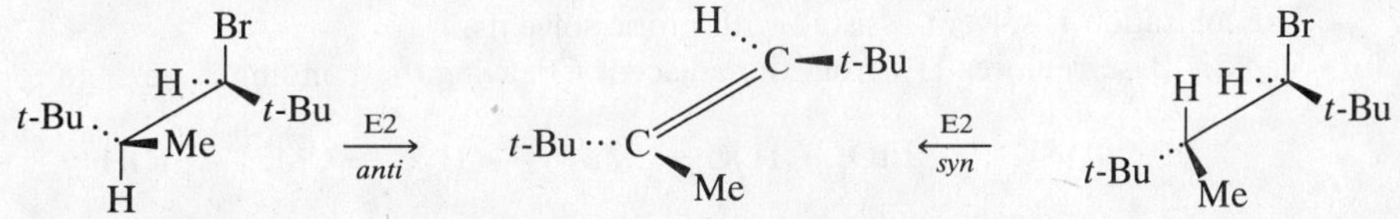

threo isomer   (*E*)-2,2,3,5,5-Pentamethyl-3-hexene (**A**)   *erythro* isomer

8.113   Predict the product from an E2 reaction of (*a*) an *exo*- and (*b*) an *endo*-2-bromo-*exo*-3-deuteriobicyclo[2.2.2]octane.

The rigidity of the bicyclic system prevents Br and an adjacent H or D from ever being *anti*-coplanar. *Syn*-coplanarity prevails and this is the mode of elimination.

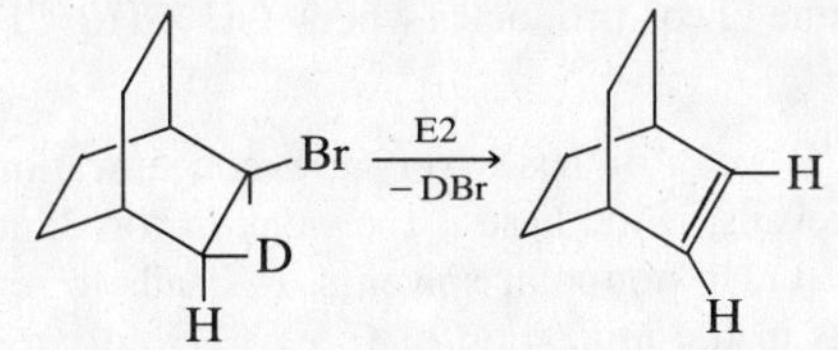

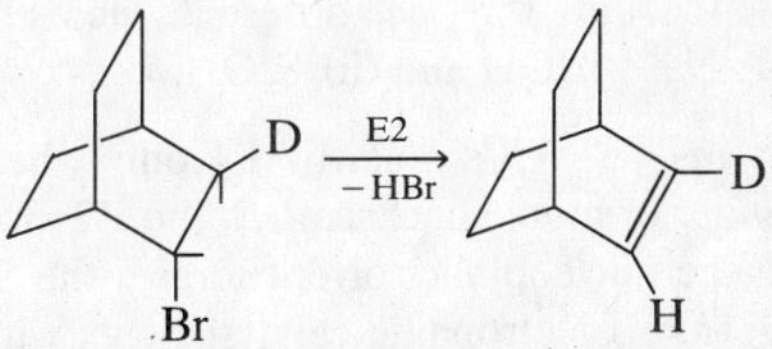

8.114   (*a*) Dehalogenation of *vic*-dihalides with active metals or I$^-$ has an E2-like TS. With the aid of Newman projections predict the products from reaction of I$^-$ with (i) *meso*- and (ii) (S, S)-2,3-dibromobutane.   (*b*) Refer to Fig. 8-15. Account for the fact that **A** readily forms an alkene with I$^-$ but **B** does not.

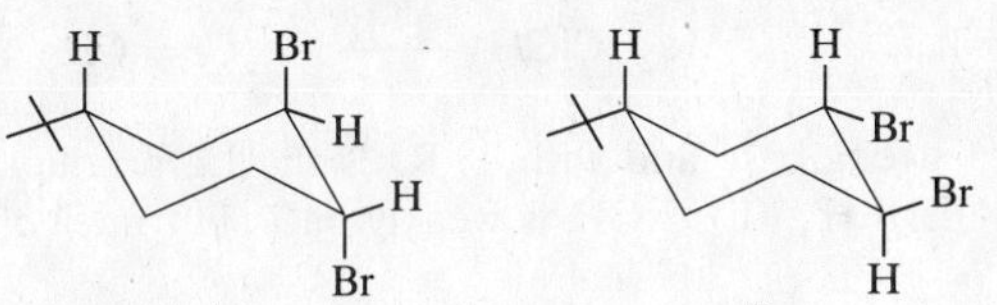

A   B   Fig. 8-15

(*a*)   Instead of B:$^-$ displacing on H as in dehydrohalogenation, I$^-$ displaces on X in dehalogenation.

(i)

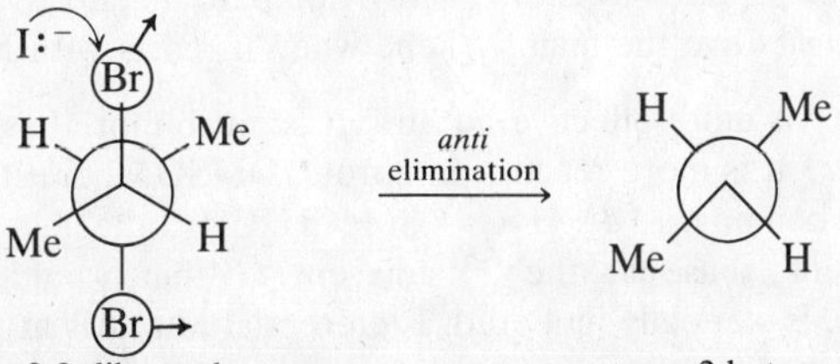

meso-2,3-dibromobutane   *trans*-2-butene

(ii)

(S,S)-2,3-dibromobutane   *cis*-2-butene

The initially formed IBr reacts with more I^- forming I_2 and a second Br^-. This last reaction is an S_N2-like displacement by I^- on I of IBr.

(*b*) In each diastereomer, the Br's are *trans*. However, in **A** the Br's are *trans-axial* and capable of E2 elimination, but in **B** the Br's are both equatorial and incapable of being eliminated. The presence of the *t*-Bu, that demands an equatorial position, freezes the ring conformation, preventing flipping of the BR's to axial positions from which E2 could occur.

8.115 (*a*) Outline the steps in the E1 reaction of Me_3CBr in EtOH with low $[EtO^-]$. (*b*) What other product will be formed? (*c*) Compare the rates of formation of the two products.

▰ (*a*) *Step 1.*

$$Me_3C\!-\!Br \xrightarrow[\text{(ionization)}]{\text{slow}} Me_3C^+ + Br^- \text{ (same as } S_N1)$$

t-Butyl
carbocation

The ionization is solvent-assisted with protic solvents.

Step 2. Base removes H^+ from the adjacent C leaving the bonding e^- pair to form the π bond:

$$EtO^- + H_2C\!-\!\overset{+}{C}Me_2 \xrightarrow{\text{fast}} H_2C=CMe_2 + EtOH$$
$$\overset{|}{H}$$

(*b*) The competitive S_N1 reaction of Me_3C^+ with the nucleophilic solvent EtOH gives ethyl *t*-butyl ether, Me_3COEt. In fact, the S_N1 route dominates the reaction of the substrate.

(*c*) Since the slow dissociation step is common to both, the rates are the same; rate $= k_1[Me_3CBr]$.

8.116 (*a*) Why do even 3° alkyl halides rarely undergo E1 reactions? (*b*) How can the E1 reaction be promoted? (*c*) Account for the different yields of the same two products when $CH_3CHBrCH_3$ reacts with (i) EtO^-Na^+/EtOH and (ii) EtOH.

▰ (*a*) 3° RX's react by E1 only when the base is weak or has a very low concentration. As the base gets stronger or more concentrated, the E2 mechanism prevails. If the base is too weak or too dilute, either R^+ reacts with the nucleophilic solvent to give the S_N1 product or, in nonpolar solvents, RX fails to react.

(*b*) Electrophilic catalysis, e.g., with Ag^+, aids in the ionization of $C\!-\!X$. Even here the counter anion (An^-) of Ag^+ can bond to R^+ to give R-An or can act as a base and remove the β-H to give the alkene. Ideally, An^- should be basic, yet a poor nucleophile. $AlCl_3$ in benzene avoids this problem:

$$Me_2CClCH_3 \xrightarrow{AlCl_3} Me_2C=CH_2 + HCl$$

(*c*) (i) EtO^- is a strong base and with 2° RX's the E2 product, $CH_3CH=CH_2$ predominates over the S_N2 product, $CH_3CH(OEt)CH_3$. (ii) EtOH is weakly basic but nucleophilic, and S_N1 is favored to give mainly $CH_3CH(OEt)CH_3$.

8.117 $Me_3CO^-K^+$ is used as a base in E2 reactions. (*a*) How does it compare in effectiveness with $EtNH_2$? (*b*) In what way may it be superior to EtO^-? (*c*) Compare its effectiveness in the solvents dimethylsulfoxide (DMSO) and Me_3COH. (*d*) Give the major alkene when it reacts with $Me_2CClCH_2CH_3$.

▰ (*a*) Me_3CO^- is more effective because it is much more basic. (*b*) Its large size precludes the competitive S_N2 reaction. (*c*) It is more reactive in aprotic DMSO where it is not solvated. Its effectiveness in Me_3COH is reduced by H—bonding. (*d*) $H_2C=CMeCH_2CH_3$, the less substituted *Hofmann* product forms, because attack by the bulky base at the 2° adjacent H that would give the more substituted Sayzteff product, $Me_2C=CHCH_3$, is sterically hindered. Preferential attack is at the less hindered 1° H.

8.118 Compare E1 and E2 reactions of RX with respect to the following mechanistic factors: steps (number and kind); TS; kinetics; driving force, stereospecificity; effect of R; rearrangements; the H/D isotope effect; competing reactions; orientation.

▮ See Table 8-3.

TABLE 8-3

		E1	E2
(a)	Steps	1. $H-\overset{\|}{\underset{\|}{C}}-\overset{\|}{\underset{\|}{C}}-X \longrightarrow H-\overset{\|}{\underset{\|}{C}}-\overset{\|}{\underset{\|}{C}}{}^{+}+X^{-}$ 2. $H-\overset{\|}{\underset{\|}{C}}-\overset{\|}{\underset{\|}{C}}{}^{+} \xrightarrow{-H^{+}} \diagdown C=C \diagup$	$B:^{-}+H-\overset{\|}{\underset{\|}{C}}-\overset{\|}{\underset{\|}{C}}-X \longrightarrow B:H + \diagdown C=C\diagup + :X^{-}$
(b)	Transition state	1. $H-\overset{\|}{\underset{\|}{C}}-\overset{\|}{\underset{\|}{C}}{}^{\delta+}---X^{\delta-}----HS:$ 2. $HS:{}^{\delta+}---H---\diagdown C \cdots C {}^{\delta+}\diagup$	$B:{}^{\delta-}--H--\diagup C \cdots C \diagdown --X^{\delta-}---HS:$
(c)	Kinetics	First-order, unimolecular Rate $= k_1[RX]$; rate of ionization	Second-order, bimolecular Rate $= k_2[RX][:B^{-}]$
(d)	Driving force	Ionization of R—X	Attack by $B:^{-}$ on H
(e)	Stereospecificity	Nonstereospecific	*anti* elimination but *syn* if *anti* not possible. (Both coplanar)
(f)	Effect of R	Stability of R^{+}; $3° > 2° > 1°$ $3° > 2° > 1°$ RX	Alkene stability (Saytzeff Rule)
(g)	Rearrangement	Common	None, except for allylic (S_N2')
(h)	H/D isotope effect	None	Observed
(i)	Competing reaction	S_N1, S_N2	S_N2
(j)	Regioselectivity	Saytzeff	Usually Saytzeff, but Hofmann with bulky bases (Me_3CO^{-})

8.119 Point out how the following factors favor E1 and E2 reactions with RX: (a) nature of R, (b) base, (c) nature of X, and (d) catalyst.

▮ See Table 8-4.

TABLE 8-4

		Favors E1	**Favors E2**
(a)	Alkyl group	$3° > 2° > 1°$	$3° > 2° > 1°$
(b)	Base strength	Weak	Strong
(c)	Leaving group	Weak base $I^{-} > Br^{-} > Cl^{-} > F^{-}$	Weak base $I^{-} > Br^{-} > Cl^{-} > F^{-}$
(d)	Catalysis	$Ag^{+}, AlCl_3$	Phase transfer (see Problem 8.131)

8.120 Compare how (a) competing E2 and S_N2 reactions ($RX + Nu^{-}$) are favored by the following factors: structure of R and of X, reagent, solvent; and (b) competing E2 and S_N1 reactions are favored by the following factors: structure of R and X, properties of base.

▮ (a) and (b) See Table 8-5

TABLE 8-5

(a)		Favors E2	Favors S_N2
(1)	Alkyl group	$3° > 2° > 1°$	$1° > 2° > 3°$
(2)	Leaving group	$I^- > Br^- > Cl^- > F^-$	$I^- > Br^- > Cl^- > F^-$
(3)	Reagent	Strong, bulky Brönsted base	Strong nucleophile
(4)	Solvent		
	(i) Low polarity	Favored	Slightly favored
	(ii) Protic polar	Disfavored	Disfavored
	(iii) Aprotic polar	Strongly favored	Favored
	(iv) Phase transfer	Strongly favored	Favored
(b)		Favors E2	Favors S_N1
(1)	R group	$3° > 2° > 1°$	$3° > 2° > 1°$
(2)	X	$I^- > Br^- > Cl^- > F^-$	$I^- > Br^- > Cl^- > F^-$
(3)	Base		
	Strength	Strong	Very weak
	Concentration	High	Low

SYNTHESES AND ANALYSIS

8.121 From propane synthesize (*a*) $CH_3CH_2CH_2F$ without using AgF [Problem 8.25(*b*)], (*b*) cyclopropane, and (*c*) 2,3-dimethylbutane. Do not repeat a prior synthesis.

◢ (*a*) $CH_3CH_2CH_3 \xrightarrow[\Delta]{Cl_2} \{CH_3CH_2CH_2Cl + CH_3CHClCH_3\} \xrightarrow{\text{alc. KOH}} CH_3CH = CH_2 \xrightarrow[\text{ROOR}]{HBr,}$

$CH_3CH_2CH_2Br \xrightarrow{\text{LiF/DMF, a polar aprotic solvent}} CH_3CH_2CH_2F$

(*b*) $CH_3CH = CH_2 \xrightarrow{\text{NBS}} BrCH_2CH = CH_2 \xrightarrow[\text{ROOR}]{HBr} BrCH_2CH_2CH_2Br \xrightarrow{\text{Mg}}$ cyclopropane

(*c*) $CH_3CH = CH_2 \xrightarrow{HBr} CH_3CHBrCH_3$ (**A**) $\xrightarrow[\text{2. CuI}]{\text{1. Li}} [(CH_3)_2CH]_2CuLi \xrightarrow{+A} (CH_3)_2CHCH(CH_3)_2$

8.122 From bromoethane, (**B**), prepare 1-butene.

◢ $CH_3CH_2Br \xrightarrow[\text{2. Cu}]{\text{1. Li}} (CH_3CH_2)_2CuLi \xrightarrow{\text{B}} CH_3CH_2CH_2CH_3 \xrightarrow{Cl_2, h\nu}$

$(CH_3CH_2CH_2CH_2Cl + CH_3CH_2CHClCH_3) \xrightarrow{Me_3CO^-K^+} CH_3CH_2CH = CH_2$

8.123 From $CH_3CHOHCH_2CH_3$ prepare (*a*) $ICH_2CH_2CH_2CH_2I$, (*b*) $CH_3CH_2CH_2CH_2SMe$, and (*c*) $H_2CBrCHBrCHBrCH_3$. (How many stereoisomers are formed?)

◢ (*a*) $CH_3CHOHCH_2CH_3 \xrightarrow{H_2SO_4} CH_3CH = CHCH_3$ (**D**) $\xrightarrow{\text{2NBS}} BrCH_2CH = CHCH_2Br^* \xrightarrow{2I^-}$

$ICH_2CH = CHCH_2I \xrightarrow{H_2NNH_2/O_2} ICH_2CH_2CH_2CH_2I^{**}$

*Little or no *gem*-dibromide is formed because Br deactivates —C̲HBr.

**Allylic halides undergo hydrogenolysis (C—X → C—H) with H_2/Pd.

(*b*) (**D**) $\xrightarrow{\text{NBS}} BrCH_2CH = CHCH_3 \xrightarrow[-HBr]{\text{MeSH}} CH_3CH = CHCH_2SMe \xrightarrow{H_2NNH_2/O_2}$

$CH_3CH_2CH_2CH_2SMe^{***}$

***C—S bonds undergo catalytic hydrogenolysis.

(*c*) $CH_3CHOHCH_2CH_3 \xrightarrow{HBr} CH_3CHBrCH_2CH_3 \xrightarrow{Me_3CO^-K^+} H_2C = CHCH_2CH_3 \xrightarrow{\text{NBS}}$

$H_2C = CHCHBrCH_3 \xrightarrow{Br_2} H_2CBrCHBrCHBrCH_3(\textbf{E})$

E has two different stereocenters and exists as two racemates.

8.124 (*a*) From *E*-2-butene prepare $CH_3CHBrCHBrCH_2CH_2CHBrCHBrCH_3$ (**G**). (*b*) Which diastereoisomers of **G** are products of this synthesis? (*c*) Which diastereomers of **G** are obtained if *Z*-2-butene is used? To simplify drawing all the structures, describe them in terms of *R/S* designations of the stereocenters.

(a) To go from a 4-carbon to a 8-carbon compound requires a coupling of alkyl halide.

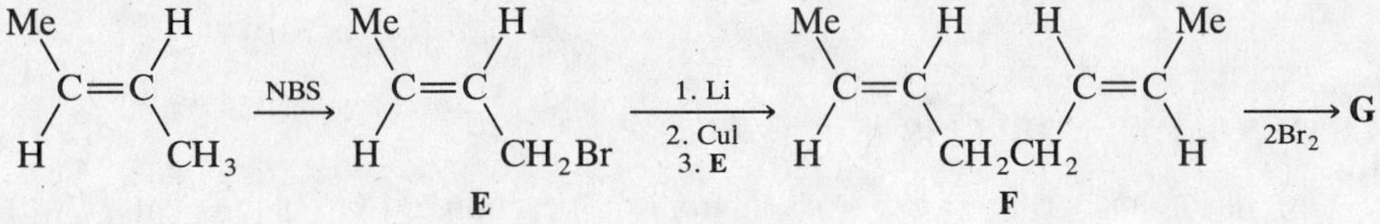

Br$_2$ adds *anti* to each double bond in **F**, engendering four stereocenters. Going from left to right, to get the diastereomer shown, the Br's add from top, bottom, bottom, top giving the *meso* (SRSR) isomer. Adding the Br's in the sequence bottom, top, top, bottom, gives the same *meso* isomer. Adding the Br's in the sequence top, bottom, top, bottom gives an enantiomer (SRRS), while the sequence bottom, top, bottom, top gives the mirror image (*RSSR*). The products are a *meso* and a racemate.

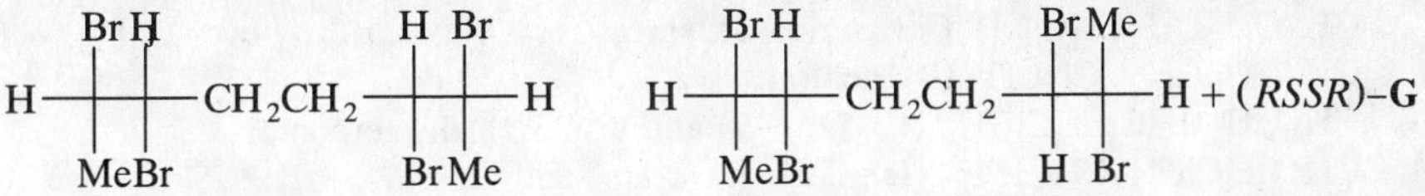

(c) The products from *cis*-2-butene are a *meso* (*RRSS*) and a racemate (*RRRR*) and (*SSSS*).

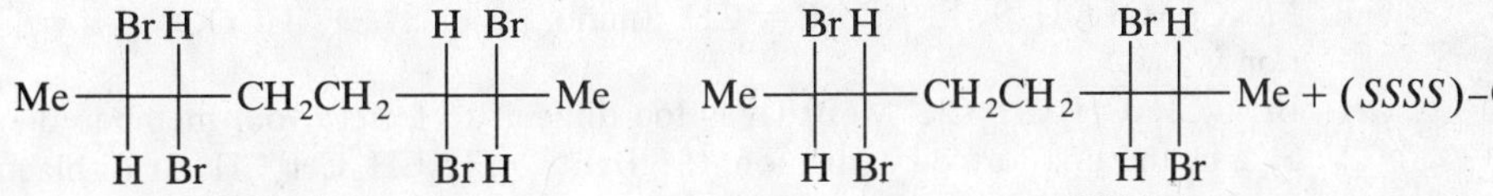

8.125 From cyclohexyl-OH prepare (a) 1,2,3-trideutereocyclohexane (with at least one pair of adjacent *cis* D's) and

(b) (**A**). Do not repeat syntheses.

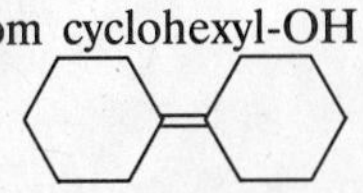

(b)

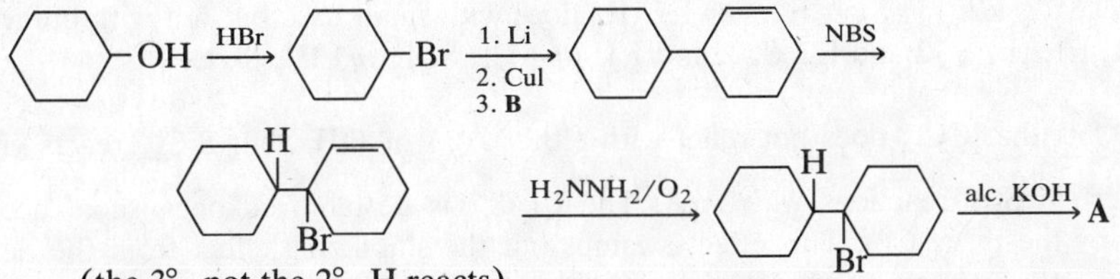

(the 3°, not the 2°, H reacts)

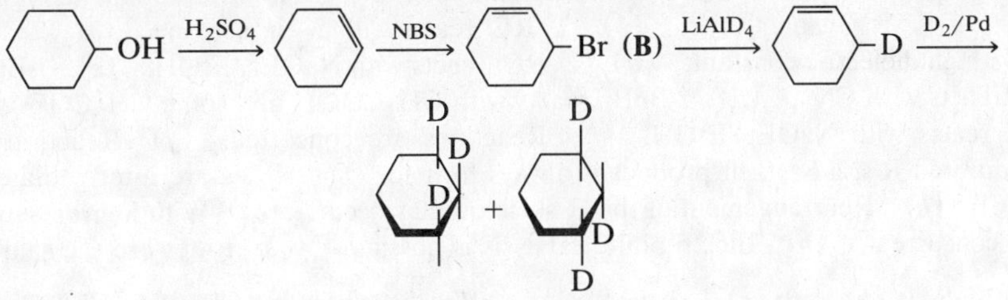

8.126 (a) Give simple tests to distinguish among hexane, CH$_3$CH=CHCl, CH$_3$CH$_2$CH$_2$Cl, and CH$_2$=CHCH$_2$Cl. (b) Distinguish among RCl, RBr, and RI.

(a) CH$_2$=CHCH$_2$Cl is an allylic chloride that reacts rapidly with AgNO$_3$ in the cold to give a white precipitate of AgCl, insoluble in HNO$_3$. CH$_3$CH$_2$CH$_2$Cl gives the same precipitate but after being warmed, because it is a less reactive alkyl chloride. CH$_3$CH=CHCl, a vinyl chloride, is inert even when heated, as is hexane which lacks Cl. The alkane and vinyl halide are distinguished by adding Br$_2$ in CCl$_4$ to each; the red-brown Br$_2$ color persists in (does not react with) the alkane, but disappears in (reacts with) the alkene.

(b) They all form an insoluble silver halide but with distinguishable properties. AgCl is white, and dissolves in conc. NH$_3$; AgBr is pale yellow; and AgI is deep yellow. To better distinguish between RBr and RI, they are fused with Na, and the X$^-$'s thereby formed are oxidized with H$_2$O$_2$ to the corresponding X_2's. I_2 is unequivocally detected by producing a deep purple color when a few drops of starch solution is added.

SUPPLEMENTARY PROBLEMS

8.127 Give all the monochlorinated products from the reaction of (S)-2-chloropentane with Cl_2 and light, and supply their (RS) identity.

▰ There are five dichlorinated pentanes:
1. $CH_3CH_2CH_2CHClCH_2Cl$ (**A**); now R, since CH_2Cl has priority over C_3H_7.
2. $CH_3CH_2CH_2CCl_2CH_3$ (**B**); achiral.
3. $CH_3CH_2CHClCHClCH_3$ (**C**); $(2S,3S)$ and $(2S,3R)$ (diastereomers).
4. $CH_3CHClCH_2CHClCH_3$ (**D**); $(2S,4R)$, *meso*, and $(2S,4S)$.
5. $CH_2ClCH_2CH_2CHClCH_3$ (**E**); (S).

8.128 Complete, where possible, the following reactions and point out the mechanisms as S_N2, S_N1, E2, E1, or none of these: (*a*) $CH_3CH_2CH_2Br + LiAlD_4$, (*b*) $Me_3CBr + HCOOH$, (*c*) $Me_3CBr + HCOOH$ with small amount of $HCOO^-$, (*d*) $BrCH_2CH_2CH_2CH_2Br$ with Mg (ether), (*e*) $I^- + BrCH_2CH_2CH_2Br$, (*f*) $CH_3CH_2Br + :PMe_3$, (*g*) $Me_2C=CHCl + Na^+ :NH_2^-$.

▰ (*a*) $CH_3CH_2CH_2D$, S_N2. ($LiAlD_4$ is a source of $D:^-$, as $LiAlH_4$ is a source of $H:^-$.)
  (*b*) $Me_3C-OCOH$, a formate ester, S_N1.
  (*c*) $Me_3C-OCOH$, S_N1, $+ Me_2C=CH_2$ (minor product) E1. ($HCOO^-$ is a weak base and its concentration is low.)
  (*d*) $BrMgCH_2CH_2CH_2CH_2MgBr$ (It is too difficult to form a four-membered ring by an intramolecular S_N2 by the first formed carbanion, $(MgBr)^+ {}^- :CH_2CH_2CH_2CH_2Br$ displacing Br^-.)
  (*e*) Cyclopropane, intramolecular S_N2. (The reacting carbanion, $^-:CH_2CH_2CH_2Br$, is engendered by an S_N2-type displacement by I^- on Br. Some $ICH_2CH_2CH_2I$ may also form by typical S_N2.)
  (*f*) $CH_3CH_2-\overset{+}{P}Me_3$ Br^- (a phosphonium salt), S_N2.
  (*g*) No reaction.

8.129 Give the symbol S_N1, S_N2, E1, E2 most consistent with each of the following statements. More than one symbol may be used. (*a*) MeX cannot react. (*b*) 2° RCl reacts with I^- in acetone. (*c*) 2° RCl reacts in formic acid that has a high dielectric constant. (*d*) 2° RCl reacts with NaOEt/EtOH. (*e*) *t*-BuBr reacts in EtOH. (*f*) *t*-BuBr reacts with CN^-. (*g*) *t*-BuBr reacts with CH_3COOH and some $CH_3COO^-Na^+$. (*h*) Unhindered 1° RX reacts with NaOEt/EtOH. (*i*) Reactions are concerted. (*j*) Reactions are stereospecific. (*k*) With saturated R's, a Saytzeff product is always formed. (*l*) R^+'s are intermediates. (*m*) RI reacts faster than RCl. (*n*) Rearrangement of the R skeleton may occur. (*o*) With a given substrate some pairs of these may be concurrent. (*p*) Electrophilic catalysis is possible. (*q*) Rates are the same.

▰ (*a*) E1, E2, S_N1; (*b*) S_N2; (*c*) S_N1; (*d*) E2, S_N2; (*e*) S_N1, very little E1; (*f*) E2; (*g*) S_N1, E1; (*h*) mainly S_N2, little E2; (*i*) S_N2, E2; (*j*) S_N2, E2; (*k*) E1 (E2 does with small base but not with bulky base); (*l*) E1, S_N1; (*m*) all; (*n*) S_N1, E1; (*o*) S_N2 and E2, S_N2 and E1; (*p*) E1, S_N1; (*q*) E1, S_N1.

8.130 Account for the fact that CCl_4 does not react with either Ag^+ or OH^- but $SiCl_4$ reacts vigorously with H_2O.

▰ CCl_4 is inert in S_N1 reactions with Ag^+. The Cl_3C^+ is destabilized because of accumulative electron-withdrawal by the three Cl's. This effect swamps out the stabilizing effect from the delocalization of e^-'s from Cl to C^+ through extended π overlap. One reason for this is the disparity of the size of the $2p$ AO of C and the $3p$ AO of Cl. CCl_4 is also inert by S_N2 because the three remaining Cl's on C sterically hinder the approach of OH^-. Because Si, unlike C, has available empty d AO's, it can rapidly undergo the addition-elimination mechanism, whereby H_2O adds to give the unstable intermediate, $Cl_4Si^- -\overset{+}{O}H_2$, that then loses HCl. Stepwise additions of H_2O eventually leads to replacement of the four Cl's by OH's

$$SiCl_4 + 4H_2O \longrightarrow Si(OH)_4 \text{ (or } SiO_2(H_2O)_x) + 4HCl \text{ (Forms a thick moist white cloud.)}$$
$$\text{silicic acid}$$

8.131 (*a*) How do small amounts of *phase-transfer catalysts*, such as quarternary ammonium salts $R_4N^+X^-$, accelerate reactions between water-insoluble organic substrates such as alkyl halides and water-soluble inorganic salts, such as $M^+:Nu^-$? (*b*) Illustrate their application by writing equations for the reaction between NaCN and n-$C_8H_{17}Cl$ with the catalyst n-$Bu_4N^+Cl^-$.

▌ (*a*) The cation of the phase transfer catalysts Q^+X^- ($Q^+ = R_4N^+$) is water soluble and slightly soluble in nonpolar solvents because of its nonpolar R groups. Q^+ transfers between the two immiscible layers taking $:Nu^-$ from H_2O as $Q^+:Nu^-$ into the nonpolar solvent, where it reacts rapidly with RX because it does not suffer from solvation. The cation then returns to the polar solvent with the leaving group $:L^-$ as the salt $Q^+:L^-$. This shuttling back and forth continues until the reaction is complete.

(*b*) In water: $\quad\quad\quad Na^+:CN^- + n\text{-}Bu_4N^+Cl^- \longrightarrow n\text{-}Bu_4N^+:CN^- + Na^+Cl^-$

In nonpolar solvent: $n\text{-}C_8H_{17}Cl + n\text{-}Bu_4N^+:CN^- \longrightarrow n\text{-}C_8H_{17}CN + n\text{-}Bu_4N^+Cl^-$.

$n\text{-}Bu_4N^+Cl^-$ goes back into H_2O and the two steps repeat.

8.132 (*a*) Outline a plausible mechanism for a nucleophilic displacement on a vinyl halide by the two step addition-elimination mechanism (Problem 8.48). (*b*) What structural features must the vinyl compound have to make this mechanism viable? Give an example.

▌ (*a*)

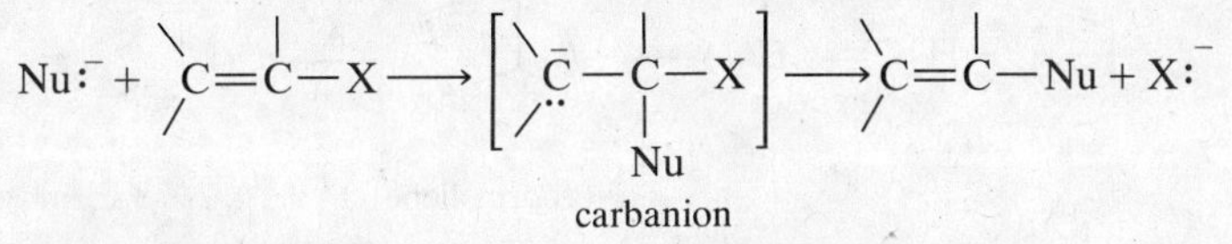

(*b*) This reaction cannot take place unless the carbanion is stabilized by having electron-withdrawing groups on the C^-. For example, $F_2C{=}CHBr$ could react by this route because of the electron-withdrawing F's.

8.133 Suggest a three-step mechanism for formation of LiR from RX.

▌ The reaction occurs on the metal surface, which is true for most metal reactants. Since $Li\cdot$ is a radical we should expect to find radical intermediates.

Step 1. $\quad R{-}X: + Li\cdot \longrightarrow [R{-}X:]^{\bar{\cdot}} + Li^+$
$\quad\quad\quad\quad\quad\quad\quad\quad$ a radical anion

Step 2. $\quad [R{-}X:]^{\bar{\cdot}} \longrightarrow R\cdot + X:^-$

Step 3. $\quad R\cdot + Li\cdot \longrightarrow R:Li$

Net equation:

$$RX + 2Li \longrightarrow RLi + Li^+X^-$$

The extra e^- of the radical anion occupies a σ^*MO^*.

8.134 Prepare (*S*)-2-bromobutane from (*S*)-2-chlorobutane.

▌ Cl cannot be replaced by Br in one step. Two S_N2 steps are required, each proceeding with inversion, resulting in overall retention.

$$(S)\text{-}CH_3CHClCH_2CH_3 \xrightarrow{\text{aq. } OH^-} (R)\text{-}CH_3CHOHCH_2CH_3 \xrightarrow{\text{TsCl}} (R)\text{-}CH_3CH(OTs)CH_2CH_3$$

$$\xrightarrow{Br^-} (S)\text{-}CH_3CHBrCH_2CH_3$$

8.135 (*a*) Give a preparation of hexachlorocyclopentadiene (**A**) from cyclopentane. (*b*) From **A**, ethylene and cyclopentadiene, prepare the insecticides (i) Chlordane (**B**) and (ii) Aldrin (**C**).

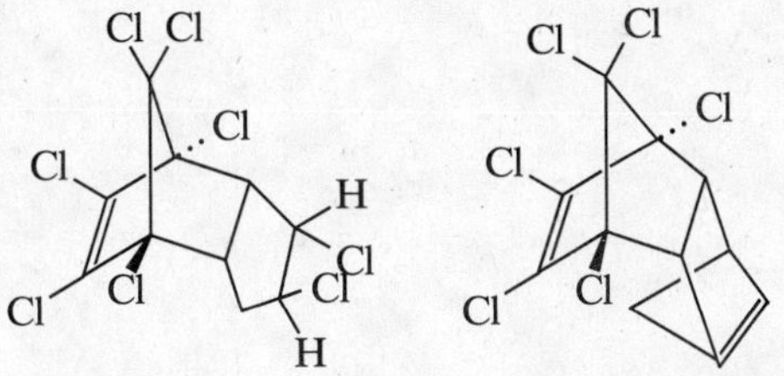

B   **C**

▌ (*a*) Cyclopentane $\xrightarrow{\text{Cl}_2,\ \text{light}}$ $\xrightarrow[-2\text{Cl}_2]{\text{Zn or } I^-}$

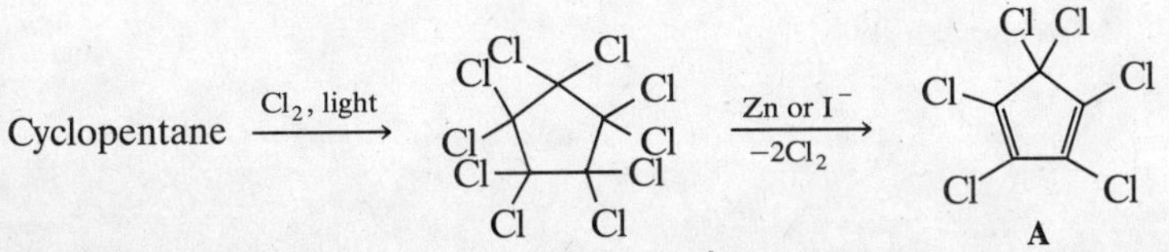

A

(*b*) **B** and **C** are prepared using Diels–Alder reactions.

(i)

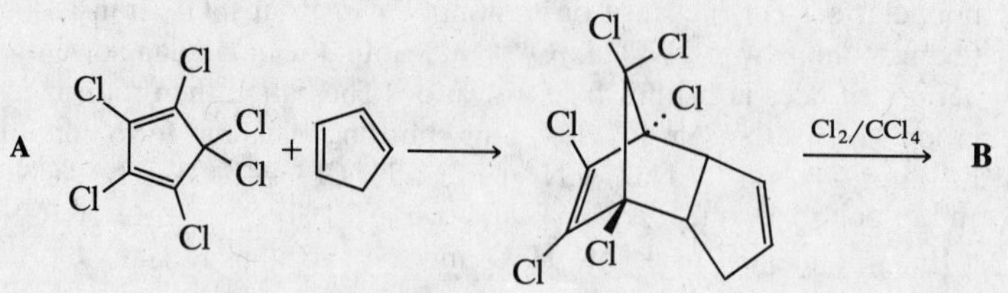

(ii)

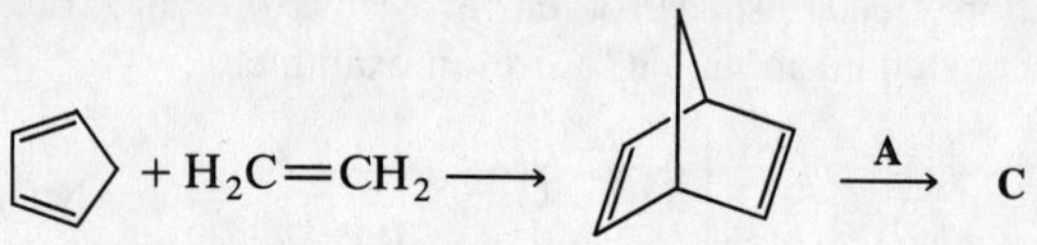

Norbornadiene

C

CHAPTER 9
Alkynes, Dienes, and Orbital Symmetry

STRUCTURE OF ALKYNES

9.1 Give (*a*) the general formula and (*b*) the degree (index or element) of unsaturation for an alkyne.

▰ (*a*) C_nH_{2n-2} and (*b*) 2°.

9.2 (*a*) What functional group is typical of alkynes? (*b*) Give the suffix used in the IUPAC system to name an alkyne.

▰ (*a*) A triple bond between C's, $-C\equiv C-$, as in $R-C\equiv C-R$. (*b*) *-yne*.

9.3 Give the kinds of compounds that have the same general formula as alkynes.

▰ Dienes, cycloalkenes, and bicyclics.

9.4 Give an example of each type of isomer listed in Problem 9.3 for C_4H_6 and name each.

▰

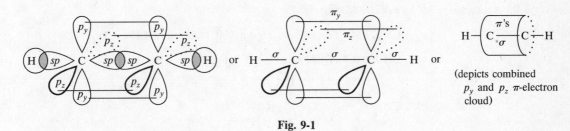

$$H_2C=CHCH=CH_2 \qquad \begin{matrix} HC-CH_2 \\ \| \quad | \\ HC-CH_2 \end{matrix} \qquad \begin{matrix} H_2C-CH \\ | / | \\ HC-CH_2 \end{matrix} \qquad H_3CC\equiv CCH_3$$

two C=C's	C=C and ring	two rings	C≡C
1,3-Butadiene	Cyclobutene	Bicyclobutane	2-Butyne

9.5 Use the hybrid orbital number rule (Problem 2.40) to determine the kind of HO's used by the triply-bonded alkyne C's.

▰ Each C has two σ bonds and no unshared pairs, and uses *sp* HO's, leaving two *p*'s on each C.

9.6 Give the relative bond lengths and bond strengths of $-C\equiv C-$ and $>C=C<$ and rationalize your answer.

▰ The triple bond is shorter and stronger than the double bond. The C atoms of C≡C are shielded by six e^-'s (from three bonds), whereas the C's of C=C are shielded by four e^-'s (from two bonds). With more shielding e^-'s present, the triply-bonded C's can get closer to each other (shorter bond length) to give more orbital overlap (stronger bond).

9.7 Draw a model for the structure of acetylene (ethyne), $H-C\equiv C-H$, showing the overlapping orbitals.

▰ See Fig. 9.1.

Fig. 9-1

9.8 Explain how the orbital picture of $-C\equiv C-$ accounts for the absence of geometric isomers in $CH_3C\equiv CCH_2CH_3$.

▰ The *sp* HO's are linear, ruling out *cis-trans* stereoisomers in which substituents must be on different sides of the multiple bond.

9.9 Compare the C—H bond lengths and bond dissociation enthalpies of an alkyne, alkene, and alkane.

▮ As a rule, "the more s character in the HO used by an atom, the closer are the bonding e^-'s to the atom, and the shorter and stronger is any of its σ bonds." The decreasing order of C—H bond lengths is

$$\underset{sp^3}{-C-H} \quad > \quad \underset{sp^2}{=C-H} \quad > \quad \underset{sp}{\equiv C-H}$$

The decreasing order of bond enthalpies is

$$\underset{sp}{\equiv C-H} \quad > \quad \underset{sp^2}{=C-H} \quad > \quad \underset{sp^3}{-C-H}$$

9.10 (*a*) Explain why cyclohexyne does not exist. (*b*) What is the smallest size ring that can accommodate a triple bond?

▮ (*a*) The linear structural unit —C—C≡C—C— cannot be bridged with only two C's. (*b*) This unit can be bridged with four C's; hence, cyclooctyne is the simplest cycloalkyne.

9.11 Why has 1-butyne a larger dipole moment (0.80 D) than 1-butene (0.30 D)?

▮ A $C-C_{sp}$ bond is more polarized than a $C-C_{sp^2}$ bond because the C with more s character is more electronegative.

9.12 Compare the physical properties of alkanes, alkenes, and alkynes.

▮ They all have similar properties. They are nonpolar and have very low water solubility but high solubility in nonpolar solvents. Alkynes are slightly more soluble in water because they are somewhat more polar (see Problem 9.11). They go from gases to liquids to solids with increasing molecular weights. In fact, there is little difference in the boiling points of these hydrocarbons with similar carbon skeletons.

9.13 The enthalpy of formation of acetylene (ΔH_f^0) is +54.3 kcal/mol. (*a*) What might happen to acetylene when it is stored? (*b*) How is acetylene stored in commercial cylinders, e.g., when needed for an oxyacetylene torch?

▮ (*a*) The positive value signals that acetylene is thermodynamically unstable and is readily (explosively) converted to its elements.

$$C_2H_2(g) \longrightarrow 2C(s) + H_2(g), \qquad \Delta H^0 = -54.3 \text{ kcal/mol}$$

(*b*) Since the liquid is also unstable, the cylinders contain pumice saturated with acetone which adsorbs acetylene. Unlike other alkynes, C_2H_2 can be dissolved in water to give a 0.5 M solution. When dissolved or adsorbed, acetylene is stable.

NOMENCLATURE OF ALKYNES

9.14 Name the structures below by the IUPAC system:

(*a*) $CH_3C\equiv CCH_3$ (*d*) $HC\equiv C-CH_2CH=CH_2$

(*b*) $CH_3C\equiv CCH_2CH_3$ (*e*) $HC\equiv C-CH_2CH_2Cl$

(*c*)

$$CH_3 - \underset{\underset{H}{|}}{\overset{\overset{CH_3}{|}}{C}} - C\equiv C - \underset{\underset{CH_3}{|}}{\overset{\overset{CH_3}{|}}{C}} - CH_3$$

▮ (*a*) 2-Butyne (*d*) 1-Penten-4-yne

(*b*) 2-Pentyne C=C has priority over C≡C and gets the smaller number.

(*c*) 2,2,5-Trimethyl-3-hexyne (*e*) 4-Chloro-1-butyne

9.15 Give the structural formulas for each of the following compounds: (*a*) 1,3-butadiyne, (*b*) 4-methyl-1-nitro-2-pentyne, (*c*) (*E*)-3-penten-1-yne (not 2-penten-4-yne; numbers as low as possible are given to double and triple bonds although this may give the yne a lower number than the ene.), (*d*) (*Z*)-5-hepten-1,3-diyne.

$\blacksquare$ (*a*) $HC\equiv C-C\equiv CH$ (*b*) $(NO_2)CH_2C\equiv CCH(CH_3)_2$ (*c*) $\underset{H}{\overset{CH_3}{}}C=C\underset{C\equiv CH}{\overset{H}{}}$ and

(*d*) $\underset{H}{\overset{CH_3}{}}C=C\underset{H}{\overset{C\equiv C-C\equiv CH}{}}$

9.16   Name the compounds in (*a*) to (*d*) of Problem 9.14 and (*e*) $H_2C=CHC\equiv CH$ as derivatives of acetylene.

    $\blacksquare$ Name the alkyl groups attached to $C\equiv C$ in alphabetical order as one word, ending with acetylene. (*a*) Dimethylacetylene, (*b*) ethylmethylacetylene, (*c*) *t*-butylisopropylacetylene, (*d*) allylacetylene, (*e*) vinylacetylene.

9.17   Name the following radicals: (*a*) $-C\equiv CH$, (*b*) $-CH_2C\equiv CH$, (*c*) $-C\equiv CCH_3$, and (*d*) $-C\equiv CCH_2CH_3$.

    $\blacksquare$ (*a*) Ethynyl, (*b*) propargyl or 2-propynyl, (*c*) 1-propynyl, and (*d*) 1-butynyl.

9.18   (*a*) Give the structural formulas for the seven alkynes of the formula C_6H_{10}. (*b*) Give the IUPAC and derived name for each isomer. (*c*). Which isomers in (*a*) are terminal alkynes?

    $\blacksquare$ (*a*)   First insert the triple bond into different positions of the six-carbon chain:

$$HC\equiv CCH_2CH_2CH_2CH_3 \ (\mathbf{A}), \quad H_3CC\equiv CCH_2CH_2CH_3 \ (\mathbf{B}), \quad CH_3CH_2C\equiv CCH_2CH_3 \ (\mathbf{C})$$

Then insert the triple bond into the two possible methyl-branched chains, noting that the triple bond cannot be on a branched C:

$$(CH_3)_2CHC\equiv CCH_3 \ (\mathbf{D}), \quad (CH_3)_2CHCH_2C\equiv CH \ (\mathbf{E}), \quad CH_3CH_2CH(CH_3)C\equiv CH \ (\mathbf{F})$$

Finally, work with a dimethyl branched chain:

$$(CH_3)_3CC\equiv CH \ (\mathbf{G})$$

    (*b*)   (**A**) 1-Hexyne, butylacetylene; (**B**) 2-hexyne, methylpropylacetylene; (**C**) 3-hexyne, diethylacetylene; (**D**) 4-methyl-2-pentyne, methylisopropylacetylene; (**E**) 4-methyl-1-pentyne, isobutylacetylene; (**F**) 3-methyl-1-pentyne, *sec*-butylacetylene; and (**G**) 3,3-dimethyl-1-butyne, *tert*-butylacetylene.

    (*c*)   Terminal alkynes have the triple bond at the end of a carbon chain; **A, E, F,** and **G**. The other alkynes are called *internal* alkynes.

9.19   Write the Fischer projection formulas and give the *R/S* designation for the enantiomers of all chiral isomers in Problem 9.18

    $\blacksquare$ Only isomer **F** is chiral.

$$CH_3CH_2\overset{\displaystyle H}{\underset{\displaystyle CH_3}{-\!\!\!+\!\!\!-}}C\equiv CH \qquad HC\equiv C\overset{\displaystyle H}{\underset{\displaystyle CH_3}{-\!\!\!+\!\!\!-}}CH_2CH_3$$

$$S \qquad\qquad\qquad\qquad R$$

9.20   Write the structural formula for an alkyne hydrocarbon having the fewest number of C's which has geometric isomers, and give the IUPAC name for both geometric isomers.

$$\blacksquare \qquad \underset{H}{\overset{HC\equiv C}{}}C=C\underset{H}{\overset{CH_3}{}} \qquad \underset{H}{\overset{HC\equiv C}{}}C=C\underset{CH_3}{\overset{H}{}}$$

          (*Z*)-3-Penten-1-yne   (*E*)-3-Penten-1-yne

9.21   Write the structural formula for a cyclic alkyne hydrocarbon with the fewest number of C's which has geometric isomers. Give only one enantiomer. Name the geometric isomers.

    $\blacksquare$ To keep the number of C's as few as possible, use a disubstituted cyclopropane ring. The substituents are ethynyl and methyl.

        cis-1-Ethynyl-2-methylcyclopropane   *trans*-1-Ethynyl-2-methylcyclopropane

9.22 Write the structural formulas for a cyclic alkyne hydrocarbon with the fewest number of C's which has two *meso* stereoisomers. Just give the structures of the *meso* stereoisomers. Name the compounds.

◢ Again use a cyclopropane ring which now must be trisubstituted with one ethynyl and two methyl groups in order to have planes of symmetry.

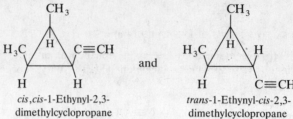

cis,cis-1-Ethynyl-2,3-   and   trans-1-Ethynyl-cis-2,3-
dimethylcyclopropane   dimethylcyclopropane

9.23 Give the IUPAC names for each of the following

(*a*) [cyclopentyl]—C≡CH,   (*b*) [cyclohexyl structure with CH₃] C≡CCH₃,

(*c*) [cyclobutyl]—C≡C—[cyclopropyl],   (*d*) [cyclohexadiene]—CH₂C≡CH

◢ (*a*) Cyclopentylethyne
(*b*) *cis*-1-Methyl-2-(1-propynyl)cyclohexane
(*c*) Cyclobutylcyclopropylethyne (note that numbers are not necessary.)
(*d*) 5-(2-Propynyl)-1,3-cyclohexediene

ACIDITY OF TERMINAL ALKYNES

9.24 (*a*) Give the equations for the reactions of propyne with (i) Na (in hexane), (ii) $Na^+NH_2^-$ (in liquid NH_3), (iii) $Ag(NH_3)_2^+OH^-$, and (iv) $Cu(NH_3)_2^+OH^-$. (*b*) On which chemical property of propyne do these reactions depend?

◢ (*a*) (i) $2CH_3C{\equiv}CH + 2Na \longrightarrow 2\,[CH_3C{\equiv}C{:}^-Na^+]$ (sodium propynide) $+ H_2$
an alkynide anion

(ii) $CH_3C{\equiv}CH + NaNH_2 \xrightarrow{\text{liq. } NH_3} CH_3C{\equiv}C{:}^-Na^+ + NH_3$

(iii) $CH_3C{\equiv}CH + Ag(NH_3)_2^+OH^- \longrightarrow CH_3C{\equiv}CAg(s) + 2NH_3 + H_2O$

(iv) $CH_3C{\equiv}CH + Cu(NH_3)_2^+OH^- \longrightarrow CH_3C{\equiv}CCu(s) + 2NH_3 + H_2O$

(*b*) The acidity of the terminal H of a terminal alkyne.

9.25 Give the products of each of the following acid-base reactions using the approximate pK_a values given in parentheses: H_2 (> 35), CH_4 (> 40), CH_3OH (17), C_2H_2 (25), HCN (9), CH_3CO_2H (5). Write NR if no reaction occurs.

(*a*) $HC{\equiv}CNa + CH_3OH$,   (*b*) $HC{\equiv}CH + CH_3Li$,   (*c*) $HC{\equiv}CH + NaH$,

(*d*) $HC{\equiv}CH + NaCN$,   (*e*) $HC{\equiv}CNa + CH_3CO_2H$

◢ Acid-base reactions always go from the stronger acids and bases to the weaker ones. Therefore acetylene will only react with bases that are converted to acids weaker than acetylene, and acetylide ion will only react with acids that are converted to bases weaker than acetylide ion. Thus,

(*a*) $HC{\equiv}CH + CH_3ONa$,   (*b*) $HC{\equiv}CLi + CH_4$,   (*c*) $HC{\equiv}CNa + H_2$,

(*d*) NR,   (*e*) $HC{\equiv}CH + CH_3CO_2Na$

9.26 Explain why the Grignard (or lithium organometallic) of $BrCH_2C{\equiv}CH$ cannot be prepared.

◢ Any Grignard formed would instantaneously react with the terminal acidic H.

$BrCH_2C{\equiv}CH + Mg \longrightarrow [BrMgCH_2C{\equiv}CH] \xrightarrow{BrCH_2C{\equiv}CH} CH_3C{\equiv}CH + BrCH_2C{\equiv}CMgBr$

9.27 Give the preparation of $CH_3C\equiv CMgBr$ without using $CH_3C\equiv CBr$.

$$CH_3C\equiv CH + RMgBr \longrightarrow CH_3C\equiv CMgBr + RH$$

9.28 Give a simple (test tube) reaction to distinguish 1-butyne from 2-butyne.

Addition of an alcoholic solution of $Ag(NH_3)_2^+$ (from $AgNO_3 + NH_3$) to the terminal alkyne, 1-butyne, gives a white precipitate of $CH_3CH_2C\equiv CAg$ [see (iii) of Problem 9.24]. 2-Butyne is an internal alkyne, has no acidic H, and does not react to give a precipitate.

9.29 (a) Describe how a mixture of 1-butyne and 2-butyne can be separated chemically into two pure components. (b) What precautions must be taken?

(a) Addition of $AgNO_3$ and NH_3 converts 1-butyne to the insoluble silver acetylide [see (iii) of Problem 9.24 and Problem 9.28] which is filtered, leaving the easily recoverable unreacted 2-butyne in solution. 1-Butyne is regenerated by treating its Ag acetylide with HCl.

$$CH_3CH_2C\equiv CAg + HCl \longrightarrow CH_3CH_2C\equiv CH + AgCl_{(s)}$$

(b) Dry heavy-metal acetylides are explosive—they must be handled only when moist.

9.30 List alkanes, alkenes, and terminal alkynes in order of decreasing acidity of their terminal $C-H$.

The order of decreasing acidities is: alkyne > alkene > alkane.

9.31 Account for the order of acidities in Problem 9.30.

This is an example of the principle "The more s character in the orbital used by the C bonded to the H, the more acidic is the H." In the conjugate base, the alkynide anion, the more s character in the HO containing the unshared pair, the less basic is the anion.

9.32 Are the orders of acidities in Problem 9.30 and bond enthalpies in Problem 9.9 compatible?

They are not related. Bond dissociation requires a homolytic cleavage, each bonded atom getting one e^-. Acidity requires a heterolytic cleavage, C getting both e^-'s, H ending up with none (it becomes H^+). Hence, it is possible for a $C-H$ bond to be the strongest, and the most acidic.

9.33 Write the products of the reaction of propynide ion, $Me-C\equiv C:^-$ with (a) H_2O, (b) CH_3OH, (c) NH_3 (liquid), (d) 1-hexene, and (e) hexane. Write NR if no reaction occurs.

(a) $Me-C\equiv CH + OH^-$, (b) $Me-C\equiv CH + CH_3O^-$, (c) $Me-C\equiv CH + H_2N:^-$, (d) and (e) NR.

9.34 Write equations for the preparation of (a) $HC\equiv CD$ and (b) $DC\equiv CD$.

(a) $HC\equiv CH \xrightarrow{NaNH_2} HC\equiv C^- \xrightarrow{D_2O} HC\equiv CD$

(b) $HC\equiv CH + 2Na \longrightarrow {}^-:C\equiv C:^- \xrightarrow{D_2O} DC\equiv CD$

9.35 Write an equation for the reaction of one mole of 1-butyne with two moles of a very strong base such as butyllithium.

Two moles of a very strong base, such as butyllithium (BuLi), convert an alkyne into a dianion by removal of the terminal H and a propargylic H.

$$CH_3CH_2C\equiv CH \xrightarrow[-2H^+]{2BuLi} CH_3\overset{..}{\overset{-}{C}}H-C\equiv C:^-$$

9.36 Account for the acidity of propargylic H's.

Extended π bonding (resonance) delocalizes the negative charge as shown:

$$\left[-\overset{..}{\overset{-}{C}}-C\equiv C- \longleftrightarrow -C=C=\overset{..}{\overset{-}{C}}- \right] \quad \text{or} \quad \left[-\overset{\delta^-}{C}\overline{=\!=\!=}C\overline{=\!=\!=}\overset{\delta^-}{C}- \right]^-$$

Furthermore, because of the sp character of the triply-bonded C, alkynyl groups ($-C\equiv CR$) are electron-withdrawing and, therefore, acid-strengthening.

PREPARATION

9.37 (*a*) Write the reactions for the industrial preparation of acetylene from CaO (lime), C (coke) and water, writing the Lewis structure for CaC$_2$. (*b*) Formulate the reaction of CaC$_2$ and water as a Brönsted acid-base reaction.

◢ (*a*) CaO + 3C $\longrightarrow$ CaC$_2$ + CO; CaC$_2$ + 2H$_2$O $\longrightarrow$ HC$\equiv$CH + Ca(OH)$_2$

(*b*) (:C$\equiv$C:)$^{2-}$ + 2H$_2$O $\longrightarrow$ HC$\equiv$CH + 2OH$^-$
  base$_1$ acid$_2$ acid$_1$ base$_2$

(Ca^{2+} is the spectator ion and is omitted.)

9.38 Give the major industrial synthesis of acetylene.

◢
$$2CH_4 \xrightarrow{1500°\,C} C_2H_2 + 3H_2$$

9.39 Explain why (*a*) the reaction in Problem 9.38 proceeds although it is highly endothermic and (*b*) the optimum time for this reaction is a mere 0.01 s.

◢ (*a*) There are twice as many moles of products as reactants. This causes a significant increase in entropy and at this high temperature the $T\Delta S$ term in the equation $\Delta G = \Delta H - T\Delta S$ predominates, making ΔG negative even though ΔH is positive. (*b*) If kept too long at this high temperature, C$_2$H$_2$ would decompose (see Problem 9.13).

9.40 Prepare propyne from propene.

◢   CH$_3$CH$=$CH$_2$ + Br$_2$ $\longrightarrow$ CH$_3$CHBrCH$_2$Br $\xrightarrow[-2HBr]{3NaNH_2}$ [CH$_3$C$\equiv$C$^-$] $\xrightarrow{+H^+}$ CH$_3$C$\equiv$CH
          a *vic*-dihalide

vic-Dihalides undergo a double dehydrohalogenation, requiring two moles of NaNH$_2$. The terminal alkyne is converted to the alkynyl anion as soon as it forms; thus three moles of the base are used in the overall reaction.

9.41 Account for the fact that a much stronger base (NaNH$_2$) is used in the double dehydrohalogenation in Problem 9.40 than in alkene formation from alkyl halides (alc. KOH).

◢ Double dehydrohalogenation of *vic*-dihalides occurs by two discrete steps:

R — CHBrCHBr — R $\xrightarrow{-HBr}$ R — CBr $=$ CH — R (a vinyl halide) $\xrightarrow{-HBr}$ R — C$\equiv$C — R

It is more difficult to dehydrohalogenate the intermediate vinyl bromide than an alkyl bromide.

9.42 Explain why CH$_3$CHBrCH$_2$Br reacts with one equivalent of alcoholic KOH to give mainly CH$_3$CH$=$CHBr (**A**) rather than CH$_2$=CHCH$_2$Br (**B**) or CH$_3$CBr$=$CH$_2$ (**C**).

◢ In E2 eliminations the more acidic H is removed preferentially. The inductive effect of the Br's increases the acidity of the H's on the C's to which the Br's are bonded. **B** is not obtained because its formation would require removal of H from the CH$_3$ group which has the least acidic H's. A little **C** is formed because its formation requires removal of H from C^2. Since R groups on a C decrease the acidity of its H's, C^2—H is less acidic than the C^1—H's. In addition there is the statistical effect (two H's available on C^1 versus one on C^2). **A**, the major product, requires loss of H from C^1.

9.43 What other kind of dihalide can undergo a double dehydrohalogenation to give an alkyne?

◢ A *gem*-dihalide as shown:

$$-CH_2-CBr_2- \xrightarrow{NaNH_2} -C\equiv C-$$

9.44 From 1,1-dibromopentane synthesize (*a*) 2-pentyne and (*b*) 1-pentyne.

◢ (*a*) CH$_3$CH$_2$CH$_2$CH$_2$CHBr$_2$ $\xrightarrow[200°C]{KOH(s)}$ CH$_3$CH$_2$C$\equiv$CCH$_3$

(*b*) CH$_3$CH$_2$CH$_2$CH$_2$CHBr$_2$ $\xrightarrow{NaNH_2}$ CH$_3$CH$_2$CH$_2$C$\equiv$C$^-$ $\xrightarrow{H_3O^+}$ CH$_3$CH$_2$CH$_2$C$\equiv$CH

9.45 Account for the different products formed in Problem 9.44.

■ In KOH(s), the initially formed terminal 1-pentyne rearranges to the internal alkyne. As in alkenes, the more highly R-substituted alkyne is more stable. The very strongly basic $NaNH_2$ removes the terminal proton in (b) to give the alkynide salt which cannot rearrange.

9.46 List the reagents used to convert (E)-2,3-dibromo-2-butene to 2-butyne.

■ Zn, Mg, or I^-; the same reagents used to dehalogenate vic-dihalides to alkenes (see Problem 7.52).

9.47 Give the product formed when Br_2 is added to $HC \equiv C:^- Na^+$.

■ The nucleophilic acetylide displaces Br^- from the electrophilic Br_2.

$$HC \equiv C:^- Na^+ + :\ddot{B}r:\ddot{B}r: \longrightarrow HC \equiv C - \ddot{B}r: + Na^+ :\ddot{B}r:^-$$

9.48 Give the organic product of the reaction of $HC \equiv C:^- Na^+$ with (a) CH_3Br, (b) $CH_3CH_2CH_2I$, and (c) $CH_2 = CHCH_2Br$.

■ (a) $HC \equiv CCH_3$, (b) $HC \equiv CCH_2CH_2CH_3$, and (c) $HC \equiv CCH_2CH = CH_2$.

9.49 Classify the reactions in Problem 9.48.

■ They are S_N2 displacements—the nucleophile is the acetylide anion.

9.50 (a) Write an equation for the reaction in Problem 9.48(b) if propyl chloride is substituted for the iodide or bromide. (b) Explain these results.

■ (a) $HC \equiv C:^- Na^+ + CH_3CH_2CH_2Cl \longrightarrow CH_3CH = CH_2 + HC \equiv CH + NaCl$
(b) Alkynides are powerful bases but mild nucleophiles. Hence E2 eliminations are very competitive with S_N2 displacements. Cl^- is a poorer leaving group than either Br^- or I^- in S_N2 reactions. Furthermore, Cl, a better acid-strengthening group than Br or I, facilitates abstraction of a β proton from the alkyl halide. Consequently, with RCl E2 elimination is the dominant reaction.

9.51 Give the product(s) of the reaction of $CH_3C \equiv C:^-$ with (a) $(CH_3)_3CBr$, (b) $CH_3CH_2CHI(CH_3)$, and (c) $(CH_3)_2CHCH_2Br$. Give a reason for your choice of product in each case.

■ (a) $CH_3C \equiv CH + (CH_3)_2C = CH_2$. 3° Halides only react by E2.
(b) $CH_3C \equiv CH + trans\text{-}CH_3CH = CHCH_3$. 2° Halides mainly react by E2.
(c) $CH_3C \equiv CH + (CH_3)_2C = CH_2$. Sterically-hindered 1° halides with an R group on the βC react mainly by E2. Some alkylation product, $CH_3C \equiv CCH_2CH(CH_3)_2$, forms in low yield.

9.52 Which of the isomeric alkynes in Problem 9.18 can be made by alkylation of an alkyne?

■ The unbranched isomers, **A**, **B**, and **C**, because their syntheses require 1° unbranched RX's. Internal alkynes with one 1° unbranched R group can also be made, i.e., **D**. Terminal alkynes with branched R groups cannot be made in good yields.

9.53 Give the syntheses of **A**, **B**, **C**, and **D** of Problem 9.18, starting with an alkynyl anion.

■ (A) $HC \equiv C^- + BrCH_2CH_2CH_2CH_3 \longrightarrow HC \equiv CCH_2CH_2CH_2CH_3$
(B) $CH_3C \equiv C^- + BrCH_2CH_2CH_3 \longrightarrow CH_3C \equiv CCH_2CH_2CH_3$
(C) $CH_3CH_2C \equiv C^- + BrCH_2CH_3 \longrightarrow CH_3CH_2C \equiv CCH_2CH_3$
(D) $(CH_3)_2CHC \equiv C^- + CH_3I \longrightarrow (CH_3)_2CHC \equiv CCH_3$

9.54 Starting with any alkyne, prepare ethylcyclohexylacetylene.

■ The derived acetylene name tells you which R groups, originating from RX's, are on the $C \equiv C$. In this case they are ethyl (1°) and cyclohexyl (2°). Since the alkylating RX must be an unbranched 1° halide, CH_3CH_2Br is the choice rather than cyclohexylbromide.

9.55 From an appropriate alkynide salt and alkyl halide, synthesize (a) 4-methyl-2-hexyne, (b) 5-methyl-2-hexyne, (c) 5,5-dimethyl-3-hexyne.

▰ In each case select the combination with an unhindered 1° RX.

(*a*) $CH_3CH_2CHC\equiv C^- + CH_3I \longrightarrow CH_3C\equiv CCHCH_2CH_3$

(with CH_3 below the first structure's CH, and CH_3 below the product's CH)

(not $CH_3C\equiv C^- + BrCH(CH_3)CH_2CH_3$)

(*b*) $(CH_3)_2CHCH_2C\equiv C^- + CH_3I \longrightarrow (CH_3)_2CHCH_2C\equiv CCH_3$ [See Problem 9.51(*c*)]

(*c*) $(CH_3)_3CC\equiv C^- + CH_3CH_2Br \longrightarrow CH_3CH_2C\equiv CC(CH_3)_3$ [See Problem 9.51(*c*)]

CH_3I is used in syntheses (caution—it is carcinogenic!) because it is a liquid and therefore more easily handled than the gaseous chloride or bromide.

9.56   Show the steps in the preparation of 2-hexyne, starting with acetylene and any alkyl halides.

▰ Acetylene is dialkylated. The derived name for this alkyne is methylpropylacetylene from which we conclude that the RX's needed for dialkylation are *n*-C_3H_7Br and CH_3I.

$$HC\equiv CH \xrightarrow{NaNH_2} HC\equiv C^{:-} \xrightarrow{n\text{-}C_3H_7Br} HC\equiv CC_3H_7 \xrightarrow{NaNH_2}$$

$$^-:C\equiv CC_3H_7 \xrightarrow{CH_3I} CH_3C\equiv CCH_2CH_2CH_3$$

9.57   Discuss the suggested synthesis of cyclodecyne from $HC\equiv CH$ and 1,8-dibromooctane.

▰ The first alkylation of acetylide (from C_2H_2) occurs with little difficulty.

$$HC\equiv C^- + Br(CH_2)_8Br \longrightarrow HC\equiv C(CH_2)_8Br$$

Problems arise in the attempted second alkylation to give the ring.

$$^-C\equiv C(CH_2)_8Br \longrightarrow$$ (ring structure)

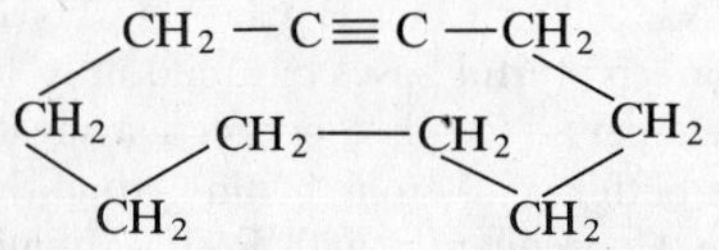

Intramolecular cyclizations leading to rings with more than six C's are difficult, and intermolecular reactions predominate. Intramolecular cyclization are encouraged by using very dilute solutions, thereby making it difficult for two molecules to collide to give the intermolecular alkylation.

9.58   Synthesize $CH_3CH_2CH(CH_3)C\equiv CH$ (compound **F** in Problem 9.18) from 1-pentyne.

▰ First form the dianion (Problems 9.35 and 9.36). Then one mole of RX is added to the dianion, alkylating the more basic propargylic carbanion.

$$CH_3CH_2CH_2C\equiv CH \xrightarrow{2BuLi} CH_3CH_2\overset{..}{C}H-C\equiv C^{:-} \xrightarrow{CH_3I}$$

$$CH_3CH_2CH(CH_3)C\equiv C^- \xrightarrow{H_3O^+} CH_3CH_2CH(CH_3)C\equiv CH \quad (\mathbf{F})$$

9.59   (*a*) What problem arises when propargylic alkylation is attempted on unsymmetrical internal alkynes?   (*b*) Give a general example of an internal unsymmetrical alkyne that can be successfully alkylated.

▰ (*a*) An unsymmetrical internal alkyne, $R'C^1H_2-C\equiv C-C^2H_2R$, has two propargylic C's (C^1 and C^2) capable of being alkylated to give a mixture of products.   (*b*) An internal alkyne with no H's on one of the propargylic C's, $R'CH_2C\equiv CCR_3$, would give a single alkylation product.

9.60   Show steps in the synthesis of 3-octyne from 1-bromobutane.

▰ $CH_3CH_2CH_2CH_2Br \xrightarrow{alc.\ KOH} CH_3CH_2CH=CH_2 \xrightarrow{Br_2} CH_3CH_2CHBrCH_2Br \xrightarrow{3NaNH_2}$

$$CH_3CH_2C\equiv C^- \xrightarrow{CH_3CH_2CH_2CH_2Br} CH_3CH_2C\equiv CCH_2CH_2CH_2CH_3$$

CHEMICAL PROPERTIES OF ALKYNES

9.61   Write equations for the stepwise reaction of 2-butyne with two moles of H_2/Pt.

▰

$$CH_3C\equiv CCH_3 \xrightarrow{H_2/Pt} CH_3C=CCH_3 \xrightarrow{H_2/Pt} CH_3CH_2CH_2CH_3$$
(with H H below the middle structure)

(*Z*)-2-butene

9.62 The ΔH's of hydrogenation of the two steps in Problem 9.61 are -42 kcal/mol and -33 kcal/mol, respectively. Why can the reaction be stopped after the alkene is formed?

◢ Since the first hydrogenation step is more exothermic, most of the alkyne will react before any alkene reacts. The Lindlar's catalyst, Pd on solid $CaCO_3$ or $BaSO_4$, deactivated (poisoned) with quinoline (a heterocyclic amine) or Ni/B, is used to ensure getting the alkene.

9.63 Account for the catalytic *syn*-addition of H_2 in Problem 9.61.

◢ The same mechanism for hydrogenation of alkenes prevails (see Problem 7.101) for alkynes; both undergo *syn* addition.

9.64 Write the equation for the reduction of 2-butyne with Na in EtOH.

◢

$$CH_3C \equiv CCH_3 \xrightarrow{\ Na\,+\,EtOH\ } \underset{(E)\text{-2-Butene}}{\overset{\displaystyle H \qquad CH_3}{\underset{\displaystyle CH_3 \qquad H}{C=C}}} \quad (+\,NaOEt)$$

9.65 *trans*-Cyclooctene is formed by the reduction of cyclooctyne with Na/EtOH. Knowing this fact answer the following: Is the stereoselective reduction (Problem 9.64) *anti* because of the mechanism or because the *trans* isomer is more stable?

◢ Cyclooctene is one of the rare alkenes whose *trans* isomer is less stable than the *cis* [see Problem 7.39(b)]. Notwithstanding this, *trans*-cyclooctene is obtained from the reaction of cyclooctyne with Na and EtOH. Consequently, the *anti* addition results from the nature of the mechanism.

9.66 Give a mechanism for the active metal (Na) reduction of an alkyne in a protic solvent (C_2H_5OH).

◢ An Na· atom transfers an e^- to the $C \equiv C$ group to give a vinyl radical carbanion intermediate, whose HO's containing the unshared pair of e^-'s and odd electron are as far away from each other as possible. The R's are now fixed *trans*. The radical anion picks up an H^+ from the protic solvent to give a *trans* vinyl radical. Another sequence of e^-/H^+ transfers occur to give the *trans*-alkene and EtO^-Na^+.

$$R-C \equiv C-R \xrightarrow{\ Na\ } \left[\overset{\displaystyle \ddot{C}=C}{\underset{\displaystyle R}{}} \overset{R}{\underset{\displaystyle .}{}} \right] \xrightarrow{\ EtOH\ } \left[\overset{\displaystyle H \qquad R}{\underset{\displaystyle R}{C=C}} \overset{}{\underset{}{.}} \right] \xrightarrow[2.\ EtOH]{1.\ Na} \overset{\displaystyle H \qquad R}{\underset{\displaystyle R \qquad H}{C=C}} + 2C_2H_5O^-Na^+$$

9.67 List the products formed when 1-butyne reacts with one equivalent of (*a*) HBr, (*b*) HBr with peroxides, and (*c*) Br_2. Characterize each reaction.

◢ (*a*) $CH_3CH_2CBr=CH_2$ a Markovnikov electrophilic addition
    (*b*) $CH_3CH_2CH=CHBr$ an anti-Markovnikov radical addition
    (*c*) $CH_3CH_2CBr=CHBr$ an electrophilic addition

9.68 Give the products formed when a second equivalent of reagent is added to the products formed in Problem 9.67 (Same as adding two equivalents to 1-butyne.)

◢ (*a*) $CH_3CH_2CBr_2CH_3$, (*b*) $CH_3CH_2CH_2CHBr_2$, and (*c*) $CH_3CH_2CBr_2CHBr_2$.

9.69 What additional factor, not present in hydrocarbon alkenes, is responsible for the orientation in the electrophilic addition to vinyl bromides leading to the product in Problem 9.68(*a*)?

◢ The Markovnikov addition of H^+ to $CH_3CH_2CBr=CH_2$ gives a carbocation that is stabilized by the inductive effect of the R groups, as was the case with alkenes. But a much more significant stabilization occurs by extended π bonding with Br.

$$CH_3CH_2\underset{:\ddot{Br}:}{C}=CH_2 + H^+ \longrightarrow [CH_3CH_2\overset{+}{\underset{:\ddot{Br}:}{C}}-CH_3 \longleftrightarrow CH_3CH_2\underset{\overset{\|}{:\underset{+}{\ddot{Br}}:}}{C}CH_3] \xrightarrow{\ Br^-\ } CH_3CH_2CBr_2CH_3$$

9.70 What additional factor, not present in hydrocarbon alkenes, is responsible for the orientation in the radical addition of HBr to vinyl bromides leading to the product in Problem 9.68(*b*)?

▮ A halogen atom destabilizes a carbon radical to which it is bonded. Hence, Br· adds as shown:

$$CH_3CH_2CH=CHBr \xrightarrow{Br·} CH_3CH_2\dot{C}HCHBr_2 \xrightarrow{HBr} CH_3CH_2CH_2CHBr_2 + Br·$$
$$\xrightarrow{Br·} \times \longrightarrow CH_3CH_2CHBr\dot{C}HBr \text{ (no reaction)}$$

9.71 (*a*) Why is double dehalogenation of a tetrahalide, i.e., —CBr$_2$CBr$_2$—, not a practical method for synthesizing alkynes? (*b*) When might this reaction be useful?

▮ (*a*) The necessary tetrabromide must usually be prepared by adding two equivalents of Br$_2$ to an alkyne. (*b*) This reaction may be used to "protect", i.e., prevent unwanted reaction of, a triple bond in a polyfunctional alkyne that is about to undergo a reaction which would also destroy the —C≡C—. Br$_2$ is first added to the alkyne to give the tetrabromo derivative. The desired reaction is carried out without affecting the tetrabromo site. Finally the alkyne is regenerated by a double debromination with Zn.

9.72 (*a*) Explain why acetylene, unlike ethylene, does not dissolve in concentrated H$_2$SO$_4$. (*b*) Why do other alkynes such as 2-butyne dissolve in conc. H$_2$SO$_4$?

▮ (*a*) Ethylene gives an alkyl carbocation salt, (H$_3$CCH$_2^+$)(HSO$_4^-$). If HC≡CH were to dissolve in H$_2$SO$_4$, a bisulfate salt of a vinyl carbocation, (H$_2$C=$\overset{+}{C}$—H)(HSO$_4^-$), would be formed. The more *s*-character in the positively-charged C, the less stable is the carbocation and the less likely it is to form. (*b*) Vinyl carbocations from other alkynes have electron-repelling R substituents, i.e, CH$_3\overset{+}{C}$=CH—CH$_3$, and thus they are more stable than the vinyl carbocation from acetylene.

9.73 Give the equation for the reaction of one equivalent of HBr with 1-pentene-4-yne.

▮ This reaction proceeds through a carbocation. Since the alkyl carbocation from the alkene group is more stable than the vinyl carbocation from the alkyne group (see Problem 9.72), the $\Delta H^‡$ for its formation is less and alkenes react at a faster rate than alkynes toward electrophilic addition.

$$H_2C=CHCH_2C≡CH \xrightarrow{H^+} H_3C-\overset{+}{C}HCH_2C≡CH \xrightarrow{Br^-} H_3CCHBrCH_2C≡CH$$
$$\xrightarrow{H^+} \times \longrightarrow H_2C=CHCH_2\overset{+}{C}=CH_2 \text{ (no reaction)}$$

9.74 Explain why alkynes are less reactive than alkenes toward addition of Br$_2$.

▮ The three membered ring bromonium ion formed from the alkyne (**A**) has a full double bond causing it to be more strained and less stable than the one from the alkene (**B**).

HC≡CH (**A**) less stable than H$_2$C—CH$_2$ (**B**)

Also, the C's of **A** that are part of the bromonium ion have more *s*-character than those of **B**, further making **A** less stable than **B** (see Problem 9.72).

9.75 Explain why catalytic hydrogenation is an exception to the generalization that alkenes are more reactive than alkynes toward addition reactions.

▮ Alkenes are adsorbed on the surface of the catalyst only when the plane of the π bond approaches perpendicularly ("head on"). Because of the cylindrical nature of the π bonds of alkynes, any approach along the axis of the cylinder can be successful (see Problem 9.7). These less constrained transition states cause alkynes to have more positive $\Delta S^‡$ values. Consequently, in this reaction alkynes react at a faster rate than alkenes.

9.76 Write an equation for the reaction of propyne with water in the presence of H$_2$SO$_4$ and HgSO$_4$. Show the intermediate.

▮ $$CH_3C≡CH + H_2O \xrightarrow{HgSO_4, H_2SO_4} [CH_3\underset{OH}{C}=CH_2] \longrightarrow CH_3\overset{O}{\underset{\|}{C}}CH_3$$

a vinyl alcohol (enol)   Acetone (a ketone)
unstable   stable

The Markovnikov addition of H$_2$O gives an unstable vinyl alcohol that rearranges, as shown, to the more stable ketone.

9.77 Use general equations to give the kinds of alkynes that are hydrated to (*a*) a single ketone, (*b*) a mixture of ketones, and (*c*) an aldehyde, by the reaction in Problem 9.76.

▮ (a) Terminal: $RC\equiv CH \longrightarrow \underset{\underset{O}{\|}}{R}CCH_3$ and symmetrical internal: $RC\equiv CR \longrightarrow \underset{\underset{O}{\|}}{R}CCH_2R$

(b) Unsymmetrical internal: $RC\equiv CR' \longrightarrow \underset{\underset{O}{\|}}{R}CCH_2R' + \underset{\underset{O}{\|}}{R}CH_2CR'$

(c) Only $HC\equiv CH \longrightarrow CH_3CHO$, the only aldehyde that can be prepared this way.

9.78 Give the structures of the products formed from the reaction of 2-hexyne with $HgSO_4$ and dilute H_2SO_4. Show the intermediate enols.

▮ $CH_3C\equiv CCH_2CH_2CH_3 \longrightarrow [CH_3CH=C(OH)CH_2CH_2CH_3] + [CH_3C(OH)=CHCH_2CH_2CH_3]$

$$CH_3CH_2\underset{\underset{O}{\|}}{C}CH_2CH_2CH_3 \qquad + \qquad CH_3\underset{\underset{O}{\|}}{C}CH_2CH_2CH_2CH_3$$

9.79 List the alkynes needed to synthesize the following ketones in the best possible yields:

(a) $(CH_3)_2CH\underset{\underset{O}{\|}}{C}CH_3$, (b) $CH_3CH_2\underset{\underset{O}{\|}}{C}CH_2CH_2CH_3$, (c) cyclopentyl–$\underset{\underset{O}{\|}}{C}CH_2$–cyclopentyl

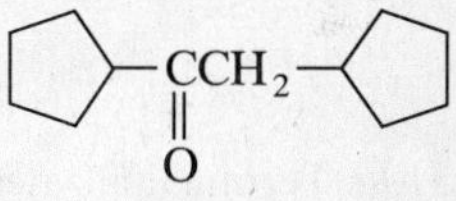

▮ (a) Methyl ketones, $CH_3\underset{\underset{R}{|}}{C}=O$, are best made from terminal alkynes; use $(CH_3)_2CHC\equiv CH$.

(b) Use the symmetrical internal alkyne $CH_3CH_2C\equiv CCH_2CH_3$ rather than the unsymmetrical $CH_3C\equiv CCH_2CH_2CH_3$, which also gives $CH_3\underset{\underset{O}{\|}}{C}CH_2CH_2CH_2CH_3$.

(c) cyclopentyl–$C\equiv C$–cyclopentyl

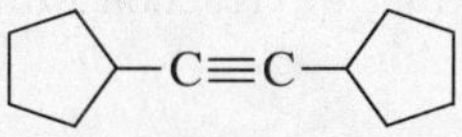

9.80 Is the conversion of an alkyne to a carbonyl compound ($HC\equiv CH \longrightarrow CH_3CHO$) a redox reaction?

▮ No. The average oxidation number of the two C's in each compound is the same (-1). Hydration is never a redox reaction. Although the C accepting the H is reduced, the C forming a bond to the OH is oxidized. The net effect is no change in the average oxidation state.

9.81 Give the equation for the reaction of 2-butyne with BH_3 complexed with tetrahydrofuran ($BH_3 \cdot THF$).

▮ A trivinylborane is formed which results from a *syn* addition.

$$3\ CH_3C\equiv CCH_3 \xrightarrow{BH_3 \cdot THF} \left(H-\underset{}{\overset{CH_3\ CH_3}{\underset{|\quad |}{C=C}}}- \right)_3 B$$

cis isomer

9.82 (a) Give the equation for the reaction of 1-butyne with $BH_3 \cdot THF$. (b) What method is employed for ensuring the addition of only one mole of borane?

▮ (a) Two moles of BH_3 add to terminal alkynes, the reaction being difficult to stop after one mole has reacted:

$$CH_3CH_2C\equiv CH \xrightarrow{BH_3 \cdot THF} [CH_3CH_2CH=CHBH_2] \xrightarrow{BH_3 \cdot THF} CH_3CH_2CH_2\underset{\underset{|}{\overset{|}{B-}}}{\overset{\overset{|}{B-}}{C}}H$$

a *gem*-diborane

(**b**) A sterically hindered dialkylborane, di-*sec*-isoamylborane or $[(CH_3)_2CHC\!-\!]_2BH$ (abbreviated
Sia_2BH), is used instead of BH_3.

$$CH_3CH_2C\!\equiv\!CH \xrightarrow{Sia_2BH} CH_3CH_2CH\!=\!CHBSia_2$$

Like all boranes, Sia_2BH gives anti-Markovnikov products when adding to triple bonds as well as to double bonds.

9.83 Give the structural formulas for the products formed on the oxidation in alkaline H_2O_2 of the product in (**a**) Problem 9.81 and (**b**) Problem 9.82(**b**).

◢ The $HC\!=\!C\!-\!B\!-$ grouping is converted to $HC\!=\!C\!-\!OH$, a vinyl alcohol, which rearranges to a carbonyl compound.

(**a**) Internal alkynes give ketones on oxidative-hydroboration.

$$\left(H\!-\!\underset{\underset{CH_3}{|}}{C}\!=\!\underset{\underset{CH_3}{|}}{C}\!-\!\right)_{\!3}\!B \xrightarrow[OH^-]{H_2O_2} [CH_3CH\!=\!\underset{\underset{OH}{|}}{C}CH_3] \longrightarrow CH_3CH_2\underset{\underset{O}{\|}}{C}CH_3$$

$$\text{unstable enol} \qquad\qquad \text{a ketone}$$

(**b**) Terminal alkynes give aldehydes

$$CH_3CH_2CH\!=\!CHBSia_2 \xrightarrow[OH^-]{H_2O_2} [CH_3CH_2CH\!=\!CHOH] \longrightarrow CH_3CH_2CH_2CHO$$

$$\text{an aldehyde}$$

9.84 (**a**) What is the product obtained from the reaction of a vinylborane with acetic acid (CH_3COOH)? (**b**) Give the structural formulas and IUPAC names for the products formed from the reaction with CH_3COOH of the product in (i) Problem 9.81 and (ii) Problem 9.82(**b**).

◢ (**a**) $RCH\!=\!CB\!\!\stackrel{|}{\diagup} \xrightarrow{CH_3COOH} RCH\!=\!CH;$ an H replaces the B.

(**b**) (i) $\left(H\!-\!\underset{\underset{CH_3}{|}}{C}\!=\!\underset{\underset{CH_3}{|}}{C}\!-\!\right)_{\!3}\!B \xrightarrow{CH_3COOH}$

$$\underset{\underset{H}{\diagup}}{\overset{\overset{CH_3}{\diagdown}}{C}}\!=\!\underset{\underset{H}{\diagdown}}{\overset{\overset{CH_3}{\diagup}}{C}}$$

$$(Z)\text{-2-Butene}$$

The net reaction is a *syn* addition of two H's to give a *cis* alkene.

(ii) $CH_3CH_2CH\!=\!CHBSia_2 \xrightarrow{CH_3COOH} CH_3CH_2CH\!=\!CH_2$

$$\text{1-Butene}$$

9.85 Use two methods to convert 2-butyne to (Z)-2,3-dideutero-2-butene.

◢ $$CH_3C\!\equiv\!CCH_3 \xrightarrow{D_2/\text{Lindlar's catalyst}} \underset{\underset{D}{\diagup}}{\overset{\overset{H_3C}{\diagdown}}{C}}\!=\!\underset{\underset{D}{\diagdown}}{\overset{\overset{CH_3}{\diagup}}{C}} \xleftarrow[\text{2. } CH_3COOD]{\text{1. } BD_3} CH_3C\!\equiv\!CCH_3$$

9.86 Use two methods to convert 2-butyne to (Z)-2-deutero-2-butene.

◢ $$CH_3C\!\equiv\!CCH_3 \xrightarrow[\text{2. } CH_3COOH]{\text{1. } BD_3\cdot THF} \underset{\underset{D}{\diagup}}{\overset{\overset{H_3C}{\diagdown}}{C}}\!=\!\underset{\underset{H}{\diagdown}}{\overset{\overset{CH_3}{\diagup}}{C}} \xleftarrow[\text{2. } CH_3COOD]{\text{1. } BH_3\cdot THF} CH_3C\!\equiv\!CCH_3$$

9.87 From 1-butyne, synthesize (**a**) (E)-1-deutero-1-butene and (**b**) 2-deutero-1-butene.

◢ (**a**) $$CH_3CH_2C\!\equiv\!CH \xrightarrow{Sia_2BH} \underset{\underset{H}{\diagup}}{\overset{\overset{CH_3CH_2}{\diagdown}}{C}}\!=\!\underset{\underset{BSia_2}{\diagdown}}{\overset{\overset{H}{\diagup}}{C}} \xrightarrow{CH_3COOD} \underset{\underset{H}{\diagup}}{\overset{\overset{CH_3CH_2}{\diagdown}}{C}}\!=\!\underset{\underset{D}{\diagdown}}{\overset{\overset{H}{\diagup}}{C}}$$

$$(b) \quad CH_3CH_2C\equiv CH \xrightarrow{Sia_2BD} \begin{array}{c} CH_3CH_2 \\ \diagdown \\ C=C \\ \diagup \quad \diagdown \\ D \qquad BSia_2 \end{array} \xrightarrow{CH_3COOH} \begin{array}{c} CH_3CH_2 \qquad H \\ \diagdown \quad \diagup \\ C=C \\ \diagup \quad \diagdown \\ D \qquad H \end{array}$$

9.88 Show the steps in the oxidative-deuteroboration with Sia_2BD of (*a*) 2-butyne and (*b*) 1-hexyne.

◢ (*a*) $CH_3C\equiv CCH_3 \xrightarrow{Sia_2BD} \begin{array}{c} CH_3C=CCH_3 \\ | \quad | \\ D \quad BSia_2 \end{array} \xrightarrow{H_2O_2, \ OH^-} \begin{array}{c} [CH_3C=CCH_3] \\ | \quad | \\ D \quad OH \end{array} \longrightarrow \begin{array}{c} CH_3CHDCCH_3 \\ \| \\ O \end{array}$

(*b*) $CH_3(CH_2)_3C\equiv CH \xrightarrow{Sia_2BD} CH_3(CH_2)_3CD=CHBSia_2 \xrightarrow{H_2O_2, \ OH^-}$

$$[CH_3(CH_2)_3CD=CH(OH)] \longrightarrow CH_3(CH_2)_3CHDCH=O$$

9.89 (*a*) Which of the following alkynes gives a single carbonyl compound on hydroboration-oxidation? (i) 1-Pentyne, (ii) 3-hexyne, (iii) 2-pentyne, (iv) 4-methyl-2-pentyne. Give the structural formulas for the carbonyl compounds formed. (*b*) Give the structural formulas for the mixture of carbonyl compounds formed from the alkynes in (*a*) which do not give single products.

◢ (*a*) The terminal alkyne (i) gives a single product which is an aldehyde.

$$CH_3(CH_2)_2C\equiv CH \longrightarrow CH_3(CH_2)_2CH_2CHO$$

The symmetrical internal alkyne (ii) gives a single product, a ketone.

$$CH_3CH_2C\equiv CCH_2CH_3 \longrightarrow \begin{array}{c} CH_3CH_2CCH_2CH_2CH_3 \\ \| \\ O \end{array}$$

(*b*) (iii) $CH_3CH_2C\equiv CCH_3 \longrightarrow \begin{array}{c} CH_3CCH_2CH_2CH_3 \\ \| \\ O \end{array} + \begin{array}{c} CH_3CH_2CCH_2CH_3 \\ \| \\ O \end{array}$

(iv) $CH_3C\equiv CCH(CH_3)_2 \longrightarrow \begin{array}{c} CH_3CCH_2CH(CH_3)_2 \\ \| \\ O \end{array} + \begin{array}{c} CH_3CH_2CCH(CH_3)_2 \\ \| \\ O \end{array}$

9.90 (*a*) How might a good yield of one ketone be obtained by the hydroboration of $CH_3C\equiv CCH(CH_3)_2$? (*b*) Give the structural formula of that ketone.

◢ (*a*) Use Sia_2BH for the hydroboration. The B of this hindered borane will form a bond to the less hindered C^2.

(*b*) $CH_3C\equiv CCH(CH_3)_2 \longrightarrow \begin{array}{c} CH_3C=CHCH(CH_3)_2 \\ | \\ BSia_2 \end{array} \longrightarrow \begin{array}{c} CH_3CCH_2CH(CH_3)_2 \\ \| \\ O \end{array}$

9.91 Give the product in each reaction: (*a*) $CH_3C\equiv CCH_3 + CH_3CH_2O^-$ in EtOH, (*b*) $CF_3C\equiv CCF_3 + CH_3CH_2O^-$ in EtOH, and (*c*) $CH_3C\equiv CH + CH_3O^-$ in MeOH.

◢ (*a*) $\begin{array}{c} CH_3C=CCH_3 \\ | \quad | \\ H \quad OCH_2CH_3 \end{array}$ (*b*) $\begin{array}{c} CF_3C=CCF_3 \\ | \quad | \\ H \quad OCH_2CH_3 \end{array}$ (*c*) $\begin{array}{c} CH_3C=CH \\ | \quad | \\ CH_3O \quad H \end{array}$

9.92 (*a*) Give the mechanism for addition of a nucleophile, RO^-, to an alkyne, $-C\equiv C-$. (*b*) Why are alkynes more reactive than alkenes toward nucleophilic addition? (*c*) Compare the reactivities in (*a*) and (*b*) of Problem 9.91. (*d*) Account for the orientation in (*c*) of Problem 9.91.

◢ (*a*) $-C\equiv C- + RO^- \xrightarrow{150\,°C} [-\overset{..}{\overset{-}{C}}=C(OR)] \xrightarrow{ROH} -CH=C(OR) + RO^-$

                       a vinyl carbanion   a vinyl ether

(*b*) Addition of RO^- to $-C=C-$ gives an alkyl carbanion, $-\overset{..}{C}-COR$, whose negative charge is on a C with sp^3 HO's. In contrast, the intermediate vinyl carbanion in (*a*) uses sp^2 HO's; it is more stable and more readily formed because it has more *s*-character. (*c*) $CF_3C\equiv CF_3$ is much more reactive because its intermediate carbanion, $CF_3\overset{..}{C}=C(OR)CF_3$, is additionally stabilized by the strong electron-withdrawing inductive effect of the $-CF_3$ group. (*d*) In a terminal alkyne, the nucleophile adds to give the more stable vinyl carbanion, the one without the electron-repelling CH_3.

9.93 (*a*) Give the product from the reaction of HCN and NaCN with HC≡CH. (*b*) Classify the reaction.

◢ (*a*) H$_2$C=CH(CN).

(*b*) The reaction is a nucleophilic addition initiated by CN$^-$,

$$HC≡CH + CN^- \longrightarrow \overset{..}{-}CH=CH(CN) \xrightarrow[-CN^-]{HCN} H_2C=CH(CN)$$

to give an anion, which then forms the product by accepting H$^+$ from HCN reforming CN$^-$.

9.94 Complete the following reactions and name the products.

$$(a)\ 2HC≡CH \xrightarrow[NH_4Cl]{CuCl} \qquad (b)\ 2HC≡CH \xrightarrow[O_2]{Cu^{2+}}$$

◢ (*a*) With CuCl under mildly acid conditions (NH$_4^+$), acetylene adds to itself (couples) to form the dimer, H$_2$C=CHC≡CH, butenyne (or vinylacetylene) (note that numbers are superfluous). Note that under basic conditions (NH$_3$) the copper acetylide is formed [see (iv) of Problem 9.24(*a*)]. (*b*) Under oxidative conditions, the dimer formed is HC≡C—C≡CH, butadiyne.

9.95 (*a*) Give the product from the reaction of propyne with NBS (N-bromosuccinimide). (*b*) Account for the product mechanistically.

◢ (*a*) Just as alkenes undergo allylic substitution, alkynes undergo propargylic halogenation. The product is HC≡CCH$_2$Br, propargyl bromide. (*b*) The propargylic radical is stabilized by extended π bonding (resonance) [H$_2$C̣—C≡C— ⟷ H$_2$C=C=Ċ—].

9.96 (*a*) Write the structural formulas for the products formed when 3-heptyne reacts with KMnO$_4$ under (i) neutral conditions at room temperature and (ii) alkaline or acidic conditions at higher temperatures. (*b*) Rationalize the formation of the product from (i) of part (*a*).

◢ (*a*) (i) CH$_3$CH$_2$C≡CCH$_2$CH$_2$CH$_3$ ⟶ CH$_3$CH$_2$C—CCH$_2$CH$_2$CH$_3$ (A, a diketone)
   with two ‖ ‖ O O groups.

(ii) CH$_3$CH$_2$COOH + HOOCCH$_2$CH$_2$CH$_3$. Oxidative cleavage to carboxylic acid(s) occurs.

(*b*) Like the alkenes, alkynes undergo hydroxylation under mild conditions; the intermediate enediol rearranges to two hydroxyketones, which are both easily oxidized further to **A**.

CH$_3$CH$_2$C≡C(CH$_2$)$_2$CH$_3$ ⟶ [CH$_3$CH$_2$C=C(CH$_2$)$_2$CH$_3$]
   with HO OH groups.

an enediol

⟶ [CH$_3$CH$_2$CH—C(CH$_2$)$_2$CH$_3$] + [CH$_3$CH$_2$C—CH(CH$_2$)$_2$CH$_3$] $\xrightarrow{[O]}$ **A**
   OH ‖ O groups / ‖ O OH groups.

hydroxyketones

9.97 Give the products formed from the reaction of each of the following compounds with KMnO$_4$ in warm acid. (*a*) 2-Methyl-3-heptyne, (*b*) 3-hexyne, (*c*) 1-pentyne, and (*d*) 2,6-nonadiyne.

◢ (*a*) (CH$_3$)$_2$CHC≡CCH$_2$CH$_2$CH$_3$ ⟶ (CH$_3$)$_2$CHCOOH + HOOCCH$_2$CH$_2$CH$_3$
(*b*) CH$_3$CH$_2$C≡CCH$_2$CH$_3$ ⟶ 2CH$_3$CH$_2$COOH. Symmetrical internal alkynes give one acid.
(*c*) HC≡CCH$_2$CH$_2$CH$_3$ ⟶ CO$_2$ + HOOCCH$_2$CH$_2$CH$_3$. C^1 of a terminal alkyne is oxidized to CO$_2$.
(*d*) CH$_3$C≡CCH$_2$CH$_2$C≡CCH$_2$CH$_3$ ⟶ CH$_3$COOH + HOOCCH$_2$CH$_2$COOH + HOOCCH$_2$CH$_3$
   The central portion of a diyne gives a dicarboxylic acid.

9.98 What is the structural formula of an alkyne that undergoes oxidative cleavage to give two moles of CH$_3$COOH and one mole of HOOC(CH$_2$)$_3$COOH?

◢ Write the products in a line so that the COOH groups point toward each other keeping the dicarboxylic acid in the middle. Then erase the OOH's and join the C's of the COOH's by triple bonds. Thus

CH$_3$COOH, HOOC(CH$_2$)$_3$COOH, HOOCCH$_3$ ⟵ CH$_3$C≡C(CH$_2$)$_3$C≡CCH$_3$

The number of C atoms in the proposed structure must be the same as the total in the oxidation products, including CO$_2$ if formed.

9.99 Deduce the structural formula of a compound, $C_{10}H_{10}$ (**A**), that gives as the only organic compound, $HOOCCH_2CHCH_2COOH$ (**B**) on oxidative cleavage.
$$\underset{\displaystyle CH_2COOH}{|}$$

❚ **A** has an index of unsaturation of 6 which is attributed to the presence of three triple bonds because of the isolation of the tricarboxylic acid **B**. Since **B** has three less C's than **A**, the three triple bonds must be terminal so that three moles of CO_2 are lost in the oxidation. Compound **A** is

$$HC\equiv CCH_2CHCH_2C\equiv CH$$
$$\underset{\displaystyle CH_2C\equiv CH}{|}$$

9.100 Give the products that result from the ozonolysis/hydrolysis of the compounds in Problem 9.97.

❚ They all give the same product as obtained on oxidative cleavage.

9.101 What is the main utility of oxidative cleavage or ozonolysis of alkynes?

❚ These cleavage reactions are rarely used for syntheses because alkynes are not readily-available inexpensive starting materials. They are used mainly to locate the position of a triple bond in an alkyne.

9.102 Write the equations for the reactions of $CH_3C\equiv C:^-$ with (**a**) $CH_3CH=O$, (**b**) $(CH_3)_2C=O$, and (**c**) ⬡$=O$, all followed by the addition of H_2O.

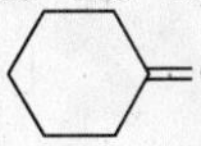

❚ The nucleophilic alkynide adds to the C of the $C=O$ group to give an intermediate alkoxide anion. Water converts the anion to an alcohol.

(**a**)
$$CH_3C\equiv C:^- + \underset{\displaystyle H}{\overset{\displaystyle CH_3}{C}}=\ddot{O}: \longrightarrow CH_3C\equiv C-\underset{\displaystyle H}{\overset{\displaystyle CH_3}{\underset{|}{\overset{|}{C}}}}-\ddot{O}:^- \xrightarrow{H_2O} CH_3C\equiv C-\underset{\displaystyle H}{\overset{\displaystyle CH_3}{\underset{|}{\overset{|}{C}}}}-OH$$

an alkoxide ion   an alkynol

(**b**)
$$CH_3C\equiv C:^- + \underset{\displaystyle CH_3}{\overset{\displaystyle CH_3}{C}}=O \longrightarrow CH_3C\equiv C-\underset{\displaystyle CH_3}{\overset{\displaystyle CH_3}{\underset{|}{\overset{|}{C}}}}-\ddot{O}:^- \xrightarrow{H_2O} CH_3C\equiv C-\underset{\displaystyle CH_3}{\overset{\displaystyle CH_3}{\underset{|}{\overset{|}{C}}}}-OH$$

(**c**)
$$⬡=O + {}^-:C\equiv CCH_3 \longrightarrow ⬡\underset{\displaystyle :\ddot{O}:^-}{\overset{\displaystyle }{-}}C\equiv CCH_3 \xrightarrow{H_2O} ⬡\underset{\displaystyle OH}{-}C\equiv CCH_3$$

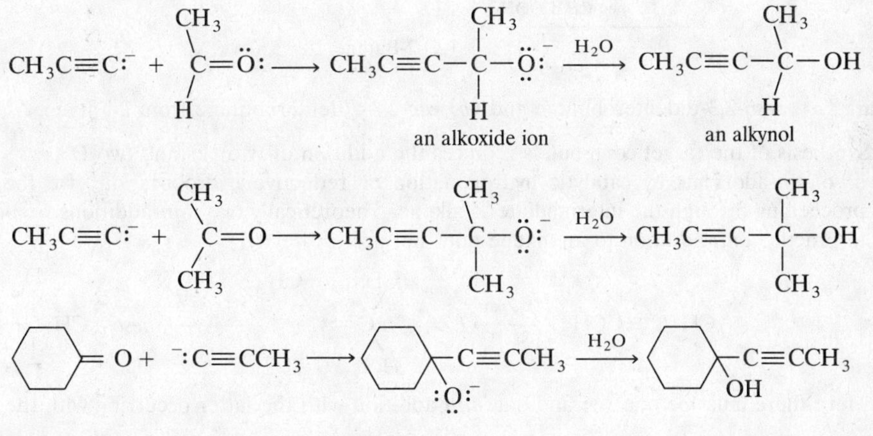

9.103 Supply the alkynide anion and carbonyl compound needed to synthesize the following alkynols:

(**a**) $CH_3C\equiv CCH(OH)CH_2CH_3$,   (**b**) $HOCH_2C\equiv CH$,   (**c**) $CH_3CH_2\underset{\displaystyle OH}{\overset{\displaystyle CH_3}{\underset{|}{\overset{|}{C}}}}C\equiv CCH_3$

❚ (**a**) $CH_3C\equiv C:^- + O=CHCH_2CH_3$,   (**b**) $HC\equiv C:^- + O=CH_2$,

(**c**) $CH_3C\equiv C:^- + \underset{\displaystyle CH_3CH_2}{\overset{\displaystyle CH_3}{C}}=O$

SYNTHESES WITH ALKYNES

9.104 Show how (**a**) 2,2-dibromopropane and (**b**) 1,1-dibromopropane can be synthesized from propane.

❚ Multistep syntheses are best solved by identifying the required functional group and then planning backwards from the desired product (the target compound), through a sequence of precursors, to the starting compound. This backwards approach is called a *retrosynthetic analysis*. The functional grouping is a *gem*-dihalide whose precursor is an alkyne made from an alkene that in turn comes from the alkane.

(*a*) $CH_3CH_2CH_3 \xrightarrow[\text{heat}]{Cl_2} CH_3CHClCH_3 + CH_3CH_2CH_2Cl \xrightarrow{\text{alc. KOH}} CH_3CH{=}CH_2 \xrightarrow{Br_2}$

$CH_3CHBrCH_2Br \xrightarrow[\text{heat}]{KOH(s)} CH_3C{\equiv}CH \xrightarrow{2\ HBr} CH_3CBr_2CH_3$

(*b*) $CH_3C{\equiv}CH\ [\text{from}\ (a)] \xrightarrow[\text{peroxide}]{2\ HBr} CH_3CH_2CHBr_2$

9.105 Prepare (*a*) (*E*)-2-butene and (*b*) (*Z*)-2-butene from 2-bromobutane.

⟋ By retrosynthetic analysis the target compounds are each prepared from the alkyne which in turn is made from the corresponding alkene.

(*a*) $CH_3CH_2CHBrCH_3 \xrightarrow{\text{alc. KOH}} CH_3CH{=}CHCH_3 \xrightarrow{Br_2}$

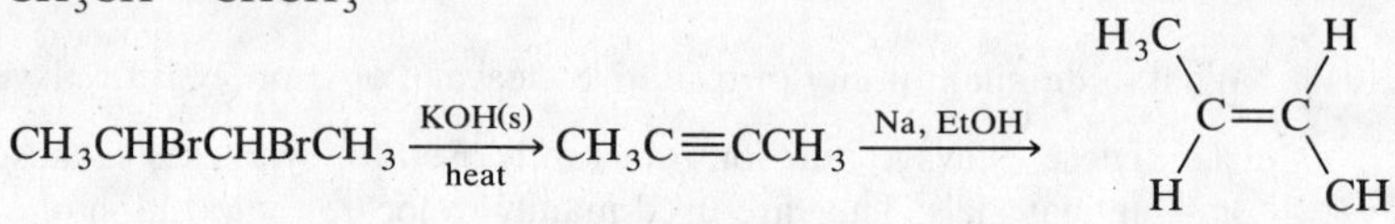

$CH_3CHBrCHBrCH_3 \xrightarrow[\text{heat}]{KOH(s)} CH_3C{\equiv}CCH_3 \xrightarrow{Na,\ EtOH}$

(*E*)-2-Butene

The double dehydrogenation is effected with hot solid KOH, rather than NaNH$_2$, to prevent isomerization to 1-butyne.

(*b*) $CH_3C{\equiv}CCH_3$ — H$_2$, Lindlar's catalyst / BH$_3$, then CH$_3$COOH — or

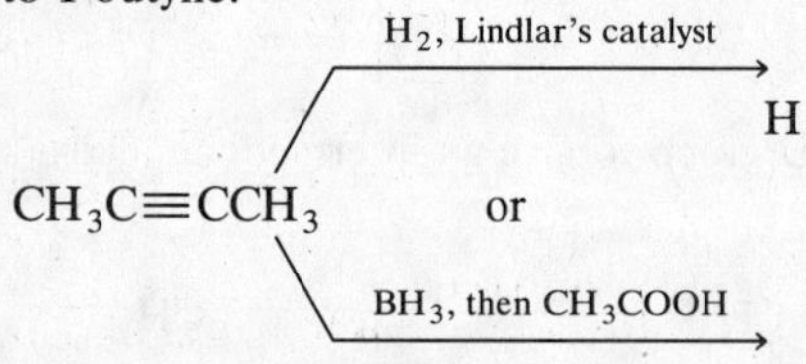

(*Z*)-2-Butene

9.106 Prepare (*a*) *meso*-2,3-dideuterobutane and (*b*) *rac*-2,3-dideuterobutane from 2-butyne.

⟋ Synthesis of the target compounds requires the addition of two H's and two D's.

(*a*) Two *syn*-additions by catalytic hydrogenation or reductive hydroboration give the target compound by proceeding through the intermediate *Z* alkene. Theoretically two *anti*-additions would give the product but in practice *anti*-addition to an alkene does not occur directly.

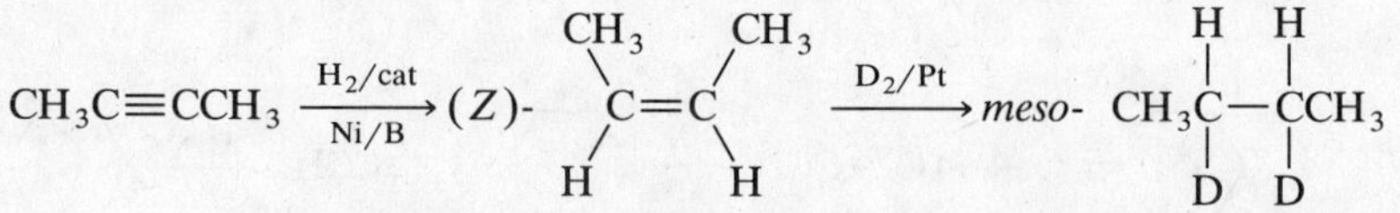

$CH_3C{\equiv}CCH_3 \xrightarrow[\text{Ni/B}]{H_2/\text{cat}} (Z)\text{-}$ $\xrightarrow{D_2/\text{Pt}} meso\text{-}$

(*b*) Here there must be one *syn* and one *anti*-addition with the latter occurring with the alkyne.

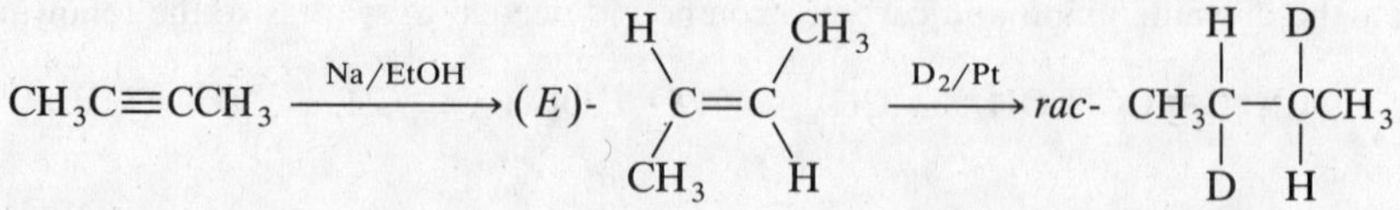

$CH_3C{\equiv}CCH_3 \xrightarrow{Na/\text{EtOH}} (E)\text{-}$ $\xrightarrow{D_2/\text{Pt}} rac\text{-}$

9.107 Synthesize (*a*) *rac*-2,3-dibromobutane and (*b*) *meso*-2,3-dibromobutane from 2-butyne.

⟋ Br$_2$ can only add *anti*, unlike H$_2$ as in Problem 9.106.

(*a*) Synthesis of this stereoisomer requires a *syn*-addition of H$_2$ and an *anti*-addition of Br$_2$ in any order.

$CH_3C{\equiv}CCH_3 \xrightarrow[\text{Ni/B}]{H_2}$ $\xrightarrow{Br_2} rac\text{-}$

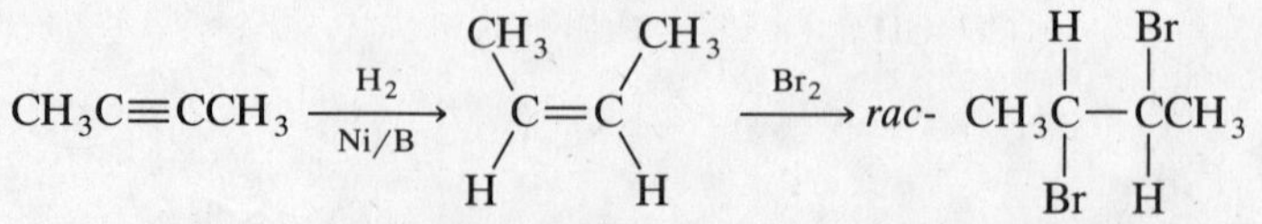

(*b*) This synthesis requires an *anti*-addition of H$_2$ and an *anti*-addition of Br$_2$ in any order.

$CH_3C{\equiv}CCH_3 \xrightarrow{Br_2}$ $\xrightarrow[\text{Ni/B}]{H_2} meso\text{-}$

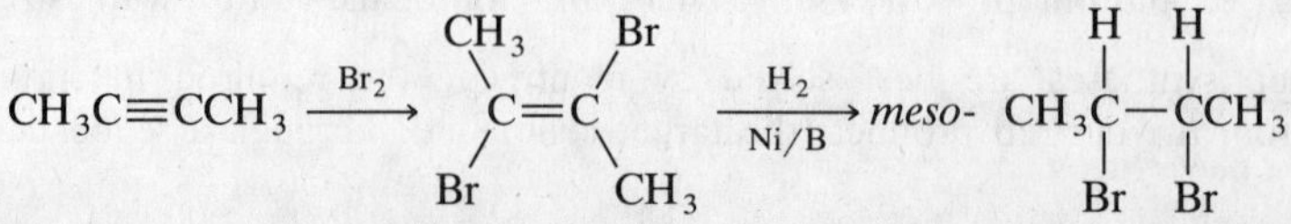

9.108 Use $HC\equiv CH$ as the only organic reactant to prepare (a) (E)-3-hexene and (b) (Z)-3-hexene.

■ Stereospecific alkenes are obtained from the corresponding alkyne.

(a) This stereoisomer results from *anti*-addition of two H's to 3-hexyne, (**A**), that is synthesized by dialkylation with CH_3CH_2Br.

$$HC\equiv CH \xrightarrow{HBr} CH_2=CHBr \xrightarrow{H_2/Pt} CH_3CH_2Br \xrightarrow{Mg, \text{ ether}} CH_3CH_2MgBr$$

$$HC\equiv CH \xrightarrow[-2\,EtH]{2\,EtMgBr} (:C\equiv C:)^{-2}\,2(MgBr^+) \xrightarrow{2\,CH_3CH_2Br} CH_3CH_2C\equiv CCH_2CH_3 \quad (\mathbf{A})$$

$$\mathbf{A} \xrightarrow[EtOH]{Na} \begin{array}{c} CH_3CH_2 \qquad H \\ \diagdown \quad / \\ C=C \\ / \qquad \diagdown \\ H \qquad CH_2CH_3 \end{array}$$

(b) $$\mathbf{A} \xrightarrow[Ni/B]{H_2} \begin{array}{c} CH_3CH_2 \qquad CH_2CH_3 \\ \diagdown \quad / \\ C=C \\ / \qquad \diagdown \\ H \qquad H \end{array}$$

9.109 Convert (a) (E)-2-butene to (Z)-2-butene and (b) (Z)-2-butene to (E)-2-butene.

■ Both isomerizations proceed through the same alkyne.

(a) (E)-$CH_3CH=CHCH_3$

(b) (Z)-$CH_3CH=CHCH_3$

$$\xrightarrow{Br_2} CH_3CHBrCHBrCH_3 \xrightarrow[\text{heat}]{KOH(s)} CH_3C\equiv CCH_3 \begin{array}{l} \xrightarrow{H_2}{}_{Ni/B} (Z)\text{-}CH_3CH=CHCH_3 \\ \\ \xrightarrow{Na}{}_{EtOH} (E)\text{-}CH_3CH=CHCH_3 \end{array}$$

9.110 Prepare (a) butane, (b) 1-butanol, $CH_3CH_2CH_2CH_2OH$, (c) butanone, $CH_3CH_2COCH_3$, from $HC\equiv CH$.

■ In each case the four-carbon chain is generated by alkylation of acetylide anion with CH_3CH_2Br prepared from acetylene. Do not repeat the synthesis of any compound needed in more than part of the question.

(a) Preparation of CH_3CH_2Br [see Problem 9.108(a)]:
Alkylation:

$$HC\equiv CH \xrightarrow{NaNH_2} HC\equiv C:^- \xrightarrow{CH_3CH_2Br} CH_3CH_2C\equiv CH \xrightarrow{2\,H_2/Pt} CH_3CH_2CH_2CH_3$$

(b) $$CH_3CH_2C\equiv CH \xrightarrow{H_2/\text{Lindlar's catalyst}} CH_3CH_2CH=CH_2 \xrightarrow[2.\,H_2O_2,\,OH^-]{1.\,BH_3\cdot THF} CH_3CH_2CH_2CH_2OH$$

(c) $$CH_3CH_2C\equiv CH \xrightarrow[HgSO_4]{H_3O^+} CH_3CH_2\overset{\overset{\displaystyle O}{\|}}{C}CH_3$$

9.111 Prepare 3-octyne from organic compounds with no more than two C's.

■ Synthesis of this eight-carbon compound requires the merging of four two-carbon units through discrete alkylation reactions. The derived name of this compound is butylethylacetylene, from which we infer that acetylene is alkylated with 1-bromobutane and bromoethane, each of which is synthesized from acetylene. See Problem 9.110(a) for the synthesis of CH_3CH_2Br and its reaction with $HC\equiv C:^-$ and Problem 9.110(b) for the synthesis of $CH_3CH_2CH=CH_2$, each from acetylene. HBr is then added to $CH_3CH_2CH=CH_2$ in the presence of peroxides to form $CH_3CH_2CH_2CH_2Br$.

$$HC\equiv C:^- + BrCH_2CH_2CH_2CH_3 \longrightarrow HC\equiv CCH_2CH_2CH_2CH_3 \xrightarrow[2.\,CH_3CH_2Br]{1.\,NaNH_2} CH_3CH_2C\equiv C(CH_2)_3CH_3$$

9.112 Synthesize (a) *cis*-1-butyl-2-ethylcyclopropane and (b) *trans*-1-butyl-2-ethylcyclopropane from 3-octyne.

■ Stereospecific cyclopropanes are synthesized by adding singlet $\ddot{C}H_2$, generated from CH_2N_2, to the appropriate geometric isomer of the corresponding alkene.

(a) $$CH_3CH_2C\equiv C(CH_2)_3CH_3 \xrightarrow[2.\,CH_3COOH]{1.\,Sia_2BH} \begin{array}{c} CH_3CH_2 \qquad (CH_2)_3CH_3 \\ \diagdown \quad / \\ C=C \\ / \qquad \diagdown \\ H \qquad H \end{array} \xrightarrow{CH_2N_2} \begin{array}{c} \qquad\quad CH_2 \\ \qquad / \diagdown \\ CH_3CH_2\overset{\displaystyle |}{C}-\overset{\displaystyle |}{C}(CH_2)_3CH_3 \\ \quad | \qquad | \\ \quad H \qquad H \end{array}$$

(b) $$CH_3CH_2C\equiv C(CH_2)_3CH_3 \xrightarrow[EtOH]{Na} \begin{array}{c} CH_3CH_2 \qquad H \\ \diagdown \quad / \\ C=C \\ / \qquad \diagdown \\ H \qquad (CH_2)_3CH_3 \end{array} \xrightarrow{CH_2N_2} \begin{array}{c} \qquad\quad CH_2 \\ \qquad / \diagdown \\ CH_3CH_2\overset{\displaystyle |}{C}-\overset{\displaystyle |}{CH} \\ \quad \diagdown \qquad \diagdown \\ \quad H \qquad (CH_2)_3CH_3 \end{array}$$

9.113 Synthesize 1-hexen-5-yne from $CH_3CH(OH)CH_3$.

/ From the structure H_2C=$CHCH_2CH_2C$≡CH we deduce that the two three-carbon fragments to be joined in a Corey–House reaction are H_2C=$CHCH_2$— and —CH_2C≡CH. Propene and propyne are intermediates from which two different three-carbon reactants are synthesized.

(a) $CH_3CH(OH)CH_3 \xrightarrow[\text{heat}]{H_2SO_4} CH_3CH$=$CH_2 \xrightarrow{Br_2} CH_3CHBrCH_2Br \xrightarrow[\text{2. } H_2O]{\text{1. } NaNH_2} CH_3C$≡$CH$

(b) CH_3C≡$CH \xrightarrow[\text{heat}]{Cl_2} ClCH_2C$≡$CH$ (**A**) (a propargylic radical halogenation)

(c) CH_3CH=$CH_2 \xrightarrow[\text{heat}]{Cl_2} ClCH_2CH$=$CH_2$ (**B**) (an allylic radical halogenation)

$$\textbf{B} \xrightarrow[\text{2. CuI}]{\text{1. Li}} (H_2C=CHCH_2)_2CuLi \xrightarrow{\textbf{A}} H_2C=CHCH_2CH_2C≡CH$$

9.114 Synthesize CH_3CH_2C≡$CCH(OH)CH_2CH_2CH_3$ from 1-butyne.

/ (a) $CH_3CH_2CH_2CHO$ (**C**) is synthesized from CH_3CH_2C≡CH [see Problems 9.82(b) and 9.83(b)].

(b) CH_3CH_2C≡$CH \xrightarrow{NaNH_2} CH_3CH_2C$≡$C$:$^- \xrightarrow[\text{then } H_2O]{\textbf{C}} CH_3CH_2C$≡$CCH(OH)CH_2CH_2CH_3$

9.115 Give a method of preparation of (S)-(E)-4-deutero-2-hexene from an alkyne and a chiral halide.

/ The precursor of this stereospecific alkene is the corresponding alkyne made by alkylating 1-propyne with 1-bromo-1-deuteropropane. Since this S_N2 alkylation goes with inversion but without change in priorities at the stereocenter, the R enantiomer of the halide must be used. The alkyne is reduced with Na/EtOH.

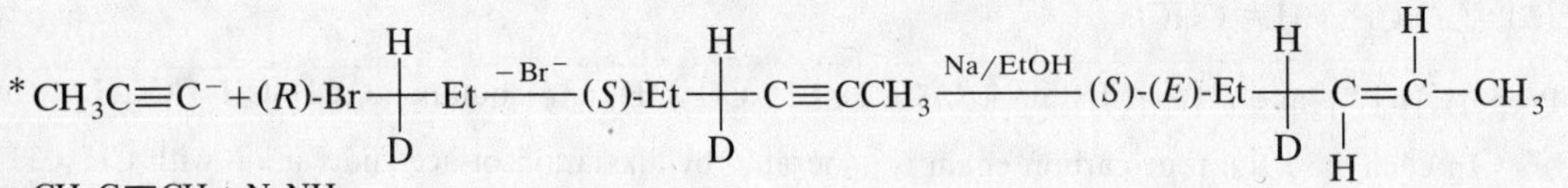

*from CH_3C≡$CH + NaNH_2$

9.116 (a) Give the structural formula of 2-methyl-1-penten-3-yne. (b) Prepare this compound from organic compounds with no more than three C's.

/ (a) H_2C=$C(CH_3)C$≡CCH_3. (b) Direct alkylation of $^-$:C≡CCH_3 with H_2C=$C(Br)CH_3$, a vinyl halide, does not occur. Hence, the C=C is introduced after the alkylation step, i.e., by dehydration of an alcohol.

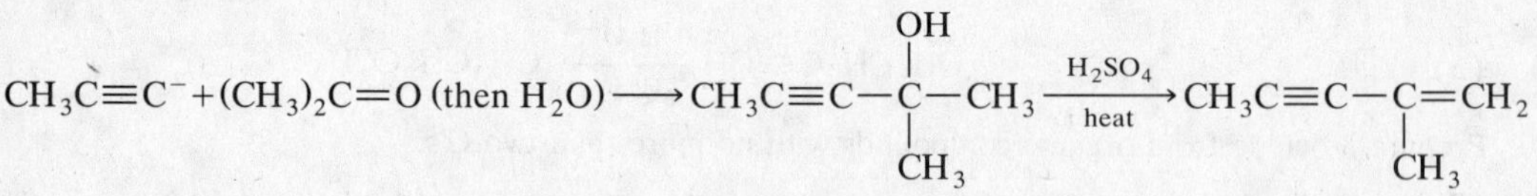

STRUCTURE AND NOMENCLATURE OF DIENES

9.117 Give the structural formulas and IUPAC names of the unbranched isomeric dienes, C_5H_8.

/ (i) H_2C=C=$CHCH_2CH_3$, 1,2-pentadiene; (ii) H_2C=CH—CH=$CHCH_3$, 1,3-pentadiene, Z and E; (iii) H_2C=$CHCH_2CH$=CH_2, 1,4-pentadiene; (iv) CH_3CH=C=$CHCH_3$, 2,3-pentadiene.

9.118 Categorize the three kinds of dienes in Problem 9.117.

/ (i) and (iv) *Cumulated* dienes (allenes) with two double bonds on the same C. (ii) *Conjugated* diene with alternating C=C and C—C bonds. (iii) *Isolated* diene with at least one sp^3 hybridized C between the C=C groupings.

9.119 Compare the stabilities of the three types of dienes in Problem 9.117 from their heats of hydrogenation, ΔH_h (in kcal/mol): (i) −70, (ii, E) −54, and (iii) −61. For comparison, ΔH_h for 1-pentene is −30.1 kcal/mol.

/ The calculated ΔH_h, assuming no interaction between the double bonds, is −60.2 (twice the value for 1-pentene with a single C=C). This is close to the value for (iii). The more negative the observed value of ΔH_h compared to −60.2, the less stable is the diene; the less negative the ΔH_h, the more stable is the diene. The decreasing order of stability of the dienes is

conjugated > isolated > cumulated

9.120   (*a*) Account for the stability of conjugated dienes by (i) extended π bonding and (ii) resonance.   (*b*) Calculate the resonance energy for 1,3-pentadiene.

   ▮   (*a*) (i) Both of the adjacent doubly-bonded C's in the conjugated diene system have a pAO, in the same plane (Fig. 9-2) and overlap side-by-side to engender an extended π system involving all four C's. This results in decreased energy and greater stability.

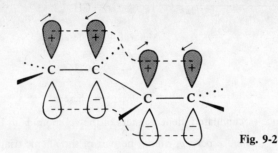

Fig. 9-2

   (ii) A conjugated diene is a resonance hybrid:

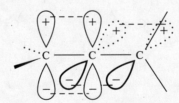

   Since the first structure has 11 bonds and no charges, it makes a more significant contribution than the charged structures, which have only 10 bonds. The hybrid "looks" most like the first structure and there is little resonance energy.
   (*c*)   Using values from Problem 9.119, $-54 - (-60.2) = 6$ kcal/mol.

9.121   Describe the bonding of the three C's of the allene system with the aid of an orbital diagram. What geometry is imposed on the three C's?

   ▮   The middle C has two σ bonds, no unshared e$^-$'s, and is sp hybridized. Its p_y AO overlaps with the p_y AO of one of the end C's to give a π bond in the xy plane. Its p_z AO overlaps with the p_z AO of the C at the other end giving a π bond in the xz plane. See Fig. 9-3.

Fig. 9-3

   The triad of C's must be linear.

9.122   Account for the observed differences in C—C single-bond lengths (in nm) in the following compounds: (i) H_3C—CH_3, 0.153; (ii) H_3C—CH=CH_2, 0.150; (iii) H_2C=CH—CH=CH_2, 0.148.

   ▮   These C—C single-bond lengths are influenced by the HO's used by the C's. As the s-character of the HO increases, the bond gets shorter. The hydridized conditions for the C's are (i) $sp^3 - sp^3$, (ii) $sp^3 - sp^2$, and (iii) $sp^2 - sp^2$ (the most s-character); (iii) has the shortest C—C bond. Additionally, the small contribution of the charged resonance structures of the conjugated diene induces some double-bond character in the C—C bond that leads to more bond shortening.

9.123   What effect does the answer to Problem 9.122 have on the relative stabilities of conjugated and isolated dienes?

   ▮   Conjugated dienes are more stable than isolated dienes. The C—C single bonds in conjugated dienes ($sp^2 - sp^2$) are shorter than the C—C single bonds in isolated dienes. Bond shortening results in greater orbital overlap and increased bond energy, making the molecule more stable.

9.124 Give the structural formulas and IUPAC names for the diene isomers, C_7H_{10}, having a cyclohexyl ring.

    ▰ The seventh C must be bonded to the six-membered ring.

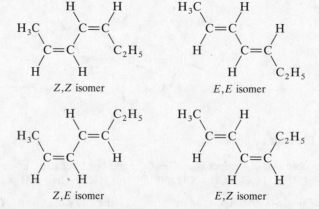

1-Methyl-1,3-cyclohexadiene   1-Methyl-1,4-cyclohexadiene   2-Methyl-1,3-cyclohexadiene

3-Methyl-1,4-cyclohexadiene   5-Methyl-1,3-cyclohexadiene

3-Methylenecyclohexene   4-Methylenecyclohexene

9.125 Account for the absence of cumulated diene isomers of the compounds in Problem 9.124.

    ▰ An external C=C, called *exocyclic*, cannot be part of the allenic triad of C's because the middle C would have to have five bonds. An allenic cyclohexadiene with internal C=C's, called *endocyclic*, cannot exist because of the linearity required for the triad. The terminal C's cannot be joined by only three C's to give a six-membered ring.

9.126 Compare the relative stabilities of isomeric alkynes, cumulated (allenes), and conjugated dienes from the fact that the order of decreasing heats of combustion ΔH_c is allenes > alkynes > conjugated dienes.

    ▰ The most stable isomer has the smallest ΔH_c. Therefore, the order of decreasing stability is conjugated dienes > alkynes > allenes.

9.127 Compare the stabilities of (i) 1,3,5-heptatriene and (ii) 1,3,6-heptatriene.

    ▰ Compound (i), $H_2C=CH-CH=CH-CH=CH-CH_3$, is more stable because it has three conjugated double bonds whereas (ii), $H_2C=CH-CH=CH-CH_2-CH=CH_2$, has only two. As the number of conjugated double bonds increases, the stability increases.

9.128 Draw and give the stereochemical designation for the geometric isomers of 2,4-heptadiene.

    ▰ Each double bond can generate geometric isomers.

Z,Z isomer   *E,E* isomer

Z,E isomer   *E,Z* isomer

9.129 Draw and give the stereochemical designation for the geometric isomers of 2,4-hexadiene.

    ▰ Since this diene is symmetrical (going from left to right is the same as going from right to left), *Z,E* and *E,Z* designate the same molecule. Hence, there are only three stereoisomers.

Z,Z   *E,E*   *Z,E*

9.130   Give the structural formulas and IUPAC names of the dienes, C_6H_{10}, other than allenes, having no geometric isomers.

     ▰   Both double bonds are terminal.

       A H_2C=$CHCH_2CH_2CH$=CH_2, 1,5-hexadiene

       B H_2C=$C(CH_3)CH_2CH$=CH_2, 2-methyl-1,4-pentadiene

       C H_2C=$C(CH_3)C(CH_3)$=CH_2, 2,3-dimethyl-1,3-butadiene

       D H_2C=$C(CH_2CH_3)CH$=CH_2, 2-ethyl-1,3-butadiene

         Note the longest chain with both C=C bonds is chosen rather than the one with more C's.

       E H_2C=$CHCH(CH_3)CH$=CH_2, 3-methyl-1,4-pentadiene

         One double bond is internal with at least one of its C's having two-like groups.

       F H_2C=$CHCH$=$C(CH_3)_2$, 4-methyl-1,3-pentadiene

9.131   (*a*) Give the two conformations of 1,3-butadiene resulting from rotation about the C—C single bond. (*b*) Discuss their relative stabilities.

     ▰   (*a*)

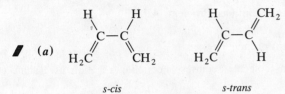

            s-cis   *s-trans*

         These are not true *cis* and *trans* forms because they are not rigid as is the case for alkenes. They are conformational isomers and are interconvertible. The prefix *s* indicates they are juxtapositions relative to the C—C σ bond.

     (*b*)   The *s-trans* conformation predominates because the bulkier methylene groups are farther apart.

9.132   (*a*) Explain why the *s-cis* conformation of 1,3-butadiene participates in the Diels–Alder reaction.   (*b*) Account for the fact that this reaction goes in a very good yield although the less stable conformation reacts.

     ▰   (*a*)   The cyclohexene product must have the *cis* orientation at its C=C; this fact requires the diene to be *s-cis*. Reaction of the *s-trans* would lead to the formation of the impossible *trans*-cyclohexene.

     (*b*)   An equilibrium exists between the two conformations, *s-cis* ⇌ *s-trans*, that favors *s-trans*. However, as the *s-cis* is consumed, it is replenished by formation from *s-trans*, and the equilibrium shifts to the left. Eventually all the diene reacts by going through the less stable *s-cis* conformation.

SYNTHESES OF DIENES

9.133   Give the industrial synthesis of 1,3-butadiene.

     ▰   Industrial syntheses require inexpensive starting materials. In this case, butane, isolated by fractional distillation of petroleum, is dehydrogenated ($-2H_2$) with a heterogeneous catalyst.

9.134   Synthesize 1,3-butadiene from 1-butene.

     ▰ H_2C=$CHCH_2CH_3 \xrightarrow{\text{NBS}} H_2C$=$CHCHBrCH_3 \xrightarrow{\text{alc. KOH}} H_2C$=$CHCH$=$CH_2$

9.135   Synthesize 1,3-butadiene from acetylene.

     ▰ $2HC$≡$CH \xrightarrow[\text{NH}_4\text{Cl}]{\text{CuCl}} H_2C$=$CHC$≡$CH \xrightarrow[\text{(BaSO}_4)]{\text{H}_2/\text{Pt}} H_2C$=$CHCH$=$CH_2$

9.136   (*a*) The addition of one equivalent of HBr to vinylacetylene gives a product **A** that does not give a precipitate with $Cu(NH_3)_2^+OH^-$. Give the structural formula of **A**.   (*b*) Give the structural formula of another product **B** that could have been formed.   (*c*) Account for the formation of **A** rather than **B**.

     ▰   (*a*) The lack of reaction with Cu^+ indicates that **A** is not a terminal alkyne. The HBr added to the —C≡CH to give a diene, H_2C=CH—CBr=CH_2, 2-bromo-1,3-butadiene.   (*b*) **B** would be CH_3CHBrC≡CH, formed from addition to the C=C.   (*c*) Although typically —C=C— is more reactive than —C≡C— in electrophilic additions (Problem 9.73), in this case the triple bond reacts because the product is the conjugated diene **A**, which is more stable than **B**, an alkyne.

9.137 Predict the product of the reaction of $(CH_3)_2CHCHClCH_2CH=CH_2$ with alc. KOH.

/ The more stable conjugated diene $(CH_3)_2CHCH=CHCH=CH_2$ is formed rather than the Sayzteff product, the isolated diene $(CH_3)_2C=CHCH_2CH=CH_2$.

9.138 (*a*) Which dihydroxybutanes can be used to prepare 1,3-butadiene?   (*b*) Why cannot a *vic*-dihydroxy compound (diol) such as $CH_3CH(OH)CH(OH)CH_3$ be used?   (*c*) Why can the *vic*-diol $(CH_3)_2C(OH)C(OH)(CH_3)_2$ be used to synthesize 2,3-dimethyl-1,3-butadiene?   (*d*) Why is the yield in (*c*) low?

/ The dienes are made by a double dehydration with an acid catalyst (Al_2O_3, P_2O_5, $KHSO_4$, etc.). Branched chain compounds cannot be used to give the unbranched target product.
(*a*) $HOCH_2CH_2CH_2CH_2OH$ and $HOCH_2CH_2CH(OH)CH_3$ both give good yields of $H_2C=CHCH=CH_2$.
(*b*) A single dehydration step gives an enol, $H_3CCH=C(OH)CH_3$ (the more stable Sayzteff product) which rearranges to the ketone, $CH_3COCH_2CH_3$ (Problem 9.76).
(*c*) There are no H's on the C's bonded to the OH's, therefore dehydration must give terminal C=C's. An intermediate enol cannot form. This diol dehydrates to give 2,3-dimethyl-1,3-butadiene, $H_2C=C(Me)C(Me)=CH_2$.
(*d*) This kind of diol undergoes a pinacol rearrangement (see Problem 14.91).

9.139 Synthesize $H_2C=CHCH_2CH_2CH=CH_2$ (**C**) from propene.

/ Going from a three-carbon to a six-carbon molecule requires a coupling reaction best achieved by a Corey–House synthesis.

$$2\,H_2C=CHCH_3 \; (\textbf{A}) \xrightarrow[\Delta]{Cl_2} 2\,H_2C=CHCH_2Cl \xrightarrow[\text{2. CuI}]{\text{1. Li}} (H_2C=CHCH_2)_2CuLi \; (\textbf{B}); \qquad \textbf{A} + \textbf{B} \longrightarrow \textbf{C}$$

9.140 Prepare 1,3-cyclohexadiene from cyclohexane.

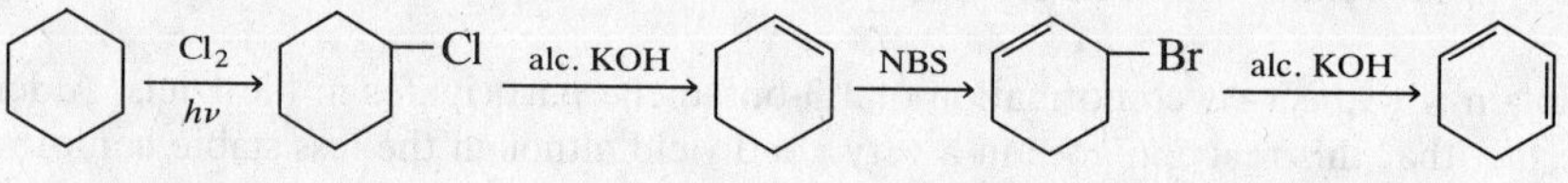

3-Bromo-cyclohexene

9.141 (*a*) Categorize the two kinds of Diels–Alder reactants.   (*b*) Prepare 1,4-cyclohexadiene from acyclic (noncyclic) compounds by a Diels–Alder synthesis.

/ (*a*) The first kind of reactant is a conjugated *diene*; the second is a *dienophile* which may be an alkene or alkyne. Electron-withdrawing groups, such as C≡N and C=O attached to the multiple bond of the dienophile, increase its reactivity.

(*b*)

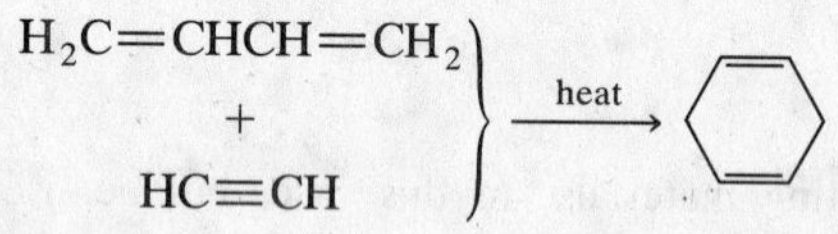

REACTIONS OF DIENES

9.142 Give the ozonolysis products from the dienes in Problem 9.130.

/ **A** $H_2C=O$, $O=CH-CH_2CH_2CH=O$, **D** $H_2C=O$, $CH_3CH_2-CO-CH=O$,
  $O=CH_2$ $O=CH_2$
  B $H_2C=O$, $CH_3-CO-CH_2CH=O$, **E** $H_2C=O$, $O=CH-CH(CH_3)-CH=O$,
  $O=CH_2$ $O=CH_2$
  C $H_2C=O$, $CH_3-CO-CO-CH_3$, **F** $H_2C=O$, $O=CH-CH=O$,
  $O=CH_2$ $O=C(CH_3)_2$

9.143 Give the mechanism for the acid-catalyzed isomerization of 1,4-cyclohexadiene to the more stable 1,3-isomer.

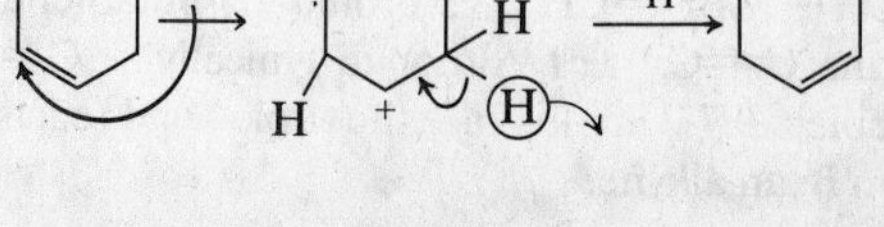

9.144 Typical of alkynes and allenes, prolonged treatment of either 2-pentyne (**A**) or 1,2-pentadiene (**B**) with solid KOH results in the following equilibrium mixture:

$$\text{(A) } CH_3C\equiv CCH_2CH_3 \text{ (96\%)} \rightleftharpoons \text{(B) } H_2C=C=CHCH_2CH_3 \text{ (4\%)}$$

(*a*) Suggest a mechanism.   (*b*) Why is 1-pentyne not formed?

◢ (*a*)   Removal of H$^+$ from C^1 of **A** or C^3 of **B** by OH$^-$ affords carbanionic contributing structures of the same resonance hybrid:

$$A \xrightleftharpoons{-H^+} \left[H_2\ddot{C}-C\equiv CCH_2CH_3 \longleftrightarrow H_2C\!=\!=\!C\!=\!=\!CCH_2CH_3 \longleftrightarrow H_2C=C=\ddot{C}-CH_2CH_3 \right]^- \xrightleftharpoons{-H^+} B$$

path to **A** \ / path to **B**

H$^+$ (from H$_2$O)

H$^+$ from H$_2$O adds mainly to C^1 of the hybrid, giving the more stable **A**, and minimally to C^3 to give **B**.

(*b*)   Were 1-pentyne to form, it would be isomerized by OH$^-$ to 2-pentyne, the more stable internal alkyne (see Problem 9.45).

9.145 (*a*) Give the two isomers (exclusive of geometric isomers) formed when one equivalent of **HBr** is added to 1,3-butadiene.   (*b*) Explain 1,4-addition in terms of the typical mechanism for electrophilic addition.

◢ (*a*)   There are two kinds of additions, $H_2C=CH-CHBr-CH_2H$, 1,2-addition, and $H_2CBr-CH=CH-CH_2H$, 1,4-addition. (Bold letters indicate the modes of the additions.)

(*b*)   The electrophile (**H**$^+$) adds to either C=C to form an allylic carbocation whose positive charge is delocalized to C^2 and C^4 (resonance forms **A** and **B**), resulting in greater stability. The nucleophile (**Br**$^-$) adds to C^2 of the hybrid **C** to give the 1,2-adduct or to C^4 to give the 1,4-adduct.

$$H_2C=CHCH=CH_2 \xrightarrow{H^+} \left[\begin{array}{c} H_2CH\overset{+}{C}HCH=CH_2 \\ \text{(A)} \\ \updownarrow \\ H_2CHCH=CHCH_2^+ \\ \text{(B)} \end{array} \right] \text{ or } \left[H_2CHCH\!=\!=\!\overset{+}{CH}\!=\!=\!CH_2 \atop \text{(C)} \right] \xrightarrow{Br^-}$$

$$H_2CHCHBrCH=CH_2 \; + \; H_2CHCH=CHCH_2Br$$

9.146 (*a*) Explain why HBr adds to 1,3-pentadiene at a faster rate than to 1,4-pentadiene.   (*b*) Is this inconsistent with the conjugated diene being more stable than the isolated diene?

◢ (*a*) When an electrophile (H$^+$) adds to the conjugated diene in the rate-controlling step, an allylic carbocation is formed (Problem 9.145). Addition to the isolated diene gives an ordinary saturated 2° carbocation, $CH_3\overset{+}{C}HCH_2CH=CH_2$. The allylic carbocation is more stable, the $\Delta H^\ddagger$ of its formation is less than the $\Delta H^\ddagger$ for the formation of the ordinary carbocation. Thus, it is formed at a faster rate.   (*b*) No! Stability is a thermodynamic property, while reactivity is a kinetic property.

9.147 (*a*) When HBr adds to butadiene at a low temperature (-80 °C), which addendum is the major product?   (*b*) Which is the major product at higher temperatures (40 °C)?   (*c*) What happens when the 1,2-adduct is warmed to higher temperatures?

◢ (*a*) $CH_3CHBrCH=CH_2$, 1,2-adduct (**A**).   (*b*) $BrCH_2CH=CHCH_3$, 1,4-adduct (**B**).   (*c*) The 1,2-adduct rearranges to give mainly the 1,4-adduct.

9.148 (*a*) Use an enthalpy diagram to illustrate the results in Problem 9.147.   (*b*) Explain the results in terms of rate and thermodynamic control of products. Identify the rate-controlled and thermodynamically-controlled products.   (*c*) Why is the 1,4-adduct more stable?

◢ (*a*)   See Fig. 9-4. The two products arise from $\Delta H^\ddagger$ differences in the second step, the reaction of Br$^-$ with the allyl R$^+$.

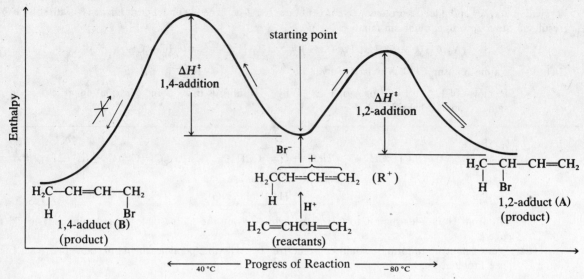

Fig. 9-4

(b) At $-80\,°C$ the 1,2-adduct has the lower $\Delta H^{\ddagger}$ and is formed at the faster rate. It is the *rate-controlled* product, **A**. As the temperature rises to $40\,°C$, the 1,2-adduct is able to reverse back to the intermediate R^{+}, and then can pass through the higher enthalpy transition state, leading to the more stable *thermodynamically-controlled* 1,4-adduct, **B**. **B** accumulates at the higher temperature because the $\Delta H^{\ddagger}$ for reversing to the R^{+} has a higher $\Delta H^{\ddagger}$ than that of **A**.

(c) **B** is a more substituted alkene than **A**.

9.149 (a) Give the products of the reactions of $H_2C{=}CHCH{=}CH_2$ with one eq of the following reagents at room temperature: (i) Cl_2, (ii) HBr with peroxide, and (iii) H_2/Pd. (b) Give the structure of the intermediate formed in reaction (ii) of (a).

⬛ (a) (i) $ClCH_2CH{=}CHCH_2Cl$ (major) + $ClCH_2CHClCH{=}CH_2$ (minor)
(ii) $CH_3CH{=}CHCH_2Br$. Radical addition gives 1,4-adduct almost exclusively.
(iii) $CH_3CH{=}CHCH_3 + CH_3CH_2CH{=}CH_2$.

(b) It is an allylic radical stabilized by resonance (delocalized π bonding):

$$\left[H_2C{=}CH{-}\overset{\cdot}{C}H{-}CH_2Br \longleftrightarrow H_2\overset{\cdot}{C}{-}CH{=}CH{-}CH_2Br \right] \quad \text{or} \quad \left[H_2\overset{\delta\cdot}{C}{\cdots}CH{\cdots}\overset{\delta\cdot}{C}H{-}CH_2Br \right].$$

9.150 (a) Write the structures of all the possible intermediate carbocations (R^{+}'s) that could be obtained from the reaction of 2-methyl-1,3-butadiene, $H_2C^{1}{=}C^{2}Me{-}C^{3}H{=}C^{4}H_2$ with one mole of HBr. Evaluate the likelihood of each R^{+} forming. (b) Give the complete mechanism for the formation of the two products, indicating the major one.

⬛ (a) $H_2HC{-}\overset{+}{C}Me{-}CH{=}CH_2$ (**A**); H^{+} adds to C^{1} to give the 3° allylic R^{+}, the most stable and most likely to form. $H_2\overset{+}{C}{-}CHMe{-}CH{=}CH_2$ (**B**) and $H_2C{=}CMe{-}CHH{-}\overset{+}{C}H_2$ (**C**), respectively; addition to C^{2} or C^{3} would give these unlikely nonallylic 1° R^{+}'s. $H_2C{=}CMe{-}\overset{+}{C}H{-}CH_2H$ (**D**), addition to C^{4} gives this 2° allylic R^{+}, less likely than **A**, more likely than **B** and **C**.

(b)

$$\underset{1\quad 2\quad 3\quad 4}{H_2C{=}\underset{|}{C}{-}CH{=}CH_2} + HBr \xrightarrow{\;\delta+\;\delta-\;} \left[H_3C{-}\underset{+}{\overset{Me}{\underset{|}{C}}}{-}CH{=}CH_2 \longleftrightarrow H_3C{-}\overset{Me}{\underset{|}{C}}{=}CH{-}\overset{+}{C}H_2 \right]$$

$$\Big\downarrow Br^{-}$$

$$CH_3{-}\overset{Me}{\underset{|}{\underset{Br}{C}}}{-}CH{=}CH_2 \quad + \quad CH_3{-}\overset{Me}{\underset{|}{C}}{=}CH{-}CH_2{-}Br$$

3-Bromo-3-methyl-1-butene   1-Bromo-3-methyl-2-butene
(minor)   (major)

9.151 Give the products (ignoring *cis/trans* isomerism) of the reaction of (*a*) cyclopentadiene and (*b*) 1-methyl-1,3-cyclohexadiene with equivalent amounts of (i) Br_2, (ii) HBr, (iii) HBr/peroxide, and (iv) H_2S/peroxide.

◢ (*a*) (i) [structure: cyclopentene ring with Br and Br] (ii) [structure with H and Br] (iii) [structure with H and Br] (iv) [structure with H and SH]

(*b*) (i) Br—[cyclohexene ring]—Me, Br (ii) H—[ring]—Me, Br (iii) Br—[ring]—Me, H (iv) HS—[ring]—Me, H

9.152 (*a*) Which additional C's in the following R^+ bear some positive charge?

$$-\overset{|}{\underset{7}{C}}=\overset{|}{\underset{6}{C}}-\overset{|}{\underset{5}{C}}=\overset{|}{\underset{4}{C}}-\overset{|}{\underset{3}{C}}=\overset{|}{\underset{2}{C}}-\overset{+}{\underset{1|}{C}}-$$

(*b*) With which of these C's will $:Nu^-$ react to yield the thermodynamically-controlled product?

◢ (*a*) C^3, C^5, and C^7. These are alternating sites.

$$\left[-\overset{|}{\underset{7}{C}}=\overset{|}{\underset{6}{C}}-\overset{|}{\underset{5}{C}}=\overset{|}{\underset{4}{C}}-\overset{+}{\underset{3}{C}}-\overset{|}{\underset{2}{C}}=\overset{|}{\underset{1|}{C}} \longleftrightarrow -\overset{|}{\underset{7}{C}}=\overset{|}{\underset{6}{C}}-\overset{+}{\underset{5}{C}}-\overset{|}{\underset{4}{C}}=\overset{|}{\underset{3}{C}}-\overset{|}{\underset{2}{C}}=\overset{|}{\underset{1|}{C}} \longleftrightarrow \overset{+}{\underset{7}{C}}-\overset{|}{\underset{6}{C}}=\overset{|}{\underset{5}{C}}-\overset{|}{\underset{4}{C}}=\overset{|}{\underset{3}{C}}-\overset{|}{\underset{2}{C}}=\overset{|}{\underset{1|}{C}} \right]$$

(*b*) Nu^- adds to equivalent C^1 or C^7 to give the conjugated triene

$$-\overset{|}{C}=\overset{|}{C}-\overset{|}{C}=\overset{|}{C}-\overset{|}{C}=\overset{|}{C}-\overset{|}{\underset{|}{C}}-Nu \quad \text{(more stable)}$$

Addition at C^3 (or C^5) gives a triene with only 2 conjugated C=C's,

$$-\overset{|}{C}=\overset{|}{C}-\overset{|}{\underset{\underset{Nu}{|}}{C}}-\overset{|}{C}=\overset{|}{C}-\overset{|}{C}=\overset{|}{C}- \quad \text{(less stable)}$$

9.153 Consider the addition of one eq of Br_2 to 1,3,5-hexatriene. (*a*) Deduce structures of possible products. (*b*) Which are the thermodynamically-controlled products?

◢ (*a*) First, Br^+ adds at C^1 to form a 2° allylic-type R^+ having + charge on C^2, C^4 and C^6. Then Br^- adds to form three dibromo addition products.

$$\overset{1}{H_2C}=\overset{2}{CH}-\overset{3}{CH}=\overset{4}{CH}-\overset{5}{CH}=\overset{6}{CH_2} \xrightarrow{Br_2}$$

$$\left[\begin{array}{l} \overset{1}{H_2C}-\overset{2}{CH}=\overset{3}{CH}-\overset{4}{\underset{+}{CH}}-\overset{5}{CH}=\overset{6}{CH_2} \\ \quad | \\ \quad Br \\ \updownarrow \\ H_2C-\overset{+}{CH}-CH=CH-CH=CH_2 \\ \quad | \\ \quad Br \\ \updownarrow \\ H_2C-CH=CH-CH=CH-\overset{+}{CH_2} \\ \quad | \\ \quad Br \end{array} \right] \xrightarrow{Br^-}$$

$$\begin{array}{l} H_2C-CH=CH-CH-CH=CH_2 \quad \textbf{(A)} \\ \;\;| \qquad\qquad\qquad\; | \\ \;\;Br \qquad\qquad\qquad\; Br \\[8pt] H_2C-CH-CH=CH-CH=CH_2 \quad \textbf{(B)} \\ \;\;| \quad\; | \\ \;\;Br \;\; Br \\[8pt] H_2C-CH=CH-CH=CH-CH_2 \quad \textbf{(C)} \\ \;\;| \qquad\qquad\qquad\qquad\; | \\ \;\;Br \qquad\qquad\qquad\qquad\; Br \end{array}$$

A fourth product (**D**), $H_2C=CH-CHBr-CHBr-CH=CH_2$, arises from addition at C^3 and C^4.

(*b*) Thermodynamic-control conditions favor the more stable products. These are the conjugated dienes **B** and **C** rather than the isolated dienes, **A** and **D**. **C** is more stable than **B** because its double bonds have more R groups.

9.154 Convert 1,3-butadiene to *rac*-1,4-dibromo-2,3-dideuterobutane.

◢ $$H_2C=CHCH=CH_2 \xrightarrow{Br_2} \underset{trans}{H_2CBrCH=CHCH_2Br} \xrightarrow{D_2/Pd} BrH_2C\overset{\overset{\displaystyle H\,D}{|}}{\underset{\underset{\displaystyle D\,H}{|}}{|\!\!-\!\!|}}CH_2Br$$

9.155 Give the major product of a peroxide-catalyzed reaction of 1,3-butadiene with $BrCCl_3$.

◢ This is a radical addition which typically gives mainly the 1,4-adduct, $BrCH_2CH=CHCH_2CCl_3$.

9.156 Give the mechanism for the electrophilic (E^+) induced polymerization of 1,3-butadiene acting as a typical conjugated diene. Indicate the repeating unit (mer) of the polymer.

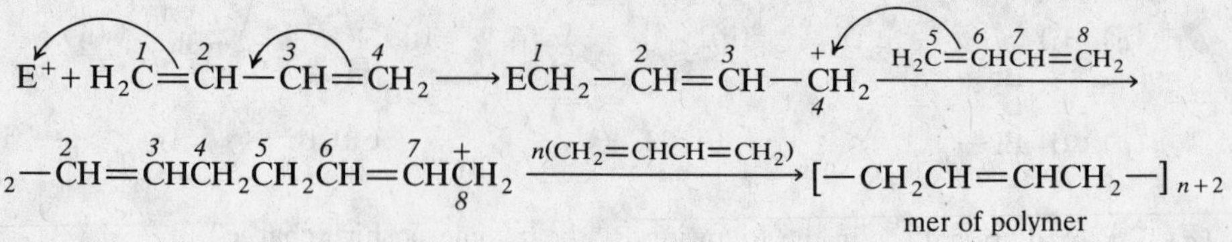

$$E^+ + H_2\overset{1}{C}=\overset{2}{CH}-\overset{3}{CH}=\overset{4}{CH_2} \longrightarrow E\overset{1}{CH_2}-\overset{2}{CH}=\overset{3}{CH}-\overset{4}{\overset{+}{CH_2}} \quad \overset{5}{H_2C}=\overset{6}{CH}\overset{7}{CH}=\overset{8}{CH_2} \longrightarrow$$

$$E\overset{1}{CH_2}-\overset{2}{CH}=\overset{3}{CH}\overset{4}{CH_2}\overset{5}{CH_2}\overset{6}{CH}=\overset{7}{CH}\overset{+}{\overset{8}{CH_2}} \xrightarrow{n(CH_2=CHCH=CH_2)} [-CH_2CH=CHCH_2-]_{n+2}$$

mer of polymer

9.157 Give the mechanism for the anionic ($Nu:^-$) induced polymerization of isoprene (2-methyl-1,3-butadiene) that affords a synthetic rubber.

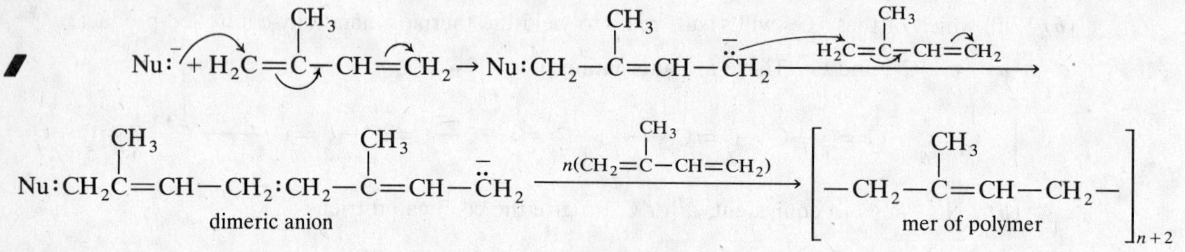

$$Nu:^- + H_2C=\overset{\overset{\displaystyle CH_3}{|}}{C}-CH=CH_2 \rightarrow Nu:CH_2-\overset{\overset{\displaystyle CH_3}{|}}{C}=CH-\overset{..}{C}H_2 \quad \overset{\overset{\displaystyle CH_3}{|}}{H_2C=C-CH=CH_2} \longrightarrow$$

$$Nu:CH_2\overset{\overset{\displaystyle CH_3}{|}}{C}=CH-CH_2:CH_2-\overset{\overset{\displaystyle CH_3}{|}}{C}=CH-\overset{..}{C}H_2 \xrightarrow{n(CH_2=\overset{\overset{\displaystyle CH_3}{|}}{C}-CH=CH_2)} \left[-CH_2-\overset{\overset{\displaystyle CH_3}{|}}{C}=CH-CH_2-\right]_{n+2}$$

dimeric anion · mer of polymer

The reaction is stereospecific in yielding a polymer with an all-Z configuration.

Conjugated dienes undergo nucleophilic attack more easily than simple alkenes because they form more stable allyl carbanions,

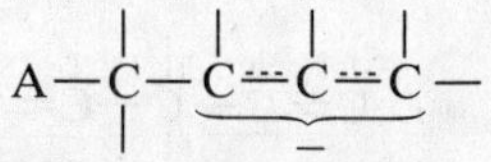

$$A-\overset{|}{\underset{|}{C}}-\underset{\underbrace{}_{-}}{\overset{|}{C}\text{---}\overset{|}{C}\text{---}\overset{|}{C}}-$$

Like the allyl cation, the allylic anion is stabilized by charge delocalization through extended π bonding.

9.158 Show the initiation and the dimerization step in the radical ($Z\cdot$) induced polymerization of a conjugated diene.

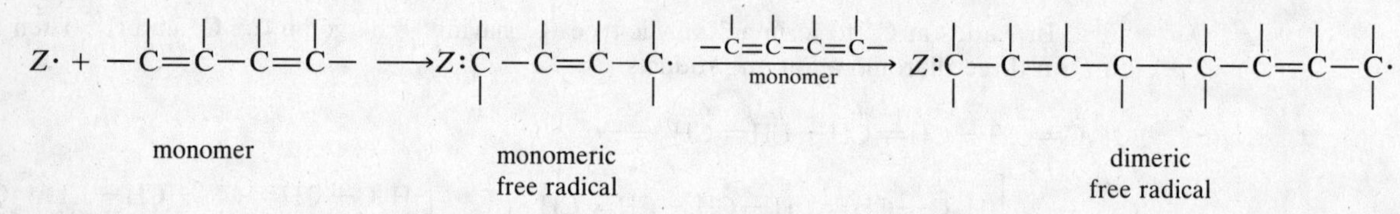

$$Z\cdot + -\overset{|}{C}=\overset{|}{C}-\overset{|}{C}=\overset{|}{C}- \longrightarrow Z:\overset{|}{C}-\overset{|}{C}=\overset{|}{C}-\overset{|}{C}\cdot \xrightarrow[\text{monomer}]{-\overset{|}{C}=\overset{|}{C}-\overset{|}{C}=\overset{|}{C}-} Z:\overset{|}{C}-\overset{|}{C}=\overset{|}{C}-\overset{|}{C}-\overset{|}{C}-\overset{|}{C}=\overset{|}{C}-\overset{|}{C}\cdot$$

monomer · · · · · · · · · · · monomeric · dimeric
free radical · free radical

ANALYSIS AND STRUCTURE PROOF

9.159 Give a simple chemical test to distinguish the following pairs of compounds:
(*a*) 1-Hexyne and 2-hexyne, (*b*) 1,4-hexadiene and hexane, (*c*) 2-bromo-1,4-pentadiene and 4-bromo-2-pentyne, and (*d*) 3-hexyne and bicyclo[2.2.0]hexane.

▮ (*a*) 1-Hexyne, a terminal alkyne, gives a precipitate, $CH_3(CH_2)_3C\equiv CAg$ with $Ag(NH_3)_2Cl$. The internal alkyne 2-hexyne does not. (*b*) Unlike hexane, the diene is oxidized with $KMnO_4$ under mild conditions to give MnO_2, a brown precipitate. (*c*) Since 4-bromo-2-pentyne is a propargyllic halide, it rapidly reacts with $AgNO_3$ in ethanol to give a precipitate of AgCl. Since the Br in 2-bromo-1,4-pentadiene is vinylic, its reactivity is diminished and it is inert towards $AgNO_3$. (*d*) The alkyne is unsaturated and decolorizes (reacts with) the reddish-brown solution of Br_2 in CCl_4. (The color is due to the Br_2; CCl_4 is merely the solvent). Bicyclo[2.2.0]hexane is inert.

9.160 Describe chemical methods (not necessarily simple tests) that would distinguish between:

(*a*) 2-Hexyne and 2-hexene
(*b*) 1,4-Pentadiene and 1-pentene
(*c*) 3-Octyne and 4-octyne
(*d*) 2,4-Hexadiene and 2-hexyne
(*e*) $CH_3CH_2CH(CH_3)C\equiv CCOOH$ (**A**) and $CH_3CH_2CH_2CH_2C\equiv CCOOH$ (**B**),

(*f*) $CH_3CH_2CH=C=CHCOOH$ (**C**) and $CH_2=CHCH(COOH)CH=CH_2$ (**D**)
(*g*) 2,4-Hexadiene (**E**) and 2,4-hexadiyne (**F**) (two ways)
(*h*) 1,3-Cyclohexadiene (**G**) and 3-methylenecyclohexene (**H**).

▮ (*a*) and (*b*) Use quantitative catalytic hydrogenation. The alkyne in (*a*) and the diene in (*b*) consume two eq of H_2, the alkenes only one eq.

(c) 4-Octyne is a symmetrical alkyne and undergoes ozonolysis to give a single acid, $CH_3CH_2CH_2COOH$. 3-Octyne gives two separable acids, CH_3CH_2COOH and $CH_3CH_2CH_2CH_2COOH$.

(d) 2,4-Hexadiene is a conjugated diene that can undergo a Diels–Alder reaction when heated with a dieneophile, such as maleic anhydride, to give a new solid product as determined by its melting point.

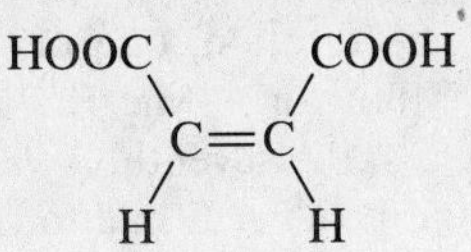

$$HOOC \quad COOH$$
$$C=C$$
$$H \qquad H$$

Maleic anhydride

(e) Unlike B, A has a chiral center and is resolvable.

(f) Unlike D, the allene C is chiral and can be resolved.

(g) Quantitative hydrogenation leads to the absorption of two eq of H_2 by E and four by F. Also, F cannot undergo a Diels–Alder reaction; the "product" would be an allenic cyclohexadiene which is too strained to exist.

(h) While G is an s-cis conjugated diene that readily undergoes a Diels–Alder reaction, e.g., with maleic anhydride [see (d)], H has a rigid s-trans arrangement and cannot undergo such a reaction.

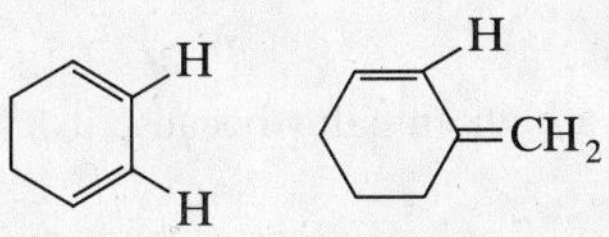

G s-cis   H s-trans

9.161 An unknown optically active hydrocarbon (A), C_8H_{12}, gives an optically inactive compound (B), C_8H_{18}, after hydrogenation. A gives no precipitate with $Ag(NH_3)_2^+$ and gives optically inactive C, C_8H_{14}, with H_2 in presence of Ni/B. (a) Determine the structures, give suitable names for A, B, and C, and give your reasoning. (b) Will an optically active C result if A is reacted with Na in EtOH? Explain and give the structure of this optically active C. (c) What would the structure of A be if on reaction with H_2, Ni/B, or Na in EtOH, it gave an optically active C?

(a) Since three eq of H_2 are consumed to get B, A has three degrees of unsaturation that arise from multiple bonds—it has no rings. A has a $-C≡C-$ because it adds one eq of H_2 with Ni/B, a reagent that reduces alkynes to alkenes. The absence of a positive test with $Ag(NH_3)_2^+$ indicates that A has an internal $-C≡C-R$ group accounting for two of the degrees of unsaturation. The third degree is due to a $-C=C-$. Since the completely hydrogenated compound B is achiral, the alkynyl and alkenyl groups attached to the stereocenter must have the same skeleton and number of C's. The position of the multiple bonds in A and C must be the same, since C, a dialkenyl compound, is achiral. Furthermore both multiple bonds cannot be terminal. In order for C to be achiral, the original alkenyl group in A must be Z, because the C=C in C, formed by syn catalytic hydrogenation of A, is Z. The eighth C in (A) is a $-CH_3$ bonded to the chiral C. The structures are:

(A) $CH_3-C=C-\underset{*}{C}H(CH_3)-C≡C-CH_3$, (Z)-4-methyl-2-hepten-5-yne
                | |
                H H

(*indicates chiral C.)

(B) $CH_3CH_2CH_2CH(CH_3)CH_2CH_2CH_3$, 4-methylheptane

(C) $CH_3C=C-CH(CH_3)-C=C-CH_3$, (Z, Z)-4-methyl-2,5-heptadiene
              | | | |
              H H   H H

(b) Yes. This anti reduction would have caused the new alkenyl group to be E, while the original one is Z. The compound is

$$CH_3-C=C-CH(CH_3)-\overset{H}{\underset{|}{C}}=C-CH_3,\quad (Z,E)\text{-4-methyl-2,5-heptadiene}$$
        | |
        H H

(c) In order for C to be chiral regardless of the method for reducing $-C≡C-$, the position of the multiple bond of the alkynyl and alkenyl groups in A must be different; $-C≡C-$ must be internal and therefore $-C=C-$ is terminal. A would be

$$H_2C=CH-CH_2-CH(CH_3)-C≡C-CH_3,\quad \text{4-methyl-1-hepten-5-yne}$$

9.162 A hydrocarbon (**D**) C_7H_{10}, is catalytically hydrogenated to C_7H_{14} but does not react with H_2, Ni/B. Vigorous oxidation with $KMnO_4$ affords $HOOC^1C^2H_2C^3H_2\overset{\overset{\displaystyle O}{\|}}{C^4}C^5H_2C^6OOH$ (**E**). Deduce all the possible structures of **D** and explain your answer.

D has three degrees of unsaturation, one of which is a ring, because only two eq of H_2 are consumed ($C_7H_{10} + 2H_2 \rightarrow C_7H_{14}$). **D** is not an alkyne (no reaction with H_2, Ni/B) and must be a diene. Since the oxidation product has only six C's, the seventh C was lost as CO_2, indicating the presence of a terminal $=CH_2$ group. The open-chain oxidation product **E** had to come from a cycloalkene. Had both C=C groups in **D** been *exo cyclic* (outside the ring), **E** would have been a cyclic compound. One of the three C's in **E** with an oxygen-containing functional group has to be bonded to the exocyclic $=CH_2$, the other two come from cleavage of the *endocyclic* (internal) C=C. If C^1 and C^6 are the C's of the endo C=C and C^4 is part of the exo C=C, **D** has the structure **D**-1. If C^1 and C^4 come from the endo bond and C^6 from the exo bond, the compound is **D**-2. The third possibility has C^4 and C^6 from the endo bond and C^1 from the exo bond with the structure **D**-3.

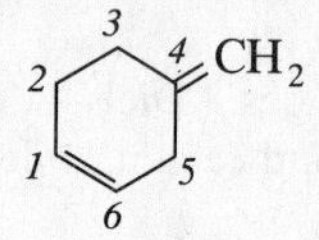
D − 1

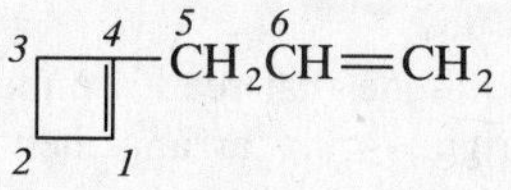
D − 2

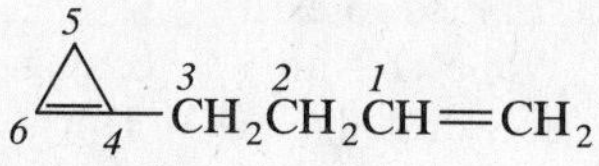
D − 3

It is noteworthy that **D**-3 has a high enthalpy because it has a very high ring strain.

9.163 (*a*) Catalytic hydrogenation of **F**, $C_{10}H_{14}$, gives butylcyclohexane. Treatment of **F** with $Cu(NH_3)_2^+$ gives no precipitate but does after treatment with hot $NaNH_2$. When **F** is first reacted with H_2, Ni/B and then oxidatively ozonized, a nonresolvable compound (**G**), $C_5H_9(COOH)_3$, is formed. Deduce the structure of **F** and account for all observations. (*b*) What would the structure of **F** be if **G** were resolvable?

(*a*) **F** has four degrees of unsaturation, one of which is a six-membered ring as deduced from the isolation of butylcyclohexane on complete hydrogenation. The butyl group indicates that four of the C's are part of a single-side chain on the ring which must have an internal C≡C which rearranges to the terminal position upon treatment with $NaNH_2$. The fourth degree of unsaturation is an endocyclic C=C. Since a two-carbon fragment is lost on oxidative ozonolysis to **G**, the side chain in **F** must be $-CH_2C \equiv CCH_3$, which cleaves to $-CH_2COOH + HOOCCH_3$. In order for **G** to be achiral, the ring-C bonded to the side chain must have two $-CH_2COOH$ groups. The position of the endocyclic C=C in **F** therefore must be one that affords a $-CH_2COOH$ group in **G**. C^6 and C^8 are equivalent and one of them is part of the endocyclic double bond, the other is part of the C≡C.

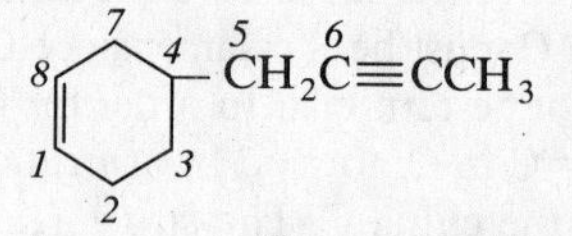
F

$$HOOC^1C^2H_2C^3H_2\underset{\underset{\displaystyle C^7H_2C^8OOH}{|}}{C^4H}-C^5H_2C^6OOH$$
G

(*b*) Optically active **G** is $HOOC^1C^2H_2C^3H_2C^4H_2\underset{\underset{\displaystyle C^8OOH}{|}}{C^5H}-C^6H_2C^7OOH$. C^5 is the stereocenter. C^1 and C^8 are part of the exocyclic C=C and **F** now would be

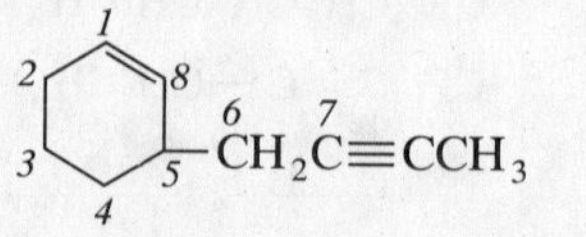

ORBITAL SYMMETRY

9.164 (*a*) Draw orbital diagrams for the π molecular orbitals of 1,3-butadiene, a typical conjugated diene. Indicate the nodes by heavy dots and show the distribution of e^-'s. Compare the relative energies of these molecular orbitals with those of ethene and isolated dienes. Simplify the graphs by showing only the signs of the upper lobes of the *p* orbitals. Superimpose standing waves onto the simplified orbital graph.

1,3-Butadiene has a *p* AO on each C. These overlap side-by-side to generate four π molecular orbitals (see Fig. 9-5). Nodes are present whenever there is a switch in signs from + to −. Note that π_1 of the diene has a lower energy than the π MO of ethene. The sum of the energy of π_1 and π_2 of 1,3-butadiene is less than twice π for two ethenes, the equivalent of an isolated diene.

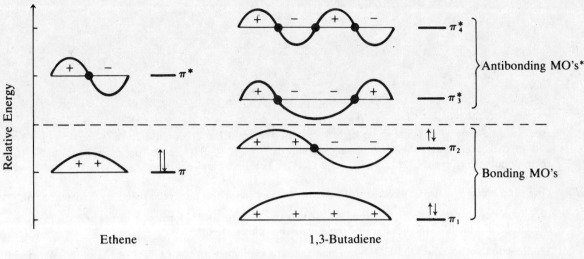

Fig. 9-5

9.165 Justify the assignment of bonding and antibonding to the molecular orbitals of conjugated dienes, i.e., 1,3-butadiene.

   In a linear π system the relative energies of the molecular orbitals are determined by considering the individual pairs of p-orbital overlap on proceeding form left to right across the chain. An excess of bonding interactions, $+$ with $+$, or $-$ with $-$, denotes a bonding MO. An excess of antibonding interactions, $+$ with $-$, denotes an antibonding MO. 1,3-Butadiene has three pairs of p orbital overlaps to consider, $C^1 - C^2$, $C^2 - C^3$, and $C^3 - C^4$. The energies are listed in decreasing order (i.e., $\pi_4^* > \pi_3^* > \pi_2 > \pi_1$):*

   π_4^*:   3 antibonding $(+-, -+, -+)$; highest energy antibonding

   π_3^*:   2 antibonding and 1 bonding $(+-, --, -+)$; next-to-highest energy antibonding

   π_2:   2 bonding and 1 antibonding $(++, +-, --)$; next-to-lowest energy bonding

   π_1:   3 bonding $(++, ++, ++)$; lowest energy bonding.

9.166 (*a*) Determine the molecular orbitals of the allyl system. Indicate their relative energies and state if they are bonding (π), nonbonding (π^n), or antibonding (π^*). (*b*) Insert the e^-s for the carbocation, $C_3H_5^+(R^+)$, the radical, $C_3H_5 \cdot (R \cdot)$, and the carbanion, $C_3H_5:^-(R:^-)$, and compare the relative energies of these species.

   (a) Three p AO's give three MO's as shown in Fig. 9-6. In linear systems with odd numbers of molecular orbitals, the middle-energy molecular orbital is nonbonding. The node point in such an MO^n is at a C indicated by a zero (0). An MO^n will always have an equal number of bonding and antibonding overlaps or no overlaps at all. The latter situation prevails for the allyl species because there is no overlap between a C designated O with the p AO on either side of it.

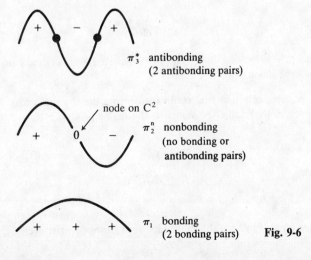

Fig. 9-6

(b)

	R^+	$R\cdot$	$R:^-$
π_3^*	——	——	——
π_2^n	——	↑	↑↓
π_1	↑↓	↑↓	↑↓

The absence or presence of e^-s in the π_2^n orbital does not appreciably affect the stabilities of these species. However, the extra e^-s in the π_2^n do slightly increase the repulsive forces between the other e^-s in the species, and so the order of the slight decreasing stability is $R^+ > R\cdot > R:^-$. Each species is more stable than the corresponding alkyl type, $C_3H_7^+$, $C_3H_7\cdot$, and $C_3H_7:^-$ because of delocalization.

9.167 Give the *Orbital Symmetry (Woodward–Hoffman)* rules as applied to pericyclic reactions (Problem 5.55).

▮ In pericyclic ring closures, i.e., the Diels–Alder reaction, the newly formed σ bonds arise from the head-on overlap of p orbitals of the unsaturated reactants. The rules state that:

1. Reaction occurs when the HOMO of one reactant overlaps with the LUMO of the other. When different molecules react, it makes no difference whose HOMO or LUMO is selected.
2. Only the terminal p AO's of the interacting molecular orbitals are considered because they overlap to form the two new σ bonds in the resulting ring.
3. The reaction is allowed only when the overlapping lobes of the HOMO and LUMO *have the same sign or shading* (same symmetry). If opposite signs face each other at any potential contact (wrong symmetry), the reaction is forbidden.

9.168 (a) Apply the Orbital Symmetry rules to a discussion of the cycloaddition reaction of two moles of $H_2C=CH_2$ to give cyclobutane (i) thermally (from the ground state) and (ii) photochemically with ultraviolet light (uv) (from the excited state). (b) Classify this cycloaddition reaction.

▮ (a) (i) When the HOMO of one ethene molecule approaches the LUMO of the other one, the signs of only one pair of lobes matches, the other pair does not—the reaction is not allowed. [See Fig. 9-7(a).]
(ii) Photochemical irradiation with uv light causes a $\pi \to \pi^*$ transition (Fig. 9-5) resulting in the proper orbital symmetry—the reaction is now allowed. [See Fig. 9-7(b).]

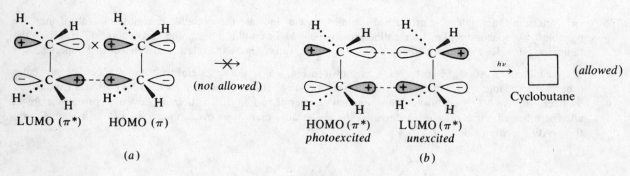

Fig. 9-7

(b) This is a [2 + 2] cycloaddition. The two bracketed numbers indicate that the cycloaddition involves two species each having two π e^-'s.

9.169 (a) Give the two possible products that could result from the thermal cycloaddition of $F_2C=CCl_2$. (b) Explain why this reaction occurs thermally. (c) Which is the major product?

▮ (a)

$$\begin{array}{cc} F_2C\!-\!CF_2 & F_2C\!-\!CCl_2 \\ | \quad\quad | & | \quad\quad | \\ Cl_2C\!-\!CCl_2 & Cl_2C\!-\!CF_2 \\ \mathbf{A} & \mathbf{B} \end{array}$$

(b) In order for this to be a thermal reaction it cannot be pericyclic; it occurs in two steps.

(c) The first step is the formation of a diradical, as shown below, with the odd e^-'s on the C's bonded to the Cl's. The Cl's help stabilize the diradical by $p-d\ \pi$ bonding, something that F's could not do. This diradical gives **A** as the major product.

$$2F_2C{=}CCl_2 \xrightarrow{\text{heat}} \begin{array}{c} F_2C\!\!-\!\!\!-\!\!\!-\!\!CF_2 \\ | \qquad | \\ Cl_2C\cdot \quad \cdot CCl_2 \end{array} \longrightarrow A$$
more stable diradical
intermediate

The less stable diradical that would lead to **B**, $\begin{array}{c} F_2C\!\!-\!\!CCl_2 \\ | \qquad | \\ Cl_2C\cdot \quad \cdot CF_2 \end{array}$, does not form.

9.170 (a) Classify the Diels–Alder reaction (see Problem 9.141) in terms of the number of interacting e^-'s. (b) Show that this reaction is thermally allowed according to the Orbital Symmetry rules. (c) Show that it is immaterial which HOMO and LUMO is used. (d) Can uv light catalyze this reaction?

▟ (a) The reaction is a [2 + 4] cycloaddition, 4 e^-'s from the diene and 2 e^-'s from the dienophile.
(b) The LUMO of the dienophile and the HOMO of the diene have the correct match and the reaction is thermally allowed (Fig. 9.8).

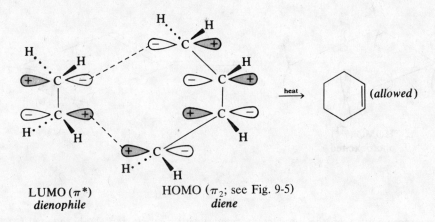

LUMO (π^*)
dienophile

HOMO (π_2; see Fig. 9-5)
diene

Fig. 9-8

(c) See Fig. 9.9(a).
(d) No. Figure 9.9(b) shows improper symmetry.

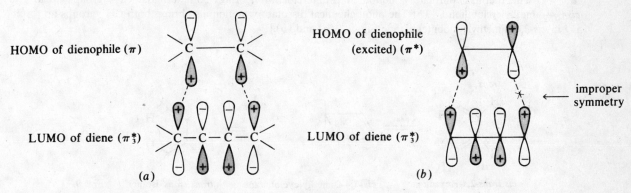

HOMO of dienophile (π)

LUMO of diene (π_3^*)

(a)

HOMO of dienophile (excited) (π^*)

LUMO of diene (π_3^*)

(b)

← improper symmetry

Fig. 9-9

9.171 (a) Name the product formed when 1,3-butadiene undergoes an intramolecular ring closure. (b) Classify this type of pericyclic reaction. (c) Give the net bonding change for this cyclization. (d) According to the Orbital Symmetry concept, how must the terminal p AO's rotate toward each other in order to get the proper symmetry if the ring closure goes (i) thermally or (ii) photochemically?

▟ (a) Cyclobutene. (b) Electrocyclic; a single molecule undergoes ring closure or opening. (c) One double bond is lost and a single bond is formed. (d) In electrocyclic reactions only the HOMO is considered and its terminal p AO's must rotate so that their lobes with like signs point toward each other. (i) Thermally, the HOMO of butadiene is π_2 with $(+\ -)$ symmetry. The rotation of the terminal orbitals must be in the *same* direction (i.e., both counterclockwise or both clockwise), called *conrotatory*, so that a proper match is achieved as shown in Fig. 9.10(*a*). (ii) Since uv light causes electron-excitation, the HOMO is now π_3^*. Now the proper match is achieved when the terminal *p*'s rotate in opposite directions (one clockwise and one counterclockwise), called *disrotatory*, as shown in Fig. 9.10(*b*).

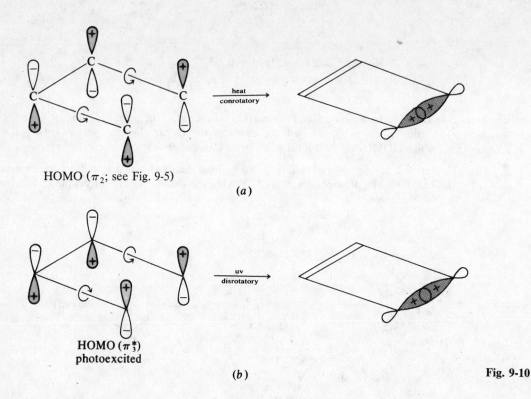

HOMO (π_2; see Fig. 9-5)

(*a*)

HOMO (π_3^*)
photoexcited

(*b*)

Fig. 9-10

9.172 Give the stereochemistry of the products formed when (*a*) *cis,trans*-2,4-hexadiene reacts thermally and (*b*) *trans,trans*-2,4-hexadiene reacts photochemically.

> (*a*) The thermal conrotatory motion, if counterclockwise, brings both terminal CH_3 groups up to give *cis*-3,4-dimethylcyclobutene. (*b*) The photochemical disrotatory motion also brings both CH_3 groups up resulting in *cis*-3,4-dimethylcyclobutene. [See Fig. 9.11(*a*) and (*b*).]

cis,trans-2,4-Hexadiene   *cis*-3,4-Dimethylcyclobutane   *trans,trans* isomer   **Fig. 9-11**

9.173 Apply the Woodward–Hoffmann rules to predict whether the following reactions would be expected to occur thermally or photochemically and give the structures of the products.
(*a*) $H_2C{=}CH_2 + [:CH_2CH{=}CH_2]^-$
(*b*) $H_2C{=}CH_2 + [CH_2{=}CH{-}CH_2]^+$
(*c*) $H_2C{=}CH_2 + (Z)\text{-}H_2C{=}CHCH{=}CHCH{=}CH_2$ (to give a ring with eight C's)

> (*a*) The terminal *p*'s of the HOMO of $H_2C{=}CH_2$ (π) are $(+\ +)$ and those of the LUMO of the allyl carbanion (π_3^*) are also $(+\ +)$. This is the correct symmetry for a thermal reaction. The product is the

cyclopentyl carbanion,

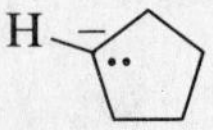

(*b*) Since the terminal *p*'s of the LUMO of the allyl carbocation (π_2^n) are $(+\,-)$, there is no match and the thermal reaction is not allowed. In the allowed photochemical reaction, the LUMO (π_3^*) symmetry for the cation is also $(+\,+)$ and now the reaction is allowed. Note that there is no need to draw the orbital pictures for the interacting molecular orbitals—it is sufficient to show the signs of the upper lobes. The photochemical product is cyclopentyl carbocation.

(*c*) The following generalization makes unnecessary the drawing of all the molecular orbitals, i.e., those of the conjugated triene: in linear systems the signs of the terminal *p*'s alternate $[(+\,+), (+\,-), (+\,+)$, etc.] as the energies of the molecular orbitals increase. The triene has six *p* e^-'s that fill the three lowest energy MO's. The HOMO is π_3 whose symmetry is $(+\,+)$. Since the LUMO of ethylene is $(+\,-)$, this cycloaddition is thermally forbidden. Photochemically, the HOMO of the triene (π_4^*) has a $(+\,-)$ symmetry and cycloaddition is now allowed, giving 1,3-cyclooctadiene.

SUPPLEMENTARY PROBLEMS

9.174 (*a*) Write Lewis structural formulas for four isolable species that are isoelectronic with C_2^{2-}. (*b*) According to the Molecular Orbital theory what do these species have in common?

(*a*) The species must have a triple bond between two atoms, each of which has an unshared pair of e^-'s.

$$:N\equiv N: \qquad :C\equiv O: \qquad :C\equiv N:^- \qquad :N\equiv O:^+$$

(*b*) Their molecular orbital electronic configurations [see Problem 2.30(*b*)] are identical. They have a bond order of 3 and have high bond dissociation energies.

9.175 Starting with acetylene (**A**) give the reagents for synthesis of each of the following industrially important compounds:

(*a*) *trans*-1,2-Dichloroethene (*d*) 1,1,2-Trichloroethene (*f*) Pentachlorethane
(*b*) 1,2-Dichlorethane (*e*) 1,1,2-Trichloroethane (*g*) 1,1,2,2-Tetrachlorethene
(*c*) 1,1,2,2-Tetrachloroethane

(*a*) 1 Cl_2, (*b*) 1 Cl_2 then 1 H_2/Pd, (*c*) 2 Cl_2, (*d*) **A** $\xrightarrow{Na}$ $HC\equiv C^-\,Na^+$ $\xrightarrow{Cl_2}$ $HC\equiv CCl$ $\xrightarrow{Cl_2}$ $Cl_2C{=}CHCl$, (*e*) compound from (*d*) $+H_2$/Pd, (*f*) compound from (*d*) $+ Cl_2$, (*g*) **A** $\xrightarrow{2NaNH_2}$ $Na^+\,{}^-C\equiv C^-\,Na^+$ $\xrightarrow{2Cl_2}$ $CCl\equiv CCl$ $\xrightarrow{Cl_2}$ $Cl_2C{=}CCl_2$.

9.176 From cyclohexane and any acyclic compound prepare (*a*) 3-ethylidenecyclohexene, (*b*) dicyclohexylacetylene, and (*c*) decalin (see Problem 5.77). Is the product from this synthesis *cis* or *trans*?

(*a*) Cyclohexane is first converted to 3-bromocyclohexene (**B**) (Problem 9.140). Then

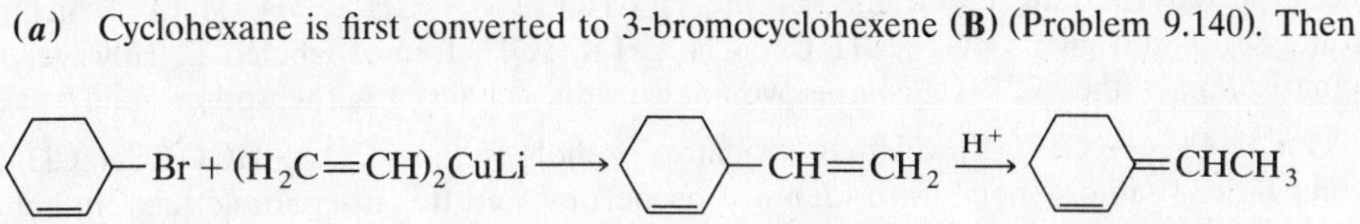

B less stable isolable diene more stable conjugated diene

(*b*) Cyclohexane (C_6H_{12}) $\xrightarrow[uv]{Cl_2}$ $C_6H_{11}Cl$ $\xrightarrow{(H_2C=CH)_2CuLi}$ $C_6H_{11}{-}CH{=}CH_2$ $\xrightarrow[2.\ NaNH_2\quad 3.\ H_2O]{1.\ Br_2}$

$$C_6H_{11}{-}C\equiv CH \xrightarrow[peroxide]{HBr} C_6H_{11}{-}CH{=}CHBr \xrightarrow[2.\ CuI]{1.\ Li} (C_6H_{11}{-}CH{=}CH)_2CuLi \xrightarrow{C_6H_{11}Cl}$$

$$C_6H_{11}{-}CH{=}CH{-}C_6H_{11} \xrightarrow{Br_2} C_6H_{11}{-}CHBrCHBr{-}C_6H_{11} \xrightarrow[200\ ^\circ C]{solid\ KOH} C_6H_{11}{-}C\equiv C{-}C_6H_{11}$$

(c) The Diels–Alder reaction is a good method for forming the second ring. See Problem 9.140 for the preparation of cyclohexene, which is then reacted with 1,3-butadiene.

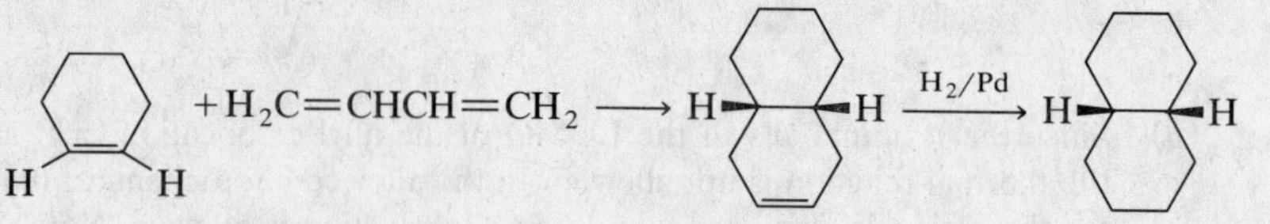

The geometry of the alkene, *cis* in the cyclohexene, is preserved in the adduct—the decalin is *cis*.

9.177 (a) Give all the possible products from 1,4-addition of HBr to 3-methylenecyclohexene at 45 °C. (b) Which intermediate carbocation (R^+) is more stable? (c) Predict the major product.

▮ (a) At 45 °C, 1,4-addition is the dominant pathway giving two possible products:

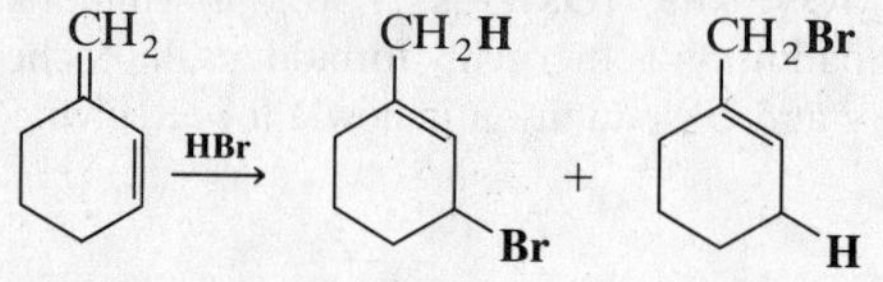

(b) Addition of H^+ to the methylene group gives **C**.

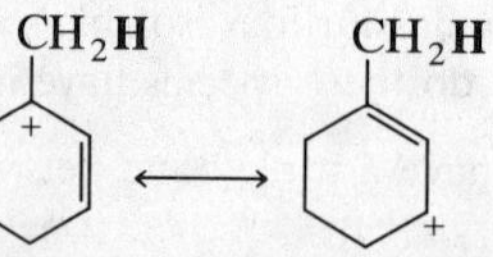

This allylic R^+ has a positive charge on a 3° and 2° C. Addition of H^+ to the ring C=C gives an allylic R^+ (**D**) having a positive charge on a 2° and 1° C:

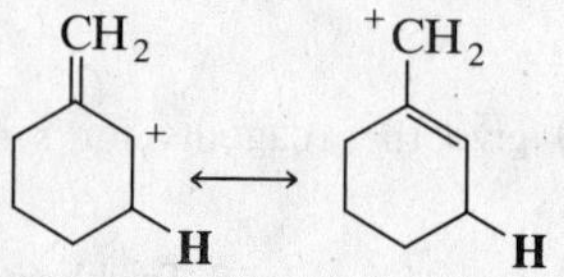

In **C** the positive charge is dispersed to more substituted C's. Thus **C** is the more stable R^+.
(c) **Br⁻** adds to **C**, the dominant R^+, to give the 1,4-trisubstituted adduct **A**.

9.178 Account for the following observations:

(a) $CH_3CH_2CH_2C{\equiv}C{-}\overset{14}{C}H_3$ when treated with $NaNH_2$, then H^+, gives the terminal alkyne isomer which, on oxidative ozonolysis, gives $^{14}CO_2$ and a carboxylic acid with some amount of ^{14}C labeling.
(b) The reaction of cyclopentadiene with $H_2C{=}CHCOOH$ gives two stereoisomers.
(c) 1,3-Butadiene and O_2 do not react unless irradiated by uv light to give the 1,4-adduct.

▮ (a) The expected rearranged terminal alkyne is $CH_3CH_2CH_2CH_2C{\equiv}\overset{14}{C}H$ (**A**) which, on oxidative ozonolysis, would give $^{14}CO_2 + CH_3CH_2CH_2CH_2COOH$, free of labeled **C**. However, by successive isomerizations, the C≡C can move down the chain to the other end to give $HC{\equiv}CCH_2CH_2CH_2{-}\overset{14}{C}H_3$ (**B**), which, on oxidative ozonolysis, gives $CO_2 + HOOCCH_2CH_2CH_2{-}\overset{14}{C}H_3$. **A** and **B** are "radioisomers" with identical properties, and this inseparable mixture behaves as if the product molecule were labeled at two sites, $^{14}CH_3CH_2CH_2CH_2C{\equiv}\overset{14}{C}H$ (**C**). Ozonolysis of **C** gives the observed mixture of labeled products.
(b) The bicyclo products are *endo* (rate-controlled) and *exo* (thermodynamic-controlled).

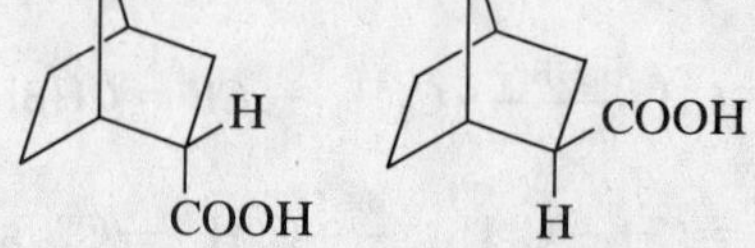

endo-stereoisomer   *exo*-stereoisomer

(c) Ordinary ground-state O_2 is a diradical, $\uparrow\ddot{O}-\ddot{O}\uparrow$, where the arrows represent e^-'s indicating their spins. It can form one bond with the diene, leaving an intermediate incapable of forming a second bond because it has two e^-'s with the same spin.

$$\uparrow\ddot{O}-\ddot{O}\uparrow \; + \; H_2C\overset{\uparrow\downarrow}{-\!\!-}CHCH\overset{\uparrow\downarrow}{-\!\!-}CH_2 \longrightarrow \; \uparrow\ddot{O}-\ddot{O}-CH_2CH=CHCH_2\uparrow$$

When irradiated, O_2 is excited to the singlet spin-paired state, $\uparrow\downarrow\ddot{O}-\ddot{O}:$, which is now capable of undergoing a pericyclic reaction to give the adduct:

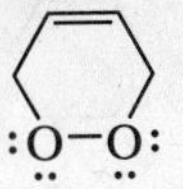

9.179 Give the structure and name of a hydrocarbon with the fewest possible number of C's (exclusive of acetylene) that is (a) a chiral alkyne; (b) an alkyne that gives the same single product on reaction with either B_2H_6 followed by H_2O_2/OH^- or $H_2O/Hg^{++}/H^+$; (c) an alkyne that gives the same product on reaction with either $Na/EtOH$ or $H_2/Ni-B$; (d) an alkyne that gives the same two products from reaction with either of the reagents in (b); (e) an alkyne with diastereomers.

▐ (a) $HC\equiv C-$ must be one of the ligands bonded to the chiral C along with a H, Me, and Et. Thus

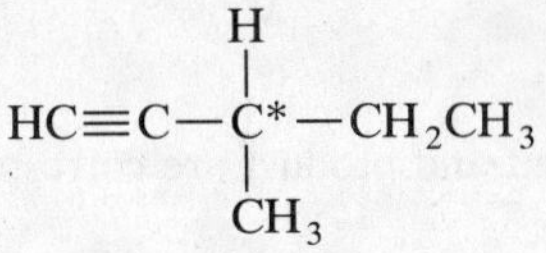

$$HC\equiv C-\overset{\displaystyle H}{\underset{\displaystyle CH_3}{C^*}}-CH_2CH_3$$

3-Methyl-1-pentyne

(b) The compound must be a symmetrical internal alkyne:

$$CH_3C\equiv CCH_3$$

2-Butyne

(c) With internal alkynes these reagents would give *trans* and *cis* stereoisomers respectively. To avoid this, the alkyne must be terminal.

$$HC\equiv CCH_3$$

Propyne

(d) Unlike the alkyne in (b), this alkyne must be internal but unsymmetrical:

$$CH_3C\equiv CCH_2CH_3$$

2-Pentyne

The products are $CH_3\overset{\displaystyle O}{\overset{\|}{C}}CH_2CH_2CH_3$ and $CH_3CH_2\overset{\displaystyle O}{\overset{\|}{C}}CH_2CH_3$.

(e)

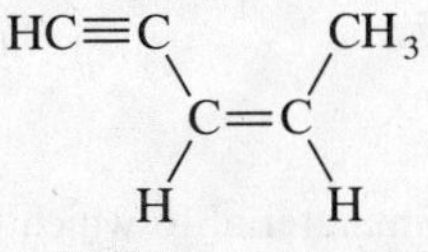

(Z)-3-Penten-1-yne 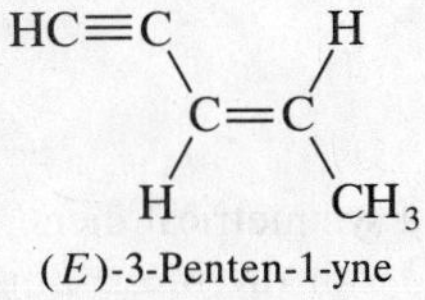   (E)-3-Penten-1-yne

9.180 Give the structure and name of the simplest hydrocarbon which is (a) a cumulative polyene with diasteromers, and (b) a diasteromeric diene with a six-C ring having no chiral C's.

▐ (a) Recall that a properly substituted three-carbon cumulated diene has two enantiomers (optical isomers, Problem 6.97) because the σ bonds on the terminal C's are in perpendicular planes (akin to the situation for a tetrahedral C). The insertion of a third cumulative double bond causes the σ bonds of the terminal C's to become coplanar, making possible *cis-trans* isomers.

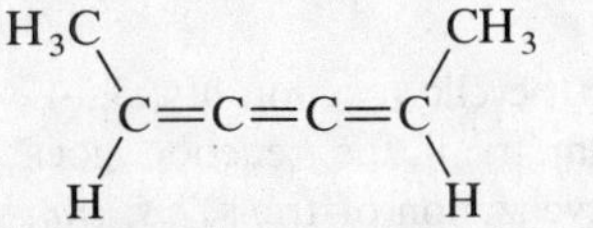

(Z)-2,3,4-Hexatriene   and   (E)-2,3,4-Hexatriene

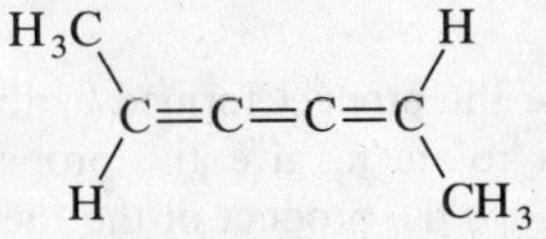

(b) There are three possibilities. One possibility is a cyclohexadiene with two Me's *cis/trans* to each other. Hence, the Me's cannot be on a C=C, thereby eliminating 1,3-disubstitution. To avoid chiral C's, the Me's cannot be 1,2-disubstituted—they must be 1,4-disubstituted. One set of diasteromers is

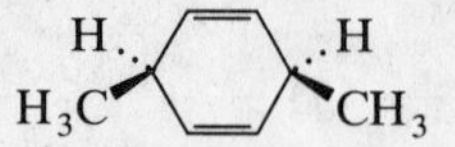

cis-3,6-Dimethyl-1,4-cyclohexadiene 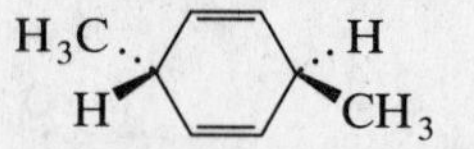   *trans*-3,6-Dimethyl-1,4-cyclohexadiene

The other two possibilities are cyclohexenes with *cis/trans* isomerism about an exocyclic C=C:

(*E*)   (*Z*)   (*E*)   (*Z*)

3-Ethylidenecyclohexene   4-Ethylidenecyclohexene

9.181 Account for the following reactions

(a) $Me_2\overset{1}{C}=\overset{2}{C}H\overset{3}{C}H_2\overset{4}{C}H_2\overset{5}{C}=\overset{6}{C}H\overset{7}{C}H_3 \xrightarrow{H^+}$

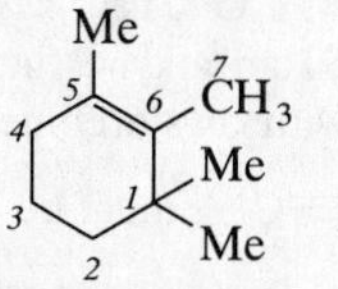

1,2,3,3-Tetramethylcyclohexene

(C's in the reactant and product are correspondingly numbered.)

(b) $Me_2C=CHCH_2CH_2CH=CMe_2 \xrightarrow{H^+}$

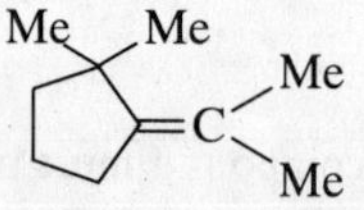

2-Isopropylidene-
1,1-dimethylcyclopentane

Why was a six-membered ring not formed in this reaction?

In both reactions H^+ adds to one of the double bonds giving an R^+ which then forms the ring by adding to the other double bond. The final product results from the formation of the more stable initial R^+ and final cyclic R^+.

(a) H^+ adds to C^2 resulting in a stable 3° R^+ on C^1 that ring closes on to C^6 leaving C^5 as the new stable 3° R^+. An H^+ is then lost from an adjacent C following Saytzeff's rule.

$$Me_2\overset{1}{C}=\overset{2}{C}H\overset{3}{C}H_2\overset{4}{C}H_2\overset{5}{C}=\overset{6}{C}H\overset{7}{C}H_3 + H^+ \longrightarrow Me_2\overset{1}{C}\overset{2}{C}H CH_2CH_2\overset{5}{C}=\overset{6}{C}H\overset{7}{C}H_3 \longrightarrow$$

$$\downarrow -H^+$$

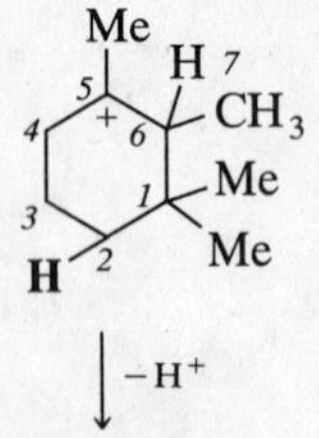

product

(b) Since this is a symmetrical diene, it is immaterial to which C=C H^+ adds. However, H^+ adds to give the 3° R^+ (the C with the Me's) which then cyclizes to a five-membered ring so as to form a 3° R^+. If it had cyclized to a six-membered ring, a less stable 2° R^+ would have formed.

$$\overset{1}{Me_2C}=\overset{2}{C}H\overset{3}{C}H_2\overset{4}{C}H_2\overset{5}{C}H=\overset{6}{C}Me_2 + H^+ \longrightarrow Me_2\overset{+}{C}-CHCH_2CH_2CH=CMe_2 \longrightarrow$$

$$\downarrow -H^+$$

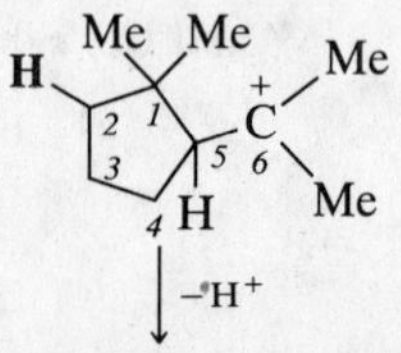

product

9.182 **(a)** Name the product formed by the electrocyclic reaction of 1,3,5-hexatriene. **(b)** How must the terminal *p* AO's rotate to give the proper symmetry if the reaction goes (i) thermally and (ii) photochemically? **(c)** Give the product of the thermal cyclization of *trans, cis, trans*-2,4,6-octatriene. **(d)** Give the product of the photochemical cyclization of *trans, cis, cis*-2,4,6-octatriene.

(a) 1,3-Cyclohexadiene. (b) The HOMO of this triene is π_3 with $(++)$ symmetry of the terminal p AO's; hence (i) requires disrotatory motion and (ii) requires conrotatory motion. (c) A disrotatory motion brings the two CH_3's up to give *cis*-5,6-dimethyl-1,3-cyclohexadiene. (d) A conrotatory motion brings the CH_3's up giving *cis*-5,6-dimethyl-1,3-cyclohexadiene.

For (c) and (d) see Problems 9.171 and 9.172 for a related discussion of the stereochemistry of an electrocyclic reaction of a conjugated diene.

9.183 (a) Write (i) the structural formula and (ii) the skeleton for isoprene, a conjugated diene, C_5H_8, that is the monomer for natural rubber. (b) Use dashed lines to pick out the isoprene units which are the building blocks for the *terpenes* such as limonene, myrcene, and *alpha*-phellandrene, and for vitamin A. The structural formulas for these natural products are shown in the answer. (c) What is the empirical formula for a terpene?

(a) (i) $H_2C{=}C{-}CH{=}CH_2$ isoprene (2-methyl-1,3-butadiene),   (ii) $C{-}C{-}C{-}C$
    | |
    CH_3 C

(b)

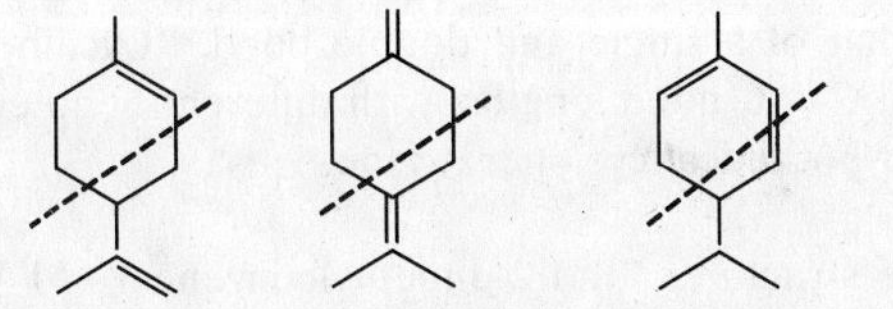

Limonene   Myrcene   α-Phellandrene

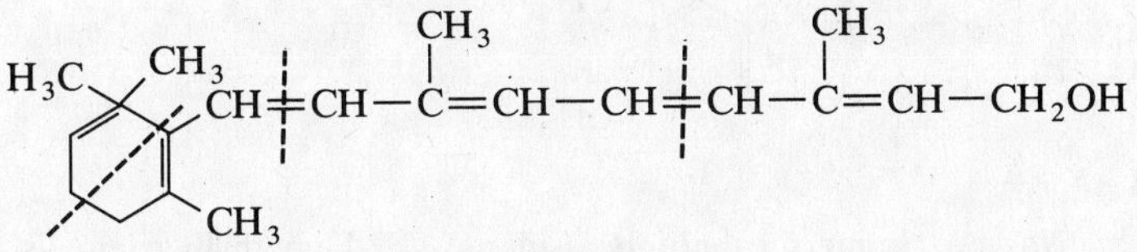

Vitamin A

(c) The three terpenes in part (b) have the molecular formula, $C_{10}H_{16}$. The empirical formula is C_5H_8; the general formula for terpenes is $(C_5H_8)_n$.

CHAPTER 10
Aromaticity and Benzene

STRUCTURE OF BENZENE

10.1 (*a*) Show (i) the Kekulé resonance structures and (ii) the resonance hybrid of benzene, C_6H_6. (*b*) What is the C-to-C bond order? (*c*) How does the resonance hybrid differ from a hypothetical cyclohexatriene?

 (*a*)

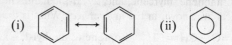

(*b*) The bond order is $1\frac{1}{2}$.

(*c*) The resonance hybrid has only one C-to-C bond length and bond energy. This length is intermediate between that of a single and double bond. "Cyclohexatriene" would have two different alternating $C-C$ and $C=C$ bond lengths, with different bond energies. The hybrid is more stable (less reactive) than the hypothetical cyclohexatriene.

10.2 (*a*) Draw the Kekulé structures for 1,2-dimethylbenzene. (*b*) Would you expect to isolate two isomers of this compound? Explain. (*c*) Write the structures of all the products of ozonolysis of 1,2-dimethylbenzene.

(*a*)

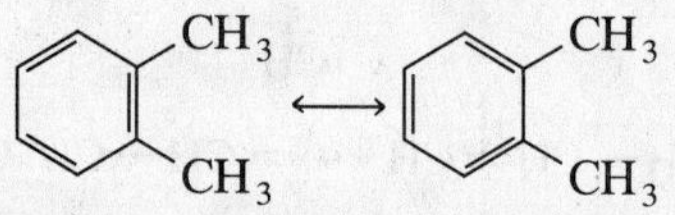

$$\underset{\textbf{A}}{\text{(structure A)}} \longleftrightarrow \underset{\textbf{B}}{\text{(structure B)}}$$

(*b*) No, two isomers cannot be isolated. 1,2-Dimethylbenzene is a resonance hybrid of the Kekulé structures **A** and **B**.

(*c*)
$$CH_3-\underset{\underset{O}{\parallel}}{C}-\underset{\underset{O}{\parallel}}{C}-CH_3, \quad CH_3-\underset{\underset{O}{\parallel}}{C}-\underset{\underset{O}{\parallel}}{C}-H \quad \text{and} \quad H-\underset{\underset{O}{\parallel}}{C}-\underset{\underset{O}{\parallel}}{C}-H$$

10.3 The experimentally determined enthalpy of hydrogenation of benzene is -49.8 kcal/mol. Given $\Delta H_h = -28.6$ kcal/mol for cyclohexene, calculate the resonance energy of benzene.

If benzene contained three noninteracting double bonds, its ΔH_h would be $3(-28.6) = -85.8$ kcal/mol. Simple conjugation would lower the value slightly (see 9.119). The extra stabilization in benzene is $-49.8 - (-85.8) = 36.0$ kcal/mol, which is the *resonance energy*. This is energy that benzene does *not* possess because of resonance.

10.4 (*a*) Calculate ΔH_h for the addition of 1 mole of H_2 to (i) benzene, and (ii) 1,3-cyclohexadiene from the data given in Problem 10.3 and the value for $\Delta H_h = -55.4$ kcal/mol for 1,3-cyclohexadiene. (*b*) List the three hydrocarbons (cyclohexene, 1,3-diene, and benzene) in order of decreasing rates of monohydrogenation. (*c*) If benzene is reacted with *one* mole of H_2, what would you expect to isolate from the reaction?

(*a*) Add the following reactions:

(i)
$$C_6H_{12} - 2H_2 \longrightarrow 1,3\text{-}C_6H_8 \quad \Delta H_h = +55.4 \text{ kcal/mol}$$
$$\underline{C_6H_6 + 3H_2 \longrightarrow C_6H_{12} \quad \Delta H_h = -49.8}$$
$$C_6H_6 + H_2 \longrightarrow 1,3\text{-}C_6H_8 \quad \Delta H_h = +5.6 \text{ kcal/mol}$$

(ii)
$$C_6H_{12} - H_2 \longrightarrow C_6H_{10} \quad \Delta H_h = +28.6 \text{ kcal/mol}$$
$$\underline{1,3\text{-}C_6H_8 + 2H_2 \longrightarrow C_6H_{12} \quad \Delta H_h = -55.4}$$
$$1,3\text{-}C_6H_8 + H_2 \longrightarrow C_6H_{10} \quad \Delta H_h = -26.8 \text{ kcal/mol}$$

(*b*) Since the change in the numbers of moles is the same for each hydrogenation, we assume that the ΔS's for the monohydrogenation of C_6H_6, C_6H_8, and C_6H_{10} are about the same, and that the ΔH_h's are directly related to the ΔH's. Therefore, the reaction with the most negative ΔH_h is the fastest,

240

and the order is cyclohexene (-28.6 kcal/mol) > 1,3-cyclohexadiene (-26.8 kcal/mol) ≫ benzene ($+5.6$ kcal/mol).

(*c*) When benzene is converted to the diene, the diene is reduced all the way to cyclohexane before more benzene reacts. For each mole of benzene, one third of a mole of cyclohexane would be isolated and two thirds of a mole of benzene would be recovered.

10.5 The experimentally determined enthalpy of combustion, (ΔH_c), of C_6H_6 is -789.1 kcal/mol. Theoretical values for the "combustion" contribution of each bond are: C=C, -117.7; C—C, -49.3; and C—H, -54.0 kcal/mol. (*a*) Write a balanced equation for the combustion of one mole of benzene. (*b*) From this data, calculate the ΔH_c for C_6H_6 and explain the difference.

▟ (*a*) $C_6H_6 + \frac{15}{2}O_2 \longrightarrow 6CO_2 + 3H_2O$
  (*b*) The contribution is calculated for each bond and then totaled for the molecule.

$$\text{Six C — H bonds} = 6(-54.0) = -324.0 \text{ kcal/mol}$$

$$\text{Three C — C bonds} = 3(-49.3) = -147.9$$

$$\text{Three C = C bonds} = 3(-117.7) = \underline{-353.1}$$

$$\text{Calculated value} = -825.0 \text{ kcal/mol}$$

The difference $[-789.1 - (-825.0) = 35.9 \text{ kcal/mol}]$ is a measure of the resonance energy, the energy that benzene does *not* have. Approximately the same value was obtained from ΔH_h in Problem 10.3.

10.6 Give an orbital picture of benzene. How does it account for benzene's extraordinary stability?

▟ The ring (skeleton) is comprised of six sp^2 hybridized C's, each σ-bonded to two C's and an H (Fig. 10-1). Each C also has a p AO with one e⁻; the AO's project above and below the plane of the ring which is a nodal plane. Rather than form three localized alternating double bonds (cyclohexatriene), these p AO's overlap laterally to form an extended π system in which the e⁻'s are symmetrically delocalized over all six C's, making the C's equivalent (Fig. 10-2). Delocalization results in less electron repulsion, greater stabilization, and lower energy.

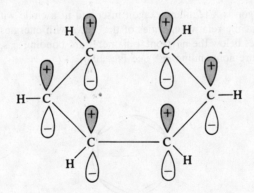

Fig. 10-1

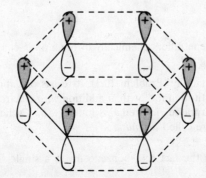

Fig. 10-2

10.7 Use molecular orbital theory to account for the greater stability of benzene.

▌ Six p AO's, one from each C, yield six π molecular orbitals—three bonding and three antibonding. Each p AO has an e^-, and the six e^-'s completely fill the three bonding MO's with two e^-'s in each, accounting for the extraordinary stability of benzene. The π^*'s are empty. Since benzene is cyclic, instead of nodal points there are nodal planes (shown as lines) that are perpendicular to the plane of the ring (Fig. 10-3).

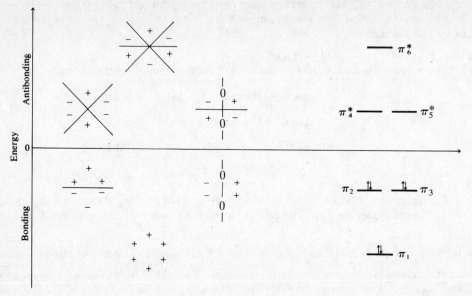

Fig. 10-3

10.8 For benzene, instead of using nodal planes as in Problem 10.7, apply the *polygon rule* to determine the relative energies of molecular orbitals of conjugated cyclopolyenes.

▌ For benzene, the polygon is a regular hexagon inscribed in a circle with *one* vertex at the bottom of the circle. The vertices represent the relative energies of the MO's with energies increasing from the bottom to the top of the circle. The vertices below the horizontal diameter are bonding π's, those above are antibonding π^*'s, and those on the diameter are nonbonding π^n. See Fig. 10-4.

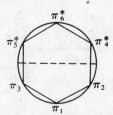

Fig. 10-4

10.9 (*a*) List the ways in which benzene differs chemically from an open-chain conjugated triene. (*b*) What class of compounds does benzene belong to?

▌ (*a*) Benzene has greater stability (Problem 10.3); it resists oxidation by mild oxidants such as aq. $KMnO_4$ and dil. HNO_3; it reacts by substitution rather than addition with electrophilic reagents, such as Br_2, HNO_3, and H_2SO_4, so that the stable unsaturated ring remains intact. (*b*) Cyclic compounds that are much more stable than their open-chain analogs are called *aromatic*.

10.10 What conclusion is drawn from the fact that benzene forms a single C_6H_5Br product when it is monobrominated?

▮   All the H's in benzene are equivalent. (Another possible conclusion, found to be incorrect based on other facts, is that only one H on the ring is easily replaceable.)

10.11   Which of the following C_6H_6 structures give only one C_6H_5Br isomer?

(i)   (ii)   (iii)   (iv)

▮   Both structures (i) and (iv) have equivalent H's; on this basis their structures would be acceptable for C_6H_6. Structures (ii) and (iii) would give two and three isomers, respectively.

10.12   Write the structures of all the (*a*) dibrominated and (*b*) tribrominated derivatives of C_6H_6.

▮   (*a*)   There are three isomers:

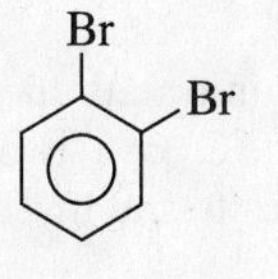

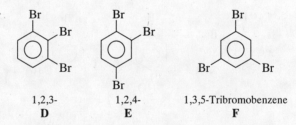

1,2- or *ortho* (*o*)   1,3- or *meta* (*m*)   1,4- Dibromobenzene or *para* (*p*)
A   B   C

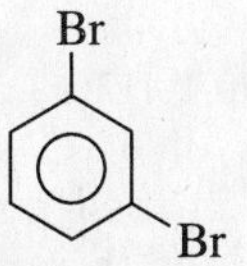

(*b*)   There are three isomers:

1,2,3-   1,2,4-   1,3,5-Tribromobenzene
D   E   F

10.13   At the time that Kekulé presented his structure for C_6H_6, the alternate structure, now called *prismane*, was proposed by Ladenburg [see Problem 10.11 (iv)].   (*a*) Draw all the isomeric dibromoprismanes. Can prismane be excluded as a possible structure for benzene on this basis?   (*b*) How many disubstituted isomers of prismane can be written if the substituents are different, e.g., Br and Cl? Can prismane be excluded on this basis?

▮   (*a*)   See Fig. 10-5. There are three possible isomers of dibromoprismane, as well as three isomers of the Kekulé structure [see Problem 10.12(*a*)]. However, one of them is chiral and exists as a pair of enantiomers. All the dibromobenzenes are achiral. Thus, the prismane structure can be excluded on this basis.

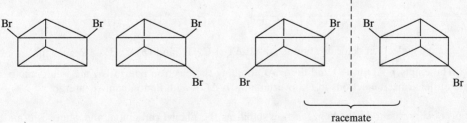

racemate   Fig. 10-5

(*b*)   There are three possible positional isomers of Br,Cl-disubstituted prismane, as is also the case for Br,Cl-disubstituted benzene. However, two of the prismane derivatives are chiral; each exists as a pair of resolvable enantiomers. This fact further eliminates a prismane as a possible structure. See Fig. 10-6.

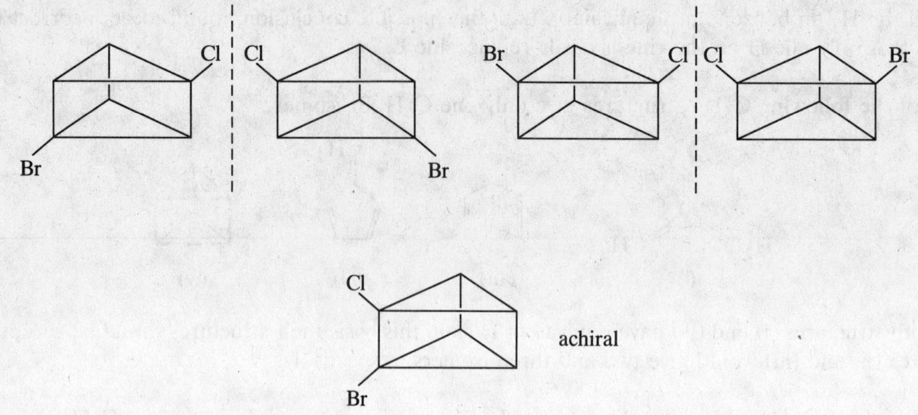

Fig. 10-6

10.14 When the three dibromobenzenes of Problem 10.12(*a*) are mononitrated, the one melting at 87 °C gives only one mononitro product, while those with mp's of 6 °C and −7 °C give two and three mononitro derivatives, respectively. These results led Körner in 1875 to assign structures to the three isomeric dibromides. What are the assignments and how may they be deduced from these results?

The only dibromide with four equivalent positions for mononitration [(i) below] is **C** in Problem 10.12—it must be the isomer melting at 87 °C. The dibromide with mp of 6 °C is **A** in Problem 10.12 because it can give the two mononitrated products (ii) and (iii). The remaining dibromide, **B** in Problem 10.12, mp of −7 °C, can yield the three isomeric dibromonitrobenzenes (iv), (v), and (vi).

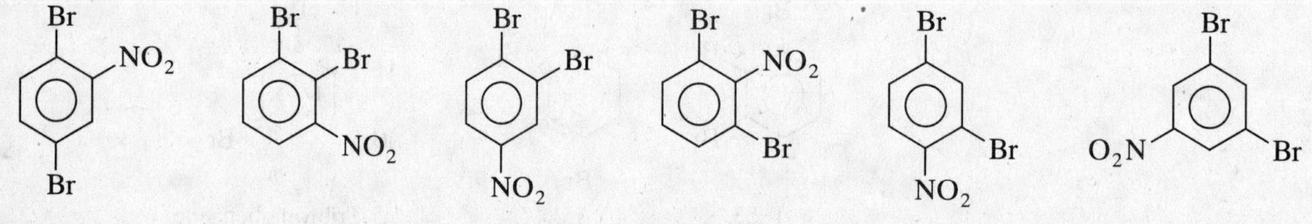

(i) (ii) (iii) (iv) (v) (vi)

10.15 Compare the stabilities of phenyl (C_6H_5) and cyclohexyl (*a*) cations and (*b*) anions.

(*a*) $C_6H_5^+$ is a vinyl carbocation and is less stable than $C_6H_{11}^+$, a 2° carbocation. (*b*) In $C_6H_5{:}^-$ the electron pair is in an sp^2 HO. This carbanion has more *s* character and is more stable than $C_6H_{11}{:}^-$ whose unshared pair is in an sp^3 HO.

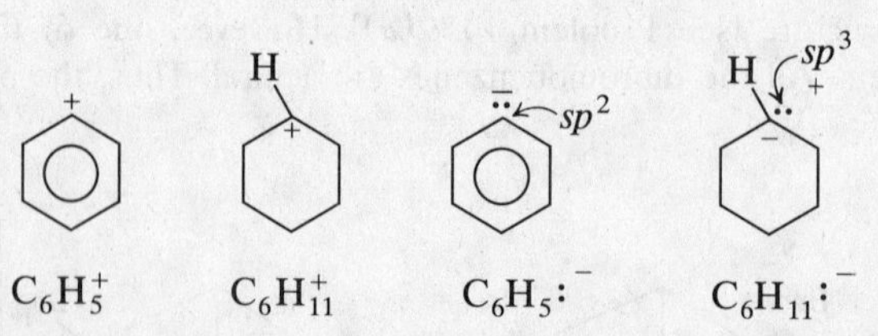

$C_6H_5^+$ $C_6H_{11}^+$ $C_6H_5{:}^-$ $C_6H_{11}{:}^-$

10.16 Would you expect electron delocalization to stabilize (*a*) $C_6H_5^+$ and (*b*) $C_6H_5{:}^-$ to a significant extent? Explain.

No. The empty *p* AO in (*a*) and the *p* AO holding the electron pair in (*b*) are in a plane perpendicular to the plane of delocalized electrons in the overlapping *p* AO's and, hence, cannot interact.

10.17 What kind of substituent on the benzene ring stabilizes the phenyl carbanion, and where is it most effective?

A strongly electron-withdrawing substituent such as F, placed on an adjacent ring C, where it is as close as possible to the C with the negative charge, stabilizes it by induction.

10.18 (*a*) What kind of substituent on the benzene ring (i) destabilizes and (ii) stabilizes the phenyl carbocation and where is it most effective? (*b*) Write the resonance structures of the carbocation and evaluate their contribution to the hybrid if there is a substituent with an unshared pair of e$^-$'s (e.g., —F:) on the adjacent atom.

(a) (i) A strongly electron-withdrawing substituent such as $-\overset{+}{N}=\overset{\cdot\cdot}{\underset{\cdot\cdot}{O}}:^{-}$ on the adjacent ring C. (The positive formal charge on N makes $-NO_2$ an even better electron-withdrawer than $-NH_2$.) (ii) An electron-donating substituent such as methyl or any R group on the adjacent ring C.

(b)

The contributing structure with the carbene makes a meager contribution because it no longer has the stable aromatic ring.

10.19 **(a)** How does an attached (i) $-F$ and (ii) $-NO_2$ affect the electron density of the benzene ring on delocalization? **(b)** Compare the orbital overlap effects with the inductive effects of these groups. **(c)** Compare the bond lengths of $C-F$ and $C-N$ in these phenyl derivatives with those in their corresponding alkyl derivatives. **(d)** What is the decreasing order of effectiveness of delocalization by extended p-p π bonding of the halogens (X)?

(a) Since F and N each has a p AO in the same plane as the π ring of benzene, extended π overlap occurs. (i) The p AO of F has an unshared pair of e^-'s which on delocalization feeds into the ring, increasing its electron density. (ii) Since the p AO of N has no e^-'s, extended π bonding diminishes electron density of the ring by spreading it towards the $-NO_2$ group. **(b)** The F is electron-withdrawing by induction but electron-donating by p orbital overlap. In this and most other cases, extended π bonding predominates over the inductive effect. The NO_2 group is electron-withdrawing by both effects. **(c)** In both cases, extended π bonding introduces some double bond character into the $C-F$ and $C-N$ bonds, making them shorter than their alkyl analogs. **(d)** The smaller the X, the shorter is the $C-X$ bond. The shorter the bond, the more effective is the overlap of the p AO's and the more extensive is the delocalization. The decreasing order is $F > Cl > Br > I$.

10.20 **(a)** Draw resonance structures for (i) C_6H_5F and (ii) $C_6H_5NO_2$ showing which C's of the ring bear the partial charges induced in the ring by extended π bonding. **(b)** Use electrostatic theory to rationalize this same charge distribution.

(a) (i)

(ii)

In each case the para and the two ortho positions bear some of the charge.

(b) Two generalizations can be made. (1) Maximize delocalization by moving the charge on to as many C's as possible. (2) Minimize electrostatic repulsion by avoiding like charges on adjacent atoms. Having the partial charges on the para and ortho positions (three positions) is consistent with these generalizations. Applying this reasoning can often obviate the need to write all the contributing structures.

NOMENCLATURE AND PHYSICAL PROPERTIES

10.21 Explain why **(a)** benzene is slightly soluble in water, while both 1,3- and 1,4-cyclohexadiene are insoluble, **(b)** benzene has a much higher mp (5.5 °C) than either of these dienes, and **(c)** 1,4-disubstituted benzenes generally have higher mp's than the corresponding 1,2- or 1,3-isomers.

(a) The delocalized e^-'s in benzene are more easily polarized, resulting in greater van der Waals attractive forces to water. **(b)** Benzene is a completely planar molecule and it can be more closely packed in the crystal. **(c)** The 1,4-isomer has a more symmetrical structure, allowing it to fit better into the crystal lattice than either of its isomers.

10.22 (*a*) What is an azeotrope? (*b*) What kind of azeotropic mixture is formed by benzene and water? (*c*) Benzene forms an azeotropic mixture with water and ethanol boiling at 65 °C. Explain how this property is used to obtain anhydrous ethanol from 95% ethanol in water (which is an azeotropic solution having a bp of 78.2 °C).

◢ An *azeotrope* is a mixture of two or more liquids that boils at a constant temperature lower (or higher) than any of its components. (*b*) The mixture is a lower boiling azeotrope because the attractive forces of benzene-to-water are less than those of benzene-to-benzene and water-to-water. (*c*) Benzene is added to 95% ethanol-water and when heated, the lowest boiling component (benzene-ethanol-water) distills at 65 °C until all the water has been removed.

10.23 Name the following substances:

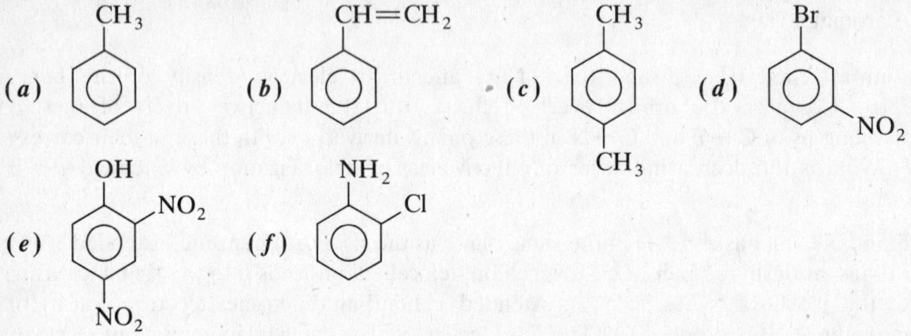

(*a*) CH_3—ring   (*b*) $CH{=}CH_2$—ring   (*c*) CH_3—ring—CH_3 (*d*) Br—ring—NO_2

(*e*) OH—ring with NO_2 and NO_2 (*f*) NH_2—ring—Cl

◢ (*a*) Toluene or methylbenzene, (*b*) styrene or ethenylbenzene (vinylbenzene), (*c*) 1,4-dimethylbenzene or *p*-xylene, (*d*) 1-bromo-3-nitrobenzene or *m*-bromonitrobenzene, (*e*) 2,4-dinitrophenol, and (*f*) *o*-chloroaniline.

10.24 Draw the structural formulas of: (*a*) benzaldehyde, (*b*) mesitylene, (*c*) cumene, (*d*) 2-chloro-4-ethylbenzoic acid, (*e*) acetophenone, (*f*) phthalic acid, and (*g*) *p*-toluenesulfonic acid.

◢ (*a*) benzaldehyde structure   (*b*) mesitylene structure   (*c*) cumene structure   (*d*) 2-chloro-4-ethylbenzoic acid structure

(*e*) acetophenone structure   (*f*) phthalic acid structure   (*g*) *p*-toluenesulfonic acid structure

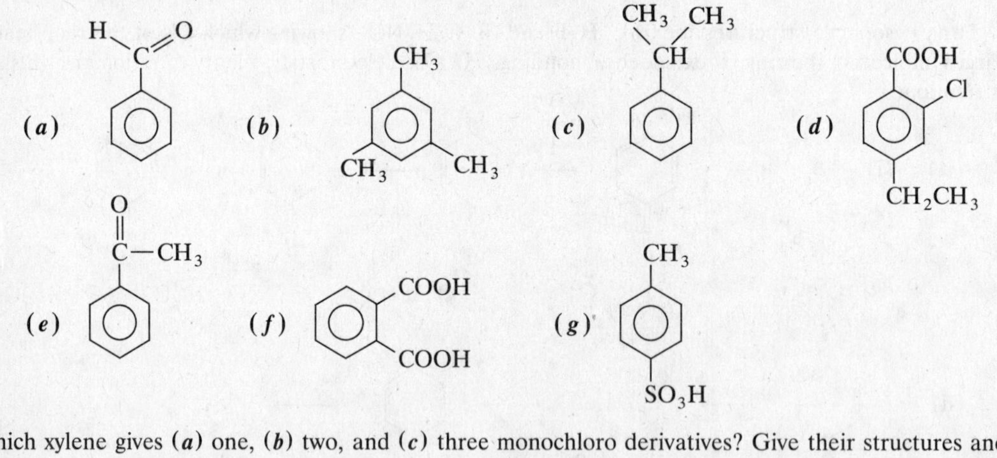

10.25 Which xylene gives (*a*) one, (*b*) two, and (*c*) three monochloro derivatives? Give their structures and names.

◢ (*a*) Monochlorination of *p*-xylene gives one monochloro derivative because all four available positions are equivalent. The product is 2-chloro-1,4-dimethylbenzene (**A**). (*b*) *o*-Xylene has two types of equivalent positions, leading to two isomeric products, 3-chloro-1,2-dimethylbenzene (**B**), and 4-chloro-1,2-dimethylbenzene (**C**). (*c*) *m*-Xylene has three types of positions giving three different derivatives, 2-chloro-1,3-dimethylbenzene (**D**), 5-chloro-1,3-dimethylbenzene (**E**), and 1-chloro-2,4-dimethylbenzene (**F**). (See Fig. 10-7.)

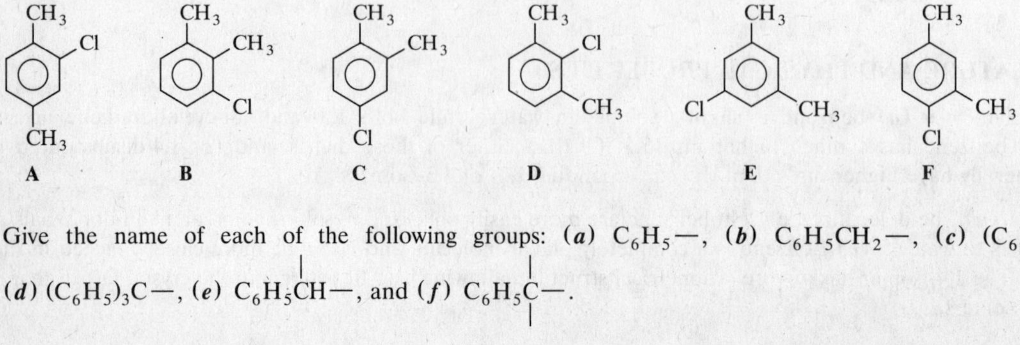

A   B   C   D   E   F   **Fig. 10-7**

10.26 Give the name of each of the following groups: (*a*) C_6H_5—, (*b*) $C_6H_5CH_2$—, (*c*) $(C_6H_5)_2CH$—, (*d*) $(C_6H_5)_3C$—, (*e*) $C_6H_5\overset{|}{C}H$—, and (*f*) $C_6H_5\overset{|}{\underset{|}{C}}$—.

▰ (a) Phenyl (Ph or φ), (b) benzyl (Bz or PhCH₂), (c) benzhydryl or diphenylmethyl, (Ph₂CH), (d) trityl or triphenylmethyl (Ph₃C), (e) benzal, and (f) benzo.

10.27 Give the name of each of the following phenyl-substituted groups: (a) $C_6H_5CHCH_3$, (b) $C_6H_5CH_2CH_2$—, (c) $C_6H_5CH{=}CH$—, and (d) $C_6H_5CH{=}CHCH_2$—.

▰ (a) α-Phenethyl, (b) β-phenethyl, (c) styryl, and (d) cinnamyl.

10.28 Write structural formulas for: (a) benzotrifluoride, (b) 2,4-dinitrobenzyl bromide, (c) biphenyl, (d) trityl chloride, (e) 2,4′-dimethyldiphenylmethane, and (f) 1,3-diphenylbutane. The prime after the second number in (e) (′) indicates that one of the substituents is in the second ring at that numbered position.

▰ (a) [structure: benzene ring with CF₃] (b) [structure: benzene ring with CH₂Br, NO₂ and NO₂] (c) [structure: biphenyl] (d) [structure: triphenylmethyl chloride, C with Cl and three phenyl groups]

(e) CH_3—⬡—CH_2—⬡(CH_3)   (f) ⬡—CH_2CH_2CH(CH_3)—⬡

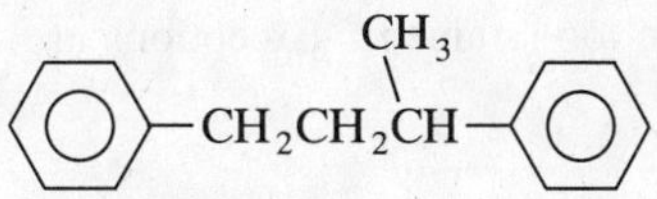

10.29 Correct each of the following and write its corresponding structure.
(a) 2,4,6-Trinitrobenzene, (b) 4-chloro-*meta*-xylene, (c) 2-aminonitrobenzene, (d) 1-ethyl-4-butylbenzene, and (e) 1-chloro-2-chloropropylbenzene.

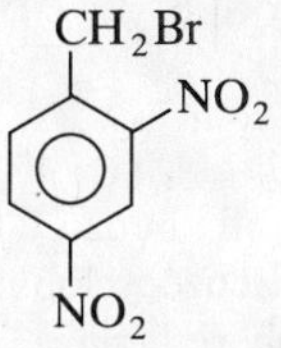

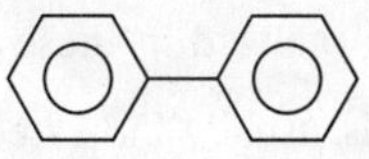

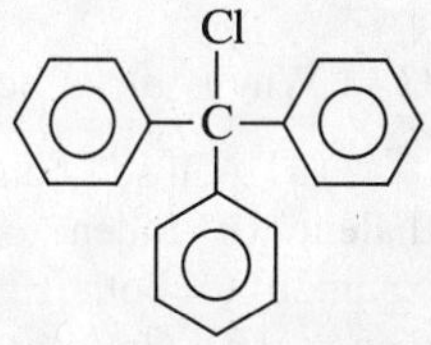

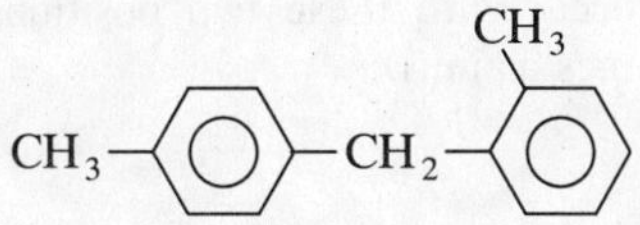

▰ (a) Wrong numbering; 1,3,5-trinitrobenzene; (b) *meta* is used only for disubstituted derivatives; 1-chloro-2,4-dimethylbenzene; (c) amino has priority over nitro; *o*-nitroaniline; (d) substituents not listed in alphabetical order; 1-butyl-4-ethylbenzene; and (e) position of the 2-chloropropyl group is uncertain; 1-chloro-2-(2-chloropropyl)benzene.

(a) [structure: benzene ring with O₂N, NO₂, NO₂]   (b) [structure: benzene ring with Cl, CH₃, CH₃]   (c) [structure: benzene ring with NO₂, NH₂]   (d) [structure: benzene ring with C₂H₅, n-C₄H₉]

(e) [structure: benzene ring with Cl and CH₂CHCH₃ with Cl]

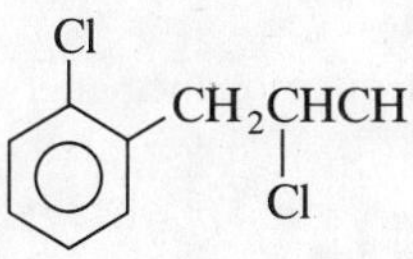

10.30 Give the structure and name of each of the following substances: (a) "TNT", (b) "DDT", (c) "DES", diethylstilbestrol, (d) "PABA".

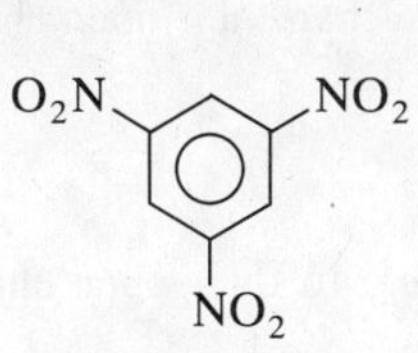

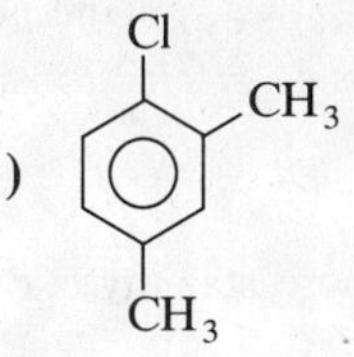

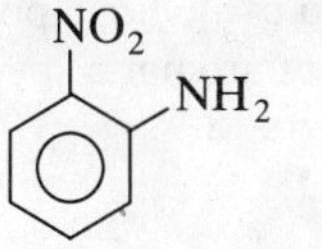

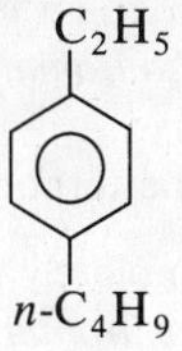

▰ (a) [structure: benzene ring with NO₂, O₂N, NO₂, CH₃]
2,4,6-Trinitrotoluene,

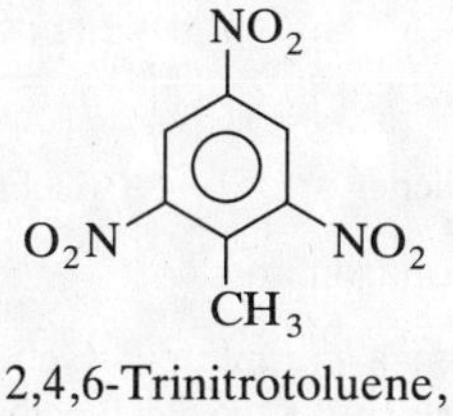

(b) [structure: two chlorophenyl rings on C—CCl₃ with H]
4,4′-dichlorodiphenyltrichloroethane,

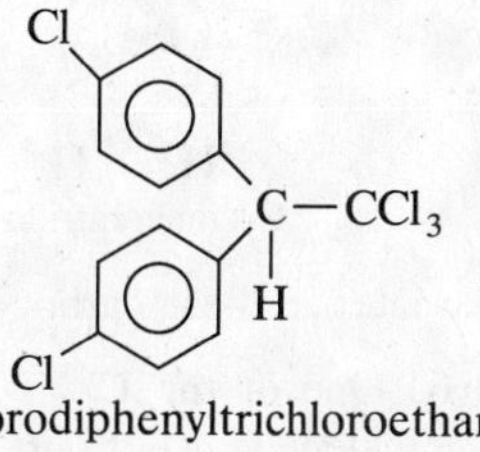

(c) HO—⬡—C(CH₃CH₂)=C(CH₂CH₃)—⬡—OH
(E)-3,4-(4,4′-dihydroxyphenyl)-3-hexene,

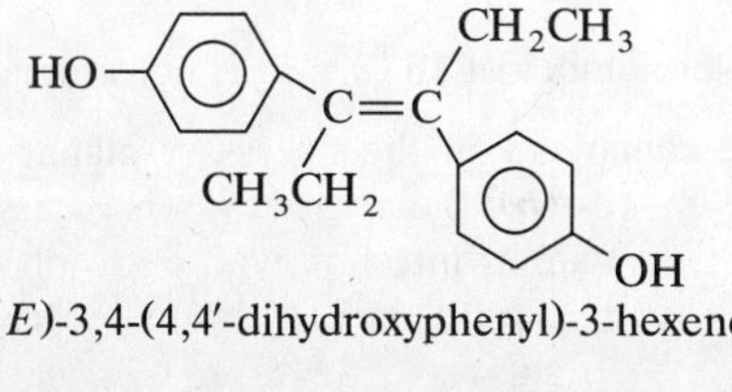

(d) [structure: benzene ring with COOH and NH₂]
p-aminobenzoic acid

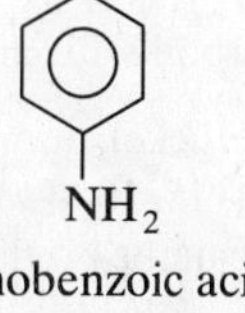

10.31   Name each of the following substituted biphenyls:

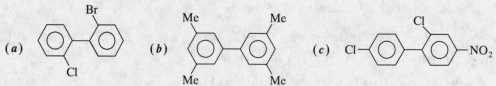

⬛   (*a*) 2-Bromo-2′-chlorobiphenyl, (*b*) 3,5,3′,5′-tetramethylbiphenyl, and (*c*) 2,4′-dichloro-4-nitrobiphenyl.

10.32   (*a*)   Name each of the following compounds:

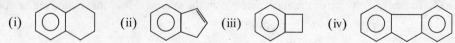

(*b*)   Why is *ortho* before benzo omitted in these names?

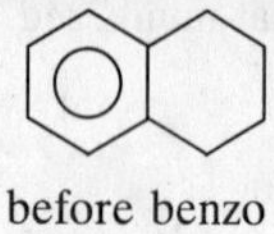

⬛   (*a*) A fused benzene ring is usually indicated by the prefix benzo.* (i) Tetralin or 1,2,3,4-tetrahydronaphthalene. (ii) Indene or benzocyclopentadiene [see (iii)]. (iii) Benzocyclobutene (cyclobut*ene*, because the C=C common to both rings counts as being in the four-membered ring). (iv) Fluorene or dibenzocyclopentadiene.   (*b*) *Ortho* is understood because fusion can only occur with these two positions. Any other fusion positions would be too strained. *Exceptions are common names as in (i).

AROMATICITY

10.33   State Hückel's rule for determining whether a molecule is aromatic.

⬛   Hückel's rule applies to flat, carbocyclic molecules, where each C in the ring is capable of being sp or sp^2 hybridized, thus providing a p orbital for extended π bonding. In order to be aromatic, such a molecule must have $(4n + 2)$ π electrons, where n equals zero or a whole number. Some *Hückel numbers* are 2, 6, 10, 14, and 18.

10.34   (*a*) Define antiaromatic.   (*b*) Apply Hückel's rule to antiaromaticity.

⬛   (*a*) Planar conjugated carbocyclic polyenes that are especially *less* stable than their open chain analogs are called *antiaromatic*. (*b*) Antiaromatic species possess $4n$ π electrons; e.g., $4, 8, \ldots$.

10.35   Define the term nonaromatic.

⬛   Completely conjugated carbocyclic polyenes whose stability is comparable to their open chain analogs are called *nonaromatic*.

10.36   List aromatic, antiaromatic, and nonaromatic compounds in decreasing order of resonance energies (stabilities).

⬛   Aromatic > nonaromatic > antiaromatic.

10.37   (*a*)   Why are the following substances not aromatic?

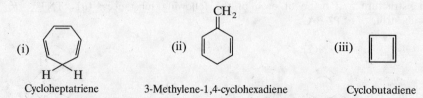

(i) Cycloheptatriene   (ii) 3-Methylene-1,4-cyclohexadiene   (iii) Cyclobutadiene

(*b*)   Characterize these carbocyclic polyenes as antiaromatic or nonaromatic.

⬛   (*a*) (i) One of the C's is sp^3 hybridized, thereby preventing a completely cyclic overlapping π system. (ii) The methylene C is not part of the ring which has one sp^3 hybridized C. (iii) There are only four π electrons ($n = 1/2$, not an integer).   (*b*) (i) and (ii) are nonaromatic while (iii) is antiaromatic.

10.38   Explain why the hydrocarbon with an acceptable Hückel number of 10 ($n = 2$) is not aromatic.

⬛   Although it has a Hückel number, the molecule cannot adopt the necessary planar conformation. If the double bonds are all *cis* [Fig. 10-8(*a*)] or one is *trans* [Fig. 10-8(*b*)] the angle strain is excessive. The isomer with two *trans* double bonds cannot be flat because two of the H atoms interfere with each other [Fig. 10-8(*c*)].

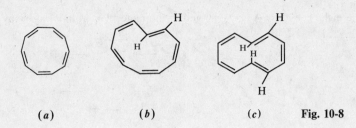

(a) (b) (c) **Fig. 10-8**

10.39 Apply the polygon rule to 3-, 4-, 5-, 7-, and 8-carbon systems (see Problem 10.8) and indicate the character of the molecular orbitals.

▌ See Fig 10-9.

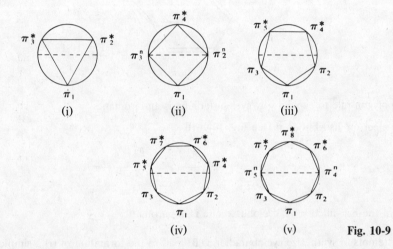

(i) (ii) (iii)

(iv) (v) **Fig. 10-9**

10.40 Explain aromaticity and antiaromaticity in terms of molecular orbital energy levels.

▌ Aromaticity is observed when all bonding MO's are filled and nonbonding MO^n's, if present, are empty or completely filled. Hückel enunciated his rule because of this requirement. A species is antiaromatic if it has e^-'s in MO^*'s or if it has half-filled MO's or MO^n's, provided it is planar.

10.41 (a) Write Kekulé-type resonance structures for cyclooctatetrene, C_8H_8 (**A**). (b) On the basis of these contributing structures, predict its stability. (c) The ΔH_h for hydrogenating **A** to cyclooctane is about four times the value for the addition of H_2 to cyclooctene. What does this tell you about the structure of **A**? (d) Is the ability to write equivalent contributing resonance structures always reliable for predicting aromaticity of conjugated carbocyclic polyenes?

▌ (a)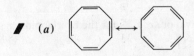

(b) Since these are equivalent energy resonance forms like those for benzene, we predict **A** to be aromatic.
(c) There is little or no π electron delocalization (resonance). If there were, ΔH_h for cyclooctatetraene would be lower, indicating lower energy and greater stability.
(d) No. MO theory, including Hückel's rule, is the best method for predicting aromaticity.

10.42 Cyclooctatetraene **A** (Problem 10.41) is nonaromatic—it undergoes reactions typical of alkenes (addition of electrophilic reagents like Br_2 and HCl, oxidation by $KMnO_4$). (a) Predict the stability of **A** in terms of Fig. 10-9(v). (b) Explain why **A** is nonaromatic.

(a) The eight π e$^-$'s of **A** are arranged in the molecular orbitals as shown:

Since the π^n's are half-filled, **A** would be predicted to be antiaromatic.

(b) Cyclooctatetraene is not planar; it is actually tub-shaped (see Fig. 10-10). The p orbitals of one C=C are not coplanar with those of a neighboring C=C, and there can be no effective overlap for delocalization. This noncoplanarity avoids the antiaromaticity which requires coplanarity.

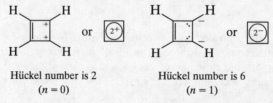

Fig. 10-10

10.43 Use the polygon rule to explain why cyclobutadiene is antiaromatic.

The electron distribution is [see Fig. 10-9(ii)]

$$\pi_3^n \underline{\;\uparrow\;} \qquad \overline{\;\;\;}\,\pi_4^* \qquad \underline{\;\uparrow\;}\,\pi_2^n$$
$$\underline{\;\uparrow\downarrow\;}\,\pi_1$$

Because of the half-filled π^n's, cyclobutadiene is antiaromatic.

10.44 (a) All attempts to synthesize cyclobutadiene (**B**) lead to the formation of (i) a simple open chain molecule and products formed from it and (ii) a dimer. Give the structures of these compounds and characterize the reactions. (b) In solid argon at a few degrees above absolute zero, **B** has been generated and its structure determined. Account for the fact that **B** has very long C—C bonds.

(a) (i)
$$\begin{array}{c} HC=CH \\ | \quad | \\ HC=CH \end{array} \longrightarrow 2HC\equiv CH \quad \text{Reverse cycloaddition}$$

(ii)
$$2\begin{array}{c} HC=CH \\ | \quad | \\ HC=CH \end{array} \longrightarrow \;\boxed{\;\;\;\;\;}\; \quad \text{Cycloaddition (Diels–Alder)}$$

(b) Molecules will always have structures with the lowest possible energies. Hence, **B** has extra long C—C bonds to localize the C=C bonds and thereby minimize the extended π-orbital overlap which induces the antiaromaticity.

10.45 Draw four-membered rings showing all C=C's, H's, unshared pairs of e$^-$'s, and charges that would result in aromatic *ions*.

It is necessary to have a p AO on each C with a total of either two or six e$^-$'s for the overlapping π system.

$$\underset{\substack{\text{Hückel number is 2} \\ (n=0)}}{\overset{\substack{H \qquad H}}{\boxed{}^{+}_{+}}} \quad \text{or} \quad \boxed{2+} \qquad\qquad \underset{\substack{\text{Hückel number is 6} \\ (n=1)}}{\overset{\substack{H \qquad H}}{\boxed{}^{-}_{-}}} \quad \text{or} \quad \boxed{2-}$$

10.46 7-Bromocycloheptatriene (tropylium bromide) completely dissociates in water and gives a precipitate of AgBr instantaneously with AgNO$_3$, unlike its open-chain analog, 3-bromo-1,4-pentadiene. Explain.

▮ The cycloheptatrienyl carbocation formed by a loss of Br^- is unusually stable. It has an empty p orbital, being sp^2 hybridized. It is aromatic, having six π electrons delocalized in seven overlapping p orbitals.

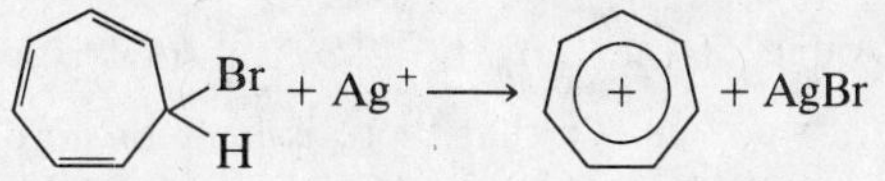

10.47 Give the electron distribution in the molecular orbitals of the cycloheptatrienyl cation.

▮ Note that the "polygon in the circle" indicates that the three lowest energy MO's are below the diameter and are bonding. The four highest energy ones are above the diameter and are MO*'s.

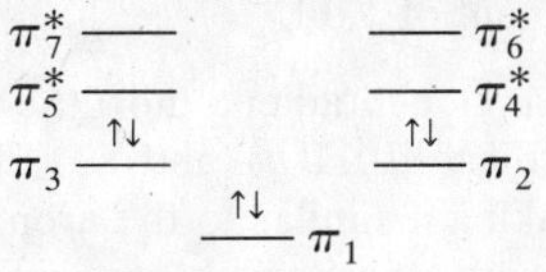

10.48 Explain why an H of the CH_2 group in cycloheptatriene is much less acidic than a typical allylic H.

▮ Removal of an H^+ leaves the cycloheptatrienyl *carbanion*. If the unshared pair were in an overlapping p AO, the cyclic π system would have eight e^-'s. The two newly introduced e^-'s would half-fill the π_4^* and π_5^* molecular orbitals, making the anion antiaromatic and unstable and the acid much weaker than its open-chain analog. The two e^-'s probably occupy an unhybridized sp^3 orbital to avoid antiaromaticity, and the acid is no stronger than an alkane.

10.49 Explain why cyclopentadiene ($K_a \cong 10^{-15}$) is much more acidic than 1,3-cyclohexadiene.

▮ Removal of an H^+ from the saturated C converts it to an sp^2 hybridized C with a pair of electrons in a p orbital that overlaps with the p orbitals on both sides, giving rise to a ring with six (a Hückel number) delocalized π electrons. This aromaticity stabilizes the cyclopentadienyl anion causing cyclopentadiene to be much more acidic than most hydrocarbons. Removal of an H^+ from the cyclohexadiene also gives an anion with six e^-'s in a ring. However, the presence of an sp^3 C prevents continuous cyclic overlap, and the anion is not aromatic.

10.50 Show the electron distribution in the MO's of the cyclopentadienyl anion.

▮ The electron distribution is

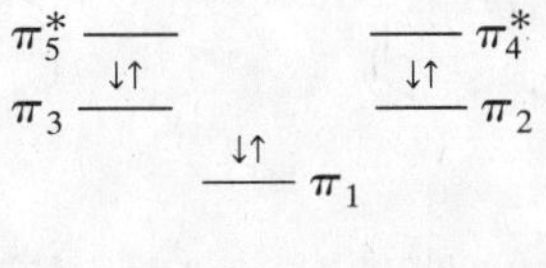

10.51 (*a*) Use (i) resonance theory and (ii) MO theory to predict whether 5-chloro-1,3-cyclopentadiene readily undergoes solvolysis. (*b*) Show that cyclopentadienyl cation is a diradical.

▮ (*a*) Solvolysis occurs through the S_N1 mechanism, giving a cation intermediate that must be relatively stable.

(i)

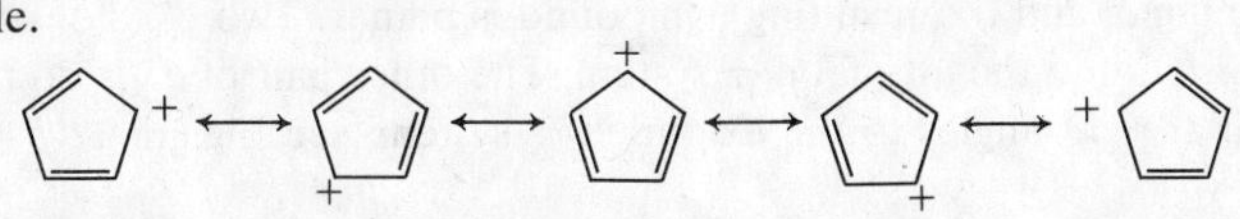

With five equivalent contributing structures, we predict stability for the cation and easy solvolysis for the chloride.

(ii) Two e^-'s must be removed from the distribution in Problem 10.50 leaving four rather than six π e^-'s. Instead of being aromatic, this cation is actually antiaromatic and the chloro compound is inert to solvolysis.

(*b*) The π_2 and π_3 MO's are half-filled.

10.52 Which species is the smallest aromatic substance? (*Hint*: It is an ion.)

▮ The cyclopropenyl cation is an aromatic substance because it has two π e^-'s ($n = 0$). It forms a stable salt that can be stored in a bottle.

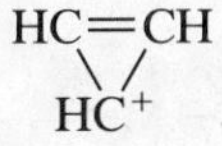

10.53 The ΔH_h biphenyl, C_6H_5—C_6H_5, to cyclohexylcyclohexane is about -100 kcal/mol. (*a*) Draw a conclusion about the extent of π orbital overlap between the two rings. (*b*) Discuss the geometry of biphenyl.

◢ (*a*) Since twice the value of the ΔH_h (-49.8 kcal/mol) for benzene $\xrightarrow{3H_2}$ cyclohexane is observed for biphenyl $\xrightarrow{6H_2}$ bicyclohexane, we conclude that there is little or no delocalization from one ring to the other. If there were, ΔH_h would be less than $2(-49.8)$ kcal/mol, because of increased stabilization. (*b*) Little π overlap between the rings results in insignificant double bond character between the σ-bonded C's joining the phenyl groups, and there is free rotation between the two flat rings.

10.54 Azulene ($C_{10}H_8$) is a deep-blue compound with the structure shown in Fig. 10-11(*a*). Account for (*a*) its aromaticity and (*b*) its dipole moment of 1.0 D.

◢ (*a*) Although neither the cyclopentadiene nor the cycloheptatriene ring alone is aromatic, charged resonance structures (Figs. 10-11(*b*) and (*c*) show a preponderance of negative charge in the five-membered ring, making it similar to the aromatic cyclopentadienyl anion. In these structures, the seven-membered ring bears a positive charge, giving it the aromatic character of the cycloheptatrienyl cation.

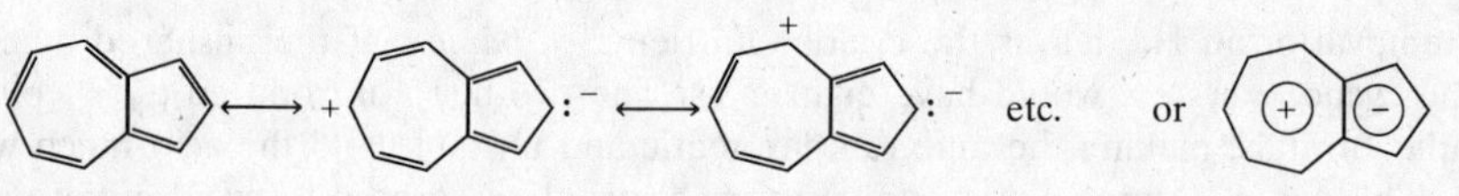

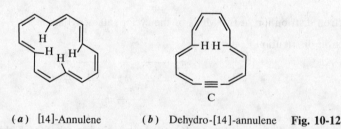

(*a*)   (*b*)   (*c*)   **Fig. 10-11**

(*b*) The main contributing structures to the hybrid show charge separation responsible for the observed dipole moment.

10.55 On the basis of its Hückel number, [14]-annulene ($C_{14}H_{14}$) is expected to be aromatic. Yet it does not undergo substitutive nitration or sulfonation. (*a*) Explain the nonaromatic behavior. (*b*) Explain why compound **C**, which has one C≡C in place of one of the C=C's is aromatic.

(*a*) [14]-Annulene   (*b*) Dehydro-[14]-annulene   **Fig. 10-12**

◢ (*a*) The H's of [14]-annulene that point to the interior of the ring interfere with each other. X-ray analysis shows that the molecule is not planar [see Fig. 10-12(*a*)]. (*b*) Two of the interfering H's are removed to form the triple bond, and the resulting compound is planar. Two e⁻'s of one of the π bonds of the C≡C are delocalized into the aromatic π system. The other pair of e⁻'s do not interact because they are in a π orbital at right angles to the extended π system [see Fig. 10-12(*b*)].

SYNTHESES AND REACTIONS

10.56 What are the common sources of benzene and alkyl benzenes?

◢ Commercially, benzene and alkylated benzenes (toluene and the xylenes) are obtained by fractional distillation of petroleum. Coal tar, one of the products of the *pyrolysis* or *destructive distillation* of coal (heating in the absence of oxygen), is also a major source of aromatic hydrocarbons. Pyrolysis produces, in addition, the large amount of coke used in the production of steel and in other metallurgical processes. A third source, also from petroleum, is *catalytic dehydrogenation* of cycloalkanes, like methylcyclohexane, into aromatic hydrocarbons:

$$\text{Cyclohexane—Me} \xrightarrow[-3H_2]{\text{catalyst, }\Delta\text{, pres.}} \text{benzene—Me}$$

10.57 Give a synthesis of benzene from (*a*) acetylene and (*b*) hexane.

◢ (*a*) $3HC \equiv CH \xrightarrow[\Delta]{Ni \text{ or } Co \text{ complex}}$ benzene

This trimerization, a [2.2.2] cycloaddition, requires passage through a hot tube.

(*b*) $CH_3(CH_2)_4CH_3 \xrightarrow[450-550\,°C]{CrO_3}$ benzene

This type of reaction and the reaction in Problem 10.56 are used to produce mixtures of aromatic hydrocarbons by cyclization and dehydrogenation of aliphatic hydrocarbons found in petroleum.

10.58 Synthesize benzene using a Diels–Alder reaction.

◢ $HC \equiv CH + CH_2 = CHCH = CH_2 \longrightarrow$ $\xrightarrow[\Delta]{Pd}$ $+ H_2$

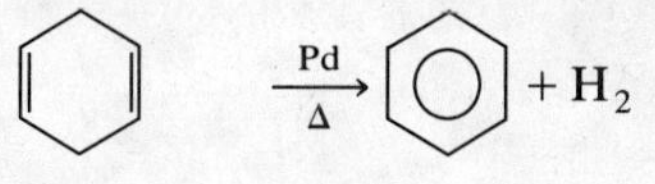

1,4-Cyclohexadiene

10.59 (*a*) Give the products of the reaction with O_2 in the presence of the catalyst V_2O_5 and heat of (i) benzene and (ii) *o*-xylene. (*b*) What are the products of oxidation of (i) and (ii) in (*a*) with $KMnO_4$ or CrO_3? (*c*) What conclusion can be drawn about the stability of the aromatic ring from the product of the oxidation in (ii)?

◢ (*a*) (i)

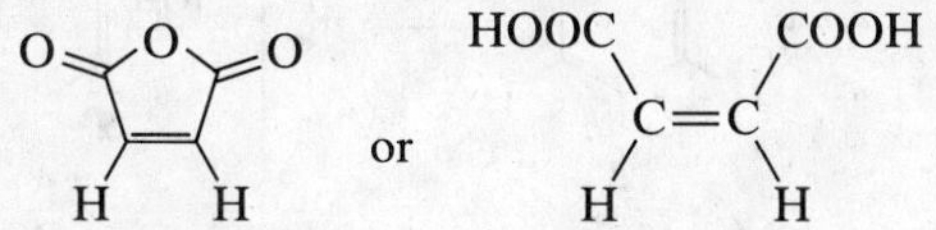

Maleic anhydride   or   Maleic acid(*cis*)

(ii)

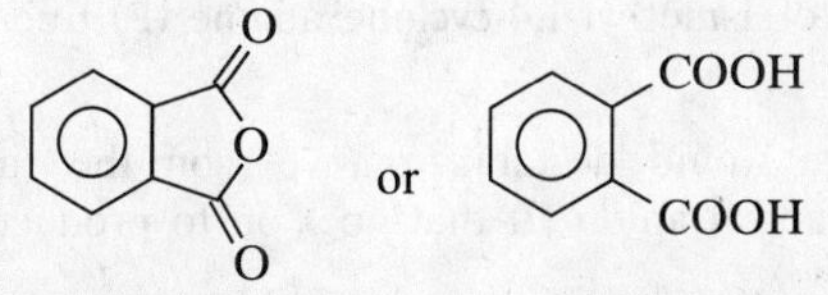

Phthalic anhydride   or   Phthalic acid

(*b*) Benzene is inert to these oxidants (recall Problem 10.9); phthalic acid is obtained from (ii).
(*c*) The extra stability of the aromatic ring is illustrated by its inertness to milder oxidants.

10.60 (*a*) Give the products of the following hydrogenation reactions:

(i) 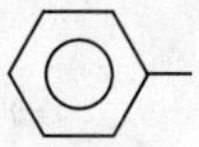 $\xrightarrow[100\,atm,\,\Delta]{H_2,\,Ni}$ (ii) 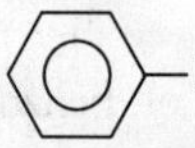 $\xrightarrow[35\,atm,\,\Delta]{H_2,\,Pt/Al_2O_3}$

(*b*) What can be concluded about the stability of the aromatic ring from these reactions?

◢ (*a*) (i) $C_6H_{11}OH$, cyclohexanol; (ii) $C_6H_{11}Me$, methylcyclohexane.
(*b*) The drastic conditions for reduction of the ring, when contrasted with the mild conditions for alkenes, again illustrate the marked stability of the aromatic ring.

10.61 Give the product of the reduction of benzene by Li or Na in liquid NH_3 and EtOH.

◢ This *Birch reduction* is related to the reduction of alkynes to alkenes (see Problem 9.66). The product is 1,4-cyclohexadiene.

$$C_6H_6 + 2M + 2EtOH \xrightarrow{liq. \ NH_3}$$ $+ 2(M^+EtO^-)$ where M = Li, Na

10.62 Give the mechanism of the Birch reduction of benzene.

◢ An alkali metal in liquid NH_3 is a source of solvated electrons. The first step is the addition of an e^- to form a benzene radical anion **A**, a strong base. Although the equilibrium lies far to the left, **A** readily accepts H^+ from the EtOH (or NH_3 in absence of EtOH) pulling the equilibrium to the right. The resulting radical **B** then accepts another e^- from M to form the anion **C**, a strong base, which reacts with a second EtOH. Protonation at the central C occurs more rapidly than at the end C's of the conjugated chain, to form the unconjugated product, **D**. **D** is thus the rate-controlled product. The thermodynamically more stable product is 1,3-cyclohexadiene.

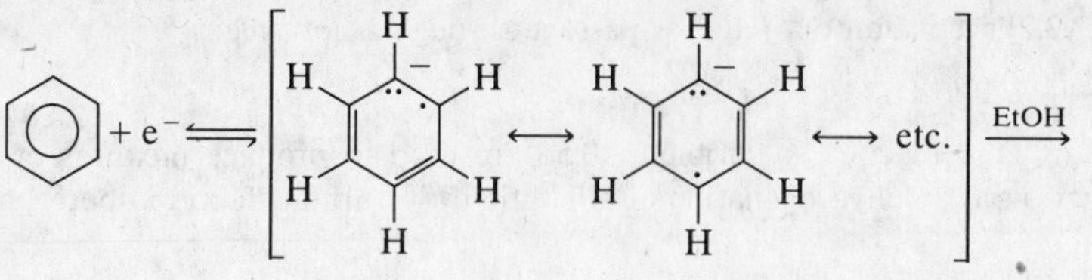

A

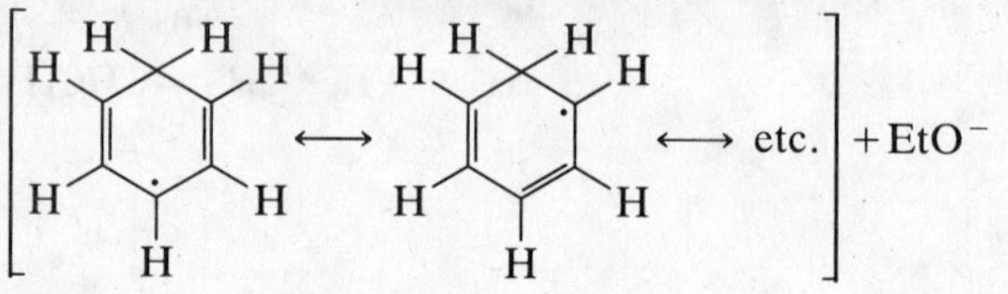

B

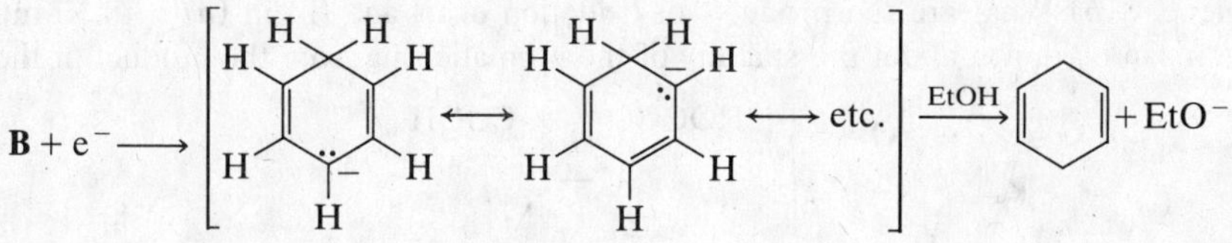

C   **D**

10.63 Birch reduction of toluene gives a 50% yield of 1-methyl-1,4-cyclohexadiene (**F**) free of the isomeric 3-methyl-1,4-cyclohexadiene (**G**). Explain.

⟋ CH_3 is electron-donating and therefore would destabilize a $(-)$ on the ring carbon bonded to it. Consequently, the more stable intermediate radical anion **H**, that goes on to product, has CH_3 on the double bond.

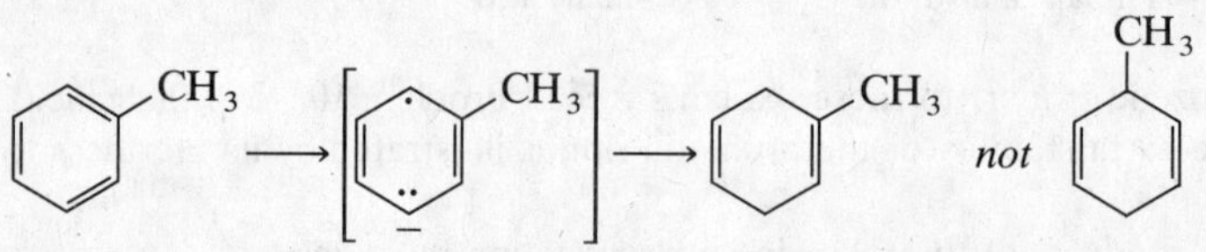

H   **F**   **G**

10.64 Explain why Birch reduction of benzoic acid gives 2,5-cyclohexadiene-1-carboxylic acid (**I**) rather than the 1,4-isomer (**J**).

⟋ COOH is electron-withdrawing and the more stable intermediate radical anion (**K**) that leads to product, has COOH attached to the negatively-charged C.

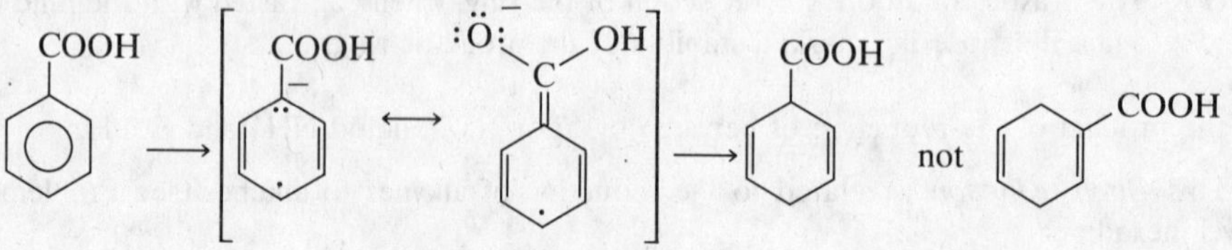

K   **I**   **J**

10.65 Referring to Problems 10.63 and 10.64, make a general statement relating the nature of the substituent on the benzene ring to (**a**) its eventual position in the product and (**b**) the rate of Birch reduction.

⟋ (**a**) Electron-releasing groups, like OCH_3 and R, end up on a double bond, and electron-withdrawing groups, like COOH, end up allylic to both double bonds. (**b**) The reactivity of the arene is increased by electron-withdrawing groups and decreased by electron-donating groups.

10.66 Explain the formation of 1,4-cyclohexadiene from the Birch reduction of bromobenzene.

◢ The expected product, 3-bromo-1,4-cyclohexadiene, is an allylic bromide which is easily converted to an organometallic, $R:^-M^+$. This strongly basic carbanion abstracts H^+ from EtOH to give the diene.

10.67 Give the structures of the products of the reactions of benzene with (*a*) HNO_3/H_2SO_4, (*b*) Cl_2/Fe, (*c*) $H_2S_2O_7$, (*d*) $CH_3CH_2Cl/AlCl_3$, (*e*) $Br_2/FeBr_3$, and (*f*) $RCOCl/AlCl_3$.

◢ Monosubstitution in each case leads to: (*a*) $Ph-NO_2$, (*b*) $Ph-Cl$, (*c*) $Ph-SO_3H$, (*d*) $Ph-CH_2CH_3$, (*e*) $Ph-Br$, and (*f*) $Ph-COR$.

10.68 Explain why the reactions in Problem 10.67 result in substitution rather than addition.

◢ Addition (of one equivalent) to the double bond would destroy the extra stability engendered by the aromatic sextet.

POLYNUCLEAR AROMATIC HYDROCARBONS

10.69 (*a*) Identify with numbers and Greek letters the C's in naphthalene. (*b*) Give the number and names of the isomers of (i) monomethylnaphthalene and (ii) dimethylnaphthalene.

◢ (*a*) See Fig. 10-13.

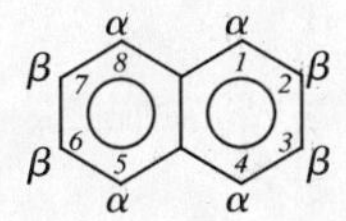

Fig. 10-13

(*b*) (i) Two isomers: α- or 1-methylnaphthalene and β- or 2-methylnaphthalene (ii) Ten isomers: 1,2-, 1,3-, 1,4-, 1,5-, 1-6, 1,7-, 1,8-, 2,3-, 2,6-, and 2,7-dimethylnaphthalene.

10.70 Draw structures for the following: (*a*) β-nitronaphthalene, (*b*) α-naphthol, (*c*) 1,5-dichloro-naphthalene, (*d*) 1-naphthalenesulfonic acid, and (*e*) 2-naphthoic aid.

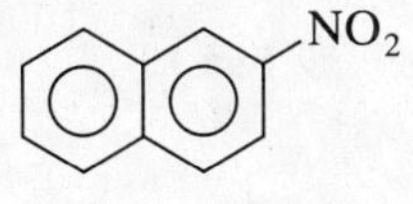

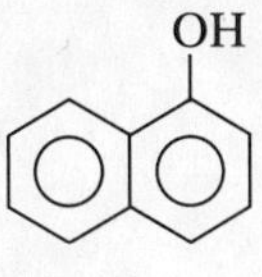

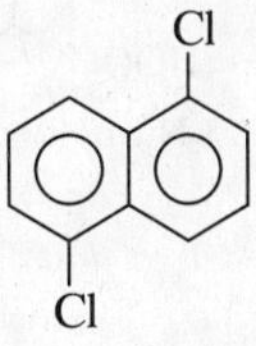

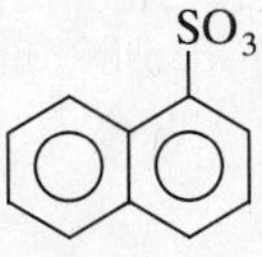

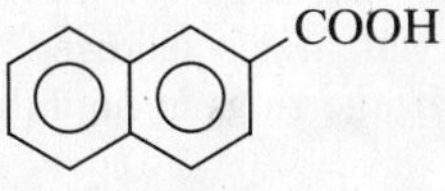

10.71 (*a*) Draw three resonance structures and the resonance hybrid for naphthalene. Which is the major contributor to the hybrid? (*b*) X-ray analysis shows that, unlike benzene, the C-to-C bond lengths in naphthalene are not all the same. Which is shorter (has more double-bond character), the C^1-C^2 or C^2-C^3 bond? Explain.

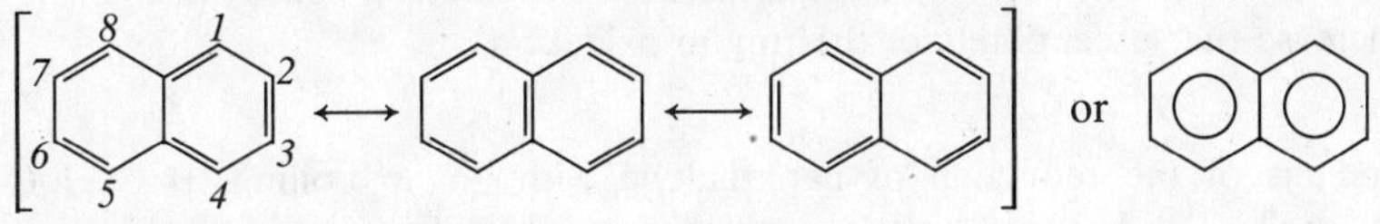

Resonance structures **A** and **C** have the Kekulé structure in only one ring and would not be expected to be as stable as **B**, with the full Kekulé structure in both rings.

(*b*) C^1-C^2- is shorter because it is a double bond in two of three resonance structures; C^2-C^3 is a single bond in two of three resonance structures.

10.72 (*a*) Give the product of oxidation of naphthalene with (i) CrO_3/acetic acid and (ii) O_2/V_2O_5, heat. (*b*) The resonance stabilization of naphthalene is 255 kJ/mol. How does this fact explain its facile oxidation as compared with the unreactivity of benzene [whose resonance energy is 151 kJ/mol]?

(a) (i)

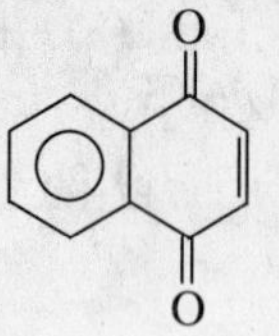

1,4-Naphthaquinone

(ii)

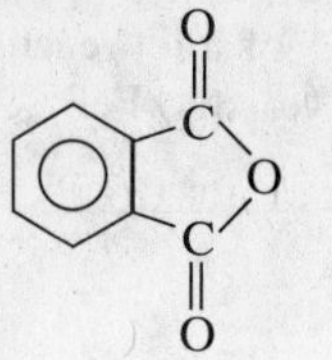

or

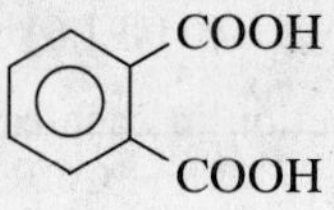

Phthalic anhydride   Phthalic acid

(*b*) Oxidation of one ring of naphthalene requires less energy than oxidation of benzene. It "costs" 104 kJ in resonance energy; oxidation of the second ring would cost 151 kJ.

10.73 Oxidation of 1-nitronaphthalene yields 3-nitrophthalic acid while oxidation of α-naphthylamine yields phthalic acid (see Fig. 10-14). How do these reactions establish the gross structure of naphthalene?

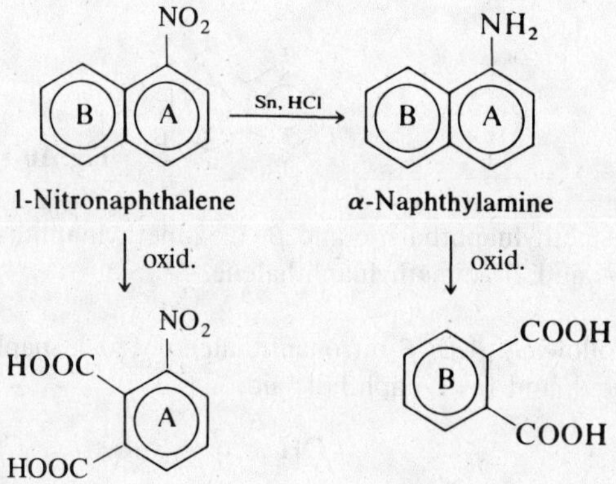

NO$_2$

B A

Sn, HCl →

NH$_2$

B A

1-Nitronaphthalene α-Naphthylamine

↓ oxid.   ↓ oxid.

NO$_2$

HOOC

A

HOOC

3-Nitrophthalic acid

COOH

B

COOH

Phthalic acid   **Fig. 10-14**

The electron-attracting —NO$_2$ stabilizes ring A of 1-nitronaphthalene to oxidation, and ring B is oxidized to form 3-nitrophthalic acid. By orbital overlap, —N̈H$_2$ releases electron density, making ring A more susceptible to oxidation, and α-naphthylamine is oxidized to phthalic acid. The NO$_2$ labels one ring and establishes the presence of two fused benzene rings in naphthalene.

10.74 Explain why different rings in the substituted naphthalenes in Problem 10.73 are oxidized.

An oxidizing agent is electron-seeking; therefore substituents like nitro, that withdraw electrons from the ring (by delocalization and/or induction), decrease the electron density in the ring, making it more resistant to oxidation. Conversely, substituents like amino, that increase the electron density in the ring (supplying e⁻'s by π delocalization), increase the susceptibility of the ring to oxidation.

10.75 (*a*) Give the products of the reduction of naphthalene with Na in boiling (i) C_2H_5OH (bp = 78 °C) and (ii) $C_5H_{11}OH$ (bp = 132 °C). (*b*) What is the significance of the difference in alcohols used in (i) and (ii)?

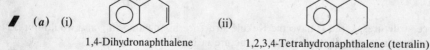

(a) (i)

1,4-Dihydronaphthalene

(ii)

1,2,3,4-Tetrahydronaphthalene (tetralin)

(*b*) The boiling point of the alcohol determines the temperature of the reaction; to achieve the necessary higher temperature in (ii), an alcohol with higher bp is used.

10.76 Use a Diels–Alder reaction to synthesize (*a*) tetralin and (*b*) naphthalene.

(*a*)

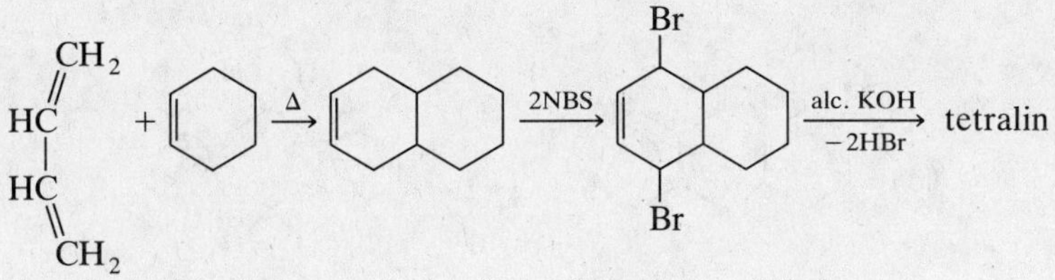

$$\begin{array}{c} CH_2 \\ \| \\ HC \\ | \\ HC \\ \| \\ CH_2 \end{array}$$ + ⬡ $\xrightarrow{\Delta}$ [fused ring] $\xrightarrow{2NBS}$ [dibromo fused ring] $\xrightarrow[-2HBr]{\text{alc. KOH}}$ tetralin

(*b*) Tetralin is dehydrogenated with S or Pd to give naphthalene.

10.77 Explain why benzene and naphthalene do not undergo a Diels–Alder reaction.

Although these compounds could be considered to be conjugated polyenes, if they behaved in this manner and underwent the Diels–Alder reaction too much resonance energy would be lost.

10.78 (*a*) Write resonance structures for anthracene and depict the resonance hybrid. (*b*) Anthracene has a resonance energy of 351 kJ/mol. On the basis of its resonance energy per ring as compared with that of benzene (see Problem 10.72) would anthracene be expected to be more or less resistant than benzene toward oxidation and reduction?

(*a*) [anthracene resonance structures] ⟷ [structure] ⟷ [structure] ⟷

[structure] or [structure]

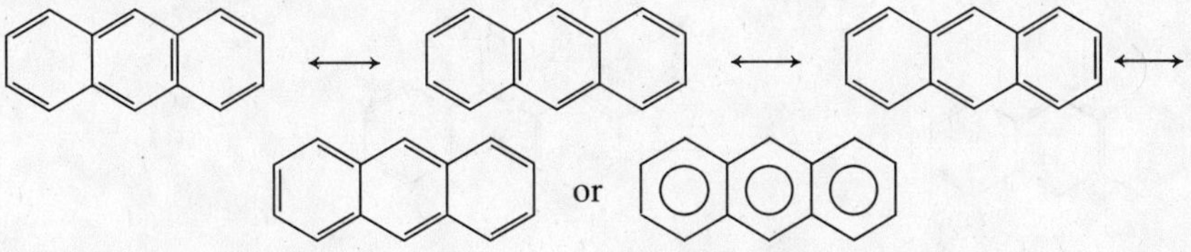

(*b*) The resonance energy per ring is $351 \div 3 = 117$ kJ/mol, somewhat less than the value for benzene of 151 kJ/mol. Anthracene is oxidized and reduced more easily than benzene.

10.79 (*a*) Identify with numbers and Greek letters the C's in anthracene. (*b*) Write the structures of (i) 1-anthranoic acid, (ii) 9,10-dibromoanthracene, (iii) 1,2,6,7-tetramethylanthracene, (iv) 1,2-benzanthracene, and (v) 9-anthrol.

(*a*) See Fig. 10-15.

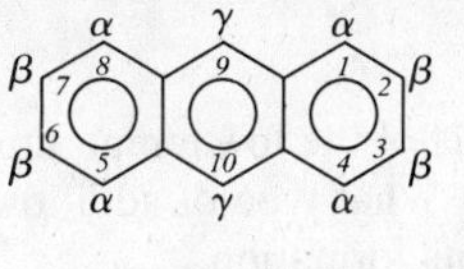

Fig. 10-15

(*b*) (i) [COOH-substituted anthracene] (ii) [Br,Br-substituted anthracene] (iii) [tetramethyl anthracene]

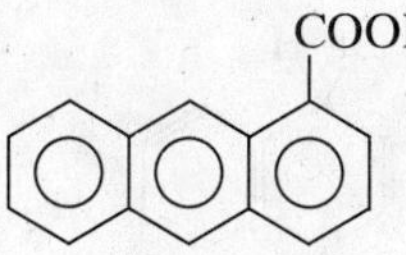

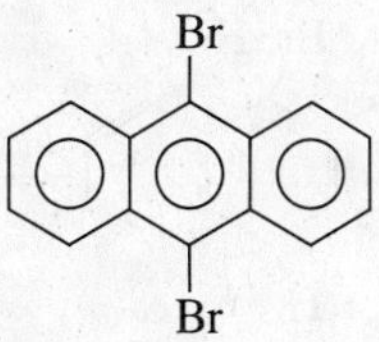

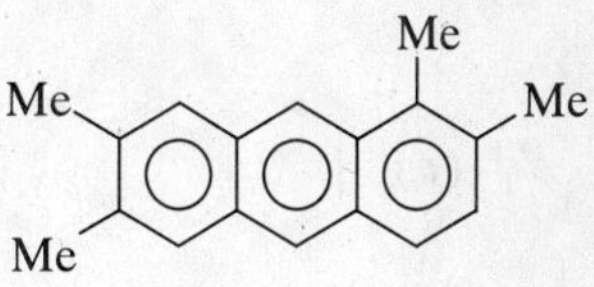

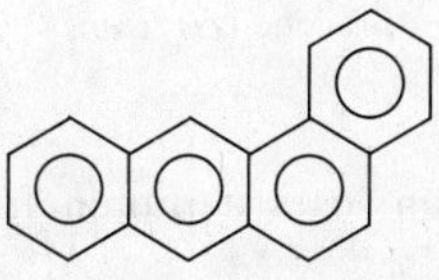

(iv) [1,2-benzanthracene] (v) [9-anthrol with OH]

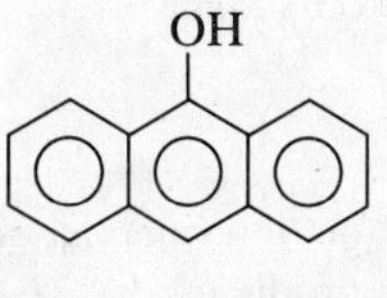

10.80 How many monochloro derivatives of anthracene are possible? Give their names.

There are three sets of equivalent positions (α, β, and γ); thus there are three different monochloroanthracenes: 1- (same as 4-, 5- and 8-), 2- (same as 3-, 6-, and 7-) and 9- (same as 10-)chloroanthracene.

10.81 How many dichloro derivatives of anthracene are possible? Give their names.

There are 15 derivatives. Four have both Cl's in the same outside ring: 1,2-, 1,3-, 1,4-, and 2,3-dichloroanthracene. Six have one Cl in each outside ring: 1,5-, 1,6-, 1,7-, 1,8-, 2,6-, and 2,7-dichloroanthracene. Four have one Cl in an outside ring and one in the inside ring: 1,9-, 1,10-, 2,9-, and 2,10-dichloroanthracene; and one with both Cl's in the inside ring: 9,10-dichloroanthracene.

10.82 What are the products of (*a*) oxidation of anthracene with $K_2Cr_2O_7/H_2SO_4$ and (*b*) reduction of anthracene with Na/C_2H_5OH?

(*a*)

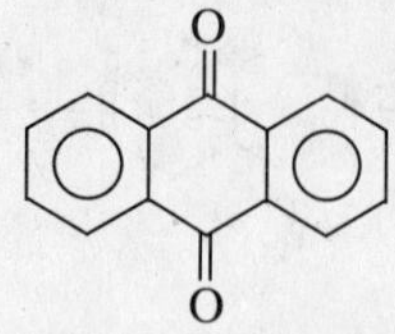

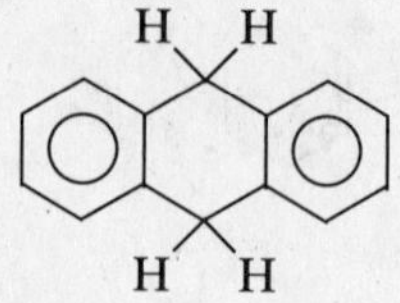

9,10-Anthraquinone

(*b*)

9,10-Dihydroanthracene

10.83 Give an explanation for both the oxidation and reduction in Problem 10.82 occurring at positions 9 and 10.

▮ Attack at the 9- and 10-positions leaves two benzene rings intact with a total resonance energy of $2(151) = 302$ kJ/mol for isolated rings. Attack at any position in the outer rings would leave a naphthalene ring intact, having only 255 kJ/mol.

10.84 What is the structure of the Diels–Alder product of anthracene with (*a*) ethene, and (*b*) maleic anhydride (see Problem 10.59)?

▮ Anthracene acts as a diene; the bonds involved are shown darkened in the structure.

(*a*) $+ H_2C=CH_2 \longrightarrow$

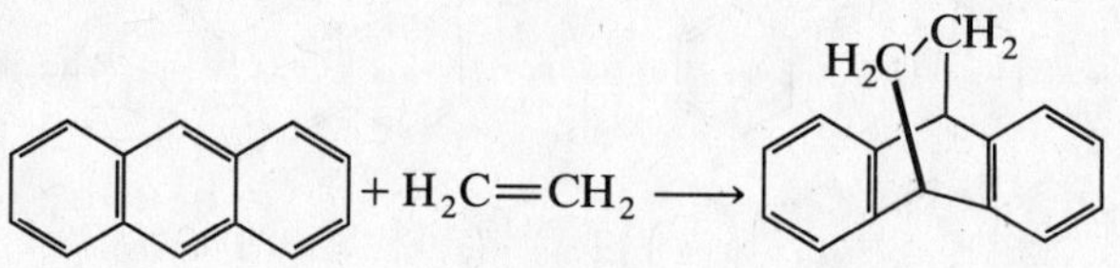

(*b*) $+$ $\longrightarrow$

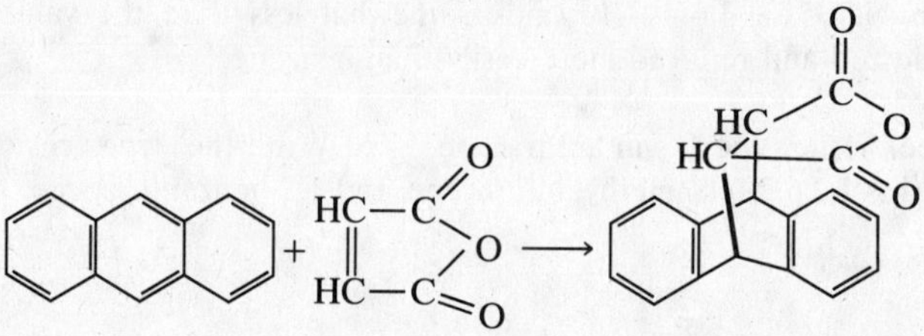

10.85 (*a*) Write the structure of the product of the low temperature reaction of anthracene with Br_2/CCl_4 and propose a mechanism for its formation. (*b*) What type of addition has occurred? (*c*) Identify the product formed at a higher temperature and rationalize its formation.

▮ (*a*) $\xrightarrow{Br^+}$ a carbocation $\xrightarrow{Br^-}$ 9,10-Dibromo-9,10-dihydroanthracene (*cis/trans*)

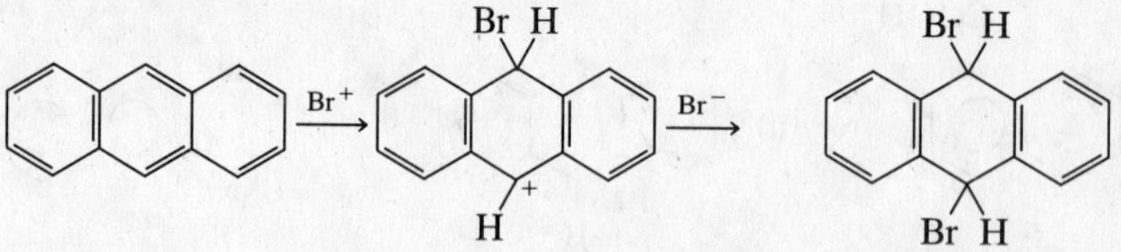

(*b*) 1,4-Addition.

(*c*) At a higher temperature, the intermediate carbocation loses a proton from C^9 giving 9-bromoanthracene, the substitution product.

10.86 Draw the five resonance structures of phenanthrene and depict the resonance hybrid.

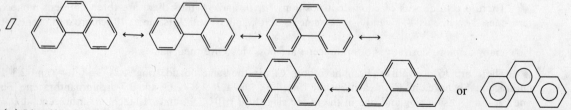
$\longleftrightarrow$ ... $\longleftrightarrow$ ... $\longleftrightarrow$ ... $\longleftrightarrow$ ... or

10.87 (*a*) Identify with numbers and Greek letters the C's in phenanthrene. (*b*) Predict which should be the shortest C-to-C bond (have the most double bond character).

▟ (*a*) See Fig. 10-16.

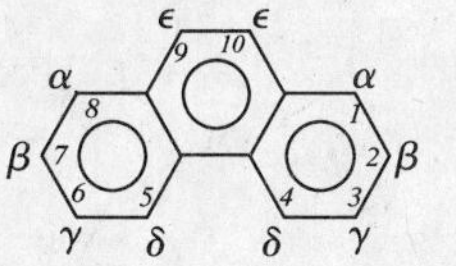

Fig. 10-16

(*b*) The C^9—C^{10} bond. Four of the five resonance forms in Problem 10.86 have the double bond here.

10.88 How many monomethylphenanthrenes are possible?

▟ There are five sets of equivalent positions: 1 and 8; 2 and 7; 3 and 6; 4 and 5; and 9 and 10. Thus there are five different monomethylphenanthrenes. These are: 1-, 2-, 3-, 4-, and 9-methylphenanthrene.

10.89 Referring to Problems 10.78 and 10.86, predict whether their respective anthracene or phenanthrene should have more resonance energy. Explain.

▟ There are more aromatic sextets in phenanthrene's resonance structures (10) than in those of anthracene (6); thus phenanthrene has more resonance energy.

10.90 Phenanthrene reacts with one equivalent of Br_2 at low temperatures to give an addition product, 9,10-dibromo-9,10-dihydrophenanthrene (**G**), which is a mixture of *cis*- and *trans*-isomers. (*a*) Write the structure of **G**, and give a mechanism for its formation. (*b*) Explain why reaction occurs to give **G**, rather than any other isomer. (*c*) Why do both *syn*- and *anti*- addition occur? (*d*) What type of addition has occurred?

▟ (*a*)

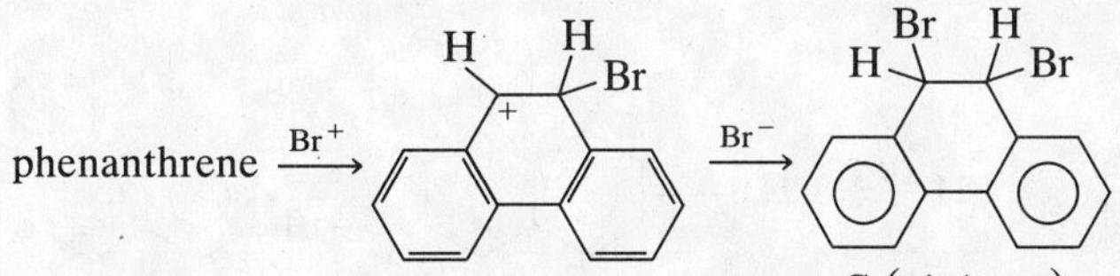

phenanthrene $\xrightarrow{Br^+}$ **F** $\xrightarrow{Br^-}$ **G** (*cis/trans*)

(*b*) The C^9—C^{10} bond has the most double bond character [see Problem 10.87(*b*)]. Addition to this bond results in a biphenyl compound (see Problem 10.53) with two benzene rings, each having 151-kJ/mol delocalization energy. The adduct from addition to an outside ring would give a naphthalene product, with less stability [see Problem 10.72(*b*)].

(*c*) The expected intermediate bromonium ion collapses to a stable carbocation (**F**) having positive charge delocalized into the attached phenyl ring. Addition of Br^- occurs from either side. (*d*) 1,2-Addition.

10.91 Referring to Problem 10.90, when **G** is heated, HBr is evolved, giving 9-bromophenanthrene. Give a mechanism for this reaction.

▟ Heat causes the reformation of **F** by reversal of the product-forming step. **F** then loses H^+ from the adjacent C to reform the aromatic ring, giving the thermodynamically more stable phenanthrene product.

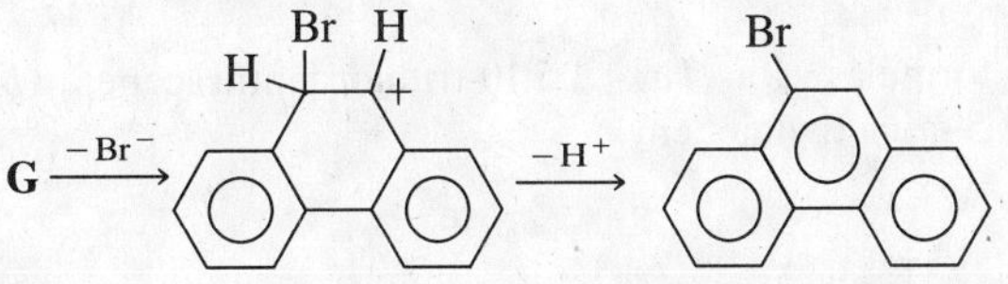

G $\xrightarrow{-Br^-}$ **F** $\xrightarrow{-H^+}$ 9-Bromophenanthrene

10.92 Give the products of the reaction of (*a*) anthracene and (*b*) phenanthrene with Na in alcohol.

▟ In each case two H's add individually to C^9 and C^{10}. The products are

(*a*) 9,10-Dihydroanthracene

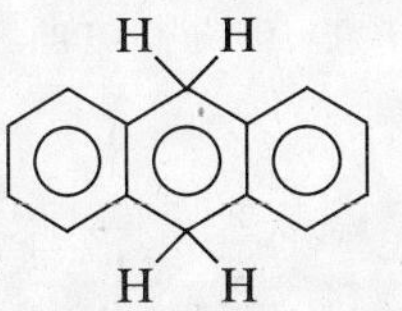

(*b*) 9,10-Dihydrophenanthrene

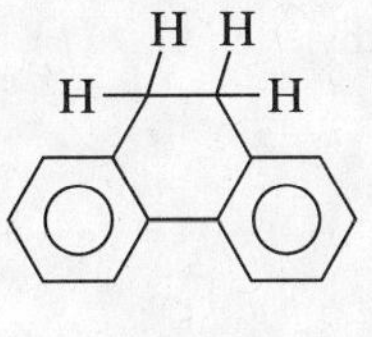

10.93 Give the product of the reaction of phenanthrene with an oxidant, e.g., $K_2Cr_2O_7$ in acid.

⬧ Oxidation occurs at C^9 and C^{10}.

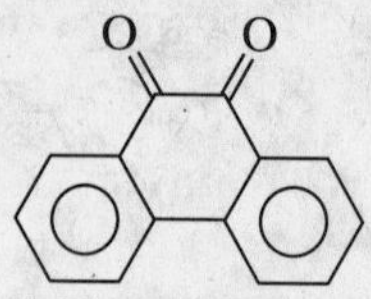

9,10-Phenanthraquinone

10.94 Compare the ability of anthracene, phenanthrene, naphthalene, and benzene to act as dienes in the Diels–Alder reaction.

⬧ Anthracene readily participates as a diene in Diels–Alder reactions (Problem 10.84) but phenanthrene does not. If the central ring of phenanthrene reacted as does the central ring of anthracene, the aromaticity of all three rings would be destroyed. If the diene portion of phenanthrene were to include the $C^9 = C^{10}$ double bond, the aromaticity of the two rings would be lost. The $\Delta H^{\ddagger}$ of such a reaction would be prohibitive. Naphthalene does not react under typical conditions but has been made to react under very high pressures; it resists losing resonance energy. Benzene does not react because its aromatic ring is too stable.

10.95 1-Ethenylnaphthalene reacts with $H_2C = CH_2$ to give a product **A** which reacts when heated with Pd or S to give **B**, $C_{14}H_{10}$. Give the structures of **A** and **B**.

⬧ The required structures are

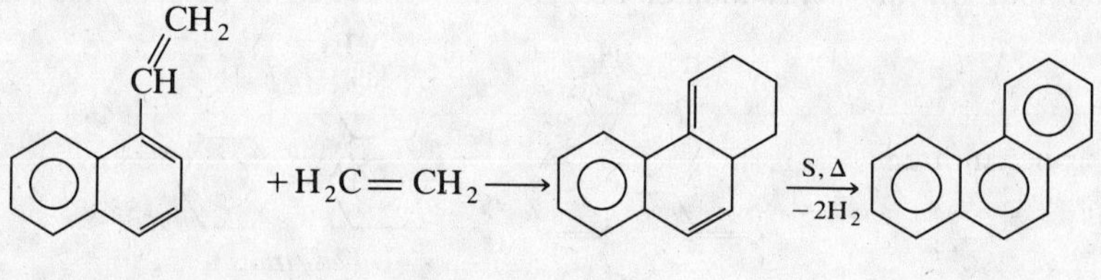

1-Ethenylnaphthalene ... **A** ... Phenanthrene, **B**

10.96 Give the product of the reaction of anthracene and O_2 with a photosensitizer in the presence of ultraviolet light. What is the purpose of the photosensitizer?

⬧ O_2 adds in a Diels–Alder-type reaction to C^9 and C^{10}. The photosensitizer helps excite O_2 from the triplet ground state to the singlet excited state needed for the *photooxidation*.

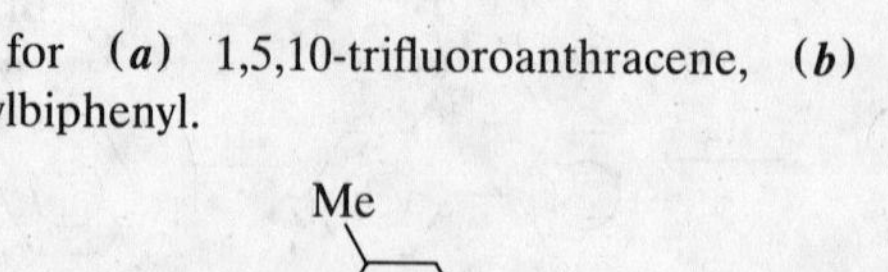

$$\text{anthracene} \xrightarrow[hv]{O_2, \text{ sensitizer}}$$

10.97 Give the structural formulas for (*a*) 1,5,10-trifluoroanthracene, (*b*) 2,6,9-trimethylphenanthrene, and (*c*) 2-chloro-3-fluoro-2′,5′-dimethylbiphenyl.

⬧ (*a*) ... (*b*) 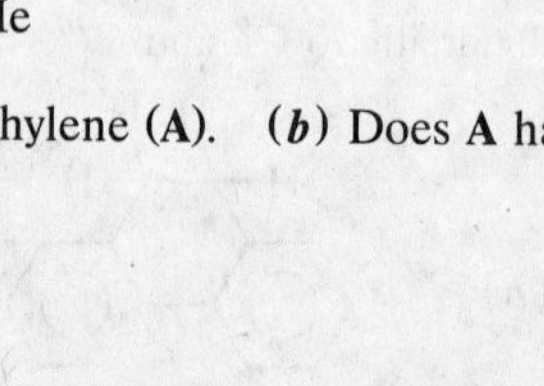 ... (*c*)

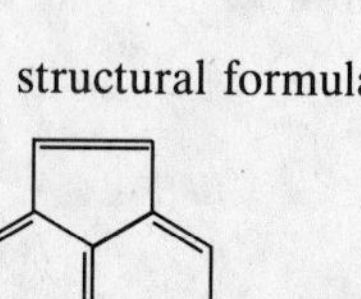

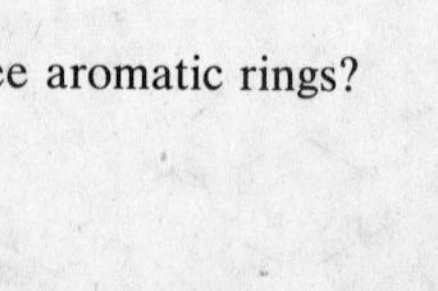

10.98 (*a*) Give the structural formula of acenaphthylene (**A**). (*b*) Does **A** have three aromatic rings?

⬧ (*a*)

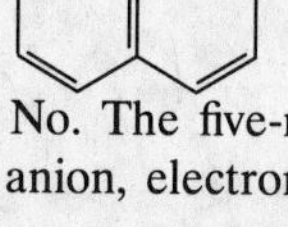

(*b*) No. The five-membered ring is not aromatic. For this ring to be aromatic like the cyclopentadienyl anion, electron density must be removed from one of the benzene rings, attenuating its aromaticity.

10.99 (*a*) Define the terms (i) "*ortho*-fused" and (ii) "*ortho*- and *peri*-fused", as applied to fused polynuclear aromatic hydrocarbons. (*b*) Apply these terms to acenaphthylene.

◢ (*a*) These are polynuclear compounds in which (i) two rings have two and only two atoms in common and (ii) one ring contains two and only two atoms in common with each of two other rings of a contiguous series of rings. (*b*) The two six-membered rings are "*ortho*-fused. The five-membered ring is "*ortho*- and *peri*-fused".

10.100 Several polynuclear aromatic hydrocarbons, many found in cigarette smoke, are potent carcinogens. Draw the structural formula for each of the following: (*a*) Benz[*a*]pyrene. Indicate the pyrene ring system. (*b*) Dibenz[*a*, *h*]anthracene. (*c*) 7,12-Dimethylbenz[*a*]anthracene. Explain the use of the bracketed italicized letters in the names.

◢ (*a*) Pyrene has four rings exclusive of the lone "*ortho*-fused ring," labeled **A**.

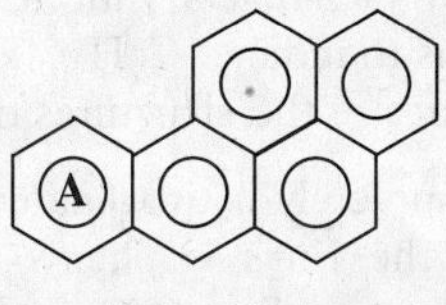

(*b*)

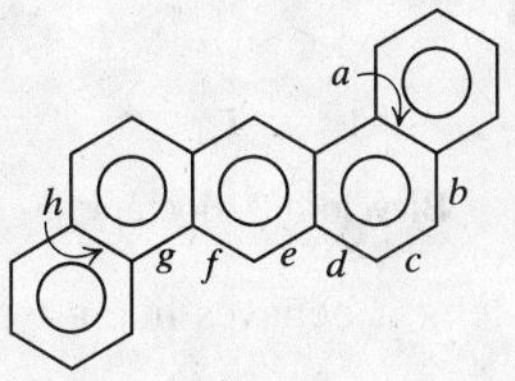

(*c*)

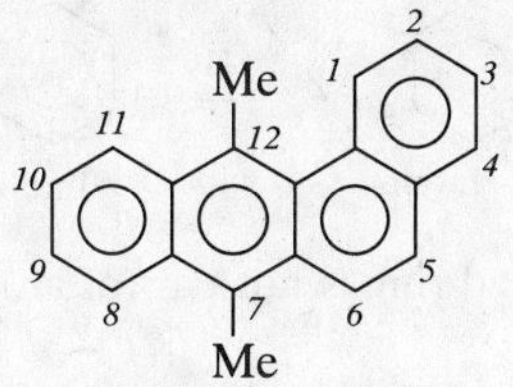

The sides of the rings of the parent compounds are designated with letters so that the position of *ortho*-fusion may be indicated as shown in (*b*).

SUPPLEMENTARY PROBLEMS

10.101 Borazine (also called borazole), $B_3N_3H_6$, has a flat, monocyclic structure of alternating B and N atoms. All B—N bond lengths are equal, and all ring angles are 120°. (*a*) Draw two Kekulé structures and depict the resonance hybrid for borazine that conforms with these data. (*b*) Should borazine be aromatic? Explain.

◢ (*a*)

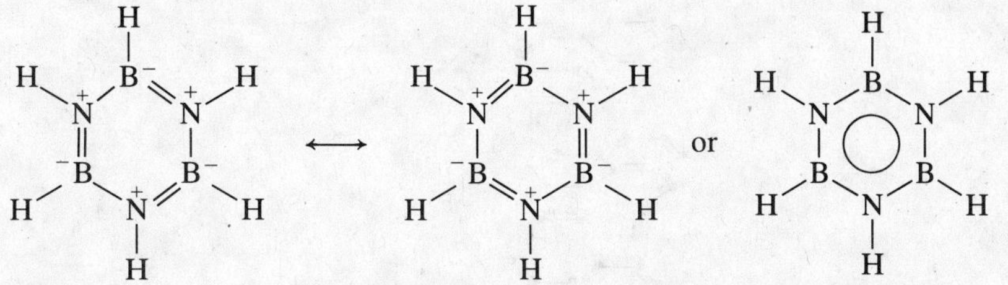

(*b*) Borazine is aromatic. Both N and B are sp^2 hybridized. Each B has an empty p orbital and each N has two nonbonding e⁻'s in a p orbital, giving a total of six delocalized e⁻'s.

10.102 Predict which of the following compounds may have aromatic character. Give your reasons.

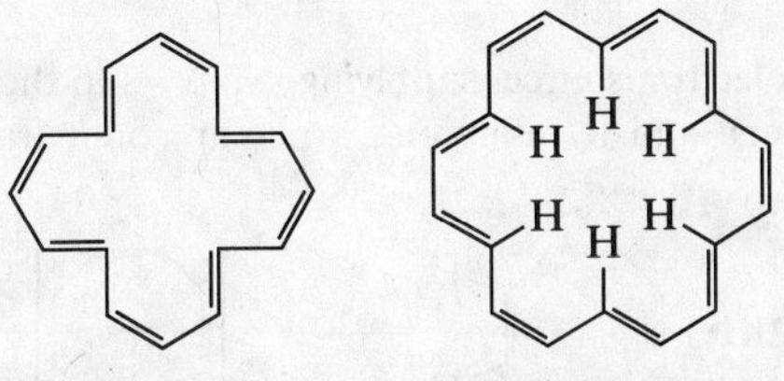

[16]-Annulene   [18]-Annulene

✐ [18]-Annulene is aromatic. It has nine conjugated double bonds and 18 e⁻'s in a cyclic structure where internal H's do not prevent it from achieving coplanarity. The [16]-annulene has $4n$ π electrons and so it is not aromatic.

10.103 How can 1,3,5,7-cyclononatetraene be converted to an aromatic anion?

✐ Removal of an H⁺ from the sp^3 hybridized C produces a planar anion with ten delocalized electrons:

10.104 Indene, C_9H_8, isolated from coal tar, reacts with $KMnO_4$ and decolorizes Br_2 in CCl_4. It is catalytically hydrogenated under mild conditions to indane, C_9H_{10} (**E**), and under vigorous conditions to C_9H_{16}, **F**. Oxidation of indene yields phthalic acid. What are the structures of indene, indane, and **F**?

✐ The molecular formula of completely hydrogenated **F** reveals the presence of two rings. The formation of phthalic acid shows that one of the rings is phenyl and that the remaining three C's must be part of a five-membered ring system fused to two adjacent C's in the ring.

Indene   Indane, **E**   Bicyclo[4.3.0]octane, **F**

The C=C in the five-membered ring is not part of an aromatic system; it behaves like a typical C=C.

10.105 (*a*) Discuss the molecular structure of graphite. (*b*) Account for its physical properties in terms of its molecular structure.

✐ (*a*) Graphite is made up of stacking layers of fused benzene-like rings (see Fig. 10.17). The atoms in any given plane are tightly bonded together by σ bonds and alternating π bonds. The forces between the planar sheets are much weaker, and are attributed to π-bond overlap similar to those found in "sandwich" compounds (see Problem 10.123). (*b*) The weak bonds between the sheets are easily deformed and slide past each other smoothly, making graphite a good lubricant. It is a good conductor of electricity and heat parallel to the atomic planes, but not perpendicular to the planes. The π electrons can move freely within the planes to conduct electricity or heat, but not across the sheets. Graphite is black, a fact consistent with its MO's being very close together, making absorption of light at all frequencies in the visible range possible.

0.142 nm

0.335 nm

Fig. 10-17

10.106 1,3,5,7-Cyclooctatetraene, a nonaromatic hydrocarbon (see Problems 10.41 and 10.42) reacts with two eq of K to form a stable compound, **A**. H_2 is not produced. What is the structure of **A**, and what is the reason for its stability?

✐ The metal acts as an electron source, supplying two e⁻'s to the cyclooctatetraene. The resulting dianion has ten e⁻'s (a Hückel number), and by assuming a planar configuration becomes aromatic and therefore more stable.

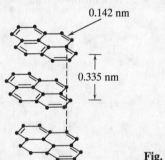

A

10.107 (*a*) Benzene reacts with diazomethane, CH_2N_2, to give C_7H_8 (**B**). **B** isomerizes to **C**, which is completely hydrogenated to cycloheptane. Give the structures of **B** and **C**. (*b*) What conclusion can be drawn about the reactivity of methylene, H_2C:? (*c*) What is the driving force for the rearrangement of **B** to **C**?

(*a*)

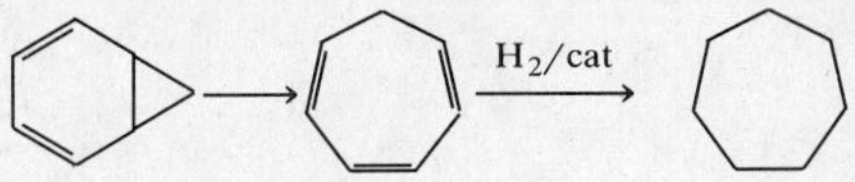

(*b*) Since H_2C: adds so readily to benzene which ordinarily withstands addition, it must be an extremely reactive species.

(*c*) The rearrangement removes the strained three-membered ring and converts a conjugated diene to a more stable conjugated triene.

10.108 (*a*) Write resonance forms of the structure of the dianion **D**, formed by the following reaction, and explain its ease of formation.

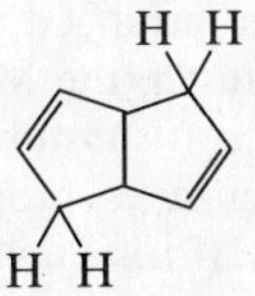

$$+ 2C_4H_9Li \longrightarrow [C_8H_6]^{2-}\, 2Li^+ + 2C_4H_{10}$$
$$\mathbf{D}$$

Loss of two protons, one in each ring, results in a relatively stable structure with a Hückel number of ten delocalized electrons.

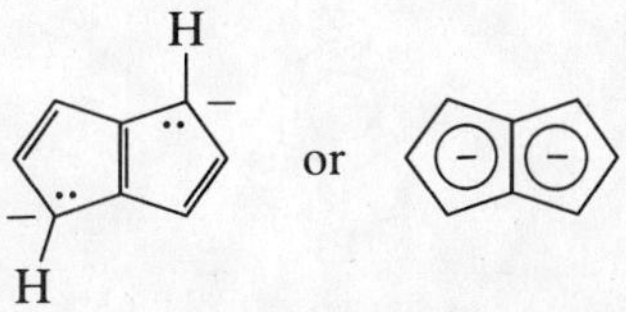

$$\mathbf{D}$$

10.109 [10]-Annulene is not aromatic although it has ten e^-'s available for delocalization (see Problem 10.38). Would you expect compound **J** below to be aromatic?

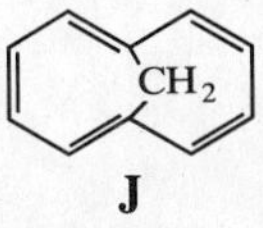

$$\mathbf{J}$$

Yes. The internal H's in [10]-annulene which prevent it from achieving coplanarity, are replaced in **J** by a methylene bridge above the molecule, permitting it to be flat. Since the bridgehead C's are still sp^2 hybridized in **J**, their p e^-'s are available for extended delocalization in a 10-electron system.

10.110 Describe simple chemical tests that can distinguish between (*a*) benzene and cyclohexadiene, (*b*) benzene and naphthalene, and (*c*) anthracene and phenanthrene.

(*a*) The diene decolorizes (reacts with) Br_2/CCl_4; benzene is unreactive. (*b*) Naphthalene is oxidized by CrO_3/acetic acid to produce naphthaquinone (Problem 10.72); benzene does not react. (*c*) Anthracene undergoes a Diels-Alder reaction with maleic anhydride (Problem 10.84); phenanthrene does not react as a diene (Problem 10.94).

10.111 Show how the three tribromobenzenes can be identified by the Körner method (Problem 10.14).

Nitration of 1,3,5-tribromobenzene gives one product (**A**), 1,2,3-tribromobenzene gives two isomeric nitro compounds (**B**) and (**C**), and 1,2,4-tribromobenzene gives three tribromonitrobenzenes, (**D**), (**E**), and (**F**).

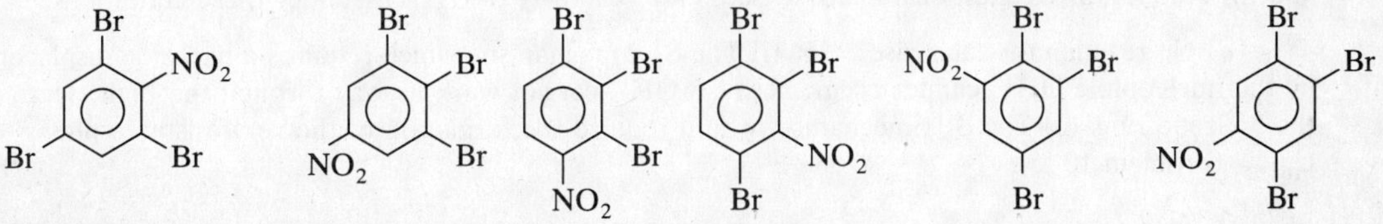

10.112 Give structures and names for all the isomers of tetrafluorobenzene.

▰ In **A**, all F's are contiguous; 1,2,3,4-tetrafluorobenzene. In **B**, three F's are adjacent and the fourth **F** is separated; 1,2,3,5-tetrafluorobenzene. **C** has two pairs of adjacent F's; 1,2,4,5-tetrafluorobenzene.

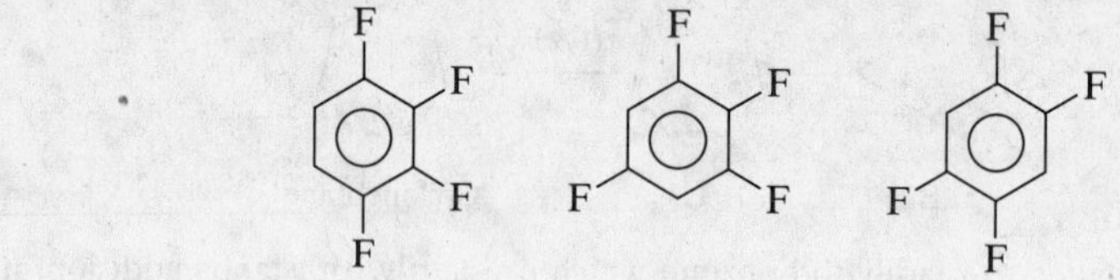

A   **B**   **C**

10.113 Give structures and names of all isomeric benzene derivatives, C_9H_{12}, that theoretically can have one of the following number of ring substituted monobromo derivatives: (*a*) one, (*b*) two, (*c*) three, and (*d*) four.

▰ Of the nine C's, six are part of the benzene ring and three are attached as alkyl groups. The three C's may be present as three Me's (a trisubstituted benzene), a Me and Et (a disubstituted benzene) or either *n*-Pr or *i*-Pr. (*a*) In 1,3,5-trimethylbenzene (mesitylene), (**A**), three Me's are arranged so the three remaining positions are equivalent, giving one monobromo derivative. (*b*) If disubstituted, the Me and Et must be *para*, leaving two kinds of free ring positions, as in 1-ethyl-4-methylbenzene, (**B**). If trisubstituted the three Me's must be adjacent, as in 1,2,3-trimethyl-benzene (**C**). (*c*) Two monosubstituted benzenes, propylbenzene, (**D**), and *i*-propylbenzene (cumene), (**E**), have three kinds of positions, as does **F**, 1,2,4-trimethylbenzene, leading to three isomeric monobromo compounds. (*d*) 1-Ethyl-2-methylbenzene, (**G**), and 1-ethyl-3-methylbenzene, (**H**), each have four different positions.

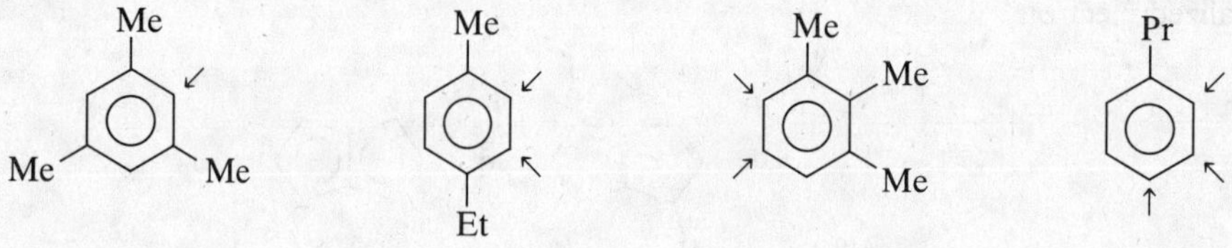

A   **B**   **C**   **D**

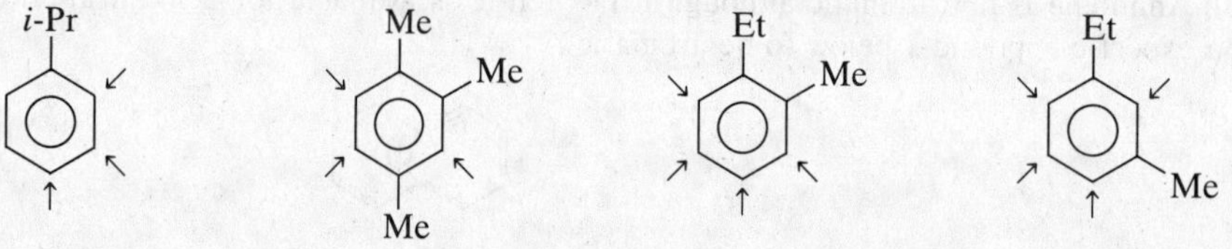

E   **F**   **G**   **H**

10.114 Name each of the following compounds:

(*a*) $CH_3CH_2CHCH_2CH_3$

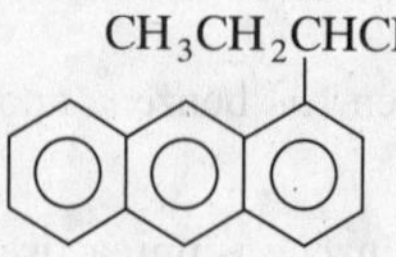

(*b*) $CH_3CHCH(CH_3)CH_2CH_3$

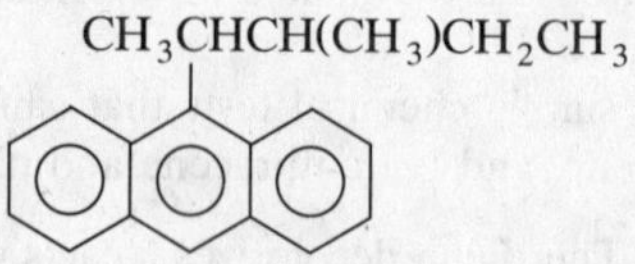

(*c*) ... NO_2 ... $CH_2CH_2CH_2CH_2$ ... NO_2

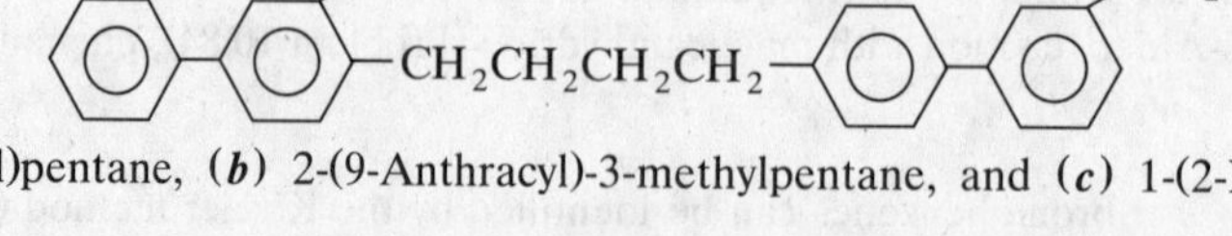

▰ (*a*) 3-(1-Anthracyl)pentane, (*b*) 2-(9-Anthracyl)-3-methylpentane, and (*c*) 1-(2-Nitrobiphenyl)-4-(3′-nitrobiphenyl)butane.

10.115 (*a*) What product, if any, is formed when C_6H_5Br is mixed with (i) OH^- at mild temperatures (S_N2 conditions), and (ii) ethanol (S_N1 conditions)? (*b*) Discuss the reactivity of C_6H_5Br under these conditions.

▰ (*a*) No reaction for each case. (*b*) (i) The S_N2 mechanism, which requires a backside displacement of Br^- by the nucleophile OH^-, cannot occur, because OH^- cannot work its way through the high electron density of the benzene ring. (ii) The S_N1 mechanism would require the formation of the very unstable phenyl carbocation, $C_6H_5^+$ (Problem 10.15).

10.116 Give simple chemical tests to distinguish cyclohexane, cyclohexene, and benzene.

◢ Add Br_2/CCl_4 to each of the three liquids. Cyclohexene, which undergoes addition, instantaneously decolorizes the red-brown color of Br_2. In presence of light, cyclohexane slowly decolorizes Br_2 but with the evolution of HBr gas, which is detected by its formation of a white cloud when in contact with moist breath. Cyclohexane, a typical alkane, undergoes free radical substitution. Benzene is unreactive under these conditions.

10.117 (*a*) Outline a synthesis of biphenyl from benzene. (*b*) Give the staring compound for the preparation of (i) 2,2′-dinitrobiphenyl and (ii) 2,2′-dimethyl-6,6′-dinitrobiphenyl. (*c*) What kind of biaryl (substituted biphenyl) can best be synthesized in good yield by this method (*Ullmann reaction*)?

◢ (*a*) $C_6H_6 \xrightarrow{Br_2/Fe} C_6H_5Br \xrightarrow[\Delta]{Cu} C_6H_5—C_6H_5$ (Ullmann reaction)

(*b*) (i) *o*-Nitroiodobenzene. Of all the halogens, I is the best leaving group in this coupling reaction.
(ii) 2-Methyl-6-nitroiodobenzene. Note that the starting material with halogen between two sizable groups is *not* subject to steric hindrance.

(*c*) Symmetrical biaryls, Ar—Ar, are best made because only one aryl halide, ArX, is needed. Unsymmetrical biaryls, Ar—Ar′, require the coupling of two different aryl halides, ArX and Ar′X. Ar′—Ar′ and Ar—Ar would also be formed. However, in some cases, with the proper mix, unsymmetrical biaryls have been made in good yield.

10.118 (*a*) How are naturally occurring terpenes converted to benzene derivatives? (*b*) Which benzene derivative(s) is/are derived from limonene, myrcene, and *alpha*-phellandrene (Problem 9.183)?

◢ (*a*) Dehydrogenation with a surface catalyst, e.g., Pd, converts the six-membered ring to a benzene ring. All exocyclic C=C bonds are reduced in this aromatization process. (*b*) Each given terpene gives *p*-isopropyltoluene (cymene).

10.119 (*a*) Give the product formed from the photochemical reaction of C_6H_6 and Cl_2. (*b*) Why does not Br_2 react in a similar fashion?

◢ (*a*) Several stereoisomers of 1,2,3,4,5,6-hexachlorocyclohexane (benzenehexachloride) are formed by free radical addition of Cl_2. One of the major stereoisomers is "lindane", a commercial insecticide. (*b*) Br·, the intermediate reactant, is much less reactive than Cl· and cannot add to the very stable benzene ring.

10.120 Compare the oxidation products of toluene and 2-methylnaphthalene with $KMnO_4$ in acid.

◢ Since the aromatic ring of benzene is very stable towards oxidation, $—CH_3$ is oxidized to $—COOH$. The product, in poor yield, is benzoic acid, C_6H_5COOH. 2-Methylnaphthalene is oxidized to 2-methyl-1,4-naphthaquinone (Problem 10.72) because on a per ring basis naphthalene is less aromatic than benzene.

10.121 Prepare mesitylene by a cycloaddition reaction.

◢ Recall the cycloaddition of three moles of acetylene to give benzene (Problem 10.57). Use propyne, $CH_3C≡CH$, to prepare mesitylene. Other isomers are not formed in good yields because they would have more crowded transition states with adjacent CH_3 groups.

10.122 When benzene is treated with DCl at low temperatures, a compound, C_6H_6DCl (**C**), is formed. On warming the reactants, C_6H_6 and DCl are re–formed. However, in the presence of $AlCl_3$, an isomer of C_6H_6DCl (**D**) is produced, which, on warming, gives mainly C_6H_5D and HCl. Discuss the structures and categorize each type of isomer.

◢ Since D is not incorporated into the benzene ring in the absence of $AlCl_3$, isomer **C** has no C—D σ bond. Instead, the D end of DCl is attracted to the π cloud of benzene to form a loosely bound *n complex*, indicated by an arrow in the structural formula. π Complexes are also called *charge-transfer* complexes, because the electron-rich benzene ring, the donor molecule, transfers some electron density to the electron-poor D of DCl, the acceptor molecule. With the catalyst $AlCl_3$, exchange of D for H occurs on warming. This exchange requires the formation of a C—D bond to give the σ *complex*, **D**. The benzene ring is re–formed by losing an H rather than the D because the C—H bond is weaker than the C—D bond. Notice the delocalization of the positive charge in the σ complex.

π complex, **C** σ complex, **D**

10.123 (*a*) Describe the structure of the *metallocene*, ferrocene $(C_5H_5)_2Fe$. (*b*) Account for its stability and aromaticity. (*c*) Predict whether ferrocene is a unique compound.

     (*a*)   Ferrocene is composed of an Fe^{2+} sandwiched between two cyclopentadienyl anions and held together by π complexation. There are no C—Fe σ bonds, as evidenced by the fact that the two rings freely rotate. The most stable conformation is a staggered one with the rings not flush.

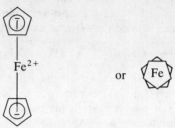

Ferrocene, a *sandwich* compound

     (*b*)   Ferrocene is stable because its Fe has a full valence shell of 18 e^-'s, six of its own (present in its five $3d$ AO's) and six from each cyclopentadienyl anion. It also retains the aromaticity of the cyclopentadienyl anions.

     (*c*)   Many transition metals form sandwich compounds with aromatic compounds providing the combined number of valence shell e^-'s totals 18, e.g., $(C_6H_6)_2Cr$, dibenzenechromium, six from Cr, and six from each benzene.

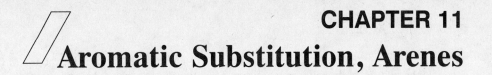

Aromatic Substitution, Arenes

ELECTROPHILIC AROMATIC SUBSTITUTION

11.1 (*a*) What types of reagents effect characteristic benzene substitution? (*b*) Why is it called *electrophilic aromatic substitution*?

◢ (*a*) Electrophilic reagents or Lewis acids. (*b*) An H is replaced by an electrophilic group, E, preserving the aromatic system.

11.2 How does the substitution in Problem 11.1 differ from (*a*) S_N1 and S_N2 reactions, and (*b*) free radical substitution?

◢ (*a*) In S_N1 and S_N2 reactions the attacking group is a nucleophile or Lewis base and the group replaced is a weaker base. (*b*) The attacking species, $X\cdot$, removes an $H\cdot$ and leaves another radical, $R\cdot$, which enters a chain reaction.

11.3 (*a*) What is the first step in the reaction of E^+ with PhH? (*b*) Compare it with the first step in the addition to an alkene.

◢ (*a*)

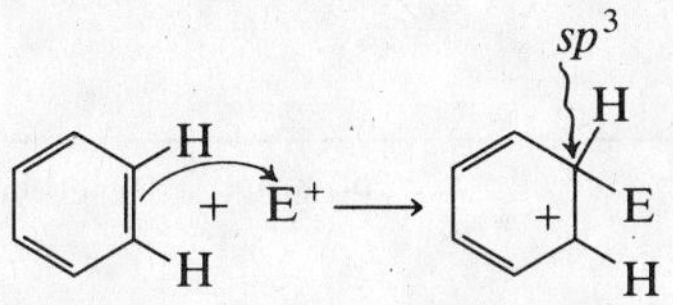

sigma complex   (*b*) 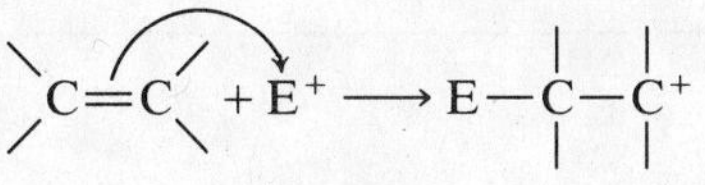   carbocation

The σ-complexed benzenonium ion (sometimes called benzenium ion) is one example of an *arenonium* ion, formed by the electrophilic attack on an arene, PhR. It is not aromatic, since the cyclic delocalization is interrupted by the sp^3 hybridized C. [In (*b*) a cyclic onium ion such as bromonium ion (7.) may substitute for the carbocation.]

11.4 (*a*) How do the second steps in Problem 11.3(*a*) and (*b*) differ? (*b*) Account for the difference.

◢ (*a*) In (*b*) of Problem 11.3, the carbocation reacts with a Lewis base: $E-\overset{|}{\underset{|}{C}}-\overset{|}{\underset{|}{C}}{}^+ + B:^- \longrightarrow$

$E-\overset{|}{\underset{|}{C}}-\overset{|}{\underset{|}{C}}-B$. The arenonium (or arenium) ion in (*a*) of Problem 11.3 loses an H^+, regenerating the stable aromatic π system:

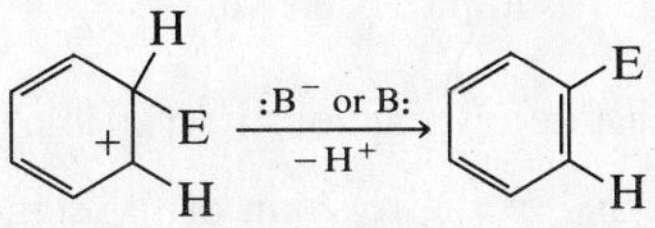

(*b*) Were the arenonium ion to add $B:^-$, a much less stable cyclohexadiene derivative would form.

11.5 (*a*) Write (i) the contributing resonance structures and (ii) the delocalized hybrid structure to account for the relative stability of the benzenonium ion. (*b*) Describe the orbital hybridization of the C's in the benzenonium intermediate.

◢ (*a*) (i)

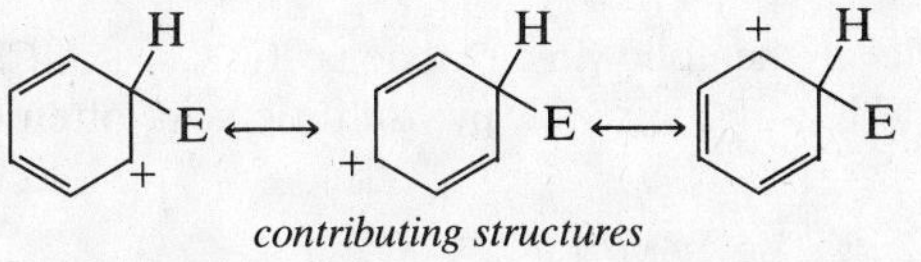

contributing structures   (ii) 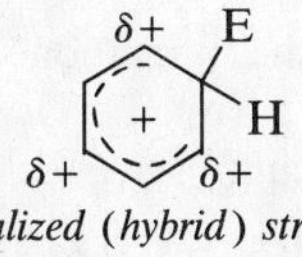   *delocalized (hybrid) structure*

(*b*) The benzenonium ion is a stable allylic carbocation. The C attacked by E^+ becomes sp^3 hybridized. The other five C's are sp^2 hybridized and their remaining p AO's overlap laterally to form a delocalized π electron cloud.

11.6 Draw an enthalpy diagram for the reaction of PhH with E^+, indicating the intermediate, In, the TS_1 and TS_2 for the two steps, the relative energies of activation for the two steps, and the heat of reaction ΔH_r.

◢ See Fig. 11-1.

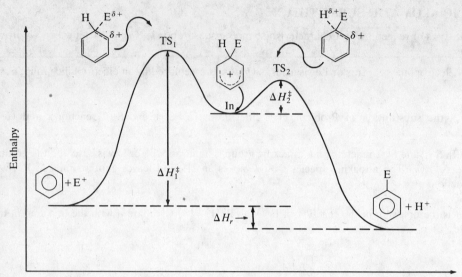

Fig. 11-1

11.7 Which is the rate-determining step in electrophilic aromatic substitution?

◢ Formation of the intermediate arenium cation is usually slow and rate-determining. Elimination of H^+ is fast since it restores aromaticity—it has no effect on the overall reaction rate.

11.8 How is the absence of a *primary isotope effect* used to (*a*) eliminate a one-step substitution of H by E and (*b*) establish that the first step is rate-determining?

◢ Recall that the isotope effect, or rate ratio k_H/k_D (Problem 8.109), is based on the more rapid breaking of a C—H than a C—D bond in the rate-determining step. The absence of an isotope effect in most aromatic electrophilic substitutions shows that breaking the C—H bond is not part of the rate-controlling step. Therefore, (*a*) a simultaneous bond-forming and C—H bond-breaking mechanism is eliminated and (*b*) the first step in which E^+ bonds to the aromatic ring without cleavage of a C—H bond is rate-determining. The C—H or C—D bond is broken in the fast second step that restores the stable aromatic system. Hence the overall rate is independent of the particular isotopic species used.

11.9 Why are most aromatic substitution reactions irreversible? (*Hint*: Refer to Fig. 11-1.)

◢ The energy barrier $\Delta H_2^\ddagger$ for the reaction of the sigma complex to form products is less than $\Delta H_r^\ddagger$ for the reverse rejection of E^+. (If it were not, the first step would be fast and reversible and not rate-determining.) To summarize:

$$\text{For ArH} + E^+ \underset{k_{-1}}{\overset{k_1}{\rightleftharpoons}} \left[\begin{array}{c} H \quad E \\ \diagdown \diagup \\ Ar \end{array} \right]^+ \xrightarrow{k_2(-H^+)} \text{ArE}, \quad k_2 \gg k_{-1}$$

11.10 (*a*) Show the formation of the **electrophile** in the following reactions: (i) $Cl_2 + AlCl_3$, (ii) $HNO_3 + H_2SO_4$, (iii) $Br_2 + Fe$, (iv) H_2SO_4, and (v) $H_2S_2O_7$ ($HOSO_2OSO_2OH$, pyrosulfuric acid, often called "fuming" sulfuric acid or "oleum"). (*b*) Identify each base.

◢ (*a*)   (i) $Cl_2 + AlCl_3 \longrightarrow [Cl^{\delta +} ---Cl---^{\delta -}AlCl_3]$
          (ii) $HONO_2 + H{:}OSO_3H \longrightarrow [H_2ONO_2]^+ \longrightarrow H_2O + NO_2^+$ (nitronium ion)
         (iii) $3Br_2 + 2Fe \longrightarrow 2FeBr_3$; $Br_2 + FeBr_3 \longrightarrow [Br^{\delta +}---Br---^{\delta -}FeBr_3]$
         (iv) $2H_2SO_4 \longrightarrow H_3O^+ + HSO_4^- + SO_3$
          (v) $HOSO_2OSO_2OH \longrightarrow H^+ + HSO_4^- + SO_3$

(**b**)   (i) $AlCl_4^-$, (ii) $HOSO_2O^-$ (from protonation of H_2O by a second H_2SO_4), (iii) $FeBr_4^-$, (iv) and (v) $HOSO_2O^-$.

11.11   Discuss the essential role of the catalysts used for aromatic electrophilic substitutions.

▌   The catalyst makes the reagent more electrophilic, thereby raising the H_{GS}, lessening the $\Delta H^{\ddagger}$ of TS_1, and enabling the substitution to proceed at a faster rate. The catalyst plays this role by either actually forming the electrophile as in (ii) and (iv) of Problem 11.10 or by polarizing the reagent as in (i) and (iii) of Problem 11.10.

11.12   Write an equation for each of following reactions and identify the electophile (E) and base (B) for each: (**a**) $HOCl + H^+$, (**b**) HNO_3, (**c**) $ICl + ZnCl_2$, (**d**) $HONO + H^+$.

▌   (**a**) $HOCl + H^+ \longrightarrow H_2OCl^+ \longrightarrow Cl^+$ (E) $+ H_2O$ (B)
      (**b**) $2HONO_2 \longrightarrow NO_3^- + H_2ONO_2^+ \longrightarrow NO_2^+$ (E) $+ H_2O$ (B)
      (**c**) $2I-Cl + ZnCl_2 \longrightarrow 2I^+$ (E) $+ ZnCl_4^{2-}$ (B) (I^+ is more stable than Cl^+.)
      (**d**) $HONO + H^+ \longrightarrow H_2ONO \longrightarrow NO^+$ (E) $+ H_2O$ (B)

11.13   (**a**) Some of the evidence for the existence of NO_2^+ [(ii) of Problem 11.10] is the four-fold depression of freezing point of H_2SO_4 ($i = 4$, where i is the number of particles formed according to the balanced equation). Give equations to illustrate this fact. (**b**) Can nitronium ion be isolated?

▌   (**a**)   1. $HONO_2 + H_2SO_4 \rightleftharpoons [H_2ONO_2]^+ + HSO_4^-$
          2. $[H_2ONO_2]^+ \rightleftharpoons H_2O + \mathbf{NO_2^+}$
          3. $H_2O + H_2SO_4 \rightleftharpoons H_3O^+ + HSO_4^-$
          Summation: $HNO_3 + 2H_2SO_4 \longrightarrow \mathbf{NO_2^+} + H_3O^+ + 2HSO_4^-$ (four particles, $i = 4$).
      (**b**)   Salts such as nitronium perchlorate, $NO_2^+ClO_4^-$ and tetrafluoroborate, $NO_2^+BF_4^-$ have been isolated and can be used for aromatic nitrations.

11.14   (**a**) Provide an enthalpy diagram for the reversible aromatic sulfonation. (**b**) Would you expect this reaction to show a moderate k_H/k_D isotope effect? (**c**) Which experimental conditions encourage desulfonation (reverse of sulfonation)?

▌   (**a**)   See Fig. 11-2. In halogenation, nitration, and other irreversible electrophilic substitutions, $\Delta H^{\ddagger}$ for formation of the σ complex is considerably greater than for its expulsion of H^+, $k_2 \gg k_{-1}$. In sulfonation, $\Delta H^{\ddagger}$ for loss of SO_3 is only slightly greater than for loss of H^+ and k_2 is slightly greater than k_{-1}.

$$ArH + SO_3 \underset{k_{-1}}{\overset{k_1}{\rightleftharpoons}} Ar\overset{+}{\underset{SO_3^-}{\diagdown}}{}^H \overset{k_2}{\longrightarrow} ArSO_3^- + H^+$$

Therefore the σ complex can react about equally well in either direction and sulfonation is reversible.

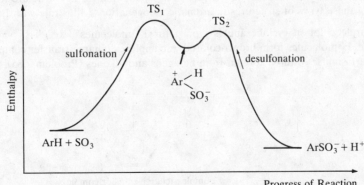

Fig. 11-2

(**b**)   Yes because k_2 affects the overall rate. The loss of D^+ from the deuterated σ complex has a greater $\Delta H^{\ddagger}$ than the comparable loss of H, is slower, and sulfonation exhibits a moderate primary isotope effect.

(**c**)   The equilibrium may be shifted toward desulfonation by employing hot dilute aq. H_2SO_4.

11.15 (*a*) Account for the following differences in the primary kinetic isotope effect: $k_H/k_D \cong 7$; $k_H/k_T \cong 10$–20, where T is tritium, ^3H. (*b*) With the aid of an enthalpy diagram compare the rates of the following reactions and explain the difference.

(*1*) $C_6D_6 + H_2SO_4 \rightleftharpoons C_6D_5SO_3H + DOH$
(*2*) $C_6T_6 + H_2SO_4 \rightleftharpoons C_6T_5SO_3H + TOH$ (Use a dashed line for this reaction.)

◢ (*a*) Isotope effects are attributed solely to mass differences, which are manifested in the vibrational frequencies of the C—H, C—D, and C—T bonds. The greater the mass of the isotope whose bond is broken in the rate-controlling step, the greater is the primary isotope effect. Since the mass of T is greater than the mass of D, $k_H/k_T > k_H/k_D$.

(*b*) See Fig. 11-3. The pathway leading to the two intermediates are practically identical for both reactions because there are no bonds broken. The second step involves breaking a C—D or C—T bond, and has a lower $H^{\ddagger}$ than the reversal of step 1 that involves breaking a C—S bond. Furthermore, $H^{\ddagger}$ for breaking the C—T bond is more than for breaking the C—D bond. Reaction (*2*) is slower than reaction (*1*).

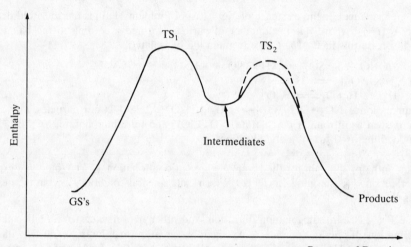

Fig. 11-3

Note that the presence of D or T has very little effect on the enthalpies of the ground states, transition states for the first step, intermediates, and products.

11.16 Typically I_2 gives purple solutions with nonpolar σ-bonded solvents such as cyclohexane. Yet its benzene solution is brown and only unreacted benzene is isolated from it with no iodobenzene. (*a*) Discuss the chemical difference in the two kinds of solutions. (*b*) Give a MO explanation for the structure formed in benzene. (*c*) What is the role of these types of structures in aromatic halogenations? Illustrate with Br_2.

◢ (*a*) The purple color in cyclohexane is typical for I_2 molecules. (Recall I_2 vapor is also purple.) In benzene, I_2 molecules form brown-colored π complexes (charge-transfer complexes, Problem 10.122). These are similar to those formed from halogens and alkenes (Problem 7.85).

π complex (charge-transfer complex)

Since no σ bonds are formed, the recovered benzene is unchanged.

(*b*) The name "charge-transfer" indicates electron transfer from the electron-rich π system of the arene (the donor) to the electrophilic I_2 (the acceptor). For this to happen the donor HOMO must have a low ionization potential (be "high-lying") and the acceptor must have a "low-lying" LUMO. Because of the e^- transfer from HOMO to LUMO, the π complex is a radical anion. The orbital picture has a pAO of an I of I_2 overlapping with the π cloud of PhH without being attached to any one ring C.

(*c*) The π complex of PhH and Br_2 precedes the σ complex. It is likely that $FeBr_3$ then removes the Br^- from the π complex which in turn collapses in the rate-determining step to the σ complex.

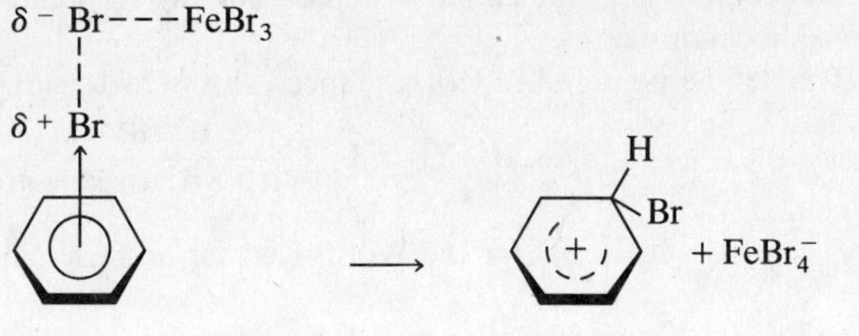

π complex with $Br_2 \cdot FeBr_3$ σ complex

11.17 (*a*) Identify the electrophile formed from the reaction of $CH_3CH_2Cl + AlCl_3$. (*b*) Show how a comparable electrophile can be formed from each of the following: (i) $CH_2{=}CH_2$ and (ii) CH_3CH_2OH. (*c*) Show the reaction of benzene with the electrophile in (*a*). (*d*) What is the product of the reaction of benzene with the electrophiles in (*b*)? (*e*) Why is HF and not HBr used with $CH_2{=}CH_2$?

   (*a*) The incipient $CH_3CH_2^+$ from $CH_3CH_2^{\delta+}{-}{-}{-}Cl{-}{-}{-}^{\delta-}AlCl_3$.

   (*b*) (i) add conc. H_2SO_4 or HF; $CH_3CH_2^{\delta+}{-}{-}{-}^{\delta-}OSO_3H$ or $\left[H_2C\overset{\displaystyle H}{\underset{}{\diagdown\diagup}}CH_2 \right]^+ F^-$; (ii) add BF_3, conc.

H_2SO_4, or H_3PO_4; $\left[CH_3CH_2^{\delta+}{-}{-}{-}\underset{H}{O}{-}{-}{-}^{\delta-}BF_3 \right]$.

   (*c*) In this *Friedel–Crafts alkylation* benzene displaces $[ClAlCl_3]^-$ from the electrophilic $C^{\delta+}$ to give the σ complex. Subsequent ejection of H^+ results in formation of $HAlCl_4$ and ethylbenzene, $Ph{-}CH_2CH_3$.

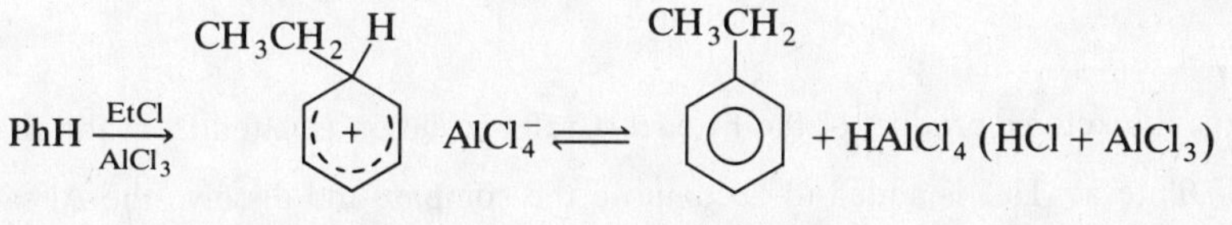

σ complex

   (*d*) PhEt.

   (*e*) The proton donor must afford a weak nucleophile (F^-); a stronger nucleophile like Br^- would add to the protonated alkene, forming CH_3CH_2Br and preventing reaction of the alkene with benzene.

11.18 (*a*) Compare the products of the reaction of benzene with *i*-PrCl and *n*-PrCl in $AlCl_3$. (*b*) Account for the products mechanistically.

   (*a*) The expected $Ph{-}CHMe_2$ is isolated from the reaction with *i*-PrCl. With *n*-PrCl, both $Ph{-}CH_2CH_2CH_3$ and $Ph{-}CHMe_2$ form. (*b*) 1° RX's are less reactive than 2° and 3° halides. At the higher temperatures required for 1° RX, some rearrangement always occurs. A possible pathway is for benzene to displace on the 2 °C while a :H shifts to the 1° carbon:

$$Ph\overbrace{H + CH_3{-}\underset{\underset{\displaystyle H}{\diagup}}{CH}{-}CH_2^{\delta+}}{-}{-}{-}Cl{-}{-}{-}^{\delta-}AlCl_3 \longrightarrow Ph{-}CHMe_2 + AlCl_4^- + H^+$$

Formation of a "free" 1° carbocation is unlikely. Rearrangement limits the scope of this reaction.

11.19 (*a*) Give the product of the reaction of benzene and $AlCl_3$ with (i) $CH_3CH_2CH_2COCl$, an acyl chloride, and (ii) $(CH_3CH_2CH_2CO)_2O$, an acid anhydride. (*b*) What is the electrophile? Show contributing resonance structures. (*c*) Why is the product in (*a*) *not* rearranged? (*d*) How can we use the acylation to synthesize unrearranged alkyl side chains on an aromatic ring? Illustrate by preparing $Ph(CH_2)_3CH_3$.

   (*a*) (i) and (ii) $PhCOCH_2CH_2CH_3$

   (*b*) $RCOCl + AlCl_3 \longrightarrow \left[R{-}C{\equiv}\overset{+}{O}{:} \longleftrightarrow R{-}\overset{+}{C}{=}\overset{..}{O}{:} \right] + AlCl_4^-$

                                  an acylium ion

                      A   **B**

A is the main contributing resonance structure for the *acylium ion* (the electrophile) because both C and O have an octet. The anhydride gives the same acylium ion and $[AlCl_3OAc]^-$.

(c) The acylium ion is much more stable than any alkyl carbocation and so it cannot rearrange to a more stable cation.

(d) The ketone prepared in (a) is reduced to the hydrocarbon:

$$PhCOCH_2CH_3 \xrightarrow[\text{or } H_2NNH_2, \text{ OH}^- \text{ (Wolff–Kishner)}]{\text{Zn/Hg, HCl (Clemmensen)}} PhCH_2CH_2CH_2CH_3.$$

See Problems 15.103 and 15.104 for the Wolff–Kishner and Clemmensen reductions, respectively.

11.20 Compare the Friedel–Crafts alkylation with RX and acylation with RCOX as to the (a) mechanism, and (b) kind and amount of catalyst.

▮ (a) Alkylation, see Problem 11.17(c). Acylation:

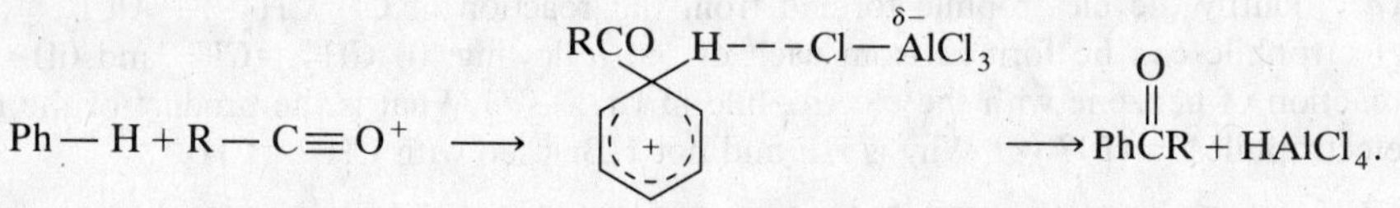

$$Ph-H + R-C\equiv O^+ \longrightarrow \underset{\text{(+)}}{\bigodot} \overset{RCO \; H\text{---}Cl\overset{\delta-}{-}AlCl_3}{} \longrightarrow PhCR + HAlCl_4.$$

(b) Both require a Lewis acid of the type MX_n, most commonly $AlCl_3$, but also BF_3, $FeCl_3$, $ZnCl_2$. In acylation, a 1:1 complex of RCOCl and catalyst forms, which then dissociates into the acylium ion:

$$R\overset{O}{\underset{\delta+}{-C}}\text{---}Cl\text{---}\overset{\delta-}{AlCl_3} \longrightarrow R-C\equiv O^+ + AlCl_4^-.$$

Acylations require more than one equivalent of catalyst because the ketonic product also complexes with $AlCl_3$: $\quad \overset{\delta+}{:O:}\text{---}\overset{\delta-}{AlCl_3}$

$$\underset{Ph \qquad R}{\overset{\|}{C}}$$

11.21 How is the ketonic product of the Friedel–Crafts acylation isolated from the reaction mixture?

▮ Dilute aq. HCl is added to decompose the complex and dissolve the Al salts. The ketone is soluble in the organic layer, from which it is isolated by distillation or crystallization.

11.22 Supply structures for the products of the reaction of benzene with (a) $CH_3CH=CH_2$ (HF, 0 °C) (b) cyclohexanol (BF_3, 60 °C), (c) $[Me_2CHCO]_2O$ ($AlCl_3$), and (d) $CH_2=CHCH_2Cl$ ($ZnCl_2$).

▮ (a) $PhCH(CH_3)_2$ (b) $Ph-\overset{H}{\underset{}{\bigcirc}}$ (c) $Ph-\overset{O}{\overset{\|}{C}}-CHMe_2$ (d) $PhCH_2CH=CH_2$

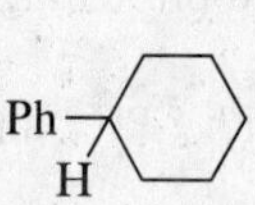

11.23 Give the product of reaction of benzene with ethylene oxide / $AlCl_3$.

▮ $$AlCl_3 + \overset{O}{\overset{}{CH_2-CH_2}} \longrightarrow \overset{\overset{\delta+}{O}\text{---}\overset{\delta-}{AlCl_3}}{CH_2-CH_2} \xrightarrow{PhH} PhCH_2CH_2OH + AlCl_3$$

11.24 Benzene reacts with covalent mercuric acetate $[Hg(OCOCH_3)_2]$ and $HClO_4$ to form $PhHgOCOCH_3$. (a) Give a mechanism for this electrophilic substitution. (b) Explain that $k_H/k_D = 6$.

▮ (a) *Step 1.* Formation of electrophile:

$$CH_3\overset{O}{\overset{\|}{C}}O-Hg-\overset{O}{\overset{\|}{O}}CCH_3 \underset{}{\overset{H^+}{\rightleftharpoons}} CH_3\overset{O}{\overset{\|}{C}}O-Hg-\overset{+OH}{\overset{\|}{O}}CCH_3 \rightleftharpoons CH_3\overset{O}{\overset{\|}{C}}OHg^+(E^+) + CH_3COOH$$

Step 2. Electrophilic substitution:

$$PhH + {}^+HgOCOCH_3 \rightleftharpoons \underset{HgOCOCH_3}{Ph+} \xrightarrow{slow} PhHgOCOCH_3 + H^+$$

Thallium (Problem 11.27) may also be introduced into the aromatic ring by this method.
(b) A C—H bond is broken in the rate-determining step 2.

11.25 (*a*) Why cannot benzene be iodinated with I_2 directly? (*b*) Show how benzene can be iodinated with I_2.

▮ (*a*) Iodination with I_2 is slow ($F_2 > Cl_2 > Br_2 > I_2$) and somewhat reversible ($\Delta H = 12$ kcal/mol).

(*b*) HNO_3 affects the reaction by oxidizing I_2 to a more powerful electrophile, hydrated I^+.

1. $\frac{1}{2}I_2 + 2H^+ + NO_3^- \longrightarrow \left[{}^{\delta+}I---{}^{\delta+}OH_2 \right]^+ + NO_2$

    electrophile

2. $PhH + [I---OH_2]^+ \xrightarrow{-H_2O} \overset{\overset{\displaystyle H\quad I}{\diagdown\diagup}}{Ph^+} \xrightarrow{H_2O} PhI + H_3O^+.$

The electrophilic $HO^{\delta-}-I^{\delta+}$ is formed when H_2O_2 is the oxidant. In direct iodination I^- would be a product, and its presence could reverse the reaction. An oxidizing agent converts I^- to I_2.

11.26 Explain why iodination of an arene occurs with ICl.

▮ ICl is more electrophilic than I_2 because it is polarized; i.e., ${}^{\delta+}I-Cl^{\delta-}$. The aromatic ring more easily displaces Cl^- from ${}^{\delta+}I$ then it displaces I^- from the nonpolar I—I.

11.27 (*a*) Why cannot fluoroarenes be prepared by direct reaction of F_2? (*b*) How may fluorobenzene be prepared by thallation? (*Hint*: see Problem 11.24.) Indicate the electrophile.

▮ (*a*) Fluorine is too reactive. Both addition and polysubstitution occur.

(*b*) $Tl(OCOCF_3)_3$ is reacted with benzene, followed by addition of KF and BF_3.

$$Tl(OCOCF_3)_3 \rightleftharpoons {}^+Tl(OCOCF_3)_2 \ (E) + CF_3COO^-$$

$$PhH + {}^+Tl(OCOCF_3)_2 \xrightarrow{-H^+} PhTl(OCOCF_3)_2 \xrightarrow{KF/BF_3} PhF$$

SUBSTITUENT EFFECTS IN ELECTROPHILIC AROMATIC SUBSTITUTION

11.28 (*a*) How do substituent groups (G) on an aromatic ring influence the course of electrophilic aromatic substitution? (*b*) Classify them by their effects.

▮ (*a*) Such G's affect the electrophilic aromatic substitution in two ways:

(1) *Reactivity* or rate of reaction. Those more reactive than benzene are *activating*, those less reactive are *deactivating*. (2) *Orientation*—whether E enters *ortho*, *meta* or *para*.

(*b*) There are three classes of substituent groups:

(1) All activating groups direct E to the *ortho* and *para* positions.

(2) Most deactivating groups direct E to the *meta* positions.

(3) A few deactivating groups, e.g., halogen, differ from (2) in being *ortho-* and *para*-directing.

11.29 (*a*) How can the Hammond postulate be used to predict the orientation of E by ArG? (*b*) How does an (i) electron-releasing, and (ii) electron-withdrawing G affect the stability of the σ complex of electrophilic substitution?

▮ (*a*) Aromatic electrophilic substitution is endothermic. The Hammond postulate states that transition states of endothermic reactions resemble their products (intermediates). By comparing the relative enthalpies of the *o*, *m*, and *p* intermediate arenonium ions, we have also compared the relative enthalpies of their TS_1's. The most stable intermediate has the TS_1 with the smallest $\Delta H^\ddagger$ and is therefore most likely to form. (*b*) (i) Stabilizes and (ii) destabilizes.

11.30 Write contributing structures for the intermediate arenonium ion from reaction of PhG with E^+ at the (*a*) *para*, (*b*) *ortho*, and (*c*) *meta* positions.

▮ (*a*)

A

(b)

ortho

B

(c)

meta

C

11.31   How do the activating and deactivating effects account for the orientation of entering E^+ referred to in Problem 11.28(b)?

▰   Activating and deactivating effects are strongest at the *ortho* and *para* positions. Activating G's stabilize all positions, but *o* and *p* more than *m*. Deactivating G's destabilize all positions, but *o* and *p* more than *m*.

11.32   (a) From the resonance forms in Problem 11.30, generalize about the distribution of the +'s in the σ complex. (b) Provide an electrostatic explanation. (c) Account for the behavior of the different categories of G's (Problem 11.28) in the reaction of PhG with an E^+.

▰   (a) There are three +'s delocalized on alternating C's. (b) The more C's bear positive charges, the more stable is the delocalized system. Any structure with like charges on adjacent C's would have too high an enthalpy. (c) This concept of *alternant polarity* says that, regardless of the nature of G, the + charge is delocalized to positions *o,o,p* to the C bonded to E^+. When G is electron-releasing, it stabilizes the + charge on the C bonded to it, lowering $\Delta H^{\ddagger}$, and increasing the reaction rate at the *o,o,p* positions. When G is electron-withdrawing, it destabilizes the + charge on the C bonded to it, raising $\Delta H^{\ddagger}$, and decreasing the reaction rate at the *o,o,p* positions. In this case, reaction occurs at the *meta* position.

11.33   (a) Account for the increased reactivity of toluene compared with benzene. (b) What is the statistical $(o+p)/m$ products ratio expected from mononitration of toluene? (c) The actual product distribution is $(o+p)/m = 97/3$. How does resonance account for this orientation?

▰   (a) The electron-releasing Me activates *all* positions in toluene, including the *meta*, which senses the electron-donating inductive effect of Me. (b) Since toluene has two *o* positions, and one *p* and two *m* positions, the statistical $(o+p)/m$ distribution should be 60/40. (c) When E^+, here NO_2^+, bonds to the *o* or *p* positions, the rate is even more enhanced because the resonance hybrids for *para* and *ortho* attack (**A** and **B** in Problem 11.30) have a 3° C^+ stabilized by the attached electron-repelling Me. The Me in the *meta* σ complex, **C** in Problem 11.30, is not bonded to a C^+; its enthalpy is higher, as is the $\Delta H^{\ddagger}$ leading to its formation.

11.34   When E^+ reacts with $PhCF_3$ the ratio of $(o+p)/m$ products is 12/88. Explain.

▰   The CF_3 group exerts a strong electron-withdrawing inductive effect due to the three F's on the alkyl C. Thus all five C's in the ring have diminished reactivity, but to a lesser extent for the *meta* C's. In *meta* attack no resonance structure can be written with a + charge on the ring C bearing the CF_3 (see **C** in Problem 11.30).

11.35   Classify electron-donating G's in terms of their structure and their electronic effects and give an example for each class.

▰   (1) G has an unshared pair of electrons on the atom bonded to the ring, which can be delocalized to the ring by extended π bonding (**D**); e.g., $-\ddot{N}H_2$, $-\ddot{O}-$, $-\ddot{X}:$, and $-\ddot{S}-$.

(2) The atom bonded to the ring participates in an electron-rich π bond (**E**); e.g., $>C=C<$, C_6H_5-, and $Ar-$.

(3) G has no unshared pair and is electron-donating by induction and or by *hyperconjugation* (**F**); e.g., alkyl groups.

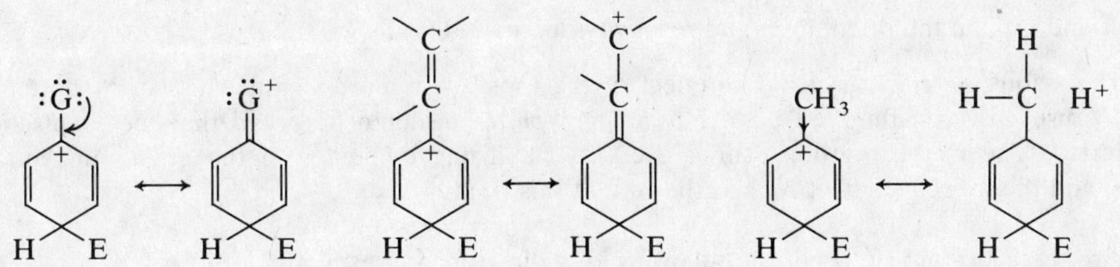

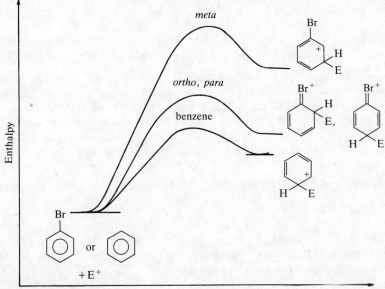

D   **E**   **F**

hyperconjugated
structure

11.36 Explain the relative stability and major contribution of resonance structure **D** in Problem 11.35.

▮ All atoms have an octet of electrons.

11.37 Classify electron-withdrawing G's in terms of their structure and electronic effects and give an example of each.

▮ The attached atom has no unshared pair and has some positive charge. The positive charge may be (i) full (**H**) or (ii) a positive formal charge (**I**), or (iii) a $\delta+$ from being π-bonded to a more electronegative atom (**J**), or (iv) σ-bonded to several electronegative atoms (**K**).

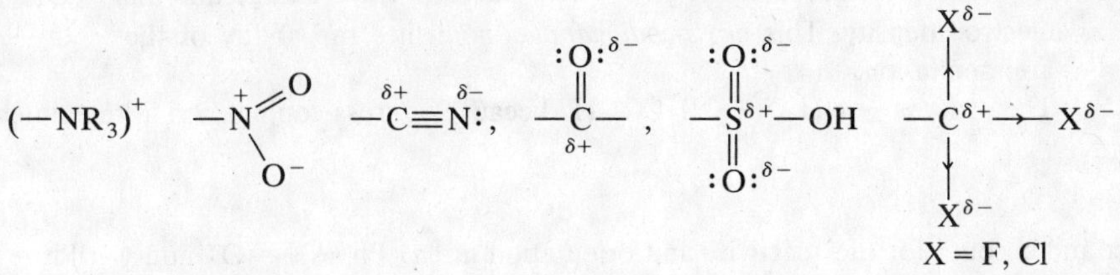

H   **I**   **J**   **K**

11.38 Explain that halogens are o-, p-directors, but are deactivating.

▮ The electronegative halogens inductively withdraw e^-'s from all ring C's of the σ complex, and the o-, p-, and m-benzenonium ions each have a higher $\Delta H^{\ddagger}$ than that of the cation from benzene. The halogens have unshared electrons and can delocalize electron density to the o- and p-C's. Halogens are said to be π-donating but σ-withdrawing.

11.39 Draw an enthalpy diagram for the reaction of E^+ with PhBr compared to the reaction with benzene.

▮ See Fig. 11-4.

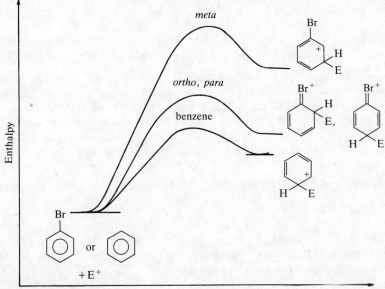

Progress of Reaction   **Fig. 11-4**

11.40 Predict and explain the orientation and reactivity due to $-\ddot{\text{O}}\text{CH}_3$.

◢ The stabilizing electron-donating effect of the $\ddot{\text{O}}$ is much more significant than its destabilizing inductive effect. Anisole is activating and orients *ortho* and *para*. It should be noted that the *m* position is somewhat deactivated. The methoxy group cannot exert its stabilizing influence on the arenonium ion when *m*-attack occurs, and the inductive effect retards the rate at this position.

11.41 Compare the activating effects of the following *o,p*-directors and explain your order.

(*a*) $-\ddot{\text{O}}\text{H}, -\ddot{\text{O}}\!\!:^-$ and $-\ddot{\text{O}}\overset{\displaystyle \|}{\underset{\displaystyle \text{O}}{\text{C}}}-\text{CH}_3$ (*b*) $-\ddot{\text{N}}\text{H}_2$ and $-\ddot{\text{N}}\text{H}-\overset{\displaystyle \|}{\underset{\displaystyle \text{O}}{\text{C}}}-\text{CH}_3$

◢ (*a*) The order of activation is $-\text{O}^- > -\text{OH} > -\text{OCOCH}_3$. The $-\text{O}^-$, with a full negative charge, is best able to donate electrons, thereby giving the very stable uncharged intermediate

In $-\text{O}\overset{\displaystyle \|}{\underset{\displaystyle }{\text{C}}}\text{CH}_3$, the C of the $^{\delta+}\text{C}{=}\text{O}^{\delta-}$ has a positive charge and makes demands on the $-\ddot{\text{O}}-$ for electron density. This *cross-conjugation* diminishes the ability of the $-\ddot{\text{O}}-$ to donate e$^-$'s to the arenonium ion.

(*b*) The order is $-\text{NH}_2 > -\text{NHCOCH}_3$ because of cross-conjugation in the amide, $\text{Ar}-\overset{\displaystyle |}{\underset{\displaystyle \text{H}}{\text{N}}}{=}\overset{\displaystyle |}{\underset{\displaystyle :\ddot{\text{O}}:^-}{\text{C}}}-\text{CH}_3$.

11.42 Predict and account for the reactivity and orientation in (*a*) $\text{Ph}-\ddot{\text{N}}{=}\ddot{\text{O}}:$ and (*b*) $\text{Ph}-\overset{+}{\text{S}}\text{Me}_2$.

◢ (*a*) The nitroso group behaves like halogen in that it deactivates the ring inductively by attracting e$^-$'s, but orients *ortho* and *para* as a consequence of delocalization of the unshared pair of e$^-$'s on N. The delocalized structure **A** for the σ complex is quite stable with all atoms having an octet.

A

(*b*) $\text{R}_2\overset{+}{\text{S}}-$ behaves like $\text{R}_3\overset{+}{\text{N}}-$ for the same reason—the positively-charged atom strongly attracts electron density from the ring.

11.43 Compare the rate of nitration under similar conditions of PhOMe and PhSMe. Explain.

◢ PhOMe > PhSMe. The π bond from O (which uses a $2p$ orbital) to the ring C is shorter and stronger than the comparable bond from S (which uses a $3p$ orbital) to the ring C.

11.44 PhNH_2 reacts with Br_2 in H_2O to give more than 90% yield of 2,4,6-tribromoaniline, while PhNMe_2 is mononitrated at the *meta* position with the more powerfully electrophilic reagent $\text{HNO}_3/\text{H}_2\text{SO}_4$. Explain.

◢ The tribromoderivative forms because NH_2 is a strongly activating *o,p*-orienting substituent (as is NMe_2). Recall that amines are also proton acceptors, so in *strong* acid they are completely protonated. Consequently, the only species present in $\text{HNO}_3/\text{H}_2\text{SO}_4$, is the conjugate acid PhNMe_2H^+, and it is the species undergoing nitration. The NR_2H^+ group, with a full + charge, is a deactivator that orients *meta*.

11.45 (*a*) Categorize the following G substituents as activating *o,p*; deactivating *o,p* or deactivating *m*, and give reasons: (i) $\text{Ph}\ddot{\text{S}}\text{R}$, (ii) $\text{Ph}\overset{\displaystyle \text{O}}{\underset{\displaystyle \|}{\ddot{\text{S}}}}\text{R}$ (sulfoxide), and (iii) $\text{Ph}\overset{\displaystyle \text{O}}{\underset{\displaystyle \|}{\overset{\displaystyle \|}{\ddot{\text{S}}}}}\text{R}$ (sulfone). (*b*) Compare the reactivity of PhSOR with PhNO.

◢ (*a*) (i) Activating, *o,p*. There is a delocalizable unshared pair of e$^-$'s on S. (ii) Deactivating, *o,p*. Like PhNO (Problem 11.42) it is π-donating and σ-withdrawing (Problem 11.38). (iii) Deactivating *m*. Lacking an unshared pair on S, the strong inductive effect of $\text{S}^{\delta+}$ makes this G behave like $-\text{SO}_3\text{H}$ (**J** in Problem 11.37).

(b) PhNO > PhSOR. The smaller N delocalizes electron density better than the larger S (Problem 11.43).

11.46 Place each of the following in decreasing order of relative $\Delta H^{\ddagger}$ for forming an arenonium ion intermediate: benzene, toluene in *meta* and *para* positions, nitrobenzene in *meta* and *para* positions.

▮ Relative $\Delta H^{\ddagger}$'s are: p-Me $< m$-Me $<$ H (in PhH) $< m$-NO$_2$ $< p$-NO$_2$. Benzene has an intermediate $\Delta H^{\ddagger}$ because it lacks the activating Me or deactivating NO$_2$ group.

11.47 Given the percentage yields of *meta*-substituted toluene from the following reactions: 0.5% bromotoluene from bromination in acetic acid; 3.5% nitrotoluene from nitration in acetic acid; and 21% ethyltoluene from reaction with CH$_3$CH$_2$Br in GaBr$_3$. Determine and account for the relative reactivities of the three reagents.

▮ The Reactivity-Selectivity principle states that *more reactive* attacking species are *less selective*, and the yields from their reactions are more nearly like those calculated from probabilities. Since Me is an o,p-director, reagents that form larger amounts of *meta* isomer are less selective; the relative reactivities are: CH$_3$CH$_2^+$ > $^+$NO$_2$ > Br$_2$ (Br$^{\delta+}$ $---$ Br $---^{\delta-}$ FeBr$_3$).

11.48 Explain the different percentages of *o*- and *p*-toluenesulfonic acids formed when PhMe is sulfonated at the following temperatures:

	0 °C	100 °C
o-toluenesulfonic acid (**A**)	43%	13%
p-toluenesulfonic acid (**B**)	53%	79%

▮ The principle of thermodynamic vs. kinetic control is applicable because sulfonation is one of the few reversible aromatic electrophilic substitutions (Problem 11.14). At 0 °C, kinetic control prevails for formation of the rate-determining TS$_1$. The somewhat higher yield of **B** indicates that, for TS$_1$, $\Delta H_{\mathbf{B}}^{\ddagger}$ is less than $\Delta H_{\mathbf{A}}^{\ddagger}$ but not enough to preclude a significant yield of **A**. As the temperature increases, thermodynamic control becomes predominant. Some initially formed **A** reverses (desulfonates) and eventually in the equilibrium mixture of products the more stable, relatively sterically unhindered *para* isomer dominates.

11.49 Why is PhNO$_2$ a suitable solvent for the Friedel–Crafts alkylation of PhBr while benzene is not?

▮ Benzene is more reactive than bromobenzene in the Friedel–Crafts reaction and would alkylate more rapidly. Nitrobenzene may be used because it does not undergo the Friedel–Crafts reaction owing to the deactivating effect of the NO$_2$ group (CS$_2$ can also be used).

11.50 Explain the following percentages of *meta* electrophilic substitutions:

(a) ArCH$_3$, ArCH$_2$Cl, ArCHCl$_2$, ArCCl$_3$ (b) ArN$^+$Me$_3$, ArCH$_2$N$^+$Me$_3$, ArCH$_2$CH$_2$N$^+$Me$_3$
   4.4%   15.5%   33.8%   64.6%   100%   88%   19%

▮ (a) Successive replacement of H's in electron-releasing CH$_3$ by electronegative Cl's makes G increasingly electron-attracting and *m*-orienting.   (b) The + charge on N in $^+$NMe$_3$ makes the substituent electron-attracting and *m*-directing by an inductive effect. Its influence wanes with increasing CH$_2$'s between $^+$N and Ar. With two CH$_2$'s, the electron-releasing effect of the alkyl group is more significant and o,p-orientation dominates.

11.51 Describe and account for the reaction, if any, of D$_2$SO$_4$ in D$_2$O with: (a) C$_6$H$_5$SO$_3$H, (b) C$_6$H$_5$OH, and (c) C$_6$H$_6$.

▮ (a) There is no ring deuteration because —SO$_3$H is deactivating. However, the acidic H is exchanged for D to give C$_6$H$_5$SO$_3$D. At elevated temperatures desulfonation can occur (Problem 11.14) giving initially C$_6$H$_5$D. (b) o,p-Orientation yields 2,4,6-triD-C$_6$H$_2$OD. The acidic H is exchanged. (c) Slow reaction produces hexadeuterobenzene because there is no activating or orienting substituent.

11.52 Give the principal monosubstitution products from the following reactions and indicate whether each reaction is faster (**F**) or slower (**S**) than with benzene:
(a) Nitration of PhNHCOMe   (d) Nitration of Ph—Ph   (g) Nitration of PhC≡N
(b) Bromination of PhCBr$_3$ (e) Nitration of PhCOOMe   (h) Bromination of PhI.
(c) Chlorination of PhCMe$_3$ (f) Sulfonation of PhCHMe$_2$

▮ (a) p-O$_2$NC$_6$H$_4$NHCOCH$_3$ (**F**); (b) m-BrC$_6$H$_4$CBr$_3$ (**S**); (c) p-ClC$_6$H$_4$CCMe$_3$ (**F**); (d) p-O$_2$NC$_6$H$_4$Ph (**F**) (Ph is an activating o,p group); (e) m-O$_2$NC$_6$H$_4$COOMe (**S**); (f) p-HSO$_3$C$_6$H$_4$CHMe$_2$ (**F**); (g) m-O$_2$NC$_6$H$_4$CN (**S**); (h) p-BrC$_6$H$_4$I (**S**).

11.53 Classify the following substituent groups by their orientation and reactivity:

(a) —CH=CHNO$_2$, (b) —OCR (c) —CNH$_2$, (d) —OAr (e) —CH$_2$OH (f) —CCH$_3$
         ‖   ‖   ‖
         O   O   O

▰ (b), (d), (e) Activating o,p; (c), (f) deactivating m; (a) deactivating (by NO$_2$) o,p (by C=C).

11.54 Give the structures, indicating by an arrow the position(s) most likely to undergo electrophilic substitution in each of the following compounds, and explain your choices. (a) Phenyl benzoate, PhOCOPh; (b) p-nitrobiphenyl, p-O$_2$N—C$_6$H$_4$—Ph; (c) phenyl-m-cyanophenylmethane; and (d) 1,4-diphenylbenzene (p-terphenyl).

▰ (a) See **A** below. The ring bonded to ⟩C=O is deactivated; the ring bonded to —O— is activated. (b) See **B**. Although the ring with NO$_2$ is deactivated, it nevertheless activates the unsubstituted ring. *Para* substitution is less hindered than *ortho*. (c) See **C**. The ring with CN is deactivated, and the —CH$_2$—Ar group activates the unsubstituted ring. *Para* is less hindered than *ortho*. (d) See **D**. Reaction occurs on the middle ring since it is bonded to two activating Ph's.

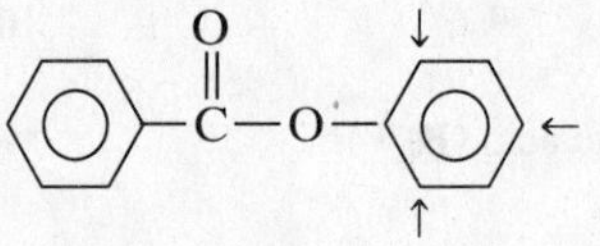

A 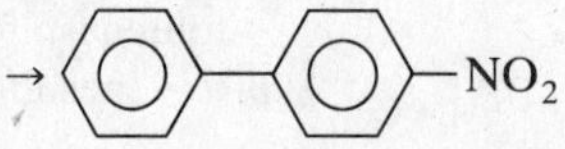   **B**

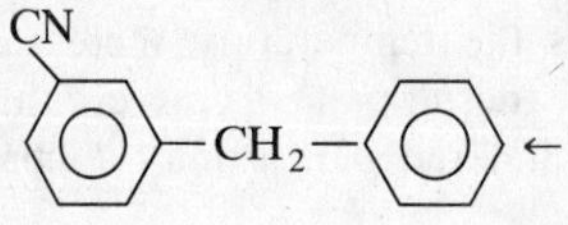

C 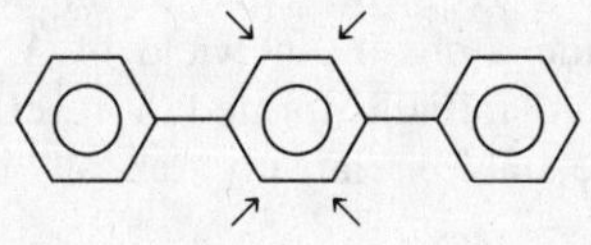   **D**

11.55 Indicate by an arrow the position(s) most likely to react in each of the following three isomeric nitrotoluenes. Explain your choices.

▰

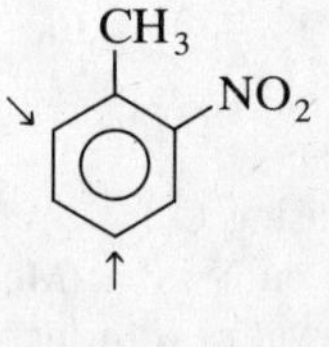

E (*ortho*) 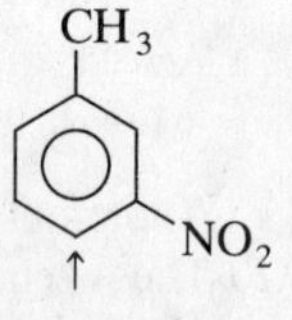   **F** (*meta*) 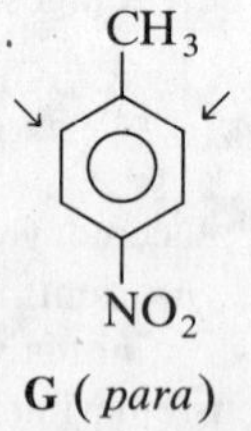   **G** (*para*)

In **E**, Me directs E$^+$ *ortho* and *para* to C^4 and C^6, positions that are also *meta* to NO$_2$—the substituents reinforce each other. In **F**, the orientation is in opposition. The o,p-director controls the orientation, but somehow E$^+$ enters mostly *ortho*, not *para*, to the *meta*-directing NO$_2$. Both G's are reinforcing in **G**, and E$^+$ is directed *ortho*, on to C^2.

11.56 Show by an arrow the preferred product of reaction with E$^+$ of each of the three isomeric methoxytoluenes and explain your choices.

▰

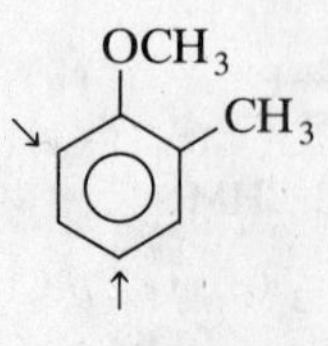

H (*ortho*) 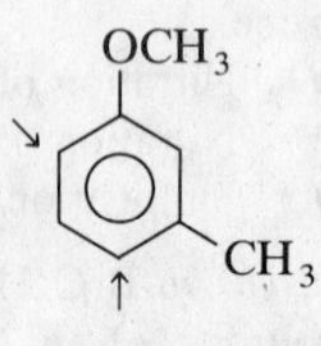   **I** (*meta*) 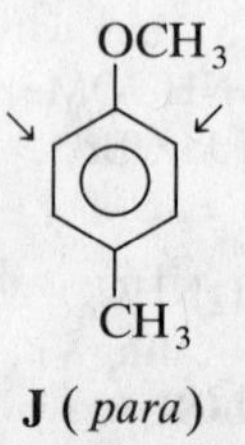   **J** (*para*)

Both groups are activating and o,p-directing. In **I**, their influence is reinforcing, and a mixture of two isomers is inevitable. Very little substitution occurs in the sterically-hindered position between the *meta* G's. In **H** and **J**, the two G's are in opposition. The more strongly activating OMe controls the orientation, and E^+ bonds mainly o and p to it.

11.57 Repeat Problem 11.56 for the isomeric methoxyacetanilides.

◢ Both G's are about equally moderate strong activators, and reaction is rapid. When these o,p-directors are reinforcing, as in **L**, a mixture of products of reaction *ortho* to both G's (but not between them) is obtained. When they compete, as in **K**, substantial amounts of all isomers are obtained, and reaction of **M** occurs at positions *ortho* to both G's.

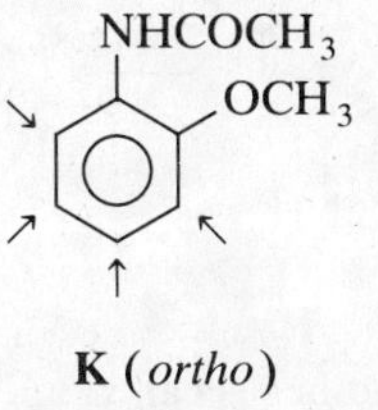

K (*ortho*) 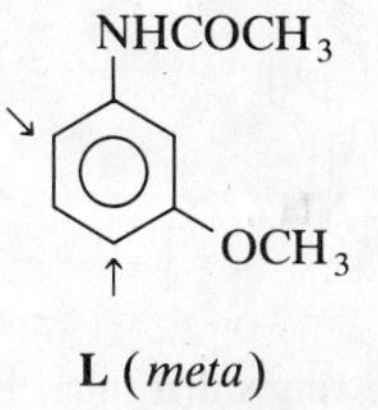   L (*meta*) 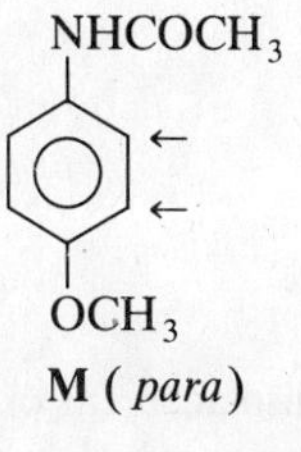   M (*para*)

11.58 Place the following compounds in the order of their relative reactivity with E^+. (*a*) p-nitrochlorobenzene, chlorobenzene, 2,4-dinitrochlorobenzene; (*b*) acetanilide ($PhNHCOCH_3$), aniline ($PhNH_2$), acetophenone ($PhCOCH_3$); (*c*) 1,3-dimethylbenzene, 1,4-dimethylbenzene, toluene, benzene, 1,3,5-trimethylbenzene; and (*d*) p-$CH_3C_6H_4COOH$, p-$HOOCC_6H_4COOH$, p-$CH_3C_6H_4CH_3$, $C_6H_5CH_3$.

◢ (*a*) Chlorobenzene > p-nitrochlorobenzene > 2,4-dinitrochlorobenzene
   (*b*) Aniline > acetanilide > benzene > acetophenone
   (*c*) 1,3,5-trimethylbenzene > 1,3-dimethylbenzene (Me's reenforcing) > 1,4-dimethylbenzene (Me's not reenforcing) > toluene > benzene
   (*d*) p-$CH_3C_6H_4CH_3$ (two A groups) > $C_6H_5CH_3$ (one A group) > p-$CH_3C_6H_4COOH$ (one A and one D group) > p-$HOOCC_6H_4COOH$ (two D groups), where A and D mean activating and deactivating, respectively.

11.59 Show with arrows the principal position(s) sulfonated by reaction of (*a*) p-$CH_3C_6H_4NH_3^+Cl^-$, (*b*) o-HOC_6H_4COOH, and (*c*) m-$C_6H_4(NO_2)_2$.

◢ (*a*)   (*b*) 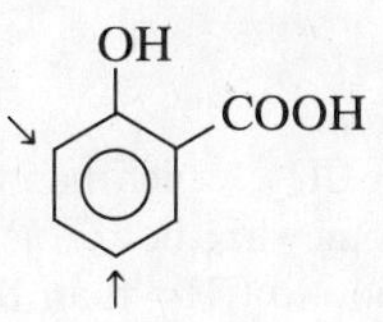   (*c*) No reaction; two strongly deactivating G's

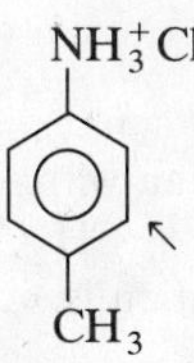

11.60 Account for the greater reactivity and the o,p-orientation in electrophilic substitution of biphenyl despite the electron-attracting inductive effect of the phenyl group.

◢ In attack at the o,p positions the unreacted ring can stabilize the $+$ charge on the attached C of the σ complex by electron-releasing delocalization that results in delocalizing the $+$ charge to both rings. Such delocalization is impossible with the intermediate from *meta* substitution which does not have the $+$ charge on the C bonded to the Ph substituent. The $+$ charge cannot be incorporated into the second ring, and delocalization is confined to one ring.

11.61 (*a*) Explain the rapid formation of 2,4,6-$Br_3C_6H_2NH_2$ (**C**) when either p-$H_2NC_6H_4SO_3H$ (**A**) or p-$H_2NC_6H_4COOH$ (**D**) is treated with bromine in H_2O. (*b*) What is the name of this type of reaction?

◢ (*a*) **A** exists as the dipolar ion, p-$H_3\overset{+}{N}C_6H_4SO_3^-$ (**A'**). Br^+ probably first attacks the ring carbon displacing SO_3 (a good leaving group). The initially formed p-bromoanilinium ion, p-$BrC_6H_4NH_3^+$ (**B**), is a strong enough acid to revert to the amino group (in **B'**), which strongly activates the ring to further substitution by additional Br^+ in the two *ortho* positions. A similar reaction occurs with **D**, which loses CO_2, also a good leaving group.

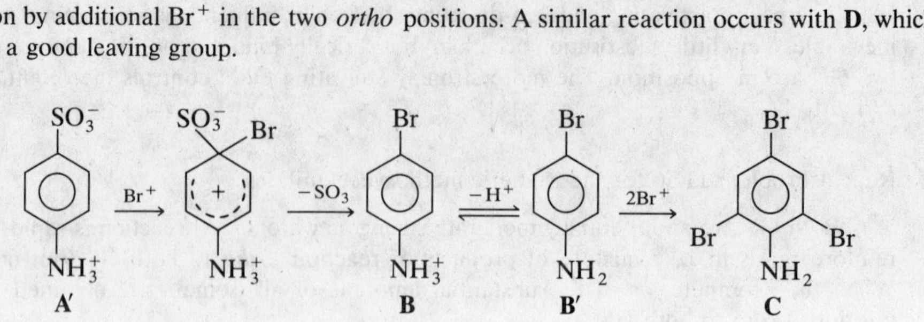

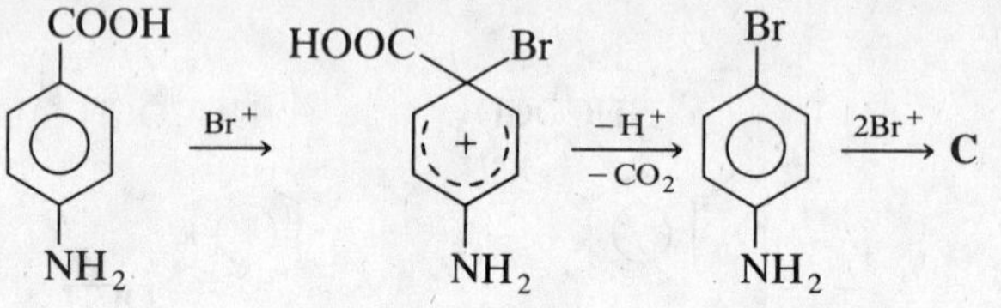

(*b*) The displacement of one ring substituent by another is called an *ipso* substitution. The *ipso* carbon is the one on which such substitution occurs.

11.62 (*a*) Give an orbital overlap explanation for the *o,p*-orientation of an activating R group such as CH_3. (*b*) Give the name for this overlap. (*c*) Why does nitration of 2-ethyltoluene yield more 4-nitro-2-ethyltoluene (**A**) than 5-nitro-2-ethyltoluene (**B**)?

▌ (*a*) The empty *p* AO of C^+ can overlap weakly with the C—H σ bond of CH_3, thereby delocalizing the + charge from C to H as shown in Fig. 11-5.

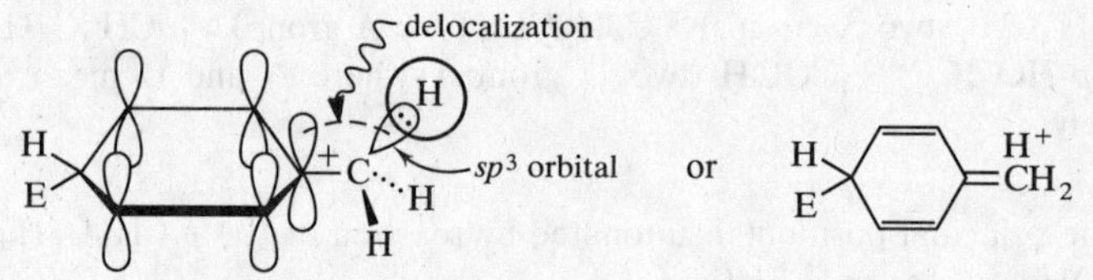

Fig. 11-5

(*b*) The orbital overlap is called *hyperconjugation*.
(*c*) Hyperconjugation is more effective with —CH_3, which has three H's, than with —CH_2CH_3, which has two H's. Consequently, —CH_3 is a somewhat better activator than —CH_2CH_3 and there is a higher yield of **A**, formed by *para* substitution to CH_3, than **B** where nitration is *para* to —CH_2CH_3.

11.63 Why can a *t*-butyl substituent be used as a *blocking group* in aromatic electrophilic substitutions?

▌ The Friedel–Crafts alkylation can be reversed, especially when a 3° alkyl group such as Me_3C is present. Dealkylation is effected with $AlCl_3$ by transfer of Me_3C^+ to another arene, used as the solvent, or at high temperatures by protonation with H^+ and loss of Me_3C as Me_2C=CH_2. Me_3C—, introduced into a ring, is used to block an active position and/or to direct another G into the ring, and then removed.

11.64 Illustrate the use of *t*-Bu as a blocking group to synthesize (*a*) *o*-benzoyltoluene from toluene, and (*b*) 1,3,-dimethyl-2-ethylbenzene from *m*-xylene.

▌ (*a*)

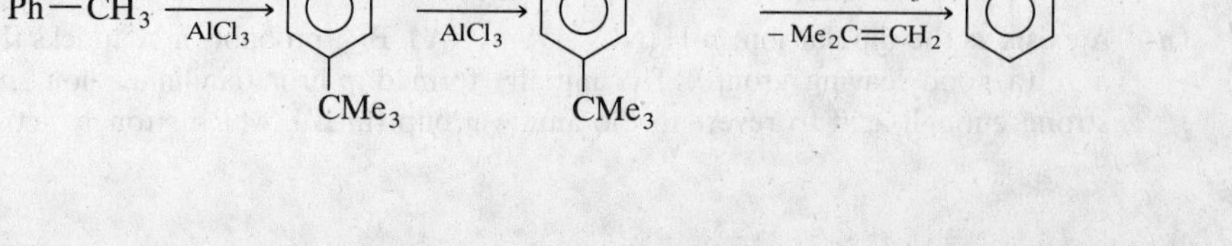

(*b*)   *m*-Xylene is first *t*-butylated, giving the less sterically-hindered thermodynamic product, **A**.

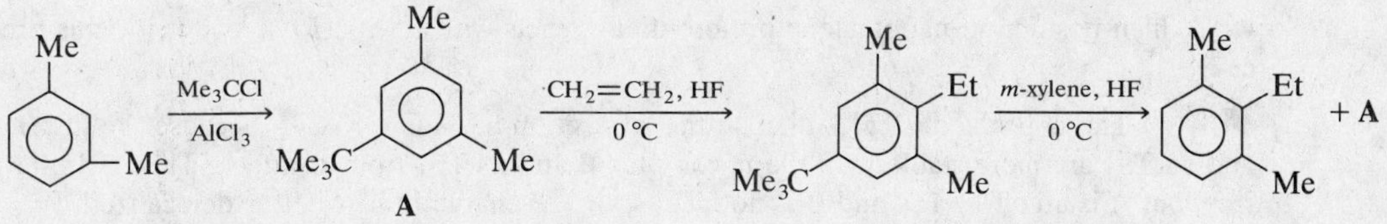

In the dealkylation, benzene or *m*-xylene may be used as an acceptor. If the latter is used, **A** is the product, and it can be recycled.

11.65   Explain the isomerization of 1,2,4-trialkylbenzenes (**B**) to the 1,3,5-isomers (**C**) during $AlCl_3$ catalyzed Friedel–Crafts alkylation reactions.

▮   A 1,2,4-tri-alkylbenzene (**B**) is first formed, rapidly but reversibly, along with $HAlCl_4$ ($AlCl_3$ + HCl), a very strong Brönsted acid. In its presence, **B** rearranges slowly but irreversibly to the less sterically-hindered, thermodynamically more stable **C**. This preference for 1,3,5-trialkyl isomers is a consequence of having the more stable σ complex, whose δ+ resides only on 3° C's bonded to R, in contrast to any other tri-R-substituted σ complex.

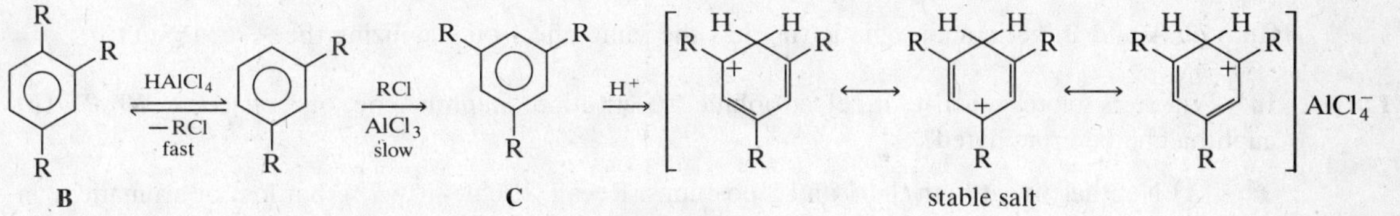

11.66   (*a*)   Give a mechanism for the following bromodealkylation:

$$ArC(CH_3)_3 + Br_2 \xrightarrow{AlBr_3} ArBr + (CH_3)_2C{=}CH_2 (+AlBr_3 + HBr)$$

(*b*)   Why does this reaction not occur with $ArCH_2CH_2CH_2CH_3$?

▮   (*a*)   In this *ipso* substitution, Br^+ displaces Me_3C^+ which loses H^+ giving isobutylene.

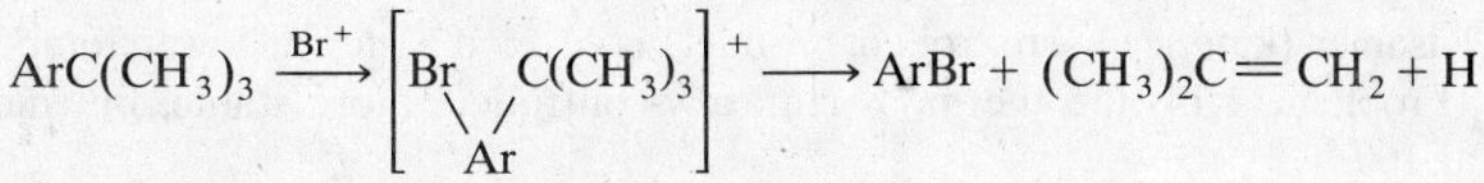

(*b*)   Ejection of the unstable 1° *n*-Bu$^+$ requires too high an energy.

11.67   Account for the products of the following reactions and explain their formation.   (*a*) Both *p*- and *o*-xylene, with large amounts of a Friedel–Crafts catalyst, are converted partly into *m*-xylene.   (*b*) Ethylbenzene, in the presence of HF—BF_3 reacts to form benzene and 1,3-diethylbenzene.

▮   (*a*) Since the Friedel–Crafts alkylation is reversible, the thermodynamically more stable *m*-isomer forms under equilibrium conditions.   (*b*) In this disproportionation the catalyst protonates C^1 and the σ complex ethylates a second molecule of PhEt to give the diethyl σ complex and benzene. Under these equilibrium conditions, the former loses H^+ to give the thermodynamically more stable 1,3-diethylbenzene. Ethylation occurs without the formation of the very high energy Et^+ as an intermediate.

11.68   Classify the substituents discussed in previous problems in the following categories: *ortho*, *para*, and very strongly activating (VSA), strongly activating (SA), activating (A), and deactivating (D); *meta* and strongly deactivating (SD) and very strongly deactivating (VSD).

▮   See Table 11-1.

TABLE 11-1

ortho, para				*meta*	
VSA	SA	A	D	SD	VSD
—OH, —NH$_2$, —NHR, —NR$_2$	—NHCOR, —OCOR, —OR	—R, —Ar, —C=C<	—I, —Br, —Cl, —F, —CH$_2$X, —NO, O=S<	—SO$_3$H, —CN, —CHO, —COOH, —COOR, —COCl	—NO$_2$, —CF$_3$, —$\overset{+}{N}R_3$

ELECTROPHILIC SUBSTITUTION IN NAPHTHALENE

11.69 (*a*) Which position in naphthalene preferentially reacts with E^+? (*b*) Account for this preference mechanistically.

◢ (*a*) The α position. (*b*) Attack at the α position has a lower $\Delta H^{\ddagger}$ because the intermediate σ complex **A** and its TS_1 are more stable than the σ complex **B** and its TS_1 from β-attack. They both have an intact benzene ring, but **A** is an allylic R^+ and **B** is not. Thus, the $+$ charge in **A** is better delocalized.

an allylic R^+
α-substitution

A

not an allylic R^+
β-substitution

B

(In both **A** and **B** the intact aromatic ring has the same effect on stabilizing the $+$ charge.)

11.70 (*a*) Which is more reactive in electrophilic substitution, naphthalene or benzene? Why? (*b*) How may naphthalene be brominated?

◢ (*a*) Napthalene, at both the 1 and 2 positions. Recall (Problem 10.72) that loss of aromaticity in one ring of naphthalene "costs" $255 - 151 = 104$ kJ/mol, much less than that for the loss of the single ring in benzene (151 kJ/mol). (*b*) Because of the significant activation of one ring by the other, naphthalene is easily brominated in CCl_4 without a Lewis catalyst like $FeBr_3$, which is required to brominate benzene.

11.71 Account for the formation of mostly 1-naphthalenesulfonic acid at 40-80 °C and ~85% of the 2-isomer at 160 °C when naphthalene is sulfonated.

◢ The 1-isomer (kinetically-controlled product) is formed faster at lower temperatures. Since the reaction is reversible (Problem 11.14) the thermodynamically-controlled, more stable, but more slowly formed 2-isomer is produced at 160 °C.

11.72 (*a*) Why is β-naphthalenesulfonic acid more stable (Problem 11.71) than the α-isomer? (*b*) Devise an experiment to confirm the relative stabilities.

◢ (*a*) The $-SO_3H$ group is about as large as a *t*-butyl group. In the 1 position it is sterically hindered, being within the van der Waals radius of the C^8H. This is called a *peri interaction*. (*b*) Subject pure α-naphathalene-sulfonic acid to the same reaction conditions (H_2SO_4, 160 °C). The same equilibrium mixture ($\approx 85\%$ β and 15% α) is obtained.

11.73 State the rules for deciding which ring reacts with E^+ in naphthyl-G under kinetically-controlled conditions.

◢ Rule 1. α-Substitution always dominates.
Rule 2. When one ring has a deactivating G on it, further substitution occurs in the unsubstituted ring at an α position if available.
Rule 3. When one ring has an activating α-G, further substitution occurs in the same ring at position 4, and to a smaller extent at position 2. An activating β-G orients E^+ to position 1.

11.74 (*a*) Discuss the concept of alternant polarity as applied to the intermediate cation from α-substitution on naphthalene by E^+. (*b*) Use this concept to predict the major product from nitration at 0 °C of (i) 1-nitronaphthalene and (ii) 2-nitronaphthalene.

◢ (*a*) When E^+ forms a bond to a C of the aromatic ring, some $+$ charges are introduced on the adjacent C's and on all other alternating C's of the ring as shown for α-substitution on naphthalene:

(*b*) In both cases the second nitro group enters according to rules 1 and 2 in Problem 11.73.
(i) 1,8-Dinitronaphthalene because attack at C^8 does not generate any + charge on C^1 bonded to NO_2, plus some 1,5-derivative, because of steric crowding in the C^8 *peri* position.

no + on C^1 better than + on C^1

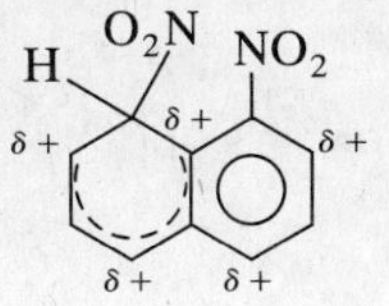

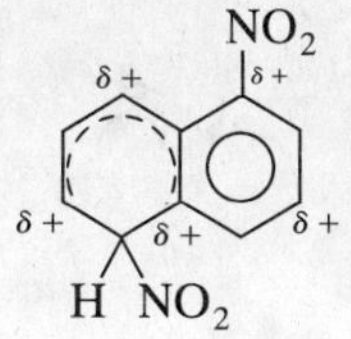

(ii) 1,6-Dinitronaphthalene for the same reason as in (i).

no + on C^2 better than + on C^2

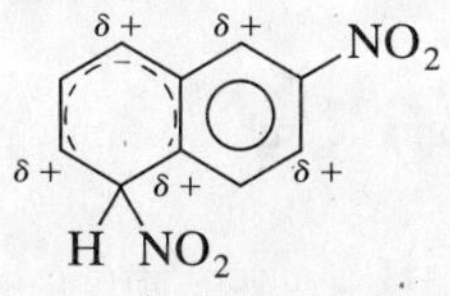

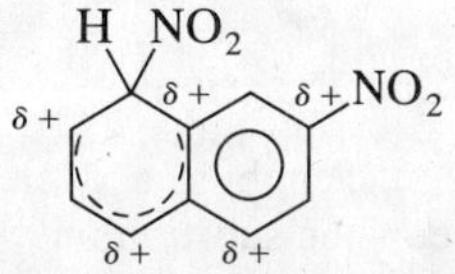

This concept makes writing many resonance structures unnecessary.

11.75 Write the structures for the product(s) of (*a*) nitration of 1-methoxynaphthalene and (*b*) bromination of 2-methylnaphthalene.

(*a*)

+ some

(*b*)

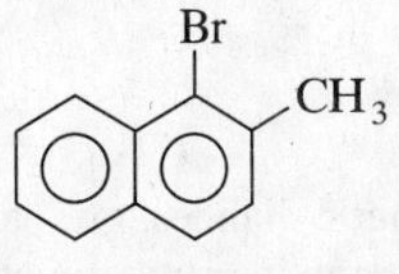

In (*b*) the activated ring has no available *p* position so substitution occurs at the more reactive *ortho* (α) position.

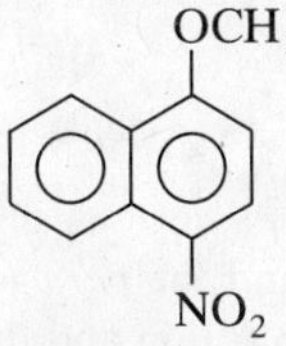

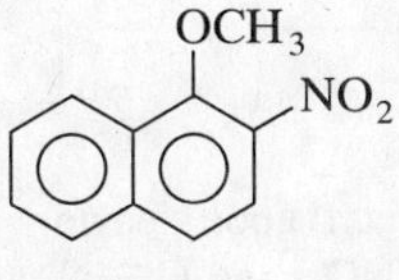

11.76 (*a*) Why is Friedel–Crafts acylation but not alkylation of naphthalene practical? (*b*) Give the product of acylation of naphthalene with CH_3COCl and $AlCl_3$ in the solvent (i) CS_2, and (ii) $PhNO_2$. (*c*) Explain the different products in (*b*).

(*a*) Acylation introduces a deactivating group (—COR) that prevents further acylation from occurring. Introduction of an activating-R group induces polyalkylations. (*b*) (i) 1-Acetylnaphthalene and (ii) 2-acetylnaphthalene. (*c*) $PhNO_2$ may form a bulky complex with $RCOCl—AlCl_3$ that can only attack the more spacious 2 position.

11.77 Provide the product(s) of the reaction of naphthalene with succinic anhydride and $AlCl_3$ in $PhNO_2$.

A separable mixture of α- and β-products is obtained:

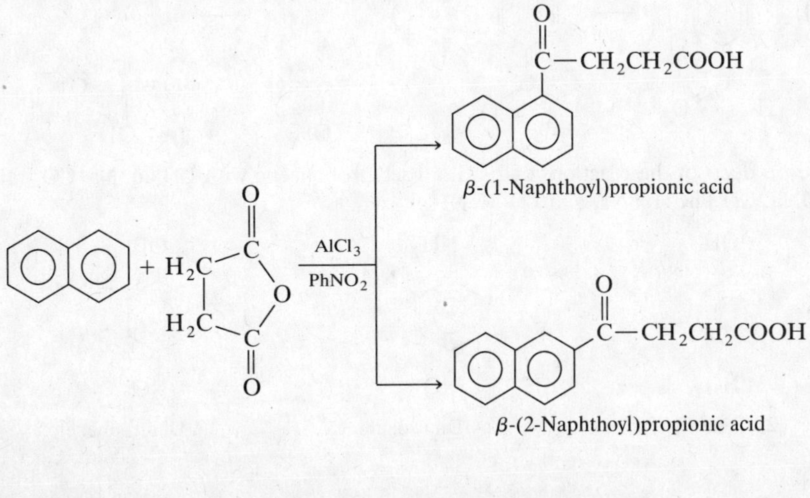

β-(1-Naphthoyl)propionic acid

β-(2-Naphthoyl)propionic acid

11.78 Contrast the CrO_3/HOAc oxidation of toluene and β-methylnaphthalene.

◢ The Me of toluene is more susceptible to oxidation than the aromatic ring and the product is PhCOOH. In β-methylnaphthalene, the reactive α positions are more easily oxidized than Me and, under these conditions of oxidation, the main product is the quinone **A**.

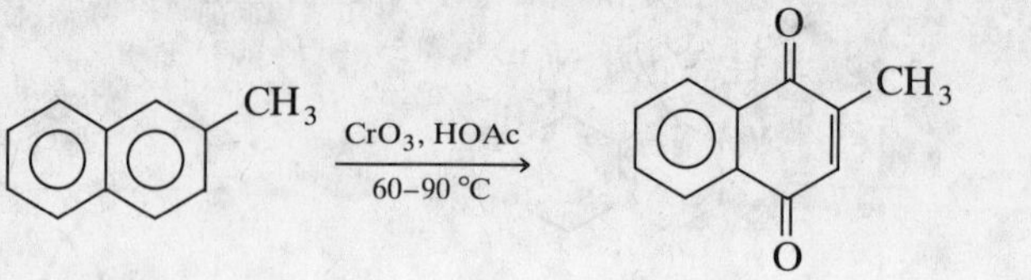

A, 2-Methyl-1,4-naphthoquinone

NUCLEOPHILIC AROMATIC SUBSTITUTION

1. Addition-Elimination Reactions

11.79 (*a*) Compare nucleophilic and electrophilic aromatic substitutions. (*b*) What kind of aromatic compounds undergo nucleophilic substitution?

◢ (*a*) Nucleophilic aromatic displacement of $:H^-$, a very strong base and extremely poor leaving group, is rare and occurs only when an oxidant that converts $:H^-$ to H_2O is present. The steps are similar except that the intermediate is a *arenanion* in which the negative charge is dispersed to the *ortho* and *para* positions.

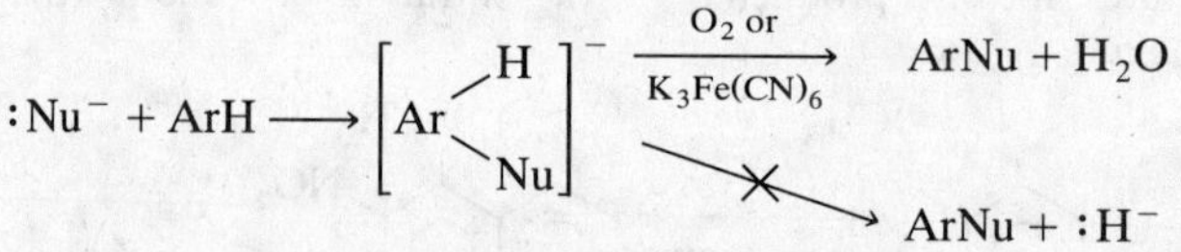

(*b*) Aromatic halides and tosylates. Such good leaving groups are more easily displaced, especially when electron-attracting substituents, such as NO_2 and $C\equiv N$, are *ortho* and/or *para* to the reacting C. The greater the number of these *ortho* and *para* substituents, the more rapid the reaction and the less vigorous the conditions required.

11.80 Show the structure of the intermediate arenanion formed from the reaction of Nu^- with $p\text{-}XC_6H_4G$, where G is (*a*) NO_2, (*b*) $C\equiv N$, (*c*) $N{-}O$, (*d*) $CH{=}O$, and (*e*) SO_3H.

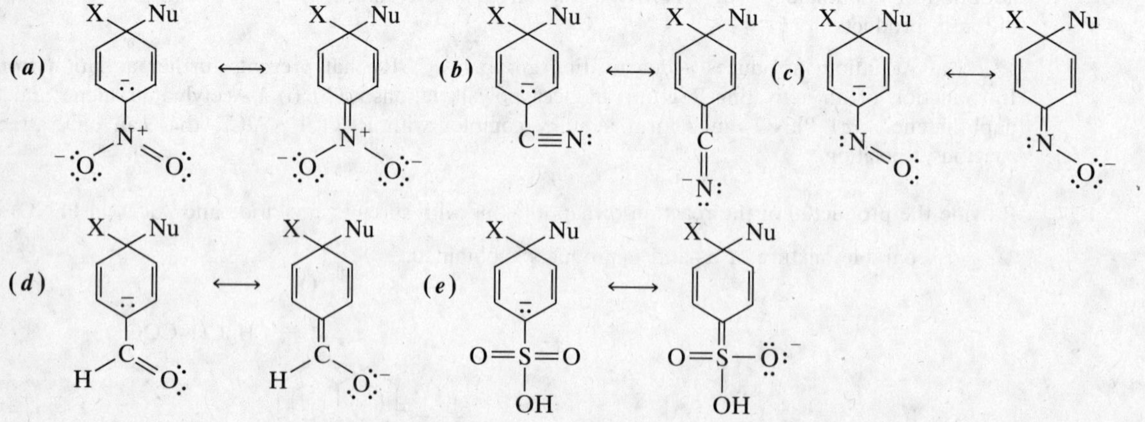

11.81 Give the products of the reactions of 2,4-dinitrochlorobenzene with (*a*) aq. Na_2CO_3, 100 °C, (*b*) NH_3, pressure, (*c*) EtONa, (*d*) $PhCH_2SNa$, and (*e*) $MeNH_2$.

(*a*) 2,4-Dinitrophenol

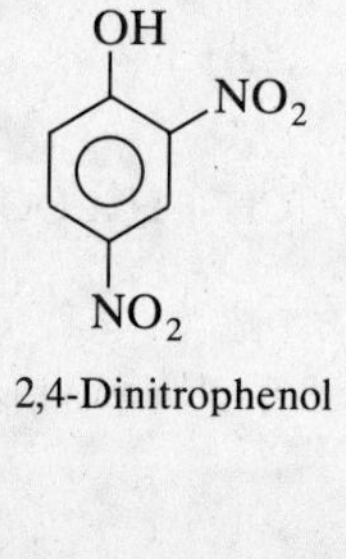

(*b*) 2,4-Dinitroaniline

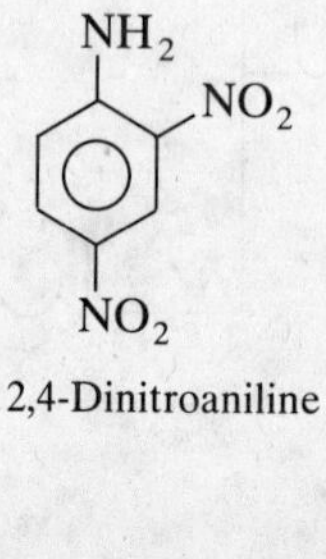

(*c*) 2,4-Dinitrophenetole

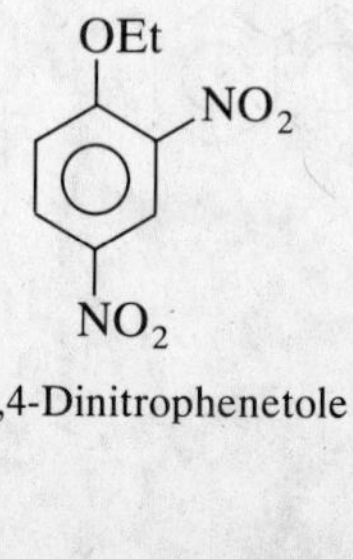

(d)

SCH₂Ph

NO₂

NO₂

2,4-Dinitrophenyl-
benzylthioether

(e)

NHMe

NO₂

NO₂

2,4-Dinitro-N-
methylaniline

11.82 For the reaction of *p*-halonitrobenzenes with MeO⁻, the experimental rate equation is rate = $k_2[p\text{-}XC_6H_4NO_2]\,[OH^-]$ and the order of reactivity for the halides is ArF ≫ ArCl, ArBr > ArI. (*a*) Give a mechanism. (*b*) Explain the order of reactivity of the halides. Why is this order evidence for the first step being rate-determining? (*c*) Provide an enthalpy diagram for the reaction.

▰ (*a*) $\quad Ar-X + MeO^- \xrightarrow{\text{slow}} \left[\begin{matrix} X \\ \diagdown \\ Ar \end{matrix} \hspace{-0.5em} \begin{matrix} OMe \\ \diagup \end{matrix} \right]^- \xrightarrow{\text{fast elimination}} Ar-OMe + X^-$

intermediate

(*b*) Since F is the most electronegative of the halogens, it best stabilizes the − charge on the neighboring C's in the TS and in the intermediate. If the second step were rate-determining, ArF would react the slowest, because F⁻ is the poorest leaving group of the halide ions.

(*c*) See Fig. 11-6.

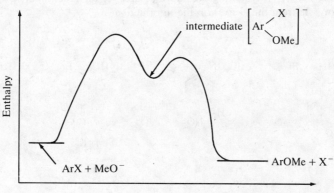

Fig. **11-6**

11.83 Give the structure for the product of the reaction of 2,4,6-trinitroethoxybenzene with NaOMe.

▰ The resulting ionic salt is called a *Meisenheimer complex* or *salt*, and its existence is taken as evidence for the formation of the tetrahedral anionic intermediate that is at the dip in the curve in Fig. 11-6.

EtO   OMe

O₂N ⟍⟋ NO₂

⟷

EtO   OMe

O₂N ⟍⟋ NO₂

(The cation is Na⁺)

$\overset{-}{\underset{N^+}{}}$
O   O⁻

N⁺
⁻O   O⁻

Meisenheimer complex (salt)

11.84 (*a*) Compare nucleophilic addition-elimination (A-E) and electrophilic (E) substitution reactions with ArX in terms of (i) number of steps, (ii) rate-determining steps, and (iii) character of intermediates. (*b*) Compare nucleophilic A-E with S_{N^2} reactions.

▰ (*a*) (i) Both types of reactions have two steps. (ii) In E reactions, the first step is rate-determining which is also usually true for A-E reactions. However, with certain nucleophiles and in some solvents, the second step may be slow. (iii) In E reactions the intermediate is a cation, variously called a σ complex, benzenium, benzenonium, arenium or arenonium ion. The intermediate in A-E reactions is an anion, sometimes isolable as a Meisenheimer salt with the countercation.

(*b*) For both, rate = k[substrate] [Nu^-]. The same nucleophiles are effective (MeO^-, RNH_2, OH^-), and the rate increases with increasing nucleophilicity of attacking reagent. S_N2 reactions go through a one-step sequence involving a TS in which the three σ-bonded nonreacting groups to the C have a trigonal planar geometry, while the nucleophile and the group being displaced are 180° from each other. In A-E there are two TS's; in the first step leading to the benzenanion, the aromatic system is destroyed, and the hybridization of the reactive C changes from sp^2 to tetrahedral sp^3. In the second step, the aromatic system is regenerated by loss of $:Nu^-$ or $X:^-$, while C regains its sp^2 hybridized state.

11.85 (*a*) Compare the rates of the reactions of piperidine, an unhindered cyclic 2° amine (R_2NH) in base, with 4-nitrobromobenzene (**A**) and 3,5-dimethyl-4-nitrobromobenzene (**B**), and explain the difference. (*b*) Do you expect a difference in the rates of the reaction of 4-cyanobromobenzene (**C**) and 3,5-dimethyl-4-cyanobromobenzene (**D**)? Explain.

▌ (*a*) In the TS and the intermediate, stabilization occurs primarily through delocalization of the − charge to the 4-nitro group. See Fig. 11-7(*a*) showing the intermediates for the reaction of R_2NH with **A** and **B**. The two Me's *ortho* to the nitro in **B** prevent it from achieving coplanarity with the ring, and delocalization is diminished. This *steric inhibition of resonance* raises the enthalpy of the TS and slows the rate compared with that of **A**. (*b*) There is little difference in the rates of **C** and **D**. The coplanarity of the CN group is hardly disturbed because of its linear shape. See Fig. 11-7(*b*) showing the intermediates for the reaction of R_2NH with **C** and **D**. (The base in (*a*) and (*b*) removes H from the N to form the intermediate.)

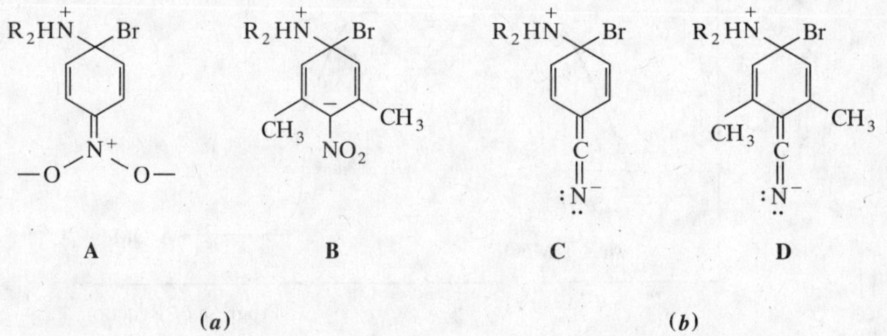

Fig. 11-7

2. Elimination-Addition Reactions

11.86 (*a*) Give the product when PhCl is treated with (i) $K^+NH_2^-$ in liquid NH_3 at −33 °C and (ii) aq. NaOH at 340 °C. (*b*) What products are formed when *p*-chlorotoluene is reacted with aq. NaOH at 340 °C? (*c*) Explain why the reactions in (*a*) and (*b*) are not considered to be addition-elimination reactions.

▌ (*a*) (i) $PhNH_2$ + KCl and (ii) PhOH + NaCl. (*b*) *m*- and *p*-hydroxytoluene + NaCl. (*c*) (1) The halogen is not activated by electron-withdrawing G's. (2) The base is much stronger ($:NH_2^-$) or the temperature is elevated (340 °C). (3) The entering group does not always occupy the vacated position (called *cine substitution*).

11.87 (*a*) PhCl labeled at C^1 with ^{14}C reacts with KNH_2 to give $PhNH_2$ labeled at both C^1 and C^2. Classify the reaction in Problem 11.86(*a*) and give a mechanism consistent with this observation. (*b*) How does the mechanism for this type of aromatic displacement account for the formation of the products in Problem 11.86(*b*)? (*c*) Which property of G, here CH_3, affects the relative yield of these products? Explain.

▌ (*a*) This reaction is an *elimination-addition* reaction. The strong base removes H^+ to give a high energy carbanion which ejects X^- to give a triple-bonded intermediate called a *benzyne* (elimination). The nucleophilic solvent adds to the very reactive benzyne (addition) giving the final product after redistribution of H's.

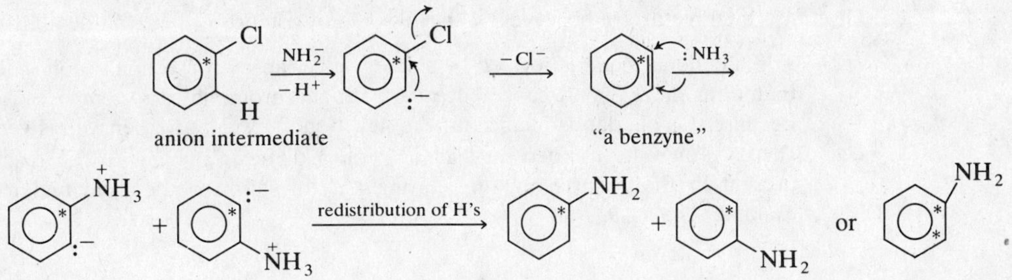

The nucleophile bonds with the labeled benzyne at either C^1 or C^2 resulting in half of the radioactivity at each position. This is the same as saying that *both* positions are labeled, because chemically the two radioisotopic isomers are indistinguishable. The radiocarbon is said to be *scrambled* between both positions.

(**b**) This reaction is also an elimination-addition reaction. The benzyne from *p*-chlorotoluene can be attacked by H_2O at C^3 giving *m*-hydroxytoluene or at C^4 giving *p*-hydroxytoluene.

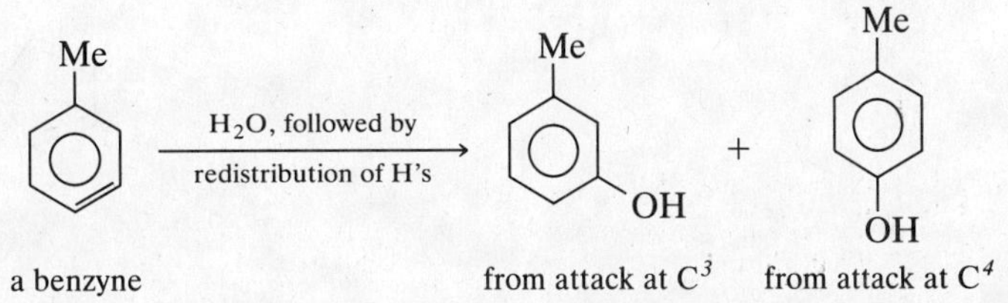

(**c**) The arene carbanion can only be affected by inductive effects, not by extended *p* orbital overlap [see Problem 11.89(*a*)]. A − charge is better stabilized when generated as close as possible to an electron-withdrawing G and as far away as possible from an electron-donating G such as CH_3. Attack at C^3 generates a − charge at C^4 and the major product is *m*-hydroxytoluene.

11.88 Show how a benzyne intermediate accounts for the formation of $m\text{-}MeOC_6H_4NH_2$ (**C**) from either $o\text{-}MeOC_6H_4Br$ (**A**) or $m\text{-}MeOC_6H_4Br$ (**B**).

Both isomers react through the same intermediate benzyne (**D**). It is the only benzyne that can arise from **A**, but one of two possibilities from **B**.

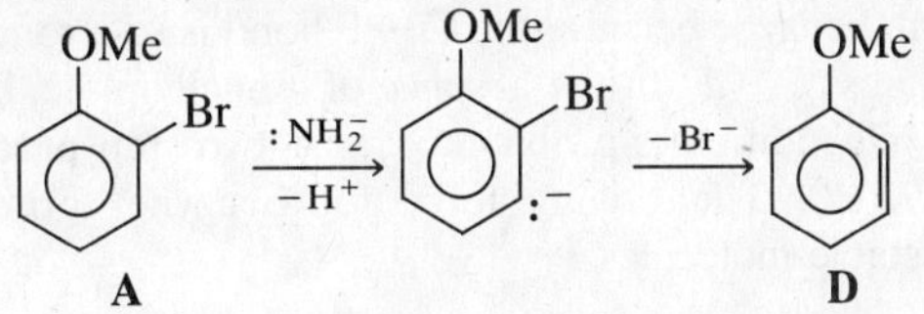

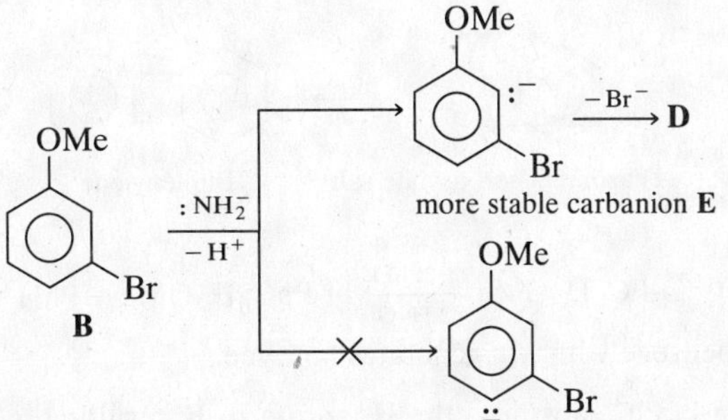

The − charge in the carbanion is better stabilized when on C^2, nearer to the electron-withdrawing MeO, as in **E**, and not on C^4. Consequently, little or no benzyne forms with the triple bond between C^3 and C^4. **C** results when NH_3 bonds to C^3 of **D**, the − charge again ending up on C^2.

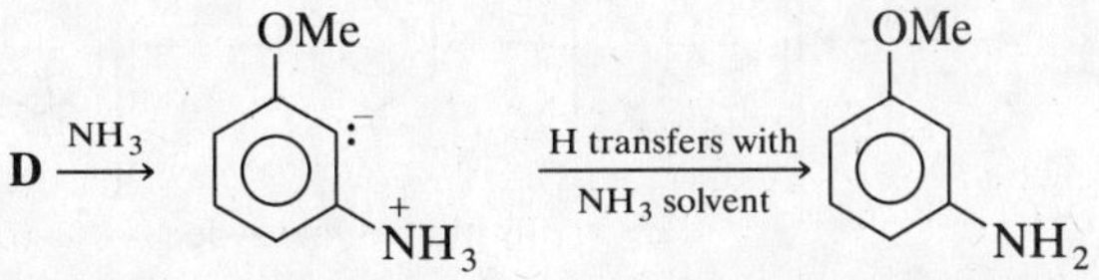

11.89 (*a*) Give an orbital picture of benzyne. (*b*) How is the existence of benzyne demonstrated?

▰ (*a*) The additional bond is formed by sideways overlap of sp^2 orbitals alongside the ring. These orbitals that form the π bond cannot overlap with the aromatic π system because they are not coplanar. Because this overlap is inefficient, the new bond is weak and benzyne is very reactive. See Fig. 11-8.

(*b*) Benzynes may be trapped by reaction with a diene in a Diels–Alder reaction. The diene must be present in the reaction mixture during the formation of benzyne under dry conditions. See, for example, Fig. 11-9.

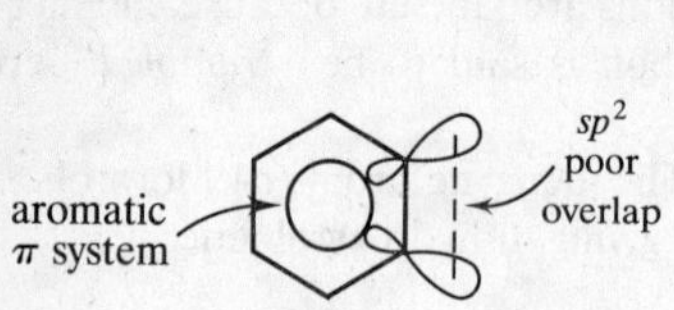

Fig. 11-8

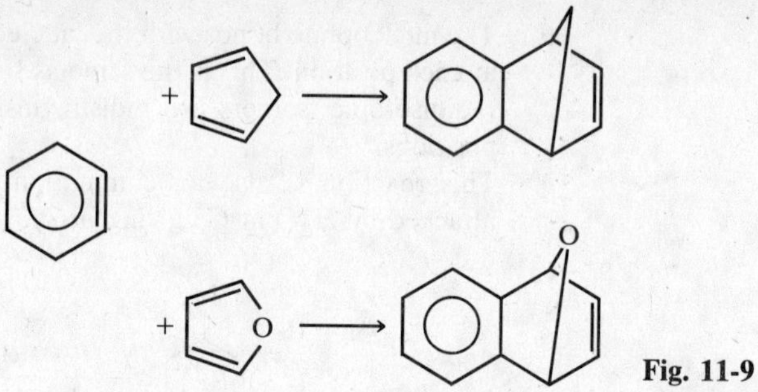

Fig. 11-9

11.90 Account for the following observations in terms of the benzyne intermediate: (*a*) 2,6-Dimethylhalobenzenes do not react. (*b*) 2,6-Dideuteriobromobenzene reacts more slowly than bromobenzene. (*c*) *o*-Deuteriofluorobenzene exchanges its D for H rapidly with KNH_2 in liq. NH_3, but forms aniline more slowly. (*d*) When benzyne is generated by thermal decomposition of the diazonium carboxylate salt, $o\text{-}^+N_2C_6H_4COO^-$ (Problem 19.80) produced from $o\text{-}NH_2C_6H_4COOH$ (anthranilic acid), it dimerizes.

▰ (*a*) Since there is no *ortho* H, benzyne cannot form. (*b*) The bond to H is broken in the slow first step (Problem 11.87). The reaction could also be a *syn* E2-type (see Problems 8.112 and 8.113) where the π bond forms as X and H leave in one-step. (*c*) The existence of an intermediate anion is indicated (Problem 11.87). Addition of H from the solvent NH_3 (containing only a trace of NH_2D) to the anion occurs faster than cleavage of the C—F bond to form benzyne because the C—F bond is so strong. D/H exchange eliminates the possibility of the *syn* E2-type mechanism. (*d*) In the absence of a nucleophile, benzyne undergoes [2 + 2] cycloaddition to give biphenylene. This cycloaddition is probably a rapid two step process and not concerted which is thermally not allowed (Problem 9.168). The driving force for benzyne formation is the loss of N_2 and CO_2, two thermodynamically very stable molecules.

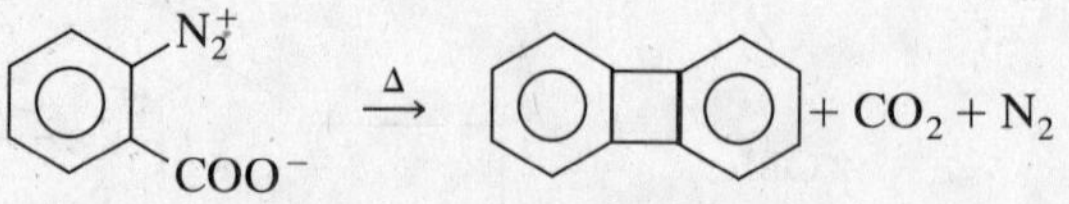

Diazonium carboxylate salt   Biphenylene

11.91 (*a*) Explain the products: $o\text{-}FC_6H_4OMe \xrightarrow[\text{2.H}_2\text{O}]{\text{1.2PhLi}} m\text{-}PhC_6H_4OMe + PhH + LiF + LiOH$. (*b*) Show that treatment of *o*-bromofluorobenzene with Mg generates benzyne.

▰ (*a*) The strong base, Ph^-, abstracts the H^+ *ortho* to F, resulting in methoxybenzyne, which reacts with a second equivalent of PhLi.

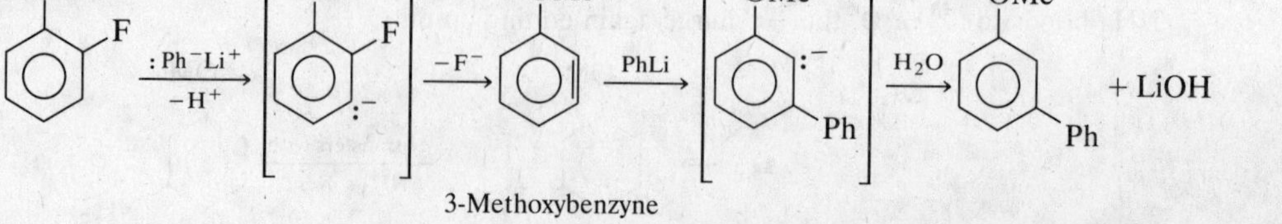

3-Methoxybenzyne

Note that Ph^- adds *meta*, inducing the − charge *ortho* to the electron-withdrawing OCH_3.

(*b*) 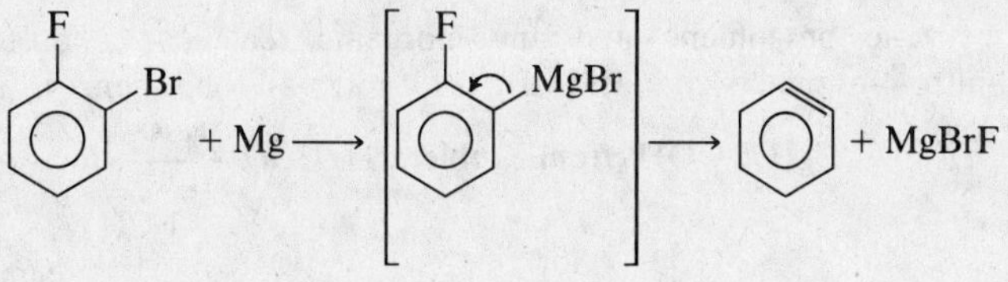

Mg forms the Grignard reagent with Br and then the carbanion ejects F^-.

SYNTHESES

11.92 Prepare (*a*) *meta*-, (*b*) *para*-, and (*c*) *ortho*-chloronitrobenzene from benzene.

(*a*) The *meta*-directing NO_2 is introduced first:

$$C_6H_6 \xrightarrow[H_2SO_4]{HNO_3} C_6H_5NO_2 \xrightarrow[FeCl_3]{Cl_2} m\text{-}ClC_6H_5NO_2$$

(*b*) The *para*-directing Cl is introduced first:

$$C_6H_6 \xrightarrow[FeCl_3]{Cl_2} C_6H_5Cl \xrightarrow[H_2SO_4]{HNO_3} p\text{-}ClC_6H_4NO_2$$

(*c*) The *para* is first blocked so that NO_2 goes exclusively to the *ortho* position:

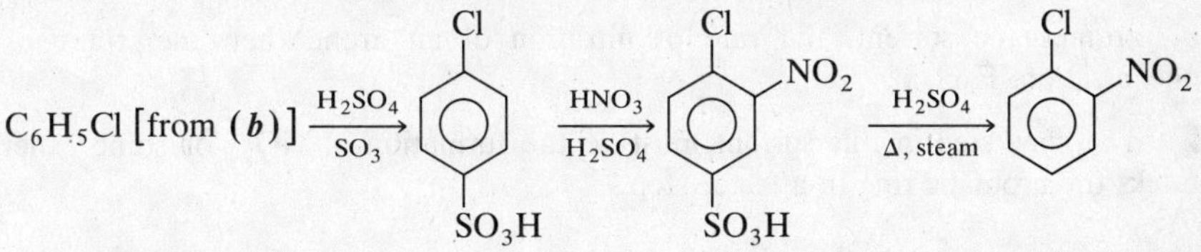

11.93 Use benzene and any inorganic or aliphatic reagents to synthesize in good yield each of the following: (*a*) *p*-bromobenzoic acid, (*b*) *o*-bromobenzoic acid, and (*c*) *m*-bromobenzoic acid.

(*a*) Bromination of toluene is more efficient than alkylation of bromobenzene, with Br deactivating.

$$C_6H_6 \xrightarrow[AlCl_3]{CH_3Cl} C_6H_5CH_3 \xrightarrow[Fe]{Br_2} p\text{-}CH_3C_6H_4Br \xrightarrow{\text{hot } KMnO_4^*} p\text{-}HOOCC_6H_4Br$$

(*b*) The *para* position of PhMe is blocked by sulfonation, as in Problem 11.92(*c*), followed by bromination.

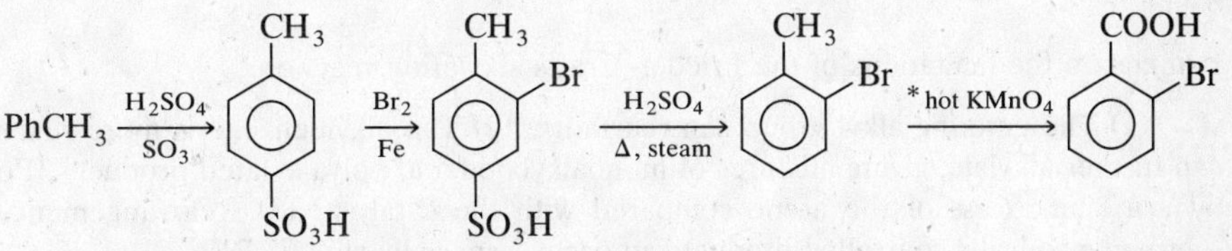

(*c*) The —COOH is introduced first to direct the —Br to the *meta* position.

$$C_6H_6 \xrightarrow[AlCl_3]{CH_3Cl} C_6H_5CH_3 \xrightarrow{^*\text{hot } KMnO_4} C_6H_5COOH \xrightarrow[Fe]{Br_2} m\text{-}BrC_6H_4COOH$$

*These two-phase oxidations are best done with phase-transfer catalysts (Problem 8.131).

11.94 Prepare (*a*) *ortho*-, (*b*) *para*-, and (*c*) *meta*-bromotoluene from benzene or toluene.

(*a*) See Problem 11.93(*b*).

(*b*) $PhMe \xrightarrow[Fe]{Br_2} p\text{-}BrC_6H_4Me$

(*c*) The Me is first converted to a *meta*-orienting G, $—CCl_3$, with Cl_2 in heat or light. After bromination, the Me is restored by reduction with Zn in acid.

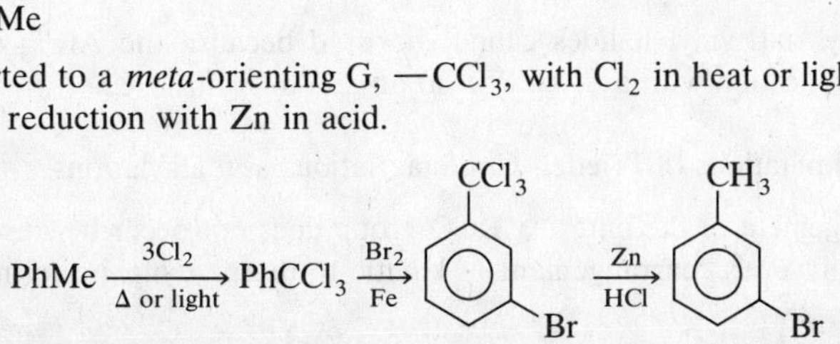

11.95 Use benzene or toluene and any inorganic reagents to prepare: (*a*) 3-nitro-4-bromobenzoic acid (**A**), (*b*) 2-nitro-4-bromobenzoic acid (**B**), (*c*) 4-nitro-2-bromo-benzoic acid (**C**), and (*d*) 3,5-dinitrobenzoic acid (**D**).

◢ (*a*) $p\text{-BrC}_6\text{H}_4\text{COOH}$ [from Problem 11.93(*a*)] $\xrightarrow[\text{H}_2\text{SO}_4]{\text{HNO}_3}$ **A**

(*b*) $CH_3C_6H_5 \xrightarrow[\text{SO}_3]{\text{H}_2\text{SO}_4} p\text{-CH}_3\text{C}_6\text{H}_4\text{SO}_3\text{H} \xrightarrow[\text{H}_2\text{SO}_4]{\text{HNO}_3}$ [benzene ring: CH₃, NO₂, SO₃H] $\xrightarrow[\text{steam}]{\text{H}_2\text{SO}_4}$

$o\text{-O}_2\text{NC}_6\text{H}_4\text{CH}_3 \xrightarrow{\text{Br}_2,\ \text{Fe}}$ [benzene ring: CH₃, NO₂, Br] $\xrightarrow{\text{hot KMnO}_4}$ **B**

(*c*) $CH_3C_6H_5 \xrightarrow[\text{H}_2\text{SO}_4]{\text{HNO}_3} p\text{-CH}_3\text{C}_6\text{H}_4\text{NO}_2 \xrightarrow[\text{Fe}]{\text{Br}_2} \text{2-Br-4-NO}_2\text{C}_6\text{H}_3\text{CH}_3 \xrightarrow[\Delta]{\text{KMnO}_4}$ **C**

(*d*) Nitration of a ring with two deactivating groups is difficult and requires more vigorous conditions.

$$CH_3C_6H_5 \xrightarrow{\text{hot KMnO}_4} C_6H_5COOH \xrightarrow[\text{H}_2\text{SO}_4]{\text{HNO}_3} m\text{-NO}_2\text{C}_6\text{H}_4\text{COOH} \xrightarrow[\text{H}_2\text{SO}_4,\ \Delta]{\text{fuming HNO}_3}$$ **D**

11.96 In nitromethane solvent, the rate of nitration of an arene (benzene, toluene, etc.) is independent of its concentration. Explain.

◢ The slow step in this solvent must be the formation of NO_2^+ or some other nitrating agent, which then attacks the aromatic ring in a faster step.

ARENES

11.97 Give three methods for introducing an alkyl side chain into the benzene nucleus and illustrate each method by preparing ethylbenzene.

◢ 1. Friedel–Crafts alkylation of benzene with (i) CH_3CH_2X, $AlCl_3$, (ii) $CH_2\!=\!CH_2$, HF, and (iii) CH_3CH_2OH, BF_3 or conc. H_2SO_4.
2. Friedel–Crafts acylation with CH_3COCl or $(CH_3CO)_2O$, $AlCl_3$ giving $PhCOCH_3$; followed by reduction of the $C\!=\!O$ to CH_2 (Problem 11.19).
3. Corey–House reaction of $Ph_2CuLi + CH_3CH_2Br$.

11.98 Summarize the limitations of the Friedel–Crafts alkylation reaction.

◢ (1) The entering alkyl group can rearrange. (2) The alkylbenzene is more reactive than benzene itself and can further alkylate, giving mixtures of monoalkylated and polyalkylated products. (Polyalkylation can be avoided by using an excess of the arene compared with the catalyst.) (3) Rearrangement of kinetically-controlled to thermodynamically-controlled product can occur, especially with 3° R's.

11.99 List the kinds of (*a*) aryl derivatives and (*b*) halides which cannot be used in Friedel–Crafts alkylations, and give your reasons.

◢ (*a*) Any substituent more deactivating than a halogen (i.e., NO_2, CF_3) makes the ring too electron-deficient to react. Amino groups are converted into strong electron-withdrawing groups by reaction with the Lewis acid catalyst:

$$\text{ArR}_2\text{N} + \text{AlCl}_3 \longrightarrow \text{ArR}_2\overset{+}{\text{N}}\!-\!\overset{-}{\text{AlCl}}_3 \qquad \text{and} \qquad \text{ArNH}_2 + \text{HF} \longrightarrow \text{ArNH}_3^+\text{F}^-$$

(*b*) Aryl and vinyl halides cannot be used because the $AlCl_3$ would have to generate a very unstable carbocation with a + charge on an sp^2 hybridized C.

11.100 Contrast the limitations of Friedel–Crafts acylations and alkylations.

◢ Rearrangement of the entering RCO group does not occur because the acylium ion is more stable than the alkyl cation; however, rearrangement of kinetic to thermodynamically more stable product can occur. Acylation gives a deactivated acylarene, which is not prone to further acylation. Aroylation with ArCOCl is a viable reaction.

11.101 (*a*) Explain why the acid chloride of formic acid, H—COCl, cannot be used to introduce the formyl group, —CH=O, into the ring by Friedel–Crafts acylation. (*b*) Give the industrial synthesis of PhCHO. (*c*) What is the electrophile in (*b*) and how is it formed?

    📕 (*a*) Formyl chloride itself is unstable, decomposing into CO + HCl.
    (*b*) In the *Gatterman–Koch* synthesis, a high pressure mixture of CO and HCl with $AlCl_3$ is used to synthesize benzaldehyde:

$$PhH + CO\,(g) + HCl\,(g) \xrightarrow{AlCl_3} PhCH=O + HAlCl_4$$

    (*c*) $HCl + AlCl_3 + :\overset{-}{C}\equiv\overset{+}{O}: \rightleftharpoons H-\overset{+}{C}=\overset{..}{O}:$ (E) $+ AlCl_4^-$

11.102 Offer a mechanism for the following *chloromethylation* reaction:

$$PhH + HCl \quad \text{and} \quad H_2C=O \xrightarrow{ZnCl_2} PhCH_2Cl + H_2O$$

    📕 The attacking species is $[H_2C=\overset{+}{O}H \longleftrightarrow H_2\overset{+}{C}-OH]$ **A**, formed by addition of H^+ to $H_2C=O$.

$$PhH + A \longrightarrow \left[\underset{Ph}{\overset{H\quad CH_2OH}{\diagdown\diagup}}\right]^+ \xrightarrow{-H^+} PhCH_2OH \xrightarrow{HCl/ZnCl_2} PhCH_2Cl + H_2O$$

11.103 (*a*) Compare the reactions of $PhCH_2CH_2CH_3$ with Br_2 (i) and Fe, (ii) with light or heat, and (iii) in the dark. (*b*) Give steps for the reaction in (ii).

    📕 (*a*) (i) Ring substitution by Br occurs at the *o* and *p* positions. (ii) Bromination of the side chain occurs at the benzylic position, the one α to Ph, giving $PhCHBrCH_2CH_3$. (iii) No reaction.
    (*b*) This is a radical chain reaction:

Initiation step: (1) $Br_2 \xrightarrow{light} 2Br\cdot$
Propagation steps: (2) $PhCH_2CH_2CH_3 + Br\cdot \longrightarrow HBr\ +$

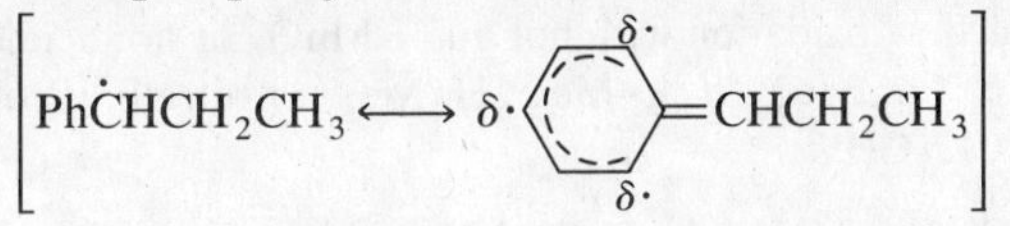

$$\left[Ph\overset{\cdot}{C}HCH_2CH_3 \longleftrightarrow \delta\cdot \underset{\delta\cdot}{\overset{\delta\cdot}{\langle\bigcirc\rangle}}=CHCH_2CH_3\right]$$

a benzylic radical with extensive π delocalization

    (3) $Ph\overset{\cdot}{C}HCH_2CH_3 + Br_2 \longrightarrow PhCHBrCH_2CH_3 + Br\cdot$

Reaction at the β or γ carbon of $PhCH_2CH_2CH_3$ would give $PhCH_2\overset{\cdot}{C}HCH_3$ or $PhCH_2CH_2\overset{\cdot}{C}H_2$ respectively, with no possible stabilization by delocalization.

11.104 How does the benzyl radical compare in stability with alkyl radicals mentioned previously?

    📕 Benzyl, allyl > 3° > 2° > 1° > Me > vinyl.

11.105 Compare the products of the reactions of $PhCH_2CH_3$ with Br_2 and Cl_2 in light, and explain any differences.

    📕 Bromination gives α-bromoethylbenzene exclusively [(ii) of Problem 11.103(*b*)]. The 2° benzylic position is only slightly favored over the 1° alkyl position in chlorination, the products being $PhCHClCH_3$ (56%) and $PhCH_2CH_2Cl$ (44%). The less reactive $Br\cdot$ is more selective than the $Cl\cdot$, which abstracts an $H\cdot$ in a more random fashion (Reactivity-Selectivity principle).

11.106 (*a*) Using the relative reactivities towards free radical chlorination of 3°:2°:1° H's as 5.0:3.8:1.0, calculate the predicted percentages of α- and β-chlorophenylethane (**A** and **B**) from $PhCH_2CH_3$. (*b*) Compare these calculated percentages yields with those reported in Problem 11.105 and give an explanation.

    📕 (*a*) $PhCHClCH_3$ (**A**): $2(3.8) = 7.6$; $7.6/(3.0 + 7.6) \times 100\% = 72\%$
            $PhCH_2CH_2Cl$ (**B**): $3(1.0) = 3.0$; $3.0/(3.0 + 7.6) \times 100\% = 28\%$
    (*b*) If abstraction of the benzylic $H\cdot$ from CH_2 had the same energy requirement as abstraction of a 2° $H\cdot$ of an alkane, the percentages would be 72% and 28%, respectively. The observed values of 56% vs. 44% indicate that in radical chlorinations the phenyl group diminishes the expected reactivity of the 2° H while leaving it more

reactive than the 1° H. Because abstraction of the benzylic 2° H· by the highly reactive Cl· is slightly exothermic, the TS more resembles the ground state reactants (Hammond postulate). In the ground state of $PhCH_2CH_3$, electron-withdrawal by Ph makes the abstraction of the benzylic H of CH_2 more difficult and less so the β-H of CH_3. Thus in $PhCH_2CH_3$ the difference in relative reactivities of 2° vs. 1° has narrowed. Note there is very little radical character in the TS, and factors that contribute to its stability by π delocalization are thus minimal. In this respect chlorination differs from bromination (Problem 11.103).

11.107 (*a*) Give the product of the reaction of *p*-xylene with NBS or with $2Br_2$, 125 °C, light. (*b*) Why does not dibromination at one Me occur? (*c*) Which reacts faster, *p*-xylene or toluene? Explain.

(*a*)

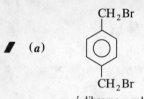

CH₂Br / CH₂Br

α-α'-dibromo-*p*-xylene

(*b*)   Electron-withdrawal by one Br makes removal of an additional H· more difficult.
(*c*)   *p*-Xylene; the electron-releasing Me provides additional stability to the radical.

11.108 Irradiation of an equimolar mixture of cyclohexane and $PhCH_3$ gives mostly cyclohexyl chloride with Cl_2, and $PhCH_2Br$ with Br_2. Explain.

In these competitive reactions the reactivities of cyclohexane and toluene are compared, Cl·, being more reactive and less selective than Br·, reacts with the kind of H present in greatest number, which in this case is one of the twelve equivalent H's of cyclohexane. The less reactive and more selective Br· reacts with the most reactive H, in this case one of the three alkyl H's of $PhCH_3$.

11.109 Give the products of the Friedel–Crafts reaction of benzene with (*a*) CH_2Cl_2, (*b*) $CHCl_3$, and (*c*) CCl_4.

It is usually impossible to stop these reactions after the addition of one equivalent of these polychloromethanes. The products are (*a*) Ph_2CH_2, (*b*) Ph_3CH, and (*c*) Ph_3CCl. In (*c*), the reaction stops after three rings have been substituted, mainly because of steric hindrance toward having four Ph's on a single C.

11.110 Provide the products of oxidation with hot alk. $KMnO_4$ or hot acidic $K_2Cr_2O_7$ of (*a*) m-$O_2NC_6H_4CH_2CH_2CH_3$, (*b*) $PhCHMe_2$, (*c*) $PhCMe_3$, (*d*) p-MeC_6H_4Me, (*e*) tetralin [Problem 10.32(*a*)(i)], and (*f*) $PhCH{=}CHCH_2CH_3$.

(*a*) m-$O_2NC_6H_4COOH$, (*b*) $PhCOOH$, (*c*) no reaction–benzylic H's are absent [see Problem 11.111(*a*)], (*d*) p-$C_6H_4(COOH)_2$, (*e*) o-$C_6H_4(COOH)_2$, and (*f*) $PhCOOH$.

11.111 (*a*) Give a general statement about the extent of the reaction in 11.110. (*b*) Explain why this oxidative process cannot be used if the ring also contains an OH or NH_2 substituent. (*c*) Why does oxidation of Me to COOH in *p*-nitrotoluene give better yields than in toluene?

(*a*) Oxidation to an aromatic acid occurs only when the alkyl side chain has a benzylic H. (*b*) These functional groups make the ring more labile to oxidative cleavage, and are themselves oxidized. (*c*) Oxidation of the ring requires electron removal and introduction of a + charge. NO_2 makes this more difficult, thereby stabilizing the ring toward oxidative cleavage.

11.112 In the oxidation of $PhCH_2Ph$ to $PhCOPh$ with CrO_3, a deuterium isotope effect of 6.4 is found. What does this say about the oxidation?

The slow step in the oxidation is cleavage of the C—H bond: $Ph_2CH_2 \rightarrow Ph_2CH\cdot$ or $PhCH_2^+$. This also explains the lack of reaction of $PhCMe_3$, with no benzylic H [Problem 11.110(*c*)].

11.113 Give the products, underlining and accounting for the major one, of dehydrohalogenation of

(*a*) $ArCH_2CHBrCH_2CH_2CH_3$,   (*c*) $CH_3CHArCHBrCH_2CH_3$,

(*b*) $CH_3CArBrCH_2CH_2CH_3$,   (*d*) $BrCH_2CHArCH_2CH_2CH_3$

(*a*) Conjugated <u>$ArCH{=}CHCH_2CH_2CH_3$</u> (more *E* than *Z*), unconjugated $ArCH_2CH{=}CHCH_2CH_3$.
(*b*) Conjugated, trisubstituted <u>$CH_3CAr{=}CHCH_2CH_3$</u> (more *E* than *Z*), conjugated disubstituted $H_2C{=}CArCH_2CH_2CH_3$.

(*c*) Conjugated $CH_3CAr{=}CHCH_2CH_3$, unconjugated $CH_3CHArCH{=}CHCH_3$.

(*d*) $H_2C{=}CArCH_2CH_2CH_3$. A 1° Br can give only a single product.

In general the most substituted, least sterically-hindered alkene (*E*) with its C=C conjugated with the ring is the major product because of its greatest stability. This stability is a factor in its faster rate of formation.

11.114 Give the principal product from dehydration of the alcohol corresponding to each bromide in Problem 11.113.

▮ (*a*) $ArCH{=}CHCH_2CH_2CH_3$ (more *E*); (*b*) and (*c*) $CH_3CAr{=}CHCH_2CH_3$ (more *E*); (*d*) after a :H shift, same as (*b*).

$$^{+}CH_2CHArCH_2CH_2CH_3 \xrightarrow{\sim H:} CH_3\overset{+}{C}ArCH_2CH_2CH_3 \xrightarrow{-H^+} CH_3CAr{=}CHCH_2CH_3$$

11.115 (*a*) Predict the order of relative reactivity of: benzyl chloride (**A**), *p*-methoxybenzyl chloride (**B**), and *p*-nitrobenzyl chloride (**C**) toward S_N1 reactions. (*b*) Repeat (*a*) for $PhCH_2Cl$ (**D**), PhCHClMe (**E**), and $PhCClMe_2$ (**F**) towards (i) S_N1 and (ii) S_N2 reactions. (*c*) Explain these relative orders.

▮ (*a*) **B > A > C**. (*b*) (i) **F > E > D** and (ii) **D > E > F**. (*c*) The order in (*a*) points to a positively-charged intermediate. The rates depend on the $\Delta H^{\ddagger}_{f}$'s of the intermediate benzylic cations, and thus on the relative energies of these cations (Hammond's principle). The benzylic cation is stabilized by virtue of its conjugation with the aromatic ring. Electron-donating CH_3O provides further stability through delocalization, and conversely, electron-withdrawing NO_2 diminishes its stability (Fig. 11-10). Adjacent + charges also increase stability. In (*b*) the typical orders for S_N1 (3° > 2° > 1°) and S_N2(1° > 2° > 3°) reactions prevail.

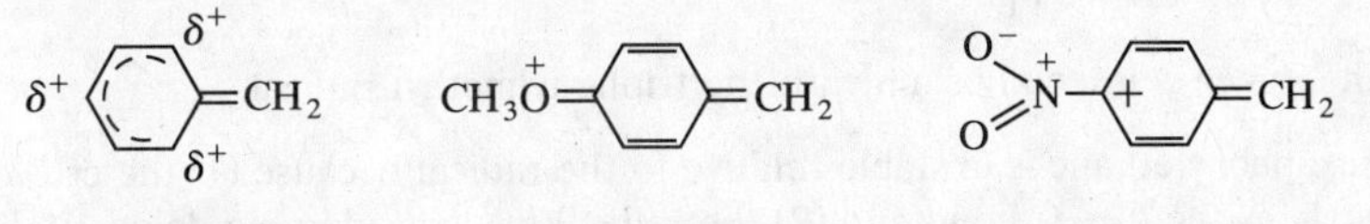

benzyl cation   *p*-methoxybenzyl cation   *p*-nitrobenzyl cation   **Fig. 11-10**

11.116 Provide the structure for the major product of each of the following reactions and justify your choice: (*a*) $PhCH{=}CHCH_2CH_3 + HBr$; (*b*) $PhCH{=}CHCH_2CH_3 + HBr$, peroxide; and (*c*) $PhCH{=}CHCH{=}CHCH_3 + H_2$, Pt (one eq. of each).

▮ (*a*) $PhCHBrCH_2CH_2CH_3$. Electrophilic addition of H^+ produces the more stable benzylic $Ph\overset{+}{C}HCH_2CH_2CH_3$ which then adds Br^-.

(*b*) $PhCH_2CHBrCH_2CH_3$. Br· adds to the *β*-C, forming the more stable benzylic $Ph\dot{C}HCHBrCH_2CH_3$ intermediate which then removes H· from HBr to propagate the chain.

(*c*) $PhCH{=}CHCH_2CH_3$. Unlike usual 1,4-additions to conjugated dienes (Problem 9.145), this is a 1,2-addition giving the product with the remaining C=C conjugated with the ring.

11.117 Provide the structures for the products of the reactions of *cis*-1-phenylpropene with: (*a*) cold, dil. $KMnO_4$, (*b*) cold, conc. H_2SO_4, (*c*) NBS, (*d*) O_3, then Zn in AcOH, (*e*) Br_2 in CCl_4, then 2 $NaNH_2$, and (*f*) BH_3/THF, then H_2O_2, OH^-.

▮ (*a*) *syn*-addition gives *erythro*-$PhCH(OH)CH(OH)CH_3$; (*b*) $PhCH(OSO_3H)CH_2CH_3$; (*c*) Allylic substitution gives *cis*-$PHCH{=}CHCH_2Br$ (the geometry of the C=C bond is preserved during allylic substitutions); (*d*) $PhCH{=}O + CH_3CH{=}O$; and (*e*) $PhC{\equiv}CCH_3$. (*f*) $PhCH_2CH(OH)CH_3 + PhCH(OH)CH_2CH_3$.

MISCELLANEOUS REACTIONS

11.118 Explain the radical addition of Cl_2 to benzene to give $C_6H_6Cl_6$.

▮

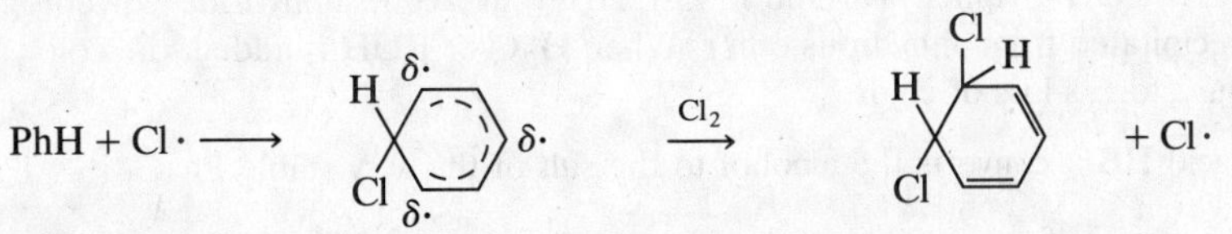

chlorocyclohexadienyl radical   1,2-Dichlorocyclohexadiene (A)

These are the chain propagating steps. **A** is no longer aromatic and, unlike PhH, rapidly adds Cl_2 to give $C_6H_6Cl_6$.

11.119 Why does Cl· not abstract an H· from PhH to give Ph· + HCl (Problem 11.118)?

▰ Delocalization of the odd e^- into the ring is not possible because the sp^2 orbital in which it is housed is at right angles to the cyclic π system and cannot overlap with it. See Problem 11.89(*a*) for a discussion of the corresponding anion. The homolytic bond dissociation energy for Ph—H is very high: ≈ 112 kcal/mol.

11.120 The reaction of Ph_3CCl with Ag or Zn gives a dimer, $(Ph_3C)_2$, originally incorrectly believed to be Ph_3CCPh_3. The dimer gives a yellow solution in benzene, which is decolorized by O_2 and X_2. (*a*) What structure is responsible for the color? (*b*) Why does the color disappear in (i) O_2 and (ii) I_2? (*c*) What is the structure of the dimer? (*d*) Account for the failure to synthesize hexaphenylethane.

▰ (*a*) $2Ph_3CCl + 2Ag \text{ (or Zn)} \longrightarrow [2Ph_3C\cdot \rightleftharpoons (Ph_3C)_2] + 2AgCl \text{ (or } ZnCl_2)$

　　　　　　　　　　　　　　　　　yellow　　　　dimer
　　　　　　　　　　　　　　　　　radical

(*b*)　(i) $2Ph_3C\cdot + O_2 \xrightarrow{0\,°C} Ph_3C—O—O—CPh_3$　　(ii) $Ph_3C\cdot \xrightarrow[0\,°C]{I_2}$　　$Ph_3C—I$

　　triphenylmethyl　　　　　a colorless peroxide　　　　　　　　　　　　colorless
　　radical　　　　　　　　　　　　　　　　　　　　　　　　　　　triphenyliodomethane

(*c*)

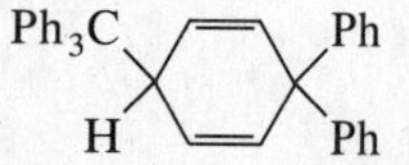

The dimer is in equilibrium with the triphenylmethyl radical.

(*d*) Hexaphenylethane is unstable relative to the radical because (1) the crowding of the six aromatic rings weakens the C—C bond and (2) the radical has considerable delocalization energy.

11.121 How may a free radical be detected instrumentally?

▰ The odd electron, by virtue of its unpaired spin, imparts a magnetic moment to the radical, making it *paramagnetic*, and attracted into a magnetic field. Also, the electron is responsible for a characteristic *electron spin resonance* or *paramagnetic resonance absorption* spectrum.

11.122 Ph· generated from benzoyl peroxide reacts with benzene to produce biphenyl (Ph—Ph) and a dimer. Show the steps in this reaction.

▰ *Step 1.* $PhCO—OCPh \longrightarrow 2PhCO\cdot \longrightarrow 2Ph\cdot + 2CO_2$
　　　　　　　　║　　║　　　　　　║
　　　　　　　　O　　O　　　　　　O

Step 2.   Ph· + PhH $\longrightarrow$

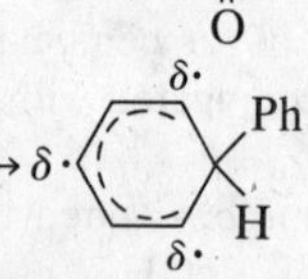

The radical intermediate from step 2 disproportionates (step 3) or combines (step 4).

Step 3.

Step 4.

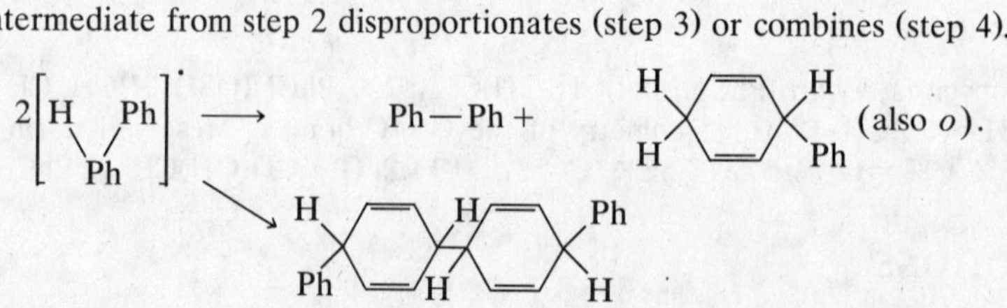

11.123 The reaction of Ph_3COH (triphenylcarbinol) with HBF_4 in acetic anhydride solvent gives a bright orange crystalline salt precipitated from anhydrous ether. When H_2O or ROH is added, the color is discharged. Identify the salt and account for its loss of color.

▰ The strong acid HBF_4 converts the alcohol to the salt of the very stable Ph_3C^+:

$$Ph_3C—OH + HBF_4 \longrightarrow Ph_3C^+BF_4^- + H_2O$$

bright orange

Ph_3C^+ owes its great stability to the delocalization of its $+$ charge into three aromatic rings. The addition of H_2O or ROH converts the ion to Ph_3COH and Ph_3COR, respectively. For example,

$$Ph_3C^+BF_4^- + ROH \rightleftharpoons Ph_3COR + HBF_4$$
$$\text{colorless}$$

11.124 Crystal violet, $(p\text{-}Me_2N\text{—}C_6H_4)_3C^+Cl^-$ (a salt), is an example of a triphenylmethane dye. Explain how the $p\text{-}NMe_2$ group further stabilize the triarylcation.

� Electron-donating groups such as NMe_2 in the *para* positions further delocalize the $+$ charge, augmenting the stability of the triarylcation (Fig. 11-11).

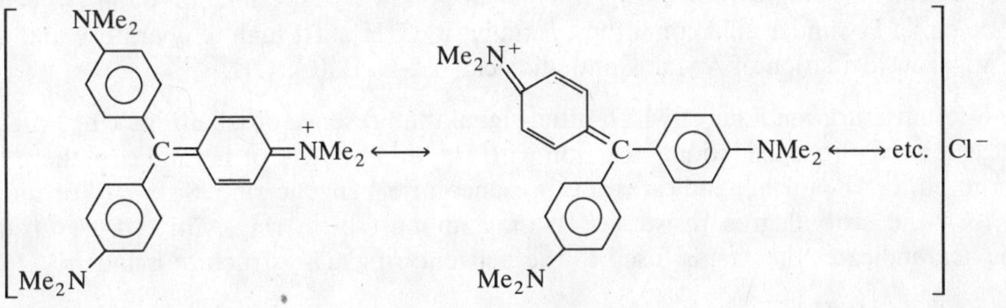

Fig. 11-11

11.125 An ether solution of Ph_3CCl, stirred with a strong reducing agent like Na/Hg (sodium amalgam), develops a deep-red color that is discharged almost immediately when H_2O or ROH is added. Account for the colored solution and its decolorization.

▌ $$Ph_3CCl \xrightarrow[-NaCl]{2Na/Hg \text{ in ether}} Ph_3C:^- Na^+ \xrightarrow{ROH} Ph_3CH + RO^-Na^+$$

$$\text{triphenylmethylsodium,} \qquad \text{colorless}$$
$$\text{red}$$

The triphenylmethyl (trityl) anion is unusually stable because of delocalization of the $-$ charge to three rings. This stabilization is analogous to that of the corresponding cation (Problem 11.123). The strongly basic carbanion accepts H^+ from either the weakly acidic H_2O or ROH giving colorless Ph_3CH.

ANALYSIS

11.126 Distinguish between $PhCH_2CH_3$ and the following compounds by simple test-tube reactions. Describe your observations.
(*a*) Ethylcyclohexane, (*b*) $PhCH=CH_2$, (*c*) $PHCHClCH_3$, and (*d*) $PhCMe_3$.

▌ (*a*) $PhCH_2CH_3$ dissolves in (is protonated by) cold conc. H_2SO_4, unlike the alkane. Alternately, see Problem 11.128. The alkane does not react. (*b*) Only the alkene decolorizes Br_2 in CCl_4 or is oxidized by purple $KMnO_4$, bleaching its color. (*c*) Only the halide gives a white precipitate of AgBr on addition of alcoholic $AgNO_3$. (*d*) PhEt, with a benzylic H, is oxidized by alc. $KMnO_4$ to PhCOOH, which may be precipitated upon acidification. The purple color of MnO_4^- disappears. If $Cr_2O_7^{2-}$ is the oxidant, the color change is from orange to green (Cr^{3+}).

11.127 Supply simple test-tube reactions to distinguish between (*a*) *m*-bromotoluene and benzyl bromide, (*b*) *p*-chloro-anisole and *p*-nitrochlorobenzene, and (*c*) phenylacetylene and styrene.

▌ (*a*) Addition of alcoholic $AgNO_3$ results in a precipitate of AgBr with benzyl bromide only. (*b*) The Cl in *p*-nitrochlorobenzene is activated by the NO_2 to nucleophilic displacement. First add NaOEt, and then the displaced Cl^- forms a white precipitate with $AgNO_3$ in EtOH. (*c*) The acetylenic H reacts with Ag^+ or Cu^+ to give a precipitate of $PhC\equiv CM$ (M = Ag or Cu). Alternately, addition of an active metal (Na or K) or $LiNH_2$ to $PhC\equiv CH$ only releases $H_2(g)$ or $NH_3(g)$, respectively.

11.128 Explain how alkylbenzene, naphthalene, anthracene, and phenanthrene can be distinguished from one another by a Friedel–Crafts reaction?

▮ Any aromatic compound that can be alkylated in a Friedel–Crafts reaction gives a distinctive color when reacted with $CHCl_3$ and $AlCl_3$. The color is due to formation of $Ar_3C^+AlCl_4^-$, possibly formed as follows:

$$ArH \xrightarrow[AlCl_3]{CHCl_3} ArCHCl_2 \xrightarrow[AlCl_3]{ArH} Ar_2CHCl \begin{cases} \xrightarrow[AlCl_3]{ArH} Ar_3CH \\ \xrightarrow{AlCl_3} Ar_2CH^+AlCl_4^- \end{cases} \longrightarrow Ar_2CH_2 + \underset{\text{colored salt}}{Ar_3C^+AlCl_4^-}$$

Benzene derivatives give an orange-to-red color; naphthalenes, blue; anthracenes, green; and phenanthrenes, purple.

11.129 Deduce the structure of compound **A**, C_9H_8, from the following experimental data: **A** decolorizes Br_2 in CCl_4, and adds one eq. of H_2 under mild conditions, forming **B**, C_9H_{10}. At high temperature and pressure, **A** adds four eq. of H_2. Vigorous oxidation of **A** yields phthalic acid, $1,2\text{-}C_6H_4(COOH)_2$.

▮ **A** has 6° of unsaturation, four of which often signal the presence of a benzene ring, as confirmed by isolation of phthalic acid on vigorous oxidation. Reaction with Br_2 and one eq. of H_2 indicate there is a C=C. Addition of three more eq. of H_2 further indicates the presence of a benzene ring. So far 5° of unsaturation have been accounted for—the sixth degree resists reduction and must be a ring with C=C. Oxidation to the *ortho*-dicarboxylic acid indicates the ring is fused to the benzene ring. The structure is indene.

Phthalic acid   Indene, **A**   Indane, **B**   Bicyclo[4.3.0]nonane

11.130 Identify (*a*) the chiral compound **C**, $C_{10}H_{14}$, that is oxidized with alk. $KMnO_4$ to PhCOOH, and (*b*) the achiral compound **D**, $C_{10}H_{14}$, inert to oxidation under the same conditions.

▮ (*a*) **C** is a monoalkyl substituted benzene with four C's in the side chain. The only R with four C's, one of which is a chiral center, is $-CH(CH_3)CH_2CH_3$; **C** is *sec*-butylbenzene, $PhCH(CH_3)CH_2CH_3$. (*b*) Any R attached to the benzene ring cannot have a benzylic H (no oxidation); **D** is *tert*-butylbenzene, $PhCMe_3$.

11.131 (*a*) Give the structures for all possible chiral compounds, $C_{10}H_{12}$, that do not decolorize Br_2 and that can be oxidized to phthalic acid. (*b*) Identify **E**, also chiral, with the same formula, but which is oxidized to PhCOOH.

▮ (*a*) The formula reveals a fifth degree of unsaturation in addition to the four of the benzene ring. This fifth degree of unsaturation must be a ring, not C=C, because the Br_2 test is negative. Production of phthalic acid means the ring is fused to the benzene ring. This fused ring has the chiral carbon and must be a mono-R-substituted five-membered or di-R-substituted four-membered ring. Only in this way can we account for the additional four C's of the formula.

1-Methylindane   *trans*-1,2-Dimethylbenzcyclobutane   1-Ethylbenzcyclobutane

(*b*) The extra unsaturation is in the single side chain: **E** is 3-phenyl-1-butene, $CH_3CHCH=CH_2$ with Ph on the CH.

11.132 Identify **F-I**, all with the formula C_8H_9Br, and **J**, C_8H_8, given that: (1) only **F** and **I** give instant precipitates with alc. $AgNO_3$; (2) both **F** and **G** react with OMe^- giving **J** that decolorizes Br_2; (3) oxidation of **H** with alkaline MnO_4^- gives the monocarboxylic acid synthesized by bromination of benzoic acid; and (4) **I** is oxidized to phthalic acid, $o\text{-}C_6H_4(COOH)_2$.

▮ Both **F** and **I** are benzylic bromides because they rapidly precipitate AgBr with $AgNO_3$. **F** and **G** are ethylbenzenes with Br in isomeric positions on the side chain. Elimination of HBr from both **F** and **G** gives the alkene (decolorizes Br_2), **J**, whose formula is $PhCH=CH_2$. **F** is $PhCHBrCH_3$ and **G** is thus $PhCH_2CH_2Br$, which only precipitates AgBr after prolonged heating. **H** is $m\text{-}CH_3CH_2-C_6H_4Br$ which on oxidation gives

m-BrC$_6$H$_4$COOH, the product of bromination of benzoic acid. **I** is o-CH$_3$C$_6$H$_4$CH$_2$Br which is oxidized to phthalic acid.

SUPPLEMENTARY PROBLEMS

11.133 (*a*) Why is the oxidation of an alkylarene to ArCOOH (Problem 11.110) difficult to carry out experimentally? (*b*) Explain how (i) a quaternary ammonium salt and (ii) a crown ether catalyzes the reaction.

◢ (*a*) The aqueous phase contains the oxidant, usually KMnO$_4$ or K$_2$CrO$_7$. The arene is usually insoluble in this phase, and is found in the organic phase—benzene, CHCl$_3$, etc. The reaction is therefore restricted to the only point of contact—the interface of the two solvents. Vigorous stirring and lengthy reaction times can slightly increase the yields.

(*b*) (i) The quaternary ammonium salt, R$_4$N$^+$X$^-$, is a phase-transfer catalyst (Problem 8.131) present in very small amounts. Because of its four large groups, R$_4$N$^+$ tends to be somewhat soluble in the organic phase to which it transports a counterion which may be X$^-$ or MnO$_4^-$, the oxidant. When R$_4$N$^+$ returns to the aqueous phase, it carries back X$^-$, ArCOO$^-$, or OH$^-$ (a product). This exchange between phases is repeated until all the arene is oxidized.

(ii) A crown ether (Problem 14.45) is a cyclic polymer of ethylene glycol, HOCH$_2$CH$_2$OH, which is soluble in organic solvents. It acts as a *host*, enclosing a cation (the *guest*) within its cavity by coordination of its O's with the M$^+$. 18-Crown-6 has a cavity of the proper size to enclose K$^+$, and in this positively-charged form attracts MnO$_4^-$ and transports it from the water into the organic phase, where it reacts.

11.134 Rank each of these species in order of decreasing reactivity to electrophilic substitution: PhMe, PhNMe$_2$, PhNMe$_3^+$, PhCH$_2$NMe$_3^+$.

◢ PhNMe$_2$ > PhMe > PhCH$_2$NMe$_3^+$ > PhNMe$_3^+$. As the number of sp^3 hybridized C's separating the aromatic ring from the positively-charged substituent increases, the deactivating effect decreases (Problem 11.50).

11.135 Prepare (*a*) PhCH$_2$Ph, (*b*) Ph(CH$_2$)$_2$Ph, (*c*) Ph(CH$_2$)$_3$Ph, and (*d*) Ph(CH$_2$)$_4$Ph from benzene, toluene, aliphatic, and inorganic reagents.

◢ (*a*) PhH + CH$_2$Cl$_2$ $\xrightarrow{\text{AlCl}_3}$ PhCH$_2$Ph

(*b*) PhCH$_3$ $\xrightarrow{\text{NBS}}$ PhCH$_2$Br $\xrightarrow[\text{2. CuI}]{\substack{\text{1. Li}\\ \text{3. PhCH}_2\text{Br}}}$ PhCH$_2$CH$_2$Ph or ClCH$_2$CH$_2$Cl + 2PhH $\xrightarrow{\text{2AlCl}_3}$ product

(*c*) PhH + CH$_2$—CH$_2$ (O) $\xrightarrow{\text{AlCl}_3}$ PhCH$_2$CH$_2$OH $\xrightarrow{\text{PBr}_3}$ PhCH$_2$CH$_2$Br $\xrightarrow[\text{2. CuI}]{\substack{\text{1. Li}\\ \text{3. PhCH}_2\text{Br}}}$ PhCH$_2$CH$_2$CH$_2$Ph

(*d*) PhCH$_2$CH$_2$Br $\xrightarrow[\text{2. CuI}]{\substack{\text{1. Li}\\ \text{3. PhCH}_2\text{CH}_2\text{Br}}}$ PhCH$_2$CH$_2$CH$_2$CH$_2$Ph

11.136 Prepare (*a*) PhCH$_2$CH$_2$D, (*b*) PhCHDCH$_3$, and (*c*) p-DC$_6$H$_4$CH$_2$CH$_3$.

◢ In each case, a halogen in the desired deuterated position is converted to the Grignard reagent and reduced with D$_2$O. In (*a*) and (*b*), reduction may also occur with LiAlD$_4$.

(*a*) PhCH$_2$CH$_2$Br [from Problem 11.135(*c*)] $\xrightarrow[\text{2. D}_2\text{O}]{\text{1. Mg, ether}}$ PhCH$_2$CH$_2$D

(*b*) PhCH$_2$CH$_3$ [from Problem 11.17(*c*)] $\xrightarrow{\text{NBS}}$ PhCHBrCH$_3$ $\xrightarrow[\text{2. D}_2\text{O}]{\text{1. Mg, ether}}$ PhCHDCH$_3$

(*c*) PhCH$_2$CH$_3$ $\xrightarrow{\substack{\text{Br}_2\\ \text{Fe}}}$ p-BrC$_6$H$_4$CH$_2$CH$_3$ $\xrightarrow[\text{2. D}_2\text{O}]{\text{1. Mg, ether}}$ p-DC$_6$H$_4$CH$_2$CH$_3$

11.137 Give the product and an explanation for the orientation in each of the following reactions.
(*a*) 1-Methylnaphthalene + (CH$_3$CO)$_2$O, AlCl$_3$, CS$_2$ (*c*) 2-Methoxynaphthalene + HNO$_3$, H$_2$SO$_4$
(*b*) 2-Nitronaphthalene + Br$_2$, Fe (*d*) 1-Bromonaphthalene + CH$_2$=CH$_2$, HF

◢ Refer to the rules in Problem 11.73 and the explanations in Problem 11.74. (*a*) 1-Methyl-4-acetonaphthalene, (*b*) 1-bromo-6-nitronaphthalene, (*c*) 1-nitro-2-methoxynaphthalene, (*d*) 1-bromo-5-ethylnaphthalene.

11.138 Prepare 1-bromo-7-methylnaphthalene (**G**) from 2-methylnaphthalene (**H**).

▸ The direct bromination of **H** produces the wrong isomer, 1-bromo-2-methylnaphthalene [Problem 11.75(*b*)]. However, the 1 position can be blocked with SO_3H, a deactivating group.

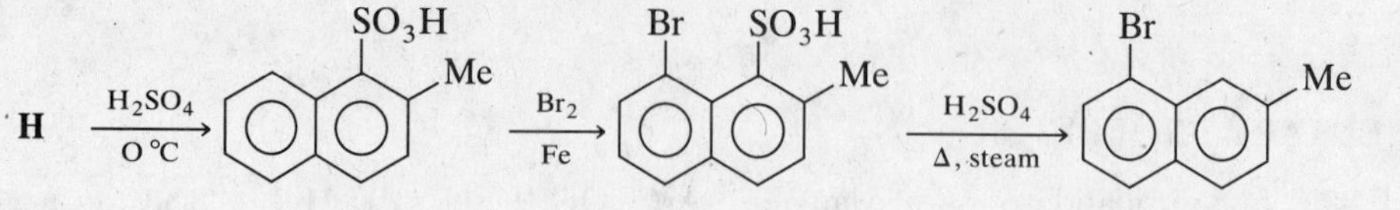

11.139 Give the structures for compounds **A–F** in the following reactions.

$$PhH + \alpha\text{-methylsuccinic anhydride} \xrightarrow{AlCl_3} A \xrightarrow[HCl]{Zn/Hg} B \xrightarrow{SOCl_2} C \xrightarrow{AlCl_3} D \xrightarrow[HCl]{Zn/Hg} E \xrightarrow[-2H_2]{Pd, \Delta} F$$

[*Hint*: See Problems 11.19(*d*) and 11.77.]

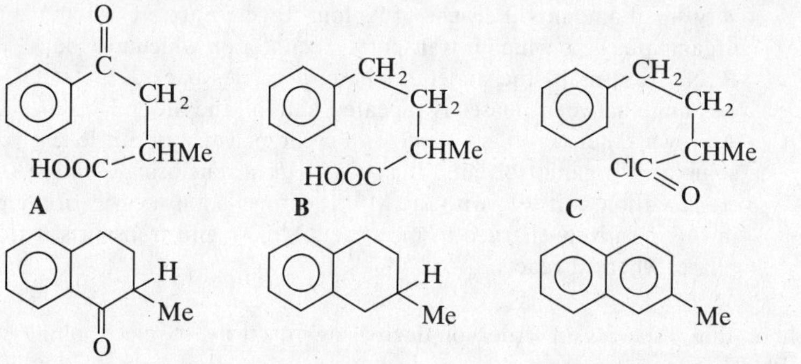

▰

Note: Benzene bonds to the less hindered acylium carbon after the anhydride is attacked by $AlCl_3$.

11.140 What is the product of heating (*a*) PhI and (*b*) $o\text{-}O_2NC_6H_4I$ with Cu?

▸ In these *Ullmann reactions* coupling occurs, giving biaryls. (*a*) Biphenyl, Ph—Ph and

(*b*) 2,2′-dinitrobiphenyl,

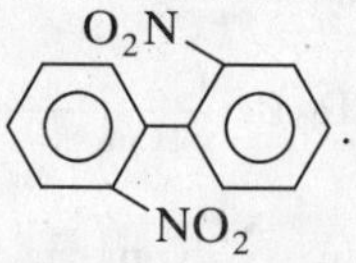

11.141 When the Ullmann reaction is carried out on 1-bromo-2-ethylnaphthalene, the product **A**, resolvable into enantiomers, is obtained. (*a*) What is **A**, and why is it chiral? (*b*) Synthesize 1-bromo-2-ethylnaphthalene.

▸ (*a*) The biaryl is sterically crowded because of the bulky *ortho*-substituents (see Problem 6.111). Therefore the aryl rings cannot be coplanar, and the energy barrier to rotation about the σ bond is too high for interconversion of enantiomers. The enantiomers are isolable at room temperatures.

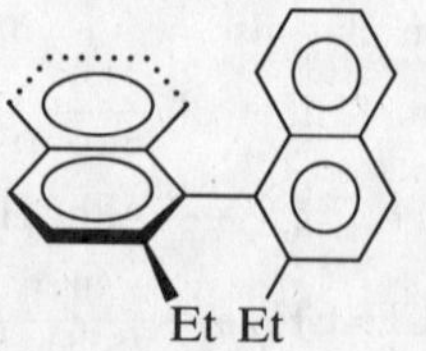

A (+ mirror image)

(*b*) $\text{Naphthalene} + CH_3COCl \xrightarrow[PhNO_2]{AlCl_3} \text{2-acetonaphthalene} \xrightarrow[HCl]{Zn/Hg} \text{2-ethylnaphthalene} \xrightarrow[Fe]{Br_2}$

1-bromo-2-ethylnaphthalene

11.142 Give the structure of DDT: $2\ PhCl + Cl_3CCH(OH)_2$ (chloral hydrate) $\xrightarrow{H_2SO_4}$ DDT.

▸ The C^+ formed in the presence of acid ($Cl_3C\overset{+}{C}HOH$) alkylates PhCl in the *p* position, giving initially $p\text{-}ClC_6H_4CH(OH)CCl_3$. This reacts further with H^+, forming $p\text{-}ClC_6H_4\overset{+}{C}HCCl_3$, which alkylates a second PhCl, giving DDT: $(p\text{-}ClC_6H_4)_2CHCCl_3$ and some *o,p*′.

11.143 Account for slow rate of addition and the anti-Markovnikov product:

$$F_3CCH{=}CH_2 + HBr(AlBr_3) \longrightarrow F_3CCH_2CH_2Br$$

▞ The two possible C^+'s from addition of H^+ are **A** and **B**. Although **A** is a $2°\ C^+$, it has a higher energy than **B**, a $1°\ C^+$, because of the proximity of its $+$ charge to the strongly electron-withdrawing CF_3 group. Note that the inductive effect of CF_3 makes the π electrons less available, and the $C{=}C$ less nucleophilic and reactive. $AlBr_3$ is needed to increase the reactivity of HBr.

$$\overset{+}{F_3CCHCH_3} \qquad\qquad F_3CCH_2CH_2^+$$

$$\textbf{A} \qquad\qquad\qquad\quad \textbf{B}$$

11.144 (*a*) What is a *partial-rate factor* as related to orientations of electrophilic substitution of benzene derivatives (PhG)? (*b*) How are partial-rate factors for PhG experimentally determined?

▞ (*a*) A partial-rate factor f is the rate of reaction at the o, m, and p positions in PhG relative to benzene for a particular electrophilic substitution. (*b*) Two kinds of information are needed: (1) The relative rates of reaction of PhH and PhG are measured by reacting an equimolar mixture of PhH and PhG with an insufficient amount of the electrophilic reagent so that the two compounds compete for the reagent under identical conditions. (2) The proportion of isomers produced from the reaction of PhG is usually determined by separation techniques followed by spectrometric procedures.

11.145 Nitration of PhMe with HNO_3 in acetic acid solvent at 45 °C occurs 25 times faster than nitration of PhH under the same conditions, and the product percentages are: *ortho*, 56.5; *meta*, 3.5; and *para*, 40.0. (*a*) Calculate the partial-rate factor for each position in toluene. (*b*) Explain these values. (*c*) Can these values be used for other electrophilic substitution reactions of toluene? Explain.

▞ (*a*) Let the rate of nitration at any one position in benzene be equal to one. Then because there are six equivalent positions, the rate for benzene as a whole is six. Since toluene reacts 25 times faster than benzene, the relative rate for toluene is $6(25) = 150$. Of the total relative rate for toluene, 56.5% is due to reaction at two equivalent *ortho* positions; thus for this position the partial-rate factor, $f_o = (150 \times 0.565)/2 = 42.4$. Similarly, $f_m = (150 \times 0.035)/2 = 2.6$; and $f_p = (150 \times 0.400)/1 = 60.0$. (*b*) An $f > 1.0$ signifies activation, and an $f < 1$ implies deactivation in replacing H at that position. Since all f's > 1, Me activates all positions relative to benzene, but *meta* less than *ortho* and *para*. The lower f_o compared to f_p may be due to steric effects. (*c*) No. Partial-rate factors differ with the kind of electrophilic substitution and even depend on the conditions used. Regardless of the reaction, the rate for benzene as a whole always equals six.

11.146 The values for nitration of *t*-butylbenzene are $f_o = 4.5$, $f_m = 3.0$, and $f_p = 75$. (*a*) How much more reactive is *t*-butylbenzene than benzene? (*b*) What are the percentage yields of the nitration isomers of *t*-butylbenzene?

▞ (*a*) Find the total reactivity of all positions in *t*-butylbenzene and divide by six, the total reactivity of benzene:

$$\frac{t\text{-BuPh}}{\text{PhH}} = \frac{2(4.5) + 2(3.0) + 75}{6(1)} = \frac{90}{6} = 15$$

Thus *t*-BuPh is nitrated 15 times faster than PhH.

(*b*) Multiply the f value for each position by the number of equivalent positions, divide by the sum of the reactivities for all three positions [see (*a*)], and convert to percentage.

$$ortho: \frac{2(4.5)}{90}100\% = 10\% \qquad meta: \frac{2(3.0)}{90}100\% = 6.7\% \qquad para: \frac{1(75)}{90}100\% = 83\%$$

11.147 In terms of electronic effects account for the following f values for nitration of benzyl chloride: $f_o = 0.290$, $f_m = 0.127$, $f_p = 0.978$ as compared to those of toluene (Problem 11.145).

▞ Whereas toluene is activated at each position because of the electron-donating inductive effect of Me, $PhCH_2Cl$ is deactivated at each position. Apparently, Cl makes the entire $-CH_2Cl$ electron-withdrawing and deactivating. However, since $f_o, f_p > f_m$, $-CH_2Cl$ is still an o-,p-director. Hyperconjugation (Problem 11.62), which is manifest when o,p positions are attacked, still prevails.

CHAPTER 12
Spectroscopy and Structure Proof

INTRODUCTION

12.1 Characterize electromagnetic radiation, commonly called light.

▮ *Electromagnetic radiation* is the transmission of energy. It has a dual nature: in some experiments it obeys wave theory and in others acts as a stream of massless particles.

12.2 What is a photon and why is it sometimes called a quantum?

▮ The *photon* is the massless particle of radiation. Radiation is emitted, transmitted, and absorbed only in whole numbers of photons. Hence, light is quantized and the photon is also called a *quantum*.

12.3 Draw a diagram of a wave, indicating the wavelength (λ), cycle, and amplitude (A).

▮ See Fig. 12-1.

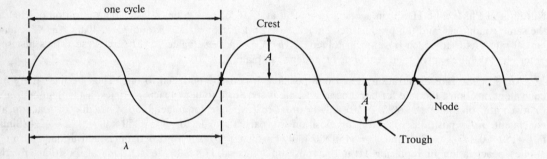

Fig. 12-1

12.4 (*a*) Define (i) the period and (ii) the frequency of a wave. (*b*) Give the mathematical relationship between frequency and wavelength.

▮ (*a*) (i) The *period* (T) is the time required to complete one full cycle; the unit is s/cycle. (ii) The *frequency* (ν) is the number of cycles that occur per second. It is also the number of waves passing through a given point in a second; the unit is cycles/s (s^{-1}) or hertz (Hz). When referring to λ, T, and ν, the word cycle is understood and often dropped. (*b*) $\nu\lambda = c$, where c = speed of light in vacuum = 3.0×10^8 m/s; the longer the wavelength, the smaller is the frequency, and vice versa.

12.5 (*a*) Give the relationship between frequency and energy (E) of a wave. (*b*) How are its wavelength and energy related?

▮ (*a*) Frequency and energy of a wave are related by the equation $E = h\nu$, where h ($= 6.63 \times 10^{-34}$ J·s/particle) is *Planck's constant*. (In this context, the particle is a photon.) Thus, the greater the frequency, the higher is the energy of the radiation. (*b*) Since wavelength and frequency are inversely related, the longer the wavelength, the smaller is the energy: $E = hc/\lambda$.

12.6 Calculate the frequencies of violet and red light if their wavelengths are 400 and 750 nm, respectively.

▮ The wavelengths are substituted into the equation $\nu = c/\lambda$ (see Problem 12.4). Thus

$$\text{Violet:} \quad \nu = \frac{3.0 \times 10^8 \text{ m/s}}{(400 \text{ nm})(10^{-9} \text{ m/1 nm})} = 7.5 \times 10^{14} \text{ s}^{-1} = 750 \text{ THz}$$

$$\text{Red:} \quad \nu = \frac{3.0 \times 10^8 \text{ m/s}}{(750 \text{ nm})(10^{-9} \text{ m/1 nm})} = 4.0 \times 10^{14} \text{ s}^{-1} = 400 \text{ THz}$$

where 1 THz = 10^{12} Hz. Violet light has the shorter wavelength and higher frequency.

12.7 (*a*) Calculate and compare the energies of the photons in Problem 12.6. (*b*) What is the energy of the red light in (i) kJ/mol and (ii) kcal/mol?

◣ (*a*) Substitute the frequencies from Problem 12.6 into the equation $E = h\nu$ [see Problem 12.5(*a*)]. Thus,

$$\text{Violet:} \quad E = (6.63 \times 10^{-34}\ \text{J}\cdot\text{s})(7.5 \times 10^{14}\ \text{s}^{-1}) = 5.0 \times 10^{-19}\ \text{J}$$

$$\text{Red:} \quad E = (6.63 \times 10^{-34}\ \text{J}\cdot\text{s})(4.0 \times 10^{14}\ \text{s}^{-1}) = 2.6 \times 10^{-19}\ \text{J}$$

(In this calculation, the particle, the photon, referred to in the unit for *h* is often omitted. The actual values have the unit of J/photon.) Photons of violet light have more energy than those of red light.

(*b*) (i) $(2.6 \times 10^{-19}\ \text{J/photon})(6.02 \times 10^{23}\ \text{photons/mol})(1\ \text{kJ}/1000\ \text{J}) = 1.6 \times 10^{2}\ \text{kJ/mol}$.

(ii) $(1.6 \times 10^{2}\ \text{kJ/mol})(1\ \text{kcal}/4.184\ \text{kJ}) = 37\ \text{kcal/mol}$.

12.8 List the regions in the spectrum of radiation in order of decreasing energy.

◣
decreasing energy
——→
γ-rays > X-rays > ultraviolet (uv) > visible > infrared (ir) > microwave > radio
(far uv > near uv)   (high > low)

Visible light is the narrowest region in the electromagnetic spectrum.

12.9 (*a*) List the colors in the spectrum of visible light in decreasing order of energy. (*b*) Give the pairs of complementary colors.

◣ (*a*)
decreasing energy
————————————————————————→
violet > blue > green > yellow > orange > red

(*b*) violet and yellow; blue and orange; red and green

12.10 (*a*) Define the term wave number, a way of often expressing frequency in infrared spectroscopy. (*b*) Given two waves with $\lambda_1 = 10^4$ nm, and $\lambda_2 = 4\ \mu$m, respectively, find the corresponding wave numbers.

◣ (*a*) The *wave number*, $\bar{\nu}$, is defined as $1/\lambda$. The most common unit of $\bar{\nu}$ is cm^{-1}, called a *reciprocal centimeter*.

(*b*) First convert the values of λ_1 and λ_2 to cm.
$\lambda_1 = 10^4$ nm $\times 10^{-9}$ m/nm $\times 10^{2}$ cm/m $= 10^{-3}$ cm; then $\bar{\nu} = 1/10^{-3}$ cm $= 10^{3}\ \text{cm}^{-1}$
$\lambda_2 = 4\ \mu$m $\times 10^{-6}$ m/μm $\times 10^{2}$ cm/m $= 4 \times 10^{-4}$ cm; then $\bar{\nu} = 1/(4 \times 10^{-4}$ cm$) = 2.5 \times 10^{3}\ \text{cm}^{-1}$

12.11 Describe the basic process used in spectroscopy.

◣ The basic process is the interaction between radiation and molecules or ions. Such species possess certain quantized energies. These energies can be raised (excited) from their ground states. This absorption is then measured in an instrument called a *spectrophotometer* (or spectrometer).

12.12 (*a*) What factor determines the wavelength of light absorbed? (*b*) Explain why the absorption spectrum for each molecule is unique. (*c*) Referring to the energy levels for a hypothetical molecule in Fig. 12-2, which transition would result from the absorption of light by the ground state (E_0) of (i) the shortest wavelength and (ii) the longest wavelength? (*d*) Which absorption from any energy level gives rise to the longest wavelength?

◣ (*a*) The difference between the lower energy level (usually the ground state) and a higher one. (*b*) Each molecule has its unique differences between its energy levels. (*c*) (i) $E_0 \rightarrow E_3$, (ii) $E_0 \rightarrow E_1$. (*d*) $E_2 \rightarrow E_3$.

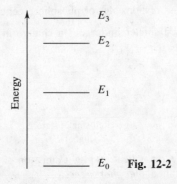

Fig. 12-2

12.13 Give a brief description of how a typical spectrophotometer functions.

▰ A compound is exposed to light with a continuous spread in wavelength (occasionally frequency) from an appropriate light source. The absorption of photons at each wavelength is detected. This procedure is called *absorption spectroscopy* and the *spectrum* of the absorbed photons is recorded on a chart against the wavelength or frequency. Absorption peaks are plotted as minima in ir spectroscopy and usually as maxima in uv spectroscopy. The spectrum may be a plot of absorbance (see Problem 12.27) or transmittance.

ULTRAVIOLET AND VISIBLE SPECTROSCOPY (ELECTRON EXCITATION)

12.14 Identify the molecular energy state which is excited by radiation in the ultraviolet and visible region.

▰ Electronic energy state. These radiations cause an electron transition from the ground state to an excited state. More specifically, the e^- goes from an occupied MO (bonding or nonbonding) to an unoccupied antibonding MO*. The larger the energy gap between the ground and excited states, the shorter must be the wavelength and the higher must be the energy and frequency of the radiation.

12.15 (*a*) Can a molecule undergo more than one electronic excitation? (*b*) Are all the molecules of a substance that are exposed to a specific radiation excited? (*c*) What happens to the excited molecules when the radiation is removed?

▰ (*a*) Yes; see Problem 12.12. (*b*) No; absorption is a random event. Relatively few molecules may be excited. *Intensity* is a measure of the concentration of excited molecules [see Problem 12.27(*c*)]. (*c*) The excited molecules give off energy and return to the ground state, or may undergo chemical change, e.g., *cis-trans* isomerism of an alkene. The return to the ground state is called *deactivation*.

12.16 Can (*a*) ionization of a molecule and (*b*) breaking of a σ bond occur in the uv region? (*c*) Bonds between what kind of atoms may break when the atoms are exposed to uv or visible radiation?

▰ (*a*) No. Ionization requires a departing excited electron to overcome the attraction of the nucleus. The energy required for this process is provided only in the high frequency X-ray and γ-ray regions of the electromagnetic spectrum. (*b*) Yes. Bonds with low bond energies may be broken. (*c*) Typically, bonds between atoms, each of which have at least one pair of unshared electrons $\left(-\overset{..}{\underset{..}{O}}-\overset{..}{\underset{..}{O}}-, :\overset{..}{\underset{..}{X}}-\overset{..}{\underset{..}{X}}:, -\overset{..}{\underset{..}{O}}-\overset{..}{\underset{..}{X}}:, -\overset{..}{\underset{|}{N}}-\overset{..}{\underset{..}{X}}:\right)$ may break.

12.17 Which spin state is observed at the instant of excitation?

▰ Since excitation occurs so rapidly ($< 10^{-13}$ s), the excited electron's spin orientation does not change. A singlet ground state (S_0) gives rise to a singlet excited state (S_1) (called the Franck–Condon effect).

12.18 Explain how an electronically excited species returns to the ground state producing only heat.

▰ It can lose all its excess energy through collisions with other molecules; the released energy appears as heat.

12.19 Describe the deactivation process responsible for fluorescence.

▰ The S_1 state releases part of its excess energy as heat and the rest by photon emission as it returns to the S_0 state. The emitted radiation has a lower energy and thus a longer wavelength than the originally absorbed radiation. This emitted radiation is called *fluorescence*. This process is the basis for *fluorescence spectroscopy*.

12.20 Describe the deactivation process responsible for phosphorescence.

▰ The initially formed excited singlet undergoes a change in spin orientation (*intersystem crossing*), to the *lower* energy excited triplet state ($S_1 \rightarrow T_1$):

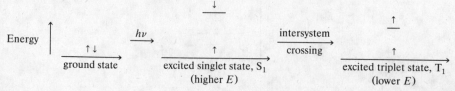

T_1 can lose energy by heat alone, or by heat and light emission of lower frequency on returning to the S_0 ground state. This emission of light is called *phosphorescence*.

12.21 (*a*) Give the observed difference between fluorescence and phosphorescence. (*b*) Account for this difference in terms of the two spin states. (*c*) Why are $S_1 \rightarrow T_1$ transitions infrequent?

◢ (*a*) A molecule fluoresces only while exposed to the exciting radiation. Fluorescence stops when the light is removed. Phosphorescence persists in the dark even after the removal of the source of absorbed radiation. (*b*) Triplet excited states have lower energy and longer lifetimes than singlet excited states because their unpaired e^-'s have the same spin. (*c*) Although $S_1 \rightarrow T_1$ is energetically favorable, it occurs slowly in accord with spectroscopic selection rules which predict that spontaneous changes of electron spin should have very low probabilities.

12.22 Describe and compare the absorbance of visible light by a (*a*) white solid, (*b*) colorless liquid or gas, (*c*) black solid, and (*d*) red gas, liquid, or solid.

◢ (*a*) and (*b*) A white substance absorbs no light in the visible region. All visible light is reflected if the substance is a solid; the light is all transmitted through a colorless gas or liquid (pure or a solution). (*c*) A black solid absorbs all colors in the visible region; no light is reflected. (*d*) A colored substance absorbs the complement of the observed transmitted or reflected color. Thus a red substance absorbs light in the green spectral region.

12.23 Given green, blue, and yellow dyes. Which dye absorbs the shortest wavelength and which the longest? Explain.

◢ Excitation is caused by the absorption of the complements (indicated in italics) of the observed colors as shown: green-*red*, blue-*orange*, and yellow-*purple*. The decreasing order of energies of the complementary colors is purple > orange > red. Therefore, the yellow dye has the highest energy gap and absorbs the shortest wavelength while the green dye has the lowest gap and absorbs the longest wavelength.

12.24 What are the different kinds of electrons in vinyl chloride, $H_2C{=}CHCl$?

◢ There are three kinds: the electrons in σ bonds, the electrons in π bonds, and the nonbonding (n) or unshared electrons, labeled as shown:

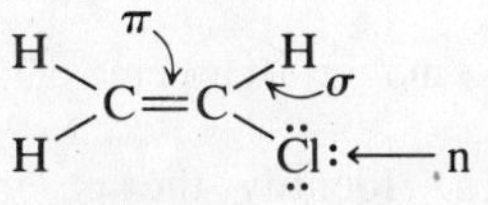

12.25 (*a*) List the possible electronic transitions in vinyl chloride. (*b*) Which transitions would be expected to be observed in the uv and visible regions of the spectrum? List them in order of increasing ΔE.

◢ (*a*) Vinyl chloride has filled σ and π MO's, filled MO^n's, and empty π^* and σ^* MO*'s. The possible transitions of an e^- are: $n \rightarrow \pi^*$, $\pi \rightarrow \pi^*$, $n \rightarrow \sigma^*$, $\pi \rightarrow \sigma^*$, $\sigma \rightarrow \pi^*$, $\sigma \rightarrow \sigma^*$. Only molecules with π bonds have π bonding and antibonding MO's, allowing for transitions to π^* MO*'s. (*b*) The $n \rightarrow \pi^* < \pi \rightarrow \pi^* < n \rightarrow \sigma^*$ (occasionally) occur in the near uv and visible regions measurable in most ordinary spectrophotometers.

12.26 List all the electronic transitions possible for (*a*) CCl_4, (*b*) $H_2C{=}O$, (*c*) cyclopentene, and (*d*) CH_3OH.

◢ Those with double bonds have excitations to a π^* and those with unshared pairs have excitations from an n MO. All have $\sigma \rightarrow \sigma^*$. In addition, (*a*) $n \rightarrow \sigma^*$, (*b*) $n \rightarrow \pi^*$, $\pi \rightarrow \pi^*$, $\sigma \rightarrow \pi^*$, $n \rightarrow \sigma^*$, $\pi \rightarrow \sigma^*$, (*c*) $\pi \rightarrow \pi^*$, $\sigma \rightarrow \pi^*$, $\pi \rightarrow \sigma^*$, and (*d*) $n \rightarrow \sigma^*$.

12.27 (*a*) What is λ_{max}? (*b*) Give the Beer–Lambert Law. (*c*) What is the meaning of ϵ_{max}, the molar extinction coefficient? (*d*) Define transmittance.

◢ (*a*) λ_{max} is a discernible wavelength at which an electronic transition occurs. (*b*) At λ_{max}, the absorbance *A* (*optical density*), which is a measure of the light absorbed through the solution, follows an exponential law (*Beer–Lambert*) of the form

$$A = \log(I_0/I) = \epsilon C l$$

where I_0 is the intensity of the incident light, I is the intensity of the emergent light, ϵ is the *molar extinction coefficient* (also called *molar absorptivity*), C is the molarity, and l is the path length (see Problem 12.31). At λ_{max}, the molar extinction coefficient is expressed as ϵ_{max}. (*c*) ϵ_{max} is related to the molecule's probability of absorbing a photon at λ_{max}, or to the intensity of excited molecules. Values for $\epsilon \geq 10^4$ are termed *high intensity absorptions*, while values $< 10^3$ are *low intensity absorptions*. (Units for ϵ_{max} are customarily omitted.) (*d*) Transmittance $T = I/I_0$ and it is often given as a percentage, i.e., $\%T = I/I_0 \times 100$.

12.28 Why is absorbance a function of C and l?

    ◢ Absorbance is a function of the number of excited molecules—the greater the number of excited molecules, the larger is A. The higher the concentration, the more molecules are exposed to and excited by the radiation. The longer the path length, the greater is the chance for the radiation to impact and excite molecules.

12.29 In a general way, explain the color of a dye solution whose visible spectrum shows more than one peak.

    ◢ If one of the peaks has a much larger ϵ_{max} than any of the others, the color will be the complement of the absorbed color with the λ_{max} having the larger ϵ_{max}. If the ϵ_{max} of two or more peaks are close in value, the color of the dye solution will be a blend of the complements of the absorbed wavelengths.

12.30 Describe the general procedure used in taking a uv or visible spectrum.

    ◢ It is usually taken on a very dilute solution (10^{-5} to 10^{-6} M), the solvent being transparent above 200 nm. The solution is placed in a 1-cm-wide silica cell (cuvette) that permits light to pass through. Alongside the solution cell is a matched cell (same value of l) containing pure solvent (the reference cell). The beam of uv or visible light, whose wavelength is continuously changing, is split into two beams, one passing through the sample solution, and the other through the reference cell. The spectrum is automatically recorded on a chart, usually as a plot of A vs. wavelength. Peaks occur at wavelengths, λ_{max}, at which light is absorbed. Actually, absorption peaks are typically broad. In most cases, only the λ_{max}'s and corresponding ϵ_{max}'s are reported. These, like a melting point, are inherent physical properties of a compound. Most instruments have two light sources, one for uv (H_2 lamp) and the other for white visible light (tungsten lamp), which have to be interchanged for a complete scan over both ranges.

12.31 A 9.37×10^{-5}M solution of **B** in a 1.0-cm cell at $\lambda_{max} = 235$ nm has an $A = 1.18$. Calculate ϵ_{max} for this transition.

    ◢ From Problem 12.27, $\epsilon_{max} = A/Cl = 1.18/(9.37 \times 10^{-5}\ \text{mol/L})(1.0\ \text{cm}) = 1.26 \times 10^4\ \text{L/mol} \cdot \text{cm}$.

12.32 What is the concentration of **B** in Problem 12.31 if its absorbance $A = 0.96$ at λ_{max}?

    ◢ $C = A/\epsilon l = 0.96/(1.26 \times 10^4\ \text{L/mol} \cdot \text{cm})(1.0\ \text{cm}) = 7.6 \times 10^{-5}\ \text{mol/L or M}$

12.33 (*a*) What is a chromophore? (*b*) Identify the chromophoric group in (i) cyclopentene, (ii) toluene, (iii) butanone, $CH_3COCH_2CH_3$, and (iv) methanethiol, CH_3SH.

    ◢ (*a*) A *chromophore* is a functional group of a molecule responsible for the absorption of light. (*b*) (i) >C=C<, (ii) $C_6H_5—$, (iii) $\text{>C=}\ddot{\text{O}}\text{:}$, (iv) $—\ddot{\text{S}}—$.

12.34 Acetone absorbs light at 154, 190, and 280 nm. (*a*) Identify the chromophore responsible for the absorption, and indicate what kind of transition causes each absorption. (*b*) Which transition(s) is(are) not observed in uv spectroscopy?

    ◢ (*a*) The chromophore is >C=O. The transitions are: $n \rightarrow \sigma^*$ (154 nm), $\pi \rightarrow \pi^*$ (190 nm) and $n \rightarrow \pi^*$ (280 nm). (*b*) 154 nm. The $\pi \rightarrow \pi^*$ (190 nm) is at the low observable limit of ordinary uv spectrometers.

12.35 The $n \rightarrow \pi^*$ transition in acetone occurs at a lower energy (lower wavelength) than the $\pi \rightarrow \pi^*$ transition, yet the $\pi \rightarrow \pi^*$ transition has a much higher ϵ_{max}. Explain.

    ◢ The $n \rightarrow \pi^*$ transition requires less energy (see Problem 12.25) but is less probable. For a transition to have a high ϵ_{max} (intensity), the orbital from which the e^- leaves and the one to which it goes must have the proper spatial juxtaposition. This is not the case for $n \rightarrow \pi^*$, which is a "forbidden" transition with a low intensity. Notwithstanding the fact that few molecules undergo these forbidden transitions, they may nevertheless require relatively less energy and occur at longer wavelengths.

12.36 Explain the following variations in λ_{max} (in nm) of MeCl (173), MeBr (204), MeI (258).

    ◢ The transition is $n \rightarrow \pi^*$. On proceeding down in the group (Cl to Br to I) absorption shifts to longer wavelengths because the n electrons are further away from the attractive force of the nucleus and are more easily excited.

12.37 Which of the following compounds would be suitable or unsuitable as a solvent for use in recording uv spectra of a solute substrate? (*a*) Cyclohexane, (*b*) iodoethane, (*c*) benzene, (*d*) diethyl ether, Et_2O. Give your reason in each case.

◢ Compounds with transitions occurring at $\lambda_{max} \geqq 190$ nm cannot be used as solvents because their absorptions would interfere with those of the sample compound. (*a*) Suitable because cyclohexane can only undergo a $\sigma \rightarrow \sigma^*$ transition whose ΔE is too large to be detected. (*b*) Unsuitable because the $n \rightarrow \sigma^*$ occurs in the detectable region (see Problem 12.36). (*c*) Unsuitable because its $\pi \rightarrow \pi^*$ transitions (> 190 nm) are detectable. (*d*) Suitable. Since O is a small atom, its unshared pair is tightly held and its $n \rightarrow \sigma^*$ transition is not detectable.

12.38 (*a*) Using MO theory, account for the following trends in λ_{max} (nm): Ethylene (175); 1,3-butadiene (217); and 1,3,5-hexatriene (250). (*b*) Explain why 1,5-hexadiene ($\lambda_{max} = 185$ nm) does not absorb light above 200 nm.

◢ (*a*) Increased conjugation of π bonds causes molecules to absorb at longer wavelengths and with greater intensity. For 1,3,5-hexatriene, the excitation is from π_3, the HOMO, to π_4^*, the LUMO. ΔE for this transition is less than ΔE for the $\pi_2 \rightarrow \pi_3^*$ (HOMO $\rightarrow$ LUMO) transition for 1,3-butadiene, which has a smaller ΔE than the corresponding $\pi \rightarrow \pi^*$ transition for ethylene. (*b*) The two double bonds are not conjugated and do not interact. λ_{max} for the unconjugated 1,5-hexadiene is very close to that of ethylene but the molar extinction coefficient is larger because there are twice as many C=C's per mole.

12.39 β-Carotene, which is the principal compound responsible for the orange color of carrots, has eleven conjugated double bonds, and absorbs light at 454 nm in the visible region of the spectrum. (*a*) Explain the shift to the visible range. (*b*) What color is absorbed?

◢ (*a*) The energy difference between the HOMO and the LUMO decreases as the number of conjugated double bonds increases. In this case, the ΔE corresponds to the energy of visible light. (*b*) Blue light, the complement of orange, is absorbed at 454 nm.

12.40 Identify the geometric isomers of stilbene, $C_6H_5CH=CHC_6H_5$, from their λ_{max} values of 294 and 278 nm.

◢ The *cis* isomer has the shorter wavelength. Steric strain prevents complete coplanarity necessary for full conjugation.

12.41 (*a*) Relate the λ_{max} values of (i) 277 and 185 nm, and (ii) 324 and 219 nm to the compounds $CH_3COCH_2CH_3$ (**A**) and $CH_3COCH=CH_2$ (**B**). (*b*) Identify the electron transitions in each case.

◢ (*a*) Conjugation in $CH_3COCH=CH_2$ causes the absorption bands to shift to longer wavelengths (with higher ϵ_{max} values); (ii) belongs to **B** and (i) to **A**. (*b*) In each case, the longer λ_{max} is the $n \rightarrow \pi^*$, and the shorter is the $\pi \rightarrow \pi^*$ transition.

12.42 Define the terms red shift and blue shift.

◢ A *red* (*bathochromic*) *shift* is a change to a longer wavelength or lower frequency and a *blue* (*hypsochromic*) *shift* is a change to a shorter wavelength or higher frequency. Increased conjugation (Problems 12.38 and 12.41) causes a red shift.

12.43 (*a*) What is an auxochrome? (*b*) What structural feature must an auxochrome possess?

◢ (*a*) An *auxochrome* is a functional group that does not itself absorb in the uv region above 200 μm but has the effect of shifting chromophore peaks to longer wavelengths with increasing intensities. (*b*) Strong auxochromes have an atom with an unshared pair of electrons attached to the chromophore. Examples are $-NH_2$, OH, F, and Cl. (See Problem 12.45 for the effect of R groups.)

12.44 Explain how an auxochrome exerts a bathochromic shift on a chromophore such as C=C.

◢ The nonbonded e^-'s become part of an extended π system by interacting with the π electrons of the C=C. This interaction has the effect of lowering the energy of both the π and π^* orbitals; the π^* to a greater extent. As a result, the $\pi \rightarrow \pi^*$ energy gap decreases giving a red shift.

12.45 (*a*) Draw a conclusion about the very slight auxochromic effect of R groups, e.g., Me, on the polyene chromophore from the following λ_{max} (in nm): 1,3-Butadiene (**A**), (217); 2-methyl-1,3-butadiene (**B**), (222); 2,3-dimethyl-1,3-butadiene (**C**), (227). (*b*) Give the Woodward–Fieser rule that pertains to these data. (*c*) Predict the λ_{max} for 2,4-dimethyl-1,3-pentadiene (**D**).

◢ (*a*) Each R group on the diene chromophore has a slight red shift. (*b*) The *Woodward–Fieser rule* assigns the value of 217 nm to the basic diene unit **A** with no attached R groups. Each R group produces a small shift of approximately 5 nm. For **B** with one R, $\lambda_{max} = 217 + 5 = 222$ nm, and for **C** with two R's, $\lambda_{max} = 217 + 2(5)$ $= 227$ nm.

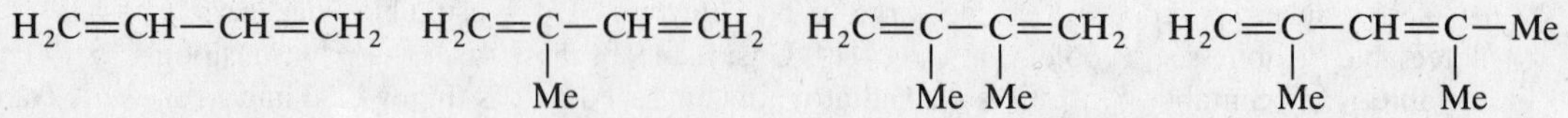

$$H_2C=CH-CH=CH_2 \quad \underset{\underset{Me}{|}}{H_2C=C}-CH=CH_2 \quad \underset{\underset{Me\ Me}{|\quad |}}{H_2C=C-C}=CH_2 \quad \underset{\underset{Me\quad\quad Me}{|\quad\quad\quad |}}{H_2C=C-CH=C}-Me$$

A   **B**   **C**   **D**

(*c*) Since **D** has three R's, $\lambda_{max} = 217 + 3(5) = 232$ nm, which is also the observed value.

12.46 From the following λ_{max} (in nm), deduce the effect of (*a*) the conformation of the diene, (*b*) an additional C=C, (*c*) the position of C=C in cyclic compounds.

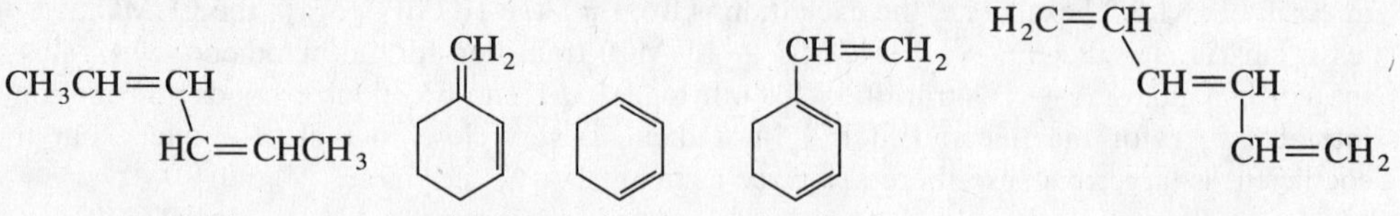

A (227)   **B** (230)   **C** (263)   **D** (293)   **E** (258)

▰ The following generalizations are extensions of the Woodward–Feiser rules. (*a*) The diene unit in **A**, *s-trans*, is assigned the base value of 217 nm and with two R's its value is $217 + 10 = 227$ nm. Note that in **B** two of the R groups are sides of a ring. The diene **C**, which also has two R's, nevertheless has a value of 263 nm. This is because it has a *s-cis* conformation which is assigned a base of 253 nm. Its predicted (and observed) value is $253 + 2(5) = 263$ nm. (*b*) The rules assign a value of 30 nm for the third conjugated C=C. This is consistent with the value for **D**, predicted and observed to be 253 (*s-cis* base) + 10 (2×5 for two R's) + 30 (for the third C=C) = 293 nm. The predicted value for the *s-trans* triene, **E**, is $217 + 30 = 247$ nm. The observed value of 258 nm proves that the predictions from the rules are not always foolproof. (*c*) **B**, a *s-trans* diene with two R's, should have a value of 227 nm. However, because one of the C=C groups of the diene is exocyclic, the rules assign another 5 units. The predicted value is $217 + 2(5) + 5 = 232$ nm, close to the observed value.

12.47 Use the Woodward–Feiser rules to predict the λ_{max} values for the following structures:

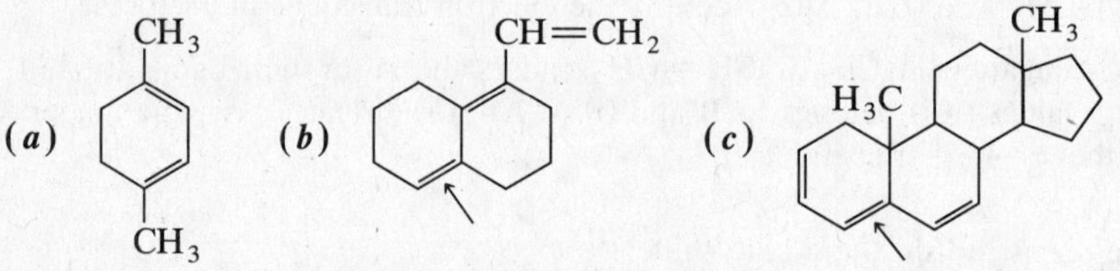

(*a*)   (*b*)   (*c*)

▰ (*a*) Adding 253 nm for the basic *s-cis* diene unit and 20 nm for the four R's (two part of a ring and two Me's) attached to the diene gives $\lambda_{max} = 273$ nm. (*b*) Adding 217 nm for the *s-trans* diene unit, 30 nm for the third C=C, 5 nm for the exocyclic C=C*, and 20 nm for the four R's gives $\lambda_{max} = 272$ nm. (*c*) Adding 253 nm for *s-cis* unit, 30 nm for the third C=C, 15 nm for the three R's, and 5 nm for the exocyclic C=C gives $\lambda_{max} = 304$ nm. *An exocyclic C=C is one attached to a ring at one end, shown by (⟵).

12.48 Hydrogenation of the triene, **A**, with one equivalent of H_2 could give three isomers of $C_{10}H_{14}$. Show how the expected λ_{max} values could distinguish among these isomers.

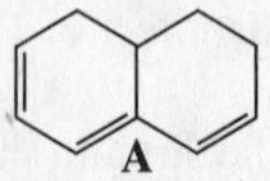

A

▰ Predicted values for the three isomers are

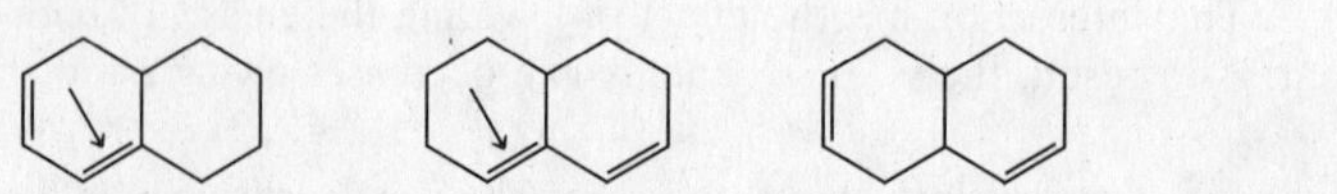

base value	(*s-cis*) 253 nm	(*s-trans*) 217 nm	< 200 nm (unconjugated)
R's × 5	(3 × 5) 15	(3 × 5) 15	—
exocyclic C=C	5	5	—
λ_{max}	273 nm	237 nm	< 200 nm (not detected)

12.49 Additional Woodward–Fieser rules predict the λ_{max} for the $\pi \rightarrow \pi^*$ transition in conjugated aldehydes and ketones. For the general structure $C{=}C{-}C{=}O$, the base values are 210 nm for aldehyde and 215 nm for ketone. Add 10 nm for an α-R, 12 nm for a β-R, 18 nm for a γ- or δ-R, and 30 nm for an additional conjugated $C{=}C$. Predict λ_{max} for the following compounds:

(**a**) $CH_3CH_2C(CH_3){=}CHCOCH_3$ (**b**) $CH_3CH{=}C(CH_3)CHO$
(**c**) $CH_3CO{-}CH{=}C(CH_3){-}CH{=}CH_2$

▮ (**a**) 215 (base value) + 24 ($2 \times \beta$-R) = 239 nm.   (**b**) 210 + 10 (α-R) + 12 (β-R) = 232 nm.
(**c**) 215 + 12 (β-R) + 30 (conj. $C{=}C$) = 257 nm.

12.50 The values for the three absorptions of benzene are (*1*) $\lambda_{max} = 184$ nm, $\epsilon_{max} = 68{,}000$ (a peak), (*2*) $\lambda_{max} = 204$ nm, $\epsilon_{max} = 8800$ (a band of several small peaks), and (*3*) 254 nm, 200-300. Give the origin of each peak.

▮ They are all $\pi \rightarrow \pi^*$ transitions. Absorption (*1*) arises from the allowed transition from either of the two benzene HOMO's to either of its two LUMO's. This peak cannot be observed in ordinary uv spectrometers and will not be referred to again. Absorption (*2*), a primary band (1°), and (*3*) a secondary band (2°), are "forbidden" low intensity bands, arising from electron transitions from different distorted higher-energy benzene rings. Absorption (*3*), the *benzenoid* band, is composed of 3–6 small sharp peaks, called *fine structure*.

12.51 Explain the effect of the following substituents on the observable 1° and 2° absorption bands of benzene: (*a*) $-NH_2$, (*b*) $-OH$, (*c*) $-COOH$, (*d*) $-Br$, and (*e*) $-CH_3$.

▮ All of these groups are auxochromes causing a red shift. They induce charge separation in both the ground and excited states. However, the energy of the excited state is diminished more than that of the ground state. The attached atoms in (*a*), (*b*), and (*d*) have unshared pairs of e^-'s capable of being delocalized into the benzene ring, making the ring negative. The CH_3 of (*e*) is a poorer electron-donor and causes a smaller red shift. The COOH of (*c*) also participates in extended π bonding but is electron-withdrawing, making the ring positive and the group negative. These groups also greatly increase the intensities of the secondary band and slightly increase the intensities of the primary band.

12.52 Predict and explain the following changes in the auxochromic red shifts: (*a*) Acidifying $ArNH_2$, (*b*) basifying ArOH, and (*c*) basifying ArCOOH.

▮ (*a*) In acid, $ArNH_2$ is converted to $ArNH_3^+$, thereby tying up the unshared pair of e^-'s and obviating the red shift. $ArNH_3^+$ absorbs at 203 nm, as does benzene. (*b*) The acidic ArOH loses H^+ giving the conjugate base, ArO^-. With a full negative charge, $-O^-$ gives a more pronounced red shift because it is a better electron-donor than $-OH$ (210 to 235 nm). (*c*) ArCOOH is also changed to its conjugate base, $ArCOO^-$, which, because of its full negative charge, becomes a poorer electron-withdrawer. There is an energetic reluctance to build up too much charge in the substituent group. Absorption shifts to shorter wavelengths, from 230 to 224 nm.

12.53 (*a*) For disubstituted benzene derivatives predict and discuss the relative red shifts when electron-donating and electron-withdrawing groups are (i) *para*, (ii) *meta*, and (iii) *ortho*. (*b*) What is the effect of two electron-donating or electron-withdrawing groups in the same ring?

▮ (*a*) (i) The red shift is greater than the sum of the individual effects of the two substituents because of resonance interaction between the groups, as demonstrated with *p*-nitroaniline. Note that the contributing structure with charge separation is relatively stable because the positive charges are on N's with octets of e^-'s and the negative charges are on electronegative O's with octets on each O. The increased stability is greater in the excited state than the ground state.

$$H_2\ddot{N}{-}\!\!\bigcirc\!\!{-}\overset{+}{N}\!\!\begin{smallmatrix}O^-\\ \| \\ O\end{smallmatrix} \longleftrightarrow H_2\overset{+}{N}{=}\!\!\bigcirc\!\!{=}\overset{+}{N}\!\!\begin{smallmatrix}O^-\\ \\ O^-\end{smallmatrix}$$

(ii) There is no interaction between the two groups and the magnitude of the shift is approximately equal to the sum of the individual shifts. (iii) The two groups interact as shown:

However, the shift is attenuated because of the steric hindrance to the coplanarity needed to achieve resonance interaction. If the groups are large enough, the *o*-substituted derivative may show the smallest red shift. (*b*) The effects are not additive because it is energetically unfavorable to introduce or to remove too much charge from the ring. The effect is similar to those for monosubstituted benzenes.

12.54 Explain why a polar (protic or aprotic) solvent usually shifts the $\pi \rightarrow \pi^*$ transition to longer wavelengths.

The excited state in most $\pi \rightarrow \pi^*$ transitions usually has more charge separation than the ground state. The polar solvent stabilizes it more strongly than it does the ground state, by dipole-dipole and H-bonding interactions. The energy of the excited state is decreased more than that of the ground state, shifting the transition to lower energy (longer wavelength, red shift).

12.55 Explain why a polar (protic or aprotic) solvent usually shifts the $n \rightarrow \pi^*$ transition to shorter wavelengths (blue shift).

The ground state in most $n \rightarrow \pi^*$ transitions is more polar than the excited state. H-bonding solvents, in particular, as well as aprotic polar solvents, interact more strongly with unshared electron pairs in the ground state (lowering its energy more) than in the excited state. The transition requires more energy and the absorption occurs at a shorter wavelength (blue shift).

12.56 Discuss the validity of the following statements: (*a*) Increasing the polarity of the solvent does not change the effects of auxochromes participating in extended π delocalization. (*b*) The three aromatic bands of polynuclear aromatic compounds, e.g., naphthalene, are shifted to longer wavelengths.

(*a*) False. Extended π delocalization induces partial charges more in the excited state than in the ground state. Thus its stability is enhanced in polar solvents because of dipole-dipole interactions. (*b*) True. Because there are more π orbitals, the HOMO $\rightarrow$ LUMO energy gap is diminished. All three peaks and bands typical of aromatic compounds are observable with ordinary uv spectrometers.

12.57 Give a statement relating absorption to the number of fused aromatic rings from the given λ_{max} values.

Naphthalene, 314 nm   Anthracene, 380 nm   Naphthacene, 480 nm, yellow   Pentacene, 580 nm, blue

As the number of linearly fused benzene rings increases, λ_{max} of the benzenoid band shifts toward longer wavelength.

12.58 Suggest structures for possible isomers with molecular formula C_4H_6O whose uv spectra show a high-intensity peak at $\lambda_{max} = 187$ nm and a very low-intensity peak at $\lambda_{max} = 280$ nm.

Functional groups with a single O are alcohols (ROH), ethers (ROR), and carbonyl compounds (aldehydes, RCH=O, and ketones, R_2C=O). The formula lacks four H's from being saturated—there are two degrees of unsaturation. This means there may be two rings, one double bond and one ring, two double bonds or one triple bond. The absorption peaks signal an unconjugated C=O. The possibilities are cyclic carbonyl compounds as shown:

Cyclobutanone   Methylcyclopropanone   Cyclopropylcarboxaldehyde

and the unconjugated 3-butenal, H_2C=CHCH$_2$CH=O.

12.59 (*a*) Which C_4H_6O isomers are possible if the uv spectrum shows a high-intensity peak at $\lambda_{max} = 215$ nm? (*b*) Predict the uv absorption peaks for any additional isomeric conjugated carbonyls.

(*a*) The uv spectrum indicates the presence of a conjugated ketone (210 nm for C=C—C=O + 5 nm for a ketone structure; see Problem 12.49). The only possible compound is H_2C=CHCOCH$_3$. (*b*) The other two isomers are Me-substituted aldehydes: **A**, CH$_3$CH=CHCH=O (210 nm for basic conjugated aldehyde + 12 for a β-R), = 222 nm, and **B**, H_2C=C(CH$_3$)CH=O (210 + 10 for an α-R), = 220 nm. These values are indistinguishable experimentally because the peaks are broad. A difference of 5 nm is usually the minimum for distinguishing two close peaks.

12.60 (*a*) Does a noncarbonyl isomer of C_4H_6O that absorbs at 217 nm exist? (*b*) Give structural formulas for isomers of C_4H_6O having a triple bond. Would these give detectable peaks in the uv spectrum?

◢ (a) No. Any such isomer would have to contain the conjugated diene unit. The O would have to be part of an OH group attached to either a terminal or an internal C. The resulting structures are the dienols C, H_2C=CH—CH=CHOH, and D, H_2C=C(OH)—CH=CH_2. Enols are unstable and rearrange to the more stable carbonyl compounds: C to the unconjugated aldehyde (Problem 12.58) and D to the conjugated ketone [Problem 12.59(a)]. (b) There are two possible alkynols: HC≡CCH_2CH_2OH and CH_3C≡CCH_2OH, and three possible alkyne ethers: CH_3OC≡CCH_3, CH_3OCH_2C≡CH, and CH_3CH_2OC≡CH, all of which absorb in the same nondetectable region as an isolated C≡C, $\lambda_{max} \cong 170$ nm.

12.61 Can the two isomers **E** and **F** be distinguished? Calculate their λ_{max} using values given in Problems 12.45 and 12.46? Assume that difference in values of 5 nm or more makes the isomers distinguishable experimentally.

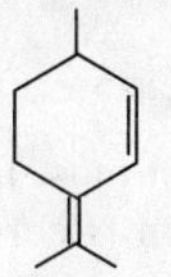

◢

	E	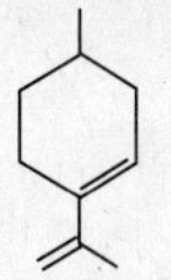 F
base value	(s-trans) 217 nm	(s-trans) 217 nm
R's × 5	(4 × 5) 20	(3 × 5) 15
exocyclic C=C	5	0
λ_{max}	242 nm	232 nm

Yes, the isomers are distinguishable.

12.62 Referring to Problem 12.49, calculate λ_{max} for compound **G**.

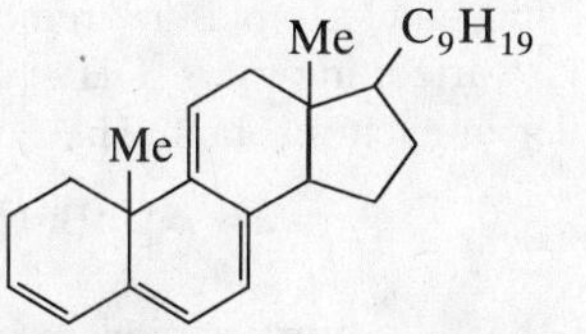

◢

base value	(s-cis)	253 nm
extended conjugation	(2 × 30)	60
exocyclic C=C	(3 × 5)	15
R's × 5	(5 × 5)	25
λ_{max}		353 nm

12.63 Dehydration of the 3° alcohol, **H**, shown below, can give three possible conjugated dienes: **I**, **J**, and **K**. (a) Give the structures of the three dienes. (b) Can the various products be distinguished by uv using the assumption in Problem 12.61? (c) Give a mechanism to account for the formation of each compound.

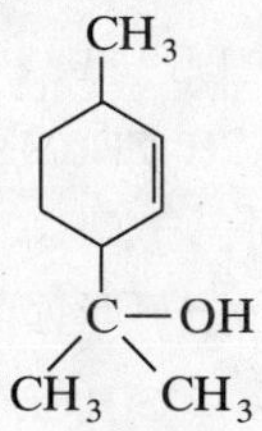

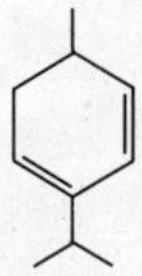

◢ (a)

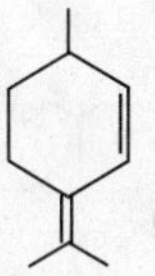

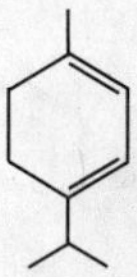

(b)

	I	J	K
base value	(s-trans) 217 nm	(s-cis) 253 nm	(s-cis) 253 nm
R's × 5	(4 × 5) 20	(3 × 5) 15	(4 × 5) 20
exocyclic C=C	5	0	0
λ_{max}	242 nm	268 nm	273 nm

The three dienes are distinguishable.

(*c*) (*a*) A 3° carbocation is formed. It can lose a proton directly, giving **I**. The C⁺ can rearrange to another 3° carbocation by a hydride shift, from which the products **J** and **K** result.

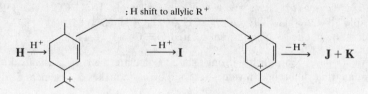

12.64   How may the rate of a reaction be measured using uv spectroscopy?

∕   Either the reactant or the product must have a distinct observable absorption. At this λ_{max}, the absorbance, *A*, is proportional to the concentration (Beer–Lambert Law). [To confirm this, a calibration curve of differing known concentrations (standard solutions) vs. *A* is first plotted.] Small samples are removed periodically from the reaction vessel, kept at constant *T*, and the absorbance of either the product or the remaining reactant is measured. If possible, the reaction is carried out in a temperature-controlled cuvette to avoid the need to remove samples. The process is repeated using different concentrations of reactants.

12.65   Apply the method of Problem 12.64 to measure the rate of the reaction of *n*-BuI with OH⁻.

∕   The reaction is *n*-BuI + OH⁻ → *n*-BuOH + I⁻. The absorbance of *n*-BuI at about 258 nm decreases as it reacts to form the alcohol, which does not absorb in the usual uv range. First, a calibration curve is determined for *n*-BuI at 258 nm. A reference cuvette with the solvent mixture is inserted in the instrument, the mixed reactants are kept at constant *T*, and small samples are removed at intervals to measure *A*. In some experiments [*n*-BuI] is unchanged and [OH⁻] is varied; in others [OH⁻] is constant and [*n*-BuI] differs. The data indicate the reaction is second order, first order in each reactant. The rate expression is (see Problem 8.50):

$$\text{rate} = k\,[n\text{-BuI}][\text{OH}^-]$$

12.66   Discuss how the rate of each of the following reactions might be determined by uv spectroscopy. Do not give experimental details.

(*a*) $CH_3CH{=}CHCH{=}CH_2 + H_2$ (1 equivalent) ⟶   (*b*) $C_6H_5CH_2CH_2OH \xrightarrow[\Delta]{H^+}$

(*c*) trans- $C_6H_5CH{=}CHC_6H_5 \longrightarrow$ *cis*-isomer

∕   (*a*) Either 1,2- or 1,4-addition converts a conjugated diene to a simple alkene. The absorption at 223 nm (217 for *s-trans* + 5 for Me) should decrease with time.   (*b*) Benzene has two important absorptions: a 1° band and a benzenoid 2° band (Problem 12.50). Both of these shift to longer wavelengths (204 to 248 nm and 254 to 282 nm) on formation of $C_6H_5CH{=}CH_2$. The absorption at either 248 or 282 nm should increase with time. (*c*) The *cis* and *trans* stilbenes have different λ_{max} values (Problem 12.40); the appearance of the *cis* or the disappearance of the *trans* peak should be effective.

12.67   Select the reactions that might be used in a uv rate study. What would you measure?

(*a*) $CH_3CH_2COCH_3 \xrightarrow[\text{cat.}]{H_2} CH_3CH_2CH(OH)CH_3$

(*b*) $CH_3CH_2CH_2Cl + NH_3 \longrightarrow CH_3CH_2CH_2NH_3^+ + Cl^-$

(*c*) $CH_3CH_2CH(OH)CH_2CH_3 \xrightarrow[\Delta]{H^+} CH_3CH_2CH{=}CHCH_3$

(*d*) $CH_3CH_2C{\equiv}CH \xrightarrow[H_2O]{H_2SO_4,\,HgSO_4} CH_3CH_2COCH_3$

(*e*) $H_2C{=}CHCH{=}CH_2 + HC{\equiv}CH \longrightarrow$ 1,4-cyclohexadiene

(*f*)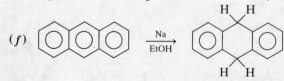

∕   Use uv spectroscopy to measure in (*a*) the decline in the absorbance of the C=O group, (*d*) the increase in absorbance of C=O, (*e*) the decrease in absorbance of the conjugated diene system and (*f*) the loss of absorbance of anthracene. Reactions (*b*) and (*c*) cannot be studied by uv because neither their reactants nor products have detectable absorptions.

12.68 (a) Describe how uv spectroscopy might be used to determine K_a for the following acid:

$$HO-\langle\bigcirc\rangle-NO_2 + H_2O \rightleftharpoons {}^-O-\langle\bigcirc\rangle-NO_2 + H_3O^+$$

(b) From information in the answer to part (a) predict whether the conjugate base of this acid is colored and, if so, give its color.

◢ (a) The major absorption of the acid is red-shifted in the conjugate base (320 to 400 nm) owing to the electronic interaction of the *para* strongly electron-donating —O$^-$ and electron-withdrawing —NO$_2$ group. The concentrations of the unionized acid HA and its conjugate base A$^-$ at equilibrium are measured at their respective λ_{max}'s, and the $[H_3O^+]$ is equal to the $[A^-]$. These values are substituted into the equation for K_a. Or the pH can be measured since $[H_3O^+] = [A^-]$.   (b) If $\lambda_{max} < 400$, colorless; if it $= 400$, yellow.

INFRARED SPECTROSCOPY

12.69 (a) Give the wavelength, frequency, and energy ranges of the most often used infrared region of the spectrum. (b) What units are customarily employed on the chart of an ir spectrum?   (c) What is the relationship between wave number and frequency?   (d) Convert 1800 cm^{-1} to Hertz.

◢ (a) The wavelength range is 2.5 to 16 μm (1 μm = 10^{-6} m). The frequency range, given by the wave number, is 4000 to 600 cm^{-1}. This corresponds to energy changes of about 1.8 to 11.4 kcal/mol (7.5 to 48 kJ/mol). (b) See Fig. 12-6. The ordinate is usually the transmittance (%) ; the abscissa indicates the wavelength (in μm) and the frequency (in cm^{-1}) (wave number), one on top and the other at the bottom of the chart. The ordinate is linear in transmittance and the abscissa is linear in wave number, although some instruments use a scale that is linear in wavelength. The horizontal scale of the usual chart changes at 2000 cm^{-1}; spacing units at higher wave numbers are half the linear distance of those of the lower values.   (c) Since $\lambda\nu = c$, [Problem 12.4(b)], $1/\lambda = \nu/c = \bar{\nu}$. Thus $\nu = \bar{\nu}c$.   (d) From (c), (1800 cm^{-1})(3.0 × 10^{10} cm/s) = 5.4 × 10^{13} Hz (1 s^{-1} = 1 Hz).

12.70 Describe the components and operation of a simple ir spectrophotometer.

◢ The light source (an electrically heated solid, e.g., a nichrome wire) produces a beam of infrared radiation which is divided (by a system of mirrors) into two parallel beams of equal intensity radiation. The sample is placed in the path of one beam and the other may be used as a reference beam when a solution is to be analyzed. A slowly rotating diffraction grating or prism varies the wavelength of radiation reaching the sample and then the detector. The detector records the difference in intensity between the two beams on a recorder chart as % transmittance. Maximum transmittance is at the top of the vertical scale, so absorbance is observed as a *minimum* on the chart even though it is called a *peak*.

12.71 Describe the ir analyses of (a) a liquid, (b) a solution, and (c) a solid.

◢ (a) Analysis of a liquid requires use of cells made of NaCl (or similar material), which is transparent to ir radiation. A thin film of pure (*neat*) liquid is placed between matching crystal plates of NaCl in a cell holder positioned in the path of one of the beams.   (b) The solution is placed in the path of the *sample* beam, and pure solvent in the *reference* beam path in special sealed NaCl cells. The solvent must not absorb ir radiation in the region of interest.   (c) The solid can be finely ground in a suitable liquid medium to make a *mull* (a two-phase mixture). Often, the suspending medium is Nujol, a heavy hydrocarbon oil. If the hydrocarbon-absorbing region is of interest, a halogenated polymer like fluorolube can be used instead. The resulting mull is placed as a film between salt plates. A popular alternative requires that a finely-ground intimate mixture of the sample and dry KBr be pressed in a special die under high pressure. A transparent pellet forms and this is placed in the light path for analysis.

12.72 (a) Why are water and ethanol not commonly used as solvents in ir spectroscopy?   (b) List the most commonly used solvents.

◢ (a) They dissolve the NaCl used for cell windows, causing fogging. (All solutes and solvents must be carefully dried before use.) In addition, they both absorb strongly in several regions, they H-bond with many solutes, and they may form dipole interactions with polar solutes, possibly shifting peaks. Water may be used if the sealed cells are constructed from water-insoluble salts like AgCl.   (b) CHCl$_3$, CCl$_4$.

12.73 What are the two fundamental vibrations for molecules?

▌ A molecule is not rigid; the covalent bond between any two atoms acts like a coiled spring with a weight at each end. Each pair of bonded atoms can be thought to vibrate by stretching and compressing, with a characteristic *stretching frequency* that is a function of the stiffness of the bond (spring) and the masses of the atoms. The assigned bond length is the average length resulting from these vibrations. In a *bending* vibration (or deformation), requiring a sequence of at least three atoms, bond lengths remain constant but bond angles change. Again the assigned bond angle is an average. Stretching and bending vibrations of a bond occur at certain quantized frequencies.

12.74 Describe the molecular processes that occur when ir radiation is absorbed by a molecule.

▌ When ir light impinges on a molecule, only certain frequencies—those corresponding to vibrational frequencies—are absorbed; the process is quantized. The absorption excites the molecule to a higher energy *vibrational* state where the amplitude of that vibration is increased. The *fundamental absorption peak* is a result of the transition from the ground state to the first excited state. Radiation in the energy range of 2-11 kcal/mol (see Problem 12.69) corresponds to the range encompassing stretching and bending frequencies in most covalent molecules.

12.75 (*a*) Compare the relative wave numbers for stretching and bending vibrations. (*b*) Define the "fingerprint" region.

▌ (*a*) Excitation of stretching vibrations requires more energy and takes place at higher frequencies (4000 to 1250 cm^{-1}) than bending frequencies (between 1400 and 675 cm^{-1}). (*b*) Because of the variety and complexity of the bending modes, the region below 1250 cm^{-1} has peaks that are characteristic of the particular molecule. This region is therefore called the *fingerprint region* and is very useful in determining whether two samples are chemically identical.

12.76 (*a*) What condition must be met for absorption of ir radiation by a molecule? (*b*) Select the diatomic molecules that do not absorb in the ir from the following: HCl, N$_2$, ClBr, O$_2$, H$_2$.

▌ (*a*) In order to absorb ir radiation a molecule must undergo a net change in dipole moment, due to its vibrational motion. (*b*) Stretching in homodiatomic molecules, e.g., N$_2$, O$_2$, H$_2$, will not change the dipole moment and so these ir *inactive* molecules do not absorb. Heterodiatomic molecules whose atoms do not have the same electronegativities, e.g., HCl and ClBr, are ir *active* and absorb.

12.77 Illustrate the stretching vibrations for a linear triatomic molecule such as CO$_2$.

▌ Each C=O bond can stretch in two modes. Both O's can alternately stretch and then contract at the same time; this is the *symmetric* mode [Fig. 12-3(*a*)]. One O can stretch while the other contracts: this is the *antisymmetric* mode [Fig. 12-3(*b*)]. Each mode gives a peak in the ir spectrum.

$$\begin{array}{cc} \rightarrow \text{ or } \leftarrow & \leftarrow \text{ or } \leftarrow \\ \leftarrow \quad \rightarrow & \rightarrow \quad \rightarrow \\ \text{O}=\text{C}=\text{O} & \text{O}=\text{C}=\text{O} \end{array}$$

(*a*) Symmetric vibration   (*b*) Antisymmetric vibration   **Fig. 12-3**

12.78 Illustrate the types of bending vibrations with a generalized sequence of three bonded atoms.

▌ There are four modes as shown in Fig. 12-4.

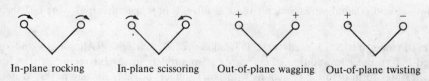

In-plane rocking   In-plane scissoring   Out-of-plane wagging   Out-of-plane twisting

(+ means coming forward, − means going backward)   **Fig. 12-4**

12.79 (*a*) Give the equation that relates the fundamental stretching frequency of a covalent bond, A—B, to the *force constant*, *k*, of the bond and the masses of atoms A and B. (*k* is related to the bond strength.) (*b*) Calculate (i) the wave number and (ii) the wavelength of the fundamental peak due to the stretching vibration of a $>$C$=$O group. ($k = 1 \times 10^6$ dyn/cm or 1×10^6 g/s^2, since 1 dyne = 1 g cm/s^2).

◢ (*a*) $\bar{\nu} = \dfrac{1}{2\pi c}\sqrt{\dfrac{k}{\mu}}$;

where *c* (speed of light) $= 3.0 \times 10^{10}$ cm/s; $\mu = m_A m_B/(m_A + m_B)$, and m_A and m_B are the masses of A and B, respectively.

(*b*) (i) The masses of the C and O atoms are $12/(6.0 \times 10^{23})$ and $16/(6.0 \times 10^{23})$ g, respectively. Substituting into the equation in (*a*) we get

$$\bar{\nu} = \frac{1}{2(3.14)(3.0 \times 10^{10} \text{ cm/s})}\sqrt{\left(1 \times 10^6 \text{ g/s}^2\right)\frac{(2.0 + 2.7)10^{-23} \text{ g}}{(2.0 \times 2.7)10^{-46} \text{ g}^2}} = 1560 \text{ cm}^{-1} \text{ or } 1600 \text{ cm}^{-1}$$

(ii) $\lambda = \dfrac{1}{\nu} = \dfrac{1}{1560 \text{ cm}^{-1} \times 10^4 \text{ cm}/\mu\text{m}} = 6.3 \ \mu\text{m}$

12.80 Summarize the relationship between the force constant *k*, the bond energy, and the vibrational frequency.

◢ *k* Is a measure of the *stiffness* of the bond. Generally, the higher the bond energy, the stiffer is the bond, and the higher is the frequency needed for excitation.

12.81 What characteristic of vibrational frequencies makes ir spectroscopy useful in determining structures of organic compounds?

◢ The various vibrational absorption frequencies are specific for a given functional group or alkyl grouping, i.e., —CH(CH$_3$)$_2$, regardless of its bonding environment. Even when there are slight changes, they are consistent. For example, the C$=$O stretch of cyclic ketones changes with ring size but is the same for different cyclic ketones with the same ring size.

12.82 Compare the relative stretching frequencies for C—C, C$=$C, and C$\equiv$C bonds. Use data in Table 12-1.

◢ Bond strength increases with increasing bond multiplicity. The increasing order of frequencies is: C—C, 1200 cm^{-1}; C$=$C, 1650 cm^{-1}; C$\equiv$C, 2150 cm^{-1}.

12.83 (*a*) How is the O—H absorption peak shifted by replacing the H by a D? The O—H and O—D bonds have approximately the same bond strength (force constants). (*b*) Predict the relative stretching frequencies for the C—F, C—Cl, C—Br, and C—I bonds. (*c*) Why do A—H (where A = C, O, N, P, etc.) stretching frequencies have the highest $\bar{\nu}$ values (3600 cm^{-1} to about 2050 cm^{-1})?

◢ (*a*) Any shift must be due to the change in mass. Since the frequencies are inversely related to the atomic masses, an increase in mass decreases the frequency of the stretching peak. For O—H, $\bar{\nu} = 3600$ cm^{-1} and for O—D, $\bar{\nu} = 2100$ cm^{-1}. (*b*) As the masses of the halogen atoms increases, the stretching frequency decreases. Thus C—F, 1400-1000; C—Cl, 800-600; C—Br, 600-500 and C—I, 500 cm^{-1}. This order is also consistent with the observed decrease in bond strength on proceeding down the halogen group. The value for C—F is much larger than the others because its bond strength is much larger than the others. (*c*) H has the smallest mass of any element.

12.84 (*a*) Summarize the relationship between the hybridized state of the C—H bond and the expected frequencies of the C—H vibration. (*b*) Compare the stretching frequencies of an aldehydic H, —CHO, and a vinylic H, C$=$CH.

◢ (*a*) Hybridization affects the bond strength in the decreasing order: $sp > sp^2 > sp^3$. Thus the frequencies decrease as follows: $\equiv$C—H, 3300; $=$C—H, 3100; —C—H, 2900 cm^{-1}. (*b*) The aldehydic H appears as a doublet at a lower frequency, 2715 and 2820 cm^{-1}, than the vinylic H. It is a distinctive peak because nothing else absorbs at this frequency.

12.85 How does conjugation affect the stretching frequency of C$=$O in a carbonyl compound?

◢ An unconjugated C$=$O has its absorption frequency of about 1715 cm^{-1} lowered to 1675-1680 cm^{-1} when conjugated with one C$=$C. Delocalization affects the length and strength of a bond. The C to O bond in the

TABLE 12-1. INFRARED ABSORPTION FREQUENCIES OF SOME COMMON STRUCTURAL UNITS

Stretching Frequencies (cm^{-1})			
Single bonds		Double bonds	
Structural unit	Frequency	Structural unit	Frequency
—O—H (alcohols)	3200–3600	$>C=C<$	1620–1680
—O—D	2100		
—O—H (carboxylic acids)	2500–3600	$>C=O$	
$>N-H$	3350–3500	Aldehydes and ketones	1710–1750
C_{sp}—H	3310–3320	Carboxylic acids	1700–1725
C_{sp^2}—H	3000–3100	Acid anhydrides	1800–1850 and
O=C—H	2715, 2820		1740–1790
C_{sp^3}—H	2850–2950	Acyl halides	1770–1815
		Esters	1730–1750
C_{sp^2}—O	1200	Amides	1680–1700
C_{sp^3}—O	1025–1200		
		Triple bonds	
—S—H	2500		
		—C≡C—	2100–2200
		—C≡N	2240–2280

Bending Frequencies (cm^{-1}) of Hydrocarbons

Alkanes	CH_3 1420–1470 1375	$=CH_2$ 1430–1470	$CH(CH_3)_2$ Doublet of equal intensities at 1370, 1385. Also 1170	$C(CH_3)_3$ Doublet at 1370 (strong) 1395 (moderate)
Alkenes Out-of-Plane	$RCH=CH_2$ 910–920 990–1000	$R_2C=CH_2$ 880–900	RCH=CHR cis 675–730 (variable) trans 965–975	
Aromatic C—H Out-of-Plane	Monosubstituted 690–710 730–770		Disubstituted ortho 735–770 meta 690–710 750–810 para 810–840	

hybrid is longer and less stiff than the isolated $C=O$ because it has more single bond character, causing a shift to a lower frequency.

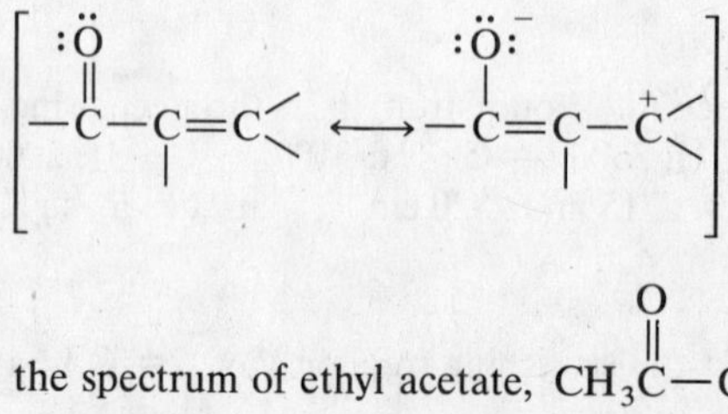

$$\left[\begin{matrix} :\overset{..}{O} \\ \| \\ -C-C=C< \\ | \end{matrix} \longleftrightarrow \begin{matrix} :\overset{..}{O}:^- \\ | \\ -C=C-\overset{+}{C}< \\ | \end{matrix} \right]$$

12.86 Identify the peaks **A-D** in Fig. 12-5, the spectrum of ethyl acetate, $CH_3\overset{\overset{O}{\|}}{C}-O-CH_2CH_3$.

/ It is extremely difficult and impractical to attempt an interpretation of each band in an ir spectrum. Only characteristic absorptions will be identified. Peak **A** below 3000 cm^{-1}, at about 2900 cm^{-1}, is due to H—C_{sp^3}

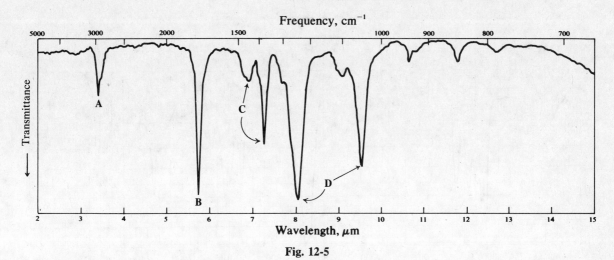

Fig. 12-5

stretching. Peak **B** at 1750 cm^{-1} is due to the characteristic C=O stretch. The bands at 1380 and 1500 cm^{-1}, labeled **C**, are due to C—H bending, and the bands labeled **D** at 1050 and 1240 cm^{-1} are due to the C—O stretching.

12.87 Match the ir spectra in Fig. 12-6(*a*) and (*b*) to the isomeric compounds 2-hexanol and di-*n*-propyl ether. Explain your reasoning.

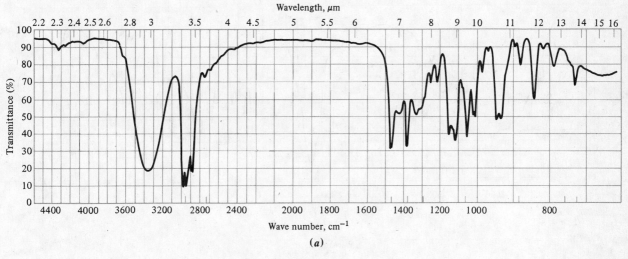

(*a*)

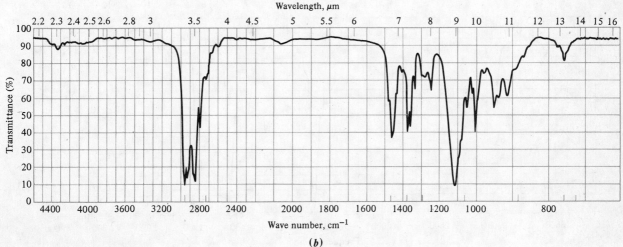

(*b*)

Fig. 12-6

Wavelength, μm

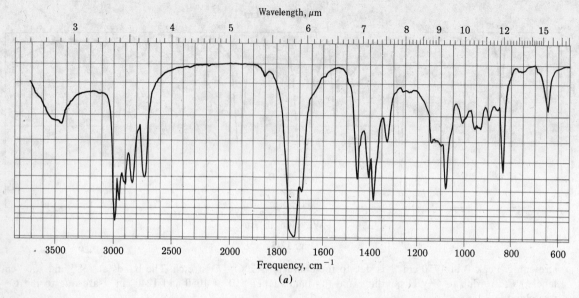

Frequency, cm⁻¹

(a)

Wavelength, μm

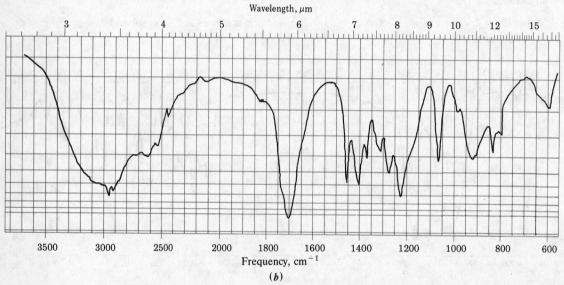

Frequency, cm⁻¹

(b)

Wavelength, μm

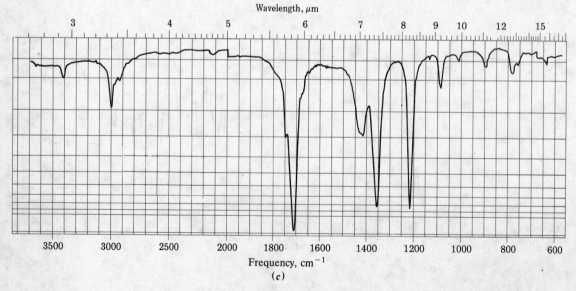

Frequency, cm⁻¹

(c)

Fig. 12-7

▰ The distinguishing feature of the alcohol, identified in Fig. 12-6(a), is the strong, broad peak at 3300 cm^{-1}, attributed to the O—H stretch of the H-bonded OH group. (In dilute solution, where there is a greater separation of individual ROH molecules, there is less H-bonding, and an additional peak at 3600-3500 cm^{-1} occurs due to the O—H stretch of alcohols not participating in H-bonding.) In addition, there is a C—O stretching peak at about 1100 cm^{-1}. This peak is very prominent in Fig. 12-6(b), the spectrum for the ether, which has no O—H stretch at all.

12.88 Match the compounds CH_3CH_2CHO, CH_3COCH_3, and CH_3CH_2COOH with the three ir spectra in Fig. 12-7(a), (b), and (c). Give your reasons.

▰ The C=O bond of all carbonyl compounds has a very high intensity peak between 1750 and 1680 cm^{-1}, present in all three spectra. The distinguishing feature of the aldehyde is the C—H doublet at 2820 and 2715 cm^{-1}, shown in Fig. 12-7(a). The acid is identified in Fig. 12-7(b) because of the very broad absorption from 3500 to 2500 cm^{-1}. By elimination, the spectrum in Fig. 12-7(c) with neither of these features is the ketone.

12.89 Match the compounds hexane, 1-hexene, and 1-hexyne with the three ir spectra in Fig. 12-8(a), (b), and (c). Give your reasons.

▰ The spectrum for 1-hexyne, a terminal alkyne, has the strong H—C$_{sp}$ stretch at 3300 cm^{-1} and the sharp, weaker C≡C at 2120 cm^{-1} in Fig. 12-8(a). The spectrum in Fig. 12-8(c) is identified as 1-hexene because it has a sharp peak at 1640 cm^{-1} (C=C stretch), and shows H—C$_{sp^2}$ stretching vibrations at 3095 cm^{-1}, both absent from the spectrum of hexane in Fig. 12-8(b). All the C—H stretching absorptions of an alkane appear at or below 3000 cm^{-1}. The alkene spectrum also has two peaks at 990 and 910 cm^{-1}, attributed to out-of-plane bending modes of the H's on the terminal C=C's.

12.90 Account for the fact that ethene and ethyne, unlike propene and propyne, have no C-to-C multiple bond stretching bands.

▰ Ethene and ethyne are symmetrical molecules and do not undergo a change in dipole moment when excited. A change in dipole moment occurs when propene and propyne are excited and a band is observed.

12.91 Which of the following vibrational modes show no ir absorption bands? (a) Symmetric CO_2 stretch, (b) antisymmetric CO_2 stretch, (c) symmetric O=C=S stretch, and (d) symmetric NC—CN (C—C) stretch.

▰ Vibrations that do not result in a change in dipole moment show no band. These are (a) and (d) which are symmetrical about the axis of the stretched bonds.

12.92 The E2 dehydrohalogenation of 2,3-dimethyl-2-chlorobutane can lead to two possible products. Give these products. How can ir spectroscopy distinguish between them?

▰ $$Me_2CHCMe_2 \xrightarrow{-HCl} Me_2C=CMe_2 \ + \ Me_2CHC=CH_2$$
$$\underset{Cl}{|} \qquad\qquad\qquad \underset{\mathbf{A}}{} \qquad\qquad \underset{\underset{\mathbf{B}}{Me}}{|}$$

The symmetrical product, tetramethylethylene, **A**, does not show C=C vibrational excitation (see Problem 12.91). The other possible product, 2,3-dimethyl-1-butene, **B**, has a C=C peak at 1640 cm^{-1}, and shows the out-of-plane bending of the terminal alkene H's of an $R_2C=CH_2$ at 890 cm^{-1}.

12.93 The dehydration of 1,2-dimethylcyclohexanol (*cis* or *trans*) can give three alkenes. Give the structure of these alkenes and explain how ir can differentiate among them.

▰

The C—H out-of-plane bending frequencies in the 800-1000 cm^{-1} region are most useful to differentiate: **A** is an example of an $R_2C=CH_2$, absorbing at 895-885 cm^{-1}, **B** is a symmetrical tetrasubstituted alkene, which shows no absorption in this region (Problem 12.90), and **C** is a trisubstituted alkene, which absorbs at 840-790 cm^{-1}.

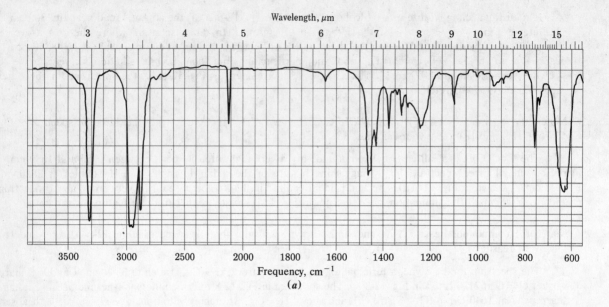

(a)

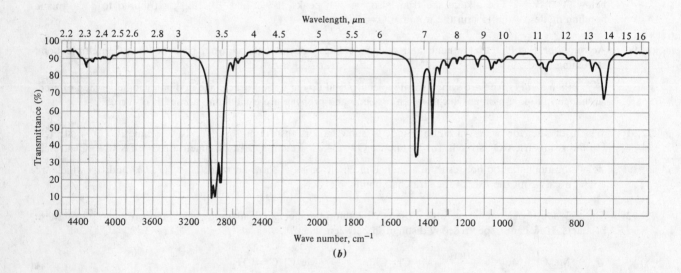

(b)

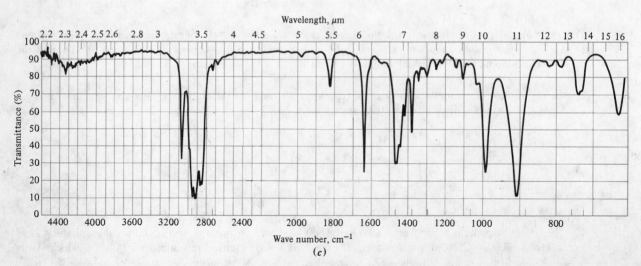

(c)

Fig. 12-8

12.94 Use ir to distinguish between (*a*) a 1° amide and a 1° amine and (*b*) a 1°, 2°, and 3° amine.

⬛ (*a*) Both have N—H stretching peaks, but the amide has the intense C═O peak as well. (*b*) At about 3300 cm^{-1} the 1° amine(RNH$_2$) has the H—N—H doublet, the 2° (R$_2$NH) has a single peak, and the 3° amine (R$_3$N), without an N—H, has no peaks.

12.95 Describe the characteristic absorption of a nitro group.

⬛ Nitro compounds are characterized by two bands: a very strong antisymmetric stretch at 1540-1615 cm^{-1} and a strong symmetric stretch at 1320-1390 cm^{-1}. As was noted for C═O groups, conjugation causes a shift to lower frequencies.

12.96 Explain the following observations. Concentrated solutions of C$_2$H$_5$OH and ethylene glycol, CH$_2$OHCH$_2$OH, have broad O—H bands near 3350 cm^{-1}. On dilution with CCl$_4$, the spectrum of the glycol does not change, but that of the alcohol shows a sharp band at 3600 cm^{-1} replacing the broad band at 3350 cm^{-1}.

⬛ The broad band at 3350 cm^{-1} is typical for the stretch of an H-bonded O—H group. H-bonding in CH$_2$OHCH$_2$OH is intramolecular and is not disturbed by dilution. H-bonding in C$_2$H$_5$OH is intermolecular. On dilution, the molecules move too far apart for H-bonding to occur and the stretching band for the non-H-bonded O—H at 3600 cm^{-1} is observed.

12.97 Match the spectra in Fig. 12-9 with the following compounds: toluene and the three C$_8$H$_{10}$ isomers, *o*-, *m*-, and *p*-xylene.

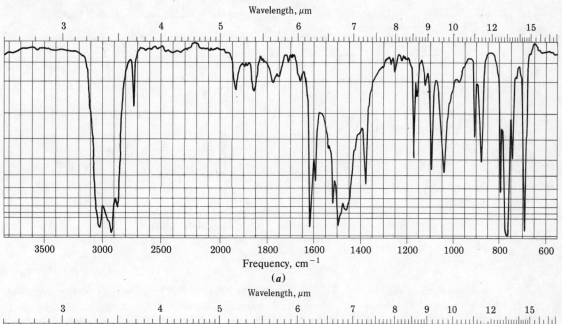

(a)

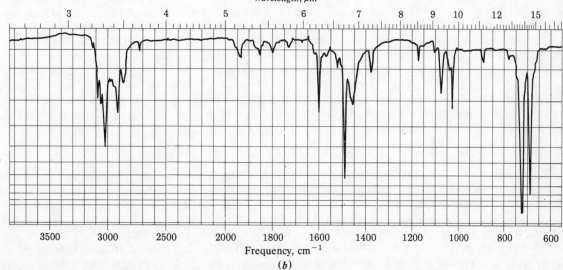

(b)

Fig. 12-9

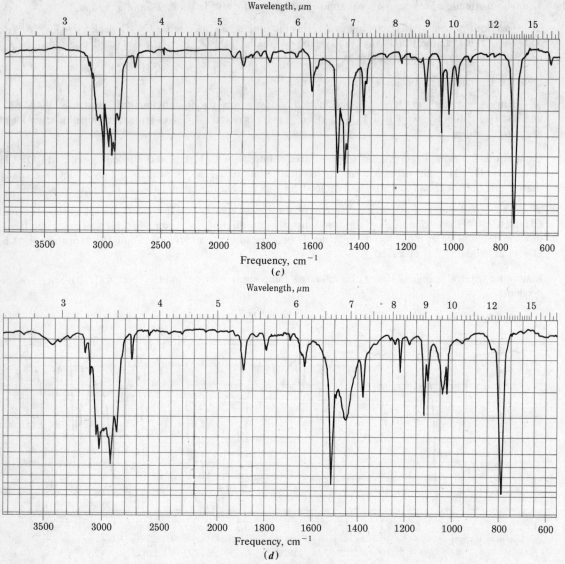

Fig. 12-9 (continued)

▌ All compounds show the aromatic H—C$_{sp^2}$ stretch at 3030 cm^{-1}. The aromatic C=C stretches appear as several bands in the 1500-1600 cm^{-1} region. The pattern varies with the orientation of the substitution. This region is little used for analysis because the bands have very low intensities and are often obscured by other nearby absorptions (especially the high intensity C=O stretch when present). The strong absorptions in the 675-870 cm^{-1} region that result from out-of-plane bending are more useful. The patterns vary with the number and position of substituents. Figure 12-9(a) has peaks at 770 and 690 cm^{-1} characteristic of *meta* disubstitution, and is tentatively identified as *m*-xylene. There is some ambiguity because monosubstituted benzene derivatives also show peaks in the same regions. Figure 12-9(b) is most likely the spectrum of toluene because its two peaks are at slightly lower frequencies, i.e., 720 and 680 cm^{-1}. The single peak at 740 cm^{-1} identifies the spectrum of Fig. 12-9(c) as that of *o*-xylene, and Fig. 12-9(d) is the spectrum of *p*-xylene, with one peak at 790 cm^{-1}.

12.98 Discuss the use of an ir spectrum for elucidating the structure of a hydrocarbon.

▌ We will move from left (high frequency) to right (low frequency) across the spectrum. The 3300-2800 cm^{-1} C—H stretch region is very instructive: 3300 cm^{-1} indicates C≡C—H, 3000-3100 cm^{-1} is due to C=C—H or Ar—H, and 2800-3000 cm^{-1} indicates the presence of C—H in saturated alkyl groups. The stretching frequencies of C-to-C multiple bonds appear in the 1450-2300 cm^{-1} region as indicated: C=C=C at 2300-2000 cm^{-1}, C≡C at 2200-2100 cm^{-1} (terminal, strong, and internal, weak), C=C at 1680-1640 cm^{-1}, C=C—C=C at 1640-1600 cm^{-1}, and aromatic C=C at 1600-1500 cm^{-1}. The C—C absorption at about 1200 cm^{-1} is useless because it is present in most organic compounds. However, the split band at 1378 cm^{-1}, referred to as the "*i*-propyl" or "*t*-butyl" split, indicates the presence of two or more Me's on a C atom. The lower frequency ranges for C—H bending for alkenes and aromatics is given in Problems 12.93 and 12.97.

12.99 Explain how the ir spectra of neat samples of phenol, C_6H_5OH, and cyclohexanol would differ.

▟ Both would show OH stretching in the 3450-3200 cm^{-1} range, with the phenol in the lower region. Phenol, however, would show the typical Ar—H absorption above 3000 cm^{-1}, and no C—H below 3000 cm^{-1}. This situation is reversed in cyclohexanol, which has C_{sp^3}—H below 3000 cm^{-1}, but no C_{sp^2}—H. Phenol would also absorb in the 1000-650 cm^{-1} range due to aromatic C—H bending.

12.100 Distinguish between the compounds in each pair by ir analysis: (*a*) *cis*- and *trans*-2-butene, and (*b*) ethylbenzene and *o*-xylene.

▟ (*a*) Both compounds show =C—H stretch at 3020 cm^{-1}, and C=C stretch around 1670 cm^{-1}. They differ in the out-of-plane bending, *cis*-2-butene absorbing in the 690 cm^{-1} region, while the *trans*-isomer absorbs strongly around 970 cm^{-1}. (*b*) Ethylbenzene, being monosubstituted, has two absorption peaks, at 750 and 700 cm^{-1}; *o*-xylene shows one band between 770-735 cm^{-1}.

NUCLEAR MAGNETIC RESONANCE (NMR) SPECTROSCOPY

1. ^1H nmr (pmr)

12.101 (*a*) What property of certain atomic nuclei is involved in nmr spectroscopy?

▟ The atomic nuclear "spin" state. Nuclei discussed in this section i.e., ^1H and ^{13}C, can exist in either of two spin states, $+\frac{1}{2}$ ($\uparrow$) or $-\frac{1}{2}$ ($\downarrow$), and are called nmr active nuclei.

12.102 Describe what happens when radiowave radiation is absorbed by ^1H nuclei in the presence of a strong applied magnetic field.

▟ The spinning nuclei generate small magnetic fields that are randomly oriented in space in the absence of an external magnetic field. In a large sample, equal numbers of nuclei are in each spin state because the states have the same energy—they are degenerate. Spin states do not have the same energy in an applied magnetic field because the nucleus is a charged particle, and a moving (in this case, spinning) charged particle generates a magnetic field of its own. The spinning nuclei align either with or against an applied magnetic field, giving rise to different quantized energy states. For the ^1H nucleus, the fields are opposed in the higher energy state (E_2) and aligned in the lower energy state (E_1) (Fig. 12-10). There are slightly more nuclei in E_1 than in E_2. When the magnetic field is removed, the energy states quickly become degenerate.

Recall that $E_2 - E_1 = \Delta E = h\nu$. The frequencies capable of "spin-flipping" the atomic nucleus from a lower to higher energy state are in the radiowave region (1–100 MHz, or wavelengths of 300–3 m), and the required frequency is directly proportional to the applied magnetic field. The stronger the field, the greater the energy required to bring about the transition. (At a field strength of 14,100 Gauss (G), a frequency of 60 MHz is required for spin-flipping the proton.) When the spin flips, the nucleus is said to be in *resonance* with the radiation; hence the name *nuclear magnetic resonance* (nmr) spectroscopy.

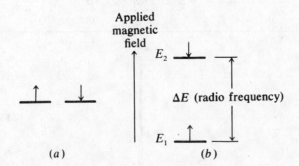

Fig. 12-10 Spin States for H.

12.103 (*a*) What property must a nucleus have to exhibit nuclear magnetic resonance? (*b*) Which atom is most studied by nmr spectroscopy in elucidating structures of organic molecules?

▟ (*a*) The nucleus must have an odd number of protons and/or neutrons. (*b*) Hydrogen; hence the name ^1H nuclear magnetic resonance (^1H nmr or pmr, *proton magnetic resonance*).

12.104 (*a*) Which of the following atoms are *not* nmr active: ^{12}C, ^{16}O, ^{14}N, ^{2}H (deuterium), ^{15}N, ^{19}F, ^{31}P, ^{13}C, ^{32}S? (*b*) With molecules having nmr active atoms other than H, how can a pmr spectrum free of absorption peaks of the other atoms be obtained?

▮ (*a*) Inactive atoms have an even number of protons *and* neutrons. These atoms are ^{12}C ($6p, 6n$), ^{16}O ($8p, 8n$), and ^{32}S ($16p, 16n$). (*b*) Ordinary spectrometers select the range of radiowave frequencies that excite only ^{1}H. Special "probes" are inserted into the instrument to get the spectra of the other nmr active atoms.

12.105 Briefly explain the technique for obtaining a nmr spectrum.

▮ In practice it is easier and cheaper to keep the frequency constant and gradually change the magnetic field strength, H_0. The sample compound is dissolved in a proton-free solvent such as CCl_4 or $DCCl_3$. (Although deuterium is nmr active, it does not interfere because it does not absorb in the frequency range set in the instrument for ^{1}H.) If a more polar solvent is needed, dry $(CD_3)_2S=O$ (perdeuterodimethyl sulfoxide) is used. The solution is placed in a long thin glass tube which is spun in the magnetic field so that all the molecules are exposed to a uniform magnetic field. A small amount of a reference compound, tetramethylsilane, $(CH_3)_4Si$ (Problems 12.108 and 12.109), is added to the sample. The spectrum is taken, and when the H_0 value is reached enabling the proton to be in resonance at the set frequency, a *signal* (peak) is traced on a calibrated chart paper that plots transmittance vs. H_0.

12.106 Explain why not all H's in a molecule spin-flip at the same *applied* magnetic field at constant frequency?

▮ At the fixed frequency of the spectrophotometer, all H's require the same field strength to spin-flip. However, the magnetic field "felt" by an H is not necessarily only that which is applied by the magnet, because the electrons in the bond to the H and those in nearby π bonds *induce* their own magnetic fields. This induced field partially *shields* the proton from the applied H_0. (The extent of the shielding depends on the neighboring electronic environment). The applied H_0 must then be increased. The field felt by the proton, the *effective field*, in a shielding situation is $H_{effective} = H_{0, applied} - H_{induced}$. The larger the shielding effect, the greater must be the applied field for resonance to occur. As shielding decreases, the applied field needed for resonance decreases. In those cases when the induced field actually deshields the proton, a smaller applied field is required to flip the proton (Problem 12.102). In this situation the effective field is the sum of the applied and induced fields. Therefore, the larger the induced field, the smaller the applied field must be.

12.107 Define the terms (*a*) downfield and (*b*) upfield as used in nmr spectra.

▮ To generate a spectrum, H_0 is increased from left to right. (*a*) The *less* shielded and the more deshielded proton signals appear *downfield* at the lower field, which is the left side of the plot. (*b*) The *more* shielded proton signals appear *upfield* at the higher field, which is the right side of the plot. See Fig. 12.11.

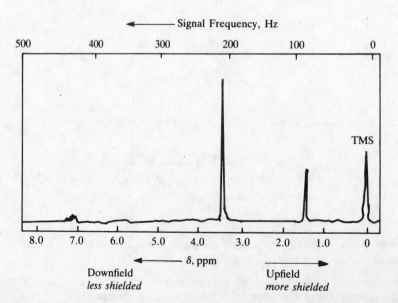

Fig. 12-11

12.108 (*a*) Define chemical shift, and (*b*) discuss how it is measured.

❙ The displacement of a signal from the hypothetical position of maximum shielding is called its chemical shift, notated as δ (delta) and measured in parts per million (ppm). Values are given on the horizontal scale at the bottom of the spectrum with the frequency scale, in Hz, at the top. The larger the δ value, the greater the chemical shift and the more downfield is the signal. Figure 12-11 illustrates a typical nmr spectrum. Chemical shifts are measured from the reference signal produced by the H's of Me_4Si (TMS), which is arbitrarily set on the bottom scale at δ = 0 ppm. Table 12-2 gives the proton chemical shift values.

TABLE 12-2 Proton Chemical Shifts

δ, ppm	Character of Underlined Proton	δ, ppm	Character of Underlined Proton
0.2	Cyclopropane: 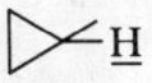 ▷H	4–2.5	Bromide: α H Br—C—H
0.9	Primary: R—CH₃	4–3	Chloride: α H Cl—C—H
1.3	Secondary: R₂CH₂	4–3.4	Alcohol: α H HO—C—H
1.5	Tertiary: R₃—CH	4–4.5	Fluoride: α H F—C—H
1.7	Allylic: —C=C—CH₃	4.1–3.7	Ester (I): α H to alkyl O R—C=O O—C⟨H
2.0–4.0	Iodide: α H I—C—H	5.0–1.0	Amine: R—NH₂
2.2–2.0	Ester (II): α H to C=O H—C—C=O OR	5.5–1.0	Hydroxyl: RO—H
2.6–2.0	Carboxylic acid: α H H—C—C=O OH	5.9–4.6	Vinylic: —C=C—H
2.7–2.0	Carbonyl: α H —C=O —C—H	8.5–6.0	Aromatic: 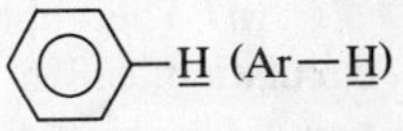 ⬡—H (Ar—H)
3–2	Acetylenic: —C≡C—H	10.0–9.0	Aldehyde: —C=O H
3–2.2	Benzylic: 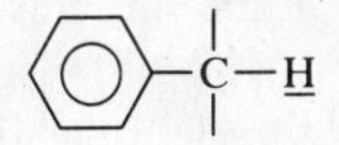 ⬡—C—H	12.0–10.5	Carboxyl: R—C=O O—H
3.3–4.0	Ether: α H R—O—C—H	12.0–4.0	Phenolic: 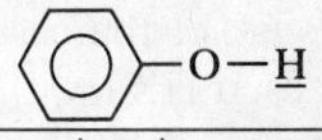 ⬡—O—H
		15.0–17.0	Enolic: —C=C—O—H

12.109 Explain why TMS is chosen as the reference compound.

▮ TMS gives a single peak because it has only one kind of H. Furthermore and most important, since its H's are more shielded than those of most other compounds, its single signal is usually isolated in the high upfield region.

12.110 (a) Is the δ value for a given kind of H an inherent constant number? (b) Find (i) the δ value and (ii) the observed shift from TMS in Hz of a signal in a 100-MHz instrument that is 162 Hz in a 60-MHz instrument.

▮ (a) Yes. The equation for δ is

$$\delta = \frac{\text{observed shift from TMS (Hz)}}{\text{frequency of spectrometer (commonly } 60 \times 10^6 \text{ Hz)}} \times 10^6 \text{ ppm}$$

The routinely-used nmr spectrometers operate at 60 MHz. For more detailed research, more expensive 100- and 200-MHz instruments are used. As the frequency of the instrument is changed, the observed shift from TMS changes accordingly and δ remains constant. The higher frequency spectrometers spread out the signals which are more accurately determined. (b) (i) Using the equation in (a),

$$\delta = 162 \text{ Hz} \times 10^6 / 60 \times 10^6 \text{ Hz} = 2.70 \text{ ppm}$$

(ii) Since δ is constant, 2.70 ppm = observed shift $\times 10^6 / 100 \times 10^6$ Hz from which observed shift = 270 Hz.

12.111 Discuss the influence of the electronegativity of A on the proton chemical shift of A—C—H.

▮ When A is an electronegative atom, e.g., O, N, X (halogen), the H is less shielded and its signal is more downfield. π-Bonded A groups, e.g., Ar (Ar—C—H), C=C (as in C=C—C—H), C≡C, C=O, and C≡N, are electronegative and also cause downfield shifts. The more electronegative is A, the greater the downfield shift. Electropositive A groups, such as Si, increase the shielding effect; this is the reason for using TMS as the reference compound.

12.112 Discuss the chemical shifts of H's attached directly to a π-bonded C and give the relative order of downfield shift of aldehydic, aryl, vinylic, and acetylenic H's compared to an alkyl H.

▮ These H's are all less shielded than those in alkanes. The order of decreasing δ values is

$$O{=}\overset{|}{C}{-}H > Ar{-}H > -\overset{|}{C}{=}\overset{|}{C}{-}H > -C{\equiv}C{-}H > -\overset{|}{\underset{|}{C}}{-}H$$

Aldehydic, aromatic, and vinylic H's are actually deshielded. An H attached to any aromatic molecule or ion appears considerably downfield, an observation that is a good criterion for aromaticity.

12.113 Account for the fact that (a) the δ value of an aromatic H (6 − 8.5 ppm) is higher than a vinylic H (4.6 − 5.9 ppm), and (b) [18]-annulene has two signals, 8.9 and −1.8 ppm.

▮ (a) The applied magnetic field induces the π e⁻'s in the aromatic ring to circulate around the ring. This circulation, called a *ring current*, generates a magnetic field which overshadows the normal shielding of the e⁻'s in any C—H bond. The net effect is to deshield the aromatic planar H's external to the ring. This effect, a kind of *anisotropy*, is called *paramagnetic deshielding*. The C=C of alkenes also has a deshielding anisotropic effect that, however, is less strong than that of the aromatic ring. As a result, vinylic H's are more upfield than aromatic H's. (b) [18]-Annulene (Problem 10.102) is aromatic. The signal at δ = 8.9 ppm arises from the 12 external H's that encounter a strong deshielding effect. The signal at δ = −1.8 ppm arises from the six internal H's that suffer a strong diamagnetic shielding effect because they lie *in* the ring current.

12.114 Why are acetylenic H's (δ = 2 to 3 ppm) more upfield (less downfield) than vinylic H's?

▮ We might expect that acetylenic H's, attached to C_{sp}, should give more downfield signals than vinylic H's. This is not the case, because the anisotropic effect of the induced circulation of the π e⁻'s shields the linearly disposed H's that lie within the ring current. Were it not for the strong electron-withdrawing effect of the C≡C group, signals for acetylenic H's would be even more upfield.

12.115 Give the relative decreasing order of δ values for 3°, 2°, 1°, and CH_4 (super 1°) H's.

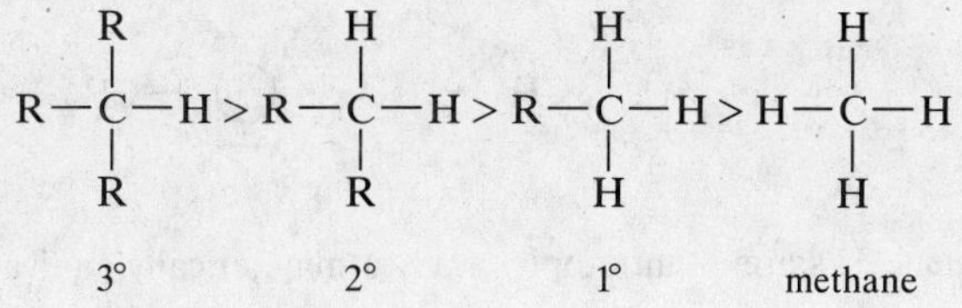

$$\overset{R}{\underset{R}{\overset{|}{R-C-H}}} > \overset{H}{\underset{R}{\overset{|}{R-C-H}}} > \overset{H}{\underset{H}{\overset{|}{R-C-H}}} > \overset{H}{\underset{H}{\overset{|}{H-C-H}}}$$

3°   2°   1°   methane

Shielding increases with the number of H's on the C.

12.116 Discuss the δ values of H's participating in H-bonding, e.g, OH and NH.

These H's exhibit δ values over a wide range, depending mainly on sample concentrations. Since H-bonding diminishes shielding, in concentrated solutions the OH signal for ROH and the NH signal for 1° and 2° amines move downfield because intermolecular H-bonding is enhanced. H-bonding is accompanied by exchange of H's from one molecule to another, resulting in signal broadening.

12.117 Give two kinds of H's that have negative δ values (more upfield than TMS).

H's attached to a cyclopropane ring and those situated in the π cloud of an aromatic system, as in [18]-annulene [see Problem 12.113(*b*)].

12.118 Describe the best way for determining the equivalence of H's. Illustrate with each H in

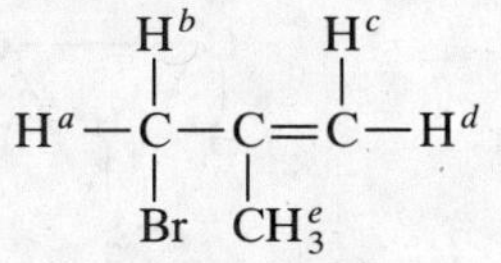

$$H^a - \overset{H^b}{\underset{Br}{\overset{|}{C}}} - \overset{H^c}{\underset{CH_3^e}{\overset{|}{C}}} = C - H^d$$

Replace one of the H's by X, and if the same product is obtained by replacement of any other H instead, the H's are equivalent. If enantiomeric products are obtained, the H's are also nmr equivalent providing the sample is in an archiral medium (which is the usual situation). If different products are obtained, including diastereomers, the H's are different. Replacement of H^a by X gives the enantiomer of the result of replacement of H^b; these H's are *enantiotopic* and they are indistinguishable by nmr. H^c and H^d give different signals; replacement of either one gives a different diastereomer. They are nonequivalent *diastereotopic* protons. All H's on the same CH_3 group are always equivalent.

12.119 How many kinds of H's are there in (*a*) CH_3CH_3, (*b*) $CH_3CH_2CH_3$, (*c*) $(CH_3)_2CHCH_2CH_3$, (*d*) $H_2C=CH_2$, (*e*) $CH_3CH=CH_2$, (*f*) $C_6H_5NO_2$, (*g*) $C_6H_5CH_3$?

(*a*) One (all equivalent).
(*b*) two: $CH_3^aCH_2^bCH_3^a$.
(*c*) four: $(CH_3^a)_2CH^bCH_2^cCH_3^d$.
(*d*) One (all equivalent).
(*e*) four:

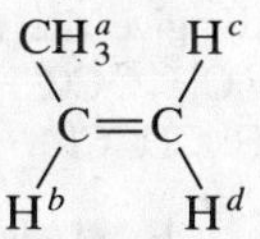

$$\overset{CH_3^a}{\underset{H^b}{\nwarrow}}C=C\overset{H^c}{\underset{H^d}{\nearrow}}$$

The $=CH_2$ H's are not equivalent since one is *cis* to the CH_3 and the other is *trans*. Replacement of H^c by X gives the *cis*-diastereomer. Replacement of H^d gives the *trans*-diastereomer.
(*f*) three: two *ortho*, two *meta*, and one *para*.
(*g*) Theoretically there are three kinds of aromatic H's, as in (*f*). Actually the ring H's are little affected by alkyl groups and are equivalent. There are two kinds: $C_6H_5^aCH_3^b$.

12.120 How many kinds of nonequivalent H's are there in (*a*) $p\text{-}CH_3CH_2C_6H_4CH_2CH_3$, (*b*) $Cl_2CHCH_2CH_2CH_2Cl$, and (*c*) $CH_3CHClCH_2CH_3$?

▰ (*a*) Three:

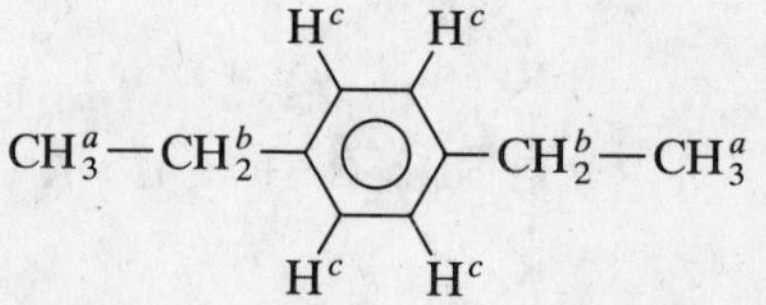

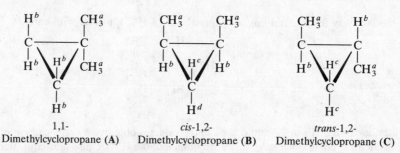

The methylene H's are enantiotopic and are magnetically equivalent.

(*b*) Four:

$$Cl_2CH^a—CH_2^b—CH_2^c—CH_2^dCl$$

(*c*) Five:

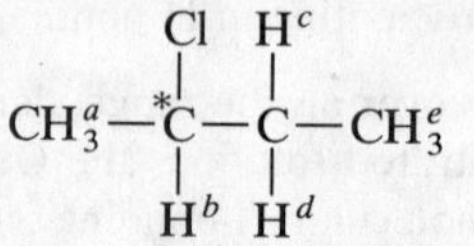

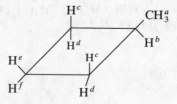

The methylene H's, H^c, and H^d are not equivalent because of the presence of the chiral C*. Replacing these diastereotopic H's separately by X (Problem 12.118) gives two diastereomers.

12.121 How many different H's are there in each of the three isomers of dimethylcyclopropane?

▰ Dimethylcyclopropane has three isomers, shown with labeled H's to indicate differences and equivalencies.

1,1- Dimethylcyclopropane (**A**)	*cis*-1,2- Dimethylcyclopropane (**B**)	*trans*-1,2- Dimethylcyclopropane (**C**)

In **B**, H^c and H^d are different since H^c is *cis* to the CH$_3$'s and H^d is *trans*. In (**C**) the CH$_2$ H's are equivalent; they are each *cis* to a CH$_3$ and *trans* to a CH$_3$.

12.122 Label the different H's in the methylcyclobutane.

▰ An H *trans* to Me is different from the *cis* H. There are six kinds of H's:

12.123 For each of the following compounds, give the number of H's with distinct NMR signals, and their relative δ values in decreasing order. (*a*) $CH_3OC(CH_3)_3$, (*b*) CH_3CH_2COOH, (*c*) *p*-xylene, 1,4-$(CH_3)_2C_6H_4$, (*d*) $(CH_3CH_2)_2O$, and (*e*) $CH_3OCH_2CH_2Cl$

▰ (*a*) Two; CH$_3$ (methoxy) > (CH$_3$)$_3$. (*b*) Three; acidic H > CH$_3$ (next to C=O of COOH) > CH$_3$. (*c*) Two; aromatic H's > CH$_3$. (*d*) Two; CH$_2$ > CH$_3$. (*e*) Three; O—CH$_2$ (2°) > O—CH$_3$ (1°) > CH$_2$—Cl (Cl is less electronegative than O).

12.124 Write a structure for each of the following compounds. Given: the corresponding number of different H's. (*a*) $C_2H_4Cl_2$, one H; (*b*) C_8H_{18}, one H; (*c*) C_9H_{12}, two H's; (*d*) noncyclic C_6H_{12}, one H; and (*e*) C_3H_7Cl, three H's.

▰ (*a*) ClCH$_2$CH$_2$Cl; the isomeric 1,1-dichloroethane has two kinds of H's. (*b*) A saturated hydrocarbon with eight C's must have only equivalent branched CH$_3$'s: (CH$_3$)$_3$C—C(CH$_3$)$_3$. (*c*) Four degrees of unsaturation points to a substituted benzene: 1,3,5-trimethylbenzene, mesitylene. (*d*) One C=C is present; all H's must be in Me's: $(CH_3)_2C{=}C(CH_3)_2$. (*e*) $CH_3CH_2CH_2Cl$; the incorrect isomer, 2-chloropropane, has only two kinds of H's.

12.125 Is it possible to distinguish among the seven isomers of $C_4H_{10}O$ by the number of distinct signals in their pmr spectra? Explain.

▮ With zero degrees of unsaturation and only a single O, the isomers must be alcohols or ethers. The seven isomers and their corresponding number of different H's are:

$CH_3^aCH_2^bCH_2^cCH_2^dOH^e$	$CH_3^aCH_2^{b,c}CH^d(OH^e)CH_3^f$	$(CH_3^a)_2CH^bCH_2^cOH^d$	$(CH_3^a)_3COH^b$
A, 5	**B**, 6	**C**, 4	**D**, 2

$CH_3^aCH_2^bCH_2^c{-}O{-}CH_3^d$	$CH_3^aCH_2^b{-}O{-}CH_2^bCH_3^a$	$(CH_3^a)_2CH^b{-}O{-}CH_3^c$
E, 4	**F**, 2	**G**, 3

A, **B**, and **G** can be distinguished from all the isomers. (In **B**, H^b and H^c are diastereotopic.)

12.126 (*a*) Explain why 1,2-dibromoethane and cyclohexane have single sharp signals although they have conformationally different H's. (*b*) Under what conditions might more than a single signal be observed for these compounds?

▮ (*a*) The H's in *gauche* and *anti* 1,2-dibromoethane and the equatorial and axial H's of cyclohexane should each give different signals. However, the conformers of each of these compounds are interconverted more rapidly than the magnetic nuclei can absorb the exciting radiation. As a result, a single signal is observed with an *average* chemical shift that reflects the relative shifts and populations of the conformers in question. The nmr sensing is much slower than that of uv and ir. (*b*) At sufficiently low temperatures to slow down the interconversions of conformers, signals for each conformationally different H might be observed. The intensities of these individual signals would correspond to the actual populations of the conformers at the attained temperature.

12.127 (*a*) How is the relative numbers of equivalent H's obtained from an ^1H nmr spectrum? (*b*) Determine the number of equivalent H's from the spectrum for $ClCH_2OCH_3$ in Fig. 12-12.

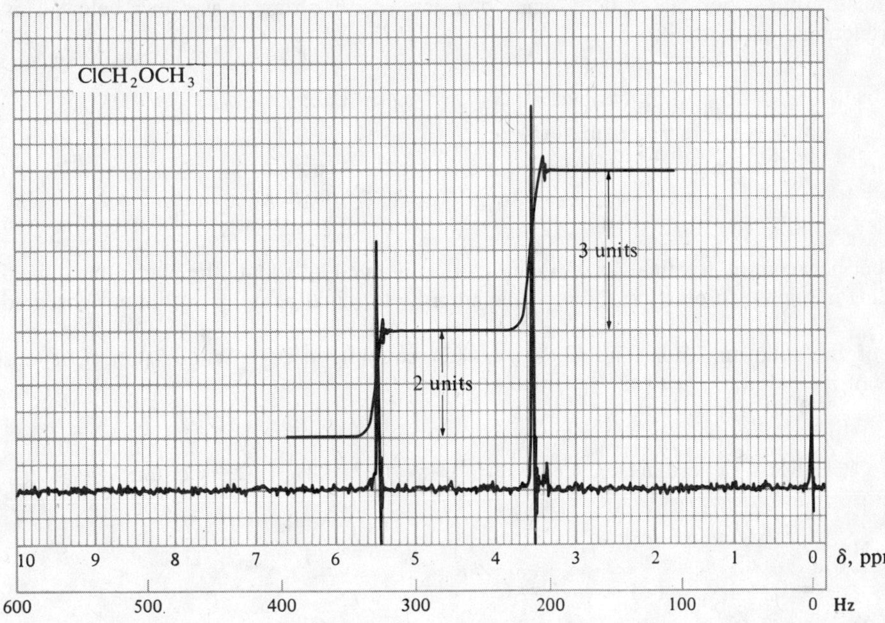

Fig. 12-12

▮ The instrument actually integrates the areas proceeding from left to right across the spectrum. If no signal is present, a horizontal line is drawn. On reaching the signal, the line ascends, leveling off when the signal ends. The vertical distances for each signal on the chart are proportional to the relative areas and number of equivalent H's giving that signal. These may be determined by counting boxes on the chart or by measurement with a ruler. (*b*) Figure 12-12 shows two peaks with a relative area of 4 : 6. This is consistent with a ratio of equivalent H's of 4 : 6 or 2 : 3.

12.128 (*a*) Give the relative signal areas for each of the compounds in Problem 12.125.   (*b*) With this information, is it possible to distinguish between **A** and **B**, **C** and **E**, and **D** and **F**? Explain.

▮ (*a*) The areas are listed in the order of the H's given: **A**, $3:2:2:2:1$; **B**, $3:1:1:1:1:3$; **C**, $6:1:2:1$; **D**, $9:1$; **E**, $3:2:2:3$; **F**, $3:2$ (not $6:4$); and **G**, $6:1:3$. (*b*) Yes, based upon the different relative integration areas.

12.129 Discuss *spin-spin coupling* with the aid of the molecular fragment $-CH^a-CH_2^b-$.

▮ The signal for a given H is shifted slightly upfield or downfield depending on how the spins of H's on adjacent atoms are aligned with the applied field. H^b appears as an approximately equal intensity *doublet* because the H^a's in about half of the molecules have a ↑ spin and the other half have a ↓ spin. The effect is reciprocal; the signal of H^a is split by the two H^b's which have four spin states of approximately equal probability:

$$\uparrow\uparrow, \{\uparrow\downarrow, \downarrow\uparrow\}, \downarrow\downarrow$$

Because the braced spin states have the same effect, the signal of H^a is split into a *triplet* with relative intensities $1:2:1$. The H^b doublet integrates for two H's, the H^a triplet for one H. Only nonequivalent H's couple; equivalent ones, e.g., the H's of CH_3, do not. In general, if n equivalent H's are affecting the signal of H's on an adjacent C, the signal is split into a *multiplet* containing $n+1$ peaks. A symmetrical multiplet is an ideal condition not always observed in practice.

12.130 Explain the splitting pattern for the $-CH^a-CH_3^b$ unit.

▮ The single H^a splits H^b into a doublet integrating for three H's. H^a appears as a *quartet* ($n = 3$; see 12.129) due to the following spinning pattern for the three H

$$\uparrow\uparrow\uparrow \quad \{\uparrow\uparrow\downarrow, \uparrow\downarrow\uparrow, \downarrow\uparrow\uparrow\} \quad \{\downarrow\downarrow\uparrow, \downarrow\uparrow\downarrow, \uparrow\downarrow\downarrow\} \quad \downarrow\downarrow\downarrow$$

Relative intensities: $1 : 3 : 3 : 1$

The entire quartet integrates for one H.

12.131 Give the ideal relative intensities for (*a*) a quintet, (*b*) a sextet, and (*c*) a septet.

▮ The relative intensities can be determined by using a Pascal triangle as shown below. This also includes a doublet, triplet, and quartet.

doubet	$1:1$
triplet	$1:2:1$
quartet	$1:3:3:1$
quintet	$1:4:6:4:1$
sextet	$1:5:10:10:5:1$
septet	$1:6:15:20:15:6:1$

Each number between the terminal 1's of a multiplet is obtained by adding the pair of numbers directly above in the preceding multiplet. In practice, the very low intensity terminal peaks are often not observed.

12.132 In which of the following molecules does spin-spin coupling occur? When splitting is observed give the multiplicity of each kind of H.

(*a*) $ClCH_2CH_2Cl$ (*b*) $ClCH_2CH_2I$ (*c*) $CH_3-\overset{\displaystyle CH_3}{\underset{\displaystyle CH_3}{C}}-CH_2Br$ (*g*)

(*d*) $\overset{H}{\underset{Br}{}}C=C\overset{H}{\underset{Br}{}}$ (*e*) $\overset{H}{\underset{Br}{}}C=C\overset{Cl}{\underset{H}{}}$ (*f*) $\overset{I}{\underset{Cl}{}}C=C\overset{H}{\underset{H}{}}$

▮ Splitting is not observed in (*a*) or (*d*), which each have only equivalent H's, or in (*c*), which has no nonequivalent H's on *adjacent* C's. The H's of CH_2 in (*b*) are nonequivalent and each is split into a triplet ($n = 2$; $2 + 1 = 3$). In (*e*) the two H's are not equivalent and each is split into a doublet. The vinylic H's in (*f*) are nonequivalent since one is *cis* to Cl and the other is *cis* to I. Each is split into a doublet. In this case the interacting H's are on the same C. Compound (*g*) gives a singlet for the four equivalent uncoupled aromatic H's, a quartet for the H's of the two equivalent CH_2 groups coupled with CH_3, and a triplet for the two equivalent CH_3 groups coupled with CH_2.

12.133 (a) Give schematic coupling patterns showing relative chemical shifts for the following alkyl groups: (i) ethyl, —CH_2CH_3; (ii) i-propyl, —$CH(CH_3)$; and (iii) t-butyl, —$C(CH_3)_3$. (b) How is the chemical shift of a multiplet signal determined?

▰ (a) See Fig. 12-13.

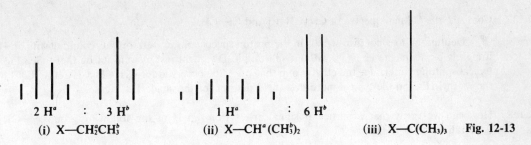

2 H^a : 3 H^b 1 H^a : 6 H^b

(i) X—$CH_2^a CH_3^b$ (ii) X—$CH^a(CH_3^b)_2$ (iii) X—$C(CH_3)_3$ **Fig. 12-13**

(b) The chemical shift is the δ value at the center of the multiplet. For an odd numbered multiplet, the center is the middle peak; if even numbered the chemical shift is midway between the two central peaks. Frequently the multiplet is not perfectly symmetrical. The peaks at one side may be higher than the corresponding ones to the other side. In such cases, the chemical shift is displaced somewhat toward the side with the larger peaks. It is at the "center of gravity" of the multiplet.

12.134 Sketch the ^{1}H nmr spectrum with integrations, using relative (not actual) chemical shifts, for: (a) 1,1-dichloroethane, (b) 1,1,2-trichloroethane, (c) 1,1,2,2-tetrachloroethane, and (d) 1-bromo-2-chloroethane.

▰ See Fig. 12-14. In (d), H^a is more downfield than H^b because Cl is more electron-withdrawing than Br.

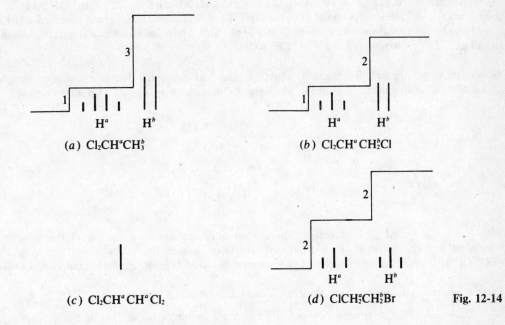

(a) $Cl_2CH^a CH_3^b$ (b) $Cl_2CH^a CH_2^b Cl$

(c) $Cl_2CH^a CH^a Cl_2$ (d) $ClCH_2^a CH_2^b Br$ **Fig. 12-14**

12.135 Why is splitting observed in 2-methylpropene (**C**) but not in neopentyl chloride (1-chloro-2,2-dimethylpropane) (**D**)?

▰ Although H^a and H^b in **C** are not on adjacent C's, they are close enough to couple because of the shorter C=C bond. In **D**, H^a and H^b on nonadjacent C's are too far away to couple, the C's being joined by longer single bonds.

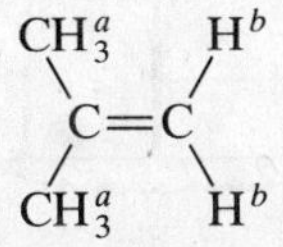

$$CH_3^a \quad H^b$$
$$\diagdown \qquad \diagup$$
$$C{=}C \qquad (CH_3^a)_3 C—CH_2^b Cl$$
$$\diagup \qquad \diagdown$$
$$CH_3^a \quad H^b$$

C   **D**

12.136 Predict the splitting of (*a*) H and (*b*) F for 2,2-difluoropropane.

▰ (*a*) F's, like H's, have half-spin ($+1/2$ and $-1/2$) nuclei and therefore split vicinal H's as predicted by the $n+1$ rule. In $CH_3^a CF_2 CH_3^a$ the two F's split the equivalent H^a's into a $1:2:1$ triplet. (*b*) F is nmr active and it's nmr spectrum can be obtained with the aid of a special probe using a different frequency than used for H. The six adjacent H's would split the F signal into a septet.

12.137 Compare the ^1H nmr spectra of CH_3CH_2Cl and CH_3CHDCl.

▰ Deuterium does not give signals in the proton spectrum. Furthermore, its coupling with an H is so weak that it merely broadens the H signal without splitting it. D's might just as well not be there. See Fig. 12-13(i) for the typical splitting pattern for the ethyl group that would be observed for CH_3CH_2Cl. CH_3CHDCl has a doublet for the methyl H's and the typical more downfield quartet for the single H.

12.138 How can we verify that a particular signal arises from an H of the following groups, —OH, —NH, —SH (generalized as —AH)?

▰ Add excess D_2O, shake the tube, and rerun the spectrum. The H's in these groups are replaced by D's:

$$R{-}A{-}H + D_2O \rightleftharpoons R{-}A{-}D + DOH$$

Since D does not resonate under the conditions used for H, the original peak for the —A—H proton practically disappears in the spectrum rerun in D_2O. A new signal for DOH appears.

12.139 (*a*) Explain why the ^1H nmr spectrum of CH_3OH in CCl_4 shows two singlets but in $(CD_3)_2S{=}O$ it shows a doublet and quartet. (*b*) Which isomeric alcohol, $C_5H_{12}O$, shows a singlet OH peak in deuterated DMSO?

▰ (*a*) H's participating in intramolecular or intermolecular H-bonding move back and forth from one OH to another so rapidly that they cannot couple with vicinal H's. This situation occurs in CCl_4; there is intermolecular H-bonding and no coupling. Thus each kind of H appears as a singlet. In deuterated DMSO H-bonding with the *solvent* occurs, and the H stays on the O of the OH. The typical coupling pattern is observed. (*b*) The technique in (*a*) can be used to distinguish 3° from 1° and 2° alcohols. Since the signal is a singlet, the alcohol in question must be 3°. The compound is $CH_3CH_2C(CH_3)_2OH$.

12.140 Generalize about the relative chemical shifts of axial and equatorial H's in substituted cyclohexanes if the chemical shifts of the encircled H in the *trans* and *cis* isomer are 4.14 and 4.54 ppm, respectively.

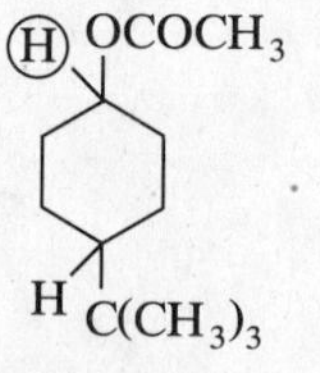

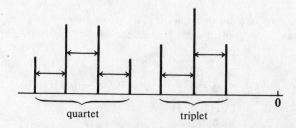

▰ The bulky *t*-butyl group "freezes" the conformation. In the *trans*-1,4 isomer the substituents are both equatorial and the encircled H is axial. In the *cis*-1,4 isomer the bulky *t*-butyl group is equatorial, the —$OCOCH_3$ is axial and the encircled H is equatorial. An *axial* H is more upfield than its equatorial counterpart.

12.141 Define the term coupling constant. Illustrate using the ethyl group pattern.

▰ See Fig. 12-15. The spacing between lines within a multiplet is constant and is independent of the field strength. Furthermore, the spacing in *each mutually coupled multiplet* is the same. This constant distance is called the *coupling constant*, J, and is expressed in Hz.

quartet   triplet   0   **Fig. 12-15**

TABLE 12-3

Type of H's	J, Hz
H—C—C—H (free rotation of C—C)	≈ 7
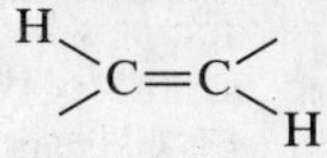 *trans*	13–18
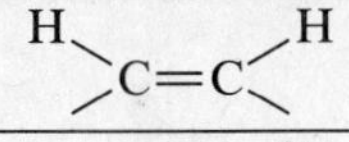 *cis*	7–12
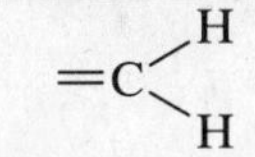	0–3
Phenyl H's *ortho* *meta* *para*	 6–9 1–3 0–1

12.142 Give the structural formula for a compound, C_2H_2BrCl, that has two doublets, $J = 16$ Hz. See Table 12-3 for J values.

▊ The three isomers and the respective J values are

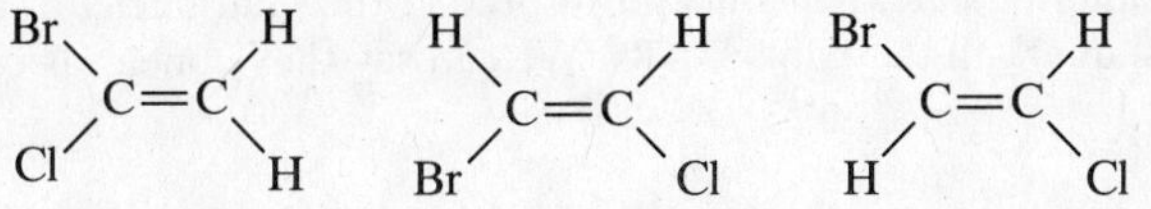

gem-vinyl H's	*cis* H's	*trans* H's
$J = 0–3$ Hz	$J = 7–12$ Hz	$J = 13–18$ Hz

The *trans* isomer fits the data. Note that J values are useful for the structure proof.

12.143 In terms of the concept of coupling constants, discuss the indiscriminate application of the $n + 1$ rule using the following information: in $CH_3^a CH_2^b CH_2^c NO_2$ (**A**) H^b appears as a sextet but in $BrCH_2^a CH_2^b CH_2^c Cl$ (**B**) H^b appears as three overlapping triplets.

▊ When applying the $n + 1$ rule to an H (or H's) flanked on more than one side by vicinal H's, a problem arises as to the number of H's to include in the value of n. Certainly, when all the vicinal H's are identical, e.g., the CH_3 groups of $(CH_3)_2CHCl$, they are totaled to give the n value (six) for finding the multiplicity of the signal (a septet) for the lone H. Although the vicinal H's are different and have different chemical shifts, they can still be combined to give n if the pairs of vicinal H's have the *same* or nearly the same coupling constants. This happens in **A** ($J_{ab} = J_{bc}$), because H^b appears as a sextet ($5 + 1 = 6$). When the coupling constants are different, the vicinal H's cannot be added and each kind of vicinal H couples independently with the H in question. This is the case for **B**. H^b's triplet from coupling with H^c is further split into a triplet due to coupling with H^a. Overlapping triplets may not always be recognizable. They may appear as a complex multiplet because peaks of each triplet may overlap with each other.

12.144 Predict the relative chemical shifts, multiplicities, and relative intensities of the H's in the following compounds (CCl_4 solvent).

(*a*) $H^a C \equiv CCH_2^b OCH_3^c$

(*d*) $BrCH_2^a CH_2^b CH_2^c Br$

(*b*) $(CH_3^a)_2 CH^b C{-}CH_3^c$, with $\|$ and O below

(*e*)

(*c*) $H^a OCH_2^b CH_2^c CH_2^d COOH^e$

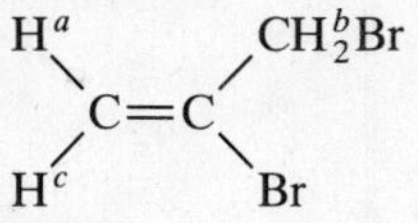

▊ H's are listed in order of decreasing chemical shifts. (*a*) Each H is a singlet (no vicinal or different geminal H's). H^b (influenced by electronegative O and $C \equiv C$) > H^c (influenced only by O) > H^a (acetylenic) with relative intensities of 2:3:1. (*b*) H^b septet (3°, influenced by C=O) > H^c singlet (1°, influenced by C=O) > H^a

doublet (most removed from C=O) with relative intensities of $1:3:6$ (c) H^e singlet > H^b triplet (influenced by O) > H^d triplet > H^c quintet if $J_{bc} = J_{cd}$, or three overlapping triplets if $J_{bc} \neq J_{cd}$. The chemical shift of H^a is unpredictable. The relative intensities are $1:2:2:2:1$. (d) H^a is equivalent to H^c and gives a triplet (influenced by Br) > H^b quintet, with relative intensities of $2:1$. (e) H^a and H^c are geminal, but not equivalent and thus they split each other. The coupling constant is small, so there is little separation between the peaks in each doublet. $H^c > H^a$ (slightly downfield because it is *cis* to the Br) > H^b, with relative intensities of $1:1:2$. Long range coupling of H^a with H^b is disregarded (Problem 12.135), because J_{ba} is so small.

12.145 Sketch the ^1H nmr spectra with integrations showing relative chemical shifts for the following compounds: (a) p-$H_3CC_6H_4CH(CH_3)_2$, (b) p-$CH_3NHC_6H_4CHO$, (c) 1,3,5-trimethylbenzene (mesitylene), (d) o-$CH_3OC_6H_4COOH$, (e) $C_6H_5OCH_2CH_2Cl$, (f) p-$CH_3CH_2OC_6H_4NH_2$, (g) m-dinitrobenzene, and (h) $C_6H_5CH(CH_3)NH_2$.

◢ See Fig. 12-16. (a) Although the aromatic H's *ortho* to Me are not identical to those *ortho* to i-Pr, they are magnetically equivalent and hence appear as a singlet integrating for four H's. (b) Each pair of equivalent aromatic H's is split into a doublet. The —CHO is strongly electron-withdrawing and the bonded N of —NHCH$_3$ is strongly electron-donating. Hence the doublet for the H's *ortho* to —CHO is more downfield than the doublet for the H's *ortho* to the amino group. (c) The Me's are equivalent as are the aromatic H's. The spectrum shows two singlets. (d) The —COOH is electron-withdrawing and —OCH$_3$ is electron-donating. Of all the aromatic H's, H^c (a doublet), *ortho* to COOH, is the most downfield, H^d (a doublet) is the most upfield and H^e and H^f are intermediate. It is difficult to predict the multiplicity of these H's because of the uncertainty of the coupling constants with the flanking H's. We can say they appear as complex multiplets. The H of COOH

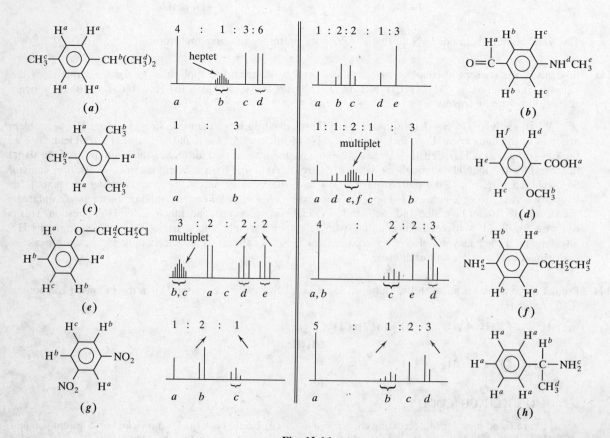

Fig. 12-16

has the most downfield chemical shift, even more than the aldehydic H. (Each peak of the H^c and H^d doublet actually appears as a doublet with very small J value because of long range splitting with the H's *meta* to them, i.e., ‖ ‖ instead of ⏐ ⏐.) (*e*) Each CH_2 appears as a triplet. As it often occurs in real situations the triplets are not symmetrical. They actually appear as

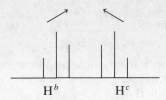

Arrows drawn from the smaller to the larger outer peak of each multiplet point towards each other. This phenomenon is called *leaning*. The *ortho* H's show as a doublet more upfield than typical aromatic H's. The other three aromatic H's appear as a complex multiplet for reasons discussed in (*d*). (*f*) Although the aromatic H's are different, because the electronic effects of —OCH_2CH_3 and —NH_2 are similar, their signal is a singlet. The signal for NH_2, which has a variable chemical shift, in this case is more upfield than the signal for —CH_2O—. The multiplets for CH_3CH_2— show leaning. (*g*) The H *ortho* to each —NO_2 has the most downfield signal, a singlet. The other equivalent *ortho* H's appear as a less downfield doublet since they couple with the lone *meta* H. The *meta* H should be a triplet since there is coupling with the two *ortho* H's. Do not be surprised if there is some overlapping of the doublet and triplet. There may also be some long range coupling between the two kinds of *ortho* H's. (*h*) Since the —NH_2 is not attached directly to the ring, its electronic effect, now electron-withdrawing, is greatly attenuated and the five aromatic H's appear as a singlet.

12.146 Use ^1H nmr spectroscopy to distinguish between the following geometric isomers **A** and **B**.

$$\underset{Br}{\overset{H^a}{}}C=C\underset{H^b}{\overset{CH_3^c}{}} \qquad \underset{H^a}{\overset{Br}{}}C=C\underset{H^b}{\overset{CH_3^c}{}}$$

           A   **B**

▰   For each isomer, the chemical shifts, relative intensities, and coupling patterns are the same. The only difference is the J_{ab} value, which is much larger in **A**, where H^a and H^b are *trans* (see Problem 12.142).

12.147 (*a*) Discuss the ^1H nmr spectrum of **C** in terms of relative chemical shifts.

$$\text{C}$$

(*b*) Explain why it is necessary to use a 100 MHz spectrophotometer for this study. (*c*) Why is undeuterated cyclohexanol not used to determine the coupling pattern observed for **C**?

▰   (*a*) H^a and H^e are diastereotopic H's (Problem 12.118). They couple each other (geminal coupling), as well as with H^c. Hence, H^a and H^e both appear as two pairs of doublets, the axial H being more upfield. The most downfield H^c is split into a triplet by the two H^a's and each signal of this triplet is further split into a triplet by the two H^e's. (*b*) With a 60 MHz instrument the two inner peaks of the H^e doublets are so close that they merge into a broad peak giving the appearance of a triplet. To show these individual triplets more distinctly, the spectrum must be taken on a 100 MHz spectrophotometer, which spreads out the signals. (*c*) The deuterated compound (**C**) is used to remove the complications arising from coupling of H^a and H^b with H's on their other flank.

12.148 Deduce the structure for each of the following compounds from the given ^1H nmr spectral data. Values of δ are in ppm and s = singlet, d = doublet, t = triplet, q = quartet, p = pentet, s = sextet, h = heptet, m = multiplet.

(The given number of H's were calculated using the relative intensities from the integration and the total number of H's from the molecular formula.)

(a) C_6H_{14}: 0.8, d, 12 H's; 1.4, h, two H's
(b) C_3H_7ClO: 2.0, p, two H's; 2.8, s, one H; 3.7, t, two H's; 3.8, t, two H's
(c) $C_3H_3Cl_5$: 4.52, t, one H; 6.07, d, two H's
(d) $C_3H_5Cl_3$: 2.20, s, three H's; 4.02, s, two H's
(e) C_4H_9Br: 1.04, d, six H's, 1.95, m, one H; 3.33, d, two H's
(f) $C_3H_5ClF_2$: 1.75, t, three H's; 3.63, t, two H's

▰ All compounds have 0° of unsaturation; they are alkanes or alkane derivatives.

(a) The 12-H doublet indicates two pairs of equivalent CH_3's coupled with equivalent vicinal methine H's that give a heptet. $(CH_3)_2CHCH(CH_3)_2$.

(b) The 1-H singlet is from OH. There are three CH_2's the middle one showing as a pentet because the different flanking CH_2's have similar J values. $HOCH_2CH_2CH_2Cl$.

(c) In the correct structure two H's are equivalent, splitting the single H into a triplet. They are bonded to a C with two Cl's causing their signal to be more downfield. $Cl_2CHCHClCHCl_2$. The isomers $Cl_3CCHClCH_2Cl$ and $Cl_3CCH_2CHCl_2$ show the correct multiplicity and relative integration, but the chemical shifts are in the wrong order.

(d) The 3-H and 2-H singlets arise respectively from a CH_3 and CH_2 with no vicinal H's—they each have only two vicinal Cl's. $CH_3CCl_2CH_2Cl$.

(e) The 6-H doublet and 1-H multiplet are typical of an *i*-propyl H vicinal to other H's. The more downfield 2-H doublet is due to the CH_2 of the $CHCH_2Br$ grouping. $(CH_3)_2CHCH_2Br$.

(f) The 3-H and 2-H signals from CH_3 and CH_2 respectively are triplets because they are split by two vicinal F's. $CH_3CF_2CH_2Cl$.

12.149 Solve Problem 12.148 for each of the following compounds.
(a) $C_4H_6Cl_2$: 2.2, s, three H's; 4.1, d, two H's; 5.7, t, one H
(b) C_6H_{12}: 0.9, t, three H's; 1.6, s, three H's; 1.7, s, three H's; 2.0, p, two H's; 5.1, t, one H
(c) $C_5H_{10}O$: 0.95, d, six H's; 2.10, s, three H's; 2.43, h, one H
(d) C_3H_5Br: 2.32, s, three H's; 5.35, broad s, one H; 5.54, broad s, one H
(e) C_4H_7BrO: 2.11, s, three H's; 3.52, t, two H's; 4.40, t, two H's

▰ Each compound has 1° of unsaturation, indicating the possible presence of C=C, C=O or a ring.

(a) The 1-H triplet at $\delta = 5.7$ ppm indicates a vinylic H split by a vicinal CH_2. The compound can be either the E or Z stereoisomer of $ClCH_2CH=C(CH_3)Cl$.

(b) Again the 1-H triplet at $\delta = 5.1$ ppm indicates a vinylic H split by a vicinal CH_2 which is also coupled with a CH_3— it is part of a CH_3CH_2— group. There are also two uncoupled CH_3's on the C=C, one *cis* and one *trans* to the vinylic H. $CH_3CH_2CH=C(CH_3)_2$

(c) Since there are no vinylic H's, the unsaturation is probably due to a C=O. This assumption is reinforced by finding a 3-H (CH_3) singlet at $\delta = 2.10$ ppm. The 6-H doublet and the 1-H heptet is typical of *i*-propyl.
$CH_3\overset{\underset{\|}{O}}{C}CH(CH_3)_2$.

(d) The broad singlets at 5.35 and 5.54 ppm indicate two geminal vinylic H's. The peaks are broad because for geminal coupling $J = 2$ Hz, a small value. $H_2C=CBr(CH_3)$.

(e) The absence of vinylic H's again indicates a C=O, confirmed by the 2.11-ppm value for the singlet CH_3. The two 2-H triplets indicate two CH_2's with the one more downfield being bonded to Br. Note that Br causes a more downfield shift than C=O. $CH_3\overset{\underset{\|}{O}}{C}CH_2CH_2Br$.

12.150 Solve Problem 12.148 for each of the following compounds.
(a) C_8H_{10}: 1.2, t, three H's; 2.6, q, two H's; 7.1, s, five H's
(b) $C_{10}H_{14}$: 1.30, s, nine H's; 7.30, s, five H's
(c) $C_{10}H_{14}$: 0.88, d, six H's; 1.86, m, one H; 2.45, d, two H's; 7.12, s, five H's
(d) C_9H_{10}: 2.04, p, two H's; 2.91, t, four H's; 7.17, s, four H's.
(e) $C_{14}H_{14}$: 2.9, s, four H's; 7.1, s, ten H's

▰ These compounds have at least 4° of unsaturation, indicating the presence of at least one benzene ring.

(a) The 5-H singlet at 7.1 ppm indicates a monosubstituted benzene compound. The 2-H quartet and 3-H triplet is typical of CH_3CH_2—. $C_6H_5CH_2CH_3$.

(*b*) The 5-H singlet in the aromatic region pinpoints a monosubstituted benzene ring. The 9-H singlet indicates three CH_3's with no vicinal H's, which is typical of a *t*-butyl group. $C_6H_5C(CH_3)_3$.

(*c*) Again there is a monosubstituted benzene ring. The 2-H doublet at 2.45 ppm shows a CH_2 with a single vicinal H, bonded to the ring. This single H also splits the signal for the six H's of two CH_3's into a doublet. $C_6H_5CH_2CH(CH_3)_2$.

(*d*) There are 5° of unsaturation. In the absence of vinylic H's, the fifth degree must be a ring as confirmed by the fact that the remaining three C's are methylene groups. The ring is fused to the benzene ring that is disubstituted at *ortho* positions.

(*e*) The 8° of unsaturation signals two benzene rings, each monosubstituted because of the ten aromatic H's. The 4-H singlet indicates two equivalent CH_2 groups. $C_6H_5CH_2CH_2C_6H_5$.

12.151 Select the cogent features of the ^1H nmr spectra that aid in distinguishing between the following pairs of isomers.

(*a*) $p\text{-}CH_3C_6H_4CH_3$ and $C_6H_5CH_2CH_3$

(*b*) $CH_3CH_2\overset{\|}{\underset{O}{C}}H$ and $CH_3\overset{\|}{\underset{O}{C}}CH_3$

(*c*) $CH_3\overset{\|}{\underset{O}{C}}OCH_2CH_3$ and $CH_3CH_2\overset{\|}{\underset{O}{C}}OCH_3$

(*d*) $CH_3CH_2CH_2C{\equiv}CH$ and $CH_3CH_2C{\equiv}CCH_3$

(*e*) $H_2C{=}CBrC_6H_5$ and (*E*) $H{-}\underset{Br}{\overset{}{C}}{=}\underset{H}{\overset{}{C}}C_6H_5$

(*f*) $H_2C{=}CHCH_2CH_3$ and $H_2C\overset{}{\underset{CH_2}{\diagdown\diagup}}CHCH_3$

(*g*) The *trans* and *cis* isomers of $\quad H_2C{-}CBrCH_3$
$\qquad\qquad\qquad\qquad\qquad\qquad\quad\; H_3CBrC{-}CH_2$

▟ (*a*) The aromatic singlet will integrate for four H's in the disubstituted *p*-xylene and for five H's in the monosubstituted ethylbenzene. Alternatively, *p*-xylene gives two singlet signals. (*b*) The triplet signal for the aldehydic H is strongly shifted downfield (9–10 ppm). The ketone has only one singlet. (*c*) Each spectrum shows a 3-H singlet for its isolated CH_3. The signal for CH_3 bonded to O is more downfield than when bonded to $C{=}O$ (3.3 vs. 2.1 ppm). (*d*) The terminal alkyne has a signal for an acetylenic H (2–3 ppm). The internal alkyne has no such signal. (*e*) In each case the signals for the different vinylic H's appear as coupled doublets but with very different J values. $J \cong 2$ Hz for the *gem* H's and $J \cong 15$ Hz for the *trans* H's. (*f*) The alkene has the characteristic peaks for vinylic H's; H's on a cyclopropane ring are greatly shifted upfield. (*g*) In the *trans* isomer each methylene H is *cis* to one Br and Me and *trans* to one Br and Me. Therefore all four methylene H's are equivalent and produce a singlet. In the *cis* isomer one H of each CH_2 group is *cis* to both Br's and *trans* to both CH_3's giving an equivalent pair. The geminal H's are *cis* to both CH_3's and *trans* to both Br's giving a different equivalent pair. Hence this isomer shows two 2-H doublets for the methylene H's.

12.152 Assign the nmr spectra shown in Fig. 12-17 to the appropriate monochlorination products of 2,4-dimethylpentane and justify your assignment. Note the integrations drawn by the spectrometer on the spectra.

▟ The three possible structures are

1-Chloro-2,4-dimethylpentane (**A**)   3-Chloro-2,4-dimethylpentane (**B**)   2-Chloro-2,4-dimethylpentane (**C**)

The best clues come from the splitting pattern and integration of the most downfield signal, arising from the H's closest to Cl. In spectrum (*b*) this is a triplet, for one H, clearly due to H^c of **B**. In addition, the most upfield signal is a doublet, integrating for the 12 H^a's of the four Me's, split by the methine H^b's. In spectrum (*a*) the signal with the highest δ value is a *doublet*, integrating for two H's, that corresponds only to $ClCH_2^a$ of structure **A**. This is confirmed by the complex multiplet due to the nine H's (H^b and H^f) of the three Me's that are most upfield and the four H's (H^c, H^d, and H^e) with signals between these. This leaves **C** for spectrum (*c*). The most downfield group of irregular signals, integrating for three H's, comes from H^b and H^c, respectively. The most upfield doublet, integrating for the six H^d's, arises from the two equivalent Me's split by H^c. The six H^a's give rise to the singlet at $\delta = 1.6$ ppm.

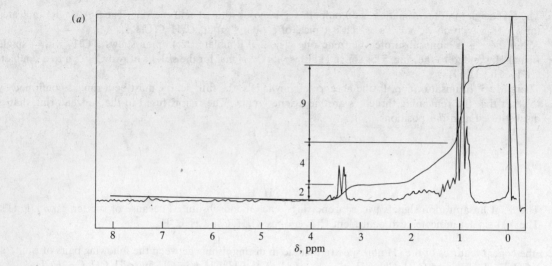

(a)

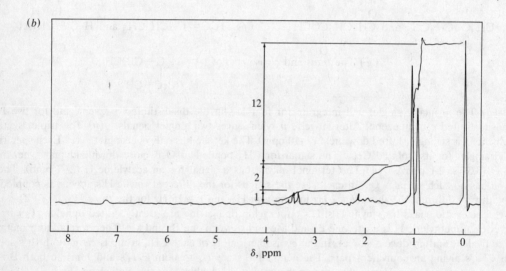

(b)

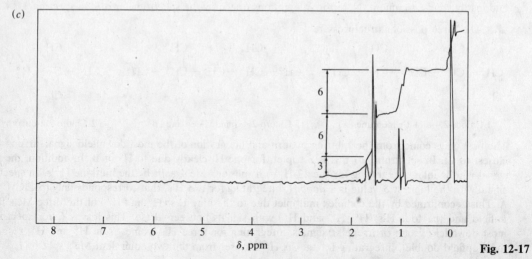

(c)

Fig. 12-17

2. ^{13}C nmr (cmr)

12.153 (*a*) Describe the difference between proton-coupled (off-resonance decoupling) and proton-decoupled cmr spectra. (*b*) Describe (i) the proton-decoupled and (ii) the proton-coupled cmr spectrum for 2-methylbutane, $(CH_3)_2CHCH_2CH_3$. (*c*) Which isomer of C_5H_{12} has an unsplit signal in its proton-coupled cmr spectrum? (*d*) How does the proton-coupled signal for tetramethylsilane, the standard also used for cmr spectroscopy, appear?

▰ (*a*) In proton-coupled spectra, splitting occurs only with H's bonded directly to the C being considered; all *other* H's are decoupled. The spectrum so obtained reveals only ^{13}C—H coupling and the observed multiplet follows the $n + 1$ rule. The technique of proton-decoupling removes splitting between the C's and all H's in the molecule, leaving singlet unsplit peaks for each type of C. (*b*) (i) Four singlets with the decreasing order of relative chemical shifts of $CH > CH_2 > CH_3$. Note the relative order is similar to ^1H nmr. (ii) The signal multiplicities are: CH, a doublet; CH_2, a triplet; and CH_3, a quartet. (*c*) A singlet appears in the proton-coupled spectrum only when the C is not bonded to any H's: $(CH_3)_4C$. (*d*) The signal is split into a quartet.

12.154 Why is coupling between bonded ^{13}C's not a factor in cmr spectroscopy?

▰ Since the natural abundance of ^{13}C is 1.1% (98.9% are ^{12}C's), this is the chance of any C in a molecule being a ^{13}C. The chances of having two ^{13}C's in any one molecule is 1.1% of 1.1%, a very small number (0.012%), and the odds of them being adjacent would be nil. Hence, we do not worry about ^{13}C—^{13}C coupling. However, a compound *synthesized* with adjacent ^{13}C's would show ^{13}C—^{13}C coupling.

12.155 (*a*) Use the following ^{13}C nmr chemical shift data (shown above the C's in ppm) obtained when a CH_3 replaces a terminal H in *n*-pentane to illustrate the α-, β- and γ-substituent effects.

$$\overset{\gamma}{\underset{13.5}{CH_3}}-\overset{}{\underset{22.1}{CH_2}}-\overset{\beta}{\underset{29.2}{CH_2}}-\overset{\beta}{\underset{32.7}{CH_2}}-\overset{\alpha}{\underset{44.3}{CH_2}}\quad \overset{}{\underset{13.7}{CH_3}}-\overset{}{\underset{22.6}{CH_2}}-\overset{\gamma}{\underset{34.5}{CH_2}}-\overset{\beta}{\underset{22.6}{CH_2}}-\overset{\alpha}{\underset{13.7}{CH_2}}\quad \overset{}{\underset{13.9}{CH_3}}-\overset{}{\underset{22.9}{CH_2}}-\overset{\gamma}{\underset{32.0}{CH_2}}-\overset{\beta}{\underset{32.0}{CH_2}}-\overset{\alpha}{\underset{22.9}{CH_2}}$$
$$\qquad\qquad\qquad\qquad\qquad (Cl) \qquad\qquad\qquad\qquad\qquad\qquad (H) \qquad\qquad\qquad\qquad\qquad\qquad (CH_3)$$

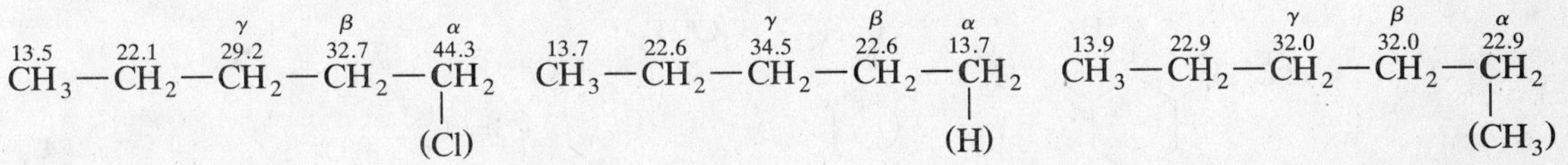

(*b*) From the data given for replacement of a terminal H by Cl in pentane, discuss the changes in the α-, β-, and γ-substituent effects that occur on substitution by Cl. (*c*) How do the chemical shifts of the CH_3's in 2-butene and propene compare? (*d*) How can the *cis* and *trans* isomers of 2-butene be distinguished?

▰ (*a*) The δ value of the **C** whose H is displaced (the α-**C**) by CH_3 increases. This typical *increase*, called the α-*effect*, is about 9 ppm (13.7 → 22.9 ppm). The once removed C, the β-C, shows a β-*effect* which typically is an *increase* of about 9.5 ppm (22.6 → 32.0). However, the twice removed C, the γ-C, shows a γ-*effect* that typically is a *decrease* of about −2.5 ppm (34.5 → 32.0). (*b*) Substitution of the electronegative Cl causes a substantial positive α-effect (+30.6 ppm), a smaller positive β-effect (+10.1 ppm), and a negative γ-effect (−5 ppm). (*c*) The values for the CH_3's in both *cis*- and *trans*-2-butene are less than in 2-propene because the CH_3's exert a mutual β-effect. (*d*) The *cis* CH_3's are more upfield by about 5 ppm. Whereas ^1H nmr distinguishes *cis* and *trans* isomers by differences in J values, cmr uses differences in chemical shifts.

12.156 (*a*) Use substituent effects to predict the *relative* values of C in $CH_3CH_2CH_3$ (**A**), $CH_3CH_2CH_2CH_3$ (**B**), and $CH_3CH(CH_3)_2$ (**D**). (*b*) Estimate the values from the data given for the substituent effects in Problem 12.155 using the value of 6 ppm for CH_3CH_3. (*c*) Predict the order of decreasing δ values for the designated C's in $C^aH_3C^bH(C^aH_3)C^cH_2C^dH_2C^eH_3$.

▰ (*a*) C of **A** feels one α- and one β-effect. C of **B** is also subject to one α- and one β-effect as well as one γ-effect. C of **D** is influenced by one α- and two β-groups. The decreasing order is **D > A > B**. (*b*) Estimations using these effects are not exact and should be made only to the nearest 0.5 ppm. Since C of ethane already has one α-effect, in making the predictions we disregard one α-effect from **A**, **B**, and **D**. For **A**, the additional β-effect adds 9.5 ppm. The predicted value is 6 + 9.5 = 15.5 ppm; the observed value is 15.6 ppm. For **B** we add 9.5 ppm for the β-effect but subtract 2.5 ppm for the γ-effect. The predicted value is 6 + 9.5 − 2.5 = 13 ppm; the observed value is 13.2 ppm. **D** has two extra β-effects and the calculated value is 6 + (2 × 9.5) = 25 ppm; the observed value is 24.3 ppm. (*c*) The effects "felt" are:

$$C^a, 1\ \alpha\text{-}, 2\ \beta\text{-}, \text{and } 1\ \gamma\text{-effect;}\quad C^b, 3\ \alpha\text{-}, 1\ \beta\text{-}, \text{and } 1\ \gamma\text{-effect;}\quad C^c, 2\alpha\text{- and } 3\ \beta\text{-effect;}$$

$$C^d, 2\ \alpha\text{-}, 1\ \beta\text{-}, \text{and } 2\ \gamma\text{-effect;}\quad C^e, 1\ \alpha\text{-} 1\ \beta\text{-}, \text{and } 1\ \gamma\text{-effect}$$

The decreasing order is $C^c > C^b > C^a > C^d > C^e$.

12.157 (*a*) Compare the relative order of chemical shifts of the different H's in the pmr spectrum with that of the different C's in the cmr spectrum. (*b*) Compare the chemical shift ranges of pmr and cmr spectra.

✒ (*a*) The relative orders are about the same since they are affected in the same way by the same three factors, namely, hybridized state of C, electronegativity of bonded atoms, and anisotropicity. Aromatic and vinylic C's, however, have δ values in the same region of the spectrum, unlike the pmr's. Ketonic and aldehydic C's are the most downfield in cmr followed slightly more upfield by acids and acid derivatives. (The anomolous position of C≡C in the pmr spectrum is due to the anisotropic effect discussed in Problems 12.112 and 12.114.) The relative order is: C=O (ketones and aldehydes) > C=O (carboxylic acids and their derivatives) > aromatics, alkenes > alkynes > C—A(O > Cl > N > Br > I) > 4°, 3 °C > 2 °C > 1 °C. The order of alkyl C's is subject to change because of the interplay of α-, β- and γ-effects. (*b*) The range for ^{13}C nmr (220–0 ppm) is much greater than the range for ^{1}H nmr (12–0 ppm). In both cases atoms that are more shielded than those in TMS have signals with negative values.

12.158 (*a*) Give the number of signals and write the structural formula for each of the following compounds. Indicate the different kinds of C's by letters *a, b, c*, etc. (i) Methylcyclohexane, (ii) cyclohexene, (iii) 1-methylcyclohexene, (iv) 1,3,5-trimethylbenzene, (v) 1,2,3-trimethylbenzene, (vi) 1-phenylpropane, and (vii) 2-methyl-2-butene. (*b*) Use the letters (see Problem 12.148) to give the multiplicity of the signals in the proton-coupled spectra.

✒ (*a*)

(i) Five   (ii) Three   (iii) Seven   (iv) Three

(v) Six   (vi) Seven   (vii) Five

(*b*) (i) $a = q$; $b = d$; $c, d, e = t$

(ii) $a = d$; $b, c = t$

(iii) $a = q$; $b = s$; $c = d$; $d, e, f, g = t$

(iv) $a = q$; $b = s$; $c = d$

(v) $a, b = q$; $c, d = s$; $e, f = d$

(vi) $a = q$; $b, c = t$; $d = s$; $e, f, g = d$

(vii) $a, b, c = q$; $d = s$; $e = d$

12.159 Identify each of the following compounds from the given molecular formulas, chemical shifts δ in ppm, and multiplicity of the proton-coupled cmr spectra.

(*a*) $C_8H_{18}O$: 71.2, *t*; 33.1, *t*; 20.3, *t*; 14.6, *q*

(*b*) $C_6H_{14}O$: 75.1, *d*; 35.3, *s*; 25.8, *q*; 18.2, *q*

(*c*) $C_6H_{14}O$; 65.5, *d*; 49.2, *t*; 25.1, *d*; 24.3, *q*; 22.7, *q*

(*d*) $C_5H_{11}ClO$: 62.2, *t*; 45.4, *t*; 32.9, *t*; 32.1, *t*; 23.7, *t*

(*e*) $C_6H_{12}O_2$:71.1, *d*; 37.9, *t*

✒ (*a*) With 0° of unsaturation, an even number (eight) of C's, and four signals, the compound must be a symmetrical ether. The multiplicity indicates that the alkyl group must have one CH_3 and four CH_2 groups. $CH_3CH_2CH_2CH_2OCH_2CH_2CH_2CH_3$.

(*b*) The singlet indicates a quarternary C that is most likely a $(CH_3)_3C$—. The doublet is a —CH bonded to an O atom. The sixth C, the quartet is a CH_3. For the compound to be an ether, the C bonded to the O would have to be a CH_2 and there would have to be two more downfield signals; it is an alcohol. $(CH_3)_3CCH(OH)CH_3$.

(*c*) There are two CH's; the downfield one is bonded to O, giving the unit HOCH—. The other CH is bonded only to C's and the occurrence of five signals for six C's indicates it is bonded to two equivalent CH_3's, i.e., —$CH(CH_3)_2$. These structural units are separated by a CH_2. The presence of a second quartet indicates another distinct CH_3. $(CH_3)_2CHCH_2CH(OH)CH_3$ or its isomer $(CH_3)_2CHCH(OH)CH_2CH_3$.

(*d*) The five triplets indicate the presence of five different CH_2's. The most downfield triplet is bonded to an O and the next most downfield triplet to Cl. $HOCH_2CH_2CH_2CH_2CH_2Cl$.

(*e*) The doublet must be a CH bonded to an O. The 1° of unsaturation and the absence of C=O and unsaturated C's indicate a cyclic compound which is substituted, leaving only equivalent CH_2's. The compound is 1,4-cyclohexanediol. In order for the CH's to be equivalent, the OH's must have the same conformation. The compound is *trans* because then both OH's are equatorial and equivalent.

12.160 Use cmr spectroscopy to distinguish among (*a*) the carbonyl isomers, C_4H_8O, (*b*) the unrearranged alkenes arising from dehydration of $CH_3CH_2CH(OH)CH_2CH_2CH_3$, and (*c*) the isomers of C_3H_8O.

⬛ (*a*) Use proton-coupled spectra. The only ketone, $CH_3\underset{\underset{O}{\parallel}}{C}CH_2CH_3$, has a strongly downfield singlet. The aldehydes, $CH_3CH_2CH_2CHO$ (**A**) and $(CH_3)_2CHCHO$ (**B**), each have a strongly downfield doublet. **A** has two triplets and a quartet whereas **B** has a second doublet and a quartet.

(*b*) Use proton-decoupled spectra. The alkenes are *E*- and *Z*-CH_3CH_2CH=$CHCH_2CH_3$ (**C**) and *E*- and *Z*-CH_3CH=$CHCH_2CH_2CH_3$ (**D**). **C** is symmetrical and has only three signals. **D** is unsymmetrical and has six signals. The *E* and *Z* stereoisomers of each pair are distinguished by the chemical shifts of the C's bonded to the C=C; the *E* isomers have the higher values.

(*c*) There are 0° degrees of unsaturation. Thus the individual isomer must be an alcohol or ether. Proton-decoupled cmr identifies the 2° alcohol $(CH_3)_2CHOH$ because it has only two signals. Both the ether, $CH_3OCH_2CH_3$, and the 1° alcohol, $CH_3CH_2CH_2OH$, have three signals. Next use proton-coupled spectra to distinguish between the ether (two quartets and one triplet) and $CH_3CH_2CH_2OH$ (one quartet and two triplets).

12.161 (*a*) Explain the single Me signal in the proton-decoupled cmr spectrum of *cis*-1,2-dimethylcyclohexane. (*b*) Use cmr to distinguish between the two diastereomers of 1,3,5-trimethylcyclohexane.

⬛ (*a*) One Me is equatorial and one is axial, and therefore they might be expected to have different signals. However, the interconversion by ring-flipping is faster than detection by the spectrophotometer. The instrument senses a time-average condition in which the Me's are equivalent. (*b*) In the *cis, cis* isomer all three Me's are equatorial. The conformation is "frozen" because interconversion would give a very high energy conformation with three axial Me's. The three Me's are equivalent, as are the three CH's and the three CH_2's, giving three signals. In the "frozen" *trans, cis* isomer the Me(e)'s are equivalent, as are the C's to which they are bonded. The two signals from Me(a)-C differ from those of Me(e)-C. The CH_2's flanking the Me(a)-C's are equivalent, and the third CH_2 is different. Six signals are observed.

12.162 In each of (*a*)–(*i*) below, suggest the structure of a compound consistent with the following spectral information: Multiplicity is disregarded when giving the numbers of signals. When more than one isomer is possible, explain what other information in the spectra can be used to distinguish them.

(*a*) C_2H_6O, a single [1]H- and ^{13}C-nmr signal.   (*f*) $C_3H_6O_2$ (an ester), two [1]H- and three ^{13}C-nmr signals.

(*b*) C_3H_9N, a single [1]H- and ^{13}C-nmr signal.   (*g*) C_4H_6(noncyclic), one [1]H- and two ^{13}C-nmr signals.

(*c*) C_5H_{12}, one [1]H- and two ^{13}C-nmr signals.   (*h*) C_5H_{10}(cyclic), four [1]H- and three ^{13}C-nmr signals.

(*d*) C_5H_{10}, a single [1]H- and ^{13}C-nmr signal.   (*i*) C_3H_3Cl, two [1]H- and three ^{13}C-nmr signals.

(*e*) $C_4H_{10}O$, two each for [1]H- and ^{13}C-nmr.

⬛ (*a*) CH_3OCH_3, (*b*) $(CH_3)_3N$, (*c*) $(CH_3)_4C$, (*d*) cyclopentane, (*e*) $CH_3CH_2OCH_2CH_3$, (*f*) CH_3COOCH_3, (*g*) CH_3C≡CCH_3, (*h*) *cis*-dimethylcyclopropane, (*i*) there are 3 possibilities:

$$HC\equiv CCH_2Cl \text{ (\textbf{E})} \qquad H_2C\!=\!C\!=\!CHCl \text{ (\textbf{F})} \qquad HC\!=\!\underset{\underset{CH_2}{\diagup}}{\overset{\diagdown}{C}}Cl \text{ (\textbf{G})}$$

The pmr of **G** has a strongly upfield cyclopropyl-type signal. The vinylic H signals of **F** are more downfield than the acetylenic H signal of **E**.

12.163 For those compounds in Problem 12.162 having more than one kind of signal for a type of spectroscopy, give their relative chemical shifts in decreasing order.

⬛ (*c*) 4° C > CH_3. (*e*) For pmr and cmr, OCH_2 > CH_3. (*f*) For pmr, CH_3O > CH_3C=O; For cmr, O=C > CH_3O > CH_3 bonded to C=O. (*g*) C≡ > CH_3. (*h*) For pmr, CH_3 > ring CH > each of the different H's of the CH_2 whose signals are close to each other. For cmr, CH_3 > CH > CH_2. Cyclopropyl [13]C's are just as strongly shielded as are cyclopropyl H's. (*i*) **E**: For pmr, CH_2Cl > HC≡; for cmr, ≡C— (senses β-effect of Cl) > HC≡ (senses γ-effect of Cl) > CH_2Cl. **F**: For pmr, =$CHCl$ > H_2C=; for cmr, =C= > =$CHCl$ > H_2C=. **G**: For pmr, HC= > CH_2; for cmr, =CCl > HC= > CH_2.

MASS SPECTROSCOPY

12.164 Use R:S as the typical generalized compound to write ionic equations for the first two steps leading to a mass spectral analysis. Identify the steps and each moiety in the equations.

Step 1. $R:S + e^- \longrightarrow R \cdot S^+ + 2e^-$ Ionization
parent   high   parent ion
         energy   a radical cation

Step 2. $R \cdot S^+$ ⟨ $R \cdot + S^+$
                          or
                         $S \cdot + R^+$ ⟩ Fragmentations
                       radicals cations

Fragmentation can also release a smaller radical cation and a nonradical molecule:

$$R \cdot S^+ \longrightarrow R + \cdot S^+ \quad \text{or} \quad \cdot R^+ + S$$

12.165 After ionization and fragmentations occur, what does the mass spectrometer do to provide a mass spectrum? Show the spectrum.

▮ The spectrometer sorts out all the cations (including the radical cations) according to their mass/charge (m/z or m/e) values and records these values (decreasing from right to left) as line signals along the abscissa of the chart, [see Fig. 12.18(a), p. 345]. At the same time the instrument records their relative abundances as signal heights plotted as intensities along the ordinate. The radicals are not detected.

12.166 (a) Why can the m/z value be assigned as the molecular weight of the cation in most cases? (b) How can the molecular weight of a compound be determined by mass spectral analysis? (c) Why is less than 1 mg of the parent compound used in the vapor state for the analysis? (d) Why do several signals appear in a typical spectrum? (e) Which fragment cations are the most abundant? (f) How are relative abundances calculated?

▮ (a) In most case the charge on the cation (the value of z) is $+1$ making $m/z = m$.
(b) If all the parent (molecular) cations do not fragment (the typical situation), the largest m/z value can be assigned as the molecular weight of the parent cation and therefore the parent itself.
(c) A relatively small number of molecules are taken in the vapor state to prevent collisions and reactions between fragments. Combination of fragments might lead to ions with larger masses than the parent cation, making it impossible to determine the molecular weight. Fragmentation patterns that are so very useful in structure proof would become confusing.
(d) The parent can fragment in several ways and each cationic fragment can further fragment to give smaller cations.
(e) The most abundant cations are the most stable ones. Hence a good understanding of cation stabilities is essential for interpreting fragmentation patterns necessary for structure proof.
(f) The most intense peak, called the *base peak*, is arbitrarily assigned a value of 100%. The smaller peak heights are measured and divided by the base peak height to give their relative percentage abundances. For example, a peak with 2/3 the height of the base peak has a relative abundance of 66.7%.

12.167 Discuss the validity of the following statements.
(a) The presence of a peak whose mass is one more than the parent, P + 1, may be due to presence of a naturally abundant D (^{2}H) replacing an H.
(b) The presence of the P + 1 peak may be attributable to the natural abundance of ^{13}C.
(c) For oxycompounds, a P + 2 peak may be attributable to the natural abundance of ^{18}O.
(d) For compounds with N atoms, some of the P + 1 peak may be due to natural abundance of ^{15}N.
(e) For organic compounds with N atoms, a P + 2 peak could arise from the presence of ^{15}N and ^{13}C.

▮ (a) False. The chance of finding a D in a molecule is miniscule because its natural abundance is only 0.016%.
(b) True. The natural abundance of ^{13}C is 1.08% and its presence in a parent molecule is detectable by the mass spectrometer.
(c) True. The natural abundance of ^{18}O is 0.20% and its presence is detectable.
(d) True. The natural abundance of ^{15}N is 0.38% and its presence is detectable.
(e) False. The chances of having one of each of these isotopes in the same molecule is practically nil (1.08% × 0.38%).

12.168 (*a*) Explain how to detect the presence in a molecule of an atom of (i) Br, (ii) Cl, and (iii) I. Illustrate with CH_3X. (*b*) Give the relative intensities of the parent cations for a compound with (i) two Br's, i.e., CH_2Br_2, and (ii) two Cl's, i.e., CH_2Cl_2.

▮ (*a*) (i) Br has two isotopes, ^{79}Br and ^{81}Br, with almost the same abundance. Therefore, two equal number parents are observed, $CH_3^{79}Br$, called P (MW = 94), and $CH_3^{81}Br$, P + 2 (MW = 96). (ii) Cl has two isotopes, ^{35}Cl (75%) and ^{37}Cl (25%) in the ratio of 3 : 1. There are two parents, $CH_3^{35}Cl$, P (MW = 50), and $CH_3^{37}Cl$, P + 2 (MW = 52), in the ratio of 3 : 1. (iii) I^+ readily cleaves from the parent cation and is detected at $m/z = 127$. When I· is lost, the next lower mass cation has an m/z value 127 less than the parent cation. (*b*) (i) There are three parents: $CH_2^{79}Br_2$, P (**A**), $CH_2^{79}Br^{81}Br$, P + 2 (**B**), and $CH_2^{81}Br_2$, P + 4, (**C**). The number of **A** and **C** molecules are equal. The chance of getting either one is 50% of 50% or 25% of each. The remaining 50% is **B**. (ii) There are three parents: $CH_2^{35}Cl_2$, P (**D**), $CH_2^{35}Cl^{37}Cl$, P + 2 (**E**), $CH_2^{37}Cl_2$, P + 4 (**F**). The relative numbers are: **D**, 75% of 75% or 56%; **F**, 25% of 25% or 6%; and the remainder, **E**, 38%. The ratios of the intensities are 56 : 38 : 6.

12.169 (*a*) Give molecular formulas of hydrocarbon cations with m/z values of (i) 29, (ii) 51, (iii) 91. (*b*) Give a combination of C, H, and N to account for m/z values of (i) 29, (ii) 57.

▮ (*a*) Divide the given values by 12 to get the number of C's; the remainder is the mass due to the H's. (i) $C_2H_5^+$, (ii) $C_4H_3^+$, (iii) $C_7H_7^+$. (*b*) (i) If one N is present, subtracting 14 leaves a mass of 15, enough for one C and three H's. The formula is CH_3N^+. (ii) One, two, or three N's can be present giving three cations: $C_3H_7N^+$, $C_2H_5N_2^+$ or $CH_3N_3^+$.

12.170 (*a*) Do parent (molecular) ions, RS^+, of hydrocarbons ever have odd m/z values? (*b*) If an RS^+ contains only C, H, and O, may its m/z value be either odd or even? (*c*) If an RS^+ contains only C, H, and N, may its m/z value be either odd or even? (*d*) Why can an ion, $m/z = 31$, not be $C_2H_7^+$? What might it be?

▮ (*a*) No. Hydrocarbons, and their parent ions, must have an even number of H's: C_nH_{2n+2}, C_nH_{2n}, C_nH_{2n-2}, C_nH_{2n-6}, etc. Since the atomic weight of C is even (12), the m/z values must be even.

(*b*) The presence of O in a formula does not change the ratio of C to H. Since the mass of O is even (16), the mass of RS^+ with C, H, and O *must be even*.

(*c*) The presence of each N ($m = 14$) requires an additional H ($C_nH_{2n+3}N, C_nH_{2n+1}N, C_nH_{2n-1}N$). Therefore, if the number of N's is odd, an odd number of H's and an odd m/z value result. An even number of N's requires an even number of H's and an even m/z value. These statements apply *only* to parent ions, *not* to fragment ions.

(*d*) The largest number of H's for two C's is six (C_2H_6). Some possibilities are CH_3O^+ and CH_5N^+.

12.171 Which electron is most likely to be lost in the ionization of the following compounds? Write an electronic structure for RS^+. (*a*) CH_4, (*b*) CH_3CH_3, (*c*) $H_2C=CH_2$, (*d*) CH_3Cl, (*e*) $H_2C=O$.

▮ Since the electron in the HOMO is most likely to be lost, the decreasing order of ionizability is $n > \pi > \sigma$. When no n or π electrons are present, the lost electron most likely comes from the highest energy σ bond. The + in each formula below shows the charge and the missing electron.

(*a*) $H:\overset{\displaystyle H}{\underset{\displaystyle H}{\overset{..}{C}}}{\overset{+}{\cdot}}H$ (+ is the charge due to the missing electron)

(*b*) $H:\overset{\displaystyle H}{\underset{\displaystyle H}{\overset{..}{C}}}{\overset{+}{\cdot}}\overset{\displaystyle H}{\underset{\displaystyle H}{\overset{..}{C}}}:H$ (the C—C bond is weaker than the C—H bond)

(*c*) $H_2C\overset{\cdot\,+}{-\!\!-\!\!-}CH_2$ (electron comes from the π bond)

(*d*) $H_3C:\overset{..}{\underset{..}{Cl}}\overset{+}{\cdot}$ (an n electron is lost)

(*e*) $H_2C=\overset{..}{O}\overset{+}{\cdot}$ (an n electron is lost)

12.172 Write equations involving the electron-dot formulas for each fragmentation used to explain the following. (*a*) Isobutane, a typical branched-chain alkane, has a lower-intensity RS^+ peak than does *n*-butane, a typical unbranched alkane. (*b*) All 1° alcohols, RCH_2CH_2OH, have a prominent fragment cation at $m/e = 31$. (*c*) All $C_6H_5CH_2R$-type hydrocarbons have a prominent fragment cation at $m/z = 91$. (*d*) Alkenes of the type $H_2C=CHCH_2R$ have a prominent fragment cation at $m/z = 41$. (*e*) Aldehydes, $RCH=O$, show intense peaks at P − 1 and 29.

(a) The weaker C—C bond cleaves more easily than the stronger C—H bond. Fragmentation of the parent cation of isobutane,

$$(CH_3)_2\overset{+}{\underset{\underset{H}{|}}{C}}CH_3 \longrightarrow (CH_3)_2\overset{+}{\underset{\underset{H}{|}}{C}} + \cdot CH_3$$

gives a 2° R$^+$ that is more stable than the 1° R$^+$ from n-butane,

$$H_3\overset{\overset{H}{|}}{\underset{\underset{H}{|}}{C}}\overset{+}{\underset{\underset{H}{|}}{C}}CH_3 \longrightarrow H_3\overset{\overset{H}{|}}{\underset{\underset{H}{|}}{C}}\overset{+}{C} + \cdot CH_2CH_3$$

Hence RS$^+$ of isobutane undergoes fragmentation more readily than does RS$^+$ of n-butane, and fewer RS$^+$ cations of isobutane survive. Consequently, isobutane, typical of branched-chain alkanes, has a lower-intensity RS$^+$ peak than has n-butane.

(b)

$$R-\overset{\overset{H}{|}}{\underset{\underset{H}{|}}{\overset{\beta}{C}}}\overset{+\cdot}{\underset{\ }{}}CH_2\overset{..}{\underset{..}{O}}H \longrightarrow R-\overset{\overset{H}{|}}{\underset{\underset{H}{|}}{\overset{\beta}{C}}}\cdot + \underset{\alpha}{\overset{+}{C}H_2\overset{..}{\underset{..}{O}}H} \longleftrightarrow H_2C=\overset{+}{\underset{..}{O}}H$$
$$\underbrace{\qquad\qquad\qquad\qquad}_{m/z = 31}$$

A C$^+$ next to an O is stabilized by extended π bonding (resonance). The RS$^+$ species of alcohols generally undergoes cleavage of the bond

$$\overset{\beta}{C}+\overset{\alpha}{C}-OH$$

(c)

$$C_6H_5:\overset{\overset{H}{|}}{\underset{\underset{H}{|}}{\overset{+}{C}}}R \longrightarrow R\cdot + C_6H_5:\overset{+}{C}H_2 \longrightarrow$$

stable benzyl R$^+$

a more stable aromatic cycloheptatrienyl cation, $m/z = 91$

(d)

$$H_2C\overset{+\overset{\cdot\cdot}{O}}{-\!-\!-}CH-CH_2\overset{\cdot\cdot}{O}R \longrightarrow H_2\overset{+}{C}-CH=CH_2 + \cdot R$$

stable allylic
cation, $m/z = 41$

(e)

$$R:\overset{+\cdot}{\underset{}{C}}=\overset{\cdot\cdot}{\underset{}{O}}: \begin{cases} \overset{-H\cdot}{\longrightarrow} & R-\overset{+}{C}=\overset{\cdot\cdot}{O}:\longleftrightarrow R-C\equiv\overset{+}{O} \\ \text{or} & \\ \overset{-R\cdot}{\longrightarrow} & \overset{+}{\underset{\underset{H}{|}}{C}}=\overset{\cdot\cdot}{O}:\longleftrightarrow H-C\equiv\overset{+}{O}: \end{cases}$$

$(m/z = (m/z)_{RS} - 1)$
stable acylonium ions
$(m/z = 29)$

12.173 Account for the major peaks of each of the following compounds. Write equations for their formation.
  (a) $CH_3OCH_2CH_2CH_3$: $m/z = 31, 45, 59,$ and 74.
  (b) $trans$-$CH_3CH=CHCH_2CH_2CH_3$: $m/z = 41, 55,$ and 84.
  (c) $CH_3CH_2NHCH_2CH_2CH_3$: $m/z = 30, 44, 58, 72,$ and 87.
  (d) $CH_3\overset{\ }{\underset{\underset{O}{\|}}{C}}-\overset{\ }{\underset{\underset{CH_3}{|}}{C}}HCH_2C_6H_5$: $m/z = 43, 91, 147,$ and 162.
  (e) $CH_3CH_2\overset{\ }{\underset{\underset{O}{\|}}{C}}OCH_3$: $m/z = 57, 59,$ and 88.

(a)

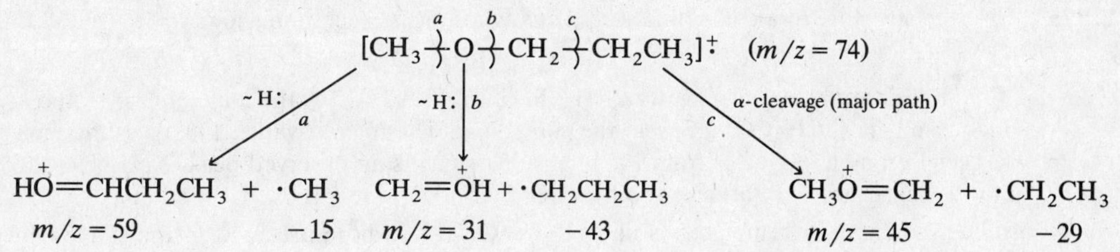

$$[CH_3 \overset{a}{+} O \overset{b}{+} CH_2 \overset{c}{+} CH_2CH_3]^{\ddagger} \quad (m/z = 74)$$

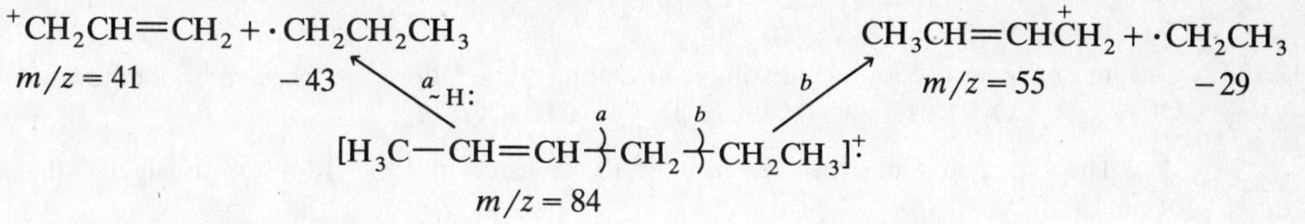

~H: a ~H: b α-cleavage (major path) c

$$H\overset{+}{O}=CHCH_2CH_3 + \cdot CH_3 \qquad CH_2=\overset{+}{O}H + \cdot CH_2CH_2CH_3 \qquad CH_3\overset{+}{O}=CH_2 + \cdot CH_2CH_3$$
$$m/z = 59 \qquad\qquad -15 \qquad m/z = 31 \qquad -43 \qquad\qquad m/z = 45 \qquad\qquad -29$$

(b)

$$^+CH_2CH=CH_2 + \cdot CH_2CH_2CH_3 \qquad\qquad\qquad CH_3CH=CH\overset{+}{C}H_2 + \cdot CH_2CH_3$$
$$m/z = 41 \qquad\qquad -43 \qquad\qquad\qquad\qquad\qquad m/z = 55 \qquad\qquad -29$$

$$^{a}\text{~H:} \qquad\qquad b$$

$$[H_3C-CH=CH \overset{a}{+} CH_2 \overset{b}{+} CH_2CH_3]^{\ddagger}$$
$$m/z = 84$$

(c)

$$H_3C\cdot + H_2C=\overset{+}{N}CH_2CH_2CH_3 \quad m/z = 72$$
$$\qquad\qquad\qquad\qquad | \atop H$$

(major) a

a d b c c $CH_3CH_2\overset{+}{N}=CH_2 + \cdot CH_2CH_3$

$$[H_3C \overset{a}{+} CH_2 \overset{d}{+} NH \overset{b}{+} CH_2 \overset{c}{+} CH_2CH_3]^{\ddagger} \qquad\qquad \text{(major)} \qquad | \atop H \quad \textbf{(A)}$$
$$m/z = 87 \qquad\qquad\qquad\qquad m/z = 58$$

(minor) b (minor) d

~H: ~H:

$$CH_3CH=\overset{+}{N}H_2 + \cdot CH_2CH_2CH_3 \qquad\qquad CH_3CH_2CH=\overset{+}{N}H_2 + \cdot CH_2CH_3$$
$$m/z = 44 \qquad\qquad\qquad\qquad\qquad m/z = 58$$

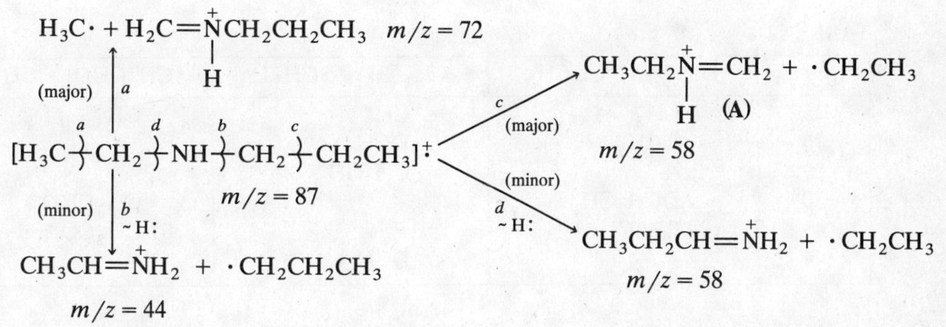

a and c are α-cleavages. **A** undergoes further cleavage to give $H_2C=\overset{+}{N}H_2$ $(m/z = 30) + H_2C=CH_2$.

(d)

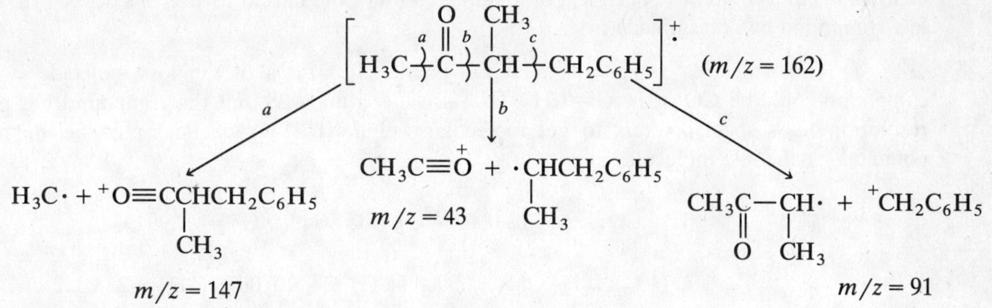

$$\left[H_3C \overset{a}{+} \overset{\overset{O}{\|}}{C} \overset{b}{+} \overset{\overset{CH_3}{|}}{CH} \overset{c}{+} CH_2C_6H_5 \right]^{\ddagger} \quad (m/z = 162)$$

a b c

$$H_3C\cdot + {}^+O\equiv CCHCH_2C_6H_5 \qquad CH_3C\equiv\overset{+}{O} + \cdot CHCH_2C_6H_5 \qquad CH_3C-CH\cdot + {}^+CH_2C_6H_5$$
$$\qquad\qquad | \atop CH_3 \qquad\qquad m/z = 43 \qquad\qquad | \atop CH_3 \qquad\qquad \|\quad| \atop O\;\;CH_3$$
$$m/z = 147 \qquad\qquad\qquad\qquad\qquad\qquad\qquad\qquad m/z = 91$$

The $^+CH_2C_6H_5$ rearranges to the more stable aromatic cycloheptatrienylium ion.

(e)

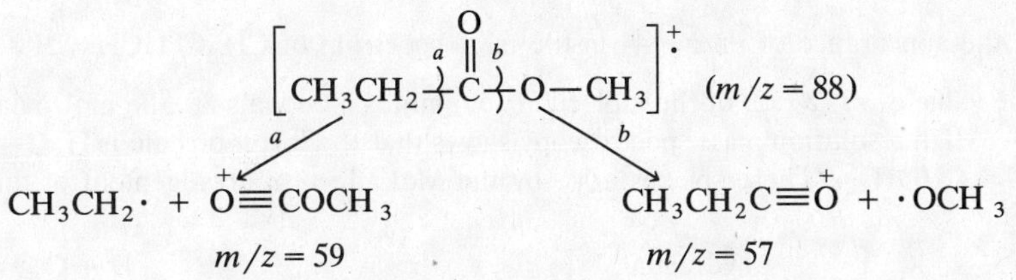

$$\left[CH_3CH_2 \overset{a}{+} \overset{\overset{O}{\|}}{C} \overset{b}{+} O-CH_3 \right]^{\ddagger} \quad (m/z = 88)$$

a b

$$CH_3CH_2\cdot + {}^+O\equiv COCH_3 \qquad CH_3CH_2C\equiv\overset{+}{O} + \cdot OCH_3$$
$$m/z = 59 \qquad\qquad\qquad m/z = 57$$

12.174 (a) Why do RSH and RSR have small but significant P + 2 peaks? (b) Why does cyclohexene have an intense peak at $m/z = 54$?

(a) ^{32}S, the major isotope of S, and ^{34}S have abundances of 95% and 4.2% respectively. Hence, the P + 2 peak is detectable. A third natural isotope, ^{33}S, whose abundance is 0.8%, adds to the intensity of the P + 1 peak. Remember that P + 1 also arises from the presence of a ^{13}C. (b) Cyclohexene radical cations undergo retro-Diels–Alder reactions. Cyclohexene itself gives $[H_2C=CH-CH=CH_2]^{\ddagger}(m/z = 54) + H_2C=CH_2$, the lost molecule.

12.175 Give the structure of a compound, $C_{10}H_{12}O$, whose mass spectrum shows m/z values of 15, 43, 57, 91, 105, and 148.

    ◢   A peak at $m/z = 15$ suggests a CH_3. Because $43 - 15 = 28$, the mass of $C=O$, the m/z value of 43 may be due to an acetyl, CH_3CO, group in the compound. The highest value, 148, gives the molecular weight. Cleaving an acetyl group ($m/z = 43$) from 148 gives 105, which is an observed peak. Next below 105 is 91, a difference of 14; this suggests a CH_2 attached to CH_3CO. So far we have CH_3COCH_2 adding up to 57, leaving $148 - 57 = 91$ to be accounted for. This peak is likely to be $[C_7H_7]^+$, whose precursor is the stable benzyl cation, $C_6H_5\overset{+}{C}H_2$. The structure is $CH_3-\underset{\underset{O}{\parallel}}{C}-CH_2-CH_2-C_6H_5$.

12.176 Use mass spectroscopy to distinguish among the following three monodeuterated methyl ethyl ketones; $DCH_2CH_2COCH_3$, $CH_3CH_2COCH_2D$, $CH_3CHDCOCH_3$.

    ◢   The expected peaks for each compound are listed in Table 12-4. Obviously each has a different combination of peaks.

TABLE 12-4

m/z	$DCH_2CH_2COCH_3$	$CH_3CH_2COCH_2D$	$CH_3CHDCOCH_3$
15	CH_3^+	CH_3^+	CH_3^+
16	DCH_2^+	DCH_2^+	—
29	—	$CH_3CH_2^+$	—
30	$DCH_2CH_2^+$	—	CH_3CHD^+
43	CH_3CO^+	—	CH_3CO^+
44	—	DCH_2CO^+	—

12.177 (*a*) The peak with the second highest m/z value in the spectrum of the compound $C_8H_{14}O_2$ is 114. List the compounds that could have been lost on fragmentation of the parent to give this peak. (*b*) How could the actual lost compound be determined?

    ◢   (*a*) The molecular weight of $C_8H_{14}O_2$ is 142. The mass of the lost molecule is $142 - 114 = 28$. This compound could be CO or $H_2C=CH_2$. (N_2 also has a mass 28, but the compound has no N.) (*b*) Use high resolution mass spectrometers to get molecular weights to four decimal places. The molecular weights so obtained for the lost molecules are:

$$CO: \qquad 12.0000(^{12}C) + 15.9949(^{16}O) = 27.9949$$

$$C_2H_4: \qquad 2 \times 12.0000\ (^{12}C) + 4 \times 1.0078\ (^1H) = 28.0312$$

Now the masses are no longer both 28 and they can be distinguished.

12.178 Explain the appearance of $m/z = 44$ in the mass spectrum of $CH_3CH_2CH_2CH=O$.

    ◢   The value of m/z (72) of the molecular ion, minus 44 equals 28, the molecular weight of the lost uncharged molecule. High resolution mass spectroscopy shows that the lost molecule is $H_2C=CH_2$ and the fragment cation is $[H_2C=CHOH]^{+\bullet}$. These species arise by the McLafferty rearrangement of the parent cation, shown below.

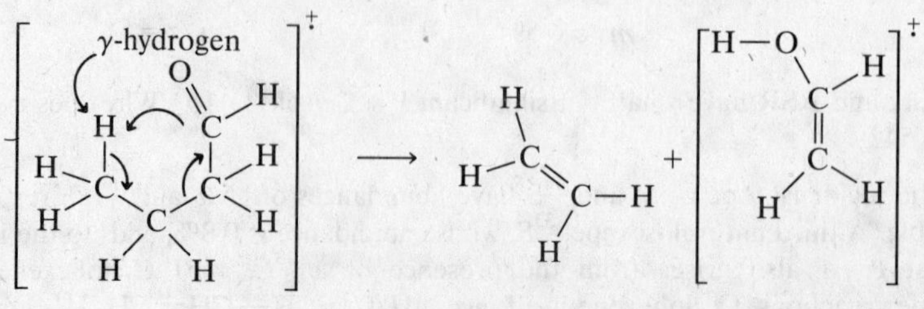

$m/z = 72$ ethene (MW = 28)   ($m/z = 44$)

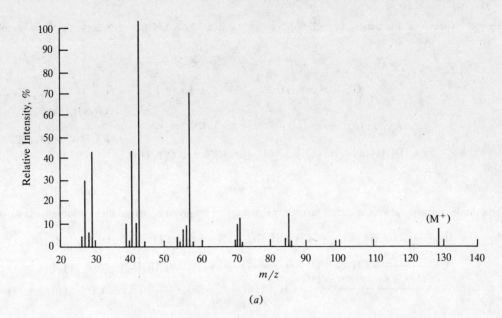

(a)

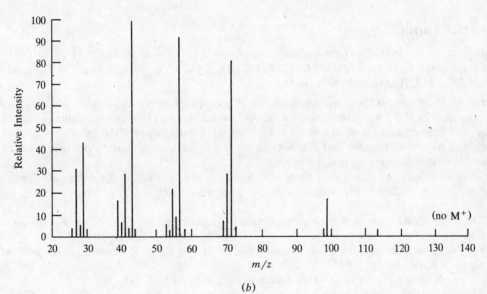

(b)

Fig. 12-18

12.179 Figure 12-18 shows the mass spectra of nonane (**A**) and isomer 3,3-dimethylheptane (**B**). Assign each given spectrum to the appropriate compound by analyzing fragmentation patterns with the aid of equations.

📕 The spectrum in Fig. 12-18(a) has a parent peak at $m/z = 128$. The next lower one at $m/z = 99$ indicates a loss of 29 $(128 - 99)$ mass units corresponding to CH_3CH_2. From this point the prominent peaks arise from a sequential loss of CH_2's. This fragmentation pattern is typical for straight chain alkanes.

$$[CH_3(CH_2)_6CH_2CH_3]^+ \xrightarrow[-29]{-\cdot C_2H_5} CH_3(CH_2)_5\overset{+}{C}H_2 \xrightarrow[-14]{-\cdot CH_2} CH_3(CH_2)_4\overset{+}{C}H_2 \xrightarrow[-14]{-\cdot CH_2}$$

$$m/z = 128 \qquad\qquad m/z = 99 \qquad\qquad m/z = 85$$

$$CH_3(CH_2)_3\overset{+}{C}H_2 \xrightarrow[-14]{-\cdot CH_2} CH_3CH_2CH_2\overset{+}{C}H_2 \xrightarrow[-14]{-\cdot CH_2} CH_3CH_2\overset{+}{C}H_2 \xrightarrow[-14]{-\cdot CH_2} CH_3\overset{+}{C}H_2$$

$$m/z = 71 \qquad\qquad m/z = 57 \qquad\qquad m/z = 43 \qquad\qquad m/z = 29$$

The spectrum in Fig. 12-18(b) has no P^+ peak. The absence of P^+ may occur with alkanes having a quarternary C because cleavage of a quaternary C-to-C bond gives a stable 3° carbocation. Three such cleavages occur, *a*, *b*, and *c*.

$$[CH_3CH_2 \overset{a}{\underset{b}{\vert}} \overset{\overset{CH_3}{\vert}}{\underset{\underset{CH_3}{\vert}}{C}} \overset{c}{\underset{}{\vert}} (CH_2)_3CH_3]^+ \qquad mw = 128 \text{ (does not persist)}$$

$- \cdot CH_2(CH_2)_2CH_3 \,(-57)$

$-\cdot CH_3\,(-15)$ $-\cdot CH_2CH_3\,(-29)$

$$CH_3\overset{+}{\underset{\underset{CH_3}{\vert}}{C}}-CH_2CH_2CH_2CH_3 \ (\textbf{A})$$
$$m/z = 113$$

$$\overset{+}{C}(CH_3)CH_2CH_2CH_2CH_3 \ (\textbf{B})$$
$$\underset{}{CH_3}$$
$$m/z = 99$$

$$CH_3CH_2\overset{+}{\underset{\underset{CH_3}{\vert}}{C}}-CH_3 \ (\textbf{C})$$
$$m/z = 71$$

These initially formed cations undergo further fragmentation to give rise to smaller cationic fragments.

$$\textbf{B} \longrightarrow CH_3CH=CH_2 + {}^+CH_2CH_2CH_2CH_3 \ (m/z = 57)$$

$$\textbf{C} \xrightarrow{-H_2C=CH_2} CH_3\overset{+}{C}HCH_3 \ (m/z = 43) \xrightarrow{-H_2} H_2C=\overset{+}{C}HCH_2 \ (m/z = 41)$$

$$\textbf{A} \xrightarrow{-CH_3CH_2CH_2CH_2CH=CH_2} CH_3\overset{+}{C}H_2 \ (m/z = 29) \xrightarrow{-H_2} [CH_2=CH]^+ \ (m/z = 27)$$

SUPPLEMENTARY PROBLEMS

12.180 Identify each of the following compounds showing a singlet in a spectrum (*a*) C_8H_{18}, (*b*) C_4H_8, (*c*) C_8H_8, (*d*) C_4H_9Br, (*e*) $C_2H_3Br_3$, (*f*) $C_5H_8Cl_4$, (*g*) $C_{10}H_{18}$, (*h*) C_5H_8, (*i*) C_3H_4, (*j*) $C_4H_8O_2$, (*k*) C_6H_2, (*l*) $C_6H_8O_2$, (*m*) $C_4H_4O_3$, and (*n*) $C_2H_6O_2$.

◢   For hydrocarbons: (i) There may be individual H atoms, especially if the number of H's is small (see *k*) or the number of H's and C's are equal (see *c*). (ii) An odd number of H's divisible by three usually indicates Me groups, and an even number of H's divisible by three indicates CH_3 or CH_2 groups. (iii) If only CH_2's are present, the compound is cyclic. (iv) When O's are present as the only heteroatom they must be ethers (*j*), ketones (*l*), anhydrides (*m*), or peroxides (*n*).

(*a*)   The compound is an alkane since there are no degrees of unsaturation. An odd number of H's divisible by three usually indicates Me groups, so there must be six CH_3's (18/3) bonded to the remaining C's. $(CH_3)_3C-C(CH_3)_3$.

(*b*)   The 1° of unsaturation is due to a ring because CH_2's are present. CH_3's are not because eight is not divisible by three. Cyclobutane.

(*c*)   Five degrees of unsaturation. Since this hydrocarbon has an H for each C, there are individual H's. Cyclooctatetraene.

(*d*)   There are three CH_3's bonded to the fourth C along with a Br. $(CH_3)_3CBr$.

(*e*)   There is no unsaturation (count X's as H's in doing this calculation) and one CH_3. CH_3CBr_3.

(*f*)   There are four CH_2's but no ring because there are no degrees of unsaturation. $C(CH_2Cl)_4$.

(*g*)   It is likely to have six CH_3's (18/3) bonded to two C's. The 2° of unsaturation indicate an internal $C\equiv C$ which does not require the presence of other kinds of H's. $(CH_3)_3CC\equiv CC(CH_3)_3$.

(*h*)   There are four CH_2's (8/2) and 2° of unsaturation, indicating two rings. The fifth C is part of a spirane.

(*i*)   Two CH_2's, 2° of unsaturation, and one C with no H's. $H_2C=C=CH_2$.

(*j*)   The four CH_2's and the 1° of unsaturation indicate a cyclic compound that includes the O's as ether linkages. The O's must be positioned to make all the H's equivalent. 1,4-dioxane.

$$\begin{array}{ccc} & CH_2-CH_2 & \\ O & & O \\ & CH_2-CH_2 & \end{array}$$

(*k*)   Two single H's are present. Three $C\equiv C$'s account for the 6° of unsaturation. $HC\equiv C-C\equiv C-C\equiv CH$.

(*l*) There are four CH_2's. The 3° of unsaturation are accounted for by a ring and two C=O groups.

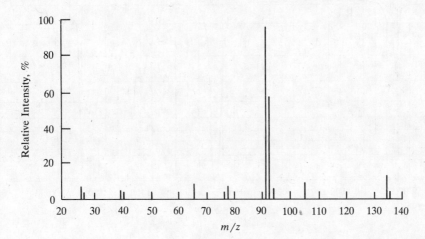

(*m*) There are two CH_2's. The 3° of unsaturation indicate a ring and two C=O groups. The third O is an ether type that is part of an anhydride group.

(*n*) Since there are no degrees of unsaturation, CH_2's are probably absent and there are two CH_3's. The O's form a peroxide linkage. $H_3C-O-O-CH_3$.

12.181 (*a*) What information can be obtained from the mass spectrum in Fig. 12-19 about the structure of an aromatic hydrocarbon? (*b*) What other spectroscopies could help pinpoint the compound?

Fig. 12-19

(a) Peaks for parent cations of aromatic compounds usually appear in mass spectra. The parent has a molecular weight of 134 and a molecular formula of $C_{10}H_{14}$. The base peak at 91 is typically $C_6H_5CH_2^+$, indicating that the compound is a monosubstituted benzene with a CH_2 attached to the ring. Two compounds, $C_6H_5CH_2CH_2CH_2CH_3$ and $C_6H_5CH_2CH(CH_3)_2$, can give this fragment. *(b)* A ^{13}C nmr spectrum would help, as *n*-butylbenzene would give eight signals, and *i*-butylbenzene would give seven signals. A pmr spectrum would show the characteristic heptet for the 3° H.

12.182 (*a*) Briefly discuss the salient similarities and differences between the following spectroscopies: (i) ir and Raman, (ii) nmr and esr (*electron spin resonance*, also called *electron paramagnetic resonance or* epr). (*b*) Discuss the origin and applications of microwave spectroscopy.

(a) (i) Like ir, Raman is a type of vibrational spectroscopy. In ir spectra all of the absorbed energy causes excitation of vibrational states, but in Raman only some of it does. The unabsorbed energy is scattered, and its changed wavelength is detected and plotted in wave numbers vs. intensity on chart paper. Unlike ir, Raman can detect vibrational absorptions even though there is no change in the dipole moment. Thus, a comparison of ir and Raman spectra affords useful information about molecular symmetry. For example the C=C stretch in tetrachloroethene is intense in Raman but absent in ir. (ii) The esr spectroscopy utilizes the fact that an odd e^- has two-spin states just as does an ^1H nucleus. In a magnetic field the e^--spin states have two different energies, and excitation from the lower to the higher is affected by lower frequency microwave radiation. The same

situation prevails for nmr spectroscopy except that *radiowaves* are used to excite the *nuclear* states. The esr spectroscopy is used to study the structures of free radicals.

(*b*) Absorption in the microwave region causes excitation of the quantized *rotational* states of molecules. The rotational levels of a molecule are related to the nuclei masses and the internuclear distances. Microwave spectroscopy is used to obtain bond angles and bond distances in simple molecules. For example, it can detect the relative amounts of *anti* and *gauche* conformations of 1-iodopropane. (In microwave cooking, the very rapid switching back and forth of the excited rotational states of H_2O molecules in the food results in heating the food.)

12.183 Summarize the kinds of information provided by the following kinds of spectral techniques: (*a*) uv, (*b*) ir, (*c*) pmr, (*d*) ^{13}C nmr, and (*e*) mass.

◢ (*a*) Conjugation; (*b*) functional groups; (*c*) environment of H's in a molecule and consequently its molecular skeleton including the H's; (*d*) carbon skeleton; and (*e*) molecular weight of the parent, and major structural features from the fragmentation pattern.

12.184 (*a*) Deduce structures of a nonreducible, noncyclic compound having the following spectral data: no uv absorption, major *m/z* values are 101 and 86, and ^{13}C has two signals. (*b*) If more than two isomers are possible, how can ir spectroscopy be used to distinguish among them?

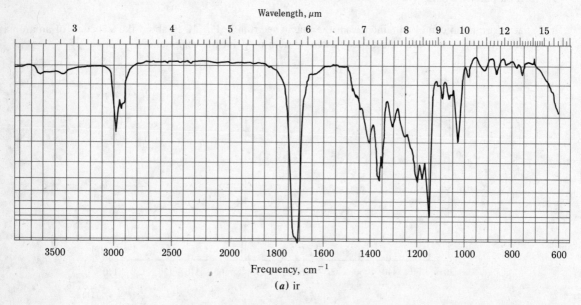

(*a*) ir

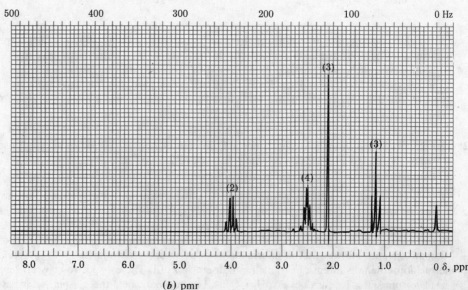

(*b*) pmr

Fig. 12-20

❚   The largest m/z value is 101, indicating the molecular weight of the parent, P. Since P has an odd mass, it must contain an odd number of N's. A reasonable formula for P = 101 is $C_6H_{15}N$. Note that with one N in the molecule the number of H's is one more than needed for an alkane with six C's. The fact that the compound is nonreducible and acyclic means it must be a saturated amine and therefore its molecular formula cannot be $C_4H_{11}N_3$ because it would then lack two H's. Fragment 86 arises from loss of CH_3 (P −15), undoubtedly by α-cleavage of an amine, e.g.,

$$[-\overset{|}{\underset{|}{N}}-\overset{|}{\underset{|}{C}}\{CH_3]^{\,\cdot+} \longrightarrow [-\overset{|}{\underset{|}{N}}-\overset{|}{\underset{|}{C}}\,]^+ + \cdot CH_3$$

Four isomeric amines can undergo this kind of cleavage:

$$\underset{\textbf{A}}{\underset{\overset{|}{H_3C}\quad\overset{|}{CH(CH_3)_2}}{CH_3\underset{\sim\!\!\!\frown}{C}HNH}} \qquad \underset{\textbf{B}}{\underset{\overset{|}{CH_2CH_3}}{CH_3CH_2N\underset{|}{C}H_2CH_3}} \qquad \underset{\textbf{C}}{\underset{\overset{|}{CH_3}\quad\overset{|}{CH_3}}{CH_3\underset{\sim\!\!\!\frown}{C}(CH_3)NCH_3}}$$

A and **B** are possible because only they have two cmr signals: **C** has three signals.   (b) **A** shows an N—H stretch of about 3300–3500 cm^{-1} whereas **B** does not.

12.185   (a) Use the spectra in Fig. 12-20 to determine the structural formula of compound $C_7H_{12}O_3$ whose uv spectrum shows absorption at $\lambda_{max} = 275$ nm ($\epsilon = 25$, ethanol).   (b) Use the spectra in Fig. 12-21 to determine the structural formula of a compound whose empirical formula is C_3H_4.

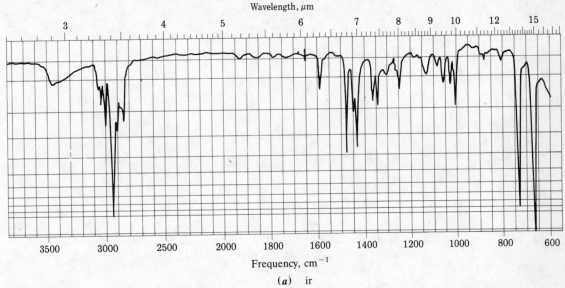

(a)   ir

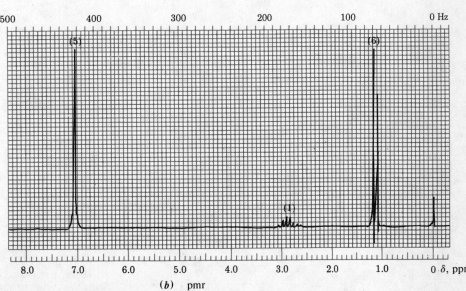

(b)   pmr

Fig. 12-21

▰ (a) There are 2° of unsaturation, at least one of which is a C=O group as indicated by the intense peak at 1730 cm^{-1} in the ir spectrum [Fig. 12-20(a)] and the low intensity $\lambda_{max} = 275$ nm in the uv spectrum. The 3-H singlet at $\delta = 2.1$ ppm is characteristic of a CH_3 attached to C=O, indicating the presence of the structural unit,

$CH_3\overset{|}{C}$=O. [See Fig. 12-20(b).] The 3-H triplet at $\delta = 1.2$ ppm and the 2-H quartet at $\delta = 4.0$ ppm is typical of an ethyl group with the CH_2 attached to an electronegative atom that must be an O in this compound. Hence, another structural unit is —OCH_2CH_3. The ir peak at about 1130 cm^{-1} is consistent with the O—C stretching frequency expected for this unit. It is now necessary to account for three C's, four H's, and one O. The 4-H complex multiplet indicates a —CH_2CH_2— unit. Since it is centered at $\delta = 2.5$ ppm, each C is bonded to a

C=O, giving the O=$\overset{|}{C}CH_2CH_2\overset{|}{C}$=O unit. The second C=O accounts for the seventh C, the third O and 2° of unsaturation. When the units are put together, the compound is the ketoester, $CH_3\underset{\underset{O}{\|}}{C}CH_2CH_2\underset{\underset{O}{\|}}{C}OCH_2CH_3$,

ethyl 4-oxopentanoate.

(b) From the mass spectrum [(Fig. 12-21(c)], we deduce that P$^+$ is $m/z = 120$ and furthermore the molecular formula is C_9H_{12} which is three times the empirical formula. There are 4° of unsaturation, from which we infer the presence of a benzene ring, confirmed by the signal near $\delta = 7$ ppm in the pmr spectrum [Fig. 12-21(b)], four signals higher than 120 ppm in the cmr spectrum [Fig. 12-21(d)], and peaks at 3000 and 3020 cm^{-1} in the ir spectrum. [Fig. 12-21(a)]. The 5-H aromatic peak in the pmr, the two ir peaks between 650 and 730 cm^{-1}, and the

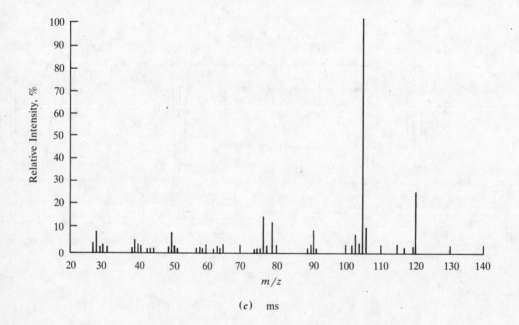

(c)   ms

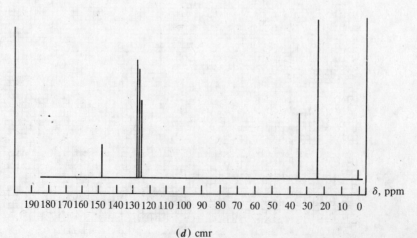

(d) cmr

Fig. 12-21 (continued)

four aromatic cmr peaks, suggest a monosubstituted benzene ring with a side chain of three C's. Since the base peak in the mass spectrum is at $m/z = 105$, we know that the C bonded to C_6H_5- is *not* a CH_2 group because, if it were, the base peak would be $m/z = 91$, for $C_6H_5CH_2^+$. $M/z = 120 - 105 = 15$ mass units, representing loss of CH_3. The base peak cation is $C_6H_5\overset{+}{C}HCH_3$, and the compound is $C_6H_5CH(CH_3)_2$. This assignment is consistent with the 6-H doublet and the less shielded 1-H heptet in the pmr spectrum and the two alkyl signals in the cmr spectrum.

12.186 Deduce the structure for a compound having the following spectral data: ir spectrum, strong peak at 1676 cm^{-1}; mass spectrum, P$^+$ at $m/z = 150$, base at $m/z = 135$; uv spectrum, $\lambda_{max} = 255$ nm; ^{1}H nmr δ values (in ppm) of (i) 7.4, *d*, two H, (ii) 6.5, *d*, two H, (iii) 3.6, *s*, three H, (iv) 2.2, *s* three H; and decoupled cmr, seven signals: one at about 210 ppm, four between 110–150 ppm and two at about 30 ppm.

 ▌ The ^{1}H nmr spectrum indicates four aromatic H's, two *ortho* to an electron-withdrawing group and two *ortho* to an electron-donating group. The compound is a *para* disubstituted benzene, as confirmed by the four

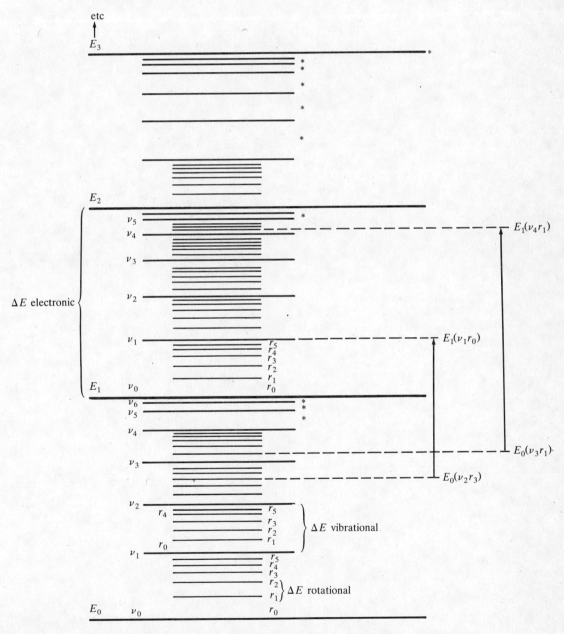

*Rotational energy levels are omitted within these vibrational levels for simplification

Fig. 12-22

aromatic signals in the cmr spectrum. The two 3-H singlets show the presence of two Me's; the more downfield Me is bonded to a strongly electronegative atom such as O, and this O is bonded to the ring. The other Me is probably attached to the $C{=}O$ which serves as the electron-withdrawing group bonded to the ring. These Me's account for the last two cmr signals. The ir spectrum indicates a $C{=}O$ group and this is confirmed by the very downfield signal in the cmr spectrum. The compound is $p\text{-}CH_3OC_6H_4COCH_3$. Its molecular weight is 150, as indicated for P^+ in the mass spectrum and the base peak results from a loss of 15 mass units (CH_3) to give the very stable cation, $CH_3OC_6H_4C{\equiv}O^+$.

12.187 Use an energy diagram to explain why uv peaks are generally broader than ir peaks.

⟋ Figure 12-22 shows that within each electronic energy level there are different vibrational energy levels. In turn, there are different rotational energy levels within each vibrational level. Consequently, there are many electronic excitations ongoing from ground state, E_0 to excited state E_1. Some typical excitations could be $E_0\nu_2r_3 \longrightarrow E_1\nu_1r_0$ or $E_0\nu_3r_1 \longrightarrow E_1\nu_4r_1$. This multitude of excitations results in a broad peak.

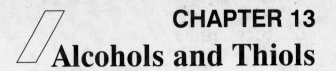

NOMENCLATURE AND STRUCTURE

13.1 Give the IUPAC name for each of the following alcohols and classify it as 1°, 2°, or 3°.

(*a*) $CH_3(CH_2)_3CHCH(CH_3)_2$ (*b*) $(CH_3)_3CCH_2OH$ (*c*) $(CH_3)_2COH$ (*d*) $BrH_2CCH_2CHC(CH_3)_3$
             | | |
            OH   Ph   OH

(*e*) $H_2C{=}CHCHCH_3$ (*f*) $PhCH_2OH$ (*g*) $HOCH_2CH_2CH_2CH_2Ph$
              |
            OH

▌ (*a*) 2-Methyl-3-heptanol, 2°; (*b*) 2,2-dimethyl-1-propanol, 1°; (*c*) 2-phenyl-2-propanol, 3°; (*d*) 5-bromo-2,2-dimethyl-3-pentanol, 2°; (*e*) 3-buten-2-ol, 2°; (*f*) phenylmethanol, 1°; (*g*) 4-phenyl-1-butanol, 1°.

13.2 Name the alcohols in Problem 13.1 by the *carbinol* system.

▌ In this older system alcohols are considered to be derived from methyl alcohol (carbinol), in which the H's are replaced by other groups. It is used mostly for naming 3° alcohols.
(*a*) *n*-Butylisopropylcarbinol, (*b*) *t*-butylcarbinol, (*c*) dimethylphenylcarbinol, (*d*) β-bromoethyl-*t*-butylcarbinol, (*e*) methylvinylcarbinol, (*f*) phenylcarbinol, (*g*) γ-phenylpropylcarbinol.

13.3 What are the common names of the following alcohols? (*a*) $(CH_3)_3COH$, (*b*) $(C_2H_5)_3COH$, (*c*) $(CH_3)_2CHCH_2OH$, (*d*) ▷$-CH_2OH$, (*e*) $ClCH_2CH_2OH$, (*f*) $CH_3(CH_2)_4OH$, (*g*) $H_2C{=}CHCH_2OH$,

(*h*) $O_2N-\langle\bigcirc\rangle-CH_2OH$, and (*i*) $HC{\equiv}CCH_2OH$.

▌ (*a*) *t*-Butyl alcohol, (*b*) triethylcarbinol, (*c*) isobutyl alcohol, (*d*) cyclopropylcarbinol, (*e*) β-chloroethanol *or* ethylene chlorohydrin, (*f*) *n*-amyl alcohol, (*g*) allyl alcohol, (*h*) *p*-nitrobenzyl alcohol, and (*i*) propargyl alcohol.

13.4 Give the IUPAC name for each of the following cyclic compounds.

(*a*)   (*b*)   (*c*)   (*d*)   (*e*)

▌ (*a*) Cyclohexanol, (*b*) (1-cyclopentenyl)methanol, (*c*) 1-methylcyclopentanol, (*d*) *trans*-2-methylcyclopentanol, (*e*) 3-cyclohexen-1-ol.

13.5 Write the structure for each of the following alcohols. (*a*) *sec*-Butyl alcohol, (*b*) cinnamyl alcohol, (*c*) 3-chloro-2-methyl-1-butanol, (*d*) *erythro*-3-chloro-2-butanol, (*e*) 3,3-dimethylcyclopentanol, and (*f*) 4,4-dimethyl-2-cyclohexen-1-ol.

▌ (*a*) $CH_3CH(OH)CH_2CH_3$ (*b*) $Ph-CH{=}CHCH_2OH$ (*c*) $CH_3CHClCH(CH_3)CH_2OH$

(*d*) $CH_3-\overset{\displaystyle H}{\underset{\displaystyle HO}{|}}\overset{\displaystyle H}{\underset{\displaystyle Cl}{|}}-CH_3$ (*e*)   (*f*)

13.6 Write structures of all the $C_5H_{12}O$ alcohols. Name each by the IUPAC, common (as alcohol), and carbinol methods. Use the alcohol method only when naming the R group is not complicated. Identify each as 1°, 2°, and 3° and indicate any chirality.

Draw the five C's in sequence and then position the OH giving three isomers.

$$CH_3CH_2CH_2CH_2CH_2OH \qquad CH_3C^*H(OH)CH_2CH_2CH_3 \qquad CH_3CH_2CH(OH)CH_2CH_3$$

1-Pentanol, *n*-pentyl alcohol,   2-Pentanol, methylpropylcarbinol, 2°   3-Pentanol, diethylcarbinol, 2°
n-butylcarbinol, 1° C^2 is chiral

Draw four C's in sequence and then position CH_3 and OH to give two isomers.

$$CH_3C^*H(OH)CH(CH_3)_2 \qquad\qquad (CH_3)_2C(OH)CH_2CH_3$$

3-Methyl-2-butanol, methylisopropylcarbinol, 2°   2-Methyl-2-butanol, *t*-pentyl alcohol,
C^2 is chiral   dimethylethylcarbinol, 3°

With three sequential C's there is one isomer:

$$HOCH_2C(CH_3)_3$$

2,2-Dimethyl-1-propanol, neopentyl alcohol, *t*-butylcarbinol, 1°

13.7 Write the structures and name all the cyclic C_4H_7OH isomers. Indicate any chirality.

(1) Cyclobutanol   (2) Cyclopropylmethanol   (3) 1-Methylcyclopropanol

(4) *cis*-2-Methylcyclopropanol, chiral   (5) *trans*-2-Methylcyclopropanol, chiral

13.8 Give the structures and explain the given names of the following alcohols: (*a*) wood alcohol, (*b*) grain alcohol, (*c*) rubbing alcohol, and (*d*) fusel oils.

(*a*) CH_3OH. Industrially, this alcohol was isolated from the liquid formed from the destructive distillation (heating in the absence of O_2) of wood during the time that charcoal was an important energy source. (*b*) C_2H_5OH. It is a product of the yeast fermentation of the sugar in grains and fruits. It is a constituent of wines, hard liquors, and beers. (*c*) $(CH_3)_2CHOH$. It is used for rubdowns and its evaporation reduces fevers. Because it is cheaper it has replaced ethanol for this purpose. (*d*) These are mixtures of alcohols obtained in small amounts along with ethanol in the fermentation of starch. The major component is $Me_2CHCH_2CH_2OH$, isopentyl (isoamyl) alcohol. In German the name means inferior oil.

13.9 Explain the following: (*a*) ROH's with three or fewer C's are H_2O-soluble; those with five or more C's are insoluble, and those with four C's are marginally soluble. (*b*) When volumes of ethanol and water are mixed, the total volume is less than the sum of the two individual volumes. (*c*) Propanol (MW = 60) has a higher boiling point than butane (MW = 58).

(*a*) The water solubility of alcohols is attributed to intermolecular H-bonding with H_2O [see Problem 2.64(*a*)]. As the molecular weights of the alcohols increase, their solubility in water decreases, because greater carbon content makes the alcohols less hydrophilic. Conversely, their solubility in hydrocarbon solvents increases. (*b*) H-bonding between ethanol and water permits the two unlike molecules to move closer together in the solution than can ethanol to ethanol and water to water molecules. (*c*) Alcohol molecules attract each other by relatively strong H-bonds and somewhat weaker dipole-dipole interactions, resulting in a higher bp. Only weaker van der Waals attractive forces must be overcome to vaporize the hydrocarbon.

13.10 (*a*) What is absolute alcohol? (*b*) How is it prepared? (*c*) What is denatured alcohol and why is it dangerous to drink? (*d*) What is the meaning of the term proof used to describe the alcohol content of wines and spirits?

(*a*) *Absolute* alcohol is pure anhydrous ethanol. (*b*) Since ethanol forms a lower boiling azeotropic mixture (see Problem 10.22) containing 95.6 : 4.4 (volume %) alcohol : water, it cannot be dried by distillation. The water can be removed chemically by treatment with Mg turnings, which react with the water forming $Mg(OH)_2$ and releasing H_2 gas. Alternatively, it can be distilled after the addition of some benzene. The benzene forms a ternary azeotrope with the alcohol-water mixture which boils at 65°, lower than the bp of the binary azeotrope. Thus it distills first, removing the water and leaving behind water-free alcohol, which is further distilled. Absolute alcohol purified in this manner should not be drunk because it contains small amounts of toxic, carcinogenic benzene. (*c*) *Denatured* alcohol is alcohol rendered undrinkable by the addition of small quantities of benzene, toxic methanol, or other poisons.   (**d**) *Proof* is defined as twice the % by volume of alcohol in an ethanol-water mixture. Thus, a wine with alcohol 12% by volume is 24 proof and an 80 proof alcoholic liquor has 40% ethanol.

13.11   (**a**) Explain why MeOH and EtOH are reasonably good solvents for many ionic substances.   (**b**) Compare the solvent properties of ethanol and pentanol toward ionic compounds.

   ▟   (**a**) They, like water, H-bond and have relatively high dielectric constants (H_2O, 78.5; MeOH, 32.6; EtOH, 24.3) for organic compounds. They are able to insulate charges by solvation, minimizing attractions between unlike ions.   (**b**) The R part in pentanol is larger than in ethanol. It can conceal the H of its O—H bond which is then not as effective in H-bonding with the anion. The ions of the salt are more extensively associated into ion-pairs and clusters, resulting in less solubility in this solvent.

13.12   Place the following compounds in decreasing order of boiling point and account for the order: 1-pentanol (**A**), 2-methyl-2-butanol (**B**), 3-methyl-2-butanol (**C**).

   ▟   **A > C > B**. As the branching increases, the shape becomes more compact and spherical. There is then less surface contact available for van der Waals attractive forces.

13.13   Explain the following trends in water solubility.   (**a**) Cyclohexanol is more soluble in water than 1-hexanol. (**b**) 1,5-Pentanediol is soluble, and 1-pentanol only slightly soluble in water.

   ▟   (**a**) The R in cyclohexanol is more compact than in 1-hexanol. Its OH group is more exposed and available for H-bonding with water. In addition, its small compact shape results in fewer water-water H-bonds being broken.   (**b**) The additional OH group increases the number of H-bonds between water and the diol.

PREPARATION

13.14   Write equations for the industrial syntheses of (**a**) methanol, and (**b**) ethanol (use two methods).

   ▟   (**a**) $CH_4 + H_2O \xrightarrow{\Delta} CO + 3H_2$; $CO + 2H_2 \xrightarrow[\text{400 °C, 200 atm}]{\text{ZnO/CrO}_3} CH_3OH$

   (**b**) (i) $H_2C{=}CH_2 + H_2O$ (steam) $\xrightarrow[\text{300–350 °C}]{H_3PO_4} CH_3CH_2OH$ (Oxo process)
   (from petroleum)

   (ii) Ethanol is also obtained commercially from *fermentation* of carbohydrates (sugars, starch, etc.) from vegetable matter [Problem 13.8(**b**)]:

$$C_6H_{12}O_6 \text{ (a carbohydrate)} \xrightarrow{\text{yeast}} 2CH_3CH_2OH + 2CO_2$$

   Since the maximum concentration obtained in this case is low ($<15\%$), a second distillation of the fermentation mixture is necessary to get a higher concentration of EtOH.

13.15   Give the synthesis of each of the following alcohols from an alkene with the same number of carbons. (**a**) 2-Butanol, (**b**) 1-methylcyclohexanol, (**c**) isobutyl alcohol, (**d**) cyclopentylcarbinol, and (**e**) 2-methyl-2-butanol.

   ▟   Markovnikov addition to a double bond can be accomplished by hydration in the presence of dilute H_2SO_4 or by oxymercuration with $Hg(OAc)_2/H_2O$ followed by reduction with $NaBH_4$ (see Problem 7.90) in preparing (**a**), (**b**), and (**e**). BH_3-THF followed by oxidation with H_2O_2 in aq. OH^- gives the anti-Markovnikov addition for the synthesis of (**c**) and (**d**). The starting materials are:

   (**a**) $CH_3CH{=}CHCH_3$ or $CH_3CH_2CH{=}CH_2$ (**b**) [cyclohexane]${=}CH_2$ or   [cyclohexene with CH_3]

   (**c**) $(CH_3)_2C{=}CH_2$ (**d**) [cyclopentane]${=}CH_2$ (**e**) $(CH_3)_2C{=}CHCH_3$ or $H_2C{=}\overset{\underset{\displaystyle |}{CH_3}}{C}CH_2CH_3$

13.16   Hydration of 3-phenyl-1-butene in dilute H_2SO_4 is not a satisfactory method for preparing 3-phenyl-2-butanol, because 2-phenyl-2-butanol is obtained instead. Explain.

   ▟   Hydration gives an intermediate 2° C^+, which undergoes a hydride shift:

$$H_2C{=}CH{-}\underset{\underset{\displaystyle Ph}{|}}{C}H{-}CH_3 \xrightarrow{H^+} H_3C{-}\overset{+}{C}H{-}\underset{\underset{\displaystyle Ph}{|}}{C}H{-}CH_3 \xrightarrow{\sim\,:H} H_3C{-}CH_2{-}\overset{+}{\underset{\underset{\displaystyle Ph}{|}}{C}}{-}CH_3 \xrightarrow[-H^+]{H_2O} CH_3CH_2{-}\overset{\overset{\displaystyle OH}{|}}{\underset{\underset{\displaystyle Ph}{|}}{C}}{-}CH_3$$

   Although phenyl is a better migrator than H, migration of H occurs leading to a more stable 3° benzylic carbocation.

13.17 Give the product and show steps in the hydration of cyclobutylethene in dilute H_2SO_4.

◢ Addition of H^+ to C^1 gives a $2°$ C^+, that rearranges by ring expansion to give ultimately 2-methylcyclo-pentanol:

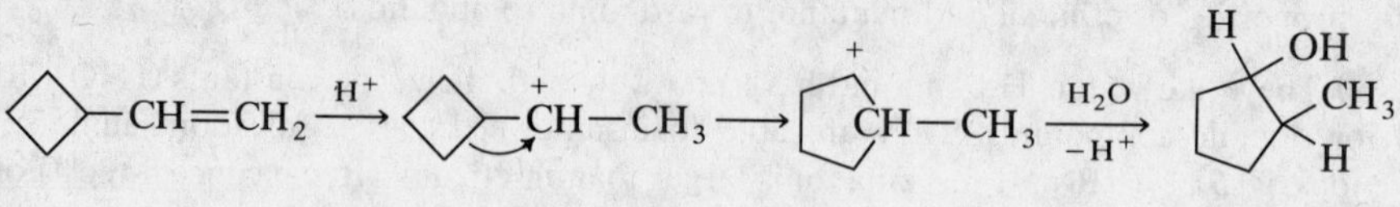

$$\square\!\!-CH\!=\!CH_2 \xrightarrow{H^+} \square\!\!-\overset{+}{C}H\!-\!CH_3 \longrightarrow \overset{+}{\text{(ring)}}CH\!-\!CH_3 \xrightarrow[-H^+]{H_2O} \text{(cyclopentane with OH, CH}_3, H, H\text{)}$$

cis and *trans*

13.18 Outline a synthesis of each alcohol from the indicated starting materials:
(*a*) Isopropyl alcohol from a hydrocarbon, (*b*) *n*-butyl alcohol from acetylene, (*c*) allyl alcohol from propane, and (*d*) *t*-butyl alcohol from *t*-butyl chloride.

◢ (*a*)

$$CH_3CH_2CH_3 \xrightarrow{Cl_2}{h\nu} CH_3CHClCH_3 \xrightarrow{aq.\ OH^-} CH_3CH(OH)CH_3$$

$$\text{or} \quad \underset{\text{alc. KOH}}{\Bigl\lfloor} CH_3CH\!=\!CH_2 \xrightarrow{H_3O^+}$$

(*b*) $H\!-\!C\!\equiv\!C\!-\!H \xrightarrow{\text{1-mol } H_2} H_2C\!=\!CH_2 \xrightarrow{HBr} CH_3CH_2Br$ (**A**)

$$\Big\downarrow NaNH_2$$

$$H\!-\!C\!\equiv\!C^- \xrightarrow{\text{A}} H\!-\!C\!\equiv\!C\!-\!CH_2CH_3 \xrightarrow[\text{2. } BH_3/H_2O_2,\ OH^-]{\text{1. 1-mol } H_2} HOH_2CCH_2CH_2CH_3$$

(*c*) From (*a*),

$$CH_3CH\!=\!CH_2 \xrightarrow{NBS} H_2BrCCH\!=\!CH_2 \xrightarrow{aq.\ OH^-} HOH_2CCH\!=\!CH_2$$

(*d*) $(CH_3)_3CCl + H_2O \longrightarrow (CH_3)_3COH$ (S_N1 solvolysis of a $3°$ halide)

13.19 Write the steps in the Grignard reaction between an alkylmagnesium halide, RMgX, and (*a*) a carbonyl compound, $>\!C\!=\!O$, and (*b*) an ethylene oxide.

◢ (*a*) $\boxed{R\!:^-}(MgX)^+ + H\!-\!\overset{H}{\underset{}{C}}\!=\!O \longrightarrow \boxed{R}\!-\!CH_2\!-\!\bar{O}(MgX)^+ \xrightarrow{H_2O} \boxed{R}\!-\!CH_2\!-\!OH$ ($1°$ alcohol)

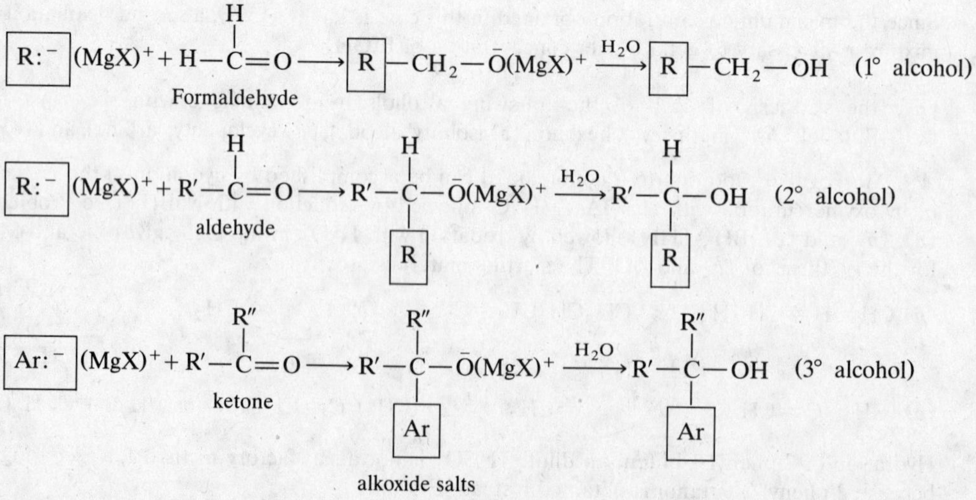

Formaldehyde

$\boxed{R\!:^-}(MgX)^+ + R'\!-\!\overset{H}{\underset{}{C}}\!=\!O \longrightarrow R'\!-\!\overset{H}{\underset{\boxed{R}}{C}}\!-\!\bar{O}(MgX)^+ \xrightarrow{H_2O} R'\!-\!\overset{H}{\underset{\boxed{R}}{C}}\!-\!OH$ ($2°$ alcohol)

aldehyde

$\boxed{Ar\!:^-}(MgX)^+ + R'\!-\!\overset{R''}{\underset{}{C}}\!=\!O \longrightarrow R'\!-\!\overset{R''}{\underset{\boxed{Ar}}{C}}\!-\!\bar{O}(MgX)^+ \xrightarrow{H_2O} R'\!-\!\overset{R''}{\underset{\boxed{Ar}}{C}}\!-\!OH$ ($3°$ alcohol)

ketone

alkoxide salts

(*b*) $\boxed{R\!:^-}(MgX)^+ + H_2\overset{:O:}{C}\!-\!CH_2 \longrightarrow \Bigl[H_2\overset{:\ddot{O}:^-}{C}\!-\!\underset{\boxed{R}}{CH_2}\Bigr](MgX)^+ \xrightarrow{H_2O} H_2\overset{OH}{C}\!-\!\underset{\boxed{R}}{CH_2}$ ($1°$ alcohol)

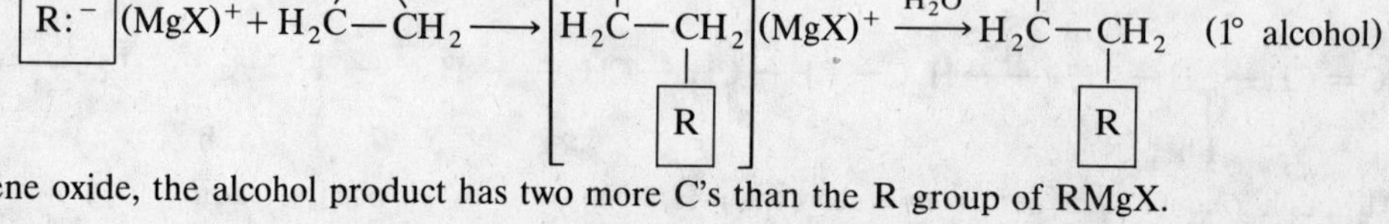

With ethylene oxide, the alcohol product has two more C's than the R group of RMgX.

13.20 Give the Grignard reagent and carbonyl compound or ethylene oxide that can be used to prepare the following alcohols. List all pairs of possible combinations.

(*a*) $CH_3CH_2CH_2OH$ (*b*) $(CH_3)_2C(OH)CH_2CH_2CH_3$ (*c*) $PhCH_2CH(OH)CH_3$ (*d*) $CH_3CH_2C(CH_3)OH$ with Ph substituent

(*e*) cyclohexane ring with $CH(CH_3)_2$ and OH (*f*) cyclopentane ring with CH_2OH and H (*g*) $(CH_3)_2CHCH_2CH_2OH$

◢ (*a*) $CH_3CH_2MgX + H_2CO$ or $CH_3MgX + H_2C\overset{O}{-}CH_2$

    (*b*) $CH_3CH_2CH_2MgX + (CH_3)_2CO$ or $CH_3CH_2CH_2COCH_3 + CH_3MgX$

    (*c*) $PhCH_2MgX + CH_3CHO$ or $PhCH_2CHO + CH_3MgX$

    (*d*) $PhCOCH_3 + CH_3CH_2MgX$ or $CH_3CH_2COCH_3 + PhMgX$ or $PhCOCH_2CH_3 + CH_3MgX$

    (*e*) $O{=}$ cyclohexane $+ (CH_3)_2CHMgX$ (*f*) $H_2C{=}O +$ cyclopentane with H and MgX

    (*g*) $H_2C\overset{O}{-}CH_2 + (CH_3)_2CHMgX$ or $H_2CO + (CH_3)_2CHCH_2MgX$

13.21 Give the structure of the alcohol synthesized when each of the following pairs of carbonyl compound and the Grignard reagent of the halide react. (*a*) Methyl phenyl ketone and chlorocyclohexane, CyCl, (*b*) acetone and bromobenzene, (*c*) formaldehyde and allyl chloride, and (*d*) cyclohexanone and benzyl bromide.

◢ (*a*) $\underset{Cy}{\overset{Me}{PhCOH}}$ (*b*) $\underset{Me}{\overset{Me}{PhCOH}}$ (*c*) $H_2C{=}CH{-}CH_2CH_2OH$ (*d*) cyclohexane ring with CH_2Ph and OH

13.22 Prepare 1-pentanol (**A**) from (*a*) an alkene, (*b*) 1-bromopentane, (*c*) 1-bromobutane, and (*d*) 1-bromopropane.

◢ (*a*) $CH_3CH_2CH_2CH{=}CH_2 \xrightarrow[\text{2. } H_2O_2,\ OH^-]{\text{1. } BH_3/THF} \mathbf{A}$ (*b*) $CH_3CH_2CH_2CH_2CH_2Br \xrightarrow{OH^-/H_2O} \mathbf{A} + Br^-$

    (*c*)   The chain must be lengthened by a Grignard reaction with $H_2C{=}O$.

$$CH_3CH_2CH_2CH_2Br \xrightarrow[Et_2O]{Mg} CH_3CH_2CH_2CH_2MgBr \xrightarrow[\text{2. } H_3O^+]{\text{1. } H_2CO} \mathbf{A}$$

    (*d*)   The chain must be lengthened by a Grignard reaction with ethylene oxide.

$$CH_3CH_2CH_2Br \xrightarrow[Et_2O]{Mg} CH_3CH_2CH_2MgBr \xrightarrow{\text{ethylene oxide}} CH_3CH_2CH_2CH_2CH_2O^-MgBr^+ \xrightarrow{H^+} \mathbf{A}$$

13.23 Outline a synthesis of 3-(*p*-chlorophenyl)-1-propanol from benzene, toluene, and any carbon compounds containing three or fewer C's.

◢ $C_6H_5CH_3 \xrightarrow[Fe]{Cl_2} p\text{-}ClC_6H_4CH_3 \xrightarrow{NBS} p\text{-}ClC_6H_4CH_2Br \xrightarrow[\text{ether}]{Mg}$

$$p\text{-}ClC_6H_4CH_2MgBr \xrightarrow[\text{2. } H_3O^+]{\text{1. ethylene oxide}} p\text{-}ClC_6H_4CH_2CH_2CH_2OH$$

Notice that Grignard formation occurs preferentially with the more active benzylic halide.

13.24 Give four limitations of the Grignard reaction.

(*1*) The halide cannot possess a functional group with an acidic H, such as OH, COOH, NH_2, SH, or $C{\equiv}C{-}H$, because the carbanion of the Grignard group would remove the acidic H and be reduced. For example:

$$HOCH_2CH_2Br + Mg \longrightarrow \underset{\text{unstable}}{[HOCH_2CH_2MgBr]} \longrightarrow (BrMg)^+\ {}^-OCH_2CH_2\mathbf{H}$$

(*2*) If the halide also has a C=O (or C=N—, C≡N, N=O, S=O, C≡CH) group, it reacts intramolecularly with itself. (*3*) The reactant cannot be a *vic*-dihalide, because it would undergo dehalogenation:

$$BrCH_2CH_2Br + Mg \longrightarrow H_2C{=}CH_2 + MgBr_2$$

(4) A ketone with two bulky R groups, e.g., $-C(CH_3)_3$, is too sterically hindered to react with an organometallic compound with a bulky R′ group.

13.25 List the reagents commonly used to reduce carbonyl functional groups to alcohols.

H_2/catalyst, $LiAlH_4$, $NaBH_4$, NaH, LiH.

13.26 (*a*) Give the product of the reaction of (i) $CH_3COCH_2CH_3$, (ii) $PhCH_2CHO$, (iii) 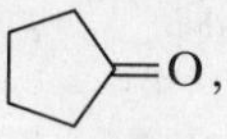, (iv) $Ph_2CHCH_2COCH_3$, with H_2/catalyst. (*b*) What catalysts are frequently used?

(*a*) (i) $CH_3CHOHCH_2CH_3$, (ii) $PhCH_2CH_2OH$, (iii) 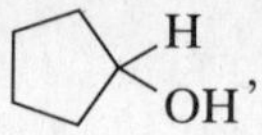, (iv) $Ph_2CHCH_2CHOHCH_3$. (*b*) Ni, Pt, Pd.

13.27 (*a*) Give the product from catalytic hydrogenation of $CH_3CH{=}CHCH_2CHO$. (*b*) Can $CH_3CH{=}CHCH_2CH_2OH$ be isolated?

(*a*) $CH_3CH_2CH_2CH_2CH_2OH$. (*b*) No. Hydrogenation of aldehyde and ketone carbonyls is usually slower than that of C—C double bonds. It is generally difficult to reduce a $>C{=}O$ when present in an alkene (or alkyne) without also reducing the multiple bond.

13.28 Give the product of reduction of (*a*) $(CH_3)_2CHCH_2CHO$, (*b*) PhCHO, (*c*) $(CH_3CH_2)_2CO$, and (*d*) 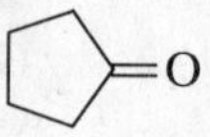 with (i) $LiAlH_4$ and (ii) $NaBH_4$. Indicate the reagent of choice.

In each case, both hydrides (i) and (ii), give the same alcohol.

(*a*) $(CH_3)_2CHCH_2CH_2OH$ (*b*) $PhCH_2OH$ (*c*) $(CH_3CH_2)_2CHOH$ (*d*) 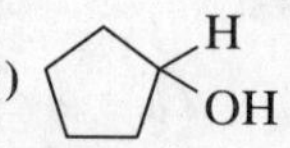

$LiAlH_4$ is a much stronger reducing agent than $NaBH_4$. It reacts almost explosively with water and alcohols giving H_2 and so it must be used in anhydrous conditions. It is often more convenient to use the less reactive borohydride, which can be used in an aqueous medium.

13.29 Write a mechanism for the metal hydride reduction of an aldehyde or ketone.

A hydride ion, H:⁻, is transferred to the C of the $>C{=}O$.

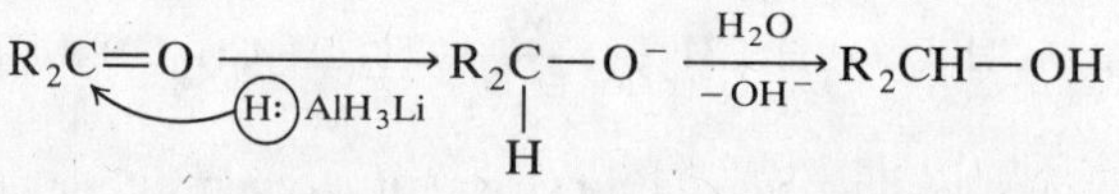

13.30 Give the expected product from the reaction of (*a*) CH_3COCH_2COOH, (*b*) $O{=}CHCH_2COOCH_3$, (*c*) $CH_3CH_2COCH_2CH_2Br$, and (*d*) $p\text{-}O_2N{-}C_6H_4{-}CHO$ with (i) $NaBH_4$ (ii) $LiAlH_4$?

$LiAlH_4$, being a more reactive reducing agent than $NaBH_4$, will also reduce carboxylic acids and esters to the corresponding 1° alcohol. Many alkyl halides are reduced to alkanes via S_N2 displacement by H:⁻. $LiAlH_4$ also reduces $-NO_2$ to $-NH_2$. (*a*) (i) $CH_3CH(OH)CH_2COOH$, (ii) $CH_3CH(OH)CH_2CH_2OH$; (*b*) (i) $HOH_2CCH_2COOCH_3$, (ii) $HOH_2CCH_2CH_2OH$; (*c*) (i) $CH_3CH_2CH(OH)CH_2CH_2Br$, (ii) $CH_3CH_2CH(OH)CH_2CH_3$; and (*d*) (i) $p\text{-}O_2NC_6H_4CH_2OH$, (ii) $p\text{-}H_2NC_6H_4CH_2OH$.

13.31 What product is expected from the reaction of 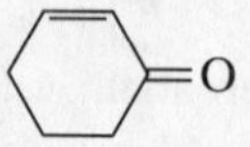 with (*a*) $LiAlH_4$ and (*b*) H_2/Pt?

(*a*) 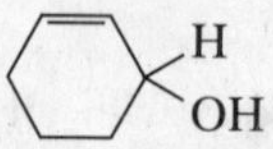 (*b*) 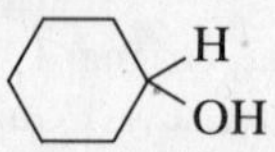

13.32 Give the carbonyl compound and reducing reagent that will produce each of the following:

(*a*) $CH_3CH(OH)CH_2CH_2OH$ (two methods), (*b*) $PhCH(CH_3)CH_2CH(OH)CH_3$, (*c*) 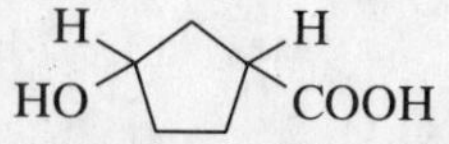 *cis* and *trans*.

(*a*) CH_3COCH_2CHO, $NaBH_4$, or CH_3COCH_2COOH, $LiAlH_4$; (*b*) $PhCH(CH_3)CH_2COCH_3$, $NaBH_4$ or $LiAlH_4$; (*c*) 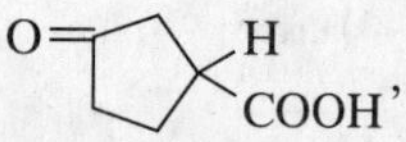, $NaBH_4$.

13.33 What is the product of the reaction of acetophenone with (*a*) LiAlD$_4$ followed by H$_3$O$^+$, (*b*) NaBD$_4$ in H$_2$O, (*c*) D$_2$/Pt in (i) aprotic solvent and (ii) protic solvent, e.g., H$_2$O?

◢ (*a*) and (*b*) PhCD(CH$_3$)OH. (*c*) (i) PhCD(CH$_3$)OD and (ii) PhCD(CH$_3$)OH. The D of ROD rapidly exchanges for the H of H$_2$O.

13.34 Write the product of the reaction of LiAlD$_4$ followed by H$_3$O$^+$ with (*a*) Ph$_2$C=O, (*b*) CH$_3$CH=CHCH=O, (*c*) CH$_2$—CH$_2$, and (*d*) CH$_3$CH—CH$_2$.
$\qquad\qquad\qquad$ \ /
$\qquad\qquad\qquad\quad$ O $\qquad\qquad\qquad\quad$ O

◢ (*a*) Ph$_2$CD(OH), (*b*) CH$_3$CH=CHCHD(OH), (*c*) HOH$_2$CCH$_2$D, and (*d*) CH$_3$CH(OH)CH$_2$D.

13.35 Synthesize the following from benzene or toluene, any alkyl halides with 3 or fewer C's, acetone and acetic anhydride (ac. anh.). (*a*) PhC(CH$_3$)(OH)CH$_2$CH$_2$CH$_3$, (*b*) (CH$_3$)$_2$C(OH)C≡CH, (*c*) (CH$_3$)$_2$C=CHCH=CH$_2$, (*d*) PhCH(CH$_3$)CH$_2$OH.

◢ (*a*)
$$PhH \xrightarrow[\text{AlCl}_3]{\text{ac.anh.}} Ph\text{—COCH}_3 \Big]$$
$$n\text{-C}_3\text{H}_7\text{Br} + \text{Mg/Et}_2\text{O} \rightarrow n\text{-C}_3\text{H}_7\text{MgBr} \Big] \rightarrow PhC(CH_3)(OH)CH_2CH_2CH_3$$

(*b*) $\quad CH_3CH_2Cl \xrightarrow[\text{alc.}]{\text{KOH}} CH_2{=}CH_2 \xrightarrow{\text{Br}_2} BrH_2CCH_2Br \xrightarrow{\text{2NaNH}_2} HC{\equiv}CH \xrightarrow[\text{from (a)}]{\text{PrMgBr}} HC{\equiv}CMgBr$

$\qquad\qquad CH_3COCH_3 + HC{\equiv}CMgBr \longrightarrow (CH_3)_2C(OH)C{\equiv}CH$

(*c*) $\quad CH_3CH_2CH_2Cl \xrightarrow[\text{alc.}]{\text{KOH}} CH_3CH{=}CH_2 \xrightarrow{\text{NBS}} BrCH_2CH{=}CH_2 \xrightarrow[\text{Et}_2\text{O}]{\text{Mg}} BrMgCH_2CH{=}CH_2$

$\quad CH_3COCH_3 + BrMgCH_2CH{=}CH_2 \longrightarrow (CH_3)_2C(OH)CH_2CH{=}CH_2 \xrightarrow[\Delta]{\text{H}_2\text{SO}_4} (CH_3)_2C{=}CHCH{=}CH_2$

(*d*) From (*a*),

$$\begin{matrix} PhCOCH_3 \Big] \\ \\ CH_3I + Mg \longrightarrow CH_3MgI \Big] \end{matrix} \rightarrow PhCOH(CH_3)_2 \xrightarrow{\text{H}_2\text{SO}_4} \underset{\underset{CH_3}{|}}{PhC{=}CH_2} \xrightarrow[\text{2. H}_2\text{O}_2,\ \text{OH}^-]{\text{1. BH}_3/\text{THF}} PhCH(CH_3)CH_2OH$$

REACTIONS

13.36 (*a*) Compare the acidity of ROH and water (in the liquid state). (*b*) List the 1°, 2°, and 3° liquid alcohols in decreasing order of acidity and give an explanation.

◢ (*a*) The electron-releasing R group makes the alcohol slightly less acidic than water. More important is the fact that water is a better solvator and stabilizer of ions, pulling the equilibrium more toward ion formation. (*b*) The decreasing order is CH$_3$OH > 1° > 2° > 3°. It is attributed to the acid-weakening electron-releasing R's.

13.37 Compare the acidities of ClCH$_2$CH$_2$OH and CH$_3$CH$_2$OH. Explain.

◢ The electron-withdrawing Cl delocalizes the negative charge of ClCH$_2$CH$_2$O$^-$ by induction making it a weaker base than CH$_3$CH$_2$O$^-$. Hence, 2-chloroethanol is more acidic.

13.38 (*a*) Write a balanced equation for the reaction of an alcohol with an alkali metal such as Na. (*b*) Place the types of alcohols into decreasing order of reactivity towards Na. (*c*) What is $^-$OR called?

◢ (*a*) 2Na + 2ROH $\longrightarrow$ H$_2$ + 2[Na$^+$ $^-$OR]. (*b*) 1° > 2° > 3°. (*c*) Alkoxide ion.

13.39 Compare and explain the relative Brönsted basicities of 1°, 2°, and 3° alcohols in the liquid state.

◢ The order of decreasing basicity is 3° > 2° > 1°, due to the electron-releasing base-strengthening effect of the R's.

13.40 Discuss the structural factors that affect the nucleophilicity of alcohols.

◢ Nucleophilicity is increased with the number of electron-repelling R groups; however this effect is counteracted by the shielding of the reactive site by the R groups.

13.41 Write equations to show why alcohols cannot be used as solvents with (*a*) Grignard reagents or (*b*) LiAlH$_4$.

▮ Alcohols are sufficiently acidic to react with the extremely strong bases, R:$^-$ and H:$^-$.

(*a*) $CH_3OH + CH_3\ddot{C}H_2MgCl \longrightarrow CH_3CH_3 + (CH_3O)^-(MgCl)^+$

(*b*) $4CH_3OH + LiAlH_4 \longrightarrow 4H_2 + LiAl(OCH_3)_4$

13.42 Explain why Na may be used to remove the last traces of H_2O from benzene but not from ethanol.

▮ Ethanol is acidic enough to react with Na whereas benzene is inert.

$$2C_2H_5OH + 2Na \longrightarrow 2C_2H_5O^-Na^+ + H_2$$

13.43 Write equations for the reactions of ROH with (*a*) $HC\equiv C^-Na^+$, (*b*) NaNH$_2$, and (*c*) aq. NaOH.

▮ (*a*) $HC\equiv C^-Na^+ + ROH \longrightarrow HC\equiv CH + RO^-Na^+$
  (*b*) $Na^+NH_2^- + ROH \longrightarrow NH_3 + RO^-Na^+$
  (*c*) $Na^+OH^- + ROH \rightleftharpoons H_2O + RO^-Na^+$

13.44 Give the product of the reaction of PrOH with (*a*) conc. HI, (*b*) PBr$_3$, (*c*) red P/I$_2$, (*d*) SOCl$_2$ in pyridine, and (*e*) PCl$_3$.

▮ (*a*) and (*c*) PrI, (*b*) PrBr, (*d*) and (*e*) PrCl.

13.45 List the hydrogen halide acids in decreasing order of reactivity in the conversion of ROH to RX.

▮ HI > HBr > HCl ≫ HF. The relative rate follows the same order as their acidity and the nucleophilicity of their conjugate base anions.

13.46 List the class of alcohols in decreasing order of reactivity towards hydrogen halide acids.

▮ 3° > 2° > 1° > MeOH.

13.47 Write a mechanism for the reaction of HBr with butanol. Label the slow step and draw its transition state.

▮ (1) $n\text{-}C_4H_9OH + HBr \rightleftharpoons n\text{-}C_4H_9OH_2^+ + Br^-$ (fast)

(2) $Br^- + n\text{-}C_4H_9OH_2^+ \xrightarrow{\text{slow}} \left[\begin{array}{c} H \quad H \\ \overset{\delta^-}{Br}\text{---}\underset{|}{C}\text{---}\overset{\delta^+}{OH_2} \\ C_3H_7 \end{array} \right]^{\ddagger} \longrightarrow Br\text{-}C_4H_9 + H_2O$ (S$_N$2)

13.48 Write a mechanism for the reaction of HBr with *t*-butyl alcohol. Label the slow step and draw its transition state.

▮ (1) $(CH_3)_3COH + HBr \rightleftharpoons (CH_3)_3COH_2^+ + Br^-$ (fast)

(2) $(CH_3)_3COH_2^+ \longrightarrow \left[\begin{array}{c} CH_3 \quad CH_3 \\ \underset{|}{C}\overset{\delta^+}{\text{---}}\overset{\delta^+}{OH_2} \\ CH_3 \end{array} \right]^{\ddagger} \xrightarrow[-H_2O]{\text{slow}} (CH_3)_3C^+ \xrightarrow[\text{fast}]{Br^-} (CH_3)_3CBr$ (S$_N$1)

13.49 Predict the *R/S* label of the product of reaction of conc. HX with (*a*) (*R*)-2-hexanol (S$_N$2 conditions), and (*b*) (*R*)-3-methyl-3-hexanol.

▮ (*a*) *S*. The slow step is concerted and at no time does a carbocation form. The Br$^-$ bonds to the back side of the C, away from the departing H$_2$O, resulting in an inversion. (*b*) *R,S* (racemate) + excess *S*. The carbocation formed when the C—O bond breaks is *sp*^{2} hybridized and flat. Bonding with Br$^-$ is equally probable from both sides. Actually, this is an oversimplification. The H$_2$O shields the incipient C$^+$ to some extent from front-side attack. Bonding from the rear is not impeded, accounting for an indeterminate additional amount of inversion.

13.50 Why is it not possible to obtain a halide by reacting ROH with X$^-$?

▮ OH$^-$ is a very poor leaving group. Acid converts it to H$_2$O, a better leaving group.

13.51 Give the stereochemical label of the chloride product of the reaction of (S)-$CH_3CHD(OH)$ with (*a*) HCl, (*b*) $SOCl_2$ with pyridine, and (*c*) $SOCl_2$ in a nonpolar solvent with no added base.

◢ (*a*) R, inversion; (*b*) R, inversion; (*c*) S; retention.

13.52 Give a mechanistic explanation for (*a*) the different results in Problem 13.51(*b*) and (*c*), and (*b*) the reaction $MeCH{=}CHCH_2OH \xrightarrow{SOCl_2} 100\%\ MeCHClCH{=}CH_2$.

◢ (*a*) In both cases, the first step is the formation of the intermediate chlorosulfite ester:

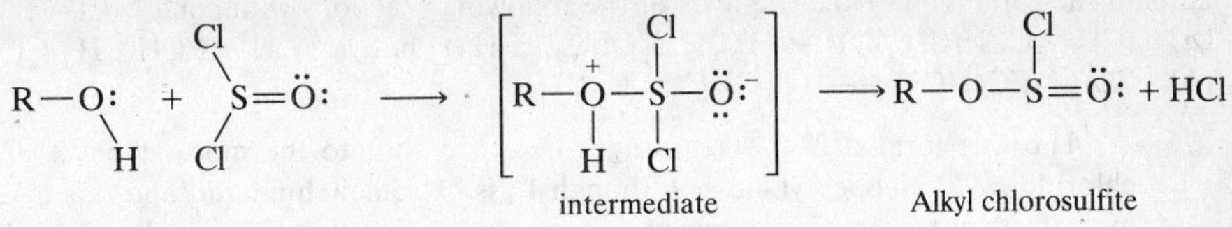

In Problem 13.51(*b*) the weak base pyridine reacts with HCl to give pyridinium ion (PyH^+) and Cl^-. The Cl^- displaces the leaving group $ClSO_2^-$, that decomposes to SO_2 and Cl^-, with inversion (S_N2).

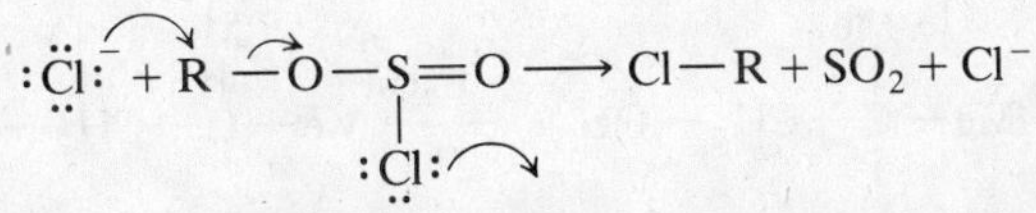

In the absence of a base and a polar solvent in Problem 13.51(*c*), the chlorosulfite ester dissociates into an *intimate ion pair*. The Cl of the anion of the ion pair attacks the front side of the C^+, with retention of configuration. Retention occurs because the Cl cannot reach the rear of the C^+ but is close to its front side. This is called the $S_N i$ (*substitution nucleophilic internal*) mechanism, in which a part of the leaving group which attacks the substrate detaches itself from the rest of the leaving group in the process.

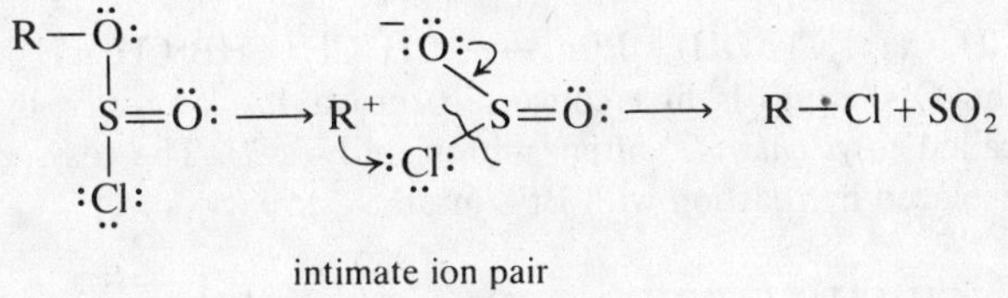

intimate ion pair

(*b*) The intermediate $MeCH{=}CHCH_2OSO_2Cl$ dissociates to an intimate ion pair whose $ClSO_2^-$ loses SO_2 while feeding Cl^- to C^3 with movement of the π e$^-$'s to give a $C^2{=}C^1$ bond. This is another example of the $S_N i$ reaction.

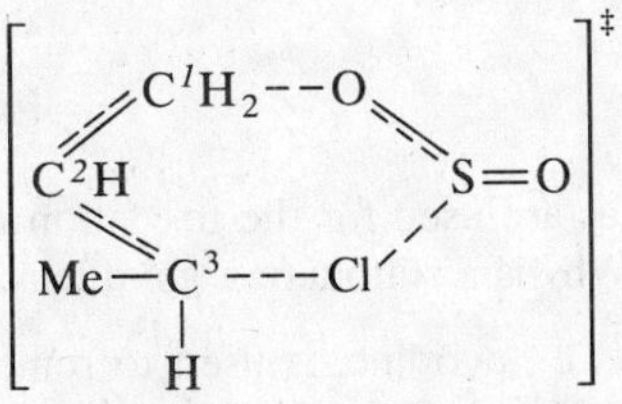

13.53 Explain the following: (*a*) 3-Pentanol reacts with HBr to give a mixture of 3- and 2-bromopentane. The exact composition of the mixture depends upon whether gaseous or aqueous HBr is used. (*b*) The same mixture of 2-chloropentane (**A**) and 3-chloropentane (**B**) is obtained when either 2- or 3-chloropentane is in contact with $ZnCl_2$ dissolved in conc. HCl.

◢ (*a*) A 2° ROH can undergo both S_N1 and S_N2 nucleophilic substitutions. 3-Bromopentane results from S_N2 attack by Br^- on the 2° C. The S_N1 pathway leaves a 2° C^+ that also gives 3-bromopentane, but, in addition, undergoes a hydride ($:H$) shift to give some 2-bromopentane.

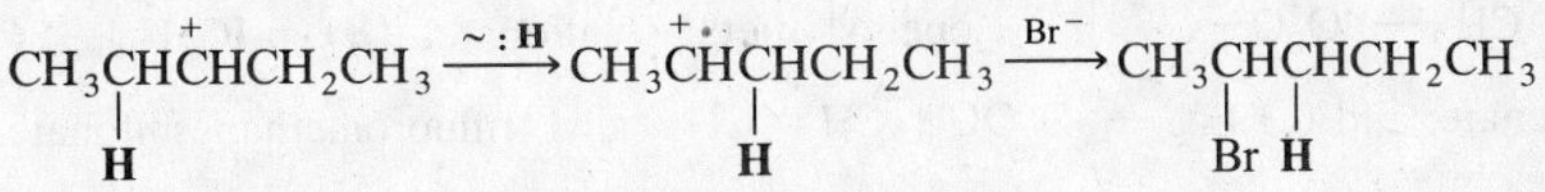

(*b*) $ZnCl_2$ is a Lewis acid that enhances formation of carbocations from RX.

$$2RCl + ZnCl_2 \rightleftharpoons 2R^+ + ZnCl_4^{2-}$$

The C^2 R^+ from 2-chloropentane is in rapid equilibrium with the C^3 R^+ from 3-chloropentane, via a hydride shift. The same equilibrium mixture results from either isomeric chloride when the mixture of R^+'s accepts a Cl^- from $ZnCl_4^{2-}$.

$$2\text{-chloropentane} \xrightarrow{-Cl^-} C^2\ R^+ \rightleftharpoons C^3\ R^+ \xleftarrow{-Cl^-} 3\text{-chloropentane}$$

$$\downarrow Cl^-$$

2- and 3-chloropentane

13.54 Explain the formation of the products of the following reactions with conc. HCl.
(*a*) $(CH_3)_3CCH(CH_3)OH \longrightarrow (CH_3)_2CClCH(CH_3)_2$ but *no* $(CH_3)_3CCH(CH_3)Cl$
(*b*) $(CH_3)_3CCH_2OH \longrightarrow (CH_3)_2CClCH_2CH_3$

▮ (*a*) The first formed 2° R^+ rearranges by a Me shift to the more stable 3° C^+, which then gives the 3° chloride. (*b*) Neopentyl alcohol, though 1°, is extremely hindered and reacts very slowly by S_N2 displacement from the rear. Formation of a neopentyl cation, via S_N1, is also unlikely. Instead, a methyl group migrating from the adjacent C acts as an intramolecular nucleophile, helping to displace H_2O. The result is a 3° C^+, from which the product is formed.

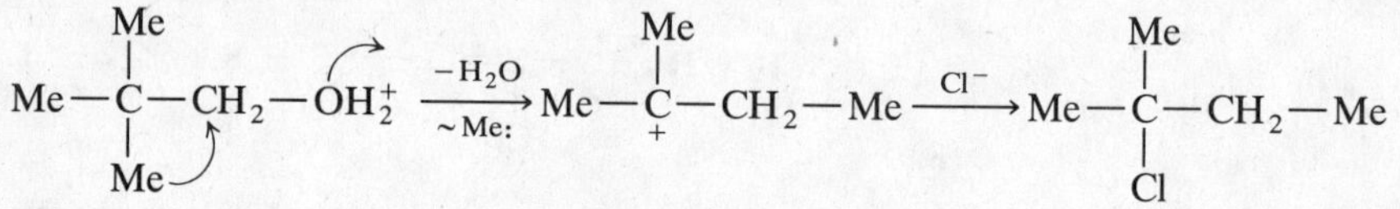

13.55 Considering that neopentyl alcohol undergoes the rearrangement in Problem 13.54(*b*), how can a neopentyl halide be synthesized from it?

▮ Use $SOCl_2$ or PBr_3; rearrangement does not occur.

13.56 Use two methods for converting 3-pentanol into 3-bromopentane with little or no 2-bromopentane.

▮ (1) $(CH_3CH_2)_2CH(OH) + PBr_3 \longrightarrow CH_3CH_2CHBrCH_2CH_3$
(2) The OH group is first converted into a *tosylate ester* by reaction with *p*-toluenesulfonyl chloride (called *tosyl chloride*, often abbreviated TsCl). The tosyl group, a good leaving group, is then easily displaced by reaction with Br^- in an S_N2 reaction.

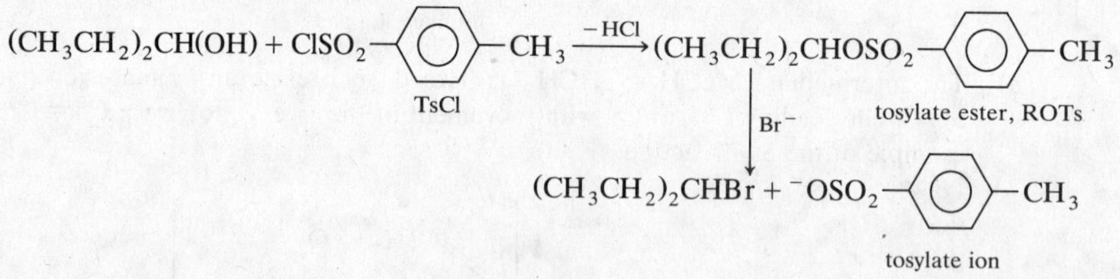

13.57 (*a*) What solvent conditions are used for the tosylation reaction? (*b*) Give the product of the reaction of tosyl chloride and water. (*c*) Why is a sulfonate a good leaving group?

▮ (*a*) An organic base, i.e., pyridine, is used to remove the HCl. It must be anhydrous because TsCl reacts with H_2O. (*b*) $p\text{-}CH_3C_6H_4SO_2OH$, *p*-toluenesulfonic acid. (*c*) The sulfonate anion is the very weak conjugate base of the very strong sulfonic acid, an acid as strong as sulfuric acid.

13.58 Give structures and names for the product of the reaction of (*a*) EtOH with benzenesulfonyl chloride, (*b*) *n*-PrOH with brosyl chloride, (*c*) cyclopentanol with mesyl chloride, (*d*) MeOH with pipsyl chloride, and (*e*) allyl alcohol with trifyl chloride.

▮ (*a*) $C_6H_5-SO_2OEt$, ethyl benzenesulfonate; (*b*) $p\text{-}BrC_6H_4-SO_2OPr$, propyl *p*-bromobenzenesulfonate;

(*c*) 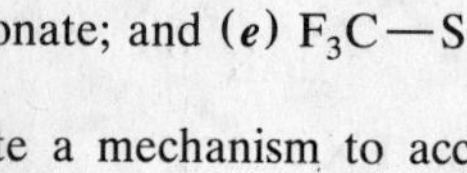 , cyclopentyl methanesulfonate; (*d*) $p\text{-}IC_6H_4-SO_2OMe$, methyl *p*-iodobenzene-sulfonate; and (*e*) $F_3C-SO_2OCH_2CH=CH_2$, allyl trifluoromethanesulfonate.

13.59 Write a mechanism to account for the following results. (*a*) When 3-buten-2-ol reacts with aq. HBr, both 3-bromo-1-butene (**C**) and 1-bromo-2-butene (**D**) are formed. (*b*) 1,4-Hexadien-3-ol (**E**) is converted into a mixture of 3,5-hexadien-2-ol (**F**) and 2,4-hexadien-1-ol (**G**) when dissolved in H_2SO_4.

▟ These reactants form allyl carbocations that are stabilized by delocalization over an extended carbon chain having more than one $^{\delta+}$C site.

(*a*) The nucleophile, Br^-, reacts at either of two electron deficient sites.

$$CH_3CHCH=CH_2 \xrightarrow{H^+} CH_3CHCH=CH_2 \xrightarrow{-H_2O} [CH_3\overset{+}{C}HCH=CH_2 \longleftrightarrow CH_3CH=CH\overset{+}{C}H_2]$$
$$\underset{OH}{|} \qquad\qquad \underset{^+OH_2}{|}$$

or $[CH_3\overset{\delta+}{C}H\text{===}CH\text{===}\overset{\delta+}{C}H_2] + Br^- \longrightarrow \mathbf{C} + \mathbf{D}$

(*b*) The double bond shifts to give an allylic conjugated diene, from which the isomer is formed.

$$H_2C=CHCHCH=CHCH_3 \xrightarrow[-H_2O]{H^+} [H_2C=CH\overset{+}{C}HCH=CHCH_3 \longleftrightarrow H_2C=CHCH=CH\overset{+}{C}HCH_3$$
$$\underset{OH}{|}$$

$$\longleftrightarrow H_2\overset{+}{C}-CH=CHCH=CHCH_3] \xrightarrow[-H^+]{H_2O} \mathbf{F} + \mathbf{G}$$

13.60 Give the product of the reaction of Ph_2CHCH_2OH with HBr and explain its formation.

▟ $PhCHCH_2OH \xrightarrow{H^+} PhCHCH_2OH_2^+ \xrightarrow[-H_2O]{\sim Ph:}$
$\underset{Ph}{|} \qquad\qquad \underset{Ph}{|}$

$$\left[PhCH\underset{\underset{Ph}{\diagdown\overset{\delta+}{\diagup}}}{\text{———}}CH_2\text{---}\overset{\overset{\delta+}{}}{O}H_2 \right]^{\ddagger} \longrightarrow Ph\overset{+}{C}H-CH_2Ph \xrightarrow{Br^-} PhCHBrCH_2Ph$$

Synchronous migration of Ph provides greater assistance in the removal of H_2O from the protonated alcohol than does a methyl group [see Problem 13.54(*b*)].

13.61 (*a*) Write an equation for the reaction of PBr_3 with an alcohol, ROH. (*b*) Does the resulting alkyl bromide show inversion, retention, or racemization?

▟ (*a*) $\qquad\qquad 3ROH + PBr_3 \longrightarrow \underset{\text{Trialkyl phosphite}}{(RO)_3 P} + 3HBr \longrightarrow 3RBr + H_3PO_3$

(*b*) The phosphite ester undergoes an S_N2 attack by Br^-, the protonated phosphite being the leaving group. The overall reaction occurs with inversion when ROH is 1° or 2°.

$$Br^- + R\overset{\overset{+}{|}}{\underset{\underset{H}{|}}{O}}-P(OR)_2 \longrightarrow Br-R + HOP(OR)_2$$

13.62 Give the stereochemical label for the product of the reaction of *cis*-4-*t*-butylcyclohexanol with (*a*) $SOCl_2$/Py, (*b*) $SOCl_2$, (*c*) TsCl, (*d*) TsCl followed by Br^-, and (*e*) PBr_3.

▟ (*a*) *trans*-Chloride, inversion; (*b*) *cis*-chloride, retention; (*c*) *cis*-tosylate, no configurational change; (*d*) *trans*-bromide, inversion at last step; and (*e*) *trans*-bromide, inversion.

13.63 List (*a*) advantages and (*b*) disadvantages of using the reagents $SOCl_2$, PBr_3, PCl_3, PI_3, and TsCl compared to using the hydrogen halide acids for converting ROH to RX.

▟ (*a*) Milder reaction conditions are required, fewer carbocation rearrangements occur, and the stereochemical results are mostly predictable. (*b*) They are not as useful with 3° alcohols, which react easily with HX and usually with no rearrangement. They must be used in anhydrous solvents because all react vigorously with water. Noxious gases (SO_2, HCl, HBr, HI) are released and must be properly ventilated.

13.64 Give the product of the reaction with conc. H_2SO_4 of: (*a*) $(CH_3CH_2)_2CHCH(OH)CH_3$, (*b*) $PhCH_2CH(OH)CH(CH_3)_2$, (*c*) $(CH_3)_3CCH(OH)CH_3$, and (*d*) 1-methylcyclohexanol.

▟ (*a*) $(CH_3CH_2)_2C=CHCH_3$. (*b*) The product is $PhCH=CHCH(CH_3)_2$ (mainly *trans*), the more stable conjugated isomer, not the Saytzeff product. (*c*) $(CH_3)_2C=C(CH_3)_2$; methyl migration occurs. (*d*) 1-Methylcyclohexene. [Note: (*a*), (*c*), and (*d*) are Saytzeff products.]

13.65 Place the following alcohols in decreasing order of rate of dehydration with H_2SO_4, and explain your order. $CH_3CH_2CH(OH)CH_2CH_2CH_3$ (**A**), $(CH_3)_2C(OH)CH_2CH_2CH_3$ (**B**), $(CH_3)_2C(OH)CH(CH_3)_2$ (**C**), $CH_3CH_2CH(OH)CH(CH_3)_2$ (**D**), and $CH_3CH_2CH_2CH_2CH_2CH_2OH$ (**E**).

▮ **C > B > D > A > E**. The alcohols **C** and **B** are both 3°, but **C** gives a more substituted C=C; **D** and **A** are both 2°, but **D** can give a more substituted C=C; **E** is 1°.

13.66 Give the product and write a mechanism for the acid dehydration of cyclobutylcarbinol.

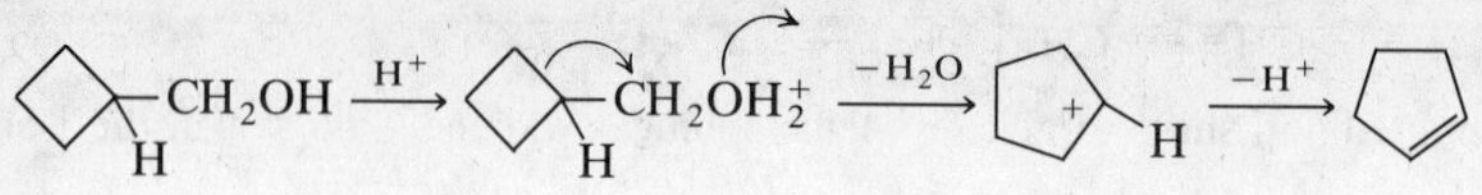

▮

Expansion of a four- to a five-membered ring which relieves ring strain is synchronous with loss of H_2O.

13.67 Place the following benzyl alcohols in decreasing order of reaction rate with HBr and explain your order: $C_6H_5CH_2OH$, $p\text{-}O_2NC_6H_4CH_2OH$, $p\text{-}CH_3OC_6H_4CH_2OH$, $p\text{-}ClC_6H_4CH_2OH$.

▮ $p\text{-}CH_3OC_6H_4CH_2OH > C_6H_5CH_2OH > p\text{-}ClC_6H_4CH_2OH > p\text{-}O_2NC_6H_4CH_2OH$.

The + charge that develops on the benzylic C in this S_N1 reaction is most effectively delocalized by the CH_3O-group [Fig. 13-1(*a*)]. The *p*-NO_2 group withdraws electron density from the ring by induction and especially by resonance interaction. Delocalization of the + charge from the benzylic carbon places the + charge in the ring adjacent to the positively charged N of NO_2, greatly destabilizing the benzylic carbocation [Fig. 13-1(*b*)]. Unlike NO_2, *p*-Cl destabilizes the + charge only by induction, not by resonance interaction, making the *p*-Cl compound less reactive than $PhCH_2OH$ but more reactive than the *p*-NO_2 compound.

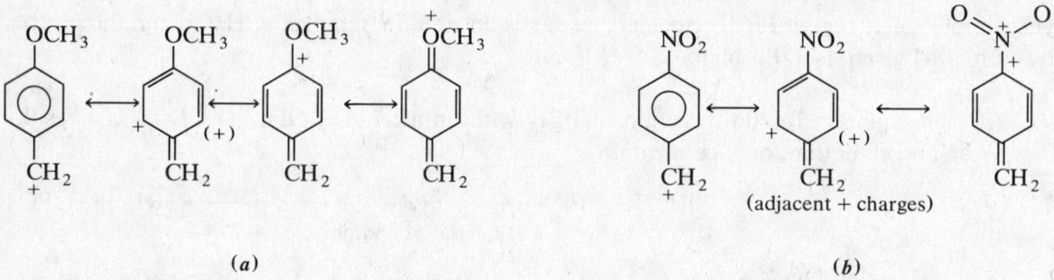

(a) (b)

Fig. 13-1

13.68 (*a*) Describe the Lucas test for distinguishing between 1°, 2°, and 3° alcohols. (*b*) What is the theoretical basis for this test? (*c*) Why is it useful only for alcohols with six or fewer C's?

▮ (*a*) The *Lucas* reagent, conc. HCl with $ZnCl_2$, converts alcohols to the corresponding alkyl chlorides, which are insoluble in the reaction mixture and appear as a cloudiness or a second more dense layer. A 3° ROH reacts immediately, a 2° ROH reacts within 5 minutes and a 1° ROH does not react at all at room temperature. (*b*) $ZnCl_2$, a strong Lewis acid, encourages an S_N1 pathway for formation of the alkyl chlorides. Thus, the rate of reaction of the alcohols is: 3° > 2° > 1°. (*c*) Initially, the alcohol must be soluble in the reagent. Alcohols having more than six C's are not soluble, so two layers are present at the start.

13.69 Alkenes dissolve in cold conc. H_2SO_4. (*a*) Write and name the structure of the product formed from propene. (*b*) What is obtained if the reaction mixture in (*a*) is diluted with H_2O?

▮ (*a*)
$$CH_3CH{=}CH_2 \xrightarrow{\text{conc. } H_2SO_4} CH_3\overset{\overset{\displaystyle OSO_2OH}{|}}{CH}{-}CH_3 \text{ (Markovnikov orientation)}$$

Isopropyl hydrogen sulfate,
a monoester of sulfuric acid

(*b*) Hydrolysis of the ester produces isopropyl alcohol.

13.70 (*a*) How do sulfonates and sulfates differ? (*b*) Compare the acid properties of (i) an alkyl hydrogen sulfate and (ii) a dialkyl sulfate. (*c*) Give the product of each in (*b*) with H_2O.

▰ (*a*) An R′ (or Ar) is attached to S in the sulfonate R′ (or Ar)—SO_2OR with the R of ROH bonded to an O. In the sulfate they are bonded to O (R′—OSO_2O—R). (*b*) Both sulfates are esters of sulfuric acid. The alkyl hydrogen sulfate, $ROSO_2OH$, is a monoester and has one acidic H; it is as strong as H_2SO_4. The dialkyl sulfate, $ROSO_2OR$, has no acidic H. (*c*) (i) $ROSO_2OH + 3H_2O \longrightarrow ROH + 2H_3O^+ + SO_4^{2-}$; (ii) $ROSO_2OR + 4H_2O \longrightarrow 2ROH + 2H_3O^+ + SO_4^{2-}$.

13.71 Write structures of (*a*) monomethyl phosphate, (*b*) triethyl phosphate, (*c*) *n*-amyl nitrite ("smelling salts"), (*d*) *t*-butyl hypochlorite, (*e*) diisopropyl fluorophosphate (a nerve gas), and give the acids from which they are derived.

▰ (*a*) CH_3O—$PO(OH)_2$ and (*b*) $(CH_3CH_2O)_3PO$, each from $(HO)_3PO$, phosphoric acid. (*c*) *n*-$C_5H_{11}ONO$, from HONO, nitrous acid. (*d*) $(CH_3)_3COCl$, from HOCl, hypochlorous acid. (*e*) $[(CH_3)_2CHO]_2\overset{\text{O}}{\underset{\|}{P}}$—F from $(HO)_2\overset{\text{O}}{\underset{\|}{P}}F$, fluorophosphoric acid.

13.72 Write the product of the reaction of ethanol with (*a*) $CH_3\overset{\text{O}}{\underset{\|}{C}}OH$ and (*b*) $C_6H_5\overset{\text{O}}{\underset{\|}{C}}Cl$.

▰ The products are esters: (*a*) $CH_3\overset{\text{O}}{\underset{\|}{C}}OEt$, ethyl acetate, and (*b*) $C_6H_5\overset{\text{O}}{\underset{\|}{C}}OEt$, ethyl benzoate.

13.73 Compare the products of oxidation of 1°, 2°, and 3° alcohols with a reagent containing Cr(VI) (CrO_3 or $K_2Cr_2O_7$) in acid.

▰ Alcohols with at least one H atom on the carbinol C (1° and 2°) are oxidized to carbonyl compounds: 2° alcohols to ketones and 1° alcohols to aldehydes which may be further oxidized to carboxylic acids. $R_2CHOH \longrightarrow R_2C=O$ and $RCH_2OH \longrightarrow RCH=O \longrightarrow RCOOH$. Under mild conditions 3° alcohols are not oxidized because they lack an H on the carbinol C.

13.74 Give the product of the oxidation of each of the following alcohols with $Cr_2O_7^{2-}$ in H_2SO_4. (*a*) $(CH_3)_2CHOH$, (*b*) $(CH_3)_2CHCH_2OH$, (*c*) Ph_2CHOH, (*d*) $Ph_2C(CH_3)OH$, and (*e*) cyclopentanol.

▰ (*a*) $(CH_3)_2C=O$, (*b*) $(CH_3)_2CHCOOH$, (*c*) $Ph_2C=O$, (*d*) no reaction, and (*e*) cyclopentanone.

13.75 How can we distinguish between 1°, 2° and 3° alcohols by the reaction with $Cr_2O_7^{2-}$ in a test tube?

▰ Dichromate in acid has a bright orange color. When it oxidizes an alcohol, it is reduced to blue-green Cr(III). The change in color indicates that the alcohol is not 3°. A distinction between 1° and 2° ROH's is not possible with this reagent.

13.76 Write a mechanism for the oxidation of a 2° alcohol with Cr(VI) as $HCrO_4^-$.

▰ A chromate ester is formed in the first step:

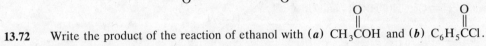

chromate ester

$$R_2\overset{\text{H}}{\underset{\text{O}}{C}} - O - Cr - OH \xrightarrow[\text{slow}]{H_2\ddot{O}:} R_2C=O + H_3O^+ + HOCr-O^- \quad [Cr(IV)]$$

E2 elimination

The Cr(IV) and Cr(VI) species react to form 2Cr(V), which in turn also oxidizes alcohols giving Cr(III) with its characteristic color.

13.77 Compare the ease of oxidation of *cis*- and *trans*-4-*t*-butylcyclohexanol with a Cr(VI) reagent.

▰ Both form a chromate ester in the fast first step. The subsequent elimination of H^+ and $HCrO_3^-$ is rate-controlling. The more hindered OH, in this case the axial OH of the *cis* isomer, gives the more sterically-hindered chromate ester which is eliminated faster because of steric acceleration (relief of strain). The *cis* isomer reacts faster than the *trans*.

13.78 How can a 1° alcohol be oxidized to an aldehyde?

▰ The oxidant pyridinium chlorochromate (PCC), made by mixing equimolar amounts of CrO_3, HCl, and pyridine, is used. It is soluble in CH_2Cl_2 and other organic solvents. In a *nonaqueous* solvent, the aldehyde is stable to further oxidation. *Collins* reagent, a variation of PCC made up of 1 mol of CrO_3 to 2 mol of pyridine in CH_2Cl_2, is also used, as is MnO_2.

13.79 What reaction(s) may occur when a 3° ROH is heated with chromic acid?

▰ (1) A chromate ester may form (and can be isolated). This ester is stable because it has no carbinol H to lose. However, treatment of the ester with H_2O causes hydrolysis and formation of the original alcohol + chromic acid. (2) Elimination can occur, resulting in an alkene.

13.80 (*a*) What is the Jones reagent? (*b*) Give the product of the oxidation of each of the following substances with

Jones reagent: (i) $CH_3CH=CHCH(OH)CH_3$ and (ii) [structure: cyclohexane ring with H and CH_2OH substituents].

▰ (*a*) The *Jones* reagent is a chromic acid in aqueous acetone solution. (*b*) The Jones reagent is sufficiently mild so that it oxidizes alcohols without oxidizing or rearranging double bonds. The products are

(i) $CH_3CH=CHCOCH_3$ and (ii) [structure: cyclohexane ring with H and CHO substituents].

13.81 Give the product of oxidation by $KMnO_4$ of 1°, 2°, and 3° alcohols in acidic and basic media.

▰ In acid, 1° ROH → RCOOH; 2° ROH → $R_2C=O$; 3° ROH is not oxidized. In base, the only difference is the formation of carboxylate ion, $RCOO^-$. RCOOH is isolated by adding H^+. In base, $KMnO_4$ is reduced to MnO_2, which precipitates as a brown sludge.

13.82 (*a*) Why is $KMnO_4$ not the reagent of choice for the preparation of methyl vinyl ketone from the corresponding alcohol? (*b*) Why can MnO_2 be used for this synthesis?

▰ (*a*) Recall that $KMnO_4$ also oxidizes alkenes, either to glycols in cold neutral solution or to ketones and acids (by cleavage of C—C) in an acidic medium. (*b*) MnO_2 is a milder oxidizing agent.

13.83 Give the product of the oxidation with MnO_2 of (*a*) $CH_3CH_2CH=CHCH_2OH$, (*b*) $PhCH_2OH$, (*c*) $PhCH(OH)CH_2CH_2OH$, (*d*) $CH_3CH=CHCH_2CH_2CH_2OH$, and (*e*) [structure: cyclopentene ring with H and OH substituents].

▰ MnO_2 selectively oxidizes the OH group of allylic and benzylic 1° and 2° alcohols to give aldehydes and ketones respectively. (*a*) $CH_3CH_2CH=CHCHO$, (*b*) PhCHO, (*c*) $PhCOCH_2CH_2OH$, (*d*) no reaction, and (*e*) [structure: cyclopentene ring with =O]. Note that only benzylic [(*b*) and (*c*)] and allylic [(*a*) and (*e*)] alcohols are oxidized.

13.84 Balance the following redox reaction (in acid) by the ion-electron (half-cell) method.

$$Me_2CHOH + K_2Cr_2O_7 + H_2SO_4 \longrightarrow Me_2C=O + Cr_2(SO_4)_3 + H_2O + K_2SO_4$$

▰ (1) Identify and write separate partial equations for the oxidation and reduction. (2) Balance H atoms by adding H^+ to the side with the fewer H's. (3) Balance O's (if necessary) in acid solution by adding H_2O to the side with the fewer O's and then balance the H's as in step (2). (4) Balance the charge by adding e^-'s to the side with less negative charge (or more positive charge). (5) Multiply each partial equation by a factor so that the number of electrons in both partials is the same. (6) Add the partials, canceling e^-'s and equal number of ions (or molecules) from both sides of the arrow. (7) Add appropriate spectator ions to give a balanced molecular equation.

Oxidation (loss of electrons): $[Me_2CHOH \longrightarrow Me_2CO + 2H^+ + 2e^-] \times 3$
Reduction (gain of electrons): $[Cr_2O_7^{2-} + 14H^+ + 6e^- \longrightarrow 2Cr^{3+} + 7H_2O] \times 1$
Addition and cancellation: $3Me_2CHOH + Cr_2O_7^{2-} + 8H^+ \longrightarrow 3Me_2CO + 2Cr^{3+} + 7H_2O$
Adding spectator ions: $3Me_2CHOH + K_2Cr_2O_7 + 4H_2SO_4 \longrightarrow 3Me_2CO + Cr_2(SO_4)_3 + 7H_2O + K_2SO_4$

13.85 Balance the following oxidation reaction (in base) by the ion-electron (half-cell) method.

$$PhCH_2OH + KMnO_4 \longrightarrow PhCOOH + MnO_2 + H_2O + OH^-$$

▰ Proceed as in Problem 13.84, except that for each needed O add $2OH^-$, and H_2O to the other side of the equation. For each H in excess, add one OH^- to that side, and one H_2O to the other side. Balance the partial by inspection and proceed to step (3). Note that $PhCOO^-$ exists in basic solution.

Oxidation (loss of electrons): $[PhCH_2OH + 5OH^- \longrightarrow PhCOO^- + 4H_2O + 4e^-] \times 3$

Reduction (gain of electrons): $[MnO_4^- + 2H_2O + 3e^- \longrightarrow MnO_2 + 4OH^-] \times 4$

Addition and cancellation: $3PhCH_2OH + 4MnO_4^- \longrightarrow 3PhCOO^- + 4MnO_2 + 4H_2O + OH^-$

Adding spectator ions: $3PhCH_2OH + 4KMnO_4 \longrightarrow 3PhCOOK + 4MnO_2 + 4H_2O + KOH$

13.86   (*a*) What reagent is used to convert a tosylate of a 1° alcohol to its aldehyde?   (*b*) Suggest a mechanism.

▰   (*a*)   Dimethyl sulfoxide and $NaHCO_3$. DMSO is reduced to dimethylsulfide.

(*b*)   (1) $Me_2\overset{+}{S}-\overset{..}{\underset{..}{O}}:^- + R-CH_2-OTs \longrightarrow Me_2\overset{+}{S}-O-CH_2R + OTs^-$ (S_N2)

(2) $Me_2\overset{..}{S}-O-CHR \longrightarrow Me_2\overset{..}{S}: + :\overset{..}{O}=CHR \ (+H_2CO_3)$ (E2)

$HCO_3^- \, H$

13.87   Give an important industrial method for converting alcohols to aldehydes or ketones.

▰   Catalytic dehydrogenation is accomplished at high temperatures with a nickel or chromium oxide-copper catalyst.

13.88   Alcohols may be dehydrated without rearrangement by heating their *xanthate* esters (*Tschugaev reaction*). (*a*) Write an equation for the formation of the xanthate ester of Ph_2CHCH_2OH.   (*b*) The pyrolysis occurs through a cyclic TS. Show a possible mechanism for this step.   (*c*) Give the alkene from pyrolysis of the xanthate of *cis*-2-phenylcyclohexanol.

▰   (*a*) $Ph_2CHCH_2OH \xrightarrow{Na} Ph_2CHCH_2O^-Na^+ \xrightarrow{S=C=S} Ph_2CHCH_2-O-\overset{\overset{S}{\|}}{C}-S^-Na^+ \xrightarrow{CH_3I}$

$Ph_2CHCH_2-O-\overset{\overset{S}{\|}}{C}-S-CH_3$, an S-methyl xanthate (Me bonded to S)

(*b*) $Ph_2C\overset{CH_2-O}{\underset{H \quad S-CH_3}{<}}C=S \longrightarrow Ph_2C=CH_2 + S=C=O + HSCH_3$

(*c*)   The mechanism shows that the xanthate group and H being eliminated must be *cis*. The product is 3-phenylcyclohexene and not the lower-energy conjugated 1-phenylcyclohexene which would have to be formed by a *trans* elimination. Such a stereochemical result led to the suggested mechanism.

13.89   What is the product of the reaction of $PhCH(OH)CH_3$ with H_2/Pd containing some $HClO_4$?

▰ $PhCH_2CH_3$. The process whereby H_2 breaks bonds is called *hydrogenolysis*.

13.90   Give the hydrogenolysis product of (*a*) $PhCH_2OH$, (*b*) $Ph_2C(OH)CH_2CH_2OH$, (*c*) $PhCOCH_2CH_3$, and (*d*) $p\text{-}HOC_6H_4CH(OH)CH_3$.

▰   (*a*) $PhCH_3$ (*b*) $Ph_2CHCH_2CH_2OH$. The nonbenzylic OH is not affected.   (*c*) $PhCH_2CH_2CH_3$. The ketone is first reduced to the alcohol with this reagent.   (*d*) $p\text{-}HOC_6H_4CH_2CH_3$. The ring OH is not reduced.

13.91   Give the product of each reaction.

(*a*) $CH_3CH_2CH=CHCH_2OH + MnO_2$ (*d*) $Ph_2C=CHCH_3 + BH_3 \cdot THF$, followed by H_2O_2/OH^-

(*b*) $Ph_2CHOH + H_2/Pd(HClO_4)$ (*e*) $PhCOCH_2CH_2Br + LiAlD_4$, followed by H_2O

(*c*) $m\text{-}O_2NC_6H_4CH_2COOH + LiAlH_4$ (*f*) $PhCH=CHCH(OH)CH_3 + PBr_3$

▰   (*a*) $CH_3CH_2CH=CHCHO$ (*c*) $m\text{-}H_2NC_6H_4CH_2CH_2OH$ (*e*) $PhCD(OH)CH_2CH_2D$

(*b*) Ph_2CH_2 (*d*) $Ph_2CH_2CH(OH)CH_3$ (*f*) $PhCH=CHCHBrCH_3$

13.92   Give the product of the reaction of ethanol with conc. H_2SO_4 at (*a*) 0 °C, (*b*) room temperature, (*c*) 130 °C, and (*d*) 180 °C.

◢ (a) $CH_3CH_2OH_2^+HSO_4^-$, ethyloxonium hydrogen sulfate; (b) $CH_3CH_2OSO_2OH$, ethyl hydrogen sulfate; (c) $CH_3CH_2OCH_2CH_3$, diethyl ether (from an intermolecular dehydration); (d) $H_2C=CH_2$, ethylene (from an intramolecular dehydration, favored by higher temperatures).

13.93 (a) Write the steps in the oxidation of $CH_3CH(OH)CH_3$ with X_2 in OH^- (the *haloform* reaction). (b) Which structural feature in an alcohol is necessary for the reaction? (c) How is this reaction utilized in the analysis of alcohols?

◢ (a) $$CH_3CH(OH)CH_3 \xrightarrow[\text{oxidation}]{X_2,\,OH^-} \underset{\text{not isolated}}{[CH_3COCH_3]} \longrightarrow \underset{\text{not isolated}}{[CH_3COCX_3]} \longrightarrow CH_3COO^- + CHX_3$$

Acidification after oxidation converts the anion to CH_3COOH,
(b) $-CH(OH)CH_3$, a methyl carbinol with at least one H on the carbinol C. (c) A distinctive precipitate of pale yellow iodoform, CHI_3, appears if I_2 is the halogen used (*iodoform* test).

13.94 Denote the alcohols giving a positive iodoform test and give their oxidation products after acidification. (a) $(CH_3)_2CHCHOHCH_3$, (b) $PhCH_2CHOHCH_3$, (c) $PhCH(OH)CH_2CH_3$, (d) CH_3CH_2OH, (e) cyclopentyl-methylcarbinol, (f) 1-methylcyclohexanol.

◢ (a) $(CH_3)_2CHCOOH$. (b) $PhCH_2COOH$. (d) CH_3COOH (CH_3CH_2OH is the only 1° ROH to give a positive test). (e) Cyclopentanecarboxylic acid. No reaction occurs in (c) and (f).

13.95 Give the structures for the unknown compounds **A** through **C**.

$$C_6H_{12}O(\mathbf{A}) \xrightarrow[\Delta]{H_2SO_4} C_6H_{10}(\mathbf{B}) \xrightarrow[\Delta]{HNO_3} C_6H_{10}O_4(\mathbf{C}) \xleftarrow[\Delta]{HNO_3} \mathbf{A}$$

◢ **A**, cyclohexanol; **B**, cyclohexene; **C**, $HOOC(CH_2)_4COOH$, adipic acid.

13.96 Select the alcohol and oxidant to best prepare the following compounds:

(a) $(CH_3)_3CCOOH$ (b) $CH_3CH_2CH=CHCHO$ (c) 1,4-cyclohexanedione (d) $CH_3COC_6H_5$

◢ (a) $(CH_3)_3CCH_2OH$ + dichromate, H^+. (b) $CH_3CH_2CH=CHCH_2OH$ + MnO_2. (c) *cis*- or *trans*-1,4-Cyclohexanediol + dichromate, H^+. (d) $CH_3CH(OH)C_6H_5$ + MnO_2 (oxidizes benzylic OH).

13.97 Write structures for **A**, **B**, and **C** in the following reaction:

$$C_6H_6 + CH_2=CHCH_2Cl \xrightarrow{AlCl_3} \mathbf{A} \xrightarrow[\text{2. }H_2O_2,\,OH^-]{\text{1. }BH_3/THF} \mathbf{B} \xrightarrow[\Delta]{HF} \mathbf{C}(C_9H_{10})$$

◢ **A** is $PhCH_2CH=CH_2$; **B** is $PhCH_2CH_2CH_2OH$; **C** is 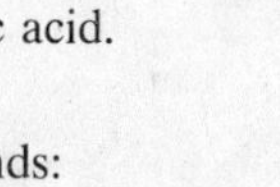 (Friedel–Crafts).

13.98 Give four methods for converting $PhCH_2OH$ to $PhCH_2D$.

◢ (1) With HCl, $PhCH_2OH$ is converted to $PhCH_2Cl$ which is then reduced to $PhCH_2D$, either directly with $LiAlD_4$ or (2) by reaction of $PhCH_2MgCl$ with D_2O. (3) With TsCl, $PhCH_2OH$ is converted to the tosylate which is then reduced with $LiAlD_4$. (4) The alcohol can be reduced catalytically with D_2/Pd, $HClO_4$. This method, although direct, is not as practical.

13.99 Write the product of hydroboration-oxidation of (E)- and (Z) 2-phenyl-2-butene.

◢ Addition of H_2O is anti-Markovnikov and *cis*. See Fig. 13-2.

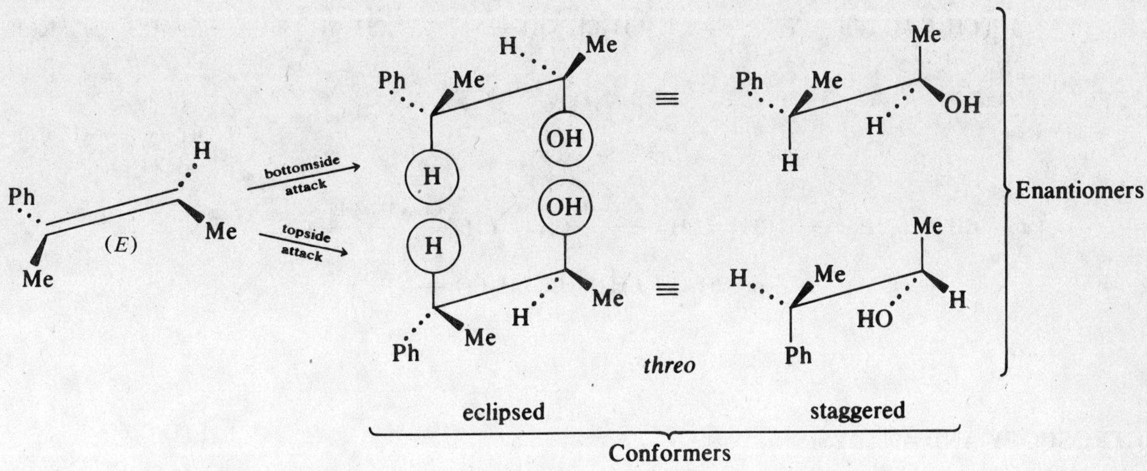

Fig. 13-2

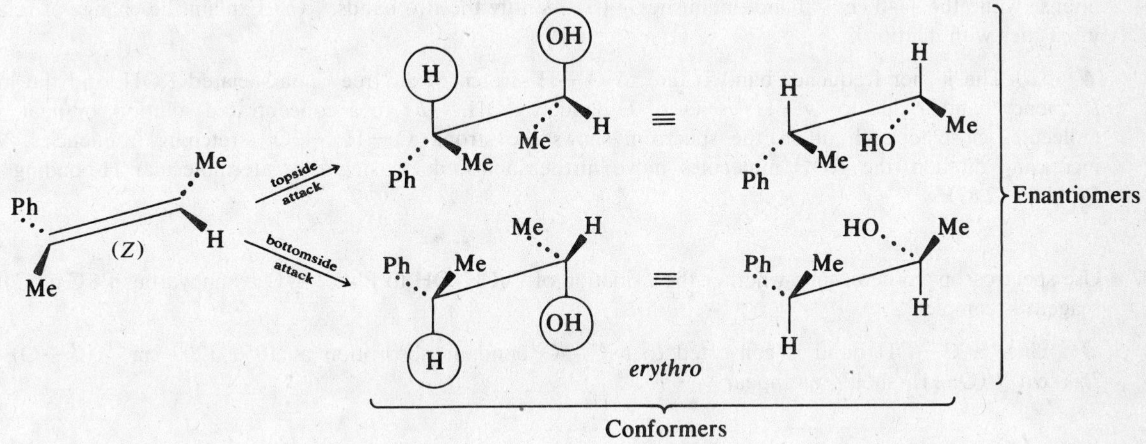

13.100 Starting with CH_3OH (where $C = {}^{14}C$), and any alcohols of three or fewer C's, synthesize
(a) $CH_3CH_2CH_2CH_2OH$ (A), (b) $CH_3CH_2CH_2CH_2OH$ (B), (c) $CH_3CH_2CH_2CH_2OH$ (D), and
(d) $CH_3CH_2CH_2CH_2OH$ (E). Do not repeat syntheses of intermediate reactants.

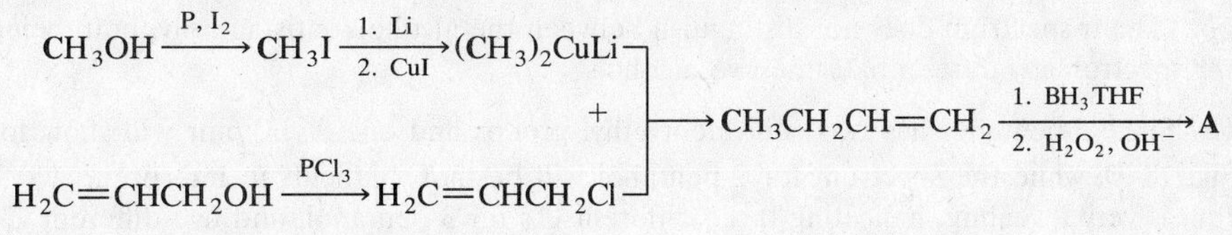

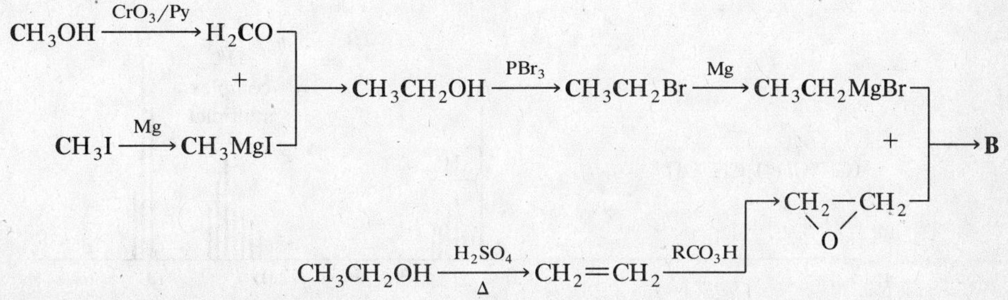

(c) $CH_3CH_2MgBr + CH_2O \longrightarrow CH_3CH_2CH_2OH \xrightarrow{SOCl_2} CH_3CH_2CH_2Cl \xrightarrow{Mg} CH_3CH_2CH_2MgCl$ ⌐
$+$
$\longrightarrow$ **D**
$CH_3OH \xrightarrow{CrO_3/Py} H_2CO$ ⌐

(d) $CH_3CH_2OH \xrightarrow{H_2SO_4} CH_2{=}CH_2 \xrightarrow{RCO_3H} CH_2{-}CH_2 \xrightarrow{CH_3CH_2MgBr} \textbf{E}$
(with epoxide O over $CH_2{-}CH_2$)

or $CH_3CH_2CH_2MgCl + H_2CO \longrightarrow \textbf{E}$

SPECTROSCOPY AND ANALYSIS

13.101 A concentrated CCl_4 solution of *t*-butyl alcohol has a broad absorption band at 3440 cm^{-1}, accompanied by a small sharp band at 3620 cm^{-1}. As the solution is progressively diluted, the 3620 cm^{-1} band becomes more intense while the 3440 cm^{-1} band diminishes. (*a*) Identify the two bands. (*b*) Explain the change of relative intensities with dilution.

▮ (*a*) The higher frequency band is due to O—H stretch of a "free" unassociated ROH, and the lower frequency band is due to O—H---O of H-bonded ROH. (*b*) In a concentrated solution, or neat, with molecules close to each other, the spectrum shows the strong O—H---O stretching frequencies. With increasing dilution, the ROH molecules move further apart, decreasing the intermolecular H-bonding (see Problem 12.87).

13.102 Use spectroscopy to determine whether the oxidation of $PhCH_2OH$ to $PhCH{=}O$ by anhydrous PCC or Collins reagent is complete.

▮ Since a C—OH bond is converted to a C=O bond, ir absorption at 1050–1200 cm^{-1} (C—O) and 3600 cm^{-1} (O—H) should disappear.

13.103 What techniques can be used to detect the H of an OH by nmr spectroscopy?

▮ (1) Shake the sample with a large excess of D_2O and retake the spectrum. The following exchange reaction occurs: $ROH + D_2O \rightleftharpoons ROD + HOD$. Since D signals are not detected by a proton nmr spectrometer (see Problem 12.105), the O<u>H</u> signal will disappear. A new signal will appear at about $\delta = 5$ ppm due to the H in DOH. (2) Since H-bonding reduces shielding, as the ROH solution is diluted (becomes less H-bonded), the OH signal becomes less broad and shifts to higher fields (see Problems 12.116 and 12.138).

13.104 Hydration of 2-pentene with H_3O^+ gives both 2- and 3-pentanol. (*a*) Use pmr to distinguish between the two alcohols. (The ir spectrum does not distinguish between the alcohols satisfactorily, both being 2°.) (*b*) How can ^{13}C nmr spectroscopy differentiate the two alcohols?

▮ (*a*) Since 3-pentanol has two equivalent ethyl groups and one 3° H, pmr will show four different protons (see Fig. 13-3), while the spectrum for 2-pentanol will be more difficult to interpret. (*b*) Uncoupled ^{13}C nmr spectrum is very revealing, indicating three different C's for 3-pentanol, and five different C's for the isomer.

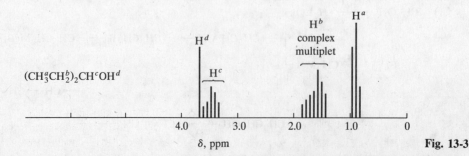

Fig. 13-3

13.105 Use mass spectrometry to distinguish the two pentanols in Problem 13.104.

◢ 3-Pentanol cleaves in one way only to give $CH_3CH_2CH{=}\overset{+}{O}H$ (mass = 59) + $CH_3CH_2\cdot$, while 2-pentanol cleaves at $C^1 - C^2$, giving $CH_3CH_2CH_2CH{=}\overset{+}{O}H$ (mass = 73) + $CH_3\cdot$, and at $C^2 - C^3$, giving $CH_3CH{=}\overset{+}{O}H$ (mass = 45) + $CH_3CH_2CH_2\cdot$.

13.106 Give a simple chemical test that can distinguish between 2- and 3-pentanol.

◢ Add I_2 in aq. KOH (the iodoform test). 2-Pentanol, having the $-CH(OH)CH_3$ group, reacts giving a yellow precipitate of CHI_3. The 3-pentanol does not react.

13.107 When 1-chloromethyl-4-methyl-1,3-cyclopentadiene (**A**) is solvolyzed in aqueous acetone, three isomeric alcohols are obtained. (**a**) Write the structures of the alcohols. (**b**) How can they be assigned structures based on nmr spectroscopy in anhydrous deuterated DMSO? (**c**) Predict which alcohol would be expected to form in the greatest and least amount and give your reason.

◢ (**a**) **A**, an allylic chloride, forms an R^+ bearing some + charges at the methylene C, at C^2 and at C^4. Thus the three alcohols, **B**, **C**, and **D**, arise from this carbocation:

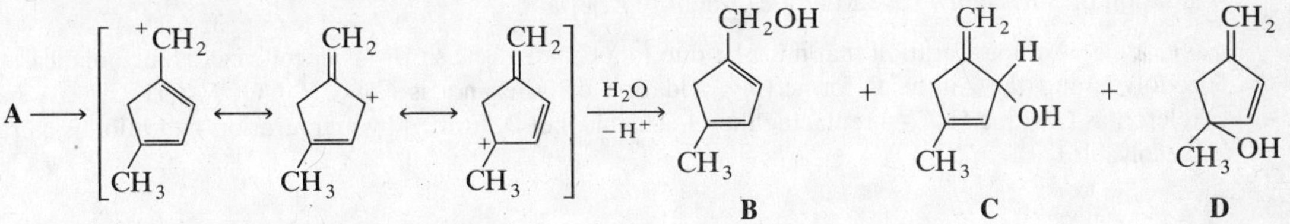

(**b**) In CCl_4, intermolecular H-bonding occurs, leading to a rapid interchange of the H of the O—H. Since the instrument only can sense an average situation, it cannot see coupling of this H with any carbinol H's. In a DMSO solution, H-bonding only occurs between the alcohol and the O of the solvent. The H stays on the O of the ROH and coupling is observed. This technique distinguishes between 1°, 2°, and 3° alcohols, whose signals for the H of OH are a triplet, a doublet, and a singlet, respectively. Thus **B** shows a triplet, **C** a doublet, and **D** a singlet. (**c**) **B** has the larger yield because it is conjugated with four substituents. Unconjugated **C** has the lowest yield.

13.108 An unknown compound with the molecular formula $C_9H_{12}O$ (i) does not decolorize Br_2 in CCl_4, (ii) is oxidized by hot $KMnO_4$ to give PhCOOH, and (iii) reacts with Na to give a colorless odorless gas. (**a**) Write the five structures (**E** to **I**) fitting these data and give your reasoning. (**b**) From the following results, deduce the correct structure and explain how each test leads to your final choice: (i) The color of $Cr_2O_7^{2-}$ changes from orange to blue-green when added to **E**, **F**, **G**, or **H**. (ii) The compound can be resolved. (iii) No precipitate of CHI_3 is observed with I_2/OH^-. (iv) Oxidation with CrO_3/Py gives a chiral compound.

◢ (**a**) The molecular formula indicates 4° of unsaturation, and from (i) and (ii) it is deduced that it is a monosubstituted Ph derivative. It has an OH in the side chain, as indicated by the reaction of Na (in iii) releasing H_2. The possible structures are

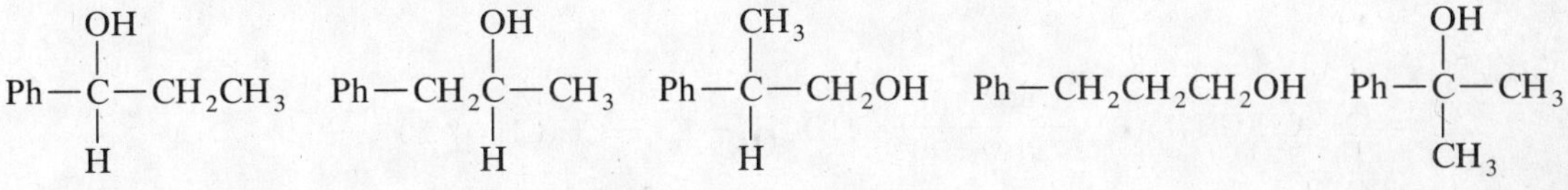

(**b**) (i) Structure **I** is a 3° alcohol and is discounted on the basis of the chromic acid test. (ii) Structure **H** is eliminated; it is not chiral. (iii) **F** would give a precipitate with I_2/OH^- because of the $-CH(OH)CH_3$ group and is therefore eliminated. Only **E** and **G** are possible at this point. (iv) The compound is **G** because on oxidation it forms the chiral aldehyde, $PhCH(CH_3)CH{=}O$.

13.109 Compounds **J**, **K**, and **L** are isomeric alcohols with the formula $C_5H_{12}O$. **J** and **K** react with chromic acid solution, **K** forming an acid **M**. The three isomers react with HBr with decreasing relative rates of **L** > **J** ≫ **K**, all giving the same $C_5H_{11}Br$ (**N**) in varying yields. **J** alone can be oxidized by I_2/OH^- to **O**. Write the structures of **J** through **O** and give explanations.

◢ There are no degrees of unsaturation—no rings or multiple bonds. The results of the chromic acid oxidation indicate that **K** is a 1° ROH, **J** is 2° ROH, and **L** is 3° ROH. The only 1° ROH that would react very slowly with HBr is the very highly hindered neopentyl alcohol, **K**, which rearranges during reaction to give 2-methyl-

2-bromobutane, **N**. **N** is obtained by the facile reaction of the 3° ROH, 2-methyl-2-butanol, **L**. The 2° ROH, **J**, is 3-methyl-2-butanol that undergoes a hydride shift in the HBr reaction to give the same 3° R^+ leading to **N**. The oxidation of **J** to the acid **O** in the haloform test confirms this assignment.

$$(CH_3)_2CHCOOH \xleftarrow[\text{oxid.}]{\text{haloform}} \overset{\overset{\displaystyle OH}{|}}{(CH_3)_2CHCHCH_3}$$
$$\mathbf{O} \qquad\qquad\qquad \mathbf{J}$$

$$(CH_3)_3CCOOH \xleftarrow{\text{oxid.}} (CH_3)_3CCH_2OH$$
$$\mathbf{M} \qquad\qquad\qquad \mathbf{K}$$

$$\text{no reaction} \xleftarrow{\text{oxid.}} (CH_3)_2C(OH)CH_2CH_3$$
$$\mathbf{L}$$

hydride shift

methyl shift $\xrightarrow{\text{HBr}}$ $\overset{\overset{\displaystyle Br}{|}}{(CH_3)_2C}-CH_2CH_3$

S_N1 displacement $\qquad\qquad \mathbf{N}$

13.110 C_7H_{14} (**A**) decolorizes Br_2 in CCl_4 and reacts with $Hg(OAc)_2$ in THF—H_2O followed by reduction with $NaBH_4$ to produce a resolvable compound **B**. **A** undergoes reductive ozonolysis to give the same compound obtained by oxidation of 3-hexanol with $KMnO_4$(**C**). Identify **A**, **B**, and **C**.

◢ **A** has 1° of unsaturation that must be due to a C=C because Br_2 is decolorized. Since one carbon is lost on ozonolysis and the ketone **C** formed by oxidation of 3-hexanol is $CH_3CH_2COCH_2CH_2CH_3$, **A** has the same skeleton as **C** with a $H_2C=$ replacing the O. The alcohol **B**, formed by mercuration-hydration is chiral because it is resolvable.

$$CH_3CH_2CH(OH)CH_2CH_2CH_3 \xrightarrow{\text{oxid.}} \underset{\underset{\displaystyle C_2H_5}{|}}{O=C}-CH_2CH_2CH_3 \text{ (C)} \xleftarrow[\text{2. Zn}]{1.\ O_3} \underset{\underset{\displaystyle C_2H_5}{|}}{CH_2=C}-CH_2CH_2CH_3 \text{ (A)}$$

$$\xrightarrow[\text{2. NaBH}_4]{1.\ Hg(OAc)_2,\ H_2O} \underset{\underset{\displaystyle C_2H_5}{|}}{CH_3-^*C(OH)}CH_2CH_2CH_3 \text{ (B)}$$

13.111 Compound **D**, an isomer of **A** in Problem 13.110, reacts with $BH_3 \cdot$ THF and then H_2O_2/OH^- to give chiral **E**. Oxidation of **E** with $KMnO_4$ or acid dichromate affords a chiral carboxylic acid, **F**. Ozonolysis of **D**, gives after reduction with Zn the same compound **G** obtained by oxidation of 2-methyl-3-pentanol with $KMnO_4$. Identify **D**, **E**, **F**, and **G**.

◢ The product of oxidation of 2-methyl-3-pentanol is **G**, $CH_3CH_2COCH(CH_3)_2$, and the double bond is attached at C^3 in this isomer as well. The chiral alcohol **E** forms on anti-Markovnikov hydration of **D**. Oxidation of **E**, 1° alcohol affords the chiral acid, **F**. **D** is thus 2-ethyl-3-methyl-1-butene.

$$\underset{\underset{\displaystyle C_2H_5}{|}}{CH_2=C}-CH(CH_3)_2 \text{ (D)} \xrightarrow[\text{2. H}_2O_2,\ OH^-]{1.\ BH_3/THF} \underset{\underset{\displaystyle C_2H_5}{|}}{HOCH_2-\overset{\overset{\displaystyle H}{|}}{C^*}}-CH(CH_3)_2 \text{ (E)} \xrightarrow{KMnO_4}$$

$$\underset{\underset{\displaystyle C_2H_5}{|}}{HOOC-\overset{\overset{\displaystyle H}{|}}{C^*}}-CH(CH_3)_2 \text{ (F)} \xrightarrow[\text{2. Zn}]{1.\ O_3} \underset{\underset{\displaystyle C_2H_5}{|}}{O=CCH(CH_3)_2} \text{ (G)} \xleftarrow{\text{oxid.}} C_2H_5CH(OH)CH(CH_3)_2$$
$$\text{2-Methyl-3-pentanol}$$

13.112 Describe how compounds **J**, **K**, and **L** in Problem 13.109 can be differentiated by pmr.

◢ Compound **K** has the simplest spectrum: it has three singlets. Going from upfield to downfield, these are: nine methyl H's, two methylene H's, as well as the (somewhat broad) hydroxyl H. Next in increasing complexity is **L**, with four signals: two of them comprise the familiar triplet and quartet of the ethyl group's five H's; the others are a singlet for six *gem* dimethyl H's and the hydroxyl H. The pmr spectrum of **J** has a doublet for the *gem* dimethyl H's of the isopropyl group, a doublet for the lone Me, a complex region integrating for the two CH—CH H's which split each other and are split by the methyl groups.

13.113 Assign structures to the three most intense peaks in the mass spectrum of 2-methyl-2-butanol at $m/z = 59, 71$, and 73.

▰

$$CH_3 \!-\!\overset{a}{|}\!-\! CH_2 \!-\!\overset{b}{|}\!-\!\underset{\substack{| \\ OH}}{\overset{\substack{CH_3 \\ |}}{C}} \!-\! CH_3$$

$\overset{a}{\longrightarrow}\ CH_3\cdot + CH_3\!-\!CH_2\!-\!\underset{\substack{| \\ CH_3}}{\overset{+}{C}}\!=\!\overset{+}{O}H \qquad m/z = 73$

$\overset{b}{\longrightarrow}\ CH_3CH_2\cdot + (CH_3)_2C\!=\!\overset{+}{O}H \qquad m/z = 59$

$\overset{c}{\longrightarrow}\ HO\cdot + CH_3\!-\!CH_2\!-\!\underset{+}{\overset{\substack{CH_3 \\ |}}{C}}\!-\!CH_3 \qquad m/z = 71$

13.114 (*a*) Using dry deuterated Me_2SO (DMSO) as the solvent, how can inspection of OH signals in the pmr spectra distinguish between *n*-, *s*-, and *t*-butyl alcohols? (*b*) Why must DMSO be dry and deuterated?

▰ (*a*) See Problem 12.139. In DMSO, coupling patterns involving the O*H* can be detected; *n*-(1°), a triplet, *s*-(2°), a doublet, and *t*-(3°), a singlet. (*b*) We must prevent intrusion in the spectrum of H's from H_2O and $(CH_3)_2SO$.

13.115 Give a simple test tube reaction that distinguishes between the compounds in each of the following pairs. What would you *do*, *see*, and *conclude*? (*a*) *t*-butyl and *n*-butyl alcohol, (*b*) ethyl and *n*-propyl alcohol, (*c*) allyl and *n*-propyl alcohol, (*d*) benzyl methyl ether and benzyl alcohol, and (*e*) cyclopentanol and cyclopentyl chloride.

▰ (*a*) Add acid $Cr_2O_7^{2-}$ (orange). The 1° *n*-butyl alcohol is oxidized; its solution changes color to green Cr(III). The 3° *t*-butyl alcohol is unchanged. Alternately, when Lucas reagent ($HCl + ZnCl_2$) is added, the 3° ROH quickly reacts to form the insoluble *t*-butyl chloride that appears as a second (lower) layer or a cloudiness. The 1° ROH does not react and remains dissolved in the reagent. (*b*) Add I_2 in OH^- until the I_2 color persists. A pale yellow precipitate of CHI_3 appears, indicating that ethyl alcohol is oxidized. *n*-Propyl alcohol does not have the $-CH(OH)CH_3$ group and is not oxidized. (*c*) Add Br_2 in CCl_4; as the Br_2 adds to the $C\!=\!C$ of the colorless allyl alcohol, its orange color disappears. The orange color persists in the unreactive *n*-propyl alcohol. (*d*) Add acid $Cr_2O_7^{2-}$. It oxidizes the alcohol, and the color changes to green. The ether is unreactive. Alternately, if the two compounds are absolutely dry, add a small piece of Na (caution, use hood and wear goggles!) to each. H_2 is released from the alcohol; the ether does not react. (*e*) The simplest test is to add conc. H_2SO_4 to each dry compound. There will be only one layer as the alcohol dissolves, evolving some heat. Two layers will be discernable for the chloride, which is not soluble in H_2SO_4.

13.116 Explain how pmr spectra can differentiate between the isomers $HOCH_2C_6H_4CH_3$ (**A**), $C_6H_5CH_2CH_2OH$ (**B**), and $C_6H_5CH(OH)CH_3$ (**C**).

▰ All have a broad singlet for the H of OH. In addition, **A** has two singlets: one for CH_3 and one for CH_2. The four phenyl H's will be a multiplet. **B** has, in addition to the five phenyl H's, two triplets for the two methylene groups that split each other. The spectrum of **C** displays five phenyl H's, a doublet for the CH_3 split by the carbinol H, and a quartet for the carbinol H split by the methyl group.

13.117 Explain that the most prominent (base) peak in the mass spectrum of allyl alcohol is at $m/z = 57$, while that of *n*-propyl alcohol is at $m/z = 31$.

▰ Because the $C\!-\!C$ bond is weaker than the $C\!-\!H$ bond, $CH_3CH_2CH_2OH$ cleaves mainly to give $CH_3CH_2\cdot + [H_2\overset{+}{C}\!-\!OH \longleftrightarrow H_2C\!=\!\overset{+}{O}H]$ ($m/z = 31$) rather than $CH_3CH_2\overset{+}{C}HOH + H\cdot$. In allyl alcohol, cleavage of the $C\!-\!H$ bond gives a resonance-stabilized cation:

$$[H_2C\!=\!CH\!-\!\underset{\substack{| \\ H}}{\overset{+}{C}}\!-\!OH \longleftrightarrow H_2C\!=\!CH\underset{\substack{| \\ H}}{C}\!=\!\overset{+}{O}H \longleftrightarrow H_2\overset{+}{C}\!-\!CH\!=\!\underset{\substack{| \\ H}}{C}\!-\!OH] \qquad (m/z = 57)$$

THIOLS

13.118 Name: (*a*) $CH_3CH_2CH_2SH$, (*b*) $(CH_3)_2CHCH(SH)CH_2CH_3$, (*c*) $CH_2\!=\!CHCH_2CH_2SH$, (*d*) $PhCH_2SH$,

(*e*) cyclopentane with Me SH substituents , (*f*) cyclohexane with Et and SH substituents .

▮ These compounds are called *thiols*, or, occasionally, *mercaptans*. (*a*) 1-Propanethiol, (*b*) 2-methyl-3-pentane-thiol, (*c*) 3-butene-1-thiol, (*d*) benzyl mercaptan (phenylmethanethiol), (*e*) 1-methylcyclopentanethiol, and (*f*) *cis*-2-ethylcyclohexanethiol.

13.119 Write the structures for (*a*) *t*-butyl mercaptan, (*b*) neopentyl mercaptan, (*c*) (*Z*)-2-penten-2-thiol, (*d*) *trans*-4-ethenylcyclohexanethiol, (*e*) allyl mercaptan, (*f*) 1-phenyl-2-propanethiol, and (*g*) 3-mercapto-1-propanol (OH has priority over SH).

▮ (*a*) $(CH_3)_3CSH$, (*b*) $(CH_3)_3CCH_2SH$, (*c*) [structure: CH_3CH_2 and SH on $C=C$; H and CH_3], (*d*) [structure: cyclohexane ring with HS, H and H, $CH=CH_2$],

(*e*) $CH_2=CHCH_2SH$, (*f*) $PhCH_2CH(SH)CH_3$, (*g*) $HSCH_2CH_2CH_2OH$.

13.120 (*a*) Which is the stronger acid, ROH or RSH? Explain. (*b*) How are the conjugate bases of thiols named? (*c*) Name $CH_3CH_2S^-Na^+$.

▮ (*a*) S is below O in the periodic table and is larger. The $-$ charge on S is more spread out in its conjugate base, RS^-, than is the $-$ charge on O in RO^-. Thus RS^- is less likely to attract an H^+ than RO^-, and RSH is the stronger acid, even though O is more electronegative than S. The pK_a of RSH is about 10^5 times that of ROH. (*b*) RS^- is a mercaptide or a thiolate (IUPAC). (*c*) Sodium ethyl mercaptide or sodium ethanethiolate.

13.121 Compare the basicity of ROH and RSH (in water), and explain any difference.

▮ Since the electron density on S is more diffuse than on O, thiols are considerably weaker bases than alcohols in a protic solvent. In addition, the greater ability of ROH_2^+ to H-bond with water compared with RSH_2^+ shifts the equilibrium towards the conjugate acid, ROH_2^+.

13.122 (*a*) Compare the position of equilibrium in the two reactions:

(*1*) $RSH + OH^- \rightleftharpoons RS^- + HOH$ (*2*) $ROH + OH^- \rightleftharpoons RO^- + HOH$

(*b*) What is formed on mixing (i) ROH with $R'S^-$ and (ii) RO^- with $R'SH$?

▮ (*a*) Acid-base equilibrium lies toward the weaker acid and weaker base. Since RSH is a much stronger acid than water, and OH^- is a much stronger base than RS^-, the equilibrium in reaction (*1*) lies completely to the right where only RS^- is present. Since alcohols are weaker acids than water and RO^- is a stronger base than OH^-, the equilibrium (*2*) lies towards the left. However, because the differences in acidities and basicities are slight, all species are present at equilibrium. (*b*) (i) No reaction. (ii) $R'S^- + ROH$.

13.123 Which is a stronger nucleophile: (*a*) RSH or RS^-, (*b*) RS^- or RO^- (in a protic solvent)? Explain.

▮ (*a*) RS^-. Anions, being charged, have a higher electron density and are stronger nucleophiles than their uncharged conjugate acids. (*b*) RS^-. In a protic solvent, the nucleophilicity of anions increases going down a group in the periodic table. The electron cloud on the larger S is more easily polarized or distorted, which makes it easier for it to attack an electrophile. Furthermore, the smaller RO^- has a higher electron density on O per unit surface area, causing it to form strong H-bonds with protic solvents, and thereby diminishing the availability of its electron pairs in displacement reactions.

13.124 Compare the $C-O-H$ and the $C-S-H$ bond angles. What does this say about the kind of HO's used by S in RSH?

▮ The $C-O-H$ angle in methanol is 109°, the expected angle for sp^3 HO's. The $C-S-H$ angle in methanethiol is 96°, much closer to the 90° value for using an unhybridized p AO's. In general, the tendency towards a 90°-bond angle for $C-X-H$ bonds increases, as we move down a group in the periodic table.

13.125 Compare (*a*) boiling points and (*b*) water solubilities of ROH and RSH. Explain the difference.

▮ (*a*) Thiols have lower bp's than the corresponding alcohols, notwithstanding their higher molecular weights. They are less polar and form weaker intermolecular H-bonds. (*b*) Since thiols are less polar and participate less effectively in H-bonding (in this case with water) than alcohols, they are less soluble in water than are alcohols.

13.126 (*a*) Write a mechanism for the reaction of RBr with SH^-. (*b*) List the types of alkyl halides in decreasing order of ease of reaction. (*c*) What is the principal product expected from the reaction of a 3° bromide?

(a) $H:\overset{..}{\underset{..}{S}}:^- + R:\overset{..}{\underset{..}{Br}}: \longrightarrow [H:\overset{..}{\underset{..}{S}}:\overset{\delta-}{---}R\overset{\delta-}{---}:\overset{..}{\underset{..}{Br}}:]^{\ddagger} \longrightarrow H:\overset{..}{\underset{..}{S}}:R + :\overset{..}{\underset{..}{Br}}:^- \quad (S_N2)$

(b) $1° > 2° \gg 3°$ (does not give a thiol)

(c) An alkene forms through an E2 elimination mechanism.

13.127 RSR is another product of the reaction in Problem 13.126. (a) Give the equations and explain its production. (b) What can be done experimentally to minimize its formation?

◢ (a) $R:\overset{..}{\underset{..}{S}}:H + HS^- \rightleftharpoons H_2S + R:\overset{..}{\underset{..}{S}}:^-$. This equilibrium makes available the good nucleophile $R:\overset{..}{\underset{..}{S}}:^-$, which displaces Br^- from another $R:Br$. $R:\overset{..}{\underset{..}{S}}:^- + R:\overset{..}{\underset{..}{Br}}: \longrightarrow R:\overset{..}{\underset{..}{S}}:R + :\overset{..}{\underset{..}{Br}}:^-$. (b) Use a large excess of HS^- to increase the probability of encounter with RBr. It is true that at the same time, the equilibrium in (a) will be shifted to the right, increasing the concentration of RS^-, a slightly better nucleophile than HS^-. Thus the use of HS^- in synthesizing thiols has been mostly replaced by thiourea (Problem 13.128).

13.128 Write an equation to show the formation of a mercaptan from an alkyl halide and thiourea, $(H_2N)_2C{=}S$.

◢ $(H_2N)_2C{=}\overset{..}{\underset{..}{S}}:\overset{\frown}{+}R:\overset{..}{\underset{..}{X}}: \longrightarrow [(H_2N)_2C{=}\overset{+}{\underset{..}{S}}:R]:\overset{..}{\underset{..}{X}}:^- \xrightarrow[2.\ H^+(-X^-)]{1.\ OH^-} R:\overset{..}{\underset{..}{S}}:H + (H_2N)_2C{=}O$

13.129 (a) Show all steps in the reaction of H_2S with $RCH{=}CH_2$ in the presence of peroxides. (b) What product is expected if the reaction is run without peroxides and with the introduction of a radical scavenger?

◢ (a) Initially, the peroxide cleaves to a radical, $R\cdot$, which initiates a chain reaction:

Initiation Step: $R\cdot + H_2S \longrightarrow R{-}H + HS\cdot$

Propagation Step 1: $HS\cdot + RCH{=}CH_2 \longrightarrow R\dot{C}HCH_2SH$

Propagation Step 2: $H_2S + R\dot{C}HCH_2SH \longrightarrow HS\cdot + RCH_2CH_2SH$

The net result is anti-Markovnikov addition of H_2S to $RCH{=}CH_2$ to give RCH_2CH_2SH. (b) The reaction yields the Markovnikov product, $RCH(SH)CH_3$.

13.130 Synthesize Me_2CHCH_2SH using (a) a Grignard reagent and (b) an alkene.

◢ (a) $Me_2CHCH_2Cl + Mg \longrightarrow Me_2CHCH_2MgCl \xrightarrow{S_8} Me_2CHCH_2SMgCl \xrightarrow{HCl} Me_2CHCH_2SH$

(b) $\qquad Me_2CH{=}CH_2 + H_2S \xrightarrow{peroxide} Me_2CHCH_2SH$

13.131 (a) Write the equation for the reaction of $EtSH$ with I_2. (b) Show by the ion-electron method that this is a redox reaction. (c) How may this reaction be reversed?

◢ (a) $2\ EtSH + I_2 \rightarrow EtS{-}SEt$ (a disulfide) $+\ 2HI$.

(b) Oxidation: $2EtSH \rightarrow EtS{-}SEt + 2H^+ + 2e^-$ Reduction: $I_2 + 2e^- \rightarrow 2I^-$

(c) Use Li in liquid NH_3: $EtS{-}SEt \xrightarrow[2.\ H_3O^+]{1.\ Li,\ NH_3} 2EtSH$.

13.132 Give the structure of the product of the reaction of $PhCH_2SH$ with (a) MeBr in OH^-, (b) $Na^{+\ -}OEt$, (c) $KMnO_4$, (d) CH_3COCl, (e) I_2, and (f) $Pb(NO_3)_2$.

◢ (a) $PhCH_2S{-}Me$, (b) $PhCH_2S^-Na^+ + EtOH$, (c) $PhCH_2{-}SO_3H$, (d) $PhCH_2S{-}\overset{\overset{\textstyle O}{\|}}{C}CH_3$, (e) $PhCH_2S{-}SCH_2Ph$, and (f) $Pb(SCH_2Ph)_2$, a black precipitate like PbS.

13.133 Synthesize propyl propanesulphonate, $PrSO_2OPr$, from n-PrBr and any inorganic reagents.

◢ $PrBr \Bigg\{ \begin{array}{l} \xrightarrow[2.\ OH^-]{1.\ Thiourea} PrSH \xrightarrow{KMnO_4} PrSO_2OH \xrightarrow{PCl_5} PrSO_2Cl \\ \qquad\qquad\qquad\qquad\qquad\qquad\qquad\qquad + \\ \xrightarrow{OH^-} PrOH \qquad\qquad\qquad\qquad\qquad PrOH \end{array} \Bigg\} \xrightarrow{pyridine} PrSO_2OPr$

13.134 Show steps in the preparation of (a) 1-phenyl-1-ethanethiol and (b) 2-phenyl-1-ethanethiol from benzene and any 2-carbon compound.

◢ Both compounds are synthesized from phenylethylene (styrene), prepared as follows:

$$C_6H_6 \xrightarrow[\text{HF}]{H_2C=CH_2} C_6H_5CH_2CH_3 \xrightarrow{\text{NBS}} C_6H_5CHBrCH_3 \xrightarrow{\text{alc KOH}} C_6H_5CH=CH_2$$

(a) $C_6H_5CH=CH_2 + H_2S \xrightarrow{H^+} C_6H_5CH(SH)CH_3$ (Markovnikov addition)

(b) $C_6H_5CH=CH_2 + H_2S \xrightarrow{\text{peroxide}} C_6H_5CH_2CH_2SH$ (anti-Markovnikov addition)

13.135 List the sequence of successively higher oxidation states of RSH.

◢
$$\underset{\text{a thiol}}{RSH} \longrightarrow \underset{\text{a disulfide}}{RSSR} \longrightarrow \underset{\substack{\text{a sulfenic}\\\text{acid}}}{RSOH} \longrightarrow \underset{\substack{\text{a sulfinic}\\\text{acid}}}{RSO_2H} \longrightarrow \underset{\substack{\text{a sulfonic}\\\text{acid}}}{RSO_3H}$$

13.136 For $CH_3S:H \rightarrow CH_3S\cdot + H\cdot$, the bond dissociation energy $\Delta H = 91$ kcal/mol and for $CH_4 \rightarrow CH_3\cdot + H\cdot$, $\Delta H \doteq 105$ kcal/mol. (a) Calculate ΔH for the reaction $CH_4 + CH_3S\cdot \rightleftharpoons CH_3\cdot + CH_3SH$ and determine in which direction the equilibrium lies. (b) Explain how CH_3SH inhibits free radical reactions.

◢ (a) $\Delta H = \Sigma$ [(bonds broken) + (bonds formed)] = $\Sigma(+105) + (-91) = +14$ kcal/mol. ΔS for this reaction is probably close to zero; thus $\Delta G \approx \Delta H$ and the equilibrium lies far to the left. (b) CH_3SH prevents alkyl radicals from propagating the chain by reacting with them. Since $CH_3S\cdot$ cannot remove H from an alkane, it persists until two $CH_3S\cdot$ radicals unite forming CH_3SSCH_3.

13.137 Distinguish between an alcohol and a thiol without using chemical or physical tests.

◢ Thiols have very distinct, unpleasant odors. 1-Butanethiol is a component of the skunk spray, and a trace of a thiol is often added to heating gas by the supplier as an aid in the detection of gas leaks.

13.138 Discuss the difference in ir absorption of RSH, which shows weak $S-H$ stretching frequencies in the 1600 to 1550 cm^{-1} region and in the 700 to 590 cm^{-1} region due to the $C-S$ stretching, and ROH.

◢ Since $S-H$ forms very weak H-bonds, its stretching frequency shifts only to a small extent due to association. (This is in contrast to the broad, strong absorption of the $O-H$ group in alcohols; see Problem 13.101.) Because S is heavier than O, $C-S$ has a smaller force constant than $C-O$ and absorbs at lower frequencies (See Problems 12.79 and 12.83). These $C-S$ absorptions are often too weak to be detected.

13.139 Compare the relative pmr δ values of (a) $-S-C-H$ in RCH_2SH with $-O-C-H$ in RCH_2OH and (b) $S-H$ with $O-H$.

◢ Differences between the O and S compounds are ascribed to their different electronegativities. S, having the lower value, causes (a) $H-C-S-$ to absorb more upfield than $-O-C-H$ and (b) $S-H$ to absorb more upfield than $O-H$. Because $S-H$ forms very weak H-bonds, its pmr absorption will not be as variable or as broad as $O-H$ absorption.

13.140 Should you expect RSH, unlike ROH, to absorb in the detectable region of the uv spectrum? Explain.

◢ Yes. Less energy is required to excite the nonbonding electrons on S compared with O, because they are farther away from the nucleus. λ_{max} for cyclohexanethiol is detected at 224 nm, while typical alcohols, with $\lambda_{max} \cong 180$ nm, are outside the range of the instrument.

13.141 (a) Give the structural formula of a compound (**A**) with the following m/z values: 90*, 61*, 47* (base peak), and 28. The peaks marked with an asterisk have detectable $m/(z+2)$ satellites with an intensity ratio of P:P+2 of about 20:1. (b) Write the structural formulas for three other isomers having the same functional group. (c) Give the key peaks expected in the mass spectra of these isomers that permit their being distinguished from each other.

◢ (a) The P:P+2 ratio of 20:1 tips off the presence of S in the compound since the ratio of $^{32}S:^{34}S$ is about 20:1. The abundance of ^{33}S (0.78%) is small but it does enhance the P+1 peak arising mainly from ^{13}C. The molecular weight of **A** is 90 and with one S, the molecular formula that fits this mass is $C_4H_{10}S$. If two S atoms were present, the formula for **A** would be $C_2H_4S_2$, which would not be consistent with the given data. The formula for the base peak is $[^+CH_2-SH \longleftrightarrow H_2C=\overset{+}{S}-H]$, arising from α, β cleavage. The peak at 61 is $^+CH_2CH_2SH$, arising from a small amount of β, γ cleavage. The peak at 28 has no S and its cation is $[H_2\overset{\cdot}{C}-\overset{+}{C}H_2]$ formed from a McLafferty rearrangement:

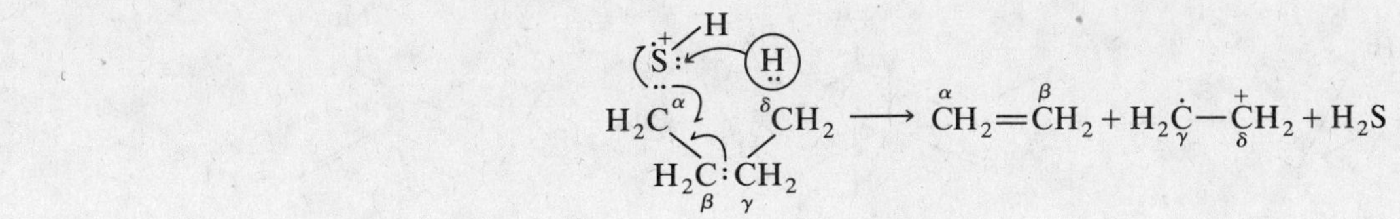

$$\text{(S:}^{\overset{+}{}}\text{H)} \quad \overset{\alpha}{H_2C} \quad \overset{\delta}{CH_2} \quad \longrightarrow \quad \overset{\alpha}{CH_2} = \overset{\beta}{CH_2} + H_2\overset{+}{\underset{\gamma}{C}} - \overset{+}{\underset{\delta}{CH_2}} + H_2S$$

$$\underset{\beta}{H_2C} \overset{}{:} \underset{\gamma}{CH_2}$$

The lost mass $(90 - 28 = 62)$ is the sum of the masses of H_2S (34) and $H_2C = CH_2$ (28).

(*b*) $(CH_3)_2CHCH_2SH$ (**B**), $CH_3CH_2CH(CH_3)SH$ (**C**), $(CH_3)_3CSH$ (**D**).

(*c*) **B** has no peak at $m/z = 28$ because it cannot undergo a McLafferty rearrangement that must proceed through a six-membered ring. Neither does it have a peak at $m/z = 75$ from β, γ cleavage. For **C**, α, β cleavage can occur in two ways, by loss of C_2H_5, the larger group, or CH_3, the smaller group. Typically the larger group is lost and the base peak cation is $CH_3\overset{+}{C}HSH$, $m/z = 61$, not 47 for **A**. **D** would be expected to have a peak at $m/z = 57$ [$90 - 33$ (SH)] with no satellite, owing to the formation of the stable 3° carbocation, $^+C(CH_3)_3$.

SUPPLEMENTARY PROBLEMS

13.142 (*a*) How many diastereomers does 2-isopropyl-5-methylcyclohexanol have? (*b*) Draw the lowest energy conformation of each. (*c*) The decreasing order of their stabilities is: menthol > neomenthol > isomenthol > neoisomenthol. Match each compound to its structure.

▐ (*a*) Because there are three chiral C's, there are four diastereomers, each with a pair of enantiomers, for a total of eight stereoisomers. (*b*) See Fig. 13-4. (*c*) Each diastereomer has an equatorial isopropyl group. Menthol is **A**, with all three substituents equatorial. Neomenthol is **B**; it is next in stability because it has an equatorial Me and axial OH. In decreasing order, are isomenthol (**C**), with OH(e) and Me(a), and neoisomenthol (**D**) with axial OH and Me.

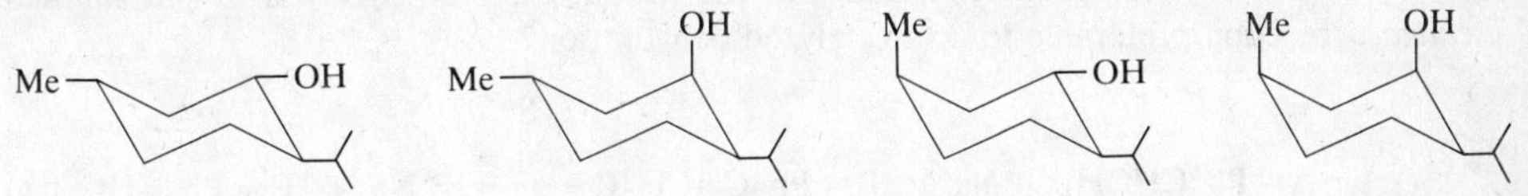

Fig. 13-4

13.143 Prepare (*a*) 1-[1-naphthyl]ethanol (**A**), (*b*) 1-[2-naphthyl]ethanol (**B**), (*c*) 2-[1-naphthyl]ethanol (**C**), and (*d*) 2-[2-naphthyl]ethanol (**D**).

▐ (*a*) and (*c*) The common intermediate to be synthesized is 1-NpCOCH$_3$

$$C_{10}H_8(NpH) + CH_3COCl \xrightarrow[CS_2]{AlCl_3} 1\text{-}NpCOCH_3 \xrightarrow{NaBH_4} 1\text{-}NpCH(OH)CH_3 \xrightarrow[\Delta]{H_2SO_4}$$
$$\overset{}{\underset{\mathbf{A}}{}}$$

$$1\text{-}NpCH = CH_2 \xrightarrow[2.\ H_2O_2,\ OH^-]{1.\ BH_3/THF} 1\text{-}NpCH_2CH_2OH$$
$$\underset{\mathbf{C}}{}$$

(*b*) and (*d*) The common intermediate, 2-NpCOCH$_3$ is prepared as in (*a*) from NpH and CH$_3$COCl, but in the solvent PhNO$_2$. Reduction with NaBH$_4$ gives **B**; dehydration of **B** followed by anti-Markovnikov hydration gives **D**.

13.144 When *trans*-2-methylcyclohexanol is treated with tosyl chloride followed by KOEt, 3-methylcyclohexene is the only product. However, this sequence with *cis*-2-methylcyclohexanol gives 1-methylcyclohexene as the main product. Account for the difference in products.

▐ Each tosylate retains the stereochemistry of the alcohol from which it came [see Problem 13.62(*c*)]. The elimination with ethoxide is E2, and it requires a coplanar, *trans* alignment of the OTs and H.

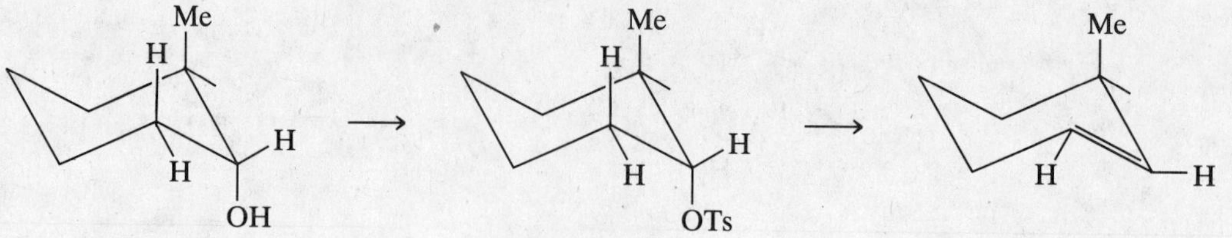

trans-alcohol   trans-tosylate   3-Methylcyclohexene

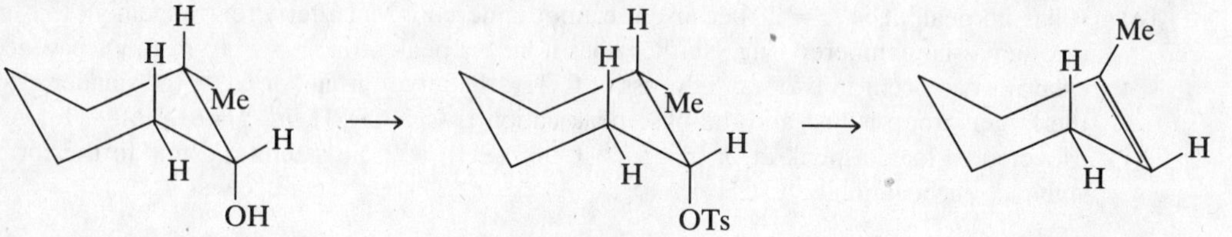

cis-alcohol   cis-tosylate   1-Methylcyclohexene

13.145 Predict and give an explanation for the products of the sequence of reactions in the preceding problem if potassium *t*-butoxide is used in the elimination step.

▰ Only one *trans*, coplanar H is available in the *trans*-tosylate for elimination, leading to 3-methylcyclohexene. There are two possible H's that are *trans* and coplanar with the tosylate group in the *cis*-compound. The bulky base removes the H from the less hindered site, producing the less substituted 3-methylcyclohexene, even though removal of the 3° H would lead to the more highly substituted 1-methylcyclohexene.

13.146 (*a*) Write structural formulas for **A**, **B**, and **C** in the following sequence of reactions.

$$Ph_2CHCH_2OH \xrightarrow{Na} A \xrightarrow{CS_2} B \xrightarrow{MeI} C \text{ (an S-methyl xanthate)}$$

(*b*) Show the cyclic transition state and give the products of the pyrolysis of the xanthate. (*c*) Why is this *Tschugaev* reaction preferable to acid-catalyzed dehydration?

▰ (*a*) $A = Ph_2CHCH_2O^-Na^+$, $B = Ph_2CHCH_2O\overset{\overset{S}{\|}}{-C}-S^-Na^+$, $C = Ph_2CHCH_2O\overset{\overset{S}{\|}}{-C}-S-Me$

(*b*) 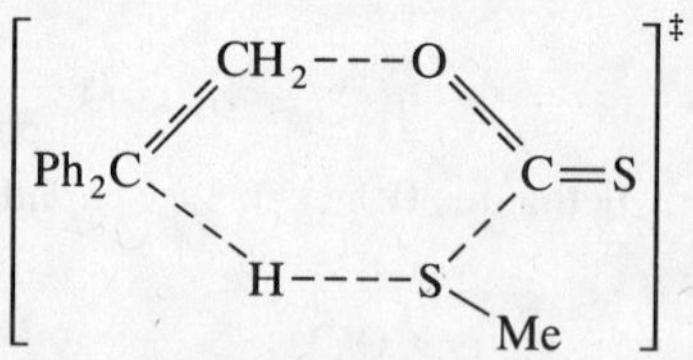
$$\left[\begin{array}{c} CH_2{-}{-}{-}O \\ Ph_2C \diagdown \qquad \diagup C{=}S \\ H{-}{-}{-}{-}S \\ \qquad\qquad Me \end{array} \right]^{\ddagger} \xrightarrow{\Delta} Ph_2C{=}CH_2 + S{=}C{=}O + MeSH.$$

The elimination is cis.

(*c*) Alcohols of the type R_2CHCH_2OH rearrange on treatment with acid.

13.147 Predict the product of the pyrolysis of the xanthate ester of (*a*) *cis*- and (*b*) *trans*-2-methylcyclohexanol.

▰ (*a*) The *cis*-xanthate can only undergo *cis*-elimination to give 3-methylcyclohexene. (*b*) There are two H's that are *cis* and coplanar in the *trans*-xanthate. Elimination goes preferentially with the 3° H to give 1-methylcyclohexene, the Saytzeff product.

13.148 (*a*) Provide a mechanism for each of the following transformations. (*b*) What other product could be formed in (ii)?

(i) 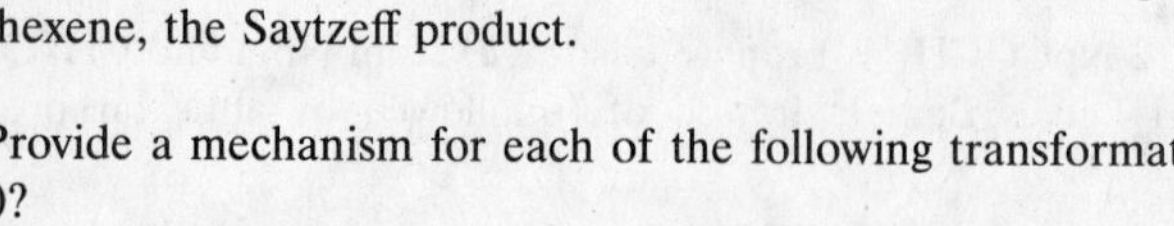 $\underset{\displaystyle\text{HO}-HC-C=CH_2 \text{ (A)}}{\overset{\displaystyle H_2C-CH_2}{\big|\qquad\quad}} \xrightarrow{H^+} \underset{\displaystyle O{=}C-CH-CH_3 \text{ (B)}}{\overset{\displaystyle H_2C-CH_2}{\big|\qquad\quad}}$

(ii) $PhCH_2CH_2CHOHC(CH_3)_3 \text{ (C)} \xrightarrow{H_2SO_4} PhCH_2CH_2\overset{\overset{\displaystyle CH_3}{\big|}}{C}{=}C(CH_3)_2$

(iii) $PhH + (CH_3)_3CCH_2OH \text{ (E)} \xrightarrow[BF_3]{} PhC(CH_3)_2CH_2CH_3 \text{ (F)}$

(a) (i) $\mathbf{A} \xrightarrow{H^+} HO-HC\overset{\overset{\displaystyle H_2C-CH_2}{|\quad\quad\;|}}{\underset{+}{-}C}-CH_3 \xrightarrow{\sim H:} HO-\overset{\overset{\displaystyle H_2C-CH_2}{|\quad\quad\;|}}{\underset{+}{C}}-CH-CH_3 \xrightarrow{-H^+} \mathbf{B}$

(ii) $\mathbf{C} \xrightarrow[H_2O^+]{H^+} PhCH_2CH_2\overset{\overset{\displaystyle CH_3}{|}}{CH}-\overset{\overset{\displaystyle CH_3}{|}}{\underset{\overset{\displaystyle |}{CH_3}}{C}}-CH_3 \xrightarrow[\sim\,:Me]{-H_2O} PhCH_2CH_2CH-\overset{\overset{\displaystyle CH_3}{|}}{\underset{\overset{\displaystyle |}{CH_3}}{\overset{+}{C}}}-CH_3 \xrightarrow{-H^+} \mathbf{D}$

(iii) $\mathbf{E} \xrightarrow{BF_3} (CH_3)_3C-CH_2\overset{+}{\underset{\overset{\displaystyle |}{H}}{O}}:\bar{B}F_3 \xrightarrow[-(HOBF_3)^-]{\sim\,:Me} (CH_3)_2\overset{+}{C}-CH_2CH_3 \xrightarrow[-H^+]{PhH} \mathbf{F}$

(b) The tetralin derivative, **G**, could have been formed from an intramolecular Friedel-Crafts alkylation of the R^+ prior to loss of H^+

G

13.149 Distinguish between each pair of compounds by a simple chemical test.
(a) $(CH_3)_2CHOH$ and $(CH_3)_2CHSH$ (c) $CH_3CH_2CH_2OH$ and $(CH_3)_2CHOH$
(b) $CH_3CH_2SCH_3$ and $(CH_3)_2CHSH$ (d) $(CH_3)_2C(OH)CH_2CH_3$ and $CH_3CH_2CH(OH)CH_2CH_3$

$\blacksquare$ **(a)** The thiol gives a precipitate with heavy metal cations like Hg^{2+}, Pb^{2+}, and Cu^{2+}. **(b)** The thiol dissolves in aqueous NaOH, forming RS^-Na^+. **(c)** The 2° ROH gives a yellow precipitate of CHI_3 with I_2/OH^- (the iodoform test). **(d)** The 2° ROH is oxidized by a Cr(VI) reagent, thus changing its color from orange to green.

13.150 Give the carbonyl compound (or ethylene oxide) and the Grignard reagent that can be used in the preparation of each alcohol in Problem 13.108.

$\blacksquare$ $PhCH{=}O + CH_3CH_2MgBr$ or $CH_3CH_2CH{=}O + PhMgBr \longrightarrow PhCHOHCH_2CH_3$, **E**
$CH_3CH{=}O + PhCH_2MgCl$ or $PhCH_2CH{=}O + CH_3MgBr \longrightarrow PhCH_2CHOHCH_3$, **F**
$PhCH(CH_3)MgCl + H_2C{=}O \longrightarrow PhCH(CH_3)CH_2OH$, **G**

$\overset{\overset{\displaystyle O}{\diagup\,\diagdown}}{CH_2{-}CH_2} + PhCH_2MgCl$ or $PhCH_2CH_2MgCl + H_2C{=}O \longrightarrow PhCH_2CH_2CH_2OH$, **H**

$\overset{\overset{\displaystyle O}{\|}}{PhCCH_3} + CH_3MgBr$ or $(CH_3)_2C{=}O + PhMgBr \longrightarrow (CH_3)_2\overset{\overset{\displaystyle OH}{|}}{C}Ph$, **I**

13.151 Outline the steps in the preparation of each alcohol in Problem 13.108 by a method other than the Grignard reaction.

$\blacksquare$ $PhH + CH_3CH_2COCl \xrightarrow{AlCl_3} PhCOCH_2CH_3 \xrightarrow{NaBH_4} \mathbf{E}$

$PhH + HOCH_2CH{=}CH_2 \xrightarrow{HF} PhCH_2CH{=}CH_2 \begin{cases} \xrightarrow[\text{2. NaBH}_4]{\text{1. Hg(OAc)}_2} \mathbf{F} \\ \xrightarrow[\text{2. H}_2O_2,\ OH^-]{\text{1. BH}_3,\ THF} \mathbf{H} \end{cases}$

$PhH + CH_3CH(OH)CH_3 \xrightarrow{HF} PhCH(CH_3)_2 \xrightarrow{NBS} PhCBr(CH_3)_2 \xrightarrow{OEt^-} Ph\overset{\overset{\displaystyle CH_3}{|}}{C}{=}CH_2 \begin{cases} \xrightarrow[\text{2. NaBH}_4]{\text{1. Hg(OAc)}_2} \mathbf{I} \\ \xrightarrow[\text{2. H}_2O_2,\ OH^-]{\text{1. BH}_3,\ THF} \mathbf{G} \end{cases}$

13.152 The carbocation salt, $Ph_3C^+BF_4^-$, oxidizes 2-heptanol to methyl pentyl ketone in 82% yield. **(a)** Write a plausible mechanism. **(b)** What is the salt reduced to?

(a) $CH_3-\overset{\overset{\overset{\displaystyle H}{|}}{|}}{\underset{\underset{\displaystyle :\overset{..}{O}H}{|}}{C}}-C_5H_{11} \xrightarrow[-HCPH_3]{+CPh_3} \left[CH_3-\overset{\overset{\displaystyle H\overset{..}{O}:^+}{\|}}{C}-C_5H_{11} \right] \xrightarrow[-HBF_4]{BF_4^-} CH_3-\overset{\overset{\displaystyle O}{\|}}{C}-C_5H_{11}$

(b) Ph_3C^+ removes H with its bonded pair of e^-'s to give Ph_3CH

13.153 Describe the resolution (separation into enantiomers) of the racemate of a chiral alcohol.

⬛ The racemic alcohols are converted to an ester by reaction with a naturally-occurring optically-active carboxylic acid. Two diastereomeric esters are formed:

$$(R)\text{-alcohol} + (R)\text{-acid} \longrightarrow (R,R)\text{-ester; and } (S)\text{-alcohol} + (R)\text{-acid} \longrightarrow (S,R)\text{-ester}$$

Diastereomers have sufficiently different physical properties that they may often be separated by fractional crystallization (if solid), by various kinds of chromatography, or by fractional distillation (if liquid). The two separated esters may be cleaved with $LiAlH_4$ to give two alcohols, one from the reduction of the carboxyl group and the other the desired enantiomeric alcohol.

13.154 Starting with benzene and any 2-carbon compound, synthesize (a) m-nitrostyrene (A) and (b) p-nitrostyrene (B).

⬛ (a) $PhH + CH_3COCl \xrightarrow{AlCl_3} PhCOCH_3 \xrightarrow[H_2SO_4]{HNO_3} m\text{-}NO_2C_6H_4COCH_3 \xrightarrow{NaBH_4}$
$$m\text{-}NO_2C_6H_4CHOHCH_3 \xrightarrow[\Delta]{H_2SO_4} \mathbf{A}$$

(b) $PhCOCH_3 \text{ [from } (a)] \xrightarrow{NaBH_4} PhCHOHCH_3 \xrightarrow[\Delta]{H_2SO_4} PhCH{=}CH_2 \xrightarrow[H_2SO_4]{HNO_3} \mathbf{B}$

13.155 List significant similarities between H_2O and ROH.

⬛ Both dissolve many ionic salts, alcohols to a lesser extent (see Problem 13.11). Because of the O—H bond, both H-bond extensively with themselves and with other congenial substances. Alcohols are slightly weaker acids than water ($K_a \cong 10^{-16}$); its H, however, is acidic enough to react with active metals (Na, Li, K, etc.), releasing H_2. The anions (OH^- and OR^-) are strong Brönsted bases, OR^- being stronger. Both are nucleophiles and good solvents for S_N1 solvolyses for which rates in alcohol are slower.

13.156 Write the product of the reaction of C_4H_9SH with (a) Pb^{2+}, (b) Hg^{2+}, and (c) Cu^{2+}.

⬛ Insoluble mercaptides form: (a) C_4H_9SPb, (b) C_4H_9SHg, and (c) C_4H_9SCu.

13.157 Explain the difference in products from the following reactions of compound **H**:

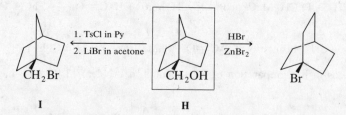

I   H

⬛ Displacement by Br^- occurs under S_N2 conditions to form **I**, regardless of the fact that this is a neopentyl alcohol. This is because the groups on the 3° bridgehead C are "tied back" and do not sterically interfere with the incoming Br^-. Under S_N1 conditions ($HBr/ZnBr_2$), the bridge methylene group moves over to bond with the incipient carbocation that forms as H_2O (a good leaving group) is lost. The result is the 3° bridgehead C^+, which then bonds to Br^-.

13.158 Write equations to show how a solution of ROH in cold, conc. H_2SO_4 gives an i (number of moles of particles formed per mole of solute) = 3, whereas for Ar_3COH, $i = 4$, as determined from measurement of freezing point depressions.

⬛ Four moles of particles (ions) are formed for each mole of Ar_3COH in solution:
   (1) $Ar_3COH + H_2SO_4 \longrightarrow Ar_3C^+ + H_2O + HSO_4^-$
   (2) $H_2SO_4 + H_2O \longrightarrow HSO_4^- + H_3O^+$

$$(1) + (2) = Ar_3COH + 2H_2SO_4 \longrightarrow Ar_3C^+ + H_3O^+ + 2HSO_4^- \qquad \text{4 particles}$$

An alkyl ROH reacts as follows (because even R_3C^+ is not stable enough to persist):

(3) $ROH + H_2SO_4 \longrightarrow ROH_2^+ + HSO_4^- \longrightarrow ROSO_2OH + H_2O$

(4) $H_2SO_4 + H_2O \longrightarrow HSO_4^- + H_3O^+$

$(3) + (4) = ROH + 2H_2SO_4 \longrightarrow ROSO_2OH + HSO_4^- + H_3O^+$ 3 particles

13.159 Suggest a method for obtaining the pure enantiomers of CH_3CHDOH from the racemate.

◢ Feed the racemate to a bacterium that metabolizes one of the enantiomers and recover the unchanged one. Convert some of this enantiomer to its tosylate; react the tosylate with OH^- to get the inverted enantiomeric alcohol.

13.160 Why is methanol more toxic than ethanol?

◢ We metabolize both alcohols to their corresponding aldehydes. $H_2C{=}O$, the product from MeOH is much more toxic than $MeCH{=}O$, the product from EtOH.

13.161 Account for the fact that the ir spectrum of a dilute solution of *cis*-3-fluorocyclohexanol (**A**) shows a broader, lower-frequency O—H stretching peak than does the *trans*-isomer.

◢ The shift in frequency indicates intramolecular H-bonding, and the closer the OH and F the greater is the shift. There is more intramolecular H-bonding in the *cis*-isomer which means that its OH and F must be closer to each other. In the *trans*-isomer the OH and F are e,a—too far apart for intramolecular H-bonding. If *cis*-3-fluorocyclohexanol were in the lower energy e,e conformation, the OH and F would be too far apart for H-bonding. Only in the a,a conformer are OH and F able to H-bond. The conformational strain of the a,a groups is extensively compensated for by the energetically favorable H-bond.

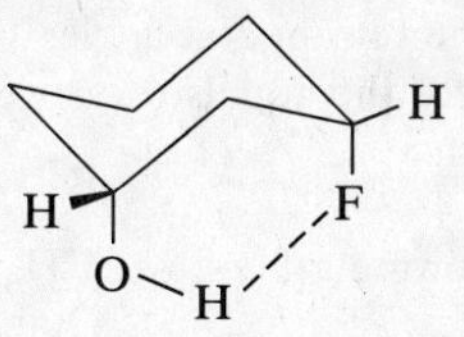

A

CHAPTER 14
Ethers, Epoxides, Glycols, and Thioethers

ETHERS

1. Introduction and Nomenclature

14.1 Give general formulas for the following kinds of ethers: (*a*) symmetrical (simple), (*b*) unsymmetrical (mixed), (*c*) aryl, (*d*) cyclic.

◢ Ethers have two hydrocarbon groups attached to an O. (*a*) The groups are identical: ROR or ArOAr. (*b*) The groups are different: ROR′, ArOR, or ArOAr′. (*c*) At least one group is Ar: ArOAr, ArOAr′, or ROAr. (*d*) The O is part of a ring: $CH_2(CH_2)_nCH_2$ (*n* can be zero); thus they are heterocyclics.

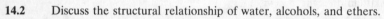

14.2 Discuss the structural relationship of water, alcohols, and ethers.

◢ Alcohols and ethers may be considered as derivatives of H—O—H. Replacement of one H affords alcohols, ROH. In ethers, R—O—R, both H's are replaced.

14.3 Compare the bond angles of H—O—H, C—O—H of alcohols, and C—O—C of ethers.

◢ In each case the O uses sp^3 HO's. When H's are bonded to hybridized heteroatoms, e.g., O, there is always a contraction of the bond angle; the bond angle in H_2O is 105° (Problem 2.39). The bond angle in alcohols is 108.5° which is very close to 109°, the tetrahedral angle. The C—O—C bond angle in ethers is 111.7°. As the groups bonded to O increase in size, the repulsive van der Waals forces between them increase, causing an expansion of the angle.

14.4 Give the common names of the following ethers: (*a*) $CH_3CH_2OCH_2CH_3$, (*b*) $(CH_3)_2CHOCH(CH_3)CH_2CH_3$, (*c*) $ClCH_2CH_2OCH_3$, (*d*) $C_6H_5OCH_3$, (*e*) $p\text{-}NO_2C_6H_4OC_2H_5$, (*f*) [cyclohexyl]—N(H)—OCH_2CH_3, and (*g*) $H_2C{=}CHOCH_2C_6H_5$.

◢ The common name is comprised of the names of the groups as separate words with the word ether. The groups are listed alphabetically. (*a*) Diethyl ether or more commonly ethyl ether, because with simple ethers the prefix di is often omitted. (*b*) *sec*-Butyl isopropyl ether. (*c*) β-Chloroethyl methyl ether. (*d*) Methyl phenyl ether, is usually called anisole. (*e*) Ethyl *p*-nitrophenyl ether, is usually called *p*-nitrophenetole. (*f*) Cyclohexyl *n*-propyl ether, (*g*) benzyl vinyl ether.

14.5 Give the IUPAC (alkoxyhydrocarbon) name to each compound in Problem 14.4.

◢ In this method the more complex R group is made the base hydrocarbon and the other group with the O (OR′) is named as a substituent alkoxy group. (*a*) Ethoxyethane, (*b*) 2-isopropoxybutane, (*c*) 1-chloro-2-methoxyethane, (*d*) methoxybenzene, (*e*) 4-ethoxynitrobenzene, (*f*) *n*-propoxycyclohexane, and (*g*) benzyloxyethene

14.6 Write the structures for each of the following compounds: (*a*) Cyclopentyl *t*-butyl ether, (*b*) *m*-diethoxybenzene, (*c*) 5-methoxy-2-pentanol, (*d*) 3-cyclohexenyl isopropyl ether, (*e*) dibenzyl ether, and (*f*) 2,4-dichlorophenyl 3-nitrophenyl ether

◢ (*a*) [cyclopentyl with H]—$OC(CH_3)_3$ (*b*) benzene with OC_2H_5 and OC_2H_5 (*c*) $CH_3CHCH_2CH_2CH_2OCH_3$ with OH

(*d*) [cyclohexenyl]—$OCH(CH_3)_2$ (*e*) $PhCH_2OCH_2Ph$ (*f*) Cl—[benzene with Cl]—O—[benzene with NO_2]

14.7 (*a*) Name (i) $CH_3OCH_2CH_2OCH_3$ and (ii) $CH_3OCH_2CH_2OCH_2CH_2OCH_3$ (*b*) Name these polyethers by the oxa method.

◢ (*a*) (i) 1,2-Dimethoxyethane, commonly called *glyme* and (ii) bis-β-methoxyethyl ether (*diglyme*). (*b*) The *oxa method* pretends that the O of the longest chain or ring is a C and it is so counted to determine either the longest carbon parent chain or the parent ring. Its presence is indicated by the prefix *oxa-* and a number to designate its position in the chain or ring. (i) The two O's and four C's are taken as six C's and the parent is hexane; thus, 2,5-dioxahexane. (ii) 2,5,8-Trioxanonane.

14.8 Give the names, both common and oxa, of the following ethers:

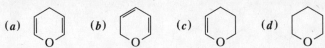

(*a*) (*b*) (*c*) (*d*)

◢ (*a*) The common name is 4H-pyran. The 4H indicates that C^4 is the CH_2 group in the pyran ring. The oxa name is 1-oxa-2,5-cyclohexadiene. (*b*) 2H-Pyran or 1-oxa-2,4-cyclohexadiene. (*c*) 2,3-dihydro-4H-pyran (DHP). The 2,3-dihydro portion of the name indicates that two H's have been added to 4H-pyran, one to C^2 and one to C^3. A correct but less used name is 3,4-dihydro-2H-pyran. The oxa name is 1-oxa-2-cyclohexene. (*d*) Tetrahydropyran or oxacyclohexane.

14.9 Name each of the following compounds:

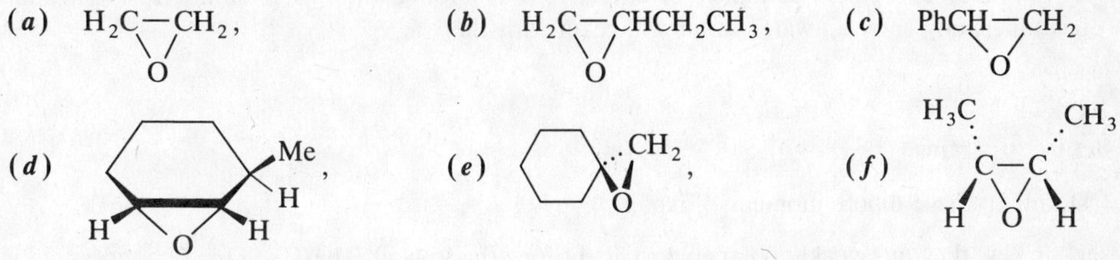

(*a*) $H_2C{-}CH_2$, (*b*) $H_2C{-}CHCH_2CH_3$, (*c*) $PhCH{-}CH_2$

(*d*) (*e*) (*f*)

◢ Three-membered cyclic ethers may be considered as being oxides of the parent alkene whose common name is used. (*a*) The common name is ethylene oxide. This type of ring is also called an *epoxide*. (*b*) 1,2-Butene oxide or 1,2-epoxybutane. (*c*) Styrene oxide or phenylethylene oxide. (*d*) *trans*-3-Methylcyclohexene oxide or *trans*-1,2-epoxy-3-methylcyclohexane. *trans* Refers to the relationship of the oxide ring, that must always be *cis*, and the Me group. (*e*) Methylenecyclohexane oxide. (*f*) *cis*-2,3-Butene oxide or (Z)-2,3-epoxybutane.

14.10 Name:

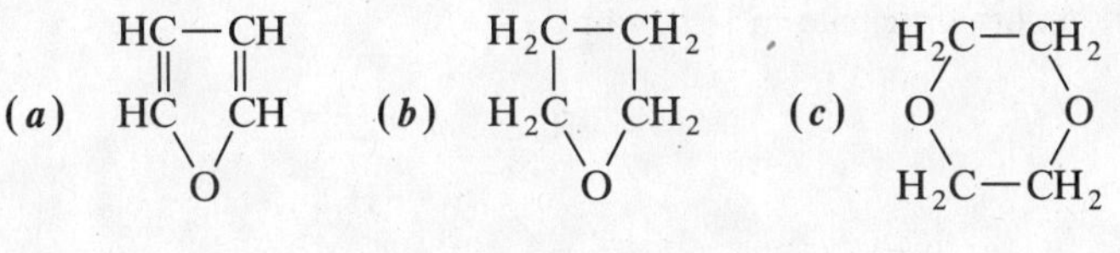

(*a*) (*b*) (*c*)

◢ (*a*) Furan. (*b*) Tetrahydrofuran. (*c*) 1,4-Dioxane (or 1,4-dioxacyclohexane).

14.11 Give the IUPAC ring names for the cyclic ethers, $(CH_2)_nO$, where $n = 2, 3, 4, 5,$ and 6.

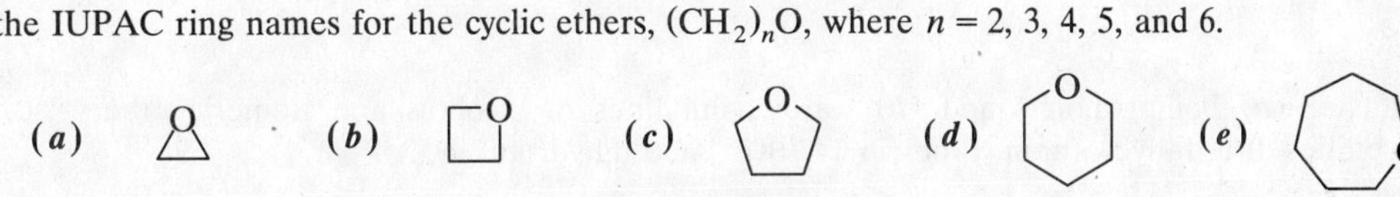

◢ (*a*) (*b*) (*c*) (*d*) (*e*)

$n = 2$ $n = 3$ $n = 4$ $n = 5$ $n = 6$
Ox*irane*   Ox*etane*   Ox*olane*   Ox*ane*   Ox*epane*

The italicized portions of these names are the suffixes used to represent the size of saturated heterocyclic rings other than those with N atoms.

14.12 Give the structural formulas for (*a*) phenyloxirane, (*b*) 3,3-dichloro-2-methyloxetane, (*c*) *trans*-2-chloro-5-ethyloxepane, and (*d*) oxetene.

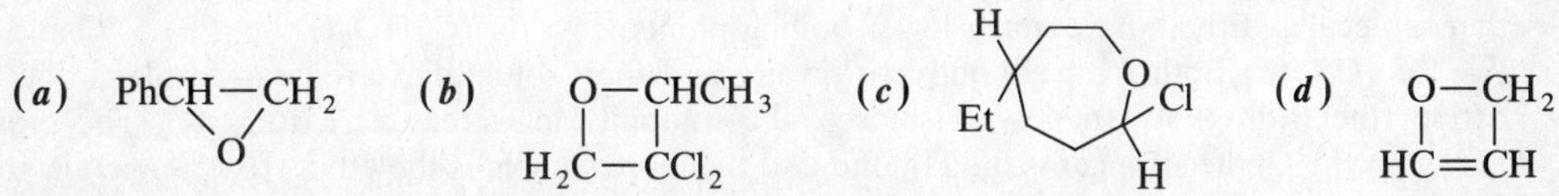

◢ (*a*) $PhCH{-}CH_2$ (*b*) $O{-}CHCH_3$ (*c*) (*d*) $O{-}CH_2$

14.13 (*a*) What is a crown ether? (*b*) Give the structural formula for (i) 12-crown-4 and (ii) 18-crown-6. (*c*) What is the repeating unit in these crown ethers?

◢ (*a*) The crown ether is a heterocyclic polyether, usually with at least four O atoms. (*b*) The first of two numbers in the name of crown ethers is the total number of atoms in the ring, the second is the number of O atoms. (*i*) The structure has 12 atoms, including four O's. (ii) There are 18 atoms, including six O's. See Fig. 14-1. (*c*) Usually a structural unit is repeated around the ring. In (i) and (ii) we have —OCH$_2$CH$_2$—.

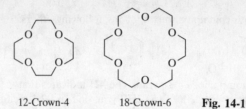

12-Crown-4   18-Crown-6   **Fig. 14-1**

14.14 (*a*) What is absolute ether? (*b*) How is its absolute quality maintained in the laboratory?

◢ (*a*) Diethyl ether is often just called ether. *Absolute* means it is absolutely free of water; i.e., it is anhydrous. (*b*) To keep an opened container of ether from absorbing water, a sodium wire is introduced. On opening the container, any entering water vapor will react with the Na.

2. Physical Properties

14.15 Do ethers have dipole moments? Explain.

◢ Yes, they are weakly polar (e.g., 1.18 D for ethyl ether). The C—O—C bond angle is 111.7° and the two C—O bond moments do not cancel.

14.16 Compare (*a*) boiling points and (*b*) water solubilities of ethers, such as diethyl ether and a hydrocarbon of comparable molecular weight and structure, e.g., *n*-pentane.

◢ (*a*) Because ethers are weakly polar, their intermolecular forces of attraction are about as weak as are those of the hydrocarbons. Hence, the bp's are about the same: for ether 34.6 °C, and for *n*-pentane 36 °C. (*b*) Ethers are much more soluble in H$_2$O because of H-bonding between the O of ethers and the H of water. Hydrocarbons do not participate in H-bonding.

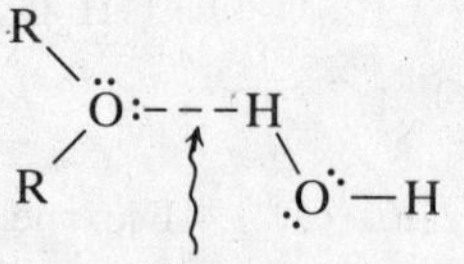

H-bond

14.17 Compare (*a*) boiling points and (*b*) water solubilities of alcohols and isomeric ethers. (*c*) Compare the solubilities of tetrahydrofuran [Problem 14.10(*b*)] and dihydrofuran (**A**).

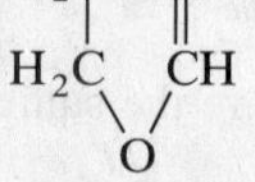

A

◢ ROH molecules have strong intermolecular attractive forces because of the H-bonding that is absent in ether molecules. Ethers have much lower boiling points, e.g., for (C$_2$H$_5$)$_2$O, bp = 34.6 °C and for *n*-C$_5$H$_{11}$OH, bp = 138 °C. (*b*) Both form H-bonds with water and their solubilities are comparable. In both cases, as the R portion (the hydrophobic moiety) increases, the solubility in water decreases. (*c*) The greater the electron density on the O, the stronger is the H-bond and the more soluble is the ether. In **A**, some electron density on the

O is drained away because of extended π-bonding with the double bond, as shown for the significant portion of the molecule:

$$[-\ddot{\underset{..}{O}}-CH=CH- \longleftrightarrow -\overset{+}{\underset{..}{O}}=CH-\bar{C}H-]$$

14.18 (*a*) Compare the O—C bond length in dicyclohexyl ether with the O—C (phenyl) bond length in anisole, PhOMe. (*b*) What are the relative chemical shifts of the *ortho* H's in anisole and the H's in benzene? (*c*) Compare the C—O stretching frequencies of the ethers in part (*a*).

▌ (*a*) Dicyclohexyl ether has the longer C—O bond length. One unshared pair of e^-'s on the O of anisole goes into a *p* AO in order to engage in extended π bonding with the benzene ring. The O—C (phenyl) bond length is shortened because the O—C has some double bond character. (*b*) The electron delocalization in anisole causes its *ortho* H's to be more upfield than those of C_6H_6. (*c*) Anisole has an $O-C_{sp^2}$ bond that has a higher stretching frequency (1200 to 1275 cm^{-1}) than the $O-C_{sp^3}$ in the alkyl ether. Recall that the stretching frequency of a bond increases as the *s*-character of the bonded atoms increases.

14.19 (*a*) Give the stable conformation of tetrahydropyran. (*b*) Whereas in cyclohexanol the OH is predominantly equatorial, in 3-tetrahydropyranol (**A**) the OH is 50% equatorial and 50% axial. Explain.

▌ (*a*) Like cyclohexane, the chair is the most stable conformation. The C—O—C bond angle of 111° is close to the tetrahedral angle. One unshared pair of e^-'s on O is axially oriented and the other is equatorial. (*b*) Some of the expected strain from an axial OH is overcome because now there is some H-bonding with the axial unshared pair of e^-'s of the ring O atom.

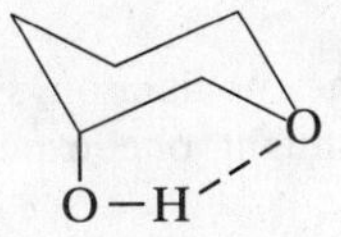

A

3. Syntheses

14.20 Write general equations for an S_N2 synthesis (Williamson synthesis) of an ether, R—O—R′.

▌ $$Na^+(R{:}\ddot{\underset{..}{O}}{:})^- + R'{:}\ddot{\underset{..}{X}}{:} \longrightarrow R{:}\ddot{\underset{..}{O}}{:}R' + Na^+ + {:}\ddot{\underset{..}{X}}{:}^- \quad (X = Cl, Br, I, OSO_2R, OSO_2Ar)$$

or $$Na^+(R'{:}\ddot{\underset{..}{O}}{:})^- + R{:}\ddot{\underset{..}{X}}{:}$$

alkoxides

14.21 Prepare the following ethers via the Williamson synthesis: (*a*) di-*n*-propyl ether (**A**), (*b*) benzyl methyl ether (**B**), (*c*) phenyl ethyl ether (**C**), and (*d*) *t*-butyl ethyl ether (**D**).

▌ (*a*) $n\text{-PrOH} \xrightarrow{Na} n\text{-PrO}^- \xrightarrow{n\text{-PrBr}}$ **A**; (*b*) $\text{MeOH} \xrightarrow{Na} \text{MeO}^- \xrightarrow{PhCH_2Br}$ **B**; (*c*) $\text{PhOH} \xrightarrow{NaOH} \text{PhO}^- \xrightarrow{EtBr}$ **C**; (*d*) $t\text{-BuOH} \xrightarrow{Na} t\text{-BuO}^- \xrightarrow{EtBr}$ **D** (This reaction produces a poor yield because of the bulkiness of t-BuO$^-$.)

14.22 Which compounds if any, in Problem 14.21 can be prepared by an alternate Williamson reaction? Give the reactions.

▌ Only **B**: $PhCH_2OH \xrightarrow{Na} PhCH_2O^- \xrightarrow{EtBr}$ **B**.

14.23 Give explanations for the inability of **A**, **C**, and **D** in Problem 14.21 to be prepared via an alternate Williamson synthesis.

▌ (*a*) **A** is a simple ether. (*b*) Unless the halide is activated (Problem 14.26), aryl halides do not undergo nucleophilic displacements. (*c*) EtO^- is a strong base as well as a nucleophile and dehydrohalogenates *t*-butyl chloride in a competing E2 reaction, giving the alkene and little or no ether.

14.24 Give six types of ethers that cannot be synthesized by the typical Williamson reaction.

▌ (*1*) $HR_2C-O-CR_2H$; both C's are secondary. (*2*) $HR_2C-O-CR_3$; one C is secondary and one is tertiary. (*3*) $R_3C-O-CR_3$; both C's are tertiary. (*4*) Ar—O—Ar; most diaryl ethers. (*5*) RCH=CHOCH=CHR′, vinyl halides do not undergo nucleophilic displacement. (*6*) $R_3CCH_2OCH_2CR'_3$; neopentyl-type halides are inert to S_N2 reactions (Problem 8.62).

14.25   Rank the following alkyl halides in decreasing order of reactivity in the Williamson reaction:

$$(CH_3)_3CCH_2Br \text{ (A)} \qquad ClCH_2CH{=}CH_2 \text{ (B)} \qquad ClCH_2CH_2CH_3 \text{ (C)} \qquad BrCH_2CH_2CH_3 \text{ (D)}$$

▰   **B**, allylic, $>$ **D**, a bromide, $>$ **C**, a chloride, $>$ **A**, neopentyl, too hindered

14.26   (*a*) Starting with C_6H_6 and C_6H_5OH, synthesize phenyl 2,4-dinitrophenyl ether (**B**).   (*b*) Could we have first prepared and then nitrated Ph_2O?

▰   (*a*) $C_6H_6 \xrightarrow[AlCl_3]{Cl_2} C_6H_5Cl \xrightarrow{HNO_3} 2,4\text{-diNO}_2C_6H_3Cl \text{ (A)}$

$\qquad\qquad\qquad\qquad C_6H_5OH \xrightarrow{OH^-} C_6H_5O^- \quad \Big\}\longrightarrow 2,4\text{-diNO}_2C_6H_3OC_6H_5 \text{ (B)}$

The Cl of **A** undergoes aromatic nucleophilic displacement because it is activated by the two NO_2 groups (see Problem 11.80).   (*b*) The ring with the first nitro group is deactivated so that the second nitro group enters the other ring. The product is ($p\text{-}NO_2C_6H_4)_2O$.

14.27   How is diphenyl ether synthesized commercially?

▰   By heating PhO^- and $PhCl$ with Cu, without a solvent, at high temperatures (>200 °C). The reaction probably proceeds by a benzyne-type mechanism (see Problem 11.87). This Cu-catalyzed reaction is the *Ullmann* reaction (see Problem 11.140).

14.28   (*a*) Synthesize tetrahydrofuran using the Williamson synthesis.   (*b*) Through which conformation does the substrate react?   (*c*) What byproduct might one expect in this synthesis?   (*d*) Why is very little of this byproduct formed?

▰   (*a*) The S_N2 reaction to prepare cyclic ethers must be intramolecular. The number of C's separating X and OH in the chain is the number in the ring. In this case enough alkoxide ion can be formed by adding NaOH to the alcohol.

4-Chlorobutanol   an alkoxide intermediate   Tetrahydrofuran

The alkoxide intermediate may not be completely formed. The incipient anion can begin to displace Cl^- as it forms, a one step reaction.   (*b*) As shown in the equation in (*a*), the substrate must be in the highest energy-eclipsed conformation   (*c*) $HOCH_2CH_2CH_2CH_2OH$.   (*d*) Formation of the diol is a bimolecular displacement, which is slower than the intramolecular ring closure.

14.29   How might an alcohol rather than an alkoxide be used in the Williamson synthesis?

▰   Add Ag_2O which catalyzes the removal of the halide ion as AgX. The OH group of ROH is then a strong enough nucleophile to effect the displacement.

$$R{-}X + Ag^+ \text{ (from } Ag_2O) \longrightarrow [R^{\delta+}{-}{-}{-}X^{\delta-}{-}{-}{-}Ag^{\delta+}]^{+\ddagger} \xrightarrow[-H^+]{R'OH} R{-}O{-}R' + AgX$$

14.30   Give general equations for the S_N2 reactions of (*a*) dimethylsulfate (**A**) and (*b*) diazomethane (**B**) in synthesizing methyl ethers. In each case indicate the leaving group.

▰   (*a*) $RO^- + CH_3OSO_2OCH_3 \longrightarrow ROCH_3 + {}^-OSO_2OCH_3$ (leaving group)

$\qquad\qquad\qquad\qquad\qquad\quad$ **A** $\qquad\qquad\qquad\qquad\qquad$ Methyl sulfate anion

(*b*) $ROH + H_2\overset{\frown}{C}N_2 \xrightarrow{HBF_4} ROCH_3 + N_2$ (leaving group)

$\qquad\qquad\qquad\qquad\qquad\qquad$ **B**

The strong acid HBF_4 first protonates CH_2N_2 to give $CH_3N_2^+$ from which N_2 (an extremely good leaving group) is displaced, ROH serving as the nucleophile. Diazomethane is used in ethyl ether solution. This reagent is very toxic and explosive and should be used with extreme caution!

14.31 (*a*) How is di-*n*-propyl ether prepared industrially?   (*b*) Why is this reaction not suitable for preparing ethers from 2° or 3° alcohols?   (*c*) What product is formed when $HOCH_2CH_2CH_2CH_2OH$ is heated with conc. H_2SO_4?

◢   (*a*) A mixture of *n*-PrOH and conc. H_2SO_4 is heated to a temperature below that required to form propylene by intramolecular dehydration. Instead intermolecular dehydration occurs.

$$2\,PrOH \xrightarrow{\text{conc. }H_2SO_4} Pr-O-Pr + H_2O$$

The ether always has a lower B.P. than the parent alcohol and is distilled off as it forms.   (*b*) Under the reaction conditions used, the products are mainly alkenes (Problem 7.55).   (*c*) Tetrahydrofuran forms by loss of H_2O from the two OH groups in the same molecule. This is the best method for forming 5-membered ring cyclic ethers.

14.32 (*a*) Offer a mechanism for the intermolecular dehydration in Problem 14.31.   (*b*) What byproduct might be expected? How could its formation be minimized?

◢   (*a*)
$$Pr-OH \underset{\text{step 1}}{\overset{H^+}{\rightleftharpoons}} Pr-\overset{+}{OH_2} \xrightarrow[\text{step 2}]{HO-Pr} Pr-\overset{+}{\underset{H}{O}}-Pr \xrightarrow[\text{step 3}]{PrOH} Pr-O-(Pr + PrOH_2^+)$$

onium ion

Step 2 is an S_N2 displacement of H_2O by the nucleophile, PrOH.   (*b*) Propene. Formation of alkene is minimized by the continuous addition of PrOH to the warmed alcohol-sulfuric acid mixture.

14.33 (*a*) Explain why a nonsymmetrical ether is not usually prepared by heating a mixture of ROH and R′OH in acid.   (*b*) Why is it possible to prepare *t*-butyl ethyl ether by heating a mixture of *t*-butanol and ethanol?   (*c*) Would you get any di-*t*-butyl ether from this reaction? Explain.   (*d*) Can *t*-butyl ethyl ether be made by heating $H_2C=CH(CH_3)_2$ and ethanol?

◢   (*a*) A mixture of three ethers, R—O—R, R—O—R′, and R′—O—R′ is obtained.   (*b*) When one alcohol is 3°, its onium ion easily loses water to form a carbocation, which is solvated by the other 2° or 1° alcohol to give the mixed ether preferentially. This is an example of an S_N1 mechanism.

$$Me_3COH_2^+ \xrightarrow{-H_2O} Me_3C^+ \xrightarrow[-H^+]{HOCH_2CH_3} Me_3COCH_2CH_3$$

(*c*) No. *t*-Butanol does not solvate the 3° carbocation readily because of steric hindrance.   (*d*) Yes. The addition of H^+ to the alkene gives the same Me_3C^+ intermediate.

14.34 Give the general equation for the alkoxymercuration-demercuration (a type of solvomercuration-demercuration, Problems 7.90 and 13.15) reaction of $RCH=CH_2$ with R′OH.

◢
$$RCH=CH_2 + R'OH \xrightarrow[\text{2. }NaBH_4]{\text{1. }Hg(OCOCF_3)_2} RCH(OR')CH_3$$

14.35 Account mechanistically for the following facts observed in solvomercuration-demercurations: absence of rearrangement, Markovnikov addition, and *anti* addition of $Hg(OCOCF_3)_2$ and R′OH, a nucleophilic solvent.

◢   A carbocation is precluded because no rearrangement occurs in the first step. *Anti* addition and Markovnikov orientation are attributed to the formation of an intermediate *mercurinium ion* (Problem 7.91), which is attacked from the backside by R′OH, (rather than HOH) on the more substituted C of the ring since that C bears more δ^+. (Front-side attack is blocked by the large $HgOCOCF_3$ group). Although the mercuration step is stereospecific, the reductive demercuration with $NaBH_4$ in the second step is not, and therefore neither is the total reaction.

14.36 Give the alkene and alcohol needed to prepare each of the following ethers by alkoxymercuration-demercuration. List alternate pairs of compounds if applicable.   (*a*) Diisopropyl ether, (*b*) di-*sec*-butyl ether, (*c*) 1-methyl-1-methoxycyclohexane, (*d*) di-*t*-butyl ether, and (*e*) 1-phenyl-1-ethoxypropane.

◢   (*a*) $CH_2=CHCH_3 + CH_3CH(OH)CH_3$.   (*b*) $CH_3CH=CHCH_3$ (*cis* or *trans*) or $CH_2=CHCH_2CH_3 + CH_3CH(OH)CH_2CH_3$.   (*c*) Methylenecyclohexane or 1-methylcyclohexene + CH_3OH.   (*d*) $(CH_3)_2C=CH_2 + (CH_3)_3COH$. (The yields of ethers with two 3° alkyl groups are poor because of severe steric hindrance.)   (*e*) $PhCH=CHCH_3$ (*cis* or *trans*) + CH_3CH_2OH. Ethanol attacks the intermediate mercurinium ion at the more positively charged benzylic C. ($CH_2=CH_2 + PhCHOHCH_2CH_3$ can also give the desired product).

14.37 Use any needed starting material to synthesize the following ethers, selecting from among inter-molecular dehydration, Williamson synthesis, or alkoxymercuration-demercuration. Justify your choice of method. (*a*) $Me_2CHCH_2CH_2OCH_2CH_2CHMe_2$, (*b*) $Me_2CHCH_2OCH_2CH_2CH_3$, (*c*) $CH_3CH_2CH(CH_3)OCH_2CH_2CH_3$, (*d*) dicyclohexyl ether, and (*e*) $H_2C=CHOCH=CH_2$ (divinyl ether)

◢ (*a*) Dehydration of $Me_2CHCH_2CH_2OH$. It is a symmetrical ether with 1° R groups. (*b*) Williamson synthesis: $CH_3CH_2CH_2O^-Na^+ + Me_2CHCH_2Cl$ or $CH_3CH_2CH_2Cl + Me_2CHCH_2O^-Na^+$. It is a nonsymmetrical ether (dehydration gives mixtures) and both alkyl groups are 1°. (Oxymercuration-demercuration of either $Me_2C=CH_2$ or $CH_2=CHMe$ yields a different isomer in each case). (*c*) Williamson synthesis: $CH_3CH_2CH(CH_3)O^- + CH_3CH_2CH_2Cl$ (1°) or oxymercuration-demercuration of 1- or 2-butene (*cis* or *trans*) + $CH_3CH_2CH_2OH$. Propene cannot be used as the alkene because it would give the *i*-propyl ether rather than the *n*-propyl ether. (*d*) Oxymercuration-demercuration with cyclohexene and cyclohexanol. Although it is a symmetrical ether, dehydration cannot be used because intramolecualr dehydration of the 2° ROH would be the dominant reaction, giving mainly cyclohexene. (*e*) Vinylic alcohol $H_2C=CHOH$ cannot serve as a substrate because it is unstable and rearranges to $CH_3CH=O$. The double bond must be introduced after the ether linkage is formed. Intermolecular dehydration of $ClCH_2CH_2OH$ leads to $ClCH_2CH_2OCH_2CH_2Cl$, which is dehydrohalogenated to give the product.

14.38 Show steps in the syntheses of (*a*) $p\text{-}NO_2C_6H_4CH_2OC_2H_5$ (**A**), (*b*) $PhCH_2CH(OCH_3)CH_3$ (**B**), and (*c*) $2,4\text{-}(NO_2)_2C_6H_3O\text{-}n\text{-}C_3H_7$ (**C**). Available starting materials are PhH, $PhCH_3$, and any alcohol of three or fewer C's.

◢ (*a*)
$$C_6H_5CH_3 \xrightarrow{\text{HNO}_3}_{\text{H}_2\text{SO}_4} p\text{-}NO_2C_6H_4CH_3 \xrightarrow{\text{NBS}} p\text{-}NO_2C_6H_4CH_2Br \xrightarrow{\text{C}_2\text{H}_5\text{ONa}} \textbf{A}$$

(*b*)
$$PhH + HOCH_2CH=CH_2 \xrightarrow{\text{HF}} PhCH_2CH=CH_2 \xrightarrow[\text{2. NaBH}_4]{\text{1. Hg(OCOCF}_3)_2,\ \text{CH}_3\text{OH}} \textbf{B}$$

(*c*)
$$PhH \xrightarrow{\text{Cl}_2}_{\text{Fe}} PhCl \xrightarrow{\text{2HNO}_3}_{\text{H}_2\text{SO}_4} 2,4\text{-}(NO_2)_2C_6H_3Cl \xrightarrow{n\text{-C}_3\text{H}_7\text{ONa}} \textbf{C}$$

14.39 (*a*) Explain why attempts to prepare $CH_3CH_2CH_2OCH=CH_2$ (**A**) using $ClCH_2CH_2OH$ (**B**) or $ClCH=CH_2$ by any of the three standard methods in Problem 14.37 prove fruitless. (*b*) Give two methods for preparing **A** from starting materials with fewer C's.

◢ (*a*) Intermolecular dehydration cannot be used because **A** is a nonsymmetrical ether. Alkoxymercuration-demercuration of $CH_3CH=CH_2$ with **B** would give the *i*-propyl ether, and the alkoxymercuration of $ClCH=CH_2$ is inhibited because of the affinity of Hg^{2+} for Cl. The Williamson pathway is not viable for the following reasons:

(1) $$ClCH_2CH_2OH \xrightleftharpoons{\text{OH}^-} [ClCH_2CH_2O^-] \longrightarrow H_2C\underset{\underset{O}{\diagdown\diagup}}{-}CH_2 \text{(ethylene oxide)}$$

[Intramolecular Williamson (Problem 14.28)]

(2) $CH_3CH_2CH_2O^- + ClCH=CH_2$, a vinyl halide, does not react.

(3) $CH_3CH_2CH_2O^- + ClCH_2CH_2OH$ does not give $CH_3CH_2CH_2OCH_2CH_2OH$ (which could be dehydrated to give **A**). Instead, a Brönsted acid-base reaction occurs giving the epoxide.

(4) $CH_3CH_2CH_2O^-$ + $ClCH_2CH_2OH$ $\longrightarrow$
 stronger base stronger acid
 (inductive effect of Cl
 is acid-strengthening)

$CH_3CH_2CH_2OH$ + $ClCH_2CH_2O^-$ ($\longrightarrow$ ethylene oxide)
 weaker acid weaker base
 (inductive effect of Cl
 is base-weakening)

(*b*) (i) By nucleophilic addition of RO^- to acetylene (Problems 9.91 and 9.92).

$$HC\equiv CH + CH_3CH_2CH_2O^-Na^+ \xrightarrow{\text{OH}^-} \textbf{A}$$

(ii) By addition of X_2 in PrOH (solvent) to ethylene (equivalent to addition of PrOX).

$$H_2C=CH_2 + Br_2 + CH_3CH_2CH_2OH \xrightarrow{-\text{HBr}} BrCH_2CH_2OCH_2CH_2CH_3 \xrightarrow{\text{alc. KOH}} \textbf{A}$$

14.40 (*a*) Give a synthesis for di-*t*-butyl ether.   (*b*) Suggest a plausible mechanism.

◢   (*a*) $2Me_3C-Cl \xrightarrow{Ag_2CO_3} Me_3C-O-CMe_3$

(*b*) Ag^+ pulls off Cl^- leaving Me_3C^+ which reacts with CO_3^{2-} to give $Me_3C-OCO_2^-$ (**C**). **C** can lose CO_2 leaving Me_3CO^- which reacts with Me_3C^+ to give the product. Because of severe steric hindrance, the yield is poor.

14.41 Outline the steps in the following syntheses:
(*a*) $H_2C=CHCH_3$ (as the only organic reactant) $\longrightarrow$ $BrCH=CHCH_2OCH_2CH_2CH_3$ (**A**)
(*b*) $H_2C=CHCH_3$ and ethylene $\longrightarrow$ $CH_3CH_2CH_2CH_2OCH(CH_3)_2$ (**B**)
(*c*) $PhCH(CH_3)OCH(CH_3)Ph$ (**C**) from PhH and any aliphatic compound.

◢   (*a*) $H_2C=CHCH_3 \xrightarrow[\text{2. } H_2O_2,\, OH^-]{\text{1. } BH_3,\, THF} HOCH_2CH_2CH_3 \xrightarrow{BuLi} {}^-OCH_2CH_2CH_3$ (**D**)

$\downarrow$ NBS

$H_2C=CHCH_2Br \xrightarrow{Br_2} H_2CBrCHBrCH_2Br \xrightarrow{\text{alc. KOH}} BrCH=CHCH_2Br$ (**E**)

$\mathbf{D} + \mathbf{E}$ (allylic, not vinylic Br reacts) $\longrightarrow \mathbf{A}$

(*b*) $H_2C=CH_2$ $\begin{cases} \xrightarrow[\text{2. Mg}]{\text{1. HBr}} CH_3CH_2MgBr \\ \xrightarrow{PhCO_3H} \underset{H_2C-CH_2}{\overset{O}{\triangle}} \end{cases} \longrightarrow CH_3CH_2CH_2CH_2OH \xrightarrow{HBr} CH_3(CH_2)_3Br$ (**F**)

$H_2C=CHCH_3 \xrightarrow[H_2SO_4]{H_2O} (CH_3)_2CHOH \xrightarrow{BuLi} (CH_3)_2CHO^- \xrightarrow[-Br^-]{\mathbf{F}} \mathbf{B}$

(*c*) $PhH + CH_3CH_2Cl \xrightarrow{AlCl_3} PhCH_2CH_3 \xrightarrow{NBS} PhCHBrCH_3 \xrightarrow{\text{alc. KOH}} PhCH=CH_2$

$\downarrow$ aq. OH^-

$PhCH(OH)CH_3 + PhCH=CH_2 \xrightarrow[\text{2. } NaBH_4]{\text{1. } Hg(OCOCF_3)_2} \mathbf{C}$

Although the ether is symmetrical, dehydration of $PhCH(OH)CH_3$ cannot be used because it would readily undergo intermolecular dehydration to give the stable conjugated alkene, $PhCH=CH_2$.

14.42 (*a*) Give (i) a general equation for the synthesis of an α-chloroether and (ii) a specific synthesis of α-chloromethyl methyl ether.   (*b*) Give the product of each of the following reactions:

(i) $(CH_3)_2C=CH_2 + ClCH_2OCH_3 \xrightarrow{AlCl_3} \mathbf{A}$ and (ii) $PhCH_2MgCl + ClCH_2OCH_3 \longrightarrow \mathbf{B}$

◢ (*a*) (i) $\underset{\underset{H}{|}}{ROH} + R'C=O + HCl\,(g) \longrightarrow \underset{\underset{H}{|}}{ROCR'Cl}$ (an α-chloroether)

(ii) $CH_3OH + H_2C=O + HCl \longrightarrow H_3COCH_2Cl$

(*b*) (i) $\mathbf{A} = \underset{\underset{Cl}{|}}{(CH_3)_2CCH_2CH_2OCH_3}$. This is a Friedel–Crafts-type addition to a double bond.

(ii) $\mathbf{B} = PhCH_2CH_2OCH_3$. This is an organometallic coupling reaction.

4. Chemical Reactions

14.43 (*a*) Give a simple chemical test to distinguish an ether, e.g., $CH_3CH_2OCH_2CH_3$, and a hydrocarbon of comparable molecular weight, e.g., $CH_3CH_2CH_2CH_2CH_3$.   (*b*) Use an equation to show why ethers separate out from solution in conc. H_2SO_4 on addition of water.

▮ (a) Like H_2O and ROH, ethers are basic by virtue of the unshared pair of e^-'s on O. Consequently, ethers dissolve in conc. H_2SO_4 with evolution of much heat.

$$R\overset{..}{O}R + H_2SO_4 \longrightarrow \left[R_2\overset{..}{O}:H\right]^+ + HSO_4^-$$
$$\text{base}_1 \quad \text{acid}_2 \qquad\qquad \text{acid}_1 \quad\quad \text{base}_2$$

Alkanes do not dissolve, two layers appear, and of course no heat is evolved.

(b) Water is a stronger base than ether and removes the proton from R_2OH^+:

$$\left[R_2OH\right]^+ + H_2O \longrightarrow R_2O + H_3O^+$$
$$\text{acid}_1 \qquad \text{base}_2 \qquad \text{base}_1 \quad \text{acid}_2$$

14.44 (a) Why are ethers such as Et_2O used as solvents for (i) BF_3, and (ii) RMgBr? (b) Compare the Lewis basicities of tetrahydrofuran, ethyl ether, and diisopropyl ether and give your reasoning. (c) Define the terms *F*-strain and *B*-strain, using *n*-propyl ether.

▮ (a) Because of their unshared e^-'s, ethers are also Lewis bases capable of reacting with Lewis acids such as BF_3 and RMgBr to form coordinate covalent bonds.

(i) $$Et_2\overset{..}{O}: + BF_3 \longrightarrow Et_2\overset{..}{\underset{}{O}}:\overset{+}{B}F_3$$

(ii) $$2Et_2\overset{..}{O}: + RMgBr \longrightarrow Et_2O:\overset{\overset{\textstyle R}{|}}{\underset{\underset{\textstyle Br}{|}}{\overset{..}{Mg}}}:OEt_2$$

Note that two molecules of ether coordinate tetrahedrally with one Mg^{2+}.

(b) In addition to the amount of electron density on the nucleophilic site, steric affects also influence basicities. The greater the steric hindrance encountered in the formation of the coordinate bond, the weaker is the Lewis basicity. In tetrahydrofuran the R groups (the sides of the ring) are "tied back" leaving a very exposed O atom free to serve as a basic site. The 2° R groups in diisopropyl ether furnish more steric hindrance than do the 1° ethyl groups in ethyl ether. The order of decreasing Lewis basicity is thus tetrahydrofuran > ethyl ether > *i*-propyl ether.

(c) If the steric hindrance is generated in the *front* of the molecule in the path of the approaching Lewis acid, as shown for *n*-propyl ether in Fig. 14-2(*a*), this hindrance is called F-strain. If the steric hindrance arises in the *back* of the molecule away from the approaching Lewis acid, as shown for *n*-propyl ether in Fig. 14-2(*b*), it is called *B-strain*.

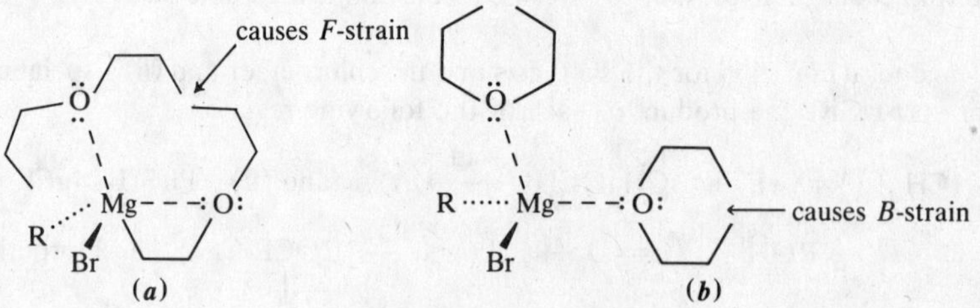

Fig. 14-2

14.45 Suggest two important synthetic uses of crown ethers.

▮ Crown ethers strongly complex metallic cations of salts in the interior (the "hole") of the ring by forming ion-dipole bonds. 18-Crown-6 (see Problem 14.13) strongly complexes and traps K^+ as shown in Fig. 14-3. In nonpolar or weakly polar solvents, salts exist as ion-pairs. Ion-pairing diminishes the reactivity of the anion which is intended to act as a nucleophile in some organic reaction. By complexing the cation, the crown ether leaves a

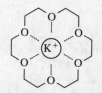

Fig. 14-3

"bare" anion with a greatly enhanced reactivity. Moreover, the crown ether acts as a *phase-transfer catalyst* by transfering an ionic salt from an aqueous medium or from a solid into a weakly polar solvent. Different size crown ethers can be tailor-made to complex different-sized cations.

14.46 Give the product(s) from the reaction of one mole of dibenzyl ether with (*a*) one mole of conc. HI and (*b*) excess of HI.

▰ Ethers are cleaved by conc. HI. (*a*) $PhCH_2OH + PhCH_2I$ and (*b*) $2PhCH_2I$. The initially formed $PhCH_2OH$ reacts with more HI to give a second mole of $PhCH_2I$.

14.47 Identify the ethers that are cleaved with excess conc. HI to yield (*a*) $(CH_3)_3CI$ and $CH_3CH_2CH_2I$, (*b*) cyclohexyl and methyl iodides, and (*c*) $I(CH_2)_5I$.

▰ Place an O atom between the C's bonded to the I's. (*a*) $(CH_3)_3COCH_2CH_2CH_3$, (*b*) cyclohexyl-O-Me, and (*c*) The presence of two I's in the same product indicates a cyclic ether, i.e., tetrahydropyran.

14.48 (*a*) Give S_N2 and S_N1 mechanisms for the cleavage of ethers with HI. (*b*) Why does S_N2 cleavage occur at a faster rate with HI than with HCl?

▰ (*a*) *Step 1*

$$R\!-\!O\!-\!R' + HI \longrightarrow R\!-\!\overset{+}{\underset{\underset{H}{|}}{O}}\!-\!R' + I^-$$

$$\text{base}_1 \qquad \text{acid}_2 \qquad\qquad \text{acid}_1 \qquad \text{base}_2$$

Step 2 for S_N2 $I^- + R\!-\!\overset{+}{\underset{\underset{H}{\overset{|}{O}}}{}}\!-\!R' \xrightarrow{\text{slow}} RI + HOR'$ (R is 1°)

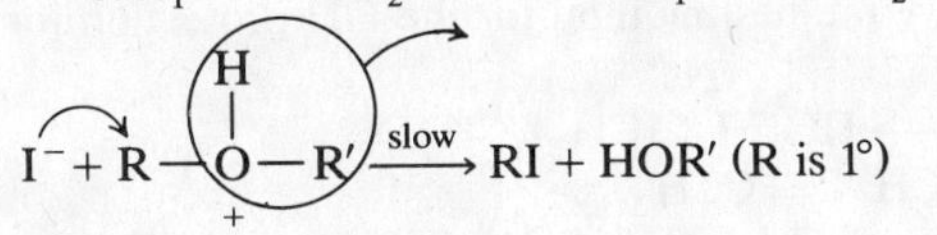

Step 2 for S_N1 $R\overset{+}{\underset{\underset{H}{|}}{O}}R' \xrightarrow{\text{slow}} R^+$ (R is 3°) $+ R'OH$

Step 3 for S_N1 $R^+ + I^- \longrightarrow RI$

(*b*) The transfer of H^+ to ROR' in step 1 is greater with HI, which is a stronger acid, than with HCl. Furthermore, in step 2, I^-, being a better nucleophile than Cl^-, reacts at a faster rate.

14.49 Account for the following observations:

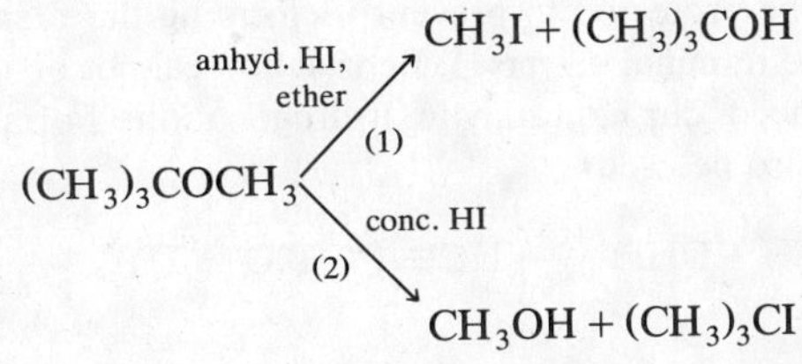

$$(CH_3)_3COCH_3 \begin{cases} \xrightarrow[\text{ether}]{\text{anhyd. HI,}} \; CH_3I + (CH_3)_3COH \quad (1) \\[2ex] \xrightarrow{\text{conc. HI}} \; CH_3OH + (CH_3)_3CI \quad (2) \end{cases}$$

▰ The high polarity of the solvent (H_2O) in reaction (2) favors an S_N1 mechanism giving the 3° R^+.

$$CH_3\overset{H}{\underset{+}{O}}C(CH_3)_3 \longrightarrow CH_3OH + (CH_3)_3C^+ \xrightarrow{I^-} (CH_3)_3CI$$

The low polarity of solvent (ether) in reaction (1) favors the S_N2 mechanism and the nucleophile, I^-, attacks the 1° C of CH_3.

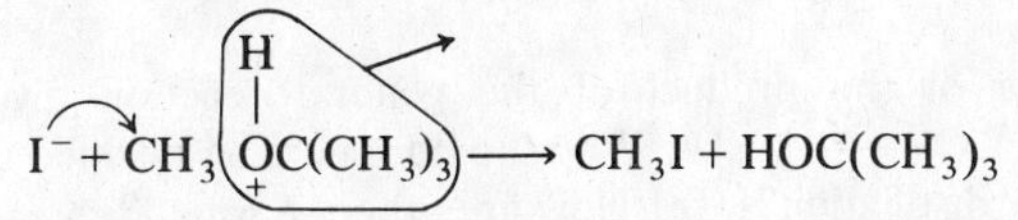

$$I^- + CH_3\overset{H}{\underset{+}{O}}C(CH_3)_3 \longrightarrow CH_3I + HOC(CH_3)_3$$

14.50 Explain why ArOR ethers are cleaved to give RI and ArOH rather than ArI and ROH.

▰ S_N2 attack on a C of a benzene ring does not occur nor does the high energy $C_6H_5^+$ form by an S_N1 reaction. Hence ArI cannot be a product even in an excess of conc. HI.

14.51 Give three methods for protecting the OH group of an alcohol by ether formation. In each case, indicate how the alcohol is liberated.

■ (1) Formation of tetrahydropyranyl ethers.

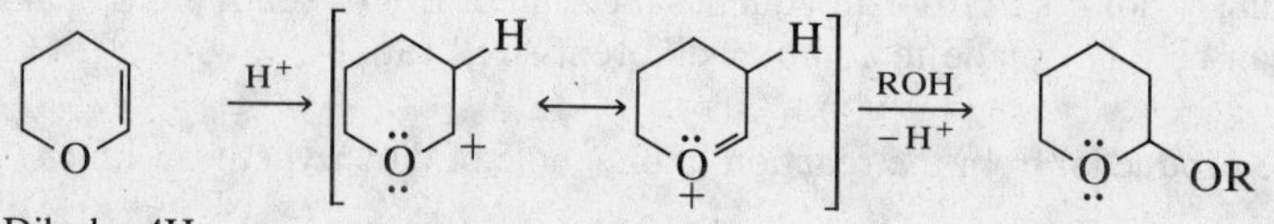

2,3-Dihydro-4H-pyran (DHP)

a tetrahydropyranyl ether (ROTHP)

followed by hydrolysis in aqueous acid: $ROTHP + H_2O \xrightarrow{H^+} ROH + DHP$.

(2) Formation of benzyl ethers (benzylation).

$$ROH + C_6H_5CH_2Br \xrightarrow{Ag_2O} C_6H_5CH_2OR \text{ (a benzyl ether)}$$

followed by catalytic hydrogenolysis: $C_6H_5CH_2OR \xrightarrow{H_2/Pd} C_6H_5CH_3 + ROH$.

(3) (a) Formation of silyl ethers

$$Me_3Si\text{—}Cl + ROH \xrightarrow{\text{amine base}} Me_3Si\text{—}OR$$

Chlorotrimethylsilane   a silyl ether

followed by hydrolysis with mild acid: $Me_3Si\text{—}OR \xrightarrow{\text{mild } H^+} ROH + Me_3Si\text{—}OH$.

14.52 Referring to Problem 14.51, give the best method for the OH protection for each of the following syntheses and rationalize your choice.
(a) $HOCH_2C(CH_3)_2CH_2Br \longrightarrow HOCH_2C(CH_3)_2CH_2D$
(b) $HOCH_2C\equiv CH \longrightarrow HOCH_2C\equiv CCH_3$
(c) $H_2C=CHC(CH_3)_2OH \longrightarrow BrCH_2CH_2C(CH_3)_2OH$

■ (a) ROTHP cannot be used because the alcohol would likely rearrange under the acidic conditions of the ether formation. Benzylation is not effective because the Ag_2O could react with the Br group of the reactant to give an OH group. Only silylation would give a good yield.

$$HOCH_2C(CH_3)_2CH_2Br + Me_3SiCl \longrightarrow Me_3Si\text{—}OCH_2C(CH_3)_2CH_2Br \xrightarrow[\text{2. } D_2O]{\text{1. Mg}}$$

$$H_2O + Me_3SiOCH_2C(CH_3)_2CH_2D \xrightarrow{\text{mild } H^+} HOCH_2C(CH_3)_2CH_2D + Me_3SiOH$$

(b) The OH must be protected to prevent its forming the reactive alkoxide anion during the attempted alkylation of the terminal alkyne H. Benzylation cannot be used because the $C\equiv C$, a typical π bond, would be reduced during catalytic hydrogenation. Formation of ROTHP is effective (although silylation may also be used).

$$HOCH_2C\equiv CH + DHP \xrightarrow{H^+} HC\equiv CCH_2O\text{—}THP \xrightarrow[\text{2. } CH_3I]{\text{1. BuLi}}$$

$$CH_3C\equiv CCH_2O\text{—}THP \xrightarrow{H^+} CH_3C\equiv CCH_2OH + DHP$$

(c) Benzylation can be used. The OH must be protected because it would be converted rapidly to Br (it is an allylic OH) when HBr (peroxide) is added.

$$H_2C=CHC(CH_3)_2OH + C_6H_5CH_2Br \xrightarrow{Ag_2O} H_2C=CHC(CH_3)_2OCH_2C_6H_5 \xrightarrow{\text{HBr, peroxide}}$$

$$BrCH_2CH_2C(CH_3)_2OCH_2C_6H_5 \xrightarrow{H_2/Pd} BrCH_2CH_2C(CH_3)_2OH + C_6H_5CH_3$$

14.53 (a) Write the structure of the product of the general reaction given and name the type of product: $RCH_2CH_2OCH_2CH_2R + O_2 \longrightarrow ?$ (b) Why should ethers be purified before being used in a synthesis where they must be removed by distillation? (c) How are ethers purified?

■ (a) $RCH_2\underset{\underset{OOH}{|}}{C}HOCH_2CH_2R$. ROOH compounds are hydroperoxides; this product is a hydroperoxide ether.

(b) Hydroperoxides, which are often solids, explode when heated or rubbed abrasively. The hydroperoxides are formed by long exposure of ethers to atmospheric O_2. They are dissolved in the ether, and are concentrated when the ether is purified by distillation. (c) Ethers are often purified by extraction with $FeSO_4$ solution, which reduces the —OOH group to the nonexplosive, innocuous —OH group.

14.54 Give a mechanism for the formation of the hydroperoxide in Problem 14.53.

▰ This reaction has a radical mechanism in which O_2, a diradical, is the initiator.

Initiation step: $RCH_2CH_2OCH_2CH_2R + \cdot \ddot{O}\!-\!\ddot{O}\cdot \longrightarrow RCH_2\dot{C}HOCH_2CH_2R + H\!:\!\ddot{O}\!-\!\ddot{O}\cdot$

Propagation step 1: $RCH_2\dot{C}HOCH_2CH_2R + \cdot\ddot{O}\!-\!\ddot{O}\cdot \longrightarrow RCH_2CHOCH_2CH_2R$

$$\underset{\textstyle :\ddot{O}-\ddot{O}\cdot}{\mid}$$

Propagation step 2: $RCH_2CHOCH_2CH_2R + RCH_2CH_2OCH_2CH_2R \longrightarrow$

$$\underset{\textstyle :\ddot{O}-\ddot{O}\cdot}{\mid}$$

$$RCH_2CHOCH_2CH_2R + RCH_2\dot{C}HOCH_2CH_2R$$
$$\underset{\textstyle OOH}{\mid}$$

14.55 (*a*) Write the structures of the products formed from a reaction of O_2 with (i) allyl n-propyl ether and (ii) benzyl n-propyl ether. (*b*) Explain why oxidation occurs to give the products.

▰ (*a*) (i) $\underset{\textstyle OOH}{H_2C\!=\!CHCH\!-\!O\!-\!CH_2CH_2CH_3}$ (ii) $\underset{\textstyle OOH}{PhCH\!-\!O\!-\!CH_2CH_2CH_3}$

(*b*) The intermediate radicals, allyl, $[H_2C\!=\!CH\dot{C}H\!-\!O\!-\!CH_2CH_2CH_3]$, in (i) and benzyl, $[Ph\dot{C}H\!-\!O\!-\!CH_2CH_2CH_3]$, in (ii), are more stable.

14.56 Which ether, *n*-propyl or *i*-propyl, is more prone to hydroperoxide formation?

▰ *i*-Propyl ether; its intermediate is the more stable 2° radical, $(CH_3)_2\dot{C}OCH(CH_3)_2$. *n*-Propyl ether forms a 1° radical, $CH_3CH_2\dot{C}HOCH_2CH_2CH_3$.

14.57 Give the *major* products of (*a*) mononitration of *p*-methylanisole and (*b*) monobromination of *p*-ethoxyphenol.

▰ (*a*) Since OR is a stronger activator than R towards electrophilic substitution, NO_2^+ attacks *ortho* to $-OCH_3$, giving 2-nitro-4-methylanisole. (*b*) OH is a somewhat stronger activator than OR; 2-bromo-4-ethoxyphenol is the major product but some of the 3-Br isomer is formed.

14.58 Distinguish ethers from alcohols by (*a*) two simple chemical tests and (*b*) one spectral method.

▰ (*a*) 1° and 2° alcohols are oxidizable and give positive tests with $K_2Cr_2O_7$ in acid (orange color turns green). *Dry* alcohols (including 3°) of moderate molecular weights readily evolve H_2 gas on addition of Na. All alcohols emit a gas (ethane) when EtMgBr is added. Dry ethers give negative results to both tests. (*b*) When taken in dilute solutions, the IR spectra of alcohols, but *not* ethers, show an $O-H$ stretching band at $\approx 3500\ cm^{-1}$. Comparing the IR spectra is the best way to spectroscopically distinguish these functional groups.

EPOXIDES (OXIRANES)

14.59 The enthalpies of combustion of isomeric 1,2-epoxybutane and tetrahydrofuran are 597.8 and 609.1 kcal/mol, respectively. Assign the heats to the respective compounds.

▰ The epoxide has the higher value because the three-membered ring is more strained.

14.60 Give two syntheses of propylene oxide from propylene.

▰ (*1*) Add a peroxy acid, $\overset{\textstyle O}{\overset{\textstyle \|}{RC}}-OOH$ to $CH_3CH\!=\!CH_2$. Any of the following, F_3CCO_3H, $PhCO_3H$, CH_3CO_3H, $m\text{-}Cl\!-\!C_6H_4CO_3H$ (*m*-chloroperoxybenzoic acid, MCPBA), are suitable.

(*2*) $CH_3CH\!=\!CH_2 \xrightarrow{Cl_2,\,H_2O} CH_3CH(OH)CH_2Cl \xrightarrow{aq.\,NaOH}$ product

14.61 (*a*) Give the stereochemical structures and names of the epoxides formed from the reaction of MCPBA (**A**) (Problem 14.60) with (i) *cis*- and (ii) *trans*-2-butene. (*b*) Discuss the stereochemistry of the epoxidation. (*c*) Why is a carbocation *not* an intermediate? (*d*) Give the mechanism (use ArCOOOH for **A**).

(a) (i)

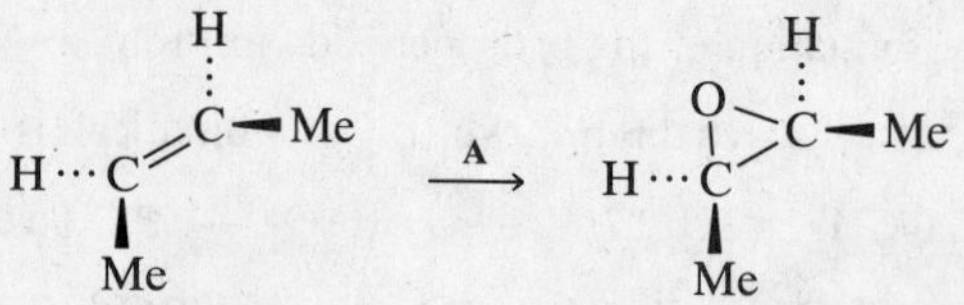

cis-2-Butene → cis-2,3-Butene oxide

(ii)

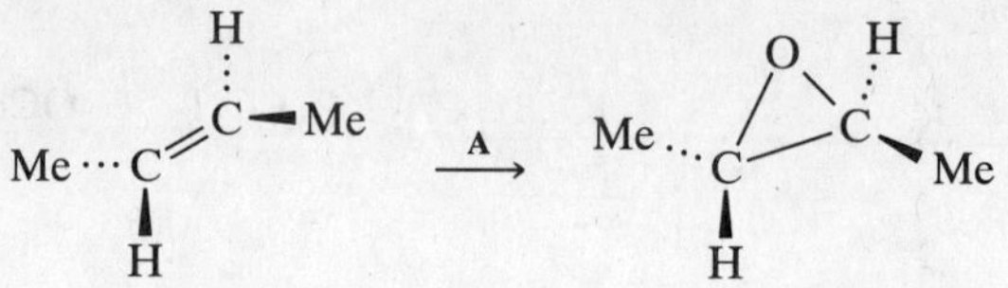

trans-2-Butene → trans-2,3-Butene oxide

(b) The stereochemistry of the alkene is retained in the epoxide. This is a stereospecific reaction.

(c) The *cis*- and *trans*-alkenes would give the same carbocation which then would proceed to give the *same* product(s).

(d) The mechanism involves an S_N2 attack by the π electrons of the double bond on the O of the OH of the peroxyacid, displacing ArCOOH. The result is a transfer of O from ArCOOOH to C=C to give the epoxide.

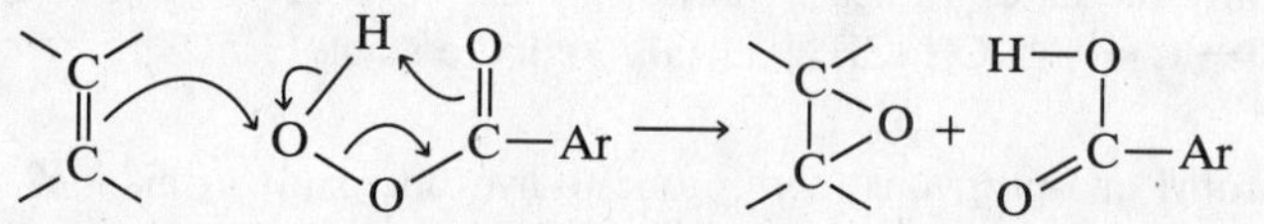

14.62 Suggest a mechanism for the conversion of a halohydrin, $>C(OH)—C(X)<$, to an epoxide.

▮ It is an intramolecular S_N2-type reaction that proceeds through an intermediate alkoxide anion.

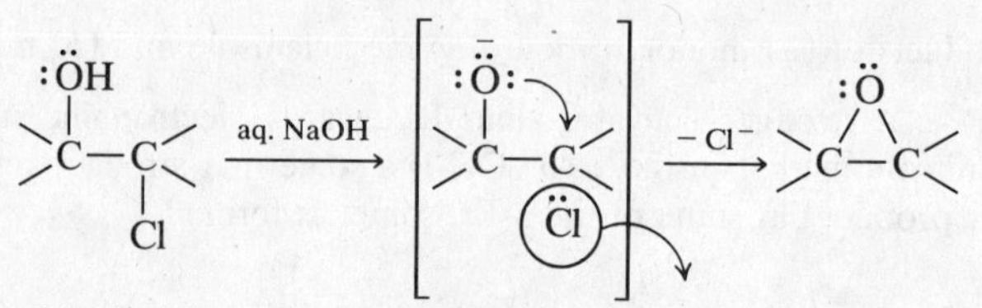

a chlorohydrin   an alkoxide anion   an epoxide

14.63 **(a)** Explain why *trans*-2-chlorocyclohexanol gives an excellent yield of epoxycyclohexane but the *cis*-isomer gives none. **(b)** What is the name given to this action of the O^- group?

▮ **(a)** Typical of all S_N2 displacements, the nucleophilic O^- must displace Cl (as Cl^-) by a back-side attack. In the *trans* isomer, O^- and Cl are properly positioned in the diaxial *anti*-coplanar conformation for such a displacement, and the epoxide is formed. In the *cis* isomer, O^- and Cl are not coplanar [one is (a) and the other is (e)], back-side attack is impossible, and no epoxide forms. **(b)** This role is called *neighboring group participation*. It has an S_N2-type transition state which always leads to inversion of configuration if the attacked C is a stereocenter.

14.64 What is the expected product from the reaction of the *cis*-isomer in Problem 14.63 with OH^-?

▮ In one conformation, the Cl and H^I are diaxial and coplanar, a situation that easily leads to dehydrochlorination. The product, a vinyl alcohol, rearranges to a ketone (Problem 9.76).

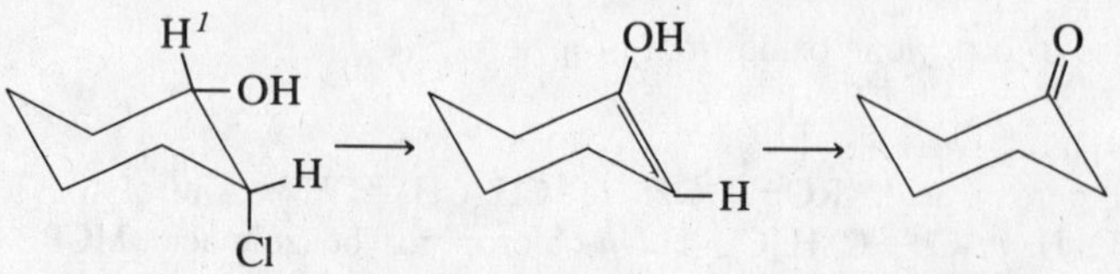

Cyclohexanone

14.65 **(a)** Give the product of the acid-catalyzed reaction of propylene oxide with (i) H_2O and (ii) MeOH. **(b)** What isomer of the product from (ii) is *not* formed in any reasonable yield? **(c)** Suggest a mechanism for the acid-catalyzed ring opening with MeOH. **(d)** Why do ring-openings of epoxides proceed at much faster rates than those of larger size cyclic ethers?

▰ (*a*) (i) $CH_3CH(OH)CH_2OH$ and (ii) $CH_3CH(OH)CH_2OMe$. (*b*) $CH_3CH(OMe)CH_2OH$. (*c*) The key steps are protonation of the epoxide followed by an S_N2 attack by the nucleophilic solvent molecule, MeOH, at the less hindered C:

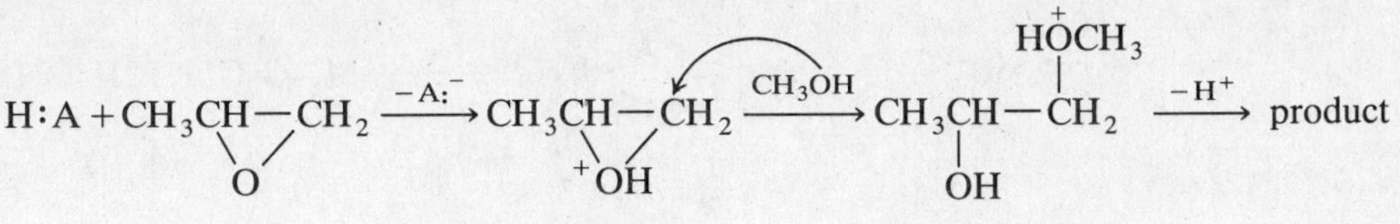

$$H:A + CH_3CH-CH_2 \xrightarrow{-A:^-} CH_3CH-CH_2 \xrightarrow{CH_3OH} CH_3CH-CH_2 \xrightarrow{-H^+} product$$

onium ion   protonated ether

We know that an S_N2 attack leads to the ring-opening because the nucleophile forms a bond to the less substituted C. Had it been an S_N1-type reaction, the nucleophile would have been attached to the more substituted C, giving the isomer in (*b*) that was not observed. (*d*) The strain in the three-membered ring (see Problem 14.59) induces less stability and greater reactivity than larger ring ethers.

14.66 (*a*) Give the products formed from the base-catalyzed reaction of CH_3CH-CH_2 (with O) with (i) aqueous NaOH and (ii) MeO^- in MeOH. (*b*) Suggest a mechanism for this base-catalyzed ring opening with MeO^-. (*c*) Why cannot MeOH cause ring-opening by itself in the absence of acid?

▰ (*a*) (i) $CH_3CH(OH)CH_2OH$, (ii) $CH_3CH(OH)CH_2OMe$. Note that the products in both the acid and base-catalyzed reactions are the same.

(*b*) $$CH_3CH-CH_2 + {}^-OMe \longrightarrow CH_3CH-CH_2OMe \xrightarrow{MeOH} CH_3CH(OH)CH_2OMe (+ {}^-OMe)$$

(with O)   (with O^-)

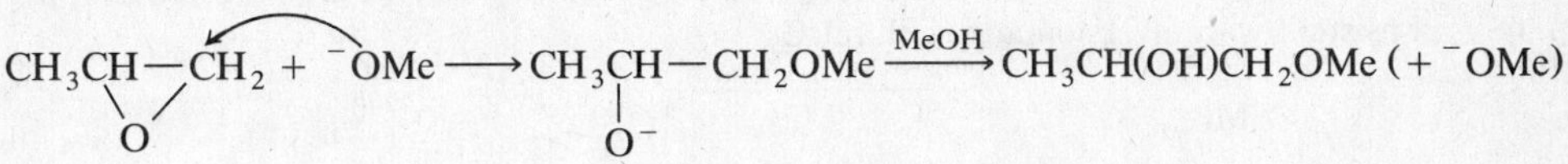

(*c*) In the absence of acid, MeOH, an extremely weak base, would have to displace the strongly basic alkoxy oxygen, $-O^-$, on ring-opening. This reaction cannot occur. In acid, the weakly basic $-OH$ group formed from protonation of the O atom of the epoxide is displaced as part of the alcohol portion of the product. This reaction can occur.

14.67 (*a*) Give the product and show the mechanism for the reaction of EtMgBr with ethylene oxide. (*b*) What is the synthetic utility of the reaction of RMgX or RLi with ethylene oxide?

▰ (*a*) This is an S_N2 reaction in which the R group of the Grignard acts as the nucleophile while the MgBr coordinates with the O.

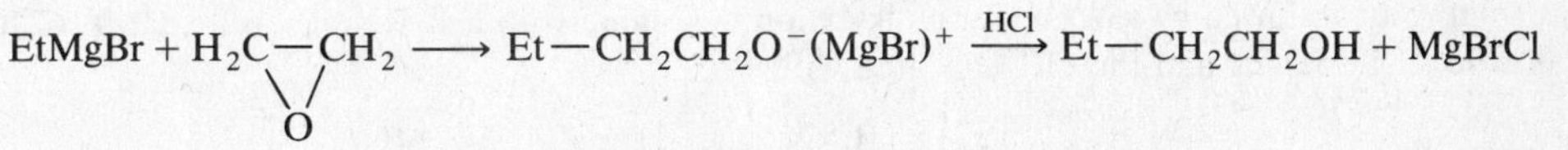

$$EtMgBr + H_2C-CH_2 \longrightarrow Et-CH_2CH_2O^-(MgBr)^+ \xrightarrow{HCl} Et-CH_2CH_2OH + MgBrCl$$

(with O)

(*b*) It is a good method for extending the R group of the organometallic by $-CH_2CH_2OH$ in one step $(RX \longrightarrow RCH_2CH_2OH)$. It avoids using $H_2C=O$ twice.

14.68 Account for the ^{14}C-labeled product from the following reaction:

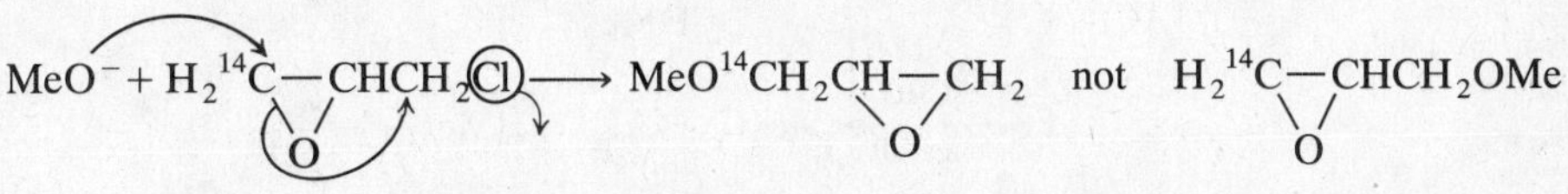

$$MeO^- + H_2{}^{14}C-CHCH_2Cl \longrightarrow MeO^{14}CH_2CH-CH_2 \quad not \quad H_2{}^{14}C-CHCH_2OMe$$

(with O)   (with O)   (with O)

▰ This is not a direct Williamson reaction. Instead the reaction is initiated by an S_N2 displacement by CH_3O^- on the less substituted ^{14}C of the epoxide, giving an intermediate alkoxide ion. The O^- then acts as a neighboring group participant to displace Cl^- by a second S_N2 reaction, forming the product.

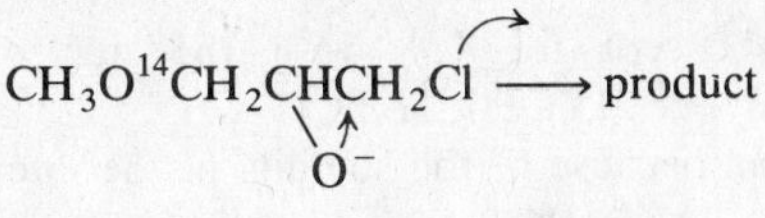

$$CH_3O^{14}CH_2CHCH_2Cl \longrightarrow product$$

(with O^-)

14.69 (*a*) Give the products formed when Me_2C-CH_2 (with O) reacts with MeOH in (i) acid, H^+, and (ii) base, MeO^-. (*b*) In terms of the mechanisms, explain why different isomers are formed.

◢ (a) (i) Me$_2$CH(OMe)CH$_2$OH and (ii) Me$_2$CH(OH)CH$_2$OMe. (b) In acid the protonated isobutylene oxide undergoes an S$_N$1-type ring-opening to give the more stable 3° carbocation which is then bonded to CH$_3$OH.

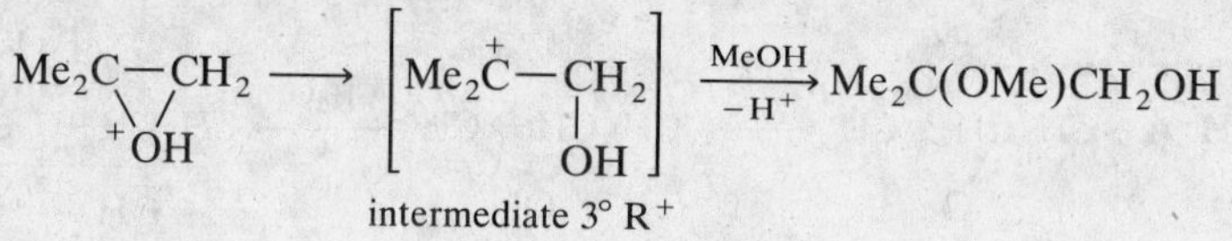

$$Me_2C\!-\!CH_2 \longrightarrow \left[Me_2\overset{+}{C}\!-\!CH_2 \right] \xrightarrow[-H^+]{MeOH} Me_2C(OMe)CH_2OH$$

$$\underset{+OH}{} \qquad\qquad \underset{OH}{}$$

intermediate 3° R$^+$

The base-catalyzed reaction proceeds in the typical S$_N$2 fashion with attack on CH$_2$.

14.70 Explain why (R)-CH$_3$CH$_2$C$-$CH$_2$ (A) reacts with CH$_3$OH in acid to give a mixture of optically pure

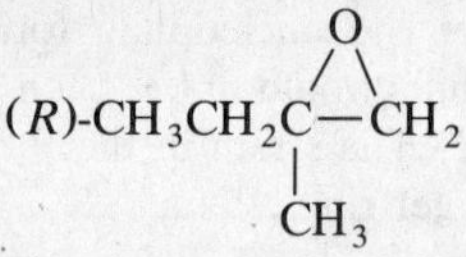

$$\overset{O}{\overset{\diagup\diagdown}{CH_3CH_2\underset{CH_3}{\overset{|}{C}}\!-\!CH_2}}$$

(R)-CH$_3$CH$_2$C(OH)CH$_2$OCH$_3$ (B) and (S)-CH$_3$CH$_2$C(OCH$_3$)CH$_2$OH (C) with very little racemization.

(B) $\underset{CH_3}{|}$ (C) $\underset{CH_3}{|}$

◢ **B** arises from an S$_N$2 reaction on the less substituted C of the ring. There is no change in the configuration or group priorities of the chiral C and the product is the R stereoisomer. **C** arises from an S$_N$1 ring-opening to give a 3° carbocation which undergoes bonding almost exclusively from the back side. This occurs because the OH group has not moved out of the way and blocks approach from the front side. It is likely that in the transition state for the S$_N$1 displacement, the leaving group has not completely left as the ROH approaches the C. Such a TS is consistent with inversion at the chiral C.

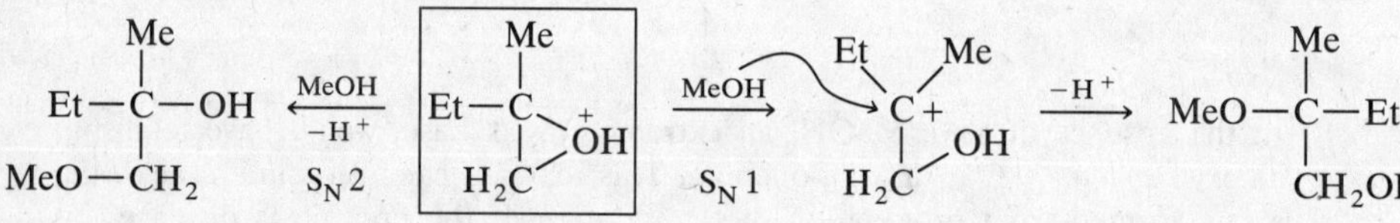

14.71 Synthesize (a) (CH$_3$)$_2$CCH$_2$OPr (D) and (b) (CH$_3$)$_2$CCH$_2$O-i-Pr$_2$ (E) from (CH$_3$)$_3$COH and any organic

$$\underset{O\text{-}i\text{-}Pr}{|} \qquad\qquad \underset{OPr}{|}$$

compound of three or fewer C's.

◢ Both compounds are best made from ring-opening of isobutylene oxide; **D** via an S$_N$1, and **E** via an S$_N$2 pathway, followed by a Williamson alkylation best done with a 1° RX. Therefore, Me$_2$CHOH should be used for the ring-opening and the OH alkylated with PrCl.

$$Me_3COH \xrightarrow{H_2SO_4} Me_2C\!=\!CH_2 \xrightarrow{ArCO_3H} \underset{\overset{|}{O}}{Me_2C\!-\!CH_2} \text{ (F)}$$

(a)

$$F \xrightarrow[Me_2CHOH]{H^+} \underset{OCHMe_2}{Me_2C\!-\!CH_2OH} \xrightarrow[2.\ PrCl]{1.\ NaH} D$$

(b)

$$F \xrightarrow[Me_2CHOH]{Me_2CHO^-} \underset{OH}{Me_2C\!-\!CH_2OCHMe_2} \xrightarrow[2.\ PrCl]{1.\ NaH} E$$

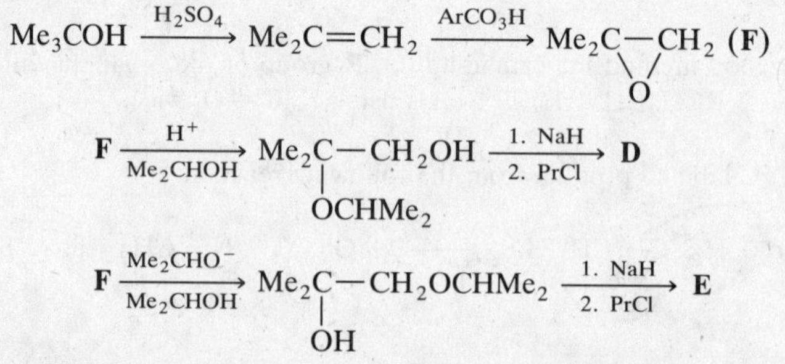

14.72 Give the products of the reactions of styrene oxide with (a) excess NH$_3$, (b) CH$_3$CH$_2$SH, followed by base, (c) dry HCl, (d) LiAlD$_4$, then H$_2$O, (e) aq. NaCN, and (f) aq. NaN$_3$.

◢ All are S$_N$2 reactions except for (c), with the nucleophile bonding to the less substituted C. (a) PhCH(OH)CH$_2$NH$_2$. (b) PhCH(OH)CH$_2$SCH$_2$CH$_3$. (c) PhCH(Cl)CH$_2$OH. This acid-catalyzed ring-opening has an S$_N$1 mechanism because of the stability of the intermediate benzyl carbocation, Ph$\overset{+}{C}$HCH$_2$OH. (d) PhCH(OH)CH$_2$D. (e) PhCH(OH)CH$_2$CN. (f) PhCH(OH)CH$_2$N$_3$.

14.73 Give structures of the major products of the reaction of 1-methyl-1,2-epoxycyclohexane (A) with (a) MeO$^-$ in MeOH and (b) H$_2$SO$_4$ in MeOH.

(a) This is an S_N2 reaction in which MeO^- forms a bond with the less substituted C.

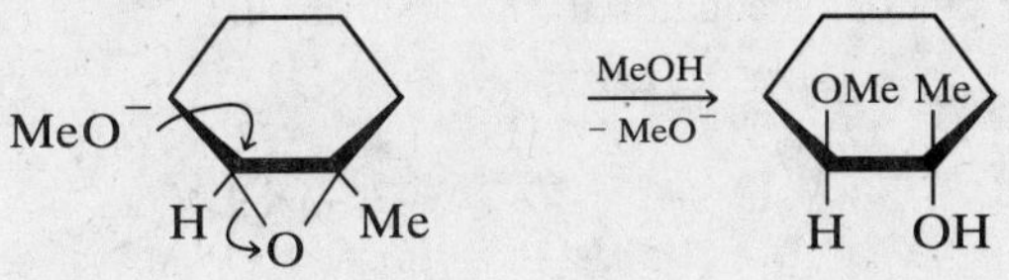

(b)

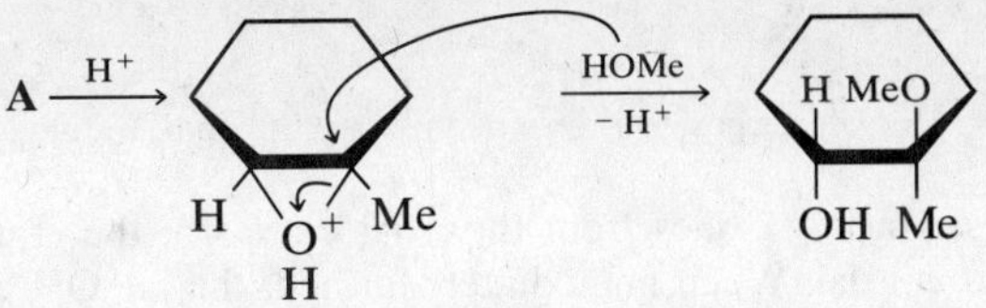

This is an S_N1 reaction in which CH_3OH bonds to the more substituted C.

14.74 Show how ethylene oxide is used to manufacture the following water soluble organic solvents:
- **(a)** Carbitol $(C_2H_5OCH_2CH_2OCH_2CH_2OH)$
- **(b)** Diethylene glycol $(HOCH_2CH_2OCH_2CH_2OH)$
- **(c)** Diethanolamine $(HOCH_2CH_2NHCH_2CH_2OH)$
- **(d)** 1,4-Dioxane [see Problem 14.10(c)]
- **(e)** 18-Crown-6

(a) $C_2H_5\overset{..}{\underset{..}{O}}H + H_2C\!-\!CH_2 \xrightarrow[]{\;H^+\;} C_2H_5OCH_2CH_2\overset{..}{O}H \longrightarrow C_2H_5OCH_2CH_2OCH_2CH_2OH$

(b) $H_2\overset{..}{\underset{..}{O}} + H_2C\!-\!CH_2 \xrightarrow{\;H^+\;} HOCH_2CH_2\overset{..}{\underset{..}{O}}H \longrightarrow HOCH_2CH_2OCH_2CH_2OH$

(c) $\overset{..}{N}H_3 + H_2C\!-\!CH_2 \longrightarrow HOCH_2CH_2\overset{..}{N}H_2 \longrightarrow HOCH_2CH_2\!-\!NH\!-\!CH_2CH_2OH$

(d)

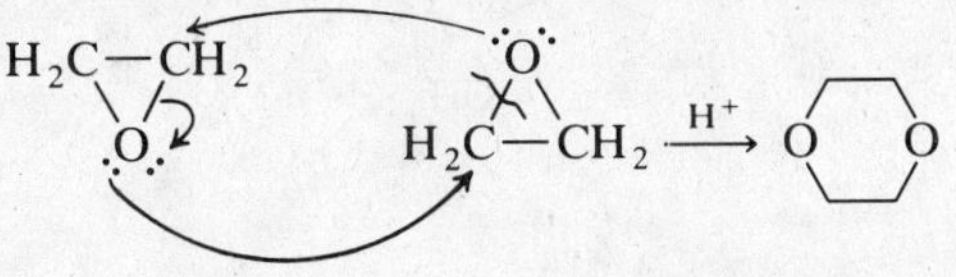

(e) $3H_2C\!-\!CH_2 \xrightarrow{\;HCl\;} HOCH_2CH_2OCH_2CH_2OCH_2CH_2OH\;(\mathbf{A}) \xrightarrow{\;HCl\;}$
$\qquad\qquad\underset{O}{}\qquad\qquad\qquad$ Triethylene glycol

$ClCH_2CH_2OCH_2CH_2OCH_2CH_2Cl\;(\mathbf{B}).$

Then $\mathbf{A} + \mathbf{B} \xrightarrow{\text{aq. KOH}}$ 18-crown-6.

14.75 From organic compounds of three or fewer C's prepare $cis\text{-}CH_3CH(OCH_3)CH_2CH\!=\!CHCH_3$ (**H**).

The precursor of a cis-alkene is an alkyne. Acetylides add to epoxides by an S_N2 pathway.

$CH_3CH\!-\!CH_2 \xrightarrow{\;{}^-C\equiv CCH_3\;} CH_3CHCH_2C\equiv CCH_3 \xrightarrow{\;CH_3I\;} CH_3CHC\equiv CCH_3 \xrightarrow{\;H_2/Pd/BaSO_4\;} \mathbf{H}$
$\qquad\underset{O}{}\qquad\qquad\qquad\underset{O^-}{|}\qquad\qquad\qquad\underset{OCH_3}{|}$

14.76 From benzene and any aliphatic compound prepare 1,2-diphenylethanol *via* styrene oxide.

$PhH + CH_3CH_2Cl \xrightarrow{\;AlCl_3\;} PhCH_2CH_3 \xrightarrow{\;NBS\;} PhCHBrCH_3 \xrightarrow{\;alc.\ KOH\;}$

$PhCH\!=\!CH_2 \xrightarrow{\;ArCOOOH\;} PhCH\!-\!CH_2 \xrightarrow[\;2.\ H_3O^+\;]{\;1.\ PhMgBr\;} PhCH(OH)CH_2Ph\ \text{(1,2-diphenylethanol)}$
$\qquad\qquad\qquad\qquad\qquad\underset{O}{}$

14.77 **(a)** Draw structures, labeling bonds (e) or (a) for the two isomers formed when 4-t-butylcyclohexene reacts with MCPBA. **(b)** Give the stereochemical structures of the products formed when the isomers in **(a)** react with (i) OH^-, (ii) $LiAlH_4$, and (iii) dry HBr, assuming that nucleophiles attack epoxides axially.

▮ (*a*) Two epoxides are formed, one *cis* and the other *trans* to the *t*-butyl group. In each, since the oxide ring is *cis*, one bond to the O atom is equatorial, the other axial.

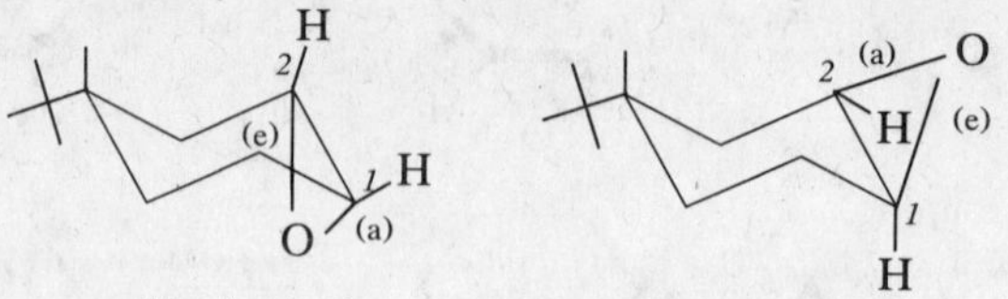

epoxide ring is *cis*   epoxide ring is *trans*

(*b*) Since nucleophiles attack epoxides from the axial direction, the equatorial C—O bond is broken and the remaining C—O bond is axial. When immediately formed, the *vic*-OH and nucleophile are axial and coplanar. When permitted, the ring flips to give the more stable diequatorial conformation. However, the bulky *t*-butyl group must be equatorial, thereby "freezing" the conformation. In the *cis* isomer the equatorial O—C^2 bond is broken; in the *trans* isomer the equatorial O—C^1 is broken.

(i)   Both isomers react with OH$^-$ to give the same diol product with *trans* diaxial OH's. The C^1 OH is *cis* and the C^2 OH is *trans* to the *t*-butyl group [Fig. 14-4(*a*)].

(ii) The nucleophile is considered to be H$^-$. *cis* epoxide ⟶ *cis*-4-*t*-butylcyclohexanol; *trans* ⟶ *trans*-3-*t*-butylcyclohexanol [Fig. 14-4(*b*)].

(iii) Br$^-$ is the nucleophile and the product is a bromohydrin. A different diastereomer is obtained from each epoxide [Fig. 14-4(*c*)].

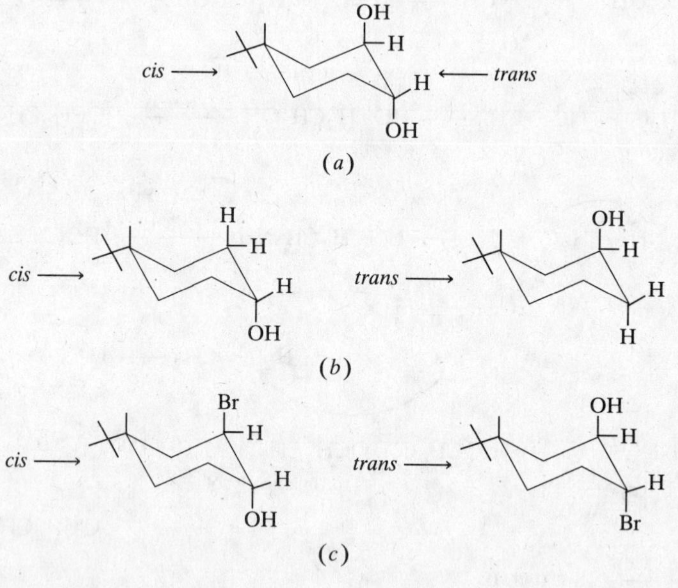

(*a*)

(*b*)

(*c*)   **Fig. 14-4**

14.78 Give the reactants for the following conversions: (*a*) 3-Methyl-1-butanol from ethylene oxide, and (*b*) 1-phenyl-cyclohexanol from 1-phenylcyclohexene oxide.

▮ (*a*) *i*-propylMgBr and (*b*) LiAlH$_4$.

14.79 Give the product of the reaction and account for the use of lithium organocuprate.

$$CH_2-CH-(CH_2)_8-C-CH_3 \xrightarrow[\text{2. H}_2\text{O}]{\text{1. (CH}_3)_2\text{CuLi, 1 mol}} ?$$

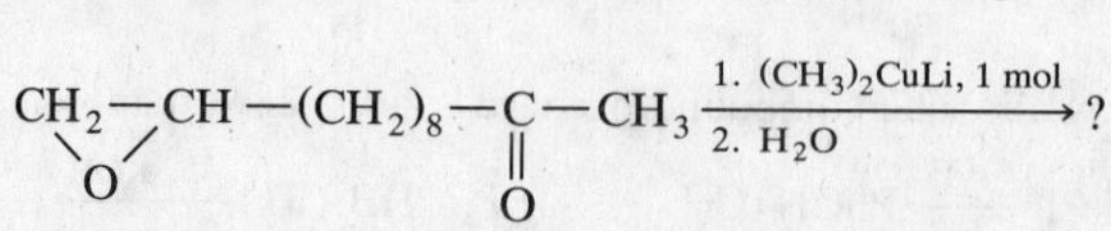

▮ Since lithium organocuprates are less reactive than organomagnesium compounds, the carbonyl group is unaffected. Reaction of one mole occurs exclusively at the epoxide ring. The product is

$$CH_3-CH_2-CH-(CH_2)_8-C-CH_3.$$
$$\quad\quad\quad\;\; OH \quad\quad\quad\quad\; O$$

14.80 Optically active $(2S,3R)$-3-bromo-2-butanol (**D**) reacts with KOH in MeOH to give **E**, an optically active epoxide. **E** is then treated with KOH in H_2O, giving 2,3-butanediol (**F**). (*a*) Write three-dimensional structures of **D**, **E**, and **F**. (*b*) Do you expect **F** to show optical rotation? Explain.

　▟ (*a*) **E** must be *trans*-butene-2-oxide; the *cis*-isomer has a plane of symmetry.

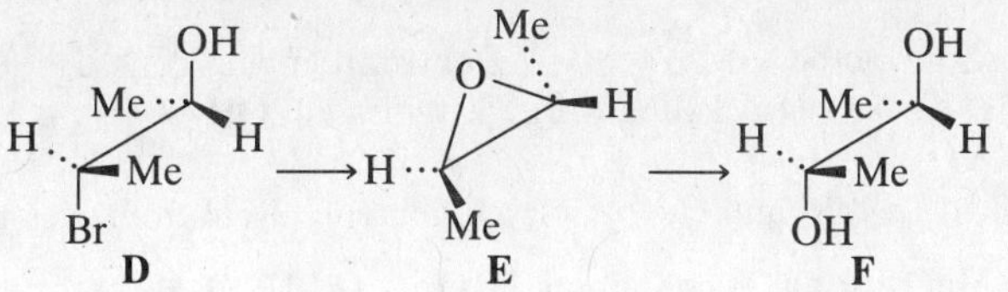

　(*b*) Ring-opening with OH^- is an S_N2 reaction, giving the inactive *meso*-glycol.

GLYCOLS

14.81 Write the structure of (*a*) propylene glycol, (*b*) glycerol (glycerin), (*c*) sorbitol, and (*d*) pentaerythritol.

　▟ (*a*) $CH_3CH(OH)CH_2OH$, (*b*) $HOCH_2CH(OH)CH_2OH$, (*c*) $HOCH_2(CHOH)_4CH_2OH$, and (*d*) $C(CH_2OH)_4$.

14.82 The ir spectrum of "neat" ethanol has a strong, broad band in the 3200 to 3600 cm^{-1} region, which changes to a sharp band in the 3610 to 3640 cm^{-1} region on dilution with CCl_4. On the other hand, ethylene glycol shows a broad band in the O—H region that is unrelated to concentration. Explain.

　▟ The band is broad because of the variable O—H stretching absorptions due to intermolecular H-bonding. As dilution increases, the molecules become separated and this H-bonding eventually disappears. In the glycol, intramolecular H-bonding is always present, regardless of dilution.

14.83 (*a*) Draw the conformational structures of the four isomeric 4-*t*-butyl-1,2-cyclohexane-diols. (*b*) Which isomer cannot H-bond intramolecularly? Why not?

　▟ (*a*) See Fig. 14-5. (*b*) **E**, because the two OH groups are diaxial and point away from each other.

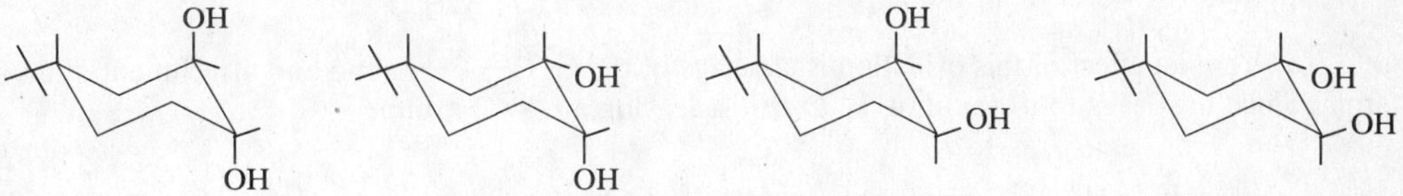

Fig. 14-5

14.84 (*a*) Explain why *cis*-1,3-cyclohexanediol has a greater fraction of its molecules in the diaxial conformation than does *cis*-1,3-dimethylcyclohexane. (*b*) Unlike the isomeric 1,2-dimethylcyclohexanes, the *cis*-1,2 diol is more stable than the *trans*. Explain.

　▟ (*a*) In the *cis* conformation the two OH's, pointing in the same direction, are close enough to H-bond, lowering the energy of this conformation somewhat (Fig. 14-6). Alkyl groups do not H-bond. (*b*) Since in the

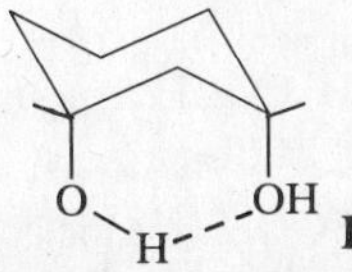

Fig. 14-6

cis-diol the two OH groups (a, e) are closer and form stronger H-bonds than those in the *trans*-diol (e, e), its energy is lowered relative to the *trans*-diol. Since Me's do not H-bond, an (e, a) conformer is not stabilized relative to the (e, e) conformer.

14.85 Prepare $HOCH_2CH_2OH$ from (*a*) ethylene, (*b*) ethanol, (*c*) ethylene oxide, and (*d*) 1,2-dibromoethane.

◢ (*a*) Oxidation with cold aq. $KMnO_4$. (*b*) Dehydration with conc. H_2SO_4, followed by oxidation as in (*a*). (*c*) Hydrolysis with H_3O^+. (*d*) Alkaline hydrolysis with aq. OH^-.

14.86 What reagent will yield (*a*) *cis*- and (*b*) *trans*-cyclopentene glycol from cyclopentene?

◢ (*a*) Cold aq. $KMnO_4$ or OsO_4 containing H_2O_2. (*b*) HCO_3H (peroxyformic acid) (Problem 7.108).

14.87 Give the structure of the glycol, called a *pinacol*, formed by the reductive coupling of each of the following using Mg in ether: (*a*) MeCOMe, (*b*) PhCOPh, and (*c*) PhCOMe.

◢ (*a*)
$$\underset{\text{HO} \quad \text{OH}}{Me_2C-CMe_2}$$
(*b*)
$$\underset{\text{HO} \quad \text{OH}}{Ph_2C-CPh_2}$$
(*c*)
$$\underset{\text{HO} \quad \text{OH}}{MeC(Ph)-C(Ph)Me}$$

14.88 (*a*) Give a mechanism for the bimolecular reductions in Problem 14.87. (*b*) What compound would you use to prepare the pinacol EtC(Ph)(OH)C(OH)(Ph)Et? (*c*) How many stereoisomers of the pinacol are possible?

◢ (*a*) Electron transfer occurs from Mg to the $\,{>}C{=}O$, giving a radical anion, or *ketyl*, followed by dimerization and hydrolysis:

$$2\,\overset{\ddot{O}}{\underset{}{R_2\overset{\|}{C}}} + \cdot Mg \cdot \longrightarrow \left[2\,R_2\overset{:\ddot{O}:^-}{\underset{}{\dot{C}}} + Mg^{2+} \right] \longrightarrow \left[\overset{Mg^{2+}}{\underset{R_2C-CR_2}{\overset{-:\ddot{O}:\;:\ddot{O}:^-}{|\quad\quad|}}} \right] \xrightarrow{2H_2O} \underset{R_2C-CR_2}{\overset{HO\quad OH}{|\quad\quad|}} + Mg(OH)_2$$

(*b*) PhCOEt. (*c*) There are two chiral centers. However, a plane of symmetry between C^2 and C^3 reduces the number of stereoisomers to three: one *meso* and one pair of enantiomers (*rac*).

14.89 (*a*) Predict the products of periodic acid (or lead tetraacetate) oxidation of (i) $HOCH_2CH_2OH$, (ii) $CH_3CH_2CH(OH)CH(OH)CH_2CH_3$, (iii) $PhCH_2CH(OH)CH(OH)CH_3$, and (iv) 1,2-cyclopentanediol. (*b*) Give the HIO_4-reduction product. (*c*) Use this reaction to test for 1,2-glycols.

◢ (*a*) The net effect of this oxidation is cleavage of the $\underset{\text{HO}\quad\text{OH}}{-\overset{|}{C}-\overset{|}{C}-}$ bond and attachment of an OH to each C atom. Since this leads to a *gem*-diol, H_2O is lost leaving a $C{=}O$ group.

$$-\underset{\text{HO}}{\overset{|}{\underset{|}{C^1}}}-\underset{\text{OH}}{\overset{|}{\underset{|}{C^2}}}- \longrightarrow -\underset{\text{HO}}{\overset{|}{\underset{|}{C^1}}}-OH + HO-\underset{\text{OH}}{\overset{|}{\underset{|}{C^2}}}- \longrightarrow -\overset{|}{C^1}{=}O + -\overset{|}{C^2}{=}O$$

(i) $2H_2C{=}O$ (ii) $2CH_3CH_2CH{=}O$ (iii) $PhCH_2CH{=}O + CH_3CH{=}O$

(iv) $O{=}CH(CH_2)_3CH{=}O$

(*b*) HIO_3. (*c*) Add Ag^+; a precipitate of $AgIO_3$ forms. One mole of HIO_4 is consumed for cleavage of the C—C bond and oxidation of the C—O bond to the next higher state.

14.90 Identify the compound that gives each of the following products on oxidative cleavage with HIO_4.

(*a*) $PhCH{=}O + CH_3COCH_3$ (*b*) Cyclopentanone + $H_2C{=}O$

(*c*) $2H_2C{=}O + HCOOH$ (formic acid)

(a) PhCH(OH)C(OH)(CH$_3$)$_2$, (b)

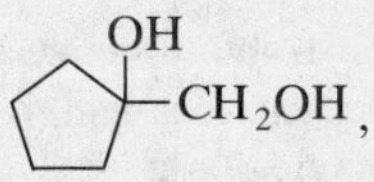

(c) HOCH$_2$CH(OH)CH$_2$OH, where HCOOH forms from the middle C.

14.91 (a) Give the ketonic product of the pinacol rearrangement of the following glycols in acid:

(a) Me$_2$C(OH)C(OH)Me$_2$ (b) PhCMe(OH)C(OH)MePh

(c) Ph$_2$C(OH)C(OH)MePh (d) PhCH(OH)CH(OH)Me

◢ (a) Me$_3$CCOMe, (b) Ph$_2$MeCCOMe, (c) Ph$_3$CCOMe, (d) PhCH$_2$COMe.

14.92 (a) Give a mechanism of the pinacol rearrangement consistent with the product formed in Problem 14.91(c). (b) Write the structure for the intermediate carbocation for Problem 14.91(d) and show how the product is formed. (c) From the products in (c) and (d) of Problem 14.91, give the relative migratory aptitudes (*ease of migration*) for Ar, R, and H.

◢ (a)

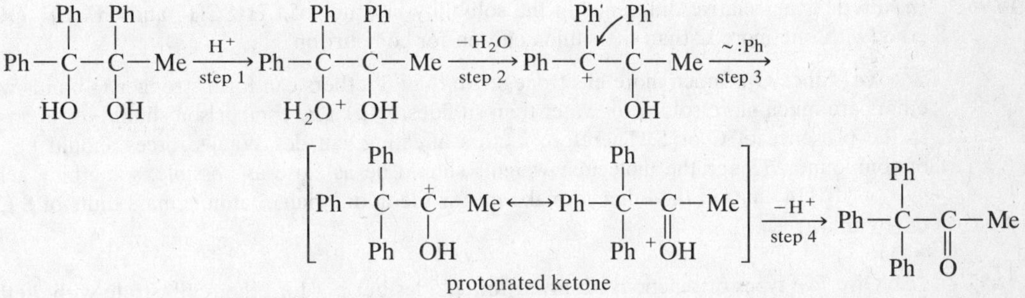

With nonsymmetrical glycols, the product obtained is determined mainly by which OH is lost as H$_2$O to give the more stable carbocation, and thereafter by which is the better migrating group. Although protonation of either OH can occur, the more stable 3° C$^+$ is formed (two Ph's vs. one Ph and one Me) in step 2. In step 3, Ph rather than Me migrates to form the product.

(b)

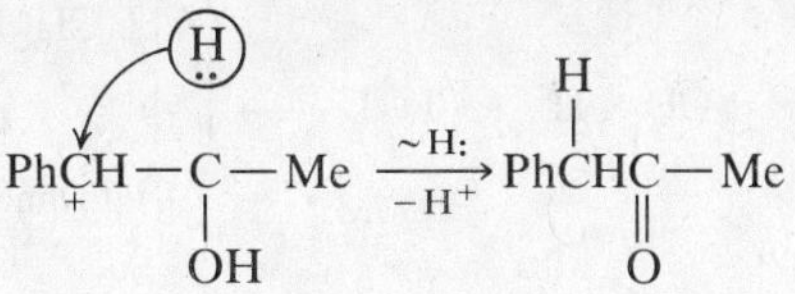

(c) The order of *migratory aptitudes* is Ar ≫ H > R.

THIOETHERS (SULFIDES) AND THEIR DERIVATIVES

14.93 (a) Give three ways of naming (CH$_3$)$_2$CHSCH$_2$CH$_2$CH$_2$CH$_3$. (b) Name:

(i) CH$_3$SCH$_2$CH$_2$CH$_2$OH (ii) PhSCH$_2$CH$_3$ (iii) ClCH$_2$CH$_2$SCH$_2$CH$_2$Cl

(iv) CH$_3$SCH(CH$_3$)SCH$_3$ (v) 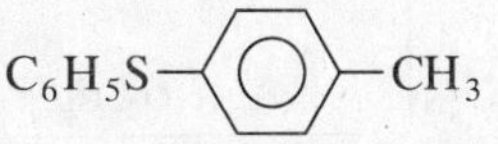 C$_6$H$_5$S—⬡—CH$_3$ (vi) 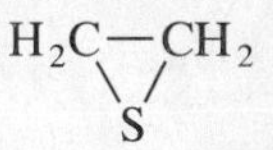 H$_2$C—CH$_2$ \ S /

(vii) 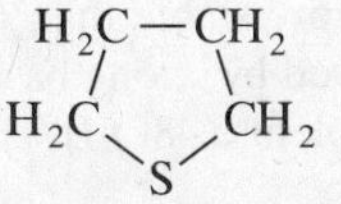 H$_2$C—CH$_2$ / H$_2$C CH$_2$ \ S /

◢ (a) The common name as a sulfide (similar to naming an ether) is *n*-butyl isopropyl thioether; as an alkylthioalkane, the IUPAC name is 1-isopropylthiobutane; the *thia* method, like the oxa method for ethers (see Problem 14.7), gives 2-methyl-3-thiaheptane. (b) (i) 3-Methylthio-1-propanol (OH has priority). (ii) Ethyl phenyl sulfide or ethylthiobenzene or thiophenetole. (iii) Bis(2-chloroethyl) sulfide, commonly called mustard gas, a powerful vesicant used as a poisonous gas. (iv) 3-Methyl-2,4-dithiapentane. The thia method is best used for compounds with more than one sulfide linkage. (v) Phenyl *p*-tolyl sulfide. (vi) Ethylene episulfide or thirane. (vii) Tetrahydrothiophene or thiolane or thiacyclopentane (see Problem 14.11).

14.94 Synthesize the following thioethers: (i) Isobutyl benzyl sulfide, (ii) dibenzyl sulfide, (iii) cyclohexyl phenyl sulfide, (iv) tetrahydrothiophene, (v) 1,4-dithiacyclohexane, (vi) 2,4-dinitrophenyl phenyl sulfide, (vii) t-butyl ethyl sulfide, (viii) di-t-butyl sulfide, (ix) i-butyl t-butyl sulfide.

◢ Analogous to the synthesis of ethers, sulfides may be made by Williamson reactions from RS^- or ArS^- and RX; (i) through (vii). Sulfides are also made by adding RSH to alkenes; (viii) and (ix). (i) $(CH_3)_2CHCH_2S^-$ (from RSH and OH^-) + $PhCH_2Cl$ or $(CH_3)_2CHCH_2Cl$ + $PhCH_2S^-$. (ii) Symmetrical sulfides are made from RX and Na_2S; $PhCH_2Cl$ + S^{2-}. (iii) PhS^- + chlorocyclohexane (no S_N2 displacement on nonactivated benzene rings). (iv) $ClCH_2CH_2CH_2CH_2Cl$ + 1 mol of S^{2-} from Na_2S. (v) $BrCH_2CH_2Br$ + $^-SCH_2CH_2S^-$ (from 1,2-ethane-dithiol and OH^-). (vi) 1-Chloro-2,4-dinitrobenzene + PhS^- (a nucleophilic aromatic substitution on an activated benzene ring). (vii) Me_3CS^- + EtBr. (viii) Markovnikov addition in conc. H_2SO_4; $Me_2C{=}CH_2$ + Me_3CSH. (ix) Same reagents in (viii) undergo anti-Markovnikov addition in presence of peroxides.

14.95 Give the main difference in using RS^- and RO^- as nucleophiles in S_N2 reactions.

◢ RS^- is a better nucleophile than RO^- and a much weaker base. Consequently, elimination with RS^- is not as serious a problem as with RO^-.

14.96 (*a*) Predict the relative difference in the solubility in water of CH_3SCH_3 and $CH_3CH_2OCH_3$. (*b*) Why is an ether with one more C than the sulfide chosen for comparison?

◢ (*a*) Since O is much more electronegative than S, ethers can form stronger H-bonds with H_2O. As a result, ethers are much more soluble in water than sulfides. (*b*) The comparison should focus on the differences owing to the presence of C or S. Therefore factors affecting van der Waal's forces should be similar in both types of compounds. Hence the molecular weights should be as close as possible, something achieved by having one more CH_2 (14 amu) in the ether to make up for the additional 16 atomic mass units of S (32 amu) compared to O (16 amu).

14.97 (*a*) Give five types of reactions observed for sulfides but not for ethers. Illustrate with diethyl sulfide. (*b*) Give two types of reactions observed for ethers but not for thioethers.

◢ (*a*) 1. Thioethers are much better nucleophiles and react with RX to give sulfonium salts.

$$CH_3CH_2SCH_2CH_3 + CH_3I \longrightarrow \left[\begin{array}{c} CH_3CH_2SCH_2CH_3 \\ | \\ CH_3 \end{array} \right]^+ I^- \text{ (sulfonium salt)}$$

Diethylmethylsulfonium
iodide

2. Thioethers are oxidized to *sulfoxides* and with excess oxidant to *sulfones*.

$$CH_3CH_2SCH_2CH_3 \xrightarrow[CH_3COOH]{H_2O_2} \underset{\underset{O}{\|}}{CH_3CH_2SCH_2CH_3} \xrightarrow[CH_3COOH]{H_2O_2} \overset{\overset{O}{\|}}{\underset{\underset{O}{\|}}{CH_3CH_2SCH_2CH_3}}$$

a sulfoxide ·   a sulfone
(diethyl sulfoxide)   (diethyl sulfone)

excess H_2O_2, CH_3COOOH

Because of p-d π bonding, S—O bonds are much more stable than O—O bonds.

3. H's on C α to the S are sufficiently acidic to be removed by strong bases to give the corresponding carbanion which is stabilized by p-d π bonding [Problem 3.48(*f*)]. H's α to two S atoms have a more enhanced acidity (Problem 18.6).

$$CH_3CH_2SCH_2CH_3 \xrightarrow{BuLi} [CH_3CH_2S\ddot{C}HCH_3]^- Li^+$$

4. Chlorination on S:

$$CH_3CH_2SCH_2CH_3 + Cl_2(\text{in } CCl_4) \longrightarrow \overset{\overset{Cl}{|}}{[CH_3CH_2SCH_2CH_3]}^+ Cl^-$$

a chlorosulfonium salt

5. Desulfurization by hydrogenolysis with *Raney* Ni:

$$CH_3CH_2SCH_2CH_3 \xrightarrow{\text{Raney Ni (H}_2\text{)}} 2CH_3CH_3 + H_2S$$

Raney Ni is prepared by adding conc. NaOH to a Ni/Al alloy. Al reacts emitting H_2 that is adsorbed by the unreacted Ni. The adsorbed H_2 hydrogenolyzes the C—S—C bonds.

(*b*) Since S is a much less basic site than O, thioethers are much less reactive towards acids in forming R_2SH^+. Partly as a result of this, sulfides are not cleaved by HI as are ethers.

14.98 Supply structures and names for compounds **A** through **K**. Different letters may indicate the same compound.

(*a*) $2CH_3CH_2CH_2Cl \xrightarrow{\text{Na}_2\text{S}_2} \textbf{A} \xrightarrow[\text{H}_2\text{SO}_4]{\text{Zn}} \textbf{B} \xrightarrow{\text{I}_2} \textbf{C} \xrightarrow[-20°\text{C}]{\text{Cl}_2} \textbf{D} \xrightarrow{\text{CH}_3\text{CH}_2\text{S}} \textbf{E}$; or $\textbf{C} \xrightarrow{\text{CH}_3\text{CH}_2\text{S}} \textbf{E}$

(*b*) $CH_3CH\!\!-\!\!CH_2 \xrightarrow{\text{KSCN}} \textbf{F} \xrightarrow[\text{2. H}_3\text{O}^+]{\text{1. PhMgBr}} \textbf{G}$; $\textbf{F} \xrightarrow[\text{2. H}_2\text{O}]{\text{1. LiAlH}_4} \textbf{H}$

(with O bridging)

(*c*) $CH_3SCH_3 \xrightarrow[100°\text{C}]{\text{H}_2\text{O}_2} \textbf{I} \xrightarrow{\text{C}_2\text{H}_5\text{O}^-} \textbf{J} \xrightarrow{\text{EtBr}} \textbf{K}$

◤ (*a*) **A** = $CH_3CH_2CH_2S$—$SCH_2CH_2CH_3$, dipropyl disulfide; **B** = $CH_3CH_2CH_2SH$, propanethiol (disulfides are reduced to thiols); **C** = **A** (thiols are oxidized to disulfides); **D** = $CH_3CH_2CH_2SCl$, propylsulfenyl chloride; **E** = $CH_3CH_2CH_2SSCH_2CH_3$, ethyl propyl disulfide (a preferred method to produce mixed disulfide).

(*b*) **F** = $CH_3CH\!\!-\!\!CH_2$, propylene episulfide; **G** = $CH_3CH(SH)CH_2Ph$, 1-phenyl-2-propanethiol; (with S bridging)

H = $CH_3CH(SH)CH_3$, 2-propanethiol. (Episulfides and epoxides undergo ring openings in the same manner.)

(*c*)
$$\textbf{I} = \begin{matrix} :O: \\ \| \\ H_3CSCH_3 \\ \| \\ :O: \end{matrix} \qquad \textbf{J} = \left[\begin{matrix} :O: \\ \| \\ H_3CSCH_2^- \\ \| \\ :O: \end{matrix} \longleftrightarrow \begin{matrix} :\ddot{O}:^- \\ \| \\ H_3CS\!=\!CH_2 \\ \| \\ :O: \end{matrix} \right] \qquad \textbf{K} = \begin{matrix} :O: \\ \| \\ H_3CSCH_2Et \\ \| \\ :O: \end{matrix}$$

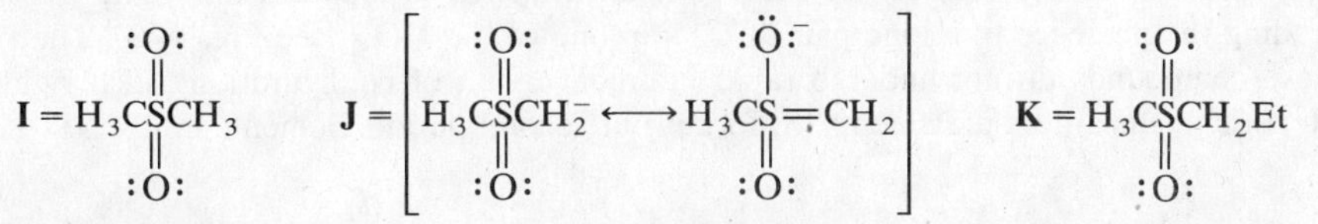

Dimethyl sulfone   a carbanion of dimethyl sulfone   Methyl propyl sulfone

The carbanion is stabilized by delocalization of the negative charge from the C to each O. One of several possible resonance structures shows the delocalization to one of the O atoms.

14.99 (*a*) Suggest a mechanism for the reaction $CH_3SCH_2CH_2Cl$ (**A**) $+ OH^- \longrightarrow CH_3SCH_2CH_2OH$ that is consistent with the following observations: (*1*) $\text{rate}_S = k_1$ [**A**] whereas, with the corresponding ether [$CH_3OCH_2CH_2Cl$ (**B**)], $\text{rate}_O = k_2$ [**B**] [OH^-]; (*2*) $\text{rate}_S \gg \text{rate}_O$; (*3*) $CH_3SCH_2CH(Cl)CH_3 \longrightarrow CH_3SCH(CH_3)CH_2OH$ (for the most part), not $CH_3SCH_2CH(OH)CH_3$. (*b*) Compare the rate of reaction of *trans*- and *cis*-1-chloro-2-(phenylthio)cyclohexane.

◤ (*a*) Unlike the ether that undergoes a typical S_N2 reaction, the thioether reacts in two steps. First the S atom of the sulfide acts as neighboring group participant to intramolecularly displace Cl⁻. This gives an intermediate cyclic sulfonium ion:

$$Step\ 1. \qquad \begin{matrix} H_2C\!\!-\!\!CH_2 + Cl^- \\ \diagdown \ \diagup \\ CH_3S^+ \end{matrix}$$

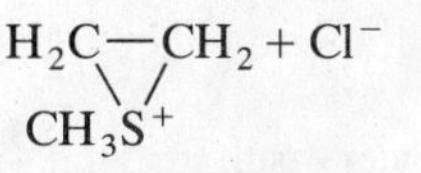

intermediate cyclic sulfonium ion

This unimolecular first step is rate-controlling, which accounts for first order kinetics and the faster rate than the bimolecular ether reaction. In the faster second step, the ring is opened by OH^- in a typical S_N2 manner:

$$Step\ 2\ (fast):\quad \text{sulfonium ion} + OH^- \longrightarrow \text{product}$$

In (*3*) the rearranged product is obtained because OH^- attacks the less substituted C of the episulfide ring. (*b*) Rate-enhancing neighboring group participation requires the participant and leaving group to be anti-coplanar. This geometry prevails only in the *trans* stereoisomer accounting for its faster rate compared with the *cis* isomer, which can only react by the slower S_N2 pathway.

14.100 (*a*) Give the two isomers that can result from the S_N2 methylation of $Me_2S\!=\!O$ (DMSO) with MeI. (*b*) What type of spectroscopy can be used to distinguish between the isomers? (*c*) Select the almost exclusive isomer and justify your choice.

▮ (a) DMSO is an ambident nucleophile owing to the presence of O and S with unshared pairs of electrons. The isomers are $[Me_3\overset{+}{S}=O]I^-$ (A), from S-methylation, and $[Me_2\overset{+}{S}-OMe]I^-$ (B), from O-methylation. (b) Use pmr spectroscopy. A shows a lone singlet because all of its H's are equivalent. Notice that ^{16}S has an even number of protons and neutrons and is nmr inactive. B has two different kinds of H's and two signals would be observed. (c) Since S is a better nucleophilic site, A is the major isomer.

14.101 (a) Give the equation for the preparation of methylcyclopropane by using A in Problem 14.100. (b) Which species in (a) is an example of an *ylid*?

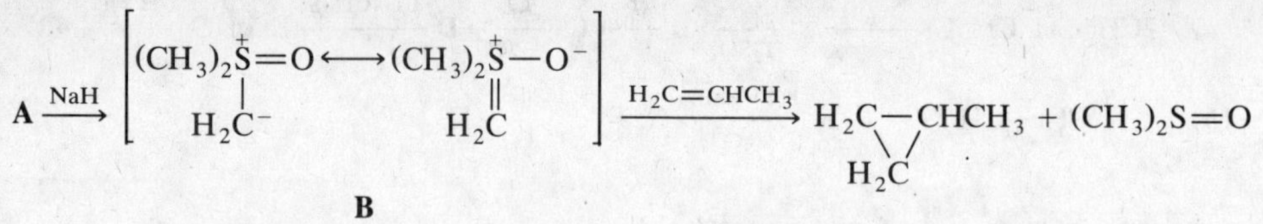

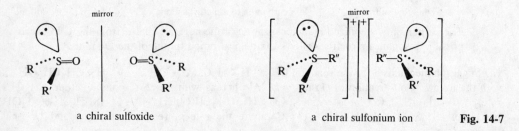

The H's of A are acidic and can be removed by a strong base (H^- of NaH) to give a stabilized carbanion as shown with contributing resonance structures. The last step can be conceived as an S_N2 displacement of DMSO, an excellent leaving group, by the π bond of the alkene on the carbanion carbon. (b) B is an *ylid* which is defined as a species with a negatively charged C bonded to a positively charged heteroatom.

14.102 (a) Explain why sulfonium salts and sulfoxides with different R or Ar groups attached to S are resolvable into enantiomers.

▮ Each compound has an S with an unshared pair of e⁻'s and three σ bonds. According to the HON rule (Problem 2.40), these S atoms use sp^3 HO's. If all attached groups are different, the S is a stereoatom, not withstanding the presence of a lone pair of e⁻'s in one of the HO's (see Fig. 14-7). Their resolvability indicates that these compounds do not undergo rapid interconversion of configuration. Such rigidity of configuration is characteristic of third-period elements (S, P) but not second-period elements of (C, N).

mirror

R····S=O   O=S····R

R'   R'

a chiral sulfoxide

R····S—R''   R''—S····R

R'   R'

a chiral sulfonium ion   **Fig. 14-7**

SUPPLEMENTARY PROBLEMS

14.103 Write the formulas of (a) ethylene sulfate, and (b) nitroglycerine, and explain why the latter commonly-used name is chemically incorrect.

▮ (a) Ethylene sulfate is an inorganic ester of ethylene glycol and sulfuric acid. The formula is

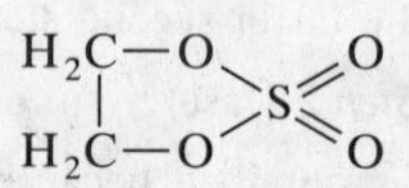

$$\begin{array}{c} H_2C-O \\ \quad\quad\quad\quad\ \ \diagdown \\ \quad\quad\quad\quad\ \ \ S \\ \quad\quad\quad\quad\ \ \diagup \\ H_2C-O \end{array} \begin{array}{c} \diagup O \\ \diagdown O \end{array}$$

(b) Glyceryl trinitrate, commonly-called nitroglycerin, is an ester of glycerol and HNO_3. The formula is

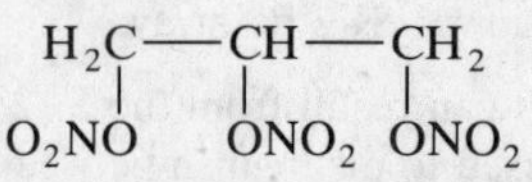

$$\begin{array}{ccc} H_2C & -CH- & CH_2 \\ | & | & | \\ O_2NO & ONO_2 & ONO_2 \end{array}$$

14.104 Starting with cyclohexane, synthesize *cis*- and *trans*-1,2-dimethoxycyclohexane.

Both syntheses require cyclohexene (C_6H_{10}): $C_6H_{12} \xrightarrow[hv]{Cl_2} C_6H_{11}Cl \xrightarrow[\text{alc.}]{KOH} C_6H_{10}$. Then

$$C_6H_{10} \begin{cases} \xrightarrow{\text{aq. KMnO}_4} \textit{cis}\text{-glycol} \xrightarrow[\text{OH}^-]{2Me_2SO_4} \textit{cis}\text{-1,2-dimethoxycyclohexane} \\ \xrightarrow[\substack{\text{1. Peroxyacid} \\ \text{2. H}_3\text{O}^+}]{} \textit{trans}\text{-glycol} \xrightarrow[\text{OH}^-]{2Me_2SO_4} \textit{trans}\text{-1,2-dimethoxycyclohexane} \end{cases}$$

14.105 From $CH_3CH{=}CH_2$ (**A**), synthesize (*a*) $(CH_3)_2CHOCH_2CH(CH_3)SO_2CH_2CH_2CH_3$ (**I**), and (*b*) 3-propoxyhexane (**J**).

(*a*) $\mathbf{A} \xrightarrow[\text{2. H}_2\text{O}_2,\ \text{OH}^-]{\text{1. B}_2\text{H}_6} CH_3CH_2CH_2OH$ (**B**); $\quad \mathbf{A} \xrightarrow[\text{2. NaBH}_4]{\text{1. Hg(OAc)}_2,\ \text{H}_2\text{O}} CH_3CH(OH)CH_3 \xrightarrow{\text{BuLi}} CH_3\overset{\overset{\displaystyle O^-}{|}}{C}HCH_3$ (**C**)

$\mathbf{A} \xrightarrow{\text{RCOOOH}} CH_3CH{-}CH_2 \text{ (over O)} \xrightarrow{\text{KCNS}} CH_3CH{-}CH_2$ (**D**) (over S);

$$\mathbf{C} + \mathbf{D} \longrightarrow CH_3CH{-}CH_2OCH(CH_3)_2 \text{ (} S^- \text{)} \quad (\mathbf{E})$$

$\mathbf{B} \xrightarrow{\text{HCl}} CH_3CH_2CH_2Cl$ (**F**); $\quad \mathbf{F} + \mathbf{E} \longrightarrow (CH_3)_2CHOCH_2CH(CH_3)SCH_2CH_2CH_3 \xrightarrow[\text{HOAc}]{\text{H}_2\text{O}_2} \mathbf{I}$

(*b*) $\mathbf{B} \xrightarrow[\text{Py}]{\text{CrO}_3} CH_3CH_2CH{=}O$ (**G**); $\quad \mathbf{F} \xrightarrow[\substack{\text{2. G} \\ \text{3. H}^+}]{\text{1. Mg}} CH_3CH_2CH(OH)CH_2CH_2CH_3$ (**H**) $\xrightarrow[\text{2. F}]{\text{1. BuLi}} \mathbf{J}$

14.106 Use nmr spectroscopy to distinguish (*a*) among $PhOCH_2CH_3$ (**A**), $PhCH_2OCH_3$ (**B**), $p\text{-}CH_3C_6H_4OCH_3$ (**C**), and (*b*) between cyclopropane and ethylene oxide.

(*a*) **A** has the characteristic ethyl splitting pattern, absent from **B** and **C**. The integration for aryl H's differs for **B** (five H's) and **C** (four H's). Also, **B** shows two benzylic H's, **C** integrates for three H's. (*b*) The singlet of ethylene oxide's H's is at the usual field strength for H in $H{-}C{-}OR$; the signal of cyclopropane's H's is very upfield, close to that of TMS.

14.107 Use mass spectrometry to distinguish between *n*-butyl ethyl ether (**D**) and methyl *n*-pentyl ether (**E**).

The parent P^+ for both ethers is $m/z = 102$. Fragmentations of P^+ ions of ethers occur mainly at the $\overset{\alpha}{C}{-}\overset{\beta}{C}$ bonds. Peaks for **D** would be at $m/z = 87$ for $H_2\overset{+}{C}{-}OCH_2CH_2CH_3$ and $m/z = 59$ for $CH_3CH_2O{-}CH_2^+$. The only cleavage of such a bond in **E** would give $CH_3O{-}CH_2^+$, $m/z = 45$.

14.108 Describe simple chemical tests to distinguish between (*a*) an ether and an alkyl bromide, (*b*) an ether and an alkene, (*c*) an ether and a 3° alcohol, and (*d*) divinyl ether and chloromethyl vinyl ether.

(*a*) The ether dissolves in conc. H_2SO_4, the halide does not. Alternatively, AgBr precipitates when alc. $AgNO_3$ is added to the halide. (*b*) Br_2 (in CCl_4) is decolorized by (reacts with) the alkene. (*c*) The *dry* alcohol liberates H_2 gas on addition of K. (*d*) The chloromethyl ether with $AgNO_3$ gives a precipitate of AgCl.

14.109 Predict the products of these reactions:

(*a*) $PrOH + Et_3O^+BF_4^- \longrightarrow$? (*c*) *cis*-1-Methyl-4-methoxycyclohexane + HI $\longrightarrow$?
Triethyloxonium
tetrafluoroborate
(Meerwein's reagent)

(*b*) $PhOCH_3 \xrightarrow[\text{2. H}_2\text{O}]{\text{1. BBr}_3}$? (*d*) Epoxide **A** $\xleftarrow{\text{MCPBA}}$ [norbornene] $\xrightarrow[\text{2. NaOH}]{\text{1. Br}_2/\text{H}_2\text{O}}$ epoxide **B**

(*a*) Trialkyloxonium salts are good alkylating agents; an S_N2 reaction occurs with the nucleophile, PrOH, displacing Et_2O, an excellent leaving group giving PrOEt + EtOEt + HBF_4.

(*b*) BBr_3 plays a similar role to the H in HI, by forming a complex with the ether, $PhMe\overset{+}{O}BBr_2Br^-$. The liberated Br^- attacks Me, displacing $PhOBBr_2$, which ultimately is hydrolyzed to give the products PhOH + MeBr + H_3BO_3.

(c) I⁻ attacks the Me of the protonated ether group, displacing *cis*-4-methylcyclohexanol with the retention of configuration + MeI.

(d) The axial-like encircled H's in Fig. 14-8 hinder endo approach of MCPBA; epoxide **A** is *exo*. The intermediate bromonium ion is also *exo*. It is opened by attack by H_2O from the *endo* side, giving a *trans* bromohydrin with the OH *endo*. This can only give rise to endo epoxide **B**.

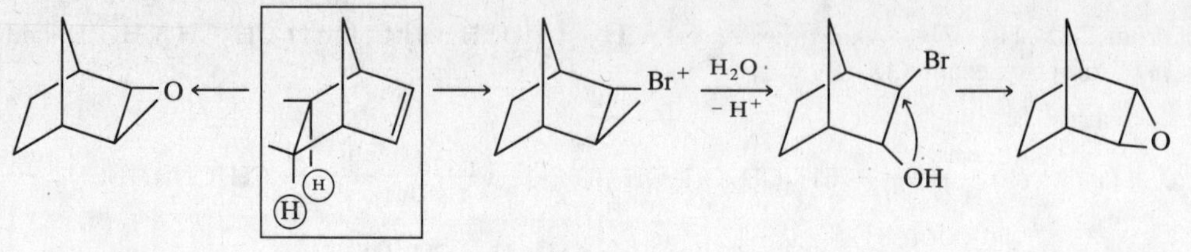

| *exo* epoxide **A** | Norbornene | a bromonium ion | Bromohydrin | *endo* epoxide **B** |

Fig. 14-8

14.110 Supply structural formulas for compounds **A** through **L**.

(a) $2\ H_2C{=}CH_2 + A \longrightarrow 2\ ClCH_2CH_2OH \xrightarrow{H_2SO_4} B \xrightarrow[\Delta]{alc.\ KOH} C$

(b) $Me_3CBr \xrightarrow{alc.\ KOH} D \xrightarrow{Cl_2/H_2O} E \xrightarrow{NaOH} F \xrightarrow[2.\ H_2O]{1.\ LiCHMe_2} G$

(c) $Propene \xrightarrow[h\nu]{Cl_2} H \xrightarrow{OH^-} I \xrightarrow{Cl_2/H_2O} J \xrightarrow[\Delta]{Ca(OH)_2} K \xrightarrow{H_3O^+} L\ (glycerol)$

▰ (a) **A** = aq. Cl_2; **B** = $ClCH_2CH_2OCH_2CH_2Cl$ (intermolecular dehydration); **C** is $CH_2{=}CHOCH{=}CH_2$ (dehydrohalogenation).

(b) $D = Me_2C{=}CH_2$; $E = Me_2C(OH)CH_2Cl$; $F = Me_2\overset{\displaystyle O}{\overset{\displaystyle \diagup\!\!\diagdown}{C{-}CH_2}}$; $G = Me_2C(OH)CH_2CHMe_2$.

(c) $H = CH_2{=}CHCH_2Cl$; $I = CH_2{=}CHCH_2OH$; $J = ClCH_2CH(OH)CH_2OH$;

$$K = H_2\overset{\displaystyle O}{\overset{\displaystyle \diagup\!\!\diagdown}{C{-}CHCH_2OH}};$$

$L = CH_2(OH)CH(OH)CH_2OH$. This sequence is the commercial synthesis of glycerol.

14.111 Give the names and structural formulas for **A** through **M**. In some cases more than one structural isomer may be possible for a given letter.

(a) Saturated ether (**A**) and unsaturated ether (**B**), each with the fewest C's that cannot be prepared by a Williamson synthesis.

(b) An ether, $C_6H_{14}O$ (**C**), reacts with excess HI to give a single alkyl iodide (**D**).

(c) A compound, $C_5H_{12}O_2$ (**E**) with no stereoatoms, reacts with conc. H_2SO_4 to give $C_5H_{10}O$ (**F**), which is inert towards $KMnO_4$.

(d) Optically active C_4H_8O (**G**) does not add H_2/Pt, and with H_3O^+ gives achiral $C_4H_{10}O_2$ (**H**).

(e) Optically active $C_5H_{12}O_2$ (**I**) reacts with Na and CH_3I to give optically inactive $C_6H_{14}O_2$ (**J**).

(f) *meso*-$C_5H_{10}S$ (**K**) with Raney Ni affords C_5H_{12} (**L**) with no stereoatoms.

(g) $C_5H_{10}S$ (**M**), with four stereoisomers, affords **L** with Raney Ni. **L** has no stereoisomers.

▰ (a) Both R groups must be 3°: **A** is $Me_3C{-}O{-}CMe_3$, di-*t*-butyl ether and **B** is $H_2C{=}CHOCH{=}CH_2$, divinyl ether. (b) Both R groups must be identical: **C** is di-*n*-propyl ether, Pr_2O, or di-isopropyl ether, *i*-Pr_2O and **D** is PrI or *i*-PrI. (c) **F** cannot be an alkene because it is inert to $KMnO_4$; it must be the cyclic ether tetrahydropyran [see Fig. 14-9(a)]. **E** is the diol 1,5-pentanediol, $HOH_2C(CH_2)_3CH_2OH$. **E** cannot be $HOCH_2C(CH_3)_2CH_2OH$ because this dineopentyl glycol would probably form an alkene via formation of a carbocation and a methyl shift, followed by elimination of H^+, and also cannot be $HOCH_2CH(CH_3)CH_2CH_2OH$ because it has a stereoatom. (d) **G** has 1° of unsaturation and is an epoxide [Fig. 14-9(b)]. It must be *trans*-butene-2-oxide, since the *cis* is achiral. The epoxide ring opens in

H_3O^+ to give *meso*-2,3,-dihydroxybutane (**H**) [Fig. 14-9(*c*)].   (*e*) **I** must be a monomethyl ether of a glycol, which loses its chirality upon methylation of the second OH group to form **J** [Fig. 14-9(*d*),(*e*)]. Another pair of possibilities is $HOCH_2CH(CH_3)CH_2OCH_3$ (**I′**) $\longrightarrow$ $CH_3OCH_2CH(CH_3)CH_2OCH_3$ (**J′**).   (*f*) **K** is a cyclic thioether and must be *cis*-2,4-dimethylthietane [Fig. 14-9(*f*)]. Raney Ni desulfurizes **K**, giving pentane, **L**. **K** cannot be 3,3-dimethylthietane because it has no stereoatom. Prove that it cannot be a dialkylepisulfide or a monoalkylthiacyclopentane.   (*g*) 4-Pentene-2-thiol, $CH_3CH{=}CHCH(SH)CH_3$ (**M**), exists as four stereoisomers: *cis-R* and *S*, and *trans-R* and *S*. Hydrogenation occurs along with desulfurization to give pentane, **L**.

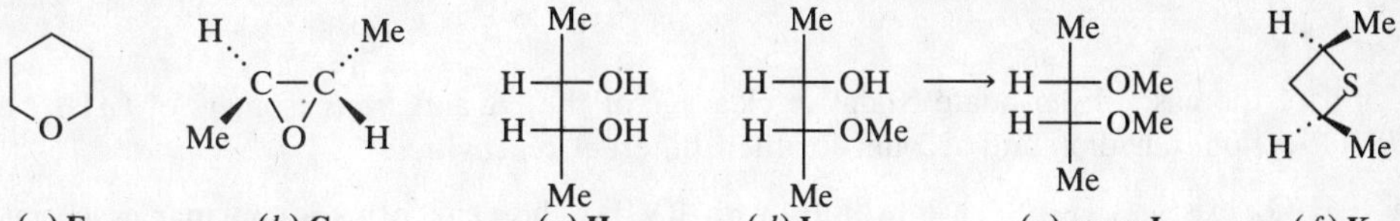

(*a*) **F**   (*b*) **G**   (*c*) **H**   (*d*) **I**   (*e*) *meso*-**J**   (*f*) **K**   **Fig. 14-9**

14.112   Synthesize the industrial solvent, sulfolane (the sulfone of thiacyclopentane).

▰   1,3-Butadiene undergoing a 1,4-addition of SO_2 is the key step.

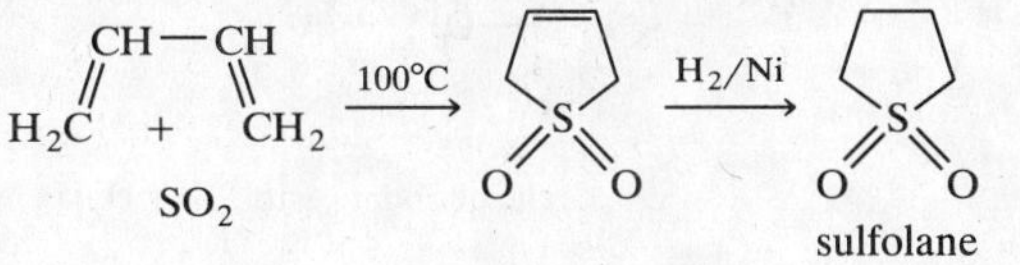

sulfolane

14.113   Compare and explain the reactions of EtO^- and EtS^- with $CyCH_2CH_2Cl$ (Cy = cyclohexyl).

▰   Both anions react by the Williamson-type S_N2 reaction to give the corresponding ether, $CyCH_2CH_2OEt$, and thioether, $CyCH_2CH_2SEt$, respectively.

14.114   Solve Problem 14.113 for $PhCH_2CH_2Cl$.

▰   The E2 and S_N2 reactions are competitive because the E2 product $PhCH{=}CH_2$ is stabilized by conjugation. On one hand, since EtO^- is a strong base and only a moderate nucleophile, it favors the E2 product. On the other hand EtS^- is a weak base and a strong nucleophile and favors the S_N2 product, $PhCH_2CH_2SEt$.

14.115   An optically active isomer of 5-bromo-2-hexanol reacts with alcoholic KOH to give optically inactive **A** while another optically active isomer gives optically active **B**, both $C_6H_{12}O$. Discuss the stereochemistry of the products and reactants for each case.

▰   The product, with 1° of unsaturation, is a cyclic ether formed from an intramolecular Williamson synthesis. From the position of the Br and OH in the reactant, the products are either the *cis* or *trans* stereoisomers of 2,5-dimethyltetrahydrofuran. Note that in naming cyclic ethers the O is given the number 1. Furthermore, the reactant has two stereocenters, C^2 and C^5. Since **A** is optically inactive, it is the achiral *cis* isomer having a plane of symmetry. Its stereoatoms are (2*S*, 5*R*) [or the identical (2*R*, 5*S*)] and, since an inversion occurs during the S_N2 cyclization, its precursor must be either (2*S*, 5*S*) or its (2*R*, 5*R*) enantiomer as shown in Fig. 14.10. Optically active **B** is the *trans* isomer whose stereoatoms are either (2*R*, 5*R*) or (2*S*, 5*S*). It is formed from either the (2*R*,

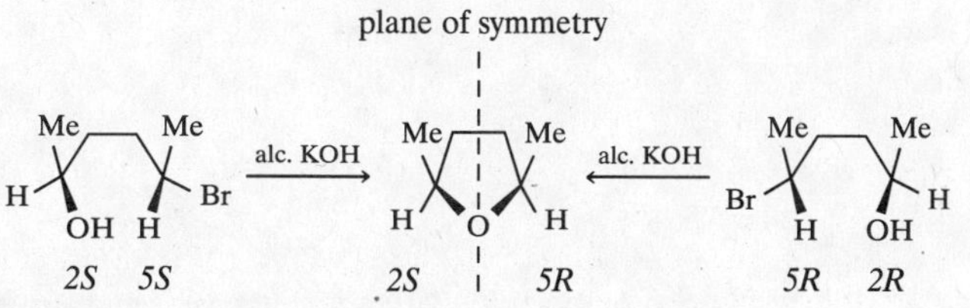

plane of symmetry

2*S*   5*S*   2*S* | 5*R*   5*R*   2*R*

meso-2,5-Dimethyltetrahydrofuran, **A**   **Fig. 14-10**

$5S$) or ($2S, 5R$) reactant. The stereochemistry is shown in Fig. 14-11 for formation of the ($2S, 5S$) enantiomer of **B** from the ($2S, 5R$) bromoalcohol; the ($2R, 5S$) alcohol gives the ($2R, 5R$) enantiomer.

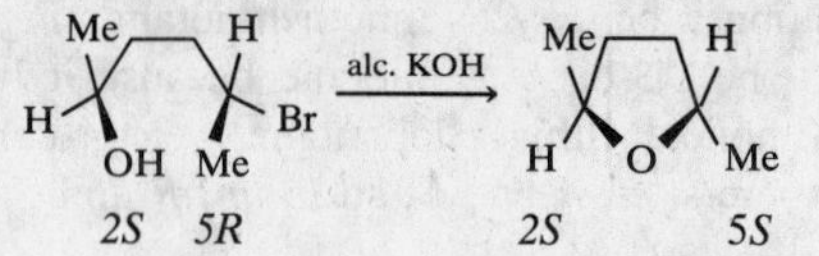

trans-2,5-Dimethyltetrahydrofuran, **B**   **Fig. 14-11**

14.116 Compare the ease of periodate oxidative cleavage of the *cis* and *trans* isomers of (*a*) 1,2-cyclopentanediol and (*b*) 1,2-cyclohexanediol, and account for their different reactivities.

◢ HIO_4 exists as H_5IO_6, a dihydrate, with I(VII). The acid forms a coplanar cyclic intermediate periodate ester (Fig. 14-12), which breaks down to products. This intermediate is attainable in (*a*) only with the *cis*-diol. The *trans*-diol doesn't react. In (*b*) this condition is attained more easily from the cis(e,a)- than the *trans*(e,e)-diol; the *cis*-diol reacts faster.

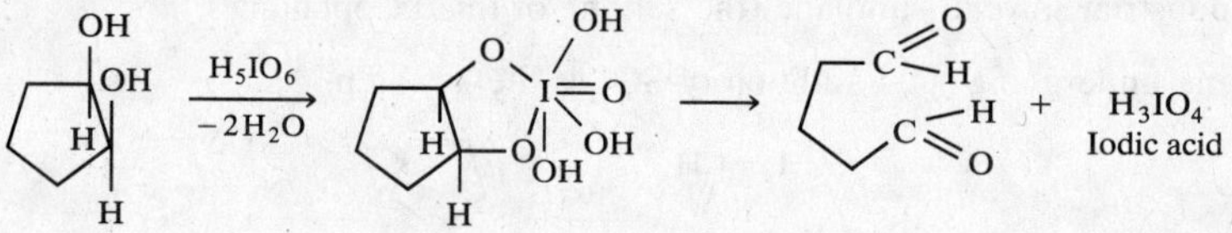

Cyclic periodate ester [I(VII)]   **Fig. 14-12**

14.117 Identify the compound (**A**) having the following m/z ms data: 90*, 61* (base peak), and 75* (low intensity). The asterisks indicate the presence of significant $m/z + 2$ satellites in ratio of 20:1.

◢ The satellites show the presence of sulfur because of the 20:1 ratio of ^{32}S: ^{34}S isotopes. The 90-peak cation is the parent, $C_4H_{10}S^+$, and the base-peak cation, $C_2H_5S^+$ arises from α,β cleavage. Since the base peak has two C's, the ion must be $^+CH_2SCH_3$ (not $^+CH_2CH_2SH$) and **A** is a methyl thioether. The cation with the low-intensity peak is $^+CH_2CH_2SCH_3$ arising from β,γ cleavage. **A** is $CH_3CH_2CH_2SCH_3$.

14.118 (*a*) Draw flat structural formulas for the stereoisomers of 4-ethyl-1,2-cyclohexanediol. (*b*) Which is the most stable isomer?

◢ (*a*) There are 4 stereoisomers (see Fig. 14-13). The designations in the figure are given relative to the C^1OH.

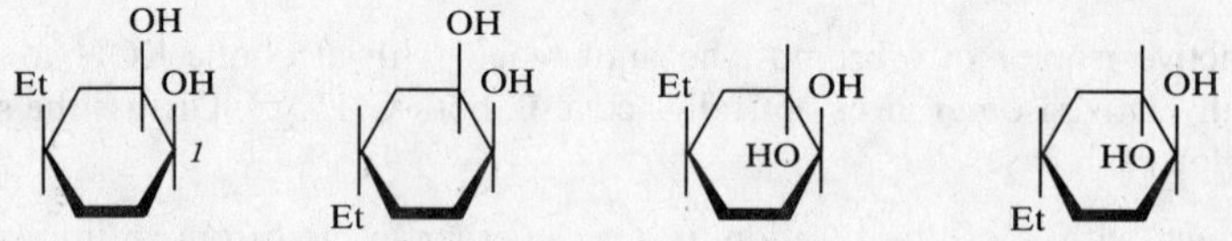

cis, cis (**A**)   cis, trans (**B**)   trans, cis(**C**)   trans, trans (**D**)   **Fig. 14-13**

(*b*) **D**; all groups are equatorial.

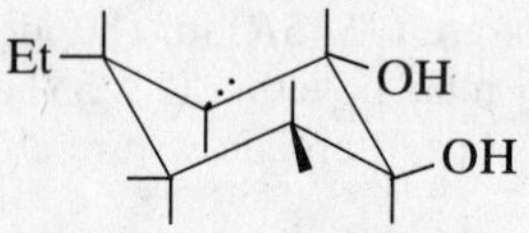

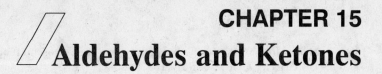

STRUCTURE AND NOMENCLATURE

15.1 Give the common names for (*a*) CH₃CHO, (*b*) CH₃CHClCHO, (*c*) (CH₃)₂CHCHO, (*d*) CH₂=CHCHO, (*e*) CH₃CH₂CH(OH)CH₂CHO, and (*f*) *trans*-CH₃CH=CHCHO.

▌ (*a*) Acetaldehyde, (*b*) α-chloropropionaldehyde, (*c*) isobutyraldehyde, (*d*) acrolein, (*e*) β-hydroxyvaleraldehyde, and (*f*) *trans*-crotonaldehyde.

15.2 Give the IUPAC names for the compounds in Problem 15.1.

▌ (*a*) Ethanal, (*b*) 2-chloropropanal, (*c*) methylpropanal, (*d*) propenal, (*e*) 3-hydroxypentanal, (*f*) (*E*)-2-butenal.

15.3 Give the common names for (*a*) PhCHO, (*b*) Ph—C=CCHO (with H on each carbon), (*c*) Ph₂CHCHO, (*d*) [structure: 3,5-dichlorobenzaldehyde], and

(*e*) OCHCH₂CH₂CH₂CHO.

▌ (*a*) Benzaldehyde, (*b*) *trans*-cinnamaldehyde, (*c*) diphenylacetaldehyde, (*d*) 3,5-dichlorobenzaldehyde, and (*e*) glutaraldehyde.

15.4 Give the IUPAC names for the compounds in Problem 15.3.

▌ (*a*) Benzenecarbaldehyde and benzaldehyde, (*b*) (*E*)-3-phenylpropenal, (*c*) diphenylethanal, (*d*) same as the common name or 3,5-dichlorobenzenecarbaldehyde (rare), and (*e*) 1,5-pentanedial.

15.5 Give the common names for (*a*) CH₃COCH(CH₃)₂, (*b*) Cl₂CHCOCH₃, (*c*) ClCH₂COCH₂Cl, (*d*) CH₂=CHCOCH=CH₂, and (*e*) CH₂=CHCH₂COCH₂CH₃.

▌ (*a*) Methyl isopropyl ketone, (*b*) α,α-dichloroacetone, (*c*) α,α′-dichloroacetone, (*d*) divinyl ketone, and (*e*) allyl ethyl ketone.

15.6 Give the IUPAC names for the compounds in Problem 15.5.

▌ (*a*) 3-Methyl-2-butanone, (*b*) 1,1-dichloropropanone, (*c*) 1,3-dichloropropanone, (*d*) 1,4-pentadien-3-one, and (*e*) 5-hexen-3-one.

15.7 Give names for each of the following compounds:
(*a*) PhCH₂COCH₂Ph   (*b*) *m*-ClC₆H₄COCH₃   (*c*) PhCOPh   (*d*) PhCOCH(Cl)CH₃

(*e*) [cyclohexenone structure]   (*f*) [di-(p-chlorophenyl) ketone structure]   (*g*) [2,3-dimethylcyclopentanone structure]

▌ (*a*) Dibenzyl ketone, (*b*) *m*-chloroacetophenone, (*c*) benzophenone, (*d*) α-chloropropiophenone, (*e*) cyclohexen-3-one, (*f*) di-(*p*-chlorophenyl) ketone, and (*g*) *cis*-2,3-dimethylcyclopentanone.

15.8 Write the formula for each of the following compounds: (*a*) Biacetyl, (*b*) chloral, (trichloroacetaldehyde), (*c*) pinacolone (3,3-dimethyl-2-butanone), (*d*) benzoin, (*e*) deoxybenzoin (benzyl phenyl ketone), (*f*) (*Z*)-3-hexenedial, and (*g*) cyclopentanecarbaldehyde.

▌ (*a*) MeCOCOMe, (*b*) Cl₃CCHO, (*c*) Me₃CCOMe, (*d*) PhCHOHCOPh, (*e*) PhCH₂COPh (deoxy indicates a missing OH), (*f*) OCHCH₂C=CCH₂CHO (with H H on the double bond), and (*g*) [cyclopentane]—CHO.

15.9 Name the following compounds by the oxo method. (*a*) $HOCH_2CH_2COCH_2CH(CH_3)_2$, and (*b*) $CH_3CH_2COCH_2CH(Cl)CHO$

✔ Oxo indicates $=O$. (*a*) 5-Methyl-3-oxo-1-hexanol, and (*b*) 2-chloro-4-oxohexanal.

15.10 Write structures for each of the following: (*a*) 3-Formylcyclohexanol, (*b*) γ-bromobutyrophenone, (*c*) 1,3-cyclopentanedione, (*d*) 4,4-dimethylcyclohexanecarbaldehyde.

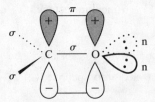

✔ (*a*)   (*b*) $PhCOCH_2CH_2CH_2Br$ (*c*)   (*d*)

15.11 (*a*) Describe the bonding of the carbonyl group in H_2CO. (*b*) What are the expected $H—C—O$ and $H—C—H$ bond angles?

✔ Carbon uses three sp^2 hybrid bonds to form three σ bonds, two bonds to the H's and one to the O. An unhybridized *p* AO on C overlaps laterally with a *p* AO of O to form the π bond in a plane perpendicular to the plane of the σ bonds. $H_2C=O$ is a planar molecule. The $H—C—O$ bond angle is slightly greater than the expected 120° (121.8°), as a consequence of the repulsion by the electronegative O on the electrons in the $C—H$ bonds. The $H—C—H$ angles are thus 116.5°, slightly less than 120°.

15.12 (*a*) Compare the polarities of the $C=O$ and the $C=C$ bonds. (*b*) How does this difference influence the reactivity of each bond as a nucleophilic site for reaction?

✔ (*a*) The $C=C$ group has no significant polar character. Since O is much more electronegative than C, $C=O$ is polarized with $C^{\delta+}$ and $O^{\delta-}$. (*b*) The π bond of $C=C$ is an electron source, and is a nucleophilic site. The polarity of the π bond in the $C=O$ causes C to be an electrophilic site and O to be a nucleophilic site.

15.13 Draw (*a*) resonance structures and (*b*) an atomic orbital representation of the $C=O$ group.

✔ (*a*) $>C=\ddot{O}: \longleftrightarrow >\overset{+}{C}-\ddot{\underset{..}{O}}:^-$. In this exceptional case the polar resonance structure makes a considerable contribution to the hybrid and has a significant effect on the chemistry of the $C=O$ group. (*b*) See Fig. 15-1.

Fig. 15-1

15.14 Account for the following: (*a*) The boiling points of 2-propanol, propanone, and 2-methylpropene (their molecular weights are approximately the same) are 82 °C, 57 °C and −7 °C, respectively; (*b*) the dipole moment of propanal (2.52 D) is greater than that of 1-butene (0.3 D); (*c*) carbonyl compounds are more soluble in water than the corresponding alkanes but less than the corresponding alcohols.

✔ (*a*) The high bp of the alcohol is due to intermolecular H-bonding, $R—O—H---\overset{\overset{\textstyle H}{|}}{O}—R$. Carbonyl compounds and alkenes have no H's for H-bonding. The dipole-dipole attractive forces of carbonyl compounds cause them to have higher bp's than alkenes. (*b*) The larger dipole moment of the $C=O$ is due to the large contribution of the polar resonance structure [see Problem 15.13(*a*)] to the hybrid. (*c*) H-bonding between an H of H_2O and the O of the $C=O$ makes carbonyl compounds more water soluble than corresponding hydrocarbons. The lack of H's able to H-bond with the O of H_2O makes the carbonyl compounds less water soluble than the alcohols.

15.15 Explain why 2-butanone has a lower ΔH^0 of combustion than butanal.

✔ Alkyl substituents stabilize $C=O$ as they do $C=C$ by releasing electrons toward the sp^2 hybridized C. The enthalpy of the ketone is lower because it has two R groups while the aldehyde has only one.

15.16 (*a*) Give (i) resonance structures and (ii) an atomic orbital representation for 3-penten-2-one. (*b*) Which should have a smaller ΔH^0 of hydrogenation, 3-penten-2-one or 4-penten-2-one? Explain.

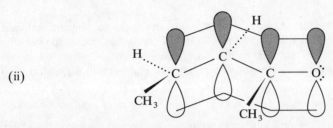

(*a*) (i)
$$\begin{bmatrix} CH_3-\overset{\overset{\displaystyle :O:}{\|}}{C}-CH=CH-CH_3 \longleftrightarrow CH_3-\overset{\overset{\displaystyle :\ddot{O}:^-}{|}}{\underset{+}{C}}-CH=CH-CH_3 \longleftrightarrow \\[2em] CH_3-\overset{\overset{\displaystyle :\ddot{O}:^-}{|}}{C}=CH-\overset{+}{C}H-CH_3 \end{bmatrix}$$

(ii)

(*b*) 3-Penten-2-one is thermodynamically more stable than 4-penten-2-one because its conjugation permits electron delocalization. Its ΔH_h^0 is lower.

15.17 (*a*) What is formalin? (*b*) How is dry $H_2C{=}O\,(g)$ prepared? (*c*) Write structures for (i) trioxane, a trimer of formaldehyde, and (ii) paraformaldehyde, a polymer.

(*a*) *Formalin* is a 40% aqueous solution of formaldehyde, $H_2C{=}O$. (*b*) It is generated by heating either trioxane or paraformaldehyde. (*c*) (i)

$$\underset{\displaystyle H_2C \underset{\displaystyle O}{\diagdown} \diagup CH_2}{\overset{\displaystyle CH_2}{\overset{\displaystyle O \diagup \diagdown O}{}}}$$

and (ii) $HO-CH_2[-O-CH_2]_n-O-CH_2-OH$.

15.18 Give the structures of (*a*) paraldehyde, a trimer, and (*b*) metaldehyde, a tetramer of acetaldehyde, $CH_3CH{=}O$.

(*a*)

$$\underset{\displaystyle CH_3CH \underset{\displaystyle O}{\diagdown} \diagup CHCH_3}{\overset{\displaystyle \overset{CH_3}{\overset{|}{CH}}}{\overset{\displaystyle O \diagup \diagdown O}{}}}$$

(*b*)

$$\begin{matrix} & \overset{CH_3}{\overset{|}{CH}}{-}O & \\ O{-}\overset{|}{CH} & & \diagdown CHCH_3 \\ CH_3CH & & O \\ & O{-}CH \diagup & \\ & \underset{CH_3}{|} & \end{matrix}$$

15.19 (*a*) What is a ketene? (*b*) Give (i) the structural formula and (ii) an atomic orbital representation of ketene.

(*a*) *Ketenes* have the general formula $R_2C{=}C{=}O$. (*b*) (i) $H_2C{=}C{=}O$, (ii) See Fig. 15-2.

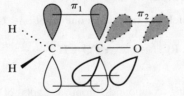

Fig. 15-2

SPECTRA

15.20 Predict the effect of $C{=}O$ on the chemical shift of (*a*) the aldehyde H and (*b*) the αH in pmr.

(*a*) The $O{=}\overset{|}{C}{-}H$ has a characteristic, very low field signal ($\delta \cong 9.5$ ppm) because the circulating π e$^-$'s in the magnetic field induce a field that effectively lowers its shielding. (In this case the induced field may actually deshield the H.) In addition, the $C^{\delta+}$ enhances the downfield shift. (*b*) The αH only feels the strong electron-withdrawing effect of $C^{\delta+}$; the range of the δ values is approximately 2.0–2.5 ppm.

15.21 Discuss the ^{13}C nmr chemical shifts of carbonyl compounds.

◢ Carbonyl C's absorb more downfield than any other type of C (about 200 ppm from TMS) because (*1*) sp^2-hybridized C's resonate more downfield from sp^3-hybridized C's and (*2*) the polar nature of C=O causes additional diminished shielding. These effects diminish for C's further away from the C=O.

15.22 Summarize the important features, including similarities and differences, in the ir spectra of aldehydes and ketones.

◢ Stretching of the polar C=O bond causes a large change in the dipole moment, resulting in a strong band at about 1725 cm^{-1} for RCHO's and 1715 cm^{-1} for R'COR's. In cyclic ketones, as the size of the ring decreases from 7 to 3, the frequency increases from 1705 to 1850 cm^{-1}. Conjugation shifts the carbonyl absorption to lower frequencies. Aldehydes also have a characteristic C—H stretching absorption doublet at 2720 and 2820 cm^{-1}.

15.23 Summarize the important similarities and differences in the mass spectra of aldehydes and ketones.

◢ Since O effectively stabilizes a + on an adjacent atom, cleavage occurs mainly at the carbonyl C. In the case of ketones, the smaller R invariably stays as part of the cation:

$$CH_3COCH_2CH(CH_3)_2 \xrightarrow{-e^-} \cdot CH_2CH(CH_3)_2 + \left[CH_3C\equiv O^+ \longleftrightarrow CH_3\overset{+}{C}=O \right]$$

Since the C—H bond in aldehydes is too strong to be cleaved, R· comes off.

$$CH_3CH_2CHO \xrightarrow{-e^-} CH_3CH_2\cdot + \left[H-C\equiv O^+ \longleftrightarrow H-\overset{+}{C}=O \right]$$

15.24 Summarize the important features of the uv spectra of aldehydes and ketones.

◢ The C=O group gives rise to two absorption peaks in the uv spectrum. The $\pi \rightarrow \pi^*$ peak, with a large extinction coefficient, is observable only when the C=O is conjugated with a double bond. The energetically more favorable $n \rightarrow \pi^*$ transition, at longer wavelengths, is observable, although it has a smaller extinction coefficient.

PREPARATION

15.25 Give an industrial preparation of (*a*) formaldehyde, (*b*) benzaldehyde, and (*c*) acetaldehyde.

◢ (*a*) $CH_3OH + O_2 \xrightarrow[\text{Ag}]{600\,°C} H_2CO$,　(*b*) $PhCH_3 \xrightarrow[\Delta]{Cl_2} PhCHCl_2 \xrightarrow[OH^-]{H_2O} PhCHO$

(*c*) $HC\equiv CH \xrightarrow[H_3O^+]{HgSO_4} CH_3CHO$ or $H_2C=CH_2 + O_2 \xrightarrow[H_2O]{PdCl_2,\ CuCl_2} CH_3CHO$ (Wacker process)

15.26 Write an equation for making aldehydes by the oxo process.

◢ Alkenes are converted to aldehydes containing one additional C atom.

$$RCH=CH_2 + CO + H_2 \xrightarrow{Co_2(CO)_8} RCH_2CH_2CHO$$

15.27 Synthesize each of the following compounds from alcohols of three or fewer carbons and acetylene: (*a*) 3-Hexanone, (*b*) pentanal, (*c*) 2-methyl-3-pentanone. You may reuse any intermediate or product once made.

◢ (*a*)

$$CH_3CH_2CH_2OH \left\{ \begin{array}{l} \xrightarrow[ZnCl_2]{HCl} CH_3CH_2CH_2Cl \xrightarrow{Mg/ether} CH_3CH_2CH_2MgCl\ (\mathbf{A}) \\[2ex] \xrightarrow[Py]{CrO_3} CH_3CH_2CHO\ (\mathbf{B}) \xrightarrow{\mathbf{A}} CH_3CH_2\underset{\underset{OH}{|}}{C}HCH_2CH_2CH_3 \xrightarrow[OH^-]{KMnO_4} CH_3CH_2\overset{\overset{O}{\|}}{C}CH_2CH_2CH_3 \end{array} \right.$$

(b) $HC \equiv CH \xrightarrow[\text{liq. } NH_3]{NaNH_2} HC \equiv C:^- \xrightarrow{CH_3CH_2CH_2Cl}$

$CH_3CH_2CH_2C \equiv CH \xrightarrow[\text{2. } H_2O_2, \, OH^-]{\text{1. Sia}_2BH} CH_3CH_2CH_2CH_2CHO$

(c) $(CH_3)_2CHOH \xrightarrow{SOCl_2} (CH_3)_2CHCl \xrightarrow{Mg/ether} (CH_3)_2CHMgCl \xrightarrow{+\mathbf{B}} (CH_3)_2CHCHOHCH_2CH_3 \xrightarrow[H^+]{Cr_2O_7^{2-}}$

$(CH_3)_2CHCOCH_2CH_3$

15.28 Give steps in a preparation of each of the following from benzene, alcohols and acids of three or fewer C's, acetylene, and inorganic reagents. Reuse compounds once made. (*a*) Propiophenone (two methods), (*b*) *p*-chlorobenzaldehyde, and (*c*) phenylacetaldehyde.

◢ **(a)** *1.* $CH_3CH_2COOH \xrightarrow{SOCl_2} CH_3CH_2COCl \xrightarrow[AlCl_3]{PhH} PhCOCH_2CH_3$

2. $CH_2 = CHCH_2OH \xrightarrow{PhH/HF} PhCH_2CH = CH_2 \xrightarrow{H_2/Pt} PhCH_2CH_2CH_3 \xrightarrow{NBS}$

$PhCHBrCH_2CH_3 \xrightarrow[\text{acetone } (S_N1)]{H_2O} PhCH(OH)CH_2CH_3 \xrightarrow{MnO_2} PhCOCH_2CH_3$

(b) $PhH \xrightarrow[\text{2. Mg/ether}]{\text{1. } Br_2/Fe} PhMgBr \xrightarrow{H_2CO^*} PhCH_2OH \xrightarrow{Cl_2/Fe} p\text{-}ClC_6H_4CH_2OH \xrightarrow{CrO_3/Py} p\text{-}ClC_6H_4CHO$

(c) $CH_3CH_2OH \xrightarrow[\Delta]{H_2SO_4} CH_2 = CH_2 \xrightarrow{peracid} H_2C \underset{O}{-} CH_2 \xrightarrow[\text{ether}]{PhMgBr} PhCH_2CH_2OH \xrightarrow{CrO_3/Py} PhCH_2CHO$

$^*CH_3OH \xrightarrow{CrO_3/Py} H_2CO \text{ (C)}$

15.29 Synthesize the following compounds, starting with cyclopentane, C_5H_{10}, alcohols of three or fewer C's, H_2CO and inorganic reagents. (*a*) Cyclopentanecarbaldehyde, (*b*) 1,5-pentanedial, and (*c*) 5-oxohexanal.

◢ **(a)** $C_5H_{10} \xrightarrow{Cl_2 \atop h\nu} C_5H_9Cl \xrightarrow{Mg/ether} C_5H_9MgCl \xrightarrow{H_2CO} C_5H_9CH_2OH \xrightarrow{CrO_3/Py} C_5H_9CHO$

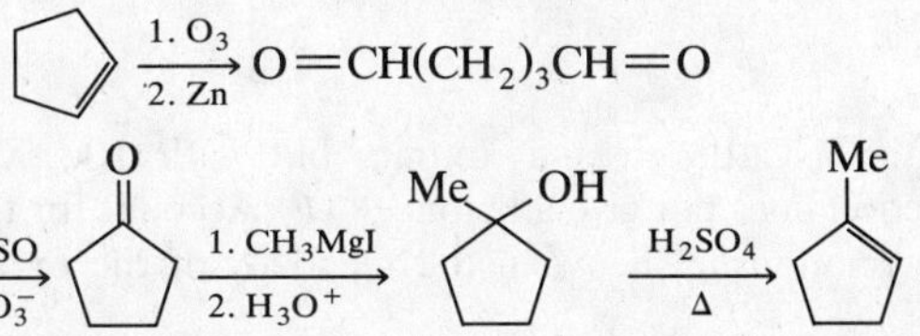

(b) $C_5H_9Cl \xrightarrow[EtOH]{KOH}$ ⬠ $\xrightarrow[\text{2. Zn}]{\text{1. } O_3} O = CH(CH_2)_3CH = O$

(c) $C_5H_9Cl \xrightarrow[\text{2. } HCO_3^-]{\text{1. DMSO}}$ (cyclopentanone) $\xrightarrow[\text{2. } H_3O^+]{\text{1. } CH_3MgI}$ (1-methylcyclopentanol) $\xrightarrow[\Delta]{H_2SO_4}$ (1-methylcyclopentene) $\xrightarrow[\text{2. Zn}]{\text{1. } O_3} OCH(CH_2)_3COCH_3$

15.30 (*a*) Give the product of the reaction of *cis*-1,2-cyclohexanediol with HIO_4. (*b*) Why is the *trans*-glycol almost inert to this reagent? (*c*) List another reagent that can bring about the same transformation.

◢ (*a*) $OCHCH_2CH_2CH_2CH_2CHO$. (*b*) The necessary cyclic TS forms easily from the *cis*-glycol but not from the *trans*-glycol. (*c*) $Pb(OCOCH_3)_4$, lead tetraacetate.

15.31 Write the structure of the product **A** and explain its formation: $H_2 + PhCH_2CH_2COCl \xrightarrow[\text{S or quinoline}]{Pd/C} \mathbf{A}$.

◢ **A** is $PhCH_2CH_2CHO$. The reduction stops at the aldehyde stage because the catalyst is *poisoned* (partially deactivated) by adding sulfur or quinoline. This is called the *Rosenmund* reaction.

15.32 (*a*) Write structures for **B** and **C** in the following reactions:

$$\mathbf{B} \xleftarrow[0\,°C]{LBAH} \boxed{CH_3CH(CH_3)COCl} \xrightarrow{LiAlH_4} \mathbf{C}, \qquad \text{where LBAH is lithium tri-}t\text{-butoxyaluminum hydride}$$

(*b*) Account for the different products. (*c*) Give an equation for the preparation of LBAH.

◢ (*a*) $\mathbf{B} = CH_3CH(CH_3)CHO$, $\mathbf{C} = CH_3CH(CH_3)CH_2OH$. (*b*) LBAH is a less active reducing agent than $LiAlH_4$. (*c*) $LiAlH_4 + 3Me_3COH \rightarrow Li(OCMe_3)_3AlH + 3H_2$.

15.33   Prepare an aldehyde by reduction of a carboxylic acid ester.

◢   Reduction of RCOOR' with $LiAlH_4$ gives RCH_2OH, since the intermediate aldehyde RCHO is generally susceptible to further reduction. If one equivalent of the *less* reactive $(i\text{-}C_4H_9)_2AlH$, diisobutylaluminum hydride (DBAH), is used at $-70\ °C$ followed by hydrolysis, RCHO is obtained in good yield.

15.34   Prepare $CH_3CH_2CH_2CHO$ from (*a*) an ester, (*b*) a nitrile, and (*c*) an acid chloride.

◢   (*a*) $CH_3CH_2CH_2COOEt$ + DBAH, (*b*) $CH_3CH_2CH_2CN$ + DBAH, (*c*) $CH_3CH_2CH_2COCl$ + LBAH.

15.35   Outline a synthesis of $PhCH_2CH_2CHO$ (**A**) from benzene, any two-C compound, and inorganic reagents.

◢   The reduction of a nitrile is used because it is easily prepared from an alkyl halide or tosylate and CN^-. The aldehyde product has *one more C* than the reactant alkyl halide.

$$PhH + H_2C\!\!-\!\!CH_2 \xrightarrow{AlCl_3} PhCH_2CH_2OH \xrightarrow{SOCl_2} PhCH_2CH_2Cl \xrightarrow{CN^-} PhCH_2CH_2CN \xrightarrow[\text{2. }H_2O]{\text{1. DBAH}} \mathbf{A}$$

(with the epoxide O bridging the $H_2C\!\!-\!\!CH_2$)

15.36   Under what circumstances may an aldehyde be prepared by oxidation of a 1° ROH with acid dichromate?

◢   If the aldehyde product is more volatile than the reactant alcohol and H_2O, it may be removed from the reaction flask by distillation as it is formed. Propionaldehyde (bp = 49 °C) can be similarly prepared from *n*-propyl alcohol (bp = 97 °C) but in poorer yields.

15.37   Prepare $Me_2CHCH_2COCH_3$ from (*a*) an alcohol, (*b*) an alkyne, (*c*) an acid chloride (two methods), (*d*) a carboxylic acid, (*e*) a nitrile, and (*f*) a nitro compound.

◢   (*a*) $Me_2CHCH_2CH(OH)CH_3$ + $KMnO_4$ or a Cr(VI) reagent
   (*b*) $Me_2CHCH_2C\equiv CH$ + H_2O in $HgSO_4$, H_2SO_4
   (*c*)   *1.* Me_2CHCH_2COCl + Me_2CuLi (from MeMgI + Li, then CuI)
           2. Me_2CHCH_2COCl + Me_2Cd (from MeMgI + $CdCl_2$)
   (*d*) Me_2CHCH_2COOH + 2 MeLi
   (*e*) Me_2CHCH_2CN + MeMgI or MeLi
   (*f*) $Me_2CHCH_2CH(NO_2)CH_3$ (**A**) + OH^-, then H_3O^+ via the sequence shown below.

$$\mathbf{A} \xrightarrow{OH^-} \left[\underset{\text{}}{Me_2CHCH_2\overset{H_3C}{\underset{}{C}}\!\!-\!\!\overset{:\ddot{O}:^-}{\underset{+}{N}}\!\!=\!\!\ddot{O}:} \longleftrightarrow Me_2CHCH_2\overset{H_3C}{\underset{}{C}}\!\!=\!\!\overset{:\ddot{O}:^-}{\underset{+}{N}}\!\!-\!\!\ddot{O}:^- \right] \xrightarrow{H^+} Me_2CHCH_2\overset{H_3C}{\underset{}{C}}\!\!=\!\!\overset{OH}{\underset{+}{N}}\!\!-\!\!\ddot{O}:^- \xrightarrow[-N_2O]{H_2O} \text{Product}$$

15.38   The reaction of R'COCl with R_2CuLi gives a ketone, but with RMgX gives a 3° alcohol, $R_2R'COH$. (*a*) Explain why the latter reaction does not give a ketone.   (*b*) Account for the difference in behavior of RMgX and R_2CuLi. (*c*) What is the relationship between the reactivity of the organometallic and the activity of the metal?

◢   (*a*) Initially a ketone is formed: $R'COCl + RMgX \rightarrow R'COR + MgX(Cl)$. However, since the ketone is more reactive than R'COCl, it reacts further with RMgX to form the 3° alcohol.   (*b*) Since the C-to-Mg bond has more ionic character than the C-to-Cu bond, its R group is more like $R:^-$ and is much more reactive.   (*c*) The more electropositive the metal, the more active and the more apt it is to bear a + charge and its R group a − charge.

15.39   Explain why organocopper and cadmium reagents react with the less reactive acid chlorides even though they don't react with the more reactive ketones.

◢ R_2CuLi and Ar_2CuLi (also R_2Cd and Ar_2Cd) do not react by the typical nucleophilic addition of an $R:^-$ to C=O. Instead Cu (and Cd) complex with the Cl, $\left[R\!-\!\overset{\delta+}{\underset{\parallel\ O}{C}}\!-\!-\!-\overset{\delta-}{\ddot{\underset{\cdot\cdot}{Cl}}}\!-\!-\!-CuR_2Li \right]$, engendering an acylium-like ion,

with greater $\delta+$ on the C. This strongly electrophilic ion can form a bond even with the weakly nucleophilic R of R_2CuLi.

15.40   Give the products **A** through **C**:

(*a*)   4-Bromocyclohexanone + $(H_2C=CH)_2CuLi \longrightarrow \mathbf{A}$ and

(*b*) $C_2H_5CH=CHCOCH_3 \xrightarrow[-78\ °C]{Me_2CuLi} \mathbf{B} \xrightarrow{H_3O^+} \mathbf{C}$

▰   (*a*)   **A** = 4-vinylcyclohexanone. The cuprate does not add to C=O but does couple.

      (*b*)   **B** = $C_2H_5CHCH=C-O^-Li^+$. This is an example of a 1,4- or *conjugate addition* to an α,β-

                        | |

                        Me CH_3

unsaturated carbonyl compound. **C** = $C_2H_5CHMeCH_2COCH_3$. The net result is a 3,4-addition.

15.41   Give the product of each of the following reactions:

    (*a*) $C_6H_5CH_3 + CrO_3$ in $(CH_3CO)_2O \rightarrow A \xrightarrow{H_2O} B$ (*c*) $C_6H_5CH_2CH_2NO_2 \xrightarrow[\text{2. }H_3O^+]{\text{1. }OH^-} D$

    (*b*) $C_6H_5CH_3 + CO + HCl \xrightarrow[\text{AlCl}_3]{\text{CuCl}} C$

▰   (*a*)   **A** = $C_6H_5CH(OCOCH_3)_2$, **B** = C_6H_5CHO; (*b*) **C** = p-$CH_3C_6H_4CHO$; (*c*) **D** = $C_6H_5CH_2CHO$. In **A**, the formation of the acetal ester prevents oxidation of the intermediate aldehyde to $-COOH$.

15.42   (*a*) Identify compounds **E** and **F**, given $C_6H_5CH_2CHMe_2 \xrightarrow{2NBS} E \xrightarrow[\text{or }OH^-]{H_3O^+} F$.   (*b*) Give a synthesis of **F** from benzene and any 4-carbon compound.

▰   (*a*) **E** = $C_6H_5CBr_2CHMe_2$, **F** = $C_6H_5COCHMe_2$; (*b*) $Me_2CHCOCl + PhH \xrightarrow{AlCl_3} F$.

15.43   Synthesize each of the following, starting with cyclohexane.   (*a*) 2-methylcyclohexanone, (*b*) cyclohexyl ethyl ketone, and (*c*) dicyclohexyl ketone.

▰   (*a*) $C_6H_{12} \xrightarrow[h\nu]{Cl_2} C_6H_{11}Cl \xrightarrow[\text{2. }HCO_3^-]{\text{1. DMSO}}$ $\xrightarrow[\text{2. }H_3O^+]{\text{1. }CH_3MgI}$ $\xrightarrow[\Delta]{H_2SO_4}$

             $\xrightarrow[\text{2. }H_2O_2, OH^-]{\text{1. }BH_3/THF}$ $\xrightarrow{CrO_3/Py}$

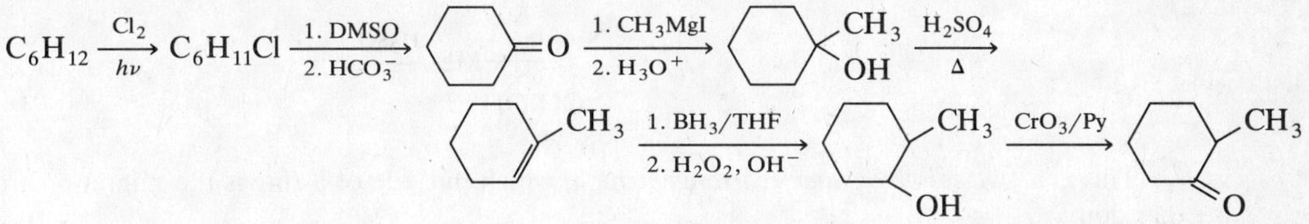

    (*b*) $C_6H_{11}Cl \xrightarrow[\substack{\text{2. Li} \\ \text{3. CuCl}}]{\text{1. }Mg/Et_2O} [C_6H_{11}]_2LiCu \xrightarrow{CH_3CH_2COCl} C_6H_{11}COCH_2CH_3$

    (*c*) $C_6H_{11}Cl \xrightarrow{\text{alc. KOH}} \text{cyclohexene} \xrightarrow{BH_3/THF} [C_6H_{11}]_3B \xrightarrow[\text{2. }H_2O_2, OH^-]{\text{1. }CO, H_2O} (C_6H_{11})_2C=O$

15.44   Write the products of reaction for (*a*) *m*-chlorobenzyl alcohol + pyridinium chlorochromate (PCC); (*b*) *cis*-3-*t*-butylcyclopentyl tosylate + DMSO, and then HCO_3^-; (*c*) $PhCH=CHCH_3 + 2NBS$, and then H_3O^+; (*d*) 1,2-dimethylcyclohexene + O_3, and then Zn; (*e*) $PhCOCl + (CH_3CH=CHCH_2)_2LiCu$; (*f*) $(CH_3)_3CCH_2CN + DBAH$; (*g*) cyclobutanol + $Cr_2O_7^{2-}$, H^+.

▰   (*a*)   *m*-ClC_6H_4CHO,   (*b*) 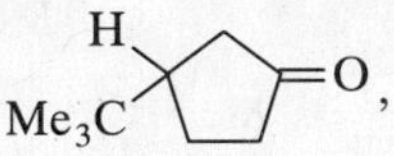   ,   (*c*) $PhCH=CHCHO$,   (*d*) $CH_3CO(CH_2)_4COCH_3$,

    (*e*) $PhCOCH_2CH=CHCH_3$, (*f*) $(CH_3)_3CCH_2CHO$, (*g*) 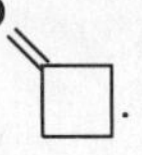 .

15.45   Suggest a mechanism for the acylation of benzene with $RCOCl$ in $AlCl_3$.

▰ $RCOCl \xrightarrow[-Cl^-]{AlCl_3} \left[R-\overset{+}{C}=\overset{..}{O}: \longleftrightarrow R-C\equiv O:^+ \right] \text{(an acylium ion)} \xrightarrow{PhH} \left[H \diagdown_{Ph} \diagup COR \right]^+ \xrightarrow{-H^+} Ph-\underset{\underset{O}{\|}}{C}-R$

15.46   Give the product of the reaction of $RCOCl$ and an alkene, $R'CH=CH_2$, in the presence of BF_3 and formulate a mechanism.

▰ $RCOCl \xrightarrow[-Cl^-]{BF_3} \left[R\overset{+}{C}=\overset{..}{O}: \right] \xrightarrow{H_2C=CHR'} \left[\underset{\underset{O}{\|}}{R}CCH_2\overset{+}{C}HR' \right] \xrightarrow{H^+} \underset{\underset{O}{\|}}{R}CCH=CHR'$

                                                                 α,β-unsaturated ketone

This is a Markovnikov addition initiated by the acylium ion.

15.47   Which acid chloride and alkene, when reacted in the presence of BF_3, will produce the following? (*a*) $PhCOCH=CHCH_2CH_3$ and (*b*) $CH_3CH_2COCH=C(CH_3)_2$.

▰   See Problem 15.46.   (*a*) $PhCOCl + H_2C=CHCH_2CH_3$ and (*b*) $CH_3CH_2COCl + H_2C=C(CH_3)_2$.

15.48 (*a*) Write an equation for the reaction of RCOOH with two moles of R'Li. (*b*) Why are two moles of organometallic necessary in this reaction?

$$(a) \quad RCOOH + 2R'Li \longrightarrow RCOR' + R'H + LiOH$$

(*b*) The first mole of R'Li reacts with the acidic H of the acid: $RCOOH + R'Li \rightarrow RCOO^-Li^+ + R'H$. A second mole of R'Li reacts as follows:

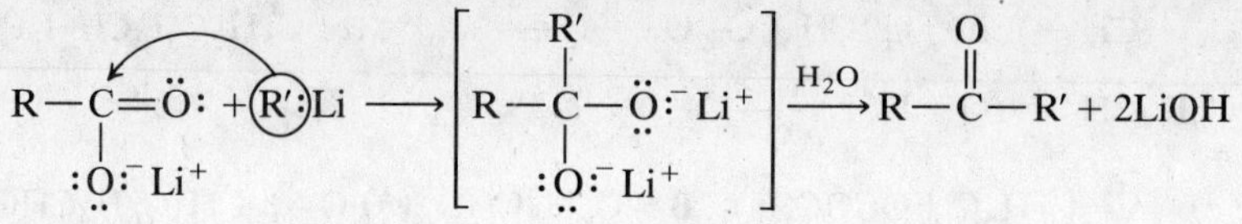

15.49 Give the product of the reaction of each of the following with conc. H_2SO_4 and explain your choice if more than one product is possible. (*a*) Me_2C-CMe_2, (*b*) $PhC(Me)-CPh(Me)$, (*c*) Me_2C-CH_2.
(with HO OH, HO OH, HO OH respectively)

◢ (*a*) Pinacolone, $Me_3C-COMe$. (*b*) $Ph_2MeC-COMe$; Ph migrates in preference to Me. (*c*) Me_2CHCHO; the 3 °OH is lost to give the more stable 3 °C$^+$, followed by H migration.

15.50 Predict the product for the following reaction and explain its formation.

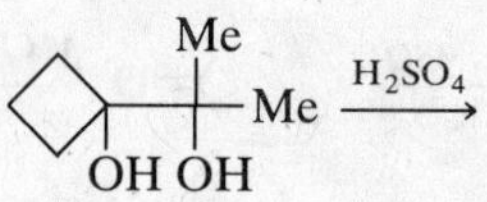

◢ This is a *pinacol-pinacolone rearrangement* in which the side of a ring is the migrating group leading to ring expansion.

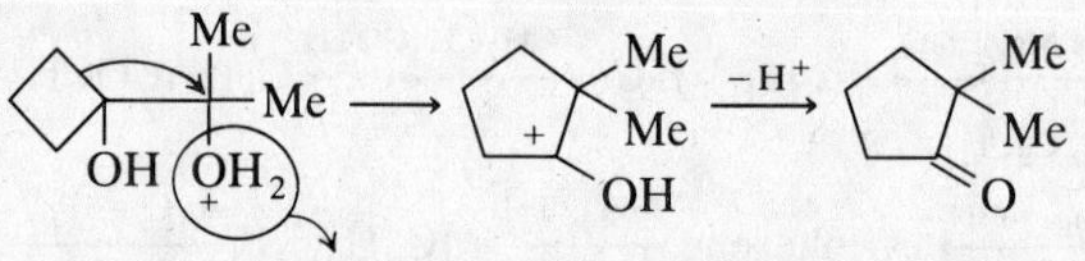

Formation of the cyclobutyl C$^+$ is unlikely because the ring strain increases in going from 90° to 120°.

15.51 Write the product of the reaction of $Me_2COHCOHMe_2$ with BF_3 and give a mechanism for its formation.

◢ The product is pinacolone, Me_3COMe. Initially, BF_3, a Lewis acid, bonds with the O of one of the OH's:

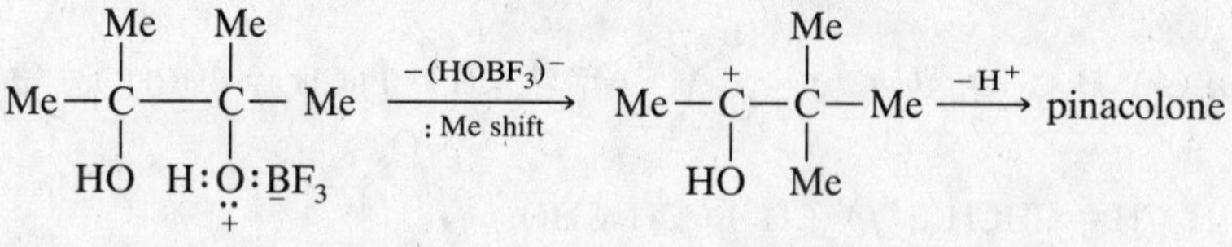

15.52 Write the structure and give a synthesis of (*a*) 1,3-dithiane, (*b*) 2-methyl-1,3-dithiane, and (*c*) 2-phenyl-1,3-dithiane.

◢ 1,3-Dithianes are prepared by the reaction of 1,3-propanedithiol, $HSCH_2CH_2CH_2SH$ (**A**), with a carbonyl compound.

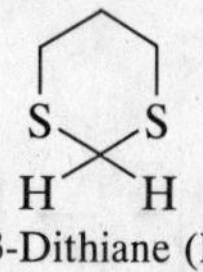

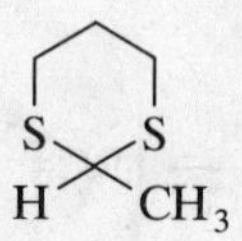

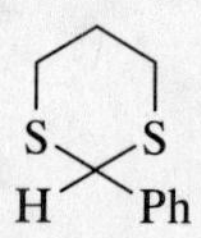

15.53 Account for the enhanced acidity of the H's on C^2 of 1,3-dithianes.

◢ The negative charge in the carbanion is stabilized by delocalization to each S by *p-d* π bonding.

15.54 Prepare (*a*) $(CH_3)_2CHCH_2CHO$, (*b*) $PhCH_2CHO$, (*c*) cyclopentylcarbaldehyde from 1,3-dithiane (**B**) (see Problem 15.52).

▌ Aldehydes are prepared by alkylating 1,3-dithiane at C^2 and by hydrolyzing the resulting thioacetal. The product RCHO has one more C from C^2 of dithiane. The general equation is

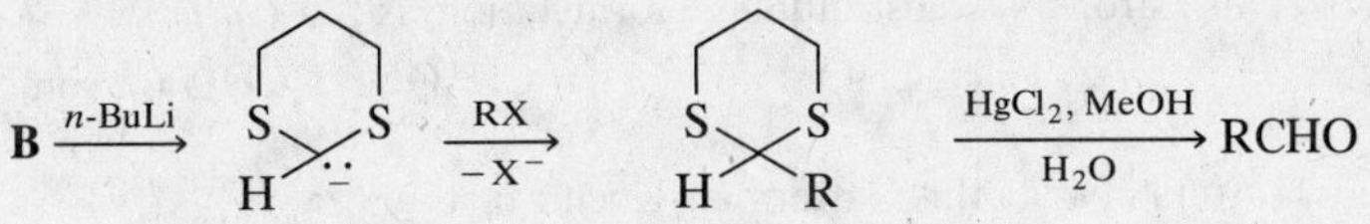

carbanion **C** alkylated product **D**

Alkylate with (*a*) $(CH_3)_2CHCH_2Cl$, (*b*) $PhCH_2Br$, (*c*) cyclopentyl chloride.

15.55 Prepare the following ketones from 1,3-dithiane (**B**): (*a*) Et_2CO (two methods), (*b*) *i*-PrCOEt, and (*c*) PhCOMe.

▌ Ketones can be prepared by (*1*) dialkylating **B** or (*2*) forming a substituted dithiane from RCHO and then alkylating it with R′X; both (*1*) and (*2*) are followed by hydrolysis.
(*a*) Dialkylate **B** with EtBr, then hydrolyze or:

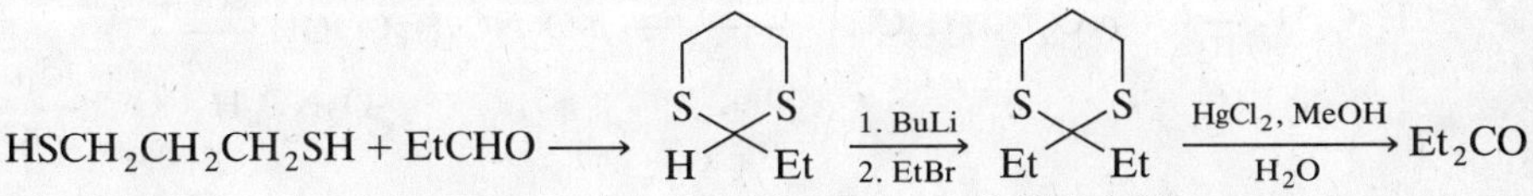

2-Ethyl-1,3-dithiane 2,2-Diethyl-1,3-dithiane

(*b*) Alkylate 2-ethyl-1,3-dithiane with *i*-PrCl, then hydrolyze with $HgCl_2$.
(*c*) Prepare 2-phenyl-1,3-dithiane from dithiane + PhCHO, alkylate with MeI, then hydrolyze.

15.56 (*a*) Use the dithiane method to synthesize PhCDO. (*b*) Why cannot the 1,3-dithiane anion be reacted with PhBr to prepare 2-phenyl-1,3-dithiane?

▌ (*a*)

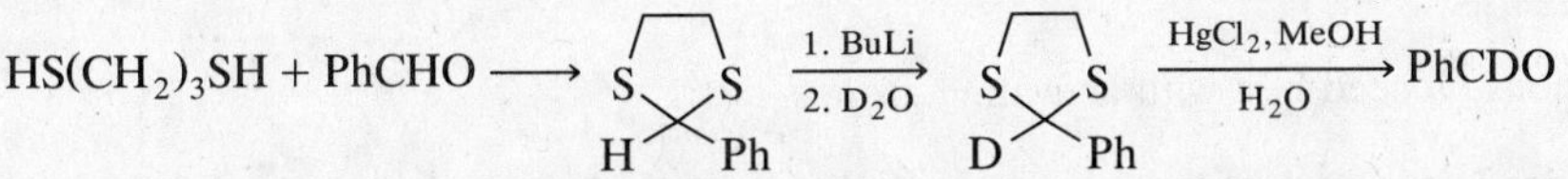

(*b*) The reaction would have to involve displacement by dithiane anion on PhBr. Nucleophilic displacement on aryl halides is not possible unless the aromatic ring is activated by electron-repelling substituents *ortho* and/or *para* to the halogen atom.

15.57 Dithiane anion is mixed with 1-Mecyclohexyl iodide in an attempt to prepare the 1,3-dithiane. Instead, a compound, C_7H_{12} (**C**) is isolated. Give the structure of **C** and explain its formation.

▌ The basic dithiane anion generates an E2 reaction, not an S_N2 reaction, with the 3° halide; **C** is 1-methylcyclohexene.

15.58 Write structures for **D**, **E**, and **F**, given dithiane + BuLi, then $Cl(CH_2)_3I \longrightarrow$ **D** $\xrightarrow{BuLi}$ **E** $\xrightarrow[H_2O]{HgCl_2,\ MeOH}$ **F**.

▌ **D** = 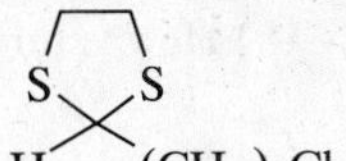 (I^- is a better leaving group.) **E** = 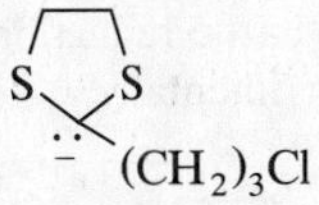 **F** = 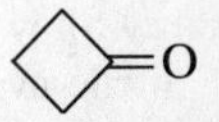

Cyclobutanone

15.59 (*a*) How is the Meerwein–Ponndorf–Verley reaction used to prepare a ketone? (*b*) Which alcohol is required to prepare the following ketones? (i) $PhCH_2CH{=}CHCOCH_3$, (ii) $(CH_3)_2CHCH_2COCH_2CH_3$, (iii) $CH_3CH_2COCH_2COOCH_3$.

▌ (*a*) In the *Meerwein–Ponndorf reaction*, an Al alkoxide of a 2° ROH is heated with a ketone. The 2° ROH is oxidized to a ketone and the original ketone is reduced to the salt of its corresponding 2° alcohol. The equilibrium between reactants and products can be shifted in either direction by varying experimental conditions, i.e., adding an excess of a reactant or distilling off a product. The reaction is called the *Oppenauer* oxidation if a ketone is desired, and it involves transfer of H: from the carbinol C to the carbonyl C.

$$3R_2C{=}O + (R'_2CHO^-)_3Al^{3+} \rightleftharpoons (R_2CHO^-)_3Al^{3+} + 3R'_2C{=}O$$

(*b*) (i) $PhCH_2CH{=}CHCH(OH)CH_3$, (ii) $(CH_3)_2CHCH_2CH(OH)CH_2CH_3$, (iii) $CH_3CH_2CH(OH)CH_2COOCH_3$

15.60 Give the product of the reaction of $CO + HCl$ in the presence of $CuCl/AlCl_3$ with (*a*) C_6H_6, and (*b*) $CH_3OC_6H_5$.

▌ This electrophilic aromatic substitution, a formylation, is the *Gatterman–Koch* reaction.

(*a*) C_6H_5CHO (*b*) $p\text{-}CH_3OC_6H_4CHO$ (+some *ortho*)

15.61 Suggest a sequence of steps for the Gatterman-Koch reaction.

▌ Since formyl chloride, HCOCl, is unstable, it is introduced into the ring indirectly in a Friedel–Crafts type of reaction.

Step 1. $^-{:}C{\equiv}O^+ + HCl \xrightarrow{\text{AlCl}_3} [H{-}C{\equiv}O{:}^+ \longleftrightarrow H{-}\overset{+}{C}{=}\overset{..}{O}{:}]AlCl_4^-$

Step 2. $ArH + [H{-}C{\equiv}O^+ AlCl_4^-] \longrightarrow \left[Ar\begin{smallmatrix}\diagup CHO \\ \diagdown H\end{smallmatrix} \right]^+ \xrightarrow{-H^+} ArCHO + HCl + AlCl_3$

15.62 Prepare *p*-nitrobenzophenone from benzene, toluene, and inorganic reagents.

▌ $CH_3C_6H_5 \xrightarrow[\text{H}_2\text{SO}_4]{\text{HNO}_3} p\text{-}O_2NC_6H_4CH_3 \xrightarrow[\Delta]{\text{KMnO}_4,\ \text{H}^+} p\text{-}O_2NC_6H_4COOH \xrightarrow{\text{SOCl}_2}$

$p\text{-}O_2NC_6H_4COCl \xrightarrow[\text{AlCl}_3]{\text{C}_6\text{H}_6} p\text{-}O_2NC_6H_4COC_6H_5$

15.63 Write the product of each of the following reactions:

(*a*)   Resorcinol $\xrightarrow[\text{ZnCl}_2]{\text{1. HCN}}$ **A**   and   (*b*) $Me_2NC_6H_5 + HCONMe_2 \xrightarrow{\text{POCl}_3}$ **B**

▌ (*a*)

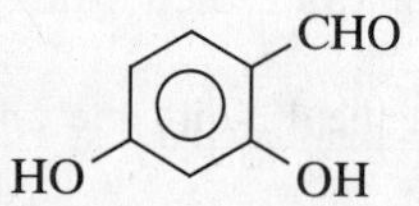

[structure: benzene ring with CHO, and HO, OH substituents]   (*Gatterman reaction*)

(*b*)

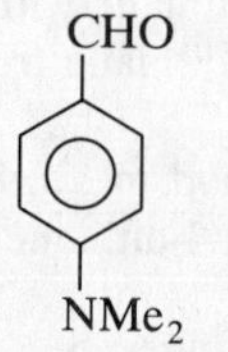

[structure: benzene ring with CHO and NMe₂]   (*Vilsmeyer reaction*, Problem 19.106)

These reactions proceed best with activating groups.

15.64 Predict the product of each of the following reactions after hydrolysis: (*a*) $EtCN + BuLi$ and (*b*) $o\text{-}BrC_6H_4CN + EtMgBr$.

▌ A Grignard or organolithium reagent adds to the $C{\equiv}N$ group of RCN to form a ketimine salt. If the temperature is lowered to $-60\ ^\circ C$, this salt precipitates. After removal from the reaction mixture, it is hydrolyzed to give a ketone.   (*a*) $EtCOBu$ and (*b*) $o\text{-}BrC_6H_4COEt$.

15.65 Show the steps in the reaction of RCN with $R'MgX$ (Problem 15.64).

▌ $R{-}C{\equiv}N{:} + \bar{R}'\overset{+}{Mg}X \longrightarrow \underset{\text{ketimine salt}}{RR'C{=}\overset{..}{N}{:}^- MgX^+} \xrightarrow[\text{MgX(OH)}]{\text{H}_3\text{O}^+} \underset{\text{ketimine}}{[RR'C{=}NH]} \xrightarrow{\text{H}_3\text{O}^+} RR'C{=}O + NH_4^+$

15.66 (*a*) Show the steps in the reduction of RCN with one equivalent of $LiAlH_4$.   (*b*) How is further reduction of the nitrile avoided experimentally?

▌ (*a*) (*1*) $R{-}C{\equiv}N{:} + LiAlH_4 \longrightarrow R{-}CH{=}\overset{..}{N}{:}^- Li^+ + AlH_3$
(*2*) $R{-}CH{=}\overset{..}{N}{:}^- Li^+ + H_2O \longrightarrow R{-}CH{=}\overset{..}{N}H + LiOH$
(*3*) $R{-}CH{=}NH + H_3O^+ \longrightarrow R{-}CH{=}O + NH_4^+$

(*b*) The $LiAlH_4$ is added to the nitrile so as to avoid an excess, and the temperature is kept low, at about $-50\ ^\circ C$. Deactivated reducing agents, $LiAlH(OEt)_3$, lithium triethoxyaluminum hydride or DBAH [Problem 15.33], can be used to avoid overreduction.

REACTIONS

15.67 Write equations for the reaction of (*a*) formaldehyde and (*b*) acetone with water. What is the general name for the product?

▌ The product, formed in a fast, reversible process, is a *gem*-diol.

(*a*) $H_2C{=}O + H_2O \rightleftharpoons H_2C(OH)_2$ (*b*) $Me_2C{=}O + H_2O \rightleftharpoons Me_2C(OH)_2$

15.68 Explain the following trend in K_{eq} for the hydration of C=O (Problem 15.67):

$$K_{eq}(H_2CO) > K_{eq}CH_3CH_2CHO > K_{eq}CH_3COCH_3$$

◪ There are two factors, (*1*) steric and (*2*) inductive, responsible for this trend. (*1*) The carbonyl C changes from using sp^2 to sp^3 HO's. This change impels the C to change from less crowded bond angles of 120° to more crowded bond angles of 109°. The bulkier the groups attached to the C, the greater is this steric effect, the higher will be the energy of the change in hybrid state, and the more likely is the equilibrium to lie towards the unhydrated compound. Thus $K_{eq}(H_2CO) > K_{eq}(RCHO) > K_{eq}(R_2CO)$. (*2*) See Problem 15.13. The ability of C=O to undergo nucleophilic addition reactions, such as hydration, depends on the magnitude of the + on the C. Since the electron-donating inductive effect of alkyl groups attenuates the + charge, their presence diminishes the reactivity of the C=O. The order of reactivity is thus $H_2CO \gg RCHO > R_2CO$, as reflected in the decreasing values of K_{eq}.

15.69 Give an explanation for the stability of the *gem*-diol, chloral hydrate (a hypnotic drug), $Cl_3CCH(OH)_2$, also known as "knockout drops", once used to shanghai sailors for service on sailing ships.

◪ The Cl⟵C dipole tends to destabilize the nonhydrated C=O structure because it puts δ+ charge on the C adjacent to the carbonyl $C^{\delta+}$. In the hydrate, adjacent δ+'s are gone. The equilibrium shifts all the way to the more stable hydrated aldehyde, which is an isolable compound.

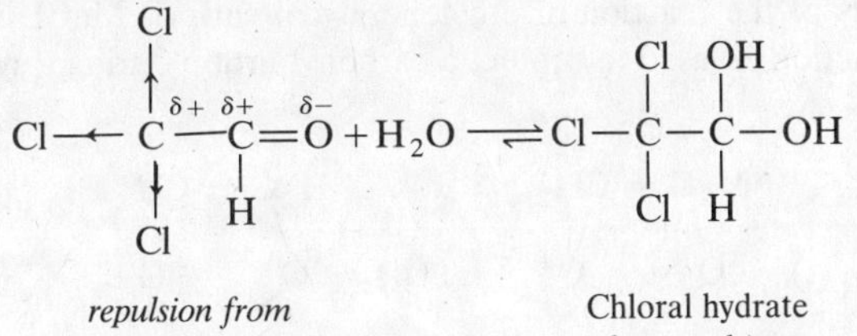

repulsion from adjacent + charges   Chloral hydrate *less repulsion*

15.70 Ninhydrin, 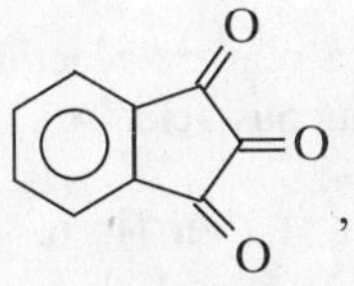 , exists as a hydrate. Which C=O is hydrated? Explain.

"nonhydrated" ninhydrin

◪ The adjacent δ+'s are separated by hydration of the center C=O.

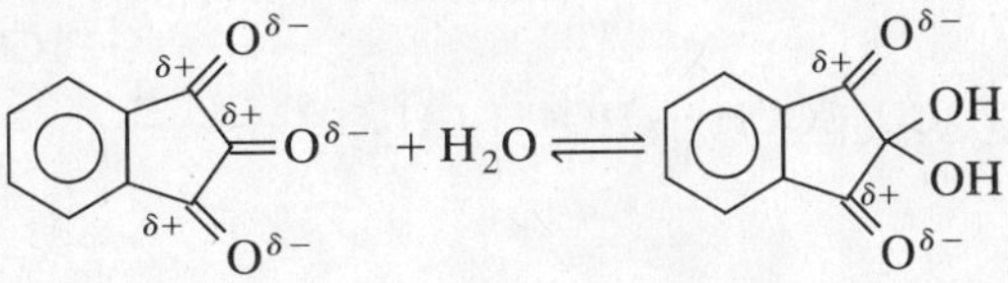

15.71 Account for the isolation of $CH_3C(^{18}O)CH_3$ from a solution of ordinary ^{16}O acetone in ^{18}O enriched H_2O.

◪ Although the equilibrium between acetone and its hydrate mostly favors the ketone, some hydrate exists in excess $H_2^{18}O$. When the hydrate loses water, there is a little more chance for ^{18}O to be retained in the ketone because the $^{18}O-C$ bond is slightly stronger than $^{16}O-C$.

$$Me_2C^{16}O + H_2^{18}O \rightleftharpoons Me_2C^{18}OH(^{16}OH) \rightleftharpoons Me_2C^{18}O + H_2^{16}O$$

15.72 (*a*) Write the steps in the formation of a *hemiacetal* from the reaction of RCHO with R'OH. (*b*) Explain the rate increase by (i) H^+ and (ii) OH^-. (*c*) Give the product of the reaction in dry HCl of equivalent amounts of (i) $CH_3CH_2CHO + MeOH$ and (ii) $PhCH_2CHO + EtOH$.

◪ (*a*)

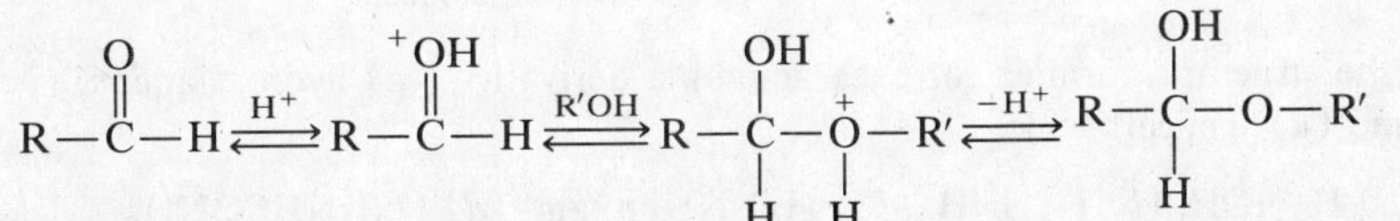

(b) Alcohols are relatively weak nucleophiles and they add slowly to aldehydes and ketones under neutral conditions. (i) Protonation of $O^{\delta-}$ places more $+$ on the carbonyl C, making it more reactive. (ii) The small amount of OR^- in equilibrium with OH^- reacts more rapidly with the carbonyl C than does ROH. (c) (i) $CH_3CH_2CH(OH)OMe$ and (ii) $PhCH_2CH(OH)OEt$.

15.73 (a) Show the steps for the addition of R'OH to the hemiacetal in Problem 15.72 to form an *acetal*. (b) How is the equilibrium shifted to favor its production?

(a)

$$R-\underset{\underset{H}{|}}{\overset{\overset{OH}{|}}{C}}-O-R' \underset{-H^+}{\overset{H^+}{\rightleftharpoons}} R-\underset{\underset{H}{|}}{\overset{\overset{+OH_2}{|}}{C}}-O-R' \overset{-H_2O}{\longrightarrow}$$

$$\left[R-\underset{\underset{H}{|}}{\overset{+}{C}}-O-R' \longleftrightarrow R-\underset{\underset{H}{|}}{C}=\overset{+}{O}-R' \right] \underset{-H^+}{\overset{R'OH}{\longrightarrow}} R-\underset{\underset{H}{|}}{\overset{\overset{O-R'}{|}}{C}}-O-R'$$

(b) The acetal is formed with R'OH in *dry* HCl and the water is distilled off as formed. The acetal is hydrolyzed in dilute aqueous acid.

15.74 (a) Give the products of the reaction of ethylene glycol with (i) MeCHO, (ii) Et_2CO, and (iii) cyclopentanone. (b) How may this reaction be used to protect a carbonyl group during a synthesis involving some other group in a molecule?

(a) (i)

$$\begin{array}{c} H_2C-CH_2 \\ | \qquad | \\ O \qquad O \\ \diagdown \;\; C \;\; \diagup \\ H \quad Me \end{array}$$

(ii)

$$\begin{array}{c} H_2C-CH_2 \\ | \qquad | \\ O \qquad O \\ \diagdown \;\; C \;\; \diagup \\ Et \quad Et \end{array}$$

(iii)

cyclopentane with $\begin{array}{c} O-CH_2 \\ | \\ O-CH_2 \end{array}$

(b) Conversion to an acetal or ketal masks the C=O, making it inert to a reagent reacting with some other group in the molecule. After the reaction, the C=O is regenerated with aqueous acid.

15.75 Show the use of a protecting group in the preparation of $PhCH_2CHOHCH_2CH_2COCH_3$ from $PhCH_2CHO$ and $BrCH_2CH_2COCH_3$ via a Grignard reaction.

If an attempt is made to convert the bromide to a Grignard reagent, the RMgX will react with the C=O in another molecule as it forms. The C=O however can be converted first to an acetal.

$$BrCH_2CH_2COCH_3 + HOCH_2CH_2OH \overset{\text{dry HCl}}{\longrightarrow} \begin{array}{c} BrCH_2CH_2 \quad O-CH_2 \\ \diagup C \diagdown \qquad | \\ H_3C \qquad O-CH_2 \end{array}$$

The Grignard reagent is then made and reacted with $PhCH_2CHO$, after which the C=O is regenerated.

15.76 (a) Write a general reaction for formation of a *Schiff base*. (b) Give the structure of the product of the reaction of (i) Me_2CO with $PhNH_2$, (ii) PhCHO with $MeNH_2$, and (iii) cyclohexanone with Me_3CNH_2.

(a) RCH=O (or R_2C=O) + R'NH$_2$ ⟶ RCH=N—R' (or R_2C=N—R') an N-substituted *imine*.

(b) (i) Me_2C=NPh, (ii) PhCH=NMe. (iii) cyclohexane ring =NCMe$_3$.

15.77 Show steps in the formation of a Schiff base.

Nucleophilic addition of the amine to the C=O gives a carbinolamine which then loses water.

$$\overset{\frown}{RCH=O} + R'\ddot{N}H_2 \rightleftharpoons \underset{\text{a carbinolamine}}{RCH(OH)\ddot{N}HR'} \rightleftharpoons RCH=NR' + H_2O$$

15.78 Write the structural formula for each ammonia derivative: (a) hydroxylamine, (b) hydrazine, (c) phenylhydrazine, and (d) semicarbazide.

(a) H_2NOH, (b) H_2NNH_2, (c) H_2NNHPh, and (d) $H_2NNHCONH_2$.

15.79 Give the structural formulas and names of the products of reaction of (*a*) benzaldehyde and (*b*) acetone with each of the ammonia-like reagents in Problem 15.78.

◢ (*a*) PhCH=NOH, benzaldehyde oxime; PhCH=NNH$_2$, benzaldehyde hydrazone; PhCH=NNHPh, benzaldehyde phenylhydrazone; PhCH=NNHCONH$_2$, benzaldehyde semicarbazone. (*b*) Me$_2$C=NOH, acetone oxime; Me$_2$C=NNH$_2$, acetone hydrazone; Me$_2$C=NNHPh, acetone phenylhydrazone; Me$_2$C=NNHCONH$_2$, acetone semicarbazone.

15.80 (*a*) Write the steps in the mechanism of reaction of a C=O with an ammonia derivative in Problem 15.78, symbolized by H$_2$N—X. (*b*) The reaction is catalyzed by weak acids, but the rate decreases in high concentrations of (i) acid and (ii) base. Explain.

◢ (*a*) These are acid-catalyzed nucleophilic additions similar to those of H$_2$O and ROH.

$$\text{>C=O:} \xrightarrow[-H^+]{H^+} \text{>}\overset{+}{\text{C}}\text{—OH} \xrightarrow{H_2N-X} \left[\underset{HO}{\text{>C}}\text{—}\overset{+}{\text{N}}\text{H}_2\text{—X} \right] \xrightarrow{-H^+} \left[\underset{HO}{\text{>C}}\text{—NH—X} \right] \xrightarrow{-H_2O} \text{>C=N—X}$$

The dehydration step could be either acid- or base-catalyzed.

(*b*) At lower pH's, the nitrogen bases are protonated, decreasing the concentration of free base available for reaction: H$_2$N—X + H$_3$O$^+$ ⇌ H$_3$$\overset{+}{\text{N}}$—X + H$_2$O. (i) There must be enough H$^+$ to catalyze the reaction, but not so much that the concentration of free base drops too low. (ii) At high pH's the H of the OH of the intermediate may be removed, thereby slowing the dehydration step. A buffering agent, such as sodium acetate is often added to maintain a favorable pH (about 5).

15.81 There are two NH$_2$ groups in semicarbazide that might react with a ketone or aldehyde. Explain why the reaction occurs as it does.

◢ The NH$_2$ group closer to the carbonyl group is deactivated (resonance-stabilized) compared with the other end NH$_2$ group:

$$\left[\overset{:\ddot{\text{O}}}{\underset{}{\text{—C—}}}\ddot{\text{N}}\text{H}_2 \longleftrightarrow \overset{:\ddot{\text{O}}:^-}{\underset{}{\text{—C=}}}\overset{+}{\text{N}}\text{H}_2 \right]$$

15.82 Cyclohexanone semicarbazone precipitates from a solution containing one equivalent each of cyclohexanone and benzaldehyde when one equivalent of semicarbazide is added. After standing for a few hours, the only product is benzaldehyde semicarbazone. Explain.

◢ The kinetically-controlled product is the derivative of cyclohexanone. Its C=O is not sterically hindered (its R groups are tied back into a ring). PhCH=NNHCONH$_2$ forms more slowly because its C=O is deactivated by the electron-releasing Ph group. However, it is the more stable semicarbazone because of conjugation, and its formation is thermodynamically controlled. In such competitive reversible reactions the equilibrium shifts with time to the more stable product.

15.83 The reaction of H$_2$NOH with a symmetrical ketone, R$_2$C=O, gives one oxime, but two isomeric oximes may form from the reaction of an aldehyde or a nonsymmetrical ketone. Explain and illustrate with structures.

◢ Rotation about the π bond in >C=N is not free and therefore geometric isomerism is possible when the two groups on the carbonyl C are different. For example,

(*Z*) *cis* (syn)   (*E*) *trans* (anti)

15.84 Compare the acidity of hydroxylamine and oximes and explain any difference.

◢ Loss of a proton from H$_2$NOH affords the conjugate base, H$_2$N—$\ddot{\text{O}}$:$^-$, in which the − charge is localized on O. The − charge in the conjugate base of an oxime is delocalized by extended π bonding:

$$\text{>C=}\ddot{\text{N}}\text{—}\ddot{\text{O}}\text{H} \xrightarrow{B:} \left[\text{>C=}\ddot{\text{N}}\text{—}\ddot{\text{O}}:^- \longleftrightarrow \text{>}\ddot{\text{C}}\text{—}\ddot{\text{N}}\text{=}\ddot{\text{O}}: \right].$$ Thus >C=NO$^-$ is a weaker base and its conjugate acid, the oxime, is more acidic.

15.85 When heated in the presence of conc. H_2SO_4, PCl_5, or $PhSO_2Cl$, oximes rearrange (*Beckmann rearrangement*). Give the product of the rearrangement of the oxime of (*a*) benzophenone, (*b*) acetone, and (*c*) propanal.

▰ Substituted amides are formed. (*a*) PhNHCOPh, (*b*) $CH_3CONHCH_3$, (*c*) $HCONHCH_2CH_3$ (*little* $CH_3CH_2CONH_2$).

15.86 Suggest a mechanism for the Beckmann rearrangement.

▰ The function of the acidic reagent is to convert the OH to a better leaving group:

$$RR'C{=}N{-}OH \xrightarrow{H_2SO_4} RR'C{=}N{-}\overset{+}{O}H_2 \quad \text{or} \quad RR'C{=}N{-}OH \xrightarrow{PhSO_2Cl} RR'C{=}N{-}OSO_2Ph$$

Loss of H_2O or $^-{:}OSO_2Ph$ occurs with simultaneous migration of the trans $:R$.

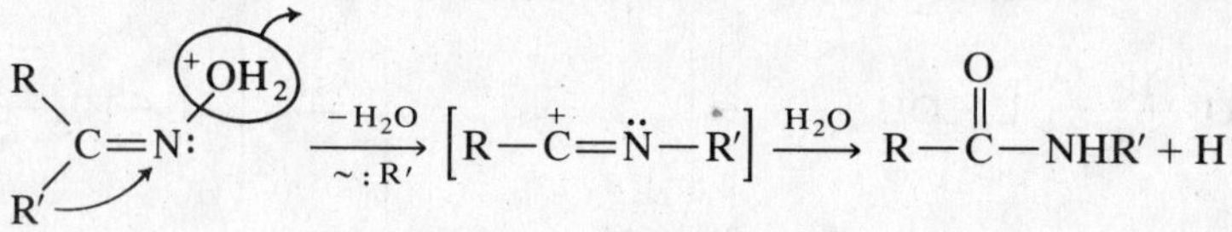

15.87 Show the Beckmann rearrangement of cyclohexanone oxime.

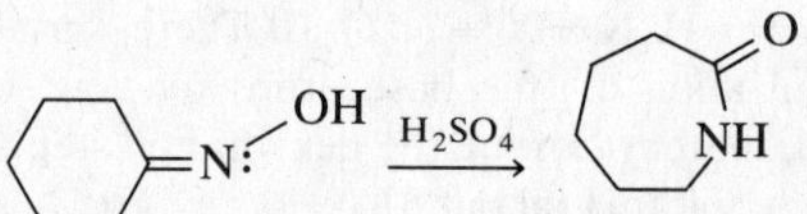

ϵ-Caprolactam
(a cyclic amide)

15.88 (*a*) Give the products of the reaction of HCN with (i) PhCHO and (ii) cyclohexanone. (*b*) Why are these reactions useful?

▰ (*a*) The products are *cyanohydrins*: (i) PhCH(OH)CN and (ii) 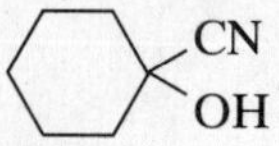 . (*b*) Cyanohydrins are easily hydrolyzed to α-hydroxyacids which are convertible to α,β-unsaturated acids.

$$RCH_2CH(OH)CN \xrightarrow{H_3O^+} RCH_2CH(OH)COOH \xrightarrow[\Delta]{H^+} RCH{=}CHCOOH$$

15.89 (*a*) Give a mechanism for the addition of HCN to R_2CO. (*b*) Why is the optimum pH of 9–10 used?

▰ (*a*) (*1*) (*2*)

(*b*) A small amount of base is necessary to convert some HCN to CN^-, after which the CN^- is regenerated. With too much base the cyanohydrin is decomposed, reversing the equilibrium.

15.90 (*a*) Write a rate expression for the mechanism in Problem 15.89 if (i) the first step is slow and the second fast and (ii) the second step is slow and the first fast. (*b*) Which is the observed rate expression?

▰ (*a*) (i) $rate_1 = k_1[R_2CO]\,[CN^-]$ and (ii) $rate_2 = k_2[R_2C(CN)O^-]\,[HCN]$. The cyanohydrin anion would be formed as a result of a fast, reversible first step for which

$$K_{eq} = \frac{[R_2C(CN)O^-]}{[R_2CO][CN^-]} \quad \text{and} \quad [R_2C(CN)O^-] = K_{eq}[R_2CO][CN^-]$$

Substitution into equation (ii) gives $rate_2 = K_{eq}k_2[R_2CO]\,[CN^-]\,[HCN] = k_2'[R_2CO]\,[CN^-]\,[HCN]$ where $k_2' = K_{eq}k_2$. (*b*) Equation in (i).

15.91 (*a*) Which is the more favorable equilibrium situation for cyanohydrin formation: RCHO + NaCN or RCHO + HCN (both in H_2O)? Explain. (*b*) Under what conditions may a cyanohydrin formation be reversed?

▰ (*a*) CN^- adds to RCHO to give $RCH(CN)O^-$, a more basic anion than itself. In this equilibrium, the side with the weaker base is favored. Thus the equilibrium lies more towards RCHO than in the HCN reaction, or K_{eq} for HCN > K_{eq} for CN^-. (*b*) With a strong base, the cyanohydrin is converted to its conjugate base from which CN^- is ejected.

$$RCH(CN)OH \xrightarrow{NaOH} RCH(CN)O^- \longrightarrow RCHO + CN^-$$

15.92 Write structures for **A** through **D** given $Me_2C=O + HCN \longrightarrow A \xrightarrow{H_3O^+} B \xrightarrow[\Delta]{H_2SO_4} C \xrightarrow[\text{2. } H_2O_2, \text{ OH}^-]{\text{1. } BH_3/THF} D.$

◢ $A = $ CH$_3$—C(OH)(CH$_3$)—CN $B = $ CH$_3$—C(OH)(CH$_3$)—COOH $C = $ CH$_2$=C(CH$_3$)—COOH $D = $ HOCH$_2$—CH(CH$_3$)—COOH

15.93 (*a*) The equilibrium constant for cyanohydrin formation is $\approx 10^3$ times greater for cyclohexanone than for cyclopentanone. Explains. (*b*) Make a general statement comparing the reactivities of a five- and six-member ring in reactions involving changes in HO's used by a ring carbon.

◢ (*a*) In cyclopentanone, the hybridized state of the C of C=O switches from sp^2 to sp^3, causing additional higher energy-eclipsing interactions with an H on each flanking C. The C=O of cyclohexanone eclipses the adjacent equatorial H's. This destabilizing effect is lost when the C acquires sp^3 HO's in the cyanohydrin. (*b*) For the five-member ring, reactions are more favorable when a ring C changes from sp^3 to sp^2 because eclipsing interactions are removed. The converse is also true: sp^2 to sp^3 is more unfavorable. Just the opposite is true for the six-member ring.

15.94 Give the product of each reaction with EtSH in H$^+$: (*a*) CH_3CH_2CHO, (*b*) cyclohexanone $=O$, (*c*) $PhCH_2COCH_3$.

◢ (*a*) CH$_3$CH$_2$CH(OH)(SEt) thiohemiacetal   (*b*) cyclohexane(OH)(SEt) thiohemiketal   (*c*) PhCH$_2$C(OH)(CH$_3$)(SEt) thiohemiketal

15.95 Give the products of the reaction in dry HCl of (*a*) $PhCHO + 2EtSH$ and (*b*) $PhCOCHO$ (phenyl glyoxal) $+ 2n\text{-PrSH}$.

◢ (*a*) In dry HCl a thioacetal is formed: $PhCH(SEt)_2$. (*b*) $PhCOCH(SPr)_2$. The internal CO is less reactive than the terminal CO because it is a ketone and is conjugated with the benzene ring.

15.96 (*a*) Write the product of the reaction of NaHSO$_3$ with a C=O and suggest a mechanism for its formation. (*b*) How can this reaction be used to purify RCHO or separate it from RCH$_2$OH?

◢ (*a*) A *bisulfite addition product*, $RCH(OH)SO_2O^-Na^+$, is formed. The nucleophile is $:SO_3^{2-}$

$$\text{C}=\text{O} + {}^-\text{O}-\text{S}(=\text{O})(\text{O}^-) \rightleftharpoons \text{C}-\text{SO}_3^-(\text{O}^-) \xrightarrow{HSO_3^-} \text{C}(\text{OH})-\text{SO}_3^- \text{ as Na}^+ \text{ salt } (+SO_3^{2-})$$

A C—S bond is formed because S is more nucleophilic than O.

(*b*) The solid bisulfite adduct is filtered from solution containing impurities or unreacted RCH$_2$OH and then decomposed by acid or base to regenerate the RCHO:

$$RCH(OH)SO_3^-Na^+ \xrightarrow[\text{or OH}^-]{H^+} \begin{array}{l} SO_2 \\ SO_3^{2-} \end{array} + RCHO \text{ (extracted with ether)}$$

15.97 (*a*) Give the product of the reaction of triphenylphosphine, Ph$_3$P:, with CH$_3$CH$_2$Br and classify the type of reaction. (*b*) Write the structure of the product of the reaction in (*a*) with NaH or *n*-BuLi.

◢ (*a*) $[Ph_3\overset{+}{P}CH_2CH_3]Br^-$, ethyltriphenylphosphonium bromide; from S_N2 displacement of Br$^-$ by the nucleophilic $:PPh_3$. (*b*) $Ph_3\overset{+}{P}\overset{..}{\overset{-}{C}}HCH_3$, a *phosphorous ylide*; by removal of an H$^+$ from the Cα to the P.

15.98 What is formed by reacting (*a*) acetone and (*b*) butanone with the product formed in Problem 15.97(*b*)?

◢ (*a*) $(CH_3)_2C=CHCH_3$. (*b*) $CH_3CH_2C(CH_3)=CHCH_3$ ($+Ph_3\overset{+}{P}-\overset{-}{O}$, triphenylphosphine oxide, in each case).

15.99 (*a*) Write and evaluate resonance structures for $Ph_3\overset{+}{P}\overset{-}{C}HCH_3$. (*b*) Show the steps in the reaction of the phosphorous ylide with a $R_2C=O$. (*c*) Why is this *Wittig reaction* particularly useful for synthesizing alkenes?

◢ (*a*) $[Ph_3\overset{+}{P}-\overset{..}{C}HCH_3 \longleftrightarrow Ph_3P=CHR]$ from expansion of the P octet and orbital overlap with its *3d* AO's. The dipolar resonance structure with an octet on each charged atom more closely resembles the hybrid. The carbanion-like character of an ylide is the result of this − charge and explains the nucleophilic nature of the C.

(*b*)

$$Ph_3\overset{+}{P}-\overset{..}{C}HCH_3 + RR'C=O \longrightarrow R-\overset{R'}{\underset{\underset{+PPh_3}{O}}{C}}-\overset{CH_3}{\underset{}{C}}-H \longrightarrow \overset{R'}{\underset{R}{}}C=C\overset{CH_3}{\underset{H}{}} + Ph_3\overset{+}{P}-\overset{-}{O}$$

a betaine or
oxaphosphetane   *E* or *Z*

The nature of the diasteromer (*E* or *Z*) can be controlled by adjusting the conditions of the reaction.
(*c*) The position of the C=C is known unequivocally.

15.100 Which phosphonium halide and carbonyl compound must be used in a Wittig reaction to synthesize (*a*) PhCH=CHCH₃, (*b*) $CH_3CH_2CH=C(CH_2CH_3)_2$, (*c*) cyclopentyl$-\underset{\underset{CH_2}{\|}}{C}-CH_3$? Give all possible combinations.

◢ (*a*) $[Ph_3PEt]^+Br^- + PhCHO$ or $[Ph_3PCH_2Ph]^+Br^- + CH_3CHO$
(*b*) $[Ph_3PCH_2CH_2CH_3]^+Br^- + CH_3CH_2COCH_2CH_3$ or $[Ph_3PCH(CH_2CH_3)_2]^+Br^- + CH_3CH_2CHO$
(*c*) $[Ph_3PCH_2]^+Br^- + CH_3CO$-cyclopentyl or $[Ph_3PCH(CH_3)$-cyclopentyl$]^+Br^- + H_2CO$
In (*b*) and (*c*) it is better to use a 1° rather than a 2° halide to prepare the phosphonium salt because the order of reactivity of RX is 1° > 2° > 3°.

15.101 (*a*) Give three ways of synthesizing methylenecyclohexane. (*b*) Why is the dehydration of cyclohexylcarbinol in acid an unsatisfactory method?

◢ (*a*) (*1*) 1-Chloromethylcyclohexane + $(Me_3CO)^-K^+$ (*2*) cyclohexylchloromethane + alc. KOH, (*3*) cyclohexanone + $[Ph_3PCH_2]^+I^-$.
(*b*) The product is 1-methylcyclohexene, formed by a hydride shift followed by H^+ elimination from a ring C.

15.102 Give the products of heating each of the following with H_2NNH_2 and strong base (Wolff–Kishner reduction): (*a*) $PhCOCH_2CH_3$, (*b*) 4,4-dimethylcyclohexanone, (*c*) p-MeOC₆H₄COCH₃, (*d*) $CH_3CH=CHCH_2CHO$.

◢ C=O is reduced to CH_2. (*a*) $PhCH_2CH_2CH_3$, (*b*) 1,1-dimethylcyclohexane, (*c*) p-MeOC₆H₄CH₂CH₃, (*d*) $CH_3CH=CHCH_2CH_3$.

15.103 Suggest steps in the Wolff–Kishner reduction.

◢
$$RCHO + H_2NNH_2 \xrightarrow{(1)} \underset{\text{a hydrazone}}{RCH=N-NH_2} \xrightarrow[OH^-]{(2)} \left[RCH=\overset{..}{N}-\overset{..}{N}H \longleftrightarrow R\overset{..}{C}H-\overset{..}{N}=\overset{..}{N}H\right]$$

$$\xrightarrow[\text{from } H_2O]{(3)\,H^+} RCH_2\overset{..}{N}=\overset{..}{N}H \xrightarrow[OH^-]{(4)} RCH_2\overset{..}{N}=\overset{..}{N}:^- \xrightarrow[\text{from } H_2O]{(5)\,H^+} RCH_3 + N_2$$

15.104 What products are formed on heating the following carbonyl compounds with zinc amalgam (Zn/Hg) and HCl (*Clemmensen reduction*)? (*a*) $PhCH_2CHO$, (*b*) $PhCO(CH_2)_3CH_3$, (*c*) CH_3COCH_2COOH, (*d*) $CH_3CH_2CH=CHCHO$.

◢ C=O is reduced to CH_2. (*a*) $PhCH_2CH_3$, (*b*) $Ph(CH_2)_4CH_3$, (*c*) $CH_3CH_2CH_2COOH$, (*d*) $CH_3CH_2CH=CHCH_3$.

15.105 Write the structures of compounds **A** and **B** in the following sequence of reactions:

$$PhCHO + HSCH_2CH_2SH \xrightarrow{\text{dry HCl}} A \xrightarrow{\text{Raney Ni}} B \text{ (Raney Ni has adsorbed } H_2)$$

◢ **A** is the cyclic thioacetal $\underset{Ph}{\overset{H}{}}C\overset{S-CH_2}{\underset{S-CH_2}{}}$. Desulfurization (a hydrogenolysis) occurs, giving **B**, $PhCH_3$.

15.106 Do each of the following transformations:

(*a*) $(CH_3)_3CCOCH_2CH_2CH_3$ from $(CH_3)_3CCOCH_2COCH_3$ (*b*) $PhCOCH_2CH_3$ from $PhCOCH_2CHO$

▮ (*a*) The unhindered keto group is converted to a cyclic thioketal. Reduction with Raney Ni completes the conversion. (*b*) In this case the aldehyde group, being more reactive, is converted to the cyclic thioacetal and then reduction is effected with Raney Ni.

15.107 How would you decide whether Clemmensen, Wolff–Kishner, or Raney Ni desulfurization is most efficacious for reducing a carbonyl compound?

▮ Carbonyl compounds, together with other functional groups that react with strong base, must be reduced by the Clemmensen method, provided they are stable in acid. If they are sensitive to acid and stable in base, the Wolff–Kishner method should be used. Raney Ni desulfurization occurs under essentially neutral conditions but it cannot be used with reactants with good leaving groups because —SH is an excellent nucleophilic group.

15.108 Select the best way for reducing the $\ce{>C=O}$ in each of the following: (*a*) $BrCH_2CH_2CHO$, (*b*) $(CH_3)_2C(OH)CH_2CH_2COCH_3$, (*c*) $PhCH(OH)CH_2COCH_2CH_3$, (*d*) $CH_3COCH_2\overset{\displaystyle O}{\overset{\diagdown\diagup}{CH-CH_2}}$.

▮ (*a*) Clemmensen reduction. Strong base causes dehydrohalogenation. $HSCH_2CH_2CH_2SH$ can displace Br^-. (*b*) and (*c*) Wolff–Kishner reduction or desulfurization. In (*b*) the 3° OH is dehydrated in acid. In (*c*) the 2° OH is easily dehydrated because the C=C formed is conjugated with the benzene ring. (*d*) None. All methods lead to opening of the epoxide ring.

15.109 In the presence of concentrated OH^-, aldehydes lacking an α-hydrogen undergo the *Cannizzaro reaction*. Give the products of the reactions of (*a*) benzaldehyde, (*b*) trimethylacetaldehyde, and (*c*) furaldehyde.

▮ (*a*) $PhCH_2OH + PhCOO^-$ (*b*) $Me_3CCH_2OH + Me_3CCOO^-$ (*c*) furyl–CH_2OH + furyl–COO^-

15.110 (*a*) Suggest a mechanism for the Cannizzaro reaction. Label the slow step. (*b*) How does the mechanism account for the fact that the product alcohol contains no carbon-bound deuterium when the reaction is run in D_2O?

▮ (*a*) (*1*) $R-\underset{\displaystyle H}{C}=O + OH^- \longrightarrow R-\underset{\displaystyle H}{\overset{\displaystyle OH}{C}}-O^-$

(*2*) $R-\underset{\displaystyle \ddot{H}}{\overset{\displaystyle OH}{C}}-O^- + R-\overset{\displaystyle H}{C}=O \xrightarrow{slow} R-\overset{\displaystyle OH}{C}=O + R-\underset{\displaystyle H}{\overset{\displaystyle H}{C}}-O^- \longrightarrow RCOO^- + RCHHOH$

(*b*) In (*2*) what was originally the aldehydic H is transferred (hydride transfer) directly from the adduct anion to a second aldehyde molecule without any intrusion by solvent (D_2O).

15.111 What are the products of the *crossed-Cannizzaro* reaction of (*a*) H_2CO and $PhCHO$ and (*b*) H_2CO and Me_3CCHO?

▮ (*a*) $PhCH_2OH + HCOO^-$ and (*b*) $Me_3CCH_2OH + HCOO^-$.

15.112 Why is H_2CO always oxidized in the crossed-Cannizzaro reactions in Problem 15.111?

▮ Since H_2CO is the most reactive aldehyde, it exists in aqueous OH^- solution mainly as the conjugate base of its hydrate, $H_2C(OH)O^-$ (Problem 15.67). There is also a statistical factor, because H_2CO has two H's available for transfer in step (*2*) of Problem 15.110; the other aldehyde hydrate anion has only one.

15.113 Give the products of the Cannizzaro reaction of $PhCOCHO$ (**A**) and $PhCOCHCl_2$ (**B**) and explain their formation.

▮ There are *internal* crossed-Cannizzaro reactions. Both **A** and **B** give $PhCH(OH)COO^-$. In **B**, prior alkaline hydrolysis gives compound **A**. The —CHO is oxidized because it has the aldehydic H needed for hydride transfer. Keto-groups can only be reduced, not oxidized, in crossed-Cannizzaro reactions.

15.114 The reaction of Me_3CMgCl and $Me_3CCOCMe_3$ after hydrolysis gives a gas, **A**, and a 2° alcohol, **B**, rather than the expected tri-*t*-butylcarbinol. Provide structures for **A** and **B** and account for their formation.

A is $Me_2C{=}CH_2$; **B** is $Me_3CCH(OH)CMe_3$. Addition to the C=O is prevented or retarded due to the presence of bulky *t*-butyl groups in both the ketone and Grignard reagent. Instead a hydride transfers from the β-position of RMgX to the carbonyl C, possibly through a cyclic TS:

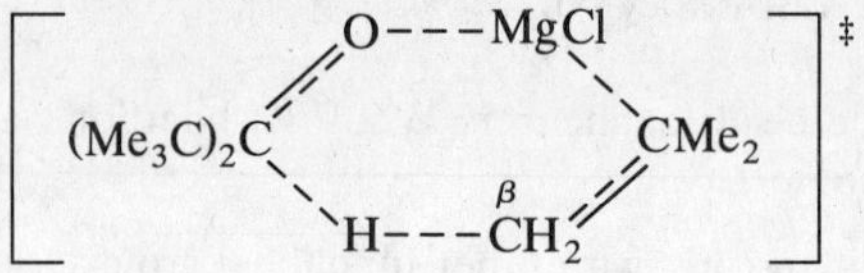
O---MgCl
$(Me_3C)_2C$
CMe_2
β
H---CH_2
‡

RMgX's without a β-H, such as MeMgX or PhMgX cannot act as reducing agents.

15.115 Show how the desired 3° ROH in Problem 15.114 can be synthesized.

Use *t*-butyllithium: $Me_3CLi + Me_3CCOCMe_3 \longrightarrow (Me_3C)_3COH$ (after hydrolysis). R is more carbanion-like in RLi than in RMgX and therefore is sufficiently reactive to overcome the steric hindrance.

15.116 (*a*) What are the essential features of the *Reformatsky reaction*? (*b*) Give the products of this reaction of $BrCH_2COOEt$ with (i) Me_2CO and (ii) cyclopentanone. (*c*) Give the product of $CH_3CHBrCOOEt + MeCHO$.

(*a*) Ketones and aldehydes are reacted with α-bromoesters (BrCHRCOOEt) and zinc in benzene to form β-hydroxyesters. First the zinc organometallic, BrZnCHRCOOEt, forms and then it adds to the C=O.

(*b*) (i) $(CH_3)_2C(OH)CH_2COOEt$, (ii) 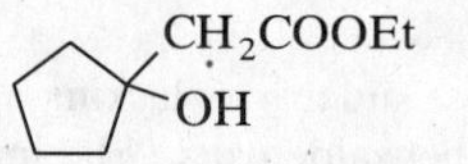 (*c*) $CH_3CH(OH)CH(CH_3)COOEt$.

CH_2COOEt
OH

15.117 Write structures for **A** through **D** given $PhH + CH_2{=}CHCH_2OH \xrightarrow{HF} A \xrightarrow[2.\ H_2O_2,\ OH^-]{1.\ BH_3/THF} B \xrightarrow{CrO_3/Py} C \xrightarrow[2.\ H_3O^+]{1.\ CN^-} D$.

A is $PhCH_2CH{=}CH_2$, **B** is $PhCH_2CH_2CH_2OH$, **C** is $PhCH_2CH_2CHO$, **D** is $PhCH_2CH_2CH(OH)COOH$

15.118 Write structures for **E** through **I** in the set of reactions

$$BrCH_2COOEt + Me_2CHCH_2CHO \xrightarrow{Zn} E \xrightarrow{CrO_3/Py} F \xrightarrow{HOCH_2CH_2OH} G \xrightarrow{LiAlH_4} H \xrightarrow{H_3O^+} I.$$

E is $Me_2CHCH_2CH(OH)CH_2COOEt$ (Reformatsky reaction), **F** is $Me_2CHCH_2COCH_2COOEt$, **G** is 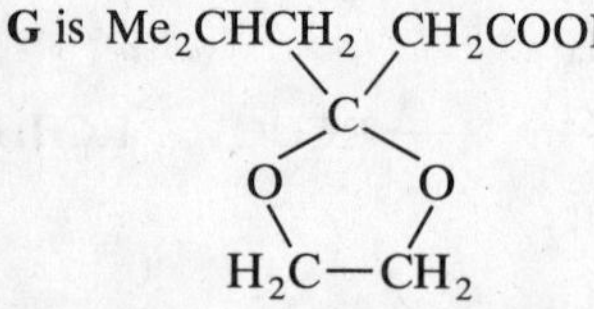 **H** is 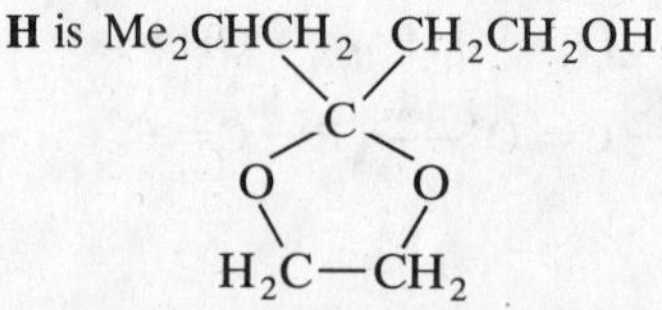 **I** is $Me_2CHCH_2COCH_2CH_2OH$

Me_2CHCH_2 CH_2COOEt
C
O O
$H_2C{-}CH_2$

Me_2CHCH_2 CH_2CH_2OH
C
O O
$H_2C{-}CH_2$

15.119 Give the product of the reaction of 1 eq of Br_2 in H_3O^+ with (*a*) acetone, (*b*) propanal, (*c*) acetophenone, and (*d*) cyclohexanone.

(*a*) CH_3COCH_2Br (*b*) $CH_3CHBrCHO$ (*c*) $PhCOCH_2Br$ (*d*) 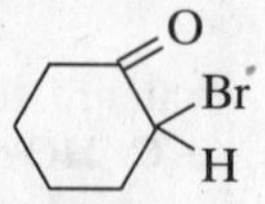

O
Br
H

15.120 How can we convert $PhCH{=}CHCOCH_3$ to (*a*) $PhCH{=}CHCOOH$, (*b*) $PhCH{=}CHCHOHCH_3$, (*c*) $PhCH_2CH_2COCH_3$, (*d*) $PhCH{=}CHCH_2CH_3$, and (*e*) $Ph(CH_2)_3CH_3$?

(*a*) Cl_2, OH^- (haloform reaction). (*b*) $Al^{3+}[Me_2CHO^-]_3$ in Me_2CHOH (Meerwein–Ponndorf reduction) or $LiAlH_4$. (*c*) To reduce only C=C of α,β-unsaturated carbonyls use dissolving metal conditions, (Birch reduction) Li, liq. NH_3, ether. (*d*) H_2NNH_2, OH^- (Wolff–Kishner reduction). (*e*) Reduce the compound in (*d*) with H_2/Pt or reduce the compound in (*c*) by Clemmensen or Wolff–Kishner method.

15.121 Write structures for the products of the reaction of PCl_5 with (*a*) propanal, (*b*) benzophenone, (*c*) propiophenone, and (*d*) cyclopentanone.

C=O is replaced by CCl_2. (*a*) $CH_3CH_2CHCl_2$, (*b*) $C_6H_5CCl_2C_6H_5$, (*c*) $C_6H_5CCl_2CH_2CH_3$, and (*d*) 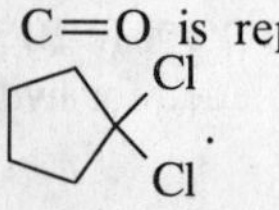.

Cl
Cl

15.122 Give the products **A** and **B** in PhCH=O + SF$_4$ $\xrightarrow{\Delta}$ **A** and cyclohexanone + MoF$_6$ ⟶ **B**.

▰ **A** is PhCHF$_2$ and **B** is ⬡$\substack{F \\ F}$.

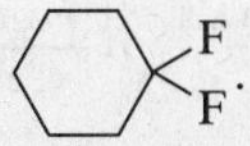

15.123 Perform each of the following transformations:
(*a*) PhCOCH$_2$CH$_3$ ⟶ PhC≡CCH$_3$ (*c*) *p*-O=CHC$_6$H$_4$COOH ⟶ *p*-O=CHC$_6$H$_4$CHO
(*b*) cyclohexanone ⟶ O=CH(CH$_2$)$_4$CH=O

▰ (*a*) PCl$_5$, then 2NaNH$_2$ (−2HCl). (*b*) NaBH$_4$, followed by dehydration with H$_2$SO$_4$/Δ to give cyclohexene; then ozonolysis and Zn reduction. (*c*) HOCH$_2$CH$_2$OH, dry HCl to protect —CHO; convert —COOH to —COCl (use SOCl$_2$) which is reduced to —CHO with H$_2$ and Pd/BaSO$_4$ (Rosenmund). Finally recover the original —CHO by decomposing the acetal group with aqueous acid.

15.124 Write structures for **E** through **I**, given

$$C_6H_6 + (CH_2CO)_2O \text{ (succinic anhydride)} \xrightarrow{AlCl_3} \textbf{E} \xrightarrow[H^+]{Zn/Hg} \textbf{F} \xrightarrow{HF} \textbf{G} \xrightarrow[H^+]{Zn/Hg} \textbf{H} \xrightarrow{Pd/C} \textbf{I}$$

▰ **E** is PhCOCH$_2$CH$_2$COOH; **F** is Ph(CH$_2$)$_3$COOH; **G** is

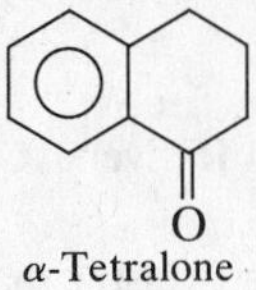

[structures: α-Tetralone, Tetralin, Naphthalene]

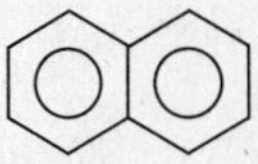

15.125 What is the product of the reaction (after acidic hydrolysis) of Mg/Hg (amalgamated Mg) in inert solvent with each of the following: (*a*) Me$_2$CO and (*b*) PhCOMe.

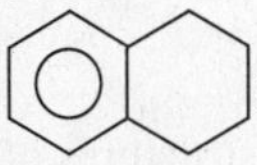

▰ (*a*) Me$_2$C(OH)C(OH)Me$_2$ (pinacol) and (*b*) PhCMeCMePh . These are *pinacol* reactions.
                                              HO OH

15.126 Two isomers are formed from the reaction of butanone with Mg/Hg. Write their structures.

▰ Two chiral C's are formed in this reaction, leading to a racemate and a *meso* structure:

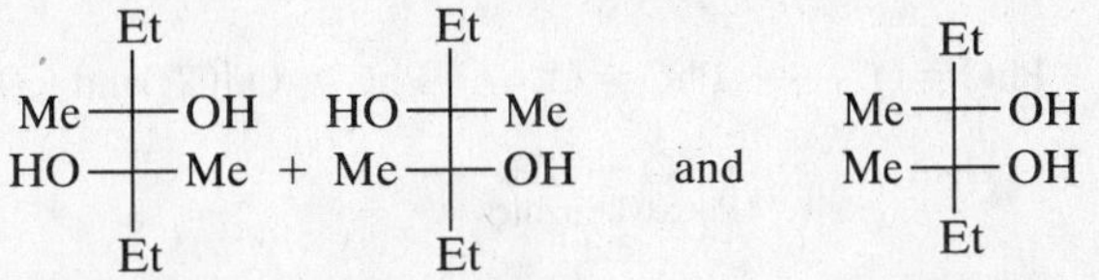

[structures: racemate, mirror image, and meso]

15.127 Given PhCH(OH)CH(OH)CH$_3$ $\xrightarrow{H^+}$ **D**, write the structure of **D** and rationalize its formation.

▰ Two factors affect the course of this pinacol-pinacolone rearrangement: (*1*) Formation of the more stable carbocation and (*2*) relative migratory aptitude of two groups. Loss of OH from C-1 leads to the more stable benzylic carbocation; this is followed by migration of H rather than Me:

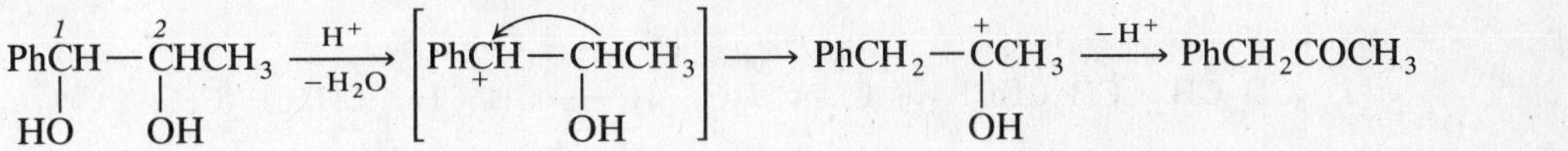

$$\underset{HO \quad\quad OH}{\overset{1 \quad\quad 2}{PhCH-CHCH_3}} \xrightarrow[-H_2O]{H^+} \left[\underset{OH}{PhCH-CHCH_3}\right] \longrightarrow \underset{OH}{PhCH_2-\overset{+}{C}CH_3} \xrightarrow{-H^+} PhCH_2COCH_3$$

15.128 Give the product of the rearrangement of the cyclopentyl glycol **E**, [structure with HO OH, C—CH$_3$, Ph], and show how it is formed.

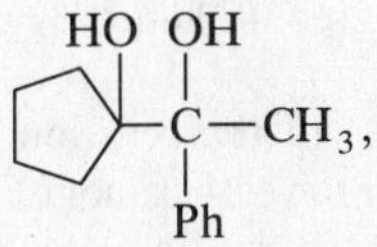

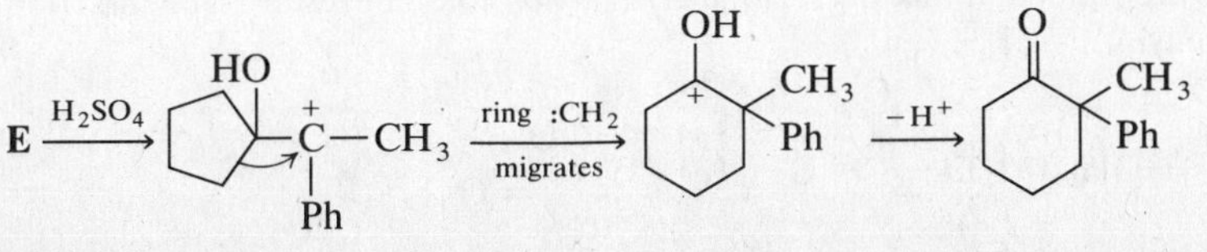

▰ **E** $\xrightarrow{H_2SO_4}$ [structure, C—CH$_3$, Ph] $\xrightarrow[\text{migrates}]{\text{ring :CH}_2}$ [structure OH, CH$_3$, Ph] $\xrightarrow{-H^+}$ [structure O, CH$_3$, Ph]

15.129 Write the structures of **A**, **B**, and **C** given

$$TsO(CH_2)_4OTs \xrightarrow[\Delta]{Ph_3P \text{ (excess)}} A \xrightarrow[\text{(2 eq.)}]{PhLi} B \xrightarrow[\text{(2 eq.)}]{PhCHO} C$$

◢ This is a Wittig synthesis of a dialkene:

$$\mathbf{A} \text{ is } \left[Ph_3\overset{+}{P}(CH_2)_4\overset{+}{P}Ph_3\right][OTs^-]_2; \quad \mathbf{B} \text{ is } \left[Ph_3\overset{+}{P}\overset{-}{C}H(CH_2)_2\overset{-}{C}H\overset{+}{P}Ph_3\right]$$

$$\mathbf{C} \text{ is } PhCH{=}CH(CH_2)_2CH{=}CHPh \left(+2Ph_3\overset{+}{P}\overset{-}{O}\right)$$

15.130 Give the structures of **D**, **E**, and **F** in the following: $Ph_2S + BrCH_2CHMe_2 \xrightarrow{BuLi} D \xrightarrow{MeCHO} E + F$.

◢ **D** is $Ph_2\overset{+}{S}{-}\overset{..}{C}H{-}CHMe_2$, a sulfur ylide; **E** is an epoxide formed by nucleophilic displacement:

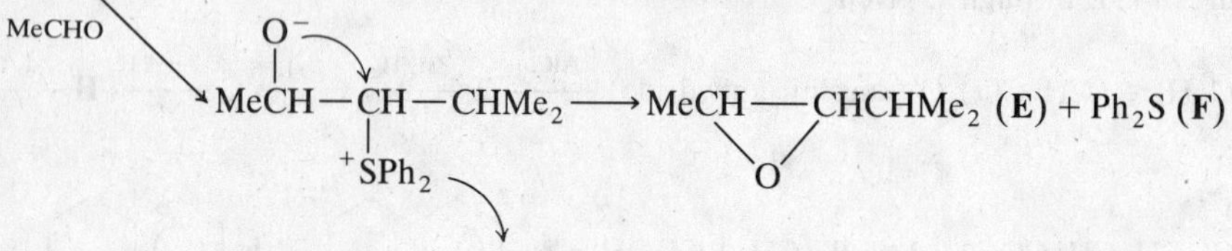

15.131 Write the structures of **G** and **H** given $\mathbf{G} \xleftarrow[\text{2. } H_2O_2,\, OH^-]{\text{1. } BH_3/THF} O{=}\bigcirc{=}CH_2 \xrightarrow{NaBH_4} \mathbf{H}.$

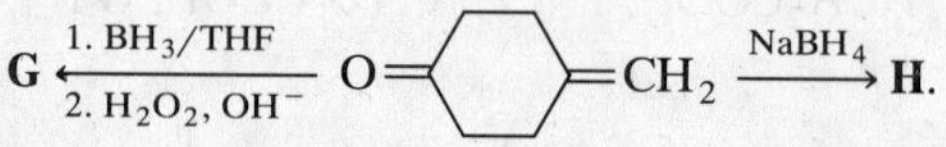

◢ BH_3 reacts with the $C{=}C$ faster than the $C{=}O$; the reverse holds for $NaBH_4$.

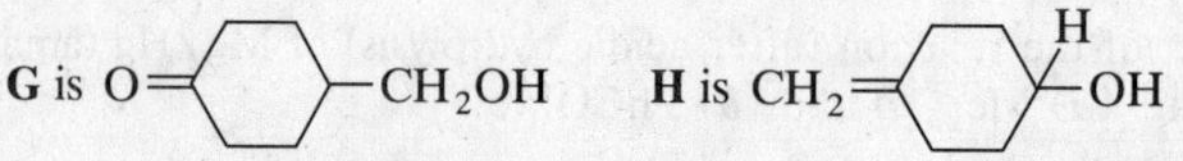

15.132 Suggest a mechanism for the free-radical oxidation of benzaldehyde by atmospheric O_2. The reaction is initiated by a radical $R\cdot$.

◢ (1) $PhCH{=}O + R\cdot \longrightarrow Ph\dot{C}{=}O + RH$ (initiation step)

(2) $Ph\dot{C}{=}O + O_2 \longrightarrow PhC{=}O$, then
$$\quad\quad\quad\quad\quad\quad\quad\quad\quad\quad | $$
$$\quad\quad\quad\quad\quad\quad\quad\quad\quad O{-}O\cdot$$

(3) $PhC{=}O + Ph\dot{C}{=}O \longrightarrow PhC{=}O \quad + Ph\dot{C}{=}O$ [(2) and (3) are propagation steps.]
$$\;\;| \quad\quad\quad\quad | \quad\quad\quad\quad\quad | $$
$$\;\;O{-}O\cdot \;\; H \quad\quad\quad\quad O{-}OH$$
$$\quad\quad\quad\quad\quad\quad\quad\quad\quad \text{Peroxybenzoic}$$
$$\quad\quad\quad\quad\quad\quad\quad\quad\quad\quad \text{acid}$$
$$O$$
$$\|$$
(4) $PhCOOH + PhCHO \longrightarrow 2\ PhCOOH$ (termination step)

15.133 Suggest a mechanism for the following reaction that occurs in the presence of uv or peroxides (free-radical initiators). $CH_3CH_2CHO + H_2C{=}CHCH_3 \longrightarrow CH_3CH_2COCH_2CH_2CH_3$

◢ (1) $CH_3CH_2CH{=}O + RO\cdot \longrightarrow CH_3CH_2\dot{C}{=}O + ROH$

(2) $CH_3CH_2\dot{C}{=}O + H_2C{=}CHCH_3 \longrightarrow CH_3CH_2\underset{\underset{O}{\|}}{C}{-}CH_2\dot{C}HCH_3$

(3) $CH_3CH_2\underset{\underset{O}{\|}}{C}CH_2\dot{C}HCH_3 + CH_3CH_2\underset{\underset{O}{\|}}{C}{-}H \longrightarrow CH_3CH_2\underset{\underset{O}{\|}}{C}CH_2CH_2CH_3 + CH_3CH_2\underset{\underset{O}{\|}}{\dot{C}}$

(1) is the initiation step. (2) and (3) propagate the chain.

15.134 What is the product of the reaction of each of the following ketones with peroxybenzoic acid? (*a*) PhCOPh, (*b*) EtCOEt, and (*c*) cyclohexanone.

◢ Esters are formed in this *Baeyer–Villiger reaction*; the net result is the insertion of the O atom of the peracid at the carbonyl C.

(*a*) $Ph{-}\underset{\underset{O}{\|}}{C}{-}OPh$ (*b*) $Et{-}\underset{\underset{O}{\|}}{C}{-}OEt$ (*c*)

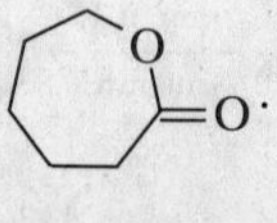

15.135 Suggest a mechanism for the Baeyer–Villiger reaction.

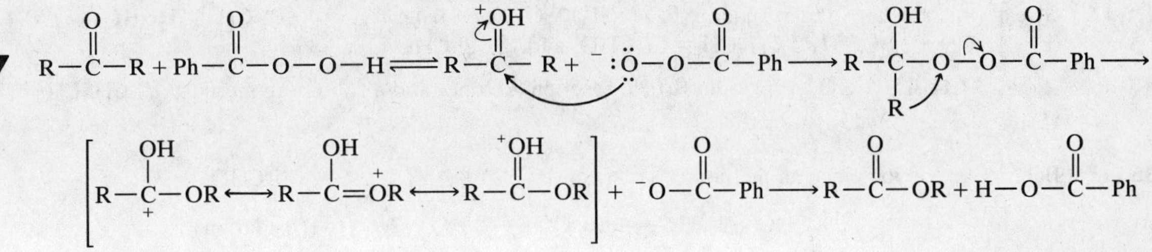

15.136 What products are formed from the Baeyer–Villager oxidation of (*a*) acetophenone, (*b*) *p*-nitrobenzophenone, and (*c*) *p*-methoxybenzophenone?

$$\blacksquare$$ (*a*) PhCOOMe + MeCOOPh, (*b*) *p*-O$_2$NC$_6$H$_4 \overset{O}{\underset{\parallel}{C}}$OPh, and (*c*) Ph$\overset{O}{\underset{\parallel}{C}}OC_6H_4OCH_3$-*p*. In (*a*) the migrating tendency of Me and Ph are similar, so two products form. In (*b*) (Ph) and in (*c*) (*p*-CH$_3$OC$_6$H$_4$), the better migrating group (with greater electron-releasing group) moves to O.

15.137 Give the product and a mechanism of the reaction PhCH=O $\xrightarrow{\text{KCN/EtOH}}$ C$_{14}$H$_{12}$O$_2$.

$$\blacksquare$$ This *benzoin condensation* competes favorably with cyanohydrin formation when aromatic aldehydes are used. The product, a dimer, is PhCH(OH)COPh.

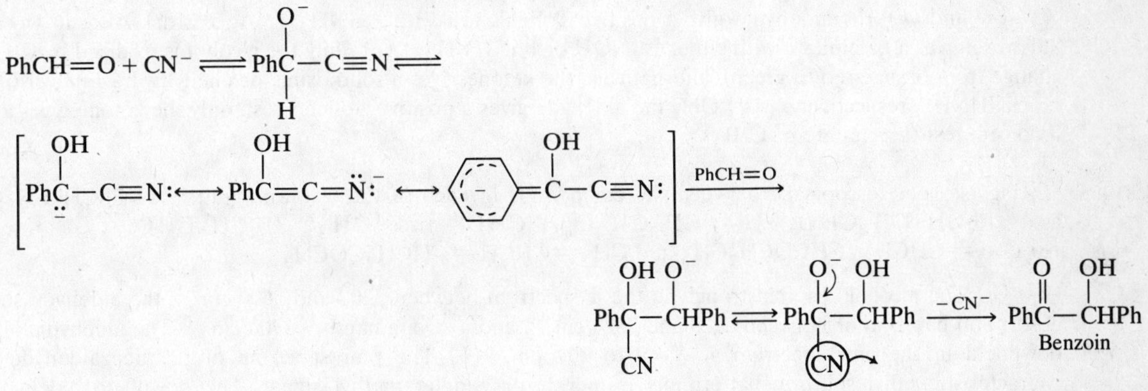

15.138 (*a*) Write the product of the rearrangement in OH$^-$ of (i) PhCOCOPh and (ii) MeCOCOMe. (*b*) Suggest a mechanism.

$$\blacksquare$$ (*a*) This is the *benzilic acid rearrangement*. (i) Ph$_2$(OH)COO$^-$ and (ii) Me$_2$C(OH)COO$^-$.

(*b*)

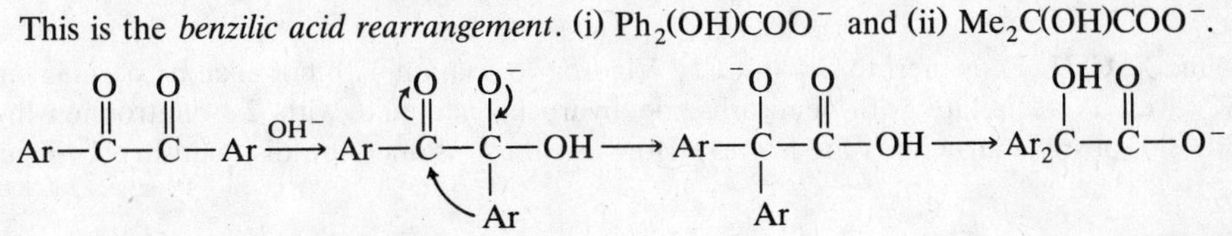

15.139 How is ketene, H$_2$C=C=O, prepared industrially?

$$\blacksquare \quad CH_3COOH \xrightarrow{\Delta} H_2C=C=O + H_2O \quad \text{or} \quad CH_3COCH_3 \xrightarrow{700\,°C} CH_2=C=O + CH_4$$

15.140 Write the products of the reaction of ketene with (*a*) H$_2$O, (*b*) EtOH, and (*c*) CH$_3$COOH.

$$\blacksquare$$ (*a*) CH$_3$COOH, (*b*) CH$_3$COOEt, (*c*) (CH$_3$CO)$_2$O (commercial synthesis of acetic anhydride).

15.141 Complete the following: (*a*) PhCOCH$_2$CH$_3$ + SO$_2$Cl$_2$, (*b*) Me$_2$⬡=O + NBS.

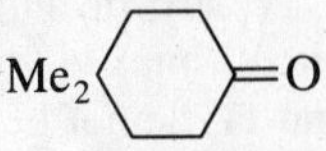

$$\blacksquare$$ Halogenation occurs at the α position to the C=O under free radical conditions. (*a*) PhCOCHClCH$_3$,

(*b*) Me$_2$⬡=O with —Br and H

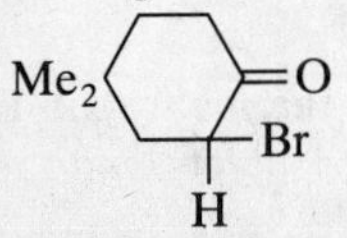

ANALYSIS

15.142 Give the products of the reaction of $Ag(NH_3)_2^+$ (*Tollens' reagent*) with (*a*) CH_3CH_2CHO, (*b*) CH_3COCH_3, (*c*) $CH_3CH_2CH_2OH$, (*d*) $CH_3CH=CHCHO$, and (*e*) $PhCHO$.

◢ (*a*) $CH_3CH_2COO^-$. (*b*) and (*c*) No reaction (ketones and alcohols are inert). (*d*) $CH_3CH=CHCOO^-$. (*e*) $PhCOO^-$.

15.143 Balance by the ion-electron method the reaction $RCHO + Ag(NH_3)_2^+ \longrightarrow RCOO^- + Ag$.

$$\left[RCHO + 3OH^- \longrightarrow RCOO^- + 2H_2O + 2e^- \right] \times 1 (\text{oxidation})$$

$$\left[Ag(NH_3)_2^+ + e^- \longrightarrow Ag + 2NH_3 \right] \times 2 (\text{reduction})$$

$$\overline{RCHO + 3OH^- + 2Ag(NH_3)_2^+ \longrightarrow RCOO^- + 2H_2O + 2Ag + 4NH_3}$$

15.144 Give the products of the reaction of I_2 in KOH with (*a*) CH_3CH_2CHO, (*b*) CH_3CH_2OH, (*c*) $PhCHO$, (*d*) $PhCH_2COCH_3$, (*e*) Me_3CCOCH_3, (*f*) $CH_3CH_2COCH_2CH_2COCH_3$, and (*g*) $PhCH_2OH$.

◢ This is the iodoform test; CHI_3, a pale yellow solid, is formed when the reaction occurs. (*a*), (*c*), and (*g*) No reaction; (*b*) $HCOO^-$; (*d*) $PhCH_2COO^-$; (*e*) Me_3CCOO^-; (*f*) $CH_3CH_2COCH_2CH_2COO^-$.

15.145 Give a simple chemical test to distinguish between the compounds in each of the following pairs:
(*a*) $PhCH=CHCH_2OH$ and $PhCH=CHCHO$ (*c*) $PhCH_2COCH_2CH_3$ and $PhCH(OH)CH_2CH_2CH_3$
(*b*) $CH_3CH_2CH_2CH_2CHO$ and $CH_3CH_2COCH_2CH_3$ (*d*) $PhCH_2CHO$ and $PHCOCH_3$

◢ (*a*) and (*b*) The aldehydes give a positive Tollen's test with $Ag(NH_3)_2^+$ (Ag mirror). Also, in (*a*) only the aldehyde gives a precipitate with either H_2NOH or $PhNHNH_2$. (*c*) Only the alcohol is oxidized by CrO_3 (color change from orange-red to green); alternatively, the ketone gives a solid oxime or phenylhydrazone with H_2NOH or $PhNHNH_2$, respectively. (*d*) Only the aldehyde gives a positive Tollen's test; only the ketone gives a positive iodoform test (precipitate of CHI_3).

15.146 Distinguish spectroscopically between the compounds in each of the following pairs: (*a*) $PhCH_2CH_2CH_2OH$ and $PhCH_2CH_2CHO$, (*b*) $CH_3CH_2C_6H_4CHO$ and $CH_3C_6H_4CH_2CHO$ (*o*, *m* or *p*), (*c*) $CH_2=CHCH=CHCOCH_2CH_3$ and $CH_2=CHCH=CHCH_2COCH_3$

◢ (*a*) The alcohol absorbs strongly in the ir spectrum between 3200 and 3600 cm^{-1}; the aldehyde shows two absorption bands at or between 2720 and 2820 cm^{-1}, and a strong band ~ 1700 cm^{-1}. The aldehydic H absorbs downfield in the pmr spectrum at $\delta = 9$ to 10 ppm. (*b*) The pmr spectrum of the benzaldehyde has the characteristic ethyl splitting pattern, its isomer has a singlet methyl signal. The downfield aldehydic H of $CH_3C_6H_4CH_2\underline{C}HO$ will appear as a triplet. (*c*) The uv absorption of the conjugated ketone is shifted by about 30 nm to longer wavelengths, in accord with the Woodward–Fieser rules. The pmr spectrum of the conjugated ketone has the ethyl pattern, its isomer has a singlet methyl signal.

15.147 Compound **X**, $C_9H_{10}O$, is inert to Br_2 in CCl_4. Vigorous oxidation with hot alkaline permanganate yields benzoic acid. **X** gives a precipitate with semicarbazide hydrochloride and with 2,4-dinitrophenylhydrazine (DNPH). (*a*) Write all possible structures for **X**. (*b*) How can these isomers be distinguished by using simple chemical tests?

◢ (*a*) The oxidation to benzoic acid reveals that there is one side chain with the three remaining C's. The formula reveals five degrees of unsaturation, four for the ring and one in the side chain. The extra degree of unsaturation must be due to a $C=O$ (positive test with DNPH) and not to $C=C$ (negative test with Br_2). The possible structures are:

$$PhCOCH_2CH_3 \qquad PhCH_2COCH_3 \qquad PhCH_2CH_2CHO \qquad PhCH(CH_3)CHO$$
$$\textbf{I} \qquad\qquad\quad \textbf{II} \qquad\qquad\quad \textbf{III} \qquad\qquad\quad \textbf{IV}$$

(*b*) The aldehydes, **III** and **IV**, are distinguished from the ketones by undergoing mild oxidation with cold $KMnO_4$. **II** can be distinguished from **I** by the haloform test; it gives a precipitate of the pale yellow CHI_3 when reacted with KI/OH^-. **III** and **IV** cannot be differentiated by any simple chemical tests.

15.148 How can pmr spectra be used to distinguish between **III** and **IV** in Problem 15.147?

◢ In **III** the aldehydic H and the benzylic H signals both appear as triplets and the methylene H's α to the $C=O$ give a multiplet. In **IV** the aldehydic H and the methyl group signals are each doublets, and the benzylic H signal is a multiplet.

15.149 (*a*) Referring to Problem 15.147, what structural feature in **IV** differentiates it from **III**? (*b*) Outline a chemical method for demonstrating the presence of this unique structural feature.

▰ (*a*) Structure **IV** is chiral. (*b*) Its chirality may be demonstrated by resolution. First oxidize it to the chiral acid, $PhCH(CH_3)COOH$, with a mild oxidizing agent (cold $KMnO_4$); then react the racemic acid with one enantiomer of a chiral amine, e.g., (*S*)-1-phenylethylamine. Two diastereomeric salts result, with different physical properties, and often they may be separated by fractional crystallization. Alternatively, the aldehyde may be reduced to the chiral alcohol with $NaBH_4$, and the alcohol then esterified with one enantiomer of a chiral acid (like lactic acid), followed by separation of the diastereomeric esters.

15.150 The mass spectrum of the chemical Mace, used as a tear gas in crowd control, has molecular ions at $m/z = 154$ and 156 in the ratio 2:1. The ir spectrum shows strong absorption in the region 1690 to 1800 cm^{-1}. Oxidation with $KMnO_4$ yields $PhCOOH$. Propose two possible isomers for the structure of Mace based on this limited data.

▰ The mass spectrum reveals one Cl (the two molecular ions having a 2:1 ratio due to ^{35}Cl and ^{37}Cl) and a molecular weight of 154. The ir spectrum shows the presence of a $C=O$. Isolation of $PhCOOH$ indicates a monosubstituted Ph accounting for 77 MW units. The remaining mass ($154 - 77 = 77$) accrues from C_2H_2ClO. The possible isomers are $PhCOCH_2Cl$ (**A**), α-chloroacetophenone, and $PhCH_2COCl$ (**B**), phenylacetyl chloride.

15.151 How can isomers **A** and **B** in Problem 15.150 be distinguished by (*a*) simple chemical tests and (*b*) spectroscopically using (i) ir and (ii) pmr spectra?

▰ The Cl in **A** does not give a precipitate of AgCl with alcoholic $AgNO_3$ but **B** reacts rapidly. Also, when shaken with acetone/H_2O, the acid chloride **B** is rapidly hydrolyzed, forming HCl that turns blue limus red. (*b*) (i) The $C=O$ peak of **B** is at a higher frequency (≈ 1800 cm^{-1}) than the $C=O$ peak of **A** that is conjugated with Ph (≈ 1700 cm^{-1}). (ii) The pmr spectrum of **B** would not show significant aromatic H splitting and its methylene H's would not be shifted downfield as much as **A**.

15.152 Explain the lack of reactivity of α-halocarbonyls (even the 3° ones like $R_2CClCHO$) in S_N1 reactions.

▰ The resulting carbocation would be too unstable due to the presence of adjacent + charges:

$$\underset{\text{Cl}}{\overset{\text{Cl}\quad\;:\!\text{O}\!:}{R_2C-C-H}} \;\xrightarrow{\;\;\;}\!\!\!\!\!\!\!\!\!\!\times\;\;\; \left[\overset{:O:}{R_2\underset{+}{C}-C-H} \longleftrightarrow \overset{:\ddot{O}\!:^{-}}{R_2\underset{+}{C}-\underset{+}{C}-H} \right]$$

S_N1 conditions

15.153 (*a*) Compare the reactivity towards KI/acetone of $CH_3CH_2CH_2Cl$ and $CH_3\overset{\text{O}}{\overset{\|}{C}}CH_2Cl$. (*b*) Explain in terms of TS theory.

▰ (*a*) In this typical S_N2 reaction, $CH_3COCH_2Cl \gg CH_3CH_2CH_2Cl$. The enhanced reactivity ($\approx 35,000:1$) is ascribed to the stabilizing effect produced in the TS of the ketone by overlap of the adjacent π bond with the p orbital of the sp^2-hybridized C (see Fig. 15-3). This type of overlap is responsible for the enhanced S_N2 reactivity of allyl halides.

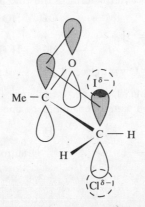

Fig. 15-3

15.154 Ozonolysis of **F**, $C_{11}H_{12}O$, gives H_2CO and **G**, $C_{10}H_{10}O_2$. Both **F** and **G** give a precipitate from reaction with I_2/OH^-. The pmr spectrum of **G** shows two singlets integrating $3:2$. Its ^{13}C spectrum has four signals. Identify compounds **F** and **G**.

◢ The pmr and ^{13}C spectra point to a symmetrically *para*-substituted benzene ring for **F**. The positive iodoform reaction identifies the substituent as $-COCH_3$, and **G** is $p\text{-}CH_3COC_6H_4COCH_3$, which has two kinds of H's, each a singlet. **G** arises from **F**, which is $p\text{-}CH_3COC_6H_4\underset{\displaystyle CH_3}{C}=CH_2$.

SUPPLEMENTARY PROBLEMS

15.155 Give structures of **A**, **B**, and **C** in $ICH_2CH_2CH_2Cl \xrightarrow[\text{2. AgBF}_4]{\text{1. Ph}_2S} A \xrightarrow{\text{NaH}} B \xrightarrow[\text{2. Acetone}]{\text{1. KOH}} C$

◢ **A** is $(Ph_2\overset{+}{S}-CH_2CH_2CH_2Cl)BF_4^-$; $AgBF_4$ assists in removal of I^- (a better leaving group than Cl^-) as AgI. **B** is $(Ph_2\overset{+}{S}-\underset{\displaystyle CH_2}{\overset{\displaystyle |}{CH}}-CH_2)Cl^-$; the intermediate carbanion displaces Cl^-, giving a cyclopropane ring.

KOH converts **B** into an ylide that reacts with acetone to give **C**, a spiranyl epoxide, as follows:

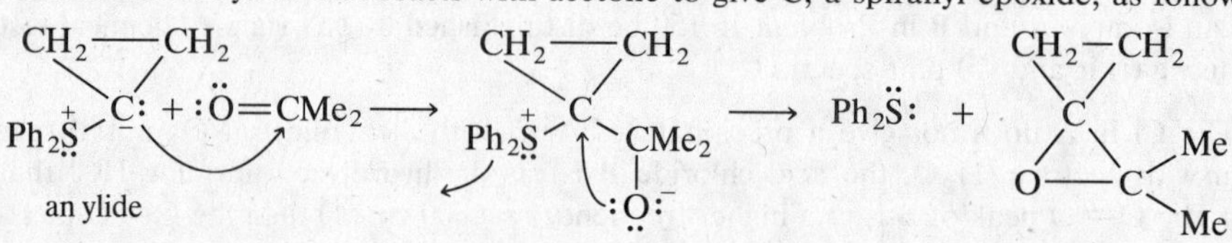

15.156 Give the product of the reaction of ethyl orthoformate, $HC(OEt)_3$, with 1 eq of RMgX.

◢ $RCH=O$. R^- displaces EtO^-, giving $HCR(OEt)_2$, an acetal, which is unreactive toward RMgX.

15.157 Give the products of the periodate oxidation of (*a*) CH_3COCHO, (*b*) 1,2-cyclohexanedione, (*c*) $PhCHOHCHO$, and (*d*) $CH_3CH_2CHOHCOCH_3$.

◢ See Problem 14.90. The net result of this oxidation is cleavage of the bond between the C's with the attached O's, with addition of OH to C of each $C-O$. The products are (*a*) $CH_3COOH + HCOOH$, (*b*) $HOOC(CH_2)_4COOH$, (*c*) $PhCH=O + HCOOH$, and (*d*) $CH_3CH_2CH=O + HOOCCH_3$.

15.158 Explain why acetals and ketals are converted to their corresponding carbonyl compounds with H_3O^+, but are stable to OH^-.

◢ The hydrolysis to $C=O$ goes via the initial formation of a half-hydrate, $>C(OH)OR$, that readily occurs in acid [see Problem 15.72(*a*)]. The half-hydrate cannot form in base, because OH^- (a weaker base) would have to displace OR^-, (a stronger base), an unfavorable process. The second part of the reaction, conversion of the half-hydrate to $C=O$, is catalyzed by both acid and base.

15.159 Write the product of the reduction of $HOCH_2CH_2CH_2COCl$ by $LiAlH(O\text{-}t\text{-}Bu)_3$, explain its formation, and account for the fact that two stereoisomers are formed.

◢ The product is a stable cyclic hemiacetal, formed from the anion of the hydroxyaldehyde product of the reduction. In the ring closure a chiral center is formed; thus the product is a racemate:

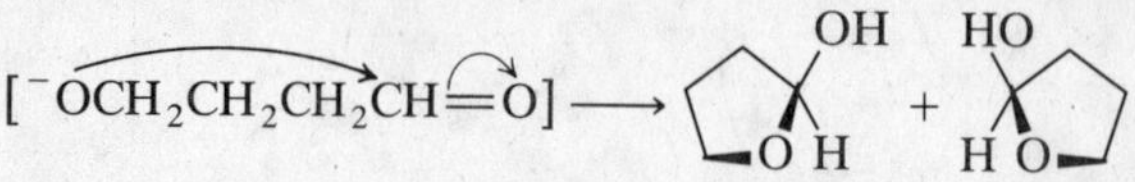

15.160 The reaction of 1 mol each of $RCH=O$ with glycerol gives six separable isomers. Write their structures.

◢ Glycerol is 1,2,3-trihydroxypropane. The cyclic acetal may form with the 1- and 2-OH's, creating in the process two chiral centers and thus two pairs of enantiomers; one pair is the *cis* and the other is *trans*.

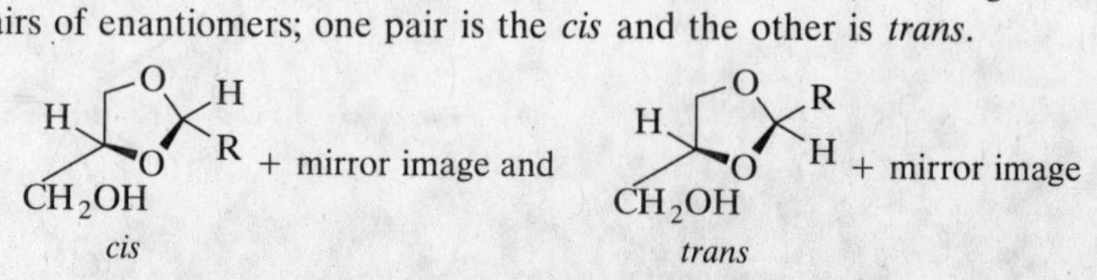

When the acetal forms from the 1- and 3-OH's, a six-membered ring is formed in which the aldehydic H is either *cis* or *trans* to the C^2 H of glycerol. These diastereomers are not chiral.

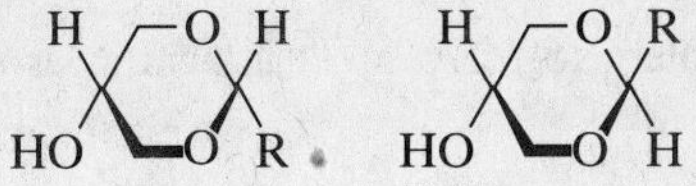

cis   *trans*

15.161 Explain the following:

$$HOCH_2(CH_2)_2CH=O \longrightarrow$$ 89% at equilibrium

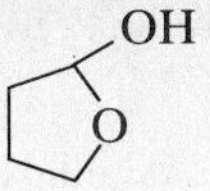

$$HOCH_2(CH_2)_3CH=O \longrightarrow$$ 94% at equilibrium

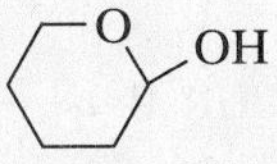

$$HOCH_2(CH_2)_7CH=O \longrightarrow$$ 9% at equilibrium

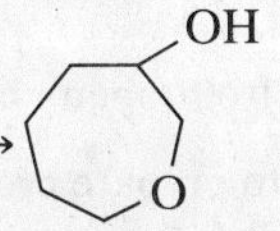

◢ Ring compounds of six or more atoms have no appreciable strain to hinder their formation. However, the ΔS factor is less favorable for ring sizes greater than six. Although ΔS is not as unfavorable in formation of rings of less than five atoms, the strain factor retards their formation.

15.162 Benzaldehyde reacts with HCN to give a mixture of two isomers that cannot be separated by physical means. (*a*) Explain. (*b*) Give a method for proving that two isomers were formed.

◢ (*a*) The product is a racemic mixture because a chiral C is created:

$$Ph—CH=O + HCN \longrightarrow Ph—C^*H(OH)CN$$

(*b*) Acid hydrolysis converts the cyanohydrin to the hydroxyacid. This chiral acid can be resolved (Problem 15.149).

15.163 Give structures for compounds **A** through **F**:

$$PhCH_3 + (CH_2CO)_2O \text{ (succinic anhydride)} \xrightarrow[\text{HCl}]{\text{AlCl}_3} \textbf{A} \xrightarrow{\text{Zn/Hg}} \textbf{B} \xrightarrow{\text{HF}} \textbf{C} \xrightarrow[\text{2. H}_3\text{O}^+]{\text{1. MeMgI}} \textbf{D} \xrightarrow[\text{—H}_2\text{O}]{\text{H}^+} \textbf{E} \xrightarrow[\text{—2H}]{\text{Se or S}} \textbf{F}$$

◢ **A** is p-MeC$_6$H$_4$COCH$_2$CH$_2$COOH   **B** is p-MeC$_6$H$_4$CH$_2$CH$_2$CH$_2$COOH

C is 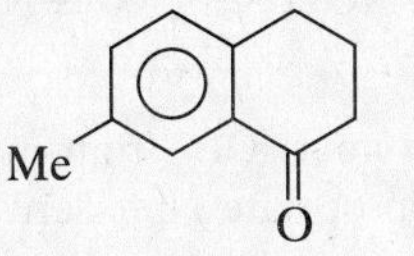   **D** is 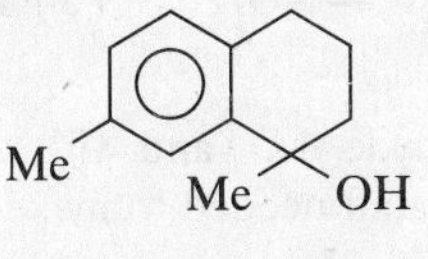   **E** is 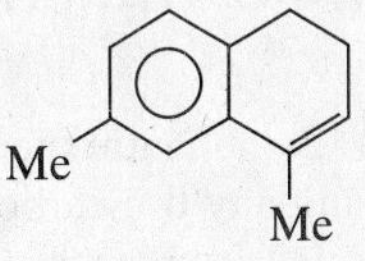   **F** is

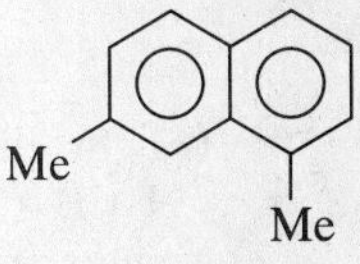

15.164 Synthesize p-D-acetophenone (**G**) from benzene, aliphatic compounds, and D$_2$O.

◢ $$PhH \xrightarrow{Br_2/Fe} PhBr \xrightarrow{Ao_2O/AlCl_3} p\text{-BrC}_6\text{H}_4\text{COCH}_3 \xrightarrow{MeOH/HCl}$$

$$p\text{-BrC}_6\text{H}_4\text{C(OMe)}_2\text{CH}_3 \xrightarrow[\text{2. D}_2\text{O}]{\text{1. Mg}} p\text{-DC}_6\text{H}_4\text{C(OMe)}_2\text{CH}_3 \xrightarrow{H_3O^+} \textbf{G}$$

15.165 The reduction of 4-t-butylcyclohexanone (**H**) with LiAlH$_4$ gives mainly the *trans* alcohol (90%), but with Sia$_2$BH, the product is mainly *cis* alcohol (88%). Draw the structures of the alcohols and explain the different product distributions.

◢ See Fig. 15-4.

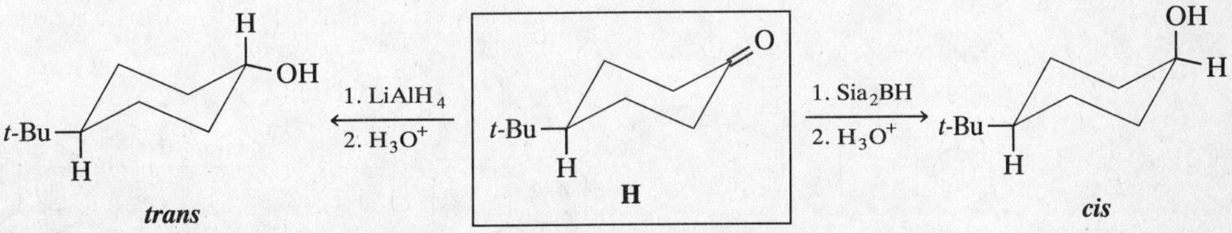

trans   **H**   *cis*

Fig. 15-4

$LiAlH_4$ approaches C=O axially to give the more stable equatorial OH (*trans*-isomer). The bulkier hydride approaches C=O from the less hindered equatorial side, resulting in the less stable axial OH (*cis*-isomer).

15.166 Reduction of ketone **H** in Problem 15.165 over Pt in acid gives *cis*- and *trans*-alcohol in a ratio of 4:1. Explain the product ratio.

Catalytic reduction on a surface involves adsorption on the catalyst and approach of the H's from the less-hindered equatorial side.

15.167 Explain how the Meerwein–Ponndorf reduction can be used to prepare an optically-active alcohol RCHOHR′ from RCOR′.

Instead of Al isopropoxide, use the Al alkoxide of an enantiomeric chiral alcohol.

$$3RCOR' + Al(O\overset{*}{C}HR^1R^2)_3 \longrightarrow \text{(after hydrolysis) } 3R\overset{*}{C}HOHR' + R^1COR^2$$

15.168 Synthesize cyclohexanecarbaldehyde from open-chain compounds.

A Diels–Alder reaction is used to prepare cyclohexene-4-carbaldehyde. The C=O is protected as an acetal, after which the C=C is reduced and the protecting group removed.

$$H_2C{=}CH{-}CH{=}CH_2 + CH_2{=}CH{-}CH{=}O \longrightarrow$$

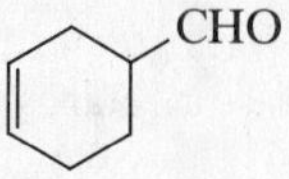

$$\xrightarrow{HOCH_2CH_2OH}$$

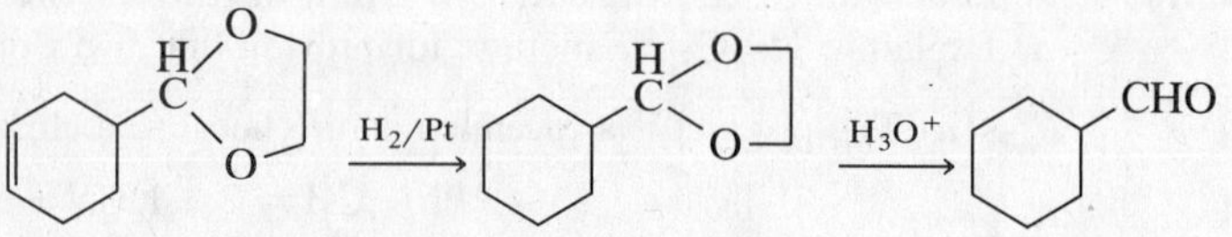

Since the Diels–Alder product is not an α,β-unsaturated aldehyde, the C=C cannot be reduced directly by the dissolving metal technique [see Problem 15.120(*c*)].

15.169 Interpret the following reaction: $RCH{=}O + H_2NOH \xrightarrow[\Delta]{HCOONa} RCN + H_2O$.

This is a combination of two reactions: oxime formation and dehydration.

$$(1)\ RCH{=}O + H_2NOH \longrightarrow RCH{=}NOH \qquad (2)\ RCH{=}NOH \longrightarrow RC{\equiv}N + H_2O$$

15.170 (*a*) Synthesize (i) 2-phenanthrenecarbaldehyde (**A**) and (ii) the 4-isomer (**B**) from naphthalene (Nph), $CH_3CH_2CH_2OH$, and any two-carbon compound needed to make the appropriate Nph derivatives. (*b*) Which isomers are also formed from each synthesis?

(*a*) The new six-membered ring may be introduced by a Diels–Alder reaction using vinylnaphthalenes as dienes and $H_2C{=}CHCHO$ (**C**) as the dienophile (see Problem 9.141). The Diels–Alder products must be isomerized to give the more stable phenanthrenes. Use two methods to introduce the vinyl group.

(i) $1\text{-}NphCH{=}CH_2$ (**D**) is needed.

$$Nph \xrightarrow{CH_3CH_2Br,\ AlCl_3} 1\text{-}NphCH_2CH_3 \xrightarrow{NBS} 1\text{-}NphCHBrCH_3 \xrightarrow{alc.\ KOH} \mathbf{D}$$

$$CH_3CH_2CH_2OH \xrightarrow{H_2SO_4} CH_3CH{=}CH_2 \xrightarrow{NBS} CH_2BrCH{=}CH_2 \xrightarrow[HCO_3^-]{Me_2SO} CH_2{=}CHCHO$$

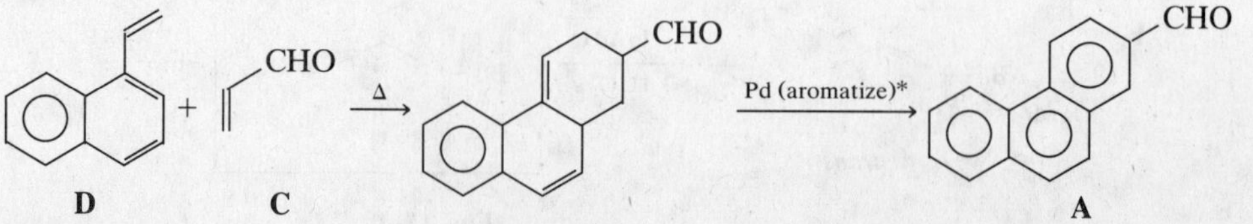

D **C** **A**

(ii) 2-NphCH=CH$_2$ (**E**) is needed.

$$\text{Nph} \xrightarrow[\text{PhNO}_2]{\text{CH}_3\text{COCl}} \text{2-NphCOCH}_3 \xrightarrow{\text{NaBH}_4} \text{2-NphCHOHCH}_3 \xrightarrow{\text{H}_2\text{SO}_4} \text{E}$$

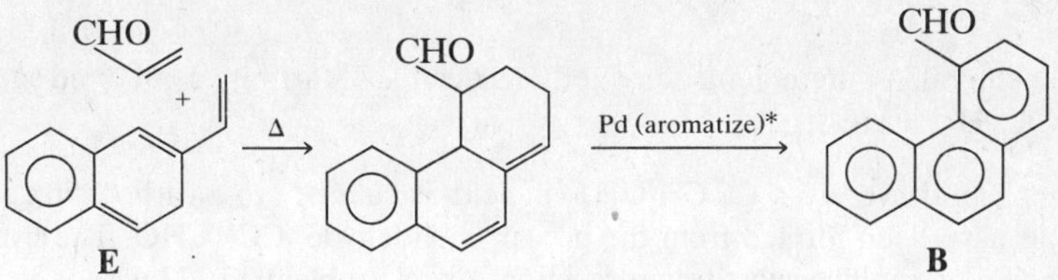

E   **B**

(*b*) The dienophile can orient itself with the vinylnaphthalenes in another way.

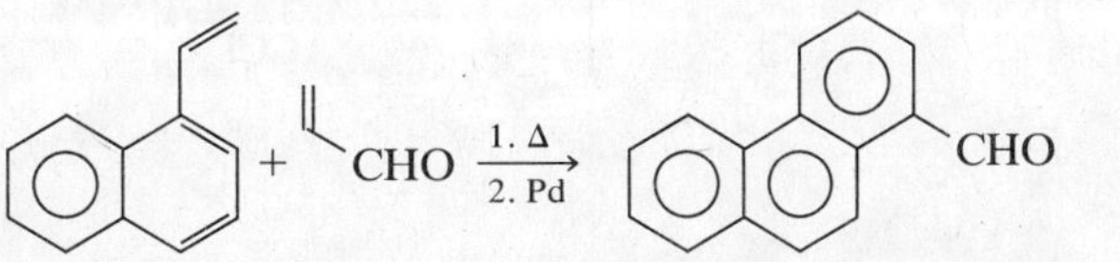

D   **C**   1-Phenanthrenecarbaldehyde

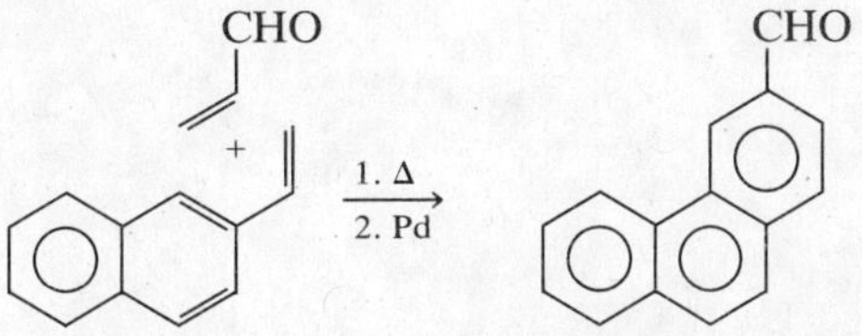

E   3-Phenanthenecarbaldehyde

*To prevent reduction of the —$\overset{\text{H}}{\text{C}}$=O during aromatization, protect it by acetal formation. The aldehyde is regenerated by H$_3$O$^+$ after formation of the phenanthrene ring.

15.171 How can we resolve racemic carbonyl compounds directly? (See Problem 15.149 for indirect methods.)

▮ The racemate may be reacted with an *R* or *S* semicarbazide or hydrazine such as a menthyl derivative (see Problem 13.142). The solid hydrazone-type carbonyl derivatives are separated by fractional recrystallization and hydrolyzed to recover the individual enantiomers. Another method involves conversion of the carbonyl compound into a semicarbazone with *p*-HOOCC$_6$H$_4$NHCONHNH$_2$. The carboxylic acid hydrazone racemate is then resolved in the typical fashion (see Problem 15.149). Again the C=O compound is recovered by hydrolysis. Unfortunately, if the α-C is the stereocenter, both methods suffer because hydrolysis causes racemization (see Problems 18.1 and 18.5).

15.172 The reaction of HCN with EtCHMeCH=O gives two isomers, **A** and **B**, in unequal amounts. Give the structures of **A** and **B**, predict which isomer predominates, and explain your choice.

▮ Two diastereomeric cyanohydrins are possible, because of the presence of a chiral C in the starting aldehyde. If the C=O orients itself to lie between the small and medium-sized groups (H and Me, respectively) on the α-C, then the incoming CN$^-$ bonds preferentially on the side of the plane with the small group. The major product is therefore **B**.

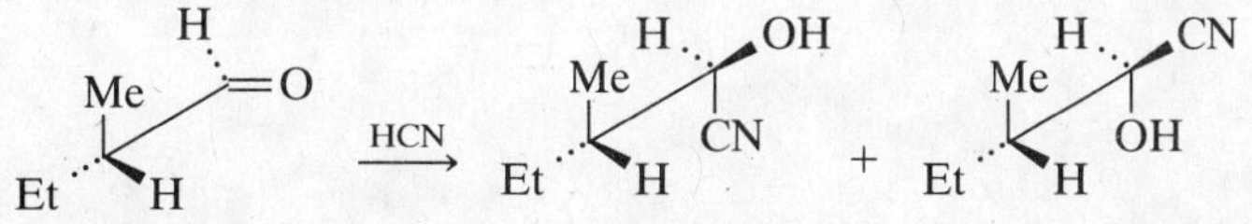

A   **B**

15.173 (*a*) Give the product of the acid-catalyzed reaction of acetone with benzene. (*b*) Discuss the mechanism.

▮ (*a*) Ph$_2$CMe$_2$. (*b*) The protonated carbonyl compound, Me$_2$$\overset{+}{C}$—OH, is essentially a carbocation that serves as an electrophile in an electrophilic-aromatic substitution. The initial product is the alcohol PhC(OH)Me$_2$ that is converted by acid to another electrophilic carbocation, PhMe$_2$C$^+$, capable of attacking a second C$_6$H$_6$ molecule to give the product.

15.174 Use chloral hydrate and any other needed starting compound to synthesize the insecticide DDT, (*p*-ClC$_6$H$_4$)$_2$CHCCl$_3$.

▮ Chloral hydrate, CCl$_3$CH(OH)$_2$ in acid, is changed to a carbocation, CCl$_3$$\overset{+}{C}$HOH, identical to the one that would have been formed from the precursor aldehyde, CCl$_3$CHO. The hydroxy carbocation undergoes the same kind of electrophilic-substitution reactions as in Problem 15.173 with 2 eq of C$_6$H$_5$Cl to give DDT.

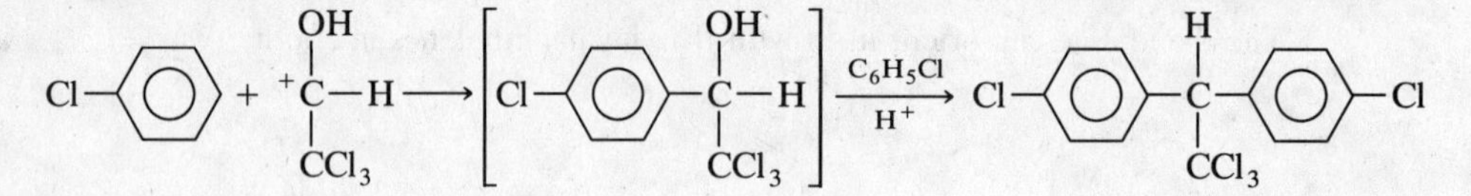

DDT

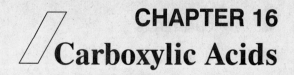

INTRODUCTION AND NOMENCLATURE

16.1 Give the general formula for an (*a*) alkyl and (*b*) aryl carboxylic acid and identify the acyl groups.

    ▰ (*a*) $RC\overset{O}{\overset{\|}{-}}OH$, (*b*) $ArC\overset{O}{\overset{\|}{-}}OH$. The acyl groups are $RC\overset{O}{\overset{\|}{-}}$ and $ArC\overset{O}{\overset{\|}{-}}$, respectively.

16.2 Give the structural formulas and common names for the first six straight chain aliphatic carboxylic acids.

    ▰ HCOOH, formic acid (from ants); CH_3COOH, acetic acid (from vinegar); CH_3CH_2COOH, propionic acid (from fat); n-$CH_3CH_2CH_2COOH$, butyric acid (from butter); n-$CH_3(CH_2)_3COOH$, valeric acid (from valerian); n-$CH_3(CH_2)_4COOH$, caproic acid (from goats).

16.3 Give the common name of the following acids: (*a*) $ClCH_2COOH$, (*b*) $O_2NCH_2CH_2COOH$, (*c*) $BrCH_2CH_2CH_2COOH$, (*d*) $CH_3C(CH_3)_2COOH$, (*e*) $O=CHCH_2CH_2CH_2CH_2COOH$, (*f*) $BrCH_2CHBrCHBrCOOH$, (*g*) $HOCH_2CH_2CHFCOOH$, (*h*) $CH_3CH_2COCH_2COOH$.

    ▰ With common names, positions of substituents are shown by Greek letters $\alpha, \beta, \gamma, \delta$. The α-C is attached to the COOH group. (*a*) Chloroacetic acid. (α is not needed here because there is only one other C in the chain.) (*b*) β-Nitropropionic acid, (*c*) γ-bromobutyric acid, (*d*) α,α-dimethylpropionic acid, (*e*) δ-formylvaleric acid. (COOH has naming priority over CHO which as a functional group is called formyl.) (*f*) α,β,γ-Tribromobutyric acid, (*g*) α-fluoro-γ-hydroxybutyric acid, (*h*) β-ketovaleric acid. (With common names *keto* indicates O= on a chain.)

16.4 Give the IUPAC name to the compounds in Problem 16.2.

    ▰ The IUPAC system replaces the *-e* of the corresponding alkane with *-oic acid*. The required names are methanoic, ethanoic, propanoic, butanoic, pentanoic, and hexanoic acids.

16.5 Give the IUPAC name to the compounds in Problem 16.3.

    ▰ The IUPAC system uses numbers to locate substituents. The C of COOH is always number 1. (*a*) Chloroethanoic acid, (*b*) 3-nitropropanoic acid, (*c*) 4-bromobutanoic acid, (*d*) 2,2-dimethylpropanoic acid. The longest chain must always have COOH. (The common name is pivalic acid.) (*e*) 6-Oxohexanoic acid, (*f*) 2,3,4-tribromobutanoic acid, (*g*) 2-fluoro-4-hydroxybutanoic acid, (*h*) 3-oxopentanoic acid.

16.6 (*a*) Give the IUPAC name to the following: (i) $PhCH_2CH_2COOH$, (ii) $CH_2=CHCOOH$, (iii) $CH_3CH=CHCOOH$, (iv) $CH_3CH_2CH(CHO)CH_2COOH$. (*b*) Name —COOH as a substituent group.

    ▰ (*a*) (i) 3-Phenylpropanoic acid; (ii) propenoic acid (the common name is acrylic acid); (iii) 2-butenoic acid, *cis* or *trans* (common name is crotonic acid); (iv) 3-formylpentanoic acid. If the CHO is not part of the longest chain, it is named as a *formyl* substituent. (*b*) Carboxy.

16.7 Give the *derived* name, as a derivative of acetic acid, of the following acids: (*a*) Me_3CCOOH, (*b*) $PhCH_2COOH$, (*c*) $Me_2CHCH_2CH_2COOH$, (*d*) $PhCH_2CH_2COOH$, (*e*) a cyclohexyl ring bonded to $\overset{CH_2COOH}{\underset{H}{\diagdown}}$, and (*f*) $Me_2C(OH)COOH$.

    ▰ The name of each group bonded to C precedes acetic as one word followed by acid. (*a*) Trimethylacetic acid; (*b*) phenylacetic acid; (*c*) isobutylacetic acid; (*d*) benzylacetic acid; (*e*) cyclohexylacetic acid; (*f*) dimethylhydroxyacetic acid.

16.8 Name the following:

(a) ⬡ COOH

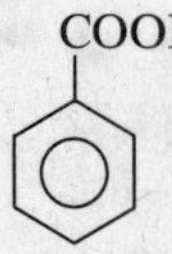

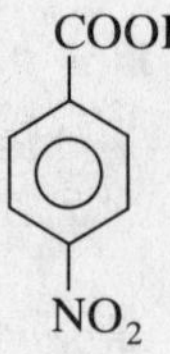

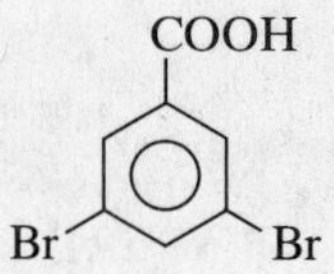

(b) ⬡ COOH with NO$_2$

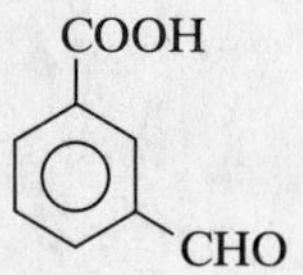

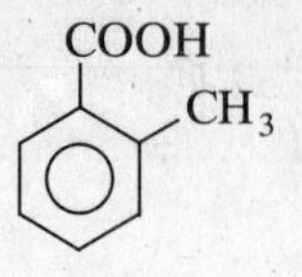

(c) ⬡ COOH with Br, Br

(d) ⬡ COOH with CHO

(e) ⬡ COOH with CH$_3$

(f) ⬡⬡ COOH

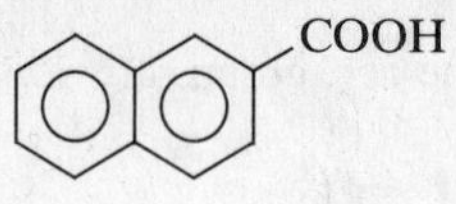

▰ Substituted phenyl carboxylic acids are named as benzoic acids. (a) Benzoic acid (the parent acid; (b) p-nitrobenzoic acid; (c) 3,5-dibromobenzoic acid; (d) m-formylbenzoic acid (COOH takes priority over CHO; thus it is named as an acid, not as an aldehyde); (e) o-methylbenzoic acid, commonly called o-toluic acid from toluene; (f) 2- (or β-) naphthoic acid.

16.9 (a) Define the term fatty acid. (b) Give the common and IUPAC names for the following fatty acids:

(i) $CH_3(CH_2)_{14}COOH$, (ii) $CH_3(CH_2)_{16}COOH$, (iii) $CH_3-(CH_2)_7-\underset{H}{C}=\underset{H}{C}-(CH_2)_7COOH$,

(iv) 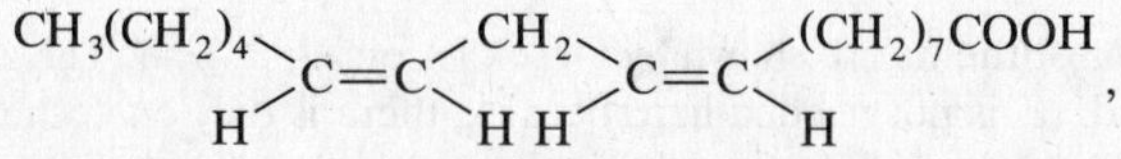 $CH_3(CH_2)_4\underset{H}{C}=\underset{H}{C}\underset{H}{CH_2}\underset{H}{C}=\underset{H}{C}(CH_2)_7COOH$,

(v) 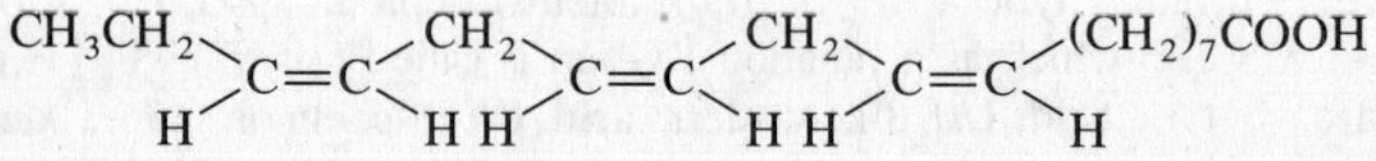 $CH_3CH_2\underset{H}{C}=\underset{H}{C}\underset{H}{CH_2}\underset{H}{C}=\underset{H}{C}\underset{H}{CH_2}\underset{H}{C}=\underset{H}{C}(CH_2)_7COOH$

▰ (a) *Fatty acids* are long chain aliphatic acids derived by hydrolysis from naturally-occurring fats and oils. (b) (i) Palmitic or hexadecanoic acid; (ii) stearic or octadecanoic acid; (iii) oleic or *cis*-9-octadecenoic acid; (iv) linoleic or *cis,cis*-9,12-octadecadienoic acid; (v) linolenic or *cis,cis,cis*-9,12,15-octadecatrienoic acid.

16.10 (a) Generalize about the numbers of C's in naturally-occurring fatty acids. (b) Explain why this kind of C content is observed. (c) Explain why unsaturated fatty acids have lower mp's than the corresponding saturated acids. (d) Compare the mp's of a *trans*- and a *cis*-isomeric fatty acid.

▰ (a) There are an even number of C's. (b) Plants and animals biosynthesize fatty acids by building up CH_3COOH units. (c) The uniform zig-zag chains of the saturated acids can pack together tightly in the solid. The kink at the *cis* position of the chain diminishes the close packing, thereby lowering the mp of the *cis* isomer. (d) A *trans* double bond does not interfere with the uniform zig-zag and close packing is permitted. The *trans* isomer has a higher mp.

16.11 Give the common and IUPAC names of the dicarboxylic acids, $HOOC(CH_2)_nCOOH$, $n = 0$ to 5.

▰ These acids are named as *dioic acids*; it is understood that the COOH's are terminal C's. (i) HOOCCOOH, oxalic or ethanedioic acid; (ii) HOOCCH$_2$COOH, malonic or propanedioic acid; (iii) HOOC(CH$_2$)$_2$COOH, succinic or butanedioic acid; (iv) HOOC(CH$_2$)$_3$COOH, glutaric or pentanedioic acid; (v) HOOC(CH$_2$)$_4$COOH, adipic or hexanedioic acid; (vi) HOOC(CH$_2$)$_5$COOH, pimelic or heptanedioic acid. A useful mnemonic for remembering these common names is: "**O**h, **m**y such **g**ood **a**pple **p**ie."

16.12 Write the structural formulas and give the IUPAC names for: (a) phthalic acid; (b) isophthalic acid; (c) terephthalic acid; (d) maleic acid; (e) fumaric acid; (f) tartaric acid; and (g) citric acid.

▰ (a) ⬡ COOH, COOH

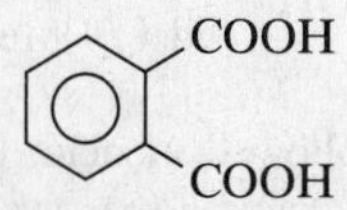

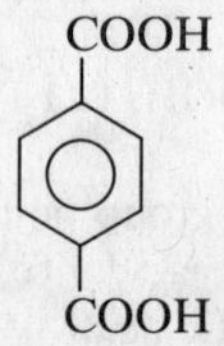

Benzene-1,2-dicarboxylic acid

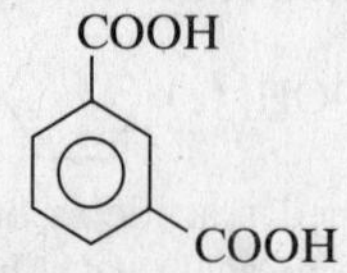

(b) ⬡ COOH, COOH

Benzene-1,3-dicarboxylic acid

(c) ⬡ COOH, COOH

Benzene-1,4-dicarboxylic acid

$$(d) \quad \begin{array}{cc} HOOC & COOH \\ \diagdown & \diagup \\ & C=C \\ \diagup & \diagdown \\ H & H \end{array} \qquad (e) \quad \begin{array}{cc} HOOC & H \\ \diagdown & \diagup \\ & C=C \\ \diagup & \diagdown \\ H & COOH \end{array}$$

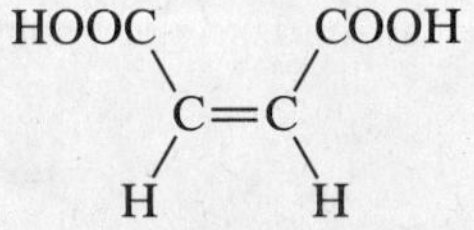

cis-Butenedioic
acid

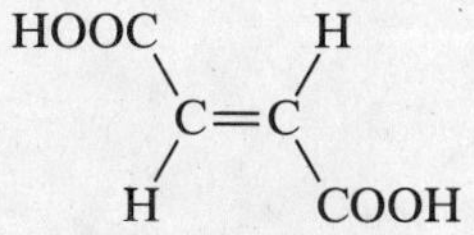

trans-Butenedioic
acid

(f) HOOCCH(OH)CH(OH)COOH (g) HOOCCH$_2$C(OH)CH$_2$COOH
$$\qquad\qquad\qquad\qquad\qquad\qquad\qquad\qquad | $$
$$\qquad\qquad\qquad\qquad\qquad\qquad\qquad COOH$$

2,3-Dihydroxybutanedioic acid   3-Hydroxy-1,2,3-propanetricarboxylic acid

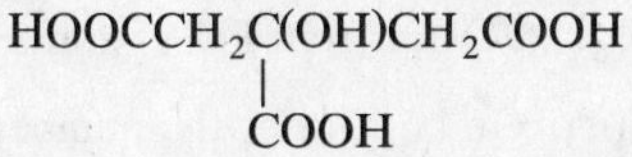

Carboxylic acids with at least three COOH's are named as alkanepolycarboxylic acids because only two COOH's can be part of the longest chain.

16.13 Account for the following physical properties of carboxylic acids: (*a*) Only those with five or fewer C's, exclusive of those in COOH, are water soluble, but many with six or more C's dissolve in alcohols. (*b*) Their boiling and melting points are higher than those of corresponding alcohols.

▮ (*a*) RCOOH's dissolve because the H of COOH can H-bond with H$_2$O in two ways (Fig. 16-1). The R portion is nonpolar and hydrophobic and this effect predominates when R possesses more than five C's, thereby diminishing the solubility of the acid. Alcohols are less polar than H$_2$O and less antagonistic than water toward the less polar carboxylic acids of higher C content. (*b*) The intermolecular forces (H-bonding and dipole-dipole attraction) are greater for RCOOH.

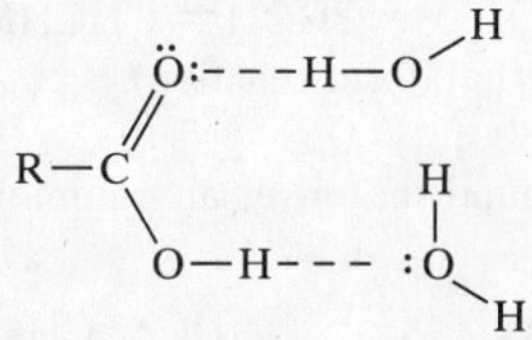

$$\begin{array}{c} \ddot{O}\text{:}\text{ - - -}H\text{—}O^{\diagup H} \\ R\text{—}C \qquad\qquad\qquad H \\ \qquad\qquad\qquad | \\ O\text{—}H\text{ - - - }\text{:}O \\ \qquad\qquad\qquad \diagdown H \end{array} \quad \textbf{Fig. 16-1}$$

16.14 (*a*) What is "glacial" acetic acid? (*b*) Account for the name. (*c*) How is acetic acid often abbreviated? (*d*) What is vinegar and how is it made?

▮ (*a*) 100% acetic acid free of water. (*b*) Since the mp of anhydrous acetic acid is 17 °C, it is solid in a refrigerator and looks "icy". (*c*) HOAc, where Ac stands for acetyl, CH$_3$C=O. (*d*) *Vinegar* is a 5% aqueous solution of HOAc, and is a product of fermentation of sugars and starch; ethanol is an intermediate fermentation product.

16.15 Acetic acid in the vapor state has a molecular weight of 120. Explain.

▮ CH$_3$COOH undergoes intermolecular H-bonding and exists as the dimer

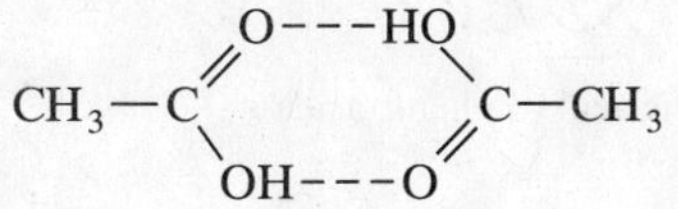

$$\begin{array}{c} O\text{ - - -}HO \\ \diagup\qquad\qquad \diagdown \\ CH_3\text{—}C \qquad\qquad C\text{—}CH_3 \\ \diagdown\qquad\qquad \diagup \\ OH\text{ - - -}O \end{array}$$

16.16 (*a*) Account for the fact that the C—O bond in RCOOH is shorter than in ROH. (*b*) How do the C=O bond lengths in RCOOH and RCHO compare? (*c*) Compare the reactivities of the C=O in RCOOH and RCHO towards nucleophiles.

▮ (*a*) The main contributing resonance structures for RCOOH are

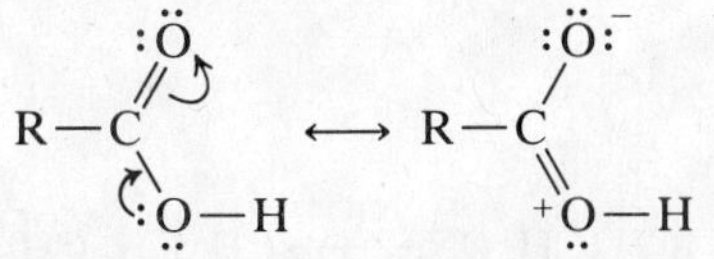

$$\begin{array}{c} \text{:}\ddot{O} \\ \diagup\!\!\!/ \\ R\text{—}C \\ \diagdown \\ \text{:}O\text{—}H \end{array} \longleftrightarrow \begin{array}{c} \text{:}\ddot{O}\text{:}^- \\ \diagup \\ R\text{—}C \\ \diagdown\!\!\!\diagdown \\ ^+O\text{—}H \end{array}$$

Because of the contribution by the charge-separated structure, there is some double-bond character in the C—O bond of the acid, which shortens its bond length. (*b*) Contribution to the hybrid of this structure also puts some single-bond character in the C=O bond, thereby making it longer than in carbonyl compounds. (*c*) In

RCOOH there is less + charge on the C=O carbon causing this C to be less electrophilic and less reactive toward nucleophiles.

PREPARATION

16.17 Synthesize (*a*) $CH_3CH_2CH_2COOH$ from (i) $CH_3CH_2CH_2CH_2OH$ and (ii) $CH_3CH_2CH_2CHO$; (*b*) $p\text{-}O_2NC_6H_4COOH$ from $PhCH_3$; and (*c*) adipic acid from benzene.

▮ (*a*) (i), (ii) In both cases the number of C's in the precursor and in the acid are the same. This signals the need for oxidation. Acidified $KMnO_4$ can be used for both.

(*b*) It is necessary to first nitrate $PhCH_3$ because —COOH is a *meta* director, and then oxidize.

$$PhCH_3 \xrightarrow[H_2SO_4]{HNO_3} p\text{-}NO_2C_6H_4CH_3 \xrightarrow[H^+, \Delta]{KMnO_4} p\text{-}NO_2C_6H_4COOH$$

The presence of the electron-withdrawing NO_2 encourages the oxidation of the phenyl-side chain.

(*c*) Adipic acid can be prepared by oxidative cleavage of cyclohexene prepared from benzene.

$$C_6H_6 \xrightarrow{H_2/Pd} \underset{\text{Cyclohexane}}{C_6H_{12}} \xrightarrow[h\nu]{Cl_2} \underset{\text{Chlorocylohexane}}{C_6H_{11}Cl} \xrightarrow{\text{alc. KOH}} \underset{\text{Cyclohexene}}{C_6H_{10}} \xrightarrow[H^+]{KMnO_4} \underset{\text{Adipic acid}}{HOOC(CH_2)_4COOH}$$

Industrially, cyclohexane is oxidized directly.

16.18 List the compounds from which $Me_2CHCOOH$ can be prepared by oxidation in good yield.

▮ Me_2CHCH_2OH, Me_2CHCHO, $Me_2CHCH=CHCHMe_2$ (oxidative cleavage), $Me_2CHC\equiv CCHMe_2$ (oxidative cleavage), $Me_2CHCOMe$ (haloform reaction).

16.19 Give the structure of a cyclic compound that gives an equimolar amount of $HOOCCH_2CH_2COOH$ on oxidative cleavage.

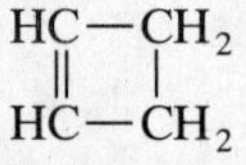

▮
$$\begin{array}{c} HC-CH_2 \\ \| \quad \ | \\ HC-CH_2 \end{array}$$
Cyclobutene

16.20 Give the structure and name of the acid formed on oxidation of (i) phenanthrene (Problem 10.87), and

(ii) acenaphthene, a coal tar derivative, 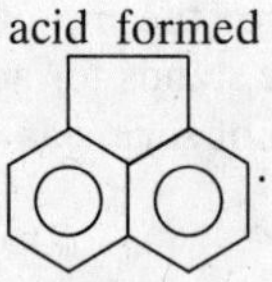 .

▮ (i)

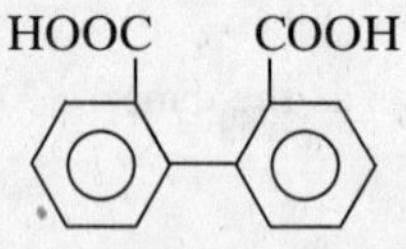

o,o'-Biphenyldicarboxylic acid (diphenic acid)

(ii)

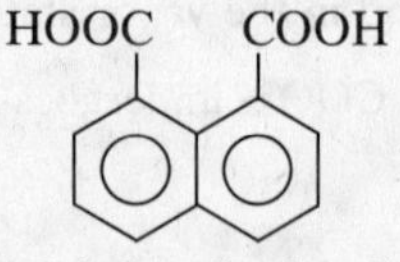

1,8-Naphthalenedicarboxylic acid

16.21 Prepare butanoic acid from 1-bromopropane. Use two methods.

▮ This synthesis requires an increase of the chain by one C (a step-up) that can be achieved in two ways. The —COOH takes the place of the —X group of the halide. The added C is shown in bold type.

$$CH_3CH_2CH_2Br \begin{cases} \xrightarrow{Mg} CH_3CH_2CH_2MgBr \xrightarrow{CO_2} CH_3CH_2CH_2COO^-(MgBr)^+ \xrightarrow{H^+} CH_3CH_2CH_2COOH \\ \\ \xrightarrow{CN^-} CH_3CH_2CH_2CN \xrightarrow{H_3O^+} CH_3CH_2CH_2COOH\ (+NH_4^+) \end{cases}$$

16.22 Give the structure and name of the acids formed by a step-up reaction of the following halides: (*a*) $PhCH_2CH_2CH_2Br$, (*b*) $CH_3CHClCH_2CH_2CH_3$, (*c*) $PhCH_2CH_2Cl$, (*d*) cyclohexyl-CMe_2Cl, (*e*) $PhCl$, (*f*) $HOCH_2CH_2CMe_2Cl$, (*g*) *trans*-4-chloromethylcyclohexane, (*h*) *Z*-$MeCH=CHBr$, and (*i*) $BrCH_2CH_2Br$.

◢ (a) $PhCH_2CH_2CH_2COOH$, 4-phenylbutanoic acid; (b) $CH_3CH_2CH_2CH(CH_3)COOH$, 2-methylpentanoic acid; (c) $PhCH_2CH_2COOH$, 3-phenylpropanoic acid; (d) cyclohexyl-CMe_2COOH, 2-cyclohexyl-2-methylpropanoic acid; (e) $PhCOOH$, benzoic acid; (f) $HOCH_2CH_2CMe_2COOH$, 4-hydroxy-2,2-dimethylbutanoic acid; (g) cis- and trans-4-methylcyclohexanecarboxylic acid; (h) Z-$MeCH{=}CHCOOH$, Z-2-butenoic acid; (i) $HOOCCH_2CH_2COOH$, succinic or 1,4-butanedioic acid.

16.23 Give the preferred method from Problem 16.21 for the syntheses in Problem 16.22 and justify your choice.

◢ (a) Either method gives good yields. (b) Carbonation is better. This is a 2° halide that could undergo some competitive E2 reaction with CN^-. (c) Carbonation is better. CN^- could initiate some E2 reaction to give the stable conjugated alkene, $PhCH{=}CH_2$. (d) Only carbonation; 3° halides do not undergo S_N2 displacements. (e) Carbonation: typical aryl halides do not undergo displacement reactions. Tetrahydrofuran must be used as the solvent for making the Grignard reagent of aryl chlorides. Ether can be used to prepare the lithium organometallic. (f) Neither method can be used because the halide is 3° and cannot react with CN^- and the acid OH group prevents the preparation of the organometallic compound. A successful synthesis can be achieved by protecting the OH group first (Problem 14.51) and then carbonating. (g) Either method can be used but carbonation is preferred because the halide is 2° and the nitrile method may give some alkene. The CN^- reaction goes with inversion to give the cis-carboxylic acid. The stereoisomer formed on carbonation depends on the counterion, MgX^+ or Li^+, the polarity of the solvent, and the temperature. The reaction will go with considerable retention or will give the more stable isomer, in both cases the trans carboxylic acid. (h) Only

carbonation; vinyl halides do not readily undergo S_N2 reactions. Since, unlike sp^3 carbanions, $-\overset{|}{\underset{|}{C}}{:}^-$, sp^2

carbanions, ${=}\overset{|}{C}{:}^-$, e.g., vinyl carbanions, cannot invert, carbonation goes with retention; the acid is the Z-isomer. Grignards of vinyl halides are best prepared in THF, Li compounds in ether. (i) Only the nitrile method; Mg would lead to loss of the vic-Br's as $MgBr_2$ to give the alkene.

16.24 (a) Review the mechanism of the carbonation reaction of RMgX and CO_2. (b) What organic product is formed when a nitrile is hydrolyzed in base?

◢ (a) CO_2 acts as a carbonyl compound toward RMgX. Thus, $RMgX + O{=}C{=}O \rightarrow R-\overset{\underset{||}{O}}{C}-O^-MgX^+$.

Acid converts the salt to RCOOH. (b) The carboxylate anion, $RCOO^-$.

16.25 Give the mechanism for the acid-catalyzed hydrolysis of a nitrile, $RC{\equiv}N$.

◢ The chemistry of $-C{\equiv}N$ is similar to that of ${>}C{=}O$ in that protonation of the basic site heteroatom increases the electrophilicity of the C of the functional group enabling H_2O to react with it.

$$RC{\equiv}N \xrightarrow{H^+} RC{\equiv}\overset{+}{N}H \xrightarrow{H_2O} RC{=}NH \xrightarrow{reshuffle\ H^+}$$
$$\underset{\underset{H_2O^+}{|}}{}$$

$$\left[\underset{\underset{HO}{|}}{RC}{=}\overset{+}{N}H_2 \longleftrightarrow R-\underset{\underset{OH}{|}}{\overset{|}{C}}-NH_2 \longleftrightarrow R-\underset{\underset{+OH}{|}}{\overset{||}{C}}-NH_2 \right] \xrightarrow{H_2O}$$

$$R-\underset{\underset{OH}{|}}{\overset{\overset{+OH_2}{|}}{C}}-NH_2 \xrightarrow{reshuffle\ H^+} R-\underset{\underset{OH}{|}}{\overset{|}{C}}-\overset{+}{N}H_3 \longrightarrow R-\overset{\underset{||}{O}}{C}-OH + NH_4^+$$

16.26 Synthesize $HOOCCH_2CH_2COOH$ from $CH_2{=}CH_2$.

◢ Here a two carbon step-up is required using $BrCH_2CH_2Br$. The nitrile method must be used [Problem 16.23(i)]. Hydrolysis of the dinitrile gives the diacid.

$$CH_2{=}CH_2 \xrightarrow{Br_2} BrCH_2CH_2Br \xrightarrow{CN^-} NCCH_2CH_2CN \xrightarrow{H_3O^+} HOOCCH_2CH_2COOH$$

16.27 Starting with C_6H_6 and $C_6H_5CH_3$ prepare: (a) C_6H_5COOH, (b) p-$CH_3C_6H_4COOH$, (c) 2-methyl-5-chlorobenzoic acid, (d) p-$HOOCC_6H_4CH_2COOH$, (e) 2-bromo-4-nitrobenzoic acid, and (f) 1,2,4-benzenetricarboxylic acid. Do not repeat the preparation of any needed intermediate compound.

▰ (*a*) In the absence of an electron-withdrawing substituent, the oxidation of toluene goes in poor yields.

$$C_6H_6 \xrightarrow{Br_2/Fe} C_6H_5Br \xrightarrow[\substack{2.\ CO_2 \\ 3.\ H^+}]{1.\ Mg} C_6H_5COOH$$

(*b*) $CH_3C_6H_5 \xrightarrow{Br_2/Fe} p\text{-}CH_3C_6H_4Br \xrightarrow[\substack{2.\ CO_2 \\ 3.\ H^+}]{1.\ Mg} p\text{-}CH_3C_6H_4COOH$

(*c*) $CH_3C_6H_5 \xrightarrow{Cl_2/Fe} p\text{-}CH_3C_6H_4Cl \xrightarrow{Br_2/Fe}$ $\xrightarrow[\substack{2.\ CO_2 \\ 3.\ H^+}]{1.\ Mg/Et_2O}$

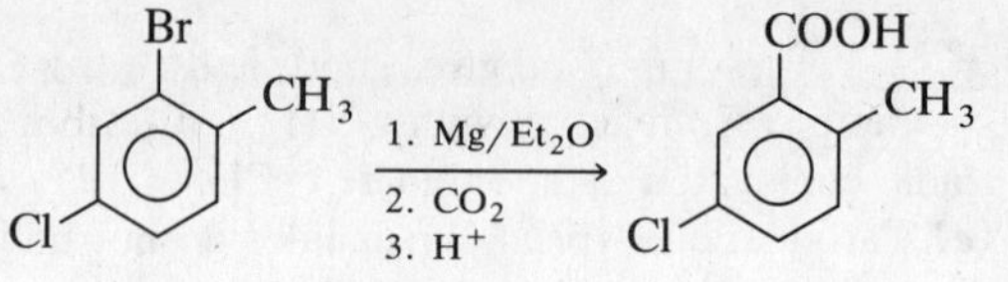

In ether, aryl chlorides are inert toward Grignard formation; aryl bromides react. In tetrahydrofuran (oxacyclopentane), ArCl reacts.

(*d*) $p\text{-}CH_3C_6H_4Br \xrightarrow{NBS} p\text{-}BrCH_2C_6H_4Br \xrightarrow{2Mg}$

$$p\text{-}BrMgCH_2C_6H_4MgBr \xrightarrow[\substack{2.\ H_3O^+}]{1.\ 2CO_2} p\text{-}HOOCC_6H_4CH_2COOH$$

(*e*) $C_6H_5CH_3 \xrightarrow[H_2SO_4]{HNO_3} p\text{-}NO_2C_6H_4CH_3 \xrightarrow{Br_2/Fe}$ $\xrightarrow[H^+]{KMnO_4}$

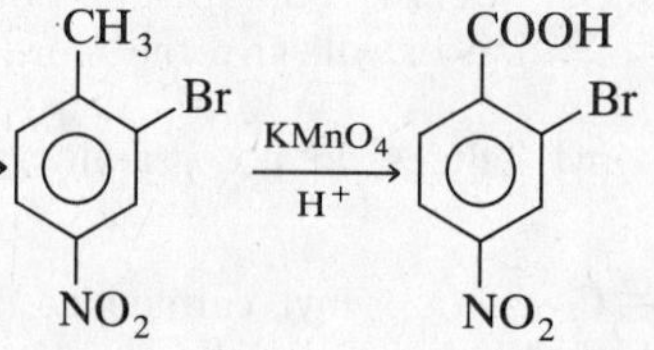

(*f*) $C_6H_5CH_3 \xrightarrow{2Br_2/Fe}$ $\xrightarrow{\text{dicarbonation}}$ $\xrightarrow[H^+]{KMnO_4}$

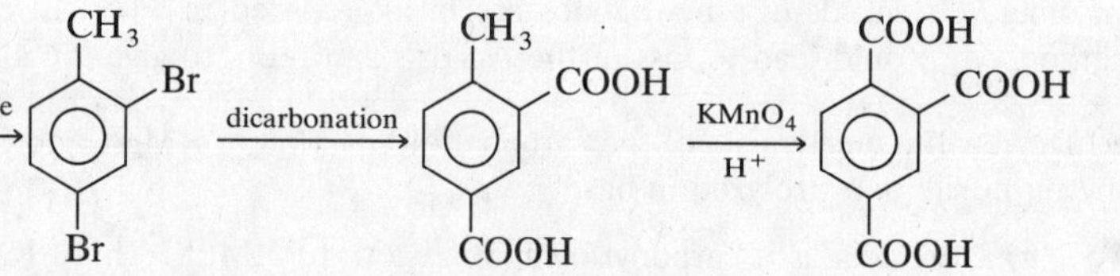

16.28 Use naphthalene to synthesize (*a*) 1-naphthoic acid and (*b*) 2-naphthoic acid.

▰ (*a*) Naphthalene $\xrightarrow{Br_2/Fe}$ 1-bromonaphthalene $\xrightarrow{\text{carbonation}}$ 1-naphthoic acid

(*b*) The 2-position of naphthalene cannot be halogenated but can be acetylated to give a methyl ketone from which the acid is obtained by the haloform reaction.

$$\text{Naphthalene} \xrightarrow[AlCl_3]{CH_3COCl/C_6H_5NO_2} \text{2-naphthylCOCH}_3 \xrightarrow[\substack{2.\ H_3O^+}]{1.\ Br_2,\ OH^-} \text{2-naphthoic acid}$$

16.29 Prepare 2-methylbutanoic acid from 2-butanol.

▰ The precursor of the acid has an X on the site of COOH. 2-Butanol is converted to this halide.

$$\underset{\underset{OH}{|}}{CH_3CH_2CHCH_3} \xrightarrow{SOCl_2} \underset{\underset{Cl}{|}}{CH_3CH_2CHCH_3} \xrightarrow{\text{carbonation}} \underset{\underset{COOH}{|}}{CH_3CH_2CHCH_3}$$

Do not use the RCN route because $CH_3CH_2CHClCH_3$ is a 2° halide subject to dehydrohalogenation.

16.30 Prepare (*a*) adipic acid and (*b*) succinic acid from tetrahydrofuran.

▰ (*a*) Tetrahydrofuran $\xrightarrow{\text{conc. HI}} I(CH_2)_4I \xrightarrow{\text{dicarbonation}} HOOC(CH_2)_4COOH$

(*b*) Tetrahydrofuran $\xrightarrow{\text{conc. HI}} I(CH_2)_4I \xrightarrow{OH^-} HO(CH_2)_4OH \xrightarrow{KMnO_4} HOOC(CH_2)_2COOH$

16.31 Prepare 2-methylbutanoic acid from ethanol.

▰ The precursor halide needed to prepare this acid is $CH_3CH_2CHClCH_3$.

(*1*) $C_2H_5OH \xrightarrow{PBr_3} C_2H_5Br \xrightarrow[\text{ether}]{Mg} C_2H_5MgBr$ [use in (*3*) below]

(*2*) $C_2H_5OH \xrightarrow{Cu,\ \Delta} CH_3CHO$ [use in (*3*) below]

(*3*) $CH_3CH{=}O + C_2H_5MgBr \longrightarrow CH_3CHOHCH_2CH_3 \xrightarrow{HCl}$

$CH_3CHClCH_2CH_3 \xrightarrow{\text{carbonation}} CH_3CH_2CHCH_3COOH$

16.32 Use any 2-carbon organic compounds to prepare butanoic acid.

$$\text{CH}_3\text{CH}_2\text{MgBr} + \underset{\overset{\displaystyle \diagdown \diagup}{\text{O}}}{\text{H}_2\text{C}-\text{CH}_2} \longrightarrow \text{CH}_3\text{CH}_2\text{CH}_2\text{CH}_2\text{O}^-\text{MgBr}^+ \xrightarrow{\text{H}_3\text{O}^+}$$

$$\text{CH}_3\text{CH}_2\text{CH}_2\text{CH}_2\text{OH} \xrightarrow{\text{KMnO}_4} \text{CH}_3\text{CH}_2\text{CH}_2\text{COOH}$$

16.33 Use three methods to prepare propanoic acid from $\text{HC}\equiv\text{CH}$ and any one-carbon compound.

1. $\text{HC}\equiv\text{CH} \xrightarrow{\text{HBr}} \text{H}_2\text{C}=\text{CHBr} \xrightarrow{\text{carbonation}} \text{H}_2\text{C}=\text{CHCOOH} \xrightarrow{\text{H}_2/\text{Pd}} \text{CH}_3\text{CH}_2\text{COOH}$

2. $\text{HC}\equiv\text{CH} \xrightarrow[\text{2. CH}_3\text{I}]{\text{1. NaNH}_2} \text{CH}_3\text{C}\equiv\text{CH} \xrightarrow[\text{2. OH}^-, \text{H}_2\text{O}_2]{\text{1. Sia}_2\text{BH}} \text{CH}_3\text{CH}_2\text{CHO} \xrightarrow{\text{KMnO}_4} \text{CH}_3\text{CH}_2\text{COOH}$

3. $\text{HC}\equiv\text{CH} \xrightarrow[\text{2. 2CH}_3\text{I}]{\text{1. 2NaNH}_2} \text{CH}_3\text{C}\equiv\text{CCH}_3 \xrightarrow[\text{H}_2\text{SO}_4]{\text{HgSO}_4} \text{CH}_3\text{CH}_2\text{COCH}_3 \xrightarrow[\text{2. Br}_2]{\text{1. OH}^-} \text{CH}_3\text{CH}_2\text{COOH}$

16.34 Prepare 6-oxo-6-phenylhexanoic acid from cyclohexanol and C_6H_6.

$$\text{Cyclohexanol} \xrightarrow[\text{H}^+]{\text{K}_2\text{Cr}_2\text{O}_7} \text{cyclohexanone} \xrightarrow{\text{PhMgBr}^*}$$

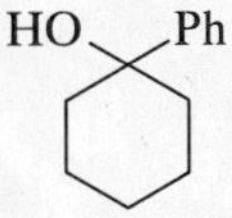

$$\xrightarrow[\Delta]{\text{CrO}_3, \text{HOAc}} \underset{\overset{\displaystyle \|}{\text{O}}}{\text{PhC(CH}_2)_4\text{COOH}}$$

1-Phenylcyclohexanol   6-Oxo-6-phenylhexanoic acid

$^*\text{PhH} \xrightarrow[\text{2. Mg/Et}_2\text{O}]{\text{1. Br}_2/\text{Fe}} \text{PhMgBr}$

Cyclanols undergo acid catalyzed oxidative cleavage, probably via the alkene.

16.35 Starting with any coal tar product give the most direct synthesis of (*a*) phthalic acid and (*b*) 3-nitrophthalic acid.

(*a*) Oxidize naphthalene with V_2O_5 and O_2 at high temperatures. (*b*) Nitrate naphthalene before the oxidation. The $-\text{NO}_2$ stabilizes the ring bearing it toward oxidation.

16.36 Give industrial methods for the manufacture of (*a*) acetic acid (use two ways, exclusive of fermentation) and (*b*) formic acid.

(*a*) $\text{CH}_3\text{OH} + \text{CO} \xrightarrow{\text{Rh/I}_2} \text{CH}_3\text{COOH}$ (major method); $\text{CH}_3\text{CHO} \xrightarrow[\text{catalyst}]{\text{O}_2} \text{CH}_3\text{COOH}$

(*b*) $\text{CO} + \text{NaOH} \longrightarrow \text{HCOO}^-\text{Na}^+ \xrightarrow{\text{H}_2\text{SO}_4} \text{HCOOH}$

16.37 (*a*) Which type of halogen-containing compound could react with OH^- to give a carboxylic acid? (*b*) Use this method to convert PhCH_3 to PhCOOH.

(*a*) $\text{R(Ar)}-\text{CX}_3 \longrightarrow \text{R(Ar)}-\text{COOH}$ (*b*) $\text{PhCH}_3 \xrightarrow[\text{h}\nu]{\text{Cl}_2} \text{PhCCl}_3 \xrightarrow[\text{2. H}^+]{\text{1. CaO}} \text{PhCOOH}$

Because of steric hindrance this is not a good general method even though RCCl_3-type compounds are readily available from the radical addition of HCCl_3 to alkenes.

ACIDITY AND CARBOXYLATE SALTS

16.38 Write balanced equations for the following reactions and name the salt that is formed. (*a*) $\text{CH}_3\text{COOH} + \text{NaOH}$, (*b*) $\text{CH}_3\text{CH}_2\text{COOH} + \text{Ca(OH)}_2$, (*c*) $\text{CH}_3(\text{CH}_2)_{16}\text{COOH} + \text{Fe(OAc)}_3$ (aq)

When naming the anion (conjugate base) of the carboxylic acid, exchange the suffix *-ate* for *-ic* and drop *acid*.

(*a*) $\text{CH}_3\text{COOH} + \text{NaOH} \longrightarrow \text{H}_2\text{O} + \text{CH}_3\text{COO}^-\text{Na}^+$, sodium acetate

(*b*) $2\text{CH}_3\text{CH}_2\text{COOH} + \text{Ca(OH)}_2 \longrightarrow 2\text{H}_2\text{O} + (\text{CH}_3\text{CH}_2\text{COO}^-)_2\text{Ca}^{2+}$, calcium propionate (a food preservative)

(*c*) $3\text{CH}_3(\text{CH}_2)_{16}\text{COOH} + \text{Fe}^{3+} + 3\text{OAc}^- \longrightarrow 3\text{HOAc} + [\text{CH}_3(\text{CH}_2)_{16}\text{COO}^-]_3\text{Fe(s)}$, ferric stearate
Heavy metal salts of fatty acids are insoluble in water.

16.39 (*a*) What is a soap? (*b*) Differentiate between a soft and hard soap.

▰ (*a*) *Soap* is a salt of a fatty acid. (*b*) Soft soaps are K^+ salts, hard soaps are Na^+ salts.

16.40 (*a*) Describe a micelle formed from a soap. (*b*) Explain why these very small micelles do not coalesce. (*c*) Describe the detergency (ability to remove oil and grease) role of these soap micelles.

▰ (*a*) A soap has two distinctly different portions. The charged COO^- polar end ("head") is hydrophilic and tends to project into the water. The large alkyl portion ("tail") is hydrophobic and tends to avoid water. In a colloidal soap solution the soap molecules form a sphere with their tails pointing inward toward each other, affording a congenial water-free environment. Their heads on the surface of the sphere face the stabilizing water medium. The sphere-like structure, shown in cross section in Fig. 16-2(*a*), is called a *micelle*. Solid dots represent the polar heads and the wavy lines the nonpolar tails buried in the interior. (*b*) The micelles do not coalesce because of the repulsions between their like-charged surfaces. (*c*) Most dirt is held to surfaces, such as skin and in clothing, by thin films of oil or grease which are nonpolar hydrophobic materials. When the dirty object is agitated with soap (or with other detergents), the oil is dispersed into very fine droplets that dissolve in the interiors of the micelles. The micelles with the trapped oil [see Fig. 16-2(*b*)], still with an affinity for water because of their ionic shells, wash away.

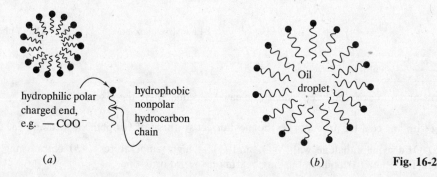

(*a*) hydrophilic polar charged end, e.g. $—COO^-$ hydrophobic nonpolar hydrocarbon chain (*b*) Oil droplet **Fig. 16-2**

16.41 Use the concept of charge delocalization (resonance) to explain why (*a*) RCOOH ($pK_a \cong 5$) is more acidic than ROH ($pK_a \cong 15$), (*b*) resonance in the acid has less influence than in the conjugate base, and (*c*) peroxy acids, RCOOH, are much weaker than RCOH.
$$\overset{\|}{\underset{O}{}} \qquad \overset{\|}{\underset{O}{}}$$

▰ (*a*) Again we compare relative acid strengths in terms of stabilities of the conjugate bases. Since the negative charge in $RCOO^-$ is delocalized to both O's with half of the charge on each O, $RCOO^-$ is more stable and a weaker base than RO^-, whose charge is localized on only one O. Consequently, RCOOH is the stronger acid.

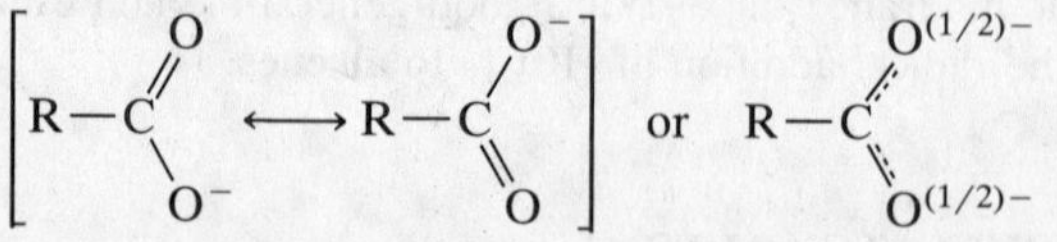

$$\left[\ \underset{O^-}{\overset{O}{R-C}} \quad\longleftrightarrow\quad \underset{O}{\overset{O^-}{R-C}}\ \right] \quad \text{or} \quad \underset{O^{(1/2)-}}{\overset{O^{(1/2)-}}{R-C}}$$

(*b*) Although resonance (Problem 16.16) should make the acid more stable, it involves contribution from a charge-separated resonance structure. Therefore there is less delocalization energy in the acid than in the anion where resonance involves two equal energy contributing structures. Delocalization in the anion has a more profound stabilization effect.

(*c*) There is no way to delocalize the $-$ charge of the peroxy anion, $RCOO O^-$ to $C=O$, as can be done with $RCOO^-$. The peroxy anion is much more basic and the peroxy acid is much less acidic.

16.42 (*a*) Write equations for the ionization of RCOOH and for K_a. (*b*) Give the thermodynamic equation relating pK_a with ΔH° and ΔS° of the ionization reaction and discuss the relationship. (*c*) Which factors influence (i) ΔH° and (ii) ΔS°? (*d*) Must H_3O^+ be taken into account in rationalizing differences in acid strengths?

(a)
$$RCOOH + H_2O \rightleftharpoons RCOO^- + H_3O^+; \qquad K_a = \frac{[RCOO^-][H_3O^+]}{[RCOOH]}$$

(b)
$$\Delta G^\circ = -2.30RT \log K_a = \Delta H^\circ - T\Delta S^\circ \qquad \text{or} \qquad pK_a = (\Delta H^\circ - T\Delta S^\circ)/2.30RT$$

A more negative ΔH° or a more positive $T\Delta S^\circ$ makes K_a larger and pK_a smaller; the acid becomes stronger.

(c) (i) Electronic effects such as induction, field effect, and resonance. (ii) Solvation effects. The better the anion is solvated, the more the equilibrium is driven to the right and the stronger is the acid. Better solvation does not necessarily mean *more* water molecules are constrained.

(d) H_3O^+ is present in the aqueous solutions of all acids; it is a common factor and can be disregarded.

16.43 Briefly discuss the relationship between $\Delta S^\circ_{\text{solvation}}$ and ionization of acids.

⬛ The ions formed as the result of ionization are much more solvated than the molecular acids themselves. Water molecules participating in solvation are in a more orderly condition than before the addition of the acid. Consequently, ionization of molecular acids invariably cause a decrease in entropy; ΔS° is negative. The smaller the number of H_2O molecules needed for solvation, the fewer water molecules are constrained and the less negative is ΔS°. Three important, but not exclusive, factors that influence solvation are the extent of charge delocalization, H-bonding, and steric effects.

16.44 **(a)** Discuss field effects and their relationship to inductive effects. **(b)** How should (i) an electron-withdrawing group (EWG) and (ii) an electron-donating group (EDG) influence acid strength?

⬛ **(a)** The transmission of the effect of the partial charge on the substituent to $-COO^-$ through the solvent or space is referred to as a *field effect*; the transmission through the σ-bonded chain is the inductive effect. Both effects operate in the same direction. **(b)** The influence of the inductive (or field) effect on acidity is best understood in terms of the conjugate base, $RCOO^-$, and can be summarized as follows:

(i) *Electron-withdrawing groups stabilize* $RCOO^-$ *and strengthen the acid.*

(ii) *Electron-donating groups destabilize* $RCOO^-$ *and weaken the acid.*

16.45 **(a)** What is being compared when the following equation is used to obtain the data in Table 16-1?
$$HX \text{ (aq)} + CH_3COO^- \text{ (aq)} \rightleftharpoons X^- \text{ (aq)} + CH_3COOH \text{ (aq) at 25 °C}$$

TABLE 16-1

Acid	pK_a	$\Delta H^\circ_{\text{rel}}$ kcal / mol	$T\Delta S^\circ_{\text{rel}}$ kcal / mol
CH_3COOH	4.756	0	0
$HCOOH$	3.752	+0.1	+1.45
$CH_2ClCOOH$	2.868	-1.0	+1.6
$PhCOOH$	4.213	+0.5	+1.3
$p\text{-}NO_2C_6H_4COOH$	3.442	+0.1	+1.9

(b) Explain the significance of giving the thermodynamic functions as $\Delta H^\circ_{\text{rel}}$ and $\Delta S^\circ_{\text{rel}}$.

⬛ **(a)** The relative acidity of HX is being compared to CH_3COOH. Since acid-base equilibria disfavor the side with the stronger acid (and base), the more this equilibrium is shifted to the right, the stronger is HX relative to HOAc. **(b)** $\Delta H^\circ_{\text{rel}}$ and $\Delta S^\circ_{\text{rel}}$ are the relative values for the acids compared to HOAc whose value is set to zero. They are not the absolute values.

16.46 **(a)** Use the data in Table 16-1 to discuss the validity of the following statements: (i) CH_3COOH is a weaker acid than HCOOH solely because of the acid-weakening, electron-donating inductive effect of R, in this case CH_3, and (ii) $ClCH_2COOH$ is a stronger acid than HOAc because Cl is strongly electronegative. **(b)** Generalize about the use of electronic effects to account for differences in acidities of HOAc and HX.

⬛ **(a)** Statement (i) is invalid. If anything, the slightly positive $\Delta H^\circ_{\text{rel}}$ (+0.1) for HCOOH should mean that electronic effects (induction and field effects) alone should make HCOOH a slightly weaker acid. Actually the difference is small and based on ΔH° the two acids should have about the same pK_a. The major difference is the positive $T\Delta S^\circ_{\text{rel}}$ (actually, the less negative $\Delta S^\circ_{\text{ionization}}$) which accounts for the greater acidity of HCOOH.

Induction and field effects only partly influence solvation. Statement (ii) is valid. The strongly electronegative Cl is a good EWG, making the anion a weaker base than OAc^- and $ClCH_2COOH$ a stronger acid. This effect is confirmed by the relatively large negative ΔH_{rel}° (-1.0). The large positive $T\Delta S_{rel}^\circ$ ($+1.6$) also is an acid-strengthening effect. (b) Electronic effects affecting ΔH° are applied with confidence and entropy effects ignored only when differences in pK_a values are relatively large (> 1.5). With small differences in pK_a values, ΔS° is often more significant than ΔH°. However, although for the wrong reason, in many cases correct comparisons can be made using inductive and field effects.

16.47 (a) Are PhCOOH and p-$NO_2C_6H_4COOH$ stronger acids than HOAc solely because of electronic factors? (b) Is p-$NO_2C_6H_4COOH$ a stronger acid than PhCOOH because of electronic effects?

◢ (a) No. Both have positive ΔH_{rel} and should be weaker acids because of electronic effects. The positive $T\Delta S_{rel}$ cause these acids to be stronger than HOAc. (b) In part, yes. The nitro acid does have a less positive ΔH_{rel}, but the dominant factor is the more positive ΔS_{rel}.

16.48 (a) Can the aromatic ring in benzoic acid stabilize the benzoate anion by π-electron delocalization? Illustrate. (b) Discuss the electronic effect of the p-NO_2 group in p-$NO_2C_6H_4COO^-$.

◢ (a) The only contributing structure (A) that delocalizes electron density from $PhCOO^-$ has a + charge on an O atom with only six e^-'s;

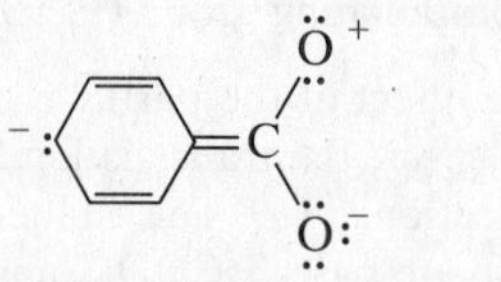

A

The contribution from this extremely-high-energy resonance structure is nil. (b) There is no direct resonance interaction between $-COO^-$ and $-NO_2$. The resonance interaction of the NO_2 with the ring induces some + on the ring C bearing the COO^- (B), from which a strong electron-withdrawing inductive effect is generated. This effect is base-stabilizing, and thus acid-strengthening.

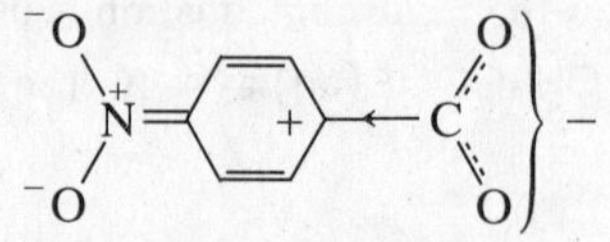

B

Refer to Table 16-2 and to the electronic effects discussed in Problem 16.48 for Problems 16.49, 16.50, and 16.51.

TABLE 16-2. pK_a Values of Monosubstituted Benzoic Acids (at 25 °C)

Group	para	meta	ortho
H (4.17)			
NO_2	3.40	3.46	2.21
Cl	4.03	3.82	2.89
Me	4.35	4.28	3.89
OH	4.54	4.12	3.00

16.49 Account for the fact that (a) p-$NO_2C_6H_4COOH$ is more acidic than the *meta* isomer and (b) the reverse is true for the Cl acids.

◢ (a) See Problem 16.48 for a discussion of the acid-strengthening role of p-NO_2. Through resonance, m-NO_2 can induce a + charge at the C's *ortho* to the C bearing the COO^-. This process is less effective because the induced charge is once removed from the C bonded to COO^-. m-Nitrobenzoic acid is thus less acidic. (b) By resonance interaction p-Cl places a − charge, not a + charge, on the p-C of the ring, an effect that is of minimal significance. Cl is an EWG by induction, and its effect is stronger from the nearer *meta* position.

16.50   (*a*) Why are both *p*-Me and *m*-Me substituted acids weaker than PhCOOH, with the *p*-acid being the weaker one?   (*b*) Why is the *p*-OH acid weaker than PhCOOH while the *m*-OH acid is stronger?

▰   (*a*) Both *p*- and *m*-Me are electron-donating and acid-weakening. Hyperconjugation (Problem 11.62) permits a *p*-Me to put a little extra $\delta -$ on the ring C bearing the —COO⁻, resulting in more effective electron-donation and acid-weakening.   (*b*) Through resonance interaction, *p*-OH places an additional − charge on the carboxyate group (see **C**), an acid-weakening effect that predominates over its electron-withdrawing, acid-strengthening inductive effect. A *m*-OH cannot do this and behaves only inductively as an EWG to increase acidity.

C

16.51   (*a*) Generalize about the acidities of the *o*-acids.   (*b*) What is this effect called?   (*c*) Speculate about the reason for this trend.

▰   (*a*) All *ortho* substituted acids are stronger than their *para* and *meta* counterparts.   (*b*) This is known as the *ortho effect*.   (*c*) Like their *para* counterparts, *ortho* substituents also induce a charge on the C binding the COO⁻. But their full role, not fully understood, is more complex because several factors are involved. It is reasonable to suggest that steric effects and occasionally H-bonding are important.

16.52   What is the correlation between the effect of a substituent on the acidity of ArCOOH and on the aromatic electrophilic substitution?

▰   *Meta* directing, deactivating substituents, such as —NO₂, are acid-strengtheners. When *ortho, para* directing activating groups such as OH and Me are *para* to —COO⁻, these acids are weaker than PhCOOH. Their effect from the *meta* position is not easily predictable.

16.53   Use the inductive effect to account for the following differences in acidity (*a*) $FCH_2COOH > ClCH_2COOH$, (*b*) $ClCH_2COOH > ClCH_2CH_2COOH$, (*c*) $Me_3CCH_2COOH > Me_3SiCH_2COOH$, (*d*) $Cl_2CHCOOH > ClCH_2COOH$, and (*e*) $NO_2CH_2COOH > ClCH_2COOH$.

▰   (*a*) Since F is more electronegative than Cl, it is a better EWG and a better acid-strengthener.   (*b*) Induction diminishes with increase in the number of σ bonds through which the effect operates. $ClCH_2COO^-$, with the closer Cl, is a weaker base than $ClCH_2CH_2COO^-$ with a more removed Cl, and so $ClCH_2COOH$ is the stronger acid.   (*c*) Si is very electropositive and is an acid-weakening EDG.   (*d*) Two Cl's are more electron-withdrawing than Cl making Cl_2CHCOO^- the weaker base and $Cl_2CHCOOH$ the stronger acid.   (*e*) There is a formal + charge on the N, $\left[-\overset{+}{N}-O^- \atop \diagdown O \right]$, making —NO₂ a better EWG than Cl, $NO_2CH_2COO^-$ a weaker base, and NO_2CH_2COOH a stronger acid.

16.54   Account for the differences in acidities: (*a*) $PhCH_2COOH$ or $H_2C{=}CHCH_2COOH > CH_3CH_2COOH$, and (*b*) $N{\equiv}CCH_2COOH$ or $CH_3COCH_2COOH > CH_3CH_2COOH$.

▰   (*a*) The sp^2 hybridized C's of Ph and —C=C— attract the bonded electrons more than do the sp^3 hybridized C's. Consequently Ph— and —C=C— are acid-strengthening EWG's.   (*b*) Because of $\delta +$ on C, the polarized $[^{\delta+}C{=}O^{\delta-}]$ and $[^{\delta+}C{\equiv}N^{\delta-}]$ are acid-strengthening EWG's. The C of C=O uses sp^2 HO's and the C of C≡N uses sp HO's, further enhancing the electron-withdrawal properties of these groups.

16.55   Would you expect 3-butenoic acid or 3-butynoic acid to be stronger?

▰   The —C≡C—, whose C's use sp HO's, is a better EWG than is $\diagup C{=}C\diagdown$, whose C's use sp^2 HO's. $HC{\equiv}CCH_2COOH$ ($pK_a = 3.32$) is a stronger acid than $H_2C{=}CHCH_2COOH$ ($pK_a = 4.35$).

16.56   *o*-Nitrobenzoic acid ($pK_a = 2.21$) is stronger than 3,5-dinitrobenzoic acid ($pK_a = 2.80$) in water, whereas in ethanolic solutions the opposite is true (their respective pK_a's in EtOH are 8.62 and 8.09). Suggest a possible reason for (*a*) the weaker acidities in ethanol and (*b*) the inversion of acidities in water.

▰   (*a*) EtOH is a weaker base and a poorer ion-solvater than is H₂O. Thus, the ionization equilibrium lies more to the left in EtOH where the acids are weaker.   (*b*) The ΔS of ionization has a greater influence on pK_a in water which is the better solvating medium. *o*-Nitrobenzoic acid is probably a stronger acid in water because of a more favorable ΔS. In ethanol, where the entropy term is less significant, 3,5-dinitobenzoic acid may be stronger because of a more favorable ΔH that can arise from the inductive effect of *two* nitro groups even though they are *meta*.

16.57 Explain why highly-branched acids such as $Me_3CCH_2\overset{\overset{\displaystyle Me}{|}}{\underset{\underset{\displaystyle CMe_3}{|}}{C}}COOH$ are less acidic than unbranched acids.

▰ The $—COO^-$ of the branched acid is shielded from solvent molecules and cannot be stabilized as effectively as can an unhindered anion.

16.58 Use conformational theory to explain why (*a*) *trans*-4-*t*-butylcyclohexanecarboxylic acid is stronger than the *cis*-isomer, and (*b*) *exo*-2-norbornanecarboxylic acid is more acidic than the *endo*-isomer.

▰ In both cases the less sterically-hindered is $—COO^-$ toward solvation, the stronger is the acid. (*a*) The COO^- in the *trans*-isomer is equatorial, less hindered and better solvated. Thus the *trans* acid is stronger. (*b*) *Exo*-COO^- is more exposed to solvent and the *exo* acid is stronger.

16.59 (*a*) Write the chemical equations for the complete dissociation of a typical dicarboxylic acid, $HOOC(CH_2)_nCOOH$. (*b*) Give a relative comparison of pK_{a1} and pK_{a2} and justify your answer.

▰ (*a*) They dissociate in two steps:

$$HOOC(CH_2)_nCOOH + H_2O \rightleftharpoons \underset{\text{monoanion}}{HOOC(CH_2)_nCOO^-} + H_3O^+ \quad pK_{a1}$$
$$HOOC(CH_2)_nCOO^- + H_2O \rightleftharpoons \underset{\text{dianion}}{{}^-OOC(CH_2)_nCOO^-} + H_3O^+ \quad pK_{a2}$$

(*b*) Since it takes more free energy to remove an H^+ from an anion than from a molecule, pK_{a1} is smaller than pK_{a2} ($K_{a1} > K_{a2}$).

16.60 (*a*) Given the pK_{a1}'s and pK_{a2}'s (respectively, in parentheses) of the following dicarboxylic acids: oxalic (1.27, 4.27); malonic (2.86, 5.70); succinic (4.21, 5.64); glutaric (4.34, 5.27); and adipic (4.41, 5.28). (*a*) Why are these acids stronger (smaller pK_{a1}) than monoalkylcarboxylic acids such as butanoic acid (4.82)? (*b*) Account for the trend in the acidities.

▰ (*a*) They are more acidic than monoalkylcarboxylic acids because COOH is an EWG for somewhat the same reason that is C=O [Problem 16.54(*a*)]. (*b*) The trend of declining acidities is in order of increasing number of sigma bonds between $HOOC—$ and $—COO^-$.

16.61 Explain the statement "If all electronic and solvation factors were the same, any dicarboxylic acid would be twice as acidic as any monocarboxylic acid."

▰ The dicarboxylic acid has two ionizable H's whereas the monocarboxylic acid has only one. On the basis of this statistical factor alone the dicarboxylic acid should be twice as strong.

16.62 (*a*) Define the term ΔpK_a as it applies to the acids in Problem 16.60. (*b*) Discuss the significance of this term as it relates to the relative acidities of the acid and its acid anion. (*c*) Find the ΔpK_a's for the dicarboxylic acids given in Problem 16.60.

▰ (*a*) $\Delta pK_a = pK_{a2} - pK_{a1}$. (*b*) The larger the value, the weaker as a proton donor is the acid anion relative to the acid or, more seldom, the stronger is the acid relative to the acid anion. (*c*) oxalic, 3.00; malonic, 2.84; succinic, 1.43; glutaric, 0.93; and adipic, 0.87.

16.63 (*a*) Discuss the trend in ΔpK_a values calculated in Problem 16.62. (*b*) What would the ΔpK_a be for a hypothetical dicarboxylic acid with an infinitely long chain of C's?

▰ (*a*) In the monoanion, $—COO^-$ exerts an acid-weakening field effect on the COOH because the presence of another nearby negative charge is destabilizing due to electrostatic repulsion. (*b*) Zero, because there would be no interaction between the acidic groups. The compound would behave as two distinct monocarboxylic acids.

16.64 What factor influences the acidity of the monoanions of malonic and succinic acids but not those of oxalic, glutaric, or adipic acids?

▮ In general, the acidity of an H is weakened if it participates in H-bonding because its ionization requires more free energy to break the H-bond. This occurs between COOH and COO⁻ of the acid monoanions of malonic, that forms a five-membered ring (not counting the very small H), and succinic, that forms a six-membered ring as shown:

Malonate monoanion   Succinate monoanion

In the oxalate monoanion the OH and O⁻ are less able to form an H-bond because they are spacially more separated than in the malonate and succinate monoanions. In the glutarate and adipate monoanions the rings formed as the result of intramolecular H-bonding are seven- and eight-membered respectively. Formation of these rings is unfavorable because of an appreciable loss in entropy. Consequently, H-bonding is less significant.

16.65 Account for the fact that (**a**) maleic acid is a stronger acid than fumaric acid but maleate monoanion is a weaker acid than fumarate monanion and (**b**) phthalic acid is stronger than either isophthalic or terphthalic acids but phthalate monoanion is weaker than isophthalate and terephthalate monoanions.

▮ In both cases H-bonding and the field effect in the monoanion are the key factors. (**a**) Maleic acid is stronger because the H-bonding between the *cis* COOH and COO⁻ stabilizes its monanion. However, this same H-bonding weakens the acidity of the monoanion. The acidity is also attenuated because of the field effect generated by —COO⁻ on the nearby —COOH. In general, the closer are the COOH's, the larger is ΔpK_a. The *trans* COOH and COO⁻ in fumaric acid are too far apart for H-bonding or any significant field effect.

Fumaric acid (weaker)   Fumarate monoanion (no H-bonding and meager field effect)   Maleic acid (stronger)   Maleate monoanion (H-bonding and strong field effect)

(**b**) In phthalic acid the *ortho* groups are close enough to participate in H-bonding and to exert a field effect as is the case in maleic acid. The *meta* groups in isophthalic acid and the *para* groups cannot exert a field-effect because they are too far apart as is the case in fumaric acid. Hence, phthalic acid is the strongest of the three acids because H-bonding stabilizes its conjugate base, the monoanion. However, this same H-bonding makes the monoanion the weakest acid.

16.66 Account for the fact that ΔpK_{a1} for *cis*-1,2-cyclohexanedicarboxylic acid (2.42) is greater than for the *trans* isomer (1.75).

▮ The higher value signals closer proximity of the COOH's, and the e,a *cis* COOH's are closer than the e,e *trans* COOH's.

16.67 Why is the field effect just as important, if not more so, than H-bonding in influencing the ΔpK_a values?

▮ A group whose negative charge is well delocalized, e.g., COO⁻, forms weaker H-bonds than, for example, an anion with localized charges, e.g., RO⁻, that forms stronger H-bonds.

16.68 Account for the fact that salicylic acid, o-HOC₆H₄COOH, is a stronger acid than o-CH₃OC₆H₄COOH.

▮ We might expect the electronic effects of —OH and —OCH₃ to be about the same. If anything, the —OCH₃ might be more acid-strengthening because it is bulkier (*ortho* effect). The answer lies in the ability of salicylate ion to undergo intermolecular H-bonding (the dominant factor) as shown, thereby stabilizing the conjugate base and enhancing acidity.

16.69 Relative acidities have been determined in the gas phase by instrumental techniques. (*a*) Give the most important advantage of these methods over studies in solvent for determining relative acidities. (*b*) Explain the following gas phase observations that are contrary to findings in solution: Propanoic acid > acetic acid; chloroethanoic acid > fluoroethanoic acid; *t*-butanol > *n*-butanol.

◢ (*a*) In the gas phase one obtains the intrinsic acidities, free of the role of base and solvent. (*b*) Since each result is opposite to what is expected from inductive effects, it appears that electronic effects are not pertinent. In each case the larger anion is more stable. Apparently the stability of the anion is directly related to the ease of polarization, which in turn is directly related to size.

16.70 (*a*) Write a chemical equation for the solution of RCOOH in conc. H_2SO_4, indicating the two possible cations. (*b*) Discuss the relative stabilities of the cations. (*c*) Which cation more readily undergoes C—O bond cleavage? (*d*) How could the determination of (*i*) (Problem 13.158) in conc. H_2SO_4 indicate which is the main cation formed?

◢ (*a*)

$$RC{\overset{\displaystyle \|}{\underset{\displaystyle O}{}}}OH + H_2SO_4 \longrightarrow HSO_4^- + \left[RC{\overset{\displaystyle \|}{\underset{\displaystyle O}{}}}OH_2^+ \text{ (A) and } RC{\overset{\displaystyle \|}{\underset{\displaystyle {}^+OH}{}}}OH \text{ (B)} \right]$$

(*b*) **B** is much more stable and is the major cation because it has equivalent contributing structures:

$$\left[RC{\overset{\displaystyle \|}{\underset{\displaystyle {}^+OH}{}}}OH \longleftrightarrow RC{\overset{\displaystyle \|}{\underset{\displaystyle OH}{}}}\overset{+}{O}H \right].$$

(*c*) **A** is more reactive. It loses H_2O to give the acylium ion, $RC\equiv O^+$, a reactive intermediate in many organic reactions such as Friedel–Crafts acylations (Problem 11.19).

(*d*) If **B** were formed along with HSO_4^-, with two ions in solution, $i = 2$. If **A** were formed, it would lose H_2O, which would accept an H^+ from H_2SO_4, and the net reaction would be

$$RCOOH + 2H_2SO_4 \longrightarrow RC\equiv O^+ + H_3O^+ + 2HSO_4^-$$

With four ions in solution, $i = 4$. The experiment shows $i \cong 2$.

CHEMICAL REACTIONS

16.71 Select the reducing agents that can reduce $RCOOH \to RCH_2OH$ from the following: $NaBH_4$; $LiAlH_4$; Na/EtOH; H_2/catalyst; BH_3/THF followed by H_3O^+.

◢ $LiAlH_4$ and BH_3/THF followed by H_3O^+.

16.72 (*a*) Which reducing agent, $LiAlH_4$ or BH_3/THF, will reduce the following carboxylic acids to their corresponding 1° alcohols? (i) $CH_3CH(CH_3)CH_2COOH$, (ii) $p\text{-}CH_3COC_6H_4COOH$, (iii) cyclohexanecarboxylic acid, (iv) $m\text{-}O_2NC_6H_4COOH$, (v) $(Z)\text{-}CH_3CH=CHCH_2COOH$, and (vi) $BrCH_2CH_2CH_2COOH$. (*b*) Give the structure of the alcohol.

◢ (*a*) (i) Both, (ii) BH_3/THF, (iii) both, (iv) BH_3/THF, (v) $LiAlH_4$, (vi) BH_3/THF.

(*b*) (i) $CH_3CH(CH_3)CH_2CH_2OH$, (ii) $p\text{-}CH_3COC_6H_4CH_2OH$, (iii)

(iv) $m\text{-}O_2NC_6H_4CH_2OH$, (v) $(Z)\text{-}CH_3CH=CHCH_2CH_2OH$, (vi) $Br(CH_2)_3CH_2OH$.

16.73 Justify your answers in Problem 16.72(*a*).

◢ (i) There is no other functional group that could be reduced. (ii) $LiAlH_4$ reduces C=O more readily than COOH. (iii) See (i). (iv) $LiAlH_4$ reduces —NO_2 whereas BH_3/THF does not. (v) BH_3/THF rapidly reduces alkenes to alkanes whereas $LiAlH_4$ does not. (vi) $LiAlH_4$ reduces halides to alkanes whereas BH_3/THF does not.

16.74 (*a*) Write the equation for the first step in the reaction of RCOOH with $LiAlH_4$. (*b*) What is the key step in the reduction of the product in (*a*)? (*c*) What is the intermediate product of the reduction and why is it not isolable?

◢ (*a*) $RCOOH + LiAlH_4 \rightarrow RCOO^-Li^+ + H_2 + AlH_3$. (*b*) A hydride is transferred from AlH_3 to the carboxylate C. (*c*) $RCH{=}O$, which is further reduced to RCH_2O^-. Acidification gives the alcohol RCH_2OH.

16.75 (*a*) Give balanced equations for the reaction of each of the following reagents with $PhCH_2COOH$: (i) $SOCl_2$, (ii) PCl_3, (iii) PCl_5, (iv) $CH_3C{-}O{-}CCH_3$, (v) CH_3OH/H_2SO_4, (vi) NH_3 then heat. (*b*) Name the organic
$\quad\quad\quad\quad\quad\quad\quad\quad\quad\quad\quad\quad\quad\quad\quad\quad\;\; \overset{\|}{O}\quad\;\; \overset{\|}{O}$
product formed from each reaction and classify its functional group.

◢ (*a*)
(i) $PhCH_2COOH + SOCl_2 \longrightarrow PhCH_2COCl + SO_2\,(g) + HCl\,(g)$
(ii) $3PhCH_2COOH + PCl_3 \longrightarrow 3PhCH_2COCl + H_2HPO_3\,(l)$
(iii) $PhCH_2COOH + PCl_5 \longrightarrow PhCH_2COCl + POCl_3\,(l) + HCl\,(g)$
(iv) $2PhCH_2COOH + (CH_3CO)_2O \longrightarrow PhCH_2\overset{\|}{C}{-}O{-}\overset{\|}{C}CH_2Ph + 2CH_3COOH$
$\quad\quad\quad\quad\quad\quad\quad\quad\quad\quad\quad\quad\quad\quad\quad\quad\quad\quad\quad\; O\quad\quad\;\; O$
(v) $PhCH_2COOH + CH_3OH \xrightarrow{H_2SO_4} PhCH_2\overset{\|}{C}OCH_3 + H_2O$ (reacts with H_2SO_4)
$\quad\quad\quad\quad\quad\quad\quad\quad\quad\quad\quad\quad\quad\quad\quad\quad\quad\;\; O$
(vi) $PhCH_2COOH + NH_3 \longrightarrow \underset{\text{ammonium salt}}{PhCH_2COO^-NH_4^+} \xrightarrow{\text{heat}} PhCH_2\overset{\|}{C}{-}NH_2 + H_2O$
$\quad\quad\quad\quad\quad\quad\quad\quad\quad\quad\quad\quad\quad\quad\quad\quad\quad\quad\quad\quad\quad\quad\quad\quad\;\; O$

(*b*) (i), (ii), and (iii) phenacetyl chloride, an acid chloride; (iv) phenylacetic anhydride, an acid anhydride; (v) methyl phenylacetate, an ester; (vi) phenylacetamide, a 1° amide.

16.76 (*a*) Give the final product with the sequence of intermediates for the reaction of propanoic acyl with Br_2 and a trace of PBr_3 followed by addition of H_2O [*Hell–Volhard–Zelinsky* (HVZ) reaction]. (*b*) What is the final product when 2 eq of reagent are used? (*c*) What is the reaction with Me_3CCOOH? (*d*) What product is formed if (i) PCl_3 replaces PBr_3 and (ii) Cl_2 replaces Br_2?

◢ (*a*) $CH_3CH_2COOH \xrightarrow{Br_2/PBr_3} \underset{\text{acid bromide}}{CH_3CH_2COBr} \xrightarrow{Br_2} \underset{\alpha\text{-bromoacid bromide}}{CH_3CHBrCOBr} \xrightarrow{H_2O} \underset{\alpha\text{-bromoacid}}{CH_3CHBrCOOH}$

(*b*) CH_3CBr_2COOH. (*c*) No reaction, the acid does not have an αH, necessary for the reaction. (*d*) (i) The same product, and (ii) 2-chloropropanoic acid. The α halogen comes from X_2.

16.77 Give the product formed when PhCOOH reacts with (*a*) Br_2/Fe and (*b*) $H_2S_2O_7$ (SO_3 dissolved in H_2SO_4).

◢ $-COOH$ is a *meta*-directing group. (*a*) $m\text{-}BrC_6H_4COOH$ and (*b*) $m\text{-}HO_3SC_6H_4COOH$.

16.78 (*a*) Compare the behavior of CH_3COOH and $HCOOH$ on being warmed in conc. H_2SO_4. (*b*) Explain the difference in terms of the mechanism. (*c*) Give the products from the warming of Ph_3CCOOH in conc. H_2SO_4 and account for their formation. (*d*) Complete the following reaction: $p\text{-}HOC_6H_4COOH \xrightarrow[Br_2]{\text{excess}}$ and account for the product. (*e*) What product is synthesized by heating glacial acetic acid to 700 °C?

◢ (*a*) CH_3COOH does not react. $HCOOH$ decomposes to H_2O and CO. (*b*) The small amount of protonated $HCOOH$ at the O of OH initiates the reaction:

$$HC\underset{\underset{\displaystyle {}^+OH_2}{|}}{=}O \xrightarrow{-H_2O} HC{\equiv}O^+\ (\mathbf{A}) \xrightarrow{-H^+} {:}C{\equiv}O{:}$$

The acylium ion (**A**) is a very unstable powerful acid that loses H^+ to give CO. The acetic acid equivalent, CH_3CO^+, cannot do this; instead it reforms the protonated acetic acid. (*c*) $Ph_3COH + CO$. The intermediate acylium ion, Ph_3CCO^+, loses CO to give the stable triaryl carbocation, Ph_3C^+, which then bonds with H_2O to eventually give Ph_3COH. (*d*) 2,4,6-Tribromophenol. With a ring-activating substituent, an *o*- or *p*-COOH is displaced as CO_2 and H^+ by the attacking electrophile, in this case Br^+. Excess Br_2 further brominates the phenol. (*e*) Ketene, $H_2C=C=O$, by dehydration.

16.79 (*a*) Compare the reactivities of CH_3COOH, *m*-toluic acid, and Cl_3CCOOH on being heated with a base-like soda lime, a solid mixture of NaOH and CaO. (*b*) Account for the difference in behavior of the three acids. (*c*) Predict the ease of decarboxylation of 2,4,6-trinitrobenzoic acid.

◢ All three acids first form mixtures of Na and Ca carboxylate salts. (*a*) CH_3COO^- does not react further. m-$CH_3C_6H_4COO^-$ decarboxylates to give a poor yield of toluene and Cl_3COO^- gives a good yield of Cl_3CH at even lower temperatures. (*b*) The reactive species, $RCOO^-$, can lose CO_2 when the resulting carbanion is stabilized. CH_3COO^- does not decompose; $H_3C:^-$ is very unstable because its C uses sp^3 HO's. (*c*) $PhCOO^-$ decomposes a little more readily because the C of $Ph:^-$ uses sp^2 HO's. Cl_3CCOO^- easily loses CO_2 because $Cl_3C:^-$ is a fairly stable carbanion.

16.80 (*a*) Synthesize $PhCH_2CH_2Br$ from $PhCH_2CH_2COOH$. (*b*) Suggest a free-radical chain mechanism for the reaction used. Use RCOOH as the acid in your mechanism.

◢ (*a*) $$PhCH_2CH_2COOH \xrightarrow{Ag_2O} PhCH_2CH_2COO^-Ag^+ \xrightarrow{Br_2} PhCH_2CH_2Br + CO_2 + AgBr$$

This brominative decarboxylation is called the *Hunsdiecker* reaction. Pb^{2+} salts are also used.

(*b*)
$$R-\overset{\overset{\displaystyle O}{\|}}{C}O^-Ag^+ + Br_2 \longrightarrow R-\overset{\overset{\displaystyle O}{\|}}{C}O-Br \text{ (acyl hypohalite)} + AgBr$$

Initiation step:
$$R-\overset{\overset{\displaystyle O}{\|}}{C}O-Br \longrightarrow R-\overset{\overset{\displaystyle O}{\|}}{C}O\cdot + Br\cdot \text{ (The O—Br bond is very weak.)}$$

Propagation step 1:
$$R-\overset{\overset{\displaystyle O}{\|}}{C}O\cdot \longrightarrow R\cdot + CO_2$$

Propagation step 2:
$$R-\overset{\overset{\displaystyle O}{\|}}{C}O-Br + R\cdot \longrightarrow RBr + R-\overset{\overset{\displaystyle O}{\|}}{C}O\cdot$$

16.81 (*a*) Compare the reaction of CH_3CH_2COOH with excess (i) CH_3MgBr and (ii) CH_3Li.

◢ (*a*) (i) $$CH_3CH_2COOH \xrightarrow{CH_3MgBr} CH_3CH_2COO^-(MgBr)^+ + CH_4$$

(ii) $$CH_3CH_2COOH \xrightarrow[-CH_4]{CH_3Li} CH_3CH_2COO^-Li^+ \xrightarrow{CH_3Li} CH_3CH_2C(O^-Li^+)_2 \overset{\displaystyle CH_3}{\underset{\displaystyle |}{}}$$

dialkoxide of a *gem*-diol

Water converts the dianion into the diol that decomposes to the ketone, $CH_3CH_2COCH_3$, the final product.

(*b*) The more electropositive the metal (M) of the R—M bond, the more ionic is the bond. Li is more electropositive than Mg. R from R—Li bears more $-$ charge than R from R—MgX, and thus is a stronger nucleophile capable of adding to the C=O of COO^-.

16.82 (*a*) Give the products from heating the first seven straight-chain dicarboxylic acids (i–vii). (*b*) Explain why adipic acid does not form a cyclic anhydride and suberic (1,8-octanedioic) acid does not form a cyclic ketone.

◢ The reactions that occur when dicarboxylic acids are heated are dependent on the number of intervening CH_2's.

(i) $HOOCCOOH \longrightarrow H_2O + CO + CO_2$ (ii) $CH_2(COOH)_2 \longrightarrow CH_3COOH + CO_2$

(iii) $HOOCCH_2CH_2COOH \longrightarrow$

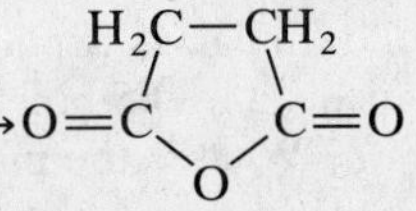

succinic anhydride

(iv) $HOOC(CH_2)_3COOH \longrightarrow$

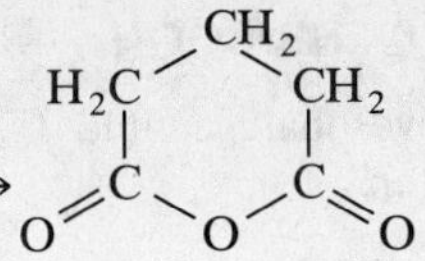

glutaric anhydride

(v) $HOOC(CH_2)_4COOH \longrightarrow$ cyclopentanone $+ CO_2$

(vi) $HOOC(CH_2)_5COOH \longrightarrow$ cyclohexanone $+ CO_2$

Ketone formation in (v) and (vi) can be encouraged by heating the Ba^{2+} salts.

(vii) $HOOC(CH_2)_6COOH \longrightarrow HOOC(CH_2)_6\overset{\parallel}{\underset{O}{C}}-O-\overset{\parallel}{\underset{O}{C}}(CH_2)_6\overset{\parallel}{\underset{O}{C}}-O-\overset{\parallel}{\underset{O}{C}}(CH_2)_6\overset{\parallel}{\underset{O}{C}}-O-$

a linear polymeric anhydride

(b) Each such reaction would give a seven-membered ring that is too difficult to form. All cyclic products have five- and six-membered rings that are easily formed.

SUBSTITUTED CARBOXYLIC ACIDS

16.83   Give two ways of synthesizing an α-hydroxycarboxylic acid such as lactic acid, α-hydroxypropanoic acid.

1. Add HCN to an aldehyde with one less C than the carboxylic acid and hydrolyze the nitrile.

$$CH_3CH{=}O + HCN \longrightarrow CH_3CH(OH)CN \xrightarrow{H^+} CH_3CH(OH)COOH$$

2. $CH_3CH_2COOH \xrightarrow{PBr_3/Cl_2} CH_3CHClCOOH \xrightarrow[2.\ H^+]{1.\ OH^-} CH_3CH(OH)COOH$

16.84   Give the products isolated from heating (a) α-hydroxy, (b) β-hydroxy, (c) γ-hydroxy, (d) δ-hydroxy, and (e) ϵ-hydroxyhexanoic acid. Give the stereochemistry of the product from (a) and (b).

(a) $CH_3(CH_2)_3CHOHCOOH \longrightarrow$

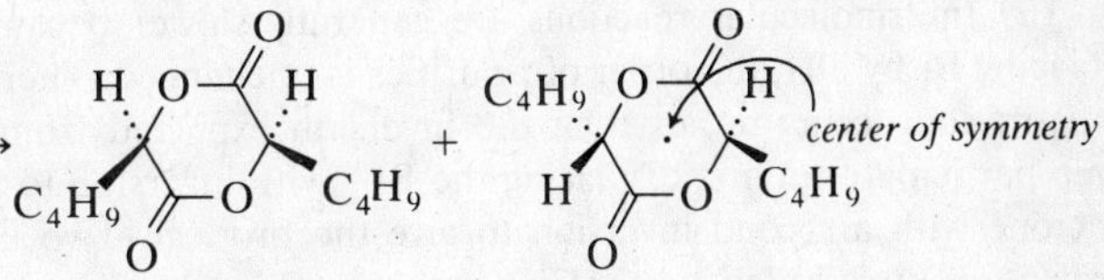

cis, racemic   trans, meso

(b) $CH_3(CH_2)_2CHOHCH_2COOH \longrightarrow CH_3(CH_2)_2CH{=}CHCOOH$ (stable conjugated molecule)

(cis + mainly trans)

(c) $CH_3CH_2CHOHCH_2CH_2COOH \longrightarrow$

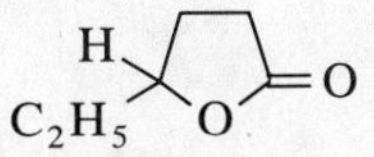

4-Ethyl-γ-butyrolactone or
4-ethyl-4-butanolide (a cyclic ester)

(d) $CH_3CHOH(CH_2)_3COOH \longrightarrow$

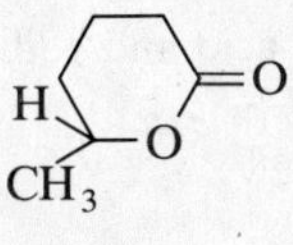

5-Methyl-δ-valerolactone or
5-methyl-5-pentanolide

(e) $HOCH_2(CH_2)_4COOH \longrightarrow HOCH_2(CH_2)_4\overset{\parallel}{\underset{O}{C}}-OCH_2(CH_2)_4\overset{\parallel}{\underset{O}{C}}-OCH_2(CH_2)_4\overset{\parallel}{\underset{O}{C}}-$

This is a small portion of a long chain polymeric ester.

16.85 (*a*) What is the product when each of the following acids is reacted with aq. NaOH? (i) 2-Bromobutanoic acid, (ii) 3-bromobutanoic acid, (iii) 4-bromobutanoic acid, (iv) 5-bromopentanoic acid. Assume that in (i) and (ii) the initially formed carboxylate salt is acidified. (*b*) What is the product from reaction of (i) with alc. KOH?

(*a*) (i) α-Haloacids typically give α-hydroxyacids by S_N2 displacements.

$$CH_3CH_2CHBrCOOH \longrightarrow CH_3CH_2CHOHCOOH$$

(ii) β-Substituted acids are dehydrohalogenated (E2). This facile reaction occurs because the product has a conjugated system.

$$CH_3CHBrCH_2COOH \longrightarrow CH_3CH{=}CHCOOH \text{ (mostly } trans)$$

(iii) γ-Haloacids undergo intramolecular S_N2-type displacement of X^- driven by the nucleophilic carboxylate anion, to yield γ-lactones.

γ-Butyrolactone
(4-butanolide)

(iv) Similar to part (*c*) to give a δ-lactone.

δ-Valerolactone
(5-pentanolide)

(*b*) $CH_3CH{=}CHCOOH$ (mostly *trans*).

16.86 (*a*) Compare the rates of a typical S_N2 intermolecular reaction ($RX + R'COO^-$) with intramolecular S_N2 lactone formation. (*b*) Explain the fact that (*R*)-$CH_3CHBrCOO^-Na^+$ reacts with NaOH to give (*R*)-$CH_3CHOHCOO^-Na^+$.

(*a*) Intermolecular reactions are generally slower because they require collision of two species. (*b*) On displacing Br by OH, the order of priorities is unchanged. Therefore, since both configurations are *R*, *retention* of configuration occurs rather than the inversion expected from S_N2 reactions. It is believed that the $-COO^-$ group participates in first displacing the Br^- with inversion to give an unstable α-lactone. Then OH^- attacks the α-lactone with a second inversion to give the product. Two inversions add up to retention. Intervention by an adjacent group is called *neighboring-group participation*.

unstable α-lactone

(*R*) (*S*) (*R*)

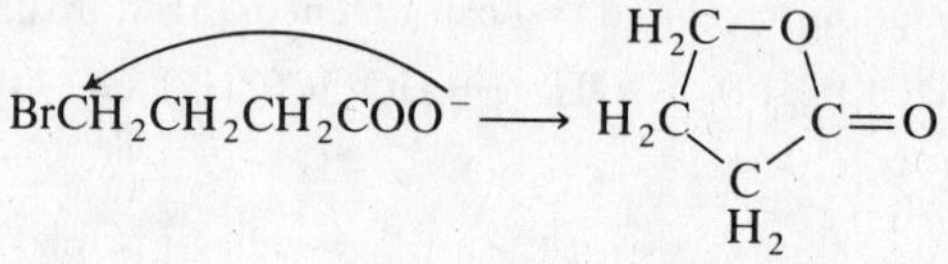

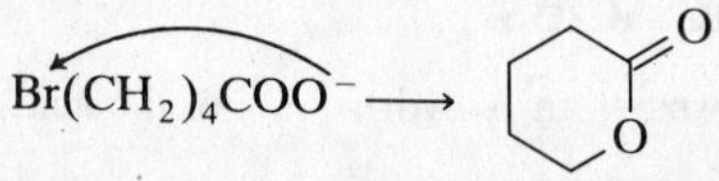

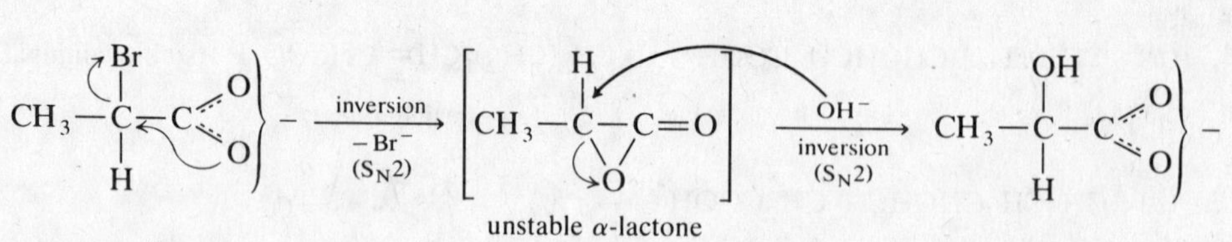

16.87 Convert 2-chlorobutanoic acid into 3-chlorobutanoic acid.

Dehydrohalogenate 2-chlorobutanoic acid and add HCl to the product, 2-butenoic acid. H^+ adds to give a + on the β-carbon, which then bonds to Cl^-.

$$CH_3CH_2CHClCOOH \xrightarrow{\text{alc. KOH}} CH_3CH{=}CHCOOH \xrightarrow{H^+} CH_3\overset{+}{C}H\overset{H}{C}HCOOH \xrightarrow{Cl^-} CH_3CHCl\overset{H}{C}HCOOH$$

The α-R^+ is not formed because its + would be next to the $C^{\delta+}$ of COOH:

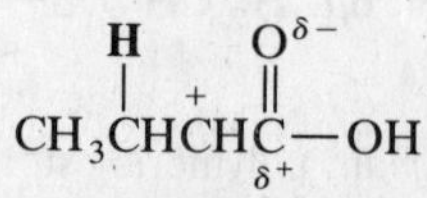

16.88 Prepare malonic acid from acetic acid.

$$CH_3COOH \xrightarrow{Br_2/PBr_3} BrCH_2COOH \xrightarrow{CN^-} NCCH_2COOH \xrightarrow{H_3O^+} CH_2(COOH)_2$$

In practice CN^- is added to the carboxylate salt to avoid emission of the very toxic HCN. The hydrolysis of the nitrile is done under controlled conditions to prevent decomposition of the malonic acid (Problem 16.90).

16.89 (*a*) Complete the following reaction: $PhCOCOOH \xrightarrow{\text{conc. } H_2SO_4} ?$ (*b*) Design a labeling experiment to determine the fate of the two C=O groups in the α-keto acid and state the result.   (*c*) Suggest a mechanism.

(*a*) $PhCOOH + CO$.   (*b*) A **C** stands for ^{14}C. Synthesize $PhCOCOOH$, collect the carbon monoxide, and determine if it is labeled. CO is obtained, indicating it originates from —COOH, not the keto group C. If $PhCOCOOH$ is used in the same experiment, unlabeled CO is collected leading to the same conclusion.   (*c*) See Problem 16.78.

$$PhCOCOOH \xrightarrow[-H_2O]{H^+} PhCOC\equiv O^+ \longrightarrow CO + PhC\equiv O^+; \quad PhCO^+ + H_2O \xrightarrow{-H^+} PhCOOH$$

16.90 (*a*) Give the products formed when (i) $HOOCCH_2COOH$ (malonic acid), a typical *gem*-dicarboxylic acid, and (ii) CH_3COCH_2COOH (acetoacetic acid), a typical β-ketoacid, are heated.   (*b*) Suggest a common mechanism.

(*a*)   (i) $HOOCCH_2COOH \xrightarrow{\Delta} CH_3COOH + CO_2$ (ii) $CH_3COCH_2COOH \xrightarrow{\Delta} CH_3COCH_3 + CO_2$
(*b*)   The crucial step is intramolecular H-bonding as shown (G = OH for malonic; G = CH$_3$ for acetoacetic).

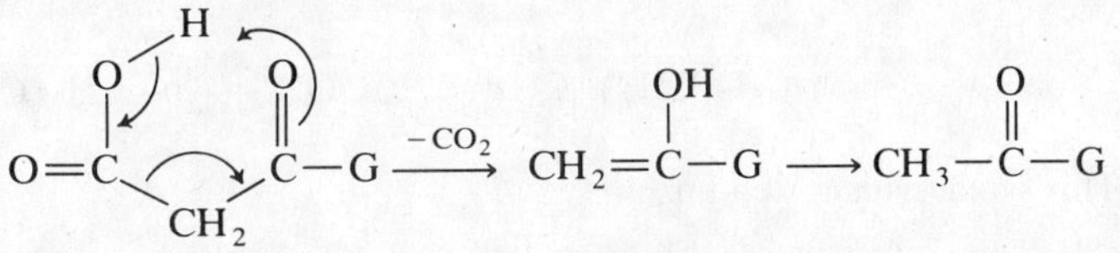

an enol (unstable)

The unstable enol rearranges to the more stable C=O group which in acetic acid is part of $-\overset{\displaystyle O}{\overset{\|}{C}}OH$.

16.91 Give the products formed on heating (*a*) 1,1,2-cyclohexanetricarboxylic acid and
(*b*) 1,1,2-cyclobutanetricarboxylic acid.

(*a*)

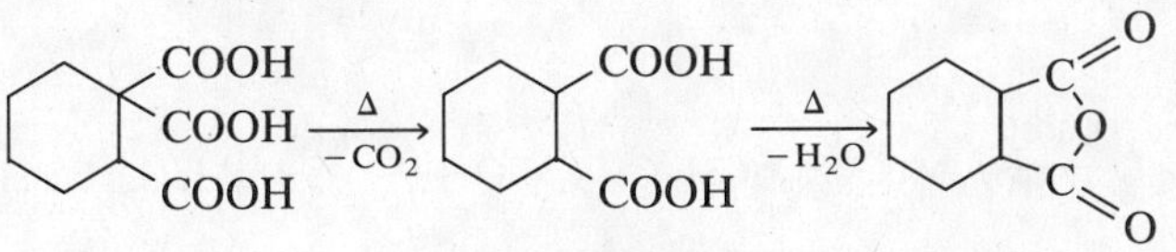

cis- and *trans-*
Cyclohexane-1,2-
dicarboxylic acid

cis- and *trans-*
anhydride

(*b*)

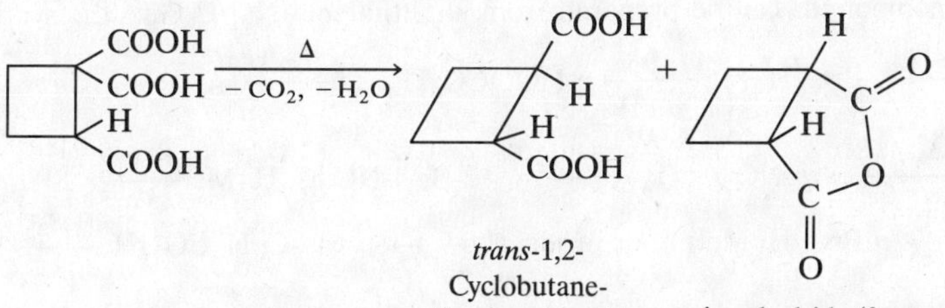

trans-1,2-
Cyclobutane-
dicarboxylic acid

cis-anhydride (from *cis* acid)

The *trans*-dicarboxylic acid cannot form the anhydride because a five- and a four-membered ring cannot be fused *trans*.

16.92 Give the product from the acidification of $PhCH=CHCH_2COOH$ and rationalize its formation.

∥ γ-Phenyl-γ-butyrolactone,

$$\begin{array}{c} Ph-CH-O \\ | \qquad \backslash \\ H_2C \qquad C{=}O \\ \backslash \quad / \\ CH_2 \end{array}$$

Protonation of C=C affords the stabilized benzyl carbocation, $Ph\overset{+}{C}HCH_2CH_2COOH$, which forms a C—O bond with the COOH affording the lactone.

16.93 Convert $CH_3CH_2COCH_2CH_2COOH$ to each of the following compounds in good yield:
(*a*) $CH_3CH_2COCH_2CH_2CHO$, (*b*) $CH_3(CH_2)_4CHO$, (*c*) $CH_3CH_2CHOHCH_2CH_2COOH$, and
(*d*) $CH_3CH_2CHOHCH_2CH_2CH_2OH$

∥ (*a*) Reduce the acid chloride, prepared from the acid with $SOCl_2$, with $LiAlH(O\text{-}t\text{-Bu})_3$. The C=O remains intact. (*b*) Reduce C=O to CH_2 with Zn/HCl (Clemmensen reduction) and then reduce the COOH to CHO as in (*a*). (*c*) Reduce C=O to CHOH with $NaBH_4$; the COOH is unchanged. (*d*) Reduce both groups with $LiAlH_4$.

SYNTHESES

16.94 Show the conversion of stearic acid to (*a*) 1-bromopentadecane and (*b*) 1-nonadecanol.

∥ Stearic acid, $CH_3(CH_2)_{16}COOH$, has 18 C's. (*a*) Three C's must be lost, two by oxidation and one by brominative decarboxylation (Hunsdiecker reaction).

$$CH_3(CH_2)_{14}CH_2CH_2COOH \xrightarrow{Br_2/PBr_3} CH_3(CH_2)_{14}CH_2CHBrCOOH \xrightarrow[\text{2. } H^+]{\text{1. alc. KOH}}$$

$$CH_3(CH_2)_{14}CH{=}CHCOOH \xrightarrow[\Delta]{KMnO_4} CH_3(CH_2)_{14}COOH \xrightarrow[\text{2. } Br_2]{\text{1. } Ag^+} CH_3(CH_2)_{14}Br$$

(*b*) This synthesis is a step-up.

$$CH_3(CH_2)_{16}COOH \xrightarrow{LiAlH_4} CH_3(CH_2)_{16}CH_2OH \xrightarrow{SOCl_2} CH_3(CH_2)_{16}CH_2Cl \xrightarrow[\substack{\text{2. } CO_2 \\ \text{3. } H^+}]{\text{1. Mg}}$$

$$CH_3(CH_2)_{16}CH_2COOH \xrightarrow{LiAlH_4} CH_3(CH_2)_{18}OH$$

16.95 Prepare 4-*p*-tolylbutanoic acid from toluene and succinic acid.

∥ Succinic anhydride made from succinic acid is used to acylate toluene. The side chain is then converted to the butanoic acid.

$$C_6H_5Me + O{=}C \underset{\substack{| \\ O}}{\overset{\substack{H_2C-CH_2 \\ / \qquad \backslash}}{}} C{=}O \xrightarrow{AlCl_3} p\text{-}MeC_6H_4\underset{\substack{\| \\ O}}{C}CH_2CH_2COOH \xrightarrow{Zn/HCl} p\text{-}MeC_6H_4CH_2CH_2CH_2COOH$$

16.96 (*a*) From PhH or PhMe and any needed aliphatic compound prepare: (i) 3-Cl-4-methylbenzoic acid (**A**), (ii) 2-bromo-4-nitrobenzoic acid (**B**), (iii) 4-sulfophthalic acid (**C**), (iv) trimellitic acid (1,2,4-benzenetricarboxylic acid) (**D**). (*b*) Which of these compounds can be prepared from naphthalene (Nap)? Give the syntheses.

∥ (*a*). (i) $PhMe \xrightarrow{Br_2/Fe} p\text{-}BrC_6H_4Me \xrightarrow[\substack{\text{2. } CO_2 \\ \text{3. } H^+}]{\text{1. Mg}} p\text{-}HOOCC_6H_4Me \xrightarrow{Cl_2/Fe} \mathbf{A}$

(ii) $PhMe \xrightarrow{HNO_3/H_2SO_4} p\text{-}NO_2C_6H_4Me \xrightarrow{Br_2/Fe} 2\text{-}Br\text{-}4\text{-}NO_2C_6H_3Me \xrightarrow[\Delta]{KMnO_4} \mathbf{B}$

(iii) $PhMe \xrightarrow{Br_2/Fe} o\text{-}BrC_6H_4Me(\text{minor product}) \xrightarrow[\substack{\text{2. } CO_2 \\ \text{3. } H^+}]{\text{1. Mg}} o\text{-}Me\text{-}C_6H_4COOH \xrightarrow{H_2S_2O_7}$

$$2\text{-}Me\text{-}5\text{-}(HO_3S)C_6H_3COOH \xrightarrow[\Delta]{KMnO_4} \mathbf{C}$$

In order to get a better yield of purer $o\text{-}BrC_6H_4Me$ use the following sequence:

$$PhMe \xrightarrow{H_2S_2O_7} p\text{-}MeC_6H_4SO_3H \xrightarrow{Br_2} 3\text{-}Br\text{-}4\text{-}MeC_6H_3SO_3H \xrightarrow[\Delta]{H_3O^+} o\text{-}BrC_6H_4Me$$

Sulfonation/desulfonation is used to block positions, in this case *para*, from an unwanted reaction.

(iv) $PhMe \xrightarrow{2Br_2/Fe} 2,4\text{-}Br_2C_6H_3Me \xrightarrow[\text{2. H}^+]{\text{1. Mg, CO}_2} 6\text{-Me-1,3-}C_6H_3(COOH)_2 \xrightarrow[\Delta]{KMnO_4} D$

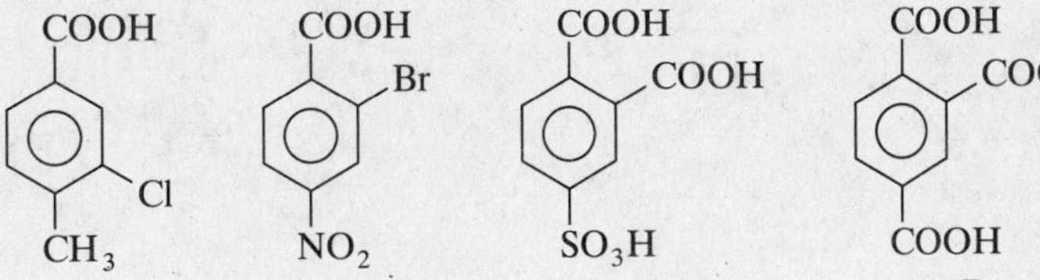

A   **B**   **C**   **D**

(*b*) The compounds having *ortho* COOH's, **C** and **D**.

(iii) $NapH \xrightarrow[\Delta]{H_2SO_4} 2\text{-}NapSO_3H \xrightarrow[\Delta]{KMnO_4} C$

(iv) $NapH \xrightarrow[PhNO_2]{CH_3COCl} 2\text{-}CH_3CONap \xrightarrow[OH^-]{Cl_2} 2\text{-}NapCOOH(\text{haloform reaction}) \xrightarrow{KMnO_4} D$

16.97   From phthalic acid prepare β-indanone (**E**), .

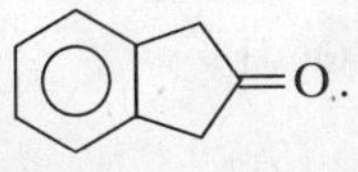

▮   The five-membered ring ketone signals a ring closure of a six-carbon chain dicarboxylic acid.

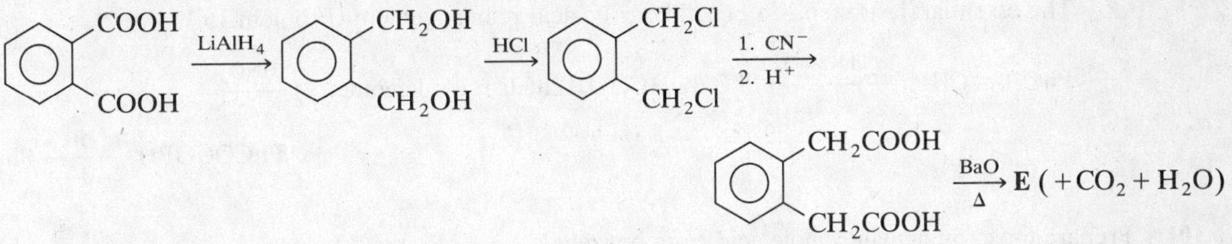

16.98   Synthesize each of the following ^{14}C-labeled compounds from any needed organic compound using CO_2 (from $BaCO_3$), CH_3OH or CH_3I ($C = ^{14}C$).   (*a*) CH_3CH_2COOH, (*b*) CH_3CH_2COOH, (*c*) CH_3CH_2COOH, (*d*) CH_3CH_2COOH, (*e*) $PhCOCH_3$, and (*f*) $PhCOCH_3$.

▮ (*a*) $CH_3CH_2Cl \xrightarrow{Mg} CH_3CH_2MgCl \xrightarrow[\text{2. H}^+]{\text{1. CO}_2} CH_3CH_2COOH$

(*b*) $CH_3OH \xrightarrow[\Delta]{Cu} H_2CO \xrightarrow[\text{2. H}^+]{\text{1. CH}_3MgI} CH_3CH_2OH \xrightarrow{HBr} CH_3CH_2Br \xrightarrow[\substack{\text{2. CO}_2 \\ \text{3. H}^+}]{\text{1. Mg}} CH_3CH_2COOH$

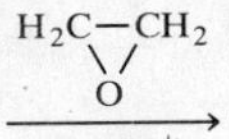

(*c*) $CH_3I + Mg \longrightarrow CH_3MgI \xrightarrow[\text{then H}^+]{\underset{O}{H_2C-CH_2}} CH_3CH_2CH_2OH \xrightarrow{KMnO_4} CH_3CH_2COOH$

(*d*) $CH_3MgI \xrightarrow[\text{2. H}^+]{\text{1. CO}_2} CH_3COOH \xrightarrow{LiAlH_4} CH_3CH_2OH \xrightarrow{HBr} CH_3CH_2Br \xrightarrow[\text{2. CO}_2, \text{H}^+]{\text{1. Mg}}$

$CH_3CH_2COOH \xrightarrow{LiAlH_4} CH_3CH_2COOH$

(*e*) $CH_3MgI + CO_2 \longrightarrow CH_3COOH \xrightarrow{SOCl_2} CH_3COCl \xrightarrow[AlCl_3]{PhH} PhCOCH_3$

(*f*)   Repeat the steps in (*e*) using CH_3MgI and CO_2.

16.99   Prepare (*a*) (i) 2-oxocyclopentanecarboxylic acid and (ii) 1-cyclopentenylmethanol from cyclopentanol, and (*b*) *cis*-1,2-cyclohexanedicarboxylic acid from any organic compound of four C's or less. Use as few steps as possible.

▮ (*a*)   (i)   Consider a Cl in place of —COOH and —OH in place of =O. Then

Cyclopentanol $\xrightarrow{H_2SO_4}$ cyclopentene $\xrightarrow{Cl_2/H_2O}$ 2-chlorocyclopentanol $\xrightarrow{CN^-}$ 2-cyanocyclopentanol $\xrightarrow{H_3O^+}$

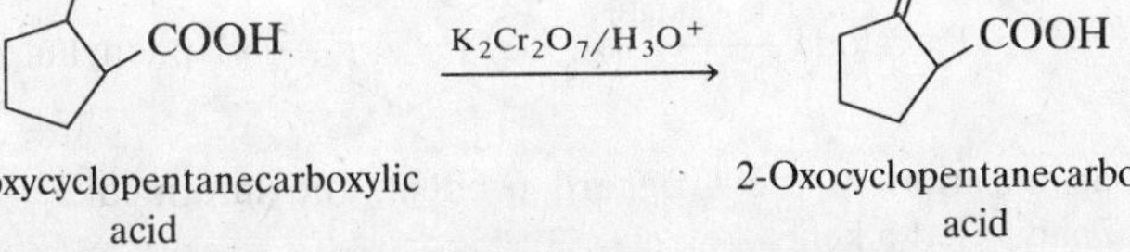

2-Hydroxycyclopentanecarboxylic acid $\xrightarrow{K_2Cr_2O_7/H_3O^+}$ 2-Oxocyclopentanecarboxylic acid

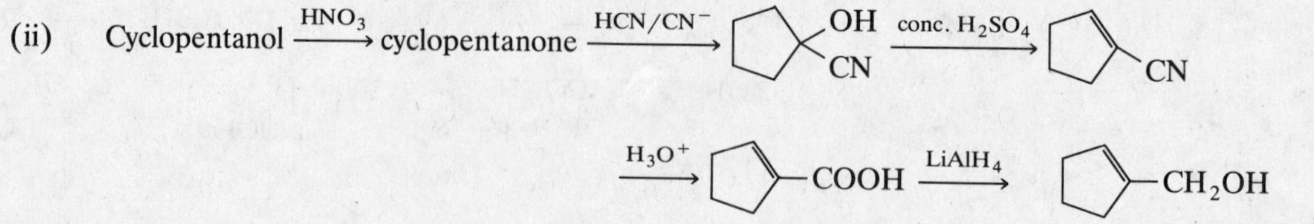

(ii)   Cyclopentanol $\xrightarrow{HNO_3}$ cyclopentanone $\xrightarrow{HCN/CN^-}$ [cyclopentane ring with OH and CN] $\xrightarrow{conc.\ H_2SO_4}$ [cyclopentene ring with CN]

$\xrightarrow{H_3O^+}$ [cyclopentene ring]—COOH $\xrightarrow{LiAlH_4}$ [cyclopentene ring]—CH$_2$OH

1-Cyclopentenylmethanol

Were the hydroxyacid made first, an attempt to dehydrate it in conc. H_2SO_4 would lead to some decarbomonoxylation.

(**b**)   Use the Diels–Alder reaction to make the cyclohexane ring. To get *cis* COOHs, use maleic acid as the dienophile with 1,3-butadiene as the diene.

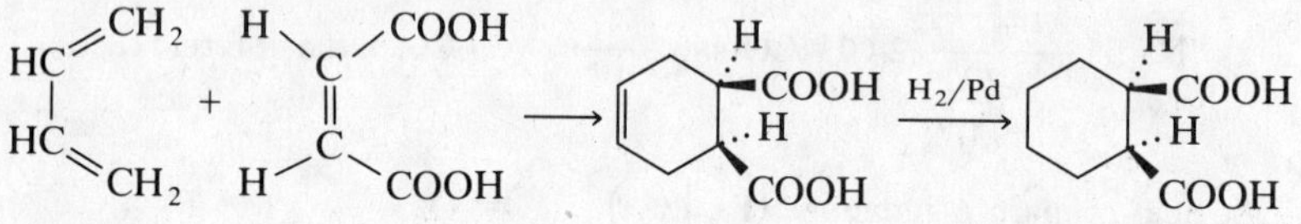

[reaction scheme: butadiene + maleic acid → cyclohexene with COOH groups $\xrightarrow{H_2/Pd}$ cyclohexane with COOH groups]

16.100   Prepare benzilic acid (1-hydroxy-1,1-diphenylethanoic acid) from either *cis*- or *trans*-stilbene.

▮   The essential (last) step is a benzil-benzilic acid rearrangement (Problem 15.138).

PhCH=CHPh $\xrightarrow{cold\ KMnO_4}$ PhCHOHCHOHPh(disregard geometry) $\xrightarrow{HNO_3}$

PhCOCOPH $\xrightarrow[2.\ H^+]{1.\ OH^-}$ Ph$_2$COHCOOH

16.101   Prepare 6-oxo-6-phenylhexanoic acid from benzene.

▮   The six-C ketoacid and the fact that PhH is the only starting material signal the need to open a six-C ring compound by oxidation of C=C or —CHOH. In order to get a phenyl ketone, Ph must be bonded to C=C and is best introduced by a Grignard reaction.

PhH $\xrightarrow{Br_2/Fe}$ PhBr $\xrightarrow{Mg}$ PhMgBr (**A**);   PhH $\xrightarrow[high\ pres.]{H_2/Pd,\ \Delta}$ cyclohexane $\xrightarrow[h\nu]{Cl_2}$

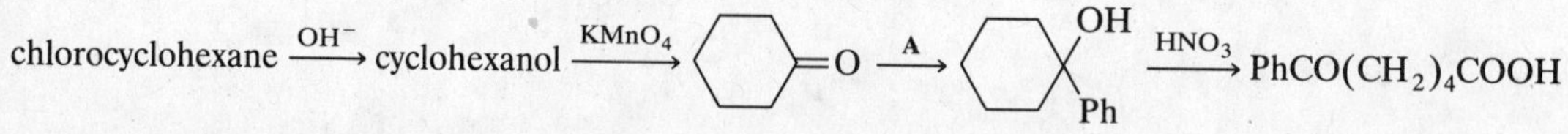

chlorocyclohexane $\xrightarrow{OH^-}$ cyclohexanol $\xrightarrow{KMnO_4}$ [cyclohexanone]=O $\xrightarrow{A}$ [cyclohexane with OH and Ph] $\xrightarrow{HNO_3}$ PhCO(CH$_2$)$_4$COOH

16.102   From PhH and any needed aliphatic and inorganic reagents synthesize (*a*) α-tetralone

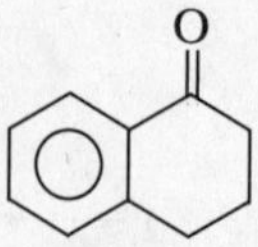

[structure of α-Tetralone]

α-Tetralone

and (*b*) 1-phenylnapthalene.

▮   In both cases the second ring is formed by acylating with succinic anhydride.

(*a*)   PhH + succinic anhydride $\xrightarrow{AlCl_3}$ PhCOCH$_2$CH$_2$COOH $\xrightarrow{Zn/Hg,\ HCl}$ Ph(CH$_2$)$_3$COOH $\xrightarrow{SOCl_2}$
Ph(CH$_2$)$_3$COCl $\xrightarrow{AlCl_3}$ α-tetralone

(*b*)   α-Tetralone $\xrightarrow[2.\ H^+]{1.\ PhMgBr}$ [structure with Ph] $\xrightarrow[\Delta]{S}$ 1-phenylnaphthalene

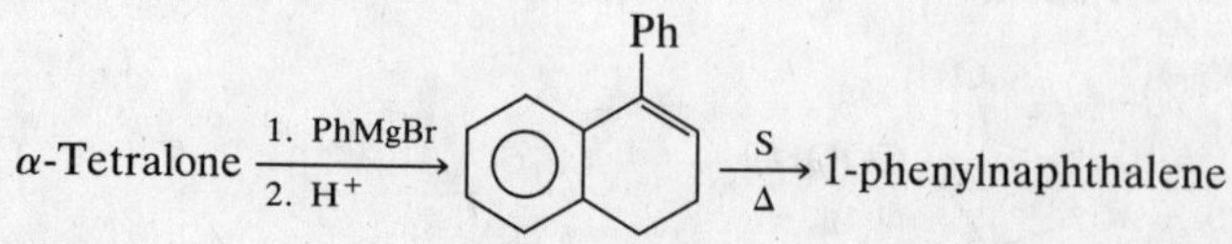

During the acidification of the Grignard product, the intermediate alcohol is dehydrated because the product is a conjugated alkene.

ANALYSIS AND SPECTROSCOPY

16.103 Use simple test tube chemical reactions to differentiate among the dry compounds: n-pentanol, pentanoic acid, pentane, pentanal, and ethyl methyl ether.

◢ Add $NaHCO_3$; pentanoic acid evolves CO_2. Add $[Ag(NH_3)_2]^+$ (a solution of $AgNO_3$ in aq. NH_3) to remaining compounds; pentanal gives a Ag mirror. Add Na metal to the three remaining compounds; n-pentanol emits H_2. Add conc. H_2SO_4 to the remaining two compounds; the ether dissolves to give a warm solution. The alkane, pentane, is inert to all tests.

16.104 With the aid of simple chemical tests differentiate among 2-chloropropanoic acid, pyruvic acid ($CH_3COCOOH$), acrylic acid ($H_2C=CHCOOH$) and propanoic acid.

◢ Pyruvic acid is also a keto compound and gives an insoluble red 2,4-dinitrophenylhydrazone with 2,4-dinitrophenylhydrazine (Problem 15.79). Acrylic acid is also an alkene and decolorizes Br_2/CCl_4. Both propanoic and 2-chloropropanoic acids give precipitates with aq. $AgNO_3$. However, $CH_3CH_2COO^-Ag^+(s)$ dissolves on acidification with HNO_3, reforming the acid. The precipitate from the chloroacid contains AgCl that does not dissolve in aq. HNO_3.

16.105 Differentiate between (**a**) MeCOOH and HCOOH and (**b**) HOOCCOOH, $HOOCCH_2COOH$, and $HOOCCH_2CH_2COOH$.

◢ (**a**) HCOOH has an aldehydic-type H, readily oxidized by acidified $KMnO_4$ whose deep-purple solution is decolorized. (**b**) HOOCCOOH is oxidized by $KMnO_4$ in H_3O^+. When heated, $(HOOC)_2CH_2$ loses CO_2 (**g**).

16.106 (**a**) Define the term neutralization equivalent of an acid. (**b**) Find the number of ionizable H's for a polycarboxylic acid (MW = 210 g/mol) with a neutralization equivalent of 70 g/eq. How many equivalents of NaOH would be neutralized by one mole of this acid? (**c**) Find the neutralization equivalent of mellitic acid, $C_6(COOH)_6$.

◢ (**a**) The *neutralization equivalent* (NE) is the equivalent weight (g/eq) of an acid as determined by titration with standardized NaOH. (**b**) The number of ionizable H's of an acid is the number of equivalents per mole, and is equal to MW/NE. Here the number of equivalents (number of ionizable H's) = (210 g/mol)/(70 g/eq) = 3 eq/mol. The number of equivalents of NaOH equals the number of ionizable H's, in this case 3 eq/mol. (**c**) The neutralization equivalent of mellitic acid is

$$NE = \frac{MW}{\text{Number of ionizable H's}} = \frac{342 \text{ g/mol}}{6 \text{ eq/mol}} = 57 \text{ g/eq}$$

16.107 Neutralization of 0.3504 g of acid **A** requires 27.24 mL of 0.1500 M NaOH, and the MW is found from mass-spectral data to be 172.1 g/mol. (**a**) Calculate the NE of **A**. (**b**) How many ionizable H's are there in **A**?

◢ (**a**) 0.1500 eq/L × 0.02724 L = 0.004086 eq $NE = \dfrac{0.3504 \text{ g}}{0.004086 \text{ eq}} = 85.76 \text{ g/eq}$

(**b**) $\dfrac{172.1 \text{ g/mol}}{85.76 \text{ g/eq}} = 2$ eq/mol or 2 ionizable H's/mol. **A** is a dicarboxylic acid.

16.108 Which carboxylic acid (**B**), NE = 52 g/eq, loses CO_2 when heated to give an acid (**C**), NE = 60 g/eq?

◢ Assume **C** is a monocarboxylic acid and NE = MW. The —COOH accounts for 45 g/mol of the molecular weight, leaving 60 − 45 = 15 g/mol for the remainder, due to —CH_3. **C** is CH_3COOH. **B** has a second COOH replacing an H of CH_3COOH; it is malonic acid, $H_2C(COOH)_2$ [(104 g/mol)/(2 eq/mol) = 52 g/eq].

16.109 (**a**) Give structures of the four optically-active structural isomers of $C_4H_8O_3$ (**D** through **G**) that evolve CO_2 with aq. $NaHCO_3$. (**b**) Find the structure of **D**, the isomer that reacts with $LiAlH_4$ to give an achiral product. (**c**) Give chemical reactions to distinguish among **E**, **F**, and **G**.

(a) The isomers have 1° of unsaturation that must be due to —COOH, since CO_2 is evolved on adding aq. $NaHCO_3$. The third O is present as —OH or —OR.

$$CH_3\overset{*}{C}HCOOH\ (\mathbf{D}) \qquad CH_3\overset{*}{C}HCH_2COOH\ (\mathbf{E}) \qquad CH_3CH_2\overset{*}{C}HCOOH\ (\mathbf{F}) \qquad CH_3\overset{*}{C}HCOOH\ (\mathbf{G})$$

with substituents below respectively: CH_2OH, OH, OH, OCH_3.

(b) $LiAlH_4$ converts —COOH to —CH_2OH. Only **D** is reduced to an achiral product, $CH_3CH(CH_2OH)_2$.

(c) The ether, **G**, differs from **E** and **F** in that it is inert to oxidation by $KMnO_4$ or CrO_3. **E** gives a positive iodoform test, distinguishing it from **F**.

16.110 Two isomeric carboxylic acids **H** and **I**, $C_9H_8O_2$, react with H_2/Pd giving compounds, $C_9H_{10}O_2$. **H** gives a resolvable product and **I** gives a nonresolvable product. Both isomers can be oxidized to PhCOOH. (a) Give the structures of **H** and **I**. (b) Mention another significant structural difference of **H** and **I**. (c) How can uv spectroscopy distinguish between **H** and **I**?

(a) The uptake of one mole of H_2 indicates the presence of a $\ce{>C=C<}$ that, along with Ph and COOH, accounts for the 6° of unsaturation. Furthermore **H** and **I** are monosubstituted phenyl compounds. **H** is $H_2C=CPhCOOH$ giving $H_3C\overset{*}{C}HPhCOOH$ with a chiral center. **I** is $PhCH=CHCOOH$, giving $PhCH_2CH_2COOH$ with no chiral center. (b) **I** exists as E, Z diastereomers. (c) **I** absorbs at the longer wavelength because the Ph, C=C, and C=O are linearly conjugated; in **H** they are cross-conjugated.

16.111 Tell how propanal and propanoic acid can be distinguished by their (a) ir, (b) pmr, (c) cmr, and (d) mass spectroscopies.

(a) Propanal has a characteristic C—H stretching doublet at 2720 and 2820 cm^{-1}. Propanoic acid has a very broad O—H band at 2500–3300 cm^{-1}. The C=O bands for both are in the same general region, about 1700 cm^{-1}.

(b) Propanal gives a singlet near $\delta = 9.7$ ppm (aldehydic H), a triplet near 0.9 (CH_3), and a multiplet near 2.5 (CH_2). Propanoic acid has a singlet in the range 10–13 (acidic H), a triplet near 0.9 (CH_3) and a quartet near 2.5 (CH_2).

(c) Carbonyl C's are sp^2-hybridized and attached to electronegative O's and hence suffer little shielding. They absorb farther downfield than any other kind of C: 190–220 for carbonyl compounds (propanal) and somewhat less downfield, 150–185, for carboxylic acids (propanoic acid).

(d) All carboxylic acids have a prominent peak at the m/z value of the acylium ion formed by fragmentation of the C—O bond:

$$\underset{\substack{\text{parent radical}\\\text{cation}}}{\overset{\displaystyle RC-H}{\underset{\displaystyle :\overset{.}{O}{}^+}{\big\|}}} \longrightarrow \underset{\text{acylium ion}}{RC\equiv O^+} + \cdot OH$$

The peak for the acylium ion, $CH_3CH_2CO^+$, from propanoic acid, is $m/z = 57$. Aldehydes typically undergo cleavage at the α-bond to give for propanal CHO^+ ($m/z = 29$).

16.112 With the aid of single chemical reaction and a quantitative chemical analysis, distinguish among $MeCH_2CH_2CH_2COOH$ (**A**), $MeCH_2CHMeCOOH$ (**B**), and Me_3CCOOH (**C**).

Treat these acids with Br_2/PBr_3. Without an α-H, **C** does not react. **B** has a single α-H and incorporates one Br (**B** → $MeCH_2CMeBrCOOH$). **A** has 2α-H's and is dibrominated (**A** → $CH_3CH_2CBr_2COOH$). The bromine content in the brominated derivatives of **A** and **B** is determined by quantitative analysis.

16.113 Distinguish among the three acids in Problem 16.112 by (a) ir, (b) pmr, (c) decoupled cmr, and (d) mass spectroscopies.

(a) **C** has the *tert*-butyl unsymmetrical doublet at 1370 cm^{-1} (strong) and 1395 cm^{-1} (moderate). **B** and **A** have no distinctive differences. (b) They all have the strongly-downfield signal for the H of —COOH. **B** has a doublet (the α-Me) and a triplet (the terminal Me), each integrating for three H's. **C** has two singlets in the ratio of nine (three Me's) to 1 (COOH). **A** has a profusion of signals and more complex coupling. (c) **A** and **B** both have five signals (all C's are different). They are best distinguished with coupled cmr to show that **A** has one Me (one quartet) while **B** has two Me's (two quartets). **C** has three signals. (*d*) **A** and **B**, typical of carboxylic acids having a —C—C—C—C—COOH unit, undergo a McLafferty fragmentation (Problem 12.178) to give cations with different m/z values as shown in Fig. 16-3. The acylium ion from **C** would likely lose CO leaving the stable 3° carbocation, Me_3C^+ ($m/z = 57$).

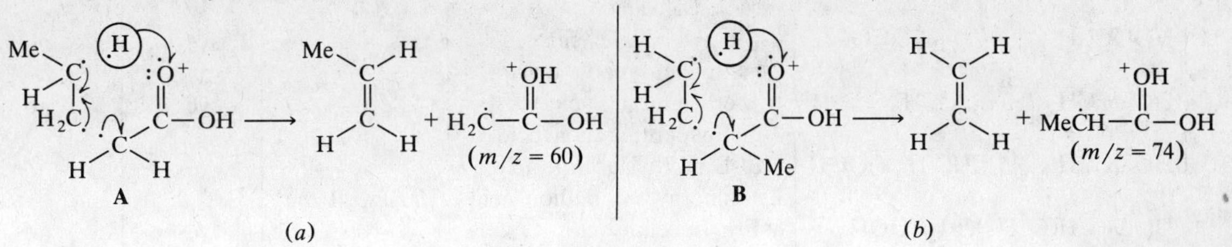

Fig. 16-3

16.114 How can the three isomeric tetracarboxylic acids, D^1, D^2, and D^3 (Fig. 16-4), be distinguished by anhydride formation?

▟ Add an equivalent amount of $SOCl_2$; D^1 gives two isomeric monoanhydrides. See Fig. 16-4(*a*). D^2 and D^3 each give only one monoanhydride. See Fig. 16-4(*b*) and (*c*). On addition of a second equivalent of $SOCl_2$ to the monoanhydrides of D^2 and D^3, only the monoanhydride of D^3 reacts to give a dianhydride [Fig. 16-4(*c*)].

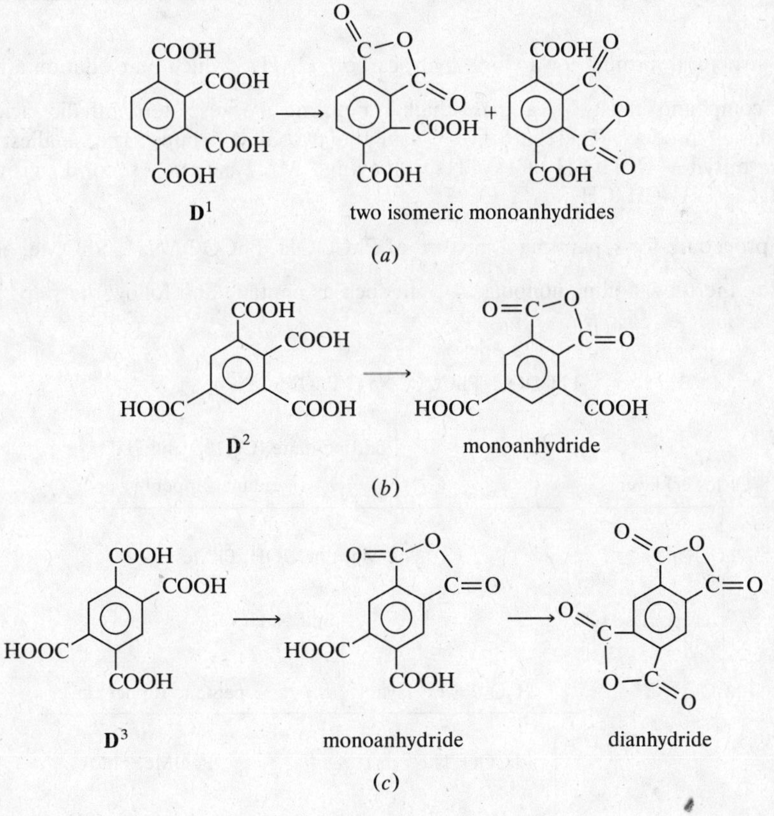

Fig. 16-4

SUPPLEMENTARY PROBLEMS

16.115 Write the structures and give the common and IUPAC names for all the isomeric dicarboxylic acids with the molecular formula $C_6H_{10}O_4$. Also list which acids have chiral C's, form cyclic anhydrides, and easily decarboxylate.

▟ See Table 16-3.

TABLE 16-3

Structure	Name (common and IUPAC)	Chirality	Anhydride	$-CO_2$ easily
$HOOCCH_2CH_2CH_2CH_2COOH$	Adipic acid, hexanedioic acid	no	yes	no
$HOOCCH(CH_3)CH_2CH_2COOH$	α-Methylglutaric acid, 2-methylpentanedioic acid	yes	yes	no
$HOOCCH_2CH(CH_3)CH_2COOH$	β-Methylglutaric acid, 3-methylpentanedioic acid	no	yes	no
$HOOCCH(CH_3)CH(CH_3)COOH$	α,α′-Dimethylsuccinic acid, 2,3-dimethylbutanedioic acid	yes (1 *meso*, 1 *rac*)	yes	no
$HOOCCH(C_2H_5)CH_2COOH$	α-Ethylsuccinic acid, 2-ethylbutanedioic acid	yes	yes	no
$HOOCC(CH_3)_2CH_2COOH$	α,α-Dimethylsuccinic acid, 2,2-dimethylbutanedioic acid	no	yes	no
$HOOCCH(C_3H_7)COOH$	*n*-Propylmalonic acid, propylpropanedioic acid	no	no	yes
$HOOCCH(i\text{-}C_3H_7)COOH$	*i*-Propylmalonic acid, isopropylpropanedioic acid	no	no	yes
$HOOCC(CH_3)(C_2H_5)COOH$	Ethylmethylmalonic acid, ethylmethylpropanedioic acid	no	no	yes

16.116 Write the structural formula for a chiral hydrocarbon, $C_{11}H_{16}$, which on oxidation affords terephthalic acid.

▮ The compound must be a *para*-dialkyl benzene because terephthalic acid (p-$HOOCC_6H_4COOH$) is the oxidation product. There are five C's in the two alkyl groups. The smallest alkyl group with a chiral C is *sec*-butyl($-C^*H(CH_3)CH_2CH_3$) leaving Me as the second group. The compound is p-$MeC_6H_4CH(CH_3)CH_2CH_3$.

16.117 Outline a procedure for separating a mixture of PhCOOH, PhCOO⁻Na⁺, PhOMe, and PhMe.

▮ Add an inert low-boiling nonpolar solvent such as pentane and follow the steps in Fig. 16-5.

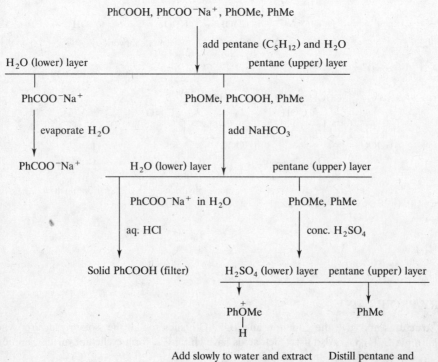

Add slowly to water and extract PhOMe with fresh pentane. Distill pentane from upper layer and recover PhOMe.

Distill pentane and isolate PhMe.

Fig. 16-5

16.118 Identify the substances **A** through **D** in the sequence:

$$\text{Palmitic acid} \xrightarrow{\text{LiAlH}_4} \textbf{A} \xrightarrow{\text{HCl}} \textbf{B} \xrightarrow[\text{2. Ethylene oxide}]{\text{1. Mg/Et}_2\text{O}} \textbf{C} \xrightarrow{\text{KMnO}_4} \textbf{D}$$

▮ **A** is $CH_3(CH_2)_{14}CH_2OH$, **B** is $CH_3(CH_2)_{14}CH_2Cl$, **C** is $CH_3(CH_2)_{16}CH_2OH$, and **D** is $CH_3(CH_2)_{16}COOH$ (stearic acid).

16.119 Identify the substances **A** through **D** in the sequence:

$$HC\equiv CH \xrightarrow[\text{2. 2CO}_2]{\text{1. 2Na}} \textbf{A} \xrightarrow{\text{Na/EtOH}} \textbf{B} \xrightarrow{\text{1,3-cyclohexadiene}} \textbf{C} \xrightarrow{\Delta} \textbf{D}$$

▮ **A** is $HOOCC\equiv CCOOH$, **B** is *trans*-butenedicarboxylic acid (fumaric acid), and **C** is the Diels–Alder adduct, which forms the *trans* anhydride, **D**, on heating.

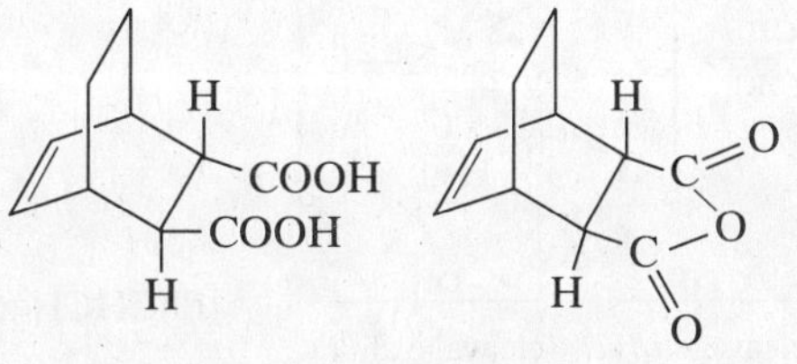

C   **D**

16.120 Give structural formulas for tropic acid (**F**), $C_9H_{10}O_3$, atropic acid (**G**), $C_9H_8O_2$, and hydrotropic acid (**H**), $C_9H_{10}O_2$, from the given information. **F**, isolated from the alkaloid atropine (used to relieve muscle spasms and pain) is oxidized to PhCOOH.

$$\textbf{F} \xrightarrow{\text{HBr}} C_9H_9O_2Br \xrightarrow[\text{alc}]{\text{KOH}} \textbf{G} \xrightarrow{\text{H}_2/\text{Ni}} \textbf{H}$$

In addition, $PhCHCH_3MgBr + CO_2 \xrightarrow{\text{H}_3\text{O}^+} \textbf{H}$, and **F** gives a positive test with CrO_3 in acid.

▮ **F** is a monosubstituted benzene compound with 1° of unsaturation in the side chain (the COOH), as indicated by the synthesis of **H**, $PhCHCH_3COOH$. Working backwards from **H**, **F** is $PhCHCOOH$, and **G** is

$\underset{\text{CH}_2\text{OH}}{|}$

$PhCCOOH$ from dehydrobromination of the corresponding bromide. **F** cannot be $Ph-\underset{\underset{CH_3}{|}}{\overset{\overset{OH}{|}}{C}}-COOH$ because 3°

$\overset{\|}{CH_2}$

alcohols are inert to CrO_3.

16.121 (*a*) Write the structural formulas and indicate the oxidation numbers of the central atoms in (i) methanesulfonic acid, (ii) methanesulfinic acid, (iii) methanesulfenic acid, and (iv) methanephosphonic acid.   (*b*) Give the relative order of acidities of these acids, including acetic acid and ethanol. Group together any acids whose acidities are of the same order.

▮ (*a*)   (i) $Me-\overset{\overset{O}{\|}}{\underset{\underset{O}{\|}}{S}}-OH$ (ii) $Me-\overset{\overset{O}{\|}}{S}-OH$ (iii) $Me-\ddot{\underset{..}{S}}-OH$ (iv) $Me-\overset{\overset{O}{\|}}{\underset{\underset{OH}{|}}{P}}-OH$

ON =   +4   +2   0   +3

(*b*) The anion with the largest number of lone O's will have the most charge delocalization and will be the weakest base. The increasing order of basicities is

$MeSO_3^-$ $< MeSO_2^-, CH_3CO_2^-, MeP(OH)O_2^-$ $< MeSO^-$ $< MeO^-$
(3 lone O's)   (2 lone O's)   (1 lone O)   (1 lone O)

Although $MeSO^-$ and MeO^- have a single lone O, $MeSO^-$ is a weaker base than MeO^- because its charge is delocalized to S by $p\text{-}d\ \pi$ bonding, $Me\overline{S}=O$. The $-$ in MeO^- is localized on O. The order of decreasing acidities is

$MeSO_2OH > MeSO(OH), CH_3CO_2H, MePO(OH)_2 > MeSOH > MeOH$

16.122 Give a method for making 2-naphthoic acid from naphthalene other than those in Problem 16.28.

⬛ High temperature sulfonation with conc. H_2SO_4 gives 2-naphthalenesulfonic acid whose salt is then fused with NaCN. The product, 2-cyanonaphthalene, is hydrolized in aq. acid giving 2-napthoic acid.

16.123 (*a*) Explain the following: both $PhCH_2COCH_2Cl$ and $PhCHClCOCH_3$ form $PhCH_2CH_2COOH$ when reacted with OH^-, followed by acidification. (*b*) Give the product and show steps: 2-chlorocyclohexanone + OH^- followed by acid → ?

⬛ (*a*) A common intermediate is required in this *Favorskii* rearrangement to get the same product. Removal of an αH by OH^- is followed by an S_N2 displacement of Cl^- to give a cyclopropanone ring. Ring-opening occurs to give the more stable benzylic carbanion.

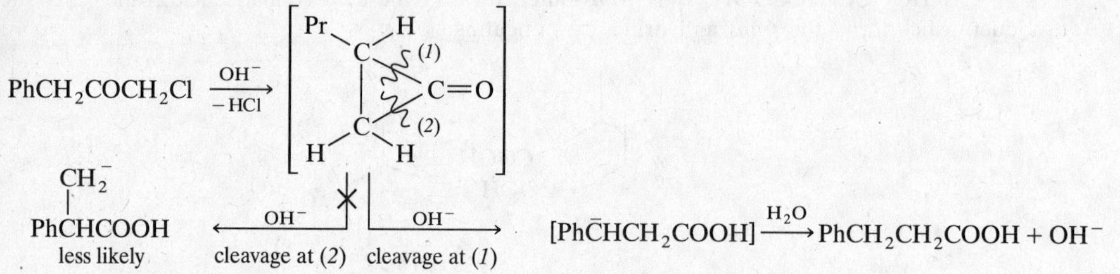

(*b*) Cyclopentanecarboxylic acid is formed in this Favorskii reaction:

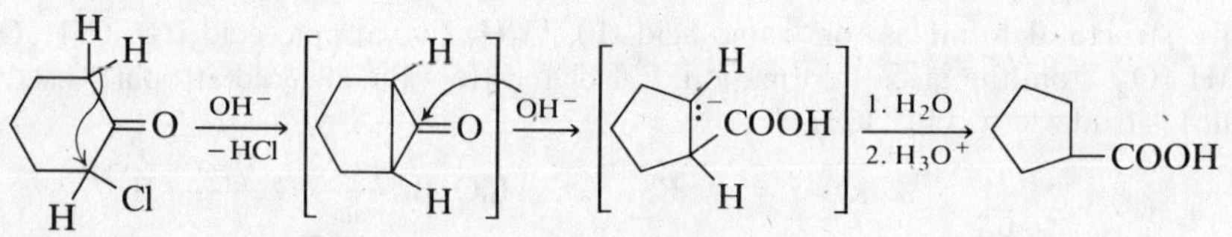

16.124 (*a*) Give the product from the reaction of cyclohexanone with perbenzoic acid. (*b*) Mention a useful aspect of this reaction.

⬛ This is an example of the Baeyer-Villiger reaction (Problem 15.134). The product is *omega*-caprolactone. (*b*) The product is a seven-membered lactone, a compound that cannot be made by an intramolecular ring closure.

16.125 Discuss the advisability of trying to prepare a single ^{18}O labeled acetic acid, $MeC\overset{\parallel}{\underset{O}{}}{}^{18}OH$, using $^{18}OH_2$ as the source of the labeled O.

⬛ We might expects to make the compound by reacting MeCOCl with $H_2{}^{18}O$. However the hoped for acid would ionize in water to give the delocalized anion, $MeC\overset{\parallel}{\underset{^{18}O}{}}-O^- \longleftrightarrow MeC\overset{|}{\underset{^{18}O^-}{}}=O$. When H^+ adds back to the anion to reverse the ionization, a mixture of radioisomers results, $MeC\overset{\parallel}{\underset{^{18}O}{}}-OH + MeC\overset{|}{\underset{^{18}OH}{}}=O$. This mixture cannot be separated and behaves as if only one compound is present, i.e., the one with both O's labeled, $MeC\overset{\parallel}{\underset{^{18}O}{}}-^{18}OH$.

16.126 Outline a typical method for resolving *rac-(R,S)* RCOOH.

⬛ $(R,S)\text{-RCOOH} + (R)\text{-base} \longrightarrow [(R)\text{-RCOO}^- (R)\text{-base H}^+ \textbf{(A)}] + [(S)\text{-RCOO}^-(R)\text{-baseH}^+ \textbf{(B)}]$

insoluble diastereomeric salts

After separation by fractional recrystallization,

$\textbf{A} \xrightarrow{\text{HX}} (R)\text{-RCOOH} + (R)\text{-baseH}^+X^-$ and $\textbf{B} \xrightarrow{\text{HX}} (S)\text{-RCOOH} + (R)\text{-baseH}^+X^-$

The base is often a naturally occurring alkaloid such as quinine or brucine (very poisonous—handle with care!).

16.127 The photochemical dimerization of cinnamic acid, $PhCH{=}CHCOOH$, can give 11 isomeric cyclobutanes; five belong to the truxillic acid group and six to the truxinic acid group. (*a*) What is the nature of this dimerization? (*b*) Give the structural difference between the two groups, aside from stereoisomers, if only a truxillic acid can have a center of symmetry.

◢ (*a*) This is a [2 + 2] cycloaddition reaction. (*b*) In order for a center of symmetry to be present, the Ph's and COOH's must be opposite (and *trans*), as in truxillic acid, not adjacent to each other.

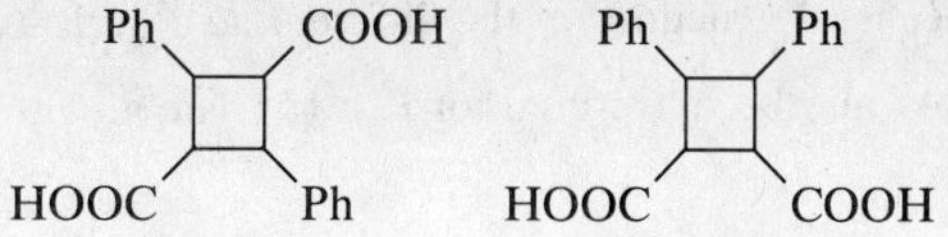

Ph   COOH   Ph   Ph

□   □

HOOC   Ph   HOOC   COOH

truxillic acid group   truxinic acid group

16.128 Give the structure of a hydrocarbon, $C_{12}H_{20}$, that gives two diastereomeric aliphatic dicarboxylic acids on oxidative cleavage.

◢ In order to get two dicarboxylic acids, the hydrocarbon must be a diene, and the 3° of unsaturation indicates that it is also cyclic. The diastereomers must be *meso* and *racemic* and the dicarboxylic acids are $HOOCCH(CH_3)CH(CH_3)COOH$. The cyclic compound is

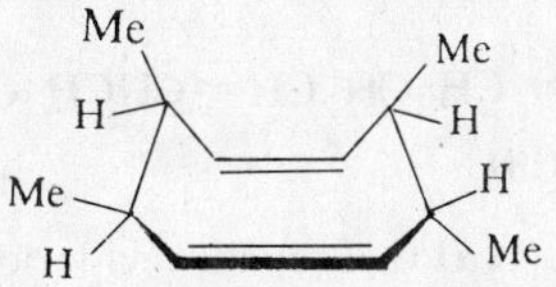

Me   Me

H   H

Me   H

H   Me

One half with the *cis* Me's gives the *meso* diacid and the other half with the *trans* Me's gives the *rac* diacid.

CHAPTER 17
Acid Derivatives

GENERAL AND NOMENCLATURE

17.1 (*a*) Write a general formula for the carboxylic acid derivatives. (*b*) Give their common structural features. (*c*) Give the names and general structures of the different acid derivatives. (*d*) Why are they studied as a unit?

◢ (*a*) RCO-G where Ar may be substituted for R. (*b*) The acyl group, $R-\overset{\overset{O}{\|}}{C}-$, and G, which has a hetero

atom bonded to the acyl C. (*c*)

$$R-\overset{\overset{O}{\|}}{C}-X \qquad R-\overset{\overset{O}{\|}}{C}-O-\overset{\overset{O}{\|}}{C}-R \qquad R-\overset{\overset{O}{\|}}{C}-OR' \qquad R-\overset{\overset{O}{\|}}{C}-NR_2$$
$$\text{acid halide} \qquad \text{acid anhydride} \qquad\qquad \text{ester} \qquad\quad \text{amide}$$

where $R = H$, alkyl, or aryl (*d*) Most of the acid derivatives are interconvertible and all can be prepared from the corresponding carboxylic acid.

17.2 (*a*) Name each of the following acid halides by the IUPAC method. (i) CH_3CH_2COCl, (ii) $(CH_3)_3CCH_2COCl$, (iii) $CH_3CH_2CH_2CHBrCOBr$, (iv) $CH_3CH_2CH=CHCH_2COCl$, and (v) 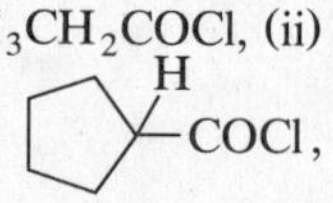 a cyclopentane ring with H and —COCl, (*b*) Give common names for compounds (i) through (iii).

◢ Replace *-ic acid* by *-yl halide*. (*a*) (i) Propanoyl chloride, (ii) 3,3-dimethylbutanoyl chloride, (iii) 2-bromopentanoyl bromide, (iv) 3-hexenoyl chloride, and (v) 2-cyclopentanecarbonyl chloride. (*b*) (i) Propionyl chloride, (ii) β,β-dimethylbutyryl chloride, and (iii) α-bromovaleryl bromide.

17.3 Name the following acid halides. (*a*) C_6H_5COCl, (*b*) $3,5\text{-}(NO_2)_2C_6H_3COBr$, (*c*) $PhCH_2COCl$,

(*d*) naphthalene ring with COCl , (*e*) $ClCOCH_2COCl$, (*f*) benzene ring with two COCl groups

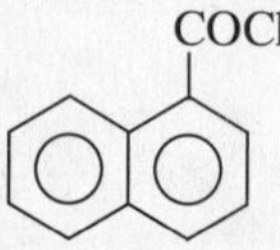

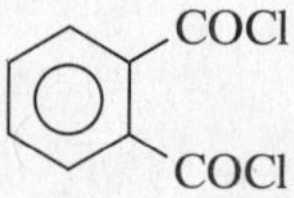

◢ (*a*) Benzoyl chloride, (*b*) 3,5-dinitrobenzoyl bromide, (*c*) phenylacetyl chloride, (*d*) α-naphthoyl chloride, (*e*) malonyl dichloride, and (*f*) phthaloyl dichloride.

17.4 Give the common name for each anhydride: (*a*) $(PhCO)_2O$, (*b*) $PhCOOCOCH_3$, (*c*) $(CH_3CHClCO)_2O$,

(*d*) $CH_3(CH_2)_4COOCOCH_2CH_3$, (*e*) nitrophthalic anhydride structure, (*f*) maleic anhydride structure.

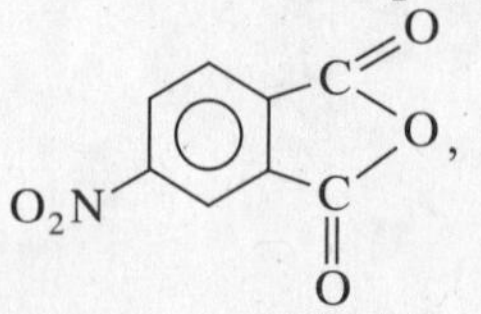

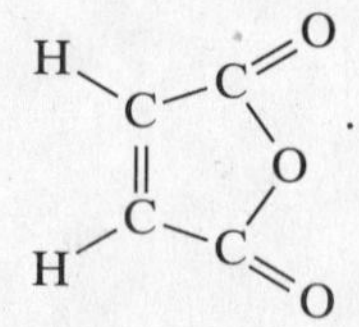

◢ Name the acid or acids, if it is a mixed anhydride, followed by the word *anhydride*. (*a*) Benzoic anhydride, (*b*) acetic benzoic anhydride, (*c*) α-chloropropionic anhydride, (*d*) hexanoic (or caproic) propionic anhydride, (*e*) 4-nitrophthalic anhydride, (*f*) maleic anhydride.

17.5 (*a*) Give common names of these esters: (i) $CH_3COOCH_2CH_2CH_3$, (ii) 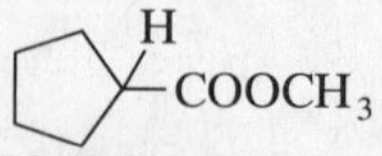 cyclopentane ring with H and —COOCH$_3$,
(iii) $CH_3CHBrCH_2COOCH(CH_3)_2$, (iv) $CH_2(COOCH_2CH_2CH_3)_2$, (v) $HOOCCOOC_2H_5$,
(vi) $H_2C=CHCOOCH(CH_3)CH_2CH_3$. (*b*) Give the IUPAC name to (i)–(iv) in (*a*).

◢ First name the group bonded to —O—; then replace *-ic acid* by *-ate*. (*a*) (i) *n*-Propyl acetate, (ii) methyl cyclopentanecarboxylate, (iii) isopropyl β-bromobutyrate, (iv) di-*n*-propylmalonate, (v) ethyl hydrogen oxalate, (vi) *sec*-butyl acrylate (or propenoate). (*b*) (i) Propyl ethanoate, (ii) same name, (iii) isopropyl 3-bromobutanoate, (iv) dipropyl propanedioate.

17.6 Give common names for the esters: (*a*) PhCOOCH$_2$CH$_2$CH$_3$, (*b*) *p*-CH$_3$OC$_6$H$_4$OCOCH$_2$Ph,

(*c*) *o*-HOC$_6$H$_4$COOCH$_3$, (*d*) 3,5-(O$_2$N)$_2$C$_6$H$_3$COOCH$_2$Ph, (*e*)

(a) *n*-Propyl benzoate, *(b)* *p*-methoxyphenyl phenylacetate, *(c)* methyl salicylate, *(d)* benzyl 3,5-dinitrobenzoate, *(e)* ethyl methyl phthalate.

17.7 Name the following amides: (*a*) CH$_3$CH$_2$CONH$_2$, (*b*) CH$_3$CONHPh, (*c*) *p*-CH$_3$C$_6$H$_4$CONH$_2$,

(*d*) H$_2$NCOCH$_2$CH$_2$CH$_2$CONH$_2$, (*e*) (CH$_3$)$_2$CHCONHC$_2$H$_5$, (*f*)

In general, change *-ic acid* to *-amide*. Amides of PhNH$_2$ are named as anilides. Amides with R's on N are named by writing N before the name of the R group. *(a)* Propionamide, *(b)* acetanilide, *(c)* *p*-toluamide, *(d)* glutaramide, *(e)* N-ethylisobutyramide, *(f)* cyclobutanecarboxamide.

17.8 (*a*) Why are "methylacetanilide" and "methylbenzamide" ambiguous names? (*b*) Name the following amides:

(i) PhCONMe$_2$, (ii) 2,4-Me$_2$C$_6$H$_3$CONH$_2$, (iii) *p*-MeC$_6$H$_4$CONHMe, (iv) PhNCOMe, (v) *p*-MeC$_6$H$_4$NHCOMe, (vi) CH$_3$CONMeEt. Label them as a 1°, 2°, or 3° amide.

(a) The position of the Me is not specified. *(b)* (i) N,N-Dimethylbenzamide, 3°; (ii) 2,4-dimethylbenzamide, 1°; (iii) N-methyl-*p*-toluamide, 2°; (iv) N-methylacetanilide, 3°; (v) *p*-methylacetanilide, 2°; (vi) N-ethyl-N-methylacetamide, 3°.

17.9 Write structures for the following compounds: (*a*) Benzanilide, (*b*) di-*n*-butyl adipate, (*c*) 5-oxohexanoyl bromide, (*d*) N-bromosuccinimide, (*e*) phthalimide, (*f*) γ-valerolactone, (*g*) methyl *cis*-2-bromocyclohexanecarboxylate, (*h*) *cis*-cinnamoyl chloride.

(a) PhCONHPh (*b*) *n*-C$_4$H$_9$OCO(CH$_2$)$_4$COOC$_4$H$_9$-*n* (*c*) CH$_3$CO(CH$_2$)$_3$COBr

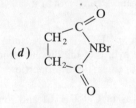

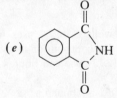

17.10 (*a*) Write a general structure for (i) an acid hydrazide, (ii) an acid azide, (iii) a thioacid, (iv) a thioester, (v) a hydroxamic acid. (*b*) Why are they classified as acid derivatives?

(a) (i) RCONHNH$_2$, (ii) RCON$_3$, (iii) RCOSH, (iv) RCOSR; (v) RCONHOH. *(b)* The acyl group
$$R-\overset{\overset{\displaystyle O}{\|}}{C}-$$
is bonded to a heteroatom, N, in (i), (ii), and (v), and S in (iii) and (iv).

17.11 (*a*) Why is a nitrile often classified as an acid derivative? (*b*) Give a common and IUPAC name for the following nitriles: (i) CH$_3$CN, (ii) PhCN, (iii) (CH$_3$)$_2$CHCH$_2$CN, (iv) NCCH$_2$COOH.

(a) Nitriles are hydrolyzed in H$^+$ or OH$^-$ to acids. *(b)* Change (*o*)*ic acid* to *onitrile*. In IUPAC add *nitrile* to the parent hydrocarbon name. (i) acetonitrile, ethanenitrile; (ii) benzonitrile, cyanobenzene; (iii) isobutyronitrile, 3-methylbutanenitrile; (iv) cyanoacetic acid, cyanoethanoic acid.

STRUCTURE AND PHYSICAL PROPERTIES

17.12 (*a*) Draw an orbital picture for a typical acid derivative, R—C(=O)—G. (*b*) Compare the extent of delocalization with that in an aldehyde or ketone.

(*a*) See Fig. 17-1. (*b*) The electron pair on G in the acid derivative is delocalized through the acyl C to the O; in the aldehyde or ketone the π e^-'s are confined to the carbonyl group.

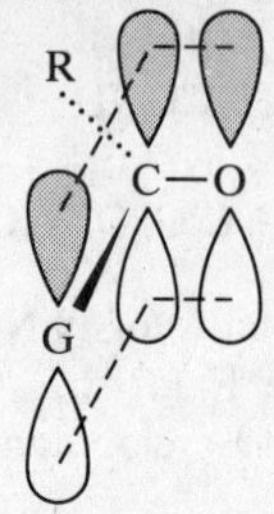

Fig. 17-1

17.13 (*a*) Give the resonance structures for RCOG. (*b*) What effect does resonance have on the stability and electrophilic character of the C=O group?

(*a*)

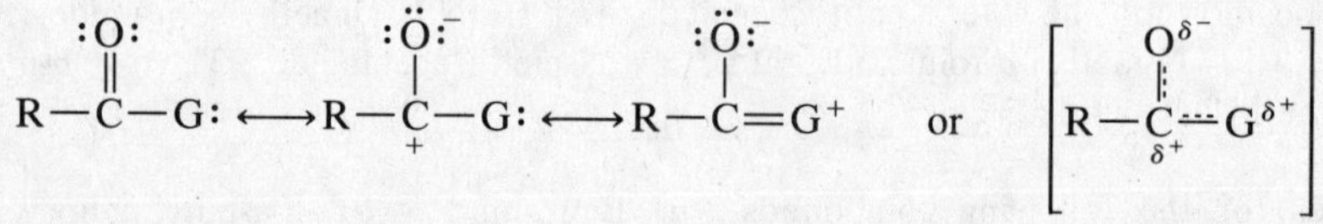

A **B** **C** the hybrid

(*b*) Electron release from G to O stabilizes C=O by diminishing the electrophilic character of C.

17.14 Explain why the C—G bond in acid derivatives is expected to be shorter and stronger than in alkyl derivatives, RG.

In RCOG, C uses an sp^2 HO to bond with G while C in RG uses an sp^3 HO. The increase in *s* character makes the bond shorter and stronger. Alternatively, the contribution to the hybrid of the dipolar structure **C** with a partial double bond between C and G (Problem 17.13) also contributes to these bond properties.

17.15 (*a*) Given that the C—Cl-bond length in CH_3COCl is about the same as in CH_3CH_2Cl and longer than in CH_2=CHCl, what may be inferred about the extent of delocalization in RCOCl's? (*b*) Evaluate the relative importance of delocalization in the following acid derivatives from their C—G=bond distances (given in nm):

G	NH_2	OCH_3	F	Cl
CH_3—G	0.147	0.142	0.138	0.178
CH_3CO—G	0.138	0.136	0.137	0.179

(*a*) The degree of delocalization, as related to the contribution of structure **C** in Problem 17.13, is very small or nonexistent. (*b*) The importance diminishes in the order $RCONH_2$ > RCOOR′ > RCOX as the electronegativity of G in the same period increases. Although Cl is less electronegative than F and might be expected to delocalize its electrons to some extent, the C—Cl bond is longer, and the π-bond overlap is not as effective.

17.16 (*a*) Give the two eclipsed conformations for N-methylacetamide about the C—N bond. (*b*) Account for the fact that, although these conformations cannot be isolated at room temperature, they can be detected by spectrochemical methods (Problem 17.115).

(*a*)

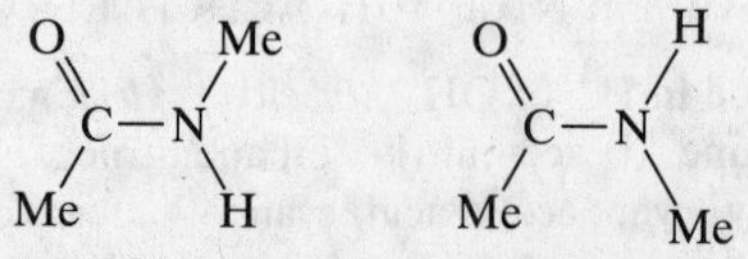

Z-form *E*-form

(*b*) There is a large energy (18–20 kcal/mol) barrier to rotation about the C—N bond in amides, indicating a high degree of double-bond character. At room temperature, interconversion of isomers is too fast to permit separation, but still very slow when compared with rotation about ordinary single bonds.

17.17   Account for the shorter C—O length in an ester compared with an anhydride.

▰   A degree of *cross-conjugation* exists in the anhydride; this competition for e⁻'s decreases the delocalization to each carbonyl O and gives the C—O σ bond less double-bond character.

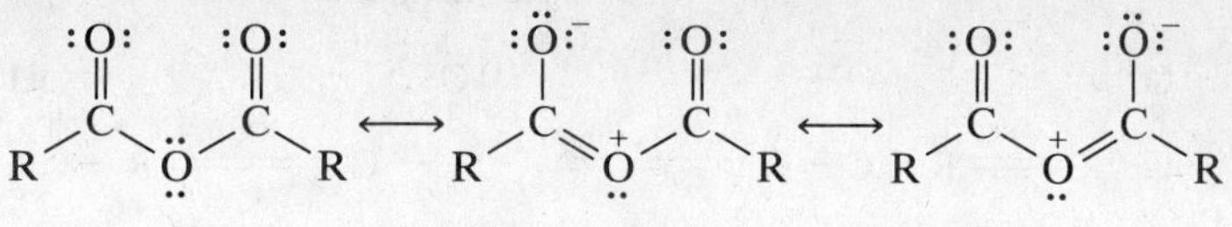

anhydride resonance structures

17.18   Explain why esters have lower bp's than (*a*) ketones and (*b*) acids of comparable molecular weight.

▰   (*a*) Because of the delocalization of e⁻'s in the ester, the + on C of C=O is more spread out, resulting in a smaller dipole moment and weaker dipole-dipole attraction than in ketones.   (*b*) Acids have strong intermolecular H-bonds, lacking in esters.

17.19   The respective bp's and MW's (in g/mol) of the following amides are: $MeCONH_2$, 221 °C and 59; MeCONHMe, 204 °C and 73; $MeCONMe_2$, 165 °C and 87. Explain.

▰   Dimethylacetamide lacks an H on N for intermolecular H-bonding; thus its bp is lowest, its highest molecular weights notwithstanding. Acetamide has two H's and is extensively H-bonded resulting in the highest bp, while methylacetamide has only one H and less H-bonding.

17.20   Primary and secondary amides tend to exist as dimers in the solid and pure liquid state. Draw a structure for the dimer of acetamide.

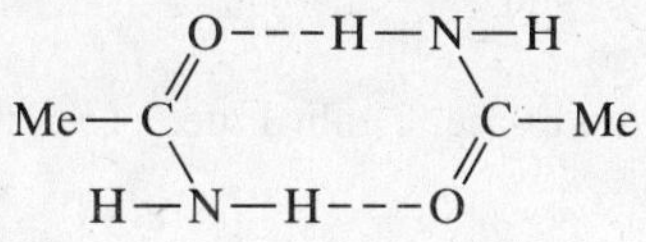

▰

17.21   Why is dimethylformamide (DMF) a useful solvent?

▰   DMF, $HCONMe_2$, is an *aprotic* solvent (has no H for H-bonding) with a moderately high dielectric constant and a high dipole moment. Thus, although it dissolves many ionic compounds, DMF does not do so by forming H-bonds with the anions. The salts are dissolved, chiefly through solvation of the cation by attraction to the end of the C—O dipole. The + end of the dipole is shielded within the molecule and can solvate the anion very weakly, if at all.

17.22   Explain the instability of the acid halides of formic acid.

▰   The large ΔH_f of CO is an indication of the stability of the C≡O bond. The decomposition reaction HCOX ⟶ C≡O + HX is favored. Formyl chloride is not stable above −60 °C.

PREPARATION

17.23   (*a*) Give the order of reactivity of acid derivatives towards a nucleophile, :Nu.   (*b*) Relate this order to the interconversion of acid derivatives (*transacylation*).   (*c*) Relate the order of reactivity of the acid derivatives to the base strength of the leaving group, G.

▰   (*a*) Acid chloride > anhydride > ester > amide.   (*b*) A more reactive derivative may be used to prepare a less reactive one by reaction with the appropriate nucleophile. For example, an ester can be made from the corresponding acid chloride or anhydride, but not from the amide, by reaction with HOR.   (*c*) The order of reactivity decreases as the base strength of the leaving group increases, i.e., $Cl^- < RCOO^- < RO^- < H_2N^-$.

17.24 Show the general mechanism of nucleophilic acyl substitution on the acyl derivative, $RC\overset{\displaystyle O}{\overset{\|}{{}}}G$, in (a) a basic and (b) an acid solution.

◢ (a)

$$R\overset{\displaystyle :O:}{\overset{\|}{-}}C-G + :Nu^- \underset{}{\overset{slow}{\rightleftharpoons}} R-\overset{\displaystyle :\overset{..}{O}:^-}{\underset{Nu}{\overset{|}{C}}}-G \overset{fast}{\rightleftharpoons} R-\overset{\displaystyle :O:}{\overset{\|}{C}}-Nu + :G^-$$

unstable intermediate

(b)

$$R\overset{\displaystyle :O:}{\overset{\|}{-}}C-G \overset{H^+}{\rightleftharpoons} R\overset{\displaystyle {}^+:OH}{\overset{\|}{-}}C-G \overset{HNu:,\ slow}{\rightleftharpoons} R-\overset{\displaystyle :\overset{..}{O}H}{\underset{HNu^+}{\overset{|}{C}}}-G \overset{-HG,\ fast}{\rightleftharpoons} R\overset{\displaystyle {}^+:OH}{\overset{\|}{-}}C-Nu \overset{-H^+}{\rightleftharpoons} R\overset{\displaystyle :O:}{\overset{\|}{-}}C-Nu$$

unstable intermediate

17.25 (a) List three reagents for converting a carboxylic acid to its acyl chloride. (b) Select the most convenient of the three reagents, give a reason for your choice, and write a balanced equation for its reaction with RCOOH. (c) What reagent can convert (i) an acid to an acyl bromide and (ii) an acyl chloride to an acyl fluoride?

◢ (a) PCl_3, $SOCl_2$, and PCl_5. (b) $SOCl_2$, because the byproducts of the reaction are the gases SO_2 and HCl, which are easily separated from the product:

$$RCOOH + SOCl_2 \longrightarrow RCOCl + SO_2\ (g) + HCl\ (g)$$

(c) (i) PBr_3, (ii) NaF + anhydrous HF.

17.26 Give structures for **A** through **F**: (a) $PhH + (CH_3CO)_2O \overset{AlCl_3}{\longrightarrow} \mathbf{A} \overset{1.\ I_2,\ OH^-}{\underset{2.\ H_3O^+}{\longrightarrow}} \mathbf{B}$

(b) $CH_3CH_2CH_2Br \underset{\substack{2.\ CO_2 \\ 3.\ H_3O^+}}{\overset{1.\ Mg}{\longrightarrow}} \mathbf{C} \overset{}{\underset{PCl_5}{\longrightarrow}} \mathbf{D} \underset{CH_3NH_2}{\longrightarrow} \mathbf{E}$

◢ (a) **A** = PhCOCH₃, **B** = PhCOOH; (b) **C** = CH₃CH₂CH₂COOH, **D** = CH₃CH₂CH₂COCl, **E** = CH₃CH₂CH₂CONHCH₃ (+HCl).

17.27 (a) Give the industrial preparation of acetic anhydride. (b) How may other anhydrides be prepared from acetic anhydride?

◢ (a) $CH_3COOH + H_2C=C=O \longrightarrow (CH_3CO)_2O$. Ketene is prepared by pyrolysis of acetone: $CH_3COCH_3 \overset{700\ ^\circ C}{\longrightarrow} CH_4 + H_2C=C=O$ (b) When heated, acetic anhydride and a carboxylic acid form an equilibrium mixture of anhydrides and acids. Since acetic acid is the most volatile component in the equilibrium mixture, the equilibrium is shifted to the right by distilling it out as it forms.

$$2RCOOH + (CH_3CO)_2O \rightleftharpoons (RCO)_2O + 2CH_3COOH$$

17.28 Write a mechanism for the reaction of acetic acid and ketene [Problem 17.27(a)].

◢ $H_2C=C=O + CH_3COOH \rightleftharpoons H_2C=C=OH^+ + {}^-OCCH_3 \overset{\displaystyle \|}{\underset{\displaystyle O}{}} \longrightarrow$

$$\left[H_2C=\overset{\displaystyle OH}{\overset{|}{C}}-O-\overset{\displaystyle O}{\overset{\|}{C}}CH_3 \right] \rightleftharpoons CH_3\overset{\displaystyle O}{\overset{\|}{C}}-O-\overset{\displaystyle O}{\overset{\|}{C}}CH_3$$

17.29 Give the product from heating each of the following acids with acetic anhydride: (a) $HOOC(CH_2)_2COOH$ and (b) $HOOC(CH_2)_4COOH$. Explain why the reactions differ.

◢ (a)

(b)

=O   + CO₂ + H₂O

Cyclopentanone

A seven-membered ring anhydride does not form because the loss of entropy is too great (Problem 5.62). Instead decarboxylation leads to a cyclic ketone.

17.30 Both *cis*- and *trans*-1,2-cyclohexanedicarboxylic acids form anhydrides on heating, but the anhydride forms from the *cis*-1,2-cyclopentanedicarboxylic acid only. Explain.

◢ The anhydride formed from the *trans*-dicarboxylic acid must have a *trans* fusion of two rings. There is too much strain when both rings are five-membered.

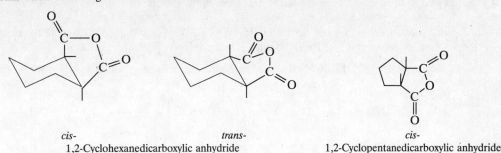

| *cis*-
1,2-Cyclohexanedicarboxylic anhydride | *trans*- | *cis*-
1,2-Cyclopentanedicarboxylic anhydride |

17.31 How can we prepare a nonsymmetrical anhydride from the acid chloride? Illustrate by preparing ethanoic benzoic anhydride from PhCOCl.

◢ The acid chloride is heated with a carboxylate salt in a polar solvent.

$$\underset{\substack{\|\\O}}{PhCCl} + \underset{\substack{\|\\O}}{CH_3CO^-Na^+} \longrightarrow \underset{\substack{\|\quad\quad\|\\O\quad\quad O}}{PhC-O-CCH_3} \quad (+NaCl)$$

ethanoic benzoic anhydride

17.32 (*a*) Formic anhydride cannot be prepared by heating formic acid. What reaction occurs? (*b*) Prepare the mixed anhydride HCOOCOR.

◢ (*a*) Dehydration occurs intramolecularly rather than intermolecularly.

$$HCOOH \longrightarrow CO + H_2O$$

(*b*) $HCOO^-Na^+ + RCOCl \longrightarrow HCOOCOR + NaCl$ (see Problem 17.31)

17.33 Prepare *n*-propyl acetate (**A**) from (*a*) an anhydride, (*b*) an acid chloride, and (*c*) an acid.

◢ (*a*) $$(CH_3CO)_2O + n\text{-PrOH} \xrightarrow[-H^+]{\text{base}} CH_3COO^- + CH_3COOCH_2CH_2CH_3 \text{ (A)}$$

(*b*) $$CH_3COCl + n\text{-PrOH} \xrightarrow[-H^+]{\text{base}} Cl^- + \mathbf{A}$$

(*c*) $$CH_3COOH + n\text{-PrOH} \underset{}{\overset{H^+}{\rightleftharpoons}} H_2O + \mathbf{A}$$

17.34 Write the structure of the products: (*a*) acetic acid + benzyl alcohol, (*b*) propionic acid + isobutanol, (*c*) acetic acid + *n*-pentanol, (*d*) salicylic acid + methanol, (*e*) oxalic acid + ethylene glycol.

◢ (*a*) CH_3COOCH_2Ph (jasmine odor) (*b*) $CH_3CH_2COOCH_2CH(CH_3)_2$ (rum flavor),

(*c*) $CH_3COO(CH_2)_4CH_3$ (*d*) [benzene ring with COOCH₃ and OH substituents] (*e*) [cyclic structure: O=C−O−CH₂ / O=C−O−CH₂]

(component of banana oil) (oil of wintergreen)

17.35 (*a*) Write an equilibrium expression for the Fischer acid esterification of acetic acid with ethanol. (*b*) Calculate K_{eq} given: at equilibrium, the concentrations of ester and water are 0.65 M each, and the concentrations of the remaining unreacted acid and alcohol are 0.35 M each. (*c*) When should [H₂O] be included in the equilibrium expression? (*d*) How may the reaction be driven to completion?

◢ (*a*) The overall equation is

$$CH_3COOH + EtOH \overset{H^+}{\rightleftharpoons} CH_3COOEt + H_2O \qquad \text{and} \qquad K_{eq} = \frac{[CH_3COOEt][H_2O]}{[CH_3COOH][EtOH]}.$$

(b) $K_{eq} = [0.65] [0.65]/[0.35] [0.35] \cong 3.4$.   (c) In cases where water is the solvent, it is present in large excess and effectively its concentration remains constant. $[H_2O]$ is then omitted from the expression, but is incorporated into the K_{eq} value. If the reaction is run in a nonaqueous solvent, H_2O is formed, its concentration is not constant and $[H_2O]$ is included.   (d) If the alcohol is inexpensive, a large amount may be used. Alternatively, the H_2O may be distilled off as a lower boiling azeotrope with benzene or toluene.

17.36   (a) Write a rate expression for the reaction in Problem 17.35.   (b) What is the order of the reaction?   (c) Write a mechanism for the reaction of RCOOH with R'OH consistent with the rate data.

◢   (a) Rate = k[RCOOH] [R'OH] [H$^+$].   (b) First order in acid, alcohol, and H$^+$, third order overall.

tetrahedral
intermediate, **B**

(All steps are reversible)

Steps 2 and 4, involving bond formation and breaking, respectively, have higher activation enthalpies and are slower than the rapid proton-transfer steps which are among the fastest chemical reactions known. The rate of the slow step 2 is consistent with the rate expression since it involves each of the species in the expression. Step 2 is slower than step 4 (Problem 17.24).

17.37   Explain the following results mechanistically: (a) PhCOOH is esterified in H_3O^+ with MeOH (where **O** means ^{18}O). The products are PhCOOMe + H_2O.   (b) In the reverse reaction, PhCOOMe (carbonyl **O** is enriched) is hydrolized in H_3O^+; the reaction is stopped before equilibrium is reached. The concentration of **O** in the recovered unreacted ester is diminished.

◢   (a) This result eliminates any mechanism in which the O in H_2O comes from the alcohol:

$$\text{PhCOOH + MeOH} \not\rightarrow \text{PhCOOMe + H}_2\textbf{O}$$

(b) This exchange points to the existence of a tetrahedral intermediate (**B** in Problem 17.36) with two indistinguishable OH groups, from which either H_2O or $H_2\textbf{O}$ can be lost in a reverse step.

17.38   (a) Devise a stereochemical experiment to determine the esterification pathway.   (b) How can the configuration of the chiral center in the ester be determined?

◢   (a) Use an enantiomer of $CH_3\overset{*}{C}HDOH$. Formation of the ester from S_N2 attack by RCOOH on $\overset{*}{R}\overset{+}{O}H_2$ leads to inversion at the chiral center. If $\overset{*}{R}OH$ bonds to the protonated acid, the configuration of the chiral center is retained.   (b) Reduce the ester with LiAlH$_4$ and separate the alcohol products. The alkyl alcohol is regenerated with its chiral center intact. For example,

$$(S)\text{-RCOO}\overset{*}{C}HDCH_3 \xrightarrow{\text{LiAlH}_4} \text{RCH}_2\text{OH} + (S)\text{-CH}_3\overset{*}{C}HDOH$$

17.39   Explain the order of the rate of esterification of the following acids with MeOH:

$$\text{MeCH}_2\text{COOH} > \text{Me}_2\text{CHCOOH} > \text{Me}_3\text{CCOOH} > \text{Et}_3\text{CCOOH} \gg (i\text{-Pr})_2\text{CHCOOH}$$

◢   As the size of the substituents on the α C increases, the tetrahedrally bonded intermediate becomes more crowded. The greater the crowding, the larger is $\Delta H^{\ddagger}$ of the TS, and the slower is the reaction.

17.40   (a) Prepare n-propyl acetate (**A**) from the appropriate R'X and RCOOH.   (b) Classify this reaction.   (c) Explain why this reaction cannot be used to prepare t-butyl acetate.   (d) Prepare t-butyl acetate.

◢   (a) (1) $CH_3COOH \xrightarrow{\text{NaOH}} CH_3COO^-Na^+$ (2) $CH_3COO^- + CH_3CH_2CH_2Br \longrightarrow \textbf{A} (+\text{NaBr})$

(b) S_N2.   (c) The carboxylate anion is sufficiently basic to bring about elimination in 3° halides.

(d) $(CH_3)_2C{=}CH_2 + CH_3COOH \xrightarrow{\text{conc. H}_2SO_4} CH_3COOC(CH_3)_3$

17.41 (*a*) Define transesterification. (*b*) Complete the following reaction:

$$CH_3COOCH_2CH_3 \xrightarrow[n\text{-}C_5H_{11}O^-/n\text{-}C_5H_{11}OH]{H^+,\ n\text{-}C_5H_{11}OH\ or} ?$$

◢ (*a*) Transesterification is the reaction of an ester with an alcohol, different from the one in the ester, to give a new ester:

$$RCOOR' + R''OH \rightleftharpoons RCOOR'' + R'OH$$

(*b*) $CH_3COOC_5H_{11}$ and CH_3CH_2OH. In this case, the lower boiling ethanol is distilled off as it forms, driving the equilibrium to the right and making the conversion feasible.

17.42 Give a mechanism for a base-induced transesterification.

◢ The reaction occurs between the ester and the alkoxide ion, $R''O^-$, in the solvent $R''OH$. $R''O^-$, a better nucleophile than $R''OH$, preferentially attacks the $C=O$ to give a tetrahedral intermediate. Loss of $R'O^-$ affords a new ester, while loss of $R''O^-$ restores the original ester.

$$\underset{\substack{O \\ \| \\ R-C-OR'}}{} + R''O^- \rightleftharpoons \underset{\substack{O^- \\ | \\ R-C-OR' \\ | \\ OR''}}{} \rightleftharpoons \underset{\substack{O \\ \| \\ R-C-OR''}}{} + R'O^-$$

17.43 Give the products of the following reaction and explain their formation:

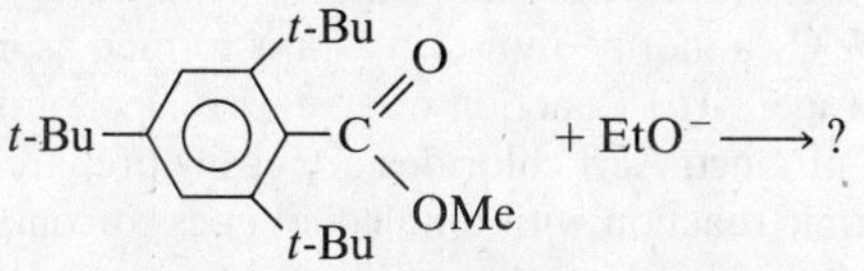

Methyl 2,4,6-tri-*tert*-butylbenzoate

◢ The rate of reaction at the $C=O$ is sufficiently hindered so that an S_N2 attack at the Me carbon dominates, giving 2,4,6-tri-*tert*-butylbenzoate anion and the ether, MeOEt.

17.44 (*a*) Write an equation for the preparation of an amide from (i) acid + $MeNH_2$, (ii) acid halide + Me_2NH, (iii) anhydride + $PhNH_2$, (iv) ester + NH_3. Label the amide 1°, 2° or 3°. (*b*) Why are two equivalents of amine used in (ii) and (iii)?

◢ (*a*)   (i) $RCOOH + MeNH_2 \longrightarrow \underset{\text{an ammonium salt}}{RCOO^-MeNH_3^+} \xrightarrow{\text{heat}} \underset{2°\ \text{amide}}{RCONHMe} + H_2O$

       (ii) $RCOCl + 2Me_2NH \longrightarrow \underset{3°\ \text{amide}}{RCONMe_2} + Me_2NH_2^+Cl^-$

       (iii) $(RCO)_2O + 2PhNH_2 \longrightarrow \underset{2°\ \text{amide}}{RCONHPh} + RCOO^-PhNH_3^+$

       (iv) $RCOOR' + NH_3 \rightleftharpoons \underset{1°\ \text{amide}}{RCONH_2} + R'OH$

     (*b*)   The acid produced as the reaction proceeds would convert half of the amine to amine salt preventing further reaction. For example, in (iii) the molar ratios at the end of the reaction with one eq of $PhNH_2$ would be $\frac{1}{2}(RCO)_2O + \frac{1}{2}RCONHPh + \frac{1}{2}PhNH_3^+{}^-OOCR$.

17.45 Describe the procedure for making amides from ArCOCl.

◢ The reaction of ArCOCl with an amine releases one eq of HCl, which must be removed. If the amine is inexpensive and readily available, a second equivalent is used to react with the HCl. As an alternative, one eq of NaOH can be used (the *Schotten-Baumann* procedure). A 3° amine, such as pyridine (Py) or Me_3N, is often employed. It forms an acylammonium salt (**A**), which undergoes displacement of Me_3N by RNH_2 to give the N-substituted amide.

$$PhCOCl + :NMe_3 \longrightarrow \underset{(\mathbf{A})}{PhCONMe_3^+Cl^-} \xrightarrow{RNH_2} PhCONHR + Me_3NH^+Cl^-$$

17.46 Prepare N-methyl-N-phenylformamide.

◢ Formic anhydride and formyl chloride are unstable (Problems 17.22 and 17.32) and cannot serve as starting materials. Formamides may be produced by heating the corresponding ammonium salt of formic acid:

$$HCOOH + PhNHMe \longrightarrow HCOO^-(PhNH_2Me^+) \xrightarrow{\Delta} HCONPhMe + H_2O$$

17.47 Show the steps in the reaction of RCOCl with conc. NH_3.

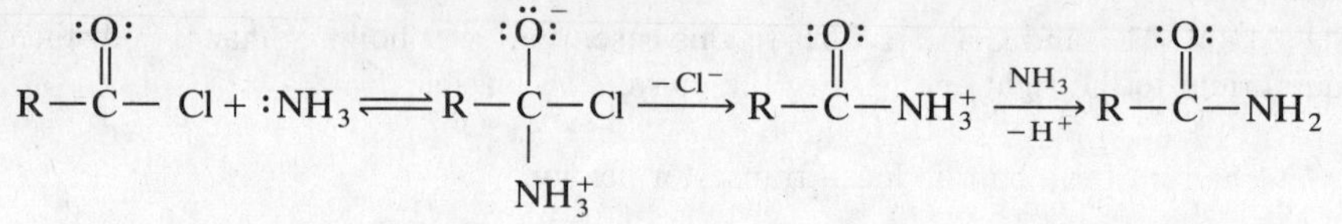

◢

17.48 Give the structure and general name of the product of the reaction of RCOCl with each of the following reagents: (*a*) NH_3, (*b*) $MeNH_2$, (*c*) Et_2NH, (*d*) $PhNH_2$, (*e*) H_2NNH_2, (*f*) H_2NOH, and (*g*) $Na^+N_3^-$.

◢ (*a*) $RCONH_2$, amide; (*b*) RCONHMe, N-substituted amide; (*c*) $RCONEt_2$, N,N-di-substituted amide; (*d*) RCONHPh, anilide from aniline, $PhNH_2$; (*e*) $RCONHNH_2$, hydrazide; (*f*) RCONHOH, hydroxamic acid, and (*g*) $RCON_3$, acyl azide.

17.49 (*a*) Why cannot HCl convert RCOOH to RCOCl? (*b*) Why is it more efficient to prepare an ester by the sequence: acid $\longrightarrow$ acyl chloride $\longrightarrow$ ester, rather than acid $\longrightarrow$ ester?

◢ (*a*) If the reaction were to occur, the acyl chloride and water products would react rapidly with each other to give starting material. H_2O cannot be removed as it is formed as in the case of ester formation (Problem 17.36) because HCl (*g*) would escape. (*b*) Reaction of acid with alcohol is slower, and the equilibrium must be shifted to the right by removing a product. Acyl chlorides are easily prepared under nonequilibrium conditions (if $SOCl_2$ is used), and their exothermic reaction with an alcohol goes to completion (HX being evolved).

17.50 Prepare 2-hydroxypropanamide from the corresponding acid.

◢ $$CH_3CH(OH)COOH + EtOH \xrightarrow{H^+} CH_3CH(OH)COOEt \xrightarrow{NH_3} CH_3CH(OH)CONH_2 + EtOH$$

Reaction of the acid with $SOCl_2$ is unfeasible because of the presence of the OH group, which would also react rapidly. If the acid chloride were to form, it would react with the OH of a second molecule:

$$CH_3CH(OH)COCl + CH_3CH(OH)COCl \longrightarrow CH_3CHCOCl$$
$$| $$
$$OCOCH(OH)CH_3$$

17.51 Give the product of each of the following reactions: (*a*) Succinic anhydride + MeOH $\longrightarrow$ **A** $\xrightarrow{PCl_3}$ **B** $\xrightarrow{MeNH_2}$ **C**, (*b*) phthalic acid + $NH_3 \longrightarrow$ **D** $\xrightarrow{300\,°C}$ **E**, (*c*) $MeCH(CH_2COOH)_2 \xrightarrow[\Delta]{(CH_3CO)_2O}$ **F**.

◢ (*a*) **A** is $HOOCCH_2CH_2COOMe$; **B** is $ClCOCH_2CH_2COOMe$; **C** is $MeNHCOCH_2CH_2COOMe$

(*b*) **D** is

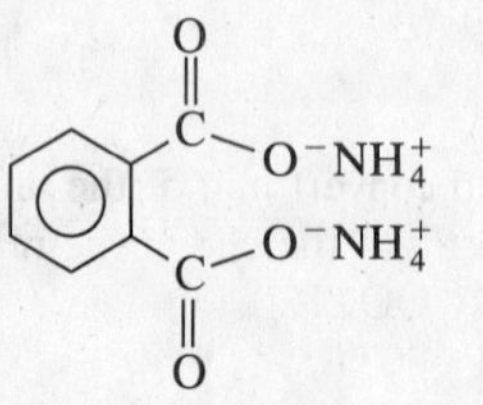

E is

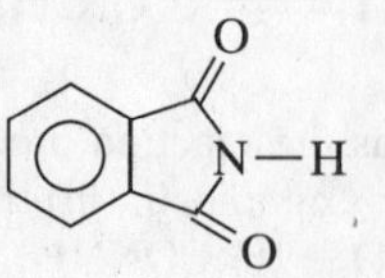

(*c*) **F** is

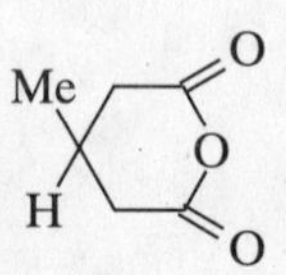

Ammonium phthalate   Phthalimide (a cyclic imide) β-Methylglutaric anhydride

17.52 (*a*) Prepare an amide from a nitrile. (*b*) Supply a mechanism for the acid-catalyzed hydration of RCN to give an amide.

◢ (*a*) The hydrolysis of a nitrile can give either an amide or a carboxylic acid. The amide is the initial product, but more often it is further hydrolyzed to the acid or carboxylate ion. It may be isolated in acid by keeping the temperature low. In base, H_2O_2 is often added, and O_2 is formed: $RCN + 2H_2O_2 \xrightarrow{OH^-} RCONH_2 + O_2 + H_2O$.

(b) The nitrile is protonated on N, making the C more electrophilic, and water acts as a nucleophile:

$$R-C\equiv N: \overset{H^+}{\rightleftharpoons} [R-\overset{+}{C}\equiv N:H^+ \longleftrightarrow R-\overset{+}{C}=\overset{..}{N}:H] \xrightarrow{+H_2O} R-\underset{\underset{H_2O^+}{|}}{C}=N:H \overset{-H^+}{\rightleftharpoons} R-\underset{\underset{HO}{|}}{C}=NH \text{ (imino acid)}$$

In a series of H^+ transfers, the imino acid is converted to an amide, $RCONH_2$.

17.53 (a) Write the products of the reactions of diazomethane, CH_2N_2, with (i) PhCOOH, (ii) CH_3CH_2COOH, (iii) $PhCH_2COOH$, (iv) $PhCH=CHCOOH$. (b) Give a mechanism for the reaction of CH_2N_2 with RCOOH. (c) What product would you expect from the reaction of CH_2N_2 with 2-hydroxybutanoic acid? Explain.

◢ (a) These reactions produce Me esters. (i) $PhCOOCH_3$, (ii) $CH_3CH_2COOCH_3$, (iii) $PhCH_2COOCH_3$, (iv) $PhCH=CHCOOCH_3$.

(b) $$RCOOH + {}^-:CH_2-\overset{+}{N}\equiv N: \longrightarrow RCOO^- + CH_3(\overset{+}{-N}\equiv N:) \xrightarrow{S_N2} RCOOCH_3 + :N\equiv N:$$

Protonation of CH_2N_2 is a necessary first step, giving the methyldiazonium ion. Although a weak nucleophile, $RCOO^-$ displaces the excellent leaving group, N_2.

(c) $CH_3CH_2CH(OH)COOCH_3$. Alkylation of ROH cannot compete with that of RCOOH because $\underset{-}{ROH}$ is much less acidic than $RCOOH$.

17.54 Write structures and names of the products of: (a) $CH_3COOEt + H_2NNH_2$, (b) $PhCH_2COCl + NaN_3$, (c) $PhCOOEt + H_2NOH$.

◢ (a) $CH_3CONHNH_2$, acetyl hydrazide; (b) $PhCH_2CON_3$, phenylacetyl azide; (c) $PhCONHOH$, benzoyl hydroxamic acid.

REACTIONS

17.55 Summarize the transacylation reactivities of RCOG's.

◢ The order of reactivity, $RCOCl > (RCO)_2O > RCOOR' > RCONH_2$ implies that a more reactive derivative can be converted to any less reactive derivative, although the reverse conversions do not occur. Anhydride exchange (Problem 17.33(a)) and transesterification also occur. All the acyl derivatives are hydrolyzed to the carboxylic acid.

17.56 Indicate the features of the mechanism of hydrolysis of acyl derivatives with regard to (a) ease of hydrolysis, (b) catalysis, (c) rate-determining step, (d) intermediate(s).

◢ (a) See Problem 17.55. (b) All show both acid and base catalysis. (c) The slow step is the addition of :Nu to the carbonyl C (Problem 17.24). (d) The tetrahedral intermediates are

$$\underset{\underset{Nu}{|}}{\overset{\overset{:\ddot{O}:^-}{|}}{R-C-G}} \text{ (basic catalysis)} \qquad \underset{\underset{HNu^+}{|}}{\overset{\overset{:\ddot{O}H}{|}}{R-C-G}} \text{ (acid catalysis)}$$

17.57 Criticize the statement: The decreasing order of reactivity of RCOG results from the increasing order of basicity of the leaving group.

◢ Although this rationale gives the correct answer, it overlooks the fact that the step in which G leaves cannot influence the rate because it is faster than the addition step. The first step, the slow nucleophilic addition, determines the rate, and the resonance stabilization of the $-CO-G$ group is important here:

$$\underset{}{\overset{\overset{:O:}{||}}{R-C-G:}} \longleftrightarrow \underset{}{\overset{\overset{:\ddot{O}:^-}{|}}{R-C=G^+}}.$$ The greater the degree of delocalization, the less reactive is RCOG. NH_2 has the greatest degree, thus $RCONH_2$ is least reactive, while X has little or no delocalization (Problem 17.15) and RCOX is the most reactive. Therefore the statement correctly predicts the order of reactivity, albeit for the wrong reason.

17.58 (a) Why does an acyl chloride undergo nucleophilic attack more rapidly than does an alkyl chloride? (b) What is the essential difference between nucleophilic attack on the $C=O$ of an aldehyde or ketone and on an acyl derivative?

▰ (a) RCl's are much less reactive than RCOCl's because (1) of the tendency of the O of C=O to attract e^-'s making the C more positive and electrophilic; (2) the TS of the acid derivative leading to the tetrahedral intermediate is less sterically hindered than the TS with pentavalent C in the S_N2 reaction of RX; (3) a σ bond must be partially broken to form the alkyl TS, and a weaker π bond is broken in the acyl case.
(b) In each case, the addition step leads to a tetrahedral intermediate. However, the intermediate from the carbonyl compound would have to eliminate the very strong bases H:$^-$ or R:$^-$ from RCHO and RCOR′, respectively, to restore the C=O. Instead, the intermediate alkoxide accepts an H$^+$ to give the adduct. The intermediate from the acyl derivative easily eliminates G:$^-$ (or GH).

17.59 Given $K_a = 2.6 \times 10^{-5}$ for hydrazoic acid, HN$_3$, and $K_a = 1.8 \times 10^{-5}$ for CH$_3$COOH. Place acyl azides (RCON$_3$) in the order of acyl-derivative reactivities (Problem 17.23).

▰ HN$_3$ is slightly more acidic than CH$_3$COOH. N$_3^-$ is slightly less basic than CH$_3$COO$^-$, and is a slightly better-leaving group. RCON$_3$ is thus less reactive than RCOCl but a little more reactive than the anhydride (RCO)$_2$O.

17.60 Explain why strong bases such as OR$^-$ and NH$_2^-$ can be leaving groups (from esters and amides, respectively) in nucleophilic transacylations and hydrolyses.

▰ The elimination step for breaking the C—G bond is exothermic because the resonance-stabilized C=O is being reformed. According to the Hammond principle, its TS more closely resembles the reactant, which for this step is the intermediate. Consequently, little breaking of the C—G bond occurs in the TS of the elimination step, and the basicity of the leaving group is of little or no consequence. The strong bases are probably assisted in elimination by H-bonding with the H of the solvent.

17.61 Give the products of heating each of the following with NaOH, followed by acidification with HCl:

(a) CH$_3$CH$_2$COOCH$_2$Ph, (b) m-ClC$_6$H$_4$COOCH$_3$, (c) ,

(d) CH$_3$CH=CHCH$_2$COOCH$_2$CH$_2$Br

▰ (a) CH$_3$CH$_2$COOH + PhCH$_2$OH; (b) m-ClC$_6$H$_4$COOH + CH$_3$OH; (c) MeCH(OH)CH$_2$CH$_2$COOH;
(d) CH$_3$CH=CHCH$_2$COOH + H$_2$C—CH$_2$ by intramolecular displacement of Br$^-$ by $^-$O— of $^-$OCH$_2$CH$_2$Br.

17.62 (a) For the hydrolysis of an ester, give the key steps leading to (i) acyl-O, (ii) alkyl-O cleavage of RCOOR′ under acidic and basic conditions. (b) Compare the reversibility and rates of acid and alkaline hydrolysis.

▰ (a) (i) In acid, H$_2$O attacks the protonated ester, R—C(=$\overset{+}{O}$H)—OR′, and after shuffling H$^+$'s, R′OH is displaced. In base, OH$^-$ attacks C=O, and R′O$^-$ is displaced. (ii) In acid, a stable R′$^+$ can form via an S_N1 reaction from the protonated ester, R—C(=O)—$\overset{+}{O}$(H)R′. In base, OH$^-$ participates in an S_N2 reaction by attacking R′ to displace RCOO$^-$.
(b) Alkaline hydrolysis (saponification) is faster and irreversible because of the stability of the RCOO$^-$ formed by proton exchange of the products: RCOOH + RO$^-$ ⟶ RCOO$^-$ + ROH. Acid hydrolysis is slower and reversible (Problem 17.36).

17.63 Discuss the feasibility of using each of the following experiments to determine unequivocally whether acyl or alkyl cleavage occurs in ester hydrolysis. Decide what further experiment should be done in those cases where it would be necessary. (a) RCOOR′; (b) RCOOR′ + OH$^-$ in H$_2$O, (c) RCOOR′ + D$_2$O + OD$^-$, (d) s-RCOOR′*; (e) s-RCOOR′*, (f) RCOOR′ where R′ is 3° (g) RCOOCH$_2$C(Me)=CHCH$_3$. [O means ^{18}O]. (a), (d), and (e) react in aq. OH$^-$; (f) and (g) in H$_3$O$^+$.

▰ (a) If the products are R′OH and RCOOH acyl cleavage occurs. If the products are RCOOH and R′OH, alkyl cleavage occurs. (b) Absence of R′OH indicates acyl cleavage; if present, alkyl cleavage is indicated. However, if R′OH were isolated, it would have to be shown that it did not originate from the first formed R′OH. This is done by subjecting R′OH to the same reaction conditions as used for the hydrolysis. (c) No information is obtained since both RCOOH and ROH would exchange with D_2O. (*d*) If the configuration in $\overset{*}{R}OH$ is unchanged, acyl cleavage occurs; an inverted configuration indicates alkyl cleavage by S_N2 attack on the alkyl C. (*e*) No pertinent information is obtained. The chiral C in R* is not involved in any plausible mechanism. (*f*) Formation of an alkene indicates an S_N1 alkyl cleavage with formation of a stable C^+ that eliminates H^+. (*g*) Alkyl cleavage in acid gives an allylic C^+ that rearranges to R″OH:

$$[{}^+H_2C{-}C(Me){=}CHMe \longleftrightarrow H_2C{=}C(Me)\overset{+}{C}HMe] \longrightarrow H_2C{=}C(Me)CH(OH)Me$$

In acid, the formation of only $HOCH_2C(Me){=}CHCH_3$ signifies acyl cleavage.

17.64 Give the products of the reactions of $LiAlH_4$ with (*a*) $PhCH_2COOCH_3$, (*b*) $(CH_3CO)_2O$, (*c*) PhCOCl, (*d*) 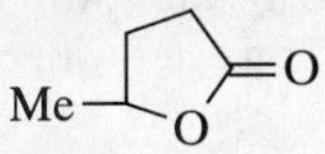, (*e*) $(CH_3)_2CHCH_2CN$.

▌ (*a*) $PhCH_2CH_2OH + CH_3OH$, (*b*) 2 eq of CH_3CH_2OH, (*c*) $PhCH_2OH$, (*d*) $MeCH(OH)CH_2CH_2CH_2OH$, (*e*) $(CH_3)_2CHCH_2CH_2NH_2$.

17.65 Write the products of the reactions of $LiAlH_4$ with (*a*) $PhCH_2CONH_2$, (*b*) $Me_2CHCONMe_2$,

(*c*) 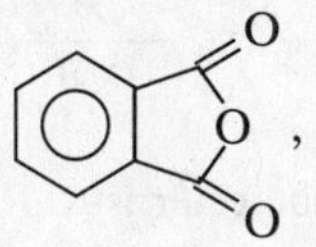, (*d*) 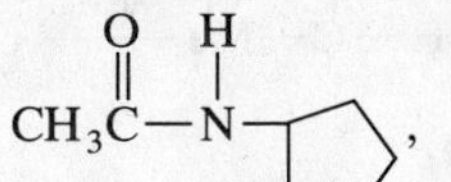, (*e*) $CH_3CH{=}CHCH_2CONHPh$, (*f*) 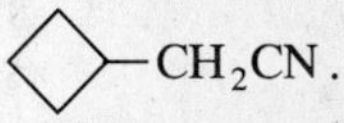.

▌ (*a*) $PhCH_2CH_2NH_2$, (*b*) $Me_2CHCH_2NMe_2$, (*c*) 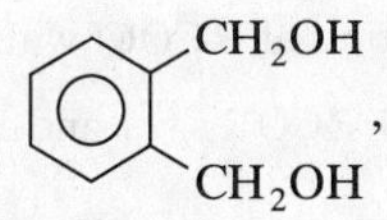, (*d*) 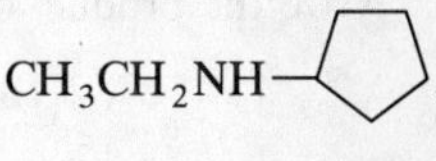,

(*e*) $CH_3CH{=}CHCH_2CH_2NHPh$, (*f*) 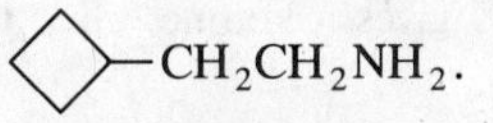.

17.66 Outline ways of preparing an aldehyde from (*a*) an acyl halide (two methods), (*b*) an ester, (*c*) an N,N-dialkylamide, and (*d*) a nitrile.

▌ Reduction with H_2 or $LiAlH_4$ usually goes all the way to the alcohol in both (*a*) and (*b*) unless special conditions are used. (*a*) See Problem 15.31. (*1*) The Rosenmund reduction uses H_2 and a poisoned Pd on $BaSO_4$ catalyst. (*2*) The less active reducing agent $LiAlH(O\text{-}t\text{-}Bu)_3$ (LBAH) is used. (*b*) and (*d*) Reduce with the less reactive $(i\text{-}Bu)_2AlH$ (DBAH) (Problem 15.33). (*c*) N,N-Dialkylamides may be reduced to the aldehyde, avoiding reduction to the amine, by using a modified hydride such as $LiAlH(OEt)_3$.

17.67 Describe the *Bouvealt-Blanc* method for reducing an ester.

▌ The ester is reduced with Na in EtOH to an alcohol. The reaction is not a reduction by H_2 that can be liberated from the reaction of Na with EtOH, but is believed to involve initial electron transfer from Na to the C=O.

17.68 (*a*) Give the product from reaction of H_2 with (i) $PhCOOCH_2Ph$ using Pd/C, and (ii) $NC(CH_2)_4CN$ using Raney Ni. (*b*) Give a synthetic application of reaction (i).

▌ (*a*) (i) $PhCOOH + PhCH_3$. This hydrogenolysis is similar to the reaction of benzyl ethers. (ii) $H_2N(CH_2)_6NH_2$, hexamethylenediamine, an intermediate in the synthesis of nylon (Problem 17.92). (*b*) It is used to protect COOH's as benzyl ethers protect OH's.

17.69 Give steps for the following conversion.

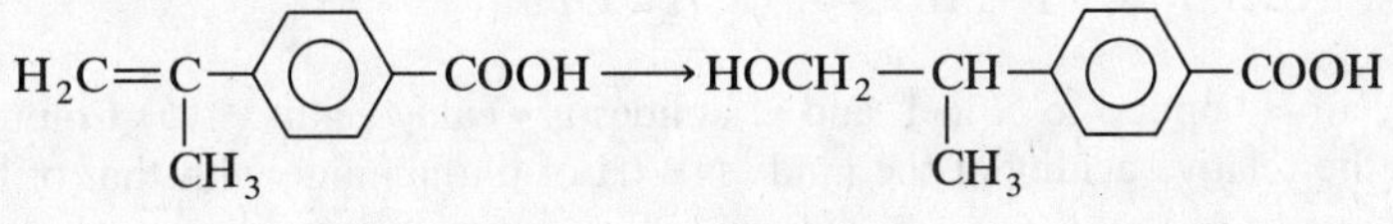

▌ The C=C is hydrated anti-Markovnikov with $BH_3 \cdot THF$. Because this reagent reacts with acids, the COOH group must be converted to an unreactive group that is removed afterwards. [C_3H_5 is $H_2C{=}C(CH_3)$.]

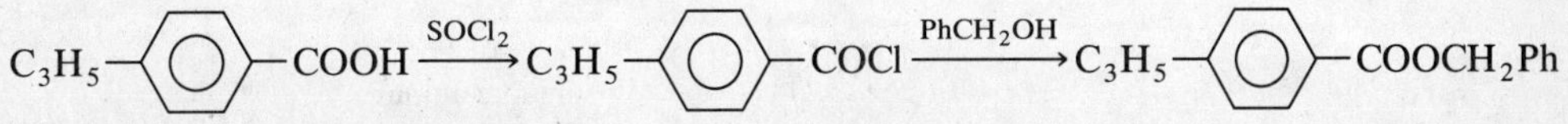

The C=C is hydrated and the resulting ester is hydrogenolyzed. A *t*-butyl ester can't be used because the removal of *t*-Bu as isobutylene by H$^+$ would dehydrate the ROH giving starting material [Problem 17.63(*f*)].

17.70 List the reagent for converting benzoyl chloride to (*a*) benzaldehyde, (*b*) benzylamine, (*c*) benzyl alcohol, (*d*) benzoyl benzoate, (*e*) benzoic anhydride, (*f*) N-benzylbenzamide.

◢ (*a*) Pd/C, poisoned with quinoline and S (Rosenmund reaction) or LBAH. (*b*) NH$_3$ to form amide, followed by LiAlH$_4$. (*c*) LiAlH$_4$. (*d*) PhCH$_2$OH from (*c*), H$^+$. (*e*) aq. NaOH to form PhCOO$^-$Na$^+$, followed by reaction with PhCOCl or heat with (CH$_3$CO)$_2$O. (*f*) PhCH$_2$NH$_2$ from (*b*).

17.71 (*a*) Write an equation for the reaction of CH$_3$COOEt with MeMgI. (*b*) Why are two equivalents of organometallic reagent used? (*c*) Why is a ketone not isolated from the reaction of an ester with one equivalent of RMgX?

◢ (*a*) CH$_3$COOEt + 2MeMgI $\xrightarrow[\text{2. H}_3\text{O}^+]{\text{1. ether}}$ CH$_3$C(OH)Me$_2$ + EtOH. (*b*) A ketone is formed as an intermediate, and it reacts with the second equivalent of MeMgI to form the 3° ROH.

$$CH_3-\overset{\overset{\text{O}}{\|}}{C}-OEt \xrightarrow{\text{MeMgI}} CH_3-\overset{\overset{-\text{O(MgI)}^+}{|}}{\underset{\underset{\text{Me}}{|}}{C}}-OEt \xrightarrow{-\text{MgI(OEt)}} CH_3-\overset{\overset{\text{O}}{\|}}{C}-Me \xrightarrow{\text{MeMgI}} CH_3-\overset{\overset{-\text{O(MgI)}^+}{|}}{\underset{\underset{\text{Me}}{|}}{C}}-Me \xrightarrow[-\text{(MgI)}^+]{\text{H}^+} CH_3-\overset{\overset{\text{OH}}{|}}{\underset{\underset{\text{Me}}{|}}{C}}-Me$$

(*c*) A ketone is formed initially. It reacts further because it is more reactive than the ester is to RMgX.

17.72 Give the product of reaction of RCOCl with (*a*) R′MgX, (*b*) R′$_2$CuLi, and (*c*) R′$_2$Cd.

◢ (*a*) RC(OH)R′$_2$, (*b*) RCOR′, (*c*) and RCOR′.

17.73 The reaction of RCN with R′MgX gives a ketone. Give the reaction steps and explain why a 3° alcohol is not obtained.

◢ R—C≡N: + R′MgX $\longrightarrow$ R—$\overset{\overset{:\text{N}^{-}\,\text{(MgX)}^+}{\|}}{C}$—R′ $\xrightarrow{\text{hydrolysis}}$ R—$\overset{\overset{\text{O}}{\|}}{C}$—R′. A second equivalent of R′MgX does not react because the intermediate imine salt bears a − charge. Unlike the ester intermediate, where elimination of OR′$^-$ leads to ketone, loss of the charge by elimination of R′ merely reverses the reaction.

17.74 Give the products of reaction of (CH$_3$)$_2$CuLi (after hydrolysis) with (*a*) N≡C(CH$_2$)$_8$COCl,

(*b*) CH$_3$CH$_2$CO—⬡—COCl, (*c*) EtOOC(CH$_2$)$_4$COCl.

◢ In each case, the less-reactive organometallic (CH$_3$)$_2$CuLi reacts with the more-reactive COCl group:

(*a*) N≡C(CH$_2$)$_8$COCH$_3$ (*b*) CH$_3$CH$_2$CO—⬡—COCH$_3$ (*c*) EtOOC(CH$_2$)$_4$COCH$_3$

17.75 Give the structures of **A** through **F**.

(*a*) CH$_3$CH$_2$COCl + PhH $\xrightarrow{\text{AlCl}_3}$ **A**   (*d*) PhCH$_2$COOCH$_3$ $\xrightarrow[\text{2. H}^+]{\text{1. 2 eq of }n\text{-BuLi}}$ **E**

(*b*) *i*-BuBr $\xrightarrow[\text{2. CuI}]{\text{1. Li}}$ **B** $\xrightarrow{\text{PhCOCl}}$ **C**   (*e*) H$_2$C=CHCH$_2$CN $\xrightarrow[\text{2. H}^+]{\text{1. PhMgBr}}$ **F**

(*c*) PhH + (CH$_3$CO)$_2$O $\xrightarrow[\text{2. H}^+]{\text{1. AlCl}_3}$ **D**

◢ (*a*) **A** is PhCOCH$_2$CH$_3$; (*b*) **B** is (*i*-Bu)$_2$CuLi, **C** is PhCOCH$_2$CH(CH$_3$)$_2$; (*c*) **D** is PhCOCH$_3$; (*d*) **E** is PhCH$_2$C(OH)(*n*-C$_4$H$_9$)$_2$; (*e*) **F** is H$_2$C=CHCH$_2$COPh.

17.76 (*a*) Show why an H bonded to N in 1° and 2° amides is weakly-acidic. (*b*) Compare the acidity to that of NH$_3$. (*c*) Compare the relative acidity of the imide N—H of phthalimide with that of benzamide.

◢ (*a*)

$$R-\overset{\overset{:\text{O}:}{\|}}{C}-\ddot{N}H_2 + B^- \rightleftharpoons \left[R-\overset{\overset{:\text{O}:}{\|}}{C}-\ddot{N}H^- \longleftrightarrow R-\overset{\overset{:\ddot{\text{O}}:^-}{|}}{C}=\ddot{N}H \right] + BH$$

amidate anion

The amidate anion is stabilized by delocalization. (*b*) Amides ($K_a \cong 10^{-16}$) are much more acidic than NH_3 ($K_a = 10^{-33}$) because the $-$ of $H_2N:^-$ is localized. (*c*) Phthalimide has two C=O's to stabilize the imide anion. Its acidity is so much greater than that of benzamide that it is converted to the conjugate base in conc. aq. NaOH.

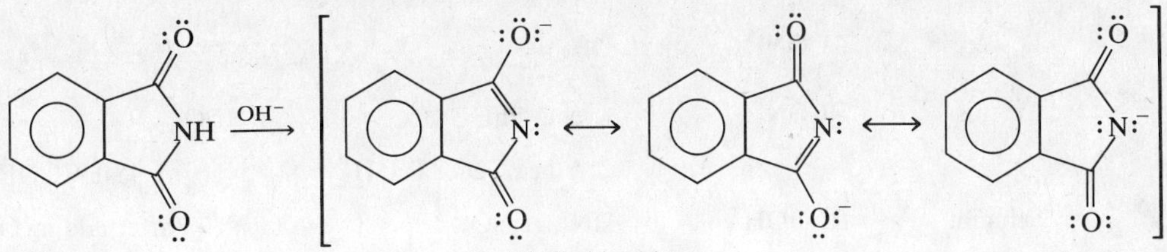

phthalimide anion

17.77 How do amides react with organometallic reagents?

▮ If the amide N has an H, as in 1° and 2° amides, an acid-base reaction occurs, producing a metal salt. These often precipitate out of solution, and no further reaction occurs.

$$RCONH_2 + R'Li \longrightarrow RCONH^-Li^+ + R'H$$

N,N-disubstituted amides give good yields of carbonyl compounds:

$$RCONR'_2 + R''Li \longrightarrow RCOR'' + R'_2NLi$$

17.78 Write equations for the reaction of (*a*) a 1°, (*b*) a 2°, and (*c*) a 3° amide with nitrous acid.

▮ (*a*) $RCONH_2 + HONO \longrightarrow RCOOH + N_2 + H_2O$

(*b*) $$R-\overset{O}{\overset{\|}{C}}-NHR' + HONO \longrightarrow R-\overset{O}{\overset{\|}{C}}-\overset{R'}{\overset{|}{N}}-N=O \text{ (an N-nitrosoamide)}$$

(*c*) $RCONR'_2$ does not react.

17.79 Give the organic product of the reaction of $PhCH_2CONH_2$ with any of the following reagents: P_2O_5, $SOCl_2$, $POCl_3$, or PCl_5.

▮ $PhCH_2CN$. Dehydration occurs with all of these reagents.

17.80 Carry out the following transformations: (*a*) C_2H_5OH to CH_3CN, (*b*) $PhCH_3$ to $PhCH_2CN$, and (*c*) $PhCH_3$ to $p\text{-}O_2NC_6H_4CN$

▮ (*a*) $CH_3CH_2OH \xrightarrow[H^+]{Cr_2O_7^{2-}} CH_3COOH \xrightarrow{PCl_5} CH_3COCl \xrightarrow{NH_3} CH_3CONH_2 \xrightarrow{P_2O_5} CH_3CN$

(*b*) $PhCH_3 \xrightarrow{NBS} PhCH_2Br \xrightarrow{CN^-} PhCH_2CN$

(*c*) $PhCH_3 \xrightarrow[H_2SO_4]{HNO_3} p\text{-}O_2NC_6H_4CH_3 \xrightarrow[H^+]{MnO_4^-} p\text{-}O_2NC_6H_4COOH \xrightarrow[2.\ NH_3]{1.\ SOCl_2} p\text{-}O_2NC_6H_4CONH_2 \xrightarrow{P_2O_5}$
$p\text{-}O_2NC_6H_4CN$

17.81 Give the product of the reaction of (*a*) $Me_2CHCH_2CONH_2$, (*b*) $PhCH_2CONH_2$, and (*c*) $m\text{-}BrC_6H_4CONH_2$ with Br_2 in NaOH.

▮ This *Hofmann* rearrangement results in formation of an amine with one less C.

(*a*) $Me_2CHCH_2NH_2$ (*b*) $PhCH_2NH_2$ (*c*) $m\text{-}BrC_6H_4NH_2$

17.82 What are the structures of **A** through **E**?
(*a*) $CH_3CH_2COCl \xrightarrow{HN_3} A \xrightarrow{\Delta} B\ (C_3H_5NO) \xrightarrow{H_2O} C\ (C_2H_7N)$
(*b*) $CH_3CH_2COOCH_3 \xrightarrow{H_2NOH} D\ (C_3H_7NO_2) \xrightarrow{OH^-} C$

▮ (*a*) $A = CH_3CH_2CON_3$; $B = CH_3CH_2NCO$; $C = CH_3CH_2NH_2$ This *Curtius* rearrangement occurs with loss of CO_2. (*b*) $D = CH_3CH_2CONHOH$. In this *Lossen* reaction, the hydroxamic acid rearranges to give the isocyanate **B**, which forms the amine **C** on reacting with H_2O. (See Problem 19.66 for the mechanism.)

17.83 Compare the reactants, conditions, and products of the Hofmann, Lossen, Curtius, and Schmidt reactions.

	Reactant	Condition	Product
Hofmann	$RCONH_2$	Br_2, OH^-	RNH_2
Lossen	$RCONHOH$	OH^-	$RNCO$ ($\xrightarrow{H_2O}$ RNH_2)
Curtius	$RCON_3$	1. Δ in PhH	$RNCO$
		2. Δ in H_2O or R'OH	RNH_2 or $RNHCOOR'$
Schmidt	$RCOOH$	HN_3, H_2SO_4	RNH_2 (after adding OH^-)

17.84 Show how a 2° alcohol can be prepared from an ester and an organometallic reagent. Illustrate by preparing di-*n*-butylcarbinol.

◢ A formate ester is reacted with 2 eq of *n*-BuMgBr. Only 2° alcohols with two identical R groups are possible. $HCOOEt \xrightarrow[\text{2. hydrolysis}]{\text{1. 2\textit{n}-BuMgBr}} (n\text{-Bu})_2CHOH$

17.85 (*a*) Write the products from the pyrolysis of $CH_3CH_2COOCH_2CH_2CH_2CH_3$ and give a mechanism for the reaction. (*b*) Give the products from heating (i) $CH_3COOCH(CH_3)CH_2CH_3$, (ii) 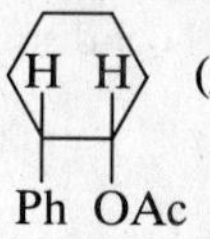 (**A**), and

(iii) 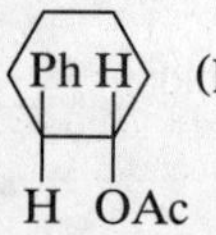 (**B**), and rationalize their formation. (*c*) The ΔH of the pyrolysis in (i) of (**B**) is $\cong +13$ kcal/mol, yet it is a useful synthetic reaction. Explain.

◢ (*a*) $CH_3CH_2COOH + H_2C\!=\!CHCH_2CH_3$. The reaction is believed to proceed through a cyclic six-center TS, and involves simultaneous *syn* elimination of a β H of the alcohol and the acetoxy group:

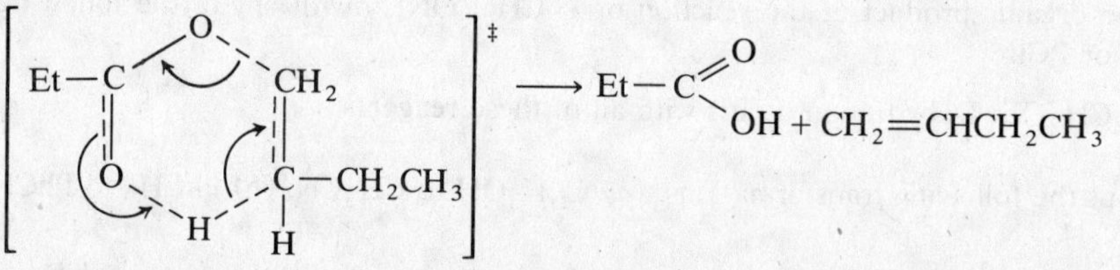

(*b*) (i) CH_3COOH + a mixture of $H_2C\!=\!CHCH_2CH_3$ (**C**) and $CH_3CH\!=\!CHCH_3$ (**D**). Since there are three β H's that may be eliminated to give **C** and two to give **D**, a near statistical (3:2) mixture of **C** and **D** is obtained.

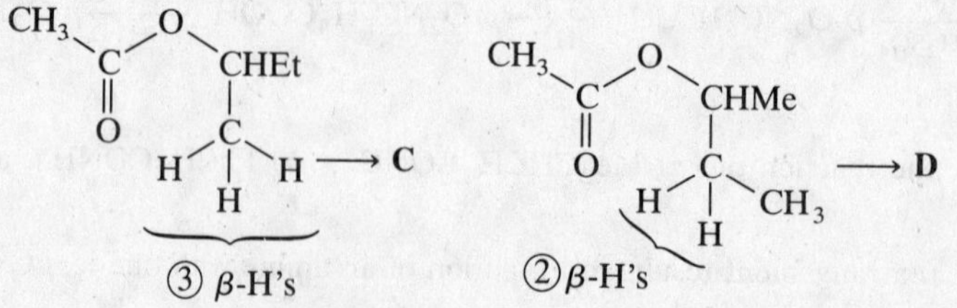

(ii) 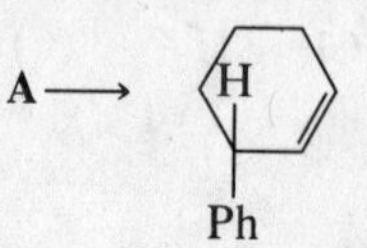 **A** $\longrightarrow$ **E**   (iii) 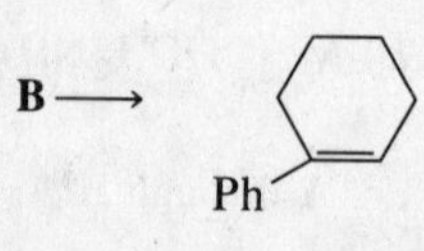 **B** $\longrightarrow$ **F**

Compound **A** cannot form the more stable **F** (Saytzeff product, conjugated) because this reaction would require the removal of an *anti* H. The Hofmann product **E** is formed instead.

(*c*) ΔS is favorable, two products being formed from one. When the reaction is run at higher temperatures, the $T\Delta S$ term overcomes the unfavorable ΔH term and ΔG becomes negative.

17.86 (*a*) Write the products of the reaction of peroxybenzoic acid with (i) acetone and (ii) cyclopentanone. (*b*) When ^{18}O-benzophenone (written as PhCOPh) is reacted, **O** is found only in the C=O of the ester. Supply a mechanism. (*c*) The migratory aptitude of the different R and Ar groups in this reaction is: $3°R >$ $2°R > Ph > 1°R > Me$. Give the products of the reaction of the unsymmetrical ketones (i) PhCOEt, (ii) PhCH$_2$COMe, and (iii) Me$_2$CHCOEt.

▐ (*a*) Esters are formed in this Baeyer-Villiger rearrangement (Problem 15.134): (i) CH$_3$COOCH$_3$ and

(ii) (cyclohexanone with O) =O.

(*b*) $Ph-\overset{O}{\overset{||}{C}}-Ph \xrightarrow{PhCOOH} Ph-\underset{Ph}{\overset{OH}{\underset{|}{\overset{|}{C}}}}-O-O-\overset{O}{\overset{||}{C}}-Ph \xrightarrow{-PhCOO^-} \left[Ph-\overset{OH}{\underset{+}{\overset{|}{C}}}-O-Ph \right] \xrightarrow{-H^+} Ph-\overset{O}{\overset{||}{C}}-O-Ph$

(*c*) (i) EtCOOPh, (ii) MeCOOCH$_2$Ph, (iii) EtCOOCHMe$_2$.

17.87 Give the product of each reaction. (*a*) RCOCl or (RCO)$_2$O + R'SH, (*b*) ArH + RSCN (in HCl), (*c*) H$_2$C=C=O + RSH, (*d*) RNCS + R'MgX.

▐ (*a*) $\overset{O}{\overset{||}{RCSR'}}$ (*b*) $\overset{O}{\overset{||}{ArCSR}}$ (*c*) $\overset{O}{\overset{||}{CH_3CSR}}$ (*d*) $\overset{S}{\overset{||}{R'CNHR}}$

17.88 (*a*) Explain why the more stable form of a thioester is the one with C=O and S—R rather than C=S and O—R. (*b*) Which would you expect to be more reactive to nucleophilic reagents, ethyl thioacetate or ethyl acetate? Explain.

▐ (*a*) Overlap of *p*-orbitals in C=O is more effective than in C=S because the bond is shorter and both are 2*p* AO's. In addition, the dipolar resonance structure with − on the more electronegative O has a lower energy than the one with − on S, making C=O more stable. (*b*) The thioester is more reactive. Delocalization is not as important as in the O-ester because (*1*) the C—S σ-bond is longer than the C—O σ-bond and (*2*) overlap of a 3*p* AO of S and a 2*p* AO of *C* is not as effective as overlap of two 2*p* AO's in the O-ester. This results in a more electrophilic C in the S-ester than in the O-ester. (*3*) If the leaving groups are compared (Problem 17.28), loss of the less basic RS$^-$ is favored over the more basic RO$^-$, and RCOSR' fits in between the anhydride and O-ester in reactivity.

17.89 (*a*) Give the products of CH$_3$COSCH$_2$CH$_2$OPh + MeOH. (*b*) How is this reaction related to the mechanism by which coenzyme A facilitates acyl transfers in living systems? Illustrate using the abbreviated structure CH$_3$CO—S—CoA for coenzyme A.

▐ (*a*) CH$_3$COOMe + HSCH$_2$CH$_2$OPh. (*b*) S-esters do not transfer acyl groups, i.e., react with a nucleophile, as easily as do anhydrides, but they are more reactive than O-esters. This makes them good acylating agents. Acetyl coenzyme A (**B**) is a large molecule bearing an acetylated thiol group at its reactive end. The presence of S in the ester group activates the acetyl group for attack by a nucleophile, and in the process the CH$_3$CO group is transferred to the nucleophile.

$\underset{\textbf{B}}{CH_3-\overset{O}{\overset{||}{C}}-S-CoA} + :NuH \xrightarrow{enzyme} CH_3-\underset{\overset{+}{N}uH}{\overset{O^-}{\overset{|}{\underset{|}{C}}}}-S-CoA \longrightarrow CH_3-\overset{O}{\overset{||}{C}}-Nu + HS-CoA$

17.90 (*a*) Define (i) lipid, (ii) triglyceride, (iii) fat, (iv) oil, and (v) wax. (*b*) What is the important chemical difference between a fat and an oil? (*c*) What nonester compounds are classified as lipids?

▐ (*a*) (i) A *lipid* is a water-insoluble substance extracted from cells by nonpolar organic solvents. (ii) A triglyceride, also called *triacylglycerol*, is a triacylated ester of glycerol. (iii) *Fat* is a triglyceride that is solid at room temperature. It is usually derived from animal fats like beef fat or butter. (iv) *Oil* is a triglyceride that is liquid at room temperature, and is extracted from plants (like corn or peanuts) or cold-blooded animals (fish). (v) *Wax* is an ester made up of a long-chain fatty acid ($\geq C_{16}$) or a long-chain alcohol ($\geq C_{16}$) e.g., beeswax. (*b*) The carboxylate parts of an oil usually have one or more *cis*-oriented double bonds, whereas those of fats have little or no unsaturation. (*c*) Steroids, like cholesterol and terpenes.

17.91 How many different triglycerides having (*a*) two identical and (*b*) three different acyl groups are possible? Draw their structures.

▮ (*a*) **A** exists as a pair of enantiomers because the center C of glycerol is chiral; thus there are three isomers. See Fig. 17-2(*a*). (*b*) All three triglycerides have a center chiral C and there are three racemates or six isomers. See Fig. 17-2(*b*).

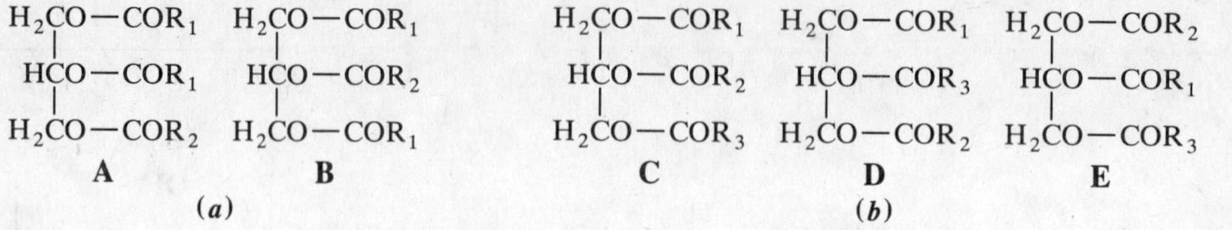

$$H_2CO—COR_1 \quad H_2CO—COR_1 \qquad H_2CO—COR_1 \quad H_2CO—COR_1 \quad H_2CO—COR_2$$
$$HCO—COR_1 \quad HCO—COR_2 \qquad HCO—COR_2 \quad HCO—COR_3 \quad HCO—COR_1$$
$$H_2CO—COR_2 \quad H_2CO—COR_1 \qquad H_2CO—COR_3 \quad H_2CO—COR_2 \quad H_2CO—COR_3$$

$$\textbf{A} \qquad\qquad \textbf{B} \qquad\qquad\quad \textbf{C} \qquad\qquad \textbf{D} \qquad\qquad \textbf{E}$$

(*a*)   (*b*)   **Fig. 17-2**

17.92 (*a*) Define condensation polymers. (*b*) Write a portion of the polymeric structure showing the *mer* of (i) Nylon-66, formed from adipic acid and hexamethylene diamine, and (ii) Nylon-6, formed from alkaline polymerization of ε-caprolactam.

▮ (*a*) *Condensation* polymers are formed when usually one or two monomers react with the elimination of simple molecules such as H_2O and EtOH.

(*b*) These linear *polyamides* form with elimination of H_2O.

(i) $HOOC(CH_2)_4COOH + H_2N(CH_2)_6NH_2 \longrightarrow [^-OOC(CH_2)_4COO^-]\ [H_3\overset{+}{N}(CH_2)_6\overset{+}{N}H_3] \longrightarrow$

Nylon-66

(ii) Heat opens the lactam ring to give the amino acid salt, which reacts further to give the polyamide.

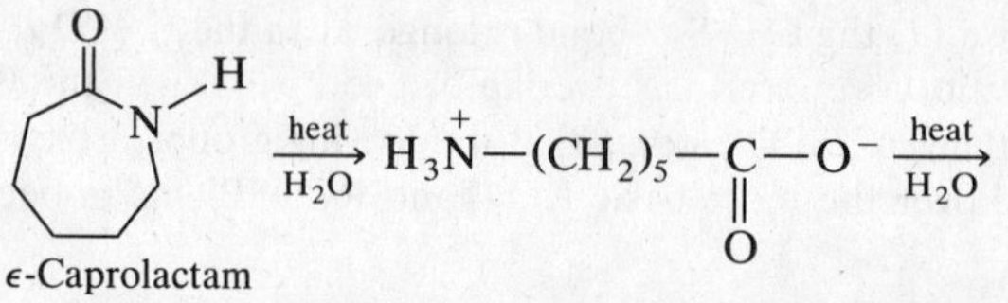

Nylon-6

17.93 (*a*) Give a partial structure of the polymer formed by treatment of β-propiolactone with base and suggest how it might be formed. (*b*) What is the partial structure of *Dacron*, the polymer formed from reaction of dimethyl-terephthalate and ethylene glycol? (*c*) Explain, using structures, how a *glyptal*, a *cross-linked* thermosetting resin, is formed from phthalic anhydride and glycerol.

▮ (*a*) A polyester is formed from successive ring-openings by alkoxide anion:

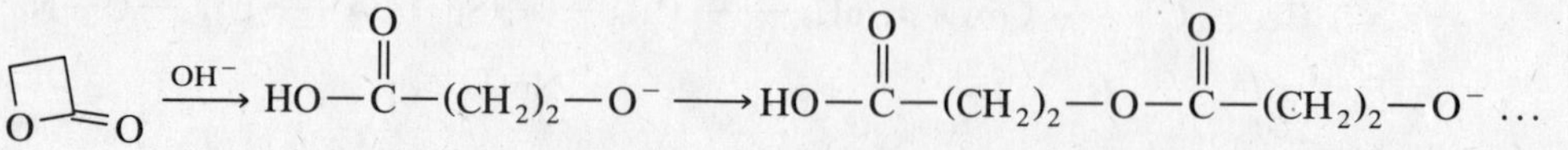

(*b*) $HOCH_2CH_2OH + HOOC\!-\!\!\langle\bigcirc\rangle\!-\!COOH + HOCH_2CH_2OH + HOOC\!-\!\!\langle\bigcirc\rangle\!-\!COOH \xrightarrow[-CH_3OH]{heat}$

Teraphthalic acid

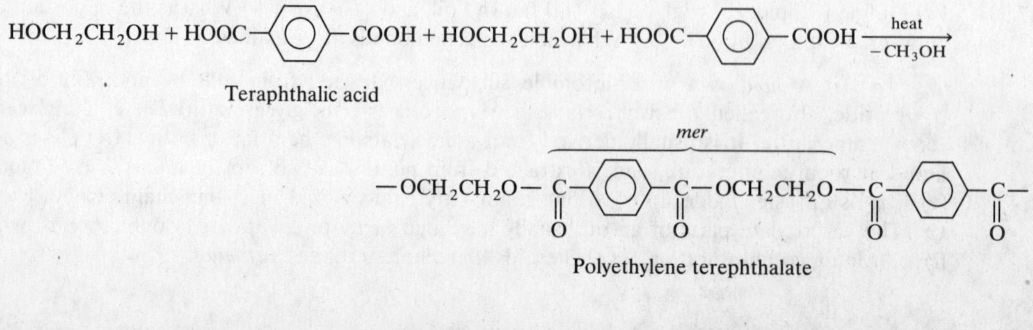

Polyethylene terephthalate

(c) Glycerol reacts initially at its more reactive 1° OH groups to give a linear polymer. The 2° OH groups are free to form cross-linked ester bonds with more phthalic anhydride molecules.

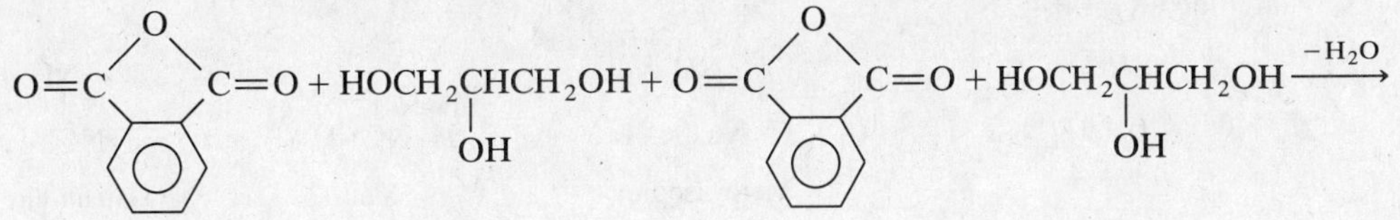

Phthalic anhydride

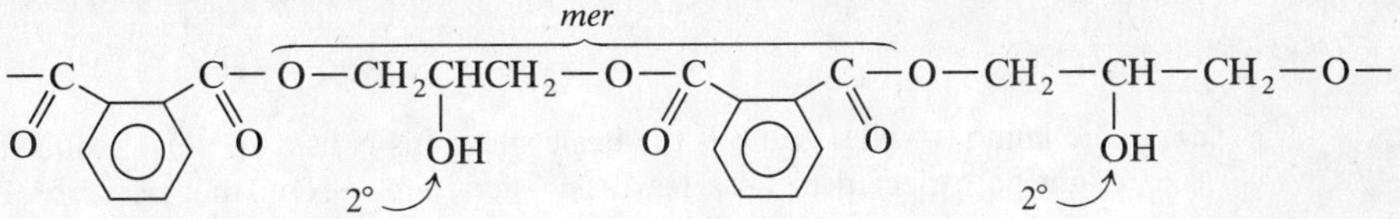

17.94 (a) Give the structure and name of the product of R—N=C=O + R'OH. (b) Show a portion of the polymer formed from the reaction of HOCH$_2$CH$_2$OH and 2,4(OCN)$_2$C$_6$H$_3$Me.

(a) RNH—C(=O)—OR', a urethane.

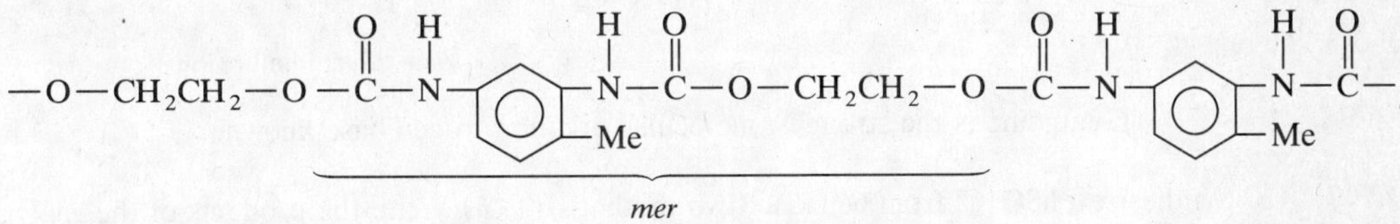

DERIVATIVES OF CARBONIC, S, AND P ACIDS

17.95 (a) Give the structures and names of the following derivatives of carbonic acid: (i) acid chloride, (ii) amide, (iii) ethyl ester, (iv) anhydride. (b) Give the structures of (i) ethyl chlorocarbonate, (ii) ethyl carbamate, (iii) cyanamide. (c) Name the acid which each of the compounds in (b) is related to.

(a) (i) O=CCl$_2$, phosgene; (ii) O=C(NH$_2$)$_2$, urea; (iii) O=C(OEt)$_2$, diethyl carbonate; (iv) CO$_2$. (b) (i) ClCOOEt, (ii) H$_2$NCOOEt, (iii) H$_2$NC≡N. (c) (i) chloroformic acid, (ClCOOH); (ii) and (iii) carbamic acid, [H$_2$NCOOH]. Both acids in (c) are unstable.

17.96 Give an industrial preparation of (a) phosgene and (b) urea.

(a) $$CO(g) + Cl_2(g) \xrightarrow[200\,°C]{activated\ C} ClCOCl$$

(b) $$CO_2(g) + 2NH_3(g) \rightleftharpoons H_2NCOO^-NH_4^+ \xrightarrow[pressure]{\Delta} H_2NCONH_2$$

Ammonium carbamate

17.97 (a) Write the structures of the *ureides* formed from the reaction of urea with (i) CH$_3$COCl and (ii) CH$_2$(COOEt)$_2$, diethylmalonate, in OEt$^-$. (b) Show the steps in the reaction in (ii) of part (a). (c) What starting material is reacted with urea to form (i) 5,5-diethylbarbituric acid (Veronal) and (ii) 5-ethyl-5-phenylbarbituric acid (Phenobarbital)?

(a) (i) CH$_3$CONHCONH$_2$, acetylurea, and (ii)

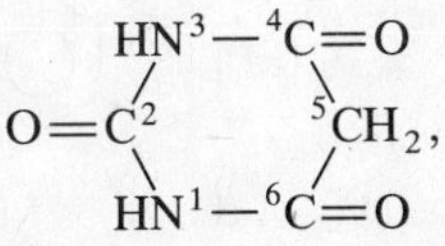

barbituric acid. (b) OEt$^-$ con-

verts urea to the base H$_2$NCONH:$^-$, which displaces $^-$OEt from CH$_2$(COOEt)$_2$, a transacylation. The sequence of reactions is repeated with the second H$_2$N of urea. (c) (i) Et$_2$C(COOEt)$_2$ and (ii) EtCPh(COOEt)$_2$.

17.98 (a) Write the structure of the anaesthetic sodium 5-ethyl-5-(1-methylbutyl)-2-thiobarbiturate (sodium pentothal). (b) Give the reactants needed for its synthesis.

(a)

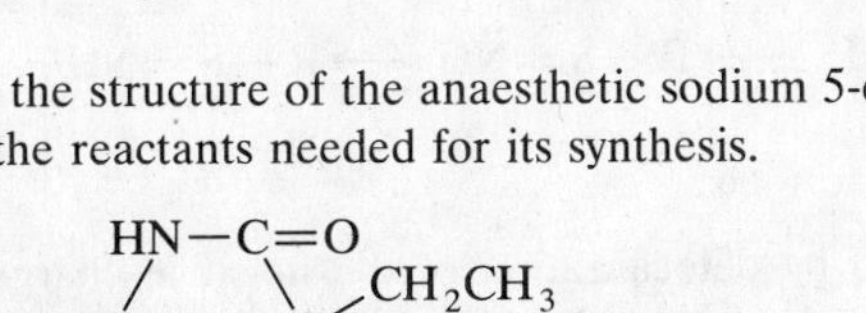

(b) (H$_2$N)$_2$C=S + (EtOOC)$_2$C—CH(Me)CH$_2$CH$_2$CH$_3$ with Et branch

17.99 (*a*) Give the products of the reaction of cyanamide, $H_2NC\equiv N$, with (i) H_2O/H^+, (ii) CH_3OH/H^+, (iii) H_2S, (iv) NH_3. (*b*) Give a general mechanism for (i) of part (*a*). (*c*) Account for the extraordinary basicity of guanidine ($K_b = 0.4$).

◢ (*a*) (i) $\overset{\overset{\displaystyle O}{\|}}{H_2NCNH_2}$ (ii) $\overset{\overset{\displaystyle NH}{\|}}{H_2NCOCH_3}$ (iii) $\overset{\overset{\displaystyle S}{\|}}{H_2NCNH_2}$ (iv) $\overset{\overset{\displaystyle NH}{\|}}{H_2NCNH_2}$

   Urea   Methylisourea   Thiourea   Guanidine

(*b*) $H_2N{-}C\equiv N: \xrightarrow{H^+} H_2N{-}\overset{+}{C}{=}NH \xrightarrow{H_2O} [H_2N{-}C{=}NH]$. Shifts of H^+ give urea.
$$\underset{\displaystyle H_2O^+}{\overset{\displaystyle |}{}}$$

(*c*) The imino ($=NH$) group is the basic site. This N uses sp^2 HO's, and since it has more s-character, it might be expected to be a less basic site than $-NH_2$ that uses sp^3 HO's. However, the conjugate acidic cation is greatly stabilized by electron delocalization among its three equivalent contributing resonance structures:

$$\underset{\displaystyle H_2N}{\overset{\displaystyle H_2N}{}}C{=}NH \xrightarrow{H^+} \left[\underset{\displaystyle H_2N}{\overset{\displaystyle H_2N}{}}C{=}\overset{+}{N}H_2 \longleftrightarrow \underset{\displaystyle H_2N}{\overset{\displaystyle H_2\overset{+}{N}}{}}C{-}NH_2 \longleftrightarrow \underset{\displaystyle H_2\overset{+}{N}}{\overset{\displaystyle H_2N}{}}C{-}NH_2 \right]$$

Guanidinium ion

Guanidine is the strongest molecular organonitrogen base known.

17.100 (*a*) Synthesize $PhSO_2Cl$ from benzene (two methods). (*b*) Write the products of the reaction of $PhSO_2Cl$ with (i) EtOH/pyridine, (ii) NH_3, (iii) Me_2CHNH_2, (iv) $PhH/AlCl_3$.

◢ (*a*) (*1*) $PhH \xrightarrow{H_2S_2O_7} PhSO_3H \xrightarrow{PCl_5} PhSO_2Cl$ (*2*) $PhH \xrightarrow{HOSO_2Cl} PhSO_2Cl$

(*b*) (i) $PhSO_2OEt$ (ii) $PhSO_2NH_2$ (iii) $PhSO_2NHCHMe_2$ (iv) $PhSO_2Ph$

17.101 Suggest a mechanism for the reaction: $RH + SO_2 + Cl_2 \xrightarrow{h\nu} RSO_2Cl + HCl$.

◢. The Reed reaction goes through a free radical chain mechanism.

(*1*) $Cl_2 \xrightarrow{h\nu} 2Cl\cdot$ (*2*) $Cl\cdot + RH \longrightarrow HCl + R\cdot$ (*3*) $R\cdot + SO_2 \longrightarrow RSO_2^{\cdot}$

(*4*) $RSO_2^{\cdot} + Cl_2 \longrightarrow RSO_2Cl + Cl\cdot$

(*2*), (*3*), and (*4*) are propagation steps.

17.102 Write structures for (*a*) ethyl methanesulfinate, (*b*) diethyl sulfate, (*c*) benzyl *p*-toluenesulfonate, (*d*) N,N-dimethylbenzenesulfonamide, (*e*) β-naphthylsulfonyl chloride.

◢ (*a*) $CH_3{-}\overset{\overset{\displaystyle O}{\|}}{S}{-}OEt$,   (*b*) $EtOSO_2OEt$,   (*c*) $p\text{-}MeC_6H_4SO_2OCH_2Ph$,

(*d*) $PhSO_2NMe_2$,   (*e*)

17.103 Compare and explain the acidity of the N—H in an acyl amide and a sulfonamide.

◢

$$R{-}\overset{\overset{\displaystyle :O:}{\|}}{\underset{\underset{\displaystyle :O:}{\|}}{S}}{-}\overset{..}{N}H_2 \rightleftharpoons \left[R{-}\overset{\overset{\displaystyle :O:}{\|}}{\underset{\underset{\displaystyle :O:}{\|}}{S}}{-}\overset{..}{N}H^- \longleftrightarrow R{-}\overset{\overset{\displaystyle :\overset{..}{O}:^-}{|}}{\underset{\underset{\displaystyle :O:}{\|}}{S}}{=}\overset{..}{N}H \longleftrightarrow R{-}\overset{\overset{\displaystyle :O:}{\|}}{\underset{\underset{\displaystyle :\overset{..}{O}:^-}{|}}{S}}{=}\overset{..}{N}H \right]$$

The conjugate base of the sulfonamide is stabilized by delocalization of the negative charge to the two O's, making a sulfonamide more acidic than the acyl amide, where delocalization is possible to only one O. (See Problem 17.76).

17.104 (*a*) Alkyl sulfonate esters undergo nucleophilic attack at the alkyl C, unlike carboxylic esters. Explain. (*b*) Give the products of reaction of $^{18}OH^-$ (written as OH^-) with (i) $CH_3SO_2OCH_2Ph$ and (ii) CH_3COOCH_2Ph. (*c*) The reaction of CH_3SO_2Cl with optically active 2-butanol gives an active methanesulfonate which is treated with aq. NaOH. The recovered 2-butanol is active and has the opposite configuration. Explain.

◤ (*a*) Attack at S would result in a more hindered pentacovalent TS than the less hindered tetracovalent TS from attack at C of the carboxylic ester. In addition, an S_N2 attack on R releases RSO_2O^-, an excellent leaving group.

$$R'SO_2\overset{\frown}{OR} + :Nu^- \longrightarrow RSO_2O^- + R:Nu$$

(*b*) (i) $CH_3SO_2O^- + PhCH_2OH$ (S_N2 on C) (ii) $CH_3CO_2^- + PhCH_2OH$ (acyl attack)

(*c*) Reaction of the alcohol with the CH_3SO_2Cl occurs by addition to S of R^*OH, followed by loss of Cl^-. The configuration about the chiral C is unchanged in this step. OH^- then attacks with inversion at the chiral C displacing $CH_3SO_2O^-$.

17.105 (*a*) Write structures for (i) trimethyl phosphate, (ii) dimethyl ethylphosphonate, and (iii) cyclopentyl pyrophosphate. (*b*) Write an equation for the preparation of a trialkyl phosphate.

◤ (*a*) (i) $O=P(OMe)_3$ (ii) $EtP(OMe)_2$ (iii)

(*b*) $3ROH + O=PCl_3 \longrightarrow (RO)_3P=O + 3HCl$

17.106 When phosphate esters react with OH^-, the first alkyl group is easily hydrolyzed. The hydrolysis becomes increasingly more difficult for the second and then the third R group. Why?

◤
$$(RO)_3P=O \xrightarrow[-ROH]{OH^-} (RO)_2\overset{O}{\overset{\|}{P}}-O^- \xrightarrow[-ROH]{OH^-} RO-\overset{O}{\overset{\|}{\underset{O^-}{P}}}-O^- \xrightarrow[-ROH]{OH^-} {}^-O-\overset{O}{\overset{\|}{\underset{O^-}{P}}}-O^- \text{ (phosphate ion)}$$

Attack by OH^- on a substrate becomes more difficult as the negative charge on the substrate increases.

17.107 (*a*) What is a phosphoglyceride? (*b*) Give the structure of phosphatidyl ethanolamine. (*c*) From what kind of acid is a phosphoglyceride derived?

◤ (*a*) *Phosphoglycerides* are mixed triesters of glycerol in which there are two acyl groups and one phosphate group on a terminal $H_2CO—$.

(*b*)
$$\begin{array}{l} H_2CO—COR \\ | \\ HCO—COR' \\ | \\ H_2CO-\overset{\,}{\underset{O}{\overset{\diagup}{P}}}\overset{\,}{\underset{O^-}{\overset{\diagdown}{O}}}-CH_2CH_2NH_3^+ \end{array}$$

(*c*) A phosphatidic acid
$$\begin{array}{l} H_2CO—COR \\ | \\ HCO—COR' \\ | \\ H_2CO—PO(OH)_2 \end{array}$$

ANALYSIS AND SPECTROSCOPY

17.108 Distinguish by simple chemical tests the following: (*a*) RCOOH and RCOCl, (*b*) RCOOR' and $RCONH_2$, (*c*) RCOOR' and $(RCO)_2O$, (*d*) RSO_2NHR' and RCONHR', and (*e*) RCN and RCOOR'.

◤ (*a*) RCOCl reacts with H_2O to release Cl^-. Addition of $AgNO_3$ gives AgCl (*s*), insoluble in HNO_3. The acid forms a precipitate of RCOOAg, soluble in HNO_3. (*b*) $RCONH_2$ emits odorous NH_3 (*g*) when heated in aq. NaOH, whereas the ester saponifies to give R'OH and $RCOO^-Na^+$. (*c*) If the anhydride is warmed in H_2O, it hydrolyzes readily to RCOOH, which is acid to litmus. Under these conditions, the ester is not hydrolyzed. (*d*) The sulfonamide dissolves in aq. NaOH forming $[RSO_2NR']^-Na^+$; the corresponding H in the amide is not acidic enough to react with NaOH. (*e*) Basic hydrolysis of the nitrile releases NH_3.

486 ∅ CHAPTER 17

17.109 (*a*) Describe the hydroxamic acid test for esters. (*b*) What other functional group gives a positive test?

⬛ (*a*) A *hydroxamic acid* (RCONHOH) is formed by reacting an ester with H_2NOH; the addition of $FeCl_3$ to its solution produces a red-to-violet colored complex. (*b*) An anhydride.

17.110 The stretching frequencies of $C{=}O$ (in cm^{-1}) in an *ir* spectrum decrease as follows: acyl chloride, ≈ 1800; ester, ≈ 1735; amide, ≈ 1690; and for reference, a ketone $C{=}O$, ≈ 1715. Explain the trend.

⬛ The effect of G on carbonyl absorptions can be explained in terms of the contributions of the two resonance

forms: $\left[\begin{array}{c}\diagdown\\ \diagup\end{array}C{=}\ddot{O}: \longleftrightarrow -\overset{+}{\underset{|}{C}}-\ddot{O}:^-\right]$. Factors that increase the $C{=}O$ character of the carbonyl bond (more input

$\quad\quad\quad$ **A** $\quad\quad\quad$ **B**

from **A**) raises the stretching frequency. An increase in the single-bond character of the bond (more input from **B**) lowers the frequency. The contribution of each resonance form is influenced by three effects: (*1*) electron-withdrawal by G tends to increase the contribution of **A**; (*2*) delocalization of e^-'s from G to O (Problem 17.13) increases the contribution of **B**; and (*3*) H-bonding to the carbonyl bond, which is stronger when there is greater contribution from **B** because of the increased negative charge on O. From consideration of the C—Cl bond length (Problem 17.15) in RCOCl, it is concluded that delocalization is not significant, and since there is no H-bonding, acid chlorides absorb at higher frequencies due to the dominance of the electron-withdrawal effect (*1*). In esters, there is no H-bonding. Effects (*1*) and (*2*) occur, influencing the frequency in opposite ways; O being more electronegative than Cl, but also contributing its e^-'s to delocalization. Effect (*1*) dominates, and esters absorb at frequencies higher than ketones but lower than acyl chlorides. N is not as electronegative as is O, thus effect (*1*) is diminished in the amide. Its e^-'s are however more easily delocalized, and amides absorb at lower frequencies than the other acyl derivatives, and below ketones. In 1° and 2° amides, where H-bonding occurs, the frequency is still lower (effect *3*).

17.111 Give reasons for the following observations: (*a*) Anhydrides have *two* strong $C{=}O$ bands and a broad band in the region from 1300 to 900 cm^{-1}. (*b*) In very dilute solutions, the absorption of the $C{=}O$ band of 1° and 2° amides shift to higher frequencies. (*c*) The frequency increases as the ring size of a lactone or lactam decreases from 5 to 4 atoms. (*d*) Dilute solutions of 1° amides have two sharp bands at ≈ 3350 and 3150 cm^{-1}; 2° amides and lactams show only one band; and 3° amides do not absorb in this region. (*e*) The $C{=}O$ in methyl salicylates is shifted down to 1680 cm^{-1}, whereas in methyl benzoate it is 1720 cm^{-1}.

⬛ (*a*) The higher-frequency (≈ 1800 cm^{-1}) absorption is attributed to the asymmetric stretch, and the lower frequency (≈ 1760 cm^{-1}) is due to the symmetric stretch. The broad band to the right is due to C—O stretch. (*b*) Intermolecular H-bonding disappears in very dilute solutions, and the $C{=}O$ bond strength increases, leading to a higher frequency (Problem 17.110). (*c*) With decreasing ring size and increasing angle strain, the delocalization of e^-'s from the singly-bonded heteroatom decreases, the $C{=}O$ bond strength increases, as does the stretching frequency. (*d*) The two bands are due to asymmetric and symmetric H—N—H stretches. 2° Amides and lactams have only one N—H stretch, and there is no N—H bond in a 3° amide. (*e*) H-Bonding between the *ortho* OH and COOMe decreases the $C{=}O$ stretching frequency in methyl salicylate.

17.112 Use ir spectroscopy to distinguish among RSO_2Cl (**A**), RSO_2OR' (**B**), RSO_2NH_2 (**C**), and RSO_2NHR' (**D**).

⬛ All four compounds exhibit strong asymmetric and symmetric $S{=}O$ stretching absorptions between 1375-1325 cm^{-1} and 1200-1140 cm^{-1}. The values decrease from **A** to **B** to **C** (or **D**), due to the same opposing factors that affect the acyl derivatives (Problem 17.110). **B** also has several strong bands at ≈ 1000 to 750 cm^{-1} assigned to S—O stretch. **C** has asymmetric and symmetric N—H stretching bands at 3350 and 3250 cm^{-1}, while **D** has only one band in this frequency range.

17.113 Use ir spectroscopy to differentiate a nitrile from a 3° amide and an alkyne.

⬛ Nitriles lack the $C{=}O$ stretch at ≈ 1680 cm^{-1} of the amide. They show $C{\equiv}N$ absorption at frequencies slightly higher than 2200 cm^{-1}, while alkynes absorbs slightly below (at lower frequencies) 2200 cm^{-1}. The alkyne absorption is weaker because $C{\equiv}N$ is more polar than $C{\equiv}C$.

17.114 Discuss the features of the pmr of (*a*) HCOOR, (*b*) $RCONH_2$, (*c*) RCH_2COX (acyl halide, ester, anhydride, amide), (*d*) RCH_2CN, (*e*) $RCOOCH_2R'$, and (*f*) $RCONHCH_2R'$.

▮ (*a*) Less than RC$\underline{H}$O, $\delta \cong 8$ ppm. (*b*) Similar to amine H's, variable ($\delta = 5$ to 8 ppm), often broad. (*c*) In the same region as H's of ketones, $\delta \cong 2$ to 2.5 ppm. (*d*) Similar to (*c*), $\delta \cong 2.5$ ppm. (*e*) In the same region as RC$\underline{H}_2$OH, $\delta \cong 4$ ppm. (*f*) In the same region as RC$\underline{H}_2$NH$_2$, at $\delta \cong 3$ ppm.

17.115 Figure 17-3 represents the pmr spectrum of N-methylformamide. Assign δ values to each H, and explain the origin of the two signals at $\delta = 2.9$ ppm.

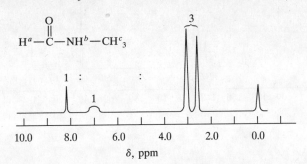

Fig. 17-3

▮ Moving from higher to lower δ values, the formyl H^a absorbs at about $\delta = 8$ ppm, and the amide H^b barely appears as a broad signal at $\delta = 7$ ppm. The considerable delocalization of electron density from N to O engenders enough double character in the C to N bond to hinder free rotation, creating two conformational diastereomers: In one diastereomer Me is *cis* and in the other it is *trans* to the C=O. (See Problem 17.16.) The two singlets at $\delta \cong 2.9$ ppm integrating for the three H^c's, arise from each of these different positional Me's. The interconversion of these isomers is slow enough for them to be detected by pmr spectroscopy.

$$\underset{\text{``cis''}}{\text{(cis structure)}} \rightleftharpoons \underset{\text{``trans''}}{\text{(trans structure)}}$$

17.116 Deduce the structure of each of the following compounds from the given pmr spectral data. Values of δ are in ppm.
(*a*) **A**, C$_8$H$_{12}$O$_4$, an ester: $\delta = 6.83$, *s*, one H; $\delta = 4.27$, *q*, two H's; $\delta = 1.32$, *t*, three H's
(*b*) **B**, C$_{10}$H$_{13}$NO$_2$, an amide: $\delta = 7.90$, broad, *s*, one H; $\delta = 7.20$, four H's (AB pattern); $\delta = 3.98$, *q*, two H's; $\delta = 2.10$, *s*, three H's; $\delta = 1.38$, *t*, three H's

▮ (*a*) There are 3° of unsaturation in **A**, which gives a positive hydroxamic ester test. Each signal corresponds to twice the number of given H's because the spectrum integrates for just half the number of H's in the formula. The quartet and triplet indicate an ethyl ester, and the two H's at $\delta = 6.83$ ppm are equivalent vinylic H's, (no splitting). **A** is either diethyl maleate or diethyl fumarate, and nmr spectroscopy can decide between the two on the basis of *J* values.

$$\underset{\text{diethyl maleate}}{\begin{array}{c} \text{H—C—COOCH}_2\text{CH}_3 \\ \| \\ \text{H—C—COOCH}_2\text{CH}_3 \end{array}} \qquad \underset{\text{diethyl fumarate}}{\begin{array}{c} \text{CH}_3\text{CH}_2\text{OOC—C—H} \\ \| \\ \text{H—C—COOCH}_2\text{CH}_3 \end{array}}$$

(*b*) Compound **B** has 5° of unsaturation. (Recall that the presence of an N requires removal of one H from the formula when calculating degrees of unsaturation.) The four-H AB pattern at $\delta = 7.20$ ppm arises from the presence of two pairs of equivalent H's indicating a *para*-substituted benzene ring. The broad signal at $\delta = 7.90$ ppm is due to an amide N—$\underline{H}$. The two-H quartet and three-H triplet is characteristic of an ethyl group. The methylene H's at $\delta = 3.98$ ppm means that Et is bonded to O not N. The chemical shift for the Me singlet arises from an acetyl group. Compound **B** is

$$p\text{-CH}_3\text{CH}_2\text{OC}_6\text{H}_4\text{NHCOCH}_3, \text{ phenacetin (an analgesic)}$$

17.117 Match the C's in $PhCH_2COOCH_2CH_3$ with their signals in the proton decoupled ^{13}C nmr spectrum in Fig. 17-4.

◢ Reading from left to right: $A = $ $C=O$; $B, C, D,$ and E are the six phenyl carbons, identified as follows: $B = C^1$, $C = C^2$ and C^6, $D = C^3$ and C^5, and $E = C^4$; $F = O\underline{C}H_2$; $G = \underline{C}H_2CO$; and $H = \underline{C}H_3$.

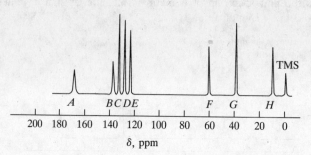

Fig. 17-4

17.118 (*a*) Predict the m/z values and structures for the fragments expected in the mass spectrum of methyl butyrate and explain their origin. (*b*) Which peak is missing in the mass spectrum of methyl isobutyrate? (*c*) Which of the following compounds do not undergo McLafferty rearrangements? (i) $PhCH_2CH_2COOCH_3$, (ii) $CH_3(CH_2)_3CONH_2$, (iii) $CH_3(CH_2)_2CN$, (iv) $(CH_3)_3CCH_2CH_2COOCH_3$.

◢ (*a*) The loss of $CH_3O\cdot$ gives the acylium ion, $CH_3CH_2CH_2C\equiv O^+$, $m/z = 71$; α cleavage on the other side of the $C=O$ affords $CH_3CH_2CH_2\cdot$ + $CH_3OC\equiv O^+$, $m/z = 59$. Peak at $m/z = 74$ represents the cation **A** from the McLafferty rearrangement [Problems 12.178 and 16.113(*d*)].

$$CH_3O\underset{\underset{parent\ ion}{}}{\overset{H}{\underset{\|}{O}}}\begin{array}{c}CH_2\\C\\CH_2\end{array}CH_2 \longrightarrow CH_3O\underset{\mathbf{A}}{\overset{H}{\underset{\|}{O^+}}}\dot{C}H_2 + \begin{array}{c}CH_2\\\|\\CH_2\end{array}$$

(*b*) $m/z = 74$ would be missing because there can be no McLafferty rearrangement. (*c*) A γ H is needed for the McLafferty rearrangement. Both (i) and (iv) do not have a γ H.

17.119 (*a*) Use uv spectroscopy to distinguish between ethyl propenoate (acrylate) and vinyl propanoate. (*b*) Suggest a synthesis of vinyl propanoate.

◢ (*a*) Ethyl propenoate has a conjugate $C=C-C=O$ unit and its π to π^* ($C=C$) and n to π^* ($C=O$) transitions occur at longer wavelengths than those for the vinyl ester.

(*b*) $CH_3CH_2COOH + HC\equiv CH \xrightarrow{H^+} CH_3CH_2COOCH=CH_2$

7.120 (*a*) Give the structure of the fragment resulting from a McLafferty rearrangement of (i) $CH_3CH_2CH_2CONH_2$ with $m/z = 59$, and (ii) $CH_3CH_2CH_2CN$ with $m/z = 41$. (*b*) 1° Amides show a strong peak in their mass spectra at $m/z = 44$. Provide the structure of the fragment that might give this peak, and suggest how it might form.

◢ (*a*) (i) $\left[H_2N-\overset{\overset{+\ddot{O}H}{\|}}{C}-\dot{C}H_2 \longleftrightarrow H_2N-\overset{\overset{+\cdot\ddot{O}H}{|}}{C}=CH_2 \right]$ (ii) $\left[H\overset{+}{N}\equiv C-\dot{C}H_2 \longleftrightarrow H\overset{+}{\underset{\cdot}{N}}=C=CH_2 \right]$

(*b*) This peak arises from α cleavage: $[R-CO-NH_2] \longrightarrow R\cdot + O=C=\overset{+}{N}H_2$, $m/z = 44$.

17.121 Identify the following compounds: (*a*) Compound **A**, MW = 113, gives a positive hydroxamic acid test and emits NH_3 on heating with NaOH.

Spectral data: ir peaks at 2237, 1733, and 1200 cm^{-1}
nmr signals at $\delta = 1.33$ ppm (*t*, three H's, $J = 7$ Hz); $\delta = 3.45$ ppm (two H's);
$\delta = 4.27$ ppm (*q*, two H's, $J = 7$ Hz)

(*b*) Compound **B** has ir absorptions at 1050, 1786, and 1852 cm^{-1} and a single nmr signal at $\delta = 3.00$ ppm. Gentle heating with MeOH gives **C**, $C_5H_8O_4$, which shows the following spectral data: ir (in cm^{-1}): 2500–3000(broad), 1730, and 1710; pmr in D_2O: $\delta = 2.7$ ppm (*s*, four H's), $\delta = 3.7$ ppm (*s*, three H's). Identify **B** and **C**.

◢ (*a*) A positive hydroxamic acid test denotes an ester and evolution of NH_3 either a 1° amide or a nitrile. The ir peak at 2237 cm^{-1} denotes CN. The odd molecular weight is consistent for the presence of an N. That the compound is an ester is also indicated by the C=O peak at 1733 cm^{-1} and the C—O peak at 1200 cm^{-1} in the ir spectrum. The coupled three-H triplet and two-H quartet at $\delta = 4.27$ ppm indicates an ethyl ester. The two-H singlet arises from an uncoupled —CH_2 *alpha* to two electron-withdrawing groups. The compound is $NCCH_2COOCH_2CH_3$, ethyl cyanoacetate. (*b*) **B** has two C=O's (1786 and 1852 cm^{-1}) that may be nonequivalent or equivalent with one peak from the symmetric and the other antisymmetric stretching frequency, and a C—O bond (1050 cm^{-1}). The mild reaction with MeOH signals that **B** is an anhydride. **C** is a carboxylic acid (ir peaks at 2500–3000 cm^{-1} broad for OH and at 1710 cm^{-1} for C=O), but also an ester (ir peak at 1730 cm^{-1} for C=O). Since reaction with 1 mol of MeOH gives a half-ester carboxylic acid, **B** is a cyclic anhydride, i.e., succinic anhydride. This anhydride would have only one singlet in the nmr spectrum because all H's are equivalent. The three-H singlet in **C** is from the $OC\underline{H}_3$ of the ester group and **C** is $HOOCCH_2CH_2COOCH_3$. Note that although the two CH_2's are not chemically equivalent, since they are each bonded to a C=O, they are pmr equivalent.

17.122 (*a*) Define saponification equivalent (SE) of an ester. (*b*) When is the SE equal to the molecular weight of an ester? (*c*) What is the SE of diethyl fumarate? (*d*) Identify **D** as methyl or ethyl cinnamate from the following data: 0.750 g of **D** is refluxed with 100.0 mL of 0.125 M KOH, and the excess KOH is neutralized by back-titrating with 27.50 mL of 0.300 M HCl.

◢ (*a*) The saponification equivalent (SE) is the weight of an ester that reacts with 1 mol of KOH.
 (*b*) If the ester is derived from a monocarboxylic acid, its MW and SE are identical.
 (*c*) It is a diester, and SE = MW/2 = (172.2 g/mol)/(2 eq/mol) = 86.1 g/eq.
 (*d*) Moles of KOH used = (0.1000 L × 0.125 mol/L) − (0.02750 L × 0.300 mol/L) = 0.00425 mol. This is the number of moles of ester that reacted, and for a monocarboxylic ester, is the number of equivalents of ester. MW = (0.750 g)/(0.00425 mol) ≐ 176 g/mol. **D** is PhCH=CHCOOEt with MW = 176.2 g/mol, rather than PhCH=CHOOMe with MW = 162.2 g/mol.

SUPPLEMENTARY PROBLEMS

17.123 (*a*) Give the steps in the Arndt–Eistert synthesis of RCH_2COOH from RCOCl. (*b*) Describe two ^{14}C-labeling experiments that would substantiate this mechanism. (*c*) What is the stereochemistry of the product when this reaction is performed with (*R*)-2-methylbutanoyl chloride? (*d*) Prepare (i) Me_3CCH_2COOH (**A**) from Me_3CBr, (ii) $PhCH_2COOEt$ (**B**) from PhCOOH by the method in (*c*).

◢ (*a*) RCOCl from RCOOH is converted to RCH_2COOH via the diazoketone;

α-diazoketone

The diazoketone undergoes the Wolff rearrangement. Ag^+, light, or heat catalyzes the loss of N_2 leaving a carbene that undergoes ∼ :R (alkyl shift) to form an intermediate ketene. The ketene readily adds a nucleophilic solvent molecule, which may be H_2O to give an acid, ROH to give an ester, or RNH_2 to give an amide.

a carbene   a ketene

(*b*) If the C of COCl is labeled, it will be found in the $\diagdown\!C\!=\!O$ of the product. If CH_2N_2 is labeled, the labeled

C is the α C of the acid or its derivatives.   (*c*) The acid product is $(R)\text{-}CH_3CH_2\overset{*}{C}HMeCH_2COOH$. When R migrates, it begins to form a bond to the new site as the bond from the old site is breaking. As a result there is retention of configuration.

(*d*)   (i) $3Me_3CBr \xrightarrow[\text{2. } CO_2]{\text{1. Mg}} Me_3CCOOH \xrightarrow{PCl_5} Me_3CCOCl \xrightarrow{CH_2N_2} Me_3CCOCHN_2 \xrightarrow{Ag_2O/H_2O} \mathbf{A}$

(ii) $PhCOOH \xrightarrow{SOCl_2} PhCOCl \xrightarrow{CH_2N_2} PhCOCHN_2 \xrightarrow[\text{EtOH}]{Ag_2O} \mathbf{B}$

17.124 β-Lactams are found in two important classes of antibiotics, the penicillins and cephalosporins.   (*a*) Draw the structure of β-propiolactam.   (*b*) Account for its unusual reactivity to nucleophiles.   (*c*) Penicillins react with the amino group of a key enzyme involved in the synthesis of the bacterial cell wall protein, thus deactivating it. Show the reaction between β-propiolactam and the enzyme, designated Enz-NH$_2$.

◢   (*a*) 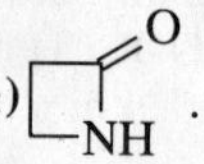 .   (*b*)   Attack by :Nu on C=O induces opening of the four-membered ring, relieving the ring strain.

(*c*)

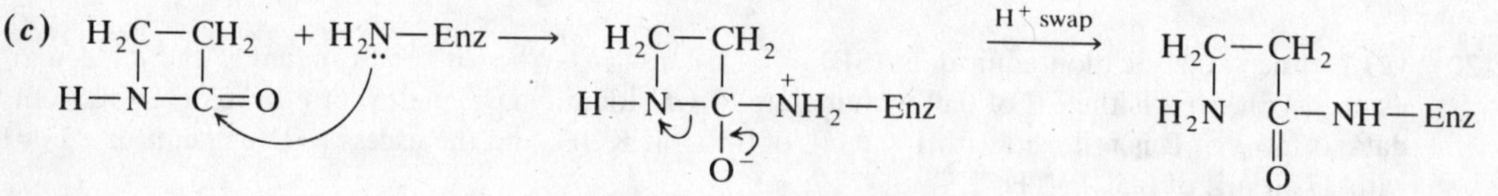

acylated, deactivated enzyme

17.125   The Beckmann rearrangement of an oxime occurs with PCl_5, H_2SO_4, or $ArSO_3H$.   (*a*) Give the products of the reaction of

(i) $Me_2C\!=\!NOH$,   (ii) $\underset{\underset{\displaystyle NOH}{\|}}{Ph\!-\!C\!-\!Me}$,   (iii) $\underset{\underset{\displaystyle HON}{\|}}{Ph\!-\!C\!-\!Me}$,   (iv) 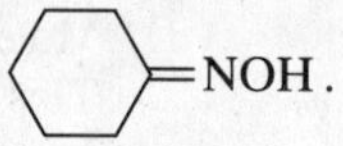 .

(*b*) Suggest a mechanism.

◢   (*a*)   (i) MeCONHMe,   (ii) MeCONHPh,   (iii) PhCONHMe,   (iv)

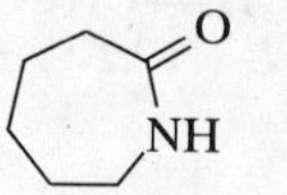

(*b*) PCl_5 or acid converts the OH of the oxime into a better leaving group by forming —Cl, —OH$_2^+$, or —OSO$_2$Ar. An internal S_N2-type reaction follows.

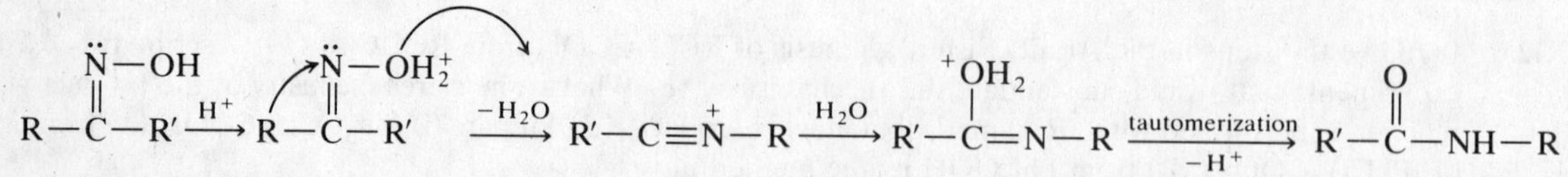

The products of the rearrangement of the *syn* and *anti* oximes in (ii) and (iii) of (*a*) indicate that the group that migrates is *anti* to OH.

17.126   (*a*) The equilibrium for formation of an ester from RCOOH and R'OH is not very favorable. Biologically, addition of *adenosine triphosphate* (ATP), the triphosphate ester of adenosine, makes the esterification process much more favorable thermodynamically. In the process, ATP is converted to *adenosine monophosphate* (AMP) and $H_2P_2O_7^{2-}$. Provide a mechanism.   (*b*) Is ATP acting as a catalyst in this reaction? Explain.

◢   (*a*)   ATP converts RCOOH to a more reactive acyl phosphate intermediate (**B**).

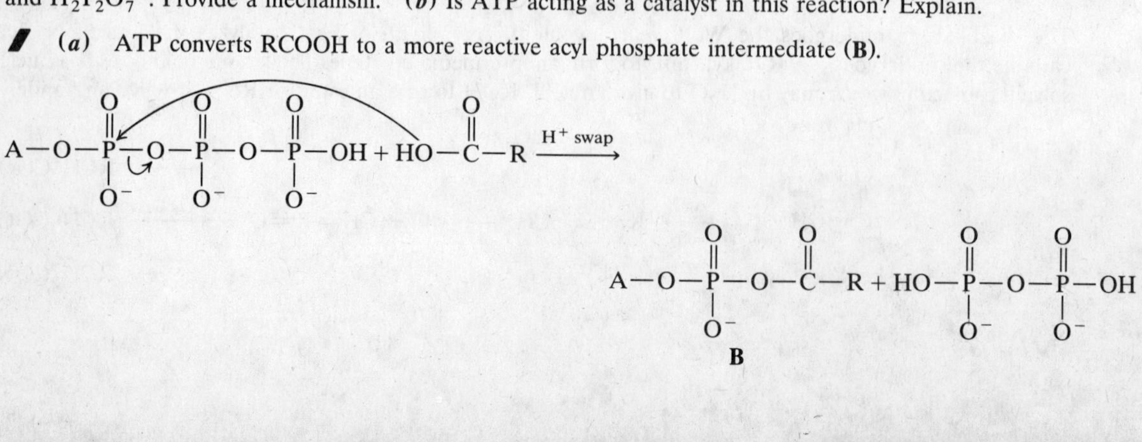

When reacted with an alcohol, a much better leaving group (adenosine monophosphate, AMP) is displaced from **B** than OH from RCOOH itself. The net result is esterification.

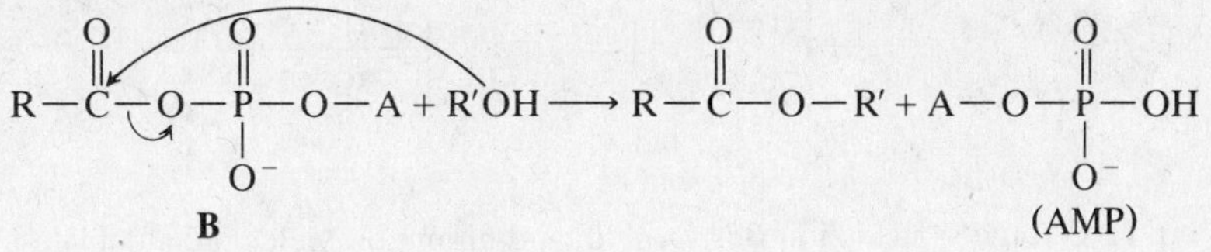

$$R-\overset{\overset{\displaystyle O}{\|}}{C}-O-\overset{\overset{\displaystyle O}{\|}}{\underset{\underset{\displaystyle O^-}{|}}{P}}-O-A + R'OH \longrightarrow R-\overset{\overset{\displaystyle O}{\|}}{C}-O-R' + A-O-\overset{\overset{\displaystyle O}{\|}}{\underset{\underset{\displaystyle O^-}{|}}{P}}-OH$$

$$\qquad\qquad\qquad\quad \mathbf{B} \qquad\qquad\qquad\qquad\qquad\qquad\qquad\qquad (\text{AMP})$$

(*b*) No; one ATP is converted to AMP + diphosphate for each RCOOR′ formed.

17.127 *Diisopropyl fluorophosphate* (DFP), a potent nerve gas, inhibits cholinesterase, an enzyme involved in transmission of nerve impulses. Representing the enzyme by En—CH_2OH, provide a mechanism for the deactivation of the enzyme.

$$En-CH_2OH + (i\text{-PrO})_2\overset{\overset{\displaystyle O}{\|}}{P}-F \overset{*}{\longrightarrow} En-CH_2O-\overset{\overset{\displaystyle O}{\|}}{P}(O\text{-}i\text{-Pr})_2 + F^- + H^+$$
$$\text{deactivated enzyme}$$

*This goes by an addition-elimination mechanism.

17.128 (*a*) Define an ortho ester. Give a general formula. (*b*) Ethyl orthoformate may be prepared by the reaction of chloroform with NaOEt. Give a reasonable mechanism. (*c*) Give the product of mild acid hydrolysis of ethyl orthoformate.

   (*a*) An *ortho ester* has three alkoxy groups attached to the same C; i.e., $RC(OR')_3$.
   (*b*) Dichlorocarbene is formed (Problem 5.61), which then inserts between the H and O of EtOH. The intermediate formed is an α-(di)chloroether, which solvolyzes rapidly via S_N1 in EtOH.

$$CHCl_3 \overset{EtO^-}{\underset{-HCl}{\longrightarrow}} :CCl_2 \overset{EtOH}{\longrightarrow} EtO-CHCl_2 \overset{-Cl^-}{\longrightarrow}$$
$$\alpha,\alpha\text{-dichloroether}$$

$$[EtO-\overset{+}{C}HCl \longleftrightarrow Et\overset{+}{O}=CHCl] \overset{EtOH}{\underset{-H^+}{\longrightarrow}} HC(OEt)_2 \overset{EtOH}{\underset{-HCl}{\longrightarrow}} HC(OEt)_3$$

(with Cl on the central carbon of $HC(OEt)_2$)

   (*c*) HCOOEt, ethyl formate.

17.129 (*a*) Place the acid chlorides PhCOCl (**A**), *p*-$O_2NC_6H_4COCl$ (**B**), and *p*-$CH_3OC_6H_4COCl$ (**C**) in decreasing order of reactivity to hydrolysis and give your reasoning. (*b*) Compare the reactivity of benzoyl chloride with cyclohexanecarbonyl chloride (**D**).

   (*a*) **B** > **A** > **C**. Assuming that the energies of the TS's of the three acyl halides are very similar, any differences in reactivity are attributed to differences in the ground states. In the three ArCOCl's the GS energy is lowered (compared with RCOCl's) because Ar is conjugated with C=O; thus e⁻'s are delocalized from the ring toward the C=O. The GS of **C**, however, is lower than that of the parent aryl compound **A**, because the O of CH_3O delocalizes its e⁻'s to C=O, further enhancing the stabilizing conjugative effect. **C** has the lowest GS, the largest $\Delta H^\ddagger$, and is least reactive. In **B**, e⁻'s are delocalized from the ring towards NO_2, curtailing the stabilizing-delocalizing effect of the ring towards the C=O (see Fig. 17-5). **B** has the highest GS, the smallest $\Delta H^\ddagger$, and is most reactive. (*b*) An alkyl group cannot delocalize e⁻'s towards or away from the C=O; it can affect the reactivity only by the weaker inductive effect. Thus **D** will react faster than **A**.

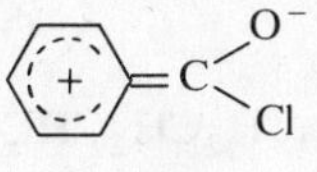

Fig. 17-5

17.130 Dihydropyran (DHP) reacts with RCOOH in $PhSO_2OH$ to give a tetrahydropyranyl ester (**A**). (*a*) Give the structure of **A** and show how it forms. (*b*) **A** is stable in base, but is easily hydrolyzed in dilute H_3O^+. Account for the hydrolysis mechanistically. (*c*) Indicate how DHP can be used to protect COOH groups. (*d*) Show how this reaction may be used to convert *p*-$HOOCC_6H_4CH_2CH=O$ to *p*-$HOOCC_6H_4CH_2COOCH_3$.

▰ (a) Addition of H⁺ to DHP gives the relatively stable cation **B**, which adds RCOOH.

(b) In H_3O^+, the same cation **B** is formed, and ultimately yields the aldehyde-alcohol **E** through hydrolysis of the hemicacetal **D**.

(c) A COOH group is converted to the THP ester to render it unreactive in base. A reaction is carried out on another functional group in the same molecule, after which the COOH group is recovered upon hydrolysis of the pyranyl ester.

(d) Convert the COOH to the THP ester; then oxidize the —CH=O group to COOH with $Ag(NH_3)_2^+$. (Acid oxidation would hydrolyze the pyranyl ester.) Convert COOH to the Me ester with CH_2N_2; then hydrolyze the pyranyl ester with dil. H_3O^+. The carboxylic ester hydrolyzes much slower under these conditions.

17.131 A pleasantly smelling optically active compound **F** has an SE = 186. It does not react with Br_2 in CCl_4. Hydrolysis of **F** gives two optically active compounds, **G**, which is soluble in NaOH, and **H**. **H** gives a positive iodoform test, and on warming with conc. H_2SO_4 gives **I** with no diastereomers. When the Ag⁺ salt of **G** is reacted with Br_2, racemic **J** is formed. Optically active **J** is formed when **H** is treated with tosyl chloride (TsCl) and then NaBr. The ir spectrum of **F** shows a single C=O stretching peak. Give structures of **F** through **J** and explain your choices.

▰ **F** is a saturated monoester with MW = 186 (no Br_2 reaction). We can logically determine the number of C's and the molecular formula by subtracting the mass of the two O's and dividing the remainder by 14, the mass of CH_2: (186 − 32)/14 = 11. To complete the mass there must be 22 H's. The molecular formula is $C_{11}H_{22}O_2$. The acid **G** has one more **C** than the alcohol **H** because it is degraded by one C in the Hunsdiecker reaction ($RCOO^-Ag^+ + Br_2$) to **J** which is also made from **H** with no change in C content. **H** is a methyl carbinol, $CH_3CH(OH)R$, because it gives a positive iodoform reaction and in order to be chiral must have at least four C's. However, **H** has five C's because the alkene, **I**, obtained on dehydration (warm conc. H_2SO_4), must have two Me's on one of the doubly-bonded C's to avoid cis-trans isomerism. **I** is $CH_3CH=C(CH_3)_2$ with five C's and **G** had six C's. **H** is $CH_3CHOHCH(CH_3)_2$ and is converted to **J**, $CH_3CHBrCH(CH_3)_2$, through the tosylate,

$$\underset{\underset{OTs}{|}}{CH_3CHCH(CH_3)_2},$$

with no change in configuration, by an S_N2 reaction with Br⁻. Consequently, **H** and **J** have inverted configurations. The skeleton of the alkyl group of **G** is the same as **H**. Replacing Br of **J** by COOH gives the structure of **G**, $(CH_3)_2CHCH(CH_3)COOH$. **F** is one of the four possible enantiomers of

$$\underset{\underset{CH_3}{|}}{(CH_3)_2CH\overset{*}{C}H}\overset{\overset{O}{\|}}{C}-O\underset{\underset{CH_3}{|}}{\overset{*}{C}HCH(CH_3)_2}.$$

17.132 How do the structures of **F** through **J** in Problem 17.131 change if (a) **I** exists as diastereomers and (b) **H** gives a negative iodoform test?

▰ (a) **I** is cis or trans $CH_3CH=CHCH_2CH_3$, **H** is $CH_3CHOHCH_2CH_2CH_3$ (3-pentanol would give **I** but it is achiral), **J** is $CH_3CHBrCH_2CH_2CH_3$, **G** is $CH_3CH_2CH_2CH(CH_3)COOH$ and **F** is

$$\underset{\underset{CH_3}{|}}{CH_3CH_2CH_2\overset{*}{C}H}\overset{\overset{O}{\|}}{C}O\underset{\underset{CH_3}{|}}{\overset{*}{C}HCH_2CH_2CH_3}.$$

(b) Since **H** is chiral and gives a negative iodoform test, it is $HOCH_2CH(CH_3)CH_2CH_3$. **I** is $H_2C=C(CH_3)CH_2CH_3$, **J** is $BrCH_2CH(CH_3)CH_2CH_3$, **G** is $HOOCCH_2CH(CH_3)CH_2CH_3$ and **F** is

$$\underset{\underset{CH_3}{|}}{CH_3CH_2CHCH_2}\overset{\overset{O}{\|}}{C}O\underset{\underset{CH_3}{|}}{CH_2CHCH_2CH_3}.$$

17.133 List all the stereoisomeric diesters formed by esterification of each stereoisomer of tartaric acid with *rac s*-BuOH. Simply indicate the different stereoisomers using *R* and *S* for the tartaric acid moiety and *R* and *S* for the alcohol portions but first give the Fischer formula for the *R*, *R*, *R*, *S* stereoisomer. Designate the racemates and *meso* forms.

◢ From *rac*-tartaric acid:

(1)

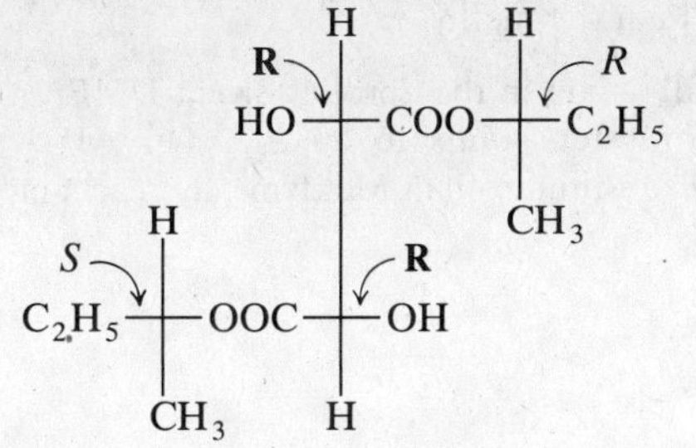

RR, RS and its enantiomer SS, SR (rac_1)
RS, RR is the same as RR, RS

(2) **RS**, **RS** and its enantiomer **SR**, **SR** (rac_2), (3) **RR**, **RR** and its enantiomer **SS**, **SS** (rac_3) From (**R**,**S**)-*meso*-tartaric acid:
(4) **RR**, **SR** and its enantiomer **SS**, **RS** (rac_4),
(5) **RS**, **SR** ($meso_1$), (6) **RR**, **SS** ($meso_2$).

17.134 (*a*) Synthesize saccharin from toluene. (*b*) Why can saccharin be sold as its Na^+ salt?

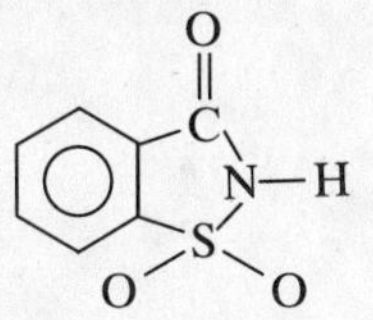

Saccharin

◢ (*a*) $PhCH_3 \xrightarrow{H_2SO_4} p\text{-} + o\text{-}H_3CC_6H_4SO_3H \xrightarrow{PCl_5} p\text{-} + o\text{-}H_3CC_6H_4SO_2Cl$

The *p*-isomer is removed by freezing, and the liquid *o*-isomer reacted further:

$o\text{-}H_3CC_6H_4SO_2Cl \xrightarrow{NH_3} o\text{-}H_3CC_6H_4SO_2NH_2 \xrightarrow{KMnO_4} [o\text{-}HOOCC_6H_4SO_2NH_2]$

which rapidly cyclizes, losing H_2O to give saccharin. (*b*) The imino group ⟩N—H̲ is acidic because the − on its conjugate base is delocalized to the ⟩C=O and ⟩SO₂ groups.

17.135 Pyrolysis of *erythro*-1-acetoxy-2-deutero-1,2-diphenylethane (**A**) gives *trans*-stilbene that retains 95% of its original deuterium, while reaction of the *three*-isomer (**B**) gives *trans*-stilbene containing only 26% D. Explain.

◢ The reaction requires a *syn* elimination of H(D) and OCOMe. The more favorable TS leading to the alkene cannot have eclipsing bulky Ph groups. This is called the *cis* or *eclipsing* effect.

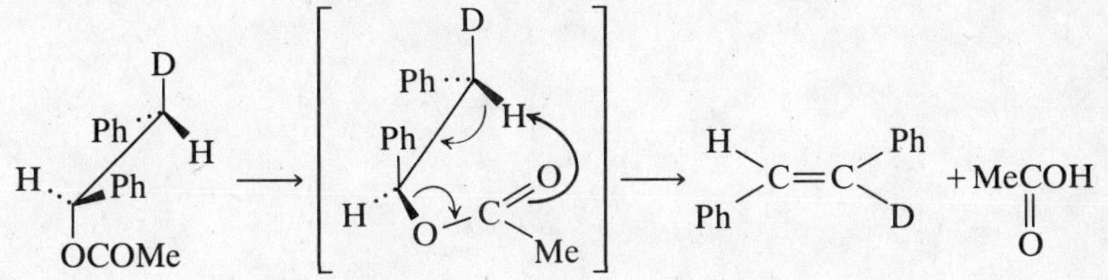

erythro-isomer (**A**)
(racemate)

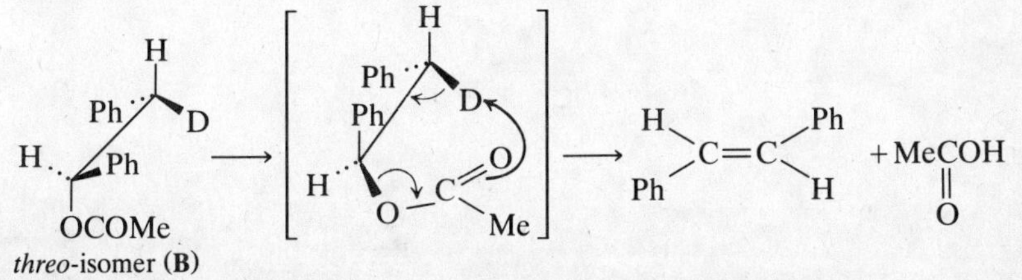

threo-isomer (**B**)
(racemate)

The *threo* product retains more than 5% D because of the isotope effect (Problem 8.112).

17.136 Cleavage of methyl cycloclohexanecarboxylate (Cy—COOMe) in LiI occurs as follows:

$$\text{Cy}-\overset{\overset{\displaystyle O}{\|}}{\text{C}}-\text{OMe} \xrightarrow{\text{LiI}} \text{Cy}-\overset{\overset{\displaystyle O}{\|}}{\text{C}}-\text{O}^-\text{Li}^+ + \text{MeI}$$

Supply a mechanism that accounts for the following: (*1*) the reaction is much faster in DMF than in EtOH; (*2*) the ethyl ester reacts about ten times slower than the methyl ester.

◢ I⁻ becomes a highly nucleophilic "naked" anion in the aprotic solvent DMF. In EtOH, it is H-bonded and less nucleophilic. The slower rate of the Et ester points to an S_N2 O-alkyl cleavage where I⁻ displaces Cy—COO⁻ from Me. Et, being more highly substituted than Me, typically reacts more slowly.

CHAPTER 18
Carbanion-Enolates and Enols

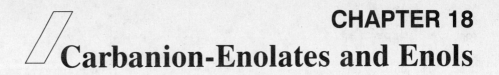

TAUTOMERISM; ACIDITY OF α H'S

18.1 Give the product and identify the type of reaction of optically active $CH_3CH_2CH(CH_3)CHO$ with (*a*) aq. NaOH, (*b*) X_2 such as Br_2 in aq. NaOH, and (*c*) NaOD in D_2O.

(*a*) *rac*-$CH_3CH_2CH(CH_3)CHO$, racemization; (*b*) $CH_3CH_2CBr(CH_3)CHO$, halogenation; (*c*) $CH_3CH_2CD(CH_3)CHO$, deuterium-exchange. The products in (*b*) and (*c*) are also racemic.

18.2 (*a*) What salient feature of the mechanisms in Problem 18.1 is indicated by the fact that all three reactions take place on the α C, and have the same rate which is directly proportional to the concentration of OH^-? (*b*) Predict the rate expression.

(*a*) Each reaction has the same rate-controlling step involving OH^- that leads to a common intermediate involving the α C, the reactive site. (*b*) Rate = k[aldehyde] [OH^-].

18.3 (*a*) What is the common intermediate in these reactions? (*b*) Account for its relative ease of formation. (*c*) Classify this anion. (*d*) Which atom bears more of the negative charge?

(*a*) It is the *carbanion-enolate anion* (**A**) formed when OH^- removes H^+ from the α-C.

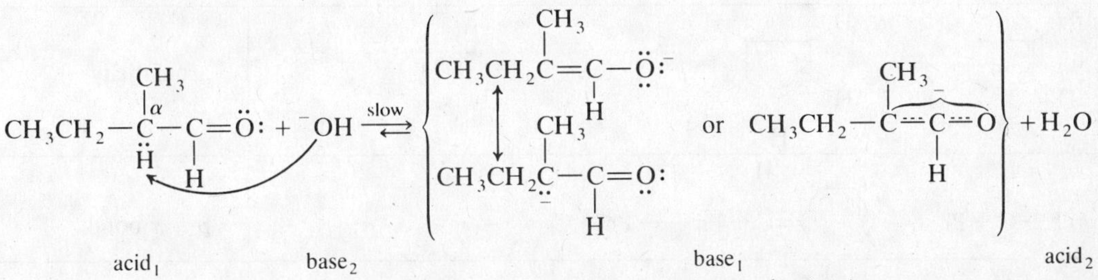

slow
acid₁
base₂
base₁
acid₂

stable carbanion-enolate ion **A**

(*b*) The α H is much more acidic than one typically bonded to C using sp^3 HO's because the negative charge is delocalized by extended π bonding to the more electronegative O atom. (*c*) It is an ambident ion since it has charge on two different atoms, C and O. (*d*) The more electronegative O bears more of the charge. We could say that the enolate resonance structure makes more contribution to the resonance hybrid than does the carbanion structure.

18.4 Draw an orbital picture of a carbanion-enolate ion.

See Fig. 18-1.

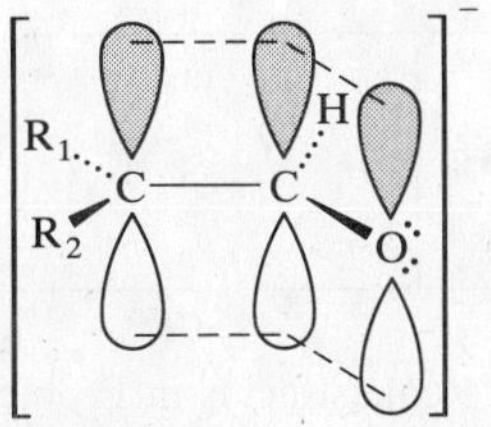

Fig. 18-1

18.5 Discuss the formation of the products of Problem 18.1 from the carbanion-enolate ion.

The α C of **A** (Problem 18.3) has considerable double bond character, causing it to lose its chirality. **A** has enantiotopic faces (Problem 6.81), and attachment of H^+ to one or the other face, that occurs with equal ease, affords a racemic mixture. **A** can react with Br_2 (X_2) or D_2O to give the product with Br(X) or D respectively on the α C.

18.6 The following compounds do not have C=O groups, yet have H's with enhanced acidity bonded to carbon. Show the carbanions (conjugate bases) and give a reason for their stability. (*a*) CH_3NO_2, (*b*) CH_3CN, (*c*) $HCCl_3$, (*d*) $CH_3C{\equiv}CH$, (*e*) cyclopentadiene, (*f*) Ph_2CH_2, (*g*) 2,4-dinitrotoluene, (*h*) $RSCH_2SR$, (*i*) Me_3S^+, (*j*) Ph_3PMe^+ (*k*) $CH_3SO_2CH_3$ (dimethyl sulfone).

◢ See Table 18-1.

TABLE 18-1

	Stable Carbanions	Reason for Stability
(*a*)	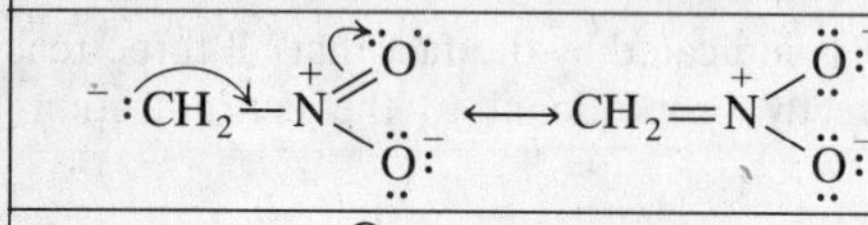	*p-p* π bond
(*b*)		*p-p* π bond
(*c*)	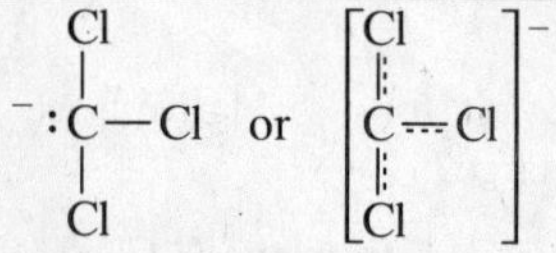	*p-d* π bond
(*d*)	$CH_3C{\equiv}C:^-$	*sp* hybrid
(*e*)	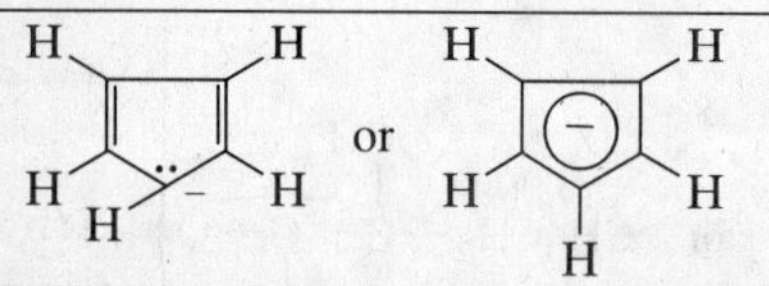	aromaticity
(*f*)	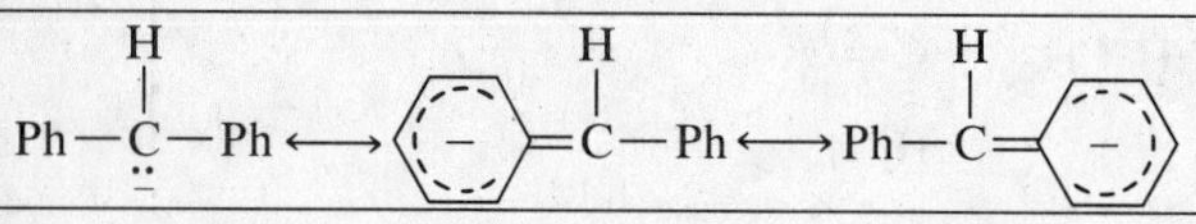	*p-p* π bond
(*g*)	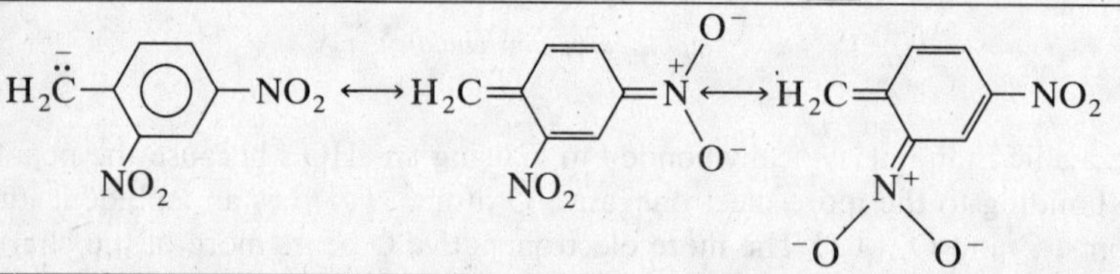	*p-p* π bond
(*h*)	$RS-\ddot{C}H-SR$ or $(RS{=}CH{=}SR]^-$	*p-d* π bond
(*i*)	$Me_2\overset{+}{S}-\ddot{C}H_2$ or $Me_2S{=}CH_2$	Electrostatic attraction and *p-d* bond
(*j*)	$Ph_3\overset{+}{P}-\ddot{C}H_2$ or $Ph_3P{=}CH_2$	Electrostatic attraction and *p-d* π bond
(*k*)	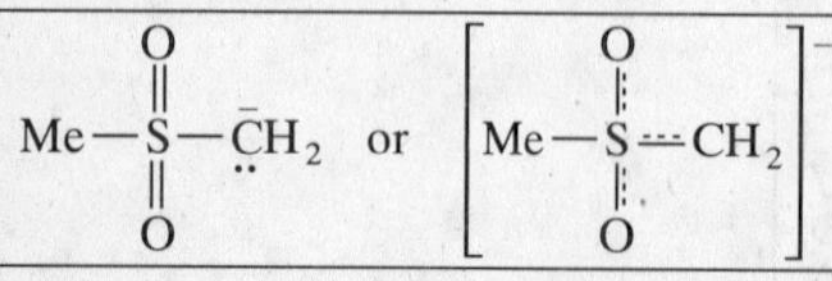	Electrostatic attraction and *p-d* π bond

18.7 Select (*a*) the strongest and (*b*) the two weakest acids in Problem 18.6 and justify your choices.

◢ (*a*) CH_3NO_2. The more electronegative the atom, in this case O, to which the − charge is delocalized, the more stable is the base and the more acidic is the parent. The − charge in (*g*) is also dispersed to O but the delocalization is less effective because some aromaticity of the benzene ring is lost. (*b*) $CH_3C{\equiv}CH$ and Ph_2CH_2 because the − charge is only on very weakly electronegative C's. The anion of cyclopentadiene (*e*) also has a − charge on C, but its attainment of aromaticity is a good stabilizing effect.

18.8 (*a*) Account for the fact that nitroform, $HC(NO_2)_3$ (trinitromethane), and cyanoform, $HC(CN)_3$ (tricyanomethane), are both strong acids ($K_a > 1$) but chloroform is a very weak acid. (*b*) Why is $CH_3SO_2CH_3$ ($pK_a \cong 31$) much less acidic than CH_3NO_2 ($pK_a \cong 10$)?

◢ (a) The conjugate bases of $HC(NO_2)_3$ and $HC(CN)_3$ are extremely weak (stable) because their negative charges are delocalized by extended p-p π-bonding to electronegative atoms in each of three groups. Hence the acids are strong. Typically, p-d π delocalization, as in $Cl_3C:^-$, is far less significant than p-p π bonding. The overlap is less effective because of the longer bond length and difference in size of the $2p$ and $3d$ orbitals. (b) p-d π bonding in $^-:CH_2SO_2CH_3$ is less effective for the same reason.

18.9 Compare the acidities of the $CH_3\overset{+}{N}-O^-$ (**A**), $CH_3\overset{\overset{O}{\|}}{C}-H$ (**B**), and $CH_3\overset{\overset{O}{\|}}{C}-OR$ (**C**), and justify your choice.

◢ **A > B > C.** The − charge of each conjugate base is delocalized to the more electronegative O. The delocalization in the anion of **A** is most extensive because two O's participate and additional stabilization arises from the strong inductive effect of N because of its formal + charge. In the anion of **C**, cross-conjugation with the O of OR competes with delocalization of the − charge to O (see Fig. 18-2), thereby attenuating the delocalization from C and making the anion a stronger base than the one from **B**.

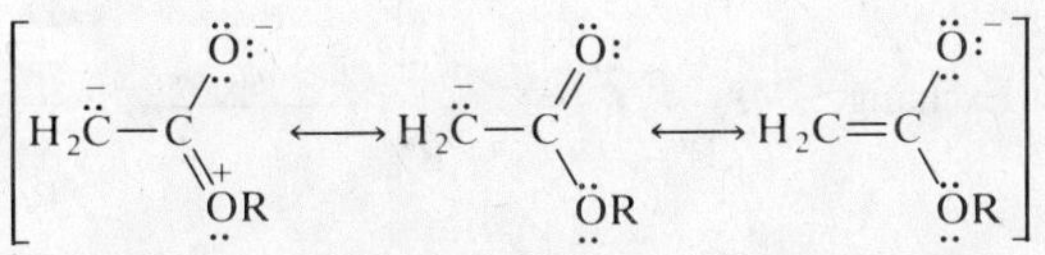

cross-conjugated resonance
structures

Fig. 18-2

18.10 (a) Write the structure of another product that can be formed when H^+ from H_2O adds to a carbanion-enolate anion. (b) What are the names given to the isomeric products and to the equilibrium in (a)?

keto form   carbanion-enolate anion   enol form

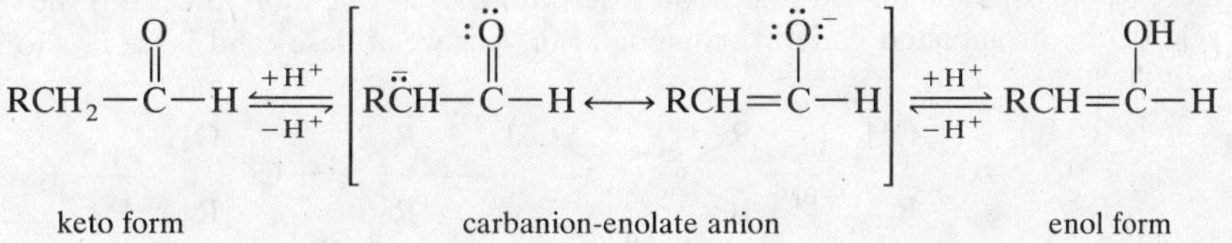

(b) The keto and enol isomers are called *tautomers* and the equilibrium is called *tautomerism*.

18.11 (a) Why is the keto tautomer so much more stable than the enol tautomer? (b) Is there any inconsistency in the fact that the keto tautomer is the major product although the O in the anion bears more of the − charge?

◢ (a) The resonance energy of the carbonyl group $\left[\rangle C=\ddot{O}: \longleftrightarrow \rangle\overset{+}{C}-\ddot{O}:^- \right]$ is greater than that of the

enol $\left[\rangle C=\overset{..}{C}-\overset{..}{O}-H \longleftrightarrow \rangle\overset{..}{C}-\overset{..}{C}=\overset{+}{O}-H \right]$. Furthermore, in general, H's attached to heteroatoms, as in

the enol form, are more acidic than C—H's, as in the keto form. Equilibrium always favors the side with the weaker acid, in this case the keto form. (b) No. The less electronegative C is the more reactive site because it can less readily bear even the small amount of − charge. Furthermore, the site with more of the − charge is more attracted to the cation present (counter cation) and loses reactivity.

18.12 Tautomerism also occurs in aqueous acid. Show the mechanism.

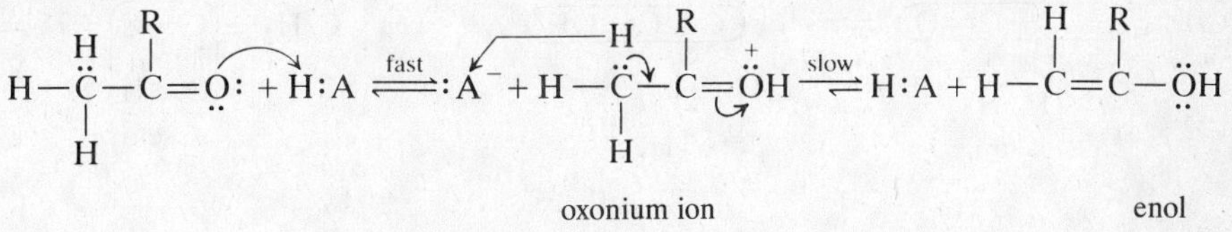

oxonium ion   enol

18.13 The three reactions in Problem 18.1 are also acid-catalyzed. (a) Referring to Problem 18.12, suggest mechanisms. (b) Would you expect the rate expression to be the same for the three reactions? Give the rate expression. (c) Why do enols not add X_2, such as Br_2, as do alkenes?

(a) The common intermediate is the enol (Problem 18.12).

Racemization:

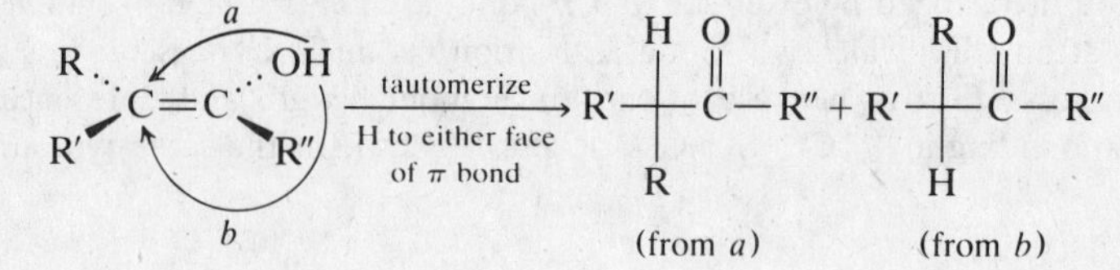

Bromination:

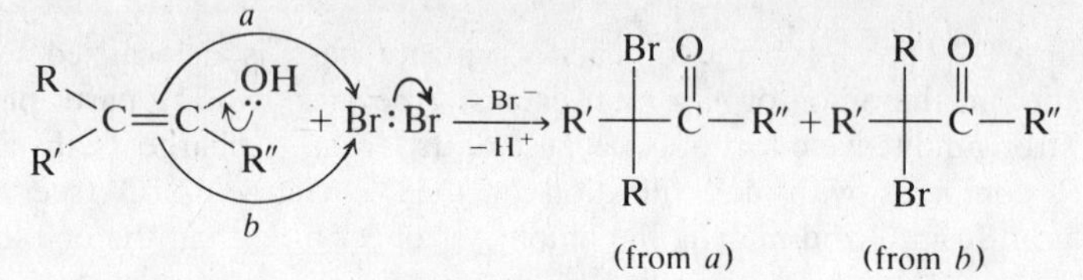

Deuterium Exchange:

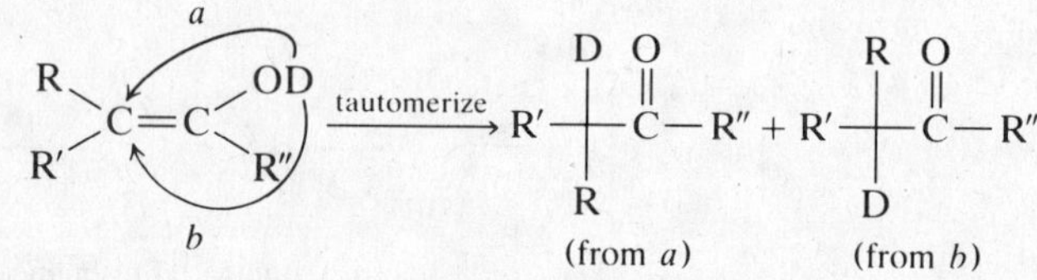

The source of D that bonds to C is more likely the solvent D_2O than OD^-.

(b) Since enol formation is rate-determining, these three reactions have the same rate expression, rate = k[carbonyl compound] [H^+].

(c) The intermediate in the reaction of C=C with Br_2 is the bromonium ion **A** which collapses to the more stable oxonium ion **B** rather than react with Br^- to give dibromide. **B** is the very strong conjugate acid of the brominated carbonyl compound (a very weak base) and loses H^+ to give the product **C**.

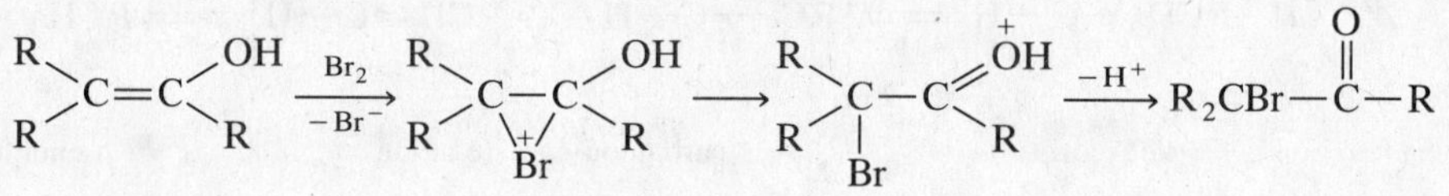

18.14 What is the essential structural unit needed for tautomerism?

X=Y–Z–H, where X is an electronegative heteroatom such as O and N. A triple bond could replace the double bond.

18.15 Show structures for the tautomer of each of the following compounds: (a) CH_3CHO, (b) $C_6H_5COCH_3$, (c) CH_3NO_2, (d) $Me_2C=NOH$, and (e) $CH_3CH=NCH_3$.

The structural unit needed for tautomerism is encircled in each case.

(a) keto ⇌ enol

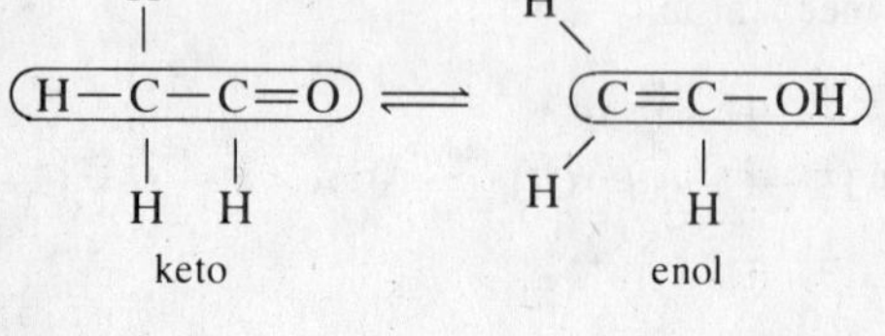

(b) keto ⇌ enol

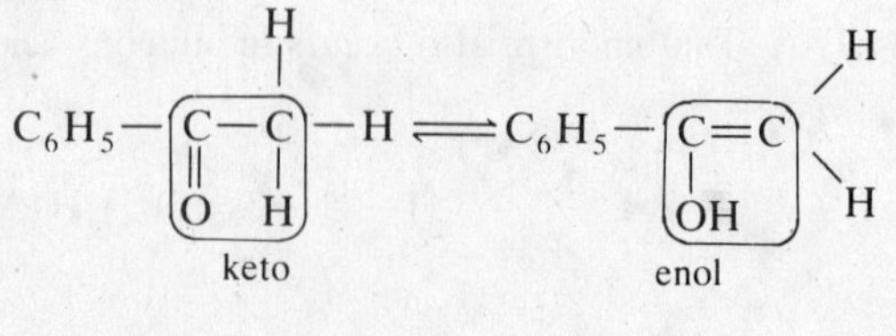

(c) nitro form ⇌ aci form

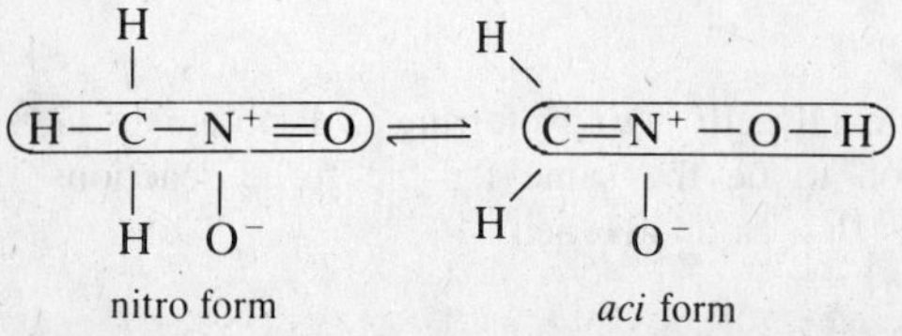

(d) oxime ⇌ nitroso

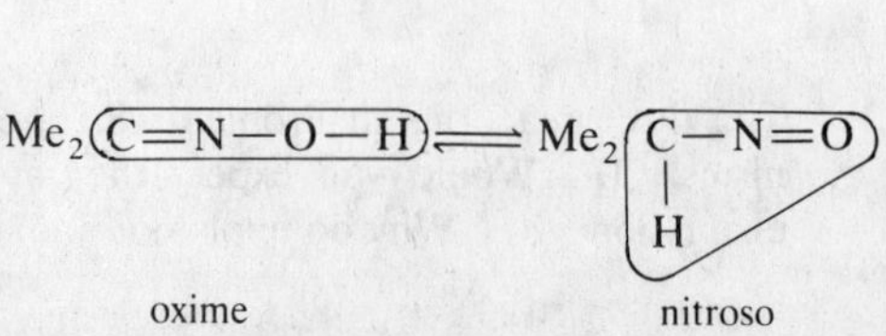

$$(e) \quad \boxed{\underset{\underset{\text{H}}{|}}{\overset{\overset{\text{H}}{|}}{\text{H}-\text{C}-\text{C}}}=\underset{\underset{\text{CH}_3}{|}}{\text{N}} \quad \rightleftharpoons \quad \boxed{\underset{\underset{\text{H}}{|}}{\text{C}}=\underset{\underset{\text{CH}_3}{|}}{\overset{\overset{\text{H}}{|}}{\text{C}}-\text{N}-\text{H}}}$$

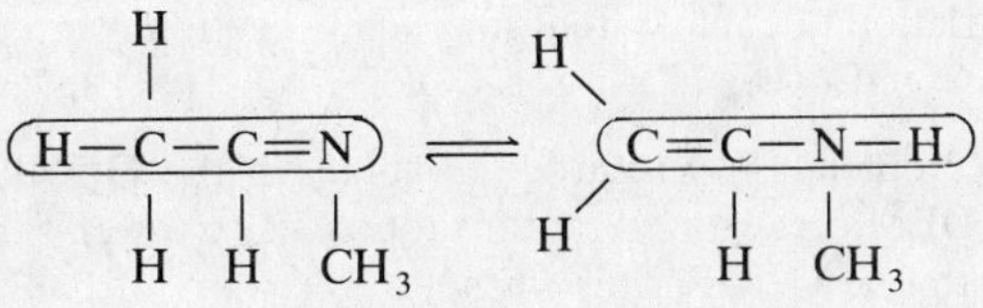

imine   enamine

18.16 Which two enols are in equilibrium with (**a**) 2-butanone, (**b**) 1-phenyl-2-butanone, (**c**) p-O$_2$NC$_6$H$_4$CH$_2$-COCH$_2$Ph, and (**d**) bicyclo[4.1.0]-2-heptanone? Which is more stable? Why?

▮ In each case, the first written enol is more stable.

(**a**) $\underset{\underset{\text{OH}}{|}}{\text{CH}_3-\text{C}}=\text{CHCH}_3$ and $\underset{\underset{\text{OH}}{|}}{\text{H}_2\text{C}=\text{CCH}_2\text{CH}_3}$. The first enol has the more substituted double bond.

(**b**) $\underset{\underset{\text{OH}}{|}}{\text{PhCH}=\text{CCH}_2\text{CH}_3}$ and $\underset{\underset{\text{OH}}{|}}{\text{PhCH}_2\text{C}=\text{CHCH}_3}$. C=C and Ph are conjugated.

(**c**) $\underset{\underset{\text{OH}}{|}}{\text{p-O}_2\text{NC}_6\text{H}_4\text{CH}=\text{CCH}_2\text{Ph}}$ and $\underset{\underset{\text{OH}}{|}}{\text{p-O}_2\text{NC}_6\text{H}_4\text{CH}_2\text{C}=\text{CHPh}}$. The p-O$_2$N extends the delocalization of the conjugated system.

(**d**) and 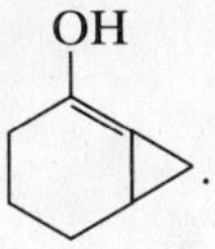 . The exocyclic C=C increases the strain in the cyclopropyl ring.

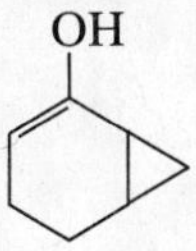

18.17 C$_6$H$_5$OH, an enol, is much more stable than its keto isomer. Show the keto form and explain this exception.

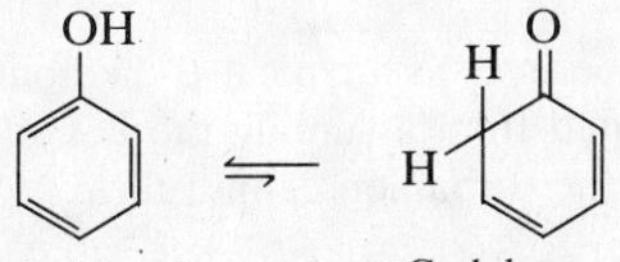

▮

Phenol (enol)   Cyclohexa-
2,4-dienone (keto)

Phenol has a stable aromatic ring.

18.18 (**a**) Write structures for the stable keto and enol tautomers of 2,4-pentanedione (**A**), a typical dicarbonyl compound. (**b**) Why are such enols of β-dicarbonyl compounds more stable than those of monocarbonyl compounds? (**c**) Account for the fact that the enol content of **A** is 15% in H$_2$O and 92% in hexane. (**d**) How can the enol be chemically detected and separated?

▮ (**a**)

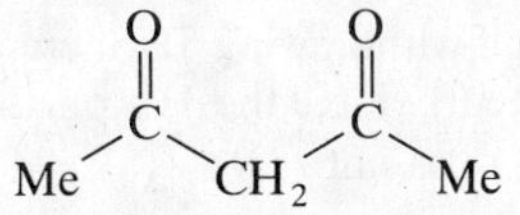

keto form 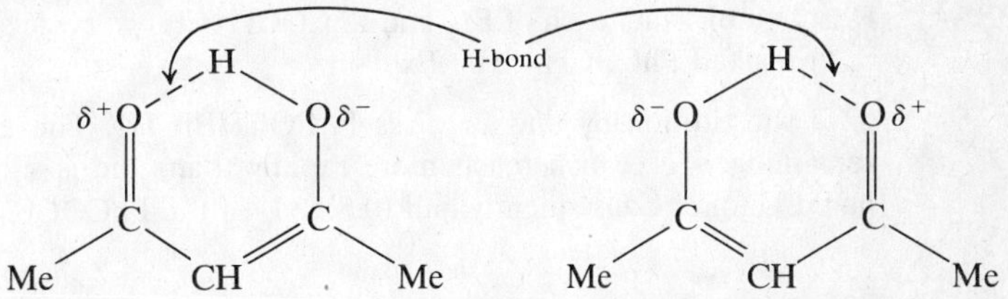   enol form

(**b**) This enol is more stable because it has a conjugated (C=C—C=O) π system and intramolecular H-bonding (chelation). (**c**) Water forms H-bonds with the C=O's, thereby inhibiting the intramolecular H-bonding that helps stabilize the enol. (**d**) The enol decolorizes a solution of Br$_2$ in CCl$_4$. The more volatile enol tautomer is separated by careful distillation of the mixture in a fused quartz apparatus (eliminates base from glass).

18.19 Discuss the application of pmr spectroscopy for determining the ratio of enol:keto tautomers.

▮ The relative intensities of the isolated signals characteristic of an exclusive H for the enol (the vinylic H) and of the keto form (the α H) are measured. The enolic H signal, like all acidic H signals, appears far downfield ($\delta = 15$–20 ppm). The ratio of the intensities is also the ratio of the tautomers. If there are two α C's, the intensity of their signal is halved to make the comparison of intensities on a per-H basis.

18.20 Account for the given variation in enol content for each of the following β-dicarbonyl compounds: $(EtOCO)_2CH_2$ (**A**), $< 1\%$; CH_3COCH_2COOEt (**B**), 7.7%; $CH_3COCH_2COCH_3$ (**C**), 76%; and $PhCOCH_2COCH_3$ (**D**), 89%.

◢ Cross-conjugation (Problem 18.9) retards the ability of the $C{=}O$ of the ester group to help stabilize the enol. Diethyl malonate (DEM), **A**, with two ester groups, has a lower enol content than acetoacetic ester (AAE), ethyl acetoacetate, **B**, with one COOR which has a lower content than the diketone **C**. The Ph group stabilizes the enol by extending the conjugation for π-bond delocalization as shown:

$$\underset{\substack{| \\ OH}}{Ph-C}=CH-\underset{\substack{\| \\ O}}{C}-CH_3$$

Note that extended conjugation is achieved by preserving the $CH_3-\underset{\substack{| \\ }}{C}{=}O$ group.

18.21 Account for the pmr spectrum of $PhCH_2COCH_3$ that shows four main types of signals roughly in the ratio of $1:5:1:3$ in decreasing order of chemical shift.

◢ The keto form has only three types of H's while the enol has four types (Problem 18.20). In the solvent used for pmr spectroscopy the enol is the almost exclusive tautomer.

18.22 Account for the fact that 1,3-cyclohexanedione readily undergoes base- or acid-catalyzed deuterium-exchange whereas 2,6-bicyclo[2.2.2]octanedione does not.

2,6-Bicyclo[2.2.2]octanedione

◢ 1,3-Cyclohexanedione behaves as a typical β-diketone. The α C of the bicyclic compound is at a bridgehead where it is sterically prevented from assuming the flat geometry needed for extended π delocalization (Bredt's rule). Without stabilization the carbanion cannot form.

18.23 Explain why the enol content of biacetyl, MeCOCOMe, is (**a**) somewhat higher than that of butanone and (**b**) much less than that of 1,2-cyclohexanedione.

◢ Adjacent $C{=}O$'s are destabilizing because of the δ^-'s on the O's of $C{=}O$. (**a**) MeCOCOMe relieves much of this electrostatic repulsion by acquiring the conformation with *anti* $O^{\delta-}$'s. Some repulsion is further relieved in the enol but the enol content is still small because this relief is associated with a loss of $C{=}O$ resonance energy. (**b**) The cyclohexane ring is rigid and the $O^{\delta-}$'s must be *syn*. The only way to avoid the repulsion is for one of the $C{=}O$'s to completely enolize.

18.24 Reaction of 1 mol each of Br_2 and $PhCOCH_2CH_3$ in basic solution yields 0.5 mol of $PhCOCBr_2CH_3$ and 0.5 mol of unreacted $PhCOCH_2CH_3$. Explain.

◢ Substitution by one Br gives $PhCOCHBrCH_3$. The electron-withdrawing Br increases the acidity of the remaining α H, which reacts more rapidly than, and is substituted before, the H's on the remaining unbrominated ketone. Consequently half (0.5 mol) of the $PhCOCH_2CH_3$ does not react.

$$\underset{(0.5\ mol)}{PhCO\overset{\frown}{C}H_2CH_3} \xrightarrow[OH^-]{0.5\ mol\ Br_2} \underset{\substack{(0.5\ mol) \\ not\ isolated}}{[PhCO\overset{\frown}{C}HBrCH_3]} \xrightarrow[OH^-]{0.5\ mol\ Br_2} \underset{(0.5\ mol)}{PhCOCBr_2CH_3}$$

less acidic ⌢   more acidic ⌢

18.25 Describe the steps in the formation of HCI_3 from the haloform reaction of $PhCOCH_3$ with NaOH and I_2 (NaOI).

◢ A three step α-C halogenation, proceeding through carbanion-enolate intermediates, results in the intermediate $PhCOCI_3$.

$$\underset{\substack{\| \\ O}}{Ph\overset{}{C}}-CH_3 \xrightarrow[NaOH]{I_2} \underset{\substack{\| \\ O}}{Ph\overset{}{C}}-CI_3$$

Then, OH^- adds to the carbonyl group, and $I_3C:^-$ is eliminated because this anion is stabilized by electron-withdrawal by the three I's. Finally, H^+-exchange occurs.

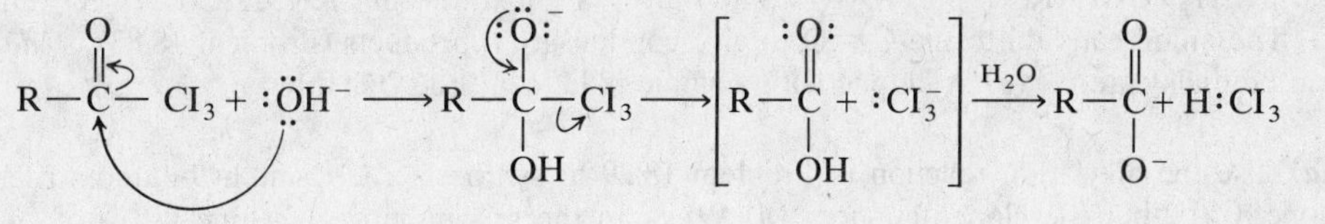

18.26 Account for the given relative rates on a per-H basis of base-catalyzed D-exchange for the **H**'s of the following compounds: $MeCOCH_3$ (**A**), 100%; $MeCOCH_2Me$ (**B**), 42%; $MeCOCH_2CMe_3$ (**C**), 0.45%; $CH_3COCH_2CMe_3$ (**D**), 5.1%; $MeCOCHMe_2$ (**E**), < 0.1%. Assume that all other α H's in these compounds are already replaced by deuterium.

◢ Both inductive and steric effects contribute to this ordering. R's are electron-repelling and destabilize the C^- to which they are bonded. The order of reactivity is 1°**A** > 2°**B** > 3°**E**. Steric hindrance retards the approach of the base and solvation of the developing negative charge. This effect accounts for the diminished rates of **C**, inhibited by the adjacent t-butyl, and **D**, inhibited by the neopentyl group on the other side of C=O. Rate retardation is more dramatic when the bulky group is attached directly to C^- as in **C**.

18.27 Should cyclobutenone (**F**) or triketocyclobutane (**G**) be more easily enolized?

◢ Hypothetical enol of **F**: 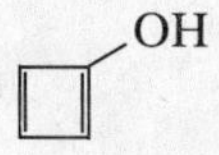   Enol of **G**:

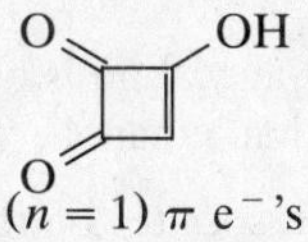

F doesn't enolize because its enol is a flat ring with $4n$ ($n = 1$) π e^-'s and is antiaromatic. **G** enolizes because its enol has $4n + 2$ ($n = 0$) π e^-'s and is stabilized by its aromaticity.

18.28 Explain the fact that cis-5-t-butyl-2-methylcyclohexanone in base is isomerized to the $trans$-isomer.

◢ The $trans$ diastereomer with (e,e) alkyl groups has a lower energy than the cis isomer whose Me is axial. Inversion of Me occurs through the intermediate carbanion-enolate involving the C to which it is attached.

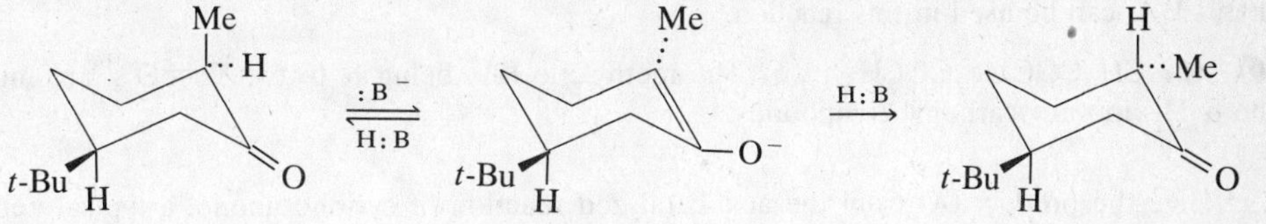

ALKYLATION

18.29 Give formulas for **A** through **D** in the following reactions.

$$RCH_2 - \overset{|}{C} = O + (i\text{-Pr})_2N^-Li^+ \longrightarrow A + B \qquad A + R'X \longrightarrow C + D$$

Lithium diisopropylamide, LDA

◢ **A** is the carbanion-enolate; $\left[R\overset{..}{\overset{-}{C}}H - \overset{|}{C} = \overset{..}{O}: \longleftrightarrow RCH = \overset{|}{C} - \overset{..}{\overset{..}{O}}:^- \right]$; **B** is $(i\text{-Pr})_2NH$; **C** is the C-alkylated product, $RCHR'\overset{|}{C} = O$; **D** is the O-alkylated product, an enol ether, $RCH = \overset{|}{C} - OR'$.

18.30 (*a*) Why is LDA rather than NaOEt used as the base in Problem 18.29? (*b*) Give the type of reaction with R'X and the limitations on the kind of R'X that can be used. (*c*) Why is this type of alkylation unsuitable for (i) unsymmetrical ketones and (ii) aldehydes? (*d*) Give another drawback of this type of synthesis. (*e*) What type of compound is best suited for monoalkylation?

◢ (*a*) LDA is a bulky base capable of abstracting H^+ but incapable of displacing X^- from R'X and thereby nullifying the alkylation. NaOEt would react with R'X. (*b*) S_N2. Only 1° R'X can be used—the others undergo elimination because the anion is a strong base. (*c*) (i) If the ketone has two different α C's, each with an H, in most cases two products can form in good yield:

$$RCH_2COCH_2R' \text{ with } R''X \text{ would give a mixture of } RR''CHCOCH_2R' \text{ and } RCH_2COCHR'R''.$$

(ii) The anion can add to the C=O to give condensation products (Problem 18.83). (*d*) An α C with two H's can be dialkylated. (*e*) A ketone with a single α H, e.g., PhCOCHMe$_2$.

18.31 (*a*) Use the alkylation reaction in Problem 18.29 to synthesize: (i) 2-methylbutanonitrile, (ii) 3-phenyl-2-pentanone, (iii) 2-benzylcyclopentanone. (*b*) Why can the unsymmetrical ketone in (ii) of (*a*) be alkylated in good yield?

(*a*) (i) $CH_3CH_2CH_2C\equiv N \xrightarrow[\text{2. MeI}]{\text{1. LDA}} CH_3CH_2CHMeC\equiv N$

(ii) $CH_3COCH_2Ph \xrightarrow[\text{2. EtBr}]{\text{1. LDA}} CH_3COCHPhEt$

(iii)

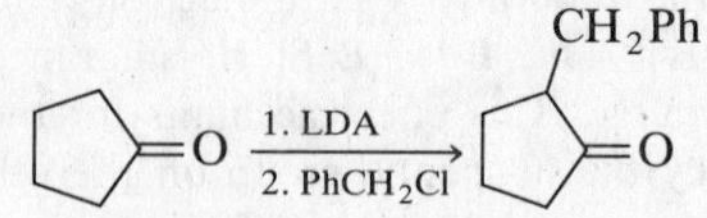

(*b*) The carbanion that is alkylated is stabilized by both the adjacent $>C=O$ and Ph, and is therefore more easily formed and reacted.

18.32 Account for the fact that more O-alkylation is observed when (*a*) the counter cation is K$^+$ rather than Li$^+$ and (*b*) the solvent is DMSO rather than ethanol.

(*a*) Li$^+$, the smaller cation, associates better with the O$^-$ site than does K$^+$, inhibiting reaction at O$^-$ and promoting reaction at C$^-$. (*b*) Protic solvents H-bond with the more electronegative O$^-$ site, leaving the C$^-$ site to react. In aprotic solvents (DMSO), the negative sites are free and O$^-$, having most of the $-$ charge, is more reactive.

18.33 (*a*) Complete the following reaction: $CH_3COCH_2COCH_3 \xrightarrow[\text{K}_2\text{CO}_3]{\text{2MeI}}$. (*b*) Explain why K$_2CO_3$, a weaker base than LDA, can be used in this reaction.

(*a*) $CH_3COCMe_2COCH_3$. (*b*) The methylene H's, being α to two C=O's, are much more acidic than the α H's in monocarbonyl compounds.

18.34 (*a*) Give the product (**A**) from the acid-catalyzed reaction of cyclohexanone, a typical ketone, with pyrrolidine (azacyclopentane), a typical 2° amine. (*b*) To what class of compounds does **A** belong?

(*a*)

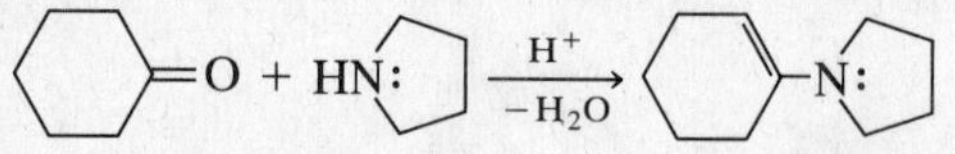

(*b*) Enamine, an N analog of an enol.

18.35 (*a*) Supply the structures for compounds **B**, **C**, and **D** formed from **A** in Problem 18.34 in the following sequence, called the *Stork-enamine* reaction. $A \xrightarrow{\text{PhCH}_2\text{Cl}} B \xrightarrow{\text{H}_3\text{O}^+} C + D$. (*b*) What structural feature of **A** permits its use in formation of **B**?

(*a*)

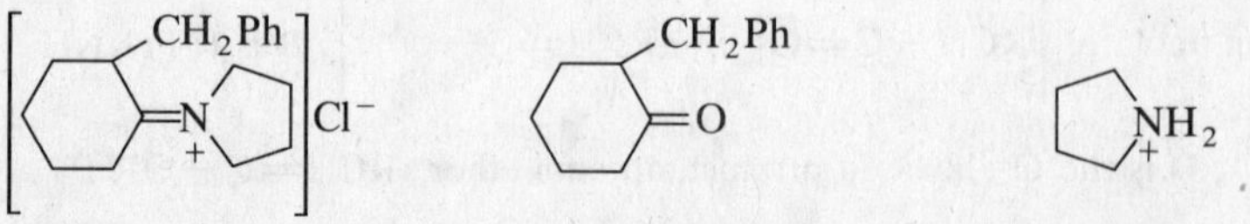

B, an immonium salt   C, an alkylated ketone   D, an ammonium cation

(*b*) The α C of the enamine is a nucleophilic site with considerable negative charge, as shown by the following contributing resonance structure, and undergoes S$_N$2 reactions.

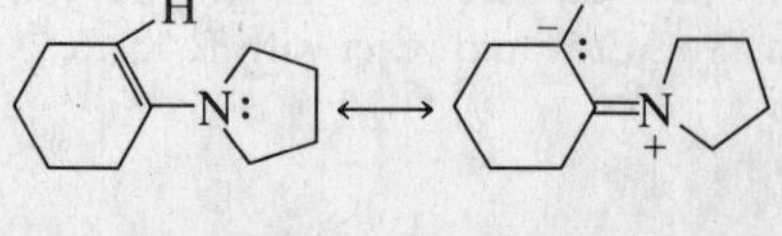

18.36 (*a*) List the types of halides that can be used in the alkylation step. (*b*) Why is the Stork alkylation reaction superior to direct alkylation of carbonyl compounds? (*c*) Illustrate the side reaction that can diminish the yield of product. (*d*) How may the main product be separated from the side product?

▮ (*a*) Only S_N2 active halides can be used: MeI, allyl, propargyl, benzyl halides, *alpha*-halo derivatives of ethers, carbonyls and esters, acid chlorides, and activated aryl halides. (*b*) The Stork reaction is run under less strongly basic conditions and results in good yields of monoalkylation products. It can also be used to alkylate aldehydes. (*c*) N-alkylation competes with C-alkylation, especially with ordinary 1° and 2° halides. With active halides this side reaction is minimized. (3° Halides undergo E2 elimination.) The products are

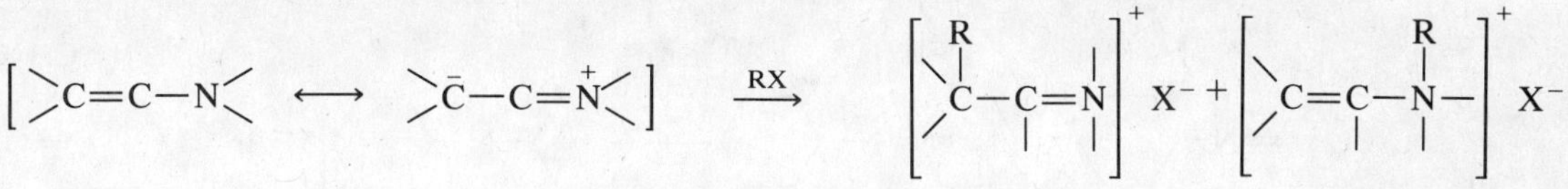

C-alkylation main product   N-alkylation side product

(*d*) The C-alkylated product hydrolyzes in dilute acid, and the resulting ketone is extracted into an organic solvent, from which it is recovered. The N-alkylated product, a salt, is inert to hydrolysis and remains in the aqueous layer.

18.37 Why cannot 1° amines (RNH_2) be used in the Stork reaction?

▮ 1° Amines react with C=O to give a mixture of tautomers:

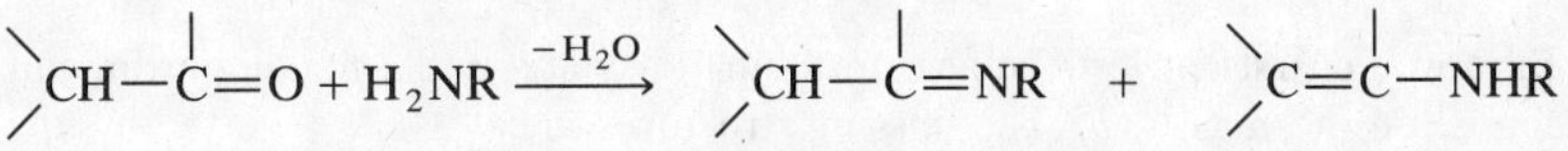

imine (major tautomer, more stable)   enamine (minor tautomer, less stable)

The major product, an imine, is more stable than the enamine (see Problem 18.15) and cannot be alkylated.

18.38 (*a*) Give the two possible enamines and C-alkylation products resulting from the Stork reaction, using 2-methylcyclohexanone and $PhCH_2Cl$. (*b*) Predict the major product and explain your choice.

▮ (*a*)

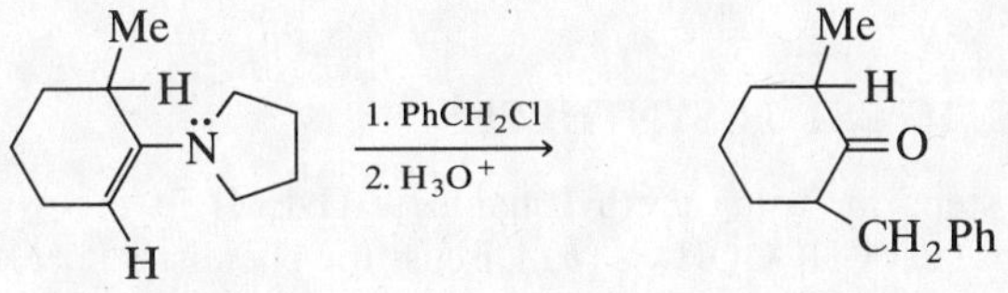

enamine A′   2-Benzyl-6-methylcyclohexanone, **A**

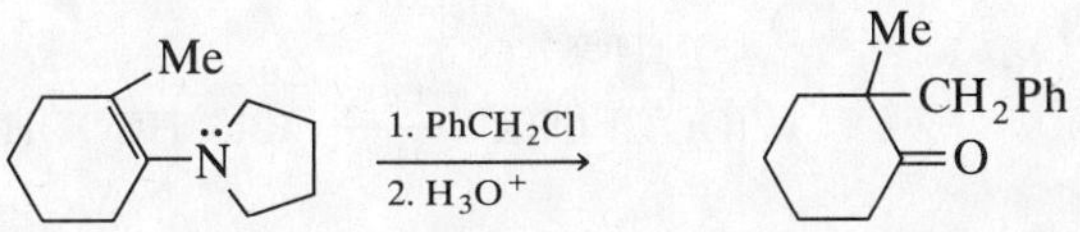

enamine B′   2-Benzyl-2-methylcyclohexanone, **B**

(*b*) We might expect **B**′ with Me on C=C to be more stable because it is more substituted and should go to **B**. However, this does not happen because **B** is more sterically hindered and A′ affords the major product, **A**, instead.

18.39 Give the final products from enamine syntheses using acetone and (*a*) allyl chloride, (*b*) chlorodimethyl ether, (*c*) methyl chloroacetate, (*d*) chloroacetone, (*e*) PhCOCl, and (*f*) 2,4-dinitrochlorobenzene.

▮ (*a*) $MeCOCH_2CH_2CH{=}CH_2$, (*b*) $MeCOCH_2CH_2OCH_3$, (*c*) $MeCOCH_2CH_2COOMe$, (*d*) $MeCOCH_2CH_2COCH_3$, (*e*) $MeCOCH_2COPh$ (a β-diketone), and (*f*) $MeCOCH_2$— 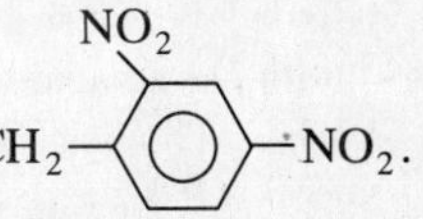

18.40 Give the carbonyl compound and halide needed in the enamine reaction to produce (*a*) 2-acetylcyclohexanone, (*b*) 2-methyl-1-phenyl-3-pentanone, and (*c*) 2,2-dimethyl-4-pentenal.

◢ (*a*) Cyclohexanone + CH_3COCl, (*b*) $CH_3CH_2COCH_2CH_3$ + $PhCH_2Cl$, and (*c*) $(CH_3)_2CHCHO$ + $CH_2{=}CHCH_2Cl$.

18.41 Give structural formulas of **A** through **C** in this modified enamine synthesis:

$$\text{Cyclohexanone + cyclohexylamine} \longrightarrow \mathbf{A}\ (C_{12}H_{21}N) \xrightarrow{\text{EtMgBr}} \mathbf{B}\ (C_{12}H_{20}NMgBr) \xrightarrow[\text{2. H}^+]{\text{1. ethylene oxide}} \mathbf{C}\ (C_8H_{14}O_2)$$

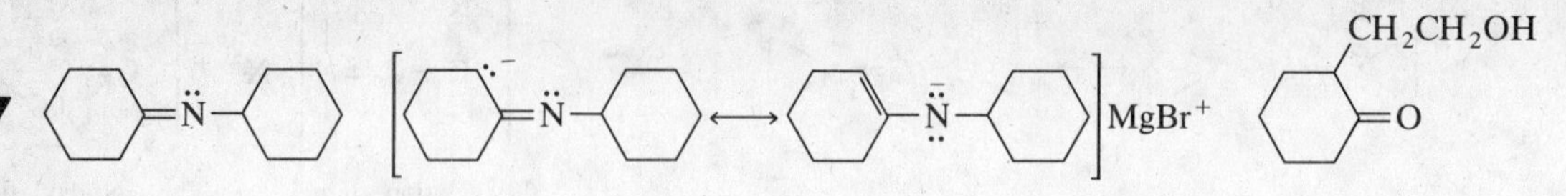

◢

18.42 (*a*) Why is it more difficult to alkylate a carboxylic acid than a ketone? (*b*) Supply the missing structural formulas in the following sequence:

$$\text{Me}_2\text{CHCOOH} \xrightarrow{\text{NaH in THF}} \mathbf{D} \xrightarrow{\text{LDA}} \mathbf{E} \xrightarrow[\text{2. H}_3\text{O}^+]{\text{1. PhCH}_2\text{CH}_2\text{Br, RT}} \mathbf{F}$$

(*c*) Why does a disodium salt of **E** not react in contrast to a half lithium salt? (*d*) What side reaction can occur if the alkylation step is attempted at higher than room temperature?

◢ (*a*) Base would first convert the acid to the carboxylate anion, making it difficult to engender an additional negative charge on the α C. (*b*) The missing structures are

D is $Me_2CHCOO^-Na^+$,   **E** is $\left[Me_2C{=}\underset{\underset{OLi}{|}}{C}{-}O^- \longleftrightarrow Me_2\bar{C}{-}\underset{\underset{OLi}{|}}{C}{=}O \right]Na^+$,   **F** is $PhCH_2CH_2CMe_2COOH$

(*c*) The Li—O bond has more covalent character, thereby diminishing the − charge on O and facilitating the generation of the − on C. (*d*) At higher temperatures, an E2 reaction of $PhCH_2CH_2Br$ occurs, giving $PhCH{=}CH_2$.

MALONIC AND ACETOACETIC ESTER SYNTHESES

18.43 (*a*) Show the general steps for using diethyl malonate (DEM) in the synthesis of mono-(RCH_2COOH) and disubstituted acetic acids ($RR'CHCOOH$). (*b*) Discuss the chemistry. (*c*) Why cannot R_3CCOOH be made by this synthesis?

◢ (*a*)

$$\underset{\text{DEM}}{(EtOOC)_2CH_2} \xrightarrow[\text{RX}]{\text{NaOEt}} (EtOOC)_2CHR \xrightarrow[\text{2. H}_3\text{O}^+]{\text{1. OH}^-} RCH_2COOH + CO_2$$

$$ \underset{\text{NaOEt}}{\Big\downarrow} \text{R'X}^*$$

$$(EtOOC)_2CRR' \xrightarrow[\text{2. H}_3\text{O}^+]{\text{1. OH}^-} RR'CHCOOH + CO_2$$

*If **RX** is used again, the product is $R_2CHCOOH$.

(*b*) The methylene H's have appreciable acidity because they are flanked by two C=O's. EtO⁻ removes one of these H's leaving a stable carbanion,

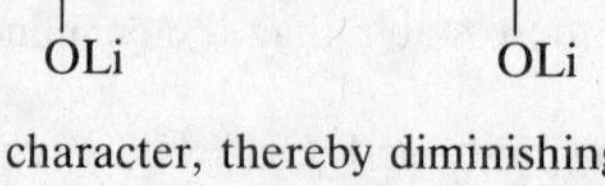

$$\overset{\displaystyle \overset{-}{\overbrace{}}}{\underset{\displaystyle EtO{-}C{\cdots}CH{\cdots}C{-}OEt}{\underset{\displaystyle \|}{O}\underset{\displaystyle \|}{O}}}$$

that acts as a nucleophile in an S_N2 reaction with RX (or ROTs). The process can be repeated to form a dialkylated derivative. The mono or dialkylated malonic ester is then hydrolyzed to the corresponding intermediate malonic acid which readily loses CO_2 to give the substituted acetic acid. (*c*) DEM has only two replaceable α H's. The α H in the dialkylated acetic acid product arises from decarboxylation of $HOOCCR_2COOH$.

18.44 Answer the following questions concerning the DEM synthesis. (*a*) What solvent is used for the reaction with NaOEt? (*b*) Why cannot malonic acid itself be used in the synthesis? (*c*) Can NaOH replace NaOEt? (*d*) What product might be isolated if diethyl malonate were reacted for a short period of time with some NaOMe? (*e*) What are the relative yields of product from reaction of DEM with 1°, 2°, and 3° RX?

◢ (*a*) EtOH is the solvent for NaOEt. A weighted amount of Na is added to excess anhydrous EtOH. (*b*) Base would convert both COOH's to COO⁻'s and the carbanion could never be formed because this would introduce a third negative charge requiring an inordinate expenditure of free energy. (*c*) No, OH⁻ would saponify the ester. (*d*) EtOOCH$_2$COOMe from transesterification. (*e*) The reaction of the carbanion with RX is S_N2. The order is 1° > 2° ≫ 3°. 3° RX's give no S_N2 product; they undergo elimination by E2.

18.45 Use DEM to prepare (*a*) 3-methylbutanoic acid, (*b*) 2-ethylbutanoic acid, and (*c*) 2-methylbutanoic acid.

◢ In each case, analyze the origin of the different pieces of the product acid (the parts derived from the halide are shown in boldface):

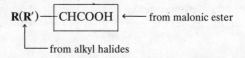

(*a*) In **Me$_2$CH**—CH$_2$COOH, there is a single R, Me$_2$CH, coming from RX which must be Me$_2$CHCl.

$$CH_2(COOEt)_2 \xrightarrow[\text{2. Me}_2\text{CHCl}]{\text{1. NaOEt}} Me_2CHCH(COOEt)_2 \xrightarrow[\text{2. H}_3\text{O}^+]{\text{1. OH}^-, \Delta}$$

$$[Me_2CHCH(COOH)_2] \xrightarrow{-CO_2} Me_2CHCH_2COOH$$

(*b*) In (**CH$_3$CH$_2$**)$_2$CHCOOH, there are two Et's attached to the α C, indicating the need for two sequential alkylations with EtBr.

$$CH_2(COOEt)_2 \xrightarrow[\text{2. EtBr}]{\text{1. NaOEt}} EtCH(COOEt)_2 \xrightarrow[\text{2. EtBr}]{\text{1. NaOEt}} Et_2C(COOEt)_2 \xrightarrow[\text{2. H}_3\text{O}^+, \Delta]{\text{1. OH}^-} Et_2CHCOOH$$

(*c*) **CH$_3$CH$_2$CH(CH$_3$)**COOH has Et and Me bonded to the α C, signaling the need for dialkylation with MeI and EtBr. (These halides are used because they are liquids that are easier to handle than gases such as MeCl and EtCl.) The larger R is introduced first to minimize steric hindrance in the second alkylation step.

$$CH_2(COOEt)_2 \xrightarrow[\text{2. EtBr}]{\text{1. NaOEt}} EtCH(COOEt)_2 \xrightarrow[\text{2. MeI}]{\text{1. NaOEt}} EtCHMe(COOEt)_2 \xrightarrow[\text{2. H}_3\text{O}^+, \Delta]{\text{1. OH}^-} EtCHMeCOOH$$

18.46 Use DEM to prepare (*a*) 2-benzylbutanedioic acid and (*b*) 4-pentenoic acid.

◢ (*a*) **PhCH$_2$**CHCOOH is a disubstituted acetic acid whose R's are PhCH$_2$– and –CH$_2$COOH. Use a
           |
           CH$_2$COOH
two-step alkylation with PhCH$_2$Cl and ClCH$_2$COOEt to get PhCH$_2$C(COOEt)$_2$. Hydrolysis and
                                         |
                                       CH$_2$COOEt
decarboxylation affords the product.

(*b*) **H$_2$C=CHCH$_2$**CH$_2$COOH is a monosubstituted acetic acid whose R is H$_2$C=CHCH$_2$–, introduced by H$_2$C=CHCH$_2$Cl, and the product is obtained after hydrolysis and decarboxylation.

18.47 Explain why each of the following cannot be synthesized from DEM in the usual fashion: (*a*) Me$_3$CCH$_2$COOH, (*b*) MeCH=CHCH$_2$COOH, (*c*) HOCH$_2$CH$_2$CH$_2$COOH, (*d*) PhCH$_2$COOH, and (*e*) Me$_3$CCH$_2$CH$_2$COOH.

◢ (*a*) R is *t*-Bu, and *t*-BuX typically undergoes elimination rather than an S_N2 reaction. (*b*) CH$_3$CH=CHCl, a vinyl chloride, does not undergo S_N2 displacement. (*c*) HOCH$_2$CH$_2$Cl cannot serve as the halide directly because the carbanion would remove the acidic alcoholic H and return to the malonate ester. The OH can be protected before the alkylation step and then released during the decarboxylation step. [See Problem 18.124(*b*) for an alternative synthesis using ethylene oxide.] (*d*) Ph is the substituent and aryl halides such as PhX do not undergo S_N2 reactions unless activated (see Problem 11.79 and also Problem 18.49 for another method.) (*e*) Although 1°, neopentyl halides are unreactive because of steric hindrance (Problem 8.62).

18.48 Prepare (*a*) cyclopentanecarboxylic acid and (*b*) 1,1-cyclopentanedicarboxylic acid from DEM.

■ (*a*) In a cyclic acid the sides of the ring are the R's of RR′CHCOOH and come from a dihalide.

$$\text{from } X(CH_2)_4X \longrightarrow \quad \begin{matrix} H_2C—CH_2 \\ | \qquad | \\ H_2C—CH_2 \end{matrix} \rangle \boxed{CHCOOH} \longleftarrow \text{from malonate ester}$$

The four C's of the ring are supplied by $ClCH_2CH_2CH_2CH_2Cl$. One Cl is displaced intermolecularly, and the other intramolecularly to create the ring. Mix equivalent amounts of DEM, NaOEt, and the dihalide to give $Cl(CH_2)_4CH(COOEt)_2$, to which another equivalent of NaOEt is added to close the ring. The product is the diester of 1,1-cyclopentanedicarboxylic acid. The desired product is obtained after hydrolysis and decarboxylation. (*b*) Saponification of the alkylated malonic ester gives the dicarboxylate salt of malonic acid which on careful acidification at low temperatures gives the *gem*-dicarboxylic acid which can be isolated. Decarboxylation requires heating the diacid.

18.49 Under what conditions can DEM be phenylated with PhBr?

■ With $NaNH_2$ in liq. NH_3, PhBr reacts with the malonate carbanion by the benzyne mechanism (Problems 11.86 and 87), giving $PhCH(COOEt)_2$. Hydrolysis and decarboxylation leads to $PhCH_2COOH$.

18.50 (*a*) Prepare succinic acid, $HOOCCH_2CH_2COOH$, using DEM as the only source of C's. (*b*) Synthesize α,β-dimethylsuccinic acid.

■ (*a*) $HOOCCH_2CH_2COOH$ can be thought of as a $HOOCCH_2$-substituted acetic acid. This substituent comes from a second molecule of DEM. The two malonate pieces are merged by adding I_2.

$$H_2C(COOEt)_2 \xrightarrow{NaOEt + I_2} [ICH(COOEt)_2] \xrightarrow[H_2C(COOEt)_2]{NaOEt}$$

$$\qquad\qquad\qquad\qquad \text{an RX-type}$$

$$(EtOOC)_2CHCH(COOEt)_2 \xrightarrow[-2CO_2]{hydrolysis} HOOCCH_2CH_2COOH$$

The intermediate halide, $ICH(COOEt)_2$, is not isolated. (*b*) For $HOOC—CHMeCHMeCOOH$, first methylate DEM with MeI, then couple it with I_2 as in (*a*). Decarboxylative hydrolysis gives the required product.

18.51 (*a*) Which alkylating agents are needed for the DEM synthesis of: (i) pentanedioic (glutaric) acid, (ii) hexanedioic (adipic) acid, and (iii) heptanedioic (pimelic) acid? (*b*) Give the relative number of equivalents of the three reactants in each of these syntheses.

■ (*a*) With few exceptions (see Problem 18.46 where α-haloesters serve as alkylating agents), syntheses of dicarboxylic acids require the merging somehow of 2 mol of DEM. We saw in Problem 18.50 that for 1,4-dicarboxylic acids the merging is achieved with I_2. For $HOOCCH_2(CH_2)_nCH_2COOH$, the alkylating agent is a dihalide with the requisite number of C's to give the chain of correct length. The $HOOCCH_2$ group at each end of the chain comes from DEM accounting for two C's at each end of the chain, for a total of four C's. All intermediate C's come from the dihalide.

$$\text{from DEM} \longrightarrow \boxed{HOOC—CH_2}—(CH_2)_n—\boxed{CH_2—COOH} \longleftarrow \text{from DEM}$$

$$\text{from } X(CH_2)_nX$$

(i) Glutaric acid has a five-C chain, $n = 1$; the alkyl halide is CH_2I_2. (ii) Adipic acid has six C's, $n = 2$; $Br(CH_2)_2Br$ is used. (iii) Pimelic acid has seven C's, $n = 3$; $Cl(CH_2)_3Cl$ is used. (*b*) Two eq each of DEM and NaOEt and one eq of the dihalide. In these syntheses the choice of halogen of the halide is not specified: use the cheapest and easiest-to-handle substrate, if time is not of the essence.

18.52 (*a*) Which alkylating agents are needed for the DEM synthesis of: (i) 1,2-cyclopentanedicarboxylic acid (**A**), (ii) 1,3-cyclopentanedicarboxylic acid (**B**), and (iii) 1,4-cyclohexanedicarboxylic acid (**C**). (*b*) Give the relative number of equivalents of reactants used.

❚ (*a*) Coupling of two DEM's is essential in each synthesis to give the two CH_2COOH units.

(i) Since this is a *vic*-dicarboxylic acid, I_2 is used for coupling. But first the remaining three C's in the ring are introduced by coupling two DEM's with $ClCH_2CH_2CH_2Cl$. Thus

$$(EtOOC)_2CH_2 + Cl(CH_2)_3Cl + H_2C(COOEt)_2 \xrightarrow{2\ EtO^-} (EtOOC)_2CH(CH_2)_3CH(COOEt)_2 \quad \mathbf{A'}$$

$$\mathbf{A'} \xrightarrow[2EtO^-]{I_2} \begin{array}{c}EtOOC \\ EtOOC\end{array}\!\!\!\big\langle\!\!\!\begin{array}{c}COOEt \\ COOEt\end{array} \xrightarrow[2.\ H_3O^+,\ \Delta]{1.\ OH^-} \begin{array}{c}HOOC\end{array}\!\!\!\big\langle\!\!\!\begin{array}{c}COOH\end{array} \quad \mathbf{A}$$

(ii) $2DEM + BrCH_2CH_2Br \xrightarrow{2OEt^-} (EtOOC)_2CHCH_2CH_2CH(COOEt)_2$ (**B'**)

$$\mathbf{B'} + CH_2I_2 \xrightarrow{2OEt^-} \begin{array}{c}EtOOC \\ \\ EtOOC\end{array}\!\!\!\big\langle\!\!\!\begin{array}{c}COOEt \\ \\ COOEt\end{array} \xrightarrow[2.\ H_3O^+,\ \Delta]{1.\ OH^-} \begin{array}{c}HOOC\end{array}\!\!\!\big\langle\!\!\!\begin{array}{c}COOH\end{array} \quad \mathbf{B}$$

(iii) $2DEM + 2BrCH_2CH_2Br \xrightarrow{4OEt^-} \begin{array}{c}EtOOC \\ EtOOC\end{array}\!\!\!\big\langle\!\!\!\begin{array}{c}COOEt \\ COOEt\end{array} \xrightarrow[2.\ H_3O^+,\ \Delta]{1.\ OH^-} HOOC\!\!-\!\!\big\langle\!\!\!\big\rangle\!\!-\!\!COOH \quad \mathbf{C}$

(*b*) (i) Two eq of DEM, four eq of NaOEt, and one eq each of RX and I_2. (ii) Two eq of DEM, four eq of NaOEt, one eq of each dihalide. (iii) Two eq of DEM, four eq of NaOEt, and two eq of dihalide.

18.53 Convert DEM to 2-oxobutanoic acid.

❚ Nitrosation of alkyl-substituted DEM is one method of producing α-ketocarboxylic acids.

$$DEM \xrightarrow[CH_3CH_2Br]{NaOEt} CH_3CH_2CH(COOEt)_2 \xrightarrow{HONO} CH_3CH_2C(NO)(COOEt)_2 \text{ (nitrosation)} \xrightarrow[hydrolysis]{decarboxylative}$$

$$\begin{bmatrix} \overset{N=O}{\underset{|}{}} \\ CH_3CH_2CHCOOH \end{bmatrix} \longrightarrow CH_3CH_2\overset{NOH}{\overset{\|}{C}}COOH \xrightarrow{H_3O^+} CH_3CH_2\overset{O}{\overset{\|}{C}}COOH + (H_3NOH)^+$$

unstable   stable
nitroso tautomer   oxime tautomer

18.54 Use PhH, PhMe, xylenes, NapH (naphthalene), and DEM to prepare: (*a*) $PhCH_2CH_2CH_2CH_2COOH$, (*b*) $p\text{-}HOOCC_6H_4CH_2CH_2COOH$, (*c*) $p\text{-}HOOCCH_2CH_2C_6H_4CH_2CH_2COOH$, (*d*) $\alpha\text{-}NapCH_2CH_2COOH$, and (*e*) $\beta\text{-}NapCH_2CH_2COOH$.

❚ (*a*) $PhH \xrightarrow{ClCH_2CH=CH_2/AlCl_3} PhCH_2CH=CH_2 \xrightarrow[peroxide]{HBr} PhCH_2CH_2CH_2Br$ (**A**). Then

$$DEM \xrightarrow[2.\ \mathbf{A}]{1.\ NaOEt} Ph(CH_2)_3CH(COOEt)_2 \xrightarrow[\Delta\ (-CO_2)]{hydrolysis} Ph(CH_2)_4COOH$$

(*b*) Alkylate DEM with $p\text{-}MeOOCC_6H_4CH_2Cl$ (**B**). Decarboxylative hydrolysis gives the product. To prepare **B**:

$$PhCH_3 \xrightarrow{Br_2/AlCl_3} p\text{-}BrC_6H_4CH_3 \xrightarrow[3.\ H_3O^+]{\substack{1.\ Mg \\ 2.\ CO_2}} p\text{-}HOOCC_6H_4CH_3 \xrightarrow[H_2SO_4]{MeOH} p\text{-}MeOOCC_6H_4CH_3 \xrightarrow{Cl_2} \mathbf{B}$$

(*c*) Couple two DEM's with $p\text{-}ClCH_2C_6H_4CH_2Cl$ (**C**). Decarboxylative hydrolysis gives product. To prepare **C**: $p\text{-}CH_3C_6H_4CH_3 \xrightarrow[h\nu]{Cl_2} \mathbf{C}$

(*d*) Alkylate DEM with $\alpha\text{-}NapCH_2Cl$ (**D**). Decarboxylative hydrolysis gives product. To prepare **D**: $NapH \xrightarrow{CH_3I/AlCl_3} \alpha\text{-}NapCH_3 \xrightarrow[h\nu]{Cl_2} \mathbf{D}$

(*e*) $NapH \xrightarrow[PhNO_2]{CH_3COCl/AlCl_3} \beta\text{-}NapCOCH_3 \xrightarrow[2.\ H_3O^+]{1.\ Br_2,\ OH^-} \beta\text{-}NapCOOH \xrightarrow[2.\ H_3O^+]{1.\ LiAlH_4} \beta\text{-}NapCH_2OH \xrightarrow{HCl} \beta\text{-}NapCH_2Cl$ (**E**).
(**E**) Alkylate DEM with **E**.

18.55 Give general equations for use of acetoacetic ester (AAE) to prepare CH_3COCH_2R and $CH_3COCHRR'$. (*b*) Discuss the chemistry. (*c*) Why cannot CH_3COCR_3 be made this way?

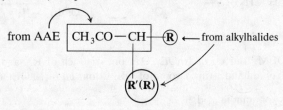

(*b*) The chemistry is the same as that for DEM (Problem 18.43). (*c*) The ^3C of the ketonic product must have at least one H which comes from replacement of the COOH in the last steps of the synthesis.

18.56 Use AAE to prepare (*a*) 4-methyl-2-pentanone (**A**), (*b*) 3-methyl-2-pentanone (**B**), and (*c*) 4-phenyl-2-butanone (**C**).

For a generalized methyl ketone, the parts are assembled as follows:

$$\text{from AAE} \longrightarrow \boxed{CH_3CO - CH - \textcircled{R}} \longleftarrow \text{from alkylhalides}$$
$$\textcircled{R'(R)}$$

(*a*) $CH_3COCH_2 - \mathbf{CHMe_2}$ (**A**) has one R, i.e., $-CHMe_2$. Monoalkylate with Me_2CHCl:

$$AAE \xrightarrow[Me_2CHCl]{NaOEt} CH_3COCH(CHMe_2)COOEt \xrightarrow[\Delta]{hydrolysis} \mathbf{A}$$

(*b*) $CH_3COCH - \mathbf{Et}$ (**B**) has two R's, Me and Et. The dialkylation introduces the larger Et first.
      |
     Me

$$AAE \xrightarrow[EtBr]{NaOEt} CH_3COCH(Et)COOEt \xrightarrow[MeI]{NaOEt} CH_3COC(Me)(Et)COOEt \xrightarrow[\Delta]{hydrolysis} \mathbf{B}$$

(*c*) $CH_3COCH_2 - \mathbf{CH_2Ph}$ (**C**) has one R, $PhCH_2-$. Monoalkylate with $PhCH_2Cl$:

$$AAE \xrightarrow[PhCH_2Cl]{NaOEt} CH_3COCH(CH_2Ph)COOEt \xrightarrow[\Delta]{hydrolysis} \mathbf{C}$$

18.57 Which alkylating agents are needed for the AAE synthesis of (*a*) $CH_3COCH_2CH_2COOH$ and (*b*) $CH_3COCH_2CH_2COPh$, a γ-diketone?

(*a*) The R group is $-CH_2COOH$. Alkylate with $ClCH_2COOEt$. Only the β-carboxyl group decarboxylates after hydrolysis of $CH_3COCH(COOEt)CH_2COOEt$ to give the product. (*b*) The R group is $-CH_2COPh$. Alkylate with $ClCH_2COPh$.

18.58 (*a*) Which side reaction prevails with AAE but not with DEM? (*b*) Discuss the influence of the following factors on the ratio of C- vs. O-alkylation: (i) solvent, (ii) countercation, (iii) leavability of X of RX, (iv) size of R.

(*a*) O-alkylation (Problem 18.29) competes to give enol ethers:

$$\text{enolate-carbanion of AAE} \xrightarrow{RX} \underset{\substack{| \\ OR}}{CH_3C=CHCOOEt} + \underset{\substack{\| \\ O}}{CH_3CCHRCOOEt}$$

$$\text{O-alkylation (enol ether)} \qquad \text{C-alkylation (keto form)}$$

(*b*) (i) Nonpolar and especially protic solvents favor C-alkylation because the O^- is deactivated by ion pairing in nonpolar solvents and by H-bonding in protic solvents. In aprotic solvents, there is an increase in O-alkylation because M^+ is coordinated with the aprotic solvent, and the O^- is set free to react. (ii) Since Li^+ coordinates with O^-, C-alkylation is encouraged. Na^+ and K^+ are poorer coordinators of O^- and there is an increase in

O-alkylation. (iii) See (ii) of Problem 8.46(*a*). The more easily polarized nucleophile (soft base) reacts faster with RX when X is easily polarized (RX is a soft acid). Conversely, the less easily polarized nucleophile (hard base) reacts faster with RX when X is not easily polarized (RX is a hard acid). A carbanion is a soft base and reacts better with RI, the softest RX acid. The order of decreasing C-alkylation is RI > RBr > RCl > $ROSO_2OR$ > $ROSO_2OAr$. O^- is a hard base and the order of O-alkylation is just the reverse. (iv) As the size of R increases, slightly more O-alkylation occurs.

18.59 Use AAE to prepare the β-diketone $CH_3COCH_2COCH_2CH_3$.

▰ The R is the acyl group, $—COCH_2CH_3$, introduced by the acid chloride, $ClCOCH_2CH_3$. Since acyl halides react with ethanol, aprotic solvents must be used. The carbanion is prepared with NaH, a source of the strong base $H:^-$.

$$AAE \xrightarrow[-H_2]{1.\ NaH\ 2.\ ClCOCH_2CH_3} CH_3COCH(COOEt)COCH_2CH_3 \xrightarrow[\Delta\ (-CO_2)]{hydrolysis} product$$

18.60 Use AAE to prepare (*a*) $PhCH_2CH_2COCH_2COOH$ (**A**) and (*b*) $PhCH_2CH_2COCH_2CH_3$ (**B**).

▰ Neither of the required products are methyl ketones. Their syntheses depend on the formation of a dianion when the very strong base, LDA, is used:

(*a*) $AAE \xrightarrow{2LDA} [\ ^-:CH_2CO\ddot{C}HCOOEt] \xrightarrow{PhCH_2Cl} PhCH_2CH_2CO\ddot{C}HCOOEt$ (**C**) $\xrightarrow{H_3O^+}$ **A**

(*b*) **C** [from (*a*)] $\xrightarrow{CH_3I} PhCH_2CH_2COCH(CH_3)COOEt \xrightarrow{hydrolysis,\ -CO_2}$ **B**

18.61 Indicate the halide or dihalide needed with AAE and give the number of eq of each reactant needed to prepare (*a*) 3,5-dimethyl-2-hexanone, (*b*) cyclobutyl methyl ketone, (*c*) 2,6-heptanedione, (*d*) 1,3-diacetylcyclopentane, (*e*) 1,2-diacetylcyclopropane, (*f*) 1,4-diacetylcyclohexane, and (*g*) 3-acetyl-5-hexenoic acid.

▰ In each case the halide fragments are boldfaced.

(*a*)

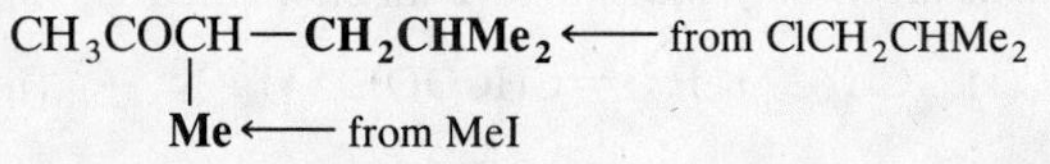

$$CH_3CO\overset{|}{C}H—\mathbf{CH_2CHMe_2} \longleftarrow from\ ClCH_2CHMe_2$$
$$\mathbf{Me} \longleftarrow from\ MeI$$

Use one eq of AAE and each halide and two eq of NaOEt. Introduce the larger group first.

(*b*)

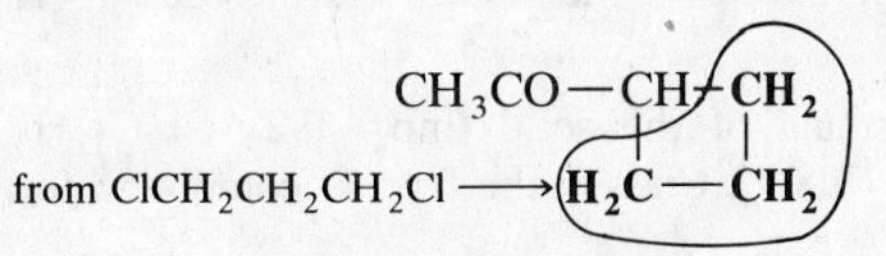

$$CH_3CO—CH{-}\mathbf{CH_2}$$
$$\quad\quad\quad\quad |\quad\quad |$$
$$from\ ClCH_2CH_2CH_2Cl \longrightarrow \mathbf{H_2C—CH_2}$$

Use one eq each of AAE and the dihalide and two eq of NaOEt.

(*c*)

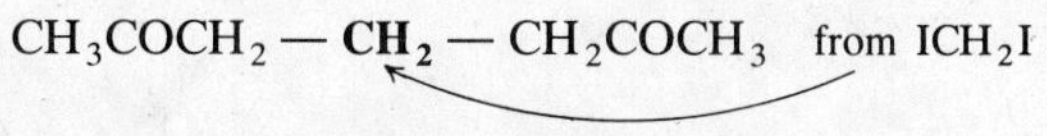

$$CH_3COCH_2—\mathbf{CH_2}—CH_2COCH_3 \quad from\ ICH_2I$$

Use two eq each of AAE and NaOEt and one eq of CH_2I_2.

(*d*)

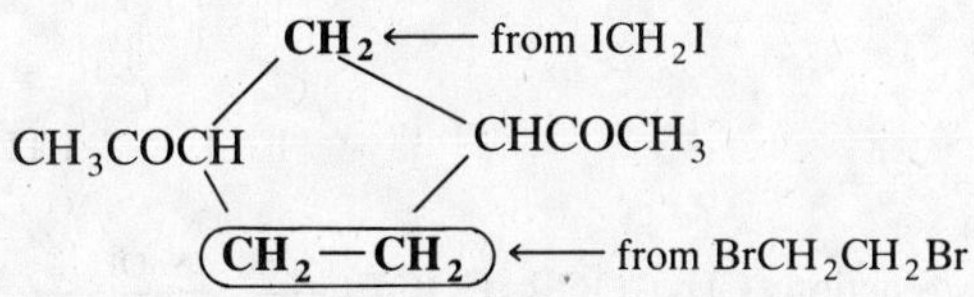

$$\mathbf{CH_2} \longleftarrow from\ ICH_2I$$
$$CH_3CO\overset{|}{C}H \quad\quad CHCOCH_3$$
$$\mathbf{CH_2—CH_2} \longleftarrow from\ BrCH_2CH_2Br$$

Use two eq each of AAE and NaOEt and one eq of each dihalide.

(*e*)

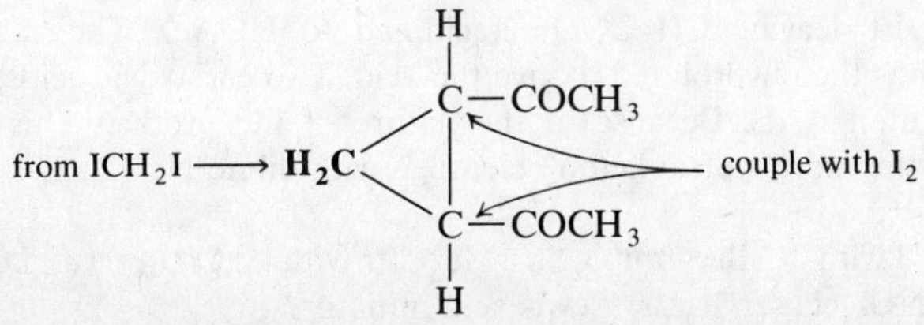

$$\quad\quad\quad\quad\quad\quad\quad H$$
$$\quad\quad\quad\quad\quad\quad\quad |$$
$$\quad\quad\quad\quad\quad\quad\quad C{-}COCH_3$$
$$from\ ICH_2I \longrightarrow \mathbf{H_2C} \quad\quad\quad\quad couple\ with\ I_2$$
$$\quad\quad\quad\quad\quad\quad\quad C{-}COCH_3$$
$$\quad\quad\quad\quad\quad\quad\quad |$$
$$\quad\quad\quad\quad\quad\quad\quad H$$

Use two eq each of AAE and NaOEt and one eq each of I_2 and CH_2I_2.

(f)

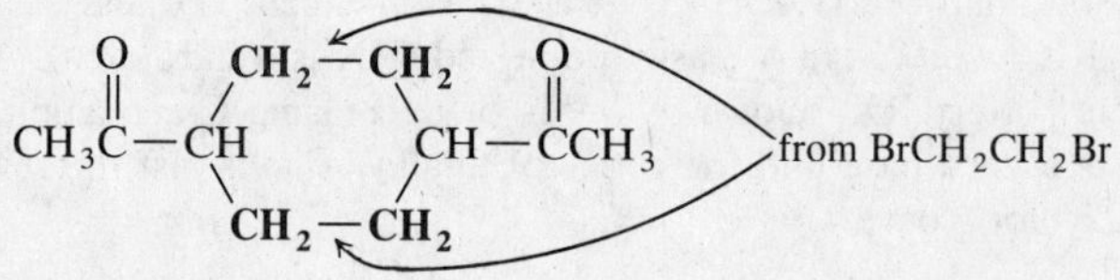

from $BrCH_2CH_2Br$

Use two eq of each reagent.

(g) from $H_2C=CHCH_2Cl \longrightarrow CH_2=CH-CH_2-\underset{\underset{COCH_3}{|}}{CH}-CH_2COOH \longleftarrow$ from $ClCH_2COOEt$

Use two eq each of NaOEt and AAE and one eq of each halide.

18.62 Give the structure and name of the product from the following combinations of reactants. (a) DEM, 2NaOEt, $2H_2C=CHCH_2Cl$; (b) AAE, 2NaOEt, s-BuBr, MeI; (c) AAE, 2NaOEt, MeI, t-BuCl; (d) AAE, 2NaOEt, $ClCH_2OPh$, CH_3Br; and (e) DEM, 2NaOEt, $BrCH_2CH_2Br$.

▰ (a) $(H_2C=CHCH_2)_2CHCOOH$, 2-allyl-4-pentenoic acid

(b) $CH_3COCH(CH_3)CH(CH_3)CH_2CH_3$, 3,4-dimethyl-2-hexanone

(c) $CH_3COCH_2CH_3$, butanone (t-BuCl forms isobutylene; no alkylation occurs.)

(d) $CH_3COCH(CH_3)CH_2OPh$, 3-methyl-4-phenoxy-2-butanone

(e) ▷—COOH, cyclopropylcarboxylic acid

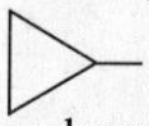

18.63 (a) Give the products of the following reactions: (i) AAE + CH_2N_2 and (ii) sodioacetoacetate + $HC(OMe)_3$(methyl orthoformate). (b) Suggest a mechanism for reaction (ii) involving an S_N2 step.

▰ (a) Both reactions are O-alkylations to give an enol ether.

(i) $CH_3C(OCH_3)=CHCOOEt$ (A) + N_2 (ii) A + NaOMe + HCOOMe

(b) $CH_3\underset{\underset{O^-}{|}}{C}=CHCOOEt + Me-O-\underset{\underset{OMe}{|}}{CH}-OMe \xrightarrow{S_N2} A + H-\underset{\underset{O}{||}}{C}-OMe + {}^-OMe$

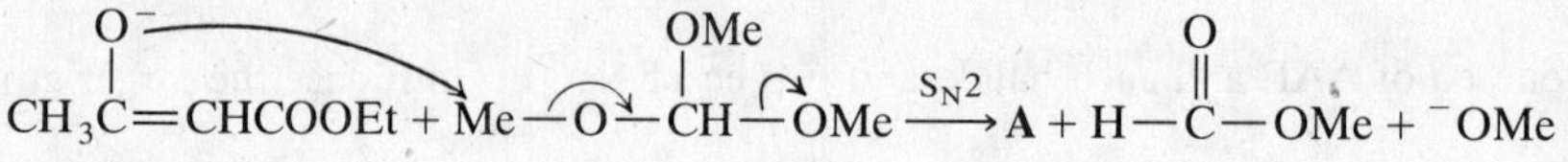

18.64 Give the structural formula of the solid (mp = 192 °C) $C_{12}H_{18}O_6Cu$, formed when AAE is added to an ammoniacal solution of $CuSO_4$. Classify the type of compound formed.

▰ The compound is a cupric chelate formed from 2 mol of the enol of AAE and Cu^{2+}:

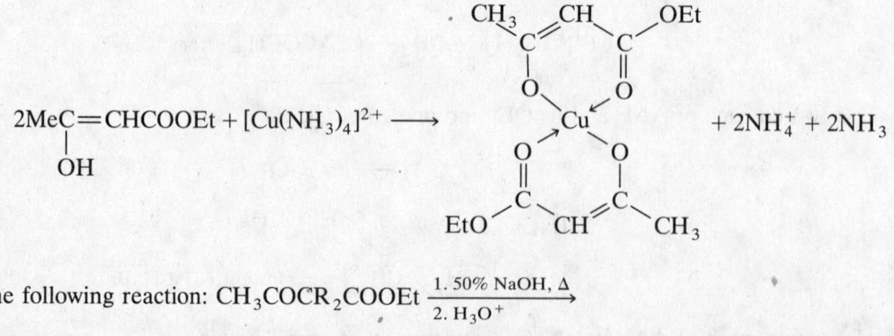

$2MeC=CHCOOEt + [Cu(NH_3)_4]^{2+} \longrightarrow$
$+ 2NH_4^+ + 2NH_3$

18.65 Complete the following reaction: $CH_3COCR_2COOEt \xrightarrow[\text{2. }H_3O^+]{\text{1. 50% NaOH, }\Delta}$

▰ $CH_3COOH + R_2CHCOOH + EtOH$. With *conc.* OH^-, attack is at the ketonic C=O leading to displacement of $:CR_2COOEt$ leaving CH_3COO^- (acidified to HOAc). The carbanion reacts with H_2O to give HCR_2COOEt, which is then hydrolyzed to give the acid. Two carboxylic acids, one of which is always HOAc, are formed from substituted AAE. Because of the nature of the product, this is known as the acid cleavage to differentiate it from the more typical ketone cleavage with dilute NaOH.

18.66 AAE can be alkylated with a t-Bu group using Me_3CBr with $AgClO_4$. (a) Discuss the mechanism. (b) Why is $AgClO_4$ and not $AgNO_3$ chosen as the Lewis acid initiator?

▮ (*a*) Ag^+ induces formation of the carbocation salt, $Me_3C^+ClO_4^-$, by forming AgBr. Me_3C^+ then adds to the $C{=}C$ of the enol in a typical fashion. When aq. $NaHCO_3$ is added to the reaction mixture, $CH_3COCH(t\text{-}Bu)COOEt$ results.

18.67 Which of the following compounds can be alkylated at $-CH_2-$ by a base that does not have to be stronger than NaOEt? (*a*) $CH_2(CN)_2$, malononitrile, (*b*) Ph_2CH_2, (*c*) $N{\equiv}CCH_2COOEt$, ethyl cyanoacetate, (*d*) O_2NCH_2COOEt, (*e*) $H_2C{=}CHCH_2CH{=}CH_2$, and (*f*) $CH_3SO_2CH_2COOEt$.

▮ (*a*), (*c*), (*d*), and (*f*). In addition to the $>C{=}O$'s, the $-CN$, $-NO_2$, and $-SO_2$ groups increase the acidities of α H's (see Table 18-1) so that they can be removed by OEt^-. Ph and $>C{=}C<$ are not good acid-strengtheners because the $-$ charge of the intermediate carbanion is delocalized to weakly electronegative C's.

α,β-UNSATURATED CARBONYL COMPOUNDS; MICHAEL ADDITION

18.68 (*a*) Write (i) the contributing resonance structures and (ii) the π-delocalized hybrid structure for $>C{=}\overset{|}{C}{-}\overset{|}{C}{=}\overset{..}{O}:$ an α,β-unsaturated carbonyl compound. (*b*) Which resonance structure is not shown because it makes very little or no contribution? Explain.

▮ (*a*) (i) $>C{=}\overset{|}{C}{-}\overset{|}{C}{=}\overset{..}{O}: \longleftrightarrow >\overset{+}{C}{-}\overset{|}{C}{=}\overset{|}{C}{-}\overset{..}{O}:^- \longleftrightarrow >C{=}\overset{|}{C}{-}\underset{+}{\overset{|}{C}}{-}\overset{..}{O}:^-$

(ii) $>\overset{\delta+}{C}{\cdots}C{\overset{\delta+}{\cdots}}\overset{|}{C}{\cdots}\overset{..}{O}:^{\delta-}$

(*b*) $>\overset{..}{C}{-}\overset{|}{C}{=}\overset{|}{C}{-}\overset{..}{O}:^+$. O has six e^-'s and a $+$ charge, resulting in a very unstable condition.

18.69 Draw the orbital picture for the resonance hybrid in Problem 18.68.

▮ See Fig. 18-3.

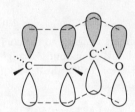

Fig. 18-3

18.70 Why do nucleophiles, $Nu{:}^-$, add to the $C{=}C$ of $-\overset{|}{C}{=}\overset{|}{C}{-}\overset{|}{C}{=}O$ but not to ordinary alkenes?

▮ $Nu{:}^-$ adds to the β C leaving a stabilized carbanion-enolate,

$$Nu{:}^- + \ >C{=}C{-}\overset{|}{C}{=}\overset{..}{O}: \longrightarrow \left[Nu{-}\overset{|}{C}{-}\overset{..}{\overset{|}{C}}{-}\overset{|}{C}{=}O \longleftrightarrow Nu{-}\overset{|}{C}{-}\overset{|}{C}{=}\overset{|}{C}{-}\overset{..}{O}:^- \right]$$

The localized carbanion from addition of $Nu{:}^-$ to $>C{=}C<$, $Nu{-}\overset{|}{C}{-}\overset{|}{C}{:}^-$, has a very high energy and doesn't form easily.

18.71 Explain the isolation of a tetradeuterated product from the reaction of $CH_3CH{=}CHCHO$ with OD^- in D_2O.

▮ The H's of CH_3 are acidic because the $-$ charge can be delocalized as shown:

$CH_3CH{=}CHC\overset{..}{H}\overset{..}{O}: + OD^- \rightleftharpoons$

$$HOD + \left[{}^-{:}CH_2CH{=}CHCH{=}\overset{..}{O}: \longleftrightarrow CH_2{=}CH\overset{..}{\overset{-}{C}}HCH{=}\overset{..}{O}: \longleftrightarrow CH_2{=}CHCH{=}CH\overset{..}{O}:^- \right]$$

There are three sites in the hybrid with some − charge that can accept D from D_2O to give three products, CH_2DCH=$CHCHO$ (A), CH_2=$CHCHDCHO$ (B), and CH_2=$CHCH$=$CHOD$ (C). The unstable enol C rearranges to A and B. Repeated reactions with OD^- reforms the carbanion-enolate and reaction with D_2O eventually produces the tetradeuterated compound, CD_3CH=$CDCHO$.

18.72 (a) Which three isomers may be present in the equilibrium mixture created when CH_2=$CHCH_2CHO$ (D) is treated with aq. NaOH? (b) Indicate the most stable isomer (99.9%).

▰ (a) $D \underset{}{\overset{OH^-}{\rightleftharpoons}} HOH + \left[CH_2=CH\overset{..}{\overset{-}{C}}HCH=\overset{..}{\overset{..}{O}}: \longleftrightarrow \right.$

$\left. {}^-:CH_2CH=CHCH=\overset{..}{\overset{..}{O}}: \longleftrightarrow CH_2=CHCH=CH\overset{..}{\overset{..}{O}}:^- \right]$.

Each site with a − charge can abstract an H^+ from H_2O to give three products: CH_2=$CHCH$=$CHOH$ (enol tautomer) of D, D (vinylacetaldehyde), and CH_3CH=$CHCH$=O (crotonaldehyde).
(b) Crotonaldehyde, the conjugated keto isomer.

18.73 Show how the isomerization of D in Problem 18.72 can also proceed in aq. acid.

▰ CH_2=$CHCH_2\underset{:\overset{..}{O}:}{\overset{\|}{CH}} \rightleftharpoons \overset{H^+}{} \left[CH_2=CHCH_2\underset{{}^+:\overset{..}{OH}}{\overset{\|}{CH}} \longleftrightarrow CH_2=CHCH_2\underset{:\overset{..}{OH}}{\overset{+}{CH}} \right] \xrightarrow{-H^+} \underset{\text{a dienol}}{CH_2=CHCH=CHOH} \xrightarrow{H^+}$

$\left[CH_3\underset{:\overset{..}{OH}}{\overset{+}{C}HCH}=CH \longleftrightarrow CH_3CH=CH\underset{:\overset{..}{OH}}{\overset{}{C}H} \longleftrightarrow CH_2CH=CHCH\underset{{}^+:\overset{..}{OH}}{\overset{\|}{}} \right] \xrightarrow{-H^+} CH_3CH=CHCHO$

18.74 (a) Which two isomers can form from the reaction of an α,β-conjugated carbonyl compound with $Nu:^-$ followed by acid? (b) Classify the reactions leading to the two products.

▰ (a) $\overset{\diagdown}{\diagup}C$=$\overset{|}{C}-\overset{|}{C}$=$O \xrightarrow[\text{2. } H^+]{\text{1. } Nu:^-} \overset{\diagdown}{\diagup}C$=$\overset{|}{C}-\underset{Nu}{\overset{|}{C}OH}$ (E) + $-\overset{|}{C}-\underset{Nu}{\overset{\overset{H}{|}}{C}}-\overset{|}{C}$=$O$ (F)

(b) The reactions are classified using numbers assigned to the conjugated atoms, $\diagup C^4$=$C^3 \diagdown C^2$=O^1. E is the 1,2-addition product typical of simple carbonyl compounds. F might have originated from the unstable intermediate enol, $NuC-C$=$C-OH$, and therefore is called the 1,4-addition product. However the net addition in F is actually 3,4- and is called a *Michael addition*.

18.75 Give the major products from the reactions of $PhCH$=$CHCOPh$ with (a) KCN/HOAc, (b) PhLi, (c) PhMgBr, (d) $(CH_2$=$CH)_2CuLi$, (e) $MeSH/OH^-$, each followed by addition of acid, and (f) $NaHSO_3$.

▰ (a) $PhCH(CN)CH_2COPh$, practically the sole product. (b) $PhCH$=$CHC(OH)Ph_2$. Organolithium compounds engage mainly in 1,2-additions. (c) Mixture of Ph_2CHCH_2COPh(3,4-addition, major) and $PhCH$=$CH(OH)Ph_2$(1,2-addition, minor). The larger the R attached to C=O, the greater the extent of 3,4-addition. (d) CH_2=$CHCHPhCH_2COPh$. (e) $PhCH(SMe)CH_2COPh$. (f) $PhCH(SO_3Na)CH_2COPh$

18.76 In general, what kinds of compounds act as Michael acceptors in reactions with carbanions?

▰ The C=C must be bonded to a functional group capable of stabilizing a − charge. Some important examples are C=$C-CHO$, C=$C-COR$, C=$C-COOR$, C=$C-NO_2$, C=$C-CN$, and C=$C-SO_2R$.

18.77 (a) Show the sequence of intermediate steps in the reaction of cyclohexanone and acrylonitrile, CH_2=$CHCN$ in aq. NaOH (the *cyanoethylation* reaction). Can the same product be obtained by a Stork-enamine reaction (Problem 18.35)?

▰ (a)

Note that under these reaction conditions the CN is not hydrolyzed to COO^-.

(*b*) Yes, enamines participate in Michael additions.

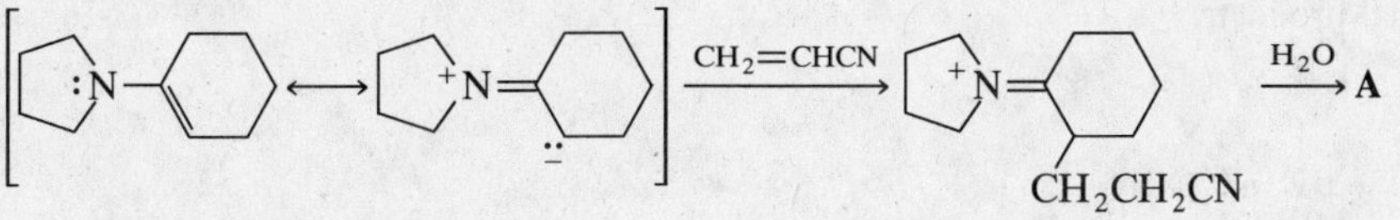

18.78 Give and name the final product from the DEM synthesis with methyl vinyl ketone and discuss the intermediate steps for its formation.

The malonate anion (from DEM and NaOEt) participates in a Michael addition with $CH_3COCH{=}CH_2$ to give the carbanion-enolate that abstracts H^+ from EtOH to furnish $CH_3COCH_2CH_2{-}CH(COOEt)_2$. This intermediate product undergoes decarboxylative hydrolysis to the final product, $CH_3COCH_2CH_2{-}CH_2COOH$, 5-oxohexanoic acid, a typical δ-ketoacid.

18.79 Provide the structures of the Michael addition products before and after hydrolysis for: (*a*) AAE and ethyl cinnamate; (*b*) DEM and mesityl oxide, $\mathbf{Me_2C{=}CHCOMe}$; (*c*) $\mathbf{H_2C{=}CHCOCH{=}CH_2}$ and two eq of $NCCH_2COOEt$; and (*d*) $CH_3COCH_2COCH_3$ and acrolein, $\mathbf{H_2C{=}CHCHO}$.

(*a*) $\mathbf{PhCH{=}CHCOOEt} + \text{AAE} \longrightarrow CH_3COCH(COOEt)\mathbf{CHPhCH_2COOEt} \longrightarrow$

$$CH_3COCH_2\mathbf{CHPhCH_2COOH}$$

(*b*) $(EtOOC)_2CH\mathbf{C(Me)_2CH_2COMe} \longrightarrow HOOCCH_2\mathbf{C(Me)_2CH_2COMe}$

(*c*) $EtOOCCH(CN)\mathbf{CH_2CH_2COCH_2CH_2}CH(CN)COOEt \longrightarrow$

$$HOOCCH_2\mathbf{CH_2CH_2COCH_2CH_2}CH_2COOH$$

The CN's are hydrolyzed and the resulting substituted malonic acids lose CO_2.

(*d*) $(CH_3CO)_2CH\mathbf{CH_2CH_2CHO}$; no change on hydrolysis.

18.80 Complete each reaction and rationalize the product:

(*a*) $Me_2CHNO_2 + CH_2{=}CHCOOEt \xrightarrow{OH^-/H_2O}$ (*b*) $\text{AAE} + CH_2{=}CHNO_2 \xrightarrow{\text{base}}$

(*a*) $Me_2C(NO_2){-}CH_2CH_2COOEt$

The intermediate carbanion, $Me_2\bar{C}NO_2$, undergoes a Michael addition to the conjugated ester.

(*b*) $CH_3COCH_2{-}CH_2CH_2NO_2$. $CH_2{=}CHNO_2$ is a good Michael acceptor.

18.81 Synthesize (*a*) $PhCOCH_2CH_2CHO$ (**A**) and (*b*) $CH_3CH_2COCH_2CH_2COPh$ (**B**) using dithiane, $CH_2{=}CHCOPh$ (**C**), and any aliphatic compound of two or fewer C's.

C is a Michael acceptor and dithiane is a way of introducing a masked C=O.

(*a*)

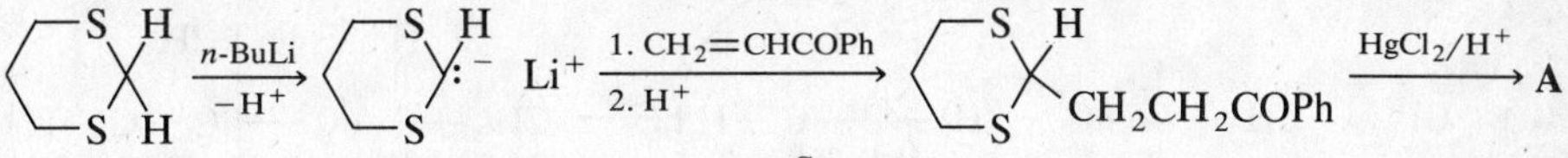

(*b*) Ethylate dithiane first with CH_3CH_2Br to give and repeat the process in (*a*).

18.82 Give the product from the addition of HBr to methyl acrylate, $H_2C{=}CHCOOMe$, and the mechanism for its formation.

Initially H^+ adds to C=O, not to C=C, to give a resonance stabilized cation:

$$\left[H_2C{=}CH{-}\overset{+:\ddot{O}H}{\overset{\|}{C}}OMe \longleftrightarrow H_2C{=}CH{-}\overset{:\ddot{O}H}{\underset{+}{\overset{|}{C}}}OMe \longleftrightarrow {}^{+}CH_2CH{=}\overset{:\ddot{O}H}{\overset{|}{C}}OMe \right] \xrightarrow{Br^-}$$

$$\left[H_2C{=}CH{-}\overset{OH}{\underset{Br}{C}}OMe \right] + H_2CBrCH{=}\underset{OH}{C}OMe$$

1,2-adduct (**D**) 1,4-adduct (**E**)

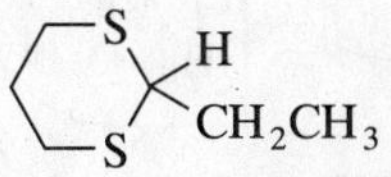

D is unstable and returns to starting material. The enol **E** tautomerizes to the more stable H_2CBrCH_2COOMe, the final product.

ALDOL-TYPE ADDITIONS

18.83 (*a*) Define the terms (i) aldol addition and (ii) mixed aldol addition. (*b*) What reagents are used as catalysts? (*c*) What kind of products are formed from these additions. (*d*) Name the bond which forms the products in (*c*). (*e*) Write a general equation for the aldol addition. (*f*) What further reaction of the product in (*c*) may occur? (*g*) What effect does the step in (*f*) have on the equilibrium of the overall reaction? (*h*) What are aldol-type additions?

◢ (*a*) (i) The addition of the nucleophilic carbanion-enolate, usually of an aldehyde, to the C=O of its parent compound is called an *aldol addition*. (ii) In a *mixed aldol addition* the carbanion-enolate adds to the C=O of a molecule other than its parent. (*b*) The bases used are typically aqueous NaOH and NaOR in the corresponding ROH. Room temperature suffices. (*c*) β-Hydroxycarbonyl compounds; hence the name *ald* for aldehyde and *ol* for alcohol. (*d*) A C—C bond forms because the C, not the O, is the more reactive site in the carbanion-enolate. In fact, the enolate contributing structure is usually omitted when writing equations even though it makes the greater contribution.

(*e*)

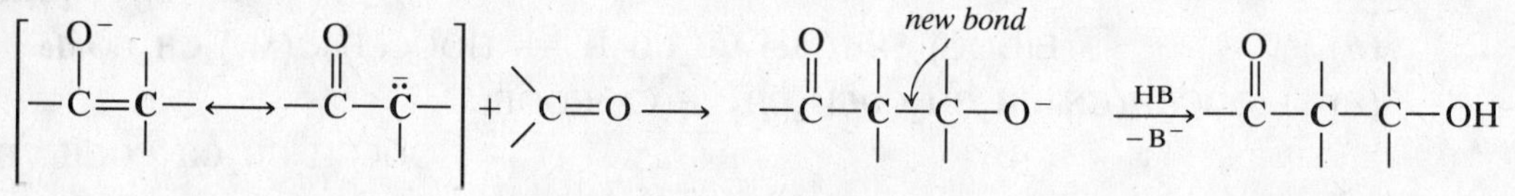

carbanion-enolate carbonyl acceptor alkoxide of β-hydroxcarbonyl compound β-hydroxcarbonyl compound

(*f*) The alcohol can lose H_2O, even in base, giving an α,β-unsaturated carbonyl compound. If more extensive conjugation is engendered, dehydration occurs on formation of the alcohol, otherwise the reaction mixture must be warmed. The reaction leading directly to the unsaturated carbonyl compound is called an *aldol condensation*. (*g*) Formation of the β-hydroxy carbonyl compound is reversible, but dehydration is irreversible under basic conditions. Formation of the alkene draws the overall reaction to completion. (*h*) When the carbanion is generated from a substrate other than a carbonyl compound (see Table 18-1), an *aldol-type* reaction occurs. Except for this fact, there are no other differences.

18.84 (*a*) Show the net reactions for the formation of the aldol adduct from (i) propanal in dilute NaOH and (ii) acetone with $Ba(OH)_2$. Name the products. (*b*) Give the major difference between these two additions. (*c*) How can we increase the poor yields of aldol-addition products from ketones?

◢ (*a*) (i)

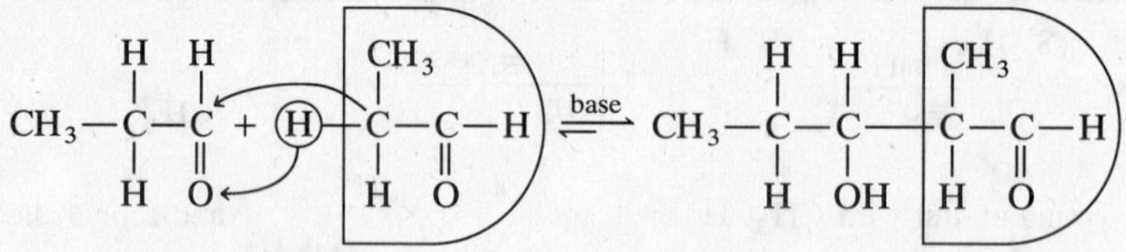

Propanal   2-Methyl-3-hydroxypentanal

(ii)

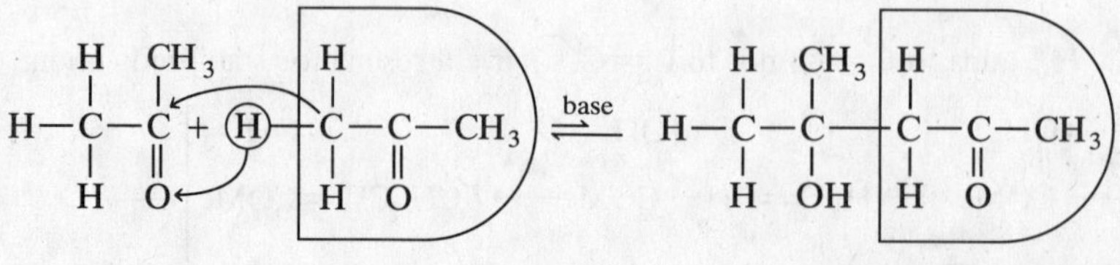

Acetone   Diacetone alcohol (4-Hydroxy-4-methyl-2-pentanone)

(*b*) Both reactions are reversible. However, reaction (i) from an aldehyde favors the product and reaction (ii) from a ketone favors the reactant. (*c*) As the product forms, continuously remove it from the basic catalyst.

18.85 Suggest a mechanism for the OH^--catalyzed aldol addition of CH_3CHO.

$\blacksquare$ *Step 1.*

$$H-\ddot{O}:^- + H:\overset{\overset{H}{|}}{\underset{\underset{H}{|}}{C}}-\overset{\overset{H}{|}}{\underset{\underset{H}{|}}{C}}=O \rightleftharpoons H_2O + {}^-:\overset{\overset{H}{|}}{\underset{\underset{H}{|}}{C}}-\overset{\overset{H}{|}}{\underset{\underset{H}{|}}{C}}=\ddot{O}:$$

Step 2.

$$CH_3\overset{\overset{H}{|}}{\underset{\underset{:O:}{||}}{C}} + {}^-:\overset{\overset{H}{|}}{\underset{\underset{H}{|}}{C}}-\overset{H}{\underset{H}{C}}=O \rightleftharpoons CH_3-\overset{\overset{H}{|}}{\underset{\underset{:O:^-}{|}}{C}}:\overset{H}{\underset{H}{C}}-\overset{H}{\underset{H}{C}}=O$$

alkoxide ion of the
β-hydroxyaldehyde

Step 3.

$$CH_3-\overset{\overset{H}{|}}{\underset{\underset{:O:^-}{|}}{C}}:\overset{\overset{H}{|}}{\underset{\underset{H}{|}}{C}}-\overset{H}{C}=O + H:\ddot{O}H \rightleftharpoons CH_3-\overset{\overset{H}{|}}{\underset{\underset{HO}{|}}{C}}-\overset{\overset{H}{|}}{\underset{\underset{H}{|}}{C}}-\overset{H}{\underset{H}{C}}=O + :\ddot{O}H^-$$

18.86 Supply a general mechanism for the H^+-catalyzed aldol additions of $C=O$ compounds.

$$\blacksquare \quad H-\overset{OH}{\underset{|}{C}}-\overset{OH}{\underset{+}{C}}{}^- + -\overset{OH}{C}=C- \rightleftharpoons \left[\begin{array}{c} H-\overset{OH}{\underset{|}{C}}-\overset{OH}{\underset{|}{C}}-\overset{|}{C}-\overset{:\ddot{O}H}{C^+} \\ \updownarrow \\ H-\overset{OH}{\underset{|}{C}}-\overset{OH}{\underset{|}{C}}-\overset{|}{C}-\overset{{}^+:\ddot{O}H}{\underset{||}{C}}- \end{array}\right] \overset{-H^+}{\rightleftharpoons} H-\overset{OH}{\underset{|}{C}}-\overset{|}{\underset{|}{C}}-\overset{|}{\underset{|}{C}}-\overset{\ddot{O}:}{\underset{||}{C}}-$$

protonated   enol   aldol
carbonyl compound   (nucleophile)
(electrophile)

The dehydration product is usually found in acid.

18.87 Show the net reactions for the formation of the aldol products and their dehydration products from (*a*) butanal, (*b*) phenylacetaldehyde, (*c*) 3-pentanone, (*d*) cyclohexanone, and (*e*) 2,2-dimethylpropanal(pivaldehyde).

$\blacksquare$ For (*a*) through (*d*) see Table 18-2. Each reactant is listed as acceptor (it has $C=O$) or carbanion source (it forms the carbanion). In (*d*) cyclic ketones are good acceptors because there is no longer any steric hindrance

TABLE 18-2

	Acceptor	Carbanion Source	Adduct	Dehydration Product
(*a*)	$CH_3CH_2CH_2\overset{H}{\underset{O}{C}}$	$+$ $\textcircled{H}-\overset{H}{\underset{C_2H_5}{C}}-\overset{H}{C}=O$	$\longrightarrow$ $CH_3CH_2CH_2\overset{H}{\underset{OH}{C}}-\overset{\overset{H}{|}}{\underset{C_2H_5}{C}}-\overset{H}{C}=O$	$\overset{-H_2O}{\longrightarrow}$ $CH_3CH_2CH_2\overset{H}{C}=\overset{\overset{H}{|}}{\underset{C_2H_5}{C}}-CH=O$ *mixture of geometric isomers*
(*b*)	$PhCH_2\overset{H}{\underset{O}{C}}$	$+$ $\textcircled{H}-\overset{H}{\underset{Ph}{C}}-\overset{H}{C}=O$	$\longrightarrow$ $PhCH_2\overset{H}{\underset{OH}{C}}-\overset{\overset{H}{|}}{\underset{Ph}{C}}-\overset{H}{C}=O$	$\overset{-H_2O}{\longrightarrow}$ *trans* $\overset{PhCH_2}{\underset{H}{}}\!\!C=C\!\!\overset{CHO}{\underset{Ph}{}}$
(*c*)	$CH_3CH_2\overset{CH_2CH_3}{\underset{O}{C}}$	$+$ $\textcircled{H}-\overset{H}{\underset{CH_3}{C}}-\overset{}{\underset{O}{C}}-CH_2CH_3$	$\longrightarrow$ $CH_3CH_2\overset{CH_3CH_2}{\underset{OH}{C}}-\overset{\overset{H}{|}}{\underset{CH_3}{C}}-\overset{}{\underset{O}{C}}-CH_2CH_3$	$\overset{-H_2O}{\longrightarrow}$ $CH_3CH_2\overset{CH_2CH_3}{C}=\overset{}{\underset{CH_3}{C}}-\overset{}{\underset{O}{C}}CH_2CH_3$
(*d*)	(cyclohexanone)	$+$ (cyclohexanone with $\textcircled{H}$)	$\longrightarrow$ (HO-cyclohexyl-cyclohexanone adduct)	$\longrightarrow$ (cyclohexylidene cyclohexanone)

to the approaching carbanion. (*e*) There is no aldol addition because Me$_3$CCHO has no α H. With concentrated NaOH at higher temperatures, the Cannizzaro reaction (Problems 15.109 and 15.110) occurs.

18.88 (*a*) Show the formation of all possible products from the aldol reaction of (i) a mixture of two aldehydes, each with an α H and (ii) a nonsymmetrical ketone with an H on each α C. (*b*) Are such reactions synthetically useful? (*c*) How can the yield of a ketone aldol adduct be improved?

◢ (*a*) (i) Each RCHO can react with itself to give two products. One RCHO can become the carbanion and react with the other as acceptor, and vice versa, affording two more products [see Table 18-3 (i)]. (ii) Two products are possible. There is a single acceptor but two different carbanion sources—one from each α C [see Table 18-3 (ii)]. (*b*) Because of the mixtures of products, these aldol reactions have limited synthetic value. (*c*) When the hindered base, LDA (lithium diisopropylamide), is used to form the carbanion, the order of ease of removal of an α H is 1° > 2° > 3°. If the α H's on the two α C's are different, only one carbanion is generated.

TABLE 18-3

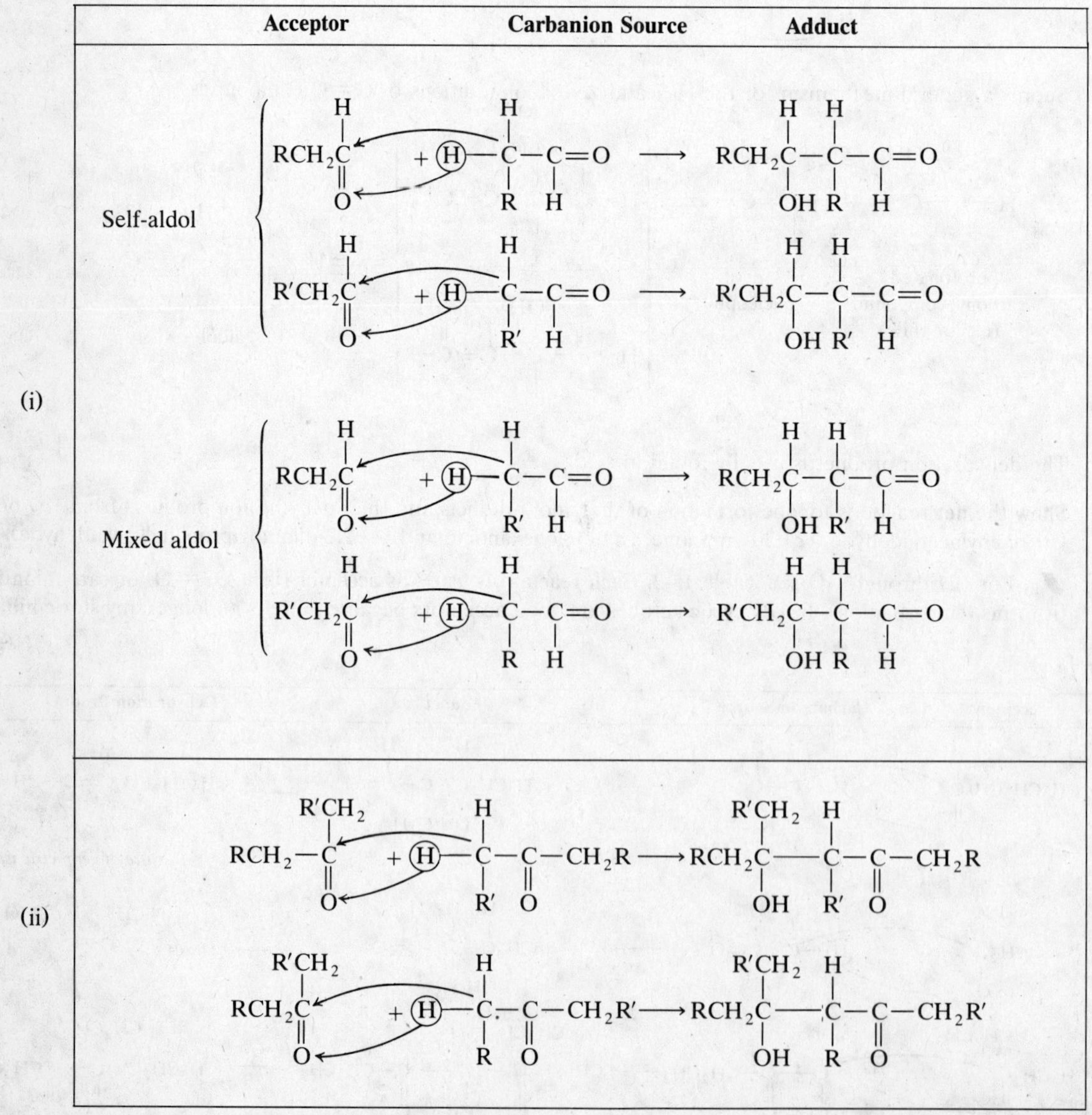

	Acceptor	Carbanion Source	Adduct
Self-aldol (i)	RCH$_2$C(H)=O + (H)—CH(R)—C=O(H)		RCH$_2$CH(OH)—CH(R)—CHO
	R'CH$_2$C(H)=O + (H)—CH(R')—C=O(H)		R'CH$_2$CH(OH)—CH(R')—CHO
Mixed aldol	RCH$_2$C(H)=O + (H)—CH(R')—C=O(H)		RCH$_2$CH(OH)—CH(R')—CHO
	R'CH$_2$C(H)=O + (H)—CH(R)—C=O(H)		R'CH$_2$CH(OH)—CH(R)—CHO

(ii)

RCH$_2$—C(CH$_2$R')=O + (H)—CH(R')—C(=O)—CH$_2$R ⟶ RCH$_2$C(CH$_2$R')(OH)—CH(R')—C(=O)—CH$_2$R

RCH$_2$C(CH$_2$R')=O + (H)—CH(R)—C(=O)—CH$_2$R' ⟶ RCH$_2$C(CH$_2$R')(OH)—CH(R)—C(=O)—CH$_2$R'

18.89 (*a*) What kinds of aldehydes can react to give a good yield of mixed aldol product? (*b*) Give the structure of aldol product from reaction of a symmetrical ketone with an RCHO (i) with an α H and (ii) without an α H.

▰ (*a*) If one of the aldehydes has no α H, it can only serve as an acceptor, thus eliminating two of the four possible aldol products in Problem 18.88 as shown:

Mixed aldol

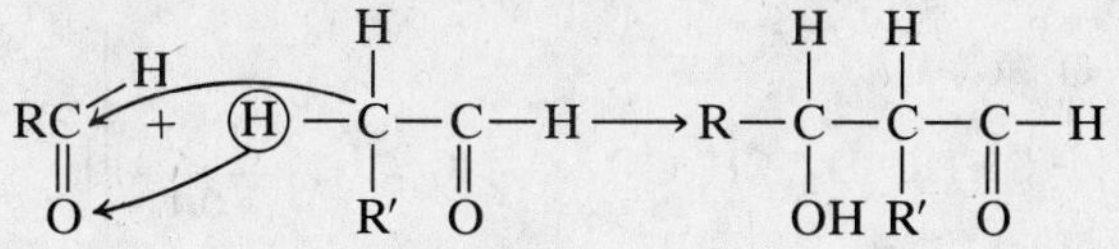

$$RC\underset{\displaystyle O}{\overset{\displaystyle H}{\|}} + \textcircled{H}-\underset{R'}{\overset{H}{C}}-\underset{O}{\overset{}{C}}-H \longrightarrow R-\underset{OH}{\overset{H}{C}}-\underset{R'}{\overset{H}{C}}-\underset{O}{\overset{}{C}}-H$$

Self-aldol

$$R'-CH_2C\underset{\displaystyle O}{\overset{\displaystyle H}{\|}} + \textcircled{H}-\underset{R'}{\overset{H}{C}}-\underset{O}{\overset{}{C}}-H \longrightarrow R'CH_2-\underset{OH}{\overset{H}{C}}-\underset{R'}{\overset{H}{C}}-\underset{O}{\overset{}{C}}-H$$

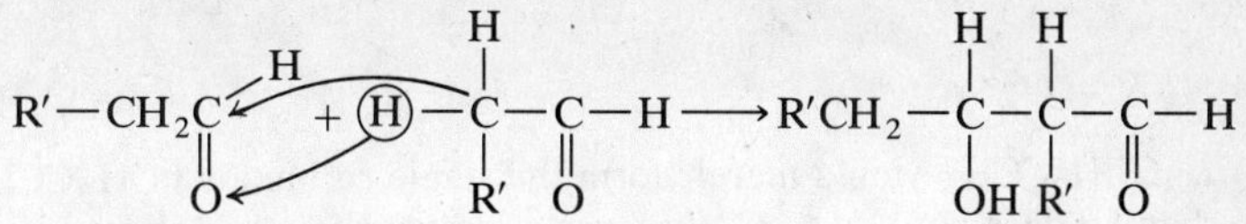

Minimize self-aldolization by adding the RCHO with the α H slowly to a large amount of the RCHO lacking the α H. (*b*) (i) Ketones are good carbanion sources but poor acceptors. Two products are possible: (*1*) the self-aldol product of RCHO which can be minimized by its proper addition to the ketone [as in (*a*)] and (*2*) the mixed aldol product:

$$RCH_2COCH_2R + R'CH_2CHO \longrightarrow RCH_2CO\underset{|}{\overset{R}{C}}H-\underset{|}{\overset{OH}{C}}HCH_2R'$$

carbanion source   acceptor   mixed aldol adduct, **A**

(ii) Self-aldolization of RCHO is impossible and only the single mixed aldol adduct, **A**, results.

18.90 Give the final products of the reaction of an aryl aldehyde PhCH=O with (*a*) CH_3CHO and (*b*) CH_3COCH_3.

▰ In these *Claisen-Schmidt reactions*, where ArCHO must be the acceptor, the first formed β-hydroxy carbonyl compound undergoes rapid dehydration to give the stable α,β-unsaturated carbonyl grouping, now further conjugated with the Ph.

(*a*)
$$\left[Ph\underset{OH}{\overset{H}{\underset{|}{\overset{|}{C}}}}-CH_2\underset{O}{\overset{}{\underset{\|}{C}}}-H \right] \longrightarrow PhCH=CHCHO$$
trans

(*b*)
$$\left[Ph\underset{OH}{\overset{H}{\underset{|}{\overset{|}{C}}}}-CH_2-\underset{O}{\overset{}{\underset{\|}{C}}}-CH_3 \right] \longrightarrow PhCH=CH\underset{O}{\overset{}{\underset{\|}{C}}}CH_3$$
trans

18.91 Give the aldol products and the corresponding alkenes (aq. NaOH or KOH used, 100 °C) from (*a*) 2,5-hexanedione, (*b*) 2,7-octanedione, (*c*) 2,8-nonanedione, and (*d*) 2,4-pentanedione.

▰ Properly constituted diketones give cyclic *intramolecular* aldol addition products. The carbanions are used to show the aldol addition leading to the hydroxy and alkene products.

(*a*)
$$C^6H_3\overset{O}{\overset{\|}{C}}{}^5C^4H_2C^3H_2\overset{O}{\overset{\|}{C}}{}^2C^1H_2:^- \xrightarrow[-OH^-]{-H_2O} \left[\text{ring with } OH, C^6H_3 \right] \xrightarrow{-H_2O} \text{cyclopentenone}$$

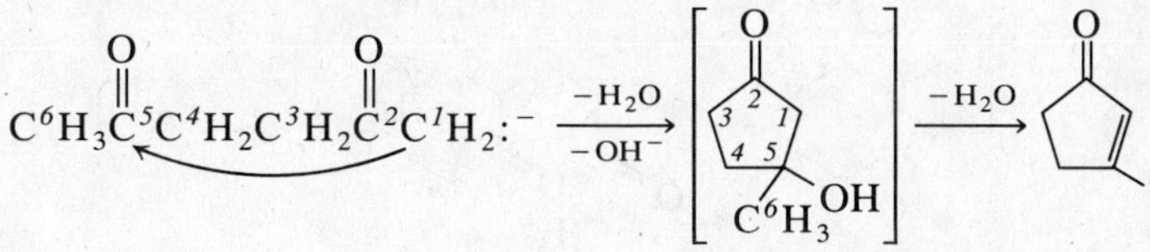

(*b*)
$$C^8H_3\overset{O}{\overset{\|}{C}}{}^7C^6H_2C^5H_2C^4H_2\bar{C}^3HC^2H_2C^1H_3 \xrightarrow[-OH^-]{H_2O} \left[\text{ring with } C-C^1H_3, OH, C^8H_3 \right] \xrightarrow{-H_2O} \text{cyclopentene with acyl}$$

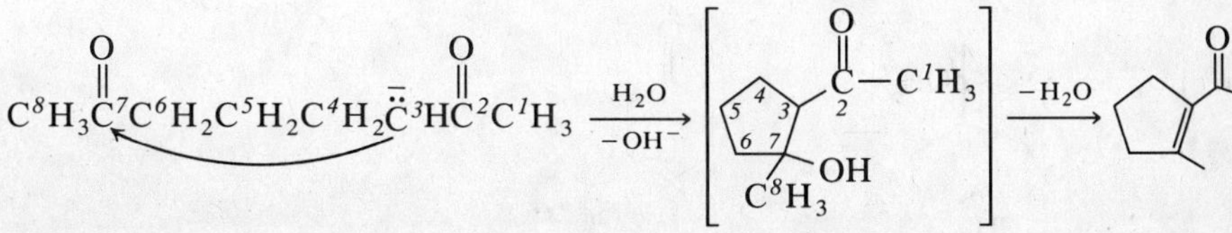

Cyclization of the carbanion from C^1 on C^7=O would lead to a seven membered ring—an improbable route because of the unfavorable ΔS of reaction (ΔS_r).

(c) $C^9H_3C^8C^7H_2C^6H_2C^5H_2C^4H_2\ddot{C}^3HC^2H_3 \xrightarrow[-OH^-]{H_2O}$ [cyclohexane ring structure with $C-C^1H_3$, OH, C^9H_3] $\xrightarrow{-H_2O}$ [cyclohexene with acetyl and methyl groups]

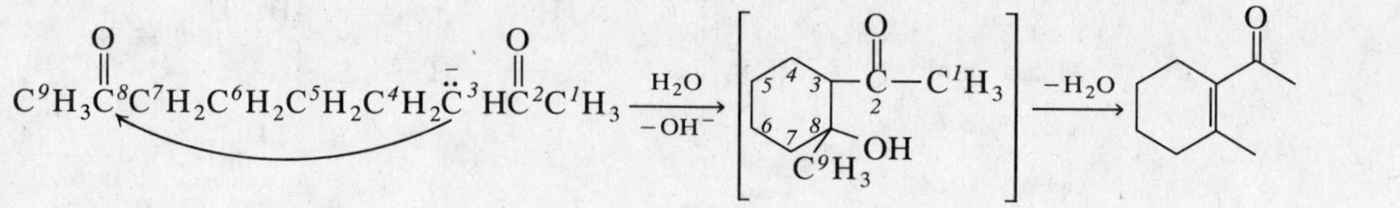

(d) $CH_3\overset{O}{\overset{\|}{C}}CH_2\overset{O}{\overset{\|}{C}}CH_3$ would merely form the stable carbanion $(CH_3\overset{O}{\overset{\|}{C}}\overset{..}{C}HCCH_3)$ and react no further. The C^1 carbanion does not add to C^4 because a strained four-membered ring would result.

18.92 Compare the ΔS_r for intermolecular and intramolecular aldolizations.

▮ The ΔS for the intermolecular reaction is less favorable because two species go to one whereas in the intramolecular reaction one reactant molecule goes to one product molecule.

18.93 (a) Identify which of the following compounds can be prepared in good yield in a one-step aldolization, and give the necessary reactants. (b) Identify those that cannot be synthesized or may be synthesized in poor yields and explain why.
(i) PhCH=CHCOCH=CHPh, (ii) PhCH=CHCH$_2$COMe, (iii) PhCH=CHCH$_2$CH$_2$COMe,
(iv) PhCOCH=CH$_2$, (v) PhCH=CHCH=CHCOMe, (vi) 3-ethyl-2-methyl-2-cyclohexenone (A), (vii) 2-methyl-

1-cyclohexenecarboxaldehyde, (viii) [structure], and (ix) 4-methylbicyclo[2.2.2]octa-3-one-1-ol.

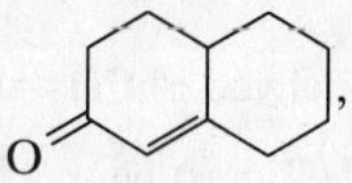

▮ Look at the hydroxy precursor of the alkene, break the α-β bond, and change C—OH to C=O.

(a) (i) PhCH$\overset{OH}{|}$╪CH$_2$COCH$_2$╪$\overset{OH}{|}$CHPh ⟵ PhCHO + CH$_3$COCH$_3$ + OCHPh

(iv) PhCOCH$_2$╪CH$_2$OH ⟵ PhCOCH$_3$ + O=CH$_2$

(v) PhCH=CHCH(OH)╪CH$_2$COMe ⟵ PhCH=CHCHO + CH$_3$COMe

Also,

PhCH(OH)╪CH$_2$CH=CHCOMe ⟵ PhCHO + CH$_3$CH=CHCOMe

because $^-$:CH$_2$CH=CHCOMe is formed more easily than $^-$:CH$_2$COCH=CHCH$_3$ (see Problem 18.95).

(vi) 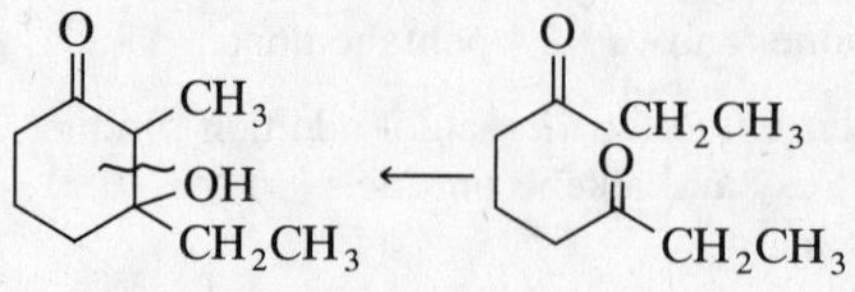 [cyclohexanone structure with CH$_3$, OH, CH$_2$CH$_3$] ⟵ [structure with CH$_2$CH$_3$, O, CH$_2$CH$_3$]

(viii) [bicyclic structure with O, OH] ⟵ [bicyclic structure with O=C, O, CH$_3$]

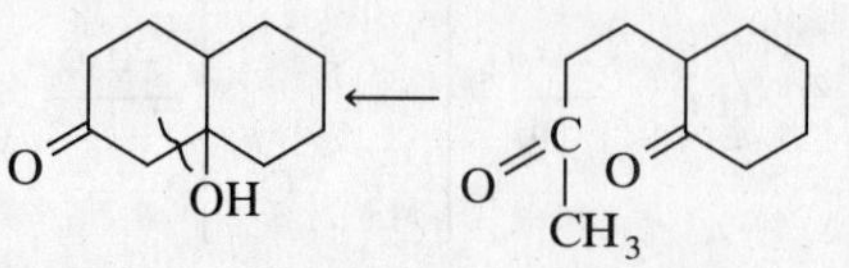

(ix) 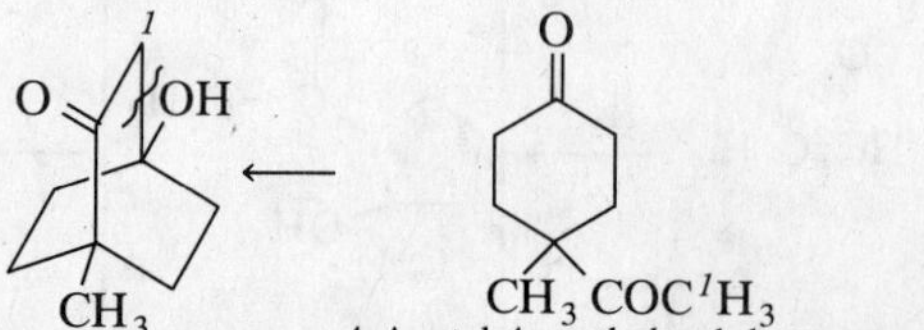 [bicyclic structure with O, OH, CH$_3$] ⟵ [cyclohexanone with CH$_3$COC^{1}H$_3$]

4-Acetyl-4-methylcyclohexanone

(*b*) (ii) $PhCH_2CH(OH)-CH_2COMe \longleftarrow PhCH_2CHO + MeCOMe$. $PhCH_2CHO$ also self-aldolizes. $PhCH(OH)-C^{\beta}H_2CH_2COMe$ is an impossible precursor because the C^- from loss of a β-H would have to react.

(iii) $PhCH(OH)-CH_2CH_2CH_2COMe$. Aldol is impossible because a γ **R**:$^-$ would have to react.

(vii)

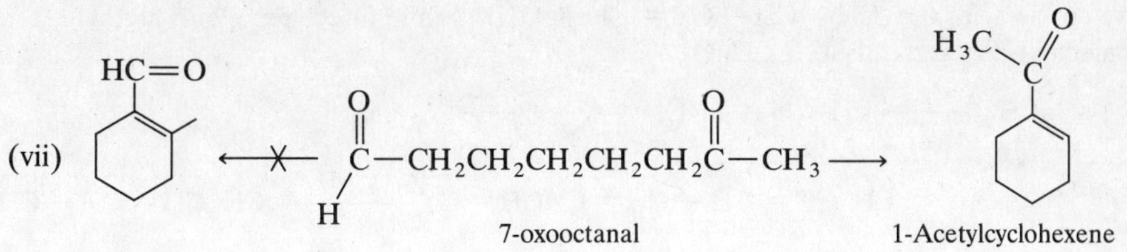

7-oxooctanal   1-Acetylcyclohexene

CHO is a better acceptor than —CO— and would cyclize to give 1-acetylcyclohexene.

18.94 Prepare the following compounds from CH_3CH_2CHO. Do not repeat precursor syntheses.
(*a*) $CH_3CH_2CH=C(CH_3)CHO$ (**A**)   (*d*) $CH_3CH_2CH_2CH(CH_3)CH_2OH$ (**D**)
(*b*) $CH_3CH_2CH_2CH(CH_3)CHO$ (**B**)   (*e*) $CH_3CH_2CH_2CH(CH_3)_2$ (**E**)
(*c*) $CH_3CH_2CH=C(CH_3)CH_2OH$ (**C**)   (*f*) $CH_3CH_2CH(OH)CH(CH_3)COOH$ (**F**)

◢ Each product has six C's, which is twice the number of C's in CH_3CH_2CHO. This suggests an aldol addition as the first step.

(*a*) $CH_3CH_2CHO \xrightarrow{OH^-} CH_3CH_2CH(OH)CH(CH_3)CHO \xrightarrow[\Delta]{H^+}$ (**A**) $+ H_2O$

(*b*) The C=C of **A** is reduced with Li, liq. NH_3, EtOH, leaving CHO untouched.
(*c*) The CHO of **A** is selectively reduced by $NaBH_4$ in EtOH.
(*d*) Both C=O and C=C are reduced by catalytic (i.e., Pt) hydrogenation;   or **B** $\xrightarrow[EtOH]{NaBH_4}$ **D**

(*e*)   **A** $\xrightarrow[OH^-,\,\Delta]{H_2NNH_2} CH_3CH_2CH=C(CH_3)_2 \xrightarrow{H_2/Pd}$ **E**;   or **B** $\xrightarrow[OH^-]{H_2NNH_2}$ **E**

(*f*) Tollens' reagent, $Ag(NH_3)_2^+$, is a specific oxidant for CHO $\longrightarrow$ COOH.

$$CH_3CH_2CH(OH)CH(CH_3)CHO \xrightarrow[2.\;H^+]{1.\;Ag(NH_3)_2^+} \textbf{F}$$

18.95 (*a*) Give the mixed aldol product from the reaction of crotonaldehyde, $CH_3CH=CHCH=O$ (**A**), with CH_3CHO. Show the mechanistic steps with explanation.   (*b*) Give one drawback to this reaction.

◢ (*a*) The − charge generated by removal of the γ H of **A** by base is delocalized to O through the conjugated system giving a stable carbanion-enolate. The anion adds to the C=O of CH_3CHO to give a δ-hydroxy alcohol that rapidly loses H_2O to give the triply-conjugated product as shown:

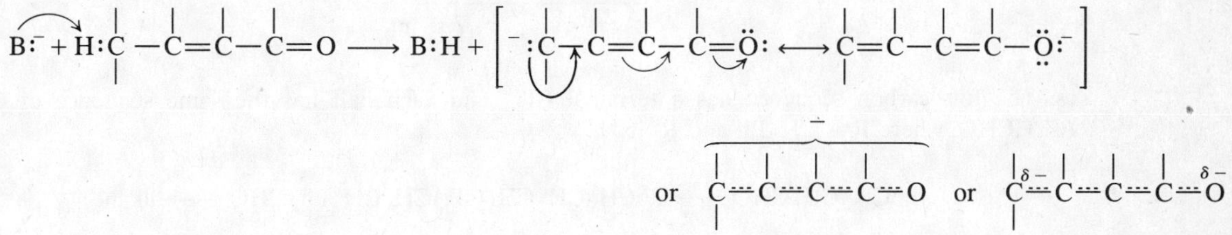

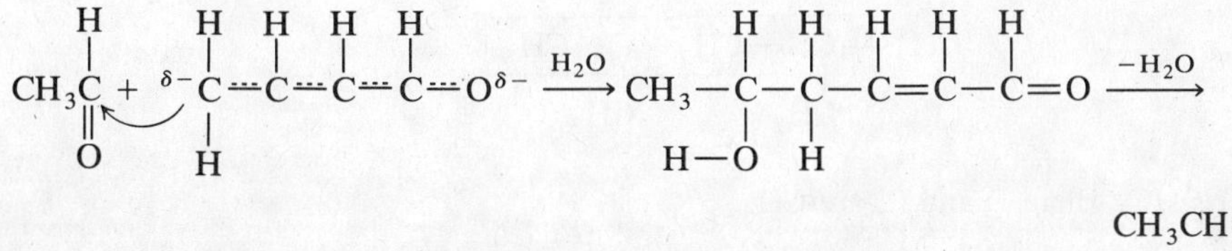

$$CH_3CH=CH-CH=CHCH=O$$

Sorbic aldehyde

(*b*) Sorbic aldehyde has an acidic H and hence is capable of reacting with more CH_3CHO to eventually give polymeric material.

18.96 Use readily available aldehydes (one to four C's) to prepare the following commercial compounds: (*a*) the food preservative sorbic acid, $CH_3CH=CH-CH=CHCOOH$, (*b*) the insect repellent, 2-ethyl-1,3-hexanediol, and (*c*) the humectant pentaerythritol, $C(CH_2OH)_4$.

◢ (*a*) $2CH_3CHO \xrightarrow[-H_2O]{OH^-} CH_3CH=CHCH=O \xrightarrow[OH^-]{CH_3CHO}$

$$CH_3CH=CH-CH=CHCH=O \xrightarrow[2.\ H^+]{1.\ Ag(NH_3)_2^+} CH_3CH=CH-CH=CHCOOH$$

(*b*) $CH_3CH_2CH_2CHO \xrightarrow{OH^-} CH_3CH_2CH_2CH(OH)\underset{\underset{\displaystyle CH_2CH_3}{|}}{C}HCHO \xrightarrow{H_2/Pd} CH_3CH_2CH_2CH(OH)\underset{\underset{\displaystyle CH_2CH_3}{|}}{C}HCH_2OH$

(*c*) CH_3CHO undergoes mixed aldol condensations with 3 mol of $H_2C=O$. A fourth mole of $H_2C=O$ then reacts with the product by a crossed-Cannizzaro reaction (Problem 15.111).

$$3H_2C=O + CH_3CHO \xrightarrow{Ca(OH)_2} (HOCH_2)_3CHO \xrightarrow[\text{conc. NaOH}]{H_2CO} C(CH_2OH)_4 + HCOO^-Na^+$$

18.97 Which of the following alkanes can be synthesized starting with a self-aldol reaction of RCHO? (*a*) $CH_3CH_2CH_2CH(CH_3)CH_2CH_3$, (*b*) $PhCH_2CH_2CH_2CH(CH_3)CH_2Ph$, (*c*) $Me_2CHCH_2CMe_3$, and (*d*) $CH_3CH_2CH_2CH_2CH_2CHMe_2$.

◢ The general formula for the aldol product of RR′CHCHO is shown in Fig. 18-4(*a*). The arrow points to the formed bond, and the carbonyl and α C's are in the rectangle. The alkane always has a terminal CH_3 in the four-carbon sequence shown in Fig. 18-4(*b*). It is formed by reduction of CHO.

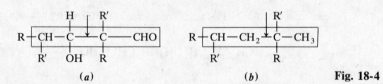

$$\text{(a)} \qquad\qquad\qquad \text{(b)} \qquad\qquad \textbf{Fig. 18-4}$$

(*a*) No. The alkane has an odd number of C's. Combining two RCHO's must give products with an even number of C's.

(*b*)

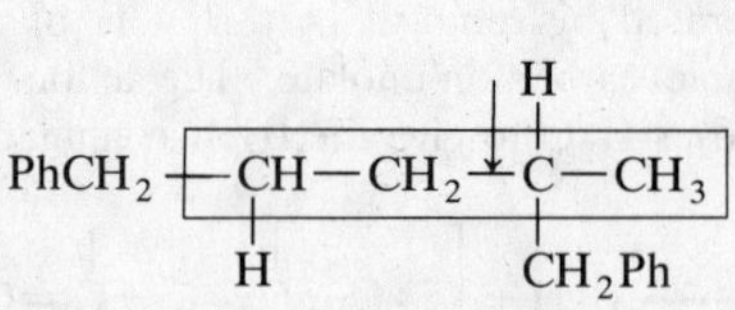

$$PhCH_2\underset{\underset{\displaystyle H}{|}}{\overset{}{C}H}-CH_2\overset{\overset{\displaystyle H}{|}}{\underset{\underset{\displaystyle CH_2Ph}{|}}{C}}-CH_3$$

Yes. The four-carbon sequence has a terminal CH_3 and each half has the same sequence of C's. Use RR′CHCHO, where R is CH_2Ph and R′ is H.

$$PhCH_2CH_2CHO \longrightarrow PhCH_2CH_2CH(OH)CH(CH_2Ph)CHO \longrightarrow \text{alkane}$$

(*c*)

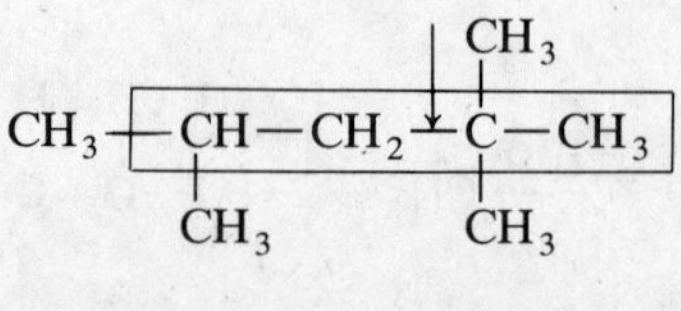

$$CH_3\underset{\underset{\displaystyle CH_3}{|}}{\overset{}{C}H}-CH_2\overset{\overset{\displaystyle CH_3}{|}}{\underset{\underset{\displaystyle CH_3}{|}}{C}}-CH_3$$

Yes. Use RR′CHCHO, where R and R′ are CH_3.

$$Me_2CHCHO \longrightarrow Me_2CH(OH)CMe_2CHO \longrightarrow \text{alkane}$$

(d)

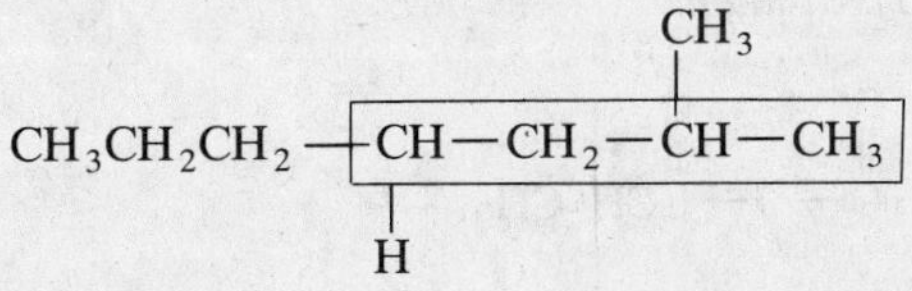

$$CH_3CH_2CH_2 \boxed{CH-CH_2-CH-CH_3}$$
$$\begin{array}{c} CH_3 \\ | \\ \end{array}$$
$$| \\ H$$

No. The two halves of the skeleton are different; one is branched and the other is not.

18.98 Give the structural formulas for the products of the aldol-type additions indicated in Table 18-4. See Table 18-1(a)–(g) for the necessary carbanions.

TABLE 18-4

	(a)	(b)	(c)	(d)	(e)	(f)	(g)
Acceptor	PhCHO	PhCHO	Me$_2$CO	Me$_2$CO	Me$_2$CO	Ph$_2$CO	PhCHO
Base	OH$^-$	OH$^-$	OH$^-$	NH$_2^-$	OH$^-$	NH$_2^-$	NHR$_2$
Carbanion source	$CH_3\overset{+}{N}\overset{O^-}{\underset{O}{\diagdown}}$	CH$_3$C≡N	CHCl$_3$	CH$_3$C≡CH	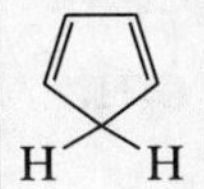 (cyclopentadiene, H H)	Ph$_2$CH$_2$	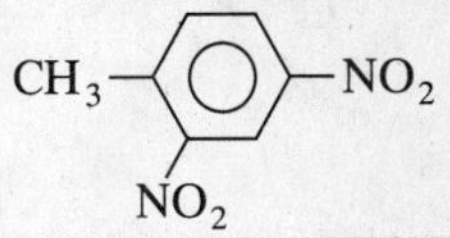 CH$_3$—(C$_6$H$_3$)(NO$_2$)—NO$_2$

▮ (a) *PhCH=CHNO$_2$ (b) *PhCH=CHCN (c) Me$_2$C—CCl$_3$
$$\qquad\qquad\qquad\qquad\qquad\qquad\qquad\qquad | \\ OH$$
(d) Me$_2$C—C≡CCH$_3$
$$\qquad\qquad | \\ \qquad\quad OH$$

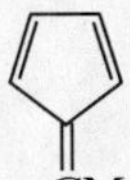

(e) (cyclopentadiene ring) CMe$_2$ (f) Ph$_2$C=CPh$_2$ (g) *PhCH=CH—(C$_6$H$_3$)—NO$_2$
$$\qquad\qquad\qquad\qquad\qquad\qquad\qquad\qquad\qquad\qquad\qquad NO_2$$

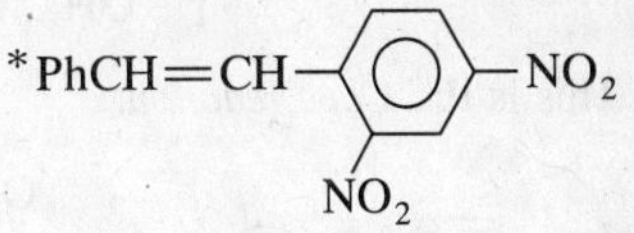

*The more stable *trans* isomer.

18.99 Prepare *trans*-cinnamic acid, PhCH=CHCOOH from benzaldehyde, PhCHO.

▮ α, β-Unsaturated carboxylic acids may be prepared from aromatic aldehydes by the Perkin condensation. The catalytic basic salt corresponds to the anhydride used.

$$PhCHO + (CH_3CO)_2O \xrightarrow{\text{NaOAc, } \Delta} trans\text{-}PhCH=CHCOOH$$

18.100 Give structures of the products from the following condensations:

(a) p-CH$_3$C$_6$H$_4$CHO + (CH$_3$CH$_2\overset{\overset{O}{\|}}{C})_2$O $\xrightarrow{\text{CH}_3\text{CH}_2\text{COO}^-\text{Na}^+}$ (b) Cyclohexanone + CH$_3$CH$_2$NO$_2$ $\xrightarrow{\text{OH}^-}$

(c) C$_6$H$_5$CHO + C$_6$H$_5$CH$_2$C≡N $\xrightarrow{\text{OH}^-}$ (d) Benzophenone + cyclopentadiene $\xrightarrow{\text{OH}^-}$

(e) CH$_3$COCH$_3$ + 2C$_6$H$_5$CHO $\xrightarrow{\text{OH}^-}$ (f) (cyclohexane)=O + N≡CCH$_2$COOCH$_3$

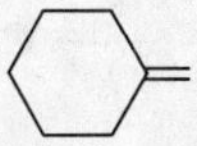

$$\xrightarrow{\text{CH}_3\text{COO}^-\text{NH}_4^+}$$

▌ (*a*) This is a *Perkin condensation.*

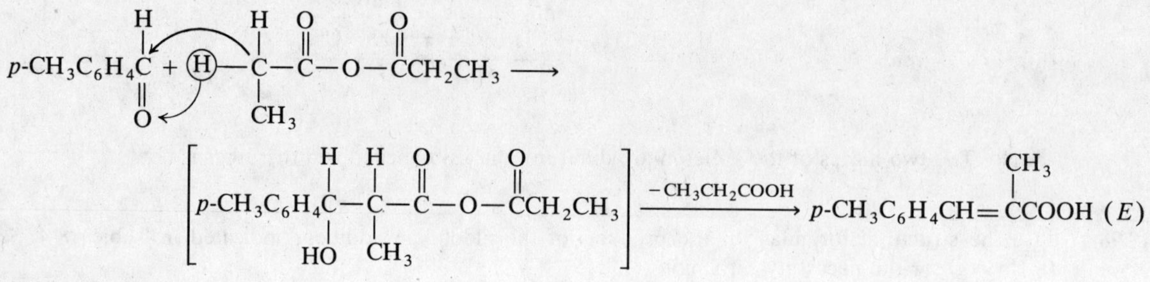

$$p\text{-}CH_3C_6H_4\overset{\overset{H}{|}}{\underset{\overset{\|}{O}}{C}} + \overset{H}{\underset{\overset{\|}{O}}{\underset{\overset{|}{CH_3}}{C}}} \overset{\overset{O}{\|}}{\underset{}{C}} - O - \overset{O}{\overset{\|}{C}}CH_2CH_3 \longrightarrow$$

$$\left[p\text{-}CH_3C_6H_4\overset{\overset{H}{|}}{\underset{\overset{|}{HO}}{C}} - \overset{\overset{H}{|}}{\underset{\overset{|}{CH_3}}{C}} - \overset{\overset{O}{\|}}{C} - O - \overset{O}{\overset{\|}{C}}CH_2CH_3 \right] \xrightarrow{-CH_3CH_2COOH} p\text{-}CH_3C_6H_4CH = \overset{\overset{CH_3}{|}}{C}COOH \ (E)$$

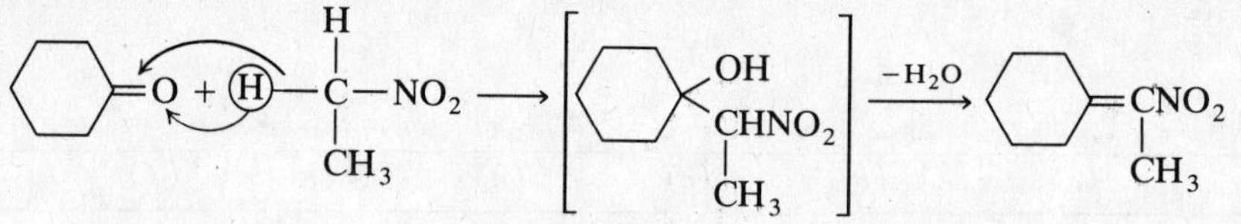

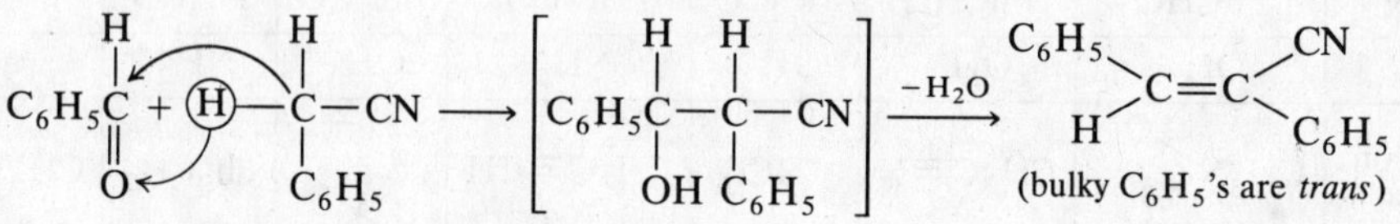

(*b*) ⬡$=O + \overset{H}{\underset{\overset{|}{CH_3}}{C}} - NO_2 \longrightarrow \left[\overset{OH}{\underset{\overset{|}{CH_3}}{⬡}}\overset{|}{\underset{CHNO_2}{}} \right] \xrightarrow{-H_2O}$ ⬡$= \overset{CNO_2}{\underset{CH_3}{}}$

(*c*) $C_6H_5\overset{\overset{H}{|}}{\underset{\overset{\|}{O}}{C}} + \overset{H}{\underset{\overset{|}{C_6H_5}}{C}} - CN \longrightarrow \left[C_6H_5\overset{\overset{H}{|}}{\underset{\overset{|}{OH}}{C}} - \overset{\overset{H}{|}}{\underset{\overset{|}{C_6H_5}}{C}} - CN \right] \xrightarrow{-H_2O} \overset{C_6H_5}{\underset{H}{}}C = C\overset{CN}{\underset{C_6H_5}{}}$

(bulky C_6H_5's are *trans*)

(*d*) $Ph_2C=O + $ ⬠ $\longrightarrow \left[Ph_2\overset{OH}{\underset{\overset{|}{H}}{C}} \text{⬠} \right] \xrightarrow{-H_2O} Ph_2C = $ ⬠

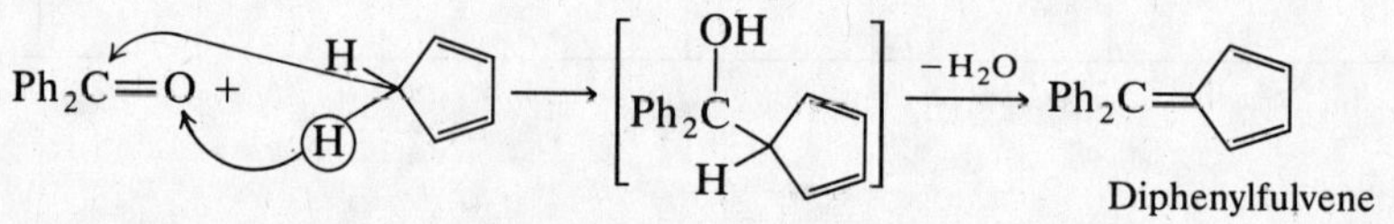

Diphenylfulvene

(*e*) Each CH_3 of $(CH_3)_2CO$ reacts with one PhCHO.

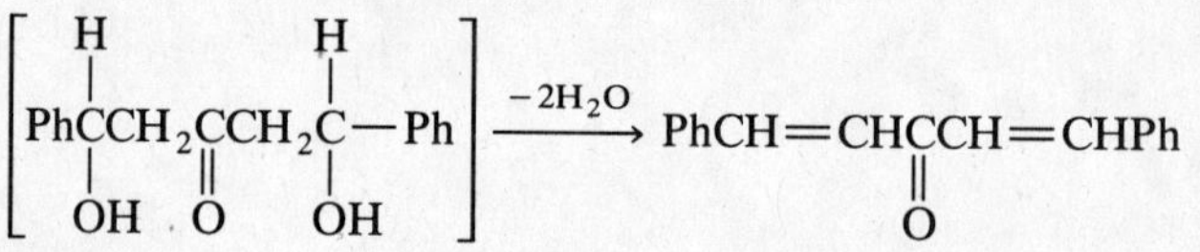

$$\left[Ph\overset{\overset{H}{|}}{\underset{\overset{|}{OH}}{C}}CH_2\overset{\overset{}{}}{\underset{\overset{\|}{O}}{C}}CH_2\overset{\overset{H}{|}}{\underset{\overset{|}{OH}}{C}}-Ph \right] \xrightarrow{-2H_2O} PhCH=CHCCH=CHPh \atop \underset{\overset{\|}{O}}{}$$

(*f*) This is the *Cope reaction.*

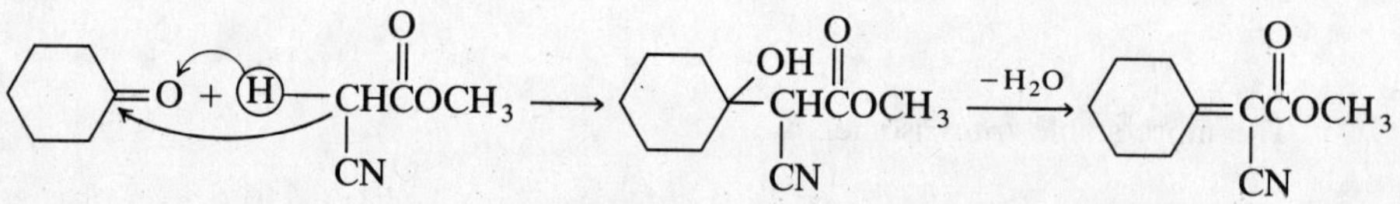

⬡$=O + \overset{H}{\underset{\overset{|}{CN}}{C}}$HCOCH_3 $\longrightarrow$ ⬡$\overset{OH}{\underset{\overset{|}{CN}}{C}}$HCOCH_3 $\xrightarrow{-H_2O}$ ⬡$=\overset{O}{\underset{\overset{|}{CN}}{C}}$CCOCH_3

18.101 Outline the steps in the base-catalyzed self-condensation of a typical nitrile, CH_3CH_2CN.

▌ The nitrile is a carbanion source and the CN is an acceptor site. The final product of this *Thorpe reaction* is a β-ketonitrile.

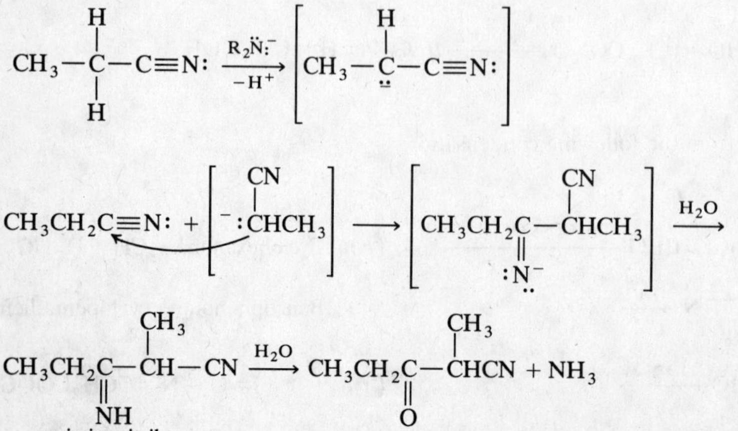

$$CH_3 - \overset{\overset{H}{|}}{\underset{\overset{|}{H}}{C}} - C \equiv N: \xrightarrow[-H^+]{R_2\ddot{N}:^-} \left[CH_3 - \overset{H}{\underset{..}{C}} - C \equiv N: \right]$$

$$CH_3CH_2C \equiv N: + \left[^-:CHCH_3 \right] \longrightarrow \left[CH_3CH_2\overset{\overset{CN}{|}}{\underset{\overset{|}{:N^-}}{C}} - CHCH_3 \right] \xrightarrow{H_2O}$$

$$CH_3CH_2\overset{\overset{CH_3}{|}}{\underset{\overset{\|}{NH}}{C}} - CH - CN \xrightarrow{H_2O} CH_3CH_2\overset{\overset{CH_3}{|}}{\underset{\overset{\|}{O}}{C}} - CHCN + NH_3$$

an iminonitrile

18.102 (*a*) Why is the typical base-catalyzed condensation of a carbonyl compound with a compound having a reactive CH_2 flanked by two $C=O$'s (DEM) unsuccessful? (*b*) What kind of catalysis is needed to promote the reaction and how is it achieved? (*c*) Outline the successful reaction (*Knoevenagel reaction*) between PhCHO and $H_2C(COOEt)_2$. (*d*) Write the structure of the product resulting from hydrolysis and decarboxylation of the initial product.

▰ (*a*) The stable carbanion from DEM is not reactive enough to add to $C=O$. (*b*) A base is needed to form the carbanion and an acid is needed to activate $C=O$. This is achieved by having a weak base ($RCOO^-$) and a weak acid ($R_2NH_2^+$) present. A strong acid and a strong base would neutralize each other.

(*c*)
$$PhCH=O \xrightarrow{Me_2NH_2^+} \underbrace{PhC\overset{H}{=}\overset{+}{O}H + {}^-:CH(COOEt)_2} \xleftarrow{OAc^-} CH_2(COOEt)_2$$

$$[PhCH(OH)CH(COOEt)_2] \xrightarrow{-H_2O} PhCH=C(COOEt)_2$$

(*d*) *trans*-Cinnamic acid, $PhCH=CHCOOH$.

18.103 Treatment of **A** with aqueous acid gives a single compound, $C_6H_{10}O$ (**B**), which forms an oxime and is oxidized to $HOOC(CH_2)_4COOH$. (*a*) Give the structure of **B**. (*b*) Outline the steps in the transformation.

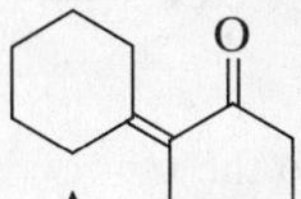

▰ (*a*) **B** gives an oxime and is a carbonyl compound. Adipic acid signals that **B** is cyclohexanone. (*b*) The first step is the reversal of the dehydration to give the β-hydroxyketone, the aldol product of **B**. The aldol addition is reversed (*retroaldol cleavage*) to eventually give **B**.

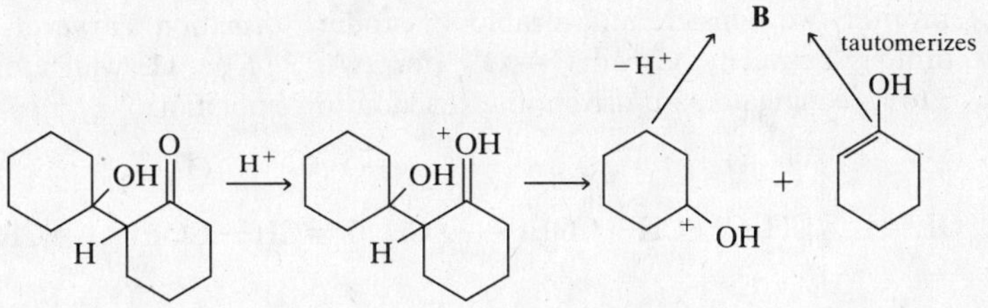

18.104 Trace the pathway for the formation of 4,4-dimethyl-2-cyclohexenone (**C**) from methyl vinyl ketone and Me_2CHCHO.

▰ With OH^-, Me_2CHCHO is converted to $Me_2\ddot{C}-CHO$ which initiates the sequence of steps:

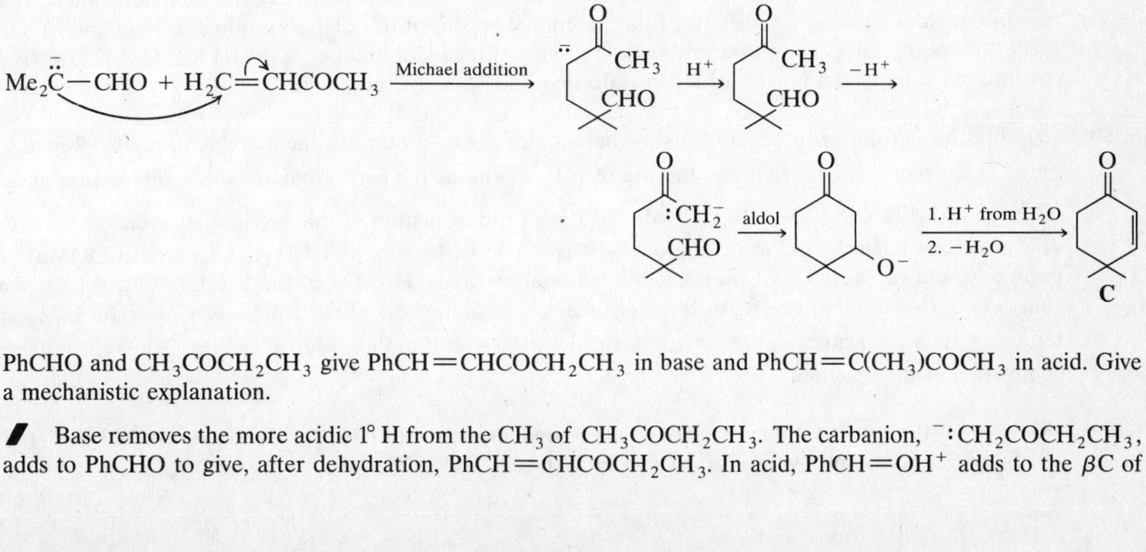

18.105 PhCHO and $CH_3COCH_2CH_3$ give $PhCH=CHCOCH_2CH_3$ in base and $PhCH=C(CH_3)COCH_3$ in acid. Give a mechanistic explanation.

▰ Base removes the more acidic 1° H from the CH_3 of $CH_3COCH_2CH_3$. The carbanion, ${}^-:CH_2COCH_2CH_3$, adds to PhCHO to give, after dehydration, $PhCH=CHCOCH_2CH_3$. In acid, $PhCH=OH^+$ adds to the βC of

the more stable (more substituted) enol $CH_3C{=}C^\beta HCH_3$ giving
|
OH

$$\left[\begin{array}{c} HO \quad CH_3 \\ Ph{-}\overset{|}{\underset{|}{C}}{-}\overset{|}{\underset{\|}{C^\beta}}{-}C{-}CH_3 \\ H \quad H \quad {}^+OH \end{array}\right] \xrightarrow[-H_2O]{-H^+} Ph{-}\overset{CH_3}{\underset{H}{C}{=}\overset{|}{C^\beta}{-}\overset{\|}{\underset{O}{C}}{-}CH_3}$$

(The less substituted, and thus less stable enol is $H_2C{=}\underset{|}{C}{-}CH_2CH_3$.)
OH

CLAISEN CONDENSATIONS

18.106 Give the product and the mechanism for the OEt^--catalyzed *Claisen* condensation of CH_3COOEt.

▰ The first step is the formation of the α-carbanion, stabilized through extended π bonding with the $C{=}O$ of $-COOR$.

$$CH_3\overset{O}{\overset{\|}{C}}OEt + OEt^- \rightleftharpoons HOEt + \left[H_2C{\cdots}\overset{O}{\overset{\|}{C}}{-}OEt\right]^-$$

In the second step, the carbanion adds to the $C{=}O$ of another molecule of ester displacing OEt^-.

$$^-{:}CH_2\overset{O}{\overset{\|}{C}}OEt + CH_3\overset{O}{\overset{\|}{C}}{-}OEt \rightleftharpoons \left[CH_3\overset{O^-}{\overset{|}{C}}{-}CH_2\overset{O}{\overset{\|}{C}}OEt \right] \rightleftharpoons CH_3\overset{O}{\overset{\|}{C}}{-}CH_2\overset{O}{\overset{\|}{C}}OEt + {}^-OEt$$
$$\text{(OEt)} \qquad\qquad AAE$$

The equilibria for the two steps are unfavorable for product formation. However, 1,3-dicarbonyl compounds have fairly acidic protons between the two $C{=}O$'s (for AAE, $pK_a \cong 11$, while for EtOH, $pK_a \cong 16$) and ^-OEt converts AAE to its conjugate base driving the reaction to completion.

$$AAE + {}^-OEt \rightleftharpoons \left[CH_3\overset{O}{\overset{\|}{C}}{-}\overset{O}{\overset{\|}{C}}H{-}\overset{}{C}OEt \longleftrightarrow CH_3\overset{O^-}{\overset{|}{C}}{=}CH{-}\overset{O}{\overset{\|}{C}}OEt \longleftrightarrow CH_3\overset{O}{\overset{\|}{C}}{-}CH{=}\overset{O^-}{\overset{|}{C}}OEt\right] + HOEt$$

18.107 Compare the Claisen condensation with the aldol addition in terms of the mechanism and nature of the product.

▰ They both involve formation of an intermediate α-carbanion which then adds to the $C{=}O$ of another molecule, generating a $-$ charge on the O. The aldol O^- accepts H^+ to give an OH. The Claisen O^- ejects ^-OR from C, reforming the resonance-stabilized $C{=}O$ group. The aldol O^- would have to eject the extremely basic $H{:}^-$ or $R{:}^-$ to reform the $C{=}O$. It is easier to eject the much less basic carbanion addendum, which is the reason the aldol addition is reversible. Both functional groups of the Claisen product, $C{=}O$ and COOR, are at higher oxidation states than the corresponding groups of the aldol product, $C{-}OH$ and $C{=}O$. This is expected because the ester is at a higher oxidation state than the carbonyl compound.

18.108 (*a*) Give the *self-Claisen* product of methyl butanoate. (*b*) Account for the inability of methyl 2-methylpropanoate (**A**) to react. (*c*) Explain why the use of $Na^+ {:}^-CPh_3$ as the base promotes the condensation of **A**.

▰ (*a*) $CH_3CH_2CH_2COCH(Et)COOMe$. Although the formation of this product is reversible, the reaction is drawn to completion by the formation of the very stable carbanion, $CH_3CH_2CH_2COC(Et)COOMe$. (*b*) The product would be $Me_2CHCOCMe_2COOMe$, without an acidic H between the two $C{=}O$'s. Rather than go to completion, this reaction reverts to the more stable reactant ester. (*c*) $Ph_3C{:}^-$ is a powerful base capable of removing the less acidic H that is α to the keto $C{=}O$, forming $Me_2\overset{..}{C}COCMe_2COOMe$ and permitting completion of the reaction.

18.109 (*a*) Give all the products from a *mixed-Claisen* condensation with $CH_3CH_2CH_2COOMe$ and $PhCH_2COOMe$. (*b*) Is this an acceptable synthesis for $CH_3CH_2CH_2COCHPhCOOMe$?

▰ (*a*) The products are listed as follows:

Acceptor	Carbanion Source	Product
CH₃CH₂CH₂COOMe	CH₃CH₂CH₂COOMe	CH₃CH₂CH₂COCH(Et)COOMe (self-Claisen)
PhCH₂COOMe	PhCH₂COOMe	PhCH₂COCHPhCOOMe (self-Claisen)
CH₃CH₂CH₂COOMe	PhCH₂COOMe	CH₃CH₂CH₂COCHPhCOOMe (mixed Claisen)
PhCH₂COOMe	CH₃CH₂CH₂COOMe	PhCH₂COCH(Et)COOMe (mixed Claisen)

(*b*) No, the yield is poor because there are so many products.

18.110 (*a*) Give the mixed Claisen product from the condensation of (i) PhCOOEt + CH₃COOEt, (ii) *p*-CH₃C₆H₄COOEt + PhCH₂COOEt, and (iii) ethyl β-naphthoate + CH₃CH₂COOEt. (*b*) Why are these syntheses reasonable for these mixed-Claisen products? (*c*) Give the technique used to improve the yield of mixed product.

▰ (*a*) (i) PhCOCH₂COOEt, (ii) *p*-CH₃C₆H₄COCHPhCOOEt, and (iii) β-NaphCOCH(CH₃)COOEt. (*b*) In each synthesis one ester has no α H and can only act as an acceptor. (*c*) Add the carbanion source ester slowly to the acceptor in an ethanolic solution of NaOEt, thereby discouraging its self-condensation.

18.111 Give the mixed products from the reactions of CH₃CH₂COOEt in NaOEt/EtOH with (*a*) HCOOEt (ethyl formate), (*b*) (EtO)₂C=O (diethyl carbonate), and (*c*) EtOOCCOOEt (diethyl oxalate). Classify each type of product.

▰ (*a*) HC(=O)CHMeCOOEt; the α-carbanion is formylated to give a β-aldehydic ester.
(*b*) EtOOCCHMeCOOEt; an EtOOC is introduced on the α-carbanion to give a malonic ester.
(*c*) EtOOCCOCHMeCOOEt, it is both a β- and α-ketodiester.

18.112 Select the esters or mixed esters needed to synthesize

(*a*) PhCH₂CH₂C(=O)—CH(CH₂Ph)COOEt   (*b*) EtOOCC(=O)C(=O)—CHMeCOOEt   (*c*) O=CH—CHPhCOOEt

▰ In the Claisen product the formed C—C bond is between the carbonyl C and the C that is α to COOR. Work backwards by breaking this C—C bond, adding OR to the carbonyl C, and adding H to the other C as shown:

(*a*) Ethyl 3-phenylpropanoate

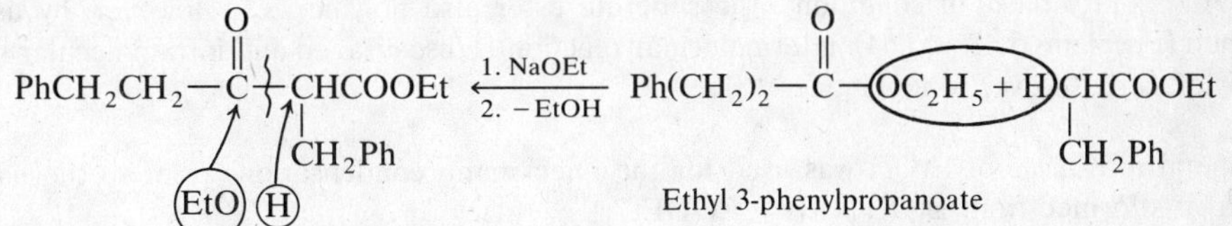

(*b*) Diethyl oxalate   Ethyl propanoate

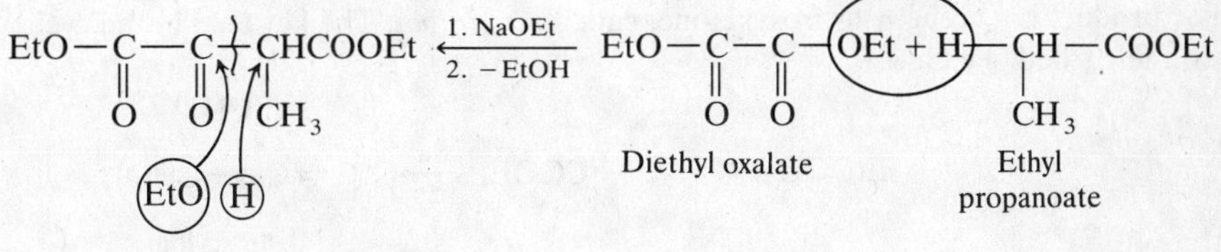

(*c*) Ethyl formate   Ethyl phenylacetate

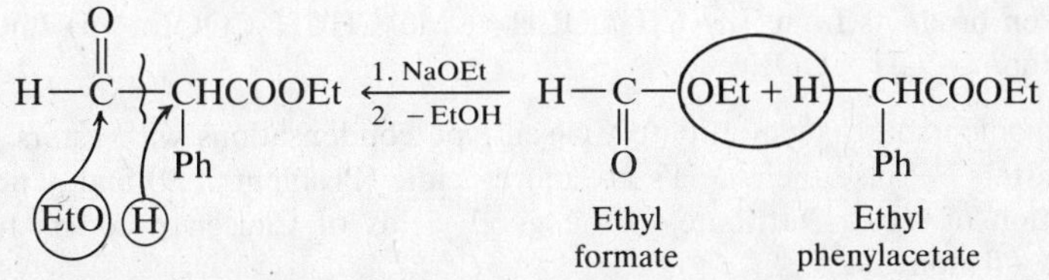

18.113 (*a*) Give the Claisen product from diethyl pimelate, EtOOC(CH₂)₅COOEt, and show the mechanism. (*b*) Why is NaH with a catalytic amount of EtOH used as the basic catalyst and not NaOEt/EtOH?

◢ (*a*) The substrate is a diester capable of undergoing an intramolecular condensation (*Dieckmann condensation*) to give a cyclic β-keto ester.

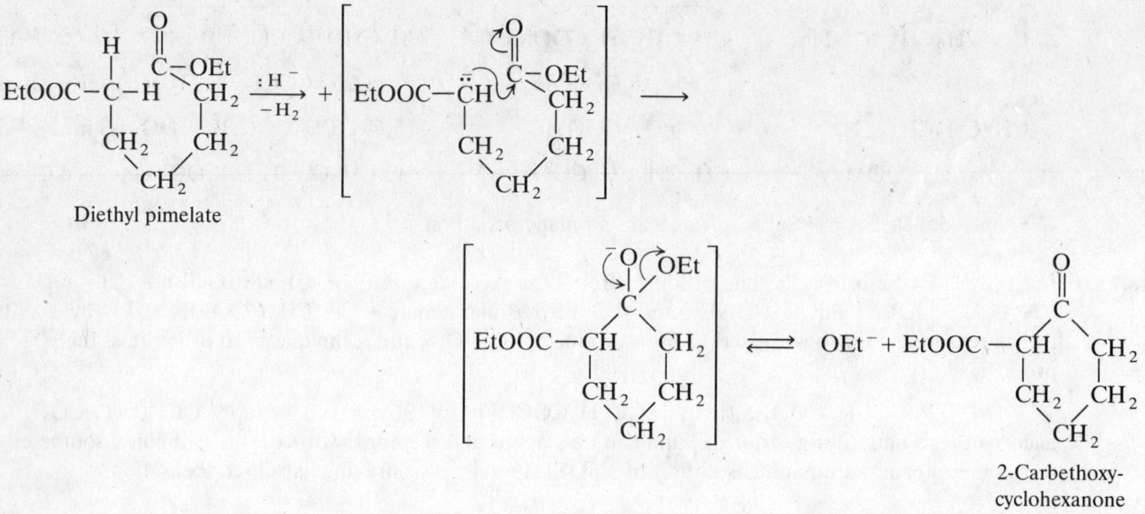

Diethyl pimelate

2-Carbethoxy-cyclohexanone

The net reaction is diester → cyclic β-keto ester + EtOH.   (*b*) Since the reaction is reversible and EtOH is a product, it is better not to have an excess EtOH as the solvent because then the equilibrium can be driven to the left towards the reactant ester.

18.114 Which of the following diesters undergo the Dieckmann condensation under usual conditions?   (*a*) Adipate, (*b*) glutarate, and (*c*) suberate [$EtOOC(CH_2)_5COOEt$].

◢ (*a*) Adipate has one less C than pimelate and reacts smoothly to give the corresponding five-membered cyclic ketone, 2-carbethoxycyclopentanone.   (*b*) An intramolecular condensation would give the highly strained four-membered ring; hence this does not happen. Instead intermolecular condensation occurs, but because the substrate is a diester, it polymerizes.

$$EtOOC(CH_2)_3C\!\!-\!\!\underbrace{CH(COOEt)CH_2CH_2C}_{mer}\!\!-\!\!CH(COOEt)CH_2CH_2C\!\!-\!\!etc.$$

(*c*) Intramolecular condensation would entail the unfavorable formation of the stable seven-membered ring. Under ordinary reaction conditions, the suberate ester also polymerizes. However, by using the high dilution method (Problems 5.63 and 64), intermolecular reaction is discouraged and intramolecular reaction is encouraged to give 2-carbethoxycycloheptanone.

18.115 Na metal in a trace of EtOH was used for the Dieckmann condensations prior to the use of NaH. What side product is formed from $EtOOC(CH_2)_nCOOEt$?

◢ The product is a cyclic α-hydroxyketone, called an *acyloin*. The key step in the cyclization is bond formation between the carbethoxy C's.

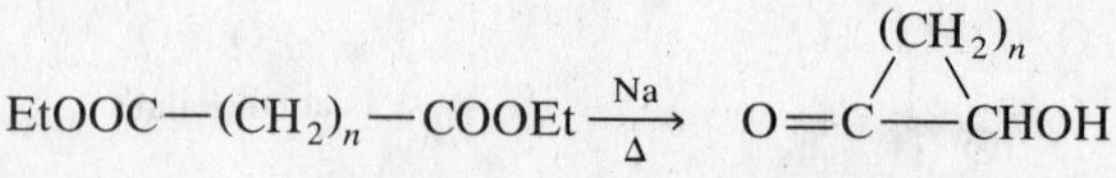

$$EtOOC\!-\!(CH_2)_n\!-\!COOEt \xrightarrow[\Delta]{Na} O\!\!=\!\!C\!-\!CHOH \;\; (CH_2)_n$$

an acyloin

18.116 Give the Claisen products from: (*a*) $CH_3COCH_3 + Me_2CHCH_2COOEt$, (*b*) $PhCOCH_3 + PhCH_2COOEt$, and (*c*) cyclopentanone + CH_3COOEt.

◢ Most carbanion sources can initiate Claisen-type condensations with esters. Ketones are better carbanion sources than esters because their α H's are more acidic (Problem 18.9) and generally they are poor acceptors. This combination of factors attribute to the good yields of Claisen products from ketones with esters. The products are β-diketones.

(*a*) $CH_3COCH_2 - COCH_2CHMe_2$ (*b*) $PhCOCH_2 - COCH_2Ph$ (*c*)

18.117 (*a*) Give structures and classify each product from the Claisen reaction of $PhCOCH_3$ with (i) HCOOEt, (ii) $(EtO)_2C{=}O$, and (iii) EtOOCCOOEt. NaOEt is basic enough to catalyze the reaction with these more reactive esters. (*b*) Can the product from (ii) react with another mole of ester?

◢ (*a*) (i) $PhCOCH_2CHO$, a β-ketoaldehyde, (ii) $PhCOCH_2COOEt$, a β-ketoester, and (iii) $PhCOCH_2COCOOEt$ an α,γ-diketoester. (*b*) No. The product, similar to AAE, forms an unreactive, stable carbanion flanked by two $C{=}O$'s.

18.118 (*a*) Give the structures and identify the kind of Claisen products obtained from the reaction of CH_3CH_2COOEt with (i) CH_3CH_2CN, (ii) $CH_3CH_2NO_2$, and (iii) CH_3SOCH_3. Stronger basic catalysts ($NaNH_2$ or NaH) must be used with this more typical ester. (*b*) What is formed when the product from (iii) is reduced with Al/Hg in aq. THF?

◢ The listed reactants are all better carbanion sources than esters and give Claisen-type products with esters. (*a*) (i) $CH_3CH(CN)COCH_2CH_3$, an α-cyanoketone, (ii) $CH_3CH(NO_2)COCH_2CH_3$, an α-nitroketone, and (iii) $CH_3SOCH_2COCH_2CH_3$, a β-ketosulfoxide. (*b*) $CH_3COCH_2CH_3$. The CH_3SO group is replaced by H in this reduction.

18.119 (*a*) Use two ways to prepare 2-carbethoxycyclohexanone by a Claisen condensation. (*b*) Suggest a method for preparing 3,6-dicarbethoxy-1,2-cyclohexanedione.

◢ (*a*) Bond 1 is formed from the Dieckmann condensation of diethyl pimelate (Problem 18.113). Bond 2 is formed by the condensation of cyclohexanone and diethyl carbonate.

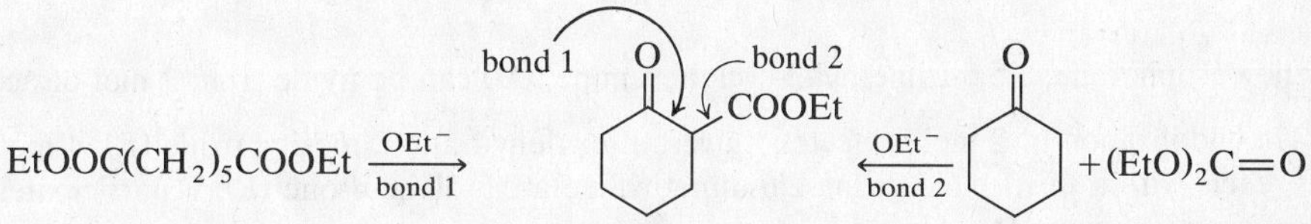

(*b*) Break both bonds joining $C{=}O$ and α C. The needed reactants are diethyl adipate, the dicarbanion source, and diethyl oxalate, the diacceptor.

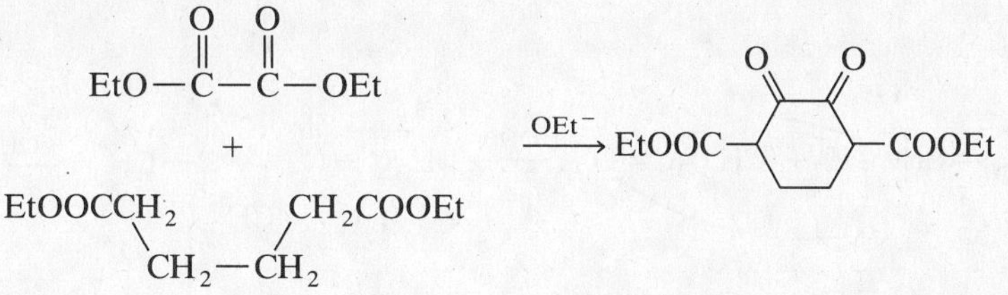

3,6-Dicarbethoxy-1,2-cyclohexanedione

SYNTHESES

18.120 Synthesize 3-ethyl-2-pentanone using acetic acid as the only organic compound.

◢ Since $CH_3COCH(C_2H_5)CH_2CH_3$ (**A**) is a methyl ketone, AAE, made as shown, is a likely intermediate.

$$CH_3COOH \xrightarrow{LiAlH_4} CH_3CH_2OH$$

Then

$$CH_3COOH + CH_3CH_2OH \xrightarrow{H_2SO_4} CH_3COOCH_2CH_3 \xrightarrow{NaOEt*}$$

$$CH_3COCH_2COOCH_2CH_3 \text{ (AAE)} \xrightarrow[2CH_3CH_2Br^{**}]{2NaOEt} CH_3COC(CH_2CH_3)_2COOCH_2CH_3 \xrightarrow[\text{2. } H^+]{\text{1. } OH^-} \textbf{A}$$

*from HOEt + Na; **from CH_3CH_2OH + HBr.

18.121 (*a*) Prepare $CH_3COCH_2CMe_3$ (**B**) from AAE. (*b*) Give a mechanism for the alkylation step. (*c*) Can DEM be alkylated under acid conditions?

▰ (a) The preparation of **B** requires the alkylation of AAE with BrCMe$_3$. This is not possible with the carbanion of AAE because of the competing E2 reaction in which Me$_2$C=CH$_2$ is formed. However, suitable Lewis acids catalyze the alkylation.

$$AAE + BrCMe_3 \xrightarrow{AgBF_4} CH_3COCH(CMe_3)COOCH_2CH_3 \xrightarrow[\text{2. H}^+]{\text{1. OH}^-} B$$

(b) Ag$^+$ removes Br$^-$ from BrCMe$_3$, leaving 3° Me$_3$C$^+$ which adds to the C=C of the enol of AAE:

$$Me_3C^+ + \overset{\overset{\displaystyle OH}{|}}{CH_3C}=CHCOOEt \longrightarrow \overset{\overset{\displaystyle ^+OH}{\|}}{CH_3C}\overset{\overset{\displaystyle }{|}}{CH}COOCH_2CH_3 \xrightarrow{-H^+} \overset{\overset{\displaystyle O}{\|}}{CH_3C}\overset{\overset{\displaystyle }{|}}{CH}COOCH_2CH_3$$
$$\qquad\qquad\qquad\qquad\qquad\qquad\quad CMe_3 \qquad\qquad\qquad\qquad CMe_3$$

(c) No. DEM has no detectable enol content.

18.122 Prepare H$_2$NCOCMe$_2$COOEt (**C**) from CH$_3$COOH and any alkyl halide.

▰ The amide moiety can be made by careful hydration of C≡N. The Me's are introduced by dialkylating N≡CCH$_2$COOEt with MeI.

$$CH_3COOH \xrightarrow{P/Br_2} BrCH_2COOH \xrightarrow[\text{2. CN}^-]{\text{1. OH}^-} N{\equiv}CCH_2COO^- \xrightarrow{H^+} N{\equiv}CCH_2COOH \xrightarrow[\text{H}^+]{\text{EtOH}}$$

$$N{\equiv}CCH_2COOEt \xrightarrow[\text{2MeI}]{\text{2EtO}^-} N{\equiv}CCMe_2COOEt \xrightarrow[\text{2. H}_2\text{O}]{\text{1. H}_2\text{SO}_4\,0,\,°C} C$$

See Problem 18.120 for conversion of CH$_3$COOH to C$_2$H$_5$OH.

18.123 Show how isophorone, 3,5,5-trimethyl-2-cyclohexenone, (**D**) can be made from 3 mol of acetone.

▰ The aldolization of 2 mol of acetone gives, after dehydration, mesityl oxide (**E**), 4-methylpenta-3-ene-2-one, which reacts with a third mole giving 2,6-dimethylhepta-2,5-diene-4-one (**F**). **F** participates in an intramolecular Michael reaction giving **D**.

$$(CH_3)_2C{=}O + CH_3COCH_3 \xrightarrow{OH^-} (CH_3)_2C{=}CHCOCH_3 \ (E)$$

$$(CH_3)_2C{=}CHC\overset{\overset{\displaystyle O}{\|}}{C}CH_2 + (CH_3)_2C{=}O \xrightarrow{OH^-} \ \cdots \xrightarrow[-H^+]{OH^-} \ \cdots$$

$$\qquad\qquad E \qquad\qquad\qquad\qquad\qquad\qquad F \qquad\qquad\qquad\qquad D$$

18.124 Use DEM to synthesize (a) PhCH$_2$CMe(CH$_2$OH)$_2$, and (b) CH$_3$CH(OH)CH$_2$CH(COOEt)$_2$.

▰ (a) The *gem* CH$_2$OH's come from reduction of COOEt's.

$$CH_2(COOEt)_2 \xrightarrow[\text{2. EtO}^-,\text{ MeI}]{\text{1. EtO}^-,\text{ PhCH}_2\text{Cl}} PhCH_2CMe(COOEt)_2 \xrightarrow{LiAlH_4} PhCH_2CMe(CH_2OH)_2$$

(b) The CH$_3$CH(OH)CH$_2$ group originates from the reaction of $^-$HC(COOEt)$_2$ with methyloxirane.

$$(EtOOC)_2CH_2 + CH_3CH{-}CH_2 \xrightarrow{NaOEt/HOEt} CH_3CHCH_2CH(COOEt)_2$$
$$\qquad\qquad\qquad\qquad\qquad \underset{O}{\diagdown\;\diagup} \qquad\qquad\qquad\qquad \underset{OH}{|}$$

In this S$_N$2 reaction the nucleophilic carbanion attacks the less substituted C.

18.125 Use DEM, readily available alkyl halides, phosgene(COCl$_2$), and any solvent and inorganic reagents to synthesize (a) the sedative drug Veronal (barbital), 5,5-diethylbarbituric acid,

$$O{=}C\underset{NH{-}CO}{\overset{NH{-}CO}{\diagup\diagdown\;\diagdown\diagup}}C\underset{Et}{\overset{Et}{\diagup\diagup}}$$

and (b) the tranquilizer Miltown, H$_2$NCOCH$_2$CMeCH$_2$OCNH$_2$.
$$\qquad\qquad\qquad\qquad\qquad\qquad\qquad\qquad\quad \overset{O}{\|}\qquad\qquad\quad\ \overset{O}{\|}$$
$$\qquad\qquad\qquad\qquad\qquad\qquad\qquad\qquad\qquad\qquad \underset{CHMe_2}{|}$$

▟ (*a*) Barbiturates are prepared by treating R-substituted DEM with ureas (Problem 17.97).

$$\text{DEM} \xrightarrow[\text{2EtBr}]{\text{2NaOEt}} (\text{EtOOC})_2\text{CEt}_2 \xrightarrow[(\text{H}_2\text{N})_2\text{C}=\text{O}]{\text{NaOEt}} \text{Veronal}$$

(*b*) Miltown is a dicarbamate whose alcohol portion is the diol formed from the reduction of a malonate diester. The R's substituted on DEM are Me and CHMe_2. (C's from DEM are boldface.)

$$\text{DEM} \xrightarrow[\text{2. NaOEt, MeI}]{\text{1. NaOEt, ClCHMe}_2} (\text{EtOOC})_2\textbf{C}(\text{Me})\text{CHMe}_2 \xrightarrow{\text{LiAlH}_4}$$

$$(\text{HOCH}_2)_2\textbf{C}(\text{Me})\text{CHMe}_2 \xrightarrow[-2\text{HCl}]{2\text{Cl}_2\text{C}=\text{O}} (\text{ClCOCH}_2)_2\textbf{C}(\text{Me})\text{CHMe}_2 \xrightarrow{\text{NH}_3} \text{Miltown}$$
$$\quad\quad\quad\quad\quad\quad\quad\quad\quad\quad\quad\quad\quad\quad\quad\quad\quad\quad\quad\quad\quad \underset{\text{O}}{\|}$$

18.126 Show the course of the *Robinson "annelation" reaction* for synthesizing fused rings in the reaction of cyclohexanone and methyl vinyl ketone.

▟ This is a Michael addition by cyclohexanone anion on the vinyl ketone followed by an intramolecular aldol reaction

The product is an α,β-unsaturated fused ring ketone.

18.127 Suggest a way of converting (*a*) $\text{CH}_3\text{COCH}_2\text{COCH}_3$ to (i) $\text{CH}_3\text{CH}_2\text{CH}_2\text{CH}_2\text{COCH}_2\text{COCH}_3$ and (ii) $\text{CH}_3\text{COCH}_2\text{COCH}_2\text{COOH}$ and (*b*) 2-acetylcyclopentanone to

▟ In each case, a less reactive CH_3 of the $\text{CH}_3\text{C}=\text{O}$ group, rather than the more reactive CH_2 of the $\text{O}=\text{CCH}_2\text{C}=\text{O}$ grouping, has to be alkylated. This is achieved by first forming the dianions with 2 eq of the very strong base KNH_2 in liq. NH_3, and then adding 1 eq of the needed RBr followed by acidification. The carbanion from CH_2 is more acidic and stable, and thus less reactive than the carbanion from CH_3 where alkylation occurs.

(*a*) (i) $\text{CH}_3\text{COCH}_2\text{COCH}_3 \xrightarrow{2\text{KNH}_2/\text{NH}_3} [^-:\text{CH}_2\text{CO}\ddot{\text{C}}\text{HCOCH}_3] \xrightarrow[\text{2. H}^+]{\text{1. }n\text{-PrCl}} n\text{-PrCH}_2\text{COCH}_2\text{COCH}_3$

(ii) CO_2 is added to the dianion to give $[^-\text{OOCCH}_2\text{CO}\ddot{\text{C}}\text{HCOCH}_3]$. Acidification affords the desired diketocarboxylic acid.

(*b*) In this case, the terminal carbanion is more reactive.

18.128 Convert PhH and any aliphatic compound to 2-(2,4-dinitrophenyl)propanoic acid (**D**).

▟ The 2-propanoic acid moeity, $-\text{CHMeCOOH}$, can originate from DEM, and the properly positioned NO_2's signal the possibility of using a nucleophilic aromatic substitution (Problems 11.79 and 11.80).

$$\text{PhH} \xrightarrow{\text{Cl}_2/\text{Fe}} \text{PhCl} \xrightarrow[\text{H}_2\text{SO}_4]{\text{HNO}_3} 2,4\text{-di-NO}_2\text{C}_6\text{H}_3\text{Cl (C)}$$

$$\text{DEM} \xrightarrow{\text{NaOEt} \atop \text{CH}_3\text{I}} (\text{EtOOC})_2\text{CHMe} \xrightarrow{\text{NaOEt} \atop \text{C}} 2,4\text{-di-NO}_2\text{C}_6\text{H}_3\text{CHMe(COOEt)}_2 \xrightarrow[\text{2. H}^+]{\text{1. OH}^-} \textbf{D}$$

18.129 Starting with cyclopentanone, use Claisen-type condensations to prepare (*a*) 2-nitrocyclopentanone and (*b*) 1,2-cyclopentanedione.

▰ These syntheses require Claisen condensations on esters of inorganic nitrogen acids, where $N=O$ assumes the role of $C=O$ of carboxylic esters. Cyclopentanone is first converted to its α carbanion.

(*a*)

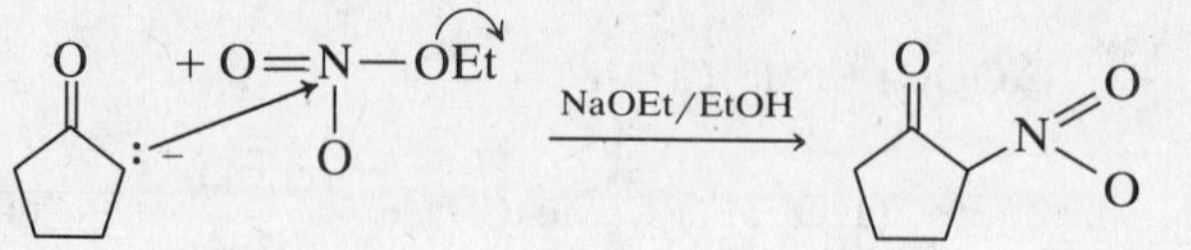

Ethyl nitrate

Alkyl nitrates tend to be explosive and they need careful handling.

(*b*)   Cyclopentanone + $O=N-OEt$ (ethyl nitrite) $\xrightarrow{\text{NaOEt/EtOH}}$

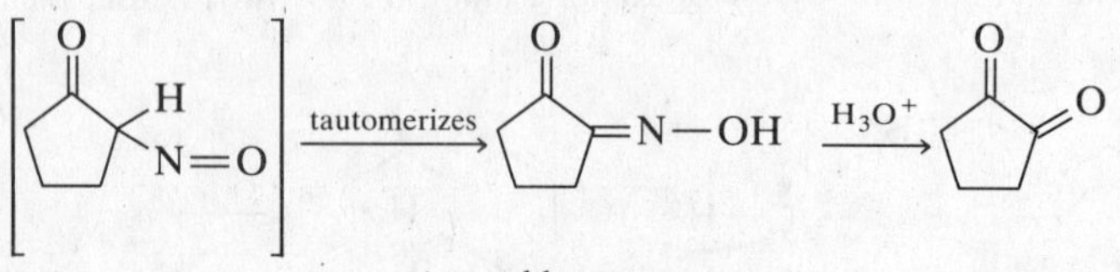

more stable tautomer

18.130 (*a*) Devise a synthesis of $PhCOCH_3$ from $PhCOCl$ and DEM.   (*b*) Can this synthesis be a general method for preparing methyl ketones?   (*c*) Convert AAE to $PhCOCH_2COOEt$.

▰ (*a*) The malonate anion can be acylated by displacing Cl from acid chlorides but the solvent for the reaction must be incapable of reacting with the acid chloride (nonnucleophilic). Often the carbanion is formed by using NaH in tetrahydrofuran (THF).

$$DEM \xrightarrow{\text{NaH/THF}} (EtOOC)_2CH^{\bar{\cdot}}\ Na^+ \xrightarrow[-\text{NaCl}]{\text{PhCOCl}} PhCOCH(COOEt)_2 \xrightarrow[\text{2. H}^+]{\text{1. OH}^-} [PhCOCH_2COOH] \longrightarrow PhCOCH_3$$

The initially formed $PhCOCH_2COOH$ is a β-ketoacid that easily loses CO_2 to give the methyl ketone.   (*b*) Yes, because DEM can be acylated with many other acid chlorides.

(*c*) $AAE \xrightarrow{\text{NaH/THF}} CH_3CO\overset{..}{C}HCOOEt \xrightarrow{\text{PhCOCl}}$

$$\underset{\underset{\textstyle CH_3COCHCOOEt}{|}}{PhC=O} \xrightarrow{\text{NH}_3/\text{NH}_4\text{Cl}} PhCOCH_2COOEt + CH_3COO^-NH_4^+$$

Acylation can be reversed under mildly acid conditions and therefore the weakly acidic buffered solution is used. Cleavage normally occurs at the more reactive carbonyl group to produce the weaker anion (from the stronger acid)—in this case acetate rather than benzoate.

18.131 Prepare

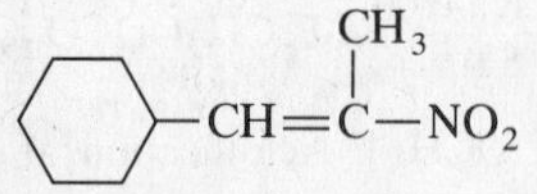

from simple acyclic compounds.

▰ The ring is assembled by a Diels–Alder reaction. The alcohol, which is the precursor of the alkene, $C=C$, is made by an aldol addition on cyclohexanecarboxaldehyde.

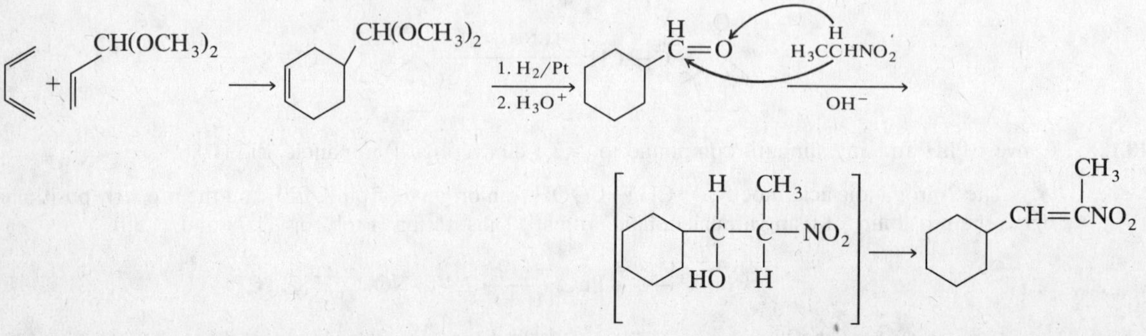

Although $H_2C=CHCH=O$ also participates in Diels–Alder reactions, it is a conjugated compound capable, to some extent, of acting as the diene. Hence the acetal is often used because better yields are obtained.

18.132 Use DEM and any carbonyl compound to prepare $HOOCCH_2CH_2CH_2COOH$ (**E**). Show the sequence of steps.

◢ The two $HOOCCH_2$— groupings come from two eq of DEM. The middle —CH_2— comes from the carbonyl compound that must be H_2C=O.

$$(EtOOC)_2CH_2 + H_2C{=}O \xrightarrow[\text{(aldol addition)}]{\text{NaOEt/EtOH}} [(EtOOC)_2CHCH_2OH] \longrightarrow$$

$$(EtOOC)_2C{=}CH_2 \xrightarrow[\text{(a Michael addition)}]{^-:CH(COOEt)_2/EtOH} (EtOOC)_2CHCH_2CH(COOEt)_2 \xrightarrow[\text{2. H}^+]{\text{1. OH}^-} E$$

18.133 Use a Claisen condensation to convert $PhCH_3$ to $PhCH_2COCH_2Ph$ (**F**).

◢ The —$COCH_2Ph$ moiety comes from $PhCH_2COOEt$ in a Claisen condensation. The $PhCH_2$— portion comes from a compound that is a good carbanion source, the same ester. The product is made from the self-condensation of $PhCH_2COOEt$ that is prepared as follows:

$$PhCH_3 \xrightarrow{\text{NBS}} PhCH_2Br \xrightarrow[\text{2. CO}_2 \text{ 3. H}^+]{\text{1. Mg/ether}} PhCH_2COOH \xrightarrow{\text{EtOH/H}_2\text{SO}_4}$$

$$PhCH_2COOEt \xrightarrow{\text{NaOEt/EtOH}} \underset{\underset{\displaystyle COOEt}{|}}{PhCHCOCH_2Ph} \xrightarrow{\text{H}_3\text{O}^+} F$$

18.134 (**a**) Prepare $PhCOCH_2CH_2Ph$ from $PhCH_3$ using a malonate ester other than DEM. (**b**) Why is the ethyl ester not used in this synthesis?

◢ (**a**) The PhCO group is introduced by acylating an active malonate —CH_2—. The —CH_2Ph group is introduced by benzylating the same malonate ester with $PhCH_2Cl$. t-Butyl malonate, $CH_2(COOC_4H_9\text{-}t)_2$, is used.

$$CH_2(COOC_4H_9\text{-}t)_2 + PhCH_2Cl^* \xrightarrow{\text{NaOEt/EtOH}} PhCH_2CH(COOC_4H_9\text{-}t)_2 \xrightarrow[\text{PhCOCl}^{**}]{\text{NaH/PhH}}$$

$$\underset{\underset{\displaystyle COPh}{|}}{PhCH_2C(COOC_4H_9\text{-}t)_2} \xrightarrow{p\text{-MeC}_6\text{H}_4\text{SO}_3\text{H/HOAc}} PhCOCH_2CH_2Ph + 2Me_2C{=}CH_2 + 2CO_2$$

$$^*PhCH_3 \xrightarrow[h\nu]{\text{Cl}_2} PhCH_2Cl \qquad ^{**}PhCH_3 \xrightarrow[\text{H}^+]{\text{KMnO}_4} PhCOOH \xrightarrow{\text{SOCl}_2} PhCOCl.$$

(**b**) OH^- would have to be used to hydrolyze the diethyl ester. This step would reverse the acylation. The t-butyl ester is hydrolyzed under mildly acidic conditions that avoid this reversal.

18.135 Prepare $(n\text{-}C_4H_9)_3CCOOH$ (**G**) from 1-bromobutane and 1-bromopentane.

◢ The C α to COOH has to be dialkylated with $n\text{-}C_4H_9Br$ since one $n\text{-}C_4H_9$ comes from $n\text{-}C_4H_9CH_2Br$. To achieve this, the C must be activated so it readily forms a carbanion. Furthermore, the activating group must be convertible to COOH. The CN group is ideal for this purpose.

$$n\text{-}C_4H_9CH_2Br \xrightarrow{\text{CN}^-} n\text{-}C_4H_9CH_2CN \xrightarrow[\text{2 } n\text{-C}_4\text{H}_9\text{Br}]{\text{NaNH}_2} (n\text{-}C_4H_9)_3CCN \xrightarrow{\text{H}_3\text{O}^+} G$$

SUPPLEMENTARY PROBLEMS

18.136 Acetone reacts with LDA ($Li^+ : \bar{N}H(i\text{-}Pr)_2$ in THF and then with trimethylsilyl chloride, Me_3SiCl, to give an *enolsilane*. (**a**) Write an equation for the reaction. (**b**) Why does O-sylation and not C-sylation occur?

◢ (**a**)
$$\underset{\displaystyle CH_3\overset{\displaystyle \overset{O}{\|}}{C}CH_3}{} \xrightarrow{\text{LDA/THF}} \left[\underset{\displaystyle CH_3\overset{\displaystyle \overset{O^-}{|}}{C}{=}CH_2}{} \longleftrightarrow \underset{\displaystyle CH_3\overset{\displaystyle \overset{O}{\|}}{C}{-}CH_2^-}{} \right] \xrightarrow{\text{Me}_3\text{SiCl}} \underset{\displaystyle CH_3\overset{\displaystyle \overset{OSiMe_3}{|}}{C}{=}CH_2}{}$$

an enolsilane

(**b**) In general, O—Si bonds are much stronger (recall the stability of sand) than C—Si bonds because of p-d π bonding between the O (furnishing a filled p AO) and Si (furnishing an empty d AO).

18.137 Enolsilanes are stable in base but are hydrolyzed in aqueous acid to reform the carbonyl compound. How is this chemistry applied to "protect" a carbonyl group during basic reactions of a functional group elsewhere in the compound?

▪ Form the enolsilane, carry out the reaction on the other functional group (e.g., replace Cl^- by OH^-), and then regenerate the $C{=}O$ group by hydrolyzing the enolsilane with aqueous acid.

18.138 Explain the isolation of 2-bromomethoxycyclohexane from the reaction of $BrCH(CN)_2$ with cyclohexene in methanol.

▪ The π bond of alkenes attacks the Br to form a bromonium ion and releasing the stable $^-{:}CH(CN)_2$ carbanion. The bromonium ion reacts with the nucleophilic MeOH in the usual manner to form the bromoether (Problem 7.83). Caution! $BrCH(CN)_2$ is very toxic probably because it is an excellent brominating agent.

18.139 Ketones and aldehydes react with diethyl succinate in the presence of strong bases such as NaH or $Me_3CO^-K^+$ to give monoesters of an α-alkylidine (or arylidene) succinic acid,

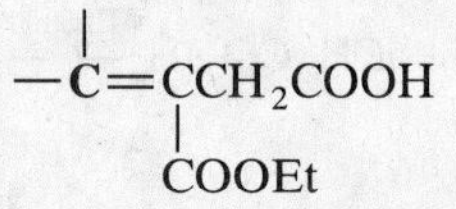

$$-\overset{|}{C}{=}CCH_2COOH$$
$$\underset{COOEt}{|}$$

The C comes from the carbonyl compound. (*a*) Use $Ph_2C{=}O$ to illustrate the steps of this *Stobbe condensation*, using arrows to show the mechanistic sequence. (*b*) Give the two products that are formed when the hydrolyzed succinic acid product formed by hydrolysis of the monoester from (*a*) undergoes a Friedel–Crafts acylation with concentrated H_2SO_4 and glacial acetic acid.

▪ (*a*)

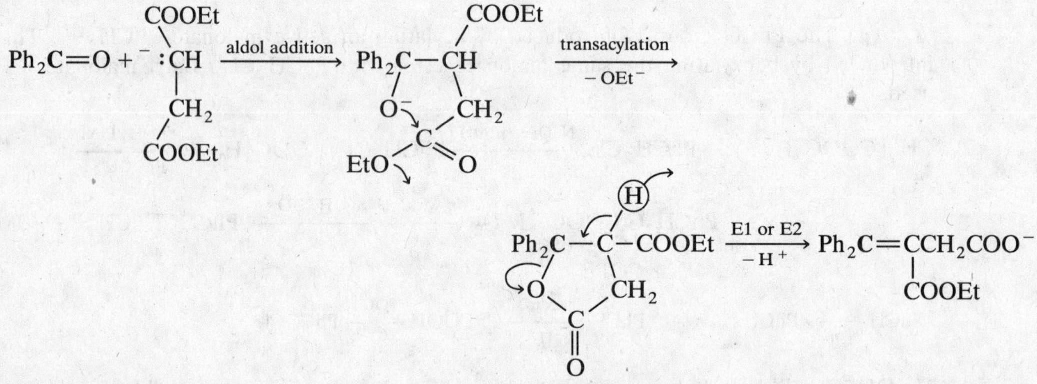

Acidification gives the product monoester carboxylic acid.

(*b*) The diacid is . Ring closure of ^1COOH on Ph^1 gives an indenone whereas

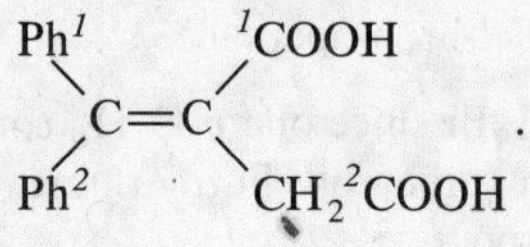

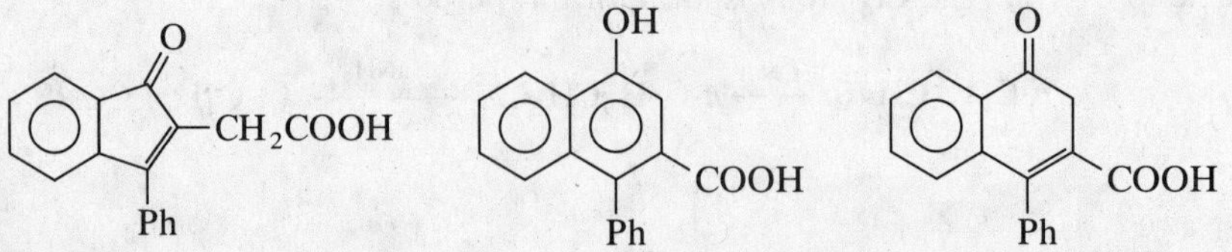

| an indenone | a naphthol | keto form of naphthol |

closure of ^2COOH on Ph^2 gives a naphthol via its keto form.

18.140 (*a*) Give the structural formulas of the two isomeric products from the Stobbe condensation of $PhCOCH_3$ and succinic acid. (*b*) Give a chemical method of distinguishing between these isomers. (*c*) What reaction might negate the reliability of the test?

▪ (*a*) They are geometric isomers,

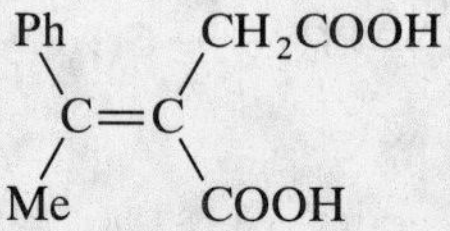

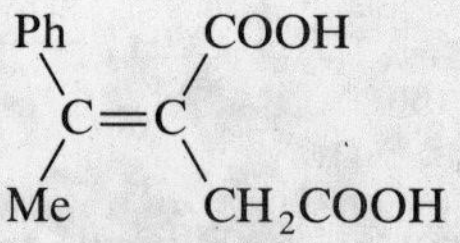

(*b*)   Carry out the acylation reaction used in Problem 18.134(*b*). Since the moeity with the COOH group must be *cis* to the Ph group for ring closure to occur, isolation of the naphthol indicates the *E* isomer, the indenone indicates the *Z* isomer. The indenone gives the typical tests for a ketone (Problem 15.79). The naphthol gives a characteristic color with $FeCl_3$ (Problem 20.77).

(*c*)   In the presence of the acid used to catalyze the ring closure, the isomers might interconvert. If the rate of isomerization is faster than cyclization, the same equilibrium mixture is obtained when starting from either pure isomer, the same mixture of ring-closed products is isolated, and the test is worthless. If the rate of cyclization is faster, the isomers retain their identity and the test is viable. Which situation prevails depends on the nature of the substrates.

18.141   Ketones or aromatic aldehydes react with α-haloesters in the presence of a strong base, e.g., $NaNH_2$ or $K^+\,{}^-O$-*t*-Bu. Give the product, $C_{10}H_{16}O_3$, of the low temperature (10 to 15 °C) reaction of cyclohexanone, ethyl chloracetate, and a dropwise added solution of *t*-BuO$^-$ in *t*-BuOH. With the aid of arrows, indicate the mechanistic steps for this *Darzen's condensation*.

▮   There are 3° of unsaturation, the cyclohexyl ring, the C=O of the ester, and a third ring or double bond formed during the reaction. The following sequence shows it to be an epoxide ring formed as the Cl$^-$ is displaced.

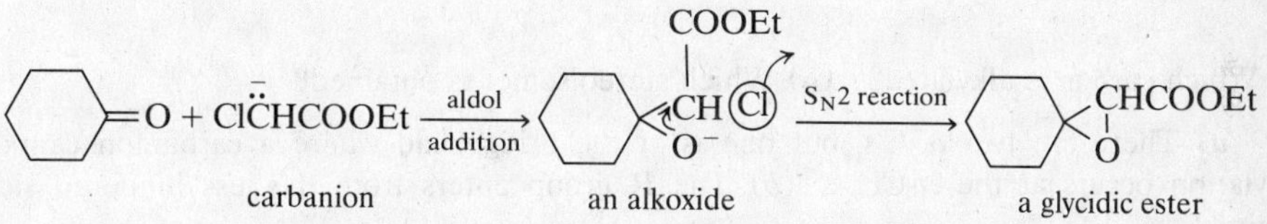

18.142   Careful saponification and subsequent acidification of glycidic esters produce thermally unstable glycidic acids which decompose to products that give oximes and dinitrophenylhydrazones. With the aid of arrows, show the sequence of steps leading from the glycidic ester in Problem 18.141 to the product. Start with the glycidic acid.

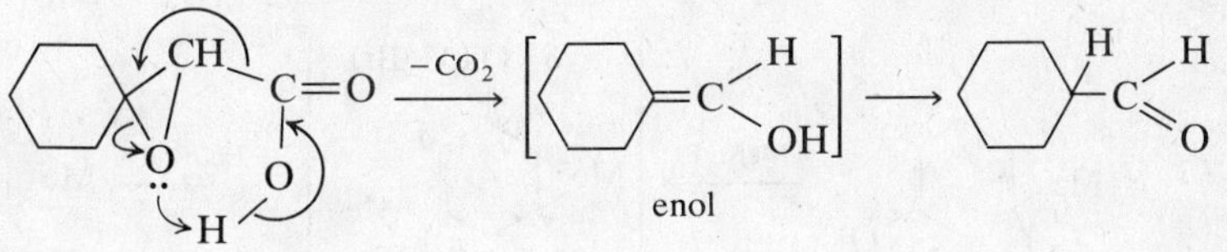

18.143   (*a*) Show the likely steps in the following transformations:

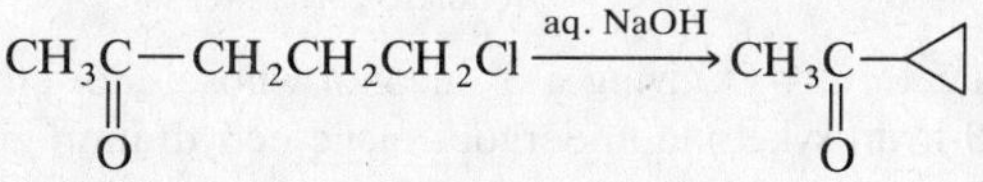

$$CH_3C{-}CH_2CH_2CH_2Cl \xrightarrow{\text{aq. NaOH}} CH_3C{-}\triangleleft$$
with O below each C

(*b*) What other product could be formed in (*a*)?

▮   (*a*) $CH_3COCH_2CH_2CH_2Cl \xrightarrow{\text{aq. NaOH}} \left[CH_3CO\ddot{C}HCH_2CH_2\,\ddot{C}l \right] \longrightarrow$ product

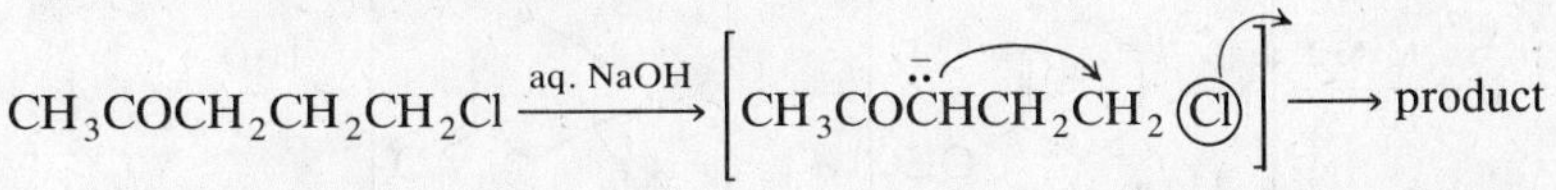

(*b*)   The carbanion from the CH_3 group could displace Cl and produce cyclopentanone.

18.144   Give the precursor needed to prepare 4-carbethoxycyclohexanone (**A**) by a Michael reaction.

▮   This compound has a 1,5-dicarbonyl grouping which is usually assembled by a Michael reaction, in this case intramolecular because there is a single precursor. The assembly is spotted by recalling that the precursor must have a C—C=C grouping. Reverse the Michael by breaking a C—C bond to reveal this group.
with O below first C

There are two ways to achieve this. If we break the $C^3{-}C^4$ bond, the vinyl group is bonded to the keto C=O. If we break the $C^2{-}C^3$ bond, the vinyl group is bonded to the ester C=O.

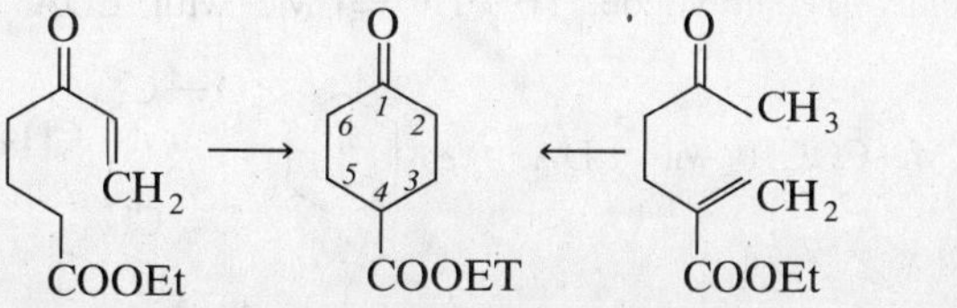

A

18.145 CH_3CH_2CHO exchanges two H's for D's with $NaOD/D_2O$. With $NaCN/D_2O$, a third H is exchanged. Which and why?

▰ As expected with $NaOD/D_2O$, the two α H's exchange to give CH_3CD_2CHO. With $NaCN/D_2O$ a cyanohydrin forms and the CN group acidifies its α H which happens to be the aldehydic H. This H is exchanged by D. Cyanohydrin formation then reverses, returning to the aldehyde. The H's α to C=O can exchange before cyanohydrin formation or after its reversal so that a trideuterated aldehyde is isolated. The following equation presumes that exchange of the α H's preceded the reaction with cyanide.

$$CH_3CD_2CHO + CN^-/D_2O \rightleftharpoons CH_3CD_2\underset{CN}{\overset{OD}{C}}{-}H \longrightarrow CH_3CD_2\underset{CN}{\overset{OD}{C}}{-}D \rightleftharpoons CH_3CD_2CDO$$

18.146 Bicyclo[2.2.1]heptan-2-one (**A**) is alkylated.

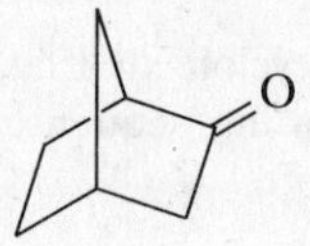

A

(*a*) Which carbon is alkylated? (*b*) Which stereoisomer is obtained?

▰ (*a*) There are two α C's, but one is at the bridgehead where a carbanion cannot form (Bredt's rule). Alkylation occurs at the α-CH_2. (*b*) The R group enters from the less hindered side—the *exo* isomer is obtained.

18.147 5,5-Dimethyl-3-ethoxycyclohex-2-enone (**B**) reacts with MeMgI followed by H^+ to give 3,5,5-trimethylcyclohex-2-enone (**C**). Give (*a*) a 1,4-addition and (*b*) a 1,2-addition pathway for the reaction.

▰ (*a*) Me:$^-$ could add to C^3 of **B** giving an enolate-carbanion salt of $^+(MgBr)$ that ejects ^-OEt.

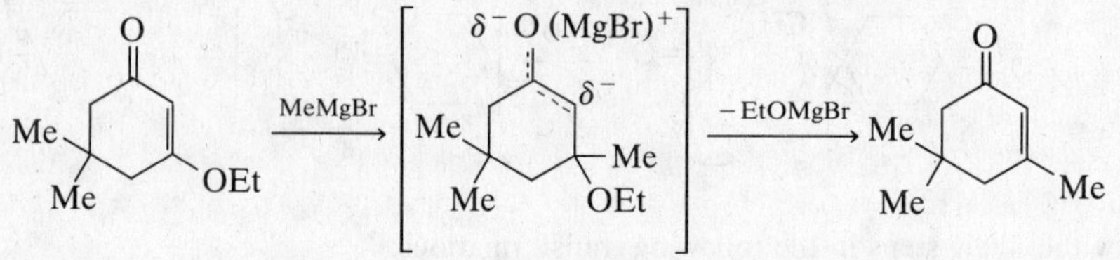

(*b*) Me:$^-$ could add 1,2 to C=O giving a 3° alcohol whose enol ether O—Et bond is hydrolyzed by H^+ to C=O. The resulting β-hydroxyketone undergoes facile dehydration giving **C**.

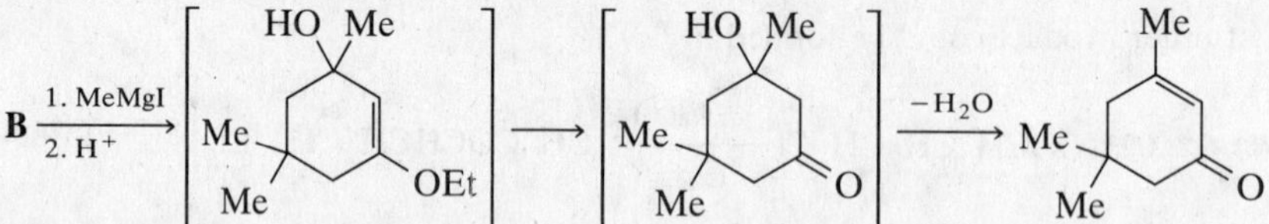

18.148 Discuss and illustrate how the following two kinds of experiments could indicate the correct pathway in Problem 18.147. Use (*a*) ^{14}C labeling and (*b*) a structural change that leaves the essential grouping intact.

▰ (*a*) Label the carbonyl C of **B**. If 1,4-addition occurs, the carbonyl C is labeled in the product. If 1,2-addition occurs, the C bonded to Me in the product is labeled, not the carbonyl C. (*b*) Start with 5,5,6-trimethyl-3-ethoxycyclohex-2-enone. 1,4-Addition gives the product 3,5,5,6-tetramethylcyclohex-2-enone while 1,2-addition leads to 3,4,5,5-tetramethylcyclohex-2-enone. Actually the pathway is 1,2-addition.

18.149 Complete the following reactions, indicating the sequence of events.
(*a*) δ-Valerolactone (5-pentanolide, **D**) + HC≡CMe with LDA at $-78\ °C$ and followed by acid. (*b*)

$BrCH_2CH_2CH_2CMe_2COCH_3$ with LDA. (*c*)

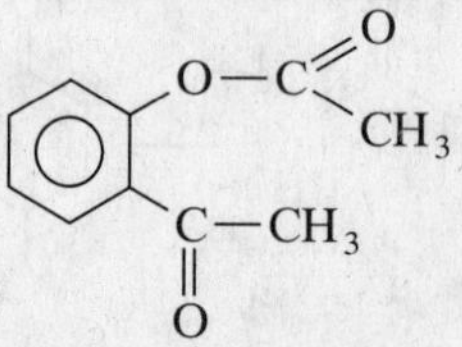

+aq.KOH followed by HOAc.

(a)

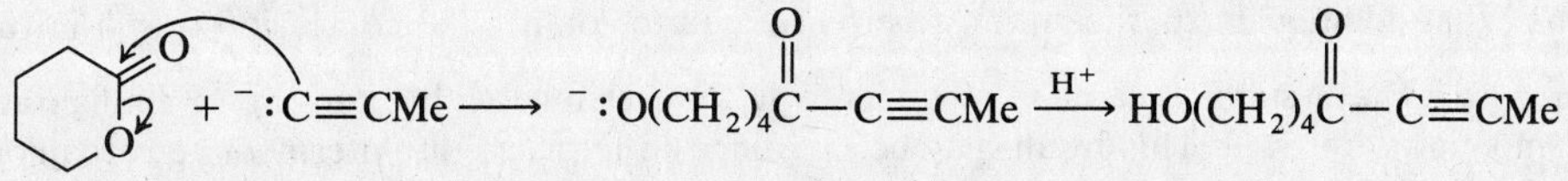

This is a Claisen-type reaction in which an acetylide is the carbanion and the alkoxy group remains as part of the product compound.

(b) The carbanion formed from the CH_3 participates in an intramolecular S_N2 reaction.

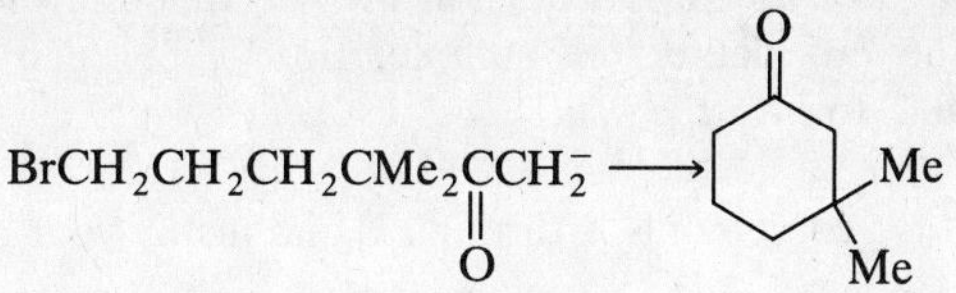

$$BrCH_2CH_2CH_2CMe_2CCH_2^- \longrightarrow$$

(c) This is a Claisen-type reaction in which the alkoxy group remains as part of the product compound.

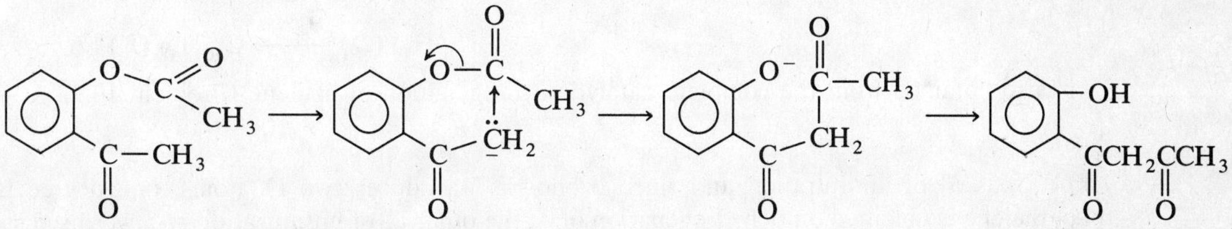

18.150 Identify and discuss the salient peaks in *(a)* the ir spectrum, and *(b)* the uv spectrum of the keto and enol tautomers of a typical β-diketone.

◢ Refer to Problem 18.18 for the structures discussed in this problem. *(a)* The keto form will show two typical intense $C=O$ bands at ≈ 1725 cm^{-1}, one for the symmetrical and one for the asymmetrical stretch. It shows no $O-H$ absorption. The resonance hybrid of the enol has diminished double-bond character in the carbonyl bonds. Consequently, the intense carbonyl-stretching absorption is shifted to lower frequency, 1640–1580 cm^{-1}. The peak is broad because of the many chelated structures differing mainly in the position of H in the H-bond. Typical of an H-bonding system, the $O-H$ stretch appears as a broad shallow band at 3000–2700 cm^{-1}. *(b)* The keto form shows the typical $C=O$ absorptions, an intense peak near $\lambda_{max} = 150$ nm ($\pi \rightarrow \pi^*$) and a low intensity peak in the 270 to 300 nm (n $\rightarrow \pi^*$) region. The enolic form shows strong absorptions in the 230 to 260 nm region due to the $\pi \rightarrow \pi^*$ transition, which is typical for α,β-unsaturated carbonyl compounds.

18.151 Show the formation of two possible products when 2-acetylcyclopentanone (**A**) reacts with NaOEt followed by H_3O^+.

◢ These reverse Claisen reactions are initiated when EtO$^-$ adds to a $C=O$. Since there are two $C=O$'s, two products are possible.

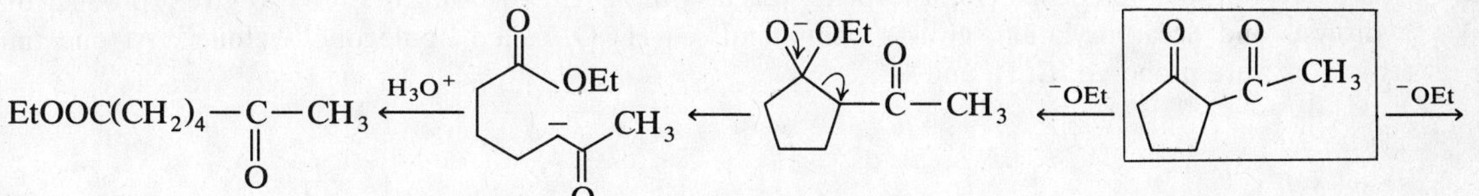

$$EtOOC(CH_2)_4 - \underset{O}{\overset{}{C}} - CH_3$$

B

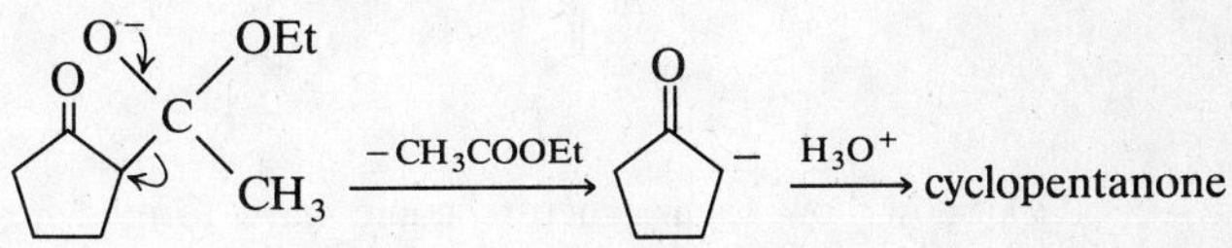

(The yield of the ketoester **B** is 90%.)

18.152 *(a)* Explain the following observation:

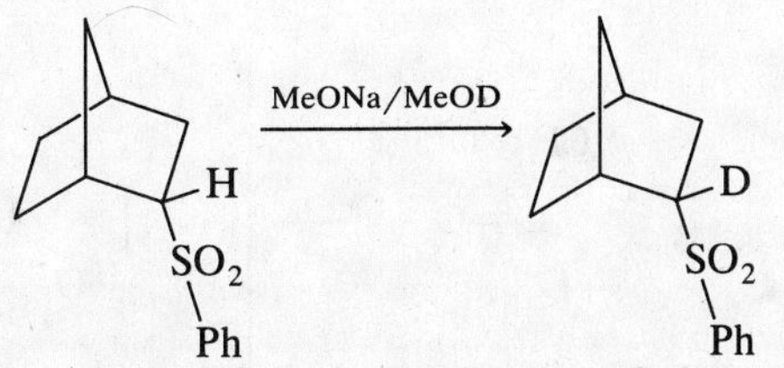

endo → *endo*

(*b*) What additional experiment must be performed to confirm the conclusion drawn in (*a*)?

▰ (*a*) The α-sulfonyl carbanions undergo H/D exchange with retention of configuration. In this case both compounds are *endo*. This result may be explained in terms of the intermediate carbanion being pyramidal but with a substantial energy barrier to inversion. (*b*) The carbanion may be planar and this result would be obtained if attack by MeOD were faster from the *exo* face. It is necessary to repeat the experiment with the *exo* sulfone. This sulfone should give the same planar carbanion that was formed from the *endo* isomer, which should again give the *endo* isomer. Now inversion occurs. If, however, the carbanion is pyramidal, there should be retention, giving the *exo* deuterated sulfone. Both experiments show retention, indicating the carbanion is pyramidal, but unable to invert.

18.153 Give the structures for compounds **A** through **E** and justify your answers.

$$C_{10}H_{16} \text{ (A)} \xrightarrow[\text{Zn or H}_2O_2]{O_3} C_{10}H_{16}O_2 \text{ (B)} \xrightarrow{\text{aq. OH}^-} C_{10}H_{14}O \text{ (C)} (\lambda_{max} = 300 \text{ nm}) \xrightarrow{\text{Zn/Hg, HCl}}$$

$$C_{10}H_{16} \text{ (D)} \xrightarrow{H_2/Pd} C_{10}H_{18} \text{ (E)}$$

E is also obtained from the complete catalytic hydrogenation of azulene (Problem 10.9). **A** $\xrightarrow[\Delta]{S}$ naphthalene, $C_{10}H_8$.

▰ **A** has 3° of unsaturation and since ozonolysis introduces two O atoms, one degree is a C=C. Since naphthalene is obtained on dehydrogenation of **A**, the other 2° of unsaturation are two fused six-membered rings with no R side chains. Likewise, **B**, **C**, **D**, and **E** have no R side chains. Since the same product is obtained on reductive or oxidative ozonolysis of **A**, the 3° of unsaturation of **B** are two C=O's and a ring. In order to get a diketone, the C=C in **A** is tetrasubstituted and must be at the fusion position of the two rings. **B** is 1,6-cyclodecanedione. **E** has the same ring system as azulene, a fused seven- and five-membered ring, and so must **C** and **D**, its precursors. The uv absorption of **C** at $\lambda_{max} = 300$ nm means that it is an α, β-unsaturated ketone, formed when **B** undergoes base-catalyzed intramolecular aldolization with NaOH to give the intermediate alcohol which dehydrates. The fact that only a single aldol product is formed substantiates that the two C=O's of **B** are equivalent and symmetrical and it is immaterial which acts as the acceptor. The Clemmenson reduction (Zn/Hg, HCl) of **C** reduces C=O to CH$_2$ to give **D** whose C=C is hydrogenated to give **E**. The structures are:

| A | B | C | D | E |

18.154 The natural product pulegone (**F**), a terpene, reacts with AAE and NaOEt/EtOH to give a product that, after hydrolysis and decarboxylation, gives a compound, $C_{13}H_{20}O$, called "pulegone acetone". At one time three structures were proposed, **G**, **H**, and **I**.

| F | G | H | I |

(*a*) Show how each structure could have formed. (*b*) Use the following spectral data to select the correct structure. ir spectrum: 1675, 1640 cm^{-1}. pmr spectrum: $\delta = 0.97$ ppm, *d*, three H's; $\delta = 1.1$ ppm, *s*, six H's; $\delta = 2.0$–2.2 ppm, complex multiplet, eight H's; $\delta = 2.3$ ppm, *s*, two H's; and $\delta = 6$ ppm, *s*, one H.

▰ (*a*) For **G**: an aldol addition in which pulegone furnishes the carbanion and the keto group of AAE is the acceptor.

F (as anion)

For **H**, AAE furnishes the carbanion and the C=O of pulegone is the acceptor. The aldol product, the precursor of **H**, can undergo dehydration and then an intramolecular Michael addition to give **I** after hydrolysis and decarboxylation.

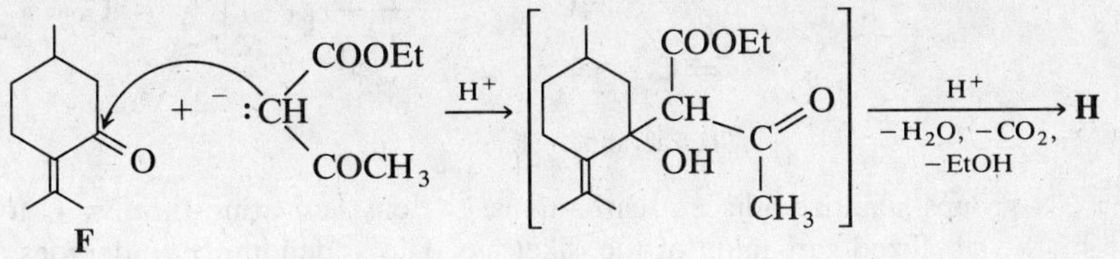

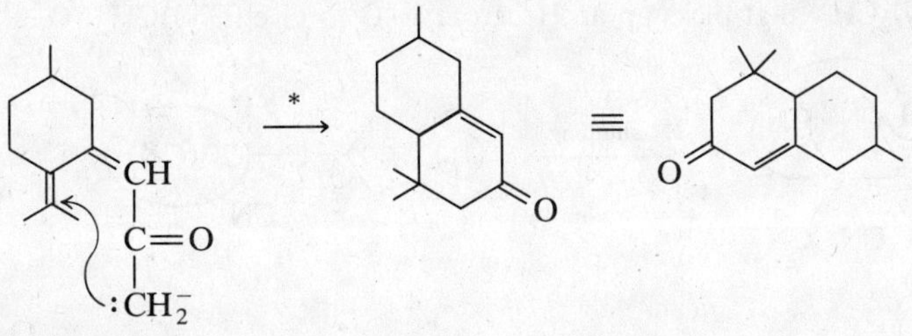

*H⁺ added after ring closure.

(*b*) **G** is eliminated because it lacks the lone uncoupled vinylic H, whose presence is revealed by the signal at $\delta = 6.1$ ppm. The two-H singlet at $\delta = 2.3$ ppm signals an isolated (uncoupled) CH_2 α to a C=O. This grouping is present only in **I**, the correct structure. Further confirmation is provided by the six-H singlet at $\delta = 1.1$ ppm because with this chemical shift the *gem* methyls are not bonded to a C=C.

18.155 Supply the structural formulas for **J** through **L** and characterize the reactions.

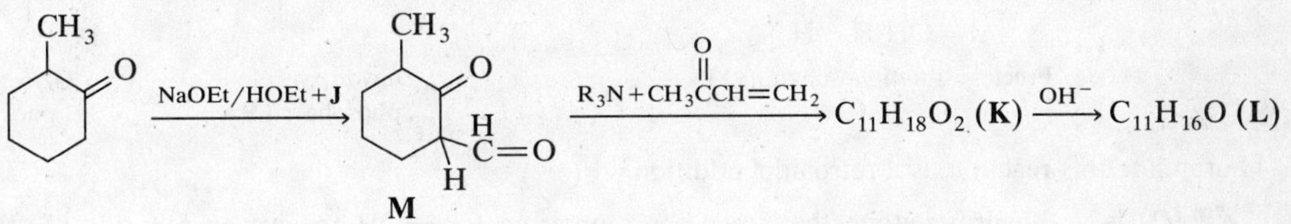

Use the following abbreviated spectral data as an aid to get the answers: **K**: ir spectrum, 1710 cm⁻¹; pmr spectrum, $\delta = 1.0$ ppm, *d*, three H's; $\delta = 2.2$ ppm, *s*, three H's. **L**: ir spectrum, 1680 cm⁻¹; pmr spectrum, $\delta = 1.0$ ppm, *d*, three H's; no signal at $\delta = 2.2$ ppm. Neither **K** nor **L** have signals in the $\delta = 9\text{–}10$ ppm range.

◢ The introduction of —CHO (formylation) in the first step is achieved by using the starting cyclohexanone as the carbanion source and HCOOEt (ethyl formate), **J**, as the acceptor in a Claisen-type condensation. The formyl group is introduced to enhance the acidity of the α H that is removed in the second step, a Michael addition of **M** to methyl vinyl ketone. Since **K** shows no pmr absorption in the $\delta = 9\text{–}10$-ppm area, the —CH=O group must have been lost in its formation. In the third step, **K** undergoes an intramolecular aldol addition to give an alcohol that loses H_2O giving **L**, an α,β-unsaturated ketone.

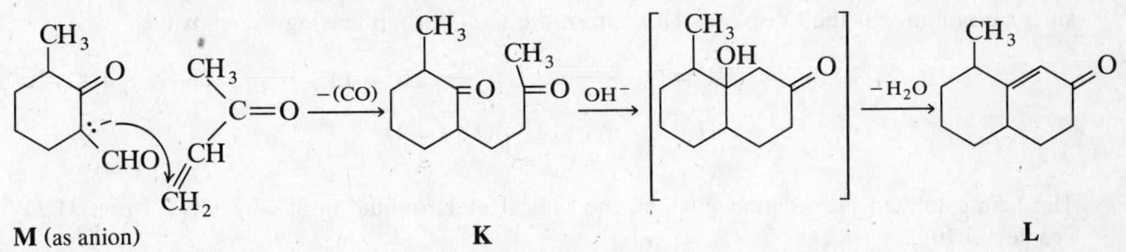

These assignments are consistent with the spectral data. The somewhat lower frequency in the ir spectrum of **L** indicates that its C=O is conjugated. **K** has two Me's: (*1*) the doublet at $\delta = 1.0$ ppm indicates one Me is removed from the C=O and is attached to a C with one H, a CH_3CH grouping, and (*2*) the singlet at $\delta = 2.2$ ppm shows a CH_3C=O grouping. The CH_3C=O methyl is gone in **L** because it was changed in the aldol cyclization.

18.156 Rationalize the following reaction and supply the structure of the missing product (**O**).

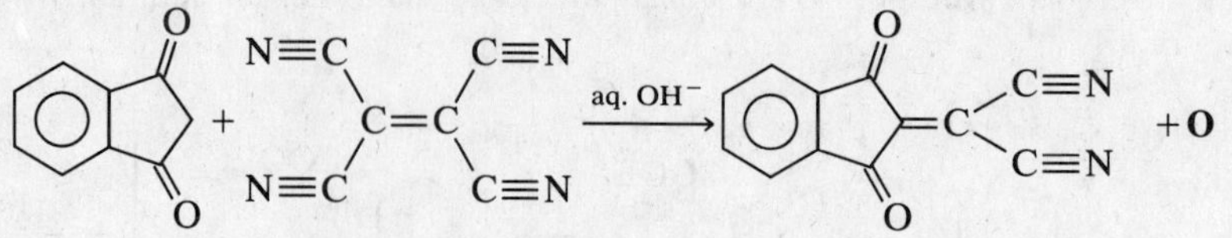

Tetracyanoethylene

◢ The CN groups stabilize adjacent carbanions, thereby activating the C=C towards Michael additions, in this case by the stabilized carbanion of the diketone. The addendum **P** undergoes an E2 reaction releasing the stabilized $(CN)_2CH^-$ that picks up an H^+ from H_2O to give $(CN)_2CH_2$, **O**.

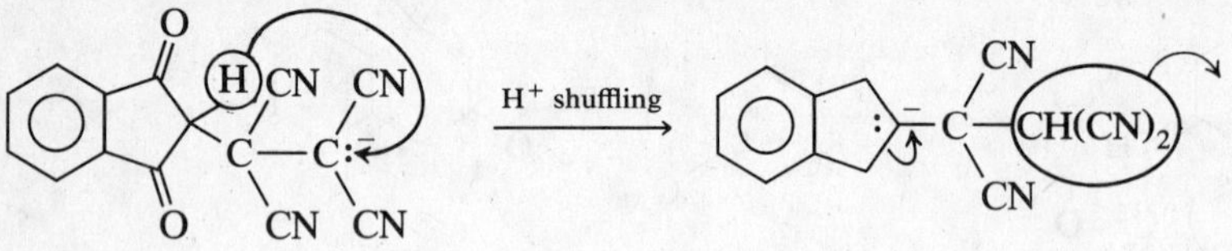

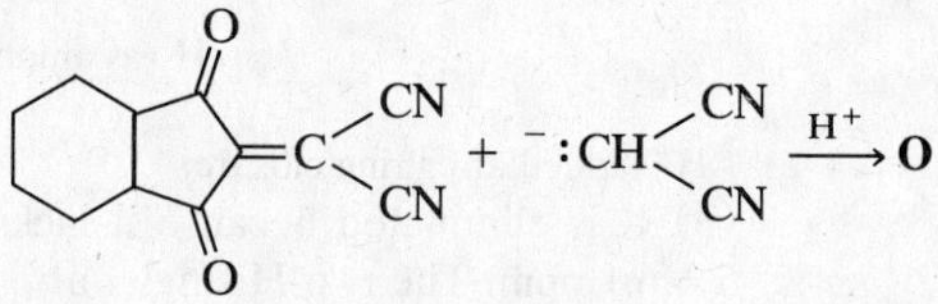

18.157 In the fermentation of the sugar glucose to ethanol a key step is

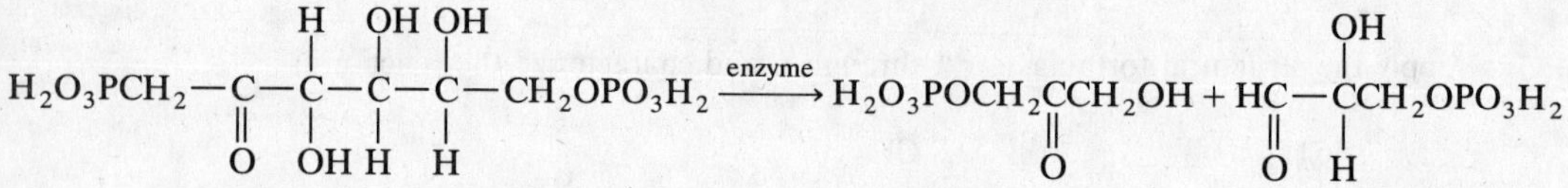

Fructose-1,6-diphosphate (**Q**)   Dihydroxyacetone phosphate (**R**)   Glyceraldehyde-3-phosphate (**S**)

Formulate this reaction as a retroaldol addition.

◢ (**Q**) is a β-hydroxyketone that loses a proton from C^β—OH to give an alkoxide (**T**) that undergoes a retroaldol addition by cleavage of the C^α—C^β bond.

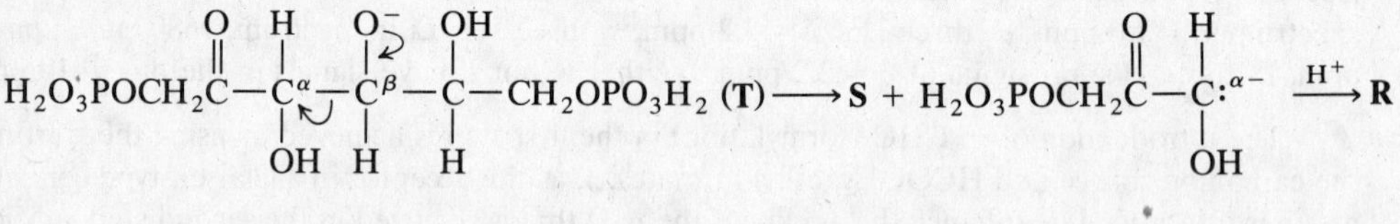

18.158 Explain why acrolein, $H_2C=CHCHO$, is epoxidized much more rapidly with a basic solution of H_2O_2 than with a peroxyacid.

◢ Base converts H_2O_2 to the conjugate base, HOO^-, that undergoes a Michael addition with acrolein to give an α-carbanion that then displaces HO^- from the HOO group leaving the epoxide.

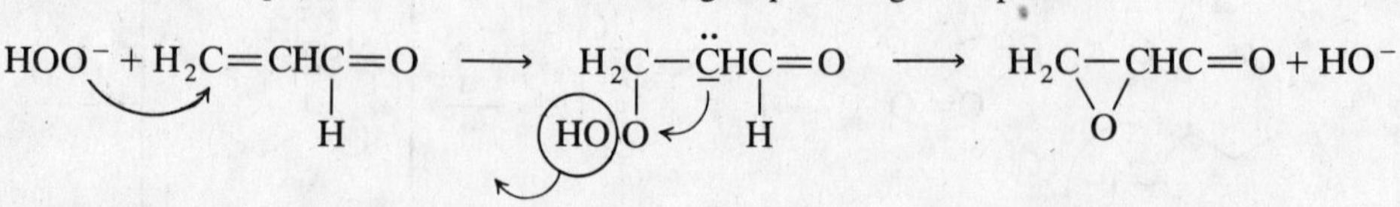

The acid-catalyzed epoxidation goes by the typical electrophilic attack by HO^+ (from H_2O_2) on C=C (see Problem 7.107).

CHAPTER 19

Amines

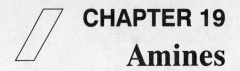

NOMENCLATURE, STRUCTURE, AND PHYSICAL PROPERTIES

19.1 Define amines and identify the following amines as primary (1°), secondary (2°), or tertiary (3°):

(*a*) $CH_3CH_2\underset{\displaystyle NH_2}{\underset{|}{C}}HCH_3$ (*b*) $(CH_3)_3N$ (*c*) $CH_3\underset{\displaystyle C_6H_5}{\underset{|}{C}}HNH_2$ (*d*) $CH_2{=}CHCH_2NHCH_3$

(*e*) 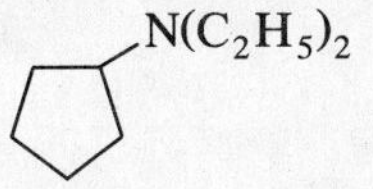 (*f*) 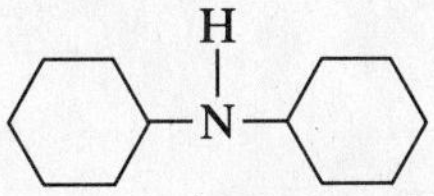

■ *Amines* are alkyl or aryl derivatives of NH_3. Replacement of one H of NH_3 by R or Ar results in a 1° amine (RNH_2), and if two or three H's are replaced, the result is a 2° (R_2NH) or 3° (R_3N), respectively. (*a*) and (*c*) 1°; (*d*) and (*f*) 2°; (*b*) and (*e*) 3°.

19.2 (*a*) Give a general structure for a quaternary (4°) ammonium ion. (*b*) Write structures for: (i) tetramethylammonium chloride, (ii) trimethylanilinium nitrate, and (iii) tetraethylammonium sulfate.

■ (*a*) $R(Ar)_3N^+$. The four H's of NH_4^+ can be replaced by some combination of R's or Ar's.
(*b*) (i) $Me_4N^+Cl^-$, (ii) $(Me_3NPh)^+NO_3^-$, (iii) $(Et_4N^+)_2SO_4^=$.

19.3 Supply common names for each of the structures in Problem 19.1.

■ Add the suffix *-amine* to the names of the groups bonded to N. (*a*) *sec*-butylamine, (*b*) trimethylamine, (*c*) α-phenylethylamine, (*d*) allylmethylamine, (*e*) diethylcyclopentylamine, and (*f*) dicyclohexylamine.

19.4 Give names for (*a*) $Me_2CHCH_2NHCHMe_2$, (*b*) $H_2N(CH_2)_4NH_2$, (*c*) $CH_3CH_2N(CHClCH_3)_2$, (*d*) $HOCH_2CH_2CH_2NH_2$, and (*e*) $CH_3CH_2\underset{\displaystyle CH_3}{\underset{|}{C}}HNMe_2$.

■ (*a*) Isobutylisopropylamine, (*b*) 1,4-tetramethylenediamine or 1,4-diaminobutane (also called *putrescine* because it is one of the putrid compounds in decaying animal matter), (*c*) 1,1'-dichlorotriethylamine, (*d*) 3-aminopropanol (alcohol has priority over amine), and (*e*) N,N-dimethyl-2-aminobutane or *sec*-butyldimethylamine

19.5 Provide names for

(*a*) 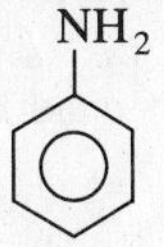 (*b*) 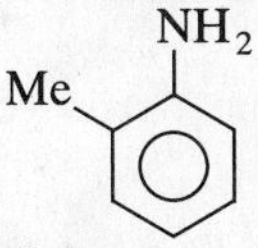 (*c*) 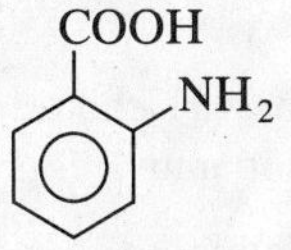 (*d*) 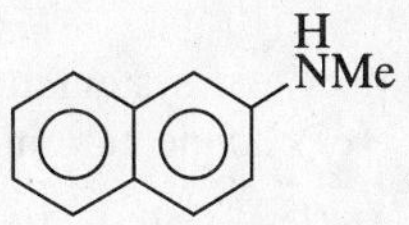

(*e*) 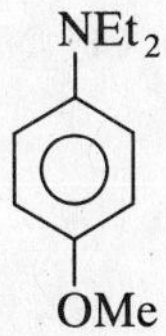 (*f*) 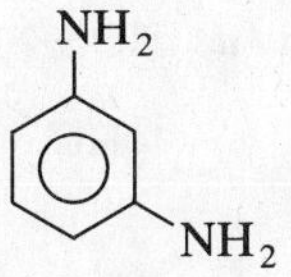 (*g*) 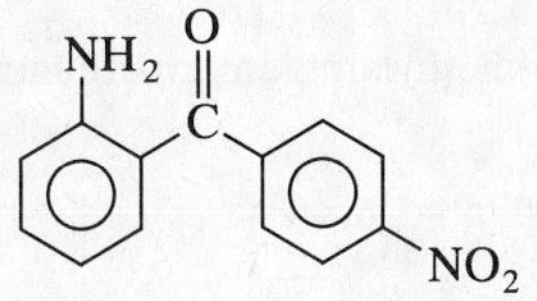

■ (*a*) Aniline, (*b*) *o*-toluidine, (*c*) *o*-aminobenzoic acid or anthranilic acid, (*d*) N-methyl-2-naphthylamine, (*e*) N,N-diethyl-*p*-anisidine, (*f*) *m*-phenylenediamine, and (*g*) 2-amino-4'-nitrobenzophenone

19.6 Give the Chemical Abstract (CA) names for (*a*) $CH_3CH_2NH_2$, (*b*) $CH_3CH_2CH_2CH_2NHCH_3$, (*c*) $H_2NCH_2CH_2NH_2$, (*d*) $PhNH_2$, (*e*) 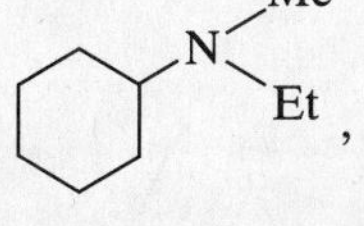, and (*f*) $CH_3CH_2N(CHClCH_3)_2$.

✐ The amino N is assigned the lowest number on the longest chain, and an N is placed before each substituent group on the nitrogen. (*a*) ethanamine, (*b*) N-methyl-1-butanamine, (*c*) 1,2-ethanediamine, (*d*) benzenamine, (*e*) N-methyl-N-ethylcyclohexanamine, and (*f*) N,N-bis(1-chloroethyl)ethanamine.

19.7 Write structures for the following compounds: (*a*) *o*-Phenetidine, (*b*) 2-ethylpyrrolidine, (*c*) piperidine-3-carboxylic acid, (*d*) *cis*-4-methyl-1-cyclohexanamine, (*e*) aziridine, and (*f*) morpholine.

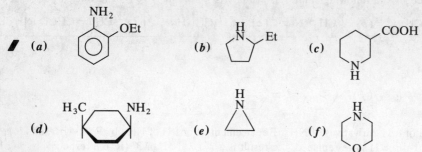

19.8 Why are the following names incorrect? (*a*) Methylaniline, (*b*) propanediamine, (*c*) N-pentyl-2-propylamine, and (*d*) *m*-xylidine.

✐ (*a*) If Me is bonded to the amino N, the correct name is N-methylaniline. If it is bonded to the ring, the correct name is *o*-, *m*- or *p*-toluidine or 2-, 3- or 4-methylbenzenamine. (*b*) The correct name must specify the positions of the amino groups; the full name is either 1,2- or 1,3-propanediamine. (*c*) The larger alkyl group is considered the parent amine; thus, N-isopropyl-1-pentylamine. (*d*) With three substituents on the ring, *o*-, *m*- and *p*-designations are inadequate. Xylidines are aminobenzenes with two Me's bonded in various positions to the ring. These positions must be specified. For example, if the Me's are *ortho* to each other, the IUPAC name is 3,4-xylidine, where the numbers refer to the positions of the Me groups. Its CA name is 3,4-dimethylbenzenamine, and it can also be named 3,4-dimethylaniline.

19.9 Name the following compounds by the *aza* system:

(*a*) [structure: 7-membered ring with ketone (=O) and N–H]   (*b*) $H_2NCH_2CH_2NHCH_2CH_3$ (*c*) $CH_3CH_2NHCH_2CH(CH_2CH_3)_2$

✐ In the aza system, N is counted in the chain as if it were C, but it is distinguished by the term *aza*, and given a position number. (*a*) 3-Azacycloheptanone, (*b*) 1,4-diazahexane, and (*c*) 5-ethyl-3-azaheptane.

19.10 Give structures and systematic names for (*a*) cadaverine (another putrid compound in dead animal matter), (*b*) PABA, (*c*) choline cation, and (*d*) dopamine.

✐ (*a*) $H_2N(CH_2)_5NH_2$, 1,5-pentanediamine; (*b*) p-$H_2NC_6H_4COOH$, p-aminobenzoic acid;

(*c*) $HOCH_2CH_2NMe_3^+$, 2-(trimethylammonium)ethanol ion; and (*d*) HO—⟨O⟩—$CH_2CH_2NH_2$, with HO on the ring,

β-(3,4-dihydroxyphenyl)ethylamine.

19.11 Place the isomeric compounds ethyldimethylamine (**A**), *n*-butylamine (**B**), and diethylamine (**C**) in order of decreasing bp's and give an explanation.

✐ **B** > **C** > **A**. 1° And 2° amines, unlike 3° amines, form intramolecular H-bonds (Fig. 19-1). **B** with two H's available for H-bonding has a higher bp than **C**.

[structure diagram: R—N(H)(H):- - -H—N:(R)(H) with H- - -:N—H- - -etc]

Fig. 19-1

19.12   (*a*) Compare the bp's of *n*-butylamine (**B**), *n*-butyl alcohol (**D**), and pentane (**E**).   (*b*) Compare their dipole moments.   (*c*) Give structures for ethanolamine showing two different intramolecular H-bonds and discuss their relative importance.

◢   (*a*) N is less electronegative than O; the H-bonds in the amine **B** are weaker than those in **D**. H-bonding is not possible with **E**. Since the MW's of the three compounds are about the same, the trend in bp's is: **D > B > E**. (*b*) This is also the decreasing order of dipole moments.

(*c*)

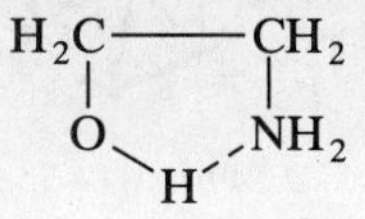

$$H_2C \text{———} CH_2 \quad \textbf{F} \quad \text{and} \quad H_2C \text{———} CH_2 \quad \textbf{G}$$

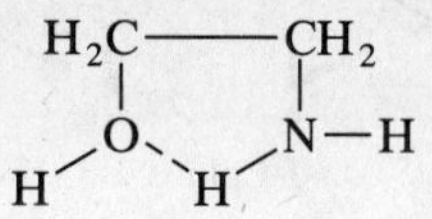

Since O is more electronegative than N, its H-bond to N is stronger than the H-bond from N-to-O; **F > G**.

19.13   Discuss the solubility of amines in (*a*) water and (*b*) alcohol.

◢   (*a*) Water solubility depends on the H-bonding between the amine and H_2O, provided the R group is not too large. Either the N—H bonds with the O of H_2O or the O—H bonds with the N of the amine, or both. 3° Amines can only H-bond through their unshared electron-pair with the H of H_2O. The amines with lower MW are water-soluble.   (*b*) Since all amines form H-bonds with hydroxylic solvents, they are very soluble in alcohols.

19.14   The C—N—C bond angle in Me_3N is 108°.   (*a*) Describe the hybridization and shape of Me_3N.   (*b*) Why is an amine of the type $R^1R^2R^3N$ chiral?   (*c*) Why is it not possible to separate the enantiomers?

◢   (*a*) N forms three sp^3 hybridized σ bonds to the C's of the Me groups and has a nonbonding electron pair in the fourth sp^3 orbital. Me_3N has a roughly pyramidal shape [Fig. 19-2(*a*)].   (*b*) Because of its pyramidal geometry, such an amine is chiral, the unshared pair being considered a fourth "different" group.   (*c*) The enantiomers rapidly interconvert, having enough kinetic energy at room temperatures, by a process called *nitrogen inversion*. For this process $H^{\ddagger} \cong 6$ kcal/mol (25 kJ/mol) and the inversion thus does not involve bond-breaking and subsequent formation. The TS for the inversion is planar, the N being sp^2 hybridized, with the unshared pair in the p_z orbital [Fig. 19-2(*b*)].

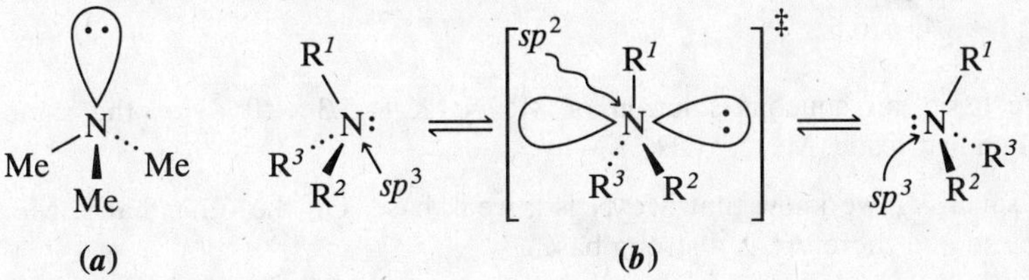

Fig. 19-2

19.15   Why are the following compounds resolvable?

(*a*) $CH_3CH_2CH_2CH(CH_3)NH_2$ (*b*) $\left[CH_2{=}CHCH_2\underset{\underset{\displaystyle Ph}{|}}{N}(CH_3)(C_2H_5) \right]^{+} I^{-}$

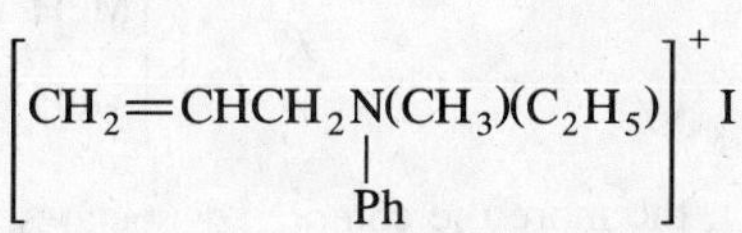

(*c*) $(CH_3)_2C \text{———} \overset{\displaystyle ..}{N}{-}CH_3$ with CH_2 bridging

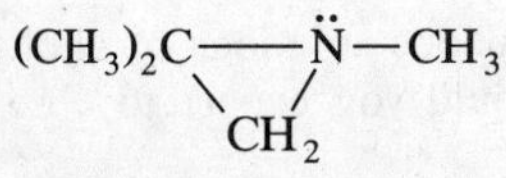

◢   (*a*) The chirality is due to the presence of the chiral 2° pentyl carbon chain.   (*b*) N uses sp^3 hybridized orbitals to form four σ bonds to four different ligands. The resulting cationic enantiomers are configurationally stable at room temperature because there is no lone pair to permit N inversion.   (*c*) N inversion requires too high an $H^{\ddagger}$ because the N in such a small ring cannot attain the 120° angles required in the TS [Fig. 19-2(*b*)].

19.16 How many isomers of 1-chloro-2-methylaziridine are possible? Draw them.

⟋ Two pairs of enantiomers, or four stereomers. There are two chiral centers: the N [recall that N inversion cannot occur, as seen in Problem 19.15(*c*)], and the 3° C. See Fig. 19-3.

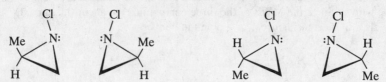

(*R* and *S*) *cis*-1-Chloro-2-methylaziridine   (*R* and *S*) *trans*-1-Chloro-2-methylaziridine   **Fig. 19-3**

BASICITY AND NUCLEOPHILICITY

19.17 (*a*) Write chemical equations for the reactions of $MeNH_2$ with (i) H_2O, (ii) gaseous HCl, (iii) $B(Me)_3$. (*b*) Characterize the chemical behavior of $MeNH_2$ in each case in (*a*).

⟋ (*a*) (i) $MeNH_2 + H_2O \rightleftharpoons MeNH_3^+ + OH^-$
methylammonium ion

(ii) $MeNH_2 + HCl(g) \longrightarrow MeNH_3^+Cl^-(s)$

(iii) $\begin{matrix} H \\ \backslash \\ Me\overset{..}{N}: \\ / \\ H \end{matrix} + BMe_3 \longrightarrow MeH_2\overset{+}{N}-\overset{-}{B}Me_3$ (The + and − are formal charges)

(*b*) (i) and (ii) Brönsted base. (iii) Nucleophile. The product is called a *complex*.

19.18 (*a*) Write the equilibrium expression (K_b) for the reaction of $MeNH_2$ in water. (*b*) Given $K_b = 4.3 \times 10^{-4}$, find the pK_b. (*c*) Find the pK_a for $MeNH_3^+$, the conjugate acid.

⟋ (*a*) $K_b = \dfrac{[MeNH_3^+][OH^-]}{[MeNH_2]}$.   (*b*) $pK_b = -\log K_b = -\log(4.3 \times 10^{-4}) = 3.4$.   (*c*) $pK_a + pK_b = 14$ from which $pK_a = 14 - 3.4 = 10.6$.

19.19 Which is more basic, an aqueous solution of Me_3N ($K_b = 5.3 \times 10^{-5}$) or the same concentration of tetra-methylammonium hydroxide, $Me_4N^+OH^-$? Why?

⟋ From its small K_b we know that Me_3N is a weak base. On the other hand, $Me_4N^+OH^-$, like NaOH, is completely ionized and therefore is a strong base.

19.20 (*a*) Write the equilibrium expression for the dissociation constant, K_{diss}, for the complex $MeH_2\overset{+}{N}-\overset{-}{B}Me_3$. (*b*) How are the values of K_{diss} and the reactivity of the amine towards the trialkylborane related?

⟋ (*a*) The chemical equation for dissociation is $MeH_2\overset{+}{N}-\overset{-}{B}Me_3 \rightleftharpoons MeH_2N: + BMe_3$ and

$$K_{diss} = \frac{[MeH_2N:][BMe_3]}{\left[MeH_2\overset{+}{N}-\overset{-}{B}Me_3\right]}$$

(*b*) The larger is K_{diss}, the more the complex dissociates, and the less nucleophilic is the amine.

19.21 (*a*) In general, the order of base strength as measured by K_b's for aqueous solutions of aliphatic amines is: $R_2NH > RNH_2 > R_3N > NH_3$. Explain the order. (*b*) What order would you expect to observe in the gas phase?

⟋ (*a*) Two effects, induction and solvation, determine the K_b of an alkyl amine. Inductively, alkyl groups, being electron-releasing, increase the electron density on nitrogen, making the amine more basic (larger K_b). Coincidentally, they stabilize the + on the conjugate acid, making the ammonium ion less acidic. [It is better to use bases for comparisons rather than the conjugate acids, as was done for carboxylic acids (see Problem 16.41)]. In terms of induction alone, increasing the number of R's should increase the basicity. Solvation through

H-bonding with H_2O is more important in the conjugate acid than in the free amine because the ammonium ion has a + charge and a greater number of H's. In terms of solvation alone, the more H's in the ammonium ion, the more it is stabilized by H-bonding, the more the equilibrium goes to the right, and the more basic should be the amine. As R's replace H's, H-bonding declines and amine basicity should decrease. Thus, induction and solvation operate in opposition, accounting for the discontinuity in K values. Induction dominates to make all three alkylamines stronger bases than NH_3 and to make dimethylamine stronger than methylamine. However, adding a third R as in R_3N does not further enhance the basicity because now the opposing solvation effect assumes more importance. (**b**) Free from solvation effects, only induction prevails and the order is $R_3N > R_2NH > RNH_2 > NH_3$.

19.22 Account for the following order of complex formation with BMe_3: $Me_2NH > MeNH_2 > NH_3 \gg Me_3N$.

◢ The first three amines are in the expected order because replacing H's by electron-donating R's makes the bases more nucleophilic. Another factor appears when Me_3N is studied. The Me's on N sterically interfere with the Me's on B, hindering close approach of the two molecules and facilitating dissociation of the complex, if formed. The net result is a sharp drop in the complexation of the 3° amine. This type of steric hindrance is called *F-strain* (front strain), since the hindrance occurs in front of the approaching molecules.

19.23 Explain why K_{diss} of the BMe_3 complex with $(CH_3CH_2)_3N\colon$ is extremely large while K_{diss} with quinuclidine is extremely small.

Quinuclidine

◢ $(CH_3CH_2)_3N\colon$ has a very large F-strain which practically prevents formation of the complex. Quinuclidine is also a 3° amine but it is a bicyclic amine whose three alkyl bonds are tied back and do not protrude in front of the molecule in the path of BMe_3. Instead, the cumulative inductive effect of the three R's enhances the nucleophilicity of the basic N.

19.24 Explain the diminished basicities of 3° amines as their R's become bulkier.

◢ The N of amines is regarded as using sp^3 HO's with the unshared electron pair occupying one tetrahedrally directed HO. As the R's get bulkier, the additional crowding can be somewhat alleviated if the bonding orbitals acquire less p character (while the lone pair HO assumes more p character). They tend to become hybridized somewhere between sp^3 and sp^2, with a concomitant increase in the bond angles. This modification is possible only when one of the HO's houses an unshared pair of electrons. Acceptance of an H^+ by the amine forces the orbitals toward the tetrahedral sp^3 configuration with a reduction of bond angles and increased steric crowding among the R's. The ammonium ion suffers a kind of strain, called *B-strain* (back strain), present in "back" of the amine and away from the entering H^+. Another contributing factor to the declining basicity is the increasing steric hindrance to the solvation of the cation. The bulkier the R's, the more B-strain there is and the weaker is the basicity.

19.25 Account for the fact that aziridine (azacyclopropane) is much less basic than piperidine or pyrrolidine.

◢ The ring strain of the three-membered aziridine ring can be partially overcome by inducing more p character in the bonding HO's and more s character in the HO with the lone pair of e^-'s. It should be noted that the basicity of a lone pair decreases as the s character of its HO increases. (Recall that bonds formed from pure p AO's have 90° bond angles.) Addition of H^+ forces N to use sp^3 HO's, reintroducing the full ring strain in the ammonium ion. Because the cation of aziridine has a much higher free energy than the base, its formation is disfavored and the basicity of aziridine is weakened. The strain in the cation is called *I-strain* (internal strain). Piperidine and pyrrolidine have no I-strain and are more basic than aziridine.

19.26 Account for the following order of increasing basicity:

$$RC{\equiv}N\colon < R'CH{=}NR < RNH_2$$
$$\text{nitrile} \qquad \text{imine} \qquad \text{amine}$$

✎ The more s character in the hybrid orbital of the N with the unshared pair of e^-'s, the less basic is the molecule. The nitrile N using sp HO's has the most s character, the imine N using sp^2 HO's has the intermediate s character, and the amine N using sp^3 HO's has the least s character.

19.27 Give (*a*) the conjugate acid and (*b*) the conjugate base of $HO(CH_2)_3NH_2$.

✎ (*a*) $HO(CH_2)_3NH_3^+$; NH_2 is a more basic site than OH. (*b*) $^-O(CH_2)_3NH_2$; H—O is more acidic than H—N.

19.28 Place ethylamine, 2-aminoethanol, and 3-amino-1-propanol in order of decreasing basicity and give your reason.

✎ $CH_3CH_2NH_2 > HO(CH_2)_3NH_2 > HO(CH_2)_2NH_2$. The electron-withdrawing inductive effect of the OH decreases the electron density on N, lowering the amine's basicity. This effect diminishes with distance from the amino group.

19.29 (*a*) In terms of s character, which N of guanidine, $HN{=}C(NH_2)_2$, is more likely to be protonated? (*b*) Account for the fact that guanidine is a strong base ($K_b \cong 1$).

✎ (*a*) The N (sp^3) of NH_2 with less s character than N (sp^2) of the imino ($=NH$) should be the more basic site and be protonated. (*b*) Actually the imino N is protonated because this leads to a symmetrical resonance stabilized cation.

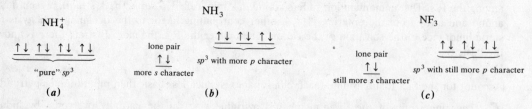

Resonance involving three equivalent contributing structures accounts for the large delocalization energy and unusual stability of the cation, resulting in the enhanced basicity of guanidine. Guanidine is probably the strongest organic N base known.

19.30 In terms of s character, explain why NH_3 with bond angles of 107° is much more basic than NF_3 with bond angles of 103°. The bond angles of NH_4^+ are 109°.

✎ The bond angle of 109° in NH_4^+ indicates that N uses pure sp^3 HO's [Fig. 19-4(*a*)]. The bond angle of 107° in NH_3 shows that, although N essentially uses sp^3 HO's, it nevertheless has slightly more p character in its bonding HO's and slightly more s character in its lone pair HO [Fig. 19-4(*b*)]. The bond angle of 103° in NF_3 indicates that N has even more p character in its bonding HO's and even more s character in its lone pair HO [Fig. 19-4(*c*)]. NF_3 is less basic than NH_3 because its lone pair orbital has more s character.

NH_4^+ NH_3 NF_3

NH_4^+	NH_3	NF_3
↑↓ ↑↓ ↑↓ ↑↓	lone pair ↑↓ / ↑↓ ↑↓ ↑↓	lone pair ↑↓ / ↑↓ ↑↓ ↑↓
"pure" sp^3	more s character / sp^3 with more p character	still more s character / sp^3 with still more p character
(*a*)	(*b*)	(*c*)

Fig. 19-4

19.31 Compare the basicities of (*a*) $H_2C{=}CHCH_2NH_2$, $CH_3CH_2CH_2NH_2$ and $HC{\equiv}CCH_2NH_2$, and (*b*) $C_6H_5CH_2NH_2$, cyclohexyl-CH_2NH_2 and p-$NO_2C_6H_4CH_2NH_2$.

✎ (*a*) The significant difference among these three bases is the kind of hybrid orbitals used by C^β—the more s character it has, the more electron-withdrawing (by induction) and base weakening it will be. The HO conditions are $H_2C{=}C^\beta HCH_2NH_2(sp^2)$, $CH_3C^\beta H_2CH_2NH_2(sp^3)$, and $HC{\equiv}C^\beta CH_2NH_2(sp)$. The increasing order of electron-attraction is propargyl > allyl > propyl, and the decreasing order of basicity is

$$CH_3CH_2CH_2NH_2 > H_2C{=}CHCH_2NH_2 > HC{\equiv}CCH_2NH_2$$

(*b*) The decreasing order is

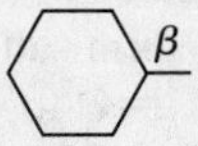

$$\langle\!\!\!\!\!\!\!\!\!\!\!\!\!\!\!\!\rangle\!-\!CH_2NH_2 > C_6H_5CH_2NH_2 > p\text{-}NO_2C_6H_4CH_2NH_2$$

The C^β in cyclohexyl-CH_2NH_2 uses sp^3 HO's while C^β in the benzylamines uses sp^2 HO's. The electron-withdrawing p-NO_2 makes the phenyl ring even more electron-withdrawing and base weakening.

19.32 Compare the basicities of $PhNH_2$, Ph_2NH, and cyclohexyl-NH_2. Explain.

 Aromatic amines are much less basic than alkylamines because the electron density from the unshared pair of e⁻'s is delocalized into the ring, mainly to the *ortho* and *para* positions (see Fig. 19-5). An increase in the number of phenyls bonded to N increases delocalization and decreases basicity. In cyclohexyl-NH_2 the electron density is localized and this amine is the most basic. The decreasing order of basicities is cyclohexyl-$NH_2 > C_6H_5NH_2 > (C_6H_5)_2NH$.

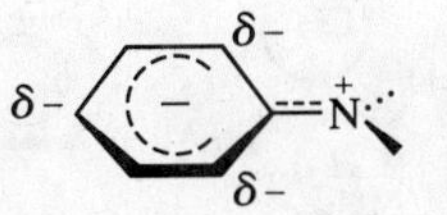

Fig. 19-5

19.33 Account for the following order of decreasing basicities:

$$C_6H_5NH_2 \text{ (A)} > m\text{-}NO_2C_6H_4NH_2 \text{ (B)} > p\text{-}NO_2C_6H_4NH_2 \text{ (C)} > o\text{-}NO_2C_6H_4NH_2 \text{ (D)}$$

 NO_2 is electron-withdrawing, by induction from all positions but mainly by extended π bonding from the *ortho* and *para* positions. Therefore all the nitroanilines are less basic than aniline, and so **C** is less basic than **B**. **D** is less basic than **C** because its NO_2 is closer and exerts a stronger inductive effect. (In Problem 19.34 we will see an additional effect that tends to cause *ortho* isomers to be less basic than *para* isomers.) Figure 19-6 shows the resonance hybrid of the *para*-NO_2 compound.

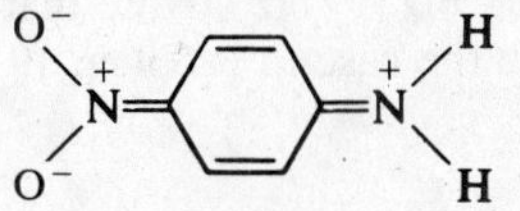

Fig. 19-6

19.34 Account for the following order of decreasing basicities:
(*a*) $p\text{-}CH_3OC_6H_4NH_2 \text{ (E)} > C_6H_5NH_2 \text{ (A)} > o\text{-}CH_3OC_6H_4NH_2 \text{ (F)} > m\text{-}CH_3OC_6H_4NH_2 \text{ (G)}$
(*b*) $p\text{-}CH_3C_6H_4NH_2 \text{ (H)} > m\text{-}CH_3C_6H_4NH_2 \text{ (I)} > C_6H_5NH_2 \text{ (A)} > o\text{-}CH_3C_6H_4NH_2 \text{ (J)}$

 (*a*) CH_3O is strongly electron-donating from the *ortho* and *para* positions by extended π bonding. This effect completely submerges the electron-withdrawing inductive effect from these positions leaving only the *meta* position where inductive withdrawal dominates. This discussion is consistent with the declining basicity order **E > A > G**. But why is **F** weaker than **A**? This is an example of the "*ortho* effect" first noted with substituted benzoic acids (see Problem 16.51). All *o*-substituted anilines are less basic than *p*-substituted anilines regardless of the electronic effect of the substituent. This effect is attributed to steric hindrance by the *o*-substituent to solvation of the cation. This steric effect destabilizes the cation making the amine a weaker base.

(*b*) CH_3, A typical alkyl group, is inductively electron-donating and base-strengthening from all positions. Moreover, if the R group has a benzylic H, as does CH_3, it is electron-donating by hyperconjugation (Problem 11.62) from the *ortho* and *para* positions. Hence the decreasing order of basicity is **H** (hyperconjugation and induction) > **I** (induction) > **A** > **J** (ortho effect).

19.35 Compare and explain the differences in the basicities of $CH_3CH_2NH_2$, $CH_3\overset{O}{\overset{\|}{C}}NH_2$, and $PhCNH_2$.

▱ The adjacent C=O weakens the basicity by aiding in the delocalization of electron density from N to O, as is the case for an α-carbanion (Problem 18.3). Hence both amides are much weaker bases than the amine. In fact, amides are not soluble in aqueous acids—unlike amines, they do not form salts. In benzamide, $PhCONH_2$, the cross-conjugation (see Problem 18.9) with Ph attenuates the ability of C=O to participate in the base-weakening extended π bonding with :NH_2. The order of decreasing basicities is: $CH_3CH_2NH_2 > PhCONH_2 > CH_3CONH_2$.

19.36 Account for the fact that although N,N-dimethylaniline is only slightly more basic than aniline, 2,6-dimethyl-N,N-dimethylaniline is much more basic than 2,6-dimethylaniline.

▱ See Fig. 19-7. Extended π bonding between the amino N and the ring requires that the σ bonds on N become coplanar with the ring and its *ortho* bonds [Fig. 19-7(*a*)]. Bulky substituents in the *ortho* 2,6-positions sterically hinder the attainment of this geometry and interfere with the base-weakening extended π bonding [Fig. 19-7(*b*)]. This effect is called *steric inhibition of resonance*.

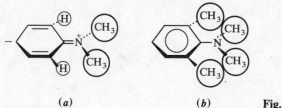

(a)   *(b)*   **Fig. 19-7**

19.37 Account for the fact that (*a*) 4-cyanoaniline is slightly more basic than 4-nitroaniline, and (*b*) 3,4,5-trinitroaniline is more basic than 4-cyano-3,5-dinitroaniline.

▱ (*a*) The NO_2 that ends up with the − charge on the more electronegative O more effectively participates in base-weakening electron delocalization with the amino N than does CN that ends up with the − charge on the less electronegative N. (*b*) In order for NO_2 to be base-weakening, its O's must become coplanar with the ring. Bulky substituents on the adjacent 3,5-positions sterically hinder the attainment of this coplanarity, thereby inhibiting the base-weakening ability of NO_2 [Fig. 19-8(*a*)]. CN is a linear group and does not encounter this steric inhibition of resonance as shown in Fig. 19-8(*b*). Note that this steric inhibition of resonance occurs at the *substituent*, not at the amino group, as is the case in Problem 19.36.

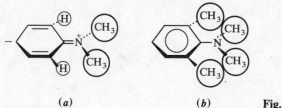

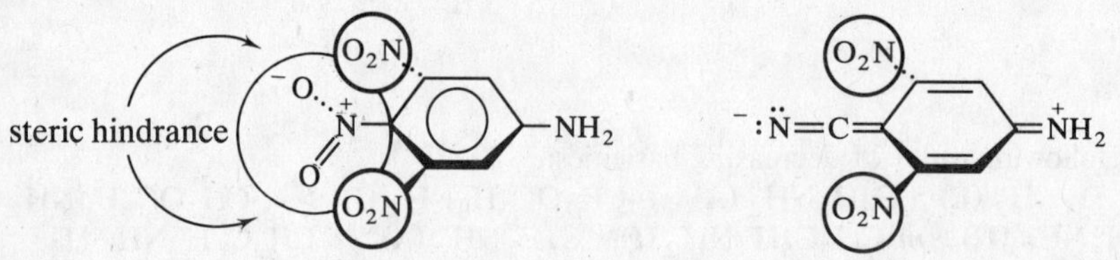

steric hindrance

(a)   *(b)*   **Fig. 19-8**

19.38 Explain why $Me_3\overset{+}{N}CH_2CH_2NH_2$ is a weaker base than $Me_3CCH_2CH_2NH_2$.

▱ Inductively the N^+ is strongly electron-attracting and base-weakening. However, the effect of the + charge is also transmitted through space and not just through the chain of σ bonds. This is an example of the field effect (see Problem 16.44).

19.39 Summarize the factors that affect relative basicities.

▱ (*1*) Electron delocalization through extended π bonding (resonance); (*2*) induction; (*3*) solvation; (*4*) steric effects towards solvation or by inhibition of resonance; (*5*) *s* character; (*6*) field effect.

19.40 Explain the insolubility of N-nitrosoamines, $R{-}\overset{\displaystyle H}{\overset{|}{N}}{-}N{=}O$ in aq. HCl.

N=O behaves like C=O in delocalizing electron density and weakening the basicity.

$$\left[RH\ddot{N}{-}\ddot{N}{=}\ddot{O}{:} \longleftrightarrow RH\overset{+}{N}{=}\ddot{N}{-}\ddot{O}{:}^{-}\right]$$

19.41 Account for the fact that, whereas carboxylic acids are about 10^5 times stronger acids in water than in ethanol, ammonium salts are only about 10 times stronger.

Compare the general equations for the dissociation of the two acids in the basic solvent HSol.

$$RCOOH + HSol \rightleftharpoons RCOO^- + H_2Sol^+ \qquad \text{and} \qquad RNH_3^+ + HSol \rightleftharpoons RNH_2 + H_2Sol^+$$

RCOOH goes from uncharged reactants to charged products. The superior ion-solvating ability of water compared to alcohol makes RCOOH a much stronger acid in water than in ethanol. With RNH_3^+ there is a cation on each side of the equilibrium, each being better solvated by water. The better ion-solvating ability of water has little or no effect on the equilibrium. RNH_3^+ is a somewhat stronger acid in water than in ethanol because H_2O is more basic than ethanol.

19.42 Give the generic name for the conjugate base of an amine.

$-\overset{|}{\underset{\cdot\cdot}{N}}:^-$ is called an *amide ion*. For example, $Me\overset{H}{\underset{\cdot\cdot}{N}}:^-$ is the methylamide ion.

19.43 What kind of reagents are used to form the conjugate base of an amine?

Active metals such as Na or K or very basic compounds such as *n*-BuLi, NaH, or RMgX.

19.44 Write equations for the reaction of the following hydrazines with aqueous acid: (*a*) $MeNHNH_2$, and (*b*) $PhNHNH_2$. Explain the difference.

(*a*) $MeNHNH_2 + H_3O^+ \longrightarrow Me\overset{+}{N}H_2NH_2 + H_2O$ (*b*) $PhNHNH_2 + H_3O^+ \longrightarrow PhNHNH_3^+ + H_2O$
Electron-donation by Me makes the adjacent N in $MeNHNH_2$ more basic. Electron-delocalization by Ph makes the adjacent N in $PhNHNH_2$ much less basic.

PREPARATION

19.45 (*a*) Give the steps in the reaction of an alkyl halide or tosylate, RX, with NH_3. (*b*) Give the side reactions which would make the method in (*a*) not useful synthetically.

(*a*) (*1*) $R{:}X + {:}NH_3 \xrightarrow{S_N2} RNH_3^+ + X{:}^-$

The fairly acidic product RNH_3^+ [$pK_a \cong 10.6$, see Problem 19.18(*c*)] exchanges an H^+ with NH_3 liberating the free amine, RNH_2.

(*2*) $RNH_3^+ + NH_3 \rightleftharpoons RNH_2 + NH_4^+$

(*b*) The nucleophilic RNH_2 can react with more RX to give 2° and 3° amines and some 4° amine salt, resulting in a complex mixture.

(*3*) $RNH_2 + RX \xrightarrow{S_N2} R_2NH_2^+ + X^-$
(*4*) $R_2NH_2^+ + NH_3 \rightleftharpoons R_2NH\ (2°) + NH_4^+$
(*5*) $R_2NH + RX \xrightarrow{S_N2} R_3NH^+ + X^-$
(*6*) $R_3NH^+ + NH_3 \rightleftharpoons R_3N\ (3°) + NH_4^+$
(*7*) $R_3N + RX \xrightarrow{S_N2} R_4N^+ + X^-$ (4° ammonium salt)

19.46 (*a*) How may the yield of RNH_2 in Problem 19.45 be enhanced? (*b*) How would you ensure a good yield of RR′NH from RNH_2 and R′X? (*c*) Give the name of the reaction between RNH_2 and an excess of CH_3I to give $RN(CH_3)_3^+$

▮ (*a*) Use a large excess of NH_3 to encourage its collisions with RX and to discourage collisions of RX with the 1° and 2° amines. (*b*) Use an excess of RNH_2. This technique is useful only when the amine is relatively inexpensive. (*c*) The sequence is called *exhaustive methylation*.

19.47 In the commercial synthesis of the methylated amines $MeNH_2$, Me_2NH, and Me_3N, MeOH and NH_3 are heated to 450 °C under pressure with Al_2O_3. What is the function of the catalyst?

▮ Al_2O_3, a Lewis acid, complexes with the O of MeOH, making OH a better leaving group.

19.48 Give the first formed amine from the reaction of (*a*) $CH_3Br + CH_3CH_2NH_2$, (*b*) $CH_2=CHCH_2Br + (CH_3)_2NH$, and (*c*) $PhCH_2Br + CH_3CH_2NHCH_3$.

▮ (*a*) $CH_3NHCH_2CH_3$, (*b*) $CH_2=CHCH_2N(CH_3)_2$, and (*c*) $PhCH_2N(CH_3)CH_2CH_3$.

19.49 What kinds of halides cannot be used to alkylate an amine? Why not?

▮ (*1*) 3° Halides form alkenes on elimination. (*2*) Vinyl and aryl halides, unless activated by *o*- or *p*-substituted electron-withdrawing groups, i.e., NO_2, do not undergo S_N2 reactions. (*3*) Halides with β-alkyl groups are sterically hindered.

19.50 (*a*) Prepare *n*-butylamine by a *Gabriel synthesis*. (*b*) Why is the synthesis in (*a*) not a viable method for preparing (i) *t*-butylamine, (ii) neopentylamine, (iii) diethylamine, (iv) *p*-toluidine from the corresponding halide or tosylate?

▮ (*a*) The acidic phthalimide ($pK_a \cong 8.3$) is first converted into its anion by OH^-.

Phthalimide anion

(*b*) Halides unreactive in S_N2 displacements cannot be used. (i) Me_3CBr is 3°. (ii) Me_3CCH_2Cl is neopentyl. (iii) 2° Amines give poor yields due to elimination. (iv) The Br in p-MeC_6H_4Br is not activated by an electron-withdrawing group.

19.51 Identify **A** through **E** in the following: $PhSO_2Cl + EtNH_2 \xrightarrow{-HCl} \textbf{A} \xrightarrow{NaOH} \textbf{B} \xrightarrow{EtBr} \textbf{C} \xrightarrow{H_3O^+} \textbf{D} + \textbf{E}$.

▮
$$PhSO_2NHEt \longrightarrow PhSO_2\overset{..}{N}Et \longrightarrow PhSO_2NEt_2 \longrightarrow PhSO_2OH + Et_2NH_2^+$$
$$\textbf{A} \qquad\qquad \textbf{B} \qquad\quad \textbf{C} \qquad\qquad \textbf{D} \qquad\quad \textbf{E}$$

19.52 (*a*) Provide the structures for the products of reaction of NH_3 with (i) oxirane and (ii) thiirane. (*b*) What kind of side reaction is expected?

▮ (*a*) A nucleophilic displacement by NH_3 opens the ring, giving first the ammonium ion $HYCH_2CH_2NH_3^+$ (Y = O or S) which then reacts with NH_3 to give the amino group. (i) Aminoethanol, $HOCH_2CH_2NH_2$ and (ii) aminothioethanol, $HSCH_2CH_2NH_2$. (*b*) The product amine is also basic and can attack the ring to give $(HOCH_2CH_2)_2NH$ and $(HOCH_2CH_2)_3N$.

19.53 (*a*) Give the starting compound to prepare *n*-propylamine by reduction with $LiAlH_4$ of (i) a nitro compound, (ii) an amide, (iii) a nitrile, (iv) an oxime, and (v) an azide. (*b*) Which of these compounds are commonly reduced to the amine with (i) H_2/Pt and (ii) Na/EtOH?

▮ (*a*) All the compounds have three C's. (i) $CH_3CH_2CH_2NO_2$ (**A**), (ii) $CH_3CH_2CONH_2$ (**B**), (iii) $CH_3CH_2C\equiv N$ (**C**), (iv) $CH_3CH_2CH=NOH$ (**D**), and (v) $CH_3CH_2CH_2N_3$ (**E**). (*b*) (i) All but **B** and (ii) **C** and **D**.

19.54 List the reducing agents that are commonly used to convert $ArNO_2$ to $ArNH_2$.

▮ Relatively inexpensive metals like Fe, Sn or Zn in dil. HCl, and $SnCl_2$ in HCl or catalytic hydrogenation. $LiAlH_4$, however, does not reduce $PhNO_2$ to $PhNH_2$.

19.55 Identify compounds **A** through **D**.

(a) $m\text{-}C_6H_4(NO_2)_2 \xrightarrow{NH_4SH} A$ and   (b) $H_2C\!=\!CHCH_2Br + N_3^- \longrightarrow B \Big[\begin{array}{l} \xrightarrow{H_2/Pt} \mathbf{C} \\[6pt] \xrightarrow[LiAlH_4]{} \mathbf{D} \end{array}$

▟ (a) **A** is *m*-nitroaniline; only one NO_2 is reduced. (b) **B** is $H_2C\!=\!CHCH_2N_3$, formed by S_N2 displacement of Br^- by N_3^-. **C** is $CH_3CH_2CH_2NH_2$; the $C\!=\!C$ is also reduced. **D** is $H_2C\!=\!CHCH_2NH_2$; $LiAlH_4$ reduces only the azide group. Note that alkyl azides are explosive! They should not be isolated, but be reacted in situ.

19.56 Give the structures for the products of the *reductive-amination* with H_2/Ni of (a) CH_3CH_2CHO with (i) NH_3, (ii) $EtNH_2$, and (iii) $EtNHMe$; and (b) $(CH_3)_2CO$ with amines in (a).

▟ (a) (i) $CH_3CH_2CH_2NH_2$, (ii) $CH_3CH_2CH_2NHEt$, (iii) $CH_3CH_2CH_2N(Me)Et$.
  (b) (i) $(CH_3)_2CHNH_2$, (ii) $(CH_3)_2CHNHEt$, (iii) $(CH_3)_2CHN(Me)Et$.

19.57 (a) Summarize the results in Problem 19.56 of the reaction of RCHO and RCOR′ with 1°, 2°, and 3° amines. (b) Discuss the advantages of reductive amination over the reaction of alkyl halides with amines (Problem 19.45).

▟ (a) $RCH\!=\!O + NH_3 \longrightarrow RCH_2NH_2$ $RCOR + NH_3 \longrightarrow R_2CHNH_2$ 1° amine
  $RCH\!=\!O + R'NH_2 \longrightarrow RCH_2NHR'$ $RCOR + R'NH_2 \longrightarrow R_2CHNHR'$ 2° amine
  $RCH\!=\!O + R'NHR'' \longrightarrow RCH_2NR'R''$ $RCOR + R'NHR'' \longrightarrow R_2CHNR'R''$ 3° amine

(b) Reductive amination produces the same kinds of products as does the reaction of amines and alkyl halides. However the tendency for successive aminations is more easily controlled. When a ketone is used, the product has a *sec*-alkyl group; these amines are not easily synthesized by ammonolysis of R_2CHX which may undergo E2 elimination.

19.58 Propose a reasonable pathway for reductive amination.

▟ In the first step a Schiff base or enamine (Problem 15.77) is formed. It is not necessarily isolated, but is reduced in situ. Its reduction is more rapid than that of the starting carbonyl compound.

$$R_2C\!=\!O + R'NH_2 \underset{-H_2O}{\rightleftharpoons} R_2C\!=\!NR' \xrightarrow{reduction} R_2CHNHR'$$

19.59 (a) Provide a structure for **A**. $CH_3CH_2CH\!=\!O + \text{piperidine} \xrightarrow{H_2/Ni} \mathbf{A}$. (b) Can the imine be an intermediate? (c) What is the intermediate that is reduced?

▟ (a) **A** is ⬡$N\!-\!CH_2CH_2CH_3$. (b) No. (c) The intermediate is either a carbinolamine or the
                                                                             iminium ion formed from it:
      N-n-propylpiperidine

      a carbinolamine   iminium ion

19.60 What makes sodium cyanoborohydride, $NaBH_3CN$, a useful alternative reducing agent in small-scale reductive aminations?

▟ Since the electron-withdrawing CN retards hydride donation, the reactant $>\!C\!=\!O$ is reduced by $NaBH_3CN$ more slowly than it reacts with amines to form imines. The protonated imine, iminium ion, formed at the pH of the reaction medium, is an electrophile, and is rapidly reduced.

19.61 Prepare $PhCH_2NHPh$ via a reductive amination from suitable reactants.

▟ $PhCH\!=\!O + PhNH_2 \longrightarrow [PhCH\!=\!\overset{+}{N}HPh] \xrightarrow{reduction} PhCH_2NHPh$

19.62 In the *Eschweiler–Clarke* synthesis of a dimethyl 3° amine ($RNMe_2$), $H_2C=O$ and conc. HCOOH are reacted with RNH_2. (*a*) Give the product of the reaction of (i) $PhCH_2NH_2$ and (ii) Et_2NH with $H_2C=O$ and HCOOH. (*b*) Give a mechanism and account for the role of HCOOH.

◢ (*a*) (i) $PhCH_2NMe_2$ (ii) Et_2NMe ($+ CO_2 + H_2O$ in both cases)

(*b*) $R_2NH + H_2C=O \rightleftharpoons R_2N-CH_2OH \overset{H^+}{\rightleftharpoons} [R_2\overset{+}{N}=CH_2 \longleftrightarrow R_2\overset{..}{N}-CH_2^+]$ (immonium ion)

$[R_2\overset{+}{N}=CH_2 \longleftrightarrow R_2\overset{..}{N}-\overset{+}{C}H_2] + \overset{O}{\underset{||}{(H:)C}} \overset{}{\longrightarrow} O^- \longrightarrow R_2N-CH_3 + CO_2$

Formic acid acts as the reducing agent by transferring a hydride to the electron-deficient C, and is oxidized to CO_2.

19.63 Provide structures for **A** through **C** in the following:

(*a*) $PhCOCH_3 + NH_4^+HCO_2^- \overset{\Delta}{\rightarrow} A$ (*b*) $Et_2C=O + HCONMe_2(DMF) \overset{\Delta}{\rightarrow} B$ (*c*) Cyclohexanone $+ DMF \overset{\Delta}{\rightarrow} C$

◢ These reductive aminations are examples of the *Leuckart* reaction.

(*a*) $PhCH(CH_3)$ with NH_2 (*b*) $Et-CH-Et$ with NMe_2 (*c*) cyclohexyl-NMe_2, H

A   B   C

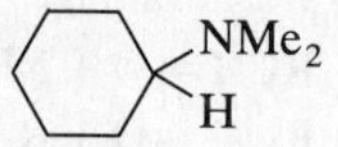

19.64 (*a*) Give the structure of **E** in the reaction $Me_2CHCONH_2$ (**D**) $\overset{NaOH}{\underset{Br_2}{\longrightarrow}}$ **E**. (*b*) Provide a mechanism for the reaction.

◢ (*a*) This is the Hofmann rearrangement (Problem 17.81). **E** is Me_2CHNH_2.

(*b*) $D \overset{OH^-}{\underset{-H^+}{\longrightarrow}} R-\overset{O}{\underset{||}{C}}-\overset{..}{N}H^- \overset{Br_2}{\underset{-Br^-}{\longrightarrow}} R-\overset{O}{\underset{||}{C}}-\overset{..}{N}HBr \overset{OH^-}{\longrightarrow}$

$\left[R-\overset{O}{\underset{||}{C}}-\overset{..}{\underset{..}{N}}-Br \longleftrightarrow R-\overset{:\overset{..}{O}:^-}{\underset{|}{C}}=\overset{..}{N}-Br \right] \longrightarrow \left[R-\overset{O}{\underset{||}{C}}-\overset{..}{N}: \right]$

F

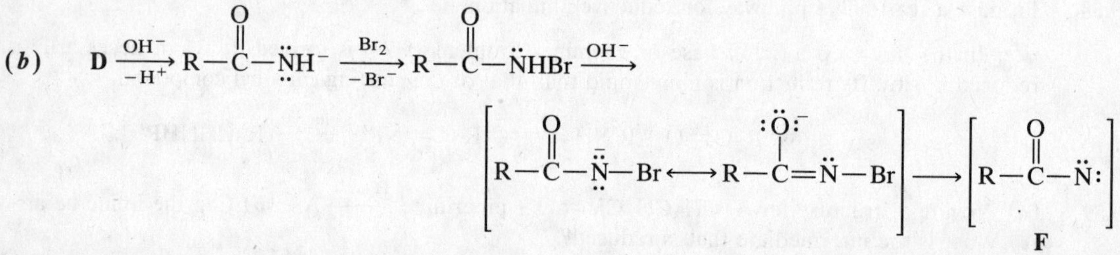

F, a nitrene, is a neutral molecule with an electron-deficient N. It is structurally similar to a carbene. Nitrenes rearrange rapidly to isocyanates which react further as shown:

$R-\overset{O}{\underset{||}{C}}-\overset{..}{N}: \overset{\sim R:}{\longrightarrow} [R-N=C=O] \overset{H_2O}{\longrightarrow} RNH_2 + CO_2$

Note that the amine has one less C than the amide and its precursor carboxylic acid.

19.65 The reaction of (*S*)-2-methylbutanamide with Br_2 and OH^- produces an optically active amine. Give the structure of the product, including its stereochemical designation and the mechanism for its formation.

◢ The product is (*S*) *sec*-butylamine. :R migrates with its electron pair to the electron-deficient :$\overset{..}{N}$, and configuration is retained because C—C is being broken at the same time that C—N is being formed in the transition state.

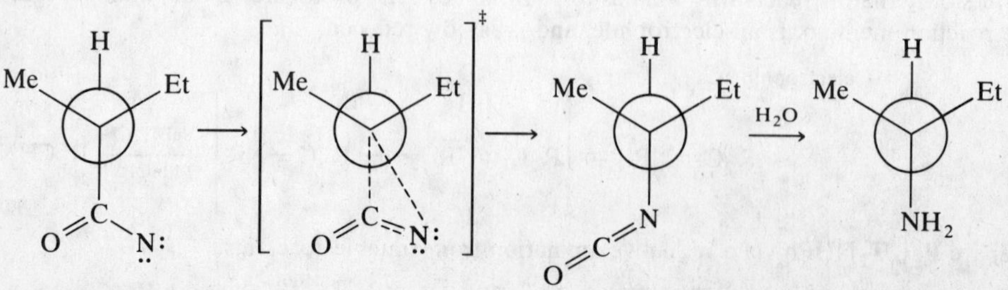

(*S*)-nitrene   (*S*)   (*S*)

19.66 Show how a nitrene intermediate may be formed in the Lossen, Curtius, and Schmidt reactions (Problems 17.82 and 17.83).

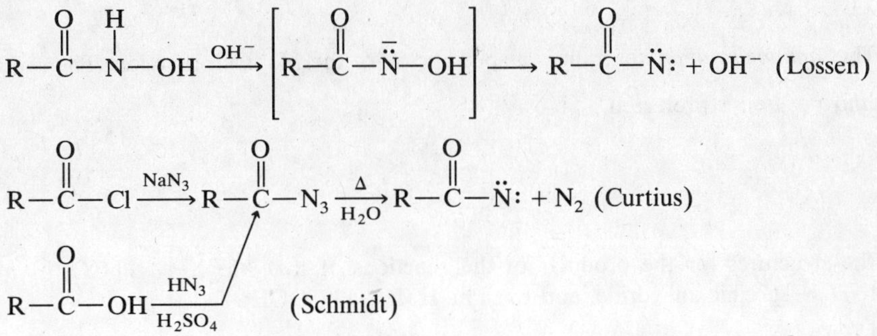

$$R-\overset{\overset{O}{\|}}{C}-\overset{\overset{H}{|}}{N}-OH \xrightarrow{OH^-} \left[R-\overset{\overset{O}{\|}}{C}-\overset{..}{\underset{..}{N}}-OH \right] \longrightarrow R-\overset{\overset{O}{\|}}{C}-\ddot{N}: + OH^- \text{ (Lossen)}$$

$$R-\overset{\overset{O}{\|}}{C}-Cl \xrightarrow{NaN_3} R-\overset{\overset{O}{\|}}{C}-N_3 \xrightarrow[H_2O]{\Delta} R-\overset{\overset{O}{\|}}{C}-\ddot{N}: + N_2 \text{ (Curtius)}$$

$$R-\overset{\overset{O}{\|}}{C}-OH \xrightarrow[H_2SO_4]{HN_3} \qquad \text{(Schmidt)}$$

19.67 (*a*) Why is dimethylation of $PhNH_2$ with MeI not a good synthesis of $PhNMe_2$? (*b*) Can $PhNMe_2$ be made by reaction of $PhNH_2$ with $H_2C=O + HCOOH$? Explain. (*c*) Give the industrial synthesis of $PhNMe_2$ from $PhNH_2$.

(*a*) $PhNMe_3^+I^-$ is a by-product (Problem 19.45). (*b*) The intermediate electrophile, H_2COH^+ (from $H_2CO + H^+$) can attack the activated ring to give $p\text{-}H_2NC_6H_4CH_2OH$. (*c*) $PhNH_2 \xrightarrow[230\,°C]{2MeOH} PhNMe_2$

19.68 Prepare *n*-propylamine (**A**) by (*a*) Gabriel synthesis, (*b*) alkyl halide amination, (*c*) nitrile reduction, (*d*) reductive amination, (*e*) Hofmann rearrangement, (*f*) amide reduction, and (*g*) Curtius reaction starting with an acid chloride.

(*a*)

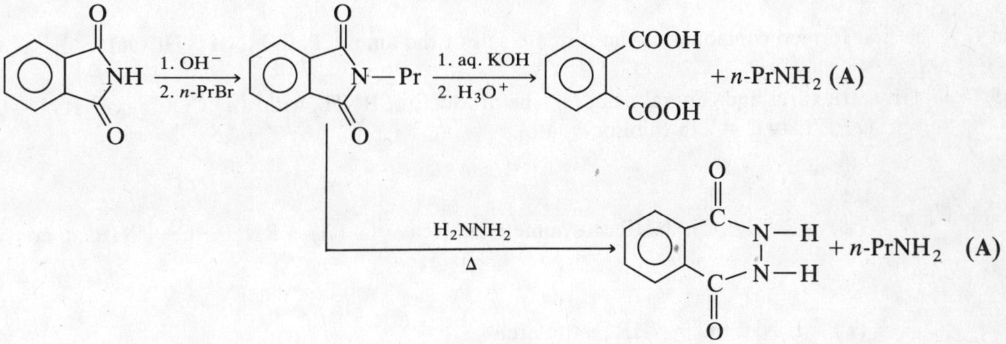

(*b*) $CH_3CH_2CH_2Br \xrightarrow{\text{excess } NH_3} A$ (*e*) $CH_3CH_2CH_2CONH_2 \xrightarrow[KOH]{Br_2} A$

(*c*) $CH_3CH_2CN \xrightarrow[2.\,H_2O]{1.\,LiAlH_4} A$ (*f*) $CH_3CH_2CONH_2 \xrightarrow{LiAlH_4} A$

(*d*) $CH_3CH_2CH=O \xrightarrow[H_2/Ni]{NH_3} A$ (*g*) $CH_3CH_2CH_2COCl \xrightarrow{N_3^-} CH_3CH_2CH_2CON_3 \xrightarrow[H_2O]{\Delta} A$

19.69 Prepare aniline from benzene via a benzyne intermediate.

$$PhH \xrightarrow[Fe]{Br_2} PhBr \xrightarrow[-33\,°C]{NaNH_2 \text{ in } NH_3} PhNH_2$$

19.70 (*a*) Give the structure of the product when aq. $H_2C=O$ and RNH_2 as its salt are reacted with $R'COCH_3$. (*b*) Provide a mechanism for this *Mannich* reaction (in acid).

(*a*) $RNHCH_2-CH_2COR'$ (**B**).

(*b*) $RNH_2 + H_2C=O \rightleftharpoons RNHCH_2OH \xrightarrow{H^+(-H_2O)} RNHCH_2^+ \xrightarrow{CH_2=C(OH)R'} \left[RNHCH_2CH_2\overset{\overset{OH}{|}}{\underset{+}{C}}R' \right] \xrightarrow{-H^+} B$

The reaction involves an electrophilic addition to the enol of the ketone. The net effect is the extension of the Me of the ketone by $-CH_2NHR$. 2° Amines can also be used.

19.71 Give the product when phenol, PhOH, is reacted with $H_2C=O + R_2NH$.

◢ This *aminoalkylation* reaction is a special case of the Mannich reaction. The product is

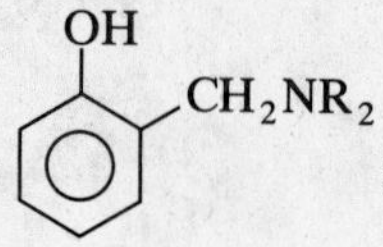

the *ortho* position is preferred.

REACTIONS

19.72 Give the structures for the products of the reactions of: (*a*) $Me_2NH + PhCOCl$, (*b*) $PhNH_2 + (CH_3CO)_2O$, (*c*) $EtNH_2$ + succinic anhydride, and (*d*) $PhNHMe + PhCOOEt$.

◢ The products are amides or anilides. (*a*) $PhCONMe_2$, (*b*) $CH_3CONHPh \, (+CH_3COOH)$,

(*c*) $EtNH\overset{\overset{\displaystyle O}{\|}}{C}CH_2CH_2\overset{\overset{\displaystyle O}{\|}}{C}O^- \, EtNH_3^+$, and (*d*) $Ph\overset{\overset{\displaystyle OMe}{|}}{\underset{\|}{C}}NPh + C_2H_5OH$ (transacylation).

19.73 Identify the products of the reactions of (*a*) $Me_2NH + PhSO_2Cl$, (*b*) $PhCH_2NH_2 + HCOOH$ followed by heat (*c*) $PhNH_2 + PhCHO$.

◢ (*a*) $PhSO_2NMe_2$, a sulfonamide (*b*) $H-\overset{\overset{\displaystyle O}{\|}}{C}-NHCH_2Ph$, a formamide

(*c*) $PhN=CHPh$, a Schiff base

In (*b*), the first formed compound is the formate salt of the amine, $PhCH_2NH_3^+ \, HCOO^-$.

19.74 Give structures and general names of the products of RNH_2 with: (*a*) $COCl_2$, (*b*) $R'N=C=O$ (an isocyanate), and (*c*) $R'N=C=S$ (a thioisocyanate).

◢ (*a*) $RNH-\overset{\overset{\displaystyle O}{\|}}{C}-NHR$, a symmetrical urea (*b*) $RNH-\overset{\overset{\displaystyle O}{\|}}{C}-NHR'$, a nonsymmetrical urea

(*c*) $R'NH-\overset{\overset{\displaystyle S}{\|}}{C}-NHR$, a thiourea

19.75 Show the steps in the formation of a diazonium cation from HONO and RNH_2.

◢ This process is called *diazotization*. Initially a nitrosonium cation is formed from HNO_2 in acid solution.

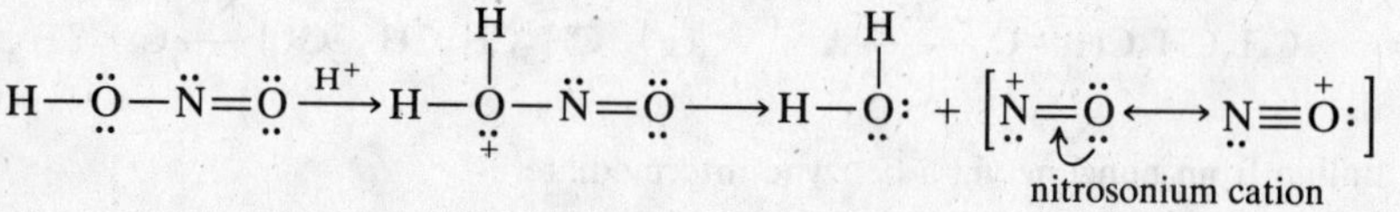

Nucleophilic attack by the electron pair of the amine on the nitrosonium ion produces an N-nitrosamine. It undergoes a series of proton transfers that produce an OH group on the second N—N bond.

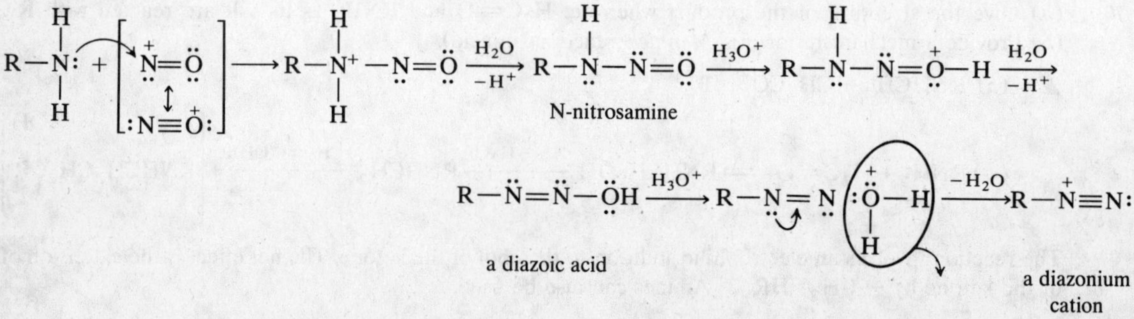

19.76 Show the course of the diazotization reaction of HONO with n-BuNH$_2$.

    ◢   The unstable n-butyldiazonium cation decomposes spontaneously, even at low temperatures, emitting N$_2$. The products probably originate from the n-Bu carbocation.

$$CH_3CH_2CH_2CH_2N_2^+ \xrightarrow{-N_2} CH_3CH_2CH_2CH_2^+ \longrightarrow CH_3CH_2CH_2CH_2OH + CH_3CH_2CH(OH)CH_3 \ (alcohols)$$

$$+ CH_3CH_2CH_2CH_2Cl + CH_3CH_2CHClCH_3 \ (alkyl \ halides)$$

$$+ CH_3CH_2CH{=}CH_2 + cis \ and \ trans\text{-}CH_3CH{=}CHCH_3 \ (alkenes)$$

19.77 (a) Name the products of the reaction of HONO with the 2° amines (i) Me$_2$NH, (ii) pyrrolidine, and (iii) PhNHMe. (b) Write the resonance forms for the product in (a) (i).

    ◢   (a) (i) Me$_2$N—N=O   (ii) [pyrrolidine]N—N=O   (iii) Ph—N—N=O, Me

N-Nitrosodimethylamine, **A**   N-Nitrosopyrrolidine, **B**   N-Methyl-N-nitrosoaniline, **C**

These compounds are commonly called *nitrosamines*.

(b) $[Me_2\ddot{N}{-}\ddot{N}{=}\ddot{O}: \longleftrightarrow Me_2\overset{+}{N}{=}\ddot{N}{-}\ddot{O}:^-]$.

19.78 Discuss the environmental and biochemical importance of nitrosamines.

    ◢   Many nitrosamines are carcinogenic. They are found in beer and in tobacco smoke. They are also formed during tanning of leather, "corning" beef, and frying bacon that has been cured with NaNO$_2$. In addition, HONO is formed in the human body by the action of gastric HCl on nitrites ingested in foods. It reacts with 2° amino groups converting them to nitrosamines (see Problems 23.118 and 23.119).

19.79 Show the course of the reaction of HONO with a 3° (a) alkylamine and (b) arylamine.

    ◢   (a) Since $R_3\overset{+}{N}{-}N{=}O$ has no amine H, it cleaves, giving a complex mixture of products. (b) NO$^+$ (*nitrosonium ion*), an electrophile, attacks the activated ring at the *para* position.

$$\langle O \rangle{-}NMe_2 + NO^+ \xrightarrow{-H^+} O{=}N{-}\langle O \rangle{-}NMe_2$$

p-Nitroso-N,N-dimethylaniline

19.80 The reaction of ethyl *p*-aminobenzoate with HONO and then with HBF$_4$ produces **A**, a crystalline ionic compound. When **A** is filtered, dried, and heated, **B**, C$_9$H$_9$O$_2$F, is formed. (a) Identify **A** and **B**. (b) What is the driving force for the formation of **B**?

    ◢   (a) **A** is the tetrafluoroborate salt, *p*-EtOOCC$_6$H$_4$—N≡N:$^+$BF$_4^-$. This explosive compound decomposes when carefully heated to give *p*-EtOOCC$_6$H$_4$F (**B**) + BF$_3$ + N$_2$. This *Schiemann* reaction affects the replacement of NH$_2$ by F. (b) The formation of molecular N$_2$.

19.81 Why are aryldiazonium ions more stable than alkyldiazonium ions?

    ◢   Electron-release from the *ortho* and *para* positions of the ring stabilizes the aryldiazonium ions.

$$\langle \rangle{-}\overset{+}{N}{\equiv}N: \longleftrightarrow \langle + \rangle{=}\overset{+}{N}{=}\ddot{N}:^-$$

The increased stability is also due to the great difficulty of forming Ar$^+$ as compared with R$^+$.

19.82 Write a general equation for the reaction of ArN$_2^+$ with a cuprous salt, CuX.

    ◢   In this reaction ArN$_2^+$ is not isolated, but is reacted *in situ* with CuX.

$$ArN_2^+ \xrightarrow{CuX} ArX + N_2$$

19.83 Give the products of the *Sandmeyer* reaction of *p*-MeC$_6$H$_4$N$_2^+$ with (a) CuBr, (b) CuCN, and (c) CuNO$_2$.

    ◢   (a) *p*-MeC$_6$H$_4$Br, (b) *p*-MeC$_6$H$_4$CN, and (c) *p*-MeC$_6$H$_4$NO$_2$.

19.84 How is an aryl amino group replaced by (*a*) OH, (*b*) H (*reductive deamination*), and (*c*) I?

◢ First convert the amine to ArN_2^+. (*a*) The phenol is formed on careful warming of ArN_2^+ in H_2O. (*b*) ArN_2^+ is reduced by EtOH. Alternatively, if HPH_2O_2 (hypophosphorous acid) is used with $NaNO_2$ in the diazotization, ArN_2^+ is reduced to ArH as it forms, HPH_2O_2 being oxidized to H_2PHO_3 (phosphorous acid). (*c*) Add KI (a modified Sandmeyer reaction without Cu^+).

19.85 Provide structures for the products of the reaction of PhN_2^+ with (*a*) $PhNMe_2$, (*b*) 2-naphthol, and (*c*) $PhCH_3$.

◢ ArN_2^+ is a weak electrophile that undergoes *diazo coupling* only with rings activated by OH, NH_2, NHR, or NR_2.

(*a*) $Ph—N=N—\bigcirc—NMe_2$.

p-N,N-Dimethylaminoazobenzene
(butter yellow)

(*b*)

1-Phenylazo-2-naphthol

(*c*) No reaction. The substrate ring is insufficiently activated.

19.86 (*a*) Explain why $2,4\text{-}(O_2N)_2C_6H_3N_2^+$ couples with anisole but PhN_2^+ does not. (*b*) Give the structure of the azo compound that forms.

◢ (*a*) The ring is not sufficiently activated by OR for it to react with most ArN_2^+. However, electron-withdrawing nitro groups make this diazonium ion less stable and thus more reactive than PhN_2^+.

(*b*) $O_2N—\bigcirc—N=N—\bigcirc—OCH_3$ (with NO_2 on the left ring)

19.87 (*a*) Prepare sodium *p*-dimethylaminoazobenzenesulfonate, methyl orange (**A**), from appropriate amines. (*b*) Explain, with structures, why methyl orange is an acid-base indicator.

◢ (*a*) $Na^{+\ -}SO_3—\bigcirc—NH_2 \xrightarrow{HONO} Na^{+\ -}SO_3—\bigcirc—N_2^+ \xrightarrow{PhNMe_2}$

$Na^{+\ -}SO_3—\bigcirc—N=N—\bigcirc—NMe_2$

A

(*b*) At pH's > 4.4, **A** exists as the yellow-colored free base. At pH's < 3.1, it is red, due to formation of **B** through protonation of an azo N and subsequent delocalization.

$\mathbf{A} \underset{\text{yellow}}{\overset{H_3O^+}{\rightleftharpoons}} \left[^-SO_3—\bigcirc—\overset{H}{\underset{+}{N}}=\ddot{N}—\bigcirc—\ddot{N}Me_2 \longleftrightarrow \ ^-SO_3—\bigcirc—\overset{H}{\underset{\cdot\cdot}{N}}—N=\bigcirc=\overset{+}{N}Me_2 \right]$
$\mathbf{B, red}$

A absorbs violet light, reflecting yellow. The color changes because the energy gap between the HOMO and LUMO in **B** is less than in **A**. Resonance interaction lowers the energy of the LUMO more than the HOMO. Thus light of a longer wavelength (lower frequency, green) is absorbed, and **B** reflects red, the complement of green. The color change is discernible near its pK_a of 3.5.

19.88 (*a*) Why are the following conditions unsatisfactory for diazo coupling: (i) strong base and (ii) strong acid? (*b*) What conditions are used to prevent coupling during diazotization of $ArNH_2$?

◢ (*a*) (i) $Ar\overset{+}{N}\equiv N: \overset{OH^-}{\rightleftharpoons} Ar\ddot{N}=\ddot{N}—OH \overset{-H^+}{\rightleftharpoons} Ar\ddot{N}=\ddot{N}—O^-.$
a diazoic$$a diazotate
acid$$anion

Neither the diazoic acid nor its anion couple.
(ii) Strong acid converts $ArNH_2$ to $ArNH_3^+$, whose ring is deactivated to coupling.
(*b*) It is necessary to avoid coupling of ArN_2^+ with unreacted $ArNH_2$. In an excess of mineral acid, most of $ArNH_2$ is converted to $ArNH_3^+$, which does not couple. However, enough free amine must be present to form ArN_2^+; hence amines couple fastest in mildly acidic solutions.

19.89 (*a*) Give the products of the reaction of $ArN{=}NAr'$ with $SnCl_2$. (*b*) Deduce the structures of the azo compounds that yield the following aromatic amines on reduction with $SnCl_2$: (i) *p*-toluidine and *p*-aminodimethylaniline, and (ii) 1 mol of 4,4′-diaminobiphenyl and 2 mol of 2-hydroxy-5-aminobenzoic acid.

(*a*) Reductive cleavage converts the azo compound to two 1° amines: $ArNH_2$ and $Ar'NH_2$. The amine N's originate from N's of the cleaved azo bond.

(*b*) (i) 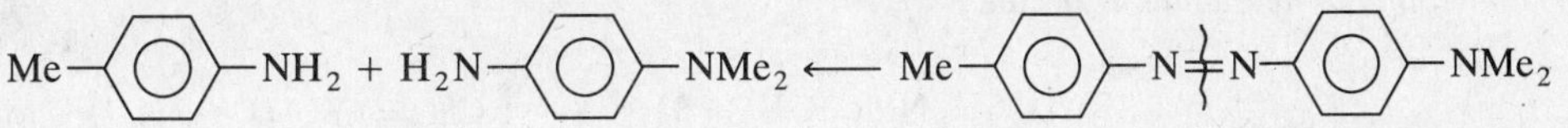

(ii) 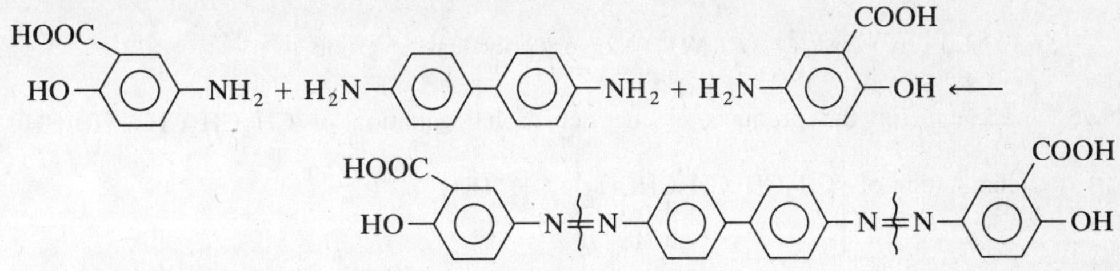

19.90 Which reactants are coupled to give the azo compounds in Problem 19.89(*b*)?

(i) 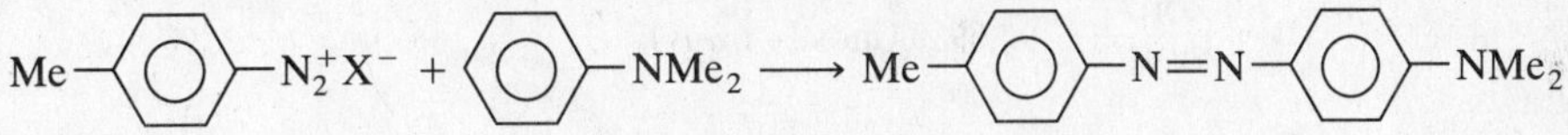

MeC_6H_5 is not active enough to couple with p-$N_2^+{-}C_6H_4{-}NMe_2$.

(ii) 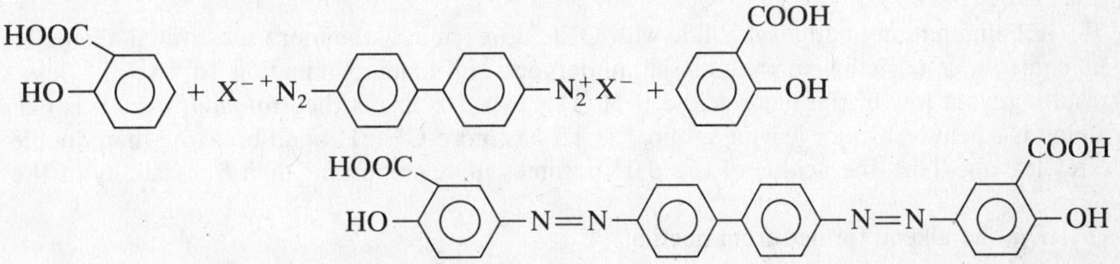

19.91 Account for the existence of two isomeric azobenzenes.

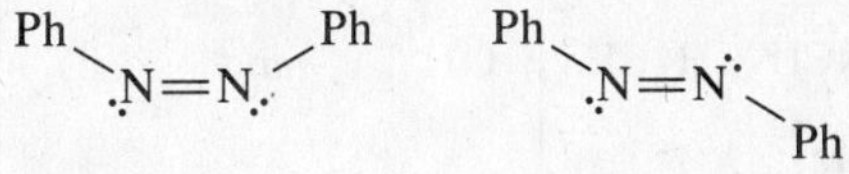

cis (*syn*) *trans* (*anti*)

The *trans* isomer is generally more stable.

19.92 In strongly acidic solution, hydrazobenzene, $C_6H_5{-}NH{-}NH{-}C_6H_5$ (**E**), rearranges to the carcinogen benzidine, p-$H_2NC_6H_4C_6H_4NH_2$-p, (**F**). Rate $= k[E]\,[H^+]^2$. (*a*) What is the reactive intermediate? (*b*) When the rearrangement is performed with a mixture of $Ar{-}NH{-}NH{-}Ar$ and **E**, the cross-coupling product 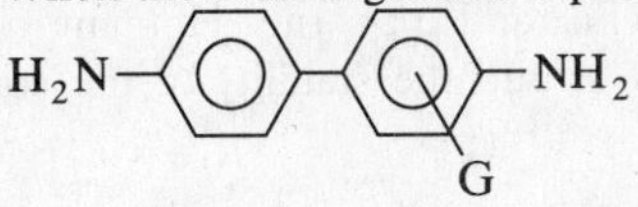 is absent. Explain.

(*a*) Since two H^+'s appear in the rate expression, diprotonated benzidine, $Ph\overset{+}{N}H_2{-}\overset{+}{N}H_2Ph$, is the rearranging intermediate. (*b*) The rearrangement is intramolecular.

19.93 (*a*) How does the oxidation of 1° and 2° amines with H_2O_2 or with a peroxycarboxylic acid differ from that of 3° amines? (*b*) Give the product from the H_2O_2 oxidation of (i) Me_3N, (ii) $PhNMe_2$, and (iii) N-methylpyrrolidine.

Amines are usually oxidized at the N, rather than at the C as in RCH_2OH.

(*a*) 1° Amines form complex mixtures of different products; 2° amines are oxidized in poor yields to N,N-dialkylhydroxylamines, R_2NOH. The product of oxidation of a 3° amine, formed in good yield, is an amine oxide, $R_3\overset{+}{N}{-}O^-$, a dipolar ion or zwitterion.

(*b*) (i) $Me_3\overset{+}{N}{-}O^-$, (ii) $Me_2\overset{+}{N}(Ph){-}O^-$, (iii) 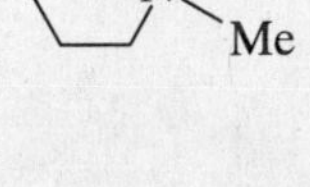

19.94 (*a*) Supply the structures for **A** through **C** in $RCH_2CH_2NH_2 \xrightarrow{\text{MeI (excess)}} A \xrightarrow{\text{AgOH}} B \xrightarrow{\Delta} C$. (*b*) Classify the reaction. (*c*) What is the leaving group in the last step? (*d*) Why does $RCH_2CH_2NH_2$ not undergo an E2 elimination?

◢ (*a*) The amine undergoes exhaustive methylation forming $RCH_2CH_2NMe_3^+I^-$, **A**, which is converted to **B**, the quaternary ammonium hydroxide, $RCH_2CH_2NMe_3^+OH^-$. When heated, a *Hofmann elimination* (also called *Hofmann degradation*) occurs:

$$RCH_2CH_2NMe_3^+OH^- \text{ (B)} \longrightarrow RCH=CH_2 \text{ (C)} + H_2O + Me_3N$$

(*b*) E2. (*c*) NMe_3. (*d*) NH_2^- is a very poor leaving group.

19.95 Account for the products of the dehydrohalogenation of $CH_3CH_2CH_2CHBrCH_3$ (**D**) and the Hofmann elimination of $\left[\begin{array}{c} CH_3CH_2CH_2\overset{|}{\underset{\underset{+NMe_3}{|}}{C}}HCH_3 \end{array}\right] OH^-$ (**E**).

$$CH_3CH_2CH=CHCH_3 \qquad CH_3CH_2CH_2CH=CH_2$$

$$\mathbf{D} \xrightarrow[\text{EtOH}]{\text{KOH}} \quad 69\% \text{ (mostly } trans) \quad + \quad 31\%$$

$$\mathbf{E} \xrightarrow{\Delta} \quad 2\% \text{ (}cis \text{ and } trans) \quad + \quad 98\%$$

◢ E2 elimination of an alkyl halide with OEt^- gives mainly the more substituted alkene by the Saytzeff's rule. In contrast, a trimethylammonium salt undergoes Hofmann elimination to give the less substituted alkene, resulting from loss of the more acidic β H ($1° > 2° > 3°$); this is the *Hofmann rule*. It is believed that since the amine is a relatively poor leaving group, the TS has more $C-\beta H$ bond-breaking than double bond formation or NR_3 leaving. Thus the acidity of the β H becomes more important than the stability of the alkene that forms.

19.96 (*a*) Give the alkene formed from heating

(i) $\left[\begin{array}{c} \overset{\overset{Me}{|}}{CH_3CH_2NCH_2CH_2CH_3} \\ \underset{Me}{|} \end{array}\right]^+ OH^-$ and (ii) $\left[\begin{array}{c} CH_3CH_2CH_2\overset{|}{\underset{\underset{CH_3}{|}}{C}}HNMe_3 \end{array}\right]^+ OH^-$.

(*b*) Predict and account for the product of Hofmann degradation of $\left[\begin{array}{c} \overset{Me\;Me}{\diagdown\diagup} \\ PhCH_2CH_2N CH_2CH_3 \end{array}\right]^+ OH^-$.

◢ (*a*) The less substituted alkene is formed. (i) $H_2C=CH_2$, not $H_2C=CHCH_3$. (ii) $CH_3CH_2CH_2CH=CH_2$, not $CH_3CH_2CH=CHCH_3$. (*b*) The Saytzeff product, $PhCH=CH_2$, and not the Hofmann product, $H_2C=CH_2$, is formed. The greatly increased acidity of the benzylic β H and the stability of the conjugated alkene influence the course of the reaction.

19.97 Rationalize these results: Thermal decomposition of

$$\left[\begin{array}{c} \overset{\overset{Me}{|}}{CH_3CH_2-N-C(CH_3)_2} \\ \underset{Me\;\;CH_3}{|\quad\;\;|} \end{array}\right]^+ OH^-$$

gives $(CH_3)_2C=CH_2 + EtNMe_2$ (93%) and $CH_2=CH_2 + t\text{-}BuNMe_2$ (7%)

◢ This result is Saytzeff, not Hofmann. There are two kinds of $1°$ β H's, one on CH_3CH_2, and the other on any CH_3 of the $3°$ Bu group. Thus, in this case, relative acidities is not a factor. Elimination from the t-Bu group is favored statistically (there are nine of these $C(CH_3)_3$ vs. three from CH_3CH_2) and also because a more stable alkene is formed.

19.98 Account for the following: The *cis* isomer of (4-*t*-butylcyclohexyl)-trimethyl-ammonium hydroxide (**F**) reacts in a Hofmann elimination while the *trans* isomer (**G**) does not react.

Refer to Fig. 19-9. In the more stable chair conformation (with the *t*-butyl group equatorial), **F** has two β H's anti to the leaving *axial* NMe_3. This is the anti-coplanar juxtaposition required for typical E2 reactions. In **G**, all β H's are *gauche* relative to the NMe_3 group—they are not anti-coplanar and there is no reaction.

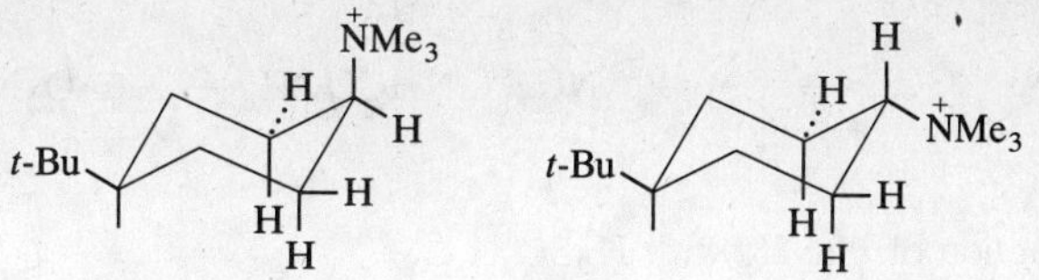

F **G** **Fig. 19-9**

19.99 Give the major alkene resulting from the thermal decomposition of the hydroxide salt of (*a*) $[(CH_3)_2CHCH_2\overset{+}{N}Me_2CH(CH_3)CH_2CH_3]$, (*b*) $Ph\overset{+}{N}Me_3$, and (*c*) 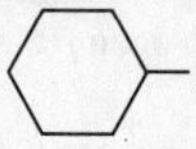 $-\overset{+}{N}Me_2CH_2CH_2CH_3$.

(*a*) There are three different kinds of β H's. The major product comes from removal of H[1].

$$(CH_3)_2CH^3CH_2\overset{+}{N}Me_2CH(CH_3^1)CH_2^2CH_3 \begin{cases} \xrightarrow{-H^1} CH_2{=}CHCH_2CH_3 \text{ (least substituted alkene)} \\ \xrightarrow{-H^2} CH_3CH{=}CHCH_3 \\ \xrightarrow{-H^3} (CH_3)_2C{=}CH_2 \end{cases}$$

(*b*) Lacking a β H, OH^- displaces on Me to give MeOH and $PhNMe_2$.
(*c*) There are two different 2° β H's, and thus, two possible products:

(i) From loss of a β H in the ring: 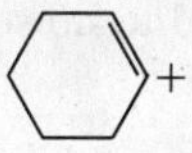 $+ Me_2NCH_2CH_2CH_3$

(ii) From loss of a β H from C_3H_7: 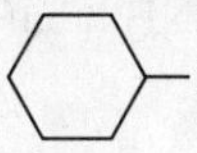 $-NMe_2 + CH_2{=}CHCH_3$

19.100 Give the product from heating (*a*) $CH_3CH_2CH_2\overset{+}{N}(O^-)Me_2$ and (*b*) cyclohexyl $CH_2\overset{+}{N}(O^-)Me_2$.

The *Cope elimination* results in an alkene and an N,N-dialkylhydroxylamine. It is an E2 reaction where the leaving groups are H and $R_2N{-}O^-$ forming $R_2N{-}OH$.

(*a*) $CH_3CH{=}CH_2 + Me_2NOH$ (*b*) 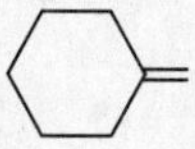 $=CH_2 + Me_2NOH$

19.101 Provide a mechanism for the Cope elimination from the following data: the N-oxide of *erythro*-2-dimethylamino-3-phenylbutane (**A**) gives mostly (*Z*)-2-phenyl-2-butene, and the *threo*-amine oxide (**B**) gives mainly (*E*)-2-phenyl-2-butene. 3-Phenyl-1-butene is a minor product in both cases.

Because this intramolecular reaction is stereospecific, the βH and the N-oxide group must be periplanar and *syn* in the TS. The more acidic βH is preferentially lost.

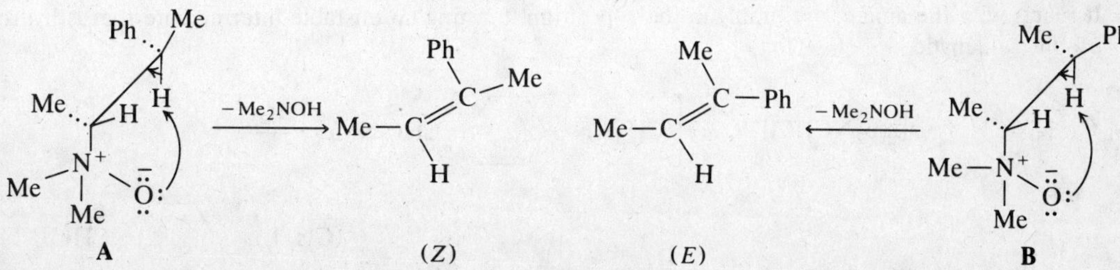

A (*Z*) (*E*) **B**

19.102 How may aniline be (*a*) monobrominated and (*b*) mononitrated?

    ▌ The NH_2 group is an extremely powerful ring activator in electrophilic substitution (Problem 11.44) and it is difficult to get just monosubstitution. To diminish its activation, it is converted to the moderately activating amide:

(*a*) $PhNH_2 \xrightarrow[\text{base}]{\text{ac. anhydride}} PhNHCOCH_3 \xrightarrow{Br_2} p\text{-}BrC_6H_4NHCOCH_4 \xrightarrow[\Delta]{OH^-} p\text{-}BrC_6H_4NH_2$

(*b*) $PhNHCOCH_3 \xrightarrow[H_2SO_4]{HNO_3} p\text{-}O_2NC_6H_4NHCOCH_3 \xrightarrow[\Delta]{OH^-} p\text{-}O_2NC_6H_4NH_2$

19.103 Give the steps in the reaction of $PhNH_2$ with H_2SO_4.

    ▌

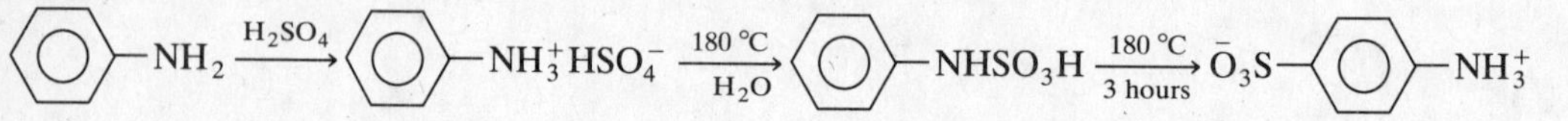

                Anilinium   Sulfamic   Sulfanilic acid
          hydrogen sulfate   acid   a dipolar ion

The last step is an example of an N-to-ring rearrangement.

19.104 How does the dipolar ion structure of sulfanilic acid account for its (*a*) high melting point, (*b*) insolubility in H_2O and organic solvents, (*c*) solubility in aqueous NaOH, and (*d*) insolubility in aqueous HCl?

    ▌ (*a*) Sulfanilic acid is ionic. (*b*) Because it is ionic, it is insoluble in organic solvents. Its solubility in H_2O is typical of dipolar salts. Not all such salts dissolve in H_2O. (*c*) The weakly acidic NH_3^+ transfers H^+ to OH^- and forms a soluble salt, $p\text{-}H_2NC_6H_4SO_3^-Na^+$. (*d*) $-SO_3^-$ is too weakly basic to accept H^+ from strong acids.

19.105 Account for the fact that 2-aminoethanoic acid (glycine) exists as a dipolar ion, as does *p*-aminobenzenesulfonic acid (sulfanilic acid) but *p*-aminobenzoic acid does not.

    ▌ The aliphatic NH_2 is sufficiently basic to accept an H^+ from COOH. The COOH is not strong enough to donate H^+ to the weakly basic $ArNH_2$, but SO_3H is a sufficiently strong acid to do so.

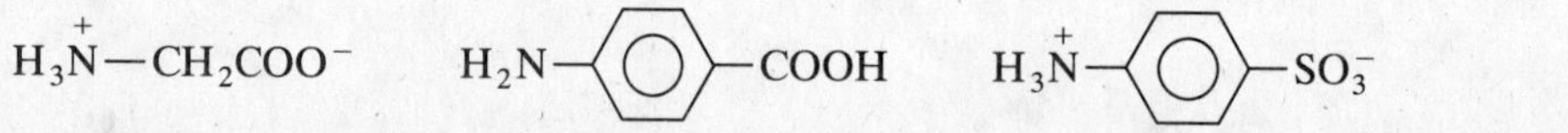

           Glycine   *p*-Aminobenzoic acid   Sulfanilic acid

19.106 In the *Vilsmeier reaction*, an aromatic 3° amine ($ArNR_2$) undergoes electrophilic substitution with Me_2NCHO (dimethylformamide) and $POCl_3$. (*a*) Give the product of the reaction with $C_6H_5NMe_2$. (*b*) Outline the steps in the reaction in (*a*), showing the electrophile.

    ▌ (*a*) Me_2N—⬡—CH=O. (*b*) A chloroimmonium ion is formed as follows:

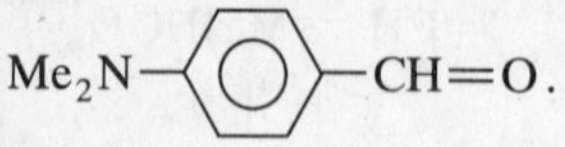

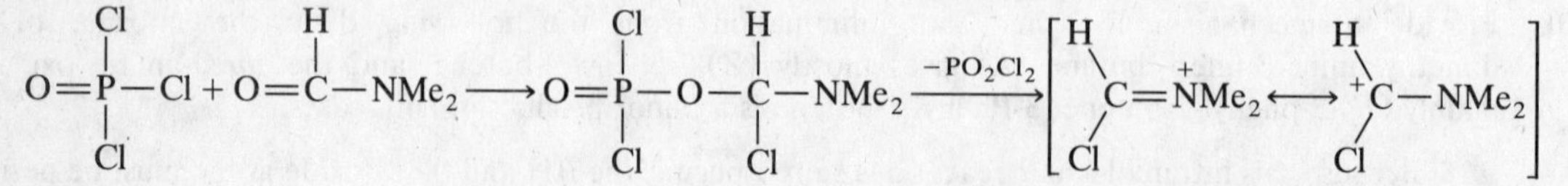

                                                 chloroimmonium ion

It reacts with the amine, preferably in the *p*-position, forming an unstable intermediate that is hydrolyzed to the product aldehyde.

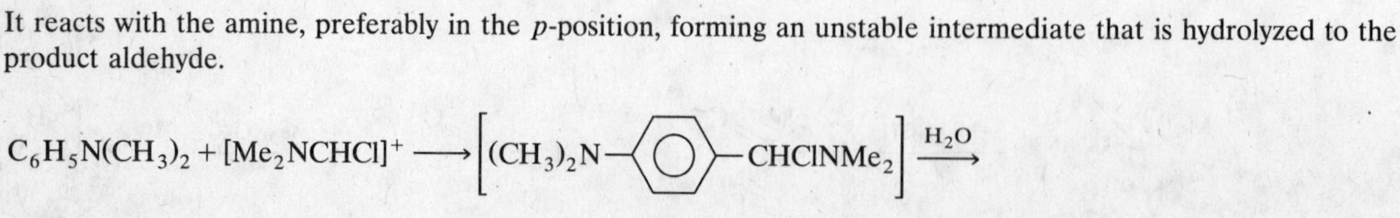

$$C_6H_5N(CH_3)_2 + [Me_2NCHCl]^+ \longrightarrow \left[(CH_3)_2N-⬡-CHClNMe_2\right] \xrightarrow{H_2O}$$

$$(CH_3)_2N-⬡-CHO + Me_2NH_2^+Cl^-$$

SYNTHESIS

19.107 Prepare $PhCH_2NH_2$ (**A**) by (*a*) Gabriel synthesis, (*b*) alkyl halide amination, (*c*) nitrile reduction, (*d*) reductive amination and (*e*) Hofmann degradation.

(*a*)

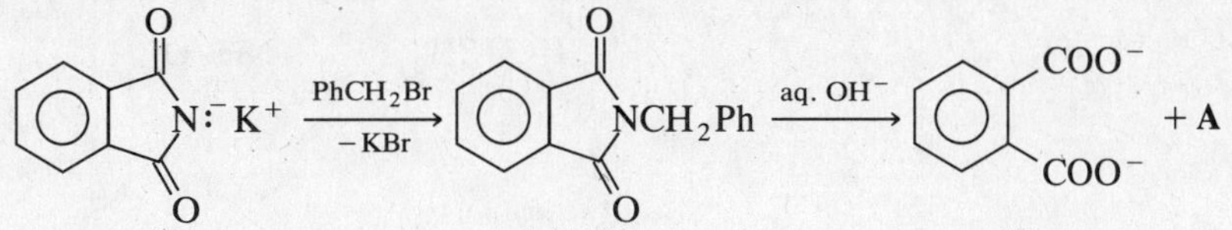

[reaction scheme: phthalimide potassium salt $\xrightarrow[-KBr]{PhCH_2Br}$ N-benzylphthalimide $\xrightarrow{aq.\ OH^-}$ phthalate dianion (COO⁻, COO⁻) $+ \mathbf{A}$]

(*b*) $PhCH_2Br \xrightarrow{excess\ NH_3} \mathbf{A}$, (*c*) $PhC\equiv N \xrightarrow[2.\ H_2O]{1.\ LiAlH_4} \mathbf{A}$, (*d*) $PhCH=O \xrightarrow[H_2/Ni]{NH_3} \mathbf{A}$

(*e*) $PhCH_2CONH_2 \xrightarrow[2.\ NH_3]{1.\ Br_2,\ KOH} \mathbf{A}$

19.108 Synthesize the following compounds from the unbranched chain $C_6H_{13}COOH$ (**B**) and inorganic reagents. Do not repeat the preparations of previously synthesized intermediates. (*a*) $C_8H_{17}NH_2$, (*b*) $C_7H_{15}NH_2$, (*c*) $C_6H_{13}NH_2$, (*d*) $C_6H_{13}CH(NH_2)C_7H_{15}$, (*e*) $C_6H_{13}NHC_7H_{15}$, and (*f*) $(C_7H_{15})_2NH$.

First note the change, if any, in carbon content. (*a*) Chain length is increased by one C:

$$\mathbf{B} \xrightarrow{LiAlH_4} C_6H_{13}CH_2OH \xrightarrow{PBr_3} C_6H_{13}CH_2Br \xrightarrow{KCN} C_6H_{13}CH_2CN \xrightarrow{LiAlH_4} C_6H_{13}CH_2CH_2NH_2$$

(*b*) Chain length is unchanged:

$$\mathbf{B} \xrightarrow{SOCl_2} C_6H_{13}COCl \xrightarrow{NH_3} C_6H_{13}CONH_2 \xrightarrow{LiAlH_4} C_6H_{13}CH_2NH_2$$

(*c*) Chain length is decreased by one C (use Hofmann degradation):

$$C_6H_{13}CONH_2\ [\text{from } (b)] \xrightarrow[2.\ H_2O]{1.\ Br_2,\ KOH} C_6H_{13}NH_2$$

(*d*) The C content is doubled:

$$C_6H_{13}CH_2Br\ [\text{from } (a)] \xrightarrow[2.\ CuI]{1.\ Li} (C_6H_{13}CH_2)_2CuLi \xrightarrow{C_6H_{13}COCl}$$

[reaction continues] $C_6H_{13}CH_2\overset{O}{\overset{\|}{C}}C_6H_{13} \xrightarrow[H_2/Ni]{NH_3} C_7H_{15}\overset{NH_2}{\overset{|}{C}}HC_6H_{13}$

(*e*) $C_6H_{13}COCl\ [\text{from } (b)] \xrightarrow[S,\ \Delta]{H_2,\ Pd/BaSO_4} C_6H_{13}CHO \xrightarrow[H_2/Ni]{C_6H_{13}NH_2} C_6H_{13}CH_2NHC_6H_{13}$

(*f*) $C_6H_{13}COCl + C_6H_{13}CH_2NH_2\ [\text{from } (b)] \longrightarrow C_6H_{13}CONHCH_2C_6H_{13} \xrightarrow{LiAlH_4}$

$$C_6H_{13}CH_2NHCH_2C_6H_{13}$$

19.109 With the aid of diazonium salts and using PhH, PhMe, and any other needed reagents and solvents, prepare (*a*) *o*-chlorotoluene, (*b*) *m*-chlorotoluene, (*c*) 1,3,5-tribromobenzene, (*d*) *m*-bromochlorobenzene (*e*) *p*-iodotoluene, (*f*) *p*-dinitrobenzene, and (*g*) *p*-cyanobenzoic acid. Do not repeat the synthesis of any intermediate compounds.

(*a*) $C_6H_5CH_3 \xrightarrow[H_2SO_4]{HNO_3}$ [*p*-nitrotoluene] $\xrightarrow[Fe]{Cl_2}$ [2-chloro-4-nitrotoluene] $\xrightarrow[2.\ OH^-]{1.\ Sn,\ HCl}$ [2-chloro-4-aminotoluene] $\xrightarrow[HCl]{NaNO_2}$

[2-chloro-4-diazonium toluene, $N_2^+Cl^-$] $\xrightarrow{HPH_2O_2}$ [*o*-chlorotoluene]

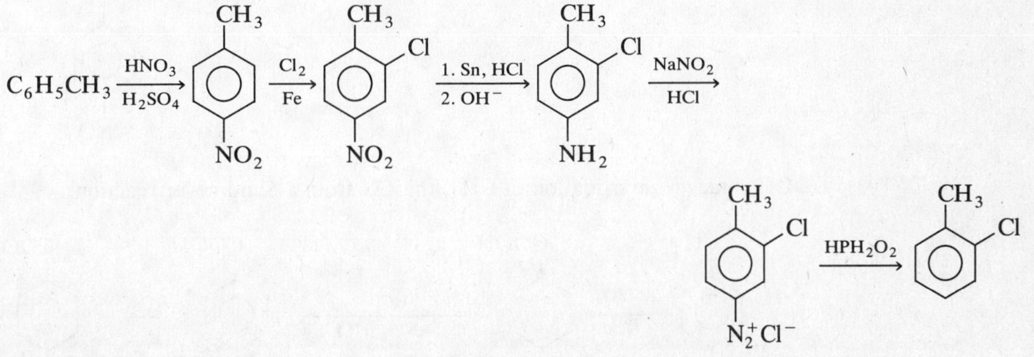

The *para* position is blocked by NO_2, ensuring that chlorination is only *ortho* to CH_3.

(b)

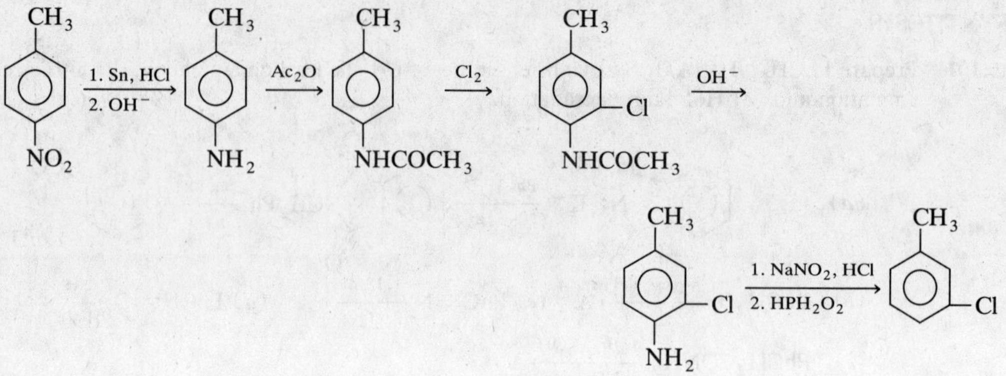

$$CH_3 \xrightarrow[\text{2. OH}^-]{\text{1. Sn, HCl}} CH_3,NH_2 \xrightarrow{\text{Ac}_2\text{O}} CH_3,NHCOCH_3 \xrightarrow{\text{Cl}_2} CH_3,Cl,NHCOCH_3 \xrightarrow{\text{OH}^-}$$

$$CH_3,Cl,NH_2 \xrightarrow[\text{2. HPH}_2\text{O}_2]{\text{1. NaNO}_2, \text{HCl}} CH_3,Cl$$

The —NHCOCH$_3$ is used to orient Cl to its *ortho* position which is *meta* to CH$_3$; it is then removed.

(c) PhNH$_2$ is rapidly tribrominated and the NH$_2$ is removed.

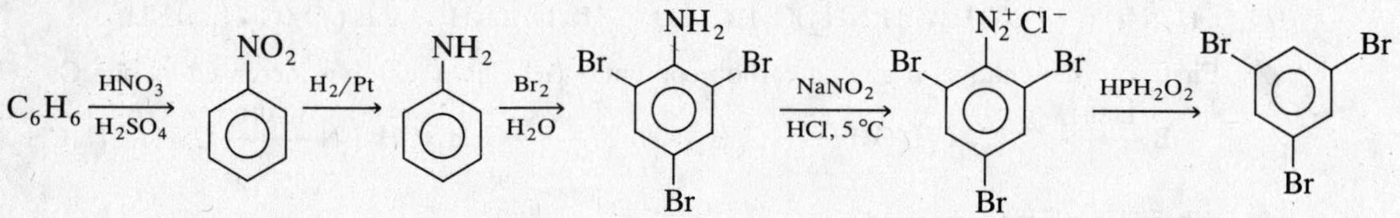

$$C_6H_6 \xrightarrow[\text{H}_2\text{SO}_4]{\text{HNO}_3} NO_2 \xrightarrow{\text{H}_2/\text{Pt}} NH_2 \xrightarrow[\text{H}_2\text{O}]{\text{Br}_2} Br,NH_2,Br,Br \xrightarrow[\text{HCl, 5 °C}]{\text{NaNO}_2} Br,N_2^+\text{Cl}^-,Br,Br \xrightarrow{\text{HPH}_2\text{O}_2} Br,Br,Br$$

(d) One halogen is introduced directly, the other by a Sandmeyer reaction.

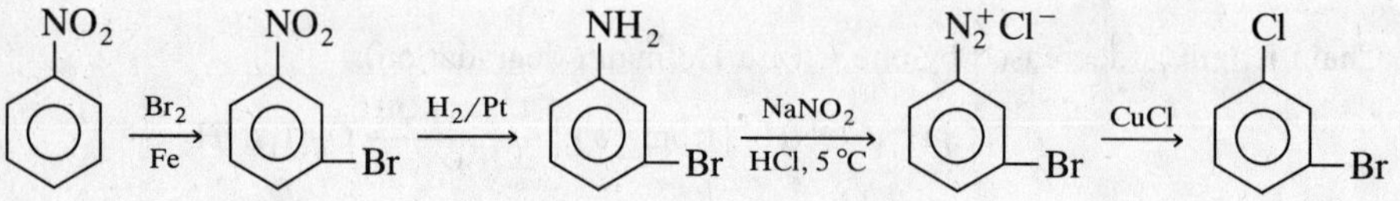

$$NO_2 \xrightarrow[\text{Fe}]{\text{Br}_2} NO_2,Br \xrightarrow{\text{H}_2/\text{Pt}} NH_2,Br \xrightarrow[\text{HCl, 5 °C}]{\text{NaNO}_2} N_2^+\text{Cl}^-,Br \xrightarrow{\text{CuCl}} Cl,Br$$

(e)

$$CH_3,NO_2 \xrightarrow[\text{2. NaNO}_2, \text{HCl, 5 °C}]{\text{1. H}_2/\text{Pt}} CH_3,N_2^+\text{Cl}^- \xrightarrow{\text{KI}} CH_3,I$$

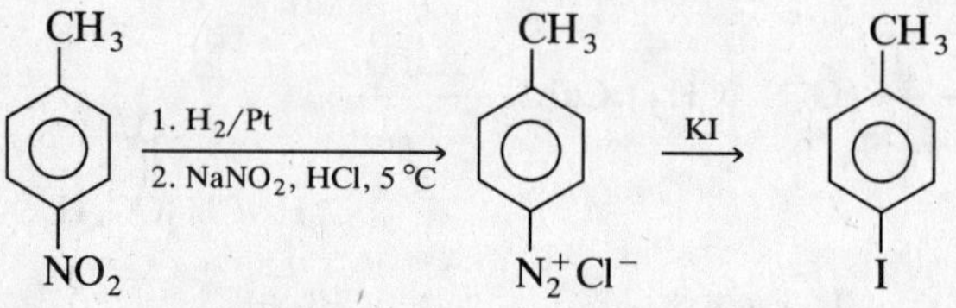

(f) One NO$_2$ is introduced directly, the other via ArN$_2^+$ by adding NaNO$_2$ with Cu$_2$O.

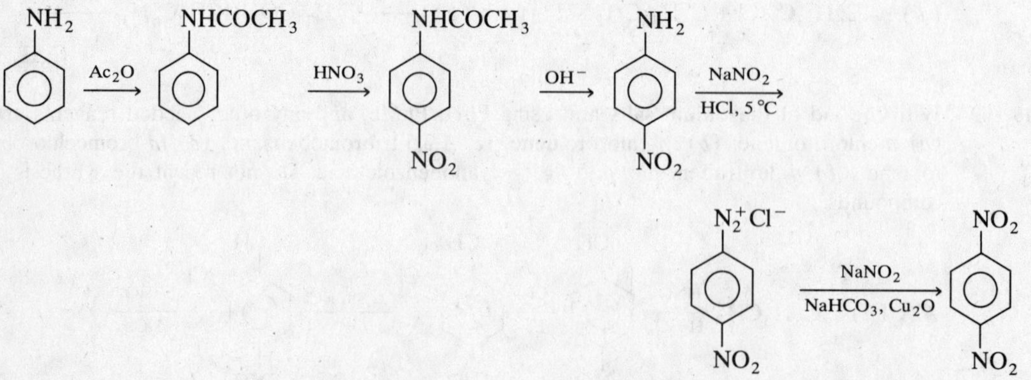

$$NH_2 \xrightarrow{\text{Ac}_2\text{O}} NHCOCH_3 \xrightarrow{\text{HNO}_3} NHCOCH_3,NO_2 \xrightarrow{\text{OH}^-} NH_2,NO_2 \xrightarrow[\text{HCl, 5 °C}]{\text{NaNO}_2}$$

$$N_2^+\text{Cl}^-,NO_2 \xrightarrow[\text{NaHCO}_3, \text{Cu}_2\text{O}]{\text{NaNO}_2} NO_2,NO_2$$

(g) COOH comes from oxidation of CH$_3$, the CN from a Sandmeyer reaction.

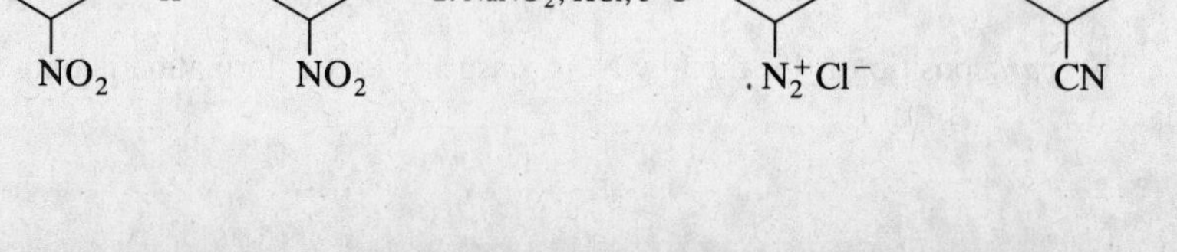

$$CH_3,NO_2 \xrightarrow[\text{H}^+]{\text{KMnO}_4} COOH,NO_2 \xrightarrow[\text{2. NaNO}_2, \text{HCl, 5 °C}]{\text{1. Zn, HCl}} COOH,N_2^+\text{Cl}^- \xrightarrow{\text{CuCN}} COOH,CN$$

19.110 Using PhH and simple aliphatics prepare (*a*) PhCH(NH$_2$)CH$_2$CH$_3$ (**A**), (*b*) *p*-H$_2$NCH$_2$C$_6$H$_4$CH$_2$NH$_2$ (**B**), (*c*) PhNHCH$_2$Ph (**C**), (*d*) 2,2′-dichlorobiphenyl (**D**), (*e*) *p*-BrC$_6$H$_4$—N≡N—C$_6$H$_4$NH$_2$-*p* (**E**), and (*f*) *p*-NO$_2$C$_6$H$_4$CH(CH$_3$)NH$_2$ (**F**).

(*a*)   PhH + ClCOCH$_2$CH$_3$ $\xrightarrow{\text{AlCl}_3}$ PhCOCH$_2$CH$_3$ $\xrightarrow[\text{H}_2/\text{Ni}]{\text{NH}_3}$ **A**

(*b*)   —CH$_2$NH$_2$ is obtained by reducing —C≡N.

PhH $\longrightarrow$ *p*-NO$_2$C$_6$H$_4$NH$_2$ [Problem 19.102(*b*)] $\xrightarrow[\text{2. NaOH}]{\text{1. Sn/HCl}}$ *p*-H$_2$NC$_6$H$_4$NH$_2$ $\xrightarrow[\text{2. CuCN}]{\text{1. HONO, 5 °C}}$

p-NCC$_6$H$_4$CN $\xrightarrow{\text{LiAlH}_4}$ **B**

(*c*)   PhNH$_2$[(Problem 19.109(*c*)] + ClCOPh* $\longrightarrow$ PhNHCOPh $\xrightarrow{\text{LiAlH}_4}$ **C**

*PhH $\xrightarrow[\text{2. Mg/Et}_2\text{O}]{\text{1. Br}_2/\text{Fe}}$ PhMgBr $\xrightarrow[\text{2. H}^+]{\text{1. CO}_2}$ PhCOOH $\xrightarrow{\text{SOCl}_2}$ PhCOCl

(*d*)   The biphenyl is made from a properly substituted benzidine via a rearrangement (Problem 19.92).

PhH $\xrightarrow[\text{2. Cl}_2/\text{Fe}]{\text{1. HNO}_3/\text{H}_2\text{SO}_4}$ *m*-ClC$_6$H$_4$NO$_2$ $\xrightarrow{\text{Sn/NaOH}}$ *m*-ClC$_6$H$_4$NHNHC$_6$H$_4$Cl-*m* $\xrightarrow[\text{2. OH}^-]{\text{1. HCl/}\Delta}$

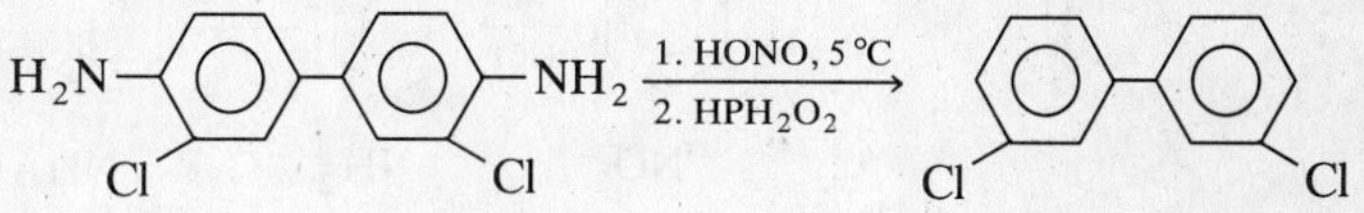

3,3′-Dichloro-4,4′-diaminobiphenyl   2,2′-Dichlorobiphenyl, **D**

(*e*)   PhNHAc [Problem 19.109(*f*)] $\xrightarrow{\text{Br}_2}$ *p*-BrC$_6$H$_4$NHAc $\xrightarrow[\Delta]{\text{NaOH}}$ *p*-BrC$_6$H$_4$NH$_2$ $\xrightarrow[\text{5 °C}]{\text{HONO}}$

p-BrC$_6$H$_4$N$_2^+$X$^-$ $\xrightarrow{\text{C}_6\text{H}_5\text{NH}_2}$ **E**

(*f*)   PhH $\xrightarrow{\text{CH}_3\text{CH}_2\text{Br/AlCl}_3}$ PhCH$_2$CH$_3$ $\xrightarrow{\text{HNO}_3/\text{H}_2\text{SO}_4}$ *p*-NO$_2$C$_6$H$_4$CH$_2$CH$_3$ $\xrightarrow{\text{NBS}}$

p-NO$_2$C$_6$H$_4$CHBrCH$_3$ $\xrightarrow[\text{NH}_3]{\text{excess}}$ product

19.111 Use *o*- or *p*-nitroethylbenzene and any inorganic reagents or solvents to synthesize the six isomeric dichloroethylbenzenes. Do not repeat preparations of intermediate products.

In these syntheses, NO$_2$ is used as a removable blocking group, as the source of Cl via the diazotized arylamine, or for conversion to NHCOCH$_3$ whose directive effect supersedes that of Me.

(i)   2,3-Dichloroethylbenzene

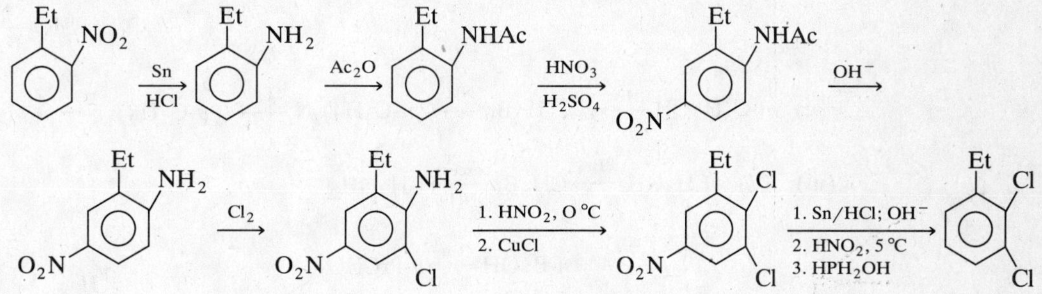

(ii)   2,4-Dichloroethylbenzene

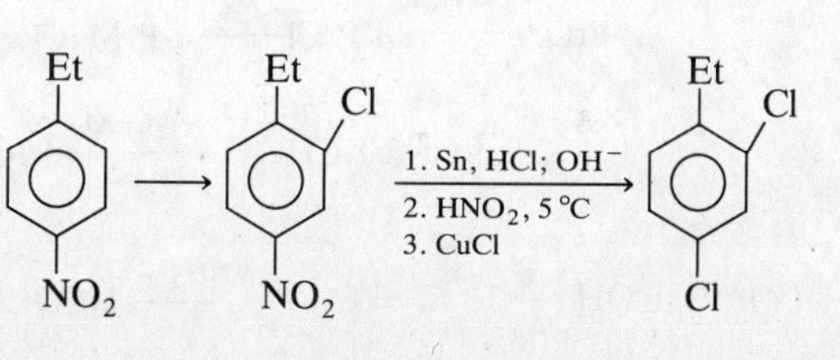

(iii) 2,5-Dichloroethylbenzene

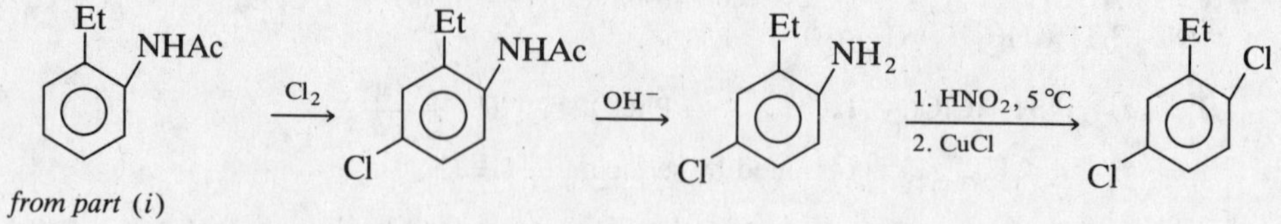

from part (*i*)

(iv) 2,6-Dichloroethylbenzene

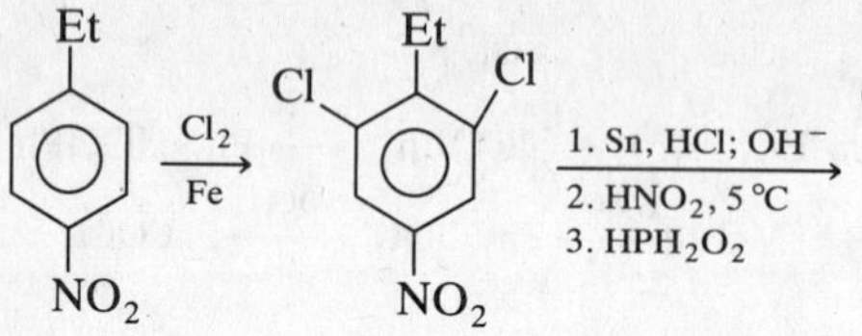

(v) 3,4-Dichloroethylbenzene

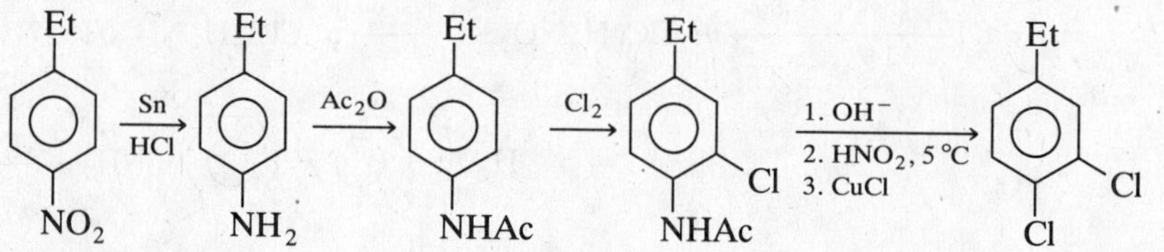

(vi) 3,5-Dichloroethylbenzene

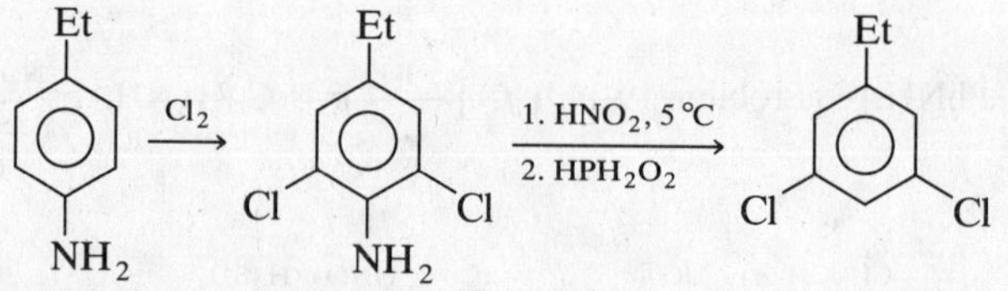

19.112 Synthesize the following compounds from alcohols of four or fewer carbons: (*a*) (i) *n*-pentylamine, (ii) tri-*n*-propylamine N-oxide, (iii) 4-(N-methylamino)heptane; and (*b*) along with cyclohexanol (i) cyclohexyldimethylamine, (ii) cyclopentylamine, (iii) 6-aminohexanoic acid.

(*a*) (i) (*1*) $C_2H_5OH \xrightarrow[\Delta]{H_2SO_4} H_2C{=}CH_2 \xrightarrow[H_2O]{Br_2} H_2CBrCH_2OH \xrightarrow{OH^-} H_2C{-}CH_2$ (**A**)
with epoxide O

(*2*) $n\text{-}C_3H_7OH \xrightarrow{SOCl_2} n\text{-}C_3H_7Cl \xrightarrow{Mg/Et_2O} n\text{-}C_3H_7MgCl \xrightarrow[2.\,H^+]{1.\,A} n\text{-}C_5H_{11}OH \xrightarrow{Cu}_{\Delta}$

$n\text{-}C_4H_9CHO \xrightarrow[H_2/Pd]{NH_3} n\text{-}C_5H_{11}NH_2$

(ii) $n\text{-}C_3H_7OH \xrightarrow{HBr} n\text{-}C_3H_7Br \xrightarrow{NH_3} (n\text{-}C_3H_7)_3N \xrightarrow{H_2O_2} (n\text{-}C_3H_7)_3\overset{+}{N}{-}O^-$

(iii) (*1*) $CH_3OH \xrightarrow{PBr_3} CH_3Br \xrightarrow[NH_3]{excess} CH_3NH_2$

(*2*)

$n\text{-}BuOH \xrightarrow[heat]{Cu} n\text{-}PrCHO$

$n\text{-}PrOH \xrightarrow{SO_2Cl} n\text{-}PrCl \xrightarrow{Mg} n\text{-}PrMgCl$

$\longrightarrow (n\text{-}Pr)_2\overset{\underset{|}{H}}{C}O^-(MgCl)^+ \xrightarrow{H_3O^+}$

$(n\text{-}Pr)_2CHOH \xrightarrow[H_2SO_4]{Na_2Cr_2O_7} (n\text{-}Pr)_2C{=}O \xrightarrow[CH_3NH_2\ from\ (1)]{H_2/Pt} (n\text{-}Pr)_2CHNHCH_3$

(*b*) (i) (*1*) $CH_3OH \xrightarrow{Cu}_{\Delta} H_2C{=}O \xrightarrow[2.\,H^+]{1.\,Ag(NH_3)_2^+} HCOOH$

(2) Cyclohexanol $\xrightarrow[\text{H}_2\text{SO}_4]{\text{Cr}_2\text{O}_7^{2-}}$ cyclohexanone $\xrightarrow[\text{H}_2/\text{Pt}]{\text{NH}_3}$ cyclohexylamine $\xrightarrow[\substack{\text{HCOOH} \\ \text{from (1) in (b)}}]{\text{H}_2\text{CO}}$

cyclohexyldimethylamine

(ii) Cyclohexanol $\xrightarrow[\Delta]{\text{H}_2\text{SO}_4}$ cyclohexene $\xrightarrow[\text{H}^+, \Delta]{\text{KMnO}_4}$ HOOC(CH$_2$)$_4$COOH $\xrightarrow[\Delta]{\text{BaO}}$ cyclopentanone

$\xrightarrow{\text{NH}_3, \text{H}_2/\text{Pt}}$ cyclopentylamine

(iii) Cyclohexanone [from (2) in (b)] $\xrightarrow{\text{H}_2\text{NOH}}$ oxime $\xrightarrow{\text{H}_2\text{SO}_4}$ [Caprolactam structure] $\xrightarrow{\text{H}_3\text{O}^+}$ 6-aminohexanoic acid

Caprolactam

The lactam forms by a Beckman rearrangement (Problem 15.87).

19.113 Prepare (a) the local anaesthetic, benzocaine p-H$_2$NC$_6$H$_4$COOC$_2$H$_5$, from p-nitrotoluene and (b) the antibiotic sulfanilamide, p-H$_2$NC$_6$H$_4$SO$_2$NH$_2$, from PhNH$_2$.

(a) p-NO$_2$C$_6$H$_4$CH$_3$ $\xrightarrow[\text{H}^+]{\text{KMnO}_4}$ p-NO$_2$C$_6$H$_4$COOH $\xrightarrow[\text{H}^+]{\text{C}_2\text{H}_5\text{OH}}$ p-NO$_2$C$_6$H$_4$COOC$_2$H$_5$ $\xrightarrow{\text{Zn/HCl}}$

$[p\text{-}\overset{+}{\text{N}}\text{H}_3\text{C}_6\text{H}_4\text{COOC}_2\text{H}_5]\text{Cl}^-$
hydrochloride salt of benzocaine

The free base can be generated by neutralizing the acidic ArNH$_3^+$ with OH$^-$.

(b) PhNH$_2$ $\xrightarrow{\text{(CH}_3\text{CO)}_2\text{O}}$ PhNHCOCH$_3$ $\xrightarrow{\text{HOSO}_2\text{Cl*}}$ p-ClSO$_2$C$_6$H$_4$NHCOCH$_3$ $\xrightarrow{\text{NH}_3^{**}}$

p-H$_2$NSO$_2$C$_6$H$_4$NHCOCH$_3$ $\xrightarrow[\text{2. OH}^-]{\text{1. H}_3\text{O}^+}$ p-H$_2$NSO$_2$C$_6$H$_4$NH$_2$

Note that the sulfonamide is much more stable than the amide and withstands hydrolysis under these conditions.

*Chlorosulfonic acid. **This reaction can be violent and NH$_3$ must be added cautiously!

19.114 Synthesize from naphthalene (NpH) and any other reagents:
(a) β-NpNH$_2$ (A), by three methods, (b) 2-NpCH$_2$NH$_2$, (c) naphthionic acid (4-amino-1-naphthalenesulfonic acid), and (d) 1,2-dinitronaphthalene. Don't repeat syntheses.

(a) NO$_2$ cannot be the precursor for NH$_2$ because NpH resists nitration at the β-position. However, —SO$_3$H and —COCH$_3$, which can be introduced at the β position, can serve as precursors.

(1) NpH $\xrightarrow[\text{2. NaOH}]{\text{1. H}_2\text{SO}_4, 150\,°\text{C}}$ β-NpSO$_3^-$Na$^+$ $\xrightarrow[\Delta]{\text{NaNH}_2}$ A

(2) β-NpSO$_3^-$Na$^+$ $\xrightarrow[\Delta]{\text{NaCN}}$ β-NpCN $\xrightarrow{\text{H}_3\text{O}^+}$ β-NpCOOH $\xrightarrow[\text{2. NH}_3]{\text{1. SOCl}_2}$ β-NpCONH$_2$ $\xrightarrow[\text{Br}_2]{\text{KOH}}$ A

(3) NpH $\xrightarrow[\text{PhNO}_2]{\text{CH}_3\text{COCl, AlCl}_3}$ β-NpCOCH$_3$ $\xrightarrow[\text{2. H}_3\text{O}^+]{\text{1. NaOH/I}_2}$ β-NpCOOH [then continue as in (2)]

(b) β-NpCN [from (2) in (a)] $\xrightarrow{\text{LiAlH}_4}$ 2-NpCH$_2$NH$_2$

(c) $\xrightarrow[\substack{\text{2. Sn, HCl} \\ \text{3. OH}^-}]{\text{1. HNO}_3, \text{H}_2\text{SO}_4}$ [naphthalene-NH$_2$] $\xrightarrow[\text{2. heat}]{\text{1. H}_2\text{SO}_4}$ [naphthalene-NH$_3^+$, SO$_3^-$]

$-SO_3^-$ blocks C^4
position

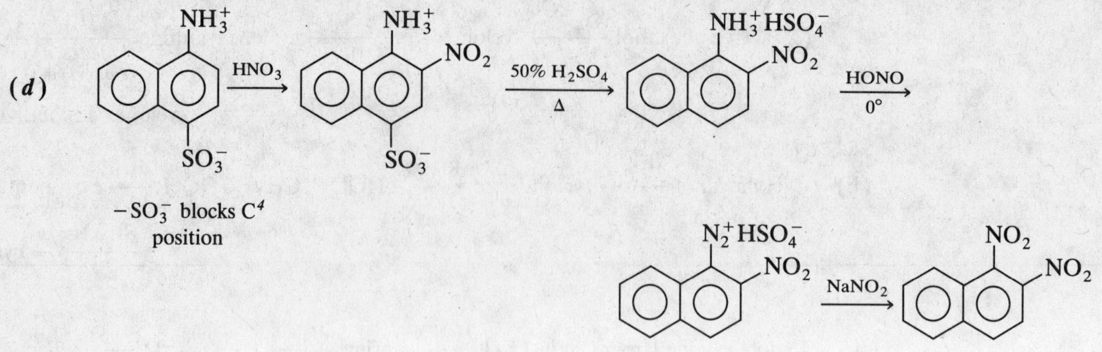

19.115 Prepare (*a*) PhD from $PhNH_2$ and (*b*) optically active *sec*-butylbenzene from an amine intermediate.

◢ (*a*) $C_6H_5NH_2 \xrightarrow[5\ °C]{HONO} C_6H_5N_2^+ \xrightarrow{DPH_2O_2} C_6H_5D$

(*b*) $C_6H_6 + CH_3CH_2CH(CH_3)Cl \xrightarrow{AlCl_3} C_6H_5CH(CH_3)CH_2CH_3 \xrightarrow[\substack{2.\ Sn/HCl \\ 3.\ OH^-}]{1.\ HNO_3/H_2SO_4}$

rac. $p\text{-}H_2NC_6H_4CH(CH_3)CH_2CH_3$ which is resolved with an optically active carboxylic acid such as tartaric acid (Problem 6.66). Then deaminate via diazonium salt and HPH_2O_2.

19.116 (*a*) Prepare $PhCH(OH)CH_2NH_2$ (**B**) from PhCHO.   (*b*) Prepare $PhCH=CHNH_2$ from PhCHO by a different method.   (*c*) Account for the formation of the mixture of $PhCH_2CHO$ and $PhCOCH_3$ when **B** is treated with HONO.

◢ (*a*) $PhCHO + HCN \longrightarrow PhCH(OH)CN \xrightarrow{LiAlH_4} B$

(*b*) $PhCHO + CH_3NO_2 \xrightarrow{OH^-} PhCH=CH_2NO_2 \xrightarrow{Fe,\ FeSO_4,\ H^+} PhCH=CHNH_2$

(*c*)   HONO converts **B** into a carbocation $PhCH(OH)CH_2^+$ (**C**) which may rearrange as follows:

$$PhCH_2CHO \xleftarrow[-H^+]{H_2O} \left[PhCH_2\overset{+}{C}HOH\right] \xleftarrow{\sim Ph:} \boxed{PhCH(OH)CH_2^+\ (C)} \xrightarrow{\sim H:} \left[Ph\overset{+}{C}(OH)CH_3\right] \xrightarrow[-H^+]{H_2O} PhCOCH_3$$

19.117 Synthesize $PhCH_2CH_2NHMe$ from PhH and any aliphatic compound.

◢ The two carbon chain can come from ethylene oxide which also provides a useful terminal functional group.

$PhH \xrightarrow[2.\ Mg]{1.\ Br_2/Fe} PhMgBr \xrightarrow[2.\ H^+]{1.\ Ethylene\ oxide} PhCH_2CH_2OH \xrightarrow{KMnO_4} PhCH_2COOH \xrightarrow[2.\ MeNH_2]{1.\ SOCl_2}$

$PhCH_2CONHMe \xrightarrow{LiAlH_4} PhCH_2CH_2NHMe$

19.118 Give structural formulas for **C** through **F** in the following reactions. **F** is the local anaesthetic Novocaine.

(*1*) $Et_2NH + H_2C\!\!-\!\!CH_2 \longrightarrow C,$ (*2*) $p\text{-}NO_2C_6H_4COOH \xrightarrow{SOCl_2} D \xrightarrow{+C} E \xrightarrow[RT]{H_2/Ni} F$
        $\diagdown O \diagup$

◢ $C = HOCH_2CH_2NEt_2;$ $D = p\text{-}NO_2C_6H_4COCl;$ $E = p\text{-}O_2NC_6H_4COOCH_2CH_2NEt_2;$

$F = p\text{-}H_2NC_6H_4COOCH_2CH_2NEt_2.$

19.119 Synthesize (*a*) pyrrolidine (azacyclopentane) from 1,3-propanediol, (*b*) $PhN(CH_2CH_2CH_2CH_3)_2$ from $PhNH_2$ and $CH_3CH_2CH_2CH_2OH$, and (*c*) morpholine (1-oxa-4-azacyclohexane) from ethylene oxide and NH_3.

◢ (*a*)   The carbon chain must be extended by one carbon. This is done by incorporating a CN group which also furnishes the amino nitrogen.

$HOCH_2CH_2CH_2OH \xrightarrow{1\ eq\ of\ SOCl_2} HOCH_2CH_2CH_2Cl \xrightarrow{KCN} HOCH_2CH_2CH_2CN \xrightarrow{SOCl_2}$

$ClCH_2CH_2CH_2CN \xrightarrow{H_2/Ni} ClCH_2CH_2CH_2CH_2NH_2 \xrightarrow[S_N2]{NaOH\ (-HCl)}$ N—H
Pyrrolidine

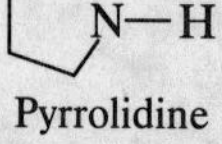

(b) $\quad CH_3CH_2CH_2CH_2OH \xrightarrow[\text{chlorochromate}]{\text{Pyridinium}} CH_3CH_2CH_2CHO \xrightarrow{PhNH_2} CH_3CH_2CH_2CH=NPh \xrightarrow[H_2O]{NaBH_4}$

$$CH_3CH_2CH_2CH_2NHPh \xrightarrow{CH_3CH_2CH_2CH_2Cl^*} PhN(CH_2CH_2CH_2CH_3)_2$$

$$^*CH_3CH_2CH_2CH_2OH \xrightarrow{HCl} CH_3CH_2CH_2CH_2Cl$$

(c) $\quad$ 2 eq of $H_2C-CH_2 + NH_3 \longrightarrow HOCH_2CH_2NHCH_2CH_2OH \xrightarrow{P_2O_5}$

$\qquad\qquad\qquad$ Morpholine

ANALYSIS

19.120 (a) How can RNH_2 (1°), R_2NH (2°) and R_3N (3°) be distinguished using (i) ir and (ii) pmr spectroscopy? (b) What technique must be used in (i) of (a) to ensure a correct conclusion? (c) How can a monoamine and diamine containing no other N's be easily distinguished by mass spectroscopy?

◢ (a) (i) A 1° amine has two peaks, symmetric and antisymmetric, in the 3300 to 3350 cm^{-1} N—H stretching region. 2° Amines have a single peak in this region and 3° amines have none since they lack an N—H bond. (ii) 1° And 2° amines have broad NH signals at $\delta = 1$ to 5 ppm whereas 3° amines lack such signals. The broad signal for a 1° amine integrates for two H's, that for the 2° amine for one H. (b) To ensure that the very broad flat signal is truly owing to an N—H, the sample is shaken with D_2O. This operation exchanges N—H for the nondetectible N—D, but a new signal appears for DHO. If this new signal does not appear, N—H is absent. (c) The parent peak for a monoamine has an odd mass; for a diamine the mass is even (Problem 12.170).

19.121 Using succinic anhydride (A), distinguish among RNH_2, R_2NH, and R_3N.

◢ $\qquad A + RNH_2 \longrightarrow RNHCOCH_2CH_2COO^-RNH_3^+ \xrightarrow{\Delta}$

$\qquad\qquad\qquad\qquad\qquad\qquad\qquad\qquad\qquad\qquad$ an imide, insoluble
$\qquad\qquad\qquad\qquad\qquad\qquad\qquad\qquad\qquad\qquad$ in H_2O and H_3O^+

$A + R_2NH \longrightarrow R_2NCOCH_2CH_2COO^-R_2NH_2^+$, a salt, which does not form an imide when heated, and is soluble in water.

$A + R_3N$, no reaction. The unreacted amine dissolves in H_3O^+.

19.122 (a) How can the *Hinsberg test* with $PhSO_2Cl$ be used to distinguish among RNH_2, R_2NH, and R_3N? (b) What are the limitations of the test?

◢ (a) R_3N does not react, but it dissolves in acid. In NaOH, RNH_2 reacts to give a sulfonamide salt, $[PhSO_2NR]^-Na^+$ (Problem 17.103) that is soluble in the basic reagent, while R_2NH gives a precipitate, $PhSO_2NR_2$. (b) The amines must be water-insoluble liquids.

19.123 With simple test-tube reactions, distinguish between (a) $PhNH_2$ and $PhNHCOMe$, (b) cyclohexylamine and $PhNH_2$, (c) $p\text{-}ClC_6H_4NH_2$ and $PhNH_3^+Cl^-$, (d) $Me_4N^+OH^-$ and Me_2NCH_2OH, (e) $PhNHMe$ and $PhNMe_2$, (f) $Me_4N^+Cl^-$ and $Me_3NH^+Cl^-$, and (g) $(PhNH_3)_2^+SO_4^{2-}$ and $p\text{-}H_3\overset{+}{N}C_6H_4SO_3^-$. Explain the steps and results.

◢ (a) Unlike the anilide, $PhNH_2$ is basic and dissolves in aq. HCl. (b) With the test tube immersed in an ice-bath, add $NaNO_2$ and aq. HCl. Both compounds form a diazonium salt but the compound from $PhNH_2$ is more stable and gives a highly colored *azo* compound on addition of β-naphthol. (All *azo* compounds are deeply colored.) Cyclohexyl-N_2^+ is unstable and emits N_2 detected by its bubbles. (c) Add a solution of $AgNO_3$; the chloride salt immediately gives a white precipitate of AgCl. (d) $Me_4N^+OH^-$ is a strong base and its solution turns red litmus blue. It also gives a white precipitate of $Ba(OH)_2$ when $BaCl_2$ is added. The other compound is a covalent aminoalcohol. (*e*) Add $NaNO_2$ and aq. HCl. The 2° amine, PhNHMe, gives a precipitate of the acid-insoluble nitrosamine. The aryl 3° amine, $PhNMe_2$, undergoes ring nitrosation to give the still basic and thus acid-soluble $p\text{-}ONC_6H_4NMe_2$. (*f*) Add conc. NaOH and heat the mixture. $Me_3NH^+Cl^-$ is changed into the volatile free base, Me_3N, detected by its typical ammonia-like odor. The other compound does not react. (*g*) Add a $BaCl_2$ solution. $(PhNH_3)_2SO_4$ is a sulfate salt and gives a white precipitate of $BaSO_4$. The other compound is a sulfonate that gives no precipitate with Ba^{2+}.

19.124 Suggest a structural formula for a chiral compound, $C_8H_{11}N$ (**A**), that dissolves in dilute HCl and releases N_2 with HONO.

▰ The compound has 4° of unsaturation indicating it has a benzene ring (a saturated compound with eight C's would have the formula $C_8H_{19}N$). **A** is a 1° amine since it dissolves in HCl and emits N_2 with HONO. The two remaining C's and the NH_2 must form the chiral moiety. **A** is $PhCH(NH_2)CH_3$.

19.125 Deduce the structure of the following amines from the following exhaustive methylation and Hofmann elimination data. (*a*) A resolvable amine is subjected to exhaustive methylation with 3 eq of MeI, followed by a Hofmann elimination. On reductive ozonolysis, the isolated alkene yields an equimolar mixture of $H_2C{=}O$ and $O{=}CHCH_2CH_2CH_3$. (*b*) $C_5H_{13}N$ (**B**) reacts with 1 eq of MeI and eventually gives propene. (*c*) $C_5H_{13}N$ (**C**) reacts with 2 eq of MeI and Ag_2O/Δ to give $H_2C{=}CH_2$ and a 3° amine. The amine reacts further with 1 eq of MeI to eventually give $H_2C{=}CHCH_3$

▰ (*a*) By pointing the carbonyl groups toward each other as given, the alkene is shown to be $H_2C{=}CHCH_2CH_2CH_3$. The amine is 1° because 3 eq of MeI were required to give the 4° ammonium ion. Since the amine is resolvable, NH_2 is bonded to a chiral C; the compound is $CH_3CH(NH_2)CH_2CH_2CH_3$. The other amine, $NH_2CH_2CH_2CH_2CH_2CH_3$, that would give the same alkene, is achiral. (*b*) (**B**) is a 3° amine because it reacts with only 1 eq of MeI. Since $H_2C{=}CHCH_3$ is the alkene, there is a three-carbon chain attached to N, either as *n*- or *i*-Pr along with two Me's to account for the two additional C's. **B** is $C_3H_7NMe_2$; the structure of C_3H_7 is uncertain. (*c*) **C** reacts with 2 eq of MeI; it is a 2° amine. Stepwise formation of $H_2C{=}CH_2$ and $H_2C{=}CHCH_3$ shows **C** is $C_3H_7NHCH_2CH_3$ with the same uncertainty about the structure of C_3H_7 as in (*b*).

19.126 Identify the compound, $C_6H_{13}N$ (**D**), and all intermediates involved in the following sequence of exhaustive methylations and Hofmann degradations. **D** reacts with 2 eq of MeI and Ag_2O/Δ giving (**E**) $C_8H_{17}N$. After reaction with MeI and further Hofmann degradation, **E** gives $H_2C{=}CH{-}\underset{\underset{Me}{|}}{C}{=}CHCH_3$ (**F**) and NMe_3.

▰ See Fig. 19-10. **D** has 1° of unsaturation and, since the alkene **E** retains N and all the C's, **D** is a heterocyclic 2° amine (reacts with 2 eq of MeI). Since **F** has a five carbon chain, **D** is a six-membered ring with a substituent Me. The position of the side chain Me on C^3 of the diene tells us the ring has an Me attached to the third C of the five-carbon ring sequence. We might expect the diene to be $H_2C{=}CHCHMeCH{=}CH_2$ but OH^- catalyzes its rearrangement to the more stable conjugated diene, **F**.

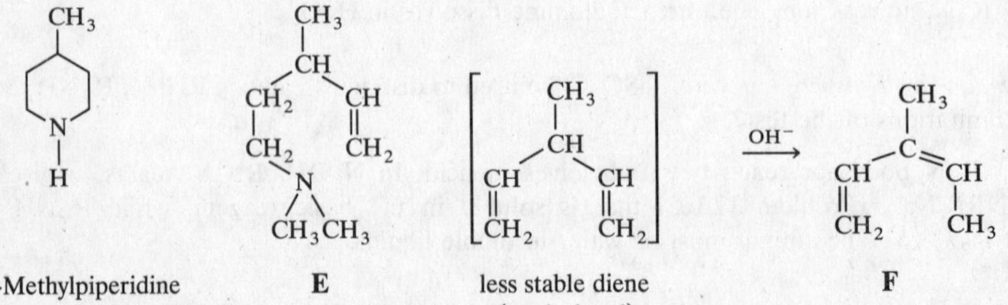

D, 4-Methylpiperidine   E   less stable diene   F
                                (not isolated)   **Fig. 19-10**

19.127 (*a*) Define alkaloids. (*b*) Optically active (*S*)-coniine, $C_8H_{17}N$ (**G**), the toxic liquid alkaloid in hemlock that supposedly caused Socrates' death, dissolves in aq. HCl and emits no gas with HONO. It gives a precipitate with $PhSO_2Cl/NaOH$. Exhaustive methylation and Hofmann elimination gives alkenes, one of which is $C_{10}H_{21}N$ (**H**). **H** goes through the Hofmann degradation sequence to give a mixture of 1,4-octadiene and 1,5-octadiene. Give all possible structures of **G** and **H**.

(*a*) *Alkaloids* are amines that occur naturally in plants. Many are toxic, e.g., strychnine and brucine, and some, when properly prescribed and used, are useful medicines, e.g., quinine, codeine, and morphine. (*b*) **G** is a 2° amine (no gas with HONO and precipitate with $PhSO_2Cl/NaOH$). Since two degradations give dienes, **G** has no C=C; its 1° of unsaturation arises from a ring. Since two sequences are needed to release the N, **G** is a nitrogen heterocyclic compound. The isolation of unbranched dienes means that any R groups on the ring must be on the α C's and unbranched. There are two possibilities: one is 2-Me and 6-Et, and the other is 2-*n*-Pr. The following sequences show that coniine is 2-*n*-propylpiperidine.

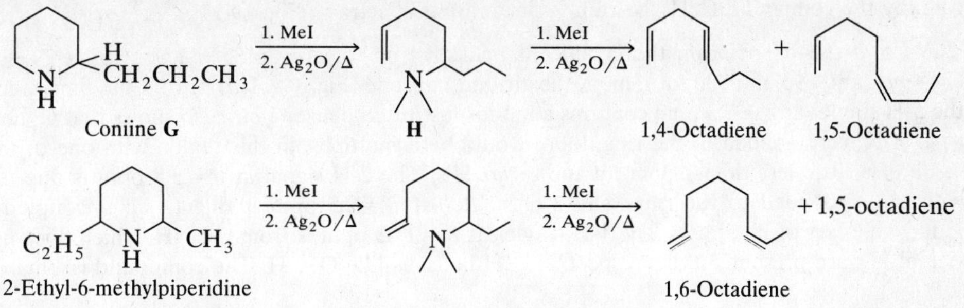

This incorrect isomer would yield 1,6- and 1,5-octadiene but not 1,4-octadiene.

19.128 Amines **I**, **J**, **K**, and **M** each have their parent cation peaks at $m/z = 59$. The highest intensity peaks are at $m/z = 44$ for **I** and **J**, 30 for **K**, and 58 for **M**. Give the structures for the amines and the cations accounting for the most prominent peak for each.

With the parent peak at $m/z = 59$, the molecular formula for the isomers is C_3H_9N. Amines fragment mainly at the α C, preferably at the weaker C—C, not at the stronger C—H bond.

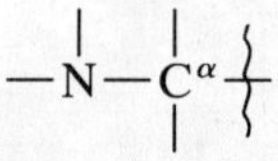

Amines **I** and **J** both lose CH_3 ($m/z = 15$); $59 - 15 = 44$. Hence, each has a CH_3 bonded to the α C. **I** and **J** are, respectively,

$$CH_3\ddot{N}HCH_2CH_3 \xrightarrow{-e^-} [CH_3\dot{N}HCH_2 \vdots CH_3]^+ \longrightarrow \left[CH_3\overset{H}{\overset{|}{N}}{=}CH_2\right]^+ + \cdot CH_3 \qquad m/z = 44$$

$$H_2\ddot{N}\overset{CH_3}{\overset{|}{C}}HCH_3 \xrightarrow{-e^-} \left[H_2\dot{N}\overset{CH_3}{\overset{|}{C}}H \vdots CH_3\right]^+ \longrightarrow [H_2N{=}CHCH_3]^+ + \cdot CH_3 \qquad m/z = 44$$

Amine **K** loses CH_2CH_3 ($59 - 29 = 30$); CH_2CH_3 is bonded to the α C.

$$H_2\ddot{N}CH_2CH_2CH_3 \xrightarrow{-e^-} [H_2\dot{N}CH_2 \vdots CH_2CH_3]^+ \longrightarrow [H_2N{=}CH_2]^+ + \cdot CH_2CH_3 \qquad m/z = 30$$

Amine **L** loses H ($59 - 1 = 58$).

$$(CH_3)_3\ddot{N} \xrightarrow{-e^-} [(CH_3)_2\dot{N}CH_2 \vdots H]^+ \longrightarrow [(CH_3)_2N{=}CH_2]^+ + \cdot H \qquad m/z = 58$$

19.129 Deduce the structure of a compound ($C_9H_{11}NO$) that is soluble in dilute HCl and gives a positive test with $Ag(NH_3)_2^+$. Its ir spectrum has a strong band at 1695 cm^{-1} and a smaller one at 2720 cm^{-1}, but no bands in the 3300 to 3500 cm^{-1} region. The proton-decoupled ^{13}C spectrum shows six signals which display the following splitting patterns in the proton-coupled spectrum: one quartet, two singlets, and three doublets, one of which is very downfield.

✐ Basicity and absence of N—H stretching bands indicate a 3° amino group, —N(CH$_3$)$_2$; the equivalent CH$_3$'s account for the quartet. The positive Tollens' test, the bands at 1695 and 2720 cm^{-1} and the very downfield doublet reveals a CHO. The 5° of unsaturation means the presence of a benzene ring along with a HC=O, and the two singlets indicate the ring is disubstituted. Since the two more upfield doublets must arise from the four unsubstituted ring C's, they must come from two equivalent pairs; the substituents are *para*. The compound is *p*-(CH$_3$)$_2$NC$_6$H$_4$CHO.

19.130 Identify the compound C$_8$H$_{11}$N from its ir and pmr spectra in Fig. 19-11.

✐ From the ir spectrum the significant peaks, in cm^{-1}, are: ≈ 3500 for a single N—H, 3000–3100 for a C$_{sp}$—H, and 690 and 730 for a monosubstituted benzene [Fig. 19-11(*a*)]. From the pmr spectrum [Fig. 19-11(*b*)], the 5-H singlet at δ = 7.3 ppm confirms a monosubstituted benzene but also shows that C, not N, is bonded to the ring. If N were bonded to the ring, there would be a multiplet in this region with one of the signals having a δ value of a little less than 7 ppm for the *ortho* H's. The 2-H signal at δ = 3.8 ppm is due to an uncoupled CH$_2$ with the C bonded to the ring. The 3-H singlet at δ = 2.5 ppm is due to an uncoupled CH$_3$ that feels the inductive effect of Ph and N. The 1-H singlet at δ = 1.43 ppm is from the NH, which does not couple even when vicinal H's are present. In this respect, N—H behaves like O—H. The compound is PhCH$_2$NHCH$_3$.

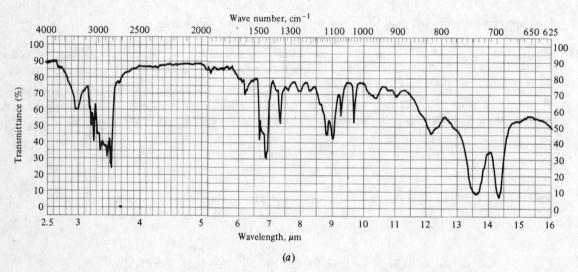

(*a*)

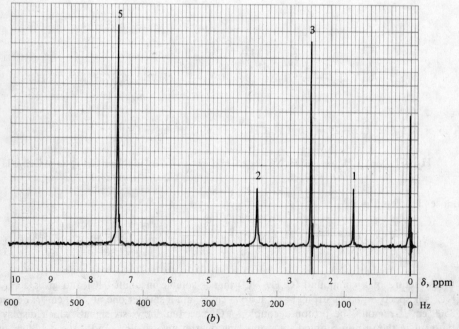

(*b*)

Fig. 19-11

SUPPLEMENTARY PROBLEMS

19.131 (*a*) Discuss the difficulties of synthesizing Me_3CNH_2 by (i) Gabriel synthesis or amination of RX and (ii) reduction of N-containing compounds. (*b*) Show how Me_3CNH_2 can be made from either Me_3COH or $Me_2C=CH_2$ (*Ritter reaction*) in good yield.

◢ (*a*) (i) These S_N2 methods would require starting with Me_3CX which would rather undergo an E2 reaction. (ii) Reduction of an amide, $RCONH_2$ must give an amine with two H's on the α C, RCH_2NH_2. Reduction of an imine, $RH(R')C=NH$ formed from $RH(R')C=O$ and NH_3 or an oxime must give an amine with at least one H on the α C, $RH(R')CHNH_2$. Although Me_3CNO_2 and Me_3CN_3 can be reduced, neither reaction gives good yields; reaction of Me_3CX with $NaNO_2$ or NaN_3 would again give E2 products. Some Me_3CNO_2 can be made by vapor-phase nitration of Me_3CH but the yields are poor, especially because chain-degradation occurs.
(*b*) In conc. H_2SO_4 these substrates are converted to Me_3C^+ which then reacts with HCN:

$$Me_3C^+ + N\equiv CH \longrightarrow [Me_3C\overset{+}{N}\equiv CH] \xrightarrow{H_2O} [Me_3CNHCH=O] \xrightarrow{H_2O} Me_3CNH_2 \,(+HCOOH)$$

a nitrilium cation   a formamide

To avoid using the very toxic HCN, nitriles are used and the corresponding nitrilium ions that form

$$\left(Me_3C\overset{+}{N}\equiv CR\right)$$

hydrolyze in a similar fashion.

19.132 (*a*) Complete the following reaction and suggest a mechanism.
$$RNH_2 + CHCl_3 + 3KOH \longrightarrow$$

(*b*) Describe an analytical use for this reaction. (*c*) Give the product for the reaction of the organic product in (*a*) with a reducing reagent such as Na/EtOH.

◢ (*a*) The products are $R\overset{+}{N}\equiv C{:}^-$ (an isonitrile) $+3KCl + 3H_2O$. Recall that $CHCl_3 + KOH$ afford the electrophilic carbene, $Cl_2C{:}$ that attacks the nucleophilic RNH_2.

$$R\ddot{N}H_2 + {:}CCl_2 \longrightarrow \begin{bmatrix} H & Cl \\ | & | \\ R\overset{+}{N}-C{:}^- \\ | & | \\ H & Cl \end{bmatrix} \xrightarrow[-2HCl]{2KOH} R\overset{+}{N}\equiv C{:}^-$$
an isonitrile

(*b*) This *carbylamine reaction* can be used as a test for 1° amines because isonitriles have very distinctive foul odors. (*c*) $RNHCH_3$. This is a method for making 2° methylamines.

19.133 (*a*) Complete the following reactions:

(i) $PhN_2^+Cl^- \xrightarrow{Na_2SO_3} A$ (ii) $p\text{-}MeC_6H_4N_2^+Cl^- \xrightarrow[\Delta]{\text{Cu bronze powder}} B$

(iii) cyclohexene $+ I-N=C=O \longrightarrow C \xrightarrow{hydrolysis} D$ (iv) 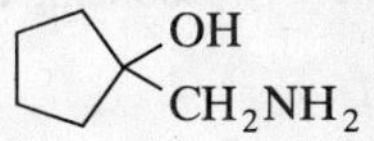 (cyclopentane with OH and CH_2NH_2) $\xrightarrow{HONO} E$

(*b*) Suggest a mechanism for (iv).

◢ (*a*) (i) **A** is $PhNHNH_2$; (ii) **B** is $p\text{-}MeC_6H_4-C_6H_4Me\text{-}p$ (this is the *Gatterman reaction* for making biphenyls); (iii) **C** is 2-iodocyclohexyl$-N=C=O$ and **D** is 2-iodocyclohexylamine; (iv) **E** is cyclohexanone. (*b*) This is a pinacol-type (Problem 15.128) ring expansion via the carbocation

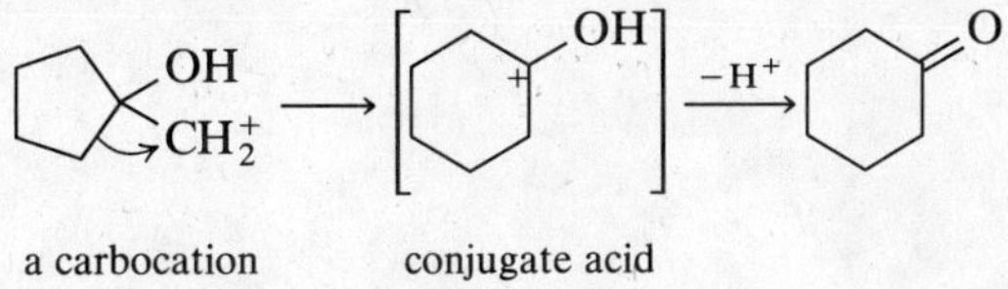

(structures: a carbocation → conjugate acid of the ketone → ketone)

a carbocation   conjugate acid of the ketone

19.134 Give the product of reduction of $PhNO_2$ with (*a*) Zn, aq. NH_4Cl; (*b*) $LiAlH_4$; (*c*) As_2O_3/aq. NaOH; (*d*) Zn, alc. NaOH; and (*e*) H_2NNH_2/Raney Ni, or excess Zn/NaOH

◢ (*a*) PhNHOH, N-phenylhydroxylamine; (*b*) and (*d*) $PhN=NPh$; (*c*) $Ph-\overset{+}{\underset{O^-}{N}}=N-Ph$, azoxybenzene;

(*e*) PhNHNHPh, hydrazobenzene.

19.135 Discuss the function of the neurotransmitter acetylcholine (Problem 19.10) in nerve transmission.

◢ When an electrical signal from, e.g., the eye, reaches the transmitting end of the first nerve cell, it liberates acetylcholine, which then migrates across a tiny gap (*synapse*) to the receptor end of the next nerve cell, activating it and permitting further transmission of the signal through many synapses on its way to the brain. In order for the activated nerve cell to be reused, the acetylcholine must be removed; it is hydrolyzed to choline and acetic acid by the enzyme cholinesterase. These components return to the transmitting end of the nerve cell where choline is reacetylated by the enzyme acetylase. The nerve cell is once again ready to transmit across a synapse. A similar process occurs to transmit signals from the brain to other parts of the body, e.g., a muscle.

19.136 The triarylmethane dye, pararosaniline $(p\text{-}H_2NC_6H_4)_2C$⸺⸺$=NH_2^+ Cl^-$, (Basic Red 9) is synthesized in three steps with the following reactants:

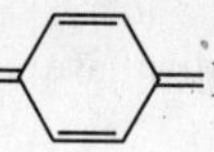

$$(1)\ 2PhNH_2 + p\text{-}H_2NC_6H_4CH_3 + PhNO_2;\quad (2)\ PbO_2;\quad (3)\ HCl.$$

(*a*) Show the steps. (*b*) Discuss the function of (i) $PhNO_2$, (ii) PbO_2, and (iii) HCl.

◢ (*a*) The final product from step *1* is the "leuco" base, formed as shown:

Step *1*

$$p\text{-}H_2NC_6H_4CH_3 \xrightarrow{PhNO_2} p\text{-}H_2NC_6H_4CHO \xrightarrow[(a)]{PhNH_2} (p\text{-}H_2NC_6H_4)_2COH \xrightarrow[(b)]{PhNH_2} (p\text{-}H_2NC_6H_4)_3CH$$

"leuco" base

The intermediate reactions (*a*) and (*b*) are electrophilic substitutions on $PhNH_2$.

Step *2*

$$(p\text{-}H_2NC_6H_4)_3CH \xrightarrow{PbO_2} (p\text{-}H_2NC_6H_4)_3COH$$

"leuco" base   carbinol color base

Step *3*

$$(p\text{-}H_2NC_6H_4)_3COH \xrightarrow[(-H_2O)]{HCl} Cl^- \left[(p\text{-}H_2NC_6H_4)_3C^+ \longleftrightarrow (p\text{-}H_2NC_6H_4)_2C=\!\!\!⟨⟩\!\!\!=NH_2^+ \right]$$

dye

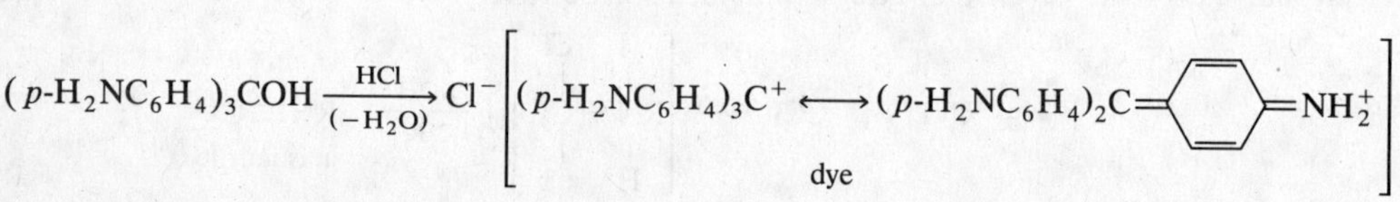

(Only one contributing structure with + on N is shown.)

(*b*) (i) $PhNO_2$ oxidizes the CH_3 of $p\text{-}H_2NC_6H_4CH_3$ to CHO and is reduced to $PhNH_2$.
(ii) PbO_2 oxidizes the triarylmethane to the carbinol.
(iii) HCl converts the carbinol to a stable cation, Ar_3C^+, whose + is delocalized to the three amino N's. This extensive delocalization narrows the HOMO ⟶ LUMO energy gap enabling excitation to occur in the visible spectrum, thereby producing color.

GENERAL, NOMENCLATURE, AND PHYSICAL PROPERTIES

20.1 Distinguish among alcohols, enols, phenols, and naphthols.

◢ Alcohols have an OH attached to an sp^3 hybridized carbon ($-\overset{|}{\underset{|}{C}}-OH$). Enols have an OH attached to a vinyl group ($-\overset{|}{C}=\overset{|}{C}-OH$). *Phenols* are a general group with an OH attached to a carbocyclic aromatic ring (ArOH). Specifically, Ar is a phenyl ring for phenols. The compound with the specific name phenol is C_6H_5OH. (In medicine, its old name carbolic acid is still sometimes used.) Naphthols are phenolic-type compounds where Ar is a naphthyl ring (NapOH).

20.2 (*a*) Account for the fact that phenols are much more stable than enols. (*b*) Give the two keto forms with type and name.

◢ (*a*) Both compounds can be considered as tautomers of a keto structure. The large resonance energy of C=O usually causes the keto tautomer to be much more stable than the enol.

$$>C=C-OH \rightleftharpoons H-\overset{|}{\underset{|}{C}}-\overset{|}{C}=O$$

However, the keto form of phenol can be attained only with loss of the stable aromatic ring making it very much less stable than phenol.

(*b*)

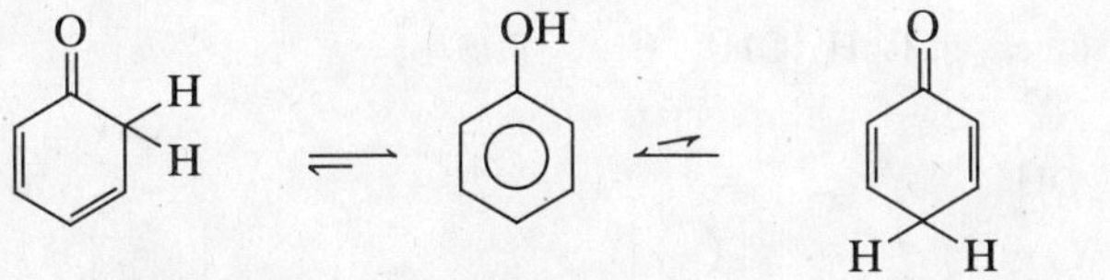

2,4-Cyclohexadienone
ortho-keto form

Phenol
"enol" form

2,5-Cyclohexadienone
para-keto form

20.3 (*a*) Account for the fact that 1,3,5-trihydroxybenzene reacts with H_2NOH to give an oximino derivative, whereas phenol and 1,3-dihydroxybenzene do not. (*b*) Explain why 1,2,4-trihydroxybenzenes (**A**) and 1,2,3-trihydroxybenzenes (**B**) do not react with H_2NOH.

◢ (*a*) The triketo tautomer of this isomer has considerable stability because of the large resonance energy of its three C=O groups. Therefore it has sufficient concentration in the phenol-keto equilibrium to react to give a trioxime.

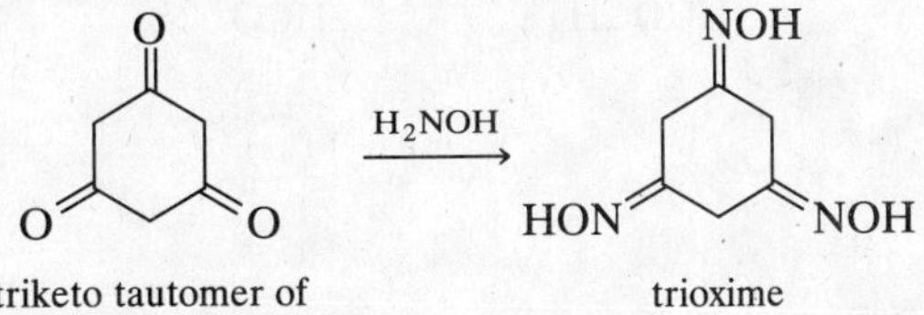

$$\xrightarrow{\text{H}_2\text{NOH}}$$

triketo tautomer of
1,3,5-trihydroxybenzene

trioxime

(*b*) The triketo tautomers of **A** and **B** are destabilized by the adjacent C=O's and have an insufficient concentration to react with H_2NOH.

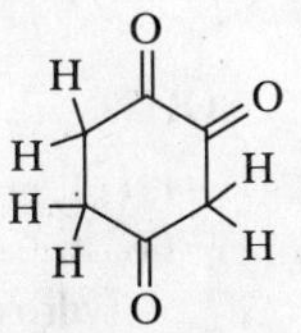

keto tautomer of **A** 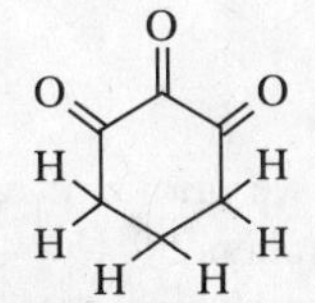   keto tautomer of **B**

20.4   Account for the position of the following equilibrium.

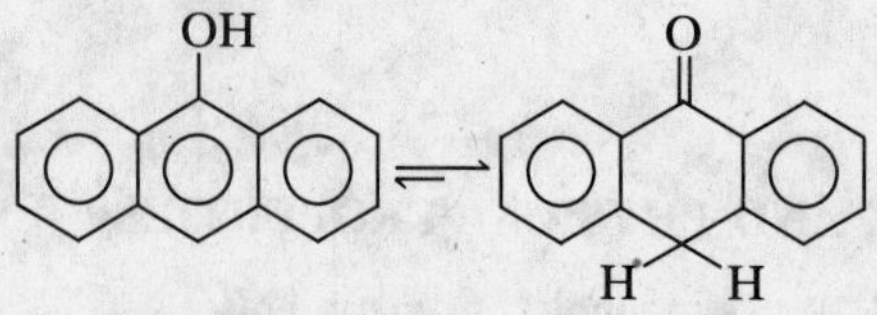

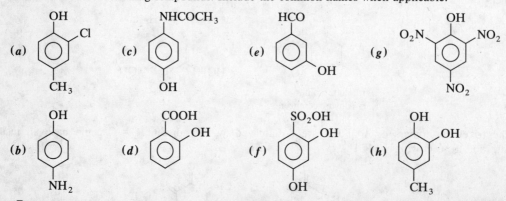

anthranol   anthrone

◢   Again the equilibrium depends on the relative resonance energies of the tautomers. Although ring aromaticity usually stabilizes the phenolic tautomer, in this case the reverse is true. Anthrone has two distinct intact aromatic rings in addition to the C=O, making it more stable than anthrol, which suffers a loss of aromaticity per ring because its three rings are fused.

20.5   (*a*) Give the structural formulas and (i) the IUPAC, (ii) the common, and (iii) the CA names of the phenyl isomers of C_7H_8O.

◢

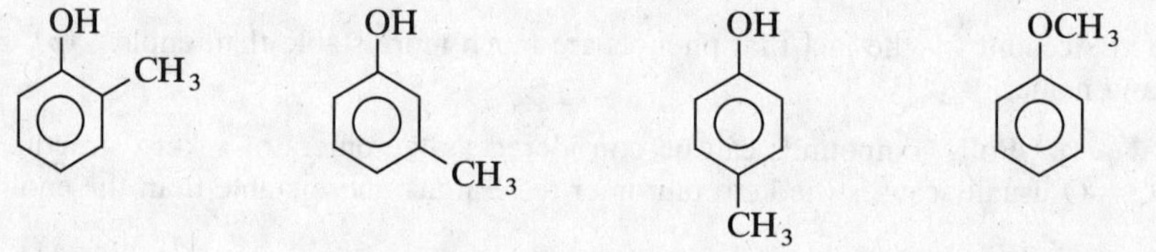

(i) *o*-Methylphenol	*m*-Methylphenol	*p*-Methylphenol	Methoxybenzene
(ii) *o*-Cresol	*m*-Cresol	*p*-Cresol	Anisole
(iii) 2-Methylbenzenol	3-Methylbenzenol	4-Methylbenzenol	Methoxybenzene

Although the CA name for C_6H_5OH is phenol, substituted phenols are abstracted as derivatives of *benzenol*.

20.6   Solve Problem 20.5 for the isomers of $C_6H_4(OH)_2$.

◢

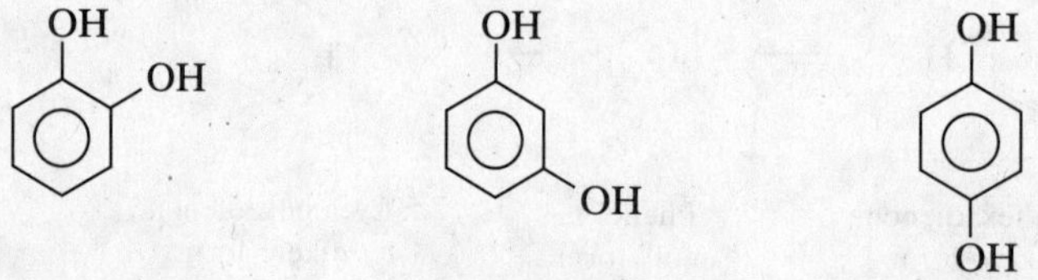

(i)	*o*-Dihydroxybenzene	*m*-Dihydroxybenzene	*p*-Dihydroxybenzene
	or 1,2-Dihydroxybenzene	1,3-Dihydroxybenzene	1,4-Dihydroxybenzene
(ii)	Catechol (pyrocatechol)	Resorcinol	Hydroquinone
(iii)	1,2-Benzenediol	1,3-Benzenediol	1,4-Benzenediol

CA names will be used infrequently for phenolic compounds.

20.7   Name each of the following compounds. Include the common names when applicable.

(*a*)   (*c*)   (*e*)   (*g*)

(*b*)   (*d*)   (*f*)   (*h*)

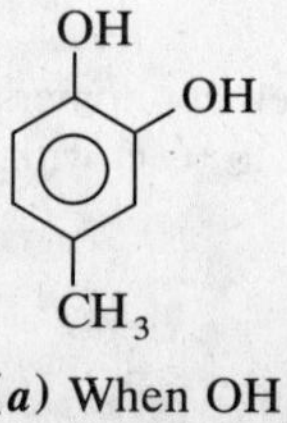

◢   COOH, CHO, SO_3H have priority over OH [see (*d*), (*e*), and (*f*)].   (*a*) When OH has priority it is given number 1; 2-Chloro-4-methylphenol.   (*b*) 4-Aminophenol or 4-hydroxyaniline. The latter name is especially used for aniline derivatives.   (*c*) *p*-Hydroxyacetanilide.   (*d*) *o*-Hydroxybenzoic acid or salicylic acid.
(*e*) *m*-Hydroxybenzaldehyde.   (*f*) 2,4-Dihydroxybenzenesulfonic acid.   (*g*) 2,4,6-Trinitrophenol or picric acid.
(*h*) 1,2-Dihydroxy-4-methylbenzene or 4-methylcatechol.

20.8 Give the structural formulas for (*a*) 2-nitro-4-acetylphenol, (*b*) *p*-vinylphenol, (*c*) 4-*n*-hexylresorcinol (an antiseptic), (*d*) ethyl salicylate, (*e*) β-naphthol, (*f*) 2-hydroxy-3-phenylbenzoic acid, (*g*) *m*-allylphenol, and (*h*) 6-bromo-1-naphthol.

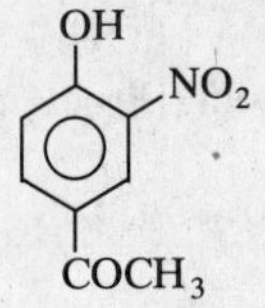

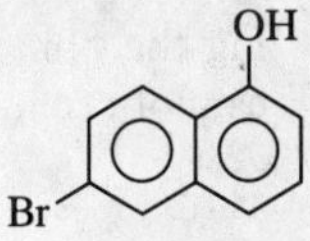

20.9 Name each of the following compounds. Include the common names when applicable.

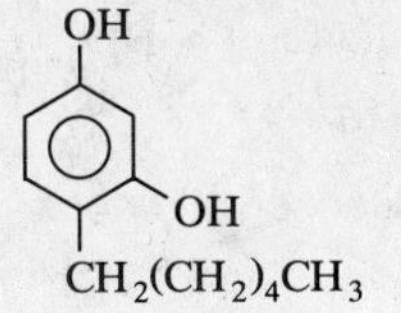

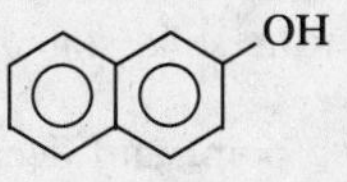

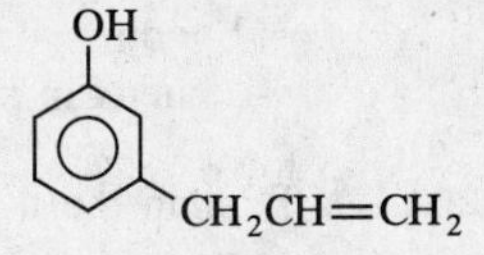

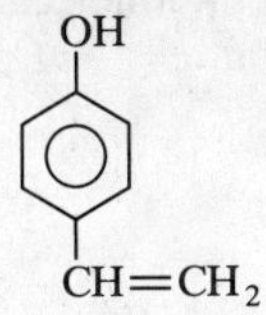

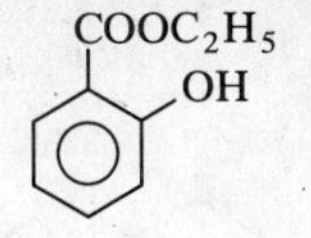

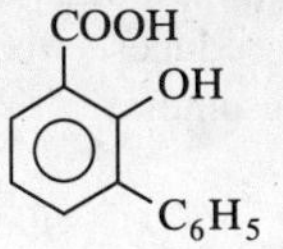

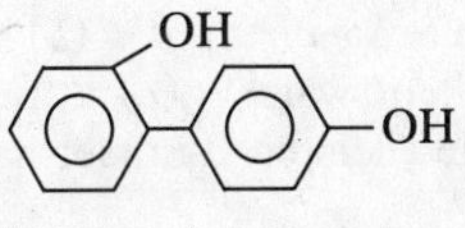

⬛ (*a*) 2-Methoxyphenol, 2-hydroxyanisole, catechol monomethyl ether, guaiacol.
   (*b*) Phenyl acetate.
   (*c*) *p*- or 4-Methylbenzenethiol or 4-methylthiophenol.
   (*d*) *m*- or 3-Mercaptophenol (or monothioresorcinol). (OH has priority over SH.)
   (*e*) 3'-Methyl-4-hydroxydiphenyl ether or 4-(3-methylphenoxy)phenol.
   (*f*) 2,4'-Dihydroxybiphenyl.

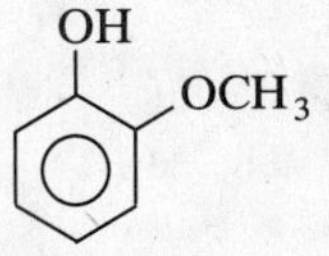

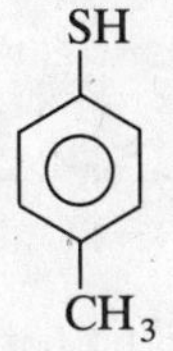

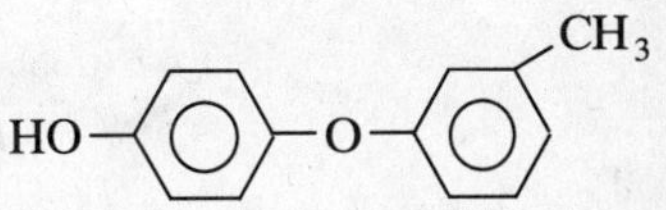

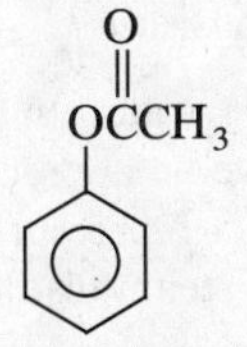

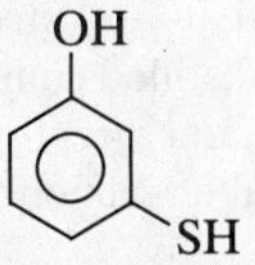

20.10 Explain why (*a*) the C—O bond in phenol is shorter than in alcohol, (*b*) the dipole moments of phenol (1.7 D) and methanol (1.6 D) are in opposite directions, and (*c*) the dipole moment of *p*-nitrophenol (5.0 D) is greater than that of phenol or nitrobenzene (4.0 D).

⬛ (*a*) C—X Bond lengths, including C—O, decrease as the *s* character of the HO used by C increases. Hence, the C_{sp^2}—O bond (more *s* character) of ArOH's is shorter than the C_{sp^3}—O bond (less *s* character) of ROH's. Also the delocalization of electron density from O to the ring by extended π bonding engenders some double bond character in the phenolic C—O bond making it shorter. (*b*) The delocalization of electron density from O to the ring causes the O of phenol to be the positive end of the molecular dipole. In alcohols the strongly electron-withdrawing electronegative O is the negative end of the dipole. (*c*) The electron-donation of OH reenforces the electron-withdrawal of NO_2.

20.11 (*a*) Compare the relative (i) boiling points and (ii) water solubilities of toluene and phenol. Explain. (*b*) Why are most other monophenolic compounds insoluble in H_2O?

⬛ (*a*) (i) The molecular weights are approximately the same. Phenol has a higher boiling point (181.8 °C) than toluene (110.6 °C) because of intermolecular attraction by H-bonding. (ii) Phenol is more water-soluble than toluene because of H-bonding with H_2O.

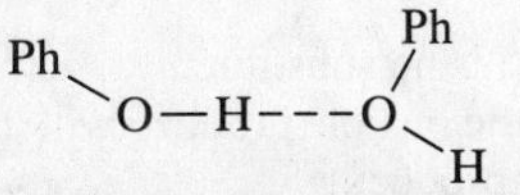

(i) Intermolecular H-bonding 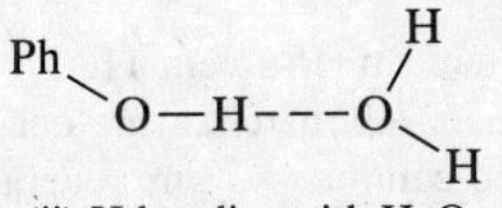   (ii) H-bonding with H_2O

(*b*) The increase in molecular weight of other phenolic compounds overshadows the solubilizing effect of H-bonding.

20.12 Account for the fact that (*a*) phenol has a higher boiling point than benzenethiol (168.7 °C) and (*b*) hydroquinone (173 °C) has a higher melting point than catechol (105 °C).

◢ (*a*) Based on molecular weight, benzenethiol should have the higher boiling point. However, S is a poor H-bonding participant; thus, intermolecular attraction in PhSH is weaker than in PhOH. (*b*) Molecules of the *p*-isomer can fit closer in the solid state causing it to have the higher melting point [Problem 10.21(*c*)].

20.13 Explain the lower boiling point and decreased water solubility of *o*-nitrophenol and *o*-hydroxybenzaldehyde as compared with their *m*- and *p*-isomers.

◢ Intramolecular H-bonding (chelation) (Fig. 20-1) in the *o*-isomers inhibits intermolecular attraction, lowering the boiling point, and reduces H-bonding with H_2O, decreasing water solubility. Intramolecular chelation cannot occur in *m*- and *p*-isomers

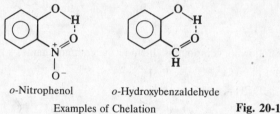

o-Nitrophenol   *o*-Hydroxybenzaldehyde

Examples of Chelation   **Fig. 20-1**

20.14 (*a*) What is meant by steam distillation? (*b*) What physical property most influences the ability of a compound to be steam distilled? (*c*) Which isomer (*o*, *m*, or *p*) of hydroxacetophenone steam distills?

◢ (*a*) When steam carries with it compounds that are mixed with boiling water but not dissolved, the compounds are said to *steam distill*. (*b*) The steam-distilled compound must have an appreciable vapor pressure at the boiling point of water. (*c*) Attraction to water greatly lowers the vapor pressure, preventing steam distillation. Only the chelated *o*-isomer has a minimal attraction with water and steam distills.

Chelate of *o*-hydroxacetophenone

20.15 Which of the following compounds exhibit chelation: (*a*) *o*-cresol, (*b*) methyl salicylate (oil of wintergreen), (*c*) *o*-cyanophenol, (*d*) *o*-fluorophenol, and (*e*) *o*-iodophenol?

◢ Chelation occurs only in (*b*) where the H of the OH H-bonds with the O of C=O, and (*d*), since F is very electronegative and is approachable to the H. In (*a*) the H of OH can only H-bond with an electronegative atom —not the C of CH_3. In (*c*), although the N of CN is electronegative, the linearity of CN places the N too far away from the OH. In (*e*), I is not sufficiently electronegative.

PREPARATION

20.16 (*a*) Give the steps for the industrial synthesis of PhOH from PhCl (*Dow process*). (*b*) Suggest a mechanism. (*c*) How would using *o*-chloroanisole help establish the proposed mechanism?

◢ (*a*) $PhCl + 2NaOH \xrightarrow[320\ atm]{360\ °C} H_2O + NaCl + PhO^-Na^+ \xrightarrow{H_3O^+} PhOH$

sodium phenoxide

(*b*) A benzyne mechanism (Problem 11.87). There is no substituent to activate the ring towards addition-elimination. (*c*) If the benzyne mechanism occurs, the major product will be the rearranged *m*-methoxyphenol. Addition-elimination cannot give any rearranged product.

20.17 (*a*) Show the steps in another industrial preparation of phenol starting with cumene, $PhCHMe_2$ (isopropylbenzene). (*b*) Give a synthesis for cumene. (*c*) How can $PhSO_3H$ be converted industrially to phenol?

(a)

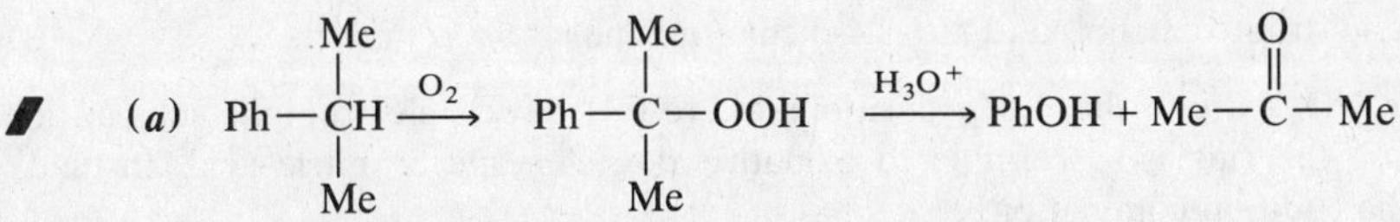

$$\underset{\substack{| \\ \text{Me} \\ \text{Cumene}}}{\overset{\substack{\text{Me} \\ |}}{Ph-CH}} \xrightarrow{O_2} \underset{\substack{| \\ \text{Me} \\ \text{Cumene hydroperoxide}}}{\overset{\substack{\text{Me} \\ |}}{Ph-C-OOH}} \xrightarrow{H_3O^+} \underset{\text{Phenol}}{PhOH} + \underset{\text{Acetone}}{Me-\overset{\overset{\textstyle O}{\|}}{C}-Me}$$

The hydroperoxide results from a free radical substitution at the active benzylic carbon.

(b)
$$PhH + CH_3CH=CH_2 \xrightarrow{H_2SO_4} PhCH(CH_3)_2$$

(c) By alkali fusion of the sulfonate salt:

$$PhH \xrightarrow{H_2S_2O_7} PhSO_3H \xrightarrow[2. \ H^+]{1. \ NaOH, \ 330 \ °C} PhOH$$

20.18 Give a mechanism for the acid-catalyzed rearrangement of cumene hydroperoxide.

In the rearrangement Ph migrates from C to O. Most acid-catalyzed rearrangements require the intermediacy of a positively-charged atom to which the group migrates. Heretofore, most of these + sites were carbocations, but in this case it is an O^+.

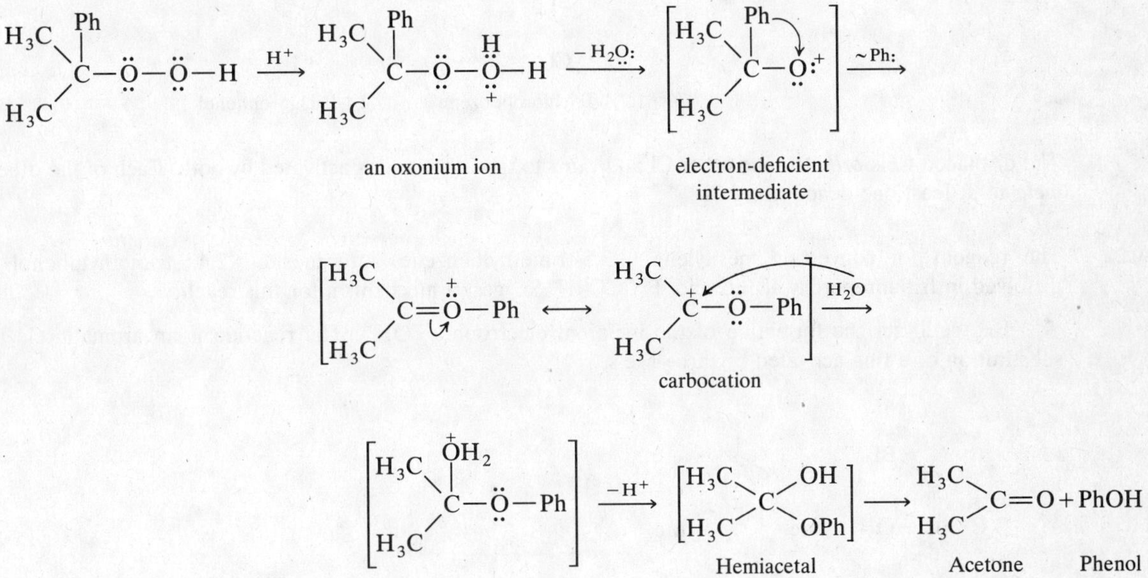

an oxonium ion   electron-deficient intermediate

carbocation

Hemiacetal   Acetone   Phenol

The rearrangement of Ph may be synchronous with the loss of H_2O.

20.19 Give a laboratory method for converting PhH to PhOH via $PhNO_2$.

Hydrolysis of the diazonium salt (Problem 19.84).

$$PhH \xrightarrow{HNO_3/H_2SO_4} PhNO_2 \xrightarrow[2. \ NaOH]{1. \ Sn/HCl} PhNH_2 \xrightarrow[0 \ °C]{NaNO_2/aq. \ HCl} PhN_2^+Cl^- \xrightarrow[\Delta]{H_2O} PhOH$$

20.20 Synthesize (a) α-naphthol and (b) β-naphthol from naphthalene.

(a) Since naphthalene is easily nitrated at the α position, this synthesis is best achieved through the diazonium salt.

$$NapH \xrightarrow{HNO_3/H_2SO_4} \alpha\text{-}NapNO_2 \xrightarrow[2. \ NaOH]{1. \ Sn/HCl} \alpha\text{-}NapNH_2 \xrightarrow[0 \ °C]{NaNO_2/H^+} \alpha\text{-}NapN_2^+Cl^- \xrightarrow[\Delta]{H_2O} \alpha\text{-}NapOH$$

(b) NapH is not nitrated at the β position, but is sulfonated there.

$$NapH \xrightarrow[180 \ °C]{H_2S_2O_7} \beta\text{-}NapSO_3H \xrightarrow[2. \ H^+]{1. \ NaOH, \ 330 \ °C} \beta\text{-}NapOH$$

20.21 Prepare (*a*) picric acid, 2,4,6-trinitrophenol, and (*b*) 2,4-dichlorophenol from benzene.

▮ (*a*) Even though the NO$_2$'s are in the *o,o,p* positions where OH directs electrophilic substitution, phenol cannot be nitrated because the ring is susceptible to oxidative ring cleavage by nitric acid. Instead, we take advantage of a nucleophilic addition-elimination.

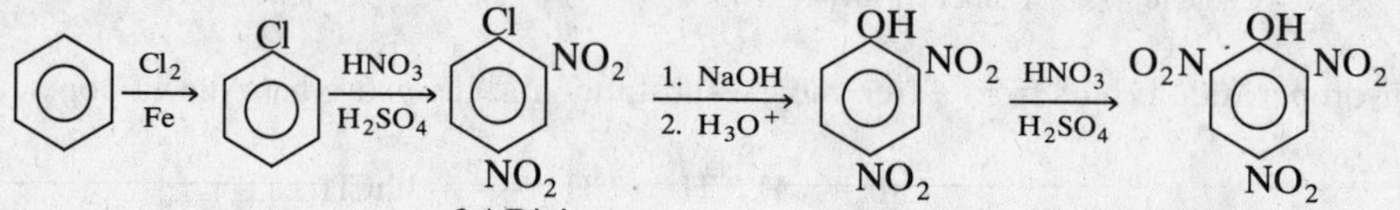

2,4-Dinitro-chlorobenzene 　 2,4-Dinitro-phenol 　 Picric acid

PhCl cannot be trinitrated because the Cl and two NO$_2$'s deactivate the ring toward further electrophilic substitution. 2,4-Dinitrophenol can be nitrated because the two deactivating NO$_2$'s prevent ring oxidation. (*b*) Phenol cannot be chlorinated because the ring is susceptible to oxidation by Cl$_2$. Again, nucleophilic addition-elimination is used.

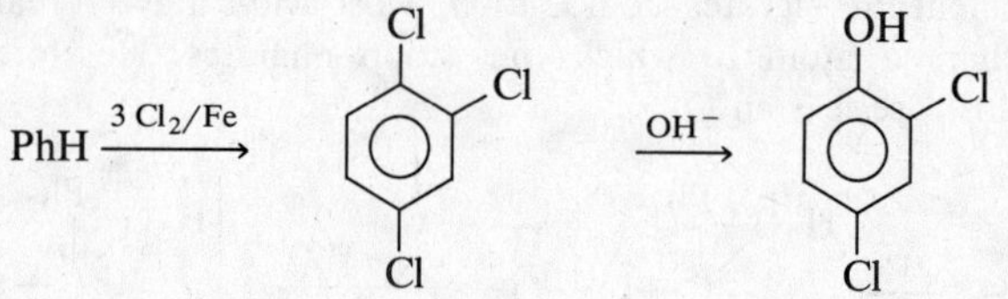

1,2,4-Trichlorobenzene 　 2,4-Dichlorophenol

The displaced Cl is *ortho* to one other Cl and *para* to the other and is activated by both. Each of the other Cl's is *meta* to at least one deactivating Cl.

20.22 The reagent for converting mesitylene (1,3,5-trimethylbenzene) into mesitol (2,4,6-trimethylphenol) is BF$_3$ dissolved in trifluoroperoxy acetic acid, F$_3$CCO$_3$H. Suggest a mechanism for this reaction.

▮ BF$_3$ catalyzes the formation of the incipient electrophile, OH$^+$. The reaction is an aromatic electrophilic substitution of a ring activated by three Me's.

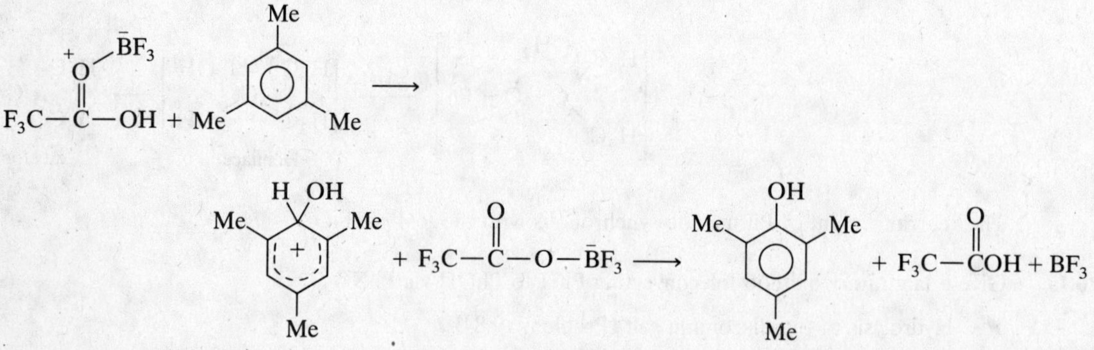

20.23 Which disubstituted benzene compound can be used to synthesize 7-methyl-1-naphthol in one step?

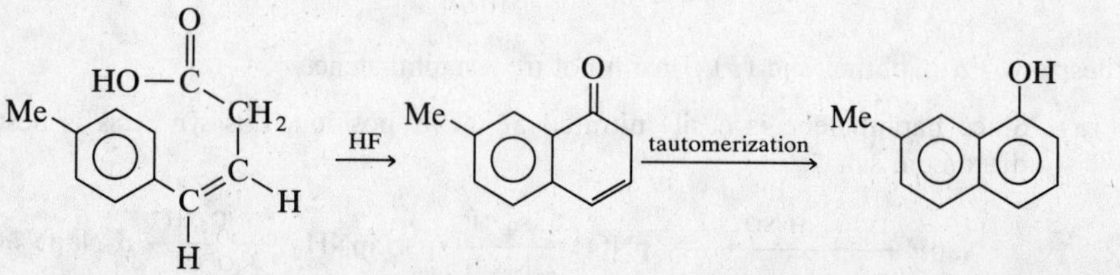

cis-4-(*p*-Tolyl)-3-butenoic acid 　 keto form 　 7-Methyl-1-naphthol

The β,γ-unsaturated ketone formed on cyclization tautomerizes instantly to the more stable naphthol. Note that only the *cis* and not the *trans*-3-butenoic acid can ring-close.

20.24 (*a*) Give a method for converting α-naphthylamine to α-naphthol other than by diazotization. (*b*) List the reagents for going the other way.

▰ (*a*) Heat α-naphthylamine with aq. $NaHSO_3$. This is an example of the *Bücherer reaction*. (*b*) The amine is prepared from the phenol by a reaction with aq. NH_3 and $(NH_4)_2SO_3$.

CHEMICAL PROPERTIES

1. Acidity

20.25 Use chemical equations to compare the reactions of EtOH, a typical alcohol, and PhOH with dilute NaOH. Name the product from PhOH.

▰
$$EtOH + Na^+OH^- \xrightarrow{\quad\times\quad} \text{no reaction}$$
$$\underset{\text{acid 1}}{PhOH} + \underset{\text{base}_2}{Na^+OH^-} \longrightarrow \underset{\underset{\text{sodium phenoxide}}{\text{base}_1}}{PhO^-Na^+} + \underset{\text{acid}_2}{H_2O}$$

20.26 Explain why PhOH ($pK_a = 10$) is much more acidic than EtOH ($pK_a = 18$).

▰ The $-$ charge on the alkoxide anion, RO^-, is completely localized, but the $-$ charge on PhO^- is delocalized by extended π bonding to the *ortho* and *para* ring positions as indicated by the starred sites in the resonance hybrid.

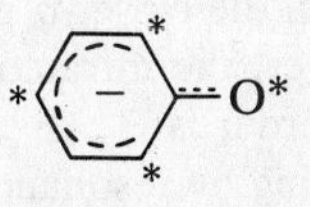

PhO^- is therefore a weaker base than EtO^- (RO^-), and PhOH (ArOH) is a stronger acid than ROH.

20.27 Use chemical equations to compare the reactions of RCOOH ($pK_a = 5$) and PhOH ($pK_a = 10$) with aqueous (*a*) $NaHCO_3$ and (*b*) Na_2CO_3 (pK_a's of H_2CO_3 and HCO_3^- are 6.4 and 10.3, respectively).

▰ The equilibria of Brönsted acid-base reactions favor the side with the weaker acid and base. In each case, write the ionic equation as if it occurs and place the pK_a values under each acid. If the weaker acid is on the right side, the reaction occurs but if the weaker acid is on the left side, the reverse reaction occurs.

(*a*)
$$\underset{pK_a=5}{RCOOH} + HCO_3^- \longrightarrow RCOO^- + \underset{pK_a=6.4\text{ (weaker acid)}}{H_2CO_3\,(H_2O+CO_2)} \qquad \text{This reaction occurs.}$$
$$\underset{pK_a=10}{PhOH} + HCO_3^- \xrightarrow{\quad\times\quad} PhO^- + \underset{pK_a=6.4\text{ (stronger acid)}}{H_2CO_3\,(H_2O+CO_2)} \qquad \text{No forward reaction.}$$

(*b*)
$$\underset{pK_a=5}{RCOOH} + CO_3^{2-} \longrightarrow RCOO^- + \underset{pK_a=10.3\text{ (weaker acid)}}{HCO_3^-} \qquad \text{This reaction occurs.}$$
$$\underset{pK_a=10}{PhOH} + CO_3^{2-} \rightleftharpoons PhO^- + \underset{pK_a=10.3\text{ (weaker acid)}}{HCO_3^-}$$

The last reaction above occurs. However, the result is borderline and any substituted phenol that has $pK_a > 10.5$ may not react.

20.28 Use ionic chemical equations to compare the reactions of $RCOO^-Na^+$ and ArO^-Na^+ with CO_2.

▰
$$RCOO^- + \underbrace{CO_2 + H_2O}_{pK_a=6.4} \xrightarrow{\quad\times\quad} \underset{\substack{pK_a=5 \\ \text{(stronger acid)}}}{RCOOH} + HCO_3^- \qquad \text{No forward reaction}$$
$$ArO^- + \underbrace{CO_2 + H_2O}_{pK_a=6.4} \longrightarrow \underset{\substack{pK_a=10 \\ \text{(weaker acid)}}}{ArOH} + HCO_3^- \qquad \text{This reaction occurs.}$$

20.29 (*a*) How do electron-attracting and electron-donating substituents affect the acidity of phenols? (*b*) List common substituents of each type.

▰ (*a*) Electron-attracting substituents disperse negative charges, making ArO^- a weaker base and the phenol a stronger acid. Electron-donating substituents concentrate negative charges, making ArO^- a stronger base and the phenol a weaker acid.

(*b*)

Electron-Attracting (EA)

$(NO_2, CN, C{=}O, COOH(R), X, SO_2R, R_3N^+)$

Electron-Donating (ED)

(Alkyl, OR, NR_2)

more acidic   charge dispersed; less basic   less acidic   charge concentrated; more basic

20.30 Place the following groups of compounds in decreasing order of acidity and justify your answers.   (*a*) Phenol (**A**), *o*-nitrophenol (**B**), *m*-nitrophenol (**C**), *p*-nitrophenol (**D**);   (*b*) phenol (**A**), *o*-chlorophenol (**E**), *m*-chlorophenol (**F**), *p*-chlorophenol (**G**); and   (*c*) (**A**), *o*-cresol (**H**), *m*-cresol (**I**), *p*-cresol (**J**).

▰ (*a*) NO_2 is electron-withdrawing and acid-strengthening by both induction and resonance. Its resonance effect is effective from only the *ortho* and *para* positions to about an equal extent. It predominates over the inductive effect which operates from all positions but at decreasing effectiveness with increasing separation of NO_2 and OH. Hence, all the nitrophenols are more acidic than phenol with *m*-nitrophenol being the weakest of the three. Since the inductive effect from the closer *o* position is the strongest, one might expect *o*-nitrophenol to be stronger than *p*-nitrophenol. However, the intramolecular H-bond in *o*-nitrophenol must be broken and this requires some energy. The decreasing order is **D > B > C > A**.

(*b*) Although Cl is electron-donating by resonance, its electron-withdrawing inductive effect that decreases with increasing separation of Cl and OH predominates, making all the chlorophenols more acidic than phenol. The decreasing order is **E > F > G > A**.

(*c*) Me is electron-donating inductively from all positions and hyperconjugatively from the *ortho* and *para* positions. The three isomers are weaker acids than phenol. *m*-Cresol is the strongest because its acidity is not weakened by hyperconjugation. The decreasing order is **A > I > H = J**.

20.31 Compare the acidities of (*a*) *p*-chlorophenol and *p*-nitrophenol, (*b*) 2,4-dinitrophenol and 2,4,6-trinitrophenol, and (*c*) *o*-aminophenol and *m*-aminophenol.

▰ (*a*) *p*-Nitrophenol is stronger because

with a + charge on N has a greater electron-withdrawing inductive effect than has Cl. Even more significantly it has an effective electron-withdrawing resonance effect.   (*b*) 2,4,6-Trinitrophenol (picric acid), a moderate acid, is more acidic because it has one more properly situated NO_2.   (*c*) In the *ortho* and *para* positions, NH_2 is electron-donating by resonance and is acid-weakening. In the *meta* position it is electron-withdrawing and acid-strengthening by induction. *m*-Aminophenol is the stronger acid.

20.32 Explain why a substituent such as NO_2 bonded *ortho* or *para* has a much greater effect on the acidity of a phenol than a benzoic acid.

▰ Charge delocalization in the nitrophenolate ion is much more effective because of the direct interaction between O^- and NO_2, which interaction is not possible in the *p*-nitrobenzoate anion.

direct extended π bonding   no direct extended π bonding

2. OH(OR) and Ring Reactions

20.33 What is the main experimental difference in the application of the Williamson synthesis for formation of alkyl (ROR′) and aryl ethers (ArOR)?

▰ Recall that the Williamson synthesis is an S_N2-type reaction of an alkoxide or phenoxide ion with an alkyl halide or sulfonate. The alkoxide is prepared from ROH with a very strong base, such as $NaNH_2$ or an active metal such as Na. Since phenols are much more acidic than alcohols, phenoxides are made by adding NaOH to the phenol.

$$ArOH \xrightarrow{NaOH} ArO^- \xrightarrow{RCl} ArOR \qquad ROH \xrightarrow{NaOH} \text{no reaction}$$

20.34 Give the structural formula and name of the principal organic product (if any) from the reaction of *p*-cresol with: (*a*) hot conc. HCl, (*b*) Me_2SO_4, aq. NaOH, (*c*) benzyl chloride, aq. NaOH, (*d*) PhCl, aq. NaOH, (*e*) CH_3COOH, H_2SO_4, (*f*) benzoyl chloride, NaOH, (*g*) acetic anhydride, (*h*) phthalic anhydride, (*i*) $PhSO_2Cl$ (benzenesulfonyl chloride), (*j*) SO_2Cl and (*k*) 2,4-dinitrochlorbenzene, aq. NaOH.

▰ Phenols are esterified and undergo Williamson syntheses like alcohols.

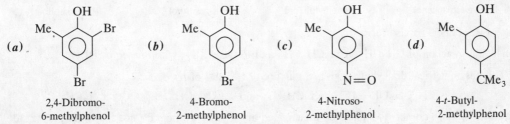

(*a*) No reaction.　(*b*) *p*-Methylanisole　(*c*) Benzyl *p*-tolyl ether

(*d*) No reaction. Unless activated, aryl halides are inert toward nucleophilic displacements.

(*e*), (*g*) *p*-Tolyl acetate　(*f*) *p*-Tolyl benzoate　(*h*) *p*-Tolyl hydrogenphthalate

(*i*) *p*-Tolyl benzenesulfonate　(*j*) No reaction.　(*k*) 2,4-Dinitrophenyl *p*-tolyl ether

20.35 Give the products for the reactions in Problem 20.34 of hexanol that are different from those of a phenol.

▰ $CH_3(CH_2)_5Cl$ is produced in (*a*) and (*j*). In (*b*), (*c*), and (*k*) a stronger base is needed to form RO^-.

20.36 Give structures and names of the principal organic product of the reaction of *o*-cresol with (*a*) Br_2/H_2O, (*b*) Br_2/CS_2, (*c*) $NaNO_2$, dilute H_2SO_4, and (*d*) $Me_2C=CH_2$, H_2SO_4.

▰ (*a*) All positions *para* and *ortho* to OH are substituted.　(*b*) Only *para* substitution occurs. (*c*) Nitrosation, a reaction that requires a very activated ring, occurs.　(*d*) Friedel-Crafts alkylation. The required structures and names follow.

(*a*) 2,4-Dibromo-6-methylphenol　(*b*) 4-Bromo-2-methylphenol　(*c*) 4-Nitroso-2-methylphenol　(*d*) 4-*t*-Butyl-2-methylphenol

20.37 (*a*) Given the molecular formula $C_6H_6SO_4$, find its isomeric products formed when phenol is treated with sulfuric acid at high (100 °C) and low (15 °C) temperatures. (*b*) Explain the isomerization of the low to the high temperature isomer.

◢ (*a*) o-$HOC_6H_4SO_3H$ is formed at low temperatures, and the *para*-isomer at high temperatures.
(*b*) Sulfonation is reversible. At higher temperatures the rate-controlled *ortho* product reverts to phenol which then reacts to give the thermodynamically controlled *para* product.

20.38 (*a*) Use resonance structures to explain why $-O^-$ is more activating than $-OH$ towards aromatic electrophilic substitution. (*b*) Account for the difference in behavior of o-cresol with Br_2/H_2O and Br_2/CS_2 (Problem 20.36).

◢ (*a*) When an electrophile, E^+, attacks PhO^-, a fairly stable uncharged intermediate is formed. When PhOH is attacked, a less stable, positively-charged intermediate is formed. The $\Delta H^{\ddagger}$ for the reaction of PhO^- is less than the $\Delta H^{\ddagger}$ for the reaction of PhOH, and PhO^- reacts at a much faster rate.

Phenol   oxonium ions   phenoxide ion   fairly stable uncharged, unsaturated ketones

(*b*) PhOH ionizes in water to give some PhO^- which is the reacting species, and complete bromination occurs. The less reactive PhOH does not ionize in nonpolar CS_2 and it monobrominates only.

20.39 Give the products of the reaction of PhOH with (*a*) H_2/Ni, 200 °C, 20 atm, (*b*) $(KSO_3)_2NO$ (*Fremy's salt*), and (*c*) Zn, heat (very poor yield).

◢ (*a*) Cyclohexanol, (*b*) p-quinone, $O{=}\!\!\!\!\!\bigcirc\!\!\!\!\!{=}O$, and (*c*) PhH.

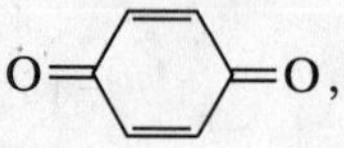

20.40 Give the products of the reaction of benzenediazonium chloride with (*a*) o-cresol, (*b*) p-cresol, (*c*) α-naphthol, and (*d*) β-naphthol.

◢ Phenolic rings are sufficiently activated to undergo electrophilic substitution by diazonium ions, ArN_2^+.

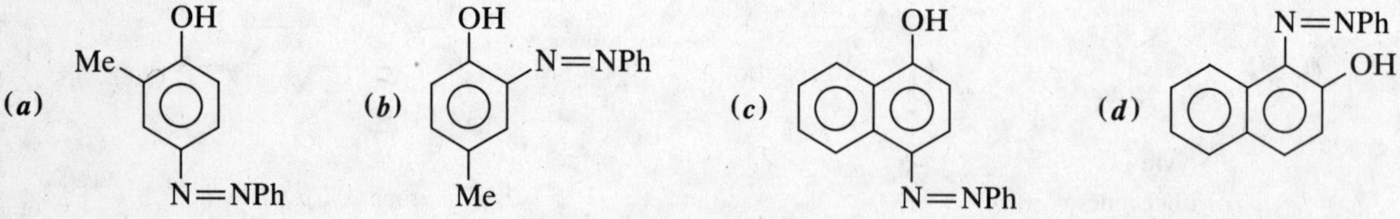

20.41 Give the structures and names of the products formed on reduction of the products in Problem 20.40 with Zn, HCl.

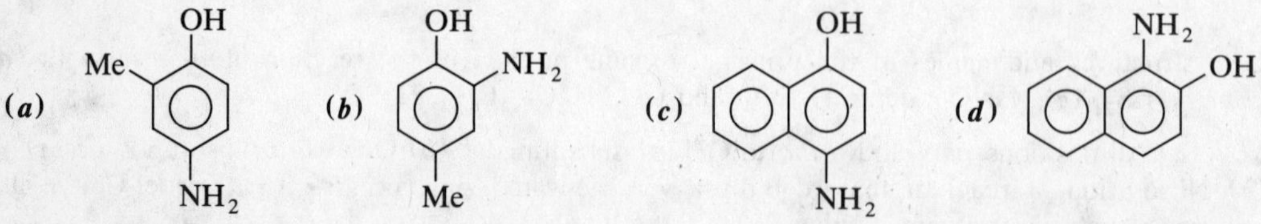

(*a*) 4-Amino-2-methylphenol   (*b*) 2-Amino-4-methylphenol   (*c*) 4-Amino-1-naphthol   (*d*) 1-Amino-2-naphthol

In each case, $PhNH_2$ is also formed.

20.42 Compare the reaction of $CH_3CH_2OCH_2CH_2CH_3$ and $PhOCH_2CH_3$ with one eq of HI.

◢ The unsymmetrical dialkyl ether gives a mixture of two sets of products:

$$CH_3CH_2OH + ICH_2CH_2CH_3 \quad\text{and}\quad CH_3CH_2I + HOCH_2CH_2CH_3$$

Since S_N2 reactions do not take place on unactivated aryl C's, aryl ethers do not cleave on the Ar side, only on the alkyl side. The products are PhOH and ICH_2CH_3.

20.43 Phenyl acetate reacts (*Fries rearrangement*) with $AlCl_3$ in an inert solvent to give two phenolic isomers, each of which reacts with H_2NOH. (*a*) Give the structures and names of the products. (*b*) Suggest a method for separating them.

▮ (*a*) Reaction with H_2NOH indicates the presence of a $-\overset{\overset{\displaystyle O}{\|}}{C}-$, in all likelihood, $-\overset{\overset{\displaystyle O}{\|}}{C}-CH_3$. Since the —O attached to the ring is an *o, p* director, this group is bonded either *ortho* or *para* to OH.

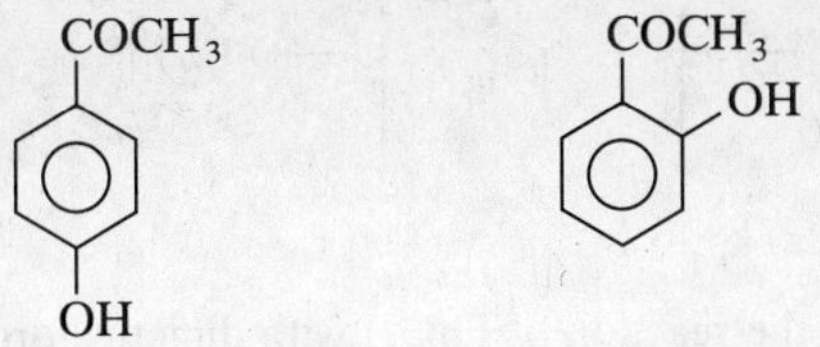

p-Hydroxyacetophenone *o*-Hydroxyacetophenone

(*b*) *o*-Hydroxyacetophenone forms a chelate and is removed from the reaction mixture by steam distillation (Problem 20.14).

20.44 (*a*) Referring to Problem 20.43, account for the fact that (i) the *para* isomer is the exclusive product at 25 °C but at 165 °C the *ortho* isomer predominates and (ii) *m*-nitrophenyl acetate does not rearrange. (*b*) Assign a role to $AlCl_3$.

▮ (*a*) (i) This is a matter of rate-controlled product (*p*-hydroxyacetophenone) and thermodynamically-controlled product (*o*-hydroxyacetophenone). It also means that the acylation is reversible. (ii) NO_2 deactivates the ring toward acylation.

(*b*) $AlCl_3$ complexes with the phenoxy O generating an incipient electrophilic acyl group:

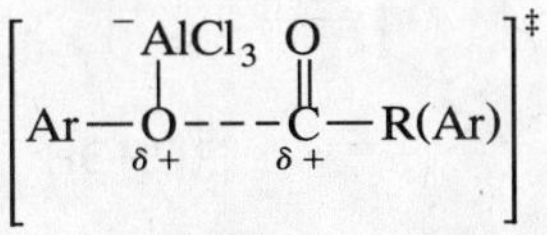

20.45 (*a*) Give the structures of the products resulting from the reaction of PhO^-Na^+ and CO_2 at 6 atm and 125 °C followed by addition of aq. acid. (*b*) Medically, why is this *Kolbe reaction* one of the most important organic syntheses? (*c*) Suggest a mechanism for this reaction.

▮ (*a*) $PhO^-Na^+ + O{=}C{=}O \xrightarrow[6\text{ atm}]{125\,°C} o\text{-}HOC_6H_4COO^-Na^+ \xrightarrow{H^+} o\text{-}HOC_6H_4COOH$

Sodium salicylate Salicylic acid

(*b*) Acetylation of salicylic acid with acetic anhydride gives aspirin, acetylsalicylic acid, the most consumed and one of the most beneficial drugs.

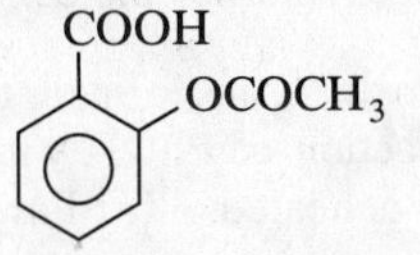

Aspirin

(*c*) CO_2 is a weak electrophile. Nevertheless, it is able to substitute on the strongly activated ring of PhO^- because there is some + charge on C.

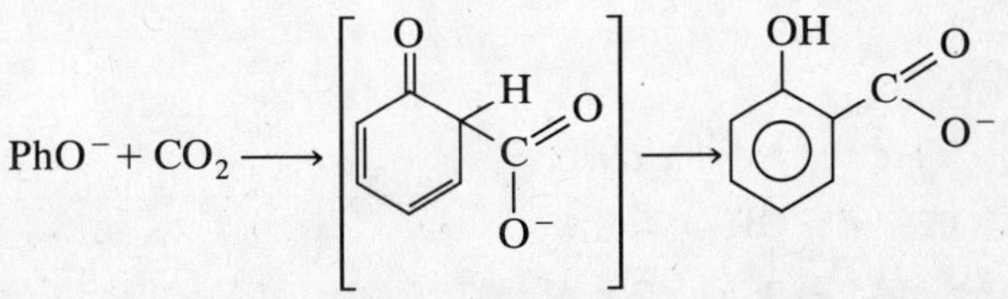

intermediate Salicylate anion

20.46 (*a*) Give the product from the reaction of PhOH with $HCCl_3$ in NaOH followed by acidification. (*b*) Suggest a mechanism for this reaction.

▮ (a) Salicylaldchydc, o-HOC$_6$H$_4$CH=O. (b) This *Reimer–Tiemann reaction* is an electrophilic substitution on PhO$^-$. The electrophile is dichlorcarbene which contains a C with only six e$^-$'s.

$$HCCl_3 \xrightarrow[-H^+]{OH^-} \ ^-:CCl_3 \longrightarrow Cl^- + \ :CCl_2$$

Dichlorocarbene

(b)

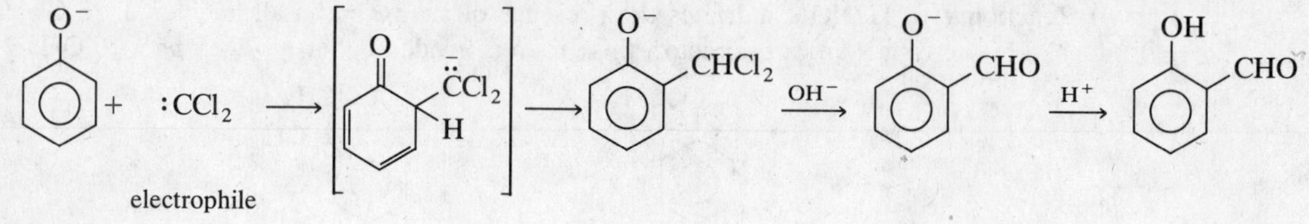

electrophile

20.47 (a) Give the product from the reaction of PhOH with dimethylformamide (HCONMe$_2$) and O=PCl$_3$ followed by addition of water. (b) Suggest a mechanism for this reaction.

▮ (a) Mainly *p*-hydroxybenzaldehyde. (b) The formylation, or *Vilsmeier reaction*, is another example of an electrophilic substitution on a highly activated ring such as PhOH. See Problem 19.108 for a possible mechanism.

20.48 (a) Give the products from the reactions of PhOH with an aldehyde RCHO, in (i) OH$^-$ followed by H$^+$ and (ii) H$_3$O$^+$. (b) In each case indicate the pathway. (c) Give the product from the acid reaction of RCHO with 2 eq of PhOH. Explain its formation.

▮ (a) The same product, *p*-HOC$_6$H$_4$CHROH (**A**) is obtained in both reactions. In (i) PhO$^-$ is the active substrate, in (ii) it is PhOH.

(b) (i)

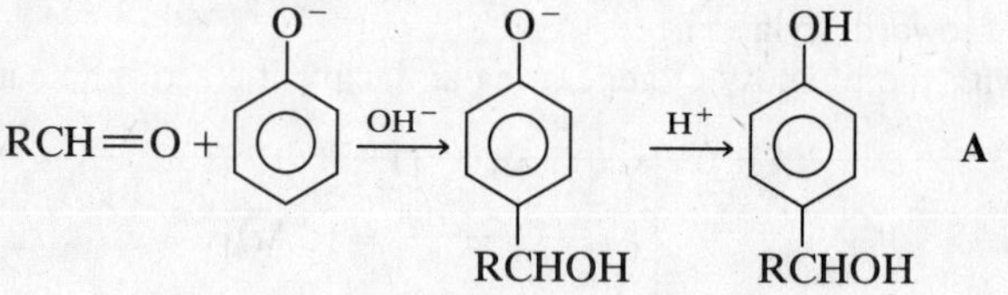

(ii) $RCH=O \xrightarrow{H^+} \left[RCH=\overset{+}{O}H \longleftrightarrow R\overset{+}{C}H-OH \right] \xrightarrow[-H^+]{PhOH} \textbf{A}$

(c)

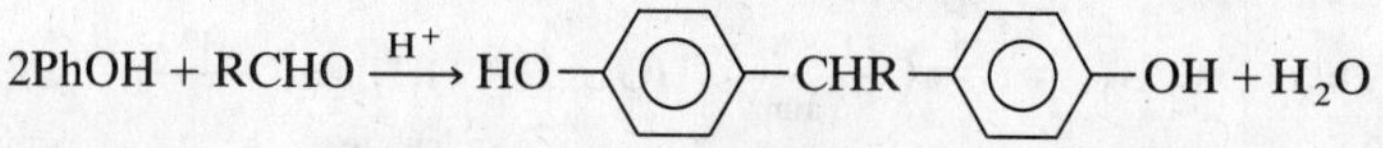

a diarylmethane

The first formed product **A** is converted by H$^+$ to a benzyl carbocation, *p*-HOC$_6$H$_4$CHR$^+$, that acts as an electrophile to attack another molecule of PhOH.

20.49 Bakelite is a phenol-formaldehyde resin formed from the base-catalyzed reaction of PhOH and H$_2$C=O. (a) Give the product of the reaction of PhOH with 2 eq of H$_2$C=O. (b) Give the structure of the dimers formed when the product in (a) is heated. (c) Further heating (*curing*) increases polymerization. Show the *mer* in the final cured resin.

▮ (a)

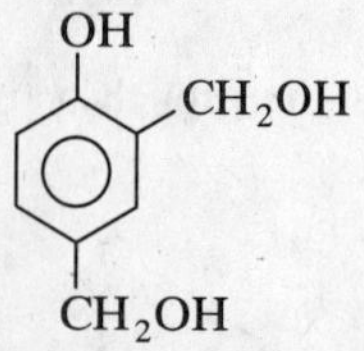

(b) There are two possible dimers:

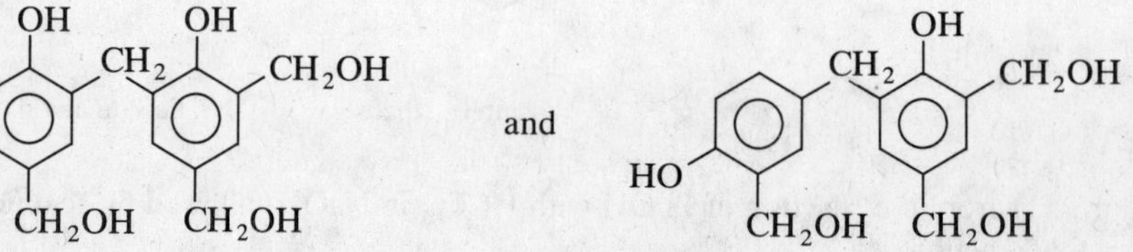

and

(c) 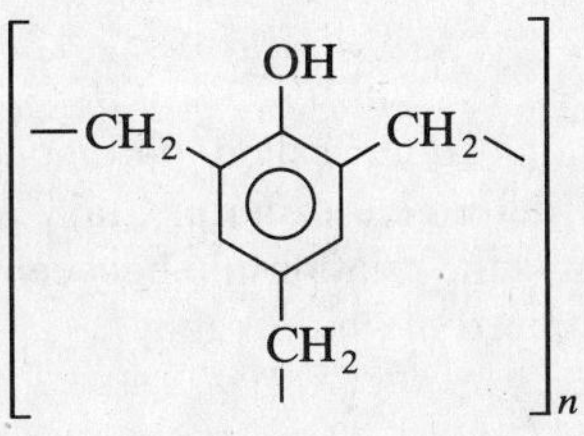 $\left[-CH_2 \underset{}{\overset{OH}{\bigcirc}} CH_2 - \right]_n$

20.50 Explain the formation of two products, one of which is a phenol, from the reaction of PhO^- with an active alkyl halide such as $H_2C=CHCH_2Cl$. ($PhCH_2Cl$ has a similar reaction.)

❚ PhO^- is actually an ambident anion with a $-$ charge on O and on the o,p-ring positions (Problem 20.26). Attack by O^- gives the ether $PhOCH_2CH=CH_2$ and attack by the *ortho* carbanion gives *o*-allylphenol, o-$HOC_6H_4CH_2CH=CH_2$. Much more *ortho* than *para* isomer is isolated.

20.51 Predict the product of the Claisen rearrangement of (a) allyl phenyl ether and (b) 2,6-dimethylphenyl allyl ether.

❚ The allyl group migrates from O to the ring, preferably *ortho* but *para* if the *ortho* positions are blocked.

(a) [structure: phenol with OH and $CH_2CH=CH_2$ at ortho position]

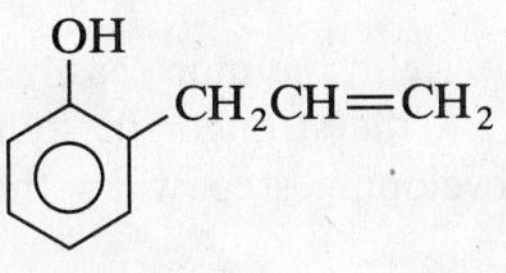

(b) [structure: phenol with OH, two CH_3 groups at 2,6 positions, and $CH_2CH=CH_2$ at para position]

o-Allylphenol   4-Allyl-2,6-dimethylphenol

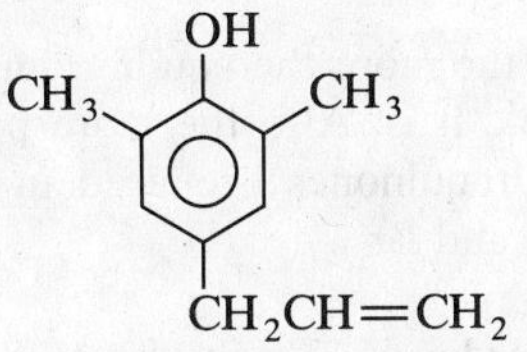

20.52 (a) Give the radioisomers obtained when the ethers in Problem 20.51 are labeled with ^{14}C, indicated as **C**, at the terminal $=CH_2$ group. (b) Explain the significance of these results as related to the mechanism of the Claisen rearrangement.

❚ (a) [structure A: phenol with OH and $CH_2CH=CH_2$ at ortho] and [structure B: phenol with OH, two CH_3 at 2,6 and $CH_2CH=CH_2$ at para]

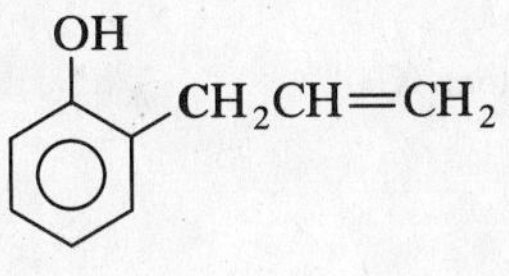

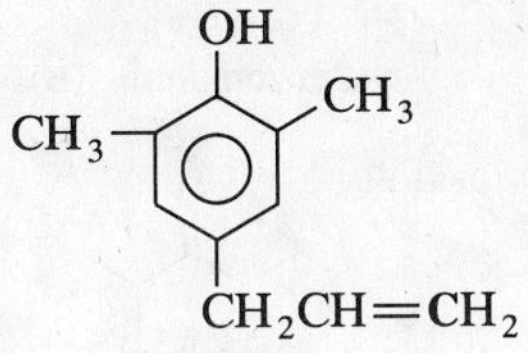

A   **B**

(b) These are concerted intramolecular rearrangements. The terminal C of the allyl group begins to bond to the ring as the O—C bond breaks giving the intermediate which rearomatizes. When the *ortho* position is blocked, the ring cannot aromatize and the allyl group then migrates from the *ortho* to the *para* position. Again the terminal C, now unlabeled in this intermediate, becomes bonded to the ring leaving the ^{14}C (**C**) in its original terminal position.

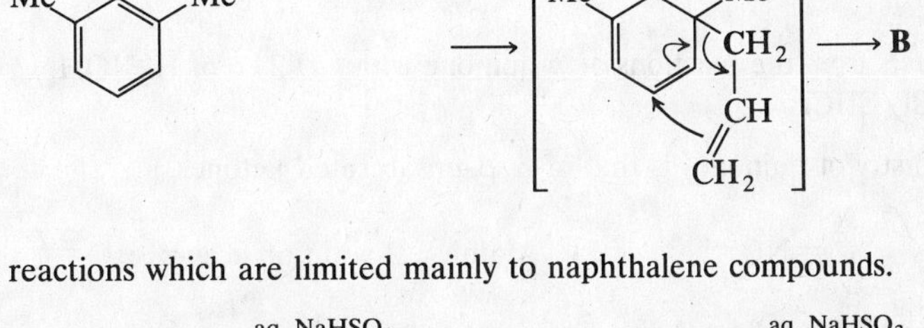

[structure: $O-\overset{\alpha}{C}H_2-\overset{\beta}{C}H=\overset{\gamma}{C}H_2$ on 2,6-dimethylphenyl ring (Me, Me)] $\longrightarrow$ [bracketed intermediate structure with O, Me, Me, CH_2, CH, CH_2] $\longrightarrow$ **B**

20.53 Complete the following reactions which are limited mainly to naphthalene compounds.

(a) α-Naphthol $\xrightarrow[NH_3]{\text{aq. NaHSO}_3}$?   (b) β-Naphthol $\xrightarrow[MeNH_2]{\text{aq. NaHSO}_3}$?

❚ These reactions are reversal of the Bucherer reaction (Problem 20.24).

(a) α-Naphthylamine   (b) N-Methyl-β-naphthylamine

3. Quinones

20.54 (*a*) Write the ionic equation for the reduction of *p*-benzoquinone (often called *p*-quinone) to hydroquinone. (*b*) The rapid reversibility of this reaction makes it possible to determine experimentally a standard electrode reduction potential, $E°$, for every quinone. Define $E°$. (*c*) What is the relationship between $E°$ and the stability of the quinone? (*d*) How is the reverse of the reaction in (*a*) utilized in photography?

(*a*)

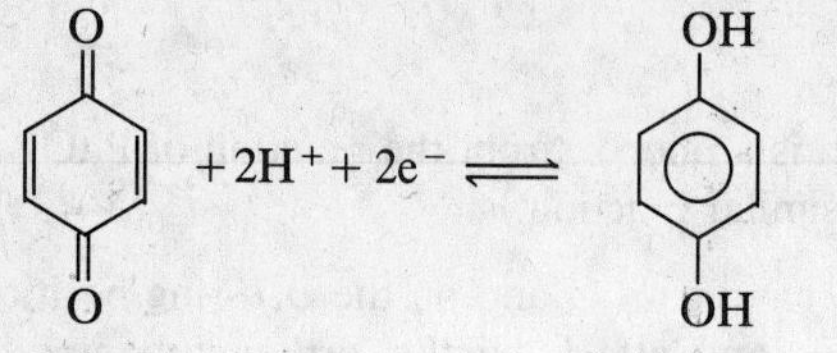

$$+2H^+ + 2e^- \rightleftharpoons$$

p-Quinone   Hydroquinone

This type of equilibrium is involved in several biochemical redox systems.

(*b*) $E°$ is the *voltage* of an electrochemical cell in which one compartment contains a 1-M solution of *p*-quinone, and the other an aqueous ethanolic solution of 1-M H^+, with a strip of platinum immersed in each solution as electrodes.

(*c*) The more positive the $E°$, the more the equilibrium shifts to the right, the more easily the quinone is reduced, and the less stable it is. Also the more positive the $E°$, the stronger the quinone is as an oxidizing agent. (*d*) Hydroquinones are used in the film-developing step when they reduce the light-activated AgBr to Ag and Br^-.

20.55 Rationalize the following decreasing order of $E°$ values: (*a*) **A** > **B** > **C**. (*b*) **D** > **E**

(*a*)

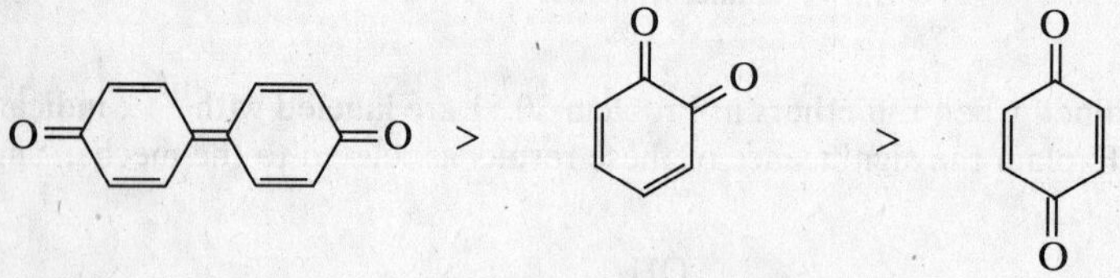

Diphenoquinone (**A**)   *o*-Benzoquinone (**B**)   *p*-Quinone (**C**)

(*b*)

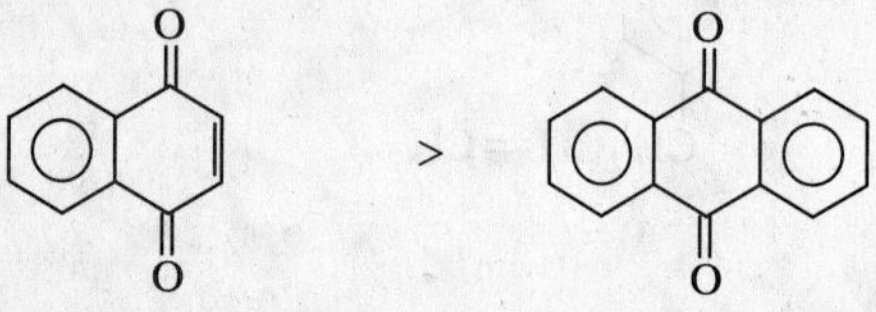

1,4-Naphthaquinone (**D**)   9,10-Anthraquinone (**E**)

(*a*) Reduction of **A** reconstitutes two aromatic rings which together have more resonance energy and stability than the conjugated diketo system of the parent quinone. Having adjacent C=O's destabilizes the *ortho* isomer relative to the *para*. Reduction of the benzoquinones only reforms a single aromatic benzene ring. (*b*) **E** has two individual benzene rings whose combined resonance energy, along with that of the two C=O's, is more than the resonance energy of the three benzene rings of the reduced product (9,10-dihydroxyanthracene) which share their delocalized π systems.

20.56 Give the products from the reactions of *p*-quinone with (*a*) 2 eq of H_2NOH, (*b*) 1 eq of MeMgI followed by H^+, (*c*) 1 eq of $HCl/CHCl_3$.

The chemistry of quinones is that of α, β-unsaturated ketones.

(*a*) HON=⟨   ⟩=NOH   (*b*) Mainly 1,2-addition occurs: O=⟨   ⟩, a quinol

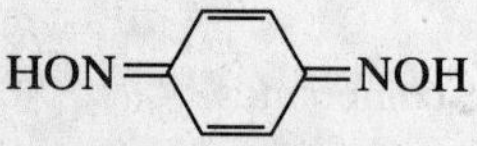

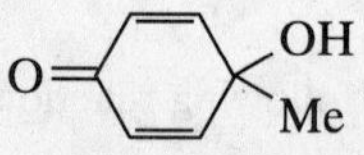

(*c*) Mostly 1,4-addition followed by tautomerization:

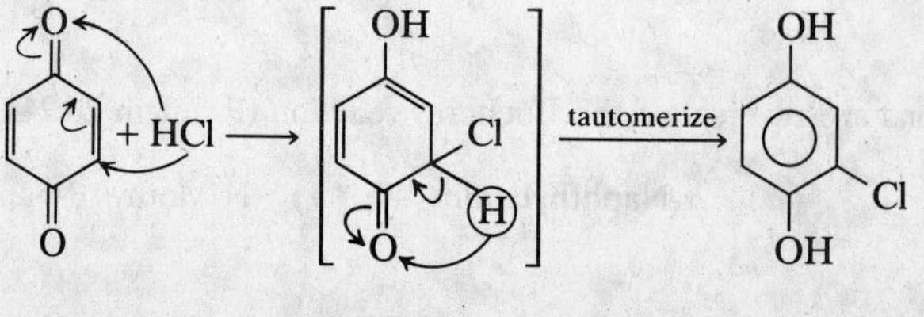

20.57 (*a*) What is (i) a quinhydrone and (ii) a semiquinone anion? (*b*) Draw a conclusion regarding electron transfer in the reduction of quinones from the detection of semiquinone anions in base.

◢ (*a*) (i) *Quinhydrone* is a green-black crystalline 1:1 charge-transfer complex of quinone, the e^- acceptor, and hydroquinone, the e^- donor.

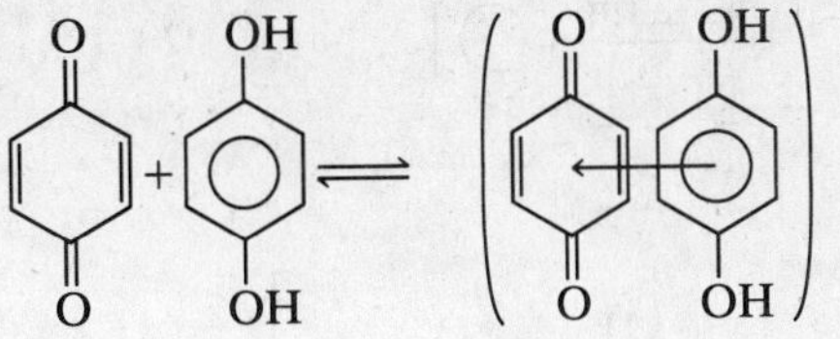

a charge-transfer complex

(ii) Alkaline solutions of quinhydrone are deeply colored and paramagnetic because of the formation of a radical anion, the *semiquinone anion*. An e^- is transferred from the dianion of the benzenediol to the quinone:

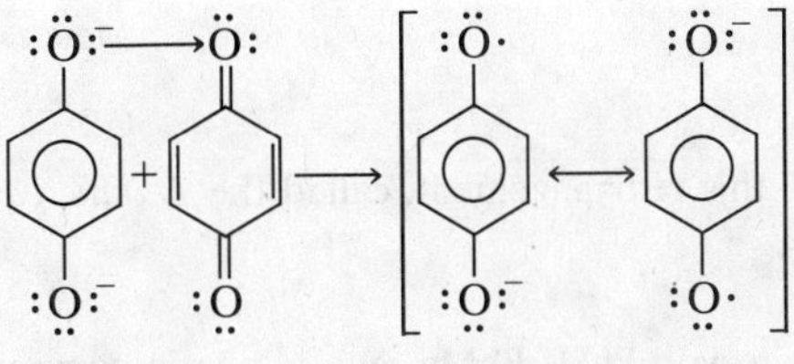

a semiquinone anion

(*b*) The two e^-'s needed to reduce the quinone are transferred singly.

20.58 (*a*) Give the product of the Diels-Alder reaction of *p*-quinone with: (i) butadiene, (ii) 1,3-cyclohexadiene, and

(iii) 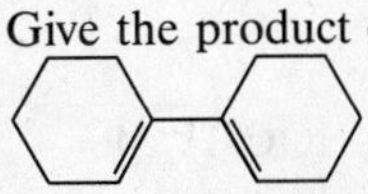 , 1,1'-bicyclohexadienyl. (*b*) Explain why 9,10-anthraquinone cannot serve as a dienophile.

◢ (*a*) In each case, the first formed product tautomerizes to the much more stable substituted hydroquinone on acidification.

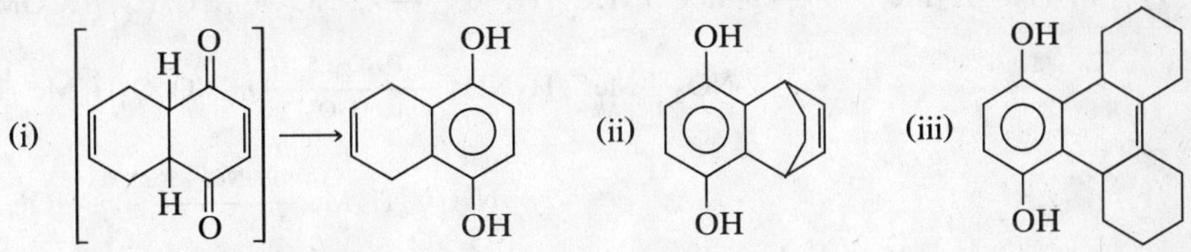

tautomers

(*b*) Were the anthraquinone to react, one of its stable benzene rings would have to lose its aromaticity—an energetically unfavorable event.

SYNTHESIS

20.59 Prepare (*a*) resorcinol and (*b*) hydroquinone from benzene.

◢ (*a*)

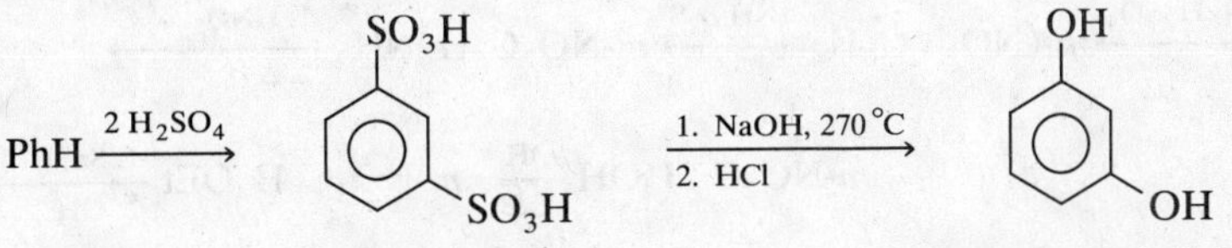

1,3-Benzenedisulfonic acid   Resorcinol

(*b*) $C_6H_6 \xrightarrow{HNO_3/H_2SO_4} C_6H_5NO_2 \xrightarrow[\text{2. NaOH}]{\text{1. Sn/HCl}} C_6H_5NH_2 \xrightarrow[H_2SO_4,\ 10\,°C]{Na_2Cr_2O_7}$

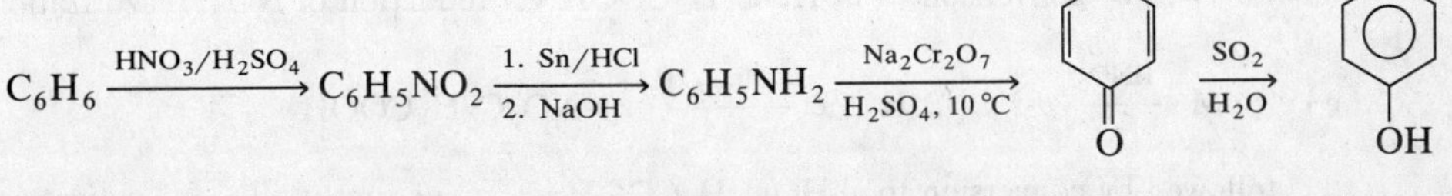

p-Quinone   Hydroquinone

20.60 Prepare catechol (**A**) from each of the following: (*a*) naturally occurring guaiacol, *o*-methoxyphenol, (*b*) *o*-dichlorobenzene, and (*c*) salicylaldehyde.

(*a*)

Guaiacol Catechol, **A**

(*b*)

o-Dichlorobenzene

(*c*)

Salicylaldehyde Monocatecholyl formate

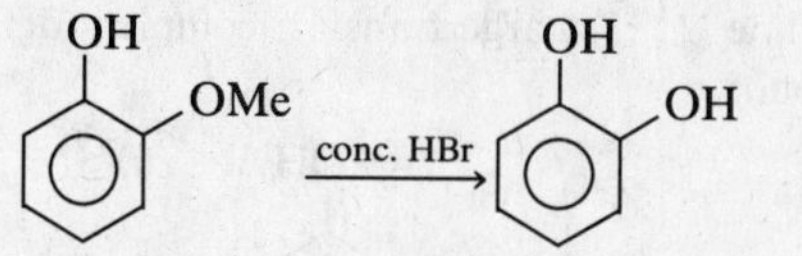

*from $H_2O_2 + OH^-$

The mechanism of this rearrangement, called the *Dakin reaction*, is reminiscent of the Baeyer-Villiger reaction (Problem 15.135).

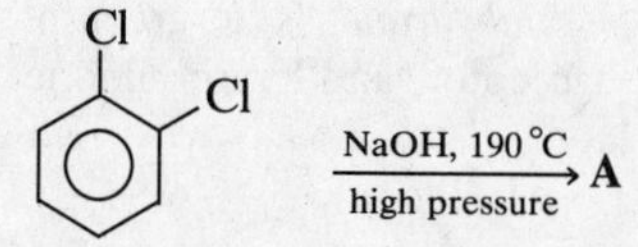

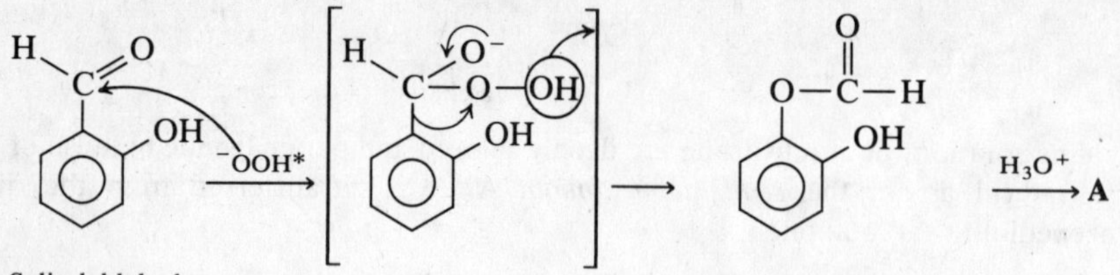

20.61 Use as starting materials PhH, PhMe, any aliphatic compounds and inorganic reagents to synthesize in good yields (*a*) *p*-cresol, (*b*) *m*-cresol, (*c*) *o*-cresol, (*d*) *p*-bromoanisole, (*e*) *m*-aminophenetole, (*f*) *m*-hydroxybenzoic acid, (*g*) *p*-hydroxybenzoic acid, (*h*) *p*-hydroxybenzaldehyde, and (*i*) *m*-hydroxybenzaldehyde. Do not repeat the synthesis of intermediate products.

(*a*) $\text{PhMe} \xrightarrow[H_2SO_4]{HNO_3} p\text{-}NO_2C_6H_4Me \xrightarrow[2.\ OH^-]{1.\ Sn,\ HCl} p\text{-}NH_2C_6H_4Me \xrightarrow[2.\ \Delta]{1.\ HNO_2,\ 5\,^\circ C} p\text{-}HOC_6H_4Me$

(*b*) $p\text{-}NH_2C_6H_4Me \xrightarrow{MeCOCl} p\text{-}MeCONHC_6H_4Me \xrightarrow{HNO_3} 2\text{-}NO_2\text{-}4\text{-}MeC_6H_3NHCOMe \xrightarrow{OH^-}$

$2\text{-}NO_2\text{-}4\text{-}MeC_6H_3NH_2 \xrightarrow[2.\ HPH_2O_2]{1.\ HNO_2,\ 5\,^\circ C} m\text{-}NO_2C_6H_4Me \xrightarrow[2.\ OH^-]{1.\ Sn,\ HCl}$

$m\text{-}NH_2C_6H_4Me \xrightarrow[2.\ \Delta]{1.\ HNO_2,\ 5\,^\circ C} m\text{-}HOC_6H_4Me$

(*c*) $\text{PhMe} \xrightarrow{H_2S_2O_7} p\text{-}HO_3SC_6H_4Me \xrightarrow{HNO_3} 4\text{-}Me\text{-}3\text{-}NO_2C_6H_3SO_3H \xrightarrow[\Delta]{H_2SO_4} o\text{-}NO_2C_6H_4Me$

Convert NO_2 to OH as in (*b*) to give $o\text{-}HOC_6H_4Me$

(*d*) $\text{PhH} \xrightarrow{H_2S_2O_7} PhSO_3H \xrightarrow[\Delta]{NaOH} PhOH \xrightarrow[Me_2SO_4]{OH^-} PhOMe \xrightarrow{Br_2} p\text{-}BrC_6H_4OMe$

(*e*) $\text{PhH} \xrightarrow{2HNO_3/H_2SO_4} m\text{-}(NO_2)_2C_6H_4 \xrightarrow{(NH_4)_2S} m\text{-}NO_2C_6H_4NH_2 \xrightarrow[2.\ \Delta]{1.\ HNO_2,\ 5\,^\circ C}$

$m\text{-}NO_2C_6H_4OH \xrightarrow[EtBr]{OH^-} m\text{-}NO_2C_6H_4OEt \xrightarrow[2.\ OH^-]{1.\ Sn,\ HCl} m\text{-}H_2NC_6H_4OEt$

(*f*) $\text{PhMe} \xrightarrow{KMnO_4/H^+} PhCOOH \xrightarrow{HNO_3/H_2SO_4} m\text{-}NO_2C_6H_4COOH$

followed by conversion to $m\text{-}HOC_6H_4COOH$ via reduction of NO_2, diazotization of NH_2, and heat.

(*g*) $\text{PhMe} \xrightarrow{HNO_3} p\text{-}NO_2C_6H_4Me \xrightarrow[\Delta]{KMnO_4/H^+} p\text{-}NO_2C_6H_4COOH$

followed by conversion to $p\text{-}HOC_6H_4COOH$ via reduction of NO_2, diazotization of NH_2, and heat.

(*h*) $C_6H_5OH + HCN \xrightarrow{HCl/ZnCl_2} p\text{-}HOC_6H_4CHO$

Prepare C_6H_5OH from PhH via nitration, reduction, diazotization and heat.

(*i*) $m\text{-}NO_2C_6H_4COOH \xrightarrow{SOCl_2} m\text{-}NO_2C_6H_4COCl \xrightarrow{LiAlH(OBu\text{-}t)_3} m\text{-}NO_2C_6H_4CHO$

20.62 Devise laboratory syntheses in good yields of the following phenols from PhH or PhMe and any aliphatic or inorganic reagents: (*a*) *m*-iodophenol, (*b*) 3-bromo-4-methylphenol, and (*c*) 2-bromo-4-methylphenol. Do not repeat a synthesis.

(*a*)

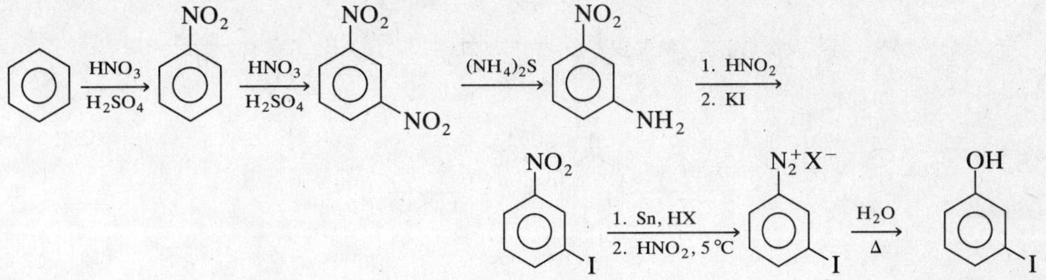

m-Iodophenol

(*b*)

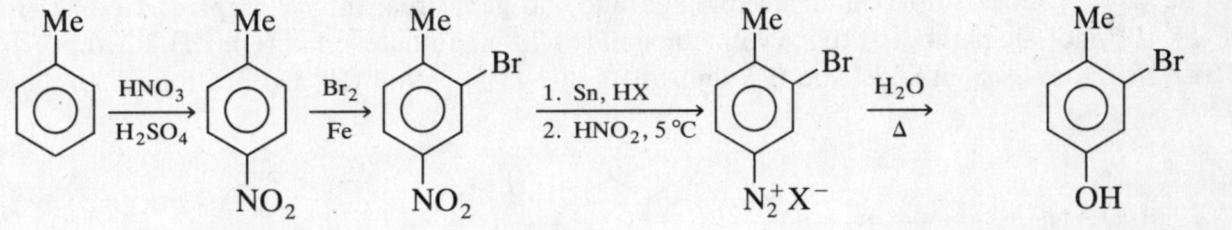

3-Bromo-4-methylphenol

(*c*)

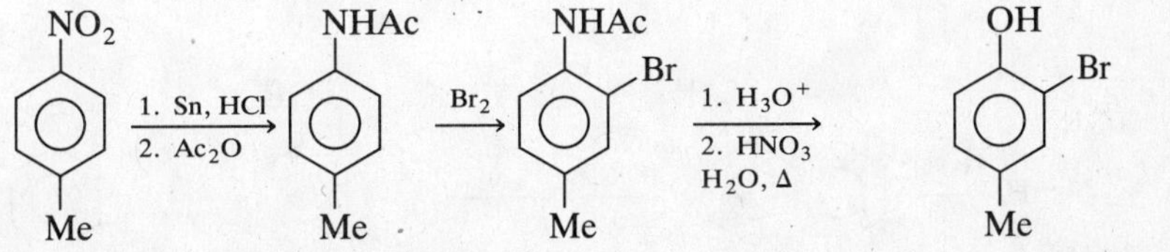

2-Bromo-4-methylphenol

20.63 Use PhOH and any aliphatic and inorganic reagent to prepare: (*a*) *o*-chloromethylphenol and (*b*) *o*-methoxy benzyl alcohol.

(*a*) $C_6H_5OH + H_2C{=}O \xrightarrow{HCl} o\text{-}HOC_6H_4CH_2Cl$

$C_6H_5OH + H_2C{=}O \xrightarrow{aq.\ OH^-} o\text{-}HOC_6H_4CH_2OH \xrightarrow{SOCl_2} o\text{-}HOC_6H_4CH_2Cl$

(*b*) From (*a*), $o\text{-}HOC_6H_4CH_2OH \xrightarrow{NaOH/Me_2SO_4} o\text{-}MeOC_6H_4CH_2OH$

Only the acidic ArOH is converted first to its conjugate base and then to the Me ether.

20.64 Synthesize (*a*) 5-bromo-2,4-dimethylphenol from *m*-xylene, (*b*) 2-hydroxy-5-methylbenzaldehyde from *p*-toluidine, (*c*) *m*-methoxyaniline from $PhSO_3H$, and (*d*) 2,4-dinitrophenyl phenyl ether from PhCl.

(*a*)

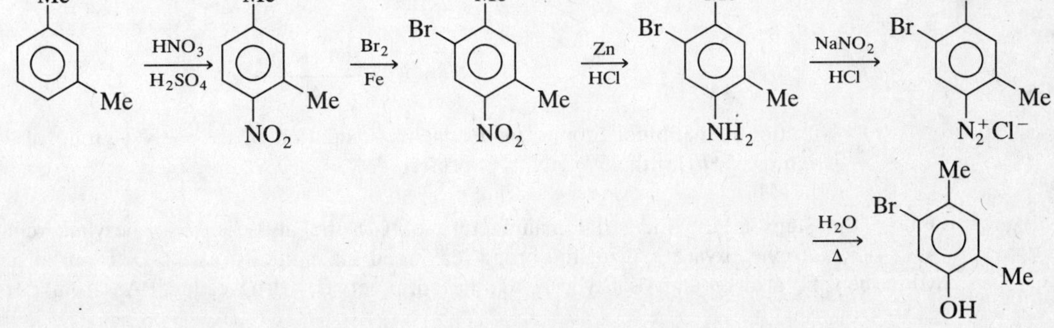

(b)

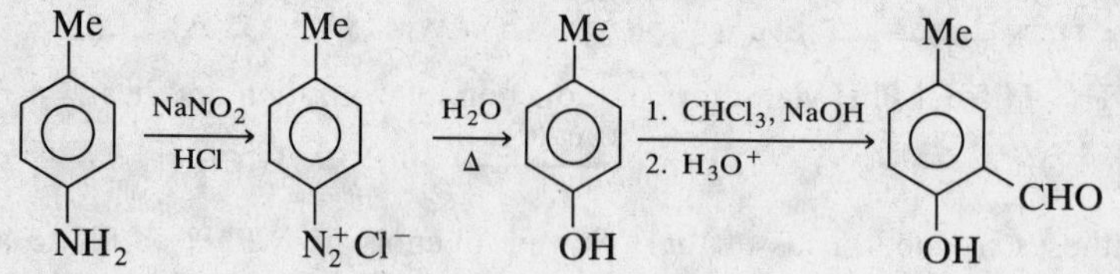

Me — NaNO₂/HCl → Me / N₂⁺Cl⁻ — H₂O, Δ → Me / OH — 1. CHCl₃, NaOH; 2. H₃O⁺ → Me / OH / CHO

(c)

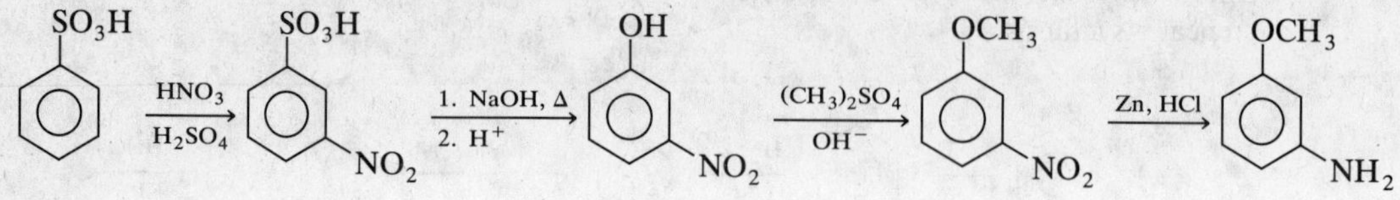

SO₃H — HNO₃/H₂SO₄ → SO₃H/NO₂ — 1. NaOH, Δ; 2. H⁺ → OH/NO₂ — (CH₃)₂SO₄/OH⁻ → OCH₃/NO₂ — Zn, HCl → OCH₃/NH₂

(d)

Cl — HNO₃/H₂SO₄ → Cl/NO₂/NO₂ — PhO⁻ / −Cl⁻ → OPh/NO₂/NO₂

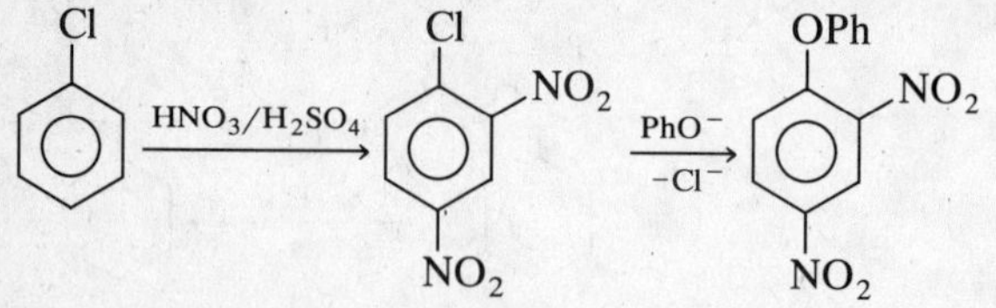

20.65 Use naphthalene (NapH) and any organic and inorganic reagent to prepare: (*a*) 4-*i*-propyl-1-naphthol (**A**), (*b*) 4-amino-1-naphthol (**B**) (use two methods), (*c*) 1,8-naphthalenediol (**C**), (*d*) 2-hydroxy-1-naphthoic acid (**D**), (*e*) 1-hydroxy-2-naphthaldehyde (**E**), and (*f*) 4-nitro-1-naphthol (**F**). Do not repeat syntheses of intermediates.

(*a*) 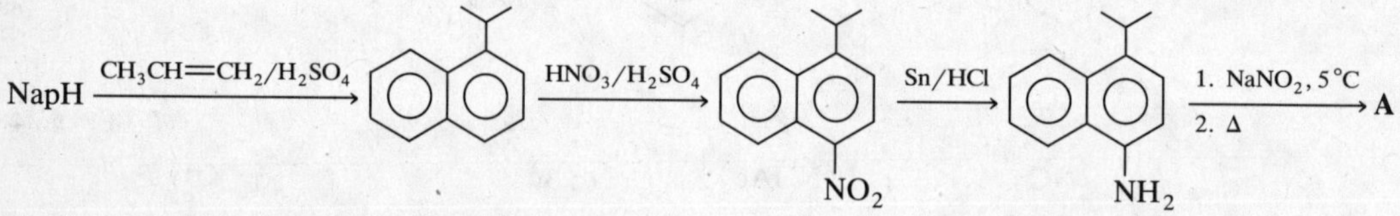 NapH — CH₃CH=CH₂/H₂SO₄ → (*i*-propyl naphthalene) — HNO₃/H₂SO₄ → (*i*-propyl-NO₂ naphthalene) — Sn/HCl → (*i*-propyl-NH₂ naphthalene) — 1. NaNO₂, 5 °C; 2. Δ → **A**

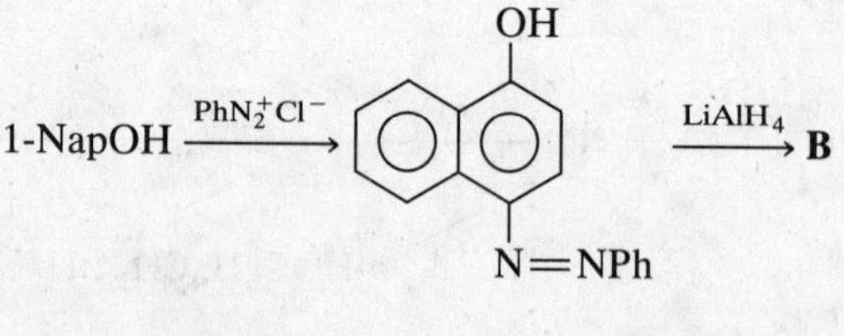

(*b*) (i) 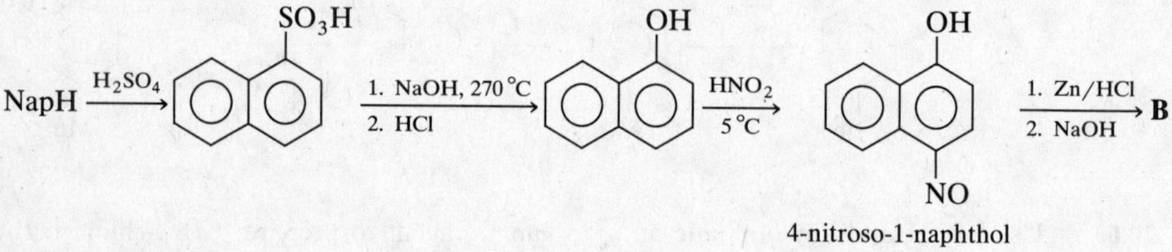 NapH — H₂SO₄ → (naphthalene-SO₃H) — 1. NaOH, 270 °C; 2. HCl → (OH naphthalene) — HNO₂, 5 °C → (OH / NO naphthalene) — 1. Zn/HCl; 2. NaOH → **B**

4-nitroso-1-naphthol

(ii) 1-NapOH — PhN₂⁺Cl⁻ → (OH / N=NPh naphthalene) — LiAlH₄ → **B**

(*c*) NapH — 2HNO₃/H₂SO₄ → (NO₂ NO₂ naphthalene) — Sn/HCl → (NH₂ NH₂ naphthalene) — 1. HNO₂, 5 °C; 2. Δ → **C**

(*d*) NapH — H₂SO₄, Δ → (naphthalene-SO₃H) — 1. NaOH, 270 °C; 2. HCl → (OH naphthalene) — 1. CO₂, 6 atm, 125 °C; 2. HCl → **D**

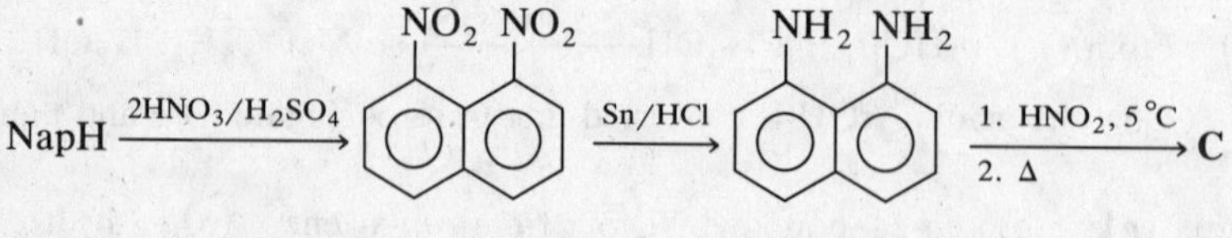

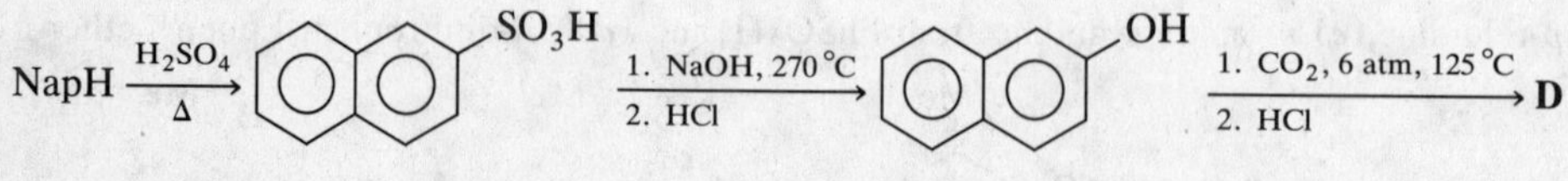

(*e*) 1-NapOH — CHCl₃, NaOH, Δ → **E**

(*f*) Nitration of naphthol produces poor yields. Oxidation of the —NO group of 4-nitroso-1-naphthol [from (i) of (*b*)] with 25% HNO₃ is preferred.

20.66 Outline the steps in the industrial manufacture of (*a*) the antiseptic, 4-*n*-hexylresorcinol from resorcinol; (*b*) 2,4-dichlorophenoxyacetic acid, the broad leaf weed killer known as 2,4-D, from benzene; (*c*) 4-amino-2-hydroxybenzoic acid (*p*-aminosalicylic acid), the antitubercular drug called PAS from nitrobenzene; (*d*) 2,4-

diaminophenol, the photographic developer, Amidol, from PhCl; (*e*) 2,6-dinitro-4-*t*-butyl-3-methylanisole (synthetic musk) from *m*-cresol; (*f*) 5-methyl-resorcinol (orcinol, constituent in litmus dyes) from *p*-toluidine; (*g*) methyl salicylate (oil of wintergreen) from PhOH; and (*h*) *m*-aminophenol from benzene.

(*a*)

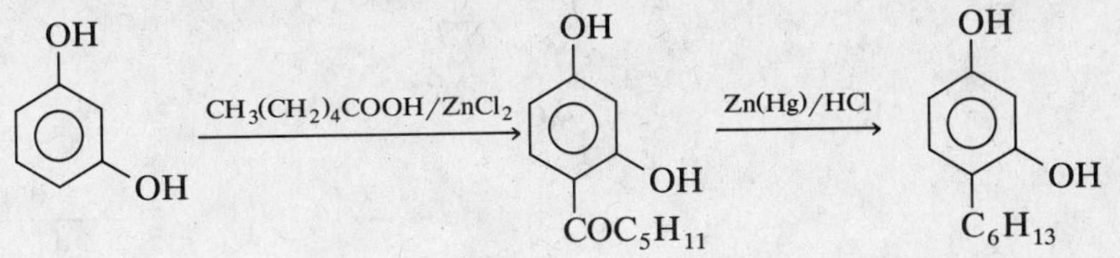

4-*n*-Hexylresorcinol

(*b*) See Problem 20.21(*b*).

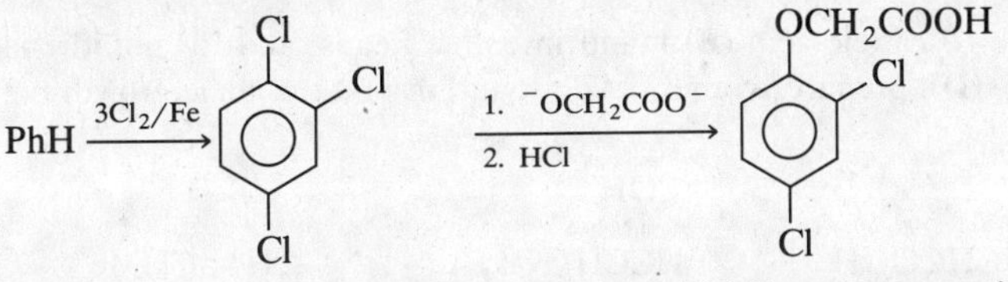

2,4-Dichlorophenoxyacetic acid

(*c*) PhNO$_2$

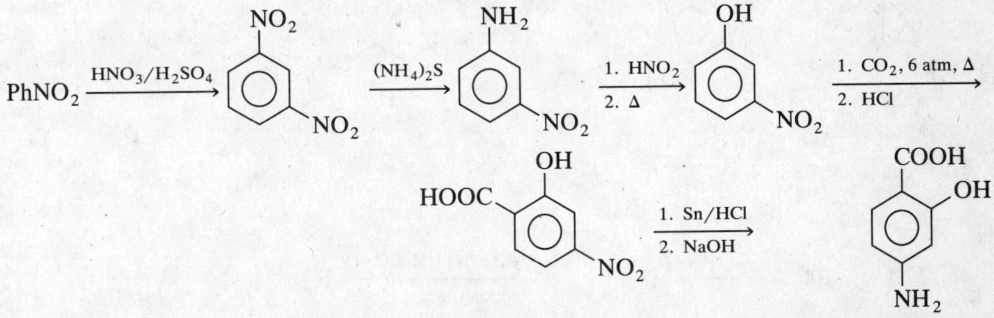

4-Amino-2-hydroxybenzoic acid

(*d*) PhCl

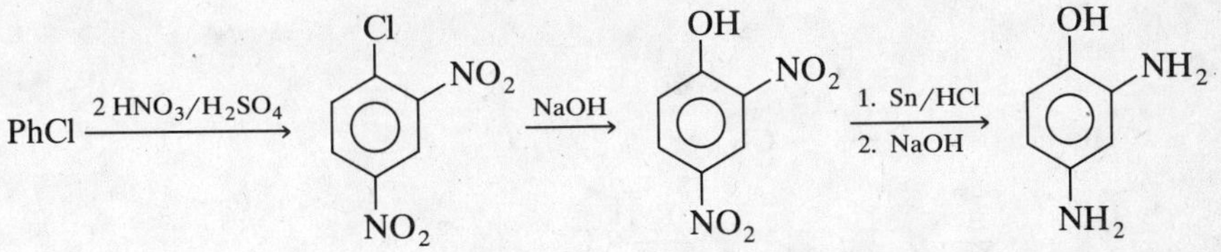

2,4-Diaminophenol

(*e*)

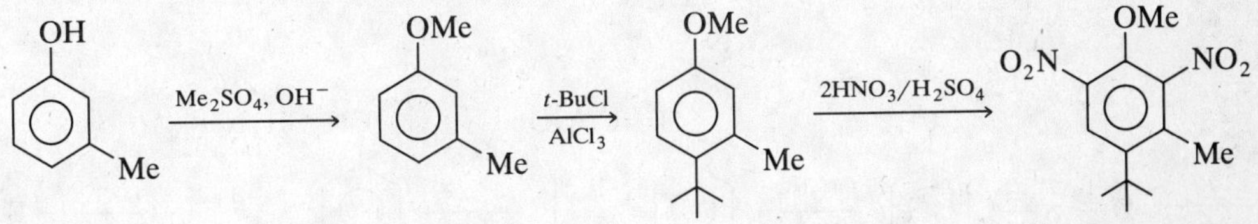

2,6-Dinitro-4-*t*-butyl-
3-methylanisole

(*f*)

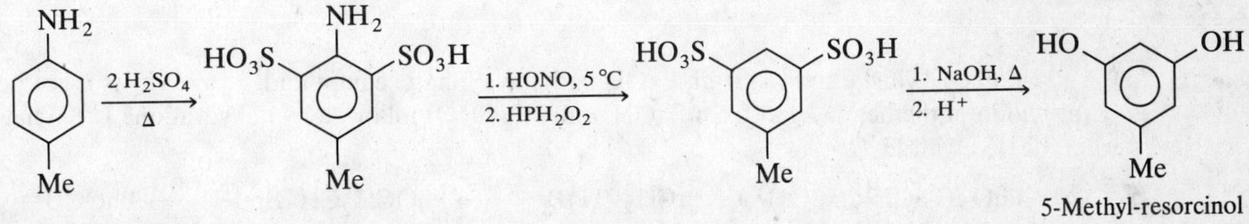

5-Methyl-resorcinol

(*g*) PhOH

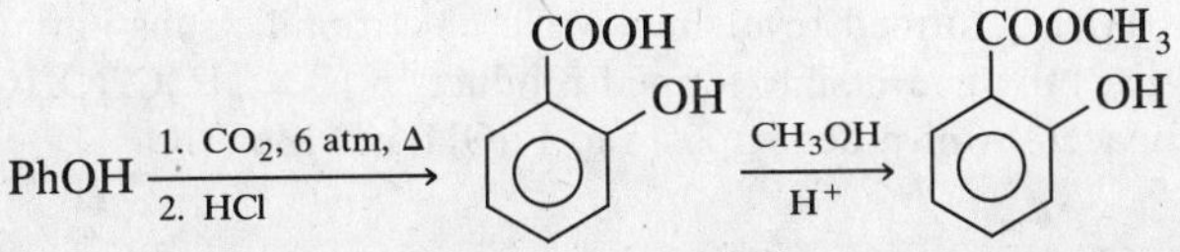

Methyl salicylate

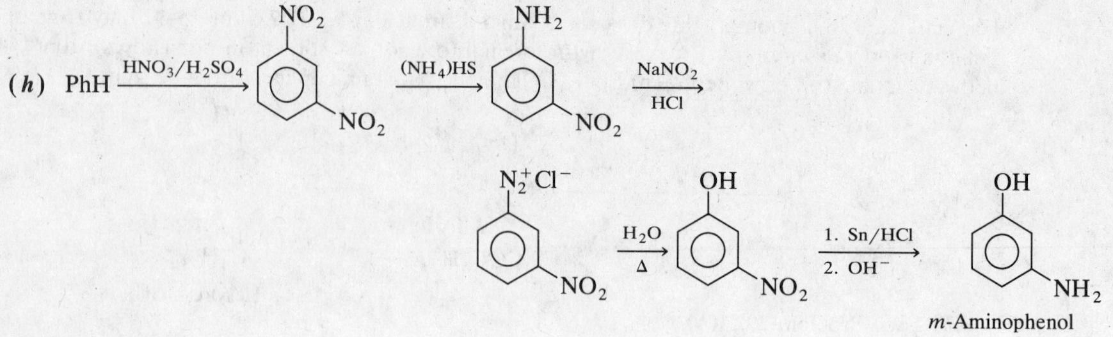

m-Aminophenol

20.67 (*a*) From vanillin, (**A**), prepare (i) caffeic acid (**B**) found in coffee beans, and (ii) noradrenaline (**C**) an adrenal hormone. (*b*) From anethole, (**D**), prepare tyramine, (**E**), found in ergot, a toxic growth on plants.

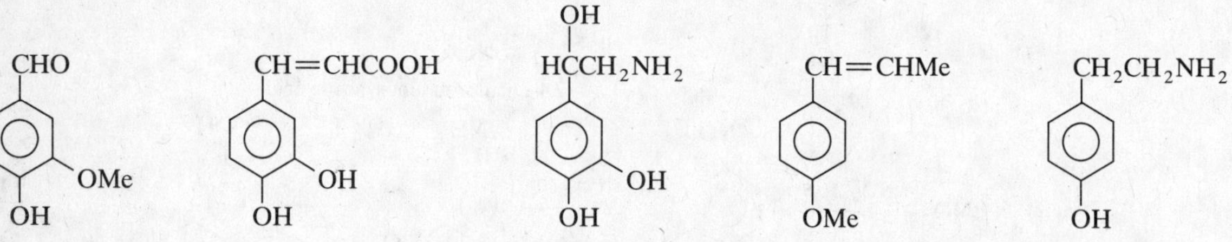

A **B** **C** **D** **E**

(*a*) (i)

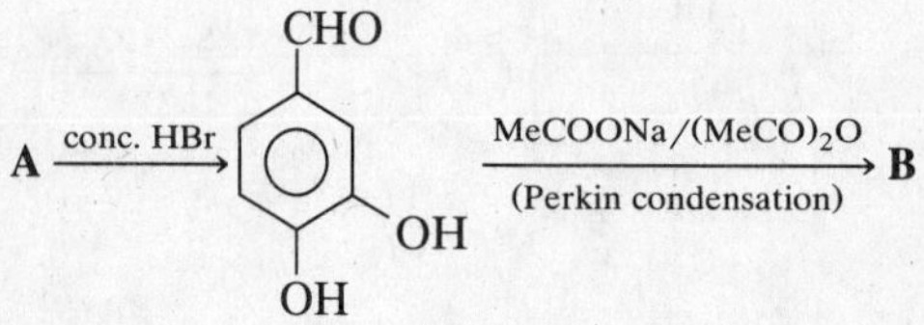

(ii)

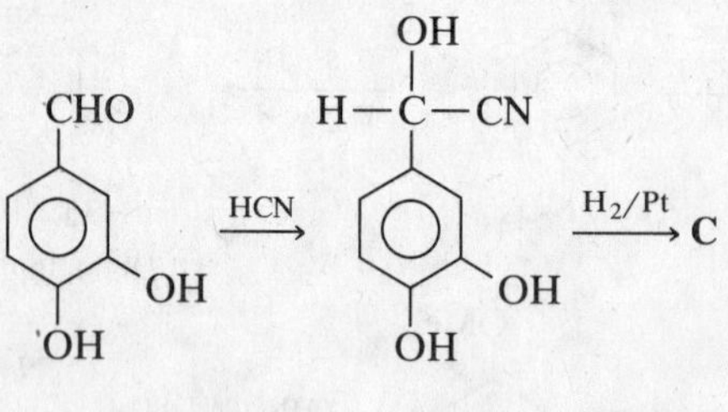

(*b*)

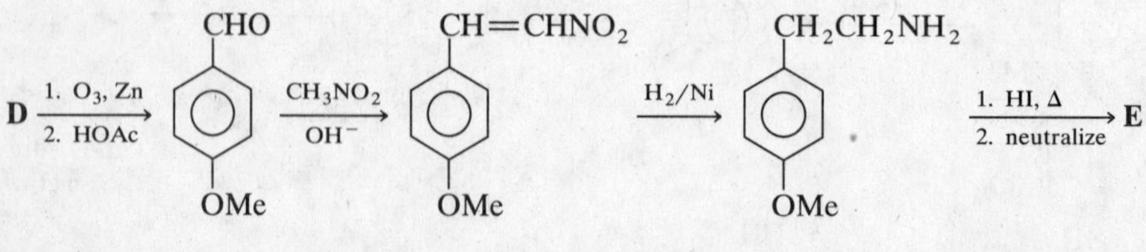

20.68 (*a*) Produce phenyl vinyl ether (**E**) from PhOH and any aliphatic compound. (*b*) Why is it not possible to make **E** by formation of the hemiacetal (from PhOH and CH_3CHO) followed by dehydration? (*c*) What is **E** converted to when heated with H_3O^+.

(*a*) $PhO^-(PhOH \text{ and } OH^-) + BrCH_2CH_2Br \xrightarrow{-Br^-} PhOCH_2CH_2Br \xrightarrow{\text{alc. KOH}} PhOCH{=}CH_2$ (**E**)

(*b*) The hemiacetal, PhOCH(OH)Me, is formed reversibly, while electrophilic substitution of phenols by carbonyl compounds in H^+ gives the irreversibly formed product, *p*-$HOC_6H_4CHOHCH_3$.

(*c*) **E** is hydrated to give the hemiacetal which decomposes to PhOH and MeCHO.

$$PhOCH{=}CH_2 \xrightarrow{H_3O^+} \underset{\text{hemiacetal}}{[PhOCH(OH)Me]} \longrightarrow PhOH + MeCHO$$

PHENOLS AND THEIR DERIVATIVES // 591

20.69 Prepare *p*-quinone from PhOH without resorting to ring oxidation.

Nitrosate PhOH [see Problem 20.36(*c*)]. *p*-Nitrosophenol is in equilibrium with its half oxime tautomer which is hydrolyzed to *p*-quinone.

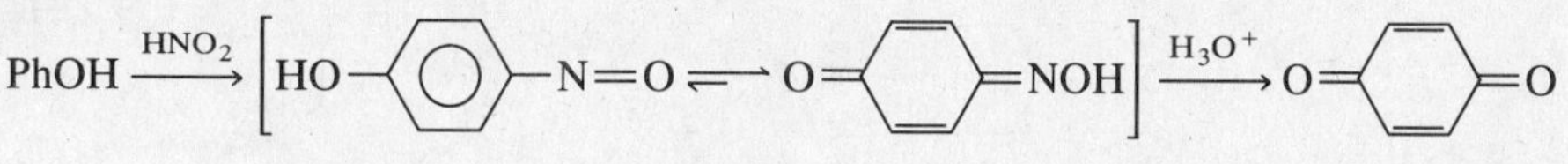

tautomers

20.70 Synthesize (*a*) thymol, 3-methyl-6-*i*-propylphenol, from any stereoisomer of menthone, and (*b*) α-naphthol from α-tetralone.

(*a*) The cyclohexanone is converted to a cyclohexadienone that tautomerizes to the phenolic compound.

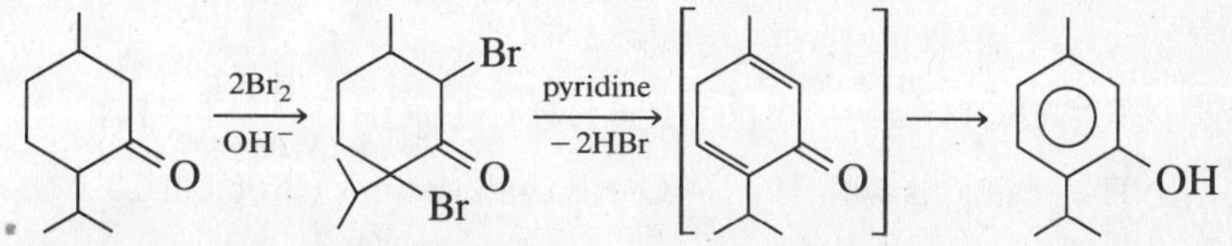

Menthone   keto tautomer   Thymol

(*b*) Hydroaromatic ketones such as the tetralones (α or β) can be dehydrogenated to the keto form which tautomerizes to the more stable phenolic form.

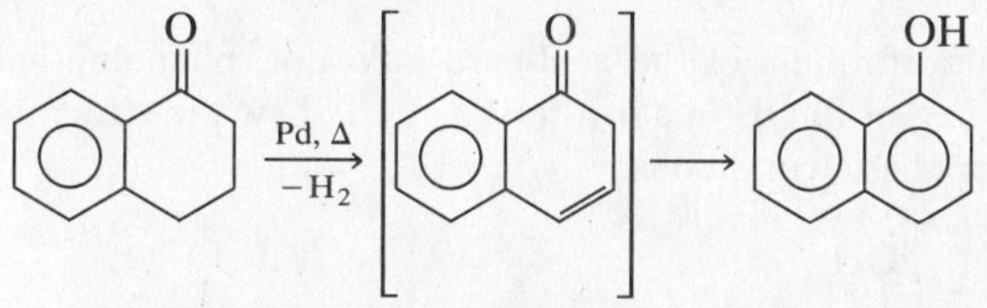

α-Tetralone   keto tautomer   α-Naphthol

20.71 Prepare phloroglucinol, 1,3,5-trihydroxybenzene, from toluene. Account for the last step. (*Hint*: Consider the triimino tautomer.)

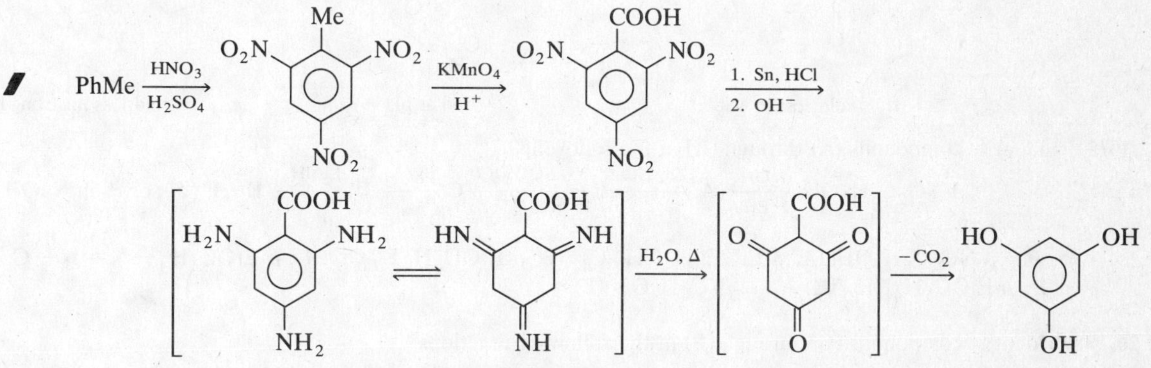

PhMe $\xrightarrow[H_2SO_4]{HNO_3}$ ... $\xrightarrow[H^+]{KMnO_4}$ ... $\xrightarrow[2.\ OH^-]{1.\ Sn,\ HCl}$

F   triimino tautomer   triketo form   Phloroglucinol

The facile hydrolysis of **F** proceeds through its triimino tautomer to give the triketo tautomer which readily decarboxylates because it is a β-keto acid.

20.72 Synthesize the antioxidant food preservatives (*a*) BHA (butylated hydroxyanisole, a mixture of 2- and 3-*t*-butyl-4-methoxyphenol) and (*b*) BHT (butylated hydroxytoluene, 2-*t*-butyl-4-methylphenol) from aliphatic and appropriate phenolic compounds.

(*a*) The Friedel–Crafts reaction of *p*-MeOC$_6$H$_4$OH with Me$_2$C=CH$_2$ gives the mixture because alkylation occurs both *ortho* to OH and to OMe.   (*b*) *p*-MeC$_6$H$_4$OH is *t*-butylated with Me$_2$C=CH$_2$.

20.73 (*a*) Synthesize **A** in one step from readily available phenolic compounds. (*b*) From PhOH and any aliphatic compound synthesize (i) **B** and (ii) the starting materials for making nylon (see Problem 17.92).

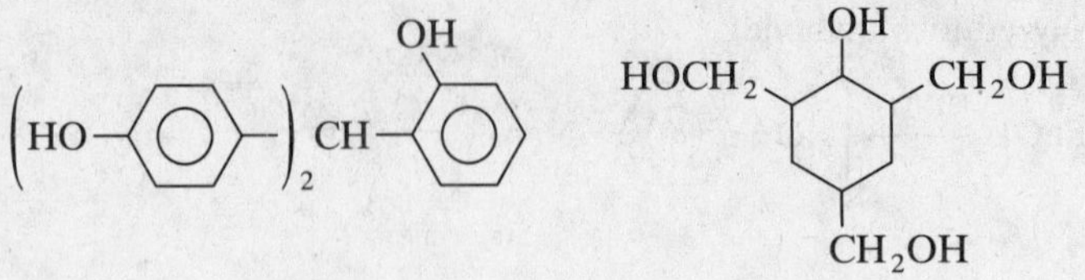

A　　　**B**

(a)

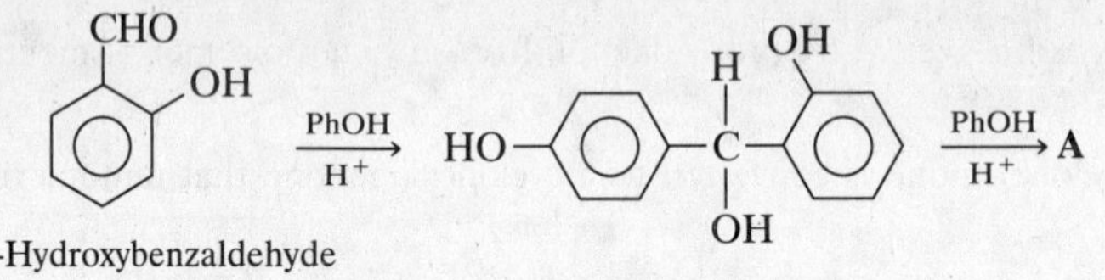

o-Hydroxybenzaldehyde

(Problem 20.48)

(b) (i) $PhOH \xrightarrow[H^+]{3H_2CO} 2,4,6\text{-}(HOCH_2)_3C_6H_2OH \xrightarrow[\Delta,\ pressure]{H_2/Ni} \textbf{B}.$

The reactions with $H_2C{=}O$ are C-alkylations [Problem 20.49(*a*)].

(ii) $PhOH \xrightarrow[200\,°C,\ 20\ atm]{H_2/Ni} cyclohexanol \xrightarrow{KMnO_4/H^+} HOOC(CH_2)_4COOH\ (\textbf{C}) \xrightarrow[2.\ Heat\ the\ salt]{1.\ NH_3}$

$H_2NCO(CH_2)_4CONH_2 \xrightarrow{P_2O_5} NC(CH_2)_4CN \xrightarrow{H_2/Ni} H_2N(CH_2)_6NH_2(\textbf{D})$

C and **D** are the starting materials.

20.74 Give the structural formula of the acid-base indicator, phenolphthalein, made by the condensation of phthalic anhydride with 2 eq of PhOH in anhydrous $ZnCl_2$. Show the structural formulas of the species in acid, at pH = 8, and more strongly basic conditions.

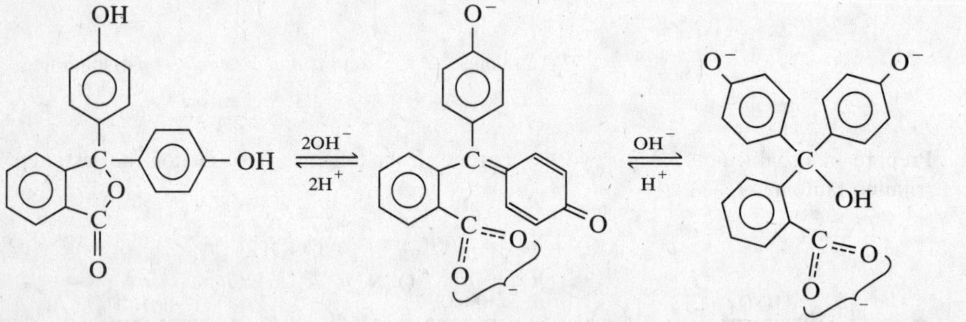

colorless in acid　　　　　red at pH = 8　　　　　colorless in strong base

20.75 Identify compounds (**A**) through (**E**) in the following.

$$p\text{-}NO_2C_6H_4OH \xrightarrow[2.\ EtBr]{1.\ OH^-} \textbf{A} \xrightarrow{Zn/HCl} \textbf{B} \xrightarrow[5\,°C]{NaNO_2/HCl} \textbf{C} \xrightarrow{PhOH} \textbf{D} \xrightarrow{LiAlH_4} \textbf{E} + \textbf{F}\ (dissolves\ in\ NaOH)$$

p-$NO_2C_6H_4OEt$, **A**; *p*-$EtOC_6H_4NH_3^+Cl^-$, **B**; *p*-$EtOC_6H_4N_2^+Cl^-$, **C**; *p*-$EtOC_6H_4{-}N{=}N{-}C_6H_4OH$-*p*, **D**; *p*-$EtOC_6H_4NH_2$ (**E**) + *p*-$H_2NC_6H_4OH$ (**F**).

20.76 Identify compounds (**G**) through (**P**) in the following reactions.

(*a*) $2,4\text{-Dinitrophenol} \xrightarrow{PhSO_2Cl} \textbf{G} \xrightarrow{NaF/DMSO} \textbf{H}$

(*b*) $p\text{-}NO_2C_6H_4OEt \xrightarrow{Sn/HCl} \textbf{I} \xrightarrow[2.\ PhOH]{1.\ NaNO_2,\ 5\,°C} \textbf{J} \xrightarrow[Et_2SO_4]{OH^-} \textbf{K} \xrightarrow{SnCl_2} \textbf{L} \xrightarrow{CH_3COCl} \textbf{M}$ ($C_{10}H_{13}O_2N$), phenacetin (an analgesic and antipyretic)

(*c*) $Catechol \xrightarrow{ClCH_2COCl/POCl_3} \textbf{N} \xrightarrow{MeNH_2} \textbf{O} \xrightarrow{H_2/Pd} rac\text{-}\textbf{P}$ ($C_9H_{13}O_3N$), adrenaline. **N** also reacts with NaOI followed by the reaction with H^+ to give 3,4-dihydroxybenzoic acid.

(*a*) $2,4\text{-diNO}_2C_6H_3OSO_2Ph$, **G**; $2,4\text{-diNO}_2C_6H_3F$, **H**. The very reactive unsolvated F^- displaces the good leaving group $PhSO_3^-$ from the ring activated by the two NO_2's.

(*b*) $EtOC_6H_4NH_3^+Cl^-$, **I**; *p*-$EtOC_6H_4N{=}NC_6H_4OH$-*p*, **J**; *p*-$EtOC_6H_4N{=}NC_6H_4OEt$-*p*, **K**; *p*-$EtOC_6H_4NH_2$, **L**; *p*-$EtOC_6H_4NHCOCH_3$, **M**.

O
‖

(c)   Since **N** reacts with NaOI, it must be a chloromethylketone 3,4-(HO)$_2$C$_6$H$_3$CCH$_2$Cl formed by acylation of the activated ring. Other possible products are an ester, o-HOC$_6$H$_4$OCOCH$_2$Cl and, less likely, an acid chloride 3,4-(HO)$_2$C$_6$H$_3$CH$_2$COCl, the alkylation product.

O is 3,4-(HO)$_2$C$_6$H$_3$COCH$_2$NHMe and **P** is 3,4-(HO)$_2$C$_6$H$_3$C̊H(OH)CH$_2$NHMe. Note that reduction of C=O engenders a chiral center.

ANALYSIS, SPECTRA, AND STRUCTURE PROOF

20.77   Give a simple test tube reaction other than an acid-base reaction that is characteristic of phenolic compounds.

▰   With Fe^{3+} salts, phenols produce complexes whose characteristic colors are green, red, blue, and purple.

20.78   Give the characteristic absorptions of phenols in (a) ir, (b) pmr, (c) uv, and (d) mass spectroscopies, especially as they differ from aliphatic alcohols.

▰   (a) Like alcohols, the OH stretching bands are at 3200 to 3600 cm^{-1} but the C—O stretching band is at 1230 cm^{-1} (attributed to its partial double-bond character), not 1050 to 1150 cm^{-1} observed for alcohols. The OH band frequency is also subject to dilution that influences intermolecular H-bonding and also intramolecular H-bonding.   (b) The OH proton of a phenol absorbs more downfield than that of an alcohol. Absorption is influenced by H-bonding—often the signal is broad. The chemical shift for phenols is 4–12 ppm. The electron-donating OH or OR shifts the ring H's more upfield.   (c) The two detectable $\pi \to \pi^*$ transitions of the phenyl ring chromophore dominate the spectrum. The auxochromic (Problem 12.43) OH causes a shift of both bands to longer wavelengths, often with intensification of the band with the longer wavelength. The detectable λ_{max}'s for phenol itself are at 210 and 270 nm in water.   (d) Unlike ROH's which often have low intensity parent peaks because of ease of dehydration, phenolic cations are relatively stable, accounting for prominent parent peaks.

20.79   In KBr pellets and in dilute CCl$_4$ solution, the O—H stretching bands in the ir spectra of o-nitrophenol are identical. However, the O—H stretch of the meta and para isomers are each different in these two media. Explain.

▰   In KBr, the OH of the three solid state compounds is H-bonded, showing the typical broad band for this condition. In dilute solution, the molecules of the meta and para isomers separate from each other, breaking the intermolecular H-bonds. Their OH stretching bands are now sharp and are at higher frequency. There is however no change in the absorption of the ortho isomer since its intramolecular H-bonding withstands dilution. Its band is broad and at a lower frequency.

20.80   Use simple chemical tests to differentiate between each member of the following pairs of compounds. Describe the results. (a) Anisole and cresol, (b) ethyl salicylate and ethyl acetylsalicylate, (c) acetylsalicylic acid and salicylic acid, (d) 2,4,6-trinitrophenol and 2,4,6-trimethylphenol, (e) PhOH and PhNH$_2$, and (f) anisole and benzyl alcohol.

▰   (a) Addition of FeCl$_3$ gives a deep color with cresol, a phenol, not with the ether. Also cresol is soluble in aq. NaOH.   (b) Ethyl salicylate has a free phenolic OH; it dissolves in NaOH and gives an intense color with FeCl$_3$.   (c) Salicylic acid has a free phenolic OH and gives an intense color with FeCl$_3$.   (d) Addition of aq. NaHCO$_3$ dissolves the more acidic nitro compound (picric acid), not the much less acidic methyl derivative.   (e) NaOH dissolves the phenol or HCl dissolves the amine.   (f) Add acidic KMnO$_4$ and warm. Benzyl alcohol is a 1° alcohol that is oxidized, decolorizing the purple color of KMnO$_4$. Under these conditions the ether resists oxidation.

20.81   (a) Compound (A), C$_7$H$_8$O, dissolves in NaOH but not in NaHCO$_3$. Br$_2$ reacts rapidly with **A** to give (**B**), C$_7$H$_5$OBr$_3$. Give the structures of **A** and **B**.   (b) What would **A** be if it did not dissolve in NaOH?

▰   (a) With 4° of unsaturation, **A** has a benzene ring. To account for the seventh C, its reactions with the bases indicates it is a phenol with a methyl substituent. We infer from the formation of a tribromo derivative that **A** is m-cresol and **B** is 2,4,6-tribromo-3-methylphenol.   (b) Anisole, C$_6$H$_5$OCH$_3$.

20.82   Find the structure of safrole (**C**), C$_{10}$H$_{10}$O$_2$, a sweet-smelling liquid isolated from oil of sassafrass, given the following properties: It does not dissolve in NaOH or give a color with FeCl$_3$. It adds one eq of H$_2$ on catalytic hydrogenation. Reductive ozonolysis affords H$_2$C=O and C$_9$H$_8$O$_3$ (**D**) that gives a positive Tollens test. Oxidation of **C** with KMnO$_4$ gives an acid (**E**) (N.E. = 166) which gives no color with FeCl$_3$. When **E** is refluxed with conc. HI, H$_2$C=O and 3,4-dihydroxybenzoic acid are isolated and identified.

▰   There are 6° of unsaturation, four of which are owing to a benzene ring. Since **C** does not dissolve in NaOH or give a color with FeCl$_3$, it is not a phenol. Formation of H$_2$C=O on ozonolysis means that **C** has a chain with a terminal =CH$_2$ grouping, and since **D** is an aldehyde (positive Tollens test), the grouping is —CH=CH$_2$.

The double bond accounts for the fifth degree of unsaturation. **E** is a monocarboxylic acid formed by complete oxidation of the alkenyl side chain and its molecular weight is 166. No other C can be directly attached to the ring because it would have oxidized giving a dicarboxylic acid. The two remaining O's must be present as ether linkages probably present as a ring, the sixth degree of unsaturation, fused to the benzene ring. This is confirmed by isolating $H_2C=O$ and 3,4-dihydroxybenzoic acid on cleavage with HI. This fused ring is actually a stable acetal. The molecular formula of **E** is $C_8H_6O_4$. The acetal ring and the benzene ring account for seven C's leaving three C's for the alkenyl side chain. The structures for **C**, **D**, and **E** are:

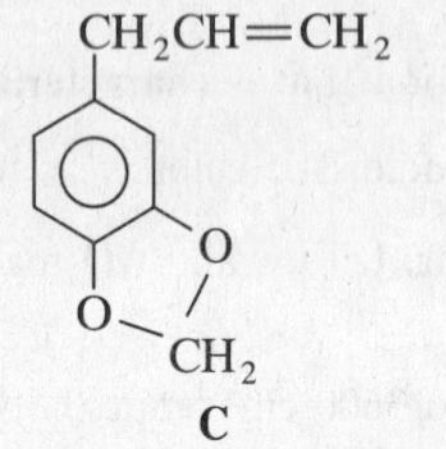

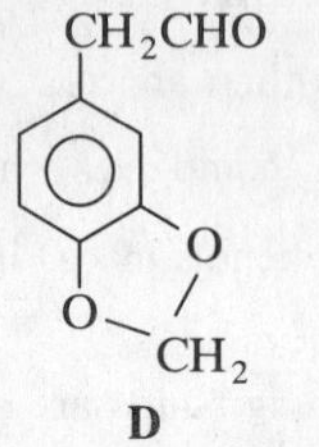

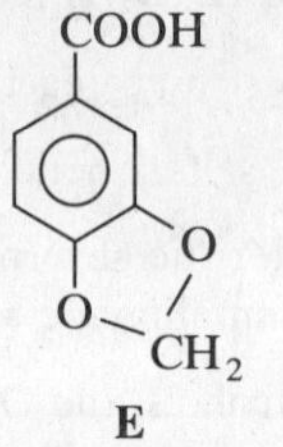

20.83 A compound, $C_{10}H_{14}O$ (**F**), dissolves in NaOH but not in $NaHCO_3$. It reacts with aq. Br_2 to give $C_{10}H_{12}Br_2O$. The ir spectrum of **F** shows a broad peak at 3250 cm^{-1} and a strong peak at 750 cm^{-1}. The pmr spectrum shows signals at the following δ values: (*1*) $\delta = 1.3$ ppm, *s*, nine H; (*2*) $\delta = 4.9$ ppm, *s* (broad), one H; and (*3*) $\delta = 7.0$, *m*, four H. Deduce the structure of **F**.

▟ The level of acidity, the facile reaction with Br_2, the broad band at 3250 cm^{-1}, and the broad singlet at $\delta = 4.9$ ppm suggests a phenolic compound. The 4-H multiplet at 7.0 ppm, the dibromination (not tribromination), and the strong ir band at 750 cm^{-1} indicate an *ortho*-substituted phenol. The nine-H singlet at $\delta = 1.3$ ppm is typical of a *t*-butyl group, which accounts for the additional four C's. **F** is $o\text{-}HOC_6H_4C(CH_3)_3$.

20.84 (*a*) Isomers **G** and **H**, $C_{10}H_{12}O$, are isolated from the oil of bay leaf. They are insoluble in aq. NaOH and decolorize Br_2/CCl_4 and $KMnO_4/H^+$. Each is vigorously oxidized to *p*-anisic acid, $p\text{-}MeOC_6H_4COOH$. Ozonolysis of **G** and **H** give the same products. (*a*) Identify **G** and **H**. (*b*) How can they be distinguished from each spectroscopically? (*c*) Give the structure of a third isomer (**I**) that is also oxidized to *p*-anisic acid and that give the same product on hydrogenation as does **G** and **H**. (*d*) Suggest a chemical reaction that can distinguish it from **G** and **H**.

▟ (*a*) Both **G** and **H** have 5° of unsaturation, four owing to a benzene ring and one to a $C=C$ bond as evidenced by positive tests with Br_2 and $KMnO_4/H^+$ for unsaturation. They are not phenolic since they are not acidic. Isolation of $p\text{-}MeOC_6H_4COOH$ shows that **G** and **H** are methyl ethers with a *para* substituted alkenyl side chain. They do not differ by the position of $C=C$ but rather are *cis-trans* isomers because they give the same ozonolysis products. Since seven C's are accounted for by the ring and the C of OCH_3, the alkenyl side chain has three C's. In order to exhibit stereoisomerism, the side chain is $-CH=CHCH_3$. **G** and **H** are *cis*- and *trans*-$p\text{-}MeOC_6H_4CH=CHCH_3$ (anethole). (*b*) Find the J values for the vinylic H's in the pmr spectrum. The *trans*-isomer has the larger value. (*c*) The structural isomer **I** is $p\text{-}MeOC_6H_4CH_2CH=CH_2$ which also gives anisic acid on oxidation and is reduced to $p\text{-}MeOC_6H_4CH_2CH_2CH_3$, as are **G** and **H**. (*d*) Reductive ozonolysis of **G** and **H** gives CH_3CHO which gives a positive test with NaOI. **I** is reductively ozonized to $H_2C=O$, which gives a negative test with NaOI.

20.85 Vanillin (**L**), $C_8H_8O_3$, is isolated from vanilla beans. It gives an intense color with $FeCl_3$ and a positive Tollens test. It is not steam-distilled and does not react with HCl. It goes through the following steps:

$$\mathbf{L} \xrightarrow[\text{one eq. of } CH_3I]{OH^-} \mathbf{M}, (C_9H_{10}O_3) \xrightarrow{KMnO_4} \mathbf{N}, (C_9H_{10}O_4) \ (HCO_3^- \text{ soluble}) \xrightarrow[\Delta]{\text{conc. HI}} \text{3,4-dihydroxybenzoic acid}$$

$$(\mathbf{L}) \xrightarrow{Ag(NH_3)_2^+} \mathbf{O} \xrightarrow{2Br_2} \mathbf{P}, (C_7H_6Br_2O_2). \text{ Identify } \mathbf{L}\text{–}\mathbf{P}.$$

▟ **L** is a phenolic (color with $FeCl_3$) aldehyde (positive Tollens test) with a single OH since it is only monomethylated. The benzene ring, CHO, and OH account for seven C's and two O's leaving an additional C and O which must be present as OCH_3, not as CH_2OH, because it does not react with HCl as would a benzylic-type compound. Inability to be steam-distilled indicates that the OH and CHO are not *ortho*. The isolation of 3,4-dihydroxybenzoic acid gives two possible juxtapositions of the three substituents:

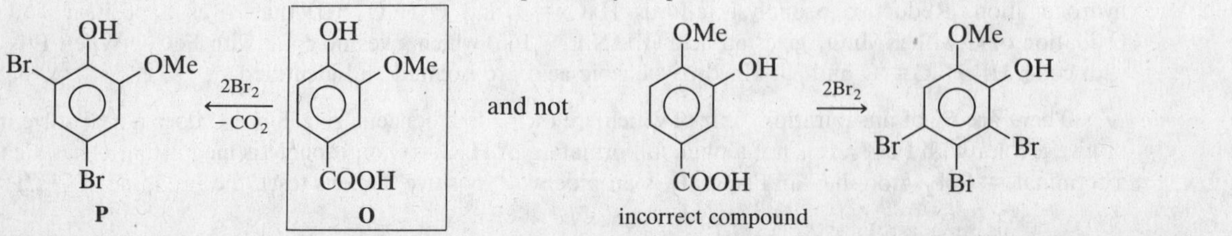

The C lost on dibromination comes from decarboxylation of COOH, meaning that COOH is *para* and not *meta* to OH—the structure on the left is correct for **O**. The remaining structures are

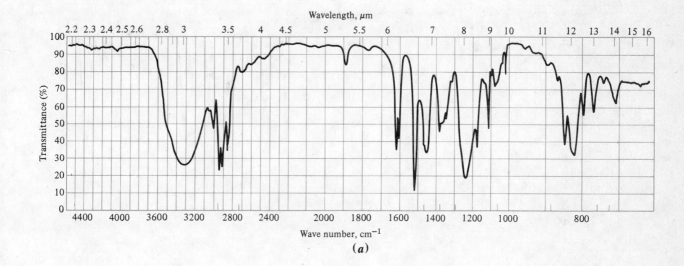

20.86 Identify the following compounds from their ir and pmr spectra: (*a*) **Q**, $C_9H_{12}O$, see Fig. 20-2(*a*) and (*b*); (*b*) **R**, $C_9H_{11}BrO$, see Fig. 20-3(*a*) and (*b*); and (*c*) **S**, $C_{10}H_{11}ClO_2$, see Fig. 20-4(*a*) and (*b*).

    (*a*) ir: The strong, broad peak at 3300 cm^{-1} arises from an OH. Absorption slightly above 3000 cm^{-1} is due to sp^2 C—H, and a *p*-disubstituted benzene is indicated by the peak at 825 cm^{-1}.

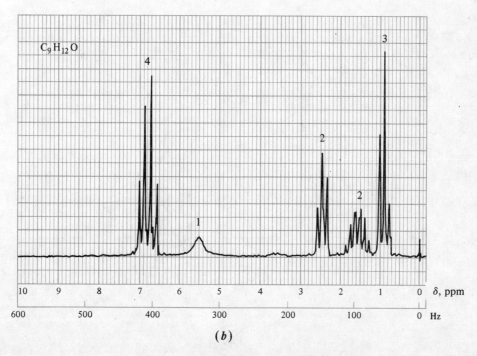

Fig. 20-2

pmr in δ: The 4 H quartet at 6.55–7.04 is due to a *p*-disubstituted benzene with an attached electron-donating group causing the upfield shift, and the broad 1 H singlet at 5.5 arises from an OH. The 3H triplet at 0.9 indicates a CH_3 bonded to CH_2, the 2H triplet at 2.5 comes from a benzylic CH_2 bonded to a second CH_2 whose signal is the 2H sextet at 2.5. These three upfield signals reveal an *n*-propyl group attached to a benzene ring. Compound **A** is *p*-$HOC_6H_4CH_2CH_2CH_3$.

(*b*) ir: The absorption > 3000 cm^{-1} (sp^2C—H) indicates an aromatic ring which is consistent with the calculated 4°'s of unsaturation. The lack of absorption at 3200–3600 cm^{-1} shows that the O cannot be present as OH, and **B** must be an ether. The peaks at 690 and 760 cm^{-1} suggest either a mono or *m*-disubstituted benzene.

pmr in δ: The 5H multiplet at 6.8–7.5 indicates a monosubstituted benzene ring with an electron-donating group, the ether O, attached to the ring. There are three CH_2 groups present as the sequence $CH_2CH_2CH_2$. The most downfield triplet is from a CH_2 attached to the O, the next most downfield triplet is from a CH_2 bonded to Br. Compound **B** is $PhOCH_2CH_2CH_2Br$.

(*c*) ir: Absorption at 3400 cm^{-1} is due to OH, and at 1675 cm^{-1} to C=O, accounting for the fifth degree of unsaturation. The peak at 860 cm^{-1} is from a *p*-disubstituted ring.

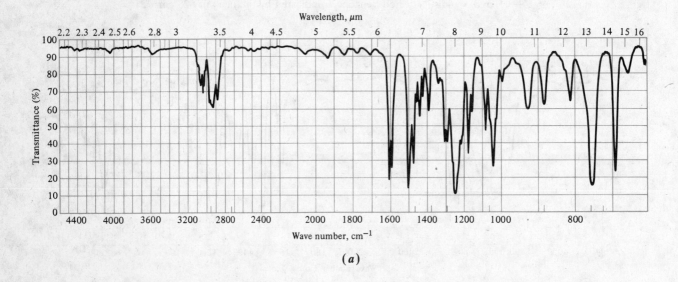

(*a*)

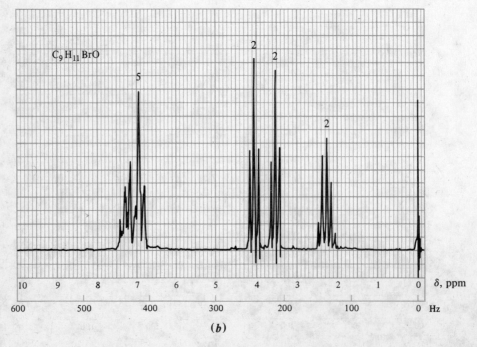

(*b*)

Fig. 20-3

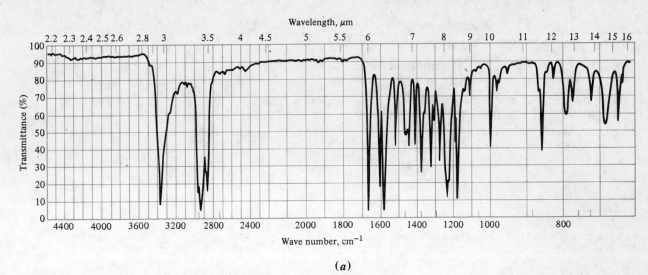

(a)

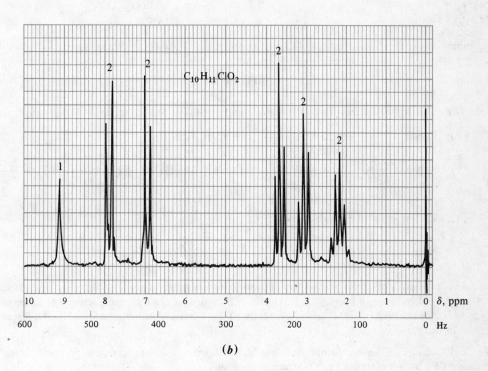

(b)

Fig. 20-4

pmr in δ: The 1H singlet at 9.1 indicates the OH is phenolic, and the 4H AB pattern at 6.9–8.0 points to a
p-disubstituted ring, with the electron-withdrawing C=O on the ring accounting for the absorption at 8. The
three 2H signals arise from a $CH_2CH_2CH_2$ group, with the most downfield CH_2 at 3.7 bonded to Cl and the one
at 3.1 bonded to C=O. Compound **C** is p-$HOC_6H_4COCH_2CH_2CH_2Cl$.

SUPPLEMENTARY PROBLEMS

20.87   Draw a flow diagram for the separation and recovery in almost quantitative yield of a mixture of the
water-insoluble compounds $PhCHO$, $PhNMe_2$, $PhCl$, p-MeC_6H_4OH, and $PhCOOH$.

▰   See Fig. 20-5.

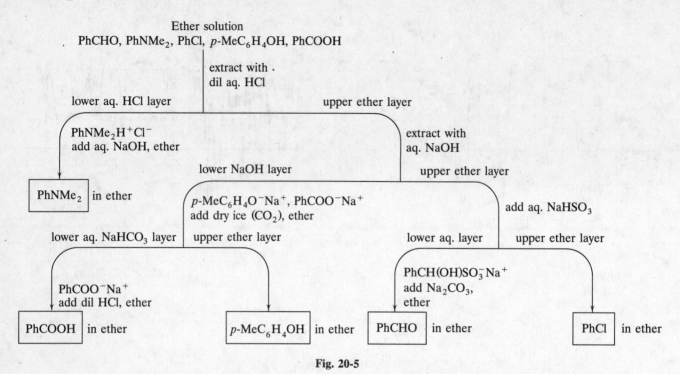

Ether solution
PhCHO, PhNMe₂, PhCl, p-MeC₆H₄OH, PhCOOH

Fig. 20-5

20.88 Convert PhNO₂ to (*a*) the bisulfate salt of *p*-aminophenol (use two steps), and (*b*) 4,4′-dihydroxybiphenyl.

▰ (*a*) $PhNO_2 \xrightarrow[\text{aq. NH}_4\text{Cl}]{\text{Zn}} PhNHOH \xrightarrow{\text{H}_2\text{SO}_4} p\text{-HOC}_6\text{H}_4\text{NH}_3^+\text{HSO}_4^-$

(*b*) $PhNO_2 \xrightarrow[\text{aq. NaOH}]{\text{excess Zn}} PhNHNHPh \xrightarrow[\Delta]{\text{HCl}} p\text{-H}_2\text{NC}_6\text{H}_4\text{C}_6\text{H}_4\text{NH}_2\text{-}p \text{ (Problem 19.93)} \xrightarrow[\text{2. }\Delta]{\text{1. 2HONO, 5°C}}$

$p\text{-HOC}_6\text{H}_4\text{C}_6\text{H}_4\text{OH-}p$

20.89 *Dioxin* (2,3,7,8-tetrachlorodibenzo-*p*-dioxin)

is a ubiquitous compound formed whenever chlorinated organic compounds are pyrolized. It causes chloracne and is believed by some to be very toxic. Dioxin is a by-product in the manufacture of the broad leaf herbicide 2,4,5-trichlorophenol (2,4,5-T), obtained by treating 1,2,4,5-tetrachlorobenzene with NaOH. Suggest a mechanism for the formation of dioxin.

▰ OH⁻ changes 2,4,5-trichlorophenol into its conjugate base which acts as a nucleophile to displace an activated Cl⁻ from unreacted 1,2,4,5-tetrachlorobenzene.

This product undergoes another aromatic nucleophilic displacement with more OH⁻, to give a phenoxide that reacts by an intramolecular displacement of Cl⁻ to give dioxin.

All of the displaced Cl's are activated to nucleophilic substitution because they are both *ortho* and *para* to other Cl's.

20.90 (*a*) Draw conclusions about migratory aptitudes of H and *p*-tolyl in migration to O⁺ from the following data: *p*-H₃CC₆H₄CH₂OOH in H₃O⁺ yields 68% methylbenzaldehyde + 38% *p*-cresol. (*b*) From the synthesis of phenol from cumene hydroperoxide (Problem 20.17), what can be concluded about the migratory aptitude of phenyl vs. methyl?

▰ (**a**) The aldehyde (68%) arises from migration of H, and cresol (38%) comes from migration of *p*-tolyl. It might appear from the yields that H is the better migrator. However, it is necessary to take into account the presence of two H's and only one aryl group. If migratory aptitudes play no role, statistically the yield of aldehyde should be about twice that of the phenol, which is approximately the observed result. Apparently, there is little difference in their migratory aptitudes. (**b**) Phenyl has a marked migratory preference to methyl, since it migrates even in the presence of two methyls.

20.91 In each of the following pairs, choose the reactant that reacts faster in the designated reaction. Account for your choice. (**a**) Nitration of PhOH or MeCOOPh (phenyl acetate) (**b**) Reaction of PhO$^-$ or *p*-N≡CC$_6$H$_4$O$^-$ with PhCH$_2$Cl. (**c**) Base-catalyzed hydrolysis of phenyl acetate or *p*-nitrophenyl acetate. (**d**) Acid-catalyzed esterification of PhOH or *p*-NO$_2$C$_6$H$_4$OH with MeCOOH.

▰ (**a**) PhOH. Because of cross-conjugation, the acetoxy group attenuates the delocalization of electron-density from O to the ring. (**b**) PhO$^-$. The *p*-CN promotes electron-density withdrawal from the O making *p*-N≡CC$_6$H$_4$O$^-$ a weaker base and, in this case, also a weaker nucleophile. (**c**) *p*-nitrophenyl acetate. The *p*-NO$_2$ promotes electron-density withdrawal from the O making *p*-NO$_2$C$_6$H$_4$O$^-$ a weaker base and a better leaving group. (**d**) PhOH. The more basic phenolic compound should be more reactive. With its electron-withdrawing *p*-NO$_2$, *p*-NO$_2$C$_6$H$_4$OH is less basic and less reactive.

20.92 Why is the ring of PhOH more easily oxidized than that of PhH?

▰ The strong electron-donating effect of OH makes the ring of PhOH very electron-rich, enabling it to readily donate electrons to oxidizing agents.

CHAPTER 21
Aromatic Heterocyclic Compounds

AROMATICITY AND NOMENCLATURE

21.1 What structural features are necessary for a heterocyclic compound to be aromatic?

▮ The structural features are the same as for a carbocyclic compound (see Problem 10.33): coplanarity of ring, each ring atom must have a *p* AO for cyclic overlap, and a Hückel number of electrons. There is one distinction from a carbocyclic compound: not all the electrons need come from π bonds, some may come from the unshared pair on the heteroatom.

21.2 Give the structure and name for a six-membered ring heterocycle with one heteroatom that is (*a*) N, and (*b*) O.

▮ Like benzene, such heterocyclic compounds have three double bonds in the ring without involving the heteroatom

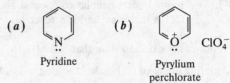

Note that in order for O to have a double bond, it must be positively charged. (Pyrylium salts are unstable.)

21.3 (*a*) Explain why pyran [Fig. 21-1(*a*)] is not aromatic. (*b*) What structural change would make it aromatic?

▮ (*a*) Pyran can get six e⁻'s in the ring, four from the two π bonds and two from the O. However, there is no cyclic overlap because the sp^3-hybridized C^4 lacks a *p* AO [Fig. 21-1(*a*)]. (*b*) Convert C^4 to a carbocation which is best done by making it part of a C=O bond as shown in Fig. 21-1(*b*).

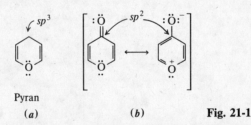

Fig. 21-1

21.4 Give the structure for a five-membered ring heterocycle with one heteroatom that is (*a*) N, (*b*) O, and (*c*) S.

▮ Stable five-membered ring heterocycles with one heteroatom can only have two double bonds in the ring. The additional two e⁻'s needed for the Hückel sextet comes from the heteroatom.

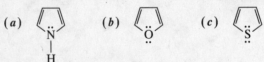

It is noteworthy that typically these heteroatoms use sp^3 HO's for bonding as in alcohols, thiols and amines. In these cases sp^2 hybridization provides a *p* AO for the aromatic system.

21.5 Give the common and ring index names for each compound in Problem 21.4.

▮ For five-membered aromatic heterocycles, the *ring index system* uses the suffix *-ole*. The prefixes *aza-* for N, *oxa-* for O and *thia-* for S are used for all ring sizes; the a is dropped when the suffix starts with a vowel. The ring index names are in parentheses. (*a*) pyrrole (azole), (*b*) furan (oxole), and (*c*) thiophene (thiole).

21.6 (*a*) Draw an orbital picture for furan. (*b*) Show the hybrid structure.

▮ See Fig. 21-2.

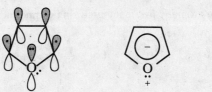

(a)   *(b)*   **Fig. 21-2**

21.7 . Discuss the difference in *(a)* dipole moments and *(b)* water solubility of pyridine and pyrrole.

▌ *(a)* The electron-withdrawing N of pyridine induces a dipole moment as shown in Fig. 21-3*(a)*. The delocalized hybrid structure of pyrrole has a considerable amount of + charge on N and a − charge in the ring causing a dipole moment [Fig. 21-3*(b)*]. The dipole moments are in opposite directions.   *(b)* The undisturbed electron-density on N in pyridine allows for H-bonding with H_2O and pyridine is miscible. In pyrrole, the lack of electron-density on N precludes H-bonding and pyrrole is only slightly soluble.

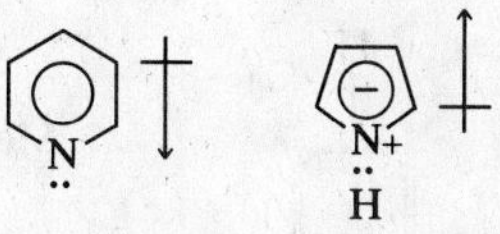

(a)   *(b)*   **Fig. 21-3**

21.8 *(a)* Give the common name for each of the following compounds using numbers and Greek letters.   *(b)* Give the ring index name for compound (iii).

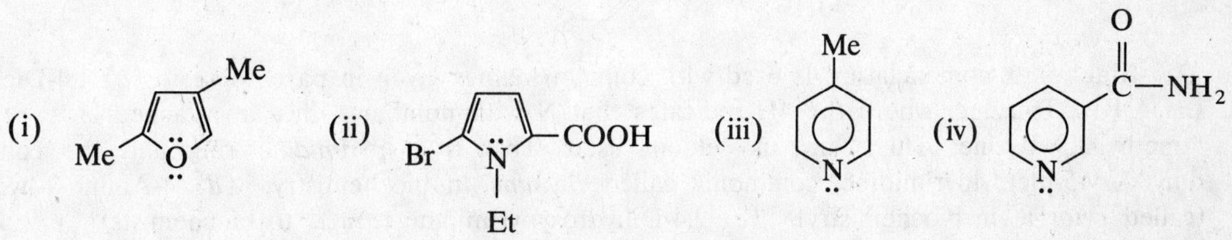

(i)   (ii)   (iii)   (iv)

▌ The numbering system and use of Greek letters are shown for a general five-membered ring and for pyridine:

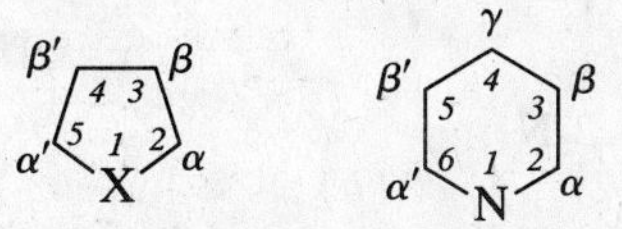

(i) 2,4-Dimethylfuran, α,β'-dimethylfuran. (ii) 1-Ethyl-5-bromopyrrole-2-carboxylic acid, N-ethyl-α'-bromo-α-pyrrolecarboxylic acid. (iii) 4-Methyl or γ-methylpyridine. The methylpyridines are also commonly called *picolines* with Greek letters to indicate position of the Me—this one is γ-picoline. (iv) 3-Pyridinecarboxyamide, pyridine-β-carboxamide. The common name is nicotinamide, and the acid, commonly called *nicotinic acid*, is Vitamin B_3, or niacin.   *(b)* The suffix for six-membered N-containing heterocycles is *-ine*. The name is 4-methylazine.

21.9 Name the following benzene-fused heterocyclic compounds:

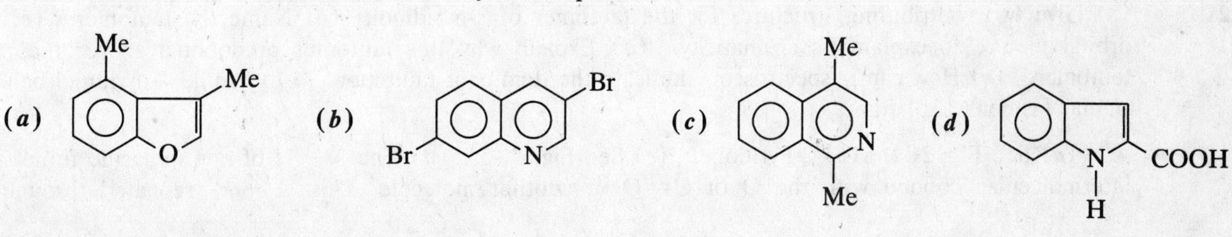

(a)   *(b)*   *(c)*   *(d)*

▌ *(a)* This ring system is called benzofuran and O is numbered 1. 3,4-Dimethylbenzofuran.   *(b)* This is the quinoline ring system, with N numbered 1. 3,7-Dibromoquinoline.   *(c)* In this isoquinoline ring system, N is numbered 2. 1,4-Dimethylisoquinoline.   *(d)* The fused ring is an indole and the N is number 1. Indole-2-carboxylic acid.

21.10 Name each of the following aromatic five-membered ring compounds with more than one heteroatom:

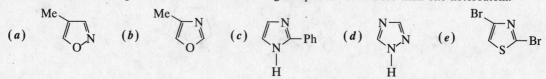

▰ The heteroatom with no double bond is named first and assigned the number 1 position. The numbering proceeds so that other heteroatoms get the lowest possible numbers. Ring index nomenclature is given with common names in parentheses.

(*a*) 4-Methyl-1,2-oxazole (4-methyloxazole since this ring is commonly called oxazole).
(*b*) 4-Methyl-1,3-oxazole, (4-methylisoxazole since this ring is commonly called isoxazole).
(*c*) 2-Phenyl-1,3-diazole (2-phenylimidazole from the common name of this ring).
(*d*) 1,2,4-Triazole.
(*e*) 2,4-Dibromo-1,3-thiazole.

21.11 Name the following monocyclic aromatic ring compounds with more than one heteroatom:

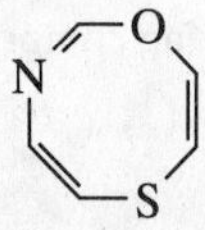

▰ Ring index nomenclature is used with common names given in parentheses. (*a*) 1,4-Diazine (pyrazine). (*b*) 4H-1,4-Thiazine, where the 4H indicates that N with number 4 has an attached H. (*c*) 2,4-Dihydroxy-5-methyl-1,3-diazine. This name is seldom used. This is a *pyrimidine* ring and the compound is 2,4-dihydroxy-5-methylpyrimidine, commonly called *thymine* in biochemistry. (*d*) 4-Amino-2-hydroxypyrimidine (called *cytosine* in biochemistry). (*e*) 2,4-Dihydroxypyrimidine (*uracil* to biochemists). (*f*) For eight-membered rings the suffix *-ocine* is used: 1-thia-4-oxa-6-azocine. Note the numbering sequence of the three heteroatoms.

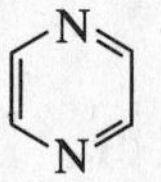

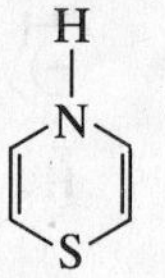

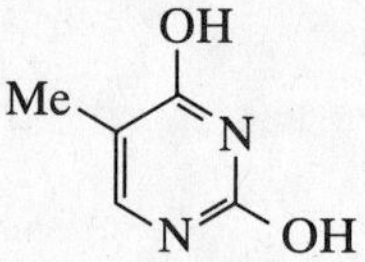

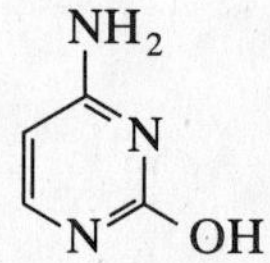

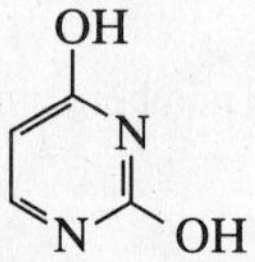

21.12 Name each of the following fused aromatic ring compounds with more than one heteroatom:

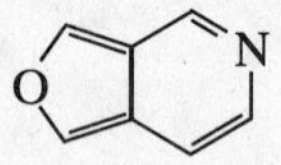

▰ The ring system in (*a*) and (*b*) with fused pyrimidine and imidizole rings is called *purine*. (*a*) 4-Amino-purine, commonly called *adenine*, (*b*) 2-amino-4-hydroxypurine, commonly called *guanine*, and (*c*) furol[3,4-*c*]pyridine. Pyridine, the larger ring, is the parent with a furan ring fused to it. The letter *c* indicates the fused side in pyridine and the 3,4 indicates the fused C's in furan. Side *a* is the C=C closest to N.

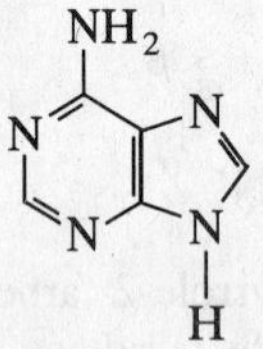

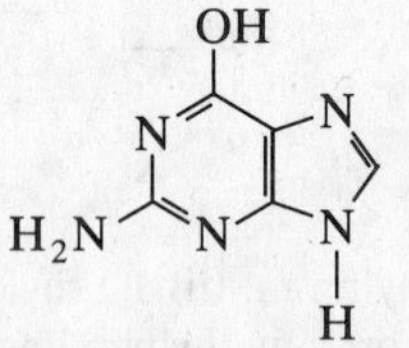

21.13 (*a*) Give two contributing structures for the tautomer of 2-pyridinol. (*b*) Name the tautomer. (*c*) Use an orbital picture to explain its aromaticity. (*d*) Explain why this tautomer predominates over the pyridinol tautomer. (*e*) How can ir spectroscopy indicate the dominant tautomer? (*f*) Would 4-pyridinol behave in a similar fashion? Explain.

▰ (*a*) See Fig. 21.4. (*b*) 2-Pyridone. (*c*) See Fig. 21-5. (*d*) The N—H of one molecule forms a strong intermolecular H-bond with the O of C=O of another molecule. This H-bond, repeated throughout the

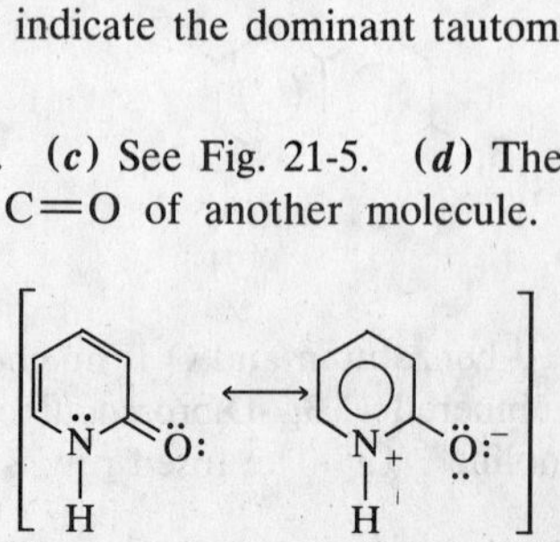

Fig. 21-4

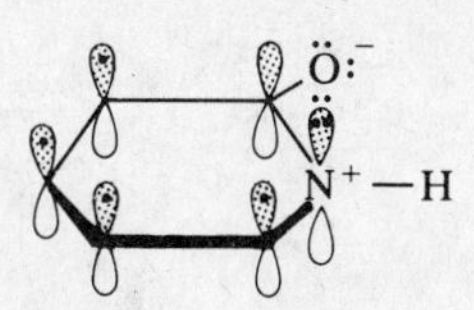

Fig. 21-5

crystalline solid, links molecules in endless helices.   (*e*) The ir spectra of solid and solution show a strong C=O stretching band.   (*f*) Yes. 4-Pyridone is the more stable tautomer.

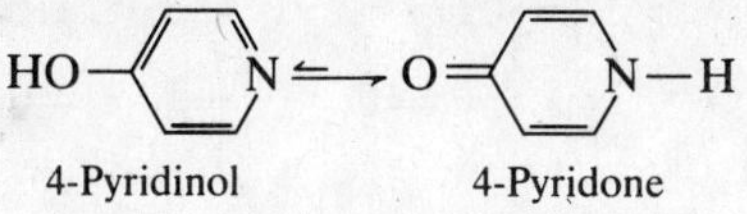

HO—⟨N⟩ ⇌ O=⟨N—H⟩

4-Pyridinol   4-Pyridone

21.14   (*a*) Write the tautomeric structures of thymine, cytosine, and uracil.   (*b*) Explain the stabilities of these tautomers.

▮   (*a*)   The keto tautomers are

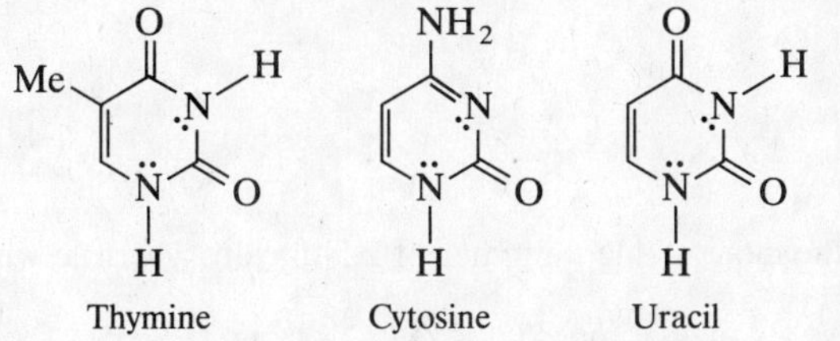

Thymine   Cytosine   Uracil

(*b*)   These keto tautomers are still aromatic; they have six e⁻'s and fit Hückel's rule. The unshared pair of e⁻'s on each HN: group is contributed to the cyclic π-overlap system and the *p* AO on each carbonyl C is devoid of e⁻'s.

PREPARATION

21.15   Give the following industrial syntheses: (*a*) thiophene from butane, (*b*) pyrrole from HC≡CH and H_2C=O, and (*c*) furan from corncobs.

▮   (*a*) Heat with sulfur at 560 °C.   (*b*) React the two compounds with Cu_2C_2 to get HOH_2CC≡CCH_2OH which is then heated with NH_3 under pressure.   (*c*) Corncobs (and other grain hulls) contain the polypentoside pentosan, $(C_5H_8O_4)_n$, which on being heated with HCl gives pentoses (see Problem 23.31). These products then are dehydrated and cyclized to form furfural (2-furancarboxaldehyde). Furfural loses CO (decarbonylation) when heated with steam and metal oxide catalysts at 400 °C and produces furan.

21.16   Prepare the following compounds by heating a 1,4-dicarbonyl compound with the appropriate inorganic reagent. (This is an often-used method for making five-membered ring heterocyclics.)   (*a*) 3,4-Dimethylfuran, (*b*) 2,5-dimethylthiophene, and (*c*) 2,3-dimethylpyrrole.

▮   The carbonyl C's become the α C's in the heterocyclic compound.

(*a*)   2,3-Dimethylbutanedial   a dienediol   3,4-Dimethylfuran

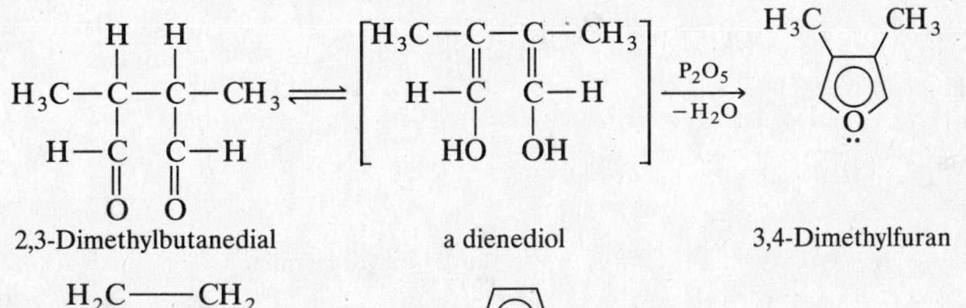

(*b*)   Acetonylacetone   2,5-Dimethylthiophene

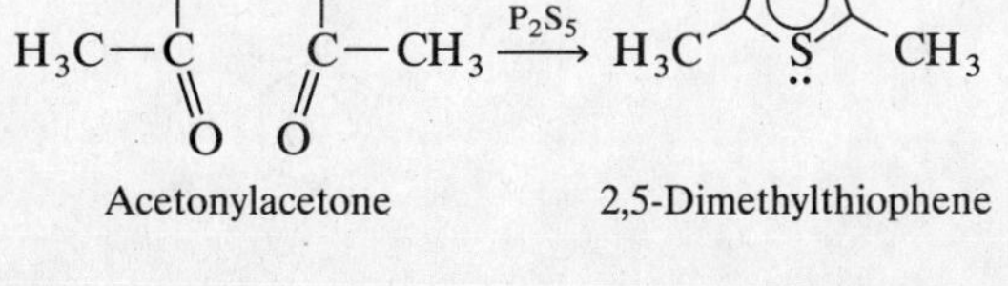

(c)

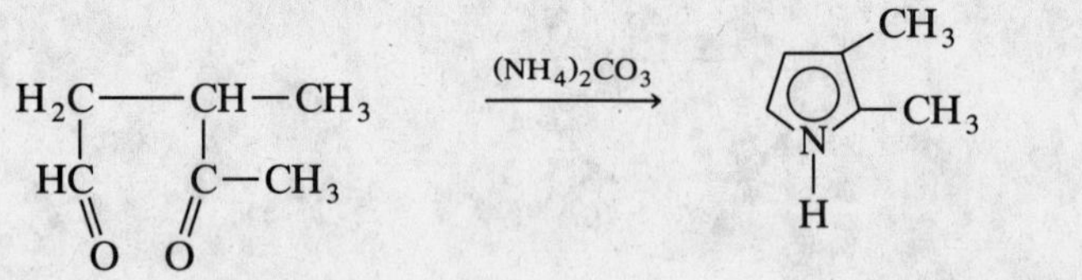

H₂C—CH—CH₃
| |
HC   C—CH₃
‖   ‖
O   O

$\xrightarrow{(NH_4)_2CO_3}$

3-Methyl-4-oxopentanal → 2,3-Dimethylpyrrole

21.17 Prepare pyrrole from succinic acid.

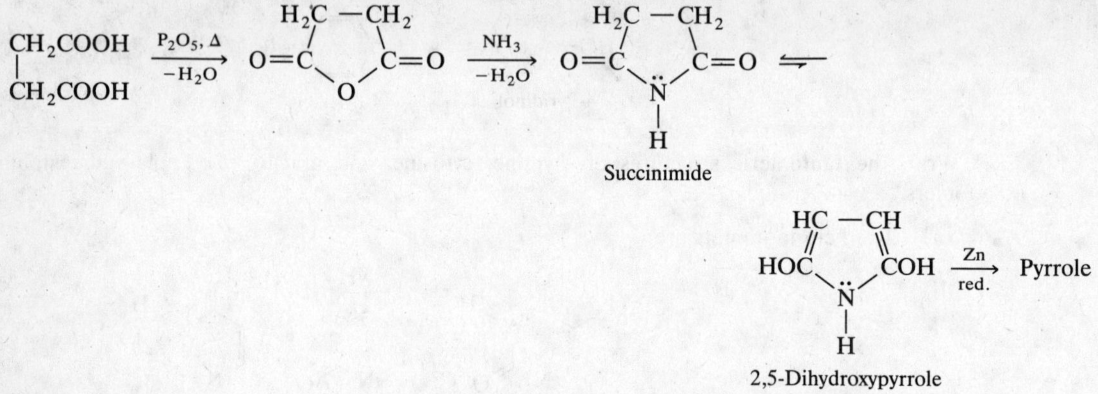

CH₂COOH
|
CH₂COOH
$\xrightarrow[-H_2O]{P_2O_5, \Delta}$
succinic anhydride $\xrightarrow[-H_2O]{NH_3}$ Succinimide $\rightleftharpoons$

2,5-Dihydroxypyrrole $\xrightarrow[red.]{Zn}$ Pyrrole

Succinimide is the more stable tautomer of 2,5-dihydroxypyrrole which is reduced with Zn.

21.18 Prepare α,α′,β,β′-tetramethylthiophene (**A**) from CH₃COOEt and any necessary reactants.

The 1,4-dicarbonyl precursor is

O Me Me O
‖ | | ‖
MeC—CH—CH—CMe (**B**) which with P₂S₅ gives **A**.

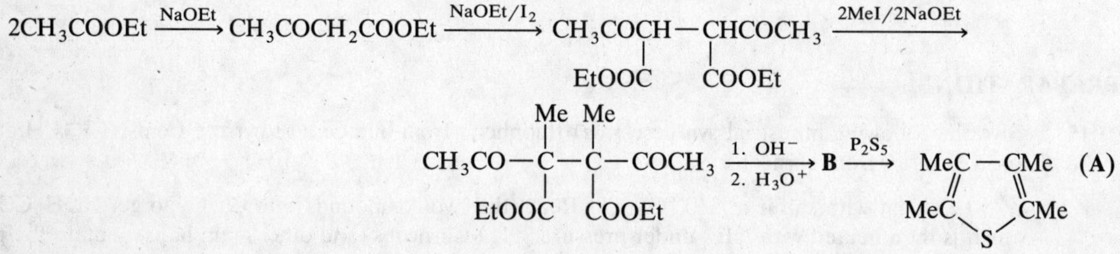

$2CH_3COOEt \xrightarrow{NaOEt} CH_3COCH_2COOEt \xrightarrow{NaOEt/I_2}$

CH₃COCH—CHCOCH₃
          | |
      EtOOC   COOEt
$\xrightarrow{2MeI/2NaOEt}$

          Me Me
            | |
CH₃CO—C—C—COCH₃
            | |
       EtOOC COOEt
$\xrightarrow[2. H_3O^+]{1. OH^-}$ **B** $\xrightarrow{P_2S_5}$

MeC—CMe
| |
MeC   CMe
   \   /
    S
(**A**)

21.19 Explain why there are no industrial syntheses of pyridine and picolines.

They are isolated from coal tar. (This is also an industrial method for obtaining pyrrole.)

21.20 Show how pyridines can be synthesized from 2RCOCH₂COOEt + R′CHO + NH₃.

This *Hantzsch pyridine synthesis* occurs as follows:

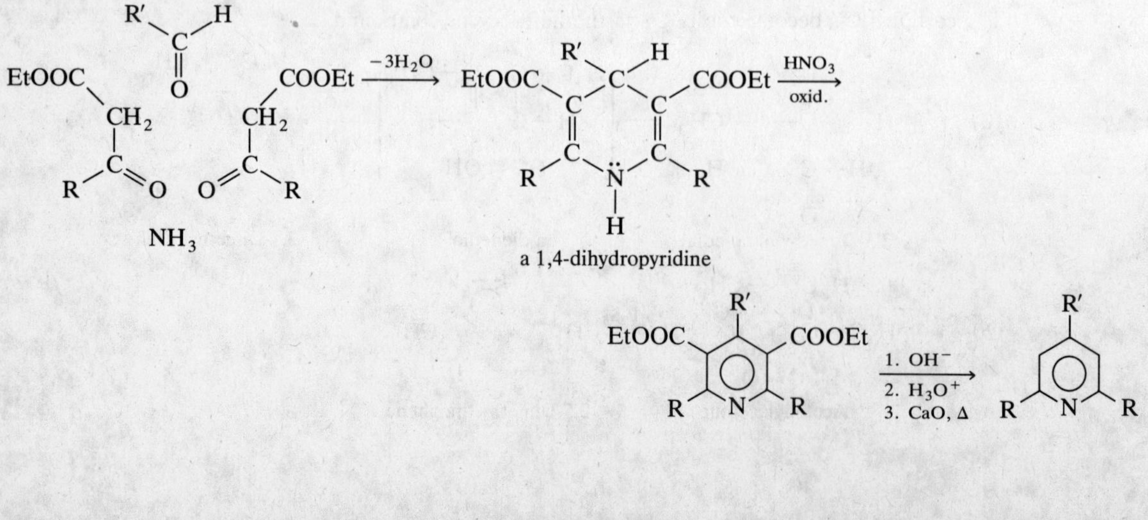

$\xrightarrow{-3H_2O}$ a 1,4-dihydropyridine $\xrightarrow[oxid.]{HNO_3}$

$\xrightarrow[3. CaO, \Delta]{\substack{1. OH^- \\ 2. H_3O^+}}$

The product must have the same R groups at C^2 and C^6, and it may also have an R at C^4 that comes from the aldehyde.

21.21 Which reactants are needed to make 2,4-diethyl-4-phenylpyridine by the Hantzsch pyridine synthesis?

▮ $C_2H_5COCH_2COOEt$ gives the C_2H_5 groups at C^2 and C^6. PhCHO gives the Ph at C^4.

21.22 (*a*) Show the reaction steps in the *Skraup quinoline synthesis* given the overall reaction

$$PhNH_2 + PhNO_2 + HOCH_2CHOHCH_2OH \xrightarrow[FeSO_4,\ \Delta]{H_2SO_4} \text{quinoline} + PhNH_2 + H_2O$$

(*b*) Why cannot $H_2C{=}CHCHO$ itself be used instead of $HOCH_2CHOHCH_2OH$?

▮ (*a*) *Step 1.* Dehydration:

$$\underset{\text{Glycerol}}{HOCH_2CHOHCH_2OH} \xrightarrow{H_2SO_4} \underset{\text{Acrolein}}{H_2C{=}CHCHO} + 2H_2O$$

Step 2. Michael addition:

$$PhNH_2 + H_2C{=}CHCHO \longrightarrow \underset{\beta\text{-(Phenylamino)propionaldehyde, } \mathbf{C}}{PhNHCH_2CH_2CHO}$$

Step 3. Electrophilic attack:

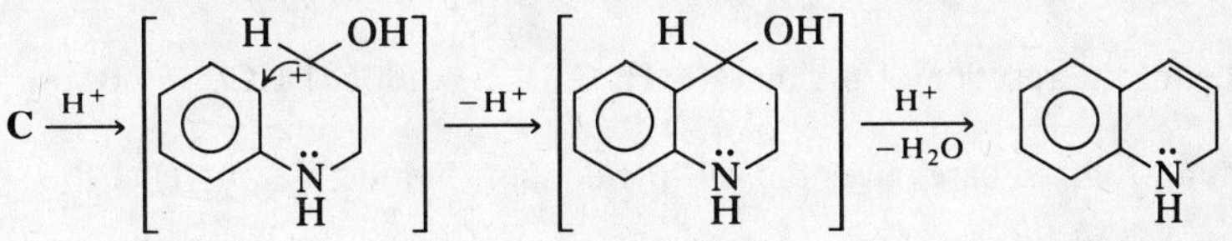

1,2-Dihydroquinoline, **D**

Step 4. Oxidation with $PhNO_2$:

$$\mathbf{D} + PhNO_2 \longrightarrow \text{quinoline} + PhNH_2$$

$PhNH_2$ formed during the oxidation step is recycled into step 2 so that $PhNO_2$ is consumed and only a small amount of $PhNH_2$ is needed to start the reaction. If oxidants other than $PhNO_2$ are used, then equimolar amounts of $PhNH_2$ are required. $FeSO_4$ moderates the potentially vigorous oxidation.

(*b*) It would polymerize in acid.

21.23 Give the products prepared by the Skraup synthesis with (*a*) *p*-nitroaniline, (*b*) *o*-methoxyaniline, and (*c*) *o*-phenylenediamine (1,2-diaminobenzene).

▮ With substituted anilines the substituents end up on the benzene ring. (*a*) 6-Nitroquinoline. (*b*) 8-Methoxyquinoline. (*c*) Ring closure will occur *ortho* to each NH_2. The product is

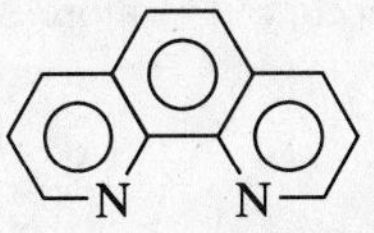

4,5-Diazaphenanthrene

21.24 A modification of the Skraup synthesis, the *Doebner–Miller synthesis* replaces glycerol with aldehydes or ketones. (*a*) Explain the formation of 2-methylquinoline from the reaction of $PhNH_2$ and CH_3CHO. (*b*) Which quinoline is formed when methyl vinyl ketone is used?

▮ (*a*) The α,β-unsaturated carbonyl compound that actually reacts is $MeCH{=}CHCHO$, the aldol condensation product of CH_3CHO. The last three steps are identical to those for the Skraup synthesis. The R attached to the β C is found at C^2 of the quinoline ring. (*b*) 4-Methylquinoline. The R attached to the $C{=}O$ is now at C^4.

REACTIONS

21.25 Compare the basicities of pyrrole, pyridine, and piperidine (azacyclohexane).

▮ The pyrrole ring needs delocalization of electron-density from N to be aromatic. The N now has insufficient electron-density to be a basic site. Pyrrole does not even dissolve in HCl. Since pyridine is aromatic without requiring the electron pair on N, N is a basic site. The *s*-character of the N is used to compare the basicities of pyridine and piperidine. Piperidine is much more basic because its N has sp^3 HO's (less s-character) while the N of pyridine has sp^2 HO's (more s-character).

21.26 Why is $PhNH_2$ ($K_b = 4.2 \times 10^{-10}$) less basic than pyridine ($K_b = 2.3 \times 10^{-9}$)?

◢ We might expect $PhNH_2$ to be more basic because its N has sp^3 HO's while the N of pyridine has sp^2 HO's. However, in $PhNH_2$ there is considerable electron-delocalization from N to the ring, providing much delocalization energy. This delocalization is destroyed when H^+ adds to the N, thereby decreasing the basicity of aniline.

21.27 (*a*) Write an ionic equation for the reaction of imidizole with aq. HCl. (*b*) Discuss the basicity of imidizole. (*c*) Why is imidizole more basic than pyridine? (*d*) How many of the N's of purine are basic sites?

◢ (*a*)

equivalent resonance structures

(*b*) The electron pair of H—N: is delocalized to provide the aromatic sextet—this N is not a basic site. The N of :N=C retains its electron density and is a basic site. This situation prevails in all nitrogen-containing aromatic systems. (*c*) The conjugate acid of imidizole is characterized by two equivalent resonance structures. (*d*) The three double-bonded N's in purine (Problem 21.12) are basic sites, the lone NH grouping is not.

21.28 Give the product of the reaction of pyridine (PyH, C_5H_5N) with (*a*) HCl, (*b*) BMe_3, (*c*) MeI, and (*d*) *t*-BuCl.

◢ (*a*) PyH, a Brönsted base, gives the salt pyridinium chloride, ⟨◯⟩NH^+Cl^- .

(*b*) PyH, a nucleophile, reacts with BMe_3, a Lewis acid, to give C_5H_5N—BMe_3.
(*c*) N-Methylpyridinium iodide, $C_5H_5NMe^+I^-$, is formed by an S_N2 reaction.
(*d*) $C_5H_5NH^+Cl^- + H_2C=CMe_2$. 3° Halides undergo E2 reactions instead of S_N2 reactions.

21.29 Give the product, if any, from mixing pyrrole and MeI.

◢ No reaction occurs because the HN: grouping is not nucleophilic (Problem 21.25).

21.30 Name the products formed when (*a*) furan, (*b*) pyrrole, and (*c*) pyridine are catalytically hydrogenated.

◢ The rings are completely reduced to the corresponding saturated heterocyclics. (*a*) Tetrahydrofuran, (*b*) pyrrolidine, and (*c*) piperidine.

21.31 Give the product formed when quinoline is reduced catalytically with 2 eq of H_2.

◢ Reduction of the pyridine ring occurs; it is more electron-deficient because of the electron-withdrawing N.

1,2,3,4-Tetrahydroquinoline

21.32 Pyrrole is reduced with Zn and MeCOOH to pyrroline, C_4H_7N. (*a*) Give two possible structures for pyrroline. (*b*) Select the correct isomer given the following findings: oxidative ozonolysis gives $C_4H_7O_4N$ which can be synthesized from 2 mol of $ClCH_2COOH$ and NH_3.

◢ (*a*) The numbers in the names show the positions of the added H's.

2,5-Dihydropyrrole (**A**)   2,3-Dihydropyrrole (**B**)

(*b*) Isomer **A** gives $HOOCCH_2NHCH_2COOH$ (**C**) and isomer **B** gives $HOOCCH_2CH_2NHCOOH$ (**D**). Since only **A** can be synthesized from 2 mol of $ClCH_2COOH$ and NH_3, pyrroline is isomer **A**.

21.33 Compare the reaction of pyrrole and pyridine with peroxybenzoic acid, $PhCO_3H$.

◢ Pyrrole is insufficiently nucleophilic to react with this oxidizing reagent. However, pyridine reacts like a typical 3° amine to give an N-oxide.

Pyridine-N-oxide

21.34 (*a*) In terms of relative stability of the intermediate, discuss the orientation of electrophilic substitution with furan, pyrrole, and thiophene. Use the general formula $C_4H_4Z:$. (*b*) Why are these heterocycles more reactive than PhH to attack by E^+? (*c*) With which kind of substituted benzenes does the reactivity of these heterocycles compare?

◢ (*a*) See Fig. 21-6. The transition state and intermediate cation (**A**) formed by the α-attack has a lower enthalpy than the one from the β-attack (**B**). **A** not only has one more contributing structure than **B**, but I and II are allylic; V is not allylic. (*b*) This is ascribed to contributing structure III, in which Z has a + charge and all C's have an octet of electrons. (*c*) They are as reactive as PhOH and $PhNH_2$.

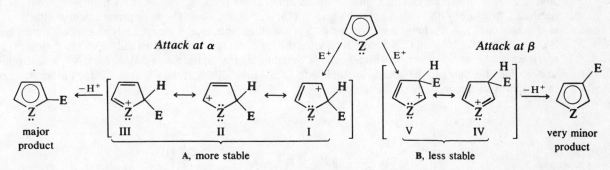

Fig. 21-6

21.35 Name the products obtained from the reaction of (*a*) furan with (i) CH_3CONO_2 (acetyl nitrate) and (ii) $(CH_3CO)_2O/BF_3$, (*b*) pyrrole with (i) SO_3/pyridine, (ii) $CHCl_3$/KOH, and (iii) $PhN_2^+Cl^-$ (give the structure), and (*c*) thiophene with (i) H_2SO_4, (ii) Br_2/PhH, and (iii) $H_2C=O$/HCl.

◢ (*a*) (i) 2-Nitrofuran, (ii) 2-acetylfuran. (*b*) (i) 2-Pyrrolesulfonic acid, (ii) 2-pyrrolecarboxaldehyde (Reimer–Tiemann reaction), and (iii) 2-phenylazopyrrole, ⌇N=N—Ph. (*c*) (i) Thiophene-2-sulfonic acid, (ii) 2,5-dibromothiophene, and (iii) 2-chlormethylthiophene.

Note that milder reagents suffice for electrophilic substitution of these heterocycles than for PhH.

21.36 Give the mononitration products of the following compounds and account for their formation: (*a*) 3-Nitropyrrole, (*b*) 3-methoxythiophene, (*c*) 2-methoxypyrrole, (*d*) 2-methoxy-5-methylthiophene, and (*e*) 5-methylfuran-2-carboxylic acid.

◢ (*a*) There are two available α positions. Attack at the 2 position gives an energetically unfavorable intermediate having a + charge on the C bonded to the electron-withdrawing NO_2. Therefore, attack occurs at the other α position giving 2,4-dinitropyrrole. (*b*) 3-Methoxy-2-nitrothiophene. The 2 position is activated more than the 5 position, being both α to the S and *ortho* to OCH_3. Here the ring and OCH_3 reenforce each other. (*c*) Here the 5 position is activated by both the ring N and the OMe, giving 2-methoxy-5-nitropyrrole. However, an appreciable amount of 2-methoxy-3-nitropyrrole (*ortho* to OMe) is also isolated. (*d*) The product is 2-methoxy-5-methyl-3-nitrothiophene. A β-ring position must undergo substitution because neither α position is available. E^+ goes *ortho* to OCH_3 which is more activating than CH_3. (*e*) 2-Methyl-5-nitrofuran is formed. E^+ displaces COOH from the activated α position.

21.37 In terms of relative stability of the intermediate, discuss the orientation of electrophilic substitution with benzo-fused five-membered ring heterocycles such as indole. Use the general formula with Z for the heteroatom.

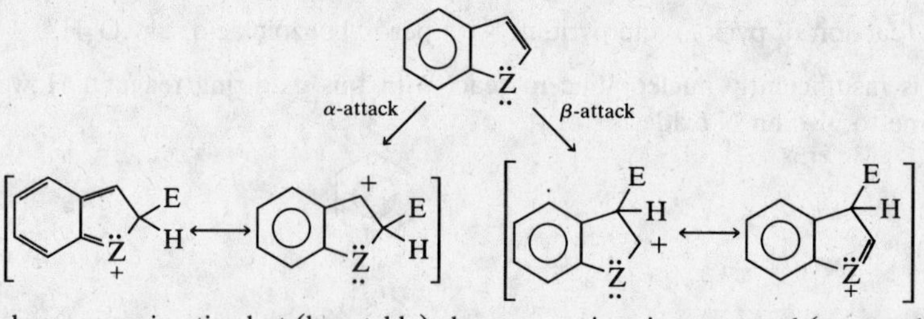

benzene conjugation lost (less stable)   benzene conjugation preserved (more stable)   **Fig. 21-7**

▮ E^+ attacks the more reactive heterocyclic ring at one of two possible positions, as shown in Fig. 21-7. β-Attack leaves a cation that has a contributing structure in which every atom has an octet of e^-'s with an intact aromatic benzene ring. To get such a cationic structure from α-attack, the benzene ring must lose its typical double-bond arrangement which accounts for its aromaticity. Attack occurs mainly at the β position, not the α position as it does on the unfused heterocycle.

21.38 (*a*) In terms of relative stability of the intermediate, discuss the orientation of electrophilic substitution on pyridine. (*b*) Compare the relative reactivities of pyridine and PhH. (*c*) With respect to attack by E^+, to which substituted benzene is pyridine related?

▮ (*a*) The intermediate cations formed by attack of E^+ at the α and γ positions have high energy contributing resonance structures with N having six e^-'s and + charge. See Fig. 21-8. The intermediate from β-attack has + charge only on C's. A + charge on C with six e^-'s is not as unstable as a + charge on N with six e^-'s, because N is more electronegative than C. β-Substitution gives the lower energy intermediate (and TS). (*b*) Pyridine is less reactive because its N inductively withdraws e^-'s, destabilizing the intermediate cation. Also, N is a nucleophilic site capable of bonding to the added electrophile to form a pyridinium cation, whose + charge further decreases the reactivity of the ring. (*c*) Nitrobenzene.

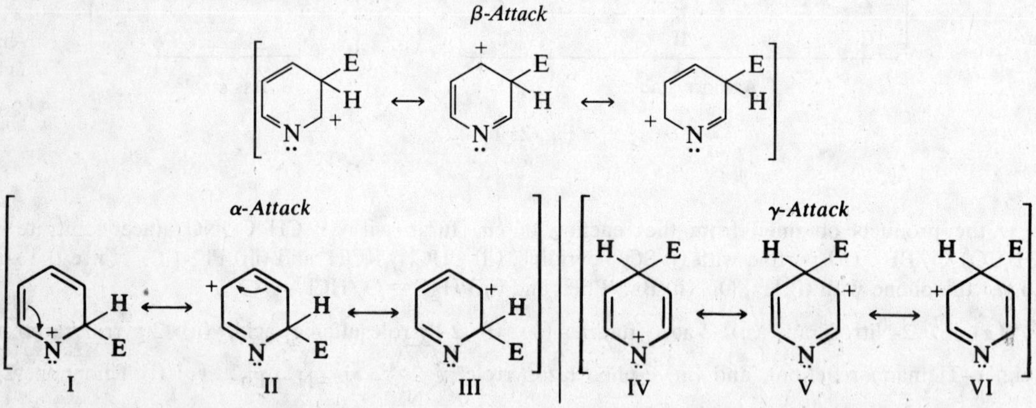

β-Attack

α-Attack   *γ-Attack*

I   II   III   IV   V   VI   **Fig. 21-8**

21.39 Name the products formed when C_5H_5N reacts with (*a*) Br_2 at 300 °C, (*b*) KNO_3/H_2SO_4 at 300 °C, followed by KOH, (*c*) H_2SO_4 at 350 °C (give the structure), and (*d*) $MeCOCl/AlCl_3$.

▮ (*a*) 3-Bromopyridine and 3,5-dibromopyridine. (*b*) 3-Nitropyridine. KOH neutralizes the pyridinium salt

that forms in acid. (*c*) 3-Pyridinesulfonic acid (a dipolar ion), 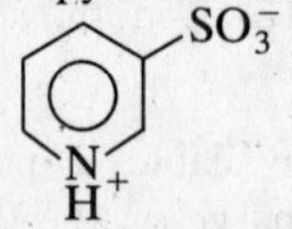 (*d*) No reaction. Pyridine is too

unreactive to undergo Friedel–Crafts acylations.

21.40 Give the expected product of the monobromination of quinoline and explain the orientation.

▮ E^+ attacks the more reactive benzene ring preferably at the α positions, giving about an equal mixture of 5- and 8-bromoquinoline.

21.41 (*a*) Give the expected product of the monobromination of pyridine-N-oxide and explain the orientation. (*b*) Name the substituted benzene analog that is electronically similar to pyridine-N-oxide.

▮ (*a*) E^+ bonds at the γ position (and somewhat at the α position) because the intermediate from such attack has a stable resonance structure with no electron-deficient atom. The intermediate from β-attack cannot be stabilized in this way. See Fig. 21-9. The ring is activated. (*b*) The very reactive phenoxide anion, PhO^-.

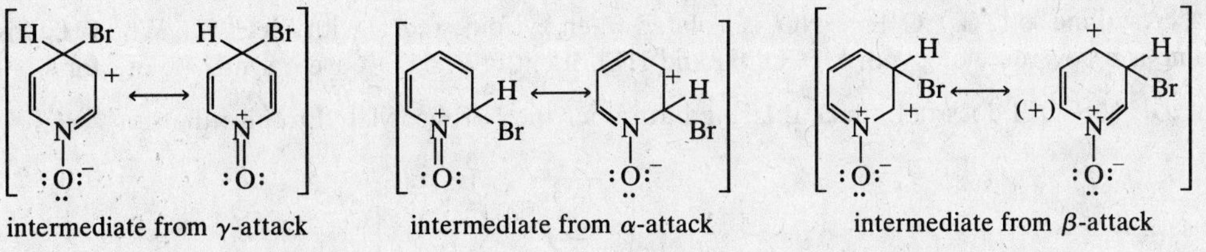

intermediate from γ-attack   intermediate from α-attack   intermediate from β-attack   **Fig. 21-9**

21.42 (*a*) Give the product from the reaction of each isomeric chloropyridine with NaOEt. (*b*) Provide a mechanism for the reaction of 2-chloropyridine and explain the behavior of 3-chloropyridine. (*c*) To which substituted benzene compound is 4-chloropyridine related?

◢ (*a*) 2-Chloropyridine → 2-ethoxypyridine; 4-chloropyridine → 4-ethoxypyridine; no reaction with 3-chloropyridine. (*b*) This is a nucleophilic aromatic displacement that proceeds by an elimination-addition mechanism (Problem 11.87).

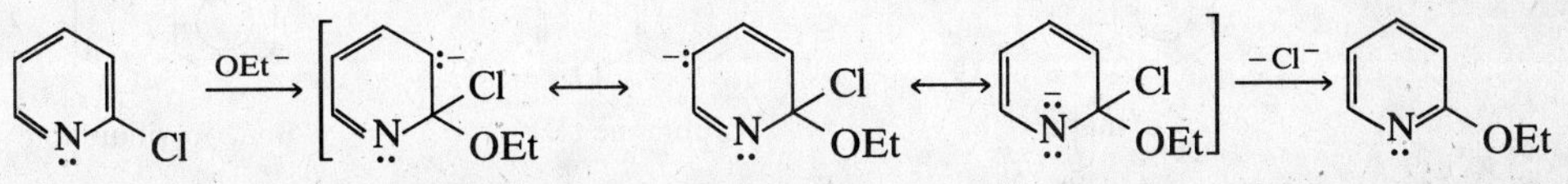

The anion intermediate is fairly stable because the $-$ charge is on N, not on C. Nucleophilic displacement at C^4 also places a $-$ charge on N. The addition of Nu: to the α and γ C is electronically akin to the addition of Nu: to C=O. Attack at C^3 gives an anionic intermediate with a $-$ charge only on C's.

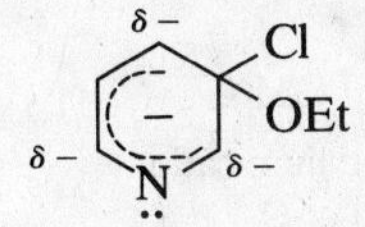

(*c*) 4-Chloronitrobenzene where the $-$ charge of the intermediate ends up on the O's of NO_2.

21.43 (*a*) Give the product resulting from heating pyridine with $NaNH_2$ followed by addition of H_2O. (*b*) Suggest a mechanism and explain the orientation of the reaction in (*a*).

◢ (*a*) 2-Aminopyridine (**A**).

(*b*) $C_5H_5N:$

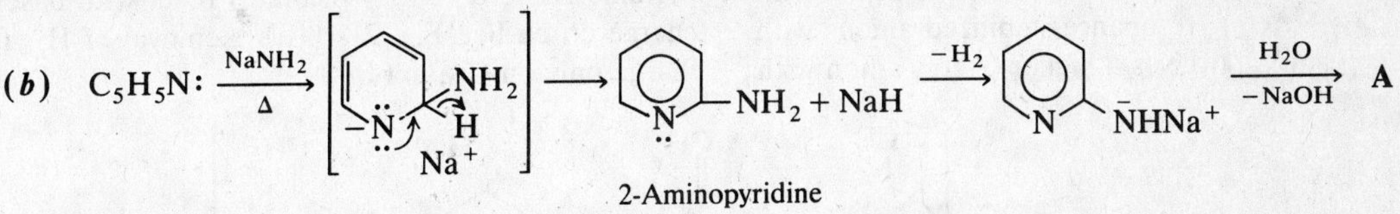

The major product results from attack at C^2 because the nearby Na^+ that is ion-paired to N^- is close enough to the α H to help remove it as $H:^-$, forming $Na^+H:^-$. The very basic $H:^-$ reacts with an H of Py—NH_2 to give α-pyridyl-NH^-Na^+ which then gives the product on addition of water.

21.44 (*a*) Give the products from reaction of OH^- and (i) pyridine, and (ii) N-methylpyridinium cation. (*b*) Compare their reactivities. (*c*) Give the product formed when an oxidant such as $K_3Fe(CN)_6$ is present in the reaction mixture (ii) of (*a*).

◢ (*a*) (i) 2-Pyridone in equilibrium with a small amount of 2-pyridinol.

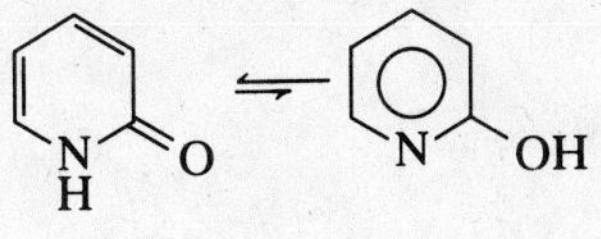

(ii)

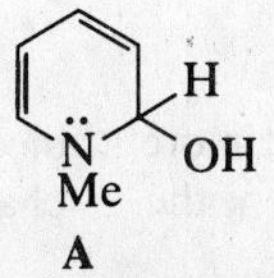

(*b*) N-methylpyridinium cation is more reactive because **A**, the first formed product, is uncharged.
(*c*) N-Methyl-2-pyridone.

21.45 (*a*) A crystalline solid (**B**), C_7H_8ClNO, is isolated when pyridine reacts with MeCOCl. When H_2O is added to **B**, pyridine is recovered along with MeCOOH and HCl. Identify **B**. (*b*) Give a synthetic use for **B**.

◢ (*a*) MeCOCl does not attack the ring but rather the N is acetylated to give the salt

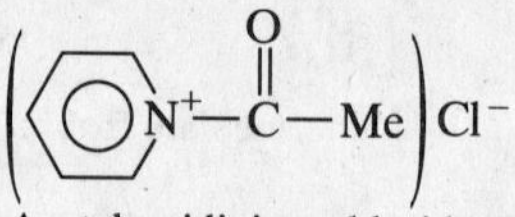

N-Acetylpyridinium chloride (**B**)

(*b*) **B** is used as an acylating reagent.

21.46 How are coumarin (**C**) and chromone (**D**) related to benzopyrylium cations?

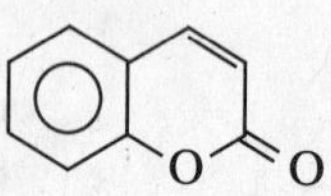

Coumarin (**C**) 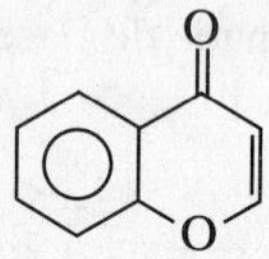   Chromone (**D**) 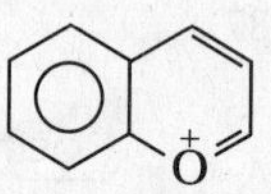   1-Benzopyrilium ion

◢ Addition of H^+ to the C=O of **C** and **D** results in a benzopyrylium cation.

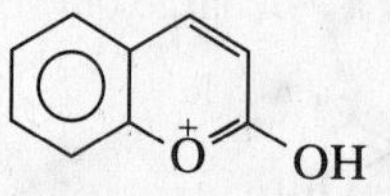

2-Hydroxy-1-benzopyrylium cation
conjugate acid of **C**

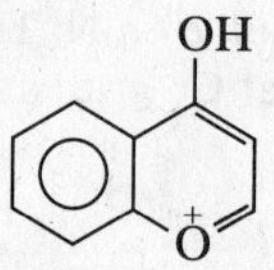

4-Hydroxy-1-benzopyrylium cation
conjugate acid of **D**

Some coumarins are useful anticoagulants, disrupting normal pathways for blood clotting.

21.47 Compare the acidities of the methyl H's of (*a*) 2-picoline and 4-picoline with those of 3-picoline, and (*b*) 2-picoline with N-methylpyridinium chloride.

◢ (*a*) Recall that the picolines are methylpyridines. The α- and γ-picolines react with base, $B:^-$, to form resonance-stabilized anions with − charge on N. See Fig. 21-10(*a*). Removal of H^+ from 3-picoline gives a higher energy anion with − charge only on C's, not on N.

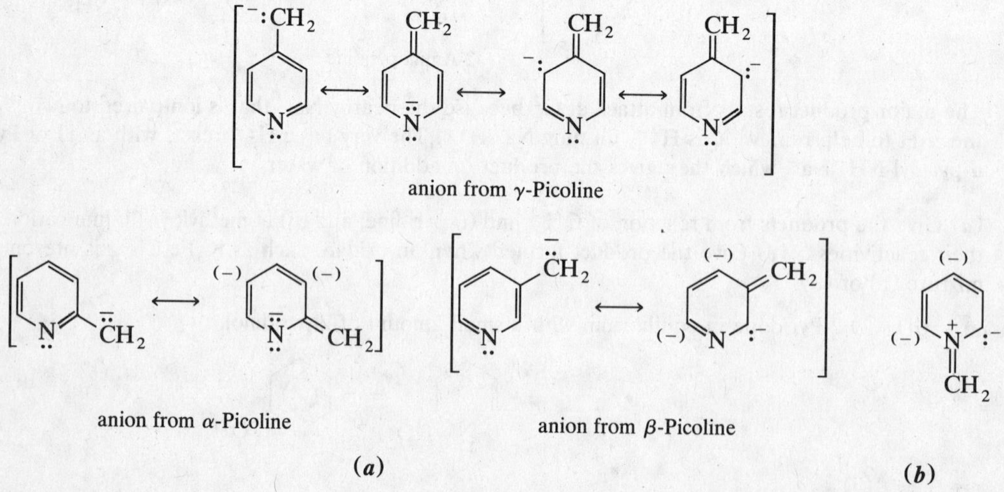

anion from γ-Picoline

anion from α-Picoline   anion from β-Picoline

(*a*)   (*b*)

Fig. 21-10

(*b*) The H's of 2-picoline are more acidic because the − charge on the conjugate base is delocalized to N. For the pyridinium cation, the − charge is delocalized only to C's; the N remains positively-charged.

21.48 2-Alkoxypyridines are readily hydrolyzed in aq. acid to give 2-hydroxypyridine (**A**) and ROH. Two mechanisms have been proposed, each starting from the pyridinium cation, (**B**); (*1*) nucleophilic aromatic displacement by water and (*2*) S_N2 attack by water on the alkyl C. (*a*) Show steps for each mechanism. (*b*) Design an experiment to distinguish between the two mechanisms.

(a) path 1:

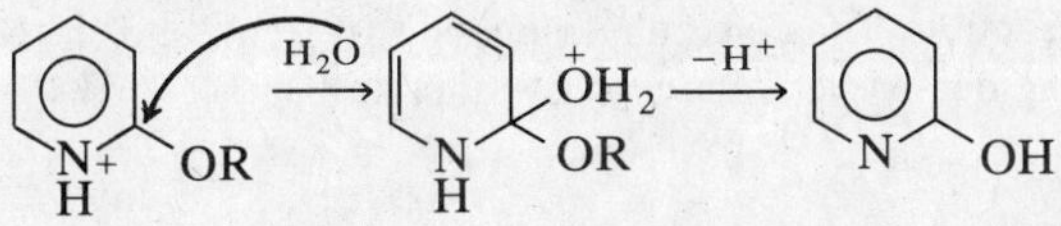

+ ROH

B   **A**

path 2:

+ ROH

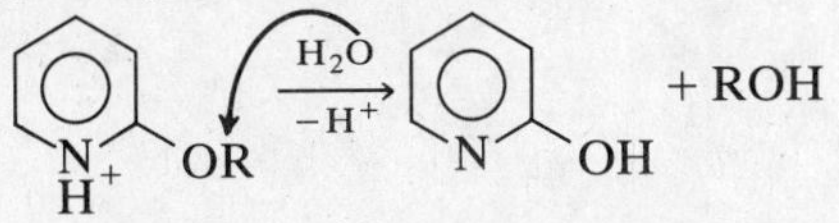

B   **A**

A tautomerizes to the more stable 2-pyridone.

(b) Use an enantiomer of the *sec*-butyl ether. The recovered *sec*-BuOH will have a retained configuration in mechanism *1* and an inverted configuration in mechanism *2*. We could also use an ^{18}O-labeled ether. The recovered ROH will be labeled if mechanism *1* is operative and unlabeled if mechanism *2* prevails.

21.49 **(a)** Complete the following reactions: (i) pyridine-N-oxide + Zn/H$_3$O$^+$ (or PCl$_5$), (ii) pyridine-N-oxide + POCl$_3$ or SO$_2$Cl$_2$, and (iii) 4-nitro-2-methylpyridine-N-oxide + HCl. **(b)** Suggest a mechanism for (iii).

⬭ **(a)** (i) Pyridine, (ii) 2-chloro and 4-chloropyridine, (iii) 4-chloro-3-methylpyridine-N-oxide.

(b)

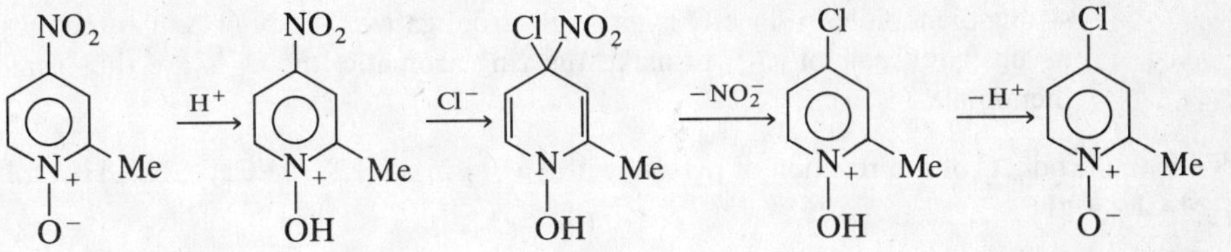

A

Protonated N-oxides readily undergo nucleophilic aromatic substitution because the intermediate, **A**, is an unchanged molecule.

21.50 Why can pyrilium perchlorate be isolated but not the I$^-$ salt?

⬭ The + charged pyrilium ring is very susceptible to nucleophilic addition at C^2 and C^4. I$^-$ is sufficiently nucleophilic to add, but ClO$_4^-$ is one of the weakest nucleophiles known and does not react. The nonaromatic products are:

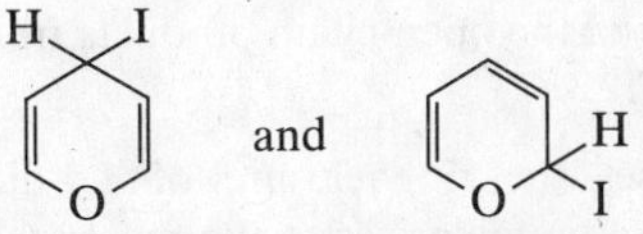

and

21.51 Account for the formation of 2,4,6-trimethylpyridine from 2,4,6-trimethylpyrilium perchlorate and NH$_3$.

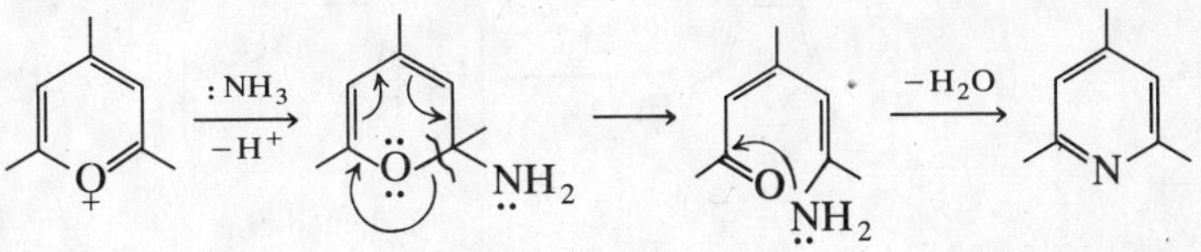

⬭

21.52 Give the oxidation product of quinoline.

⬭ The more reactive benzene ring is oxidized to quinolinic acid (2,3-pyridinedicarboxylic acid).

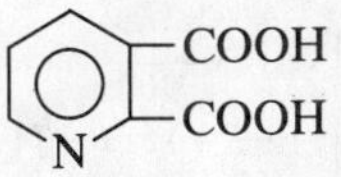

Quinolinic acid

21.53 **(a)** Prepare 2-phenylpyridine from pyridine (PyH) and PhH. **(b)** Give the oxidation product of 2-phenylpyridine.

⬭ **(a)** Ph:$^-$ displaces H:$^-$.

$$\text{Pyridine} + \text{PhLi} \longrightarrow \text{2-phenylpyridine} + \text{LiH}$$

The Ph group is closer to C^2 than to C^4 because of ion-pairing of Li$^+$ with the ring N, accounting for formation of more 2-phenylpyridine than 4-phenylpyridine.

(b) The more reactive benzene ring is oxidized giving α-picolinic acid (2-pyridinecarboxylic acid).

21.54 (*a*) Give the product from the reaction of maleic anhydride with (i) furan and (ii) N-methylpyrrole. (*b*) Why is furan the only five-membered ring heterocycle undergoing reaction (i)?

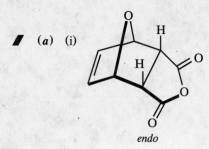

(a) (i)

endo

(ii) Electrophilic substitution occurs, giving

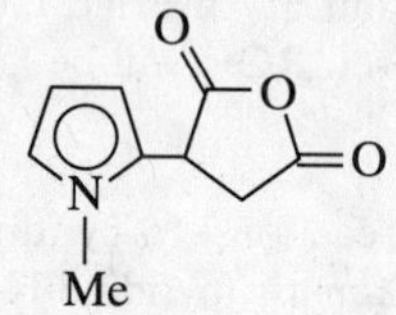

(*b*) Furan is the least aromatic five-membered ring heterocycle and can act as a diene but only towards strong dienophiles. (Since O is more electronegative than N or S, it is the most reluctant to contribute its unshared pair of e⁻'s to make the ring aromatic; the e⁻'s are thus available for reaction with a dienophile.

21.55 Give the products of the reaction of pyrrole with (*a*) I_2 in aq. KI, (*b*) CH_3CN + HCl followed by hydrolysis, and (*c*) CH_3MgI.

(a) 2,3,4,5-Tetraiodopyrrole (pyrrole is a very activated ring). (*b*) 2-Acetylpyrrole.

(c)

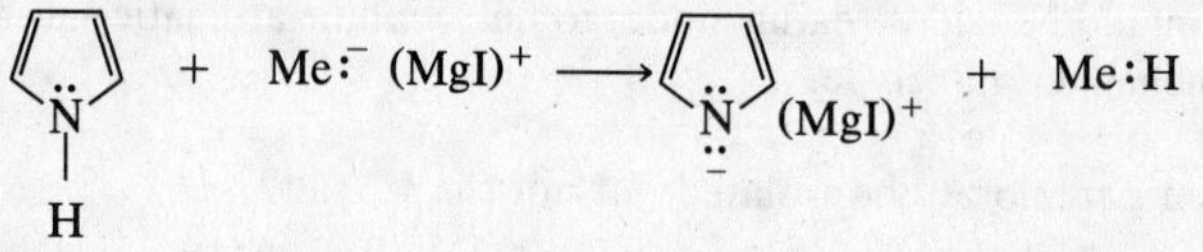

A_1 (stronger acid) B_2 (stronger base) B_1 (weaker base) A_2 (weaker acid)

21.56 Give the steps for the formation of the open-chain products from the reaction of (*a*) 2,5-diethylfuran with H_3O^+ and (*b*) pyrrole with $HONH_3^+Cl^-$.

(a) This reaction reverses the ring closure of 1,4-dicarbonyl compounds (see Problem 21.16). The intermediate dienediol tautomerizes to the more stable diketo form.

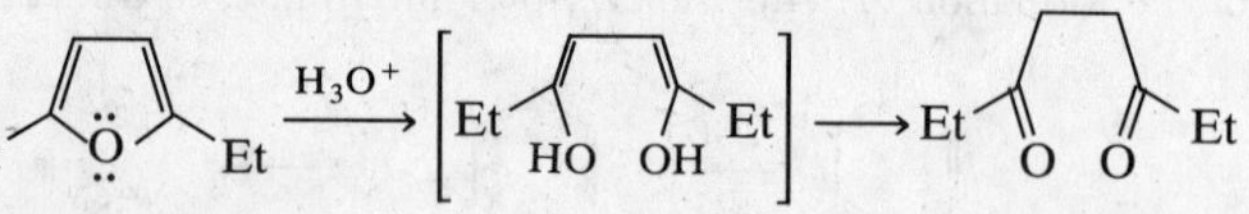

a dienediol   3,6-Octanedione

(*b*) Acid-catalyzed ring opening of pyrrole after tautomerization and hydrolysis yields butanedial that gives the dioxime with H_2NOH. The last step draws the reaction to completion and prevents recyclization to furan.

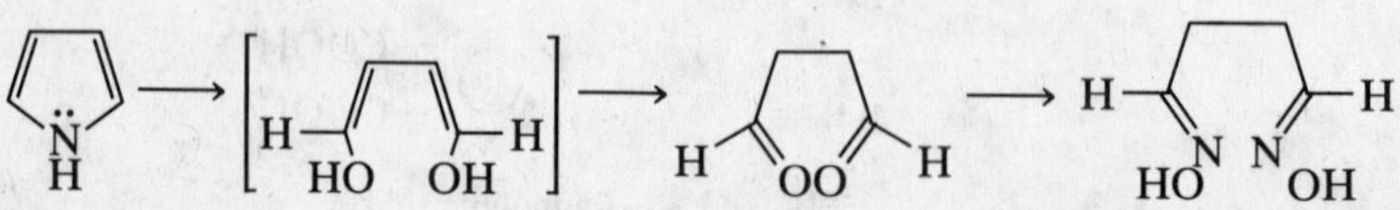

Butanediol dioxime

21.57 (*a*) Give the product of the reaction of 2-vinylpyridine and diethylmalonate in base. (*b*) Classify the type of reaction and account for the formation of the product.

(a) 2-PyCH₂CH₂CH(COOEt)₂. (*b*) A Michael addition by malonate anion to the vinyl group gives 2-PyCHCH₂CH(COOEt)₂ whose − charge is stabilized by delocalization to N (see Problem 21.47).

21.58 Provide structures for **A** and **B**: Thiophene + phthalic anhydride $\xrightarrow{\text{AlCl}_3}$ **A** $\xrightarrow{\text{H}_2\text{SO}_4}$ **B**.

▰ The first step is an acylation of thiophene to give **A** which undergoes a second acylation on the thiophene ring to give **B**.

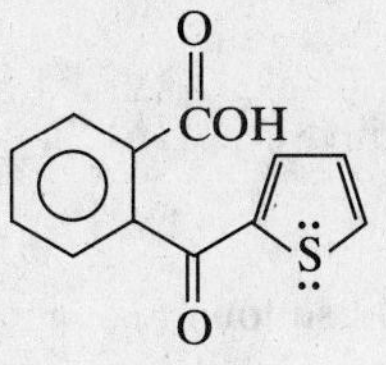

A 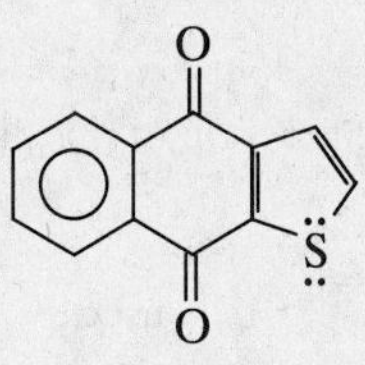   **B**

21.59 Give the structures and names of the products from the reactions of furfural, 2-furancarboxaldehyde, with (*a*) conc. aq. NaOH, (*b*) $CH_3CHO/NaOEt$, (*c*) $(CH_3CH_2CO)_2O + CH_3CH_2COO^-Na^+$, (*d*) $PhCH_2CN/OH^-$, and (*e*) cyclopentadiene/OH^-. Identify each reaction. (Disregard stereochemistry.)

▰ (*a*) Cannizzaro:

Sodium furoate   Furfuryl alcohol

(*b*) Crossed aldol:

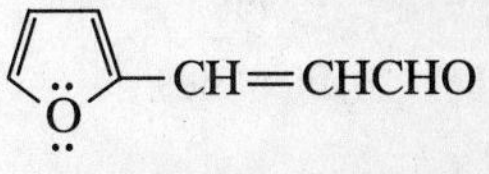

3-(2-Furyl)-propenal

(*c*) Perkin condensation:

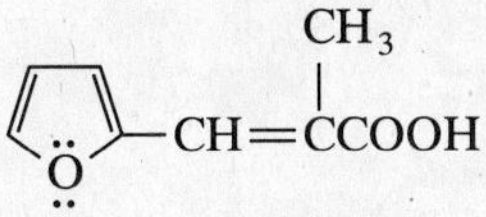

3-(2-Furyl)-2-methylpropenoic acid

(*d*) Crossed-aldol type:

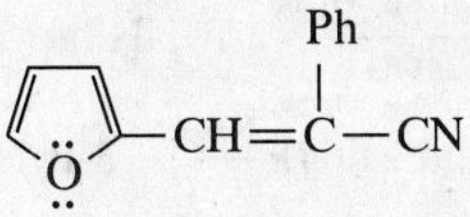

3-(2-Furyl)-2-phenylpropenenitrile

(*e*) Crossed-aldol type:

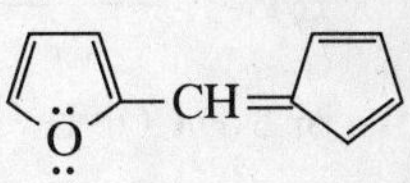

2-Furylfulvene

21.60 Compare the reaction of PhCOOH and 2-furoic acid to heating to ≈ 200 °C.

▰ PhCOOH is unreactive. 2-Furoic acid is decarboxylated giving furan.

21.61 When pyridine is reacted with metallic Na at room temperature, three deeply-colored isomeric substances, $C_{10}H_{10}N_2Na_2$(**C**), are isolated. On hydrolysis and air oxidation they give stable isomers, $C_{10}H_8N_2$(**D**), that give salts, $C_{10}H_{10}N_2Cl_2$, with aq. HCl. (*a*) Give the structural formulas for $C_{10}H_{10}N_2Na_2$ and $C_{10}H_8N_2$. (*b*) Give a mechanism for formation of one of the isomers of $C_{10}H_{10}N_2Na_2$.

▰ (*a*) The compounds are dimers of pyridine. One of the isomers of **C** is the disodium salt of the dianion of 4,4'-tetrahydrobipyridyl. The isomer of **D** formed from this isomer of **C** is 4,4'-bipyridyl.

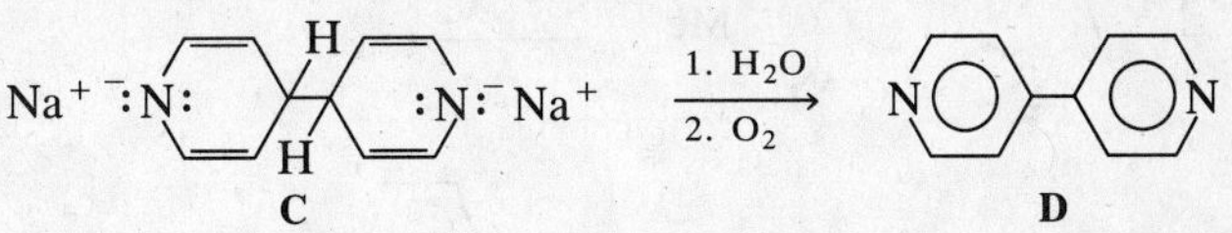

C   **D**

The other isomers are the 2,2- and 2,4-dimers. (*b*) Na· contributes an e^- to the pyridine ring, yielding a radical anion with the odd e^- at either C^2 or C^4. These radicals then couple, C^4 with C^4, C^2 with C^2, or C^2 with C^4 to give the three sets of isomeric products. The C^4 radical anion is

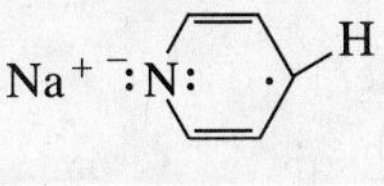

21.62 (*a*) Which two isomeric products are found when 2-pyridinol is reacted with base and $PhCH_2Cl$? (*b*) Why does the ratio of products change when 6-methyl-2-pyridinol is used?

▰ (*a*) 2-Pyridinol loses a proton to the base to give an ambident anion with some − charge on N and on O. Reaction occurs at both sites, at O giving the ether, 2-benzyloxypyridine and at N giving N-benzyl-2-pyridone.

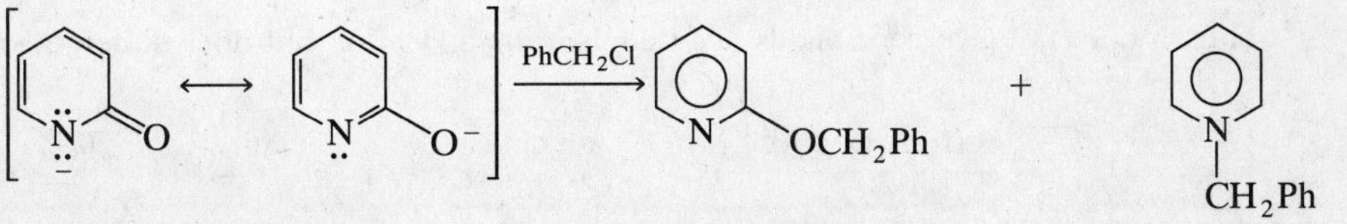

ambident anion   O-alkylation product   N-alkylation product

(b) With 2-pyridinol the pyridone is the major product (Problem 21.44). But Me at C^6 sterically hinders the approach of the large $PhCH_2$ to N in 6-methyl-2-pyridinol, and instead O is alkylated preferentially.

21.63 (a) Give the product of the reaction of pyridine with SO_3. (b) Suggest an important use of the product from the reaction in (a)

▰ (a) ⬡N^+—SO_3^- . (b) It is used as a mild sulfonating agent [see (i) in Problem 21.35(b)].

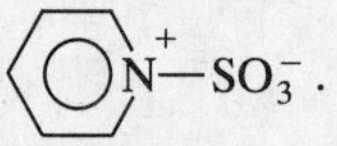

SYNTHESIS

21.64 From pyridine (PyH) or any picoline (PyMe) prepare (a) nicotinamide (Problem 21.8), and (b) the antituberculosis drug 4-pyridinecarboxylic acid hydrazide (isoniazide).

▰ (a) β-Picoline $\xrightarrow{KMnO_4}$ β-PyCOOH $\xrightarrow{SOCl_2}$ β-PyCOCl $\xrightarrow{NH_3}$ β-PyCONH$_2$ (nicotinamide)

(b) γ-Picoline $\xrightarrow{KMnO_4}$ 4-PyCOOH $\xrightarrow[\text{2. } H_2NNH_2]{\text{1. } SOCl_2}$ 4-PyCONHNH$_2$ (isoniazide)

21.65 From PyH or any PyMe prepare (a) 3-PyNH$_2$, (b) 3-PyCN (use two methods), and (c) 2-PyCN.

▰ (a) PyH $\xrightarrow{HNO_3/H_2SO_4}$ 3-PyNO$_2$ $\xrightarrow[\text{2. } OH^-]{\text{1. } Sn/HCl}$ 3-PyNH$_2$

or 3-PyCONH$_2$ (from Problem 21.64) $\xrightarrow[OH^-]{NaOBr}$ 3-PyNH$_2$

(b) 3-PyNH$_2$ $\xrightarrow[\text{2. } CuCN]{\text{1. } HONO, \, 0\,°C}$ 3-PyCN $\xleftarrow{P_2O_5}$ 3-PyCONH$_2$

(c) 2-PyNH$_2$ does not diazotize in the normal fashion and cannot be converted to the cyano compound. The CN group is best made from the amide.

2-PyCH$_3$ $\xrightarrow{KMnO_4}$ 2-PyCOOH $\xrightarrow{SOCl_2}$ 2-PyCOCl $\xrightarrow{NH_3}$ 2-PyCONH$_2$ $\xrightarrow{P_2O_5}$ 2-PyCN

21.66 From pyrrole and any acyclic compounds prepare 3-(2-pyrrolyl)-propenoic acid.

▰ Use the Vilsmeier reaction (Problem 19.106) to make 2-pyrrolecarboxaldehyde followed by the Reformatsky reaction.

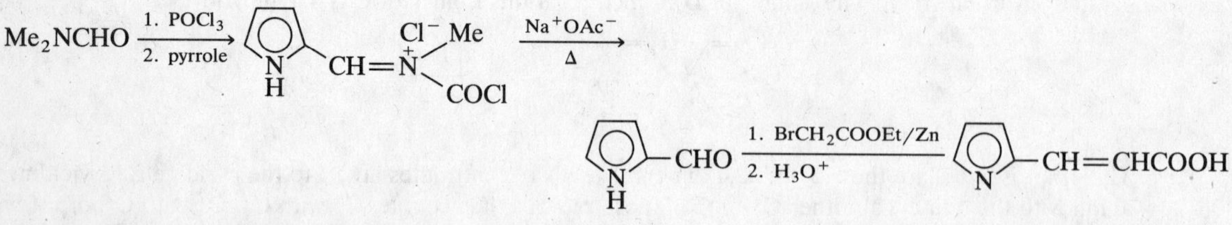

$Me_2NCHO \xrightarrow[\text{2. pyrrole}]{\text{1. } POCl_3}$ ⬡(N-H)—CH=N$^+$(Cl$^-$ Me)(COCl) $\xrightarrow[\Delta]{Na^+OAc^-}$

⬡(N-H)—CHO $\xrightarrow[\text{2. } H_3O^+]{\text{1. } BrCH_2COOEt/Zn}$ ⬡(N)—CH=CHCOOH

The aldehyde could also be made by the Reimer-Tiemann reaction [see (ii) of Problem 21.35(b)].

21.67 Prepare 4-bromopyridine from pyridine.

▰ Direct bromination of pyridine affords the 3-isomer but bromination of pyridine-N-oxide gives the 4-isomer. The oxide is then reduced.

PyH $\xrightarrow{PhCO_3H}$ Py-N-oxide $\xrightarrow{Br_2}$ 4-bromopyridine-N-oxide $\xrightarrow[\text{2. } OH^-]{\text{1. } Zn/HCl}$ 4-Br-Py

21.68 Prepare 2-propylfuran from furan and any acyclic compound.

▰ Furan does not give good yields of Friedel-Crafts alkylation but does undergo acylation.

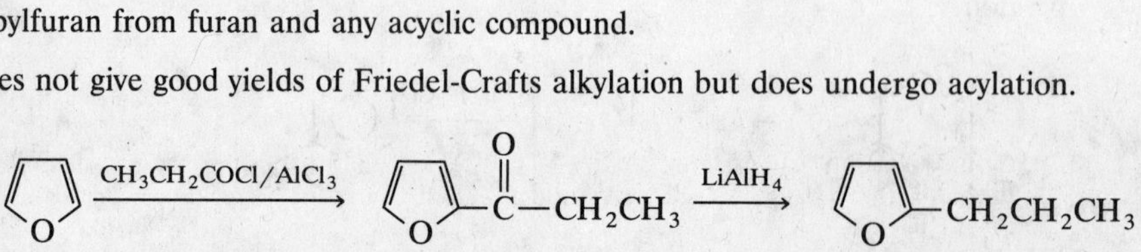

⬡(O) $\xrightarrow{CH_3CH_2COCl/AlCl_3}$ ⬡(O)—C(=O)—CH$_2$CH$_3$ $\xrightarrow{LiAlH_4}$ ⬡(O)—CH$_2$CH$_2$CH$_3$

1-(2-Furyl)-1-propanone   2-Propylfuran

21.69 Prepare β-benzothiophylacetic acid from benzothiophene and any acyclic compound.

21.70 (*a*) From quinoline (QuH) prepare **A**, . (*b*) Why cannot **A** be converted to a stable benzofuran?

    (*a*)

$$\underset{\text{2,3-Py(COOH)}_2}{} \qquad \underset{\text{2,3-Dimethylolpyridine}}{}$$

    (*b*) In order for a $C{=}C$ to be introduced into the five-membered ring, the benzene ring would have to lose its three conjugated double bonds as shown: .

21.71 (*a*) Can PyH undergo Friedel-Crafts alkylations or acylations? (*b*) Prepare 2-*n*-BuPy and 2-*n*-butylpiperidine.

    (*a*) PyH is deactivated and like $PhNO_2$ cannot be alkylated or acylated. (*b*) It can be alkylated by nucleophilic displacement by $R\!:^-$ (or $Ar\!:^-$).

$$\text{PyH} + n\text{-BuLi} \xrightarrow{-\text{LiH}} 2\text{-}n\text{-BuPy} \xrightarrow{\text{H}_2/\text{Ni}} 2\text{-}n\text{-Butylpiperidine}$$

21.72 From 2-PyMe and any acyclic compound prepare (*a*) 2-PyCOCH$_3$ (**A**), (*b*) 2-PyCH=CH$_2$ (**B**), (*c*) 2-PyCHO (**C**), (*d*) 2-cyclopropylPy (**D**), and (*e*) 2-PyC(Me)=CHCH$_3$ (**E**). Do not repeat any syntheses.

    (*a*) $\quad$ 2-MePy $\xrightarrow{\text{KMnO}_4}$ 2-PyCOOH $\xrightarrow[\text{2. NaOH (neutralize}]{\text{1. EtOH/H}_2\text{SO}_4}$ 2-PyCOOEt $\xrightarrow{\text{CH}_3\text{COOEt/NaOEt}}$

$\underset{\text{Py}^+\text{ salt)}}{}$

$$2\text{-PyCOCH}_2\text{COOEt} \xrightarrow[\text{2. H}_3\text{O}^+]{\text{1. OH}^-,\,\Delta} \textbf{A}$$

    (*b*) $\quad$ **A** $\xrightarrow{\text{NaBH}_4}$ 2-PyCHOHCH$_3$ $\xrightarrow[\Delta]{\text{P}_2\text{O}_5}$ **B** $\quad$ (*c*) **B** $\xrightarrow[\text{2. Zn/HOAc}]{\text{1. O}_3}$ **C** $\quad$ (*d*) **B** $\xrightarrow{\text{CH}_2\text{N}_2/\text{uv}}$ **D**

    (*e*) $\qquad$ Use the Wittig reaction: **A** + Ph$_3$P=CHCH$_3$ $\longrightarrow$ *cis*- and *trans*-**E**

21.73 From PyH and any acyclic compound prepare (*a*) 2-pyridone (**F**), (*b*) 2-PyCl (**G**), and (*c*) 2-PyCH$_2$CH$_2$NH$_2$ (**H**).

    (*a*) $\quad$ PyH $\xrightarrow{\text{EtO}^-}$ 2-PyOEt $\xrightarrow{\text{H}_3\text{O}^+}$ **F**

    (*b*) $\quad$ **F** $\xrightarrow{\text{PCl}_3}$ **G**. Direct hydroxylation of PyH gives inferior yields because OH$^-$ is not a strong enough nucleophile [see Problem 21.44(*a*)].

    (*c*) $\quad$ 2-PyBr + Na^{+-}:CH(COOEt)$_2$ $\longrightarrow$ 2-PyCH(COOEt)$_2$ $\xrightarrow[\text{2. H}_3\text{O}^+]{\text{1. OH}^-/\Delta}$ 2-PyCH$_2$COOH $\xrightarrow{\text{SOCl}_2}$

2-PyCH$_2$COCl $\xrightarrow{\text{NH}_3}$ 2-PyCH$_2$CONH$_2$ $\xrightarrow{\text{LiAlH}_4}$ **H**

21.74 From furfural prepare (*a*) ethyl 5-bromo-2-furoate, and (*b*) 1,2,5-tribromopentane.

    (*a*)

    (*b*)

21.75 Prepare (*a*) 8-QuOH (two ways) and (*b*) 2-QuNH$_2$ from quinoline (QuH) and any acyclic compound.

    (*a*) $\quad$ QuH $\xrightarrow{\text{HNO}_3/\text{H}_2\text{SO}_4}$ 8-NO$_2$QuH$^+$ $\xrightarrow{\text{Sn/HCl}}$ 8-QuNH$_3^+$ $\xrightarrow[\text{2. H}_2\text{O}/\Delta]{\text{1. NaNO}_2,\,0\,°\text{C}}$ 8-QuOH

    or

$$\text{QuH} \xrightarrow[\Delta]{\text{H}_2\text{SO}_4} \text{Qu-8-sulfonic acid (as dipolar salt)} \xrightarrow[\text{2. H}_3\text{O}^+]{\text{1. NaOH (fuse)}} 8\text{-QuOH}$$

Note: In the first step of both syntheses the 8-isomer must be separated from the 5-isomer.

(b) Like pyridine, quinoline undergoes nucleophilic substitution at the 2 and 4 positions.

$$QuH \xrightarrow[\text{2. } H_2O]{\text{1. } NaNH_2, \Delta} 2\text{-}QuNH_2$$

21.76 Supply the structural formulas for **A** through **C** which are involved in the *Bischler-Napieralski synthesis* of isoquinolines.

$$PhCH_2CH_2NH_2 + MeCOCl \longrightarrow \textbf{A} \text{ (acid insoluble)} \xrightarrow{P_2O_5, \Delta} \textbf{B} \text{ (acid soluble)} \xrightarrow{Pd, \Delta} \textbf{C}$$

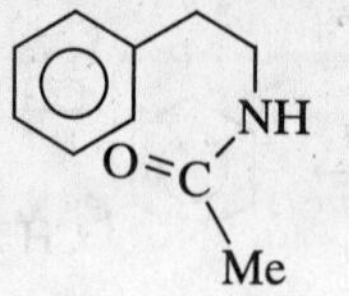

A 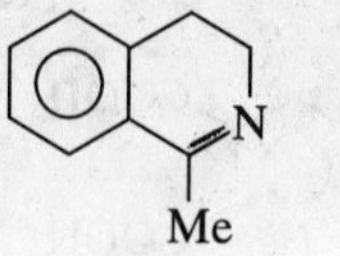   **B** 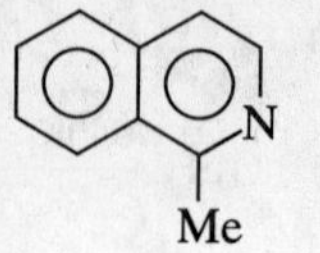   **C**

21.77 (a) Explain the difference in behavior when 1- and 3-methylisoquinoline are treated with *n*-BuLi. (b) Identify **D**.

$$1\text{-Methylisoquinoline} \xrightarrow[\text{2. 2-PyCH=O}]{\text{1. } n\text{-BuLi}} \textbf{D}$$

(a) The − charge of the 1-isomer can be delocalized to N without disrupting the stable conjugated benzene ring. This is not possible for the 3-isomer, where delocalization to N destroys the aromaticity of the benzene ring.

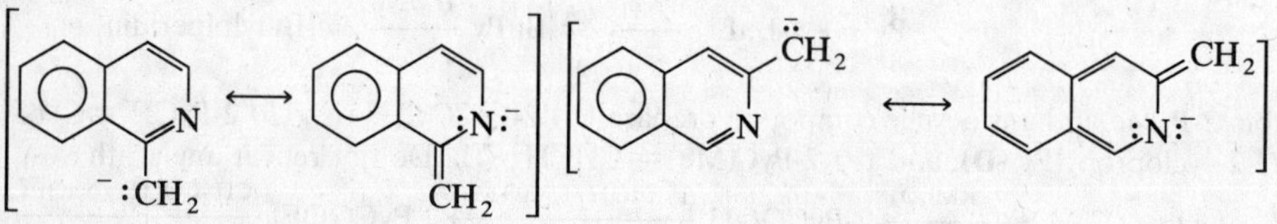

stable   not stable

(b)

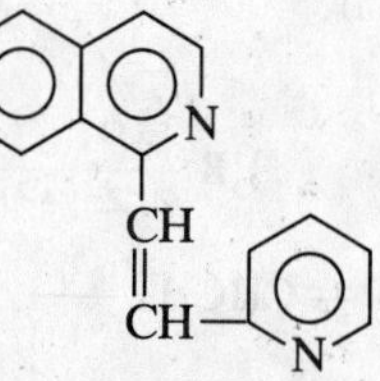

21.78 Supply the structural formulas for **E** through **L** given

(a) $o\text{-}H_2NC_6H_4COOH + ClCH_2COOH \xrightarrow{-HCl} \textbf{E} \xrightarrow[\Delta (-H_2O)]{\text{base}} [\textbf{F}] \xrightarrow{-CO_2} [\textbf{G}] \longrightarrow C_8H_7ON \textbf{(H)}$

(b) $o\text{-}H_2NC_6H_4COOEt + H_2C(COOEt)_2 \longrightarrow \textbf{I} \text{ (acid-insoluble)} \xrightarrow{NaOEt} \textbf{J} \xrightarrow[\Delta]{H^+} \textbf{K} \text{ or } \textbf{L} (C_9H_7O_2N)$

(a)

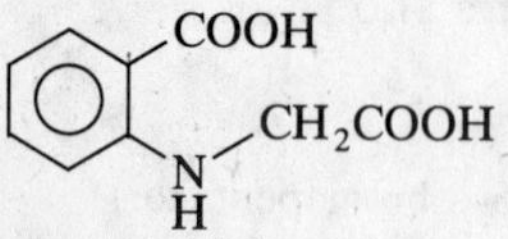

E 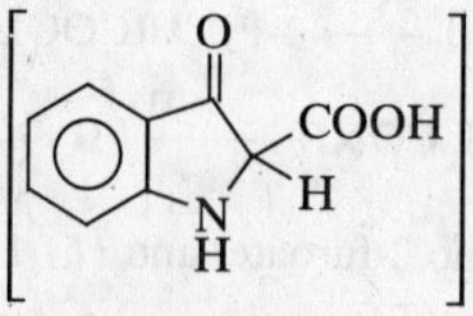   **F** 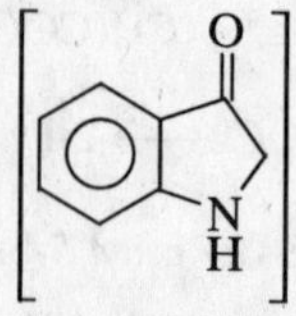   **G** 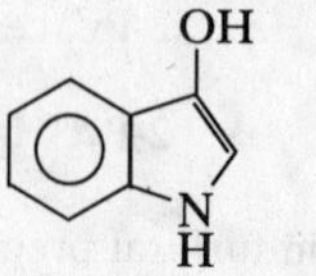   **H**

F is formed by a Dieckmann-type ring closure with carboxylic acids rather than esters.

(b) **I** is formed by a transamination, and **J** is formed by an intramolecular Claisen condensation.

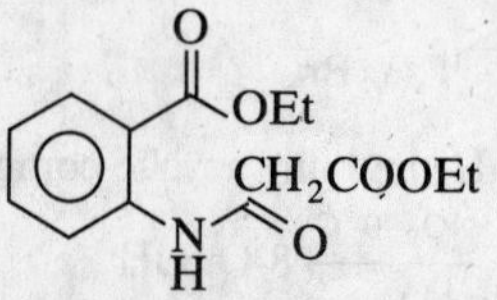

I 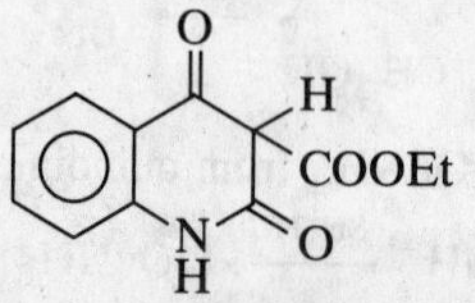   **J** 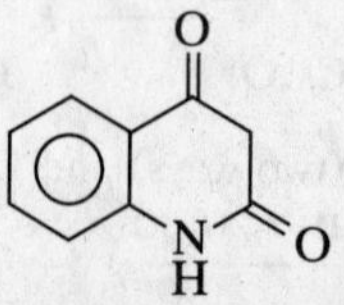   **K** 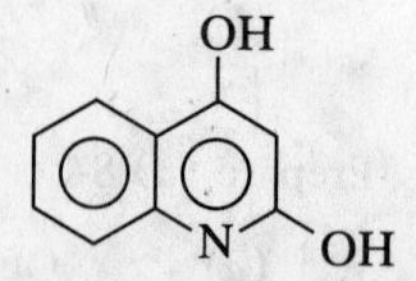   **L**

21.79 Supply the structural formulas for **M** through **R** given

(a) $o\text{-}NO_2C_6H_4C\equiv CC_6H_4NO_2\text{-}o \xrightarrow{\text{1 eq of } Br_2} \textbf{M} \xrightarrow{\text{excess Sn/HCl}} \textbf{N} \xrightarrow{\Delta (-2HBr)} \textbf{O}$

(b) $o\text{-}ClC_6H_4NHCOPh \xrightarrow{KNH_2/NH_3 (-HCl)} [\textbf{P}] \longrightarrow [\textbf{Q}] \longrightarrow \textbf{R}$

(a)

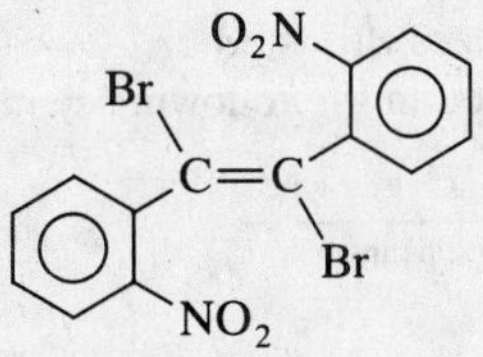

trans-M 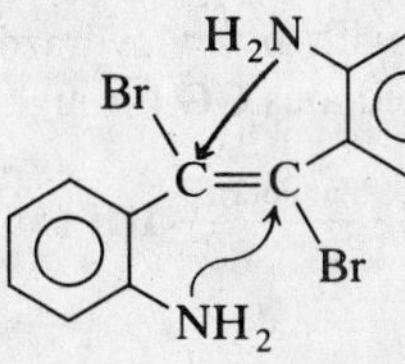   *trans*-N 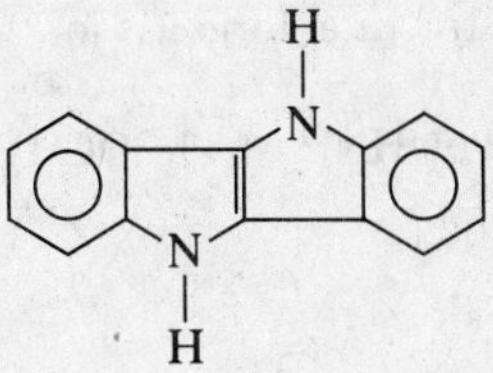   O

(b)

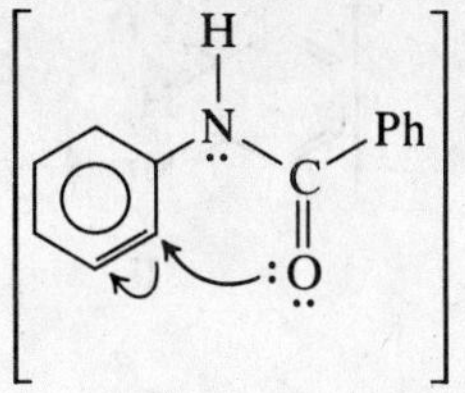

P (a benzyne) 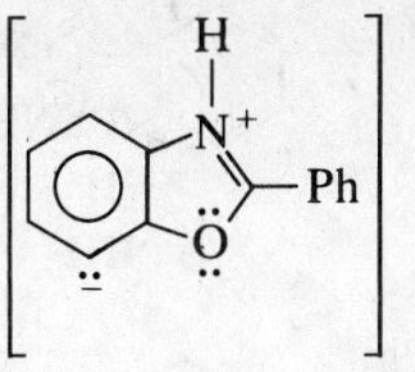   Q 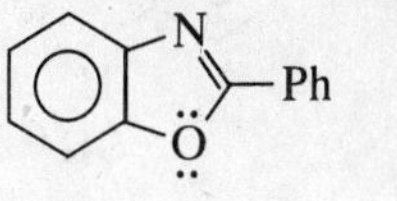   R

21.80 (a) Supply the structural formulas for **S** through **Y** which are involved in the synthesis of the opium alkaloid papaverine, $C_{20}H_{21}O_4N$ (**Y**).

$$3,4\text{-}(MeO)_2C_6H_3CH_2Cl \xrightarrow{KCN} S \xrightarrow{2\ eq\ of\ H_2/Ni} T; \qquad S \xrightarrow[\Delta]{H_3O^+} U \xrightarrow{PCl_5} V;$$

$$V + T \longrightarrow W; \qquad W \xrightarrow{P_2O_5} X \xrightarrow[\Delta]{Pd} Y$$

(b) Which heterocyclic ring is present in papaverine?

◢ (a) **S** = $3,4\text{-}(MeO)_2C_6H_3CH_2CN$, **T** = $3,4\text{-}(MeO)_2C_6H_3CH_2CH_2NH_2$,
U = $3,4\text{-}(MeO)_2C_6H_3CH_2COOH$, **V** = $3,4\text{-}(MeO)_2C_6H_3CH_2COCl$, and

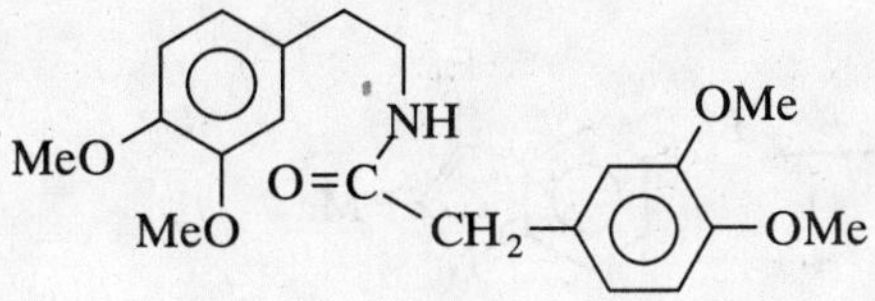

W 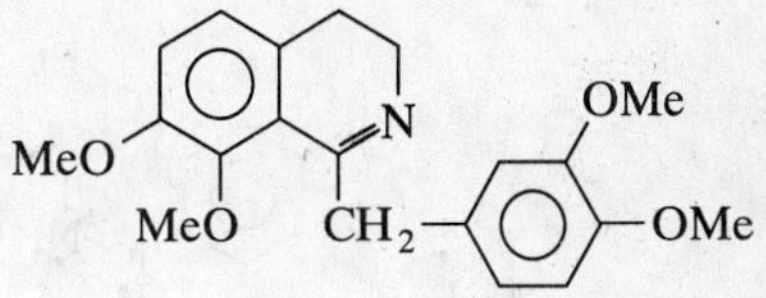   X

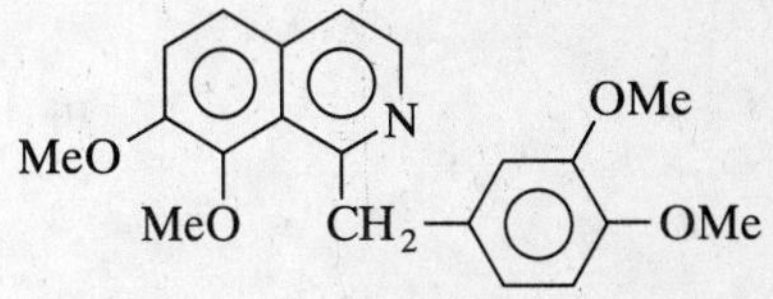

Y

(b) Isoquinoline.

21.81 (a) Supply the structural formulas for **AA** through **EE** shown below in the synthesis of the alkaloid nicotine, $C_{10}H_{14}N_2$ (**FF**). Identify each type of reaction.

$$3\text{-PyCOOH} \xrightarrow{SOCl_2} AA \xrightarrow{[EtO(CH_2)_3]_2CuLi} BB \xrightarrow[H_2/Pd]{NH_3} CC \xrightarrow{HBr} [DD] \longrightarrow EE \xrightarrow{MeI/base} FF$$

(b) How can we obtain natural nicotine from synthetic nicotine?

◢ (a) **AA** = 3-PyCOCl (acid chloride formation), **BB** = $3\text{-PyCO(CH}_2)_3OEt$ (ketone formation), **CC** = $3\text{-PyCH(NH}_2)(CH_2)_3OEt$ (reductive amination), **DD** = $3\text{-PyCH(NH}_2)(CH_2)_3Br$ (ether cleavage), and

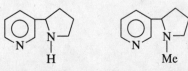

EE (intramolecular S_N2)   **FF** (N-methylation)

(b) The synthetic nicotine is racemic and it must be resolved to give the optically active natural compound.

21.82 The *Fischer indole synthesis* starts with an arylhydrazone and utilizes Brönsted or Lewis ($ZnCl_2$) acids. Supply the structural formulas for the intermediates **GG** through **KK**, involved in the following synthesis of 2-Ph-indole (**LL**).

$$PhNHNH_2 + PhCOCH_3 \longrightarrow \mathbf{GG} \xrightarrow{\text{tautomerize}} \mathbf{HH}\ (\text{an enamine}) \xrightarrow[\text{rearrangement}]{\text{Claisen-type}}$$

$$[\mathbf{II}] \xrightarrow{\text{rearomatization}} \mathbf{JJ} \xrightarrow{\text{cyclization}} \mathbf{KK} \xrightarrow{H^+(-NH_4^+)} \mathbf{LL}$$

GG **HH** **II**

JJ **KK** **LL**

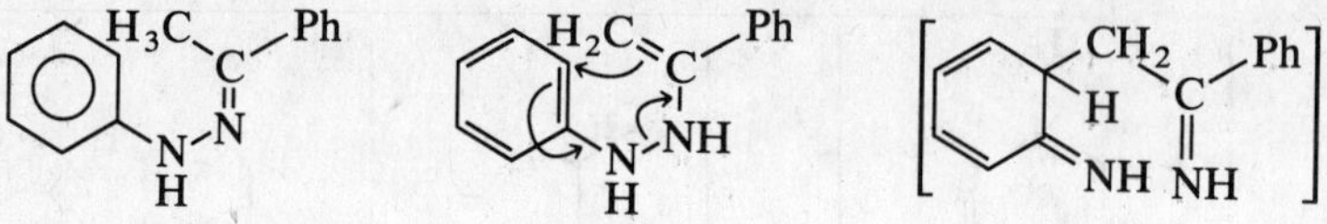

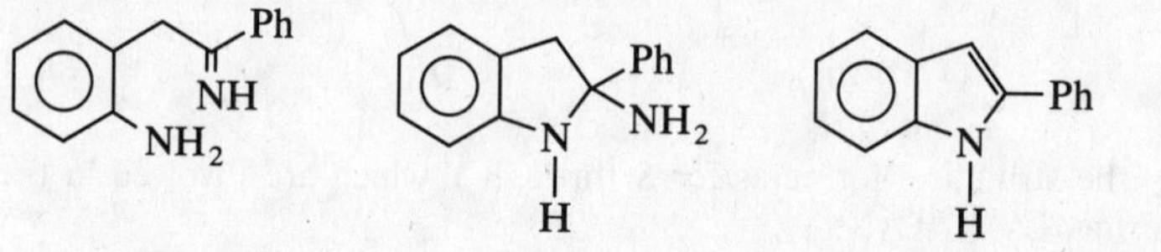

21.83 Give the phenylhydrazone needed to synthesize 3-ethyl-2-methyl-5-phenylindole (**A**) by the Fischer method and show the isomeric product that is also isolated.

A substituent on the benzene ring (Ph) must be present in the arylhydrazine. The R(Me) on C^2 of indole is bonded to the C=O and the R′(Et) on C^3 is bonded to the α C of the C=O compound. The starting materials are p-$PhC_6H_4NHNH_2 + MeCOCH_2Et$. Two enamines (**A′** and **B′**) form, each from an α C, giving the isomers **A** and **B**. The other isomer is 5-phenyl-2-*n*-propylindole (**B**).

A′ **A**

B′ **B**

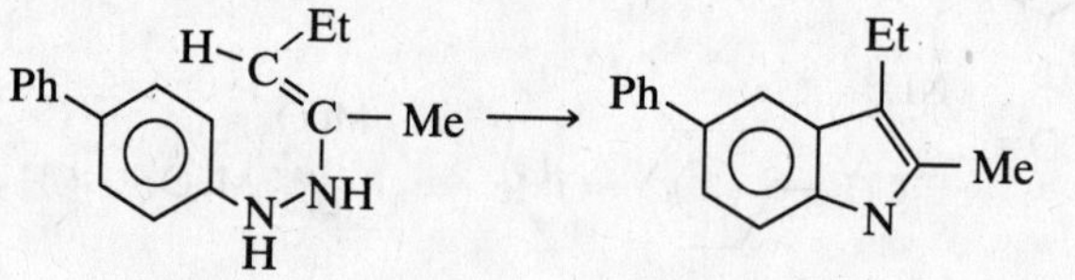

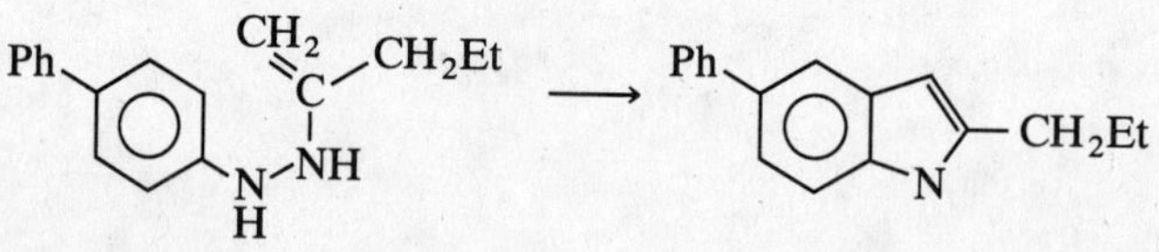

21.84 (*a*) Give the steps in preparing 1-methylisoquinoline by the Bischler-Napieralski synthesis, starting with an acid chloride. (*b*) Give the amine and acid chloride required to synthesize 1-ethyl-4,7-dimethyl-isoquinoline.

(*a*)

1-Methylisoquinoline

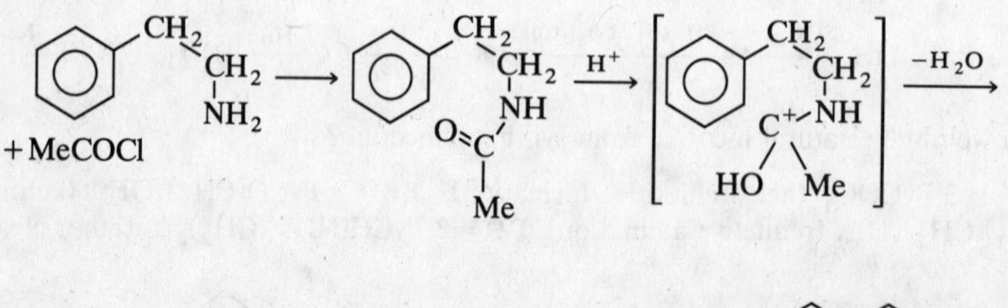

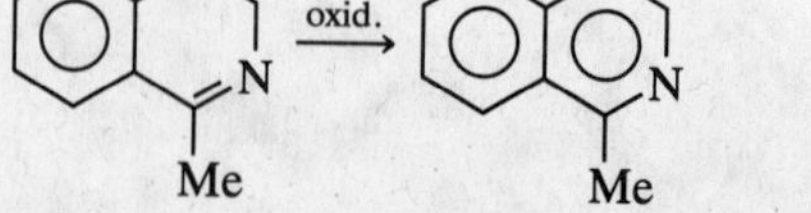

(b) The C^1 substituent (Et) of the heterocycle derives from R of RCOCl, and the two Me's come from the β-phenylethylamine. A substituent with a number > 4 is on the ring; if the number is 3 or 4, the substituent is on the side chain of the ring.

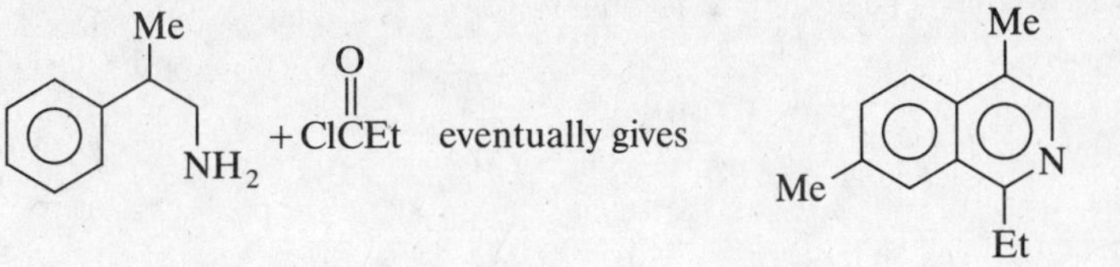

1-Ethyl-4,7-dimethylisoquinoline

SPECTRA AND ANALYSIS

21.85 How can pyridine, pyrrole, and piperidine be distinguished by ir spectroscopy? Give the key characteristic absorptions. (There is no need to give a complete analysis.)

▮ Piperidine and pyrrole have an N—H bond, absorbing at ≈ 3500 cm^{-1}, that pyridine lacks. They can be distinguished by the fact that the H—C_{sp^3} stretch in piperidine appears below 3000 cm^{-1} while in pyrrole the H—C_{sp^2} stretch appears above 3000 cm^{-1}.

21.86 How can pyridine, pyrrole, and piperidine be distinguished by pmr spectroscopy?

▮ Pyridine and pyrrole, being aromatic, have pmr signals shifted downfield. The electron-withdrawing N of PyH shifts the aromatic H's downfield (to δ = 8.5) relative to PhH. The electron pair donated by the N of pyrrole into the aromatic system shifts the aromatic H's upfield (to δ = 6.4) relative to PhH. Piperidine is not aromatic and has no signals in these downfield regions.

21.87 (a) Compare and account for the relative δ values of the H's in the α and β positions of furan and pyrrole. (b) Compare these relative values for the two rings and account for the variations. (c) Compare and account for the relative δ values of the three-ring positions of PyH.

▮ (a) The heteroatom's electron-donation is partially offset by its inductive electron-withdrawal that is felt more in the α position than in the β position. Hence, $\delta_{\alpha H}$ is more downfield than $\delta_{\beta H}$ for both rings. (b) Since O is inductively more electron-withdrawing than N, the values for both positions of furan are more downfield than the corresponding positions on pyrrole. (c) In pyridine, the N is electron-withdrawing both inductively and by resonance interaction at the α and γ positions, causing the H_α and H_γ signals to be more downfield than H_β (δ = 7.0). Since H_α is closer to the N, it is more downfield (δ = 8.61) than H_γ (δ = 7.60).

21.88 Explain why $PhNH_3^+$ absorbs in the uv spectrum at much shorter wavelength than $PhNH_2$ but protonation of pyridine has little effect.

▮ Destruction of delocalization of the unshared pair on N by protonation of $PhNH_2$ (Problem 21.26) increases the energy gap between the HOMO and the LUMO. There is practically no change in this energy gap when pyridine is protonated, because the electron pair on its N is not delocalized.

21.89 How is vigorous oxidation used to distinguish between 4- and 2-methylquinoline (MeQu)?

▮ Vigorous oxidation of 2-MeQu gives 2,3,6-pyridinetricarboxylic acid with one pair of adjacent COOH's which can form a single anhydride. Vigorous oxidation of 4-MeQu gives 2,3,4-pyridinetricarboxylic acid with two pairs of adjacent COOH's capable of forming two anhydrides, one involving the C^2 and C^3 COOH's and the other the C^4 and C^3 COOH's.

21.90 An acid-insoluble compound (A), C_6H_9N, reacts with H_2/Pd to give an acid-soluble compound (B), $C_6H_{13}N$. B reacts with 1 eq of MeI to give C which, after treatment with Ag_2O, is heated to give D, $C_7H_{15}N$. D undergoes another sequence of exhaustive methylation and Hofmann degradation to form 2-methyl-1,3-butadiene (E). Determine the structures of A through D.

▮ Compound A has 3° of unsaturation and since it is acid-insoluble and possesses an N and no O, it is likely to be a substituted pyrrole. The additional two C's are present either as two Me's or an Et. Compound B is the corresponding pyrrolidine which must be a 3° amine because it reacts with only 1 eq of MeI. Therefore, A is an

N—Me or N—Et substituted pyrrole. Compound **D** is an unsaturated amine which confirms the supposition that **B** is a cyclic amine. The butadiene portion of the final product comes from the four C's of the pyrrole ring and the presence of Me at C^2 of the chain means there is an Me on the β position of the pyrrole ring. Now we know **A** is an N—Me pyrrole. The structural formulas are:

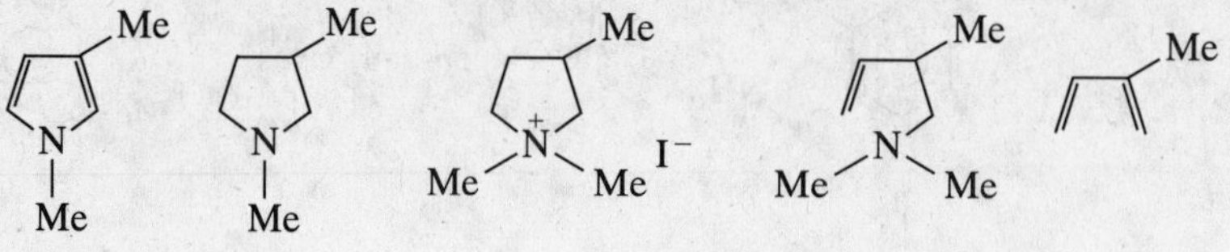

A   B   C   D   E

21.91 Two acid-soluble isomers **F** and **J** (C_9H_7N) react in the following sequences:

$$F \xrightarrow{\text{2 eq of } H_2/Pd} G \xrightarrow{\text{1 eq of MeI}} H \xrightarrow{\text{HONO}} I$$

$$J \xrightarrow{\text{2 eq of } H_2/Pd} K \xrightarrow{\text{1 eq of MeI}} L \xrightarrow{\text{HONO}} \text{no reaction}$$

All the signals in the pmr spectra of **F** and **J** have $\delta > 7$. Supply formulas for **F** through **L**.

◢ Isomers **F** and **J** are amines with 7° of unsaturation. They have fused aromatic rings since all H's are aromatic. One isomer is quinoline and the other is isoquinoline. The N-containing rings in **F** and **J** are reduced and the resulting aliphatic amines, **G** and **K**, are 2°. They are methylated to give the 3° amines, **H** and **L**. Since **L** does not react with HONO, it is a typical aliphatic-type amine. **J**, the precursor of **L**, is isoquinoline. **H** is an arylamine that undergoes ring nitrosation. **F**, the precursor of **H** is QuH. **G** is 1,2,3,4-tetrahydroquinoline and **H** is N-methyl-1,2,3,4-tetrahydroquinoline. **K** is 1,2,3,4-tetrahydroisoquinoline and **L** is N-methyl-1,2,3,4-tetrahydroiso-quinoline.

SUPPLEMENTARY PROBLEMS

21.92 Give the products of the following reactions:
(*a*) 2,6-Diethylthiophene $\xrightarrow[H_2/Ni]{\text{excess}}$; (*b*) indole $\xrightarrow[Me_2NH]{H_2CO}$; (*c*) indole $\xrightarrow{D_2SO_4}$; (*d*) isoquinoline $\xrightarrow{PhLi}$.

◢ (*a*) Octane. The intermediate cyclic sulfide is hydrogenolyzed. (*b*) β-Dimethylaminoindole. This is a Mannich-type reaction. (*c*) 1,3-Dideuterioindole. (*d*) 1-Phenylisoquinoline. C^3 is not alkylated because the − charge of the intermediate anion cannot be delocalized to N without destroying the aromaticity of the benzene ring.

21.93 Give the structures of the intermediate and aromatic heterocycle product from each synthesis. Classify each aromatic heterocycle. (*a*) 2,5-Hexanedione + H_2NNH_2 followed by air oxidation, (*b*) 2,4-hexanedione + H_2NNH_2, and (*c*) 2 mol aminoacetone followed by air oxidation, and (*d*) o-$C_6H_4(NH_2)_2$ + CH_3COOH, heat.

◢ (*a*)

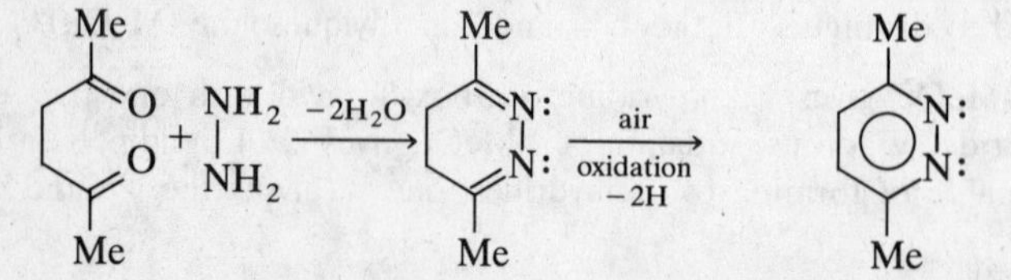

a 1,2-diazine (a pyridizine)

(*b*)

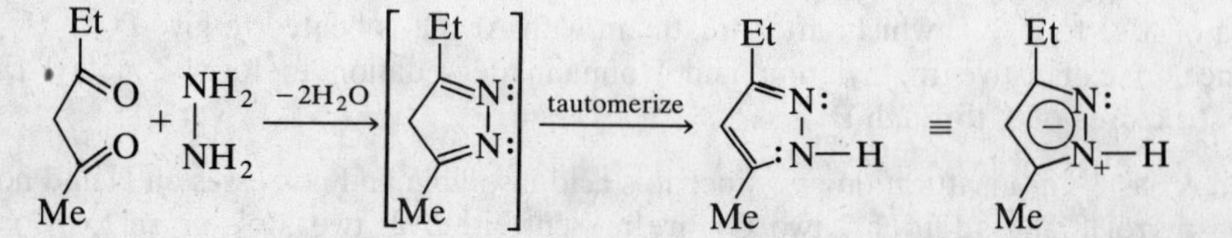

a 1,2-diazole (a pyrazole)

(c)

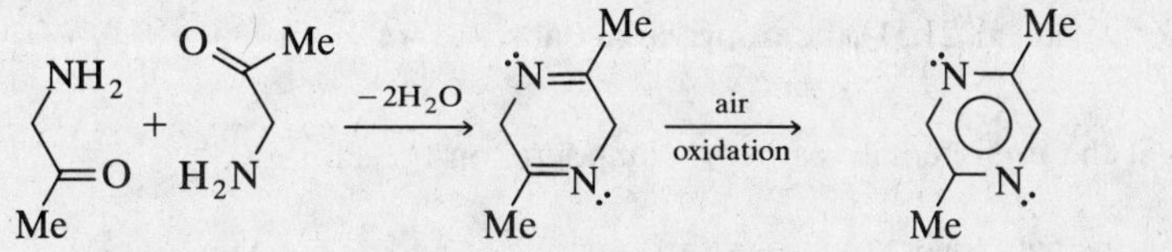

a 1,4-diazine (a pyrazine)

(d)

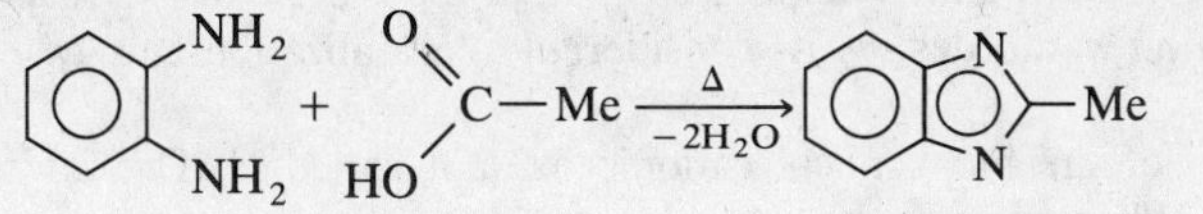

a benzimidazole

21.94 (*a*) Give the structure of the product from the reaction of PyH and $AlCl_3$. (*b*) In terms of this product explain why PyH does not participate in Friedel-Crafts reactions.

◢ (*a*)

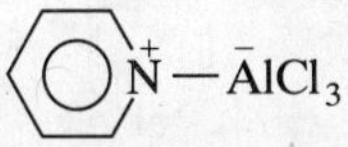

(*b*) Pyridine not only ties up $AlCl_3$ but the + charge on N greatly diminishes the reactivity towards electrophilic substitutions.

21.95 (*a*) Provide formulas for the red crystalline solids formed when PyH is reacted first with Br_2 and then with HBr. (*b*) Give a synthetic use of the final product.

◢ (*a*)

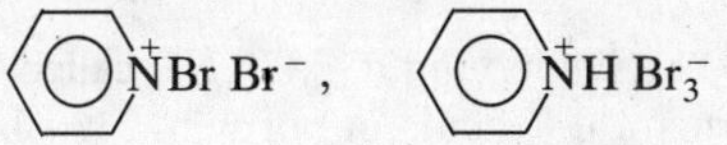

Pyridine perbromide

(*b*) It is a mild brominating agent since Br_3^- is a source of Br_2.

21.96 Give the product of the reaction of thiophene with NBS.

◢ 2-Bromothiophene. Thiophene can undergo free radical substitution.

21.97 (*a*) Give the product of the reaction of furan or thiophene with CH_2N_2. (*b*) Why does furan give a higher yield of product?

◢ (*a*) Carbenes add to the C=C of the aromatic ring, giving 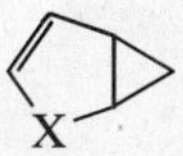 . (*b*) Furan is less aromatic (see Problem 21.54).

21.98 Supply the structures of the compound, **A**, and **B** in the following reaction.

1,2-Diethylpyridinium bromide + $OH^- \longrightarrow$ **A** $\xrightarrow{CH_3COCl}$ **B**

◢

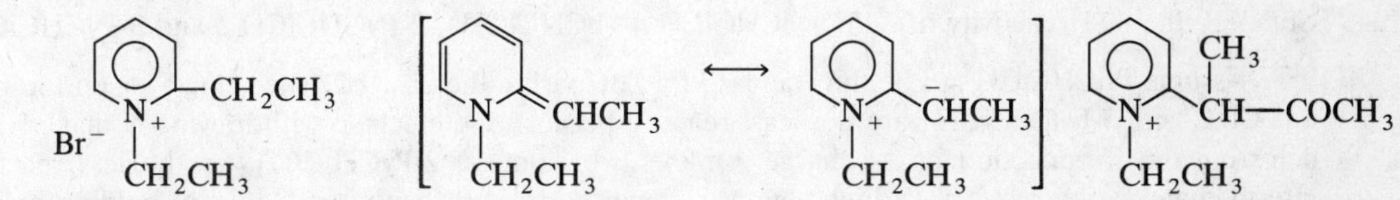

1,2-Diethylpyridinium bromide   **A**   **B**

21.99 Give the steps of the reaction of coumarin with 2 mol of the Grignard reagent, e.g., PhMgBr, followed by heating with H_2SO_4.

◢ Coumarin has the lactone grouping and behaves as an ester toward Ar(R)MgX. Dehydration of the intermediate diol leaves the cyclic ether product.

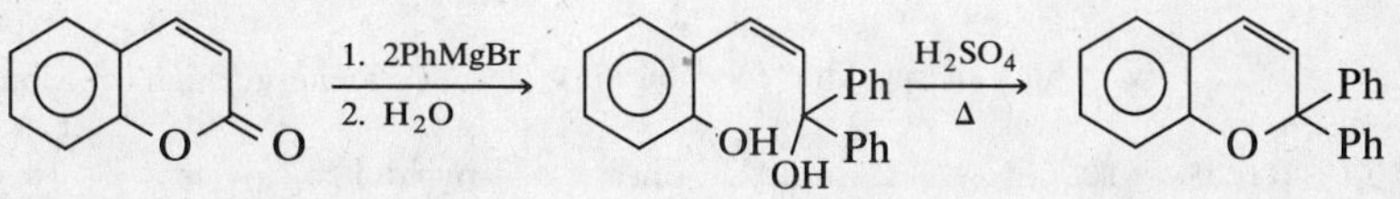

Lactone (ester-like)

21.100 Unlike pyrylium salts (see Problem 21.51), benzopyrylium salts do not react with NH_3 to give pyridine rings. Explain.

▮ It is impossible to get the intermediate carbonyl compound on the Ph ring.

21.101 Explain the difference in reactivity toward hydrolysis of 2-pyridone and a δ-lactam.

▮ A δ-lactam is readily hydrolyzed to a δ-amino acid. Even though 2-pyridone has the lactam grouping, it is not hydrolyzed because such a reaction would destroy its considerable delocalization energy.

21.102 Nicotinamide is an essential moiety of the biochemical cationic oxidant called NAD^+ (**n**icotinamide **a**denine **d**inucleotide; see Problem 23.135). When writing the formula of NAD^+ the adenine dinucleotide portion is abbreviated R. Write an equation for the role played by NAD^+ in the oxidation of CH_3CHHOH by NAD^+ in the presence of the enzyme alcohol dehydrogenase.

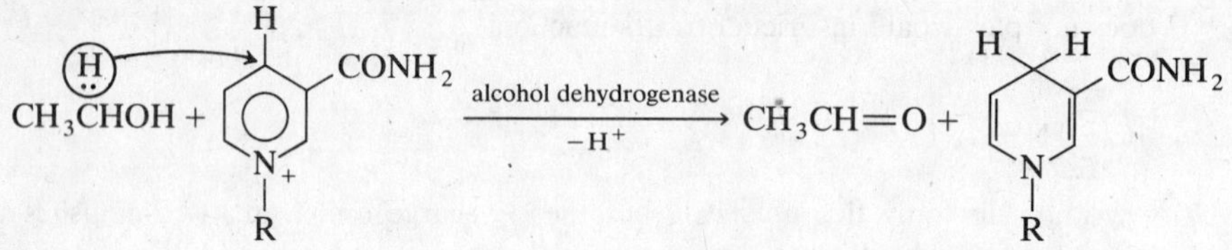

▮

The oxidation involves a hydride transfer of an α H of the alcohol to C^4 of the pyridine ring.

21.103 The base-catalyzed reaction of pyrrole with $H_2C{=}O$ gives a compound, $C_{20}H_{14}N_4$, called *porphin*, which is a structural unit in heme and chlorophyll. (*a*) Give the structural formula of porphin. (*b*) Is porphin aromatic?

▮ (*a*) The initial product is α-hydroxymethylpyrrole, formed by ring substitution on the active pyrrole ring (similar to the reaction of phenol and H_2CO, Problem 20.49), and four of these units react to form the product. Porphin has 16° degrees of unsaturation. (Recall that in this calculation we subtract an H from the molecular formula for each N.) See Fig. 21-11. (*b*) Yes. It contains a cyclic system of nine conjugated double bonds (shown in Fig. 21-11, in boldface), where $4n + 2 = 18$ and $n = 4$.

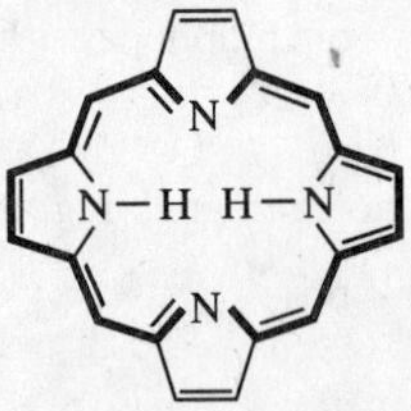

Fig. 21-11

21.104 Compare the S_N1 reactivity of 2-thienyl$CHClCH_3$, $PhCHClCH_3$, 2-Py$CHClCH_3$, and 3-Py$CHClCH_3$.

▮ Assume $PhCHClCH_3$ to be the standard for comparing the ease of generating a + on the C bonded to the lost Cl. 2- and 3-Py$CHClCH_3$ are the least reactive because the electron-withdrawing N makes the ring positive, deterring the introduction of + charge. Of the two isomers, 2-Py$CHClCH_3$ is the less reactive because its intermediate cation has a very high-energy resonance structure with the + on N holding only six e^-'s. The 3-isomer has δ +'s only on C's, and no resonance forms with an electron-deficient N. The electron-rich thienyl ring, however, can aid the formation of + charge. Furthermore, a stable resonance structure can be written with + delocalized to S with eight e^-'s.

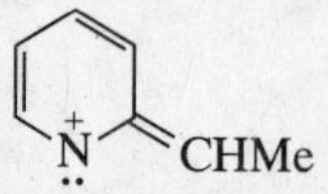

N^+ has 6 e^-'s
(very high energy, little contribution)

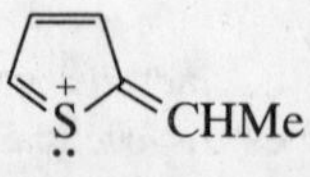

S^+ has 8 e^-'s
(low energy, high contribution)

The order of decreasing reactivity is 2-thienyl > phenyl > 3-pyridyl > 2 pyridyl.

21.105 Synthesize 2-methoxyfuran from methyl α-furoate and any other needed reagents.

▮ Typical of the aromatic five-membered monoheterocycles and unlike PyH, furan does not undergo nucleophilic displacement. However, halides can be displaced if a substituent which can stabilize the intermediate − charge is present. The activating groups of choices are —COOR(H) because of their ease of removal.

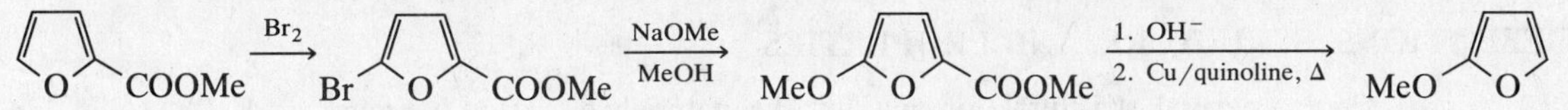

21.106 (*a*) Complete the following sequence of reactions and (*b*) account for **B** and **C**.

$$\text{Pyrrole} + \text{PhMgBr} \longrightarrow \textbf{A} \xrightarrow{\text{PhCH}_2\text{Cl}} \text{isomers } \textbf{B} \text{ and } \textbf{C}$$

▮ (*a*)

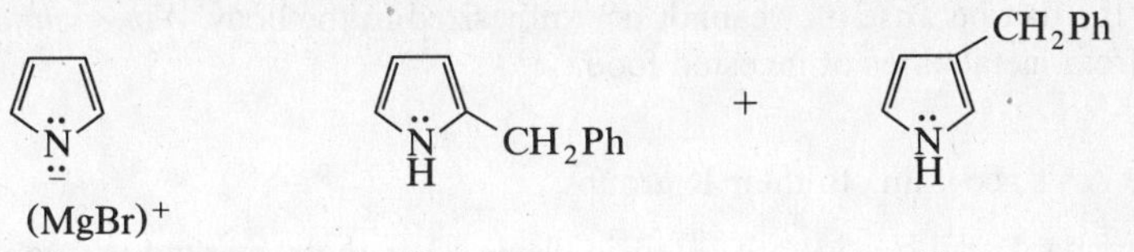

(*b*) The − charge on N can be delocalized to the 2 and 3 positions, followed by displacement of Cl⁻.

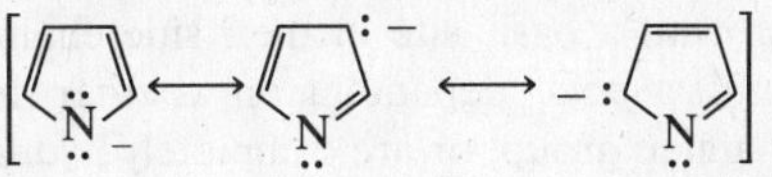

21.107 (*a*) Complete the following: Pyrrole + K ⟶ **D** $\xrightarrow{\text{PhCH}_2\text{Cl}}$ **E**. (*b*) Explain the difference in products of this sequence and the one in Problem 21.106.

▮ (*a*)

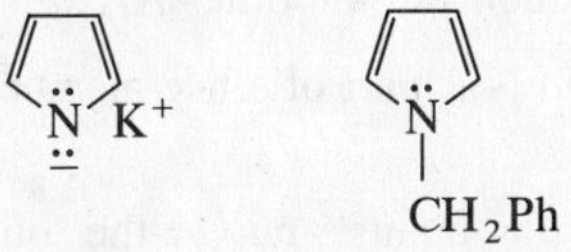

(*b*) This is a question of C- vs. N-alkylation. The more − charge on N, as is the case with the K⁺ salt, the more N-alkylation occurs. In **A** of Problem 21.106, N⁻ binds with (MgBr)⁺ and is a less reactive site.

21.108 Account for the following orders of reactivity:
(*a*) Toward aq. HCl: 2,6-Dimethylpyridine (2,6-lutidine) > pyridine
(*b*) Toward BMe₃: Pyridine > 2,6-dimethylpyridine

▮ (*a*) R's, such as Me, are electron-donating by induction and are base-strengthening. (*b*) BMe₃ is much bulkier than H₃O⁺. The Me's at C² and C⁶ flanking the N sterically hinder the approach of BMe₃, causing 2,6-lutidine to be less reactive than pyridine. This is an example of F-strain (see Problem 19.22).

21.109 Write structures for **A** through **D** and name **A** and **D** in the following reactions:

(*a*) Urea + O=CHCH₂COOEt $\xrightarrow{\text{OEt}^-}$ **A**

(*b*) H₂NCSNH₂ + MeI $\xrightarrow{-\text{HI}}$ **B** and **B** + O=CHCHMeCOOEt ⟶ **C** $\xrightarrow{\text{aq. HBr}}$ **D** (C₅H₆O₂N₂)

▮ (*a*)

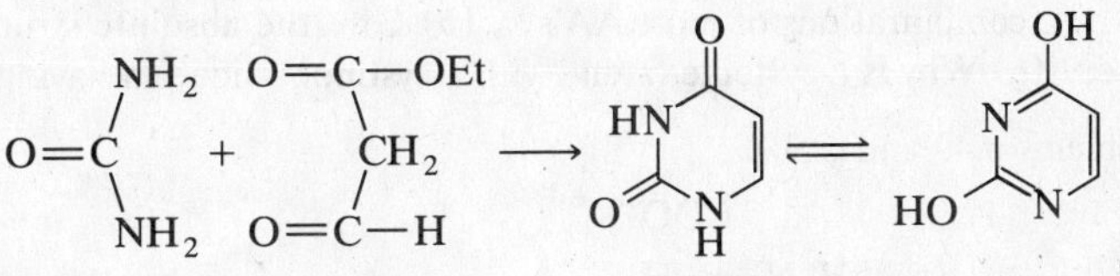

A, uracil

(*b*)

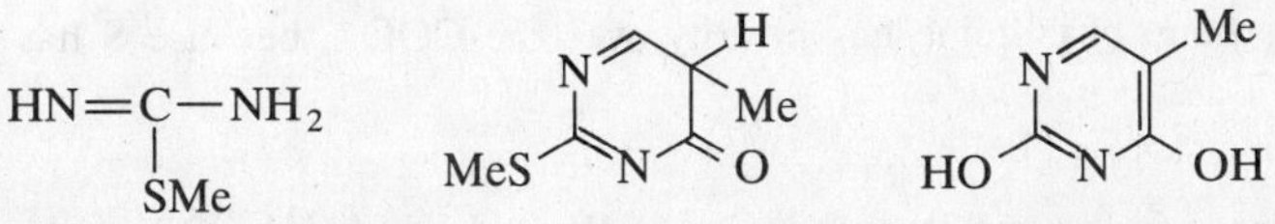

B   C   D, thymine

CHAPTER 22

Amino Acids, Peptides, and Proteins

DEFINITIONS, STRUCTURE, AND PROPERTIES

22.1 (*a*) Give a general structural formula for the naturally-occurring α-amino acids (AA) and indicate their importance. (*b*) Explain their classification as essential and nonessential.

(*a*) $RCH(\overset{+}{N}H_3)COO^-$. *α-Amino acids* are the units that comprise all *proteins*. (*b*) Ten amino acids are *essential* in the diet because they cannot be synthesized in the body. *Nonessential* amino acids are synthesized by body cells from metabolites of ingested food.

22.2 Classify the AA's according to their R groups.

The standard amino acids are listed in Table 22-1; those marked with an asterisk are the essential amino acids (see Problem 22.1). AA's are categorized as either *neutral*, *acidic*, or *basic*, depending on the nature of their R groups. Aspartic and glutamic acids, each with a second COOH in their side chain, are acidic AA's, and lysine, arginine, and histadine, each with a basic site in their side chain, are basic AA's. All others are neutral AA's, further classified as *polar* and *nonpolar* depending on whether their side chains have polar substituents, as does asparagine with an H_2NCO amido group, or are completely hydrocarbon in nature, as are alanine (R is Me) and valine (R is *i*-Pr).

22.3 What structural feature distinguishes proline from the other AA's?

Proline is a 2° amine. Also the amino N is part of a five-membered ring.

22.4 Explain (*a*) the crystallinity and high melting points, and (*b*) the solubility of the AA's.

(*a*) α-Amino acids exist as dipolar ions, $RCH(\overset{+}{N}H_3)COO^-$. The crystal structure is a consequence of the strong intermolecular electrostatic attractive forces, and unlike uncharged molecules of the same MW, most AA's decompose rather than melt. (*b*) Owing to their dipolar structure, most AA's are appreciably soluble in water (forming H-bonds and ion-dipole bonds) and insoluble in nonpolar or aprotic solvents.

22.5 (*a*) Which AA is achiral? (*b*) Give the AA's with more than one chiral center.

(*a*) Glycine, $H_3\overset{+}{N}CH_2COO^-$.

(*b*)

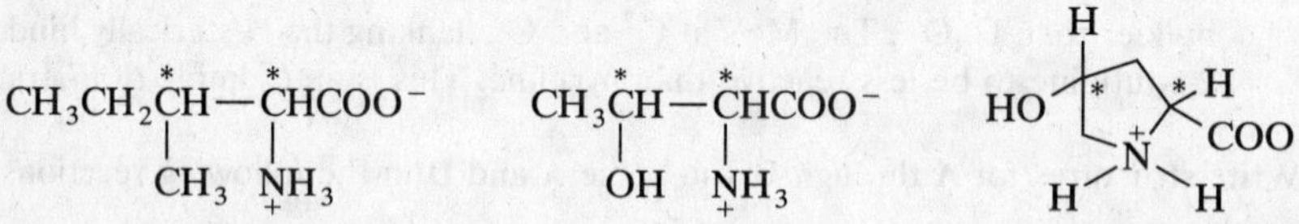

Isoleucine Threonine 4-Hydroxyproline

22.6 (*a*) What are the *R*/*S* and D/L configurations of most AA's? (*b*) Give the absolute structural configuration of (i) L-cysteine and (ii) L-serine. (*c*) Why is L-cysteine (along with L-cystine) unique in having the *R* configuration?

(*a*) *S* and L (see Problems 6.49 and 6.50).

(*b*) (i) (ii)

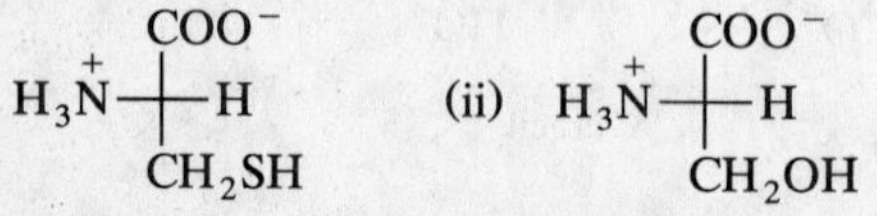

(*c*) The CH_2SH group of cysteine has priority over the COO^-, because S has a greater atomic weight than O.

22.7 (*a*) Give Fischer structures for all the stereoisomers of threonine. (*b*) Identify L-threonine and give its *R*/*S* designation.

TABLE 22-1. Natural α-Amino Acids

Name	Symbol	Formula
		Monoaminomonocarboxylic
Glycine	Gly	$H_3\overset{+}{N}CH_2COO^-$
Alanine	Ala	$H_3\overset{+}{N}CH(CH_3)COO^-$
Valine*	Val	$H_3\overset{+}{N}CH(i\text{-Pr})COO^-$
Leucine*	Leu	$H_3\overset{+}{N}CH(i\text{-Bu})COO^-$
Isoleucine*	Ileu	$H_3\overset{+}{N}CH(s\text{-Bu})COO^-$
Serine	Ser	$H_3\overset{+}{N}CH(CH_2OH)COO^-$
Threonine*	Thr	$H_3\overset{+}{N}CH(CHOHCH_3)COO^-$
		Monoaminodicarboxylic and Amide Derivatives
Aspartic acid	Asp	$HOOCCH_2CH(\overset{+}{N}H_3)COO^-$
Asparagine	Asp(NH$_2$)	$H_2NCOCH_2CH(\overset{+}{N}H_3)COO^-$
Glutamic acid	Glu	$HOOC(CH_2)_2CH(\overset{+}{N}H_3)COO^-$
Glutamine	Glu(NH$_2$)	$H_2NCOCH_2CH_2CH(\overset{+}{N}H_3)COO^-$
		Diaminomonocarboxylic
Lysine*	Lys	$H_3\overset{+}{N}(CH_2)_4CH(NH_2)COO^-$
Hydroxylysine	Hylys	$H_3\overset{+}{N}CH_2\underset{\underset{OH}{\vert}}{C}HCH_2CH_2CH(NH_2)COO^-$
Arginine*	Arg	$\underset{H_2N}{\overset{H_2\overset{+}{N}}{>}}C-NH(CH_2)_3CH(NH_2)COO^-$
		Sulfur-Containing
Cysteine	CySH	$H_3\overset{+}{N}CH(CH_2SH)COO^-$
Cystine	CySSCy	$^-OOCCH(\overset{+}{N}H_3)CH_2S-SCH_2CH(\overset{+}{N}H_3)COO^-$
Methionine*	Met	$CH_3SCH_2CH_2CH(\overset{+}{N}H_3)COO^-$
		Aromatic
Phenylalanine*	Phe	$PhCH_2CH(\overset{+}{N}H_3)COO^-$
Tyrosine	Tyr	$p\text{-}HOC_6H_4CH_2CH(\overset{+}{N}H_3)COO^-$
		Heterocyclic
Histidine*	His	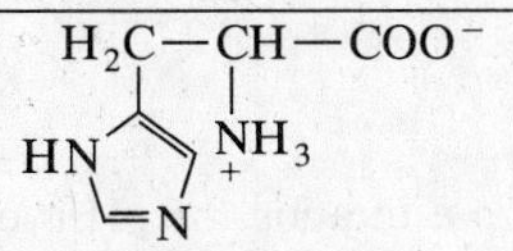
Proline	Pro	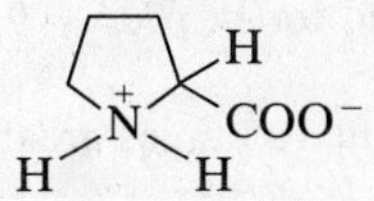
Hydroxyproline	Hypro	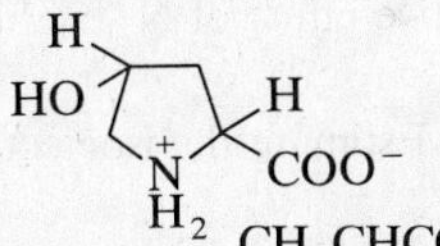
Tryptophane*	Try	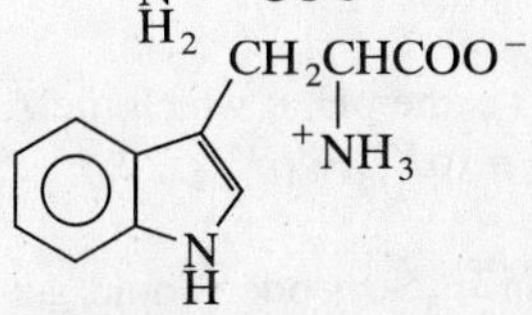

(a)

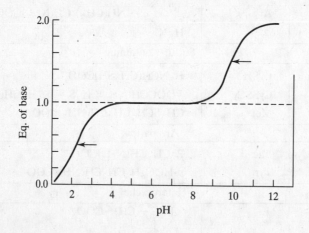

racemate₁ (*threo*) racemate₂ (*erythro*)

(b) For racemate₁, L- and D-threonine, and for racemate₂, L- and D-allothreonine. L refers only to the configuration about the α C. If, as in this problem, there is a chiral C in the R group, its configuration is not relevant to the D, L (or R, S) label. L-Threonine is (2S,3R). The diastereomer, (2S,3S)-threonine, is called L-*allothreonine*.

ACID-BASE (AMPHOTERIC) PROPERTIES

22.8 Write equilibrium equations to show the amphoteric behavior of an AA in H_2O. Include net charge of each species.

$$\overset{\text{acting as a base}}{\overset{\longleftarrow}{\qquad}} \qquad\qquad \overset{\text{acting as an acid}}{\overset{\longrightarrow}{\qquad}}$$

$$OH^- + \underset{\text{cation, }\mathbf{A}}{H_3\overset{+}{N}CHRCOOH} \rightleftharpoons \boxed{\underset{\text{ampholyte, }\mathbf{B}}{H_3\overset{+}{N}CHRCOO^- + H_2O}} \rightleftharpoons \underset{\text{anion, }\mathbf{C}}{H_2NCHRCOO^- + H_3O^+}$$

Net charge   (+1)   (0)   (−1)

22.9 Refer to Fig. 22-1 which shows the titration curve of alanine, starting with **A** (Problem 22.8, R = Me) in dilute acid. Give the approximate values of pK_a's for dissociation of **A** and **B** in Problem 22.8.

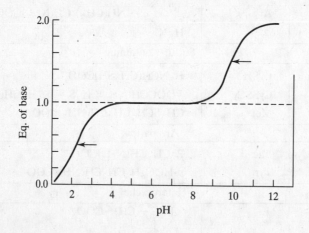

Fig. 22-1

Recall that at the midpoint in a titration the pH is equal to the pK for the titrated acid. Figure 22-1 (see arrows) shows that for **A**, $pK_{a1} = 2.3$, and for **B**, $pK_{a2} = 9.7$.

22.10 Why is the pK_a of the COOH of **A** about 10^2 times greater than that of the COOH of MeCOOH?

The electron-withdrawing inductive effect of N^+ stabilizes the COO^-.

22.11 (a) Define the isoelectric point.   (b) Estimate the isoelectric pH from the titration curve in Fig. 22-1.   (c) How is it calculated from the pK_a's?

(a) The *isoelectric point* (pI) is the pH at which the AA exists only as a dipolar ion with zero net charge (see Problem 22.8).   (b) 6.0.   (c) $pI = (pK_{a1} + pK_{a2})/2$.

22.12 In an electric field, toward which electrode would an AA migrate at a (a) pH < pI, (b) pH > pI, and (c) pH = pI? Explain.

(a) Below the pI, the cation **A** (Problem 22.8) predominates; it migrates to the cathode.   (b) Anion **C** predominates at pH's higher than its pI—it migrates to the anode.   (c) At its pI, the charges are balanced and the AA exists as the zwitterion—no migration occurs.

22.13 Write equilibrium equations for the dissociation of lysine, a basic AA, and calculate its isoelectric point. See Table 22-2 for the pK_a's.

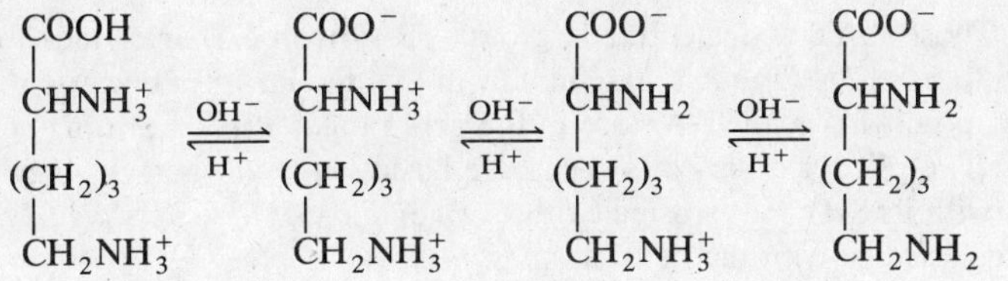

$$
\begin{array}{cccc}
\text{COOH} & \text{COO}^- & \text{COO}^- & \text{COO}^- \\
| & | & | & | \\
\text{CHNH}_3^+ & \text{CHNH}_3^+ & \text{CHNH}_2 & \text{CHNH}_2 \\
| & | & | & | \\
(\text{CH}_2)_3 & (\text{CH}_2)_3 & (\text{CH}_2)_3 & (\text{CH}_2)_3 \\
| & | & | & | \\
\text{CH}_2\text{NH}_3^+ & \text{CH}_2\text{NH}_3^+ & \text{CH}_2\text{NH}_3^+ & \text{CH}_2\text{NH}_2
\end{array}
$$

with $\overset{\text{OH}^-}{\underset{\text{H}^+}{\rightleftharpoons}}$ between each species.

Net charge   (+2)   (+1)   (0)   (−1)

The total charge on each species is given in parentheses, and the species with a zero charge exists between pH 8.95 and 10.53 which are pKa_2 and pKa_3 respectively. Thus, pI = (8.95 + 10.53)/2 = 9.74.

TABLE 22-2. Acid-base Properties of Amino Acids

With Neutral Side Chains			
Amino acid	pK_{a1}^*	pK_{a2}^*	pI
Glycine	2.34	9.60	5.97
Alanine	2.34	9.69	6.00
Valine	2.32	9.62	5.96
Leucine	2.36	9.60	5.98
Isoleucine	2.36	9.60	6.02
Methionine	2.28	9.21	5.74
Proline	1.99	10.60	6.30
Phenylalanine	1.83	9.13	5.48
Tryptophan	2.83	9.39	5.89
Asparagine	2.02	8.80	5.41
Glutamine	2.17	9.13	5.65
Serine	2.21	9.15	5.68
Threonine	2.09	9.10	5.60

With Ionizable Side Chains				
Amino acid	pK_{a1}^{**}	pK_{a2}	pK_{a3}	pI
Aspartic acid	1.88	3.65	9.60	2.77
Glutamic acid	2.19	4.25	9.67	3.22
Tyrosine	2.20	9.11	10.07	5.66
Cysteine	1.96	8.18	10.28	5.07
Lysine	2.18	8.95	10.53	9.74
Arginine	2.17	9.04	12.48	10.76
Histidine	1.82	6.00	9.17	7.59

*In all cases pK_{a1} corresponds to ionization of the carboxyl group; pK_{a2} corresponds to ionization of the ammonium ion.

**In all cases pK_{a1} corresponds to ionization of the carboxyl group of RCHCO_2H.
$\underset{+}{\overset{|}{\text{NH}_3}}$

22.14 Repeat Problem 22.13 for the dissociation of aspartic acid.

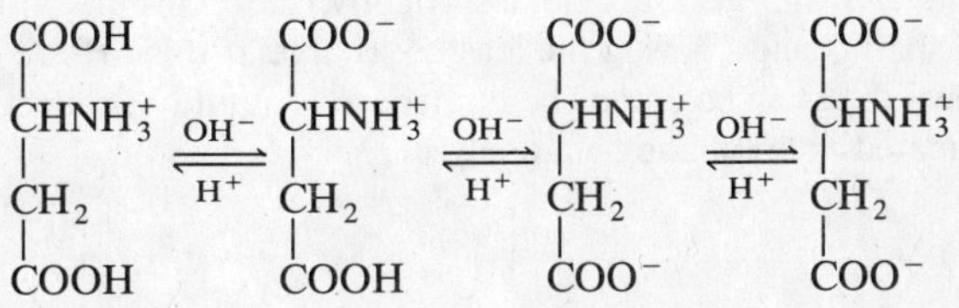

$$
\begin{array}{cccc}
\text{COOH} & \text{COO}^- & \text{COO}^- & \text{COO}^- \\
| & | & | & | \\
\text{CHNH}_3^+ & \text{CHNH}_3^+ & \text{CHNH}_3^+ & \text{CHNH}_3^+ \\
| & | & | & | \\
\text{CH}_2 & \text{CH}_2 & \text{CH}_2 & \text{CH}_2 \\
| & | & | & | \\
\text{COOH} & \text{COOH} & \text{COO}^- & \text{COO}^-
\end{array}
$$

Net charge   (+1)   (0)   (−1)   (−2)

The species with zero total charge is found to exist primarily between pH 1.88 and 3.65 (see Table 22-2). Thus, pI = (1.88 + 3.65)/2 = 2.77.

22.15 (*a*) Classify the AA's in Table 22-1 according to the effect of their R's on the pI. (*b*) The pH range in cellular fluids is 6 to 7. In what form (dipolar, cation, or anion) do the AA's in each class predominate in cells?

◢ (*a*) Those AA's with neutral R groups (R = hydrocarbon, amide, and alcohol) all have pI's in the same range, 5.5 to 6.3. (*b*) The AA's are mainly in the dipolar form because the cellular pH is very close to their pI's. Isoelectric points for acidic AA's are in the acid range; at pH's of range 6 to 7 they act as acids and exist mainly as anions. The pI's for basic AA's are in the basic range; in the cells they accept H^+ and exist mainly as cations. Cysteine (with its SH) and tyrosine (with its phenolic OH) are very weakly acidic, both having pI's between 5 and 6, and are classified with the neutral AA's.

22.16 Write the structure of histidine at pH < 1.82, and write an equation to show which proton is lost when the pH is raised above 1.82.

◢

The carboxyl-H is lost.

22.17 What is the most likely structure for monosodium glutamate (MSG), a commonly used food additive to which some people are allergic?

◢ $Na^+[^-OOCCH_2CH_2CH(\overset{+}{N}H_3)COO^-]$.

22.18 How are AA's separated and identified by *electrophoresis*?

◢ If a filter paper-strip moistened with a solution of a mixture of AA's is placed between two electrodes, the charged molecule will migrate to one electrode or the other at a rate that depends on its net charge and the applied voltage. The net charge depends on the pH. The strip is then stained with a reagent that reacts with the AA, thereby forming a color whose position on the strip is compared for identification with that of a known sample.

22.19 Choose the pH for separating a mixture of aspartic acid, threonine and histidine in an electrophoresis experiment. Explain your choice.

◢ Use a pH = 5.60. This is the pI of threonine (see Table 22-2) which has zero net charge and does not migrate. Aspartic acid (pI = 2.77) donates an H^+, is converted to an anion, and migrates to the anode. Histidine (pI = 7.59) accepts an H^+ and as a cation migrates to the cathode.

22.20 How can lysine (pI = 9.6) be separated from glycine (pI = 5.97) by electrophoresis?

◢ An aqueous solution of the mixture on a supporting medium (filter paper) is subjected to an applied voltage. The pH is adjusted to either 5.97 or 9.6. At pH = 5.97, glycine does not migrate while lysine moves to the cathode. At pH 9.6, lysine does not migrate while glycine moves to the anode.

22.21 Explain how a mixture of AA's is separated by ion-exchange *chromatography*.

◢ The column is charged with an ion-exchange resin with charged groups at its surface. A cation-exchange resin, i.e., $R—SO_3^-Na^+$ (R = resin), exchanges its cation (Na^+) for positively charged AA's in acid when most AA's are cationic. Separation depends on the rate of movement of the positively charged AA's down the column as the exchange occurs. The rate of movement is inversely proportional to the magnitude of the + charge on the AA. For example, the basic AA's, lysine, arginine, and histidine have +2 charge at pH 3.0 and displace Na^+ first. However, they are attracted more strongly, move more slowly, and are found at the top of the column. AA's with the intermediate +1 charge are held less tightly, move faster, and are absorbed further down the column. Glutamic and aspartic acids, having the least + charge at this pH are held the least, and they move at the fastest rate further down the resin column. The procedure for elution, collection, and analysis of fractions and recording of data is automated in an amino acid analyzer.

PREPARATION

22.22 Prepare valine, $Me_2CHCH(\overset{+}{N}H_3)COO^-$ (Val) by (*a*) a Hell–Volhard–Zelinsky reaction, (*b*) a reductive amination, and (*c*) a Gabriel synthesis.

◢ (*a*) $$Me_2CHCH_2COOH \xrightarrow{Br_2/P} Me_2CHCHBrCOOH \xrightarrow[NH_3]{excess} Val$$

$$(b) \qquad \underset{\substack{\|\\O}}{Me_2CHCCOOH} \xrightarrow[H_2/Pt]{NH_3} Val$$

(c)

$$Me_2CHCH_2COOEt + Br_2/P$$

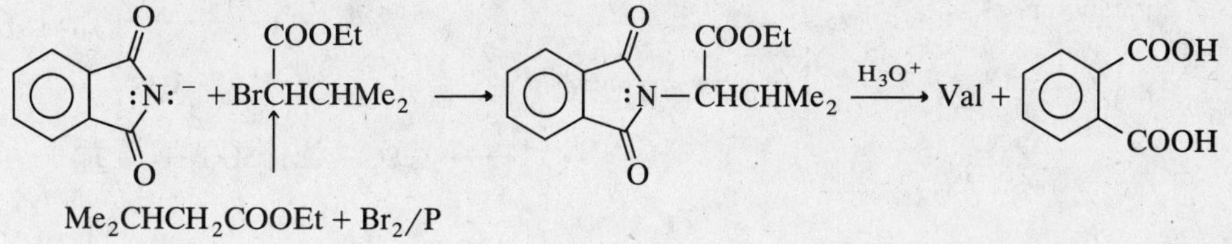

22.23 Prepare (a) methionine, $MeSCH_2CH_2CH(\overset{+}{N}H_3)COO^-$ (Met), and (b) aspartic acid, $HOOCCH_2CH(\overset{+}{N}H_3)COO^-$ (Asp), from diethyl malonate (DEM).

◆ DEM is first monobrominated and the product reacted with K phthalimidate to give N-phthalimidomalonic ester (**B**).

$$(a) \qquad (EtOOC)_2CH_2 \xrightarrow{Br_2} (EtOOC)_2CHBr \text{ (A)}$$

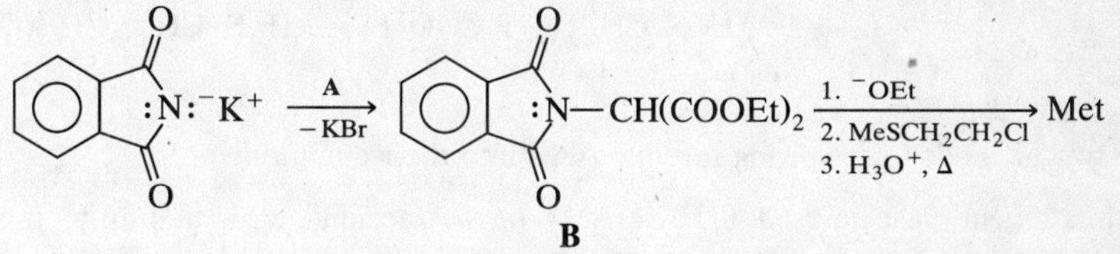

$$(b) \qquad \mathbf{B} \xrightarrow[^-OEt]{BrCH_2COOEt} \text{(phthalimide)} \xrightarrow[\Delta]{H_3O^+} Asp$$

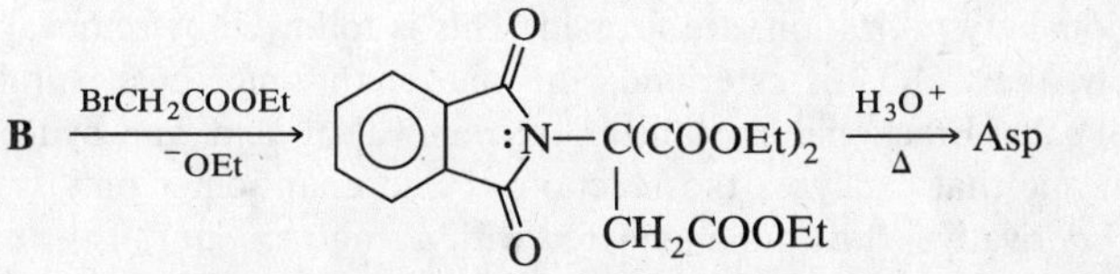

22.24 Prepare (a) leucine (Leu) and (b) tyrosine (Tyr) via diethyl acetamidomalonate (**C**).

◆ $$DEM + HONO \longrightarrow \left[O{=}N{-}CH(COOEt)_2 \right] \longrightarrow$$

$$\underset{\text{an oximino ester}}{HO{-}N{=}C(COOEt)_2} \xrightarrow[2.\ Ac_2O]{1.\ H_2/Pt} AcNHCH(COOEt)_2 \text{ (C)}$$

$$(a) \qquad \mathbf{C} \xrightarrow[BrCH_2CHMe_2]{^-OEt} \underset{\substack{|\\CH_2CHMe_2}}{AcNHC(COOEt)_2} \xrightarrow[2.\ H_3O^+,\Delta]{1.\ NaOH} Me_2CHCH_2CH(\overset{+}{N}H_3)COO^-$$

$$(b) \qquad \mathbf{C} \xrightarrow[p\text{-}AcOC_6H_4CH_2Cl]{^-OEt} \underset{\substack{|\\CH_2C_6H_4OAc\text{-}p}}{AcNHC(COOEt)_2} \xrightarrow[2.\ H_3O^+,\Delta]{1.\ NaOH} p\text{-}HOC_6H_4CH_2CH(\overset{+}{N}H_3)COO^-$$

22.25 Use the *Strecker synthesis* to prepare phenylalanine (Phe).

◆ Treatment of an aldehyde with NH_3 and CN^- produces an α-aminonitrile that is hydrolyzed to the α-amino acid.

$$PhCH_2CHO \xrightarrow[NH_3]{CN^-} PhCH_2CH(NH_2)CN \xrightarrow[2.\ H_3O^+]{1.\ OH^-,\Delta} PhCH_2CH(\overset{+}{N}H_3)COO^- \text{ (Phe)}$$

22.26 Show the steps in the Strecker synthesis of an AA.

22.27 Give structures for **G** through **I**: $MeSH + H_2C{=}CHCHO \longrightarrow G \xrightarrow[(NH_4)_2CO_3]{NaCN} [H] \xrightarrow{NaOH} I.$

■ $G = MeSCH_2CH_2CHO$, formed by a Michael-type addition; **H**, the product of a Strecker synthesis gives methionine, **I**.

$$\underset{\mathbf{H}}{\left[MeSCH_2CH_2\underset{\displaystyle NH_2}{\underset{|}{C}}HCN\right]} \longrightarrow \underset{\mathbf{I}}{MeSCH_2CH_2CH(\overset{+}{N}H_3)COO^-}$$

22.28 How can proline be synthesized from hexanedioic acid (adipic acid)?

■ One COOH is converted to NH_2 via a Hofmann rearrangement. The remaining CH_2COOH is converted to CHBrCOOH in a Hell–Volhard–Zelinsky reaction, followed by S_N2 ring-closure.

$$HOOC(CH_2)_3CH_2COOH \xrightarrow[2.\ NH_3]{1.\ 1\ eq\ of\ SOCl_2} H_2NCO(CH_2)_3CH_2COOH \xrightarrow[KOH]{Br_2}$$

$$H_2N(CH_2)_3CH_2COOH \xrightarrow[P]{Br_2} H_2N(CH_2)_3CHBrCOOH \xrightarrow{\text{intramolecular } SN_2} \text{Pro}$$

22.29 Describe two methods for resolving racemic AA's into their enantiomers.

■ A chiral agent must be used. (*1*) The NH_3^+ of the racemic AA is tied up by the conversion into an amide and the free COOH is then reacted with one enantiomer of a chiral base. Two diastereomeric salts, which are usually separable by fractional crystallization, are formed. This is followed by removal of the base and hydrolysis of the amide. Alternatively, the COO^- is esterified, and one enantiomer of a chiral acid is used to form two diastereomeric ammonium salts. Fractional crystallization, removal of acid, and hydrolysis of the ester complete the resolution. (*2*) An enzyme that catalyzes the reaction of one enantiomer only is employed. The AA is first converted into its N-acetyl derivative. It is then incubated with a small amount of the enzyme, which catalyzes the hydrolysis of the acetylated L-AA, while leaving the D-AA derivative unchanged. Separation of the L-AA from N-acetyl-D-AA is easily accomplished, the AA being amphoteric and the amide being acidic. The N-acetyl-D-AA is carefully hydrolyzed, to prevent racemization, and the D-AA is recovered.

22.30 (*a*) How can a chiral α-AA be prepared using a *transaminase* enzyme? (*b*) Give the reactant in the preparation of chiral aspartic acid by this *transamination* reaction. (*c*) Give its stereoidentity.

■ (*a*) In the presence of a transaminase enzyme, L-glutamic acid is reacted with the α-keto acid precursor of the desired L-AA in a stereospecific exchange that retains chirality (Problem 22.84). Typically, Glu is the amino group donor in transaminations.

$$\underset{\alpha\text{-ketoacid}}{RCOCOOH} + \underset{\text{L-Glutamic acid}}{HOOCCH_2CH_2CH(\overset{+}{N}H_3)COO^-} \xrightarrow{\text{transaminase}}$$

$$\underset{\text{L-amino acid}}{RCH(\overset{+}{N}H_3)COO^-} + \underset{\alpha\text{-Ketoglutaric acid}}{HOOCCH_2CH_2COCOOH}$$

(*b*) $HOOCCH_2\underset{\displaystyle O}{\underset{\|}{C}}COOH$

Oxaloacetic acid

(*c*) The aspartic acid is L since there is retention of configuration during the transamination.

22.31 (*a*) What is the relationship between reactants and products in the transamination reaction? (*b*) Which ketoacid is needed to give (i) alanine, (ii) leucine, (iii) serine, and (iv) glutamine? (*c*) Which AA's cannot be made by transamination?

■ (*a*)

$$\underset{\text{oxidant}_1}{\text{Glutamic acid}} + \underset{\text{reductant}_2}{\text{Oxaloacetic acid}} \longrightarrow \underset{\text{reductant}_1}{\alpha\text{-Ketoglutaric acid}} + \underset{\text{oxidant}_2}{\text{Aspartic acid}}$$

(*b*) (i) $CH_3COCOOH$; (ii) $(CH_3)_2CHCH_2COCOOH$; (iii) $HOCH_2COCOOH$; (iv) $H_2NCOCH_2CH_2COCOOH$.

(*c*) Proline and hydroxyproline; they are 2° amines, and only 1° amines can be made this way.

22.32 From acrylic acid prepare (*a*) γ-aminobutyric acid, the neurotransmitter called *GABA*, and (*b*) β-aminopropionic acid (β-alanine), a component of the vitamin pantothenic acid.

▮ (*a*) The NH_2 and the additional C are introduced from CN^- which reacts with the acid by a Michael-type addition.

$$CN^- + H_2C{=}CHCOO^- \xrightarrow[-OH^-]{H_2O} N{\equiv}CCH_2CH_2COO^- \xrightarrow[2.\ H^+]{1.\ H_2/Pd} H_3\overset{+}{N}CH_2CH_2CH_2COO^-$$

(*b*)
$$H_3N\!: + H_2C{=}CHCOO^- \longrightarrow H_2NCH_2CH_2COO^- \xrightarrow{H^+} H_3\overset{+}{N}CH_2CH_2COO^-$$

REACTIONS

22.33 (*a*) Give the products of the reactions of alanine $MeCH(\overset{+}{N}H_3)COO^-$ with (i) $(CH_3CO)_2O$, (ii) EtOH/HCl, (iii) $PhCOCl/NaOH$, and (iv) $Ba(OH)_2$. (*b*) Give the products of the reactions of HONO with (i) $RCH(\overset{+}{N}H_3)COO^-$ and (ii) $RCH(NH_2)COOEt$.

▮ (*a*) Amino acids undergo reactions typical of both carboxyl and amino groups.

   (i) $CH_3CONHCHMeCOOH$ (N acylation)

   (ii) $Cl^- H_3\overset{+}{N}CHMeCOOEt$ (esterification)

   (iii) $PhCONHCHMeCOO^-Na^+$ (N acylation and salt formation)

   (iv) $(H_2NCHMeCOO)_2^-\, Ba^{2+}$ (salt formation)

(*b*) (i) $HOCHRCOOH + N_2$ and (ii) $:\!\overset{..}{N}{=}\overset{+}{N}{=}CRCOOEt$, an ethyl ester of a diazoacid, by loss of the αH.

22.34 When heated, AA's are dehydrated intermolecularly to form cyclic diamides. (*a*) Write the product from the reaction of glycine. (*b*) When the Me ester of *rac*-alanine is heated, two diastereomers are obtained. One of them is not resolvable. Give their structures and account for their stereochemistry.

▮ (*a*)

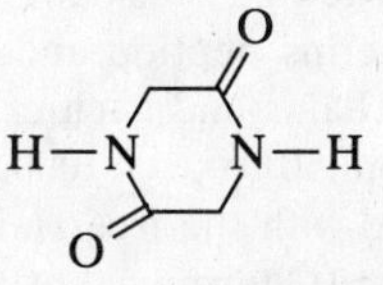

Diketopiperazine

(*b*) The *cis* is resolvable.

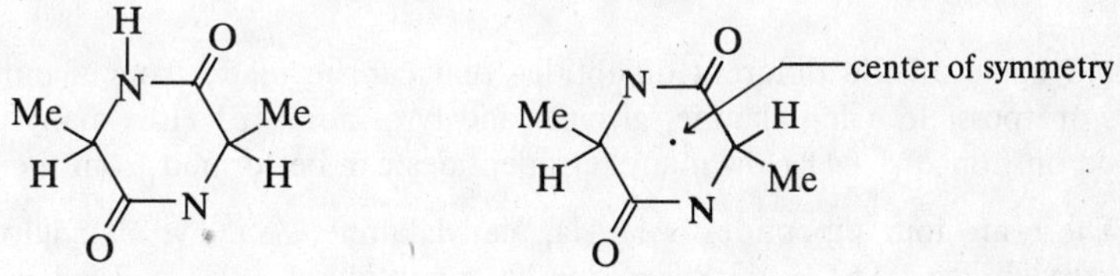

cis; racemic   *trans*; meso

22.35 Provide structures for the products formed when (*a*) β-AA, (*b*) γ-AA, (*c*) δ-AA, and (*d*) ε-AA are heated.

▮ (*a*) $RCH{=}CHCOO^-NH_4^+$

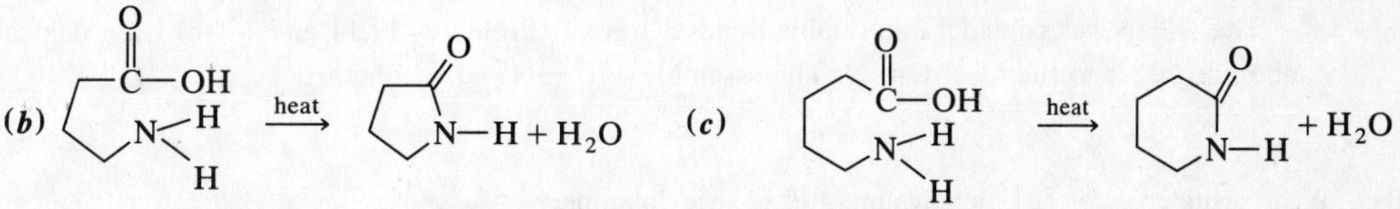

(*b*) a γ-amino acid → a γ-lactam (a cyclic amide) + H_2O

(*c*) a δ-amino acid → a δ-lactam + H_2O

(*d*) $\overset{+}{N}H_3(CH_2)_5COO^- \longrightarrow$

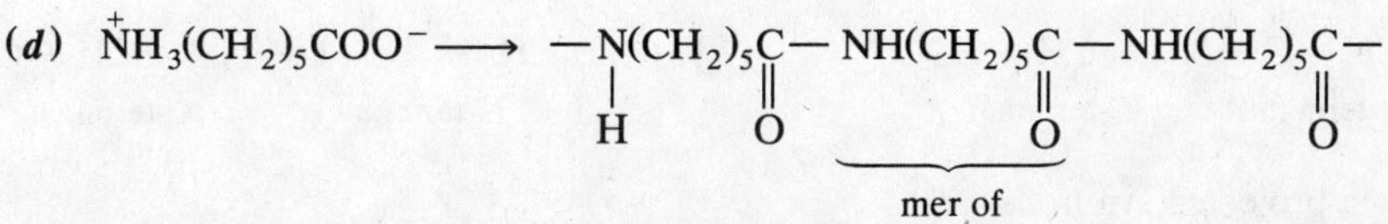

mer of
Nylon 6

Intramolecular cyclization would give a seven-membered ring, which is formed with difficulty. Hence the more facile intermolecular reaction occurs. Since the substrate is bifunctional, polymerization occurs.

22.36 Prepare (*a*) N-acetylphenylalanine ethyl ester and (*b*) N-benzoylhistidine methyl ester from the AA's.

(*a*)
$$\underset{\substack{| \\ \text{PhCH}_2\text{CHCOO}^-}}{\overset{+\text{NH}_3}{}} + \text{EtOH} \xrightarrow{\text{H}_2\text{SO}_4} \underset{\substack{| \\ \text{PhCH}_2\text{CHCOOEt}}}{\overset{+\text{NH}_3}{}} \xrightarrow{\text{Ac}_2\text{O/Py}} \underset{\substack{| \\ \text{PhCH}_2\text{CHCOOEt}}}{\overset{\text{NHCOCH}_3}{}}$$

The amino group is acylated after the esterification reaction because it would hydrolyze under the acidic esterification conditions.

(*b*)

The amino group is acylated after the esterification reaction because it would hydrolyze under the acidic esterification conditions.

Since Me esters can be made with CH_2N_2, acylation can occur first.

PEPTIDES AND PROTEINS

22.37 (*a*) What is a peptide bond or linkage? (*b*) Distinguish between a peptide, oligopeptide, polypeptide, and protein. (*c*) Give the standard way of describing the sequential order of AA's. (*d*) Name the tripeptide Tyr.Thr.Try.

(*a*)
$$\overset{\overset{\text{O}}{\|}\quad\overset{\text{H}}{|}}{-\text{C}-\text{N}-}, \text{ amide linkage}$$

(*b*) A *peptide* is an amide formed by intermolecular reaction of the amino group of one AA and the carboxyl group of a second AA. Dipeptides are made from two AA's, tripeptides from three AA's, etc., which may be the same or different. If there are four to ten AA residues, the peptide is called an *oligopeptide*. A *polypeptide* is a chain made up of many AA's. The terms peptide and polypeptide are often used interchangeably. A *protein* consists of one or more polypeptide chains and each chain can contain as much as several hundred AA's. The total number of residues may vary from 50 to over 1000.

(*c*) By convention, the amino acid with the free amino group (N-terminus) is written at the left end and the one with the unreacted carboxyl group (C-terminus) at the right end. The suffix *-ine* is replaced by *-yl* for each AA in the chain reading from left to right, followed by the full name of the C-terminal AA.

(*d*) Tyrosylthreonyltryptophan. (Note that tryptophan is the only AA without a second COOH whose name does not end in "ine".)

22.38 (*a*) List and name all the different dipeptides that can be made from alanine and glycine. (*b*) How many tripeptides are possible using alanine, glycine, and tyrosine? (*c*) How many tripeptides in (*b*) are possible if each is used only once? (*d*) How many tetrapeptides can be formed from the three AA's in (*b*)?

(*a*) There are four dipeptides: Ala.Ala, alanylalanine; Ala.Gly, alanylglycine; Gly.Ala, glycylalanine; and Gly.Gly, glycylglycine. (*b*) $3 \times 3 \times 3 = 3^3 = 27$ tripeptides. (*c*) $3 \times 2 \times 1 = 3! = 6$ tripeptides. (*d*) $3^4 = 81$ tetrapeptides.

22.39 Explain why the peptide C—N bond is stronger and shorter than the usual C—N single bond and why the rotation is restricted about this bond.

The C—N has considerable double-bond character (Problems 17.14 and 17.16) from delocalization of N's nonbonding e^-'s to the O of C=O. The assembly $\overset{\diagdown}{\underset{\overset{\|}{\text{O}}}{\text{C}}}-\text{N}\diagdown$ is coplanar.

22.40 Write structures for (*a*) alanylvaline and (*b*) valylalanine.

(*a*)
$$\underset{\substack{\\ \text{N-terminal}}}{\text{Me}-\underset{\substack{| \\ +\text{NH}_3}}{\text{CH}}-\underset{\substack{\| \\ \text{O}}}{\text{C}}-\text{NH}-\underset{\substack{| \\ \text{C-terminal}}}{\underset{\substack{\\ \text{CHMe}_2}}{\text{CH}}}-\text{COO}^-}$$

(*b*)
$$\underset{\substack{\\ \text{N-terminal}}}{\text{Me}_2\text{CH}-\underset{\substack{| \\ +\text{NH}_3}}{\text{CH}}-\underset{\substack{\| \\ \text{O}}}{\text{C}}-\text{NH}-\underset{\substack{| \\ \text{C-terminal}}}{\underset{\substack{\\ \text{Me}}}{\text{CH}}}-\text{COO}^-}$$

22.41 Criticize the following projected synthesis:

$$\text{H}_3\overset{+}{\text{N}}\text{CHRCOO}^- \xrightarrow{\text{SOCl}_2} \text{H}_3\overset{+}{\text{N}}\text{CHRCOCl}.$$

$$\text{H}_3\overset{+}{\text{N}}\text{CHRCOCl} + \text{H}_3\overset{+}{\text{N}}\text{CHR}'\text{COO}^- \longrightarrow \text{H}_3\overset{+}{\text{N}}\text{CHRCONHCHR}'\text{COO}^-$$

✔ In addition to the desired product, two molecules of acid chloride would react with one another to give another dipeptide. Also, both dipeptides would react further.

$$H_3\overset{+}{N}CHRCOCl + H_3\overset{+}{N}CHRCOCl \longrightarrow H_3\overset{+}{N}CHRCONHCHRCOCl \longrightarrow etc.$$

An AA cannot be made to react at its COOH with the amino of another AA without first protecting its own NH_2. Also, the HCl produced causes racemization at the chiral centers, and hydrolyzes amide bonds at other sites in the molecule.

22.42 Discuss the precautions in synthesizing peptides.

✔ Firstly, the amino and carboxyl groups that are not to be linked in peptide bonds must be blocked so as to be unreactive. Then all other reactive functional groups in the R's must also be protected, to prevent their participating in the coupling procedure. The coupling must be effected by a method that does not cause racemization or chemical alteration of the side chains. Finally, all protecting groups must be removed quantitatively by mild methods that do not cause rearrangements, racemization or cleavage of the peptide bonds.

22.43 (*a*) Give the product of reaction of *p*-toluenesulfonyl chloride with an AA. (*b*) How is the tosyl group removed? (*c*) What other functional group is reduced?

✔ (*a*) $H_3\overset{+}{N}CHRCOO^- \xrightarrow[\text{2. HCl}]{\text{1. TsCl, NaOH}} p\text{-}MeC_6H_4SO_2NHCHRCOOH$

(*b*) Na in liq. NH_3. The aromatic sulfonyl group is preferentially reduced.

(*c*) Any carboxylic ester: $COOR \longrightarrow CH_2OH$ ($+ HOR$). Disulfide: $S-S \longrightarrow 2\text{-}SH$

22.44 (*a*) Benzyl chlorocarbonate, $PhCH_2OCOCl$, also called carbobenzoxy chloride, (CBzCl), is a useful reagent for protecting the amino group of an AA. Write the structural formula for the product of its reaction with an AA. (*b*) How is this group removed?

✔ (*a*) $PhCH_2O-\overset{\overset{\displaystyle O}{\|}}{C}-NH\overset{\overset{\displaystyle R}{|}}{C}HCOOH$ (**A**), or $CBz-NH\overset{\overset{\displaystyle R}{|}}{C}HCOOH$. The product is a urethane (a carbamate), or half-ester and half-amide of carbonic acid. (*b*) Catalytic hydrogenolysis cleaves the benzyl$-O$ bond, forming an unstable carbamic acid, which decarboxylates:

$$\mathbf{A} \xrightarrow{H_2/Pd} PhCH_3 + [HOOCNHCHRCOOH] \longrightarrow CO_2 + RCH(\overset{+}{N}H_3)COO^-$$

If the side chain contains S, the catalyst is poisoned and Na in NH_3 is used. HBr may also be used, provided it does not hydrolyze the peptide linkages.

22.45 Another protecting group for NH_2 is the *t*-**butoxycarbonyl** (Boc) group, $t\text{-}BuO\overset{\overset{\displaystyle |}{}}{C}=O$, introduced with *t*-butyl carbonate or *t*-butoxycarbonyl azide. (*a*) Write the structure of the Boc derivative of an AA. (*b*) How is this group removed?

✔ (*a*) $t\text{-}BuO\overset{\overset{\displaystyle O}{\|}}{C}-NH\overset{\overset{\displaystyle R}{|}}{C}HCOOH$

(*b*) Since the group is a *t*-butyl ester, it is easily hydrolyzed in anhydrous acid (CF_3COOH or HBr in HOAc). Cleavage occurs to give $t\text{-}Bu^+$ and a carbamic acid, which decomposes to CO_2 and the amino acid.

$$t\text{-}BuO\overset{\overset{\displaystyle HO^+}{\|}}{C}-NH\overset{\overset{\displaystyle R}{|}}{C}HCOOH \longrightarrow t\text{-}Bu^+ + \left[O=\overset{\overset{\displaystyle HO}{|}}{C}-NH\overset{\overset{\displaystyle R}{|}}{C}HCOOH \right] \longrightarrow$$

$$CO_2 + H_3\overset{+}{N}\overset{\overset{\displaystyle R}{|}}{C}HCOO^- + Me_2C=CH_2 + H^+$$

22.46 Synthesize the dipeptide glycylproline.

✔ $CBzCl + H_3\overset{+}{N}CH_2COO^- \xrightarrow{-HCl} CBzNHCH_2COOH \xrightarrow{PCl_5} CBzNHCH_2COCl \xrightarrow[\text{OH}^-]{\text{proline}}$

$$CBzNHCH_2\overset{\overset{\displaystyle O}{\|}}{C}-N\underset{H}{\overset{\diagup}{\diagdown}}\langle\diagdown_{COOH} \xrightarrow{H_2/Pt} H_3\overset{+}{N}CH_2\overset{\overset{\displaystyle O}{\|}}{C}-N\underset{H}{\overset{\diagup}{\diagdown}}\langle\diagdown_{COO^-} + CO_2 + PhCH_3$$

22.47 How are the following side chain functional groups protected during a peptide synthesis? How are they removed? (*a*) OH as in serine, (*b*) SH as in cysteine, (*c*) COOH as in glutamic acid, (*d*) NH_2 as in lysine, (*e*) imidazyl as in histidine, and (*f*) guanadyl as in argenine.

▰ See Table 22-3.

TABLE 22-3

	Blocked Group	Blocking Group	Method of Removal
(*a*)	OH	acetyl	weak alkali
		benzyl	H_2/Pd
(*b*)	SH	benzyl	Na in liq. NH_3
(*c*)	COOH	Et, Me ester	weak alkali
		benzyl ester	weak alkali, H_2/Pd
(*d*)	NH_2	CBz	H_2/Pd
		Boc	CF_3COOH, HBr in HOAc
		p-toluenesulfonyl	Na in liq. NH_3
(*e*)	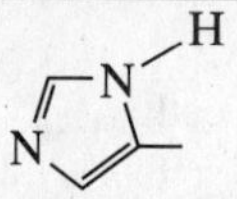	N-benzyl	Na in liq. NH_3
(*f*)	$-NH-C(NH_2)=NH$	H^+	neutralization

22.48 Discuss the activation of a terminal COOH with examples.

▰ Change COOH to an active ester, COOR, where R is a good leaving group such as p-$NO_2C_6H_4$ or to a thioester, $RCOSC_6H_4NO_2$-p. Form an active acyl compound AA-COZ, where Z is $-O-PO(OR)_2$, $-OCOR$ or $-N_3$.

22.49 Activation of the C-terminus of an AA, followed by coupling with a second AA, is accomplished with the reagent, dicyclohexylcarbodiimide (DCC), $C_6H_{11}-N=C=N-C_6H_{11}$. (*a*) Give the structure of the product of reaction of DCC with RCOOH. (*b*) Show the reaction of the product in (*a*) with an amine, $R'NH_2$. (*c*) Account for this reaction

▰ (*a*) $\underset{\underset{O}{\parallel}}{R-C}-OH + C_6H_{11}-N=C=N-C_6H_{11} \longrightarrow R-\underset{\underset{O}{\parallel}}{C}-O-\underset{\underset{NHC_6H_{11}}{|}}{C}=N-C_6H_{11}$ **(A)**

(*b*) $A + R'NH_2 \longrightarrow R-\underset{\underset{O}{\parallel}}{C}-NHR' + C_6H_{11}-NH-\underset{\underset{O}{\parallel}}{C}-NH-C_6H_{11}$ (a substituted urea)

(*c*) The reaction is a transacylation where the C=O of the acid is activated to nucleophilic attack by $R'NH_2$.

22.50 Synthesize alanylglycine Me ester using DCC.

▰ *Step 1.* Protect the N-terminus of alanine:

$$H_3\overset{+}{N}CHMeCOO^- + CBzCl \text{ (see Problem 22.44)} \longrightarrow CBzNHCHMeCOOH \text{ (B)}$$

Step 2. React with DCC:

$$B + DCC \longrightarrow CBzNHCHMe-\underset{\underset{O}{\parallel}}{C}-O-\underset{\underset{NHC_6H_{11}}{|}}{C}=N-C_6H_{11} \text{ (C)}$$

Step 3. React with glycine Me ester.

$$C + H_2NCH_2COOMe \longrightarrow CBzNHCHMeCONHCH_2COOMe \text{ (D)} + C_6H_{11}NHCONHC_6H_{11}$$

Step 4. Remove the blocking group: $D \xrightarrow{H_2/Pd} H_2NCHMeCONHCH_2COOMe$.

22.51 Describe the *Merrifield solid-phase process* for synthesizing peptides.

◢ The solid phase is beads of polystyrene whose mer is mainly $-CH_2-\overset{\overset{\displaystyle Ph}{|}}{CH}-$. However, occasional benzene rings have *p*-CH_2Cl substituents projecting out to the surface. The solid phase may be indicated as [P]—CH_2Cl (**A**), where [P] is the polystyrene backbone. The peptide chain is started at the C-terminus by bonding the Boc-protected AA to the solid phase through benzyl ester formation, followed by removal of the Boc group.

$$[P]-CH_2\overset{\frown}{Cl} + {}^-OOCCHRNHBoc \xrightarrow{-Cl^-} [P]-C_6H_4CH_2OOCCHRNHBoc \xrightarrow{CF_3COOH}$$

$$[P]-C_6H_4CH_2OOCCHRNH_2$$

A second AA (Boc-protected so that it will not self-couple) is added, along with DCC. The two steps of addition of a Boc-protected AA and regeneration of NH_2 with CF_3COOH are repeated as many times as required. In between each step, the [P]—growing peptide chain is washed with suitable solvents to remove excess reagents and undesirable products. Thus, intermediates do not have to be isolated and purified, and the yields are high. Reactant Boc-AA's, DCC, and CF_3COOH are added through an automated system. Removal of the completed peptide from the polymer is accomplished with anhydrous HF, which also removes the last Boc group.

22.52 Which α-AA can provide a cross-linkage of two peptide chains? Illustrate.

◢ Cysteine, through disulfide bonds. Cysteine linkages also occur between distant properly situated parts of the same chain.

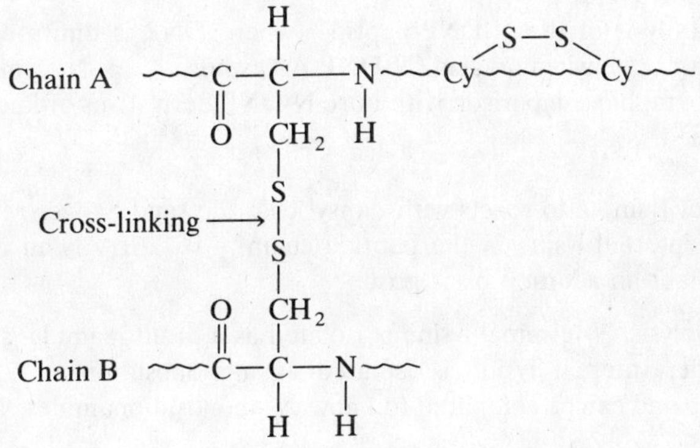

STRUCTURE DETERMINATION

22.53 How are different peptides separated from each other?

◢ Peptides contain only one free α-NH_3^+ and one free α-COO^- at their termini. In addition, the R groups of some of the AA residues in the chain have substituents that contribute to the total acid-base behavior of the peptide. Thus, each peptide has a characteristic titration curve and an isoelectric pH. Peptides are separable by ion-exchange chromatography, electrophoresis, or a combination of both.

22.54 How are peptides hydrolyzed?

◢ Heating with either strong acid or base hydrolyzes all the peptide bonds, freeing the constituent AA's. Selective partial hydrolysis may be effected by employing certain *proteolytic* (protein-breaking) enzymes. For example, trypsin only hydrolyzes a peptide bond formed from the carboxyl group of lysine or argenine, and chymotrypsin from the carboxyl group of phenylalanine, tyrosine, and tryptophan.

22.55 What products are expected from (*a*) complete and (*b*) partial hydrolysis of the tetrapeptide Ala.Met.Gly.Val?

◢ (*a*) The AA's are Ala, Met, Gly, and Val. (*b*) The dipeptides are Ala.Met, Met.Gly, and Gly.Val. The tripeptides are Ala.Met.Gly and Met.Gly.Val.

22.56 (*a*) Give the reaction of a peptide chain, Pep-NHCOCHRNH$_3^+$ with *dansyl chloride*, 5-**d**imethyl**a**mino-1-**n**aphthalene**s**ulfon**yl** chloride. (*b*) Explain how dansylation is used in *terminal (end) group analysis* of a peptide.

(a)

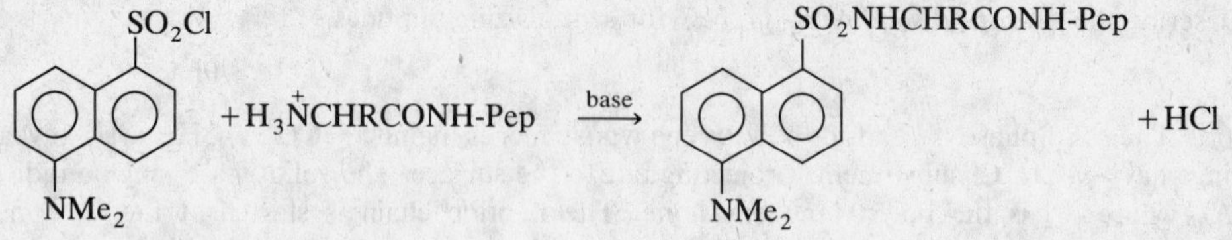

$$\text{dansyl chloride} + H_3\overset{+}{N}CHRCONH\text{-Pep} \xrightarrow{\text{base}} \text{dansyl-peptide} + HCl$$

dansyl chloride   dansyl-peptide

(b) The N-terminus is tagged as a sulfonamide. The peptide is hydrolyzed in acid to its constituent AA's and the dansyl derivative of the N-terminal AA, which is isolated and identified (sulfonamides are not hydrolyzed in acid). The dansyl group is fluorescent, making the dansylated peptide and N-terminal AA easily detected.

22.57 (a) Give the reaction of the *Sanger reagent*, 1-fluoro-2,4-dinitrobenzene (DNFB), with a peptide chain, Pep-NHCOCHRNH$_3^+$. (b) How is this reaction used to identify the N-terminal AA of the peptide chain?

(a)

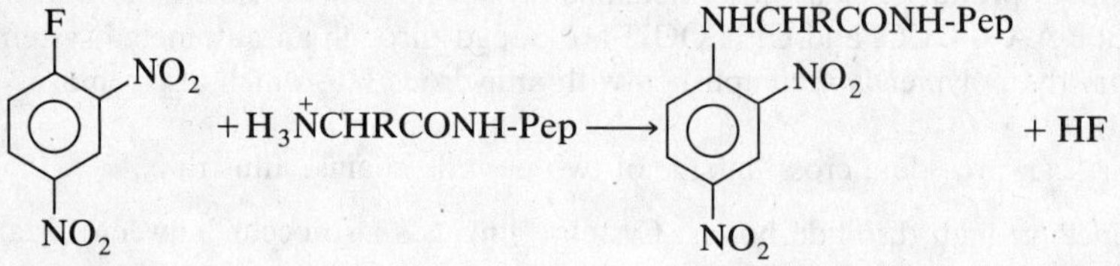

$$\text{DNFB} + H_3\overset{+}{N}CHRCONH\text{-Pep} \longrightarrow \text{N-DNP-peptide} + HF$$

DNFB   N-DNP-peptide

(b) Acid hydrolysis of the N-DNP-peptide (where DNP is **di**nitrophenyl) gives individual AA's and an N-2,4-dinitrophenylamino acid (N-DNP-AA, where AA is N-terminal), detected by its yellow color and chromatographic comparison with pure N-DNP derivatives of known AA's. In this way the N-terminus is identified.

22.58 The ϵ-NH$_2$ group of lysine also reacts with dansyl chloride (and Sanger reagent). (a) How is N-terminal lysine differentiated from internal lysine in the peptide chain? (b) How is an internal lysine differentiated from an N-terminal AA without an addition basic group?

(a) After hydrolysis, N-terminal lysine is isolated as a disulfonamide, since both amino groups have reacted with dansyl chloride. Internal lysine is isolated as a monosulfonamide. (b) The N-terminal AA has an α-sulfonamide group and can be compared to known α-monosulfonamides. The sulfonamide of the internal lysine is not on the α C.

22.59 How can the C-terminal AA be identified?

The peptide is incubated with the enzyme *carboxypeptidase*, which hydrolyzes only the C-terminal peptide bond. With prolonged incubation, each new C-terminal AA is hydrolyzed as it is exposed. A study of the rate of appearance of each newly released AA can give information about the sequence of a limited number of AA's that precede the C-terminal AA.

22.60 (a) Give the reactions in the *Edman degradation* of H$_3\overset{+}{N}$CHRCONH-Pep. (b) What is the advantage of the Edman degradation, used to determine the N-terminal AA?

(a) In the Edman degradation, PhN=C=S reacts with the NH$_2$ of the N-terminal AA.

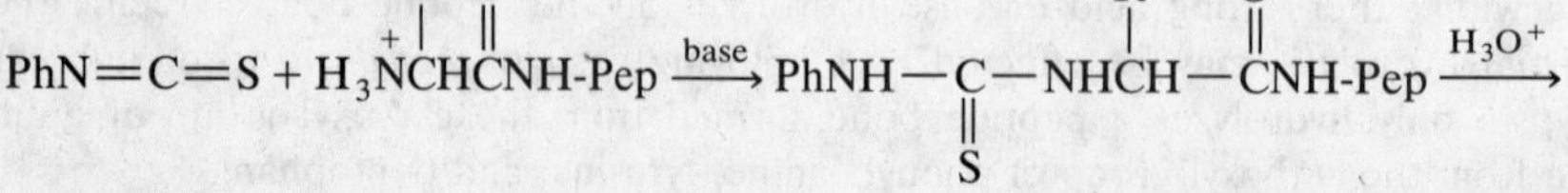

$$PhN=C=S + H_3\overset{+}{N}CHCNH\text{-Pep} \xrightarrow{\text{base}} PhNH-C-NHCH-CNH\text{-Pep} \xrightarrow{H_3O^+}$$

Phenyl   AA phenylthiourea
isothiocyanate

$$PhN-C=S,\ O=C,\ CHR,\ NH + \overset{+}{N}H_3Pep$$

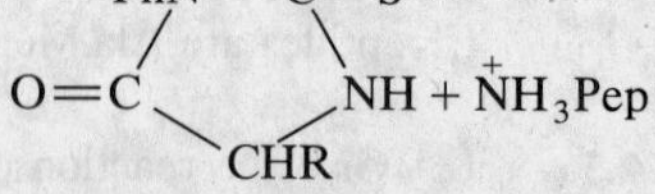

AA phenylthiohydantoin

(*b*) Since hydrolysis conditions are mild, only the terminal AA derivative is cleaved, and the rest of the peptide chain is intact. It is then recycled through further Edman degradations in an automated cycle that permits the successive cleavage and identification of a sequence of AA residues.

22.61 Show how cyanogen bromide, $Br—C \equiv N$, is used in selective cleavage of a peptide.

◢ It cleaves a peptide at the carboxyl end of each methionine residue.

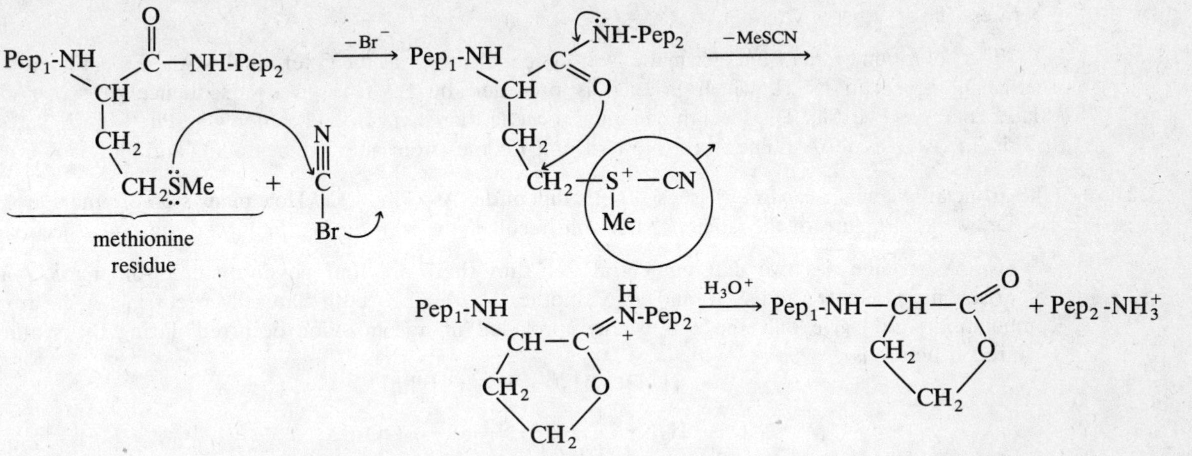

22.62 Enkephalins are pentapeptide components of endorphins, the polypeptide analgesics present in the brain. Deduce the AA sequence of an enkephalin (**A**) from the following data. The AA's identified by complete hydrolysis are: Gly, Phe, Leu, and Tyr; Gly.Gly.Phe and Tyr.Gly are isolated from its partial hydrolysis. Upon reaction of **A** with dansyl chloride, followed by peptide hydrolysis, the dansyl derivative of tyrosine is identified by thin-layer chromatography.

◢ The N-terminal AA residue is tyrosine and there are two Gly's. The two fragments are arranged in order with Tyr first, i.e., Tyr.Gly... .Gly.Gly.Phe. The cross line removes the duplicating AA, giving the sequence Tyr.Gly.Gly.Phe, to which the C-terminal Leu is added. Thus, Tyr.Gly.Gly.Phe.Leu.

22.63 A tripeptide (**B**) is hydrolyzed completely to two eq of Glu and one eq each of Ala and NH_3. **B** has only one free carboxyl group, and does not react with 2,4-dinitrofluorobenzene. Ala is released first when **B** is incubated with carboxypeptidase. Provide a structure for **B**.

◢ The AA sequence is Glu.Glu.Ala because carboxypeptidase liberates the C-terminal Ala. The N-terminal amino group is tied up with the adjacent Glu's carboxyl group in a lactam, making it unavailable for reaction with the Sanger reagent, and the other carboxyl group is part of an amide. The required structure is

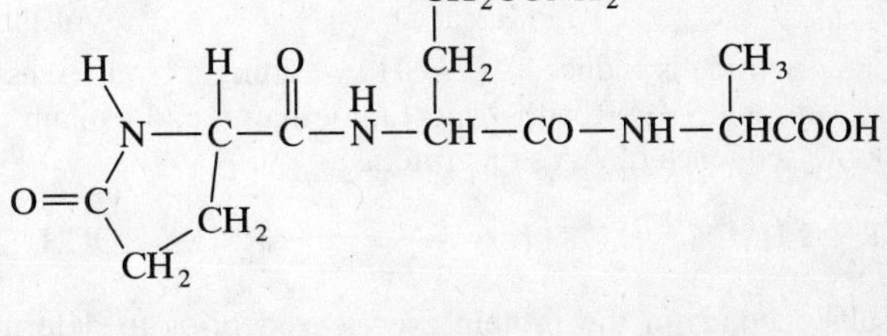

22.64 A hexapeptide (**C**) is completely hydrolyzed to give Ala, Arg, Gly, Lys, Try, Val, and NH_3. Incubation of **C** with chymotrypsin gives a dipeptide identified as Arg.Try and a tetrapeptide (**D**) containing Gly, Lys, Ala, and Val. When **C** or **D** is incubated with carboxypeptidase there is no reaction. On partial hydrolysis, **D** yields Ala.Val, Gly.Lys, Lys.Ala, and NH_3. **E**, given below, is produced when **D** is subjected to a single Edman degradation. Deduce the structure of **C**.

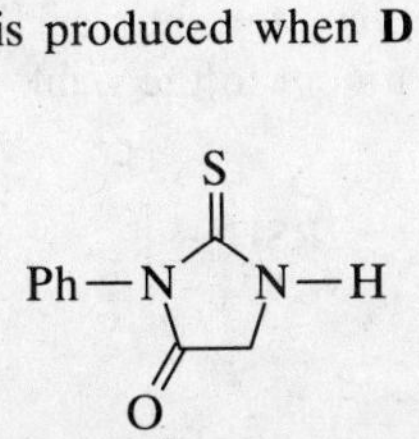

E

◢ The formation of **E** indicates that the N-terminus in **D** is Gly. Write the dipeptides with Gly first so that they overlap in a continuous way, Gly.Lys; ~~Lys~~.Ala; ~~Ala~~.Val, giving the structure of **D** as Gly.Lys.Ala.Val. The terminal carboxyl is present as the amide (no reaction with carboxypeptidase). The formation of Arg.Try by cleavage of the carboxyl peptide bond of Try with chymotrypsin means that Try is bonded to Gly of **D** (Problem 22.54). **C** is Arg.Try.Gly.Lys.Ala.Val-amide.

22.65 Provide the sequence of AA's for the heptapeptide **F** from the following information. On partial hydrolysis, Ser.Asp.Phe (**G**), Ala.His.Ser (**H**), and Phe.Ala (**I**) are identified, and limited incubation with carboxypeptidase liberates Ala.

◢ The liberation of Ala from enzymatic hydrolysis indicates that the C-terminal is Ala. **I** must be at the end of the chain, preceded by **G**, which in turn is preceded by **H**. This gives a sequence of six AA residues Ala.His.Ser.Asp.Phe.Ala. The seventh one must precede the Ala in **H**, and can only be Phe from **I**. The sequence in **F** is Phe.Ala.His.Ser.Asp.Phe.Ala. Note that unit **I** comes from both the beginning and end of **F**.

22.66 The artificial sweetener *aspartame* is a synthetic dipeptide, Asp.Phe.   (*a*) How many stereoisomers are possible? (*b*) Draw the structure of the isomer that would result if the starting materials were naturally occurring AA's.

◢ (*a*) Aspartame has two different chiral C's; thus there are four possible stereoisomers: S, S and R, R comprise one racemate, and S, R and R, S another.   (*b*) Since both naturally occurring AA's are S, their combination would give only the S, S isomer, provided no racemization occurred during the synthesis. The required structure is

$$\underset{\underset{\text{H}}{|}}{\overset{\overset{\text{HOOCCH}_2}{|}}{\text{H}_3\overset{+}{\text{N}}-\text{C}}}-\underset{\underset{\text{O}}{\|}}{\text{C}}-\underset{\underset{\text{H}}{|}}{\text{N}}-\underset{}{\overset{\overset{\text{CH}_2\text{Ph}}{|}}{\text{C}}}-\text{COO}^- (S,S)$$

22.67 The vasodilator bradykinin, a nonapeptide, contains the following AA's: 2Arg, Gly, 2Phe, 3Pro, and Ser. Carboxypeptidase incubation releases Arg first. Selective hydrolysis produces, among other products, Pro.Pro.Gly, Ser.Pro.Phe, and Pro.Gly.Phe, Arg.Pro, and Phe.Ser. Deduce the AA sequence in bradykinin.

◢ One Arg is C-terminal because of its enzymatic release. Only the fragment with Pro at the end can precede a fragment with Pro at the beginning to give Pro.Pro.Gly. This clue permits the following sequence of the units:

Arg.Pro....P~~ro~~.Pro.Gly....P~~ro~~.G~~ly~~.Phe....P~~he~~.Ser....S~~er~~.Pro.Phe...Arg

Slash lines remove overlapping AA's, and the sequence is Arg.Pro.Pro.Gly.Phe.Ser.Pro.Phe.Arg.

22.68 The pentapeptide **A**, comprised of 2Gly, Ala, Phe, and Val, gives no N_2 with HONO. Among its hydrolysis products are Ala.Gly and Gly.Ala. Give two possible structures.

◢ Since N_2 is not released, there is no free amino group at the N-terminal, and **A** must be a cyclic peptide. It has the partial sequence Gly.Ala.Gly, and the remaining Phe and Val units can be bonded in sequence in two ways, giving

(*1*) Gly.Ala.Gly   and   (*2*) Gly.Ala.Gly
　　　 ＼　 ／　　　　　　　　　 ＼　 ／
　　　Phe.Val　　　　　　　　　 Val.Phe

22.69 The disulfide bond in a peptide is reduced to —SH by adding a large excess of $HSCH_2CH_2OH$.   (*a*) Write an equation for the reaction of RS—SR with 2-mercaptoethanol and explain its action.   (*b*) How is this reaction used in determining the sequence of AA's of proteins?

◢ (*a*) $RS-SR + 2\,HSCH_2CH_2OH$ (excess) $\rightleftharpoons$ $2\,RSH + HOCH_2CH_2S-SCH_2CH_2OH$

(*b*)   Any disulfide bonds in the protein are cleaved prior to determining the AA sequence. The large excess of mercaptoethanol is used to drive the equilibrium to the right.

22.70 Dithiothreitol, $HSCH_2CH(OH)CH(OH)CH_2SH$ (**A**), functions in the same way as does 2-mercaptoethanol (Problem 22.69).   (*a*) Write an equation for the reaction of R—S—S—R with **A**.   (*b*) Explain why the equilibrium for this reaction lies much more to the right.

◢ (*a*) RS—SR +

HO＼　　＿＿＼
　　 ＼／　　 ＼SH
　　 ／＼　　 ／
HO　　 ‾‾‾‾／SH

$\rightleftharpoons$ 2RSH +

HO＼　　＿＿＼
　　 ＼／　　 ＼S
　　 ／＼　　 ｜S
HO　　 ‾‾‾‾／

$K_e \approx 10^4$

A

(*b*)   The proximity of the two SH groups increases the probability of reaction, as compared with the open chain case in Problem 22.69. The entropy factor is more favorable because in this case one molecule (the six-membered ring) is formed from one molecule of **A**, whereas when 2-mercaptoethanol is used, two molecules of thiol form from one molecule of disulfide.

22.71 Distinguish between simple and conjugated proteins.

▰ Simple proteins consist only of AA's; conjugated proteins also have a *prosthetic group*, a nonamino acid unit.

22.72 Classify conjugated proteins on the basis of their prosthetic groups.

▰ See Table 22-4.

TABLE 22-4

Class	Prosthetic Group	Example
Phosphoproteins	Phosphate groups	Casein of milk
Lipoproteins	Lipids, Cholesterol esters	HDL (High density lipoprotein in blood)
Glycoproteins	Carbohydrates	Mucin, a component of saliva; Interferon
Nucleoproteins	Nucleic acids	DNA; RNA
Metalloproteins	Heme (iron porphyrin)	Hemoglobin; Myoglobin; Cytochromes
	Zinc	Alcohol dehydrogenase (enzyme)
Flavoproteins	Flavin nucleotides	Succinate dehydrogenase (enzyme)

22.73 Categorize proteins according to (*a*) shape and (*b*) biological function.

▰ (*a*) *Globular*, somewhat spherical, and *fibrous*, long fibers or planar sheets. (*b*) Enzyme, transport, contractile, structural, hormones, antibodies, etc.

22.74 Define primary, secondary, tertiary, and quaternary structure of a protein?

▰ The *primary* structure is simply the AA sequence of the peptide chain. The *secondary* structure is a result of the different conformations that the chain can take. The *tertiary* structure is determined by any folding of the chain in on itself. A *quaternary* structure results when two or more peptide chains in some proteins are linked together by weak forces of attraction of their surface groups. Such proteins are called *oligomers* (dimers, trimers, etc.).

22.75 (*a*) What kind of bonding is greatly responsible for the secondary structure? (*b*) Describe the three types of secondary structures.

▰ (*a*) The H-bonding between an N—H of one AA residue and the O=C of another properly situated AA residue. (*b*) (*1*) The peptide sequence is coiled into a right-handed spiral in the *α-helix*, with the R groups positioned on the outside of the spiral. Each amide H—N bonds to the O=C on the next turn of the coil, four residues away by H-bonds, stabilizing this arrangement. (*2*) In the *pleated sheet* or *β-structure*, the peptide chains lie side-by-side in an open structure, with inter-chain amide H-bonding holding the chains together. *Parallel* pleated sheets have chains running in the same direction, all with their N-terminal residues starting at the same end. *Antiparallel* pleated sheets have their chains running in opposite directions. The α C's rotate slightly out of the plane of the sheet to minimize repulsions between their bulky R groups, giving rise to the crimps or pleats. In both cases, the R groups alternate positions above and below the sheet. (*3*) The *random coil* structure has no repeating geometric pattern; encompassed within it are sequences in a helical conformation, a pleated sheet conformation, and regions that appear to have no discernible repeating structure, but are actually not random conformations.

22.76 Describe the kind of bonding responsible for the tertiary structure.

▰ The unique three-dimensional shape of a protein is the result of the intramolecular forces of attraction that cause bending and coiling in the helical coil. These forces are a function of the nature of the AA side chains within the molecule. *Globular* proteins have their nonpolar R groups pointing to the interior (the hydrophobic or nonaqueous region) and their polar side chains projecting toward the aqueous environment, somewhat like a micelle. They are somewhat water soluble. *Fibrous* proteins are insoluble in water. Their polypeptide chains are held together by inter-chain H-bonds. The following are the attractive forces responsible for the tertiary structure:

(1) Ionic: bonding between COO⁻ and NH₃⁺ at different sites;
(2) H-bonding: mainly between side-chain NH_2 and COOH, also involving OH's (of serine, for example) and the N—H of tryptophane;
(3) Weakly hydrophobic van der Waals attractive forces engendered by side-chain R groups;
(4) Disulfide cross linkages between loops of the polypeptide chain.

22.77 Describe the kind of bonding responsible for quaternary structure.

▰ The same kind of attractive and repulsive forces responsible for the tertiary structure operate to hold together and stabilize the subunits of the quaternary structure.

22.78 Explain how proteins are separated by electrophoresis.

▰ Every protein has a distinct pI, based on the total number of basic and acidic side chains. When a protein mixture is subjected to an electric current, each protein migrates to an electrode at a unique rate that is a function of its MW and total net charge as determined by the pH.

22.79 Referring to Fig. 22-2, identify the three spots obtained by electrophoresis at pH = 7 of a mixture of the proteins pepsin (pI = 1.1), hemoglobin (pI = 6.7), and lysozyme (pI = 11.0).

Start

(+) Electrode   ●A   ●B   ●C   (−) Electrode   **Fig. 22-2**

▰ Pepsin, **A**, with a pI in the very acid range has many more anionic groups at pH = 7, and will migrate to the positive pole. Hemoglobin, **B**, is present mostly with net zero charge, and will move very little to the same electrode. Lysozyme, **C**, the very basic protein, exists mainly in the cationic form and migrates to the negative pole.

22.80 Collagen, a fibrous protein found in connective tissues, contains a high proportion of proline residues. (*a*) What is the consequence of the presence of proline residues in the α-helix? (*b*) As we grow older, the number of cross-links in collagen increases. How are the properties of collagen affected, and how does this change affect tendons?

▰ (*a*) The amide formed from the 2° amino N in proline lacks an H for H-bonding. This disrupts the network of H-bonds and terminates the coil of the helix at that point. In addition, the amide N is part of a rigid ring and no rotation of the ring N—C bond is possible. This results in a kink or rigid bend in the peptide chain, conferring great tensile strength. (*b*) Collagen fibers become more rigid and brittle, making tendons (connective tissues) more easily injured.

22.81 (*a*) Describe the units of hemoglobin. (*b*) How does CO cause asphixiation?

▰ (*a*) Hemoglobin has four separate peptide subunits: two identical α-chains and two identical β-chains, each bonded to heme, an iron-porphyrin (Problem 21.96) prosthetic group. Of its six coordination bonds, Fe^{2+} uses four to bond to the four N's at the center of heme, one bonds the heme to its polypeptide chain by coordination to a histidine residue, and one bonds to a molecule of O_2. (*b*) CO competes favorably (≈ 200 times) with O_2 for the sixth bonding site. In CO poisoning, since much of the hemoglobin is tied up with CO, O_2 transport to the tissues is inhibited.

22.82 Normal hemoglobin, found in disc-shaped erythrocytes (red blood cells), has a glutamic acid residue at position 6 in each of the two β-chains (Problem 22.81). In *sickle-cell anemia*, the erythrocytes assume a crescent or sickle shape. Sickle-cell hemoglobin (hemoglobin S) contains valine instead of glutamic acid, and migrates toward a positively charged electrode at a slightly lower rate than does normal hemoglobin in an electric field. How does this single error (there are 146 AA residues in the β-chain) cause sickling?

▰ The overall charge on the hemoglobin molecule is reduced by the substitution of a nonpolar Val for Glu with a COO⁻ decreasing its migration rate. The hydrophobic R groups of valine at the surface of the protein decrease its solubility, and hemoglobin S forms polymeric filaments that deform the cell into its characteristic shapes. The deformed cells are trapped in the capillaries and impair blood circulation.

22.83 In what ways do enzymes differ from typical inorganic catalysts?

▮ Enzymes are the most *efficient* catalysts known; micromolar quantities in a cell cause reactions to accelerate by a factor of 10^6 or more over noncatalyzed reactions. Most enzymes exhibit a *specificity of action*; they catalyze the reaction of only one or closely related substrates. The action of most enzymes is *regulated*; their action can be shifted from high to low activity under certain conditions (*feedback mechanism*). They operate at maximum efficiency at the organism's ambient temperature and pH, and are denatured (Problem 22.88) at higher temperatures and in extreme reaction conditions.

22.84 Account for the stereochemical specificity of enzymes with chiral substrates.

▮ Enzymes are globular proteins made up of optically active AA residues, and thus have distinct three-dimensional chiral structures that accommodate only one of a chiral enantiomer substrate.

22.85 Account for the stereochemical specificity of an enzyme with an achiral substrate whose product is chiral.

▮ When the achiral substrate fits into the contour of the protein prior to reaction, only one of the two enantiotopic faces is properly positioned and it is always the same face.

22.86 Outline the steps in an enzyme catalyzed reaction.

▮ The enzyme, E, reversibly combines with the substrate, S, to form an *enzyme-substrate complex*, E—S. E—S then decomposes to form product(s) P, releasing the enzyme.

$$E + S \underset{}{\overset{\text{step 1}}{\rightleftharpoons}} E - S \underset{}{\overset{\text{step 2}}{\rightleftharpoons}} P + E$$

22.87 Discuss the nature of the enzyme-substrate complex.

▮ The substrate binds to a specific location on or near the surface of the enzyme, usually by ionic and/or dipolar interactions. This site comprises only a small portion of the surface, and consists of a spatially ordered cluster of several AA R groups (and possibly a cofactor), some of which bind the substrate, while others participate in the reaction that leads to the product.

22.88 (*a*) Define denaturation of a protein. (*b*) List the different kinds of denaturation agents and describe the denaturation process in each case.

▮ (*a*) *Denaturation* is the alteration or loss of the unique three-dimensional conformational state of a protein. It partially or completely unfolds into random structures *without concomitant cleavage of the peptide chain*. The bonds broken are those responsible for the secondary, tertiary and, if present, quaternary structures. (*b*) See Table 22-5.

TABLE 22-5

Denaturing Agent	Process
Heat, uv radiation, shaking	Atoms vibrate more rapidly, disrupting H-bonds and van der Waals attractive forces, resulting in precipitation, e.g., hardening of egg white (albumin).
Changes in pH	Disrupts H-bonding and ionic attractive forces causing coagulation, e.g., souring of milk.
Heavy metal ions	Form precipitates with COO^- and SH groups of R side chains. The antiseptic Hg_2Cl_2 precipitates protein in infectious bacteria. (Heavy metal ions are toxic.)
Detergents, urea, H_2CO, C_2H_5OH	H-bond to protein, replacing intramolecular H-bonds, causing precipitation.

22.89 How is cysteine-cystine interconversion used in permanent-waving of hair?

▮ Protein in hair is an α-keratin peptide chain in the α-helix form. Three of these chains twist around each other forming a supercoiled "rope". The three strands are held together by covalent —S—S— cross-linkages. Firstly, the polypeptide chain is made more flexible by cleaving the disulfide linkages with a reducing agent, usually thioglycolic acid, $HSCH_2COOH$. Then, after the damp hair is set into a new shape, the disulfide cross-links are restored with a mild oxidizing agent.

$$\text{(rigid) R} - S - S - R \underset{\text{oxidation}}{\overset{\text{reduction}}{\rightleftharpoons}} 2R - SH \text{ (flexible)}$$

22.90 Distinguish between irreversible and reversible inhibition of an enzyme.

▱ Irreversible inhibitors combine chemically with or destroy a functional group on the enzyme that is necessary for catalytic activity. An example is DFP inhibition of acetylcholinesterase (Problem 17.127). There are two kinds of reversible inhibition. (*1*) In competitive inhibition, the inhibitor competes with the substrate for the active site, but once bound cannot be chemically transformed as can the normal substrate. (*2*) In noncompetitive inhibition, the inhibitor binds at a site other than the normal substrate binding site, altering the conformation of the enzyme and preventing normal activity. Removal of the inhibitor restores the enzyme activity.

22.91 The active ingredient in some meat tenderizers is papain, a proteolytic enzyme isolated from papaya. Papain hydrolyzes the peptide bonds of Arg, Lys, and Gly at their $C=O$. Explain the tenderizing process.

▱ Collagen in the connective tissue of meat makes it tough. Papain hydrolyzes some of the lysine-rich residues to shorter polypeptides, making the meat easier to chew and digest.

SPECTRA AND ANALYSIS

22.92 (*a*) Write the general structure of the violet-colored product from the reaction of an AA with ninhydrin, triketohydrindene hydrate (Fig. 22-3). (*b*) Proline and hydroxyproline give a yellow color with ninhydrin. Explain.

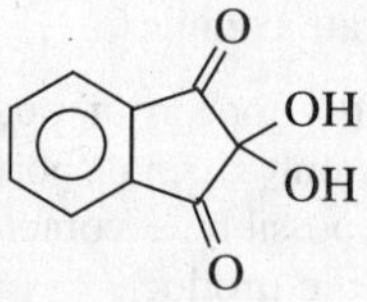

Fig. 22-3

▱ (*a*) See Fig. 22-4.

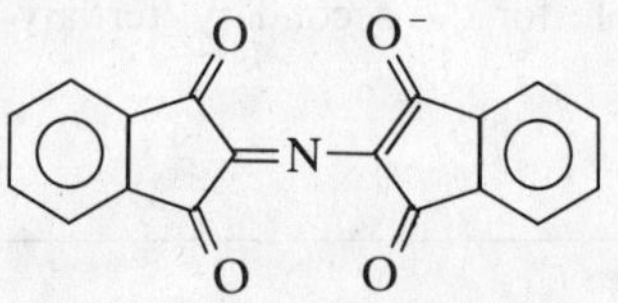

Fig. 22-4

(*b*) The same dye forms from all α-AA's with 1° amino groups because only their N is incorporated into it. The 2° amines proline and hydroxyproline give different adducts that absorb light at a different wavelength and thus have a different yellow color.

22.93 (*a*) Identify the absorption bands in the ir spectrum of AA's near 1400 and 1600 cm^{-1}. (*b*) Why does a strong peak appear at 1720 cm^{-1} in highly acidic solution?

▱ (*a*) These peaks are due to the symmetrical and antisymmetrical $C-O$ stretching in COO^-. (*b*) Acid converts COO^- to $COOH$, whose $C=O$ produces the 1720 cm^{-1} peak.

22.94 Describe the 1° amino group ir absorption.

▱ The broad strong stretching band in the 3100 to 3000 cm^{-1} region is attributed to $N-H$ stretch of NH_3^+. There are also several weak symmetric and antisymmetric $N-H$ bend absorptions near 1660–1610 cm^{-1} and 1550–1485 cm^{-1}.

22.95 Why do many proteins show appreciable absorptions in the uv spectrum at ≈ 279 nm?

▱ Proteins containing a large number of tryptophan and/or tyrosine residues absorb in this range, attributed to the aromatic rings. Phenylalanine absorbs at 259 nm, with a small ϵ_{max}.

22.96 Predict the cleavage pattern in the mass spec of an α-AA.

The molecular ion peak is very weak because AA's easily lose their carboxyl group.

$$H_3\overset{+}{N}-CHR-COO^- \xrightarrow[-45 \text{ mass units}]{-[COOH]} H_2\overset{+}{N}{=}CH-R \qquad m/z = MW - 45$$

22.97 Distinguish chemically between the following pairs of compounds: (*a*) Aspartic acid and succinic acid, (*b*) phenylalanine and tyrosine, and (*c*) serine and threonine.

(*a*) Asp gives a violet color with ninhydrin. It also evolves N_2 when reacted with HONO. (*b*) With $FeCl_3$, Ty gives a distinctive color due to the phenolic OH. (*c*) Threonine has the CH_3CHOH grouping and reacts with I_2/KOH to give CHI_3, iodoform.

SUPPLEMENTARY PROBLEMS

22.98 Treatment of (*R*)-MeCH(OH)CCl_3, first with alkaline NaN_3 and then reducing the product with H_2/Pd, yields (*S*)-alanine. Explain.

In basic solution, the O^- from OH displaces a Cl, forming an oxirane ring, which is then opened by azide ion with inversion. Hydrolysis, followed by reduction of the N_3 group, gives an (*S*)-α-amino acid.

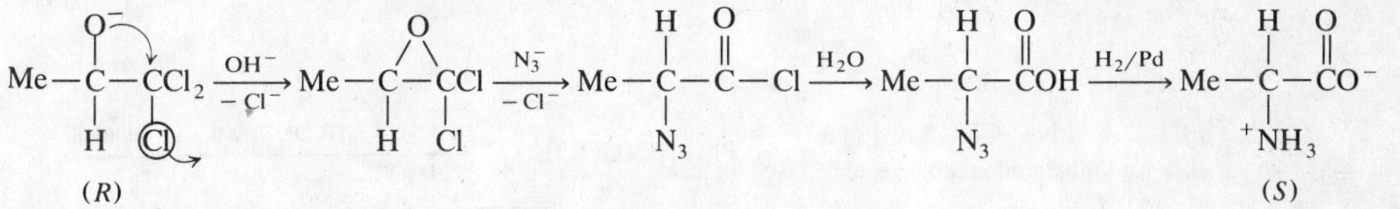

22.99 (*a*) The osmotic pressure of an aqueous solution containing 1.00 g/L of the protein bovine insulin is 4.0×10^{-3} atm at 25°C. Calculate its molecular weight. (*b*) Why is a MW calculation based upon freezing-point depressions not useful in this case?

(*a*) Osmotic pressure (Π) is the force required to oppose the net osmotic flow of solvent molecules from a dilute solution (or pure solvent) to a more concentrated solution through a superpermeable membrane. The mathematical relationship (Problem 1.67) is: $\Pi V = (g/\text{MW})(RT)$, where g = concentration in g/L, $R = 0.0821$ L · atm/mol · K, and T is in K. Rearranging terms, and substituting values,

$$\text{MW} = \frac{gRT}{\Pi} = \frac{1.00\ \text{g/L} \times 0.0821\ \text{L}\cdot\text{atm/mol}\cdot\text{K} \times 298\ \text{K}}{4.0 \times 10^{-3}\ \text{atm}} = 6116\ \text{g/mol} \cong 6.1 \times 10^3\ \text{g/mol}$$

(*b*) Solutes of high MW, like all proteins, give imperceptibly small freezing-point depressions because there are so few molecules in solution.

22.100 Hemoglobin (Problem 22.81) contains 0.35% Fe. Each molecule contains four atoms of Fe (56 g-atoms/mol). Find the MW of hemoglobin.

Four atoms of Fe weigh: 4 atoms $\times$ 56 g/atom = 224 g which is 0.35% of the MW of the protein. Therefore, MW = 224 g/mol $\div$ 0.0035 = 64×10^3 g/mol.

22.101 Outline a procedure for converting vanillin to *rac*-3,4-dihydroxyphenylalanine, whose (*S*) enantiomer is the drug L-Dopa, used for treatment of Parkinson's disease.

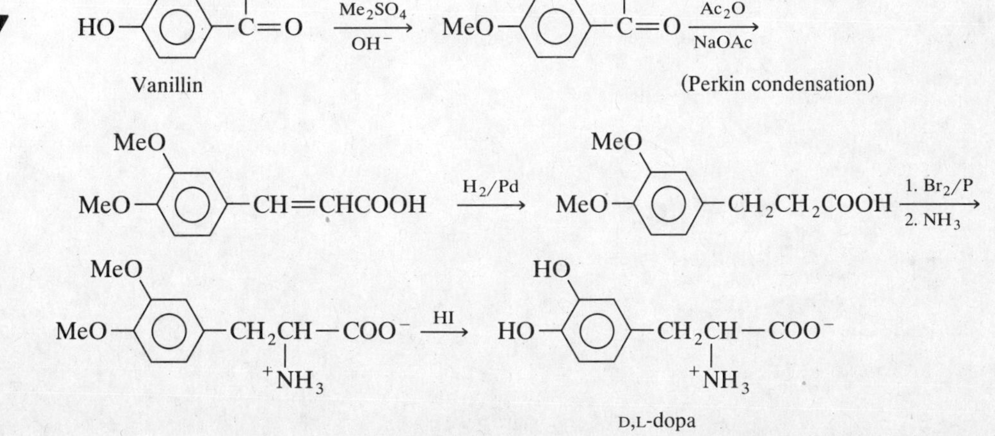

22.102 Glutathione, Glu.Cys.Gly, is a tripeptide widely distributed in plants, animals, and bacteria. The Glu residue forms a peptide bond with its γ COOH. (*a*) Give the structure of glutathione. (*b*) Explain how glutathione functions as a free radical scavenger in the cells.

▮ (*a*) $\overset{+}{H_3N}-CH-(CH_2)_2-CO-NH-CH-CO-NH-CH_2COO^-$

   | COO⁻ (below first CH) | CH₂SH (below second CH)

   the γ-COOH

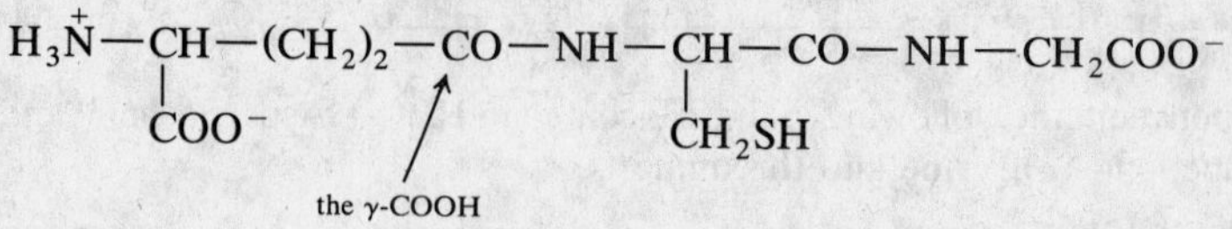

(*b*) Glutathione reduces HO· and ·O_2^- (to H_2O). In the process it is oxidized to a disulfide consisting of two tripeptide chains linked intermolecularly by an S—S bond, or

$$2P-SH \rightleftharpoons P-S-S-P+[2H\cdot]$$

22.103 Prepare (*a*) methionine from acrolein by the Strecker synthesis, and (*b*) glutamic acid *via* the phthalimidomalonic ester synthesis.

▮ (*a*) $H_2C{=}CH-CH{=}O \xrightarrow[\text{Michael}\atop\text{addition}]{CH_3SH} CH_3SCH_2CH_2CH{=}O \xrightarrow[\text{2. }H_3O^+]{\text{1. }NH_3,\ HCN} CH_3SCH_2CH_2\overset{\text{H}}{\underset{NH_3^+}{C}}-COO^-$

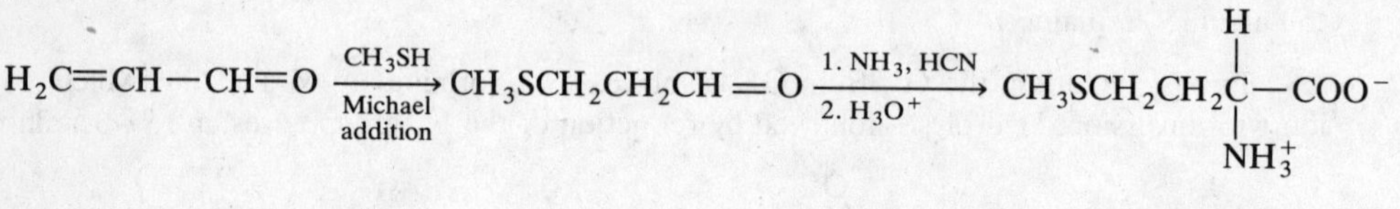

Methionine

(*b*) $\underset{\text{Phthalimidomalonic ester}}{PhthN-CH(COOEt)_2} \xrightarrow{OEt^-} PhthN\overset{..}{C}(COOEt)_2 \xrightarrow[\text{2. }H_3O^+]{\text{1. }H_2C{=}CHCOOEt,\ \text{Michael addition}}$

$\underset{COOEt}{\overset{COOEt}{PhthN-CCH_2CH_2COOEt}} \xrightarrow{H^+} \underset{COO^-}{\overset{}{\overset{+}{H_3N}-CHCH_2CH_2COOH}}$

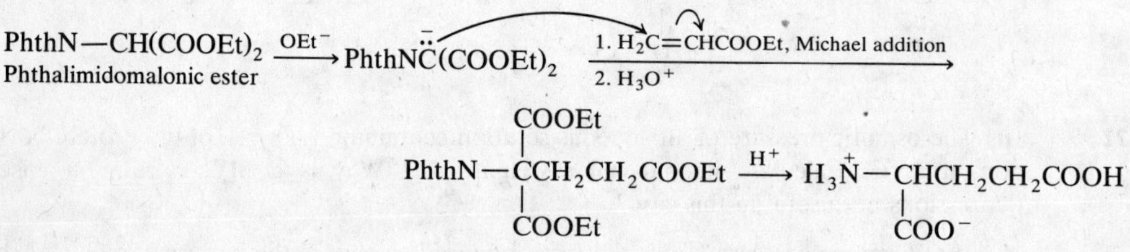

Glutamic acid

22.104 Provide structures for **A** and **B** in the reaction PhNCS + alanine $\xrightarrow{OH^-}$ **A** $\xrightarrow{H^+}$ **B**.

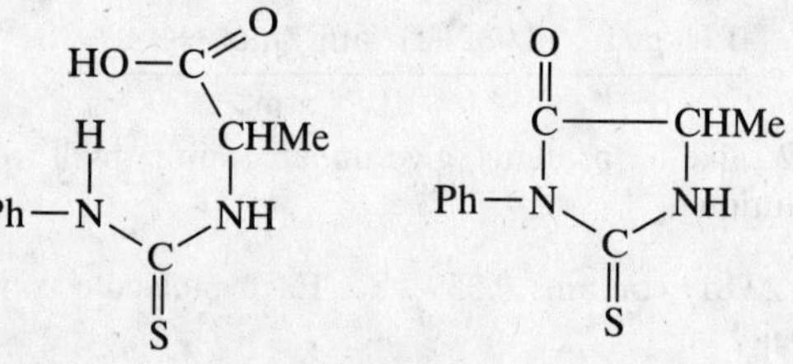

A

B

GENERAL AND NOMENCLATURE

23.1 Account for the name carbohydrate in terms of the general formula.

▟ The general formula for a carbohydrate is $C_n(H_2O)_m$. This formula, with *carbo* for carbon and *hydrate* for H_2O, accounts for the name *carbohydrate*. For simple carbohydrates, $n = m$.

23.2 Which two functional groups are present in typical carbohydrates?

▟ $C=O$ and OH. Carbohydrates are polyhydroxy aldehydes or ketones that have an OH bonded to each C other than the $C=O$.

23.3 (*a*) What is the common name for carbohydrates? (*b*) Name the suffix that indicates a simple carbohydrate.

▟ (*a*) Sugars. (*b*) The suffix *-ose*. Ketonic sugars sometimes have the suffix *-ulose*.

23.4 Define (*a*) saccharide, (*b*) monosaccharide, (*c*) disaccharide, (*d*) oligosaccharide, and (*e*) polysaccharide.

▟ (*a*) *Saccharide* is another name for carbohydrates and is used for their classification. It comes from the Latin name *saccharum* for sugar. (*b*) A *monosaccharide* is a single simple sugar. (*c*) A *disaccharide* is composed of two monosaccharide units. (*d*) *Oligosaccharides* are composed of 3-10 monosaccharide units. (*e*) Polysaccharides have more than 10 monosaccharide units.

23.5 (*a*) What is the formula relationship between two monosaccharides and a disaccharide? (*b*) Give the general formula for a disaccharide. (*c*) Write a word equation for the enzymatic hydrolysis of a trisaccharide.

▟ (*a*) The merging of two monosaccharide molecules requires the loss of a molecule of H_2O.
(*b*) $C_n(H_2O)_{n-1}$ (*c*) Trisaccharide + $2H_2O$ $\xrightarrow{\text{enzyme}}$ 3 monosaccharides.

23.6 Classify the following monosaccharides using the suffix *-ose*. (*a*) $HOCH_2CHOHCOCH_2OH$, (*b*) $HOCH_2(CHOH)_4CHO$, and (*c*) $HOCH_2(CHOH)_2CH_2CHO$.

▟ The number of C's in a chain is indicated by their prefixes *-di-*, *-tri-*, etc. (*a*) ketotetrose, (*b*) aldohexose, (*c*) deoxyaldopentose. Deoxy indicates the absence of an OH. More specifically, this is a 2-deoxyaldopentose where the number shows which C is devoid of OH.

23.7 Write molecular formulas for (*a*) a tetrose tetrasaccharide, and (*b*) a polypentoside (pentosan).

▟ (*a*) From Problem 23.5(*a*) we have $4C_4(H_2O)_4 \longrightarrow C_{16}(H_2O)_{13} + 3H_2O$. The formula is $C_{16}H_{26}O_{13}$. (*b*) This polysaccharide is a condensation polymer whose mer is the monosaccharide minus the H_2O. The formula is $[C_5(H_2O)_4]_n$ or $(C_5H_8O_4)_n$.

23.8 Deduce the molecular formula of glucose from the following data: The % composition is C = 40.0, H = 6.7, O = 53.3. A solution of 9.0 g in 100 g of H_2O freezes at 0.93 °C.

▟ The relative number of atoms of C, H, and O in 100 g of glucose would be $40.0/12 = 3.33$, $6.7/1 = 6.7$, and $53.3/16 = 3.33$, respectively. Thus, $C : H : O = 1 : 2 : 1$; the empirical formula is CH_2O, and the empirical weight (ew) = 30. The molecular weight is determined from the freezing point depression data. Thus, 9.0 g of glucose in 100 g of H_2O is equivalent to 90 g in 1 kg of water. The molality and molecular weight of the solution are, respectively,

$$m = \frac{0.93\,°C}{1.86\,°C/mol} = 0.50 \text{ mol} \quad \text{and} \quad MW = \frac{90 \text{ g}}{0.50 \text{ mol}} = 180 \text{ g/mol}$$

The molecular formula is $(CH_2O)_n$, where $n = 180 \text{ (MW)}/30 \text{ (ew)} = 6$, or $(CH_2O)_6$. Glucose is $C_6H_{12}O_6$; it is a hexose.

STEREOCHEMISTRY

23.9 (*a*) Write Fischer formulas for the D and L isomers of the simplest known aldosugar. (*b*) Give the sign of rotation of these enantiomers. (*c*) Give the *R/S* designations.

◢ (*a*) Since sugars are *polyhydroxy* compounds, the minimum number of OH's is two. Hence the simplest aldosugar is the triose, glyceraldehyde. (*b*) Fischer arbitrarily wrote the D structure for the dextrorotatory enantiomer. Therefore D is (+), L is (−). (*c*) D is *R* and L is *S*.

CHO CHO
H—OH HO—H
CH₂OH CH₂OH

D (OH on right)   L (OH on left)

23.10 Designate the following Fischer projections of glyceraldehyde as D or L.

CH₂OH OH CHO
(*a*) HO—H (*b*) HOCH₂—CHO (*c*) H—CH₂OH
CHO H OH

◢ Determine the *R/S* configuration, where *R* is D and *S* is L. The order of priorities is OH > CHO > CH₂OH. (*a*) *R* or D, (*b*) *R* or D, (*c*) *S* or L. Note that in (*a*) and (*c*) H is not on the vertical bond.

23.11 (*a*) Write the structural formula for the simplest known ketosugar. (*b*) Give a structural difference between this ketosugar and glyceraldehyde (except for the kind of C=O).

◢ (*a*) HOCH₂COCH₂OH. (*b*) The ketosugar has no stereocenter.

23.12 (*a*) How many chiral C's are there in an aldotetrose? (*b*) Give the Fischer formulas and common names for the stereoisomers of an aldotetrose and classify them as D and L sugars.

◢ (*a*) Two chiral C's: HOCH₂C*HOHC*HOHCHO. (*b*) The D sugar is arbitrarily written with the OH on the highest number stereocenter on the right side, the L sugar has this OH on the left side.

CHO CHO CHO CHO
H—OH HO—H HO—H H—OH
H—OH HO—H H—OH HO—H
CH₂OH CH₂OH CH₂OH CH₂OH

D-Erythrose   L-Erythrose   D-Threose   L-Threose

23.13 Use mild oxidation to differentiate between D-erythrose and D-threose.

◢ Under mild conditions both the CHO and CH₂OH groups are oxidized to COOH, giving diastereomers of tartaric acid. Threose gives an optical active enantiomer while erythrose gives the optically inactive *meso* isomer.

$$
\underset{\text{D-Threose}}{\overset{\overset{\displaystyle HO \quad H}{|\quad\;|}}{HOCH_2C-CCHO}} \xrightarrow{[O]} \underset{\text{D-(−)-Tartaric acid}}{\overset{\overset{\displaystyle HO \quad H}{|\quad\;|}}{HOOCC-CCOOH}} \qquad \underset{\text{D-Erythrose}}{\overset{\overset{\displaystyle HO \quad OH}{|\quad\;|}}{HOCH_2C-CCHO}} \xrightarrow{[O]} \underset{meso\text{-Tartaric acid}}{\overset{\overset{\displaystyle HO \quad OH}{|\quad\;|}}{HOOCC-CCOOH}}
$$

23.14 Use reduction to differentiate between D-erythrose and D-threose.

◢ CHO is reduced to CH₂OH to give 1,2,3,4-butanetetrol. Threose gives an optical active enantiomer while erythrose gives the optically inactive *meso* isomer.

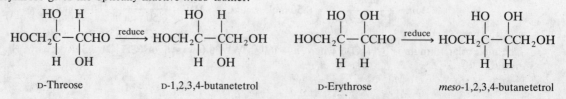

D-Threose   D-1,2,3,4-butanetetrol   D-Erythrose   *meso*-1,2,3,4-butanetetrol

23.15 Why are the optically active tartaric acid and 1,2,3,4-butanetetrol called D?

◢ Since the configurations of the chiral C's do not change during the oxidation or reduction, the D configuration is preserved.

23.16 Define the term epimer and illustrate with threose and erythrose.

◢ Diastereoisomers with more than one stereocenter that differ in the configuration about only one stereocenter are called *epimers*. D-Threose and D-erythrose are epimers because their configuration about C^2 differs.

23.17 How many chiral C's are there in an open-chain (i) aldohexose such as glucose and (ii) 2-ketohexose such as fructose? (*b*) How many stereoisomers does an aldohexose have?

◢ (*a*) (i) Four: $HOCH_2\overset{*}{C}HOH\overset{*}{C}HOH\overset{*}{C}HOH\overset{*}{C}HOHCHO$ and
(ii) three: $HOCH_2\overset{*}{C}HOH\overset{*}{C}HOH\overset{*}{C}HOHCOCH_2OH$
(*b*) There are four different chiral C's and $2^4 = 16$ stereoisomers.

23.18 What kind of open-chain aldohexose has only eight stereoisomers?

◢ A deoxyaldohexose has only three chiral C's ($2^3 = 8$).

REACTIONS

23.19 (*a*) Compare the reactions of an aldohexose and a 2-ketohexose with (i) Tollens' reagent, (ii) Fehling's solution, (iii) Benedict's reagent, and (iv) Br_2/H_2O. Describe the changes that signal a positive test and give formulas for the reagents. (*b*) Classify the product from the aldohexose.

◢ (*a*) These reagents all oxidize CHO to COOH or its salt in basic solutions. (i) Both give a positive test, the formation of a shiny silver mirror, with $Ag(NH_3)_2^+$. The ketosugar reacts because it rearranges to an aldosugar under the basic conditions (see Problem 23.23). (ii) The reagent is the Cu^{2+} tartrate complex in NaOH. The discharge of the blue color of the *Fehling*'s solution and the formation of a red precipitate of Cu_2O denotes a positive test, given by both sugars. (iii) The *Benedict*'s reagent is the Cu^{2+} citrate complex in NaOH and a positive test is indicated by the same changes as with Fehling's solution. Again both sugars react. (iv) Only the aldosugar reacts—a positive test is indicated by loss of the orange color of the aqueous Br_2 solution. (*b*) The product from both sugars, $HOCH_2CHOHCHOHCHOHCHOHCOOH$, is an example of an *aldonic* (*glyconic*) *acid*.

23.20 Give the product of the reaction of HNO_3 with an aldotetrose and classify the product.

◢ $HOOCCHOHCHOHCOOH$, an *aldaric* (*glycaric*) *acid*. Both CHO and $HOCH_2$ are oxidized to COOH.

23.21 Provide a general structure and name for the product of the reaction of an aldotetrose and ketotetrose with H_2/Ni, aq. $NaBH_4$, or Na/Hg.

◢ C=O is reduced to CHOH. The product is $HOCH_2CHOHCHOHCH_2OH$, an *alditol*.

23.22 Use Fischer projection formulas to discuss differences in the stereochemistry of the reductions of a D-aldotetrose and D-ketotetrose.

◢ The aldotetrose and the product alditol have two chiral carbons each (see Problem 23.14 for reduction products from D-threose and D-erythrose). The ketotetrose has only one chiral C but its reduction creates a second chiral center giving a mixture of two diastereomeric alditols.

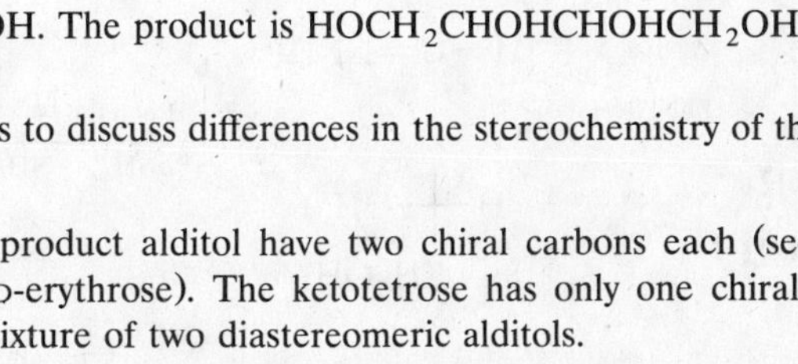

D-ketotetrose   *meso*-alditol   D-alditol

Note that the C^2 and C^3 of the D-alditol are equivalent. If we count the carbon chain from the top down, C^3 has its OH on the right side and has the D configuration. If the Fischer structure is rotated 180° in the plane of the paper, C^2 becomes C^3 with its OH on the right side of the carbon chain; its configuration is D.

23.23 (*a*) Explain the fact that in aq. NaOH a 2-ketohexose, i.e., fructose, is in equilibrium with an aldohexose, i.e., glucose, accounting for the positive Fehling's test observed with the ketohexose (see Problem 23.19). (*b*) Explain the formation of two diasteromeric aldohexoses.

◢ (*a*) The ketose and the aldose tautomerize in OH⁻ to a common intermediate enediol, establishing the following equilibrium.

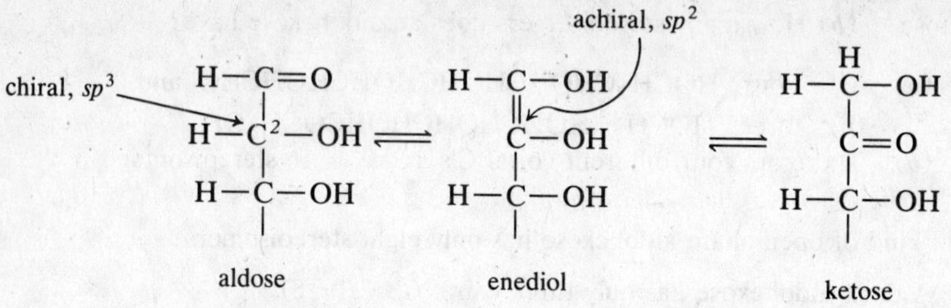

(*b*) When the aldose reforms from the enediol, H⁺ can add to C^2 from either face of the C=C to give C^2 aldohexose epimers.

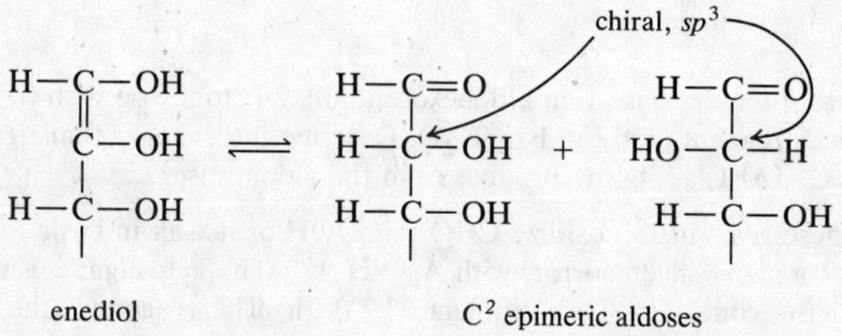

23.24 (*a*) Give the products from the reaction of HIO_4 with (i) $HOCH_2CHOHCHOHCHOHCHOHCHO$ (an aldohexose), and (ii) $HOCH_2CHOHCHOHCHOHCOCH_2OH$ (a ketohexose). (*b*) How can this reaction be used in a simple way to distinguish between these two isomers?

◢ (*a*) (i) CHO and CHOH go to HCOOH; and $HOCH_2$ to $H_2C=O$, giving $5HCOOH + H_2C=O$. (ii) C=O ends up as CO_2 and we get two $H_2C=O$'s from two $HOCH_2$'s and three HCOOH's from three CHOH's. (*b*) Collect and test for CO_2 which gives a precipitate of $CaCO_3$ with $Ca(OH)_2$. The production of CO_2 signals the presence of the ketose.

23.25 (*a*) Give the product from the reaction of D-threose with $PhNHNH_2$, show the intermediates, and classify the product. (*b*) Give the product from the same reaction with D-erythrose and account for the result. (*c*) What conclusion can be drawn about this reaction with epimers?

◢ (*a*)

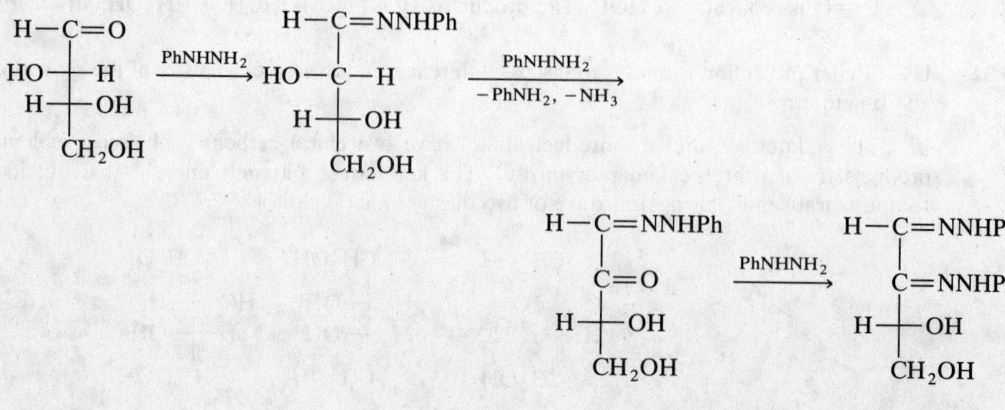

an osazone

(**b**) D-Erythrose gives the same osazone. The configuration of C^2 in the starting sugar is immaterial because this C is oxidized to C=O, and the same keto compound is formed from both diastereomeric sugars. (**c**) In general, C^2-epimers of aldosugars give the same osazone.

23.26 Give the osazone formed from a 2-ketohexose and account for its formation.

◢ PhNHNH₂ reacts with the more easily oxidized 1°-OH than with the less reactive 2°-OH.

$$
\begin{array}{c}
\text{H}-\text{C}=\text{NNHPh} \\
|\ \\
\text{C}=\text{NNHPh} \\
|\ \\
(\text{H}-\text{C}-\text{OH})_3 \\
|\ \\
\text{CH}_2\text{OH}
\end{array}
$$

23.27 (**a**) Show how the osazone of an aldohexose can be used to synthesize a 2-ketohexose. (**b**) Since glucose is converted to fructose by this method, what can you say about the configurations of C^3, C^4, and C^5 in these sugars?

◢ (**a**)
$$
\begin{array}{c}
\text{H}-\text{C}=\text{NNHPh} \\
|\ \\
\text{C}=\text{NNHPh} \\
|\ \\
(\text{H}-\text{C}-\text{OH})_3 \\
|\ \\
\text{CH}_2\text{OH}
\end{array}
\xrightarrow[(-2\text{PhCH}=\text{NNHPh})]{2\,\text{PhCHO}}
\begin{array}{c}
\text{H}-\text{C}=\text{O} \\
|\ \\
\text{C}=\text{O} \\
|\ \\
(\text{H}-\text{C}-\text{OH})_3 \\
|\ \\
\text{CH}_2\text{OH}
\end{array}
\xrightarrow{\text{Zn/HAc}}
\begin{array}{c}
\text{CH}_2\text{OH} \\
|\ \\
\text{C}=\text{O} \\
|\ \\
(\text{H}-\text{C}-\text{OH})_3 \\
|\ \\
\text{CH}_2\text{OH}
\end{array}
$$
osone

The phenylhydrazinyl group is transferred from the osazone to PhCHO giving PhCH=NNHPh and a dicarbonyl compound called an *osone*. The more reactive aldehyde group of the osone is reduced, not the less reactive keto group, and it gives the 2-ketohexose. (**b**) The configurations of these C's, which are unchanged in the reactions, must be identical in order to get the same osazone.

23.28 (**a**) Give the two isomeric products from the reaction of D-threose with NaCN/HCN. (**b**) What is the net result of this reaction?

◢ (**a**)
$$
\begin{array}{c}
\text{H}-\text{C}=\text{O} \\
\text{HO}-\!\!\!-\!\text{H} \\
\text{H}-\!\!\!-\!\text{OH} \\
\text{CH}_2\text{OH}
\end{array}
\xrightarrow{\text{NaCN/HCN}}
\begin{array}{c}
\text{CN} \\
\text{HO}-\!\!\!-\!\text{H} \\
\text{HO}-\!\!\!-\!\text{H} \\
\text{H}-\!\!\!-\!\text{OH} \\
\text{CH}_2\text{OH}
\end{array}
+
\begin{array}{c}
\text{CN} \\
\text{H}-\!\!\!-\!\text{OH} \\
\text{HO}-\!\!\!-\!\text{H} \\
\text{H}-\!\!\!-\!\text{OH} \\
\text{CH}_2\text{OH}
\end{array}
$$
D-Therose C^2 epimeric cyanohydrins

(**b**) The C chain is increased by one; this is a step-up reaction.

23.29 Why are the epimers in Problem 23.28 formed in unequal amounts?

◢ The presence of stereocenters in sugars causes their C=O groups to have diastereotopic faces that react at different rates, giving different amounts of diastereomers.

23.30 Prove the gross structure of (**a**) glucose and (**b**) fructose from the sequence of reactions (*1*) NaCN/HCN, (*2*) H₃O⁺, (*3*) HI/P.

◢ For each sugar the first step involves the addition of HCN to C=O to give the cyanohydrin, whose CN is hydrolyzed in the second step to COOH. In the third step all OH's are reduced to H's, giving an alkylcarboxylic acid. (**a**) The isolated acid is the unbranched heptanoic acid which proves that glucose is an aldohexose. (**b**) The isolated acid is the branched 2-methylhexanoic acid which proves that fructose is a ketohexose. Furthermore, since COOH is attached to the C that was originally doubly bonded to O, fructose must be a 2-ketohexose.

23.31 Give the steps for the conversion of a D-aldopentose to an aldohexose in the original version of the *Kiliani–Fischer* method, whose first step is the addition of HCN to C=O.

$$
\begin{array}{ccccccc}
\text{HC=O} & & \text{CN} & & [\text{COOH}] & \text{O=C} & \text{HC=O} \\
| & & | & & | & | \quad\rangle & | \\
\text{(HCOH)}_2 & \xrightarrow{\text{CN}^-/\text{HCN}} & \text{(HCOH)}_2 & \xrightarrow{\text{H}_3\text{O}^+} & \text{(HCOH)}_2 & \text{(HCOH)}_2 \;\text{O} & \text{(HCOH)}_2 \\
| & & | & & | & | \quad\rangle & | \\
\text{HCOH} & & \text{HCOH} & & \text{HCOH} & \text{HC} & \text{HCOH} \\
| & & | & & | & | & | \\
\text{CH}_2\text{OH} & & \text{CH}_2\text{OH} & & \text{CH}_2\text{OH} & \text{CH}_2\text{OH} & \text{CH}_2\text{OH}
\end{array}
$$

with step $\xrightarrow{\text{Na/Hg}\;\text{CO}_2}$ between the δ-lactone and the aldohexose.

a D-aldopentose   a cyanohydrin[†]   a glyconic acid[†]   a δ-lactone[*†]   a D-aldohexose[†]

[*]The γ-lactone is also formed and the mixture is reduced without separation.
[†]The C-2 epimer is also formed (see Problem 23.28).

23.32 (*a*) At which stage of the Kiliani–Fischer synthesis is it best to isolate and separate the disastereomers? (*b*) What is the present day modification? (*c*) State the stereochemical family to which the aldohexose belongs. (*d*) Can a ketose be stepped up by one C to a straight chain ketose by this method?

▮ (*a*) Since sugars are difficult to purify, the diastereomeric glyconic acids are isolated and separated as their crystalline salts. (*b*) The cyanohydrin is reduced directly to the aldose by catalytic hydrogenation in water. (*c*) D-Family. There is no change in the configuration of the OH used to indicate the family. (*d*) No. The glyconic acid will be branched (see Problem 23.30).

23.33 (*a*) Supply structures for **A** through **D** given: an aldose $\xrightarrow{\text{aq. Br}_2}$ **A** $\underset{\text{pyridine}}{\rightleftharpoons}$ **B** $\xrightarrow{\text{H}^+}$ **C** $\xrightarrow[\text{CO}_2]{\text{Na/Hg}}$ **D** where **B** is separated from the equilibrium mixture with **A**. (*b*) What is the net structural change of this sequence?

▮ (*a*) **A** is an aldonic acid [Problem 23.19(*b*)]. **B** is the C^2 epimer of **A**. **C** is the lactone which is reduced to **D**, the C^2 epimer of the initial aldose. (*b*) C^2 epimerization.

23.34 (*a*) Give structures for **E** through **G** given: an aldohexose $\xrightarrow{\text{aq. Br}_2}$ **E** $\xrightarrow{\text{CaCO}_3}$ **F** $\xrightarrow[\text{Fe(III)}]{\text{H}_2\text{O}_2}$ **G**. (*b*) What is the net structural change? (*c*) Name this overall method. (*d*) Discuss the possibility of epimer formation.

▮ (*a*) **E** is an aldonic acid, **F** is its calcium salt, $[\text{HOCH}_2\text{CHOHCHOHCHOHCHOHCOO}^-]_2\text{Ca}^{2+}$, **G** is an aldopentose, $\text{HOCH}_2\text{CHOHCHOHCHOHCHO}$. (*b*) A shortening of the carbon chain by one C. (*c*) This oxidative decarboxylation is called the *Ruff degradation*. (*d*) The α-CHOH is oxidized to —CH=O without any configurational changes of the other chiral C's. No epimers are formed.

23.35 (*a*) Supply structures for **H** through **K** given: an aldohexose $\xrightarrow{\text{NH}_2\text{OH/base}}$ **H** $\xrightarrow{\text{Ac}_2\text{O/NaOAc}}$ (**I**) $\xrightarrow{-\text{HOAc}}$ **J** $\xrightarrow{\text{NaOMe/MeOH}}$ **K**. (*b*) Explain the last step. (*c*) What is the net structural change? (*d*) Name this overall method. (*e*) Discuss the possibility of epimer formation.

▮ (*a*) **H** is an oxime, $\text{HOCH}_2(\text{CHOH})_4\text{CH=NOH}$; **I** is the completely acetylated oxime, $\text{AcOCH}_2(\text{CHOAc})_4\text{CH=NOAc}$ that loses 1 mol of HOAc to form **J**, $\text{AcOCH}_2(\text{CHOAc})_4\text{C≡N}$; **K** is an aldopentose, $\text{HOCH}_2(\text{CHOH})_3\text{CHO}$. (*b*) The acetates undergo transesterification to give methyl acetate, freeing all the sugar OH's. This is followed by the reversal of HCN addition. (*c*) There is loss of one C from the carbon chain. (*d*) *Wohl* degradation. (*e*) The α-CHOH becomes the —CH=O without any configurational changes of the other chiral C's. No epimers are formed.

STRUCTURES

23.36 Two Ruff degradations (Problem 23.34) of an aldohexose give an aldotetrose that is oxidized by HNO_3 to *meso*-tartaric acid. Give the family configuration of the aldohexose.

❚ The C^4 and C^5 are the only chiral C's remaining in the aldotetrose and they must be on the "same side" in order for *meso*-tartaric acid to be isolated. Were they on the right side, the aldohexose would be in the D-family. Were they on the left side, the aldohexose would be a member of the L-family. Both are possibilities.

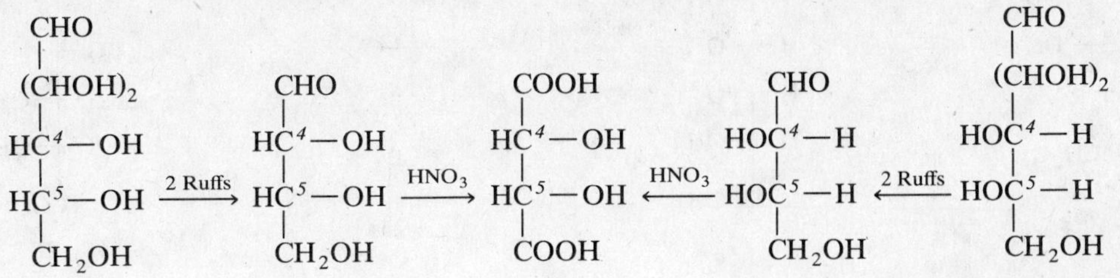

```
  CHO                CHO              COOH              CHO                CHO
   |                  |                |                 |                  |
(CHOH)₂              CHO              CHO              CHO              (CHOH)₂
   |      2 Ruffs      |      HNO₃       |      HNO₃       |      2 Ruffs      |
 HC⁴—OH  ──────→   HC⁴—OH  ──────→  HC⁴—OH  ←──────  HOC⁴—H  ←──────  HOC⁴—H
   |                  |                |                 |                  |
 HC⁵—OH            HC⁵—OH            HC⁵—OH            HOC⁵—H            HOC⁵—H
   |                  |                |                 |                  |
 CH₂OH              CH₂OH            COOH              CH₂OH              CH₂OH

D-Aldohexose    D-Aldotetrose    meso-Tartaric    L-Aldotetrose      L-Aldohexose
                                     acid
```

23.37   Which D-aldohexoses are oxidized by HNO_3 to *meso*-aldaric acids?

❚ The aldaric acids have a plane of symmetry between C^3 and C^4. Hence, the aldohexoses must also have such symmetry about the stereocenters C^2, C^3, C^4, and C^5. There are two possibilities:

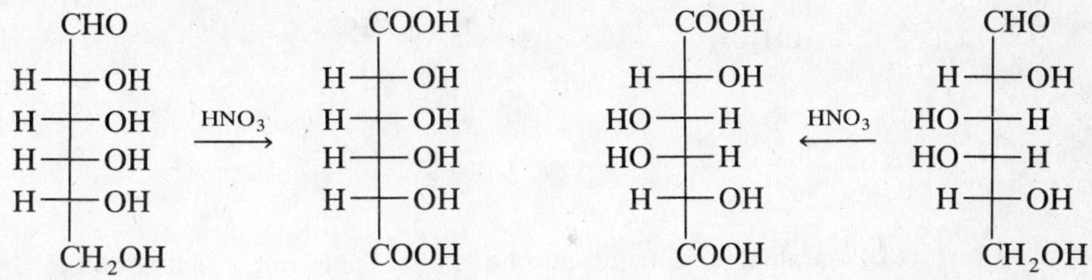

```
      CHO                  COOH                 COOH                 CHO
  H ─┬─ OH             H ─┬─ OH             H ─┬─ OH             H ─┬─ OH
  H ─┼─ OH    HNO₃     H ─┼─ OH             HO ─┼─ H    HNO₃     HO ─┼─ H
  H ─┼─ OH  ──────→    H ─┼─ OH             HO ─┼─ H  ←──────    HO ─┼─ H
  H ─┼─ OH             H ─┼─ OH             H ─┼─ OH             H ─┼─ OH
      CH₂OH                COOH                 COOH                 CH₂OH

    D-Allose         meso-Allaric acid    meso-Galactaric        D-Galactose
                                               acid
```

23.38   D-Allose and D-galactose each undergoes a Ruff degradation, followed by oxidation with HNO_3 to give a *meso*- and an optically active pentaaldaric acid, respectively. Show how this result is consistent with the structures assigned these hexoses in Problem 23.37.

❚ When C^2 of allose is changed to CHO by the Ruff reaction, C^3, C^4, and C^5 retain configurational symmetry in the resulting aldopentose that is oxidized to the *meso*-aldaric acid. Hence the OH's of these C's must all be on the same side. Since allose is a D-sugar, the OH's are on the right side. In galactose the symmetry of these C's is destroyed when C^2 is changed to CHO and hence their OH's are not all on the same side.

23.39   Which other D-aldohexoses give (*a*) an optically active and (*b*) a *meso*-pentaaldaric acid when subjected to the same sequence of reactions as in Problem 23.38?

❚ (*a*) and (*b*) See Fig. 23-1.

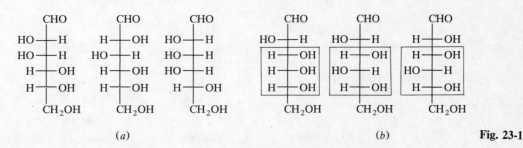

(*a*)   (*b*)   **Fig. 23-1**

23.40   Three aldohexoses, D-allose, D-glucose, and D-talose, each gives a *meso*-heptaldaric acid after oxidation of *one* of the pair of Kiliani step–up products. Assign the structures of the aldohexoses and *meso*-acids, keeping in mind that talose is the C^2 epimer of galactose. (See Problem 23.27.)

❚ There are three *meso*-heptalderic acids as shown in Fig. 23-2.

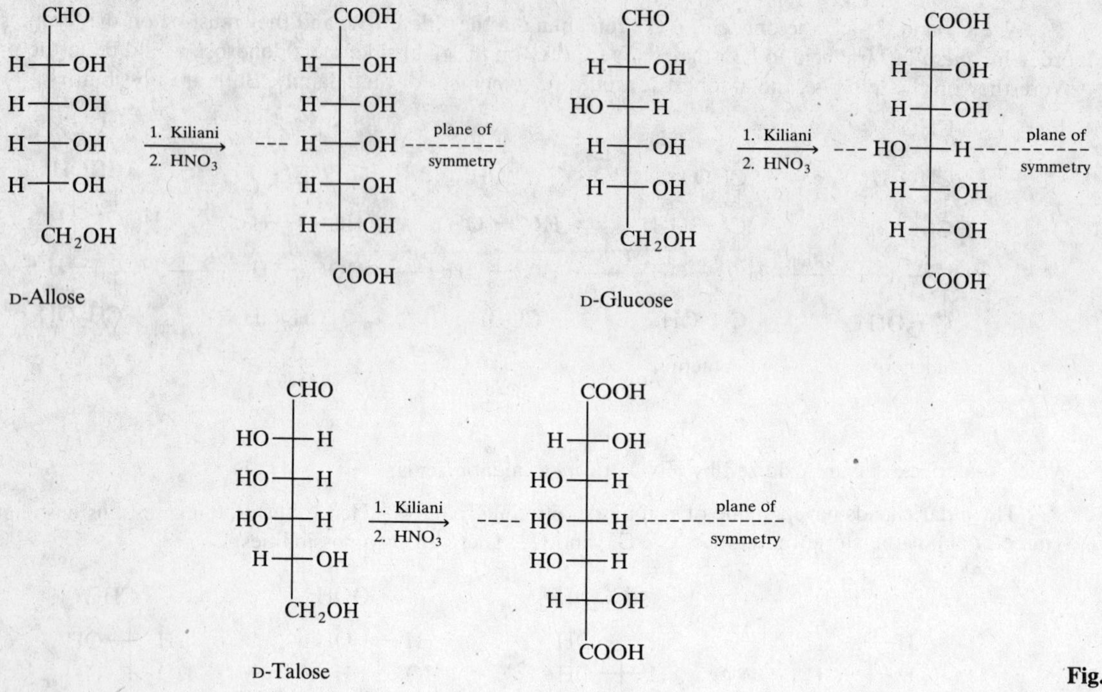

CHO
H—OH
H—OH
H—OH
H—OH
CH₂OH
D-Allose

$\xrightarrow[\text{2. HNO}_3]{\text{1. Kiliani}}$

COOH
H—OH
H—OH
H—OH
H—OH
H—OH
COOH

----- plane of symmetry

CHO
H—OH
HO—H
H—OH
H—OH
CH₂OH
D-Glucose

$\xrightarrow[\text{2. HNO}_3]{\text{1. Kiliani}}$

COOH
H—OH
H—OH
HO—H
H—OH
H—OH
COOH

----- plane of symmetry

CHO
HO—H
HO—H
HO—H
H—OH
CH₂OH
D-Talose

$\xrightarrow[\text{2. HNO}_3]{\text{1. Kiliani}}$

COOH
H—OH
HO—H
HO—H
HO—H
H—OH
COOH

----- plane of symmetry

Fig. 23-2

23.41 Give the structure of D-arabinose, the aldose isolated after subjecting D-mannose, the C^2 epimer of glucose, to a Ruff degradation.

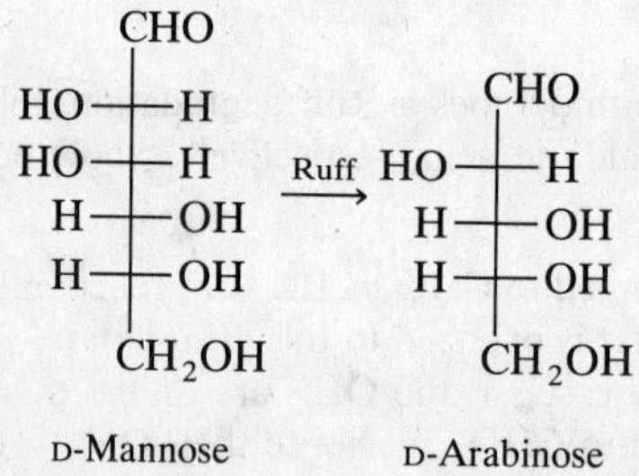

CHO
HO—H
HO—H
H—OH
H—OH
CH₂OH
D-Mannose

$\xrightarrow{\text{Ruff}}$

CHO
HO—H
H—OH
H—OH
CH₂OH
D-Arabinose

23.42 Give the structure of D-ribose, a constituent of ribonucleic acids (RNA), if it gives the same osazone as D-arabinose.

▰ D-Ribose is the C^2 epimer of arabinose since they give the same osazone.

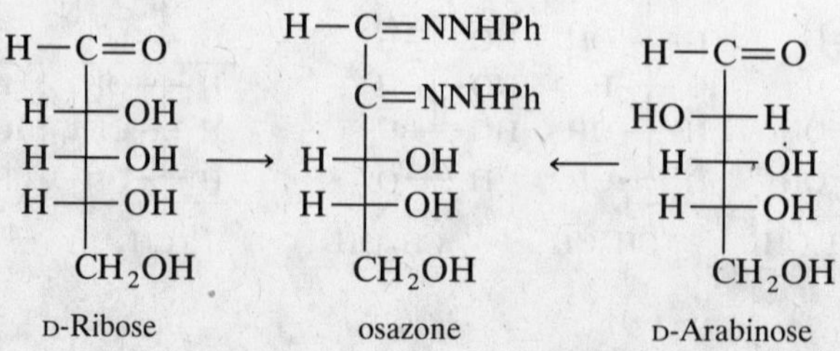

H—C=O
H—OH
H—OH
H—OH
CH₂OH
D-Ribose

$\longrightarrow$

H—C=NNHPh
C=NNHPh
H—OH
H—OH
CH₂OH
osazone

$\longleftarrow$

H—C=O
HO—H
H—OH
H—OH
CH₂OH
D-Arabinose

23.43 The aldopentoses D-xylose and D-lyxose give the same osazones and are oxidized to a *meso* and optically active aldaric acids, respectively. Give their structures.

▰ They are C^2 epimers. There is a configurational symmetry about C^2, C^3, and C^4 of xylose since xylose affords the *meso*-aldaric acid.

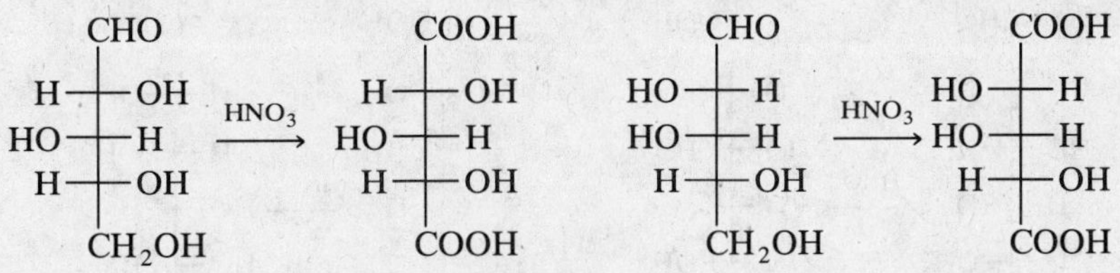

D-Xylose →(HNO₃) *meso*-Xylaric acid   D-Lyxose →(HNO₃) D-Lyxaric acid

23.44 Give the structures of two six-membered ring lactones with the same size rings, formed from glucaric acid, the aldaric acid of glucose.

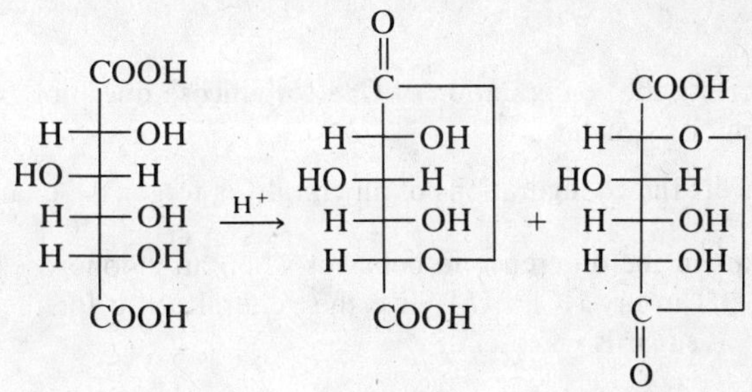

Glucaric acid →(H^+) lactone **A** + lactone **B**

23.45 Each lactone in Problem 23.44 is reduced to an aldonic acid whose lactone is treated with Na/Hg and CO_2 to give an aldohexose. Give the structure and family designation of each aldohexose.

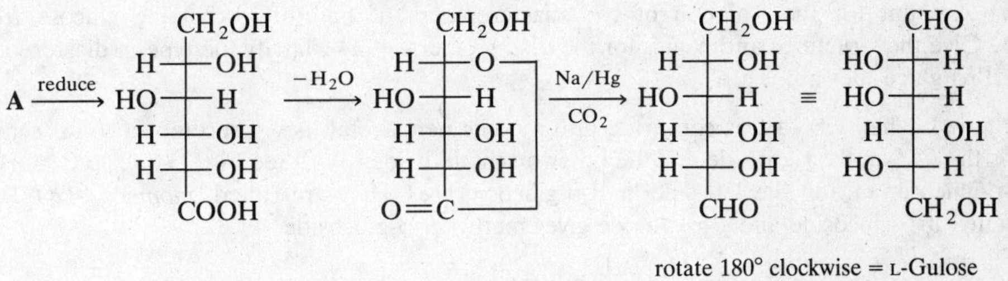

A →(reduce) ... →(−H_2O) ... →(Na/Hg, CO_2) ... ≡ ...

rotate 180° clockwise = L-Gulose

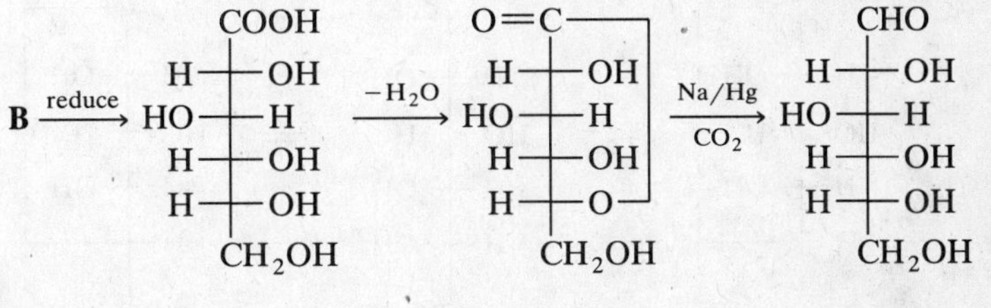

B →(reduce) ... →(−H_2O) ... →(Na/Hg, CO_2) ...

D-Glucose

23.46 Emil Fischer, the father of carbohydrate chemistry, used synthetic L-gulose (whose structure he knew) to distinguish between the known epimers D-glucose and D-mannose, whose structures were not yet established. How would he have deduced this?

L-Gulose and D-glucose were oxidized to the same aldaric acid shown in Problem 23.44. Fischer concluded that D-glucose, written with CHO on top, and L-gulose, written with CHO on the bottom (see the structure in Problem 23.45 before the 180° rotation), have the same configuration about the chiral C's. Since the structure of L-gulose was known, the structure of D-glucose was established, as well as its C^2 epimer, D-mannose.

23.47 (*a*) Which L-aldose gives the same aldaric acid as D-mannose? (*b*) How are the aldaric acids of D- and L-mannose related?

(*a*) None. (*b*) They are enantiomers, as shown in Fig. 23-3.

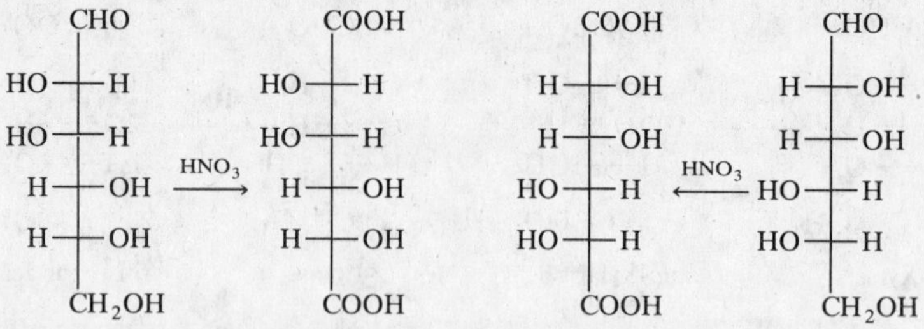

The structures are shown as Fischer projections:

D-Mannose (CHO top): HO—H, HO—H, H—OH, H—OH, CH₂OH

$\xrightarrow{\text{HNO}_3}$

D-aldaric acid (COOH top): HO—H, HO—H, H—OH, H—OH, COOH

L-aldaric acid (COOH top): H—OH, H—OH, HO—H, HO—H, COOH

$\xleftarrow{\text{HNO}_3}$

L-Mannose (CHO top): H—OH, H—OH, HO—H, HO—H, CH₂OH

Fig. 23-3

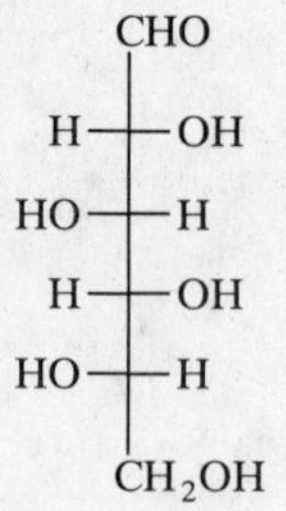

L-Idose (CHO top): H—OH, HO—H, H—OH, HO—H, CH₂OH

Fig. 23-4

23.48 (*a*) Explain why inverting the configuration of C^5 of D-glucose does not give L-glucose. (*b*) L-Idose is obtained by this inversion. Draw its structure.

▰ (*a*) We must invert the configurations of all chiral C's to get the enantiomer, L-glucose. (*b*) See Fig. 23-4.

23.49 (*a*) Compare and explain the difference in behavior when an aldohexose and a typical aldehyde (RCHO) react with an excess of R′OH in dry HCl. (*b*) Give the general name for the product from an aldohexose and the specific name when the sugar is glucose.

▰ (*a*) The aldehyde reacts with 2 eq. of ROH to give an acetal, RC(OR′)₂ whereas (see Problems 15.72 and 15.73), the aldohexose reacts with only 1 eq of ROH. The explanation is that the aldohexose actually exists as a hemiacetal formed by an intramolecular addition of one of its OH's to CH=O. Only one R′OH is needed to form the acetal. The intramolecular reaction produces a ring. Hence glucose mainly exists as a cyclic compound. (*b*) The general name is *glycoside*, and for glucose the specific name is *glucoside*.

23.50 (*a*) Account for the isolation of two diastereomers of naturally occurring glucose from a water solution. (*b*) Give the structures and names for the diasteromers. (*c*) Classify the type of diastereomers. (*d*) How many methyl glucosides are there?

▰ (*a*) When CH=O is converted into a cyclic hemiacetal its C^1 becomes a chiral center. One diastereomer has the OH on the right side and the other on the left side. (*b*) See Fig. 23-5. The C^1-OH is on the right side in α-D-glucose, and on the left side in β-D-glucose. (*c*) They are called *anomers*. (*d*) Two. α-D-Glucose gives methyl α-D-glucoside and β-D-glucose gives methyl β-D-glucoside.

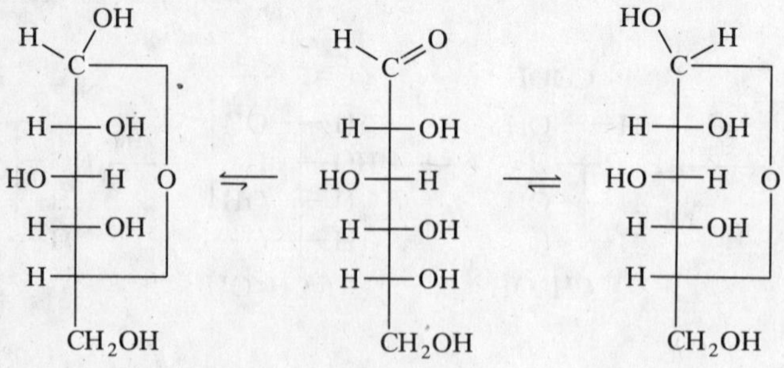

α-D-Glucose ⇌ **open-chain glucose** ⇌ **β-D-Glucose** **Fig. 23-5**

23.51 Do the anomers of D-glucose have specific rotations of the same magnitude but opposite signs?

▰ No. Only enantiomers have this characteristic property and anomers are not enantiomers.

23.52 How do epimers and anomers differ?

▰ Anomers are epimers whose conformations differ only about the C^1 (see Problem 23.16).

23.53 Name the enantiomer of α-D-(+)-glucose.

▰ α-L-(−)-Glucose. By definition the α-anomer has the OH on the same side as the OH on the C that establishes the family designation.

23.54 Why do aldoses react with Fehling's solution and $PhNHNH_2$, but not with $NaHSO_3$?

◢ These reactions are typical for the CHO group, which means that the open chain aldehyde form is in equilibrium with the cyclic hemiacetal form. Since Fehling's and osazone reactions are irreversible, the equilibrium shifts to restore the low concentration (0.02%) of the aldehyde as it is depleted through reaction, and eventually all the aldose reacts. Bisulfite addition is reversible and enough aldehyde remains in equilibrium with the bisulfite adduct to satisfy the equilibrium with the hemiacetal form. Consequently, there is no noticeable reaction.

23.55 Would you expect glycosides to react with either Fehling's or Tollens' reagents? Explain.

◢ No. Glycosides, like simple acetals, are stable in these basic solutions. There is no —CH=O present to react. Glycosides are *nonreducing*; they do not reduce Cu^{2+} to Cu^+ (as Cu_2O).

23.56 Give two products of the reaction of an aldohexose with excess $Ac_2O/NaOAc$. (*b*) Would you expect these products to react with either $PhNHNH_2$ or Fehling's solution? Explain.

◢ (*a*) The α- and β-pentaacetates of the hemiacetal are isolated, not the pentaacetate of the aldehyde. The anomeric C^1-OH is acetylated; the OH that formed the ring is not available for acetylation. (*b*) The pentaacetates do not react because they are not hydrolyzed under the basic conditions of these reagents, and thus no aldehyde form is present.

23.57 Give two products of the reaction of an aldohexose with excess $(MeO)_2SO_2$ (dimethyl sulfate) or MeI in concentrated NaOH and explain their formation.

◢ The OH's of sugars are more acidic than typical alcohols because of their mutual electron-withdrawing inductive effect. The five free OH's are changed to alkoxides which undergo a S_N2 reaction with the active methylating agents to give methyl ethers. Again, we get a mixture of the α- and β-pentamethyl glycosides.

23.58 What size rings are most frequently observed in hemiacetals? Name each type.

◢ In order for the ring to be stable and readily formed, it must have five or six atoms, one of which is an O. Hemiacetals with five-membered rings are called *furanoses*, named after furan. Those with six-membered rings are called *pyranoses*, named after pyran.

23.59 (*a*) What is the smallest aldose able to form a cyclic hemiacetal? (*b*) Which functional groups are involved in its formation?

◢ (*a*) The smallest aldose is a tetrose which has four C's and an O to form a five-membered ring. (*b*) The CHO and primary OH are incorporated into the ring.

23.60 Draw structures and label both anomers of D-threose.

◢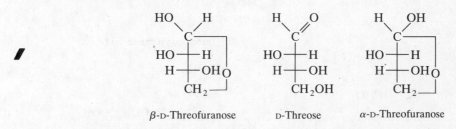

β-D-Threofuranose   D-Threose α-D-Threofuranose

23.61 The β- and α-D-glucoses have different specific rotations. When either anomer is dissolved in water, their rotations change until the same fixed value results. (*a*) What term is used for these changes? (*b*) Explain the change.

◢ (*a*) This rotation change is called *mutarotation*. (*b*) The α- and β-D-glucoses are each in equilibrium with the open chain aldehyde form and therefore with each other.

α-D-Glucose $\rightleftharpoons$ aldehyde form $\rightleftharpoons$ β-D-Glucose

As each anomer begins to establish this equilibrium, its specific rotation changes. When equilibrium is reached, the experimentally determined rotation remains constant. A base such as NaOH catalyzes the attainment of the equilibrium.

23.62 Given the following specific rotations: For glucose anomers, $\alpha = +112°$, $\beta = +19°$, and for the constant equilibrium mixture, $+52.7°$. Calculate the % composition of the anomers in the equilibrium mixture.

▮ Let a and b be the mole fractions of the α- and β-anomers, respectively. Solving the simultaneous equations

$$a + b = 1$$
$$112° a + 19° b = 52.7°$$

gives $a \times 100\% = 36.2\%$ and $b \times 100\% = 63.8\%$.

23.63 Discuss the validity of the following statements: (*a*) Glucose is the only aldose that mutarotates. (*b*) Ketoses also mutarotate. (*c*) Glycosides mutarotate. (*d*) There is a relationship between the ability of a sugar to mutarotate and reduce Fehling's reagent.

▮ (*a*) False. Mutarotation is observed for any sugar existing as a hemiacetal. (*b*) True. Ketoses exist as hemiketals and possess anomers. (*c*) False. The anomeric OH is etherified and the equilibrium with the free-carbonyl form is destroyed. (*d*) True. The reduction of Fehling's reagent and mutarotation both depend on the presence of the free carbonyl form.

23.64 Determine whether D-glucose is a furanose or pyranose from the following data and name the intermediate products.

$$\text{D-Glucose} \xrightarrow{\text{MeOH/HCl}} A \xrightarrow[\text{NaOH}]{\text{excess Me}_2\text{SO}_4} B \xrightarrow{\text{dil. HCl}} C \xrightarrow{\text{HNO}_3}$$

2,3-dimethoxysuccinic acid + 2,3,4-trimethoxyglutaric acid.

▮

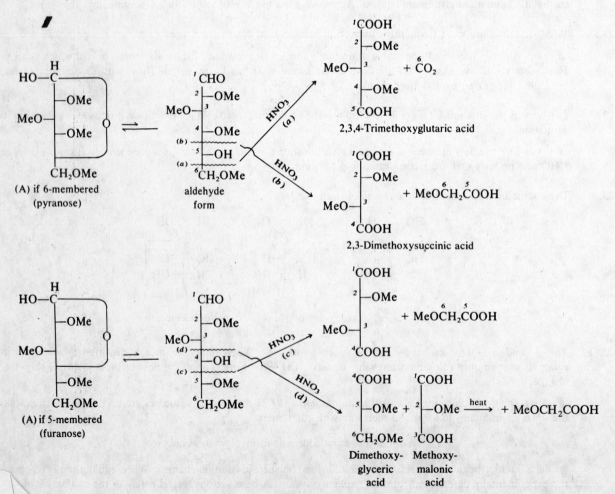

Fig. 23-6

The intermediate products are

A = methyl D-glucoside;   **B** = methyl tetra-O-methyl glucoside;   **C** = tetra-O-methyl glucose
(anomeric OH forms ether)   (other 4 OH's are etherified)   (anomeric OMe is hydrolyzed)

and the structures of the severe oxidation products are

$$HOOCCH(OMe)CH(OMe)COOH + HOOCCH(OMe)CH(OMe)CH(OMe)COOH$$

The unmethylated OH's in **C** are those participating in hemiacetal ring formation. These are C^1 and C^4 for a furanose (five-membered) and C^1 and C^5 for a pyranose (six-membered). Vigorous oxidation in the last step converts the anomeric C—OH to COOH and causes cleavage on either side of the C with the free 2° OH. See Fig. 23-6 for the possible oxidation products arising from each size ring. Routes (*a*) and (*b*) are for a pyranose and (*c*) and (*d*) are for a furanose. The six-membered ring gives the observed degradation products; hence glucose is a pyranose.

23.65 How can the sequence sugar $\xrightarrow{\text{1. HIO}_4}$ $\xrightarrow{\text{2. aq. Br}_2}$ $\xrightarrow{\text{3. H}_3\text{O}^+}$ show if a methyl glucoside has a pyranose or furanose ring?

▰ HIO_4 causes cleavage of C—C bonds with *vic.* OH's. Br_2 causes oxidation of CH_2OH to COOH, and acid promotes hydrolysis of the acetal linkage, thereby freeing the degradation units. See Fig. 23-7 for the possible oxidation products arising from each size ring.

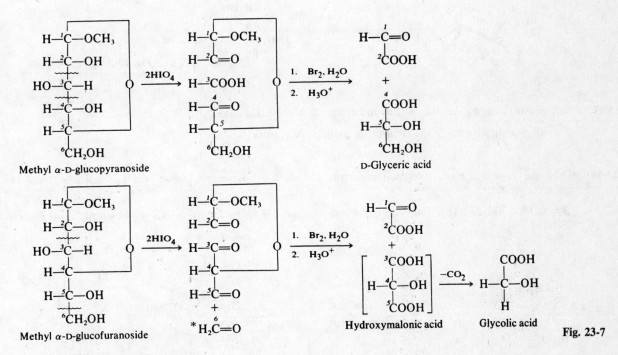

Fig. 23-7

*is oxidized to HCOOH by aq. Br_2

23.66 Draw the *Haworth* projection for α-D-glucopyranose. How does the β-anomer differ?

▰ (*a*) The Haworth structure has a flat ring perpendicular to the plane of the paper. Twist C^6 of the Fischer projection (**A**) behind the plane of the paper and rotate the C^4—C^5 bond so that the C^5OH is close enough to the C=O to form a ring (**B**). This operation points the terminal CH_2OH *upward* for all D-sugars. Invariably the ring O projects away from the viewer and the anomeric C is on the far right. As the result of this manipulation all groups on the left in a Fischer structure are up in **C** and those on the right are down. See Fig. 23-8. In the β-anomer, the anomeric OH is up.

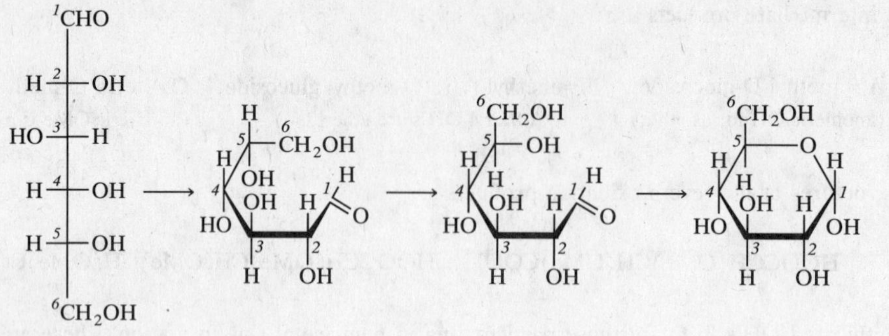

Fig. 23-8

23.67 Draw the chair conformation for β-D-glucopyranose.

◢ There are two interconverting chair forms. We select the one that has the bulkiest substituent, in most cases CH_2OH, in an equatorial position. The Haworth projection (or structure **C** in Problem 23.66) is then transformed to this chair conformation by placing the rest of the substituents in axial or equatorial positions according to their *cis-trans* and positional relationship with CH_2OH. Once we know that a β-anomeric OH is equatorial, these structural relationships can be detected directly from the Fischer structure of the hemiacetal, thereby obviating the need to draw the Haworth projection first. The structure is shown in Fig. 23-9.

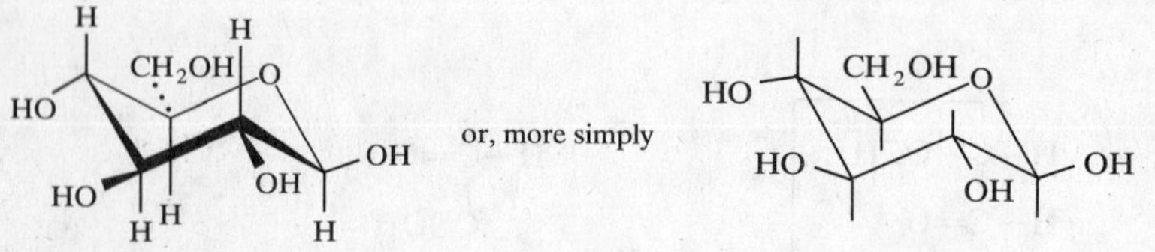

or, more simply

Fig. 23-9

23.68 Why is β-D-glucopyranose the most abundant naturally-occurring aldohexose?

◢ All ring substituents in the chair conformation are equatorial.

23.69 Draw the more and less stable chair conformations of (*a*) β-D-mannopyranose (see Problem 23.47) and (*b*) β-L-glucopyranose.

◢ (*a*) See Fig. 23-10(*a*). In the more stable conformer, CH_2OH and three OH's are equatorial. (*b*) See Fig. 23-10(*b*).

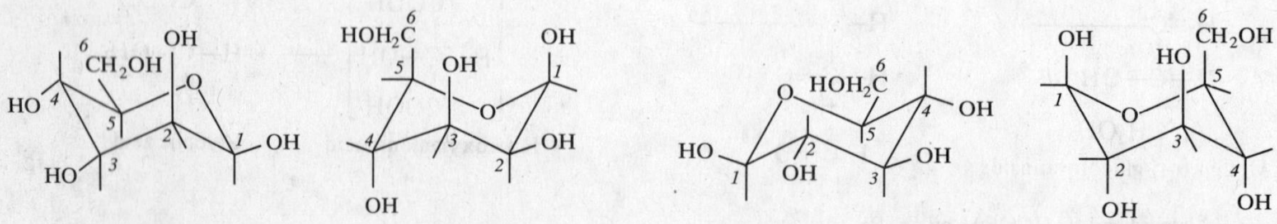

more stable   *less stable*   *more stable* (all equatorial)   *less stable* (all axial)

(*a*)   (*b*)

Fig. 23-10

'0 Draw the more and the less stable chair conformations of α-D-idopyranose, the C^2 epimer of D-gulose (see Problem 23.45). Explain your choice.

(*a*) See Fig. 23-11. Although the more stable conformer has an axial CH_2OH, this is more than compensated for by having four equatorial OH's.

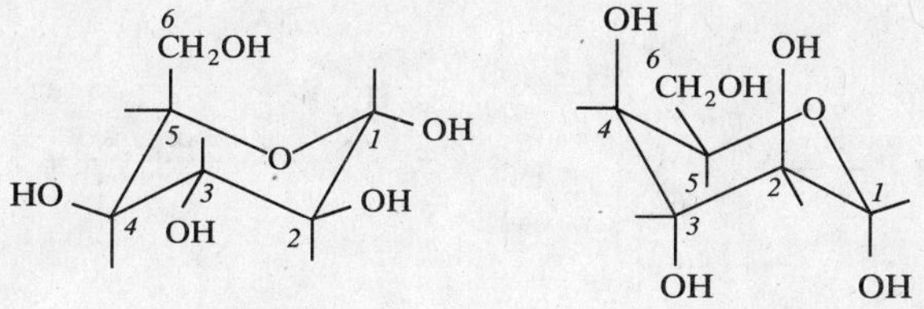

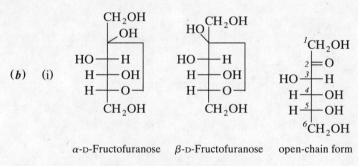

more stable   *less stable*   **Fig. 23-11**

23.71 (*a*) Which is the anomeric C in fructose? (*b*) Draw the Fischer projections of the anomers of (i) D-fructofuranose, and (ii) D-fructopyranose.

(*a*) C^2.

(*b*) (i)

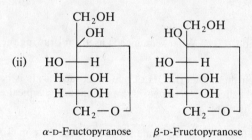

α-D-Fructofuranose   β-D-Fructofuranose   open-chain form

(ii)

α-D-Fructopyranose   β-D-Fructopyranose

23.72 Draw the Haworth projections for the anomers of D-fructofuranose.

Draw the C^6H_2OH group and the β-anomeric OH up and work out the *cis-trans* relationships of the remaining groups as shown in Fig. 23-12. The numbers are those in the keto form in Problem 23.71.

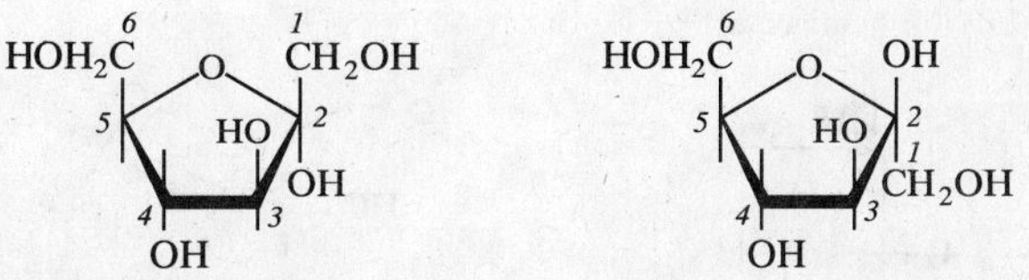

α-D-Fructofuranose   β-D-Fructofuranose   **Fig. 23-12**

23.73 Draw the Haworth projections for the anomers of D-fructopyranose and show their formation as was done in Problem 23.66.

✒ See Fig. 23-13. The numbers are those in the keto form in Problem 23.71. If the C^6-OH approaches the top face of C=O, the resulting anomeric OH is forced down. The anomeric OH is *cis* to the C^5 OH making this the α-anomer. A bottom side approach forces the anomeric OH to point up *trans* to the C^5 OH, making this the β-anomer.

α-D-Fructopyranose   topside approach ←   bottomside approach → β-D-Fructopyranose

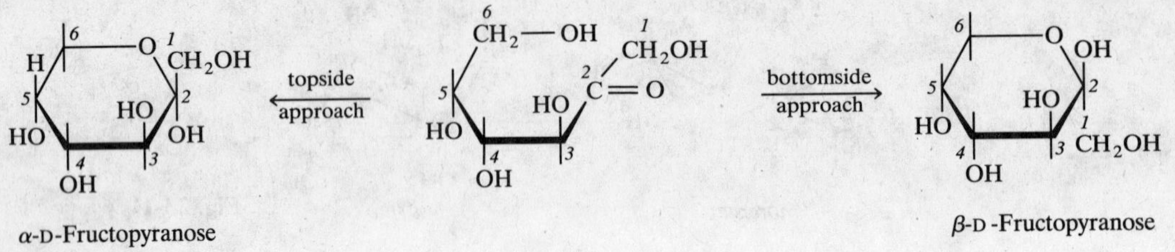

Fig. 23-13

23.74 (*a*) Draw the more stable chair conformer for α-D-fructopyranose. (*b*) How does the β-anomer differ?

✒ (*a*) See Fig. 23-14. The numbers are those in Problem 23.73. (*b*) The OH and $^1CH_2OH$ on ^2C are interchanged.

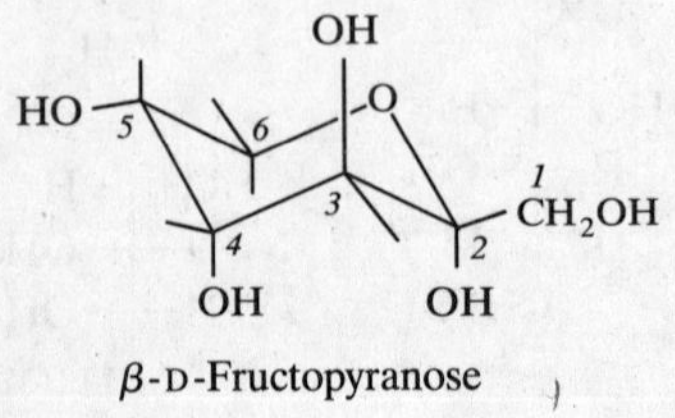

β-D-Fructopyranose   **Fig. 23-14**

DISACCHARIDES AND POLYSACCHARIDES

23.75 (*a*) Discuss the general structure of disaccharides. (*b*) What sequence is used for drawing the unit monosaccharides of the disaccharides?

✒ (*a*) A *disaccharide* is a glycoside in which the anomeric OH of one monosaccharide is bonded by an acetal linkage to an OH of a second monosaccharide, called the *aglycone*. The aglycone has a typical ether linkage. (*b*) The aglycone is the end monosaccharide on the right.

23.76 Give (*a*) the Fischer and chair structures and (*b*) the IUPAC name for the disaccharide maltose whose aglycone is a glucose unit (**A**) bonded at its C^4—OH to the α—OH of a second glucose unit (**B**). (*c*) Which structural feature in maltose is uncertain?

✒ (*a*) See Fig. 23-15. (*b*) The IUPAC name for the disaccharide maltose is 4-O-(α-D-glucopyranosyl)-β-D-glucopyranose. The 4-O indicates that the aglycone, named as a pyranosyl, is bonded at its C^4-OH. (*c*) The OH on the anomeric C of **A** is assumed to be in the more stable β-configuration, but this is not certain.

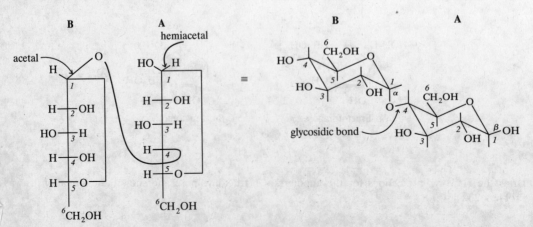

Fig. 23-15

23.77 Give the products from the reaction of maltose with (*a*) dil. HCl, (*b*) the enzyme maltase, and (*c*) the enzyme emulsin.

▰ (*a*) and (*b*) Maltose is hydrolyzed to give two equivalents of glucose. Maltase catalyzes the hydrolysis of α-glycosidic linkages only. (*c*) No reaction. Emulsin catalyzes the hydrolysis of β-glycosidic linkages only.

23.78 Discuss the behavior of maltose under the following conditions: (*a*) Fehling's solution, (*b*) dil. NaOH, (*c*) aq. Br_2, and (*d*) excess $PhNHNH_2$.

▰ Since the aglycone unit of maltose has a free anomeric OH, it is in equilibrium with the open chain aldehyde form and gives positive tests with all these reagents. The glycosidic bond is unaffected. (*a*) and (*c*) The anomeric C^1 of the aglycone is oxidized to COOH (see Problem 23.79). (*b*) Mutarotation occurs. (*d*) An osazone is formed.

23.79 Show how the following findings along with those in Problems 23.77 and 23.78 help to establish the structure of D-maltose. It is oxidized by aq. Br_2 to a carboxylic acid (**C**) that reacts with $(MeO)_2SO_2$/NaOH to give an octamethyl derivative (**D**). Then **D** is hydrolyzed by dil. HCl to 2,3,4,6-tetra-O-methyl-D-glucopyranose (**E**) and 2,3,5,6-tetra-O-methyl-D-gluconic acid (**F**). Give the structures of **C**, **D**, **E**, and **F**.

▰ We concluded from Problems 23.77 and 23.78 that maltose is an α-glucoside whose aglycone (**A**, see Problem 23.76) has a free anomeric OH of undetermined stereochemistry. The carboxylic acid **C** is formed by oxidation of the anomeric C^1 of **A**, resulting in loss of its hemiacetal ring. Methylation before hydrolysis to monosaccharides identifies the OH's not involved in any linkages in **C**. The O on C^5 of **E** is unmethylated, indicating that it was part of the pyranose ring. Since all O's of **E**, except for the anomeric OH, are methylated or part of the ring, **E** originated from **B** (Problem 23.76) and thus **F** from **A**. The fact that the C^4 OH of **F** is unmethylated tells us that this OH forms the ether linkage. See Fig. 23-16.

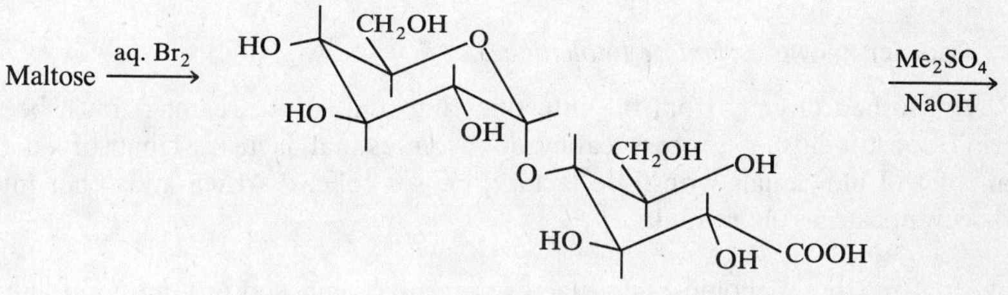

C, Maltobionic acid

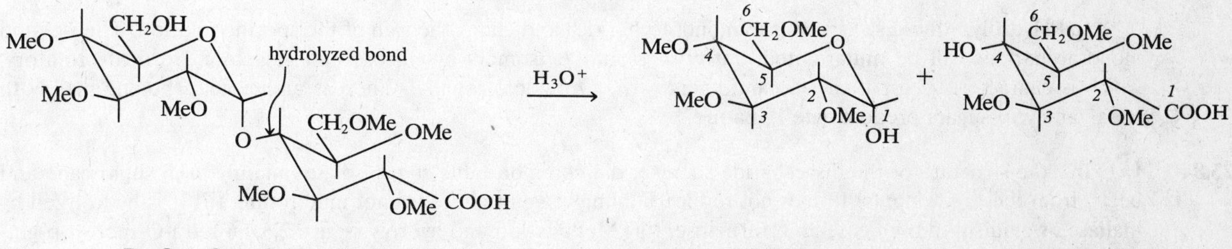

D, Octa-O-methyl-D-maltobionic acid   E, 2,3,4,6-Tetra-O-methyl-D-glucopyranose   F, 2,3,5,6-Tetra-O-methyl-D-gluconic acid

Fig. 23-16

23.80 Cellobiose, the disaccharide isolated from the polysaccharide cellulose, has the same chemistry as maltose but is hydrolyzed by emulsin. Give its chair conformational structure.

▰ Cellobiose differs from maltose only in being a β-glucoside. See Fig. 23-17.

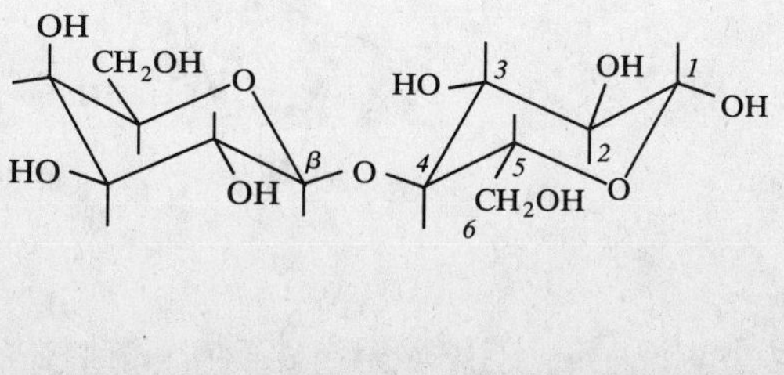

Fig. 23-17

23.81 (*a*) Deduce and give the structure of lactose, a disaccharide which is present in milk. (*1*) It is hydrolyzed by emulsin to D-glucose and D-galactose. (*2*) It is a reducing sugar that mutarotates. (*3*) Its osazone is hydrolyzed to D-galactose and D-glucosazone. (*4*) Mild oxidation, methylation, and finally hydrolysis gives results analogous to those observed for D-maltose. (*b*) Give the structural formula for the osazone of lactose.

◢ (*a*) (*1*) Lactose is a β-glycoside composed of D-glucose and D-galactose. (*2*) It has a free anomeric OH. (*3*) Since the glucose unit forms the osazone, it must be the aglycone. Lactose is a β-galactoside. (*4*) Both units are pyranoses joined through the C^4 OH of the glucose unit. See Fig. 23-18(*a*) for the structure. (*b*) See Fig. 23-18(*b*).

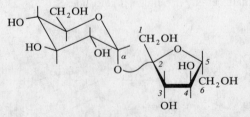

B unit **A unit**

D-Galactose unit   D-glucose unit

Lactose osazone

(*a*)   (*b*)   **Fig. 23-18**

23.82 Describe the digestive disorder known as *lactose intolerance*.

◢ Lactose cannot be absorbed directly from the intestines into the bloodstream. It must be first hydrolyzed into its monosaccharide constituents, a process catalyzed by intestinal lactase. Unabsorbed lactose, passing through the intestinal tract of individuals with little lactase, causes colic, diarrhea and other intestinal distress. Often lactose intolerance appears in older adults.

23.83 (*a*) How can we verify that maltose, cellobiose, and lactose are not composed of L-monosaccharides? (*b*) Are L-sugars observed in nature?

◢ (*a*) Hydrolyze the disaccharides to monosaccharides and check the sign of the specific rotation. The isolated monosaccharides will be mutarotated, but both α and β isomers of glucose and galactose are dextrorotatory, which is characteristic for their D enantiomers. (*b*) Only occasionally. Whereas amino acids belong mainly to the L-family, D-sugars predominate in nature.

23.84 (*a*) Give the structure of the disaccharide sucrose, the common table sugar isolated mainly from sugar cane and beets, from the following: (i) It does not reduce Fehling reagent and does not mutarotate. (ii) It is hydrolyzed by maltase or emulsin to D-glucose and D-fructose. (iii) Methylation and hydrolysis give 2,3,4,6-tetra-O-methyl-D-glucopyranose and a tetramethyl-D-fructose. (*b*) What structural features are uncertain? (*c*) Give the IUPAC name of sucrose.

◢ (*a*) (i) Sucrose has no free anomeric OH. (ii) D-Glucose and D-fructose are linked by their anomeric OH's, the α of one (hydrolysis by maltase) with the β OH of the other (hydrolysis by emulsion). (iii) The glucose unit is a pyranoside because the C^5 OH is unmethylated. See Fig. 23-19. (*b*) The fructose ring size (it is actually a

Fig. 23-19

furanoside) and the glycosidic linkage (the actual linkage is α to glucose and β to fructose). (*c*) Since either monosaccharide can be considered to be the aglycone, two names are possible: α-D-glucopyranosyl-β-D-fructofuranoside or β-D-fructofuranosyl-α-D-glucopyranoside.

23.85 (*a*) Define invert sugar. (*b*) Calculate the specific rotation of invert sugar given that $[\alpha]_D = 52.7°$ for D-glucose and $[\alpha]_D = -92.4°$ for D-fructose.

▰ (*a*) *Invert sugar* is the equimolar mixture of D-glucose and D-fructose obtained on hydrolysis of sucrose. (*b*) The specific rotation is one-half the sum of those of the individual monosaccharides: $\frac{1}{2}[+52.7° + (-92.4°)] = -19.9°$

23.86 Give the products formed from the hydrolysis of completely methylated sucrose.

▰ See Fig. 23-20. The wavy lines indicate undefined configurations.

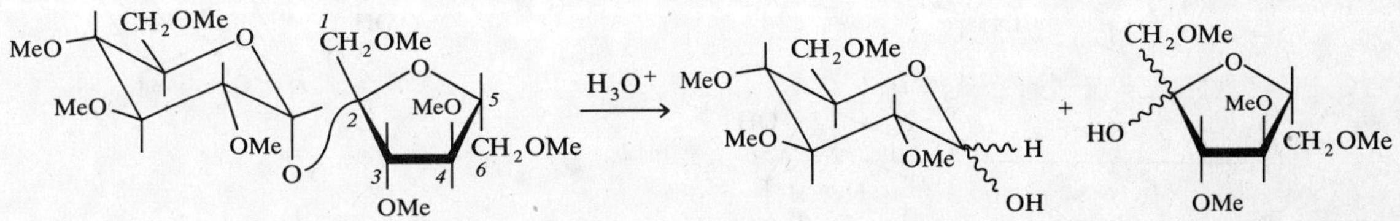

2,3,4,6-Tetra-methyl-D-glucopyranose (equilibrium mixtures of α- and β-anomers)

1,3,4,6-Tetra-O-methyl-D-fructofuranose

Fig. 23-20

23.87 Deduce the structure of a disaccharide, $C_{10}H_{18}O_9$, which, after oxidation with aq. Br_2 followed by methylation and treatment with maltase, yields 2,3,4-tri-O-methyl-D-xylose and 2,3-di-O-methyl-L-arabinonic acid.

▰ The disaccharide is an α-disaccharide (maltase hydrolysis). The unit forming the acid and having the fewer number of OMe's is the aglycone which in this case is L-arabinose. The sugar is a glycoside of D-xylose. Since the C^5 OH in both hydrolysis products is unmethylated, it is involved in the ring formation, and the two pentoses are pyranosides. Since the C^4 OH in the aglycone is unmethylated, it is the point of linkage to the α-anomeric OH of xylose. The structure is shown in Fig. 23-21.

23.88 Deduce the structure of gentiobiose, $C_{12}H_{22}O_{11}$, that undergoes mutarotation and is hydrolyzed by emulsin to D-glucose. Methylation followed by hydrolysis yields 2,3,4,6-tetra-O-methyl-D-glucopyranose and 2,3,4,-tri-O-methyl-D-glucopyranose.

▰ The gentiobiose is a β-disaccharide (emulsin hydrolysis) composed of two glucose units. The aglycone glucose has a free anomeric OH (mutarotation). Both glucose units are pyranosides because their C^5 OH's are

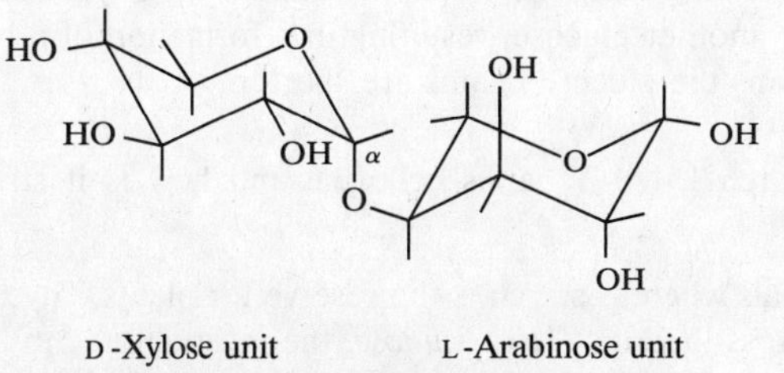

D-Xylose unit   L-Arabinose unit
4,O-(α-D-Xylopyranosyl)-L-arabinopyranoside

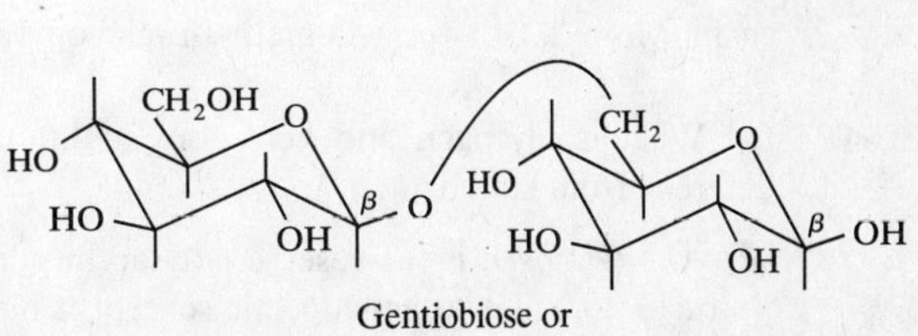

Gentiobiose or
6-O-(β-D-Glucopyranosyl)-D-β-glucopyranose

Fig. 23-21

Fig. 23-22

unmethylated. Since the C^6 OH of the aglycone is unmethylated, it is the point of attachment. The aglycone is assumed to be β-glucose. The structure of the gentiobiose is shown in Fig. 23-22.

23.89 Deduce the structures of (*a*) nonreducing trehalose, $C_{12}H_{22}O_{11}$, that is hydrolyzed by maltase to D-glucose, and (*b*) isotrehalose that is identical to trehalose except that it is hydrolyzed by either maltase or emulsin. Methylation followed by hydrolysis yields only 2,3,4,6-tetra-O-methyl-D-glucopyranose in both cases.

▞ (*a*) See Fig. 23-23(*a*). Trehalose has two glucose units each joined by their (maltase hydrolysis) anomeric α OH's (nonreducing). Since the C^5 OH is unmethylated, each glucose unit is a pyranoside. (*b*) See Fig. 23-23(*b*). Isotrehalose has the α OH of one unit bonded to the β OH of the other (maltase and emulsin hydrolysis). However, from the information given, we cannot say which.

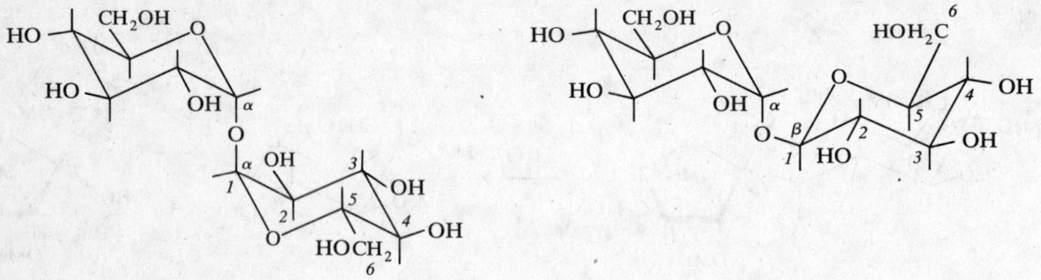

α-D-Glucopyranosyl-α-D-glucopyranoside
Trehalose
(*a*)

α-D-Glucopyranosyl-β-D-glucopyranoside
Isotrehalose
(*b*)

Fig. 23-23

23.90 Name two ubiquitous plant polysaccharides consisting of only D-glucose units.

▞ Starch and cellulose.

23.91 *Amylose*, the water soluble portion of starch, is partially hydrolyzed to maltose and α-D-glucose. When methylated, it is hydrolyzed mainly to 2,3,6-tri-O-methyl-D-glucopyranose. Describe the structure of amylose.

▞ It is composed of maltose units (see Problem 23.76) strung together in a chain where the anomeric OH of one glucose is bonded to the C^4 OH, symbolized by α (1 → 4), of another glucose. The units form a helix.

23.92 Methylation and hydrolysis of amylose also gives 0.2 to 0.4% of 2,3,4,6-tetra-O-methyl-D-glucopyranose. Explain the origin of this compound.

▞ The first glucose unit in each starch chain has a free C^4 OH and gives this compound.

23.93 *Amylopectin*, the water insoluble portion of starch, behaves like amylose on hydrolysis, except that more 2,3,4,6-tetra-O-methyl-D-glucopyranose (5%) and about 5% of 2,3-di-O-methyl-D-glucopyranose is formed. Deduce the structure of amylopectin.

▞ The linkage in most of amylopectin is identical to that in amylose. The isolation of 2,3-di-O-methyl-D-glucopyranose with an unmethylated C^6 OH means that occasionally along the chain, in addition to its typical $\alpha(1 \rightarrow 4)$ linkage, a C^6 OH forms an $\alpha(1 \rightarrow 6)$ cross-linkage with another glucose, resulting in a formation of a branched chain. More 2,3,4,6-tetra-O-methyl-D-glucopyranose means the glucose chains are shorter.

23.94 (*a*) What is glycogen and how does it differ from starch? (*b*) What is cellulose and how is it structurally different from starch?

▞ (*a*) *Glycogen* is the reserve polysaccharide of animals whereas starch is the reserve for plants. Glycogen has a structure similar to amylopectin, except it has more cross-linking. (*b*) *Cellulose*, the most abundant naturally-occurring organic compound on earth, is the chief component of wood and plant fibers; cotton is nearly pure cellulose. Cellulose differs from starch in having β-1,4-glucosidic linkages and not α. The chains are mainly linear with little branching. Cellulose also has more glucose units, giving it a higher molecular weight.

23.95 (*a*) Find the average molecular weight of starch given that an aqueous solution of 10.0 g/L of starch has an osmotic pressure $\Pi = 5.0 \times 10^{-3}$ atm at 25°C. (*b*) What is the approximate average number of glucose units in this sample of starch?

    ▰ (*a*) $\Pi = MRT$, where M is the molarity, R is the gas constant (0.082 L · atm/mol · K), and T is the absolute temperature.

$$M = \frac{\Pi}{RT} = \frac{5.0 \times 10^{-3} \text{ atm}}{(0.082 \text{ L} \cdot \text{atm/mol} \cdot \text{K})(298 \text{ K})} = 2.0 \times 10^{-4} \text{ mol/L} \quad \text{and}$$

$$MW = \frac{10.0 \text{ g/L}}{2.0 \times 10^{-4} \text{ mol/L}} = 5.0 \times 10^{4} \text{ g/mol}$$

    (*b*) Each glucose unit (MW = 180 g/mol) bonds to the starch chain with loss of one H_2O unit (18 g/mol), giving a MW of $180 - 18 = 162$ g/mol per unit. Thus, in this sample we have 5.0×10^{4} g mol^{-1}/162 g mol^{-1} unit^{-1} = 309 units or an approximate average of 300 glucose units.

23.96 (*a*) What are cyclodextrins? (*b*) How do they differ from crown ethers in terms of their catalytic behavior? (*c*) In what way are cyclodextrins used?

    ▰ (*a*) *Cyclodextrins* are oligosaccharides (see Problem 23.4) of 6–8 glucopyranose units formed by partial hydrolysis of starch. The units form a doughnut-shaped ring. (*b*) Like crown ethers, they can act as a host for guest molecules. However, unlike crown ethers, cyclodextrins have a nonpolar lyophobic inside and a polar lyophilic outside. The guests are molecules, not ions. (*c*) Since the entire structure is water soluble because of the OH's on the outside, they catalyze organic reactions, often with regiospecificity and some stereoselectivity, in the interior space. They also serve as models for enzyme action.

23.97 (*a*) Give a simple test for starch. (*b*) Describe the change that occurs when the test is performed at elevated temperatures. (*c*) Discuss the structural change that accounts for the variation in the test. (*d*) Do amylose and amylopectin give the same color? Explain.

    ▰ (*a*) Addition of I_2 gives a deep blue-black color. (*b*) The color changes to reddish-brown. (*c*) Amylose in starch traps I_2 molecules within its helix, forming a charge-transfer complex with the characteristic blue-black color. At higher temperatures the helix partially unwinds and fewer I_2 molecules are trapped. Upon cooling, the helix reforms, enclosing the I_2, and the original color returns. (*d*) Amylopectin gives a less intense red-brown color because the helical structure is disrupted by the branching of the chain.

NUCLEIC ACIDS

23.98 What are nucleic acids?

    ▰ *Nucleic acids* are high molecular-weight polymers that can be hydrolyzed to a mixture of heterocyclic bases, a pentose, and phosphoric acid. They are often combined with proteins as nucleoproteins, and are present in the nucleus and cytoplasm of all living cells.

23.99 What are the components of the bipolymer *deoxyribonucleic acid* (DNA)?

    ▰ The units comprising DNA are: the sugar 2-deoxyribose, a phosphate group, and a heterocyclic base. The prefix *deoxy* means without oxygen; in this case, the OH at C^2 of ribose is replaced by H. The base is either a purine [adenine (A) or guanine (G)] or pyrimidine [cytosine (C) or thymine (T)] derivative (see Problems 21.11 and 21.12).

23.100 How does *ribonucleic acid* (RNA) differ from DNA?

    ▰ The sugar is ribose, and the pyrimidine base uracil (U) usually replaces thymine (T).

23.101 (*a*) What are nucleosides? (*b*) Provide structures for the nucleoside of (i) deoxyribose with cytosine and (ii) ribose with guanine.

✦ (a) *Nucleosides* are β-glycosides of D-ribofuranose or D-deoxyribofuranose whose aglycones (Problem 23.75), the purine or pyrimidine bases, are bonded to C^1 of the sugar. The suffix of pyrimidine derivatives is *-idine* and of purine derivatives is *-osine*. (b) See Fig. 23-24.

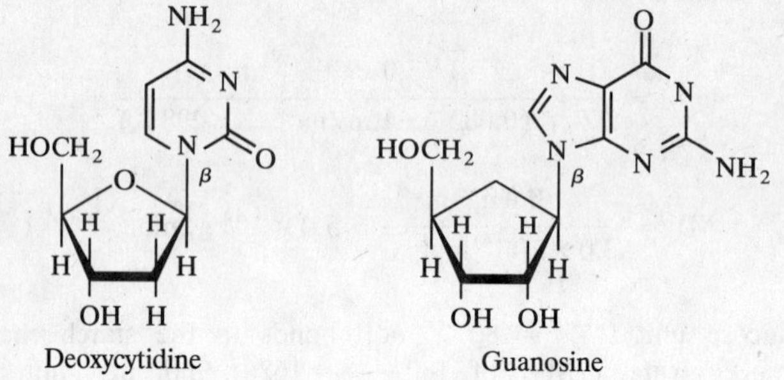

Deoxycytidine   Guanosine   **Fig. 23-24**

23.102 (a) What is nucleotide? (b) Describe the numbering system for a nucleotide. (c) Give the structural formulas for (i) 3'-deoxyuridylic acid (deoxyuridine 3'-monophosphate, *d*-UMP) and (ii) 5'-adenosine triphosphate (adenosine 5'-triphosphate, ATP).

✦ (a) A *nucleotide* is a nucleoside esterified at a sugar -OH to a phosphate group. It is comprised of a base, a sugar, and a phosphate group. Nucleotides are named either as phosphate derivatives or as acids of the heterocyclic base. (b) The base and sugar systems are numbered separately, with primes referring to the sugar C's. Deoxyribose is thus 2'-deoxyribose, and nucleotides are usually phosphorylated at the 5'-OH of the sugar, occasionally at the 3'-OH. (The prefix *mono-* is often deleted for monophosphates.) (c) See Fig. 23-25.

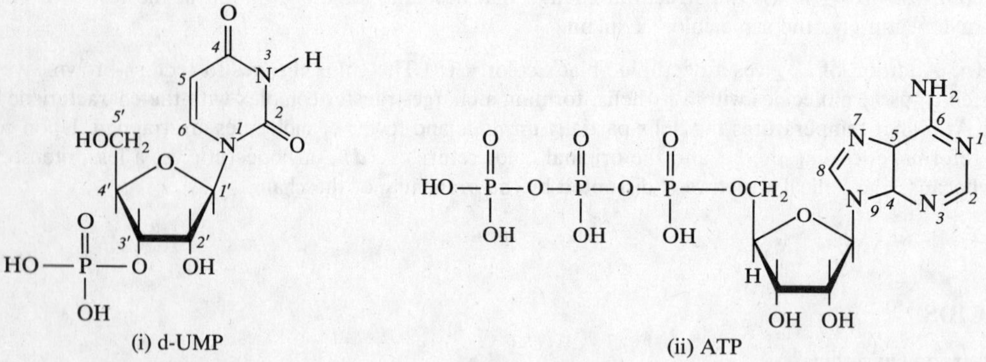

(i) d-UMP   (ii) ATP   **Fig. 23-25**

23.103 Give the structure of the *cyclic nucleotide* adenosine 3',5'-monophosphate, called cyclic AMP.

✦ Cyclic AMP is a *cyclic phosphodiester* that acts intracellularly as a *secondary messenger*, controlling the activity of cellular hormones and enzymes.

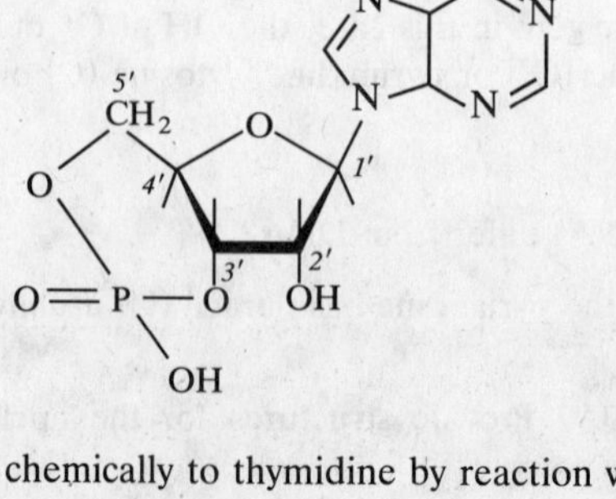

how how uridine may be converted chemically to thymidine by reaction with $H_2C=O$.

▮ This is related to the PhOH-H₂CO reaction (see Problem 20.49). The ribose group is denoted by Rib.

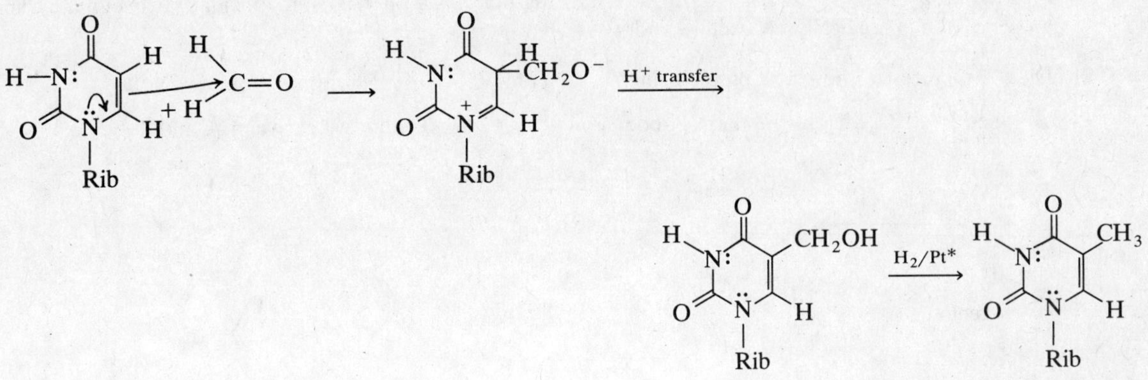

*Hydrogenolysis, as in $PhCH_2OH \longrightarrow PhCH_3$.

23.105 How may a ribonucleoside be converted chemically to a 5′-phosphorylated ribonucleotide with dibenzylphospho-chloridate, $(BzO)_2POCl$?

▮ First protect the 2′ and 3′-OH groups from phosphorylation by ketal formation with acetone (see Problem 15.74). Phosphorylation is followed by hydrolysis of the ketal and hydrogenolysis.

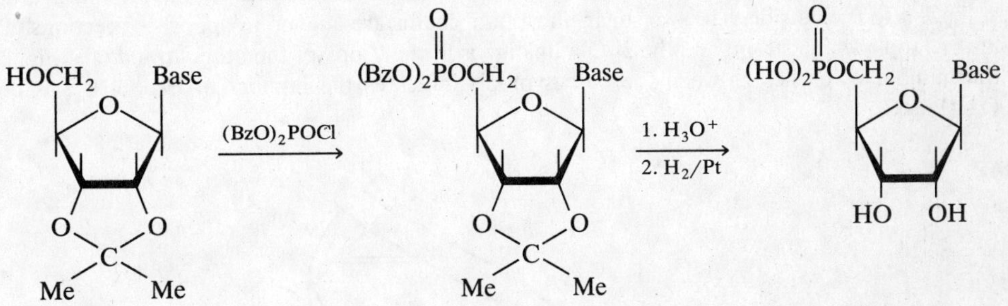

23.106 Outline the successive hydrolytic degradation products of a nucleoprotein.

▮ Nucleoprotein ⟶ nucleic acid (+ proteins) ⟶ nucleotides ⟶
                       nucleosides (+ phosphate ion) ⟶ pentose + heterocyclic amines (bases)

23.107 Give a schematic diagram for the primary structure of a nucleic acid.

▮ The "backbone" is a helix. It consists of a linear chain of sugar molecules linked via bonds from the 3′ OH to a phosphate group, which in turn continues the chain by bonding to the 5′ OH of the next sugar [see Fig. 23-26(a)]. The base is attached by its N to C^1 of the sugar [see Fig. 23-26(b)].

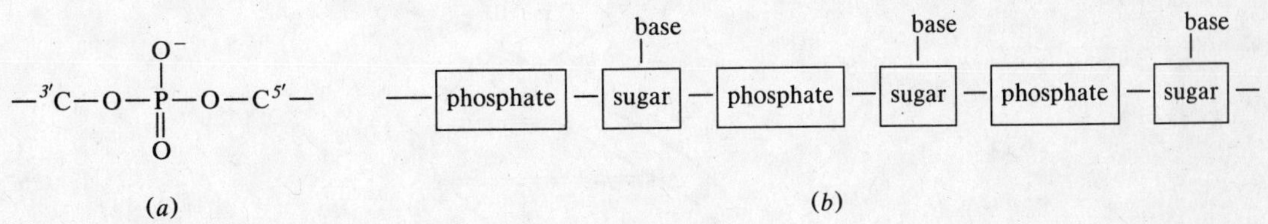

(a)   (b)

Fig. 23-26

23.108 DNA (Problem 23.99) is a dimeric polymer, in which two polynucleotide chains are entwined in a *double helix*. On hydrolysis, it is found that although the ratio of bases vary from one DNA to another, the ratios of C:G and A:T are always 1:1 (or C = G and A = T). (*a*) How are these ratios consistent with the double-helix concept? (*b*) How do the complementary bases interact with one another?

▮ (*a*) The C and A in one strand always matches the G and T respectively in the other strand. This matching is called *base-pairing*. (*b*) Base-pairing occurs by H-bonding with maximum efficiency between a pyrimidine and a purine base, specifically between A and T and between C and G.

23.109 Draw structures to show how base-pairing accounts for the ratio of bases in Problem 23.108.

▮ See Fig. 23-27. Note the three H-bonds between G and C and two between A and T.

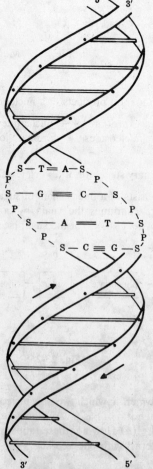

G-C base-pairing   A-T base-pairing   **Fig. 23-27**

23.110 Describe the secondary double-helix structure of DNA.

▮ The double helix has the hydrophobic bases pointing to the center of the helix in an almost planar arrangement. These base-pairs are closely stacked perpendicular to the long axis of the chain, and are attracted to each other by van der Waals forces. The hydrophilic phosphates are negatively charged at the pH of the cell and point to the outside. The two sugar-phosphate chains are aligned in opposite directions. The 5′ OH linkage is at the "top" of one strand and the 3′ OH linkage is at the "top" of the other strand (see Fig. 23-28). In the figure, the number of dashes between the base symbols indicates the number of H-bonds. S is deoxyribose and P is $O{=}P{-}O^-$.

Fig. 23-28

23.111 (*a*) How does DNA store information?   (*b*) Why are three base residues required to code for one amino acid in protein synthesis?

▮   (*a*) The sequence of bases along the DNA molecule encodes for the sequence of amino acids in every protein in all organisms.   (*b*) There are 20 AA's and only four bases, so one base cannot code for one AA. The number of possible combinations of two bases is $4^2 = 16$, still an insufficient number. With a sequence of three bases, called a *triplet*, there are $4^3 = 64$ possible combinations, providing at least one triplet for each AA. The valuable excess ($64 - 20 = 44$) allows for more than one triplet to code for the same AA (a valuable redundancy) and provides for signals to start and end the protein chain.

23.112 How many base-pairs in the gene are needed to code for the enzyme lysozyme (129 AA's) found in egg white?

▮   Three base-pairs code for one AA, and two more triplets are required for "start" and "stop" signals; or, $(3 \times 129) + (3 \times 2) = 393$ base-pairs.

23.113 How does DNA direct protein synthesis in a cell?

▮   The flow of information, which involves complementary base-pairing, is from DNA in the nucleus to *messenger* RNA (mRNA), to *transfer* RNA (tRNA) that transports the AA's for protein synthesis. The double helix of DNA separates at the required place and acts as a template for the synthesis of a shorter single strand of mRNA with complementary bases. Each triplet of bases, called a *codon*, encodes for a specific AA. For example, GCA encodes for Ala and GUG for Val. The sequence of codons in mRNA, called the *genetic code*, provides instructions for protein assembly. The mRNA migrates out of the nucleus and becomes attached to cytoplasmic ribosomes that are themselves ribonucleoproteins. A special codon signals the start of the synthesis and the next codon of mRNA base-pairs with the complementary codon (anticodon) of the tRNA that binds the N-terminal AA. The next codon initiates the approach of another tRNA whose AA forms a peptide bond with the first AA. This dipeptide moves over to the next AA brought by a tRNA, forming an attached tripeptide with no change in position of the N-terminal AA. The ribosome, acting as the factory, carries the enzymes needed to catalyze these reactions. As polypeptide build-up progresses, the ribosome moves along the length of the mRNA, releasing the now "empty" tRNA to attach another AA and enabling it to repeat its function when necessary further down the chain. This process continues until a special codon signals termination, and the synthesized protein is released from the ribosome. The COOH-terminal AA is the last one to be joined to the chain.

23.114 How is an AA bonded to its tRNA?

▮   An *aminoacyl-tRNA complex* is formed via ester linkage between the COOH of the AA and an OH of the ribose moiety of the terminal adenosine of the tRNA. Each AA has a specific tRNA to which it bonds.

23.115 How is DNA replicated during cell division?

▮   The two strands of the DNA helix separate in the region to be replicated, and each acts as a template for the formation of its complementary new strand. The new strands form from opposite directions by successive additions of deoxyribonucleoside 5′-triphosphates to the 3′ OH of the growing polynucleotide chain (*via* a phosphate bond) with release of pyrophosphate.

$$[\text{base}-\text{deoxyribose}(C^{5'})-\text{OPO}_2^- -\text{OPO}_2^- -\text{OPO}_3^{2-}] + \text{HO}-(C^{3'})\text{deoxyribose}-\text{DNA chain} \longrightarrow$$

deoxyribonucleoside 5′-triphosphate

$$\underbrace{\text{base}-\text{deoxyribose}(C^{5'})-\text{OPO}_2^-}_{\text{new base}} -\text{O}-(C^{3'})\text{deoxyribose}-\text{DNA chain} + \text{HOPO}_2^- -\text{OPO}_3^{2-}$$

DNA chain elongated by one nucleoside unit   monohydrogen diphosphate ion

The deoxyribose at the end of the elongated DNA chain has a free 3′ OH available for bonding through phosphate to another nucleoside unit.

23.116 Describe the denaturation process that occurs upon heating a solution of DNA.

▮   The H-bonds between the paired bases and the van der Waals attractive forces that hold the stacked base-pairs, aligned one pair on top of the other, are disrupted. The ordered conformation breaks and the double helix dissociates into random, disordered coils. The viscosity of the solution drops sharply.

23.117 How does a change in the base sequence in DNA cause a mutation?

◢ A change in a single base-pair in DNA can cause substitution of a different AA in the protein being synthesized, as is seen in sickle–cell hemoglobin (see Problem 22.82). In a *silent* mutation, the substitution does not significantly change the normal activity of the protein. A *lethal* mutation is characterized by production of a defective harmful protein or failure to produce an essential protein.

23.118 Account for the mutagenic activity of nitrous acid on DNA.

◢ HNO_2 converts —NH_2 to —OH, i.e., cytosine to uracil and guanine to xanthine via diazotization, thereby changing the genetic code and leading to possible mutations.

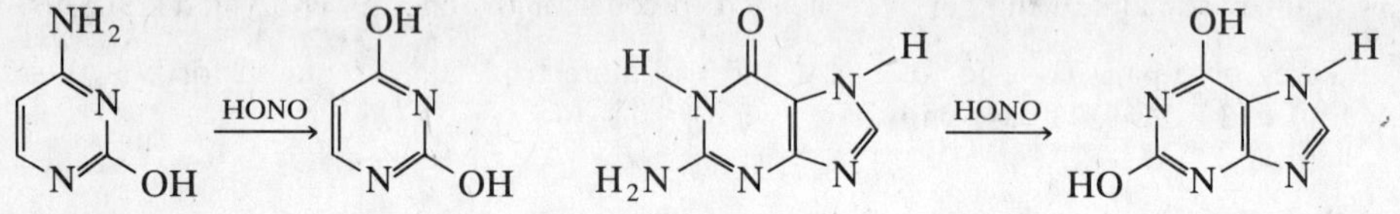

| Cytosine | Uracil | Guanine | Xanthine |

23.119 Account for the carcinogenic behavior of nitrosamines, epoxides, active halides such as MeI, and benzo[a]pyrene (BAP).

◢ Carcinogens are primarily mutagenic. By altering the base sequence in some way, they bring about a change in a protein and a corresponding change in biological function. These four classes of compounds alkylate the O and N atoms, the nucleophilic sites in the bases. Mutations arise because the alkylated bases have altered base-pairing properties. Nitrosamines act as alkylating agents, probably through formation of a diazoalkane. For example, $(CH_3)_2N$—N=O, dimethylnitrosamine, is converted to CH_2N_2. Epoxides and active halides are known to be very potent alkylating agents. BAP itself is not carcinogenic, but during partial metabolism it is converted to an epoxide derivative.

SUPPLEMENTARY PROBLEMS

23.120 (*a*) Account for the common names dextrose and levulose for D-glucose and D-fructose, respectively. (*b*) Is there a relationship between the sign of rotation and the family of the sugar?

◢ (*a*) The name *dextrose* derives from the fact that D-glucose is dextrorotatory. D-Fructose is called *levulose* because it is levorotatory. (*b*) No.

23.121 (*a*) Explain the increase in replacement of D-glucose and sucrose by invert sugar (see Problem 23.85) as a commercial sweetening agent. (*b*) Why is D-fructose used for sweetening cold drinks but not hot ones?

◢ (*a*) The D-fructose in invert sugar is sweeter than D-glucose or sucrose, and less material is needed to achieve the same level of sweetness. Thus, fewer calories are consumed. (*b*) The sweeter form is fructopyranose. Rising temperature causes a shift in the pyranose ⇌ furanose equilibrium towards the less sweet furanose.

23.122 (*a*) Name sugars **A**, **B**, and **C** in the following structures. (*b*) Give the source of **A** and **C**.

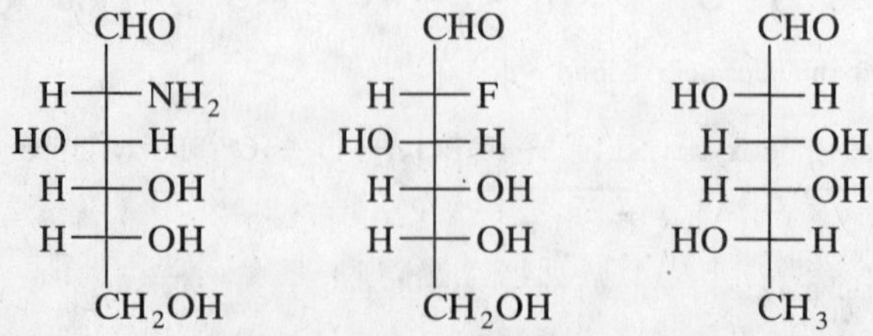

| A | B | C |

◢ (*a*) **A** is 2-amino-2-deoxy-D-glucose (D-glucosamine). **B** is 2-fluoro-2-deoxy-D-glucose. **C** is 6-deoxy-L-galactose (L-fucose). (*b*) **A** is formed by acid hydrolysis under severe conditions of the polysaccharide *chitin* that forms the hard shell of crustaceans and insects. **C** is a key sugar in several animal glycoproteins.

◢ riefly discuss the use of **B** in Problem 23.122 with ^{18}F in medical diagnoses in a process called PET (*p*ositron-mission *t*omography) scanning.

/ Atoms of ^{18}F emit positrons which annihilate nearby protons on contact, producing two photons for each collision. The distribution of the large number of generated photons is mapped by a computer, producing a colored image called a PET scan. The color is related to the concentration of the photons; yellow and orange indicate high concentrations. Compound **B** mimics glucose in the body; it goes where glucose goes. The brain is the major consumer of glucose. A PET scan of a patient suspected of having a brain disorder, such as schizophrenia, Alzheimer's disease, or a tumor, is compared to a normal brain scan. Significant differences indicates significant disorders. PET is extremely expensive and is used as a last resort for diagnosis. It is mainly a research tool.

23.124 (*a*) Draw the open-chain structures for the three D-2-ketohexose isomers of D-fructose. (*b*) Which isomer does not give a *meso* alditol on reduction? (*c*) Which isomer has the same osazone as D-galactose (see Problem 23.37)?

/ (*a*) The D-family has the C^5 OH on the right side

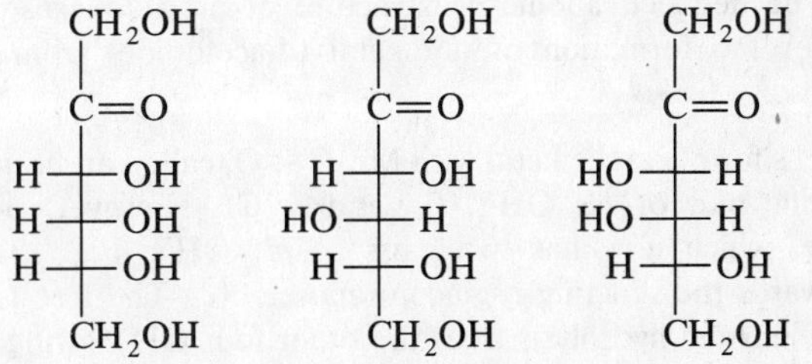

$$
\begin{array}{ccc}
\mathrm{CH_2OH} & \mathrm{CH_2OH} & \mathrm{CH_2OH} \\
\mathrm{C{=}O} & \mathrm{C{=}O} & \mathrm{C{=}O} \\
\mathrm{H{-}OH} & \mathrm{H{-}OH} & \mathrm{HO{-}H} \\
\mathrm{H{-}OH} & \mathrm{HO{-}H} & \mathrm{HO{-}H} \\
\mathrm{H{-}OH} & \mathrm{H{-}OH} & \mathrm{H{-}OH} \\
\mathrm{CH_2OH} & \mathrm{CH_2OH} & \mathrm{CH_2OH} \\
\text{D-Psicose} & \text{D-Sorbose} & \text{D-Tagatose}
\end{array}
$$

(*b*) D-Sorbose gives

$$
\begin{array}{ccc}
\mathrm{CH_2OH} & & \mathrm{CH_2OH} \\
\mathrm{H{-}OH} & & \mathrm{HO{-}H} \\
\mathrm{H{-}OH} & + & \mathrm{H{-}OH} \\
\mathrm{HO{-}H} & & \mathrm{HO{-}H} \\
\mathrm{H{-}OH} & & \mathrm{H{-}OH} \\
\mathrm{CH_2OH} & & \mathrm{CH_2OH}
\end{array}
$$

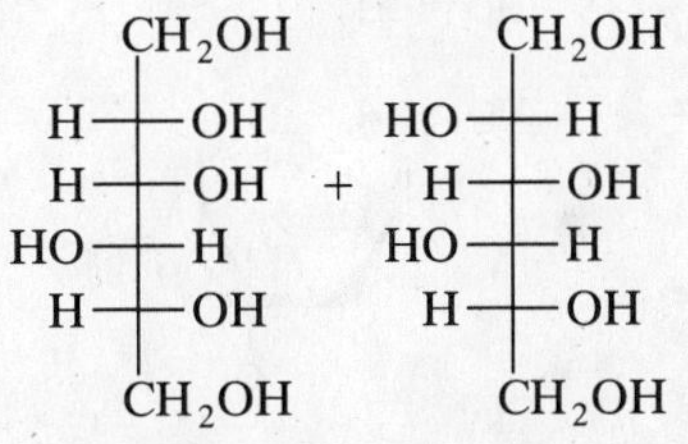

both are optically active

(*c*) D-Tagatose.

23.125 Which D-2-ketohexose has an enediol in common with D-fructose?

/ In order to have the same enediol, the $C{=}C$ must involve C^2 and C^3, and the D-2-ketohexose must have the same configuration about C^5 and C^4 as does D-fructose, e.g., both OH's on the right side. D-Psicose fits the bill. The enediol is

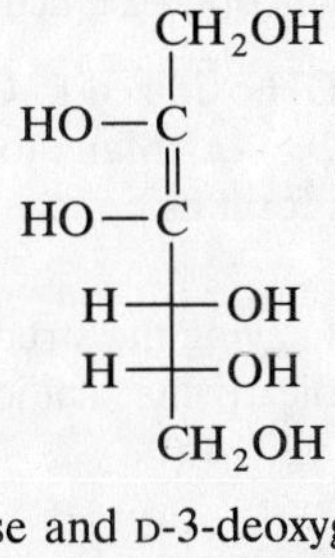

$$
\begin{array}{c}
\mathrm{CH_2OH} \\
\mathrm{HO{-}C} \\
\mathrm{\parallel} \\
\mathrm{HO{-}C} \\
\mathrm{H{-}OH} \\
\mathrm{H{-}OH} \\
\mathrm{CH_2OH}
\end{array}
$$

23.126 Distinguish chemically between D-2-deoxyglucose and D-3-deoxyglucose.

/ D-3-Deoxyglucose forms an osazone with 3 eq of $PhNHNH_2$, but D-2-deoxyglucose has no C—OH α to the $C{=}O$ and gives only a phenylhydrazone.

23.127 A hexose, **A**, forms a cyanohydrin, **B**, which is hydrolyzed and then reduced with HI/P to a carboxylic acid, **C**, which, in turn, is synthesized from PrI and $EtCH(COOEt)_2$. Give the structures of **A**, **B**, and **C** without designating the configurations of chiral C's.

/ The carboxylic acid obtained from the DEM synthesis is

$$
\mathrm{CH_3CH_2CH_2I} + {}^-\mathrm{:C(COOEt)_2} \xrightarrow{\text{after several steps}} \mathrm{CH_3CH_2CH_2CHCOOH}
$$
$$
\underset{\mathrm{CH_2CH_3}}{\qquad\qquad\qquad} \qquad\qquad\qquad \underset{\mathrm{CH_2CH_3}}{}
$$

C, 2-Ethylpentanoic acid

The COOH of **A**, which came from CN, must be attached to the C of C=O, e.g., C^3. **A** is a 3-keto sugar, HOCH₂CHOHCHOHCCHOHCH₂OH, and **B** is HOCH₂CHOHCHOHCCHOHCH₂OH.

with $\overset{\|}{O}$ under the C for A, and $HO \diagup \diagdown CN$ under the C for B.

23.128 Prepare a 2,3,4-trimethylaldopyranoside.

▮ A methyl glycopyranoside is reacted with Ph₃CCl (trityl chloride). Only the C^6H_2OH is etherified, giving the CH₂OCPh₃ group. The 2° OH's are too sterically hindered to react. In this way the C^6 OH is protected from further reaction. The free OH's of the tritylated methyl glycoside are now methylated with (MeO)₂SO₂/NaOH. Then dilute acid removes both the trityl group and the glycosidic Me leaving the C^2, C^3, and C^4 OMe's intact. The facile hydrolysis of the —O—trityl group proceeds through formation of the very stable carbocation, Ph₃C⁺.

23.129 (*a*) What can be deduced about the structure of an aldohexose from its reaction with acetone in H₂SO₄? (*b*) Account for the formation of a diketal (diacetonide) from this reaction with D-glucose. (*c*) Prepare D-3-benzylglucose.

▮ (*a*) *cis* OH's form a cyclic ketal with Me₂C=O, called an *acetonide*, Fig. 23-29(*a*). (*b*) In D-glucopyranose there is only one pair of *cis* OH's, C^2 and α C^1. However, D-glucopyranose is in equilibrium with some D-glucofuranose, which now has two pairs of *cis* OH's, Fig. 23-29(*b*). Formation of the diketal draws the equilibrium towards the reacting D-glucofuranose. (*c*) The free C^3 OH of the diacetonide is benzylated with PhCH₂Cl/NaOH. Acid hydrolysis frees the other four OH's giving the product.

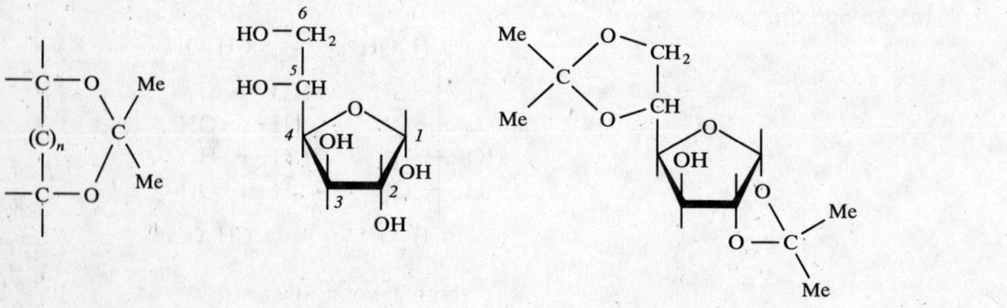

(*a*) ($n = 0$ or 1) glucofuranose (*b*) a diacetonide **Fig. 23-29**

23.130 (*a*) What is a glycuronic acid? (*b*) Why is it difficult to make a glycuronic acid from a sugar in the laboratory? (*c*) What is an important biochemical function of glucuronic acid, the glycuronic acid of glucose?

▮ (*a*) A *glycuronic acid* has its CH₂OH oxidized to COOH with CHO intact. (*b*) It is difficult to oxidize the CH₂OH without also oxidizing the CHO. (*c*) Many toxic substances are excreted in the urine as derivatives of D-glucuronic acid. Phenols and alcohols form esters called *glucuronides*, amines form glucuronate salts.

23.131 L-Ascorbic acid (vitamin C) is an enediol having the structure **E** shown in Fig. 23-30. (*a*) Account for the acidity of L-ascorbic acid (pK_a = 4.21) and indicate the acidic H. (*b*) Supply the formulas for **A** through **D** in the

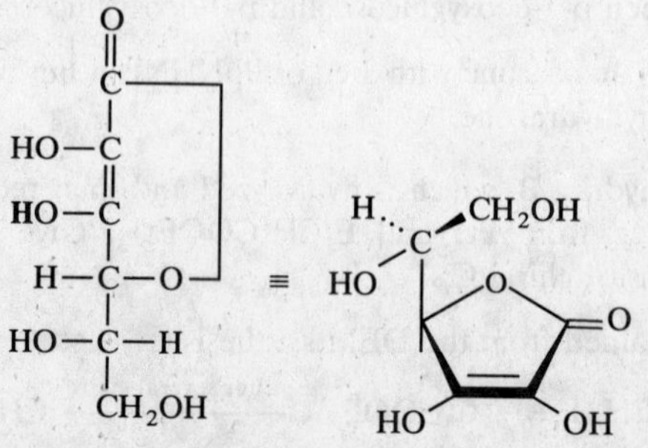

L-Ascorbic acid, **E** **Fig. 23-30**

following commercial synthesis of L-ascorbic acid:

$$\text{D-glucose} \xrightarrow{\text{NaBH}_4} \text{D-}(A) \xrightarrow{\text{[O] enzymatic}} \text{L-2-ketosugar (B)} \rightleftharpoons B' \xrightarrow{2\text{Me}_2\text{CO}} C \xrightarrow[\text{2. aq. H}^+]{\text{1. KMnO}_4/\text{OH}^-} D \xrightarrow[\Delta]{\text{H}^+} E$$

▮ (a) The anion formed by removal of the enolic **H** is stable because the − charge is delocalized to the O of the C=O through the C=C, as shown for the essential portion:

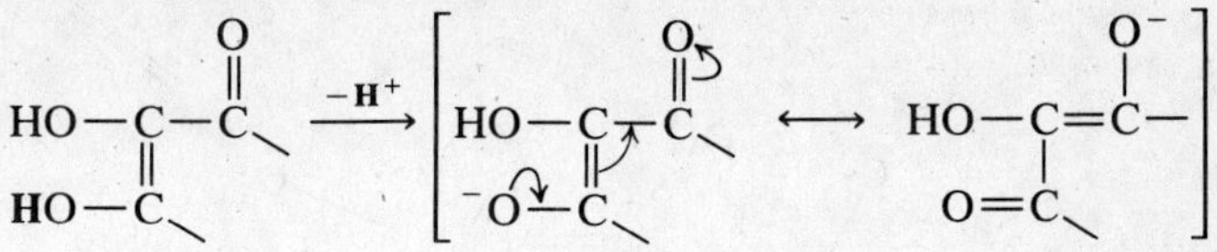

(b)

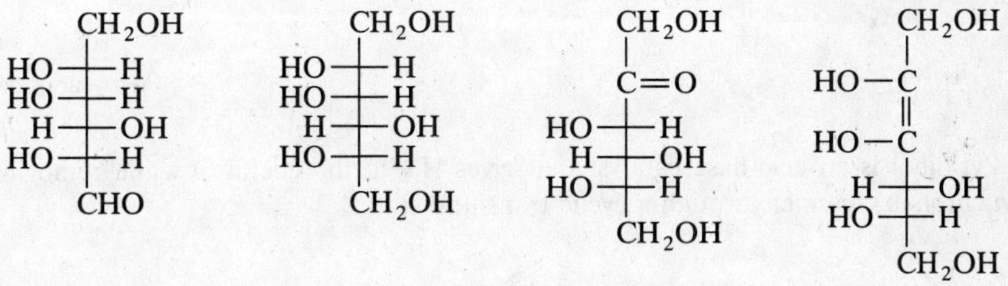

D-Glucose (turned 180°) D-Sorbitol (A) L-Sorbose (B) ene-diol of **B**

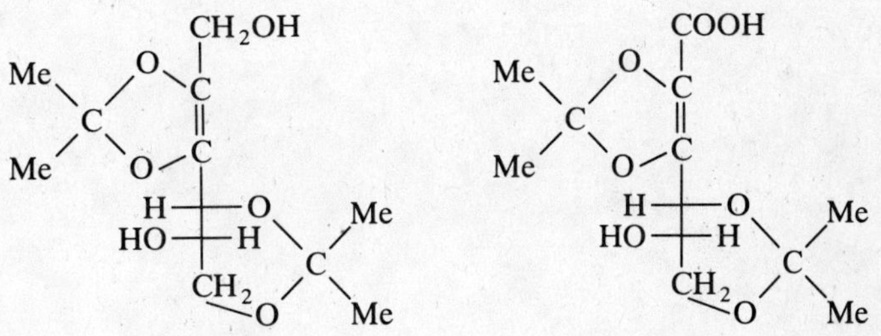

diacetonide (C) **D**

23.132 (a) What are hyaluronic acids? (b) Give their biological function.

▮ (a) Hyaluronic acids are copolymeric polysaccharides whose units are alternating D-glucuronic acid (see Problem 23.130) with a $\beta(1 \rightarrow 4)$ linkage and N-acetyl-D-glucosamine (see Problem 23.122) with a $\beta(1 \rightarrow 3)$ linkage. (b) They comprise much of the gelatinous matrix (mucin) in which collagen fibrils are embedded. This material is one of the main components of connective tissue, the lubricant of skeletal joints, filling the spaces between the cells of most tissues.

23.133 Amygdalin, $C_{20}H_{27}O_{11}N$ (**F**), is isolated from bitter almonds. Mild hydrolysis gives D-gentiobiose and a compound C_8H_7NO (**G**) which in NaOH yields NaCN and PhCHO. Hydrolysis of **F** does not occur with maltase. Suggest structures for **F** and **G**. (b) At one time some erroneously believed that **F** could serve as a cancer drug. What was their rational? (A monosaccharide analog of **F**, called *laetrile*, was actually used, but without FDA approval.)

▮ (a) **F** is the disaccharide D-gentiobiose (see Problem 23.88) β-linked to the aglycone (**G**) which is PhCH(CN)OH, the cyanohydrin of PhCHO. **F** is D-gentiobiose—$^\beta$O-CH(CN)Ph. (b) It was surmised that decomposition of the hydrolysis product **G** would release HCN which would be more toxic to the rapidly-growing cancerous tissue.

23.134 (a) Use a schematic sketch for a β-pyranoside to show the mechanism of mutarotation in (i) aq. H^+ and (ii) OH^-. (b) Show why catalysis by 2-pyridinol is greater than that of the sum of the acid and base catalysis.

⬛ **(a)** The rate depends on the conversion of the cyclic hemiacetal to the open-chain aldehyde (**A**).

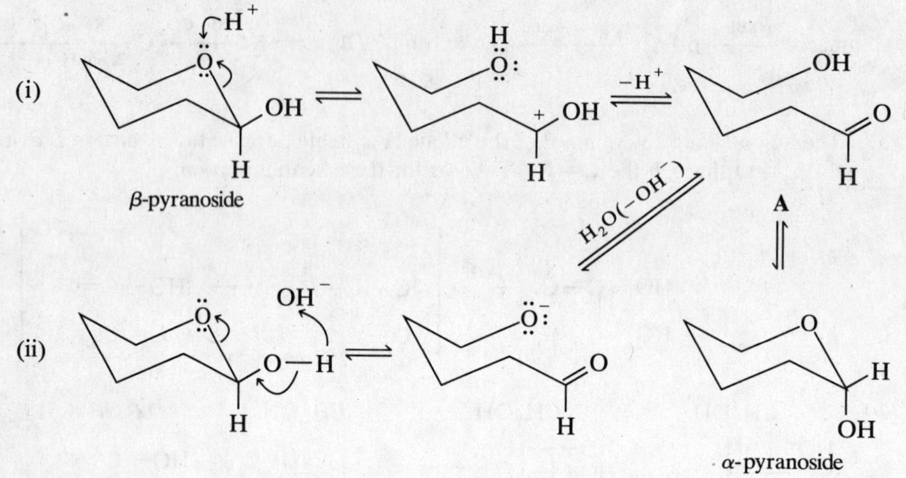

(i)

β-pyranoside

(ii)

α-pyranoside

(b) 2-Pyridinol is an acid-base catalyst that gives H⁺ to the acetal O while removing H⁺ from OH in a synchronous manner through a cyclic transition state.

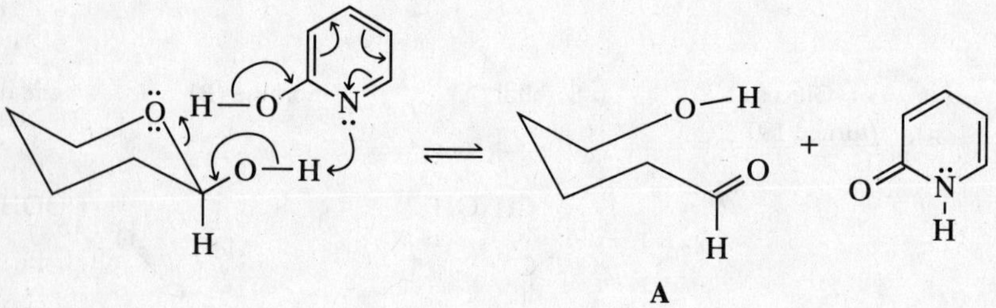

A

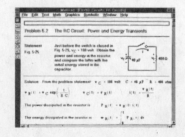

Schaum's Outlines and Solved Problems Books
in the
BIOLOGICAL SCIENCES

SCHAUM OFFERS IN SOLVED-PROBLEM AND QUESTION-AND-ANSWER FORMAT THESE UNBEATABLE TOOLS FOR SELF-IMPROVEMENT.

❊ Fried **BIOLOGY** ORDER CODE 022401-3/$12.95
(including 888 solved problems)

❊ Jessop **ZOOLOGY** ORDER CODE 032551-0/$13.95
(including 1050 solved problems)

❊ Kuchel et al. **BIOCHEMISTRY** order code 035579-7/$13.95
(including 830 solved problems)

❊ Meislich et al. **ORGANIC CHEMISTRY, 2/ed** ORDER CODE 041458-0/$13.95
(including 1806 solved problems)

❊ Stansfield **GENETICS, 3/ed** ORDER CODE 060877-6/$12.95
(including 209 solved problems)

❊ Van de Graaff/Rhees **HUMAN ANATOMY AND PHYSIOLOGY** ORDER CODE 066884-1/$12.95
(including 1470 solved problems)

❊ Bernstein **3000 SOLVED PROBLEMS IN BIOLOGY** ORDER CODE 005022-8/$16.95

❊ Meislich et al. **3000 SOLVED PROBLEMS IN ORGANIC CHEMISTRY** ORDER CODE 056424-8/$22.95

Each book teaches the subject thoroughly through Schaum's pioneering solved-problem format and can be used as a supplement to any textbook. If you want to excel in any of these subjects, these books will help and they belong on your shelf.

Schaum's Outlines have been used by more than 25,000,000 student's worldwide!

PLEASE ASK FOR THEM AT YOUR LOCAL BOOKSTORE OR USE THE COUPON BELOW TO ORDER.

Are You Suffering From

MATH ANXIETY?

Try

Bob Miller's Math Helpers

A unique new series of three class-tested books which will supplement your required texts. Bob Miller teaches Precalculus, Calculus I, and Calculus II in a friendly, personable way. You will learn through creative explanations of topics and multiple examples which are found throughout the text. Here are some comments from students who have used the CALC I HELPER:

"Without this book I'm not so sure I would have come close to passing. With it I not only passed but received an 'A'. I recommend this book highly to anyone taking a calculus course."

■

"Your book is really excellent; you explained every problem step by step. This book makes every topic seem very simple compared to other books."

Bob Miller's **PRECALC HELPER**
Bob Miller's **CALC I HELPER**
Bob Miller's **CALC II HELPER**

Affordably priced for students at $8.95 each. *

Available at your local bookstore or use the order form below.

SCHAUM'S SOLVED PROBLEMS SERIES

- Learn the best strategies for solving tough problems in step-by-step detail
- Prepare effectively for exams and save time in doing homework problems
- Use the indexes to quickly locate the types of problems you need the most help solving
- Save these books for reference in other courses and even for your professional library

To order, please check the appropriate box(es) and complete the following coupon.

❑ **3000 SOLVED PROBLEMS IN BIOLOGY**
ORDER CODE 005022-8/**$16.95 406 pp.**

❑ **3000 SOLVED PROBLEMS IN CALCULUS**
ORDER CODE 041523-4/**$19.95 442 pp.**

❑ **3000 SOLVED PROBLEMS IN CHEMISTRY**
ORDER CODE 023684-4/**$20.95 624 pp.**

❑ **2500 SOLVED PROBLEMS IN COLLEGE ALGEBRA & TRIGONOMETRY**
ORDER CODE 055373-4/**$14.95 608 pp.**

❑ **2500 SOLVED PROBLEMS IN DIFFERENTIAL EQUATIONS**
ORDER CODE 007979-x/**$19.95 448 pp.**

❑ **2000 SOLVED PROBLEMS IN DISCRETE MATHEMATICS**
ORDER CODE 038031-7/**$16.95 412 pp.**

❑ **3000 SOLVED PROBLEMS IN ELECTRIC CIRCUITS**
ORDER CODE 045936-3/**$21.95 746 pp.**

❑ **2000 SOLVED PROBLEMS IN ELECTROMAGNETICS**
ORDER CODE 045902-9/**$18.95 480 pp.**

❑ **2000 SOLVED PROBLEMS IN ELECTRONICS**
ORDER CODE 010284-8/**$19.95 640 pp.**

❑ **2500 SOLVED PROBLEMS IN FLUID MECHANICS & HYDRAULICS**
ORDER CODE 019784-9/**$21.95 800 pp.**

❑ **1000 SOLVED PROBLEMS IN HEAT TRANSFER**
ORDER CODE 050204-8/**$19.95 750 pp.**

❑ **3000 SOLVED PROBLEMS IN LINEAR ALGEBRA**
ORDER CODE 038023-6/**$19.95 750 pp.**

❑ **2000 SOLVED PROBLEMS IN Mechanical Engineering THERMODYNAMICS**
ORDER CODE 037863-0/**$19.95 406 pp.**

❑ **2000 SOLVED PROBLEMS IN NUMERICAL ANALYSIS**
ORDER CODE 055233-9/**$20.95 704 pp.**

❑ **3000 SOLVED PROBLEMS IN ORGANIC CHEMISTRY**
ORDER CODE 056424-8/**$22.95 688 pp.**

❑ **2000 SOLVED PROBLEMS IN PHYSICAL CHEMISTRY**
ORDER CODE 041716-4/**$21.95 448 pp.**

❑ **3000 SOLVED PROBLEMS IN PHYSICS**
ORDER CODE 025734-5/**$20.95 752 pp.**

❑ **3000 SOLVED PROBLEMS IN PRECALCULUS**
ORDER CODE 055365-3/**$16.95 385 pp.**

❑ **800 SOLVED PROBLEMS IN VECTOR MECHANICS FOR ENGINEERS
Vol I: STATICS**
ORDER CODE 056582-1/**$20.95 800 pp.**

❑ **700 SOLVED PROBLEMS IN VECTOR MECHANICS FOR ENGINEERS
Vol II: DYNAMICS**
ORDER CODE 056687-9/**$20.95 672 pp.**